THE
BOOK
OF THE
STATES

2016 EDITION
VOLUME 48

The Council of State Governments
Lexington, Kentucky

Headquarters: (859) 244-8000
Fax: (859) 244-8001
Internet: www.csg.org
Facebook: www.facebook.com/CSGovts
LinkedIn: www.linkedin.com/company/
council-of-state-governments
Twitter: https://twitter.com/CSGovts
YouTube: www.youtube.com/user/CSGovts

Sharing capitol ideas.

Headquarters:
David Adkins, Executive Director/CEO
1776 Avenue of the States
Lexington, KY 40511
Phone: (859) 244-8000
Internet: www.csg.org

Southern:
Colleen Cousineau, Director
P.O. Box 98129
Atlanta, GA 30359
Phone: (404) 633-1866
Internet: www.slcatlanta.org

Eastern:
Wendell M. Hannaford, Director
22 Cortlandt Street, 22nd Floor
New York, NY 10007
Phone: (212) 482-2320
Internet: www.csg-erc.org

Western:
Edgar Ruiz, Director
1107 9th Street, Suite 730
Sacramento, CA 95814
Phone: (916) 553-4423
Internet: www.csgwest.org

Midwestern:
Michael H. McCabe, Director
701 E. 22nd Street, Suite 110
Lombard, IL 60148
Phone: (630) 925-1922
Internet: www.csgmidwest.org

Washington, D.C.:

444 N. Capitol Street, NW, Suite 401
Washington, D.C. 20001
Phone: (202) 624-5460
Internet: www.csgdc.org

Publication Sales Department
1(800) 800-1910

SEP 19 2016

Paperback Price: $99.00
ISBN # 978-0-87292-703-2

Hard Cover Price: $125.00
ISBN # 978-0-87292-702-5

Foreword

Dear Friends,

"Many forms of Government have been tried, and will be tried in this world of sin and woe. No one pretends that democracy is perfect or all-wise. Indeed, it has been said that democracy is the worst form of Government except all those others that have been tried from time to time."

That was Winston Churchill's assessment of democracy and one that reminds us there are challenges inherent in every form of government, but a government of the people, by the people and for the people remains the best of the alternatives available.

For self-government to work, passionate and skillful leaders must offer themselves up as candidates, voters must be informed and select wisely, elected officials must appoint talented people of integrity and skill to conduct the business of government, and all stakeholders must work to hold the system accountable to serve the common good. Indeed, the outputs of democracy are only ever going to be as good as the inputs.

At The Council of State Governments, we are committed to helping strengthen the inputs of democracy. We provide an array of leadership development opportunities for state leaders and their staff, and we provide a myriad of ways for state leaders to learn how to best navigate the complexities of public policy. CSG believes the best solutions are data-driven and consensus-based, and so we provide the information, insights and resources that state leaders need to achieve strong policy and good governance.

As the nation's only organization of state officials representing all three branches of state government, and with a strong presence in four regional offices, CSG is uniquely positioned to serve as a catalyst for excellence in state government. Our mission is advanced by the active participation of thousands of leaders from our 56 member states and territories. We are grateful for the support provided by the states and their leaders. CSG has never been an organization that merely serves state leaders; we are an organization of state leaders. We know that when state leaders convene to compare notes, to share experiences and to study solutions, good things happen. We remain very proud of the role we play in bringing state leaders together.

This edition of *The Book of the States* is chock-full of the kind of insights and comparative data that for decades has made this publication the go-to resource for state leaders, academics, libraries, media and not-for-profit organizations. This book would not be possible without the generous assistance of our friends in the states on whom we rely to submit the data contained herein. We appreciate their partnership in this ongoing effort.

I am grateful for all of my colleagues who work throughout the year to compile this book. Under the dedicated direction of Audrey Wall, CSG has an incredible team of professionals who work to make this publication a reality. I appreciate their hard work.

For those of us in state government, 2015 was a year of change and challenge. CSG is committed to helping state leaders prepare for change and overcome challenges as their work continues to demonstrate that although democracy is not "perfect or all-wise," with skilled leadership, open exchange of ideas and the willingness to work together, it can accomplish great things. Our hope is that *The Book of the States* continues to be a key resource to help state leaders do just that.

All the best,

David Adkins
Executive Director / CEO
The Council of State Governments

The Council of State Governments is our nation's only organization serving all three branches of state government. CSG is a region-based forum that fosters the exchange of insights and ideas to help state officials shape public policy. This offers unparalleled regional, national and international opportunities to network, develop leaders, collaborate and create problem-solving partnerships.

Staff Acknowledgements

The staff wishes to thank the authors who shared their expertise and insights, the hundreds of individuals in the states who responded to surveys conducted by The Council of State Governments, national organizations of state officials, federal agencies and think tank organizations who made their most recent data and information available for this volume.

The Book of the States 2016

Managing Editor .... Audrey S. Wall

Associate Editor .... Heather M. Perkins

Lead Designer............ Chris Pryor

Graphic Designers..... Theresa Carroll
Chad Young

Copy Editors........... Carrie Abner
Shawntaye Hopkins
Lisa McKinney

Disclaimer

Table of Contents

CONTENTS

CONTENTS

Chapter Six
ELECTIONS..**265**

CONTENTS

TABLES
Taxes

ARTICLE
State Revenues from Gambling Shrinking

TABLES
Taxes

CONTENTS

Chapter Eight
STATE MANAGEMENT, ADMINISTRATION AND DEMOGRAPHICS **431**

CONTENTS

Chapter One

STATE
CONSTITUTIONS

State Constitutional Developments in 2015

By John Dinan

The level of constitutional amendment activity in 2015 was generally on par with recent odd-numbered years but somewhat lower than historical rates of activity in odd-numbered years and dramatically lower than in even-numbered years. Several measures attracted considerable attention, including two amendments on the Ohio ballot: a failed amendment that would have legalized recreational marijuana and a successful amendment changing the process for state legislative redistricting. A number of amendments in other states dealt with road building, including a failed Michigan amendment that would have increased the sales tax to boost transportation funding, a successful Texas amendment allocating excess revenue from sales taxes to a highway fund and a successful Louisiana amendment providing funding for a transportation infrastructure bank.

Constitutional amendment activity is generally much lower in odd-numbered years than even-numbered years, a pattern that continued in 2015. As is typical of odd-numbered years, Texas was responsible for a sizable portion of amendment activity, accounting for just over half of all amendments approved in 2015. Delaware, Louisiana, Ohio and Wisconsin accounted for the other successful amendments on topics such as road building, tax exemptions, redistricting and selection of the state supreme court chief justice.

Constitutional Amendment and Revision Methods

Constitutional amendments were proposed or enacted in seven states in 2015. This is on par with recent odd-numbered years. Amendments were considered in five states in 2013, nine states in 2011 and five states in 2009. This is, of course, much lower than the number of states considering amendments in recent even-numbered years: 36 states in 2014, 35 states in 2012 and 37 states in 2010.

The total number of enacted amendments in 2015—13—falls slightly below the totals for recent odd-numbered years: 19 amendments in 2013, 20 amendments in 2011 and 17 amendments in 2009. These recent totals are somewhat lower than the number of amendments enacted in several odd-numbered years earlier this century. For instance, 33 amendments were approved in 2007, and 46 amendments were approved in 2003. The data for enacted amendments in recent odd-numbered years are, of course, much lower than the number of amendments approved in recent even-numbered years: 72 amendments in 2014, 92 amendments in 2012 and 116 amendments in 2010.

Legislative Proposals and Constitutional Initiatives

All 13 amendments approved in 2015 were advanced by legislatures or proposed via the initiative process. Delaware is unique in providing that amendments take effect upon passage by the legislature in two sessions and without submission to voters. In 2015, the Delaware Legislature gave its second and final approval to one amendment. In every other state, legislature-generated amendments take effect only after they are ratified by voters. In 2015, state legislatures referred 16 amendments to voters and voters ratified 12 of them. This 75 percent passage rate is comparable to the passage rate for legislature-referred amendments in recent years. Finally, in 18 states voters can qualify amendments for the ballot via the initiative process. In 2015, voters considered two citizen-initiated amendments and defeated both of them. To put this in perspective, in recent years voters have generally approved about one-third of citizen-initiated amendments (see Table A for recent data on amendment passage).

One of the failed citizen-initiated amendments in 2015 was significant because it marked the first time Mississippi voters considered competing citizen-initiated and legislature-referred amendments. When Mississippi in 1992 became the most recent state to permit citizen-initiated amendments, it opted to create an *indirect* constitutional initiative process, rather than a direct constitutional initiative process of the sort found in 16 other states. As in Massachusetts, the only other state providing for indirect constitutional initiatives, the Mississippi Legislature can choose to place a competing legislature-referred amend-

Table A: State Constitutional Changes by Method of Initiation: 2010–11, 2012–13 and 2014–15

Method of initiation	Number of states involved			Total proposals (a)			Total adopted (b)			Percentage adopted (c)		
	2010–2011	2012–2013	2014–2015	2010–2011	2012–2013	2014–2015	2010–2011	2012–2013	2014–2015	2010–2011	2012–2013	2014–2015
All methods.................	40	37	38	191	151 (d)	122	136 (e)(f)	109	85	70.2	70.2	68.9
Legislative proposal...	37	34	37	170	132	112	124 (e)(f)	102	83	71.8	75.0	73.2
Constitutional initiative.................	9	7	8	21	19 (d)	10	12	7	2	57.1	36.8	20.0
convention..............	...	...	...	...	...	...	...	...	...	...	...	...
commission.............	...	...	...	...	...	...	...	...	...	...	...	...

Source: John Dinan and The Council of State Governments.
Key:
(a) Excludes Delaware, where proposals are not submitted to voters.
(b) Includes Delaware.
(c) In calculating the percentages, the amendments adopted in Delaware (where proposals are not submitted to voters) are excluded (one amendment was adopted in 2010 and another in 2011 and then three in 2013 and one in 2015).

(d) Excludes two Arkansas amendments that were placed on the 2012 ballot but whose results were not counted pursuant to a court order.
(e) Excludes one Alabama local amendment approved by voters in November 2010 but not certified pursuant to a court order.
(f) Includes one Oklahoma amendment that was approved by voters in 2010 but whose enforcement was permanently enjoined by a federal district court.

ment on the ballot alongside a citizen-initiated amendment.[1] However, this Mississippi procedure is complicated. When voters encounter competing amendments, they are first asked to check a box indicating on one hand whether they prefer that either or both of the amendments pass or on the other hand whether they prefer that neither pass; voters are then asked which of the two amendments they prefer.

Mississippi residents secured enough signatures to place on the 2015 ballot an amendment revising the state's education clause by guaranteeing a "fundamental right to educational opportunity" and requiring the state to establish "an adequate and efficient system of free public schools" and providing that this guarantee should be enforced by the state's chancery courts. In response, and with an eye to presenting voters with more modest changes in the education clause, the Mississippi Legislature placed on the ballot a competing amendment differing from the citizen-initiated amendment in a number of respects. The legislature-approved amendment only required the state to establish "an effective system of free public schools;" it made no mention of a "fundamental right" to educational opportunity or judicial enforcement of this provision. Mississippi voters preferred the citizen-initiated measure over the legislature-referred measure, but they indicated, by a 52 to 48 percent margin on the initial ballot question, that they preferred that

neither measure pass. As a result, neither the citizen-initiated amendment nor the legislature-referred amendment was approved.

The Ohio Legislature also placed an amendment on the 2015 ballot in response to a citizen-initiated amendment. Ohio provides for a direct constitutional initiative process, whereby amendment supporters who obtain enough signatures can place the amendment directly on the ballot with no formal opportunity for the Legislature to submit an alternative amendment. However, there is no barrier to the Ohio Legislature crafting an amendment that conflicts with a citizen-initiated amendment. In taking this route in 2015, Ohio legislators were reacting to a provision in a citizen-initiated, marijuana-legalization amendment that would have designated 10 entities as exclusively responsible for commercial marijuana growth, cultivation and extraction. In response, the Ohio Legislature placed an anti-monopoly amendment on the ballot intended to bar enforcement of this particular provision of the marijuana-legalization amendment and make it more difficult to enact future initiated amendments of this sort.[2]

In the lead up to the November 2015 vote, scholars and public officials debated whether the anti-monopoly amendment would supersede the marijuana-legalization amendment, in whole or in part, if both were approved. As it turned out, voters approved the anti-monopoly amendment, but rejected the marijuana-legalization amendment,

Table B: Substantive Changes in State Constitutions, Proposed and Adopted, 2010–11, 2012–13 and 2014–15

	Total proposed (a)			Total adopted (b)			Percentage adopted (c)		
Subject matter	2010–2011	2012–2013	2014–2015	2010–2011	2012–2013	2014–2015	2010–2011	2012–2013	2014–2015
Proposals of statewide applicability	147	130(a)(d)	116(a)	108(b)(f)	92(b)	79(b)	72.1(c)	68.5(c)	67.2(c)
Bill of Rights	22	20	15	17	13	13	77.3	65.0	86.7
Suffrage & elections	18	5(a)	10	15	3(b)	6	83.3	40.0(c)	60.0
Legislative branch	6	11	6	5	7	3	83.3	63.6	50.0
Executive branch	6	4	6	5(b)	4	4	66.7(c)	100.0	66.7
Judicial branch	7	12(a)	10(a)	5(b)(f)	7(b)	8(b)	57.1(c)	41.7(c)	70.0(c)
Local government	7	3	5	4	2	4	57.1	66.7	80.0
Finance & taxation	42	32	32	32	25	24	76.2	78.1	75.0
State & local debt	16	5	5	13	4	4	81.3	80.0	80.0
State functions	9	16	11	3	11	2	33.3	68.8	18.2
Amendment & revision	0	0	0	0	0	0	0.0	0.0	0.0
General revision proposals	0	0	0	0	0	0	0.0	0.0	0.0
Miscellaneous proposals	14	22	16	9	16	11	64.3	72.7	68.8
Local amendments	44	21	6	28(e)	17	6	63.6	81.0	100.0

Source: John Dinan and The Council of State Governments.
Key:
(a) Excludes Delaware, where amendments do not require popular approval.
(b) Includes Delaware.
(c) In calculating the percentages, the amendments adopted in Delaware (where proposals are not submitted to voters) are excluded (one amendment was adopted in 2010 and another in 2011 and then three in 2013 and one in 2015).
(d) Excludes two Arkansas amendments placed on the 2012 ballot but whose results were not counted pursuant to a court order.
(e) Excludes one Alabama local amendment approved by voters in November 2010 but not certified pursuant to a court order.
(f) Includes one Oklahoma amendment that was approved by voters in 2010 but whose enforcement was permanently enjoined by a federal district court.

which would have made Ohio the fifth state to legalize recreational marijuana, along with Colorado, Washington, Oregon and Alaska. Going forward, the anti-monopoly amendment provides that when citizen-initiated amendments are submitted, the state Ballot Board is required to determine whether a measure would grant a monopoly, which would trigger a procedure whereby a separate question would be submitted to voters, alongside of the initiated measure, stating: "Shall the petitioner, in violation of division (B)(1) of Section 1e of Article II of the Ohio Constitution, be authorized to initiate a constitutional amendment that grants or creates a monopoly, oligopoly, or cartel, specifies or determines a tax rate, or confers a commercial interest, commercial right, or commercial license that is not available to other similarly situated persons?" Voters have to approve both questions before the initiated amendment can take effect.

Constitutional Conventions and Commissions

No constitutional conventions were held in 2015, marking a full three decades since the last full-scale convention was held in Rhode Island in 1986.[3] The next opportunity for voters to call a convention is likely to occur in 2017 in New York,

one of 14 states requiring periodic submission of a convention referendum, in this case every 20 years. New York voters defeated the last convention referendum in the state in 1997, but groups and public officials are already mobilizing in anticipation of the automatically generated 2017 referendum.

The Ohio Constitutional Modernization Commission was the only constitutional commission operating in 2015. Established by the Ohio Legislature in 2011, this 32-member commission is tasked with recommending constitutional changes for legislators' consideration. Amendments securing support from two-thirds of commissioners are forwarded to the Legislature, which can decide, upon a three-fifths vote of both houses, to submit them to voters for ratification. Although the commission was originally given a 10-year charge, a provision in a biennial budget bill approved by the Legislature and signed by Gov. John Kasich in summer 2015 calls for the commission to complete its work three and a half years ahead of schedule, by Jan. 1, 2018.

Ohio voters in 2015 approved an amendment regarding state legislative redistricting that can be viewed in part as a product of the commis-

Table C: State Constitutional Changes by Legislative and Initiative Proposal: 2015

State	Legislative proposal			Constitutional initiative		
	Number proposed	Number adopted	Percentage adopted	Number proposed	Number adopted	Percentage adopted
Delaware	(a)	1	(a)			
Louisiana	4	2	50.0			
Michigan	1	0	0.0			
Mississippi	1	0	0.0	1	0	0.0
Ohio	2	2	100.0	1	0	0.0
Texas	7	7	100.0			
Wisconsin	1	1	100.0			
Totals	16	13	75.0(b)	2	0	0.0

Source: John Dinan and The Council of State Governments.
(a) Delaware does not provide for submission of amendments to voters.
(b) Excludes the one legislature-enacted amendment in Delaware.

sion's work, even if the commission had not yet recommended an amendment on this subject. In 2014, commissioners heard extensive testimony and engaged in much debate about alternatives to the current redistricting process, and in a way that further elevated the salience of an issue that had already been the subject of several failed citizen-initiated amendments in the state during the prior decade. In the midst of these discussions, the Legislature in December 2014 crafted and approved a redistricting amendment for submission to voters in 2015.

The amendment approved by Ohio voters in 2015 increases from five to seven the number of members on a reconstituted and re-named Redistricting Commission and ensures that at least two members are appointed by the minority party. Along with the governor, state auditor and secretary of state, the redistricting commission includes members designated by the house speaker and senate president as well as the minority party leaders of the house and senate. Commission-drawn maps have to secure the approval of at least two members of the minority party, or they would only remain in effect for four years, rather than the standard 10 years. This amendment only applies to state legislative districts and does not affect congressional districts.

Although an Alabama Constitutional Revision Commission established by the Alabama Legislature in 2011 completed its work in 2013, voters are still considering several commission-backed amendments. Voters in 2012 ratified several amendments recommended by the 16-member

commission and approved by the Legislature. After some discussion but no agreement in the 2014 legislative session about additional commission-recommended changes, the Legislature returned to the issue in 2015 and agreed to place several amendments on the 2016 ballot. Voters in 2016 will consider amendments regarding separation of powers, impeachment, a modest increase in the power of counties in several areas of governance, and a change in the process for enacting local constitutional amendments that apply to particular localities and make up a significant portion of the 892 amendments to the Alabama Constitution.

Constitutional Changes

Finance-related amendments outpaced amendments on other topics in 2015, as is the norm. Other amendments on the 2015 ballot dealt with constitutional rights, governing institutions, and assorted financial and non-financial policies.

Rights

Texas became the 19th state to guarantee a constitutional right to hunt and fish, when voters approved such an amendment in 2015. All but one of these hunting and fishing rights amendments have been approved in the last two decades, generally out of a desire to combat regulations on hunting and trapping supported by animal-welfare and wildlife-conservation groups. Indiana voters have an opportunity to add to this list when they consider a legislature-referred hunting and fishing rights amendment on the 2016 ballot.

Several state legislatures in 2015 debated amendments guaranteeing a right to farm, with an eye to barring restrictions on animal-confinement practices and combating nuisance lawsuits filed against farmers operating near housing developments. Although the Indiana Legislature declined, after some debate in 2015, to approve a right-to-farm amendment, the Oklahoma Legislature approved such an amendment for placement on the 2016 ballot. If voters ratify this amendment, Oklahoma would join North Dakota and Missouri in guaranteeing a right to farm in the state constitution.

One other development pertaining to rights-related amendments is worth noting regarding the same-sex marriage-ban amendments adopted in 30 states between 1998 and 2012.[4] When the U.S. Supreme Court recognized a right to same-sex marriage under the U.S. Constitution in a June 2015 case, *Obergefell v. Hodges*, this rendered unenforceable all contrary state statutes and constitutional amendments. Federal district judges had already invalidated same-sex marriage-ban amendments in a number of states in rulings generally sustained by federal circuit courts. The *Obergefell* decision barred enforcement of all same-sex marriage-ban statutes and constitutional amendments still in effect.

Institutions

Two amendments adopted in 2015 deal with the judicial branch. In an April 2015 election, Wisconsin voters approved an amendment changing the process for selecting the state Supreme Court chief justice. Prior to adoption of this amendment, the constitution specified that the longest-serving member of the court would serve as chief justice. The 2015 amendment replaces the seniority system with a majority vote of the court's members, with the chief justice serving a two-year term. After the amendment's passage, the court voted to appoint Patience Roggensack in place of long-serving Chief Justice Shirley Abrahamson. Although Abrahamson, along with several Wisconsin voters, filed a federal lawsuit seeking to retain her position as chief justice, this suit was dismissed.

The Delaware Legislature gave its second and final approval to an amendment expanding the entities that can certify questions of law to the Delaware Supreme Court. In recent years, the Delaware Legislature has enacted several amendments permitting various courts or agencies to certify questions of law to the state

Supreme Court. The 2015 amendment adds to this list, by permitting the court to hear questions certified to it by "the highest appellate court of any foreign country, or any foreign governmental agency regulating the public issuance or trading of securities."

Voters approved the only amendment on the 2015 ballot dealing with the executive branch, a Texas amendment eliminating a residency requirement for state officers elected by voters statewide. This provision had long required the comptroller of public accounts, commissioner of the General Land Office, and attorney general, among other state officials, to live in Austin; but this requirement was deemed by legislators and voters to be no longer necessary.

Voters rejected the only amendment on the 2015 ballot regarding the legislative branch, a Louisiana amendment clarifying and expanding the types of legislation that can be considered in fiscal sessions held in odd-numbered years. Louisiana is one of a number of states imposing strict limits on the types of bills considered during these sessions. This rejected amendment would have eased these limits slightly, in part by allowing legislators to consider bills regarding rebates of taxes.

Policy

Amendments dealing with road building accounted for over a quarter of all amendments appearing on the 2015 ballot. Texas voters approved two amendments of this sort. As a result of one Texas amendment, when revenue from two taxes—the sales and use tax and the motor vehicle sales, use and rental tax—exceeds certain thresholds, the excess revenue will be deposited into the State Highway Fund. This is the second Texas amendment in two years providing an infusion of transportation funding, following voter approval of a 2014 amendment stipulating that certain funds that had previously been deposited into a rainy day fund will now be deposited in the State Highway Fund. Another Texas amendment approved in 2015 gives a greater number of counties the option to construct and maintain private roads.

Louisiana voters considered two amendments in 2015 that would boost transportation funding, rejecting one and approving the other. The failed amendment would have permitted excess mineral revenue to be used for road construction and repair. The successful amendment authorizes the state treasurer to invest public funds in a new transportation infrastructure bank. Approval of this amendment came a year after voters overwhelmingly rejected an amendment that would have given even more sweeping powers to an infrastructure bank. The streamlined amendment passed by a narrow margin in 2015.

Michigan voters rejected an amendment on the May 2015 ballot that would have increased the sales tax by a penny and dedicated the increased revenue to road construction. It is unusual for a legislature-referred amendment to be defeated as soundly as this amendment, whose opponents outnumbered supporters by a four-one margin.

Voters approved three property-tax exemption amendments in 2015: two in Texas and one in Louisiana. One wide-ranging Texas amendment increases the homestead exemption from property taxes for schools. In a provision that also has been adopted in recent years in several other states, this amendment also bars imposition of a real-estate transfer tax. A second Texas amendment tweaks an earlier amendment granting a property-tax exemption for the surviving spouse of a totally disabled veteran; the 2015 amendment remedies a drafting oversight in the original amendment and ensures that the exemption can be claimed by spouses of veterans who died before 2010.

A 2015 Louisiana amendment declares that an existing property-tax exemption for "public property used for public purposes" shall not apply to "property owned by another state or owned by a political subdivision of another state." The Legislature crafted this amendment in response to a state court decision interpreting the existing constitutional provision as preventing a parish from taxing natural gas stored in that parish by a city in another state. The purpose of the 2015 amendment was to enable parishes to tax property owned by another state or its subdivision, while maintaining the tax exemption for property owned by the state of Louisiana or its subdivisions.[5]

Another amendment approved by Texas voters is one in a recent series of amendments across the country making specific exceptions to constitutional bans on lotteries, raffles or other games of chance. The Texas amendment allows professional sports team foundations to conduct charitable raffles.

Conclusion

Constitutional amendment activity in 2015 is comparable to recent odd-numbered years, but falls below historical patterns for odd-numbered years.

In terms of the subject matter of state constitutional amendments, amendments considered and adopted in 2015 generally address similar topics as those in recent years. Legislatures agreed to place on the ballot and voters occasionally approved amendments expanding rights, with a particular focus on the right to hunt and fish and the right to farm. Legislators also continue to debate various amendments altering the design of governing institutions. Although no amendments on the 2015 ballot brought about changes in the judicial retirement age, voters in 2016 will consider several amendments increasing or repealing the judicial retirement age. Finally, amendments dealing with finance and taxation continue to appear regularly on state ballots. Amendments in 2015 focused particularly on funding road construction and repair, along with the usual assortment of property-tax exemption measures.

Notes

[1] In a provision with no counterpart in Mississippi, the Massachusetts Legislature has the power to block voter consideration of a citizen-initiated amendment. In Massachusetts, a citizen-initiated amendment must obtain the support of one-fourth of the legislators in two consecutive sessions before it can be forwarded to voters.

[2] Jackie Borchardt, "What happens if both marijuana legalization and anti-monopoly amendments pass," *www.cleveland.com*, Aug. 17, 2015, *http://www.cleveland.com/open/index.ssf/2015/08/what_happens_if_both_marijuana.html*.

[3] In Louisiana in 1992, legislators organized as a limited convention to deal with spending and taxing issues and proposed an amendment that voters defeated. But this fell far short of the full-scale conventions that were once prevalent and have been held on 236 occasions since the 1770s.

[4] Thirty states adopted amendments barring recognition of same-sex marriage. In addition, Hawaii voters approved a 1998 amendment prohibiting the state judiciary from requiring legalization of same-sex marriage but allowing the legislature to decide whether or not to legalize same-sex marriage.

[5] For a discussion of the way this issue is handled in other state constitutions, see Liz Farmer, "In Louisiana, voters want other governments to pay up," *Governing*, Oct. 27, 2015, *http://www.governing.com/templates/gov_print_article?id=329780061*.

About the Author

John Dinan is professor of politics and international affairs at Wake Forest University in North Carolina. He is the author of The American State Constitutional Tradition and various articles on state constitutions.

Table 1.1
GENERAL INFORMATION ON STATE CONSTITUTIONS
(As of January 1, 2016)

State or other jurisdiction	Number of constitutions*	Dates of adoption	Effective date of present constitution	Estimated length (b) (number of words)**	Number of amendments Submitted to voters	Adopted
Alabama	6	1819, 1861, 1865, 1868, 1875, 1901	Nov. 28, 1901	388,882 (a)	1,221	892 (c)
Alaska	1	1956	Jan. 3, 1959	13,479	42	29
Arizona	1	1911	Feb. 14, 1912	45,910	275	152
Arkansas	5	1836, 1861, 1864, 1868, 1874	Oct. 30, 1874	65,700	202	102 (d)
California	2	1849, 1879	July 4, 1879	67,048	896	529
Colorado	1	1876	Aug. 1, 1876	72,860	340	158
Connecticut	2	1818 (f), 1965	Dec. 30, 1965	16,562	33	31
Delaware	4	1776, 1792, 1831, 1897	June 10, 1897	29,613	(e)	146
Florida	6	1839, 1861, 1865, 1868, 1886, 1968	Jan. 7, 1969	43,514	168	122
Georgia	10	1777, 1789, 1798, 1861, 1865, 1868, 1877, 1945, 1976, 1982	July 1, 1983	42,100	98 (g)	75 (g)
Hawaii	1 (h)	1950	Aug. 21, 1959	21,498	138	113
Idaho	1	1889	July 3, 1890	24,626	213	125
Illinois	4	1818, 1848, 1870, 1970	July 1, 1971	16,401	21	14
Indiana	2	1816, 1851	Nov. 1, 1851	11,476	79	47
Iowa	2	1846, 1857	Sept. 3, 1857	11,089	59	54 (i)
Kansas	1	1859	Jan. 29, 1861	14,097	127	97 (i)
Kentucky	4	1792, 1799, 1850, 1891	Sept. 28, 1891	27,234	76	42
Louisiana	11	1812, 1845, 1852, 1861, 1864, 1868, 1879, 1898, 1913, 1921, 1974	Jan. 1, 1975	73,224	266	184
Maine	1	1819	March 15, 1820	16,313	205	172 (j)
Maryland	4	1776, 1851, 1864, 1867	Oct. 5, 1867	43,198	266	230 (k)
Massachusetts	1	1780	Oct. 25, 1780	45,283 (l)	148	120
Michigan	4	1835, 1850, 1908, 1963	Jan. 1, 1964	31,164	74	30
Minnesota	1	1857	May 11, 1858	11,734	217	120
Mississippi	4	1817, 1832, 1869, 1890	Nov. 1, 1890	26,229	164	126
Missouri	4	1820, 1865, 1875, 1945	March 30, 1945	68,670	186	120
Montana	2	1889, 1972	July 1, 1973	12,790	57	31
Nebraska	2	1866, 1875	Oct. 12, 1875	34,934	354 (m)	230 (m)
Nevada	1	1864	Oct. 31, 1864	29,895	235	138
New Hampshire	2	1776, 1784	June 2, 1784	13,060	289 (n)	145
New Jersey	3	1776, 1844, 1947	Jan. 1, 1948	26,360	85	70
New Mexico	1	1911	Jan. 6, 1912	33,198	303 (y)	169 (x)
New York	4	1777, 1822, 1846, 1894	Jan. 1, 1895	44,397	303	227
North Carolina	3	1776, 1868, 1970	July 1, 1971	17,177	39	32
North Dakota	1	1889	Nov. 2, 1889	18,895	277	156 (o)
Ohio	2	1802, 1851	Sept. 1, 1851	56,818	291	175
Oklahoma	1	1907	Nov. 16, 1907	81,666	363 (p)	196 (p)
Oregon	1	1857	Feb. 14, 1859	49,016	498 (q)	255 (q)
Pennsylvania	5	1776, 1790, 1838, 1873, 1968 (r)	1968 (r)	26,078	36 (r)	30 (r)
Rhode Island	2	1842 (f) 1986 (s)	Dec. 4, 1986	11,407	16 (s)	13 (s)
South Carolina	7	1776, 1778, 1790, 1861, 1865, 1868, 1895	Jan. 1, 1896	27,421	689 (t)	500 (t)
South Dakota	1	1889	Nov. 2, 1889	27,774	234	118
Tennessee	3	1796, 1835, 1870	Feb. 23, 1870	13,960	66	43
Texas	5 (u)	1845, 1861, 1866, 1869, 1876	Feb. 15, 1876	86,936	669 (v)	491
Utah	1	1895	Jan. 4, 1896	20,320	172	118
Vermont	3	1777, 1786, 1793	July 9, 1793	8,565	212	54
Virginia	6	1776, 1830, 1851, 1869, 1902, 1970	July 1, 1971	21,899	57	49
Washington	1	1889	Nov. 11, 1889	32,578	180	106
West Virginia	2	1863, 1872	April 9, 1872	33,324	123	72
Wisconsin	1	1848	May 29, 1848	15,392	196	147 (i)
Wyoming	1	1889	July 10, 1890	26,349	129	100
American Samoa	2	1960, 1967	July 1, 1967	6,000	15 (y)	7 (y)
No. Mariana Islands	1	1977	Jan. 9, 1978	13,700	60 (y)	56 (w)(y)
Puerto Rico	1	1952	July 25, 1952	9,400	8 (y)	6 (y)

See footnotes at end of table.

GENERAL INFORMATION ON STATE CONSTITUTIONS — Continued
(As of January 1, 2016)

Source: John Dinan and The Council of State Governments, with research assistance from Wake Forest students Bradley Harper and Alec Papovich.

*The constitutions referred to in this table include those Civil War documents customarily listed by the individual states.

**In calculating word counts, supplemental information regarding dates of adoption and other material not formally a part of the constitution are generally excluded. In some cases, word counts are taken from the total as of January 2011.

Key:

(a) The Alabama constitution includes numerous local amendments that apply to only one county. An estimated 70 percent of all amendments are local. A 1982 amendment provides that after proposal by the legislature to which special procedures apply, only a local vote (with exceptions) is necessary to add them to the constitution.

(b) Computer word count.

(c) The total number of Alabama amendments includes one that is commonly overlooked.

(d) Eight of the approved amendments have been superseded and are not printed in the current edition of the constitution. The total adopted does not include five amendments proposed and adopted since statehood.

(e) Proposed amendments are not submitted to the voters in Delaware.

(f) Colonial charters with some alterations served as the first constitutions in Connecticut (1638, 1662) and in Rhode Island (1663).

(g) The Georgia constitution requires amendments to be of "general and uniform application throughout the state," thus eliminating local amendments that accounted for most of the amendments before 1982.

(h) As a kingdom and republic, Hawaii had five constitutions.

(i) The figure includes amendments approved by the voters and later nullified by the state supreme court in Iowa (three), Kansas (one), Nevada (six) and Wisconsin (two).

(j) The figure does not include one amendment approved by the voters in 1967 that is inoperative until implemented by legislation.

(k) Two sets of identical amendments were on the ballot and adopted in the 1992 Maryland election. The four amendments are counted as two in the table.

(l) The printed constitution includes many provisions that have been annulled.

(m) The 1998 and 2000 Nebraska ballots allowed the voters to vote separately on "parts" of propositions. In 1998, 10 of 18 separate propositions were adopted; in 2000, 6 of 9.

(n) The constitution of 1784 was extensively revised in 1792. Figure shows proposals and adoptions since the constitution was adopted in 1784.

(o) The figures do not include submission and approval of the constitution of 1889 itself and of Article XX; these are constitutional questions included in some counts of constitutional amendments and would add two to the figure in each column.

(p) The figures include six amendments submitted to and approved by the voters which were, by decisions of the Oklahoma or federal courts, rendered inoperative or ruled invalid, unconstitutional, or illegally submitted.

(q) One Oregon amendment on the 2000 ballot was not counted as approved because canvassing was enjoined by the courts.

(r) Certain sections of the constitution were revised by the limited convention of 1967–68. Amendments proposed and adopted are since 1968.

(s) Following approval of the eight amendments and a "rewrite" of the Rhode Island Constitution in 1986, the constitution has been called the 1986 Constitution.

(t) In 1981 approximately two-thirds of the proposed and four-fifths of the adopted amendments were local. Since then the amendments have been statewide propositions.

(u) The Constitution of the Republic of Texas preceded five state constitutions.

(v) The number of proposed amendments to the Texas Constitution excludes three proposed by the legislature but not placed on the ballot.

(w) The total excludes one amendment ruled void by a federal district court.

(x) The total excludes one amendment approved by voters in November 2008 but later declared invalid on single subject grounds by the state supreme court.

(y) These totals for territorial constitutions are in some cases taken from 2011 data.

Table 1.2
CONSTITUTIONAL AMENDMENT PROCEDURE: BY THE LEGISLATURE
Constitutional Provisions

State or other jurisdiction	Legislative vote required for proposal (a)	Consideration by two sessions required	Vote required for ratification	Limitation on the number of amendments legislature can submit at one election
Alabama	3/5	No	Majority vote on amendment	None
Alaska	2/3	No	Majority vote on amendment	None
Arizona	Majority	No	Majority vote on amendment	None
Arkansas	Majority	No	Majority vote on amendment	3
California	2/3	No	Majority vote on amendment	None
Colorado	2/3	No	Majority vote on amendment	(b)
Connecticut	(c)	(c)	Majority vote on amendment	None
Delaware	2/3	Yes	Not required	No referendum
Florida	3/5	No	3/5 vote on amendment (d)	None
Georgia	2/3	No	Majority vote on amendment	None
Hawaii	(e)	(e)	(f)	None
Idaho	2/3	No	Majority vote on amendment	None
Illinois	3/5	No	(g)	3 articles
Indiana	Majority	Yes	Majority vote on amendment	None
Iowa	Majority	Yes	Majority vote on amendment	None
Kansas	2/3	No	Majority vote on amendment	5
Kentucky	3/5	No	Majority vote on amendment	4
Louisiana	2/3	No	Majority vote on amendment (h)	None
Maine	2/3 (i)	No	Majority vote on amendment	None
Maryland	3/5	No	Majority vote on amendment (h)	None
Massachusetts	Majority (j)	Yes	Majority vote on amendment	None
Michigan	2/3	No	Majority vote on amendment	None
Minnesota	Majority	No	Majority vote in election	None
Mississippi	2/3 (k)	No	Majority vote on amendment	None
Missouri	Majority	No	Majority vote on amendment	None
Montana	2/3 (i)	No	Majority vote on amendment	None
Nebraska	3/5 (w)	No	Majority vote on amendment (f)	None
Nevada	Majority	Yes	Majority vote on amendment	None
New Hampshire	3/5	No	2/3 vote on amendment	None
New Jersey	(l)	(l)	Majority vote on amendment	None (m)
New Mexico	Majority (n)	No	Majority vote on amendment (n)	None
New York	Majority	Yes	Majority vote on amendment	None
North Carolina	3/5	No	Majority vote on amendment	None
North Dakota	Majority	No	Majority vote on amendment	None
Ohio	3/5	No	Majority vote on amendment	None
Oklahoma	Majority (w)	No	Majority vote on amendment	None
Oregon	(o)	No	Majority vote on amendment (x)	None
Pennsylvania	Majority (p)	Yes (p)	Majority vote on amendment	None
Rhode Island	Majority	No	Majority vote on amendment	None
South Carolina	2/3 (q)	Yes (q)	Majority vote on amendment	None
South Dakota	Majority	No	Majority vote on amendment	None
Tennessee	(r)	Yes (r)	Majority vote in election (s)	None
Texas	2/3	No	Majority vote on amendment	None
Utah	2/3	No	Majority vote on amendment	None
Vermont	(t)	Yes	Majority vote on amendment	None
Virginia	Majority	Yes	Majority vote on amendment	None
Washington	2/3	No	Majority vote on amendment	None
West Virginia	2/3	No	Majority vote on amendment	None
Wisconsin	Majority	Yes	Majority vote on amendment	None
Wyoming	2/3	No	Majority vote in election	None
American Samoa	2/3	No	Majority vote on amendment (u)	None
No. Mariana Islands	3/4	No	Majority vote on amendment	None
Puerto Rico	2/3 (v)	No	Majority vote on amendment	3

See footnotes at end of table.

CONSTITUTIONAL AMENDMENT PROCEDURE: BY THE LEGISLATURE — Continued
Constitutional Provisions

Source: John Dinan and The Council of State Governments.
Key:

(a) In all states not otherwise noted, the figure shown in the column refers to the proportion of elected members in each house required for approval of proposed constitutional amendments.

(b) Legislature may not propose amendments to more than six articles of the constitution in the same legislative session.

(c) Three-fourths vote in each house at one session, or majority vote in each house in two sessions between which an election has intervened.

(d) Three-fifths vote on amendment, except amendment for "new state tax or fee" not in effect on Nov. 7, 1994 requires two-thirds of voters in the election.

(e) Two-thirds vote in each house at one session, or majority vote in each house in two sessions.

(f) In Hawaii, the majority vote on amendment must be at least 50 percent of the total votes cast at the election; or, at a special election, a majority of the votes tallied which must be at least 30 percent of the total number of registered voters. In Nebraska the majority vote on amendment must be at least 35 percent of the total votes cast at the election.

(g) Majority voting in election or three-fifths voting on amendment.

(h) In Louisiana, if five or fewer political subdivisions of the state are affected, majority in state as a whole and also in each of affected subdivisions is required. In Maryland, if an amendent affects only the City of Baltimore or only one county, majority in state as a whole and also in affected subdivision is required.

(i) Two-thirds of both houses.

(j) Majority of members elected sitting in joint session.

(k) The two-thirds must include not less than a majority elected to each house.

(l) Three-fifths of all members of each house at one session, or majority of all members of each house for two successive sessions.

(m) If a proposed amendment is not approved at the election when submitted, neither the same amendment nor one which would make substantially the same change for the constitution may be again submitted to the people before the third general election thereafter.

(n) Amendments concerning certain elective franchise and education matters require three-fourths vote of members elected and approval by three-fourths of electors voting in state and two-thirds of those voting in each county.

(o) Majority vote to amend constitution, two-thirds to revise ("revise" includes all or a part of the constitution).

(p) Emergency amendments may be passed by two-thirds vote of each house, followed by ratification by majority vote of electors in election held at least one month after legislative approval.

(q) Two-thirds of members of each house, first passage; majority of members of each house after popular ratification.

(r) Majority of members elected to both houses, first passage; two-thirds of members elected to both houses, second passage.

(s) Majority of all citizens voting for governor.

(t) Two-thirds vote senate, majority vote house, first passage; majority both houses, second passage. As of 1974, amendments may be submitted only every four years.

(u) Within 30 days after voter approval, governor must submit amendment(s) to U.S. Secretary of the Interior for approval.

(v) If approved by two-thirds of members of each house, amendment(s) submitted to voters at special referendum; if approved by not less than three-fourths of total members of each house, referendum may be held at next general election.

(w) The legislature may, by a four-fifths vote in Nebraska or a two-thirds vote in Oklahoma, call a special election for voters to consider amendments.

(x) There is an exception for an amendment containing a supermajority voting requirement, which must be ratified by an equal supermajority.

Table 1.3
CONSTITUTIONAL AMENDMENT PROCEDURE: BY INITIATIVE
Constitutional Provisions

State or other jurisdiction	Number of signatures required on initiative petition	Distribution of signatures	Referendum vote
Arizona	15% of total votes cast for all candidates for governor at last election.	None specified.	Majority vote on amendment.
Arkansas	10% of voters for governor at last election.	Must include 5% of voters for governor in each of 15 counties.	Majority vote on amendment.
California	8% of total voters for all candidates for governor at last election.	None specified.	Majority vote on amendment.
Colorado	5% of total legal votes for all candidates for secretary of state at last general election.	None specified.	Majority vote on amendment.
Florida	8% of total votes cast in the state in the last election for presidential electors.	8% of total votes cast in each of 1/2 of the congressional districts.	Three-fifths vote on amendment except amendment for "new state tax or fee" not in effect Nov. 7, 1994 requires 2/3 of voters voting in election.
Illinois (a)	8% of total votes cast for candidates for governor at last election.	None specified.	Majority voting in election or 3/5 voting on amendment.
Massachusetts (b)	3% of total votes cast for governor at preceding biennial state election (not less than 25,000 qualified voters).	No more than 1/4 from any one county.	Majority vote on amendment which must be 30% of total ballots cast at election.
Michigan	10% of total voters for all candidates at last gubernatorial election.	None specified.	Majority vote on amendment.
Mississippi (c)	12% of total votes for all candidates for governor in last election.	No more than 20% from any one congressional district.	Majority vote on amendment and not less than 40% of total vote cast at election.
Missouri	8% of legal voters for all candidates for governor at last election.	The 8% must be in each of 2/3 of the congressional districts in the state.	Majority vote on amendment.
Montana	10% of qualified electors, the number of qualified voters to be determined by number of votes cast for governor in preceding election in each county and in the state.	The 10% to include at least 10% of qualified voters in 2/5 of the legislative districts. (d)	Majority vote on amendment.
Nebraska	10% of registered voters.	The 10% must include 5% in each of 2/5 of the counties.	Majority vote on amendment which must be at least 35% of total vote at the election.
Nevada	10% of voters who voted in entire state in last general election.	10% of voters in each of the state's congressional districts.	Majority vote on amendment in two consecutive general elections.
North Dakota	4% of population of the state.	None specified.	Majority vote on amendment.
Ohio	10% of total number of electors who voted for governor in last election.	At least 5% of qualified electors in each of 1/2 of counties in the state.	Majority vote on amendment.
Oklahoma	15% of votes cast at last general election for governor.	None specified.	Majority vote on amendment.
Oregon	8% of total votes for all candidates for governor at last election at which governor was elected for four-year term.	None specified.	Majority vote on amendment except for supermajority equal to supermajority voting requirement contained in proposed amendment.
South Dakota	10% of total votes for governor in last election.	None specified.	Majority vote on amendment.
No. Mariana Islands	50% of qualified voters of commonwealth.	In addition, 25% of qualified voters in each senatorial district.	Majority vote on amendment if legislature approved it by majority vote; if not, at least 2/3 vote in each of two senatorial districts in addition to a majority vote.

Source: John Dinan and The Council of State Governments.
Key:
(a) Initiatives can only be used to amend substantive or procedural aspects of Article IV, the Legislature Article, and cannot be used to amend any other articles.
(b) Before being submitted to the electorate for ratification, initiated measures must be approved at two sessions of a successively elected legislature by not less than one-fourth of all members elected, sitting in joint session.

(c) Before being submitted to the electorate, initiated measures are sent to the legislature, which has the option of submitting an amended or alternative measure alongside the original measure.
(d) A 2002 amendment changed this geographic-distribution rule to require at least 10% of voters in 1/2 of the counties. After this amendment was held unconstitutional by a federal district court in a 2005 ruling, the state attorney general advised that the prior rule—2/5 of legislative districts—was in effect.

Table 1.4
PROCEDURES FOR CALLING CONSTITUTIONAL CONVENTIONS
Constitutional Provisions

State or other jurisdiction	Provision for convention	Procedure for calling a convention by initiative	Legislative vote for submission of convention question (a)	Popular vote to authorize convention	Periodic submission of convention question required (b)	Popular vote required for ratification of convention proposals
Alabama	Yes	No	Majority	ME	No	Not specified
Alaska	Yes	No	No provision (c)(d)	(c)	10 years; 2012 (c)	Not specified (c)
Arizona	Yes	No	Majority	(e)	No	MP
Arkansas	No	No	No			
California	Yes	No	2/3	MP	No	MP
Colorado	Yes	No	2/3	MP	No	ME
Connecticut	Yes	No	2/3	MP	20 years; 2008 (f)	MP
Delaware	Yes	No	2/3	MP	No	No provision
Florida	Yes	Yes (m)	(g)	MP	No	3/5 voting on proposal
Georgia	Yes	No	(d)	No	No	MP
Hawaii	Yes	No	Not specified	MP	10 years; 2008	MP (h)
Idaho	Yes	No	2/3	MP	No	Not specified
Illinois	Yes	No	3/5	(i)	20 years; 2008	MP
Indiana	No	No	No			
Iowa	Yes	No	Majority	MP	10 years; 2010	MP
Kansas	Yes	No	2/3	MP	No	MP
Kentucky	Yes	No	Majority (j)	MP (k)	No	No provision
Louisiana	Yes	No	(d)	No	No	MP
Maine	Yes	No	(d)	No	No	No provision
Maryland	Yes	No	Majority	ME	20 years; 2010	MP
Massachusetts	No	No		No		
Michigan	Yes	No	Majority	MP	16 years; 2010	MP
Minnesota	Yes	No	2/3	ME	No	3/5 voting on proposal
Mississippi	No	No	No			
Missouri	Yes	No	Majority	MP	20 years; 2002	Not specified (l)
Montana	Yes	Yes (m)	2/3	MP	20 years; 2010	MP
Nebraska	Yes	No	3/5	MP (o)	No	MP
Nevada	Yes	No	2/3	ME	No	No provision
New Hampshire	Yes	No	Majority	MP	10 years; 2012	2/3 voting on proposal
New Jersey	No	No	No			
New Mexico	Yes	No	2/3	MP	No	Not specified
New York	Yes	No	Majority	MP	20 years; 1997	MP
North Carolina	Yes	No	2/3	MP	No	MP
North Dakota	No	Yes (m)	No			
Ohio	Yes	No	2/3	MP	20 years; 2012	MP
Oklahoma	Yes	No	Majority	(e)	20 years; 1970	MP
Oregon	Yes	No	Majority	(e)	No	No provision
Pennsylvania	No	No	No			
Rhode Island	Yes	No	Majority	MP	10 years; 2014	MP
South Carolina	Yes	No	(d)	ME	No	No provision
South Dakota	Yes	Yes (m)	(d)	No	No	(p)
Tennessee	Yes (q)	No	Majority	MP	No	MP
Texas	No	No	No			
Utah	Yes	No	2/3	ME	No	ME
Vermont	No	No	No			
Virginia	Yes	No	(d)	No	No	MP
Washington	Yes	No	2/3	ME	No	Not specified
West Virginia	Yes	No	Majority	MP	No	Not specified
Wisconsin	Yes	No	Majority	MP	No	No provision
Wyoming	Yes	No	2/3	ME	No	Not specified
American Samoa	Yes	No	(r)	No	No	ME (s)
No. Mariana Islands	Yes	Yes (t)	Majority	2/3	10 years	MP and at least 2/3 in each of 2 senatorial districts
Puerto Rico	Yes	No	2/3	MP	No	MP

See footnotes at end of table.

PROCEDURES FOR CALLING CONSTITUTIONAL CONVENTIONS — Continued
Constitutional Provisions

Source: John Dinan and The Council of State Governments.
Key:
MP — Majority voting on the proposal.
ME — Majority voting in the election.

(a) In all states not otherwise noted, the entries in this column refer to the proportion of members elected to each house required to submit to the electorate the question of calling a constitutional convention.

(b) The number listed is the interval between required submissions on the question of calling a constitutional convention; where given, the date is that of the most recent submission of the mandatory convention referendum.

(c) Unless provided otherwise by law, convention calls are to conform as nearly as possible to the act calling the 1955 convention, which provided for a legislative vote of a majority of members elected to each house and ratification by a majority vote on the proposals. The legislature may call a constitutional convention at any time.

(d) In these states, the legislature may call a convention without submitting the question to the people. The legislative vote required is two-thirds of the members elected to each house in Georgia, Louisiana, South Carolina and Virginia; two-thirds concurrent vote of both branches in Maine; three-fourths of all members of each house in South Dakota; and not specified in Alaska, but bills require majority vote of membership in each house.

(e) The law calling a convention must be approved by the people.

(f) The legislature shall submit the question 20 years after the last convention, or 20 years after the last vote on the question of calling a convention, whichever date is last.

(g) The power to call a convention is reserved to the people by petition.

(h) The majority must be 50 percent of the total votes cast at a general election or at a special election, a majority of the votes tallied which must be at least 30 percent of the total number of registered voters.

(i) Majority voting in the election, or three-fifths voting on the question.

(j) Must be approved during two legislative sessions.

(k) Majority must equal one-fourth of qualified voters at last general election.

(l) Majority of those voting on the proposal is assumed. Vote must take place at a special election held no less than 60 days and no more than 6 months after convention.

(m) In Montana, North Dakota and South Dakota, conventions can be called by initiative petition in the same manner as provided for initiated amendments (see Table 1.3), and with approval by a majority of voters. In Florida, conventions can be called by filing an initiative petition with signatures equal to 15 percent of the votes cast in the preceding presidential election and also equal to 15 percent of signatures in half of the congressional districts in the state and then obtaining a majority of the voters at the ensuing election.

(n) Two-thirds of all members of the legislature.

(o) Majority must be 35 percent of total votes cast at the election.

(p) Convention proposals are submitted to the electorate at a special election in a manner to be determined by the convention. Ratification by a majority of votes cast.

(q) Conventions may not be held more often than once in six years.

(r) Five years after effective date of constitutions, governor shall call a constitutional convention to consider changes proposed by a constitutional committee appointed by the governor. Delegates to the convention are to be elected by their county councils. A convention was held in 1972.

(s) If proposed amendments are approved by the voters, they must be submitted to the U.S. Secretary of the Interior for approval.

(t) The petition must be signed by 25 percent of the qualified voters or at least 75 percent in a senatorial district.

Chapter Two

FEDERALISM AND INTERGOVERNMENTAL RELATIONS

The Supreme Court and the States:
The Big Cases, Redistricting and Preemption

By Lisa Soronen

The U.S. Supreme Court will decide six big cases this term—five of them will directly impact the states. Redistricting and preemption cases are also popular with the court this term. The Supreme Court will decide four redistricting cases—including a "big" redistricting case—and four preemption cases. Justice Scalia's death is likely to impact the outcome of many of the cases important to the states.

Most U.S. Supreme Court terms have their fair share of significant cases and the court's 2015–2016 term is no exception. What is different about the big cases of this term is that there are more of them than usual. Also, this term's big cases are not as big as last term's big cases, specifically the same-sex marriage case and the Affordable Care Act—or ACA—case, which had it gone the other way might have meant the demise of the law. But what is no different about the big cases this term is that all but one of them, again involving the ACA, affect the states directly. This term the court will decide four redistricting cases. One of those cases is in the big cases category. Another noteworthy trend is that this term the Supreme Court has agreed to decide a number of preemption cases. Topics range from energy to health care claims data statutes. In the last few years the court's preemption docket has been very thin.

But the biggest difference of all this term is not the number of big cases important to the states it is, of course, the loss of Justice Scalia, who died in February. As any court-watcher knows, the Supreme Court often decides big cases 5-4. In cases where the court is now 4-4 it has two choices: affirm the lower court's decision in a non-precedential decision or wait for the new Justice to join the court and hold oral argument in the case again. Only time will tell which option the court picks in which cases.

The Big Cases

In *Reynold v. Sims* (1964) the court established the principle of "one-person, one-vote" requiring state legislative districts to be apportioned equally. The question in *Evenwel v. Abbott* is what population is relevant—total population or voter-eligible population. The maximum total-population deviation between Texas Senate districts was about 8 percent; the maximum eligible-voters deviation between dis-

tricts exceeded 40 percent. The unanimous opinion concluding Texas may redistrict using total population is "based on constitutional history, this Court's decisions, and longstanding practice." Section 2 of the 14th Amendment explicitly requires that the U.S. House of Representatives be apportioned based on total population. "It cannot be that the Fourteenth Amendment calls for the apportionment of congressional districts based on total population, but simultaneously prohibits States from apportioning their own legislative districts on the same basis." In no previous cases alleging a state or local government failed to comply with "one-person, one-vote" had the court determined if a deviation was permissible based on eligible- or registered-voter data. And states and local governments redistricting based on total population is a settled practice.

In *Friedrichs v. California Teachers Association* the court issued a non-precedential 4-4 opinion affirming by an equally divided court the lower court's decision to not overrule *Abood v. Detroit Board of Education* (1977). In *Abood* the Supreme Court held that the First Amendment does not prevent "agency shop" arrangements where public employees who do not join the union are still required to pay their "fair share" of union dues for collective-bargaining, contract administration, and grievance-adjustment. The rationale for an agency fee is that the union may not discriminate between members and nonmembers in performing these functions. So no free-riders are allowed. In two recent cases, *Knox v. SEIU* (2012) and *Harris v. Quinn* (2014), in 5-4 opinions written by Justice Alito and joined by the other conservative Justices (including Justice Scalia and Justice Kennedy), the court was very critical of *Abood*. The court heard oral argument in this case in January before Justice Scalia died, and the five more conservative Justices seemed poised to overrule *Abood*. Justice Scalia, who ultimately didn't participate in this case, likely would have voted to overrule *Abood*.

The issue in *Whole Women's Health v. Hellerstedt* is whether Texas' admitting privileges and ambulatory surgical center requirements create an undue burden on women seeking abortions and are reasonably related to advancing women's health. Texas claims, and the Fifth Circuit agreed, that women's health is advanced if doctors performing abortions have admitting privileges at a nearby hospital and if abortion clinics must comply with standards set for ambulatory surgical centers. Whole Women's Health argues that the Fifth Circuit erred in refusing to consider "whether and to what extent" Texas law actually serves its purported interest in achieving safer abortions. Whole Women's Health also argues that these requirements create an undue burden on those seeking abortions. Fewer than 10 of Texas' more than 40 abortion clinics will remain open and those that do will be inaccessible to many and will be unable to keep up with demand for abortions. The Fifth Circuit found no undue burden even though 17 percent of women of reproductive age would face travel distances of 150 miles or more to receive abortions.

For the second time the Supreme Court has agreed to decide whether the University of Texas at Austin's race-conscious admissions policy is unconstitutional in *Fisher v. University of Texas at Austin*. Per Texas' Top Ten Percent Plan, the top 10 percent of Texas high school graduates are automatically admitted to UT Austin, which fills about 80 percent of the class. Unless an applicant has an "exceptionally high Academic Index," he or she will be evaluated through a holistic review where race is one of a number of factors.

The court has held that the use of race in college admissions is constitutional if it is used to further the compelling government interest of diversity and is narrowly tailored. In the first hearing of the case, the court held that the Fifth Circuit, which upheld UT Austin's admissions policy, should not defer to UT Austin's argument that its use of race is narrowly tailored.

When the Fifth Circuit reviewed UT Austin's admissions policy it again concluded that it is narrowly tailored. The court determined that the Top Ten Percent Plan works well at increasing minority student enrollment because Texas schools are so segregated. But a number of well-qualified students are excluded—specifically minority students who performed well at majority-white schools but aren't in the top ten percent of their class. If race

wasn't considered during holistic review almost every student admitted would be white because of the test score gap between white and minority students. And as a result of holistic review, a much higher percent of white students are admitted, but generally between 25 and 30 percent of the overall number of black and Hispanic students are admitted through holistic review.

In *United States v. Texas* the Court will decide whether President Obama's deferred action immigration program violates federal law or is unconstitutional. The Deferred Action for Parents of Americans, or DAPA, program allows certain undocumented immigrants who have lived in the United States for five years and either came here as children or already have children who are U.S. citizens or permanent residents to lawfully stay and work temporarily in the United States.

The United States argues that the states lack "standing" to challenge the DAPA program. The Fifth Circuit concluded that the cost of issuing drivers licenses to DAPA program participants is a particular harm states will face, which provides the basis for standing.

States also challenged the DAPA program as violating the Administrative Procedures Act, or APA, notice-and-comment requirement and claim it is arbitrary and capricious in violation of the APA. The lower court concluded the states were likely to succeed on both claims because DAPA is a substantive rule and it is "foreclosed by Congress's careful plan" in the Immigration and Nationality Act.

The states also argue DAPA violates the Constitution's Take Care Clause because it is contrary to federal law; the president is failing to "take care" that federal law is followed.

Per the so-called "birth control mandate," the ACA has been interpreted to require employers to offer contraception coverage to women at no cost. The federal government has accommodated religious nonprofits that object to providing contraception by allowing them to complete a form objecting to the coverage. Their health insurance plan must then provide free access to contraception without the nonprofits' involvement.

The Religious Freedom Restoration Act, or RFRA, prohibits the federal government from substantially burdening a person's exercise of religion except to further a compelling interest in the least restrictive way. Religious nonprofits claim that this accommodation process makes them complicit in providing coverage to which they object and therefore substantially burdens their exercise of religion in violation of RFRA. They suggest the federal government could rely on a variety of less restrictive options to provide birth control that would not involve them at all. The court accepted seven cases, including *Zubik v. Burwell*, which the court's decision likely will be titled, involving the question of whether the birth control mandate violates RFRA. All the lower courts deciding this issue, except the Eighth Circuit, ruled in favor of the federal government.

Redistricting

In *Harris v. Arizona Independent Redistricting Commission*, the Arizona redistricting commission claims that it underpopulated some minority districts to strengthen minorities' ability to elect a candidate of their choice, so that the U.S. Department of Justice would be more likely to preclear its plan. The plaintiffs claim the commission underpopulated minority ability-to-elect districts to favor Democrats. The plaintiffs also argue that partisan gerrymandering can't justify deviating from one person, one vote and that violating one person, one vote to obtain preclearance under the Voting Rights Act, or VRA, wasn't a legitimate justification before or after the Supreme Court's 2013 decision in *Shelby County v. Holder*, holding the VRA's coverage formula unconstitutional. Two of the three judges found that the commission was *primarily* motivated by a desire to obtain preclearance. So it did not matter that the commission also was motivated by a desire to favor Democrats. A majority of the court concluded that trying to comply with the VRA could justify minor population deviations when protecting incumbent legislators can justify such deviations. A majority of the judges concluded *Shelby County* has no impact because it had not yet been decided when the map was drawn up in this case.

When the Virginia Legislature redrew congressional voting districts following the 2010 census it increased the number of minority voters in District 3, the state's only majority-minority district, from 53.1 to 56.3 percent. Plaintiffs argue in *Wittman v. Personhuballah* that the plan unconstitutionally packed minority voters into District 3, thus diluting their ability to influence races in other districts. The lower court ruled that the plan was unconstitutional, finding that race was the predominant consideration for the district. Per strict scrutiny, the lower court held that complying with the VRA is a compelling state interest, but increasing the minority population wasn't narrowly tailored as District 3 is a "safe" minority-majority district. The

Virginia legislators appealed claiming that the Supreme Court's 2001 decision in *Easley v. Cromartie* requires plaintiffs to "show a conflict between race and traditional principles, including politics, that the legislature resolved by redistricting in a way that sacrificed traditional principles to race," which plaintiffs did not and could not show in this case.

In *Shapiro v. McManus*, the Supreme Court held unanimously that a three-judge court must be convened to decide a constitutional challenge to a redistricting plan even if the judge to which the request was made doesn't think the challenger will win. Stephen Shapiro, dissatisfied with Maryland's "crazy-quilt gerrymandering," sued Maryland arguing its congressional redistricting plan violated his First Amendment right of political association. Per federal law, three judges "shall be convened" to hear challenges to the constitutionality of a congressional or statewide redistricting plan "unless [the judge whom the request for three judges is made] determines that three judges are not required." The Supreme Court reasoned that "the mandatory 'shall' … normally creates an obligation impervious to judicial discretion." The "unless [the judge whom the request for three judges is made] determines that three judges are not required" language means that the judge receiving the request for a three-judge court needs to examine the complaint to make sure it alleges a claim regarding whether a district is constitutionally apportioned, even if the claim doesn't seem particularly winnable.

Preemption Cases

In *Hughes v. PPL EnergyPlus* and *CPV Maryland v. PPL EnergyPlus*, the Maryland Public Service Commission offered the successful power plant development bidder a 20-year "contract for differences." The power plant would sell its capacity at the Federal Energy Regulatory Commission-regulated auction price. If the auction price was lower than its bid price, local utilities would make up the difference. If it was higher, the developer would rebate the utilities who would pass the cost recovery onto retail customers. Per the Federal Power Act, the Federal Energy Regulatory Commission, or FERC, has the authority to regulate interstate wholesale rates. FERC claims that Maryland's program amounts to rate-setting and is field and conflict preempted by the U.S. Constitution's Supremacy Clause. The Fourth Circuit concluded that Maryland's program is barred based on "field preemption" because it "effectively supplants the rate generated by the auction with an alternative rate preferred by the state."

It is conflict preempted because it disrupts FERC-controlled federal markets by setting the price the bidder receives for a substantial time period.

In an 8-2 decision in *FERC v. Electric Power Supply Association* the Supreme Court ruled that the Federal Energy Regulatory Commission (FERC) has the authority to regulate wholesale "demand response" and that demand response bidders may receive the same compensation as electricity producers. "Demand response" is a practice in which operators in wholesale markets pay electricity consumers to not use power at certain times. Per the Federal Power Act, FERC regulates wholesale rates of electricity but states regulate retail rates.

Electric Power Supply Association (EPSA) argued that through demand response FERC is "effectively" setting retail prices because when a consumer is deciding whether to buy electricity at retail the consumer will now consider both the cost of making the purchase *and* the cost of forgoing a demand response payment. The court disagreed stating that "the rate is what it is": "the price paid, not the price paid plus the cost of a foregone economic opportunity." No matter what they bid, successful demand response bidders receive the wholesale rate. EPSA argued that demand response bidders are receiving a "double-payment" and that they should only receive the wholesale price less the savings they net by not buying electricity on the retail market. FERC reasoned that demand response bidders should receive the same compensation as electricity generators because they are providing the same value. The court concluded that FERC's judgment wasn't "arbitrary and capricious" because regulating energy is technical and FERC provided reasons supporting its position and responded to EPSA's proposed alternative.

The Supreme Court held 6-2 in *Gobeille v. Liberty Mutual Insurance Company* that the Employee Retirement Income Security Act (ERISA) preempts Vermont's all-payers claims database (APCD) law. Seventeen other states collect health care claims data. ERISA preempts all state laws that "relate" to any employee benefits plan. Vermont's APCD law requires health insurers to report to the state information related to health care costs, prices, quality, and utilization, among other things. In an opinion written by Justice Kennedy the court concluded ERISA preempts Vermont's APCD law "to prevent States from imposing novel, inconsistent, and burdensome reporting requirements on plans." Justice Ginsburg, joined by Justice Sotomayor, dissented. She cited the State and Local Legal Center *amicus*

brief which, in her words, pointed out that APCD laws "serve compelling interests, including identification of reforms effective to drive down health care costs, evaluation of relative utility of different treatment options, and detection of instances of discrimination in the provision of care."

In *DIRECTV v. Imburgia* the Supreme Court held 6-3 that a California state court interpretation of California law that class action arbitration is unenforceable is preempted by the Federal Arbitration Act, or FAA. Two DIRECTV customers sued DIRECTV claiming its early termination fees violate California law. Their service agreement stated that all claims would be resolved by arbitration and that class arbitration would be prohibited. But, if the "law of your state" made waiver of class arbitration unenforceable, the entire arbitration provision was unenforceable. In 2008, when the DIRECTV customers sued DIRECTV, a 2005 California Supreme Court case, *Discover Bank v. Superior Court*, holding class-arbitration waivers unenforceable was good law. But in 2011 in *AT&T Mobility v. Concepcion*, the U.S. Supreme Court held that the FAA preempted and invalidated that ruling. The U.S. Supreme Court ruled that the FAA preempts the California Court of Appeals' interpretation of California law. While the Supreme Court agreed that parties could choose to have contracts governed by pre-*Concepcion* California law (or the law of Tibet or pre-revolutionary Russia), the ordinary meaning of "law of your state" is *valid* state law.

Conclusion

While not relevant to all states, this term's death penalty docket is also unusually large. But about half of the Supreme Court's death penalty cases raise issues not unique to capital punishment. Perhaps the most noteworthy case of the court's term though is the one not taken. The Supreme Court refused to hear a case holding that a city could ban assault weapons and large capacity magazines. It is just a matter of time until the court rules again on gun control. The Court's new Justice, whoever he or she may be, will have an influence on the death penalty, gun control, and many other issues of importance to the states.

About the Author

Lisa Soronen is the executive director of the State and Local Legal Center, or SLLC. In this role, Lisa files *amicus curiae* briefs to the United States Supreme Court on behalf of members of the Big Seven, including CSG, in cases affecting state and local government.

State-Federal Relations:
Lost on the Campaign Trail

By John Kincaid

Federalism is again a silent note in the presidential campaign, although some candidates advanced platforms or policies relevant to state-local relations. Despite partisan gridlock, Congress finally reauthorized the highway and education programs, with the latter increasing state and local discretionary authority, but regulatory enactments and Supreme Court diminutions of state powers continue apace. Legalized marijuana still experiences intergovernmental impediments; a revival of the Sagebrush Rebellion was a publicity failure; the federal government is poised to demand states' compliance with REAL ID while also encroaching upon state regulation of the operation of autonomous motor vehicles.

The federal government is the main driver of state-federal relations. In today's polarized political environment, the nature and direction of state-federal relations are shaped significantly by the federal government's partisan composition. Consequently, the future course of state-federal relations hinges on the outcomes of the 2016 presidential and congressional elections and on who replaces the late Justice Antonin Scalia on the U.S. Supreme Court.

The 2016 Election Campaign

The otherwise unusual 2016 presidential election campaign shares one normal trait with recent campaigns. Federalism and state-federal relations are non-issues. Some candidates have mentioned federalism or included a federalism plank in their platform, but no candidate as of early April 2016 championed federalism in stump speeches or debate appearances. Presidential candidates see little political capital in federalism and intergovernmental relations. Although Americans trust their local and state governments much more than they trust the federal government,[1] they do not translate their trust in state and local governments into demands for restoring more powers to those governments. Proposals to restore balance in the federal system and to reform state-federal relations bog down in details that ultimately bore most people.

On the Democratic side, neither Hillary Clinton nor Sen. Bernie Sanders gave attention to state-federal relations, although both support the authority of states to legalize marijuana. Some of Clinton's policy proposals, such as those concerning criminal justice, implicate state powers in positive and negative ways. For example, she advocates national guidelines for police uses of force and federal matching funds to buy body cameras for all police officers. She also would increase federal funding to states for preschool education and some other programs.

Although Sanders is a former mayor, as a Democratic Socialist, his policies would substantially increase federal fiscal and regulatory powers. "Sanders would centralize power in Washington," wrote columnist David Brooks.[2] By some estimates, his proposals would increase the fiscal size of the federal government by more than 50 percent. His proposal to make public universities tuition-free would significantly reduce states' control of their state universities. Also, unable to compete with tuition-free institutions, hundreds of private colleges would close their doors. Sanders did say, however: "States should have the right to regulate marijuana the same way that state and local laws now govern the sale of alcohol and tobacco. … It is time for the federal government to allow states to go forward as they best choose."

On the Republican side, Ben Carson, New Jersey Gov. Chris Christie and Sen. Marco Rubio were silent about federalism. Unlike most of his Republican competitors, Rubio did not even declare that the U.S. Supreme Court should have left decisions on same-sex marriage to the states. Christie proposed to cut off federal funds to sanctuary cities. Sen. Ted Cruz condemned "federal overreach" and defended the Tenth Amendment as leaving many matters, including gay marriage and marijuana legalization, to the states.

Donald Trump, who also advocated that same-sex marriage, as well as abortion policy, be decided by the states, did not highlight federalism on the campaign trail but proposed some significant federalism-relevant policies. Trump proposed to repeal the Affordable Care Act and allow the sale of health insurance across state lines. As long as a plan complies with state requirements, any vendor could offer insurance in any state. He also would block-grant Medicaid, sharply limit the state and local tax deduction from upper income taxpayers' federal income-tax liability, support states' rights to legalize marijuana, and defund sanctuary cities.

Governors Jeb Bush and John Kasich presented more developed federalism platforms. Bush vowed to increase state flexibility to manage federally funded programs such as child welfare, Medicaid, K–12 education and senior programs, but would hold states more accountable for results. Bush proposed to:

- Adhere strictly to the Constitution's limits on federal power by vetoing legislation exceeding federal authority and nominating judges who would vigorously enforce constitutional limits on federal authority.
- Nominate and appoint agency officials committed to federalism, mainly by appointing former state officials.
- Reform the regulatory process by repealing and, where necessary, replacing regulations to restore state powers.
- Enhance state enforcement of federal immigration policies by authorizing states to enforce laws that promote the goals of federal immigration law without allowing states to create their own immigration regimes.
- Promote state-driven labor and employment policies by ensuring that federal labor regulations do not unduly restrict state flexibility in responding to economic change.

Kasich, who is one of the few Republican governors to expand Medicaid under the Affordable Care Act, proposed five federalism planks:

- Return most of the federal gas tax to the states, increase state program flexibility and devote most the U.S. Department of Transportation's work to research on behalf of the states;
- Consolidate the more than 100 education programs into four large grants giving states more flexibility, reduce waivers by giving states more flexibility, and shrink the U.S. Department Education and refocus it on researching and sharing innovations that raise student achievement;
- Streamline job-training programs into several block grants, require states to focus on more useful outcome measures such as job placement and retention, and give states the ability to use existing federal training funds to help workers with jobs to upgrade their skills so as to stay employed;
- Allocate Medicaid funds to states on a per-member, per-month basis by eligibility category while allowing more flexibility around rate-setting and benefit design so as to avoid time-consuming waiver processes, and also increase the cost sharing of recipients above the poverty line and increase private-sector solutions; and
- Emphasize the case-work approach to tailoring benefits to specific low-income individuals in order to reduce dependence and remove federal obstacles to achieving positive outcomes.

Whoever is elected president is unlikely to make state-federal relations a high priority even though the 2015 lead-water crisis in Flint, Michigan, confirmed again that breakdowns in intergovernmental relations can have catastrophic consequences. Also, during this election year, Congress is unlikely to enact legislation having significant positive or negative impacts on state-federal relations. However, the Supreme Court will issue many important rulings affecting the balance of power in the federal system.

Two Congressional Achievements: Highways and Education

Surprisingly, Congress transcended partisan gridlock to enact two major intergovernmental program reauthorizations in 2015.

Congress approved a five-year, $305 billion highway bill—the Fixing America's Surface Transportation, or FAST, Act—in December. Not since 1998 had Congress passed such a long-term bill. Since 2005, there had been 35 extensions of the highway program, thus making state and local long-term planning nearly impossible. To help pay for the program, Congress took money from the Federal Reserve's "rainy day fund." Additional funds will come from reducing the amount of dividends the Federal Reserve pays to banks and from selling millions of barrels of oil from the Strategic Petroleum Reserve. Most experts agree that this is a terrible way to finance surface transportation, but Congress refuses to raise the 18.4 cent-per-gallon gas tax, which was last raised in 1993. There is, moreover, no grand vision like the one that motivated creation of the interstate highway system in 1956 under President Dwight D. Eisenhower.

In December 2015, Congress also passed the Every Student Succeeds Act, or ESSA—a major reauthorization of the Elementary and Secondary Education Act that replaces No Child Left Behind, also known as NCLB. Reauthorization should have occurred in 2007. ESSA provides more than $15 billion a year to states in formula funding and consolidates about 50 programs into a new $1.6 billion block grant but retains a maintenance-of-effort requirement, though with some flexibility. However, ESSA is authorized for only four years rather than five, thus opening the law to reauthorization under the next president.

ESSA was supported by many liberals and conservatives who believed that NCLB gave the federal government too much control over local education. ESSA restores some state and local discretionary authority but retains many federal requirements. States must still conform their standards to multiple federal statutes and gain approval from the U.S. secretary of education.

ESSA aims to achieve a 90 percent high school graduation rate by 2020. States and school districts must continue calculating four-year graduation rates the same way nationwide, and they must report data by gender, race, ethnicity, income, disability, English language learners, migrant status and homelessness. ESSA modifies rules governing periodic standardized testing, though schools must still test students in reading and math in grades 3-8 and once in high school. They also must administer science tests three times between grades 3 and 12. ESSA provides funds for schools to streamline and audit their testing programs and permits states to limit the amount of instructional time devoted to testing.

ESSA ends the federal requirement that teacher evaluations be tied to student performance on state tests, prohibits the U.S. Department of Education from telling states how to assess teacher and school performance, prohibits the federal government from mandating or giving states financial incentives to adopt particular academic standards such as Common Core, ends President Barack Obama's NCLB waivers, and enhances the Charter Schools Program while eliminating NCLB's Public School Choice program and free after-school tutoring.

ESSA requires states to go beyond test scores to determine school accountability by also considering such factors as school climate, teacher engagement and students' success in advanced coursework. States are required to intervene in the lowest performing 5 percent of schools. As such, states have more discretion over how they define school success and intervene in schools that do not demonstrate progress.

Proposed Legislation

Two bills being considered by Congress could have significant impacts on state and local governments.

One is the Voting Rights Act of 2015, which would apply the preclearance rule to every state.[3] The bill would subject any state to preclearance if a court finds that the state discriminated against voters because of race five or more times during the most recent 15 years. State officials would be required to notify the public within 48 hours of certain voting changes being made 180 days before a federal election, and local governments would need valid reasons to change voting locations or resources to be spent on an election. Passage this year seems unlikely.

A bill that could pass this year would overturn a 2014 regulation that deems state and local bonds to be of insufficient quality for banks to hold against the possibility of a financial collapse. State and local officials along with many banks are lobbying for the legislation because they believe the new rule will reduce bond buying by banks and increase borrowing costs for state and local governments. Banks are the biggest bond buyers and own about $500 billion of state and local securities. At the same time, President Obama's fiscal year 2017 budget proposed to cap the tax-free interest earned on state and local bonds for couples earning more than $250,000.

Facets of Fiscal Federalism

President Obama presented a $4.1 trillion budget to Congress for the 2017 fiscal year. The president's budget is usually dead on arrival in Congress, but for the first time in 40 years, the Republican chairs of the House and Senate budget committees refused to invite testimony from the president's budget director.

Federal aid to state and local governments will total about $667 billion in 2016, a 6.8 percent increase over 2015. Aid is expected to rise to about $694 billion in 2017, an increase of 4.1 percent. However, aid is not keeping up with inflation. Further, 73.9 percent of the aid in 2016 is for social welfare payments for individuals. Thus, the proportions of federal aid available for education, infrastructure, criminal justice, economic development and other non-welfare purposes continue to decline while states spend more on Medicaid and other mandatory social programs. In 2013, states spent 16.9 percent of all state own-source revenues on Medicaid compared to 12.2

percent in 2000. One reason for the increase was that Medicaid enrollment increased by 70 percent.[4]

Congress appears to be poised, however, to provide federal funds to states wishing to implement needle-exchange programs as one part of a spreading state and local campaign to stem the growing abuse of opiates, prescription drugs and other drugs nationwide.

The Pew Charitable Trusts estimated that federal spending in the states amounted to $3.3 trillion in 2014 and accounted for an average of 19 percent of state economic activity. The composition of this spending was 34 percent for retirement benefits, 28 percent for non-retirement benefits, 18 percent for grants, 11 percent for contracts, and 9 percent for salaries and wages.[5]

The Federal Funds Information for States advised states to try to increase their federal aid by ensuring that all residents get counted in the decennial census, identifying available grants and coordinating agency efforts to garner grants.

States are expected to spend more than $790 billion from their general funds in 2016, a 4.1 percent increase over 2015. Medicaid and education will account for about two-thirds of that spending. State revenues will be about $785 billion in 2016.

Many states could face tough economic times in 2016–17. By early 2016, Alaska, North Dakota, West Virginia and Wyoming were in recession. Louisiana, New Mexico and Oklahoma could also experience recession. Most vulnerable are states dependent on energy revenues and on manufacturers hurt by the rising dollar, as crude oil prices dropped by 72 percent from their June 2014 high. States that rely significantly on income-tax revenue from high-income residents might also experience shortfalls due to stock market volatility.

In an effort to increase revenues, Alabama and 12 other states are moving more aggressively to collect sales taxes on Internet purchases by their citizens. Alabama advanced the theory that if its residents buy more than $250,000 per year from an out-of-state business, then the seller has an "economic presence" in the state equivalent to that of a brick-and-mortar store. In January 2016, the National Conference of State Legislatures approved model legislation for states seeking to require collection and remittance of their state sales tax by remote sellers.[6] A federal appeals court upheld a Colorado law that requires out-of-state sellers that do not collect the state sales tax to send the state a list of their in-state customers. It is estimated that states lost $23.2 billion in revenue in 2012 from untaxed remote sales.[7]

The states lost a potential source of revenue in February 2016 when President Obama signed a permanent extension of the Internet Tax Freedom Act, first enacted in 1998. The law prohibits state and local governments from levying taxes on email and Internet access services.

Meanwhile, the U.S. Department of the Interior withdrew plans to allow off-shore oil and natural gas leasing between Georgia and Virginia—a decision that will cost jobs and revenue in those states as well as in North Carolina and South Carolina.

The Obama administration might seek to cut off aid to states such as Mississippi and North Carolina that pass laws granting citizens' rights to deny service to individuals requesting same-sex wedding ceremonies and related goods and laws prohibiting people from using public restrooms that do not match their birth sex. Some cities and states are boycotting such sister states by not allowing their employees to travel to them on public business. The Obama administration moved forcefully on rights of transgender people by issuing a directive to all public school systems in May 2016 that requires them to accommodate transgender students, including access to restrooms of the sex with which they identify.

Some congressional Republicans want to cut off federal funds to sanctuary cities and states that interfere with federal enforcement of immigration laws or decline to comply with U.S. Immigration and Customs Enforcement requests to detain illegal immigrants. The Obama administration also pushed back against sanctuary cities by directing the Federal Bureau of Prisons to transfer prisoners completing their sentences into immigration custody for deportation even if state or local officials who refuse to cooperate with Immigration and Customs Enforcement want the person for prosecution or incarceration.

There is continuing discussion, especially among congressional Republicans, about tax reforms that would eliminate the federal income-tax deduction for payments of state and local taxes. The deduction benefits mostly high-income people who itemize their deductions and blue states that are predominantly Democratic.[8] Many state and local officials support this deduction but might be compelled to choose during negotiations over a comprehensive tax reform between retaining that deduction or the deduction for interest earned on state and local bonds.

Another sign of unrest is that during the past several years, 27 states have passed resolutions calling for a constitutional convention to consider a balanced budget amendment. Republican presidential candidates Cruz, Kasich, and Rubio endorsed this campaign. There is a possibility that the necessary two-thirds of the states (34) will approve such resolutions by the end of this year. Constitutionally, this threshold would seem to require Congress to call a convention, but Congress will surely find a way not to do so.

Regulatory Federalism and Preemption

The Obama administration issued 82,036 pages of new and proposed regulations in the *Federal Register* in 2015 and will likely increase rulemaking as the president's tenure in office comes to a close.

The administration also has increased the use of letters of guidance, as is evident in the U.S. Department of Education's pressure on higher education institutions to enforce a "preponderance of the evidence" rule in cases arising under Title IX of the Education Amendments of 1972. While federal regulations must be issued according to the Administrative Procedure Act and must include time for "notice and comment," letters of guidance can be issued without notice and comment.

The U.S. Department of Justice issued a letter of guidance warning chief justices of state courts and their court administrators that excessive fines, arrests and imprisonment of poor people may violate the U.S. Constitution's civil rights provisions and, thus, trigger federal intervention.

This policy is closely related to the expansion of federal oversight of police departments, such as a February 2016 agreement providing federal oversight of the Miami, Florida, police force for the next four years. The 2014 police shooting of Michael Brown in Ferguson, Missouri; other police shootings of African Americans; and the rise of the Black Lives Matter movement have generated more calls for more federal oversight of local criminal justice systems.

The enactment of Vermont's genetically modified organisms, or GMO, labeling law—Act 120—due to take effect in July 2016, triggered considerable lobbying pressure on Congress to enact legislation called the Safe and Accurate Food Labeling Act of 2015, that would preempt such state labeling laws and establish standards for voluntary labeling nationwide. The principal partisan divide over the bill is that Democrats want mandatory labeling while Republicans want voluntary labeling. Meanwhile, the Grocery Manufacturers Association, along with three other trade associations, filed a lawsuit in federal court challenging the constitutionality of Vermont's law.

The federal Consumer Financial Protection Bureau, or CFPB, is expected to issue the first national rules for the $38.5 billion payday-lending industry. About 15 states have largely suppressed payday lending by placing caps on interest rates, but a few states such as Colorado regulate it and believe that their rules should be accommodated by the CFPB.

A provision in the proposed Aviation, Innovation, Reform and Reauthorization Act, which is supported by the American Trucking Association, would preempt laws in 20 states that limit truck drivers' hours, require truck drivers to be given paid meal breaks and require carriers that employ drivers to pay drivers "separate or additional compensation." This provision in the aviation bill would negate a 2014 ruling by the U.S. Court of Appeals for the 9th Circuit that carriers must comply with a California law that mandates paid meal and rest breaks for workers in the state.

A possible state-federal battle also may loom over regulation of self-driving vehicles. Although the federal government regulates car manufacturing, states regulate car operations. However, the U.S. Department of Transportation, wishing to develop operating rules, is seeking to craft a model state law governing autonomous vehicles. Some autonomous-vehicle makers such as Google dislike new state laws, including California's SB 1298, that require among other things a licensed driver to be at the wheel of a self-driving vehicle in order to correct a malfunction. Eventually, the industry will likely seek federal preemption of most or all state rules governing autonomous-vehicle operations.

Marijuana

The proliferation of state legalizations of medical and recreational marijuana continues to challenge the federal system.

Some members of Congress have responded by supporting a bill titled the Respect State Marijuana Laws Act introduced by Rep. Dana Rohrabacher (R-Calif.) in April 2015. The bill would make the federal ban on marijuana inapplicable in states that legalize the drug. Twenty-three states and the District of Columbia have legalized medical marijuana, and 13 others have legalized limited cannabis extracts for specific therapeutic use. Four states and D.C. have legalized recreational marijuana. Thus far, states that have legalized marijuana have relied on the U.S. attorney general's advice to federal prosecutors to refrain from targeting marijuana users and businesses acting legally under state laws.

Nonetheless, banking remains a significant problem for marijuana businesses because federal law prohibits banks from accepting marijuana money. Even though the federal government announced that it will not pursue financial institutions that accept legitimate marijuana money, most institutions do not wish to risk possible prosecution for inadvertently overlooking wrongdoing. The federal government will not allow states to create new financial institutions for marijuana businesses. Additionally, in 2015, the U.S. Postal Service warned newspapers that it is a crime to mail material containing marijuana advertising.

The REAL ID Hammer

REAL ID, enacted in 2005, continues to be a state-federal bone of contention reinforced by privacy advocates who object to the law's provisions governing secure driver's licenses. To date, only 22 states are compliant. Now, however, after years of enforcement postponement in deference to various states' fiscal and privacy concerns, the U.S. Department of Homeland Security appears ready to insist that the 28 non-compliant states comply with REAL ID's requirements by Oct. 1, 2020. Starting then, every traveler will need a REAL ID-compliant driver's license or other acceptable identity document such as a passport in order to board airplanes and trains, open a bank account, and engage in various other activities.

Sagebrush Rebellion Resurrection

The growth of population in Western states, especially in the mountain west, in recent decades has increased pressures on land use and economic development; yet the federal government retains ownership of huge amounts of land including, for example, 84.9 percent of Nevada's land area, 64.9 percent of Utah, 52.9 percent of Oregon and 48.1 percent of Wyoming. Furthermore, the Federal Land Policy and Management Act of 1976 declared that the remaining public domain lands would stay in federal ownership. This declaration of permanent federal ownership was a major trigger of the so-called Sagebrush Rebellion, a movement of Western citizens and local governments that began in the late 1970s to advocate state or local control over federal land and management decisions.

Bills have been introduced in Congress since 1932 to transfer ownership of various federal lands

to states. In March 2015, Sen. Lisa Murkowski (R-Alaska) sponsored yet another bill to sell, trade and transfer federal lands to states. Sen. Ted Cruz sponsored a bill in 2014 to prohibit the United States from owning more than 50 percent of a state's land area. These bills are unlikely to pass, but they reflect the unrest present in parts of the West.

A highly publicized occupation by disgruntled ranchers and other citizens of Malheur National Wildlife Refuge in Oregon in 2015 highlighted the land controversy but produced little public sympathy nationwide. The occupation began to wind down after its leader was arrested in late January 2016 and police killed one of the occupiers. Oregon Gov. Kate Brown sought federal reimbursements for the estimated $100,000 per week the state spent dealing with the occupation.

The American Lands Council, a private organization funded substantially by contributions from county governments, is seeking to require the federal government to hand over many federal lands to the states. Utah is so far the only state to pass a resolution insisting on such a land transfer. Some studies show that state takeovers of federal lands would increase costs for states. A study in Utah estimated a cost of $280 million after takeover but concluded that "from a strictly financial perspective, it is likely the state of Utah could take ownership of the lands and cover the costs to manage them."[9]

Supreme Court Rulings

The U.S. Supreme Court plays a major role in state-federal relations. The direction of federalism rulings may change, however, following the 2016 death of Justice Antonin Scalia, who was an important member of the court's conservative majority. The Republican Senate, hoping a Republican will capture the White House, has vowed not to confirm a new justice until after the presidential election. There are precedents on both sides. In 1852, the Democratic Senate ignored Whig President Millard Fillmore's nominee, and in 1868, the Republican Senate ignored President Andrew Johnson's nominee. Since 1900, the Senate has confirmed six justices during a president's last year in office, although five of those confirmations occurred when the president's party controlled the Senate. The exception was the confirmation of Justice Anthony Kennedy in February 1988, but this precedent is ambiguous because Kennedy had been nominated by President Ronald Reagan in November 1987 after the Democratic Senate had rejected his July 1987 nominee, Robert H. Bork, in a vicious confirmation process.

For now, the court is divided 4-4 between conservatives and liberals, although Justice Kennedy is an unreliable conservative. In the case of a tie vote, the justices can decide to hear the case again when a new justice joins them, or they can uphold the lower court's ruling without setting a nationwide rule. The justices often vote for re-argument when they expect a new justice to be appointed soon, but Scalia might not be replaced until 2017.

Interestingly, recent research suggests that laws enacted by more professionalized legislatures are more often struck down by the Supreme Court. The reason for this is unclear. Perhaps such legislatures push boundaries more often and also respond to citizen preferences in ways that test constitutional rules.[10]

Final Rulings

The Supreme Court issued a number of important rulings relevant to federalism during 2015 and early 2016.

Most momentous during the court's 2014–15 term was *Obergefell v. Hodges*, by which the 5-4 court struck down all state laws banning same-sex marriage or denying recognition to such marriages solemnized out of state. The majority held marriage to be a fundamental right and that same-sex marriage is protected by the Fourteenth Amendment's Due Process and Equal Protection clauses. In dissent, Chief Justice John Roberts declared: "Celebrate the availability of new benefits. But do not celebrate the Constitution. It had nothing to do with it." [11] However, the court has endorsed many rights not explicitly mentioned in the Constitution, such as rights to procreate, raise and retain custody of one's children, buy and use contraceptives, obtain an abortion, decline medical treatment, and engage in homosexual relations. Given that national public opinion had shifted in favor of gay marriage by 2015, the Supreme Court's ruling was not surprising.

In another important case in which the National Conference of State Legislatures filed an amicus brief asking the Supreme Court to affirm the constitutional role of state legislatures in redistricting, the 5-4 court held to the contrary that an independent commission does not violate the Constitution's elections clause. [12]

In a challenge to the way governments have drawn electoral districts for 50 years, the Supreme Court ruled unanimously that states can apportion legislative seats according to total population rather than only citizens or eligible voters.[13] The court had heard arguments in December 2015 in a case from Texas on the meaning of "one person, one vote," which the court has said requires political districts to be equal in population. The plaintiffs contended that counting total population discriminates against rural areas because city populations include many immigrants and children not eligible to vote. Texas contended that states have the constitutional authority not to use total population in apportioning legislative seats; the Obama administration argued that the Constitution requires states to use total population. The court decided not to settle the issue, thus leaving open the possibility for states to use different population bases, though these would likely be challenged in court. Some states already make adjustments, including Hawaii, which does not count students from out of state or military personnel registered to vote elsewhere.

The Supreme Court, however, gave states substantial leeway to control messages on automobile license plates by ruling that Texas could refuse to issue a license plate displaying the Confederate battle flag. The justices opined that license plates are government speech.[14] The court, by a 5-4 vote, also upheld a Florida law prohibiting candidates for elected judicial seats from soliciting or receiving funds personally.[15]

In *King v. Burwell*, the Supreme Court upheld, in a 6-3 decision, federal tax credits for health-insurance purchasers on exchanges established by the federal government in states that do not establish an exchange. At issue was whether the credits were limited by the Affordable Care Act to enrollments "through an Exchange established by the State under Section 1311." Writing for the majority, Chief Justice Roberts opined: "Congress passed the Affordable Care Act to improve health insurance markets, not to destroy them. If at all possible, we must interpret the Act in a way that is consistent with the former, and avoids the latter."[16]

In the field of criminal justice, the Supreme Court ruled 5-4 that Oklahoma's use of midazolam, a sedative, as its first lethal-injection drug does not violate the cruel-and-unusual-punishment provision of the Eighth Amendment.[17] In *Rodriguez v. United States*,[18] however, the court ruled that a police officer cannot prolong a traffic stop for a canine sniff without reasonable cause.

Local governments were affected especially by two rulings. In one, the court struck down an ordinance that imposed more size and duration restrictions on church-event signs than on ideological and political signs.[19] In *City of Los Angeles v. Patel*,[20] the court declared unconstitutional a city ordinance that required hotels to record and retain specific guest information onsite for 90 days and to show those records to any police officer on demand.

The Supreme Court again upheld, by a 5-4 decision, disparate-impact claims under the Fair Housing Act of 1968. This law includes a provision allowing claims not only for intentional discrimination but also for practices having a discriminatory effect, even if they were not prompted by an intent to discriminate.[21]

Overall, the 2014–15 term was a good one for the Supreme Court's liberals. They voted together on most cases and attracted support from Justice Kennedy in eight of 13 5-4 cases and also Justice Roberts in *King v. Burwell*.

In December 2015, by a 6-3 vote, the Supreme Court reversed a California Court of Appeal decision that *DirecTV* consumers were not bound by an arbitration provision requiring individual arbitration. The Federal Arbitration Act preempts California's treatment of the *DirecTV* case, and the California Court was bound by the mandate in *AT&T Mobility LLC v. Concepcion* (2011). "Lower court judges are certainly free to note their disagreement with a decision of this Court," opined Justice Stephen Breyer for the majority, "but the 'supremacy Clause forbids state courts to dissociate themselves from federal law because of disagreement with its content or a refusal to recognize the superior authority of its source.'"[22]

In December 2015, the Supreme Court also upheld an ordinance enacted by Highland Park, Illinois, that bans semiautomatic weapons and high-capacity magazines.[23] This could be an important precedent allowing state and local governments more leeway to regulate firearms in the aftermath of *McDonald v. City of Chicago* (2010), which held that the U.S. Second Amendment applies to the states and that state and local governments cannot, therefore, infringe upon the fundamental constitutional right to "keep and bear arms." However, in March 2016, the court unanimously struck down state laws and local ordinances that prohibit citizens from carrying stun guns.[24]

In January 2016, the court ruled 6-3 that juveniles sentenced to life in prison without parole can seek parole.[25] About 2,500 such inmates might now seek parole. The court also held that the Sixth Amendment requires a jury rather than a judge to determine the aggravating facts needed to impose the death penalty.[26]

The Supreme Court held by 6-2 in January 2016 that the Federal Power Act allows the Federal Energy Regulatory Commission to regulate wholesale market operators' compensation of demand-response bids despite state arguments that such regulations encroach upon state authority.[27]

In February 2016, the court, by a 5-4 vote, halted President Obama's ambitious climate change initiative by temporarily blocking an Environmental Protection Agency rule, known as the Clean Power Plan, that would require states to reduce carbon emissions from coal-fired power plants by 32 percent by 2030 from a 2005 baseline.[28] The rule required states to submit compliance plans by September 2016 unless they requested a two-year extension. The rule was challenged by 27 states and many industry groups. In March, however, the court rejected a plea from 21 states to block the U.S. Environmental Protection Agency's rule limiting emissions of mercury and other pollutants from coal-fired power plants.[29]

In March 2016, the court unanimously remanded to the lower court a case in which national park officers prohibited a moose hunter from operating a hovercraft on a state river within a national preserve in Alaska. The lower court, opined the justices, must weigh the "vital issues of state sovereignty, on the one hand, and federal authority, on the other."[30]

In another March decision, the Supreme Court held unanimously that states must recognize adoptions by same-sex parents who move from one state to another.[31]

The Supreme Court ruled 5-3 in a Medicare fraud case that seizing "untainted" assets needed to retain a defendant's chosen counsel violates the Sixth Amendment.[32] This ruling will also constrain state asset freezing and forfeiture practices. Additionally, the U.S. Department of Justice announced in December 2015 that it will no longer make "equitable sharing payments" that share assets seized from private citizens with state and local law enforcers.

By a 6-2 vote, the court declined to hear a suit brought by Nebraska and Oklahoma arguing that Colorado's legalization of marijuana violates federal law and increases drug crimes in their states. If Colorado were an entity south of the U.S. border, plaintiffs argued, the federal government would prosecute it as a drug cartel.

In March 2016, the U.S. Supreme Court struck down efforts by 18 states to track the cost and quality of health care by requiring that every health-care claim involving their residents be submitted to a statewide database. The court held, 6-2, that the Employee Retirement Income Security Act of 1974 preempts such state laws with respect to self-funded insurance plans.[33]

The Supreme Court split 4-4 over a lawsuit on whether public-sector labor unions can collect fees from government workers who choose not to join the union.[34] The case affected more than five million workers in 23 states and Washington, D.C., and sought to overturn a nearly 40-year-old Supreme Court precedent. This case would surely have gone against the unions if Scalia was still alive, but the even split let stand the lower court ruling that unions can collect such fees.

The court ruled by 6-2 that the First Amendment prohibits a government from demoting a public employee based on a supervisor's perception that the employee supported a political candidate. The employee is entitled to challenge such a demotion as being unlawful. The State and Local Legal Center filed an *amicus* brief urging the court not to find that a constitutional claim exists when an employer misperceives that an employee has engaged in political speech.[35]

Despite Scalia's death and the justices' 4-4 conservative-liberal split, the U.S. Supreme Court has been remarkably busy ruling on cases relevant to the balance of power between the states and the federal government. As of mid-April 2016, more than half of the relevant cases decided since Scalia's death preempted or otherwise altered state or local government laws or policies.

Pending Cases

A number of important cases were pending in early 2016.

For one, the Obama administration's plan to shield up to five million people from deportation was struck down by lower courts. A Supreme Court tie would leave that ruling in place.[36] The 26 states that sued to overturn the president's deportation policy argued that while the president has authority to adjust enforcement of immigration for individuals, he lacks authority to change the legal status of entire classes of illegal immigrants.

In a major abortion-rights case, the administration is backing a challenge to Texas' strict new regulations for abortion clinics.[37] A federal appeals court upheld the regulations. Thus, a tie would sustain the regulations.

The Supreme Court will decide whether a state must respect another state's sovereign immunity to the same extent as its own and whether it should overrule *Nevada v. Hall* (1979), which permits a sovereign state to be sued in the courts of another state without its consent.[38] The court also will decide whether Puerto Rico is a sovereign state with powers that go beyond its status as a U.S. territory.[39]

To be decided, as well, is whether, in the absence of a warrant, a state can criminalize a person's refusal to take a chemical test to detect alcohol in the person's blood.[40]

The Supreme Court also will decide if the Federal Power Act field-preempts a state order requiring retail utilities to enter into a contract to generate and sell wholesale power on a fixed-rate basis and whether the Federal Energy Regulatory Commission's acceptance of an annual regional-capacity auction preempts states from requiring retail utilities to enter fixed-rate contracts with sellers willing to sell in the auction on a long-term basis.[41]

Finally, the Supreme Court faces a major affirmative action case involving public universities' admission policies.[42] This case first reached the court in 2013 when it ruled that the use of race in admissions decisions must be framed narrowly to advance compelling government interests. Also, courts must examine evidence and not rely on schools' reports. The Supreme Court then remanded the case to the lower court to examine the evidence, but the result did not satisfy the Supreme Court majority. Justice Elena Kagan recused herself from the case, which means there could be a 4-3 vote to overturn affirmative action.

Conclusion

The absence of federalism on the campaign trail is consistent with the post-1980 recession of federalism as a principle from the political arena. Although state-federal relations remain the vital sinews of the operation of the American federal system of government, intergovernmental relations remain invisible to voters and often misunderstood by elected officials. Consequently, changes in state-federal relations take place in a piecemeal partisan fashion unguided by any principle of federalism, and the Supreme Court will be the main federal actor in state-federal relations until a new Congress and president are installed in January 2017. The Democratic-Republican polarization of most of the states themselves contributes to centralization trends because states cannot unite around a coherent vision of state-federal relations.

Notes

[1] Justin McCarthy, "Americans Still Trust Local Government More Than State," Gallup Poll, 22 September 2014, http://www.gallup.com/poll/176846/americans-trust-local-government-state.aspx, accessed 7 January 2016.

[2]"Livin' the Danish Dream," *New York Times*, February 12, 2016, A27.

[3]Preclearance is the administrative procedure required by the Voting Rights Act whereby states and local governments covered by the act must submit all changes affecting voting and elections for preapproval by the U.S. Department of Justice's Civil Rights Division or the U.S. District Court for the District of Columbia.

[4]The Pew Charitable Trusts, "Medicaid Consumes Growing Slice of States' Dollars," April 22, 2015, *http://www.pewtrusts.org/en/research-and-analysis/analysis/2015/04/medicaid-consumes-growing-slice-of-states-dollars, accessed April 30, 2015*.

[5]The Pew Charitable Trusts, "Where Federal Money Is Spent in States," *http://www.pewtrusts.org/en/research-and-analysis/issue-briefs/2016/03/federal-spending-in-the-states-2005-to-2014*

[6]*http://www.ncsl.org/Documents/fiscal/2016_Sales-Use_Tax%20Nexus_.pdf*

[7]Richard Rubin, "States Set Up Fight Over Web Sales Tax," Wall Street Journal, February 24, 2016, A3.

[8]Richard Rubin, "Tax Break Under GOP Fire," Wall Street Journal, January 30-31, 2016, p. A5.

[9]Stambro, Jan Elise, John C. Downen, Michael T. Hogue, Levi Pace, Paul M. Jakus, and Therese C. Grijalva, *An Analysis of a Transfer of Federal Lands to the State of Utah* (Salt Lake City: Bureau of Economic and Business Research, University of Utah, November 2014), p. xxvi.

[10]Susan M. Miller, Eve M. Ringsmuth, and Joshua M. Little, "Pushing Constitutional Limits in the U.S. States: Legislative Professionalism and Judicial Review of State Laws by the U.S. Supreme Court," State Politics & Policy Quarterly 15 (4): 476-491.

[11]576 U.S. ___ (2015), Docket No. 14-556.

[12]*Arizona State Legislature v. Arizona Independent Redistricting Commission*, 576 U.S. ___ (2015), Docket No. 13-1314.

[13]*Evenwel v. Abbott*, 576 U.S. ___ (2016), Docket No. 14-940.

[14]*Walker v. Texas Division, Sons of Confederate Veterans*, 576 U.S. ___ (2015), Docket No. 14-144.

[15]*Williams-Yulee v. Florida State Bar*, 575 U.S. ___ (2015), Docket No. 13-1499.

[16]576 U.S. ___ (2015), Docket No. 14-114.

[17]*Glossip v. Gross*, 576 U.S. ___ (2015), Docket No. 14-7955.

[18]575 U.S. ___ (2015), Docket No. 13-9972.

[19]*Reed v. Town of Gilbert*, 576 U.S. ___ (2015), Docket No. 13-502.

[20]135 S. Ct. (2015).

[21]*Texas Department of Housing and Community Affairs v. The Inclusive Communities Project, Inc.*, 576 U.S. ___ (2015), Docket No. 13-1371.

[22]*DirecTV, Inc. v. Imburgia* 576 U.S. ___ 2015), Docket No. 14-462.

[23]Adam Liptak, "Sign of Tacit Approval as Justices Turn Away Challenge to a Local Effort to Regulate Guns," *New York Times*, December 8, 2015, p. A19.

[24]*Jaime Caetano v. Massachusetts*, 576 U.S. ___ (2016), Docket No. 14-10078.

[25]*Montgomery v. Louisiana*, 576 U.S. ___ (2016), Docket No. 14-280.

[26]*Hurst v. Florida*, 577 U.S. ___(2016), Docket No. 14-7505.

[27]*Federal Energy Regulatory Commission v. Electric Power Supply Association*, U.S. 577 ___ (2016), Docket No. 14-840.

[28]Adam Liptak and Coral Davenport, "Justices Deal Blow to Obama Effort on Emissions," *New York Times*, February 10, 2016, A1 and A12.

[29]Adam Liptak and Coral Davenport, "Effort to Block Rule Set By the E.P.A. Is Rejected," *New York Times*, March 4, 2016, p. A11.

[30]*Sturgeon v. Frost*, 576 U.S. ___ (2016), Docket No. 14-1209.

[31]*V. L. v. E. L.*, 577 U.S. ___ (2016), Docket No. 15-648.

[32]*Luis v. United States*, 578 U.S. ___ (2016), Docket No. 14-419.

[33]*Gobeille v. Liberty Mutual Insurance Co.*, 576 U.S. ___ (2016), Docket No. 14-181.

[34]*Friedrichs v. California Teachers Association*, 578 U.S. ___ (2016), Docket No. 14-915.

[35]*Heffernan v. City of Paterson, New Jersey*, 578 U.S. ___ (2016), Docket No. 14-1280.

[36]*United States v. Texas*, Docket No. 15-674.

[37]*Whole Woman's Health v. Hellerstedt*, Docket No. 15-274

[38]*Franchise Tax Board of California v. Hyatt*, 578 U.S. ___ (2016), Docket No. 14-1175.

[39]577 U.S. ___ (2016), Docket No. 15-108.

[40]*Birchfield v. North Dakota*, 578 U.S. ___ (2016), Docket No. 14-1468.

[41]*Hughes v. Talen Energy Marketing*, 578 U.S. ___ (2016), Docket No. 14-614.

[42]*Fisher v. University of Texas at Austin*, Docket No. 14-981.

About the Author

John Kincaid is the Robert B. and Helen S. Meyner Professor of Government and Public Service and director of the Meyner Center for the Study of State and Local Government, Lafayette College, Easton, Pennsylvania. He is former editor of *Publius: The Journal of Federalism*; former executive director of the U.S. Advisory Commission on Intergovernmental Relations; co-editor of *Constitutional Origins, Structure, and Change in Federal Countries* (2005), *Interaction in Federal Systems* (2008), and *Local Government in Federal Systems* (2008), editor of *Federalism* (4 vols. 2011), and co-editor of the *Routledge Handbook of Regionalism and Federalism* (2013), *Intergovernmental Relations in Federal Systems: Comparative Structures and Dynamics* (2015), and *Political Parties and Civil Society in Federal Countries* (2015).

Trends in Interstate Relations

By Joseph F. Zimmerman

This article reviews developments in interstate relations pertaining to uniform state laws, interstate compacts and administrative agreements, civil union and same-sex marriage, and other pertinent interstate legal matters since 2014.

The U.S. Constitution contains five exceptionally important interstate provisions: full faith and credit, interstate commerce, intestate compacts, privileges and immunities, and rendition that are designed to make more perfect the economic union and the political union of the states. The Constitution is silent relative to the considerably larger number of interstate administrative agreements entered into by state government officers with their counterparts in sister states. Many of these agreements are of great importance.

Uniform State Laws

A federal system contains features that are improvements when compared to a unitary system, but the federal system also has disadvantages, including non-uniform state laws. The sharp growth in population and economic activity subsequent to the Civil War resulted in a proliferation of undesirable disparate laws on the same subject in states. State government officers reacted to the problem by organizing in 1892 the National Conference on Uniform State Law Commissioners to draft harmonized bills for enactment by state legislatures. Commissioners were appointed by each of the fifty states, the District of Columbia, Puerto Rico and the U.S. Virgin Islands.

Congress recognized the problems with the diversity of state laws and initiated several actions to encourage states to enter into interstate compacts and uniform state laws. To encourage states to negotiate and to enter into particular interstate compacts, Congress in 1911 initiated the practice of granting consent to specific compacts prior to their drafting. Compacts, except boundary and study commission compacts, establish a uniform state law within their respective jurisdictions and, in effect, establish a limited type of federation within the larger United States federation. Congress also has used financial incentives to encourage the adoption of more uniform laws across the states. For instance, Congress in 1974 used a cross-over sanction to encourage state legislatures to lower the maximum speed limit to 55 miles per hour to conserve gasoline and diesel fuel by stipulating a state without such a speed limit would lose 10 percent of its federal highway grants.

Hundreds of uniform laws have been drafted relating to a wide variety of subjects, with many laws enacted by only a small number of state legislatures and other laws enacted by all state legislatures after several decades. Most proposed uniform laws are private laws, based upon the English common law governing legal relationships between private individuals. In general, Midwestern and Northwestern states have the greatest propensity to enact uniform state laws, and Southern states have the least propensity to enact such laws. Recent uniform laws include the Child Custody Jurisdiction and Enforcement Act of 2013, Athlete Agents Act of 2015, and the revision in 2015 of the Fiduciary Access to Digital Assets Act. Arkansas in 2015 enacted the Uniform Partition of Heirs Property Act.

The Council of State Governments' Suggested State Legislation Committee included three uniform acts and one amended uniform act in its 2016 volume of *Suggested State Legislation*: (1) Uniform Act on the Prevention of and Remedies for Human Trafficking Act, (2) Uniform Recognition of Substitute Decision-Making Document Act, (3) Uniform Collateral Consequences of Convictions Act, and (4) amendments to the Uniform Variable Transaction Act.

Interstate Compacts and Cooperation

Based on favorable experience with intercolony compacts, the Articles of Confederation and Perpetual Union, effective in 1781, authorized states to enter into interstate compacts with the consent of Congress. A generally similar provision is included in the U.S. Constitution (art. 1, §10). There are a total of 215 active interstate compacts in the United States.

Section 10 of Article I of the U.S. Constitution grants authority to states to enter into compacts with each other provided Congress grants its consent. The U.S. Supreme Court, however, in *Virginia v.*

Tennessee in 1893 (148 U.S. 503 at 520) opined the required consent applies only to compacts encroaching upon the powers of Congress. The reader should note the Insurance Product Regulation Compact of 2004 did not need the consent of Congress to become effective because the McCarran-Ferguson Act of 1945 granted authority to the states to regulate the business of insurance and exempted the states from the national antitrust laws.

The great potential of interstate compacts to solve multistate problems was not recognized until 1921, as compacts were utilized only to settle boundary disputes between states. The New Jersey and New York state legislatures in 1921 enacted a most important compact establishing the Port Authority of New York Commission, the first use of a compact other than to solve boundary disputes between states. Subsequently, interstate compacts were developed to solve a wide variety of interstate problems. In 2004, The Council of State Governments established the National Center for Interstate Compacts to assist state governments in drafting interstate compacts.

In 2014, the Maine and New Hampshire departments of transportation reached an agreement on the replacement of the Sarah Mildred Long Bridge in Kittery, Maine, at an estimated cost of $158.5 million. The bridge, built in 1940 by agreement of the Maine-New Hampshire Interstate Bridge Authority is the second most important bridge in Maine. The new bridge will have wider shoulders for bicyclists and will improve marine navigation by straightening the navigational channel and allow larger ships to access the port and shipyard. The bridge, which began construction in the winter of 2015, is estimated to cost $158.5 million dollars and is expected to be completed in September of 2017.

U.S. Sen. Charles E. Schumer of New York in 2014 announced proposals that, if enacted by Congress, would reduce the influence of the governors of New Jersey and New York over the Port Authority of New York and New Jersey. The New Jersey governor by tradition selects the chairman of the board of directors and the New York governor selects the executive director. Sen. Schumer proposed the executive director of the authority should be chosen by the agency's board of commissioners. No action was taken on the proposal. A board of directors committee in 2014 invited a group of experts to offer suggestions to change the authority. Most of the invitees agreed the power of the governors of the two states over the authority should be reduced.

The Western Basin of Lake Erie Collaborative Agreement, signed in June of 2015, is an agreement between the states of Michigan and Ohio as well as the government of Ontario. The agreement was created to reduce phosphorus in the western Lake Erie basin by 40 percent by 2025. Excess phosphorus can result in the growth of algae blooms, including toxic strains, that disrupt the water supply to approximately 400,000 persons in southeast Michigan and the Toledo metropolitan area. The Ohio Legislature enacted a law prohibiting the spread of manure and other fertilizers on frozen ground because it frequently flows from farmers' fields into lake tributaries during rain storms and thaws.

Gov. Peter Shumlin of Vermont on March 23, 2015, announced the renewal for the seventh time of an historic agreement between his state, New York and Québec to enhance and preserve the Lake Champlain watershed. The cooperative agreement dates back to 1988. A memorandum of understanding provides for the sharing of research on water quality, protecting natural and cultural resources, reducing polluted storm water runoff and blue-green algae blooms, and protecting against invasive aquatic species.

In 2015, the Association of State and Provincial Psychology Boards released the draft of an interstate compact that would allow psychologists to practice their profession by telephone over state lines. The association formed a partnership with The Council of State Governments' National Center for Interstate Compacts to draft model language for a compact to be introduced in state legislatures in 2016. An estimated 42 million persons, 18 percent of the adult population in the United States, are in areas with a shortage of mental health service providers.

The U.S. Supreme Court resolved a dispute in 2015 involving water rights under an interstate compact entered into by Colorado, Kansas and Nebraska in 1943. Kansas had filed an original action in the Supreme Court maintaining Nebraska exceeded by a substantial margin its allocation of water in 2005 to 2006. Nebraska responded by maintaining the accounting procedures needed to be modified as the state was being charged improperly for importing water originating in the Platte River basin.

As customary, the Supreme Court appointed a special master who examined the issue and recommended a $1.8 million disgorgement. According to the special master's recommendation, Nebraska failed to comply with the compact by knowingly exposing Kansas to a substantial risk it would breach the contract since water is more valuable to Nebraska farmland than to Kansas farmland. The court found Nebraska failed to initiate many actions to stay within the allotment, including not amending the state's water law for one and a half years. The court, based upon a restatement of law, rejected Nebraska's argument holding disgorgement only may be ordered for an intentional breach of a compact. The Supreme Court acknowledged it did not know precisely how the master arrived at the $1.8 million figure, and added "what matters is that the Master took into account the appropriate considerations—weighing Nebraska's incentives, past behavior, and more recent compliance efforts—in determining the kind of signal necessary to prevent another breach." The court agreed the master was correct in holding an injunction against Nebraska was unnecessary in view of the fact Nebraska subsequently put in place compliance measures that are "up to the task" of complying with the compact.

Interstate Agreement to Elect the President by National Popular Vote

This proposed agreement is an innovative interstate compact based on Section 10 of Article I of the U.S. Constitution authorizing states to enter into interstate agreements or compacts and Section 1 of Article II of the U.S. Constitution directing state legislatures to appoint presidential-vice presidential electors. Congressional consent is not required for the proposed agreement since its activation would not encroach upon the powers of the federal government. The agreement has been enacted by states with a total of 166 electoral votes, 61 percent of the 270 electoral voters necessary to activate the agreement.

Same Sex Marriage

The question whether same-sex couples should be allowed to marry has been controversial for decades. The U.S. Supreme Court in 2015, by a 5 to 4 vote, held same-sex marriage is a constitutional right throughout the nation. Justice Anthony M. Kennedy opined: "No longer may this liberty be denied" and added: "No union is more profound than marriage for it embodies the highest ideals of love, fidelity, devotion, sacrifice, and family. In forming a marital union, two people become something greater than once they were." The four liberal justices endorsed Kennedy's opinion. Each conservative justice filed a separate dissent. Chief Justice John G. Roberts Jr. issued an opinion holding the U.S. Constitution is silent on the subject.

The North Carolina Legislature in 2015 overrode a veto by Gov. Pat McCrory and enacted a law allowing specified county officers to avoid same-sex marriage duties if they invoke a "sincerely held religious objection." The law authorizes magistrates to recuse themselves from performing all marriages and assistant and deputy registers of deeds can opt out of issuing marriage licenses. Each recusal must be in effect for at least six months.

Summary and Conclusion

Uniform state laws continue to play a role in harmonizing the laws enacted by the fifty state legislatures, and are supplemented by interstate compacts and administrative agreements. State legislators are aware their failure to harmonize laws on certain subjects may generate pressure in Congress to enact uniform laws.

About the Author

Joseph F. Zimmerman is a professor of political science at Rockefeller College of the State University of New York at Albany. He is the author of more than seventy books and numerous articles.

Table 2.1
SUMMARY OF STATE INTERGOVERNMENTAL EXPENDITURES: 1944–2013
(In thousands of dollars)

Fiscal year	Total	To Federal government (a)	To local governments Total	For general local government support	For specified purposes Education	Public welfare	Highways	Health	Miscellaneous and combined
1944	$1,842,000	…	$1,842,000	$274,000	$861,000	$368,000	$298,000	…	$41,000
1946	2,092,000	…	2,092,000	357,000	953,000	376,000	339,000	…	67,000
1948	3,283,000	…	3,283,000	428,000	1,554,000	648,000	507,000	…	146,000
1950	4,217,000	…	4,217,000	482,000	2,054,000	792,000	610,000	…	279,000
1952	5,044,000	…	5,044,000	549,000	2,523,000	976,000	728,000	…	268,000
1953	5,384,000	…	5,384,000	592,000	2,737,000	981,000	803,000	…	271,000
1954	5,679,000	…	5,679,000	600,000	2,930,000	1,004,000	871,000	…	274,000
1955	5,986,000	…	5,986,000	591,000	3,150,000	1,046,000	911,000	…	288,000
1956	6,538,000	…	6,538,000	631,000	3,541,000	1,069,000	984,000	…	313,000
1957	7,440,000	…	7,440,000	668,000	4,212,000	1,136,000	1,082,000	…	342,000
1958	8,089,000	…	8,089,000	687,000	4,598,000	1,247,000	1,167,000	…	390,000
1959	8,689,000	…	8,689,000	725,000	4,957,000	1,409,000	1,207,000	…	391,000
1960	9,443,000	…	9,443,000	806,000	5,461,000	1,483,000	1,247,000	…	446,000
1962	10,906,000	…	10,906,000	839,000	6,474,000	1,777,000	1,327,000	…	489,000
1963	11,885,000	…	11,885,000	1,012,000	6,993,000	1,919,000	1,416,000	…	545,000
1964	12,968,000	…	12,968,000	1,053,000	7,664,000	2,108,000	1,524,000	…	619,000
1965	14,174,000	…	14,174,000	1,102,000	8,351,000	2,436,000	1,630,000	…	655,000
1966	16,928,000	…	16,928,000	1,361,000	10,177,000	2,882,000	1,725,000	…	783,000
1967	19,056,000	…	19,056,000	1,585,000	11,845,000	2,897,000	1,861,000	…	868,000
1968	21,950,000	…	21,950,000	1,993,000	13,321,000	3,527,000	2,029,000	…	1,080,000
1969	24,779,000	…	24,779,000	2,135,000	14,858,000	4,402,000	2,109,000	…	1,275,000
1970	28,892,000	…	28,892,000	2,958,000	17,085,000	5,003,000	2,439,000	…	1,407,000
1971	32,640,000	…	32,640,000	3,258,000	19,292,000	5,760,000	2,507,000	…	1,823,000
1972	36,759,246	…	36,759,246	3,752,327	21,195,345	6,943,634	2,633,417	…	2,234,523
1973	40,822,135	…	40,822,135	4,279,646	23,315,651	7,531,738	2,953,424	…	2,741,676
1974	45,941,111	341,194	45,599,917	4,803,875	27,106,812	7,028,750	3,211,455	…	3,449,025
1975	51,978,324	974,780	51,003,544	5,129,333	31,110,237	7,136,104	3,224,861	…	4,403,009
1976	57,858,242	1,179,580	56,678,662	5,673,843	34,083,711	8,307,411	3,240,806	…	5,372,891
1977	62,459,903	1,386,237	61,073,666	6,372,543	36,964,306	8,756,717	3,631,108	…	5,348,992
1978	67,287,260	1,472,378	65,814,882	6,819,438	40,125,488	8,585,558	3,821,135	…	6,463,263
1979	75,962,980	1,493,215	74,469,765	8,224,338	46,195,698	8,675,473	4,148,573	…	7,225,683
1980	84,504,451	1,746,301	82,758,150	8,643,789	52,688,101	9,241,551	4,382,716	…	7,801,993
1981	93,179,549	1,872,980	91,306,569	9,570,248	57,257,373	11,025,445	4,751,449	…	8,702,054
1982	98,742,976	1,793,284	96,949,692	10,044,372	60,683,583	11,965,123	5,028,072	…	9,228,542
1983	100,886,902	1,764,821	99,122,081	10,364,144	63,118,351	10,919,847	5,277,447	…	9,442,292
1984	108,373,188	1,722,115	106,651,073	10,744,740	67,484,926	11,923,430	5,686,834	…	10,811,143
1985	121,571,151	1,963,468	119,607,683	12,319,623	74,936,970	12,673,123	6,019,069	…	13,658,898
1986	131,966,258	2,105,831	129,860,427	13,383,912	81,929,467	14,214,613	6,470,049	…	13,862,386
1987	141,278,672	2,455,362	138,823,310	14,245,089	88,253,298	14,753,727	6,784,699	…	14,786,497
1988	151,661,866	2,652,981	149,008,885	14,896,991	95,390,536	15,032,315	6,949,190	…	16,739,853
1989	165,415,415	2,929,622	162,485,793	15,749,681	104,601,291	16,697,915	7,376,173	…	18,060,733

See footnotes at end of table.

SUMMARY OF STATE INTERGOVERNMENTAL EXPENDITURES: 1944–2013—Continued
(In thousands of dollars)

Fiscal year	Total	To Federal government (a)	To local governments						
			Total	For general local government support	Education	Public welfare	Highways	Health	Miscellaneous and combined
1990	175,027,632	3,243,634	171,783,998	16,565,106	109,438,131	18,403,149	7,784,316	...	19,593,296
1991	186,398,234	3,464,364	182,933,870	16,977,032	116,179,860	20,903,400	8,126,477	...	20,747,101
1992	201,313,434	3,608,911	197,704,523	16,368,139	124,919,686	25,942,234	8,480,871	...	21,993,593
1993	214,094,882	3,625,051	210,469,831	17,690,986	131,179,517	31,339,777	9,298,624	...	20,960,927
1994	225,635,410	3,603,447	222,031,963	18,044,015	135,861,024	30,624,514	9,622,849	...	27,879,561
1995	240,978,128	3,616,831	237,361,297	18,996,435	148,160,436	30,772,525	10,481,616	...	28,926,886
1996	252,079,335	3,896,667	248,182,668	20,019,771	156,954,115	31,180,345	10,707,338	10,790,396	18,530,703
1997	264,207,209	3,839,942	260,367,267	21,808,828	164,147,715	35,754,024	11,431,270	11,772,189	15,453,241
1998	278,853,409	3,515,734	275,337,675	22,693,158	176,250,998	32,327,325	11,648,853	12,379,498	20,037,843
1999	308,734,917	3,801,667	304,933,250	25,495,396	192,416,987	35,161,151	12,075,195	13,611,228	26,173,293
2000	327,069,829	4,021,471	323,048,358	27,475,363	208,135,537	40,206,513	12,473,052	15,067,156	19,690,737
2001	350,326,546	4,290,764	346,035,782	31,693,016	222,092,587	41,926,990	12,350,136	16,518,461	21,454,592
2002	364,789,480	4,370,330	360,419,150	28,927,053	227,336,087	47,112,496	12,949,850	20,816,777	23,276,887
2003	382,781,397	4,391,095	378,390,302	30,766,480	240,788,692	49,302,737	13,337,114	20,241,742	23,953,537
2004	388,559,152	4,627,356	383,931,796	29,718,225	249,256,844	42,636,305	14,008,581	19,959,396	28,352,445
2005	405,925,287	4,620,167	401,305,120	28,320,648	263,625,820	48,370,718	14,500,232	17,515,138	28,972,564
2006	432,265,206	6,502,059	425,763,147	30,486,739	280,090,982	48,409,237	15,495,306	18,144,795	33,136,088
2007	459,742,295	4,670,648	455,071,647	31,207,065	301,062,065	56,899,141	14,881,789	20,067,198	30,953,499
2008	478,530,574	4,765,734	473,764,840	32,035,268	315,424,647	57,730,369	16,549,366	20,342,928	31,682,262
2009	490,887,391	4,894,977	485,992,414	30,421,570	324,374,036	58,741,316	16,492,780	21,019,353	34,943,359
2010	485,557,187	4,339,166	481,218,021	27,821,681	317,389,500	58,858,443	18,043,061	18,274,329	40,831,007
2011	496,832,436	4,295,922	492,536,514	27,577,126	330,482,270	56,678,841	17,243,590	18,745,863	41,808,824
2012	481,883,230	4,157,695	477,725,535	27,289,870	317,839,562	55,913,067	17,787,581	19,350,451	39,545,004
2013	488,782,863	3,392,576	485,390,287	28,412,169	324,995,548	55,565,254	18,158,521	20,242,808	38,015,987

Source: U.S. Census Bureau, Census of Governments: Finance (years ending in '2' and '7'), and Annual Survey of State Government Finances (remaining years). For information on sampling and nonsampling errors and definitions, see http://www.census.gov/govs/state/how_data_collected.html. Data users who create their own estimates from this table should cite the U.S. Census Bureau as the source of the original data only.

Note: Detail may not add to total due to rounding.
Key:
... – Not available.
(a) Represents primarily state reimbursements for the supplemental security income program.

Table 2.2
STATE INTERGOVERNMENTAL EXPENDITURES, BY STATE: 2001–2013
(In thousands of dollars)

State	2013	2012	2011	2010	2009	2008	2007	2006	2005	2004	2003	2002	2001
United States	$488,782,863	$481,883,230	$496,832,436	$485,557,187	$490,887,391	$478,530,574	$459,742,295	$432,265,206	$405,925,287	$388,559,152	$382,196,570	$364,847,087	$350,874,185
Alabama	6,476,073	6,563,313	6,800,787	6,604,013	6,535,634	6,720,814	6,088,940	5,759,949	5,281,804	4,164,719	4,074,005	4,095,562	3,892,653
Alaska	2,032,061	1,897,331	1,723,023	1,655,467	1,616,689	1,487,649	1,365,793	1,217,110	1,145,032	1,049,706	1,091,391	1,055,596	986,921
Arizona	8,209,708	8,023,697	8,668,387	9,179,514	9,618,970	10,320,506	10,341,643	9,063,746	8,028,519	7,556,518	6,936,753	6,902,301	6,439,144
Arkansas	4,937,560	5,047,345	5,151,981	5,057,598	4,698,889	4,392,649	4,300,048	4,039,533	3,886,756	3,212,815	3,210,582	3,071,214	2,941,918
California	95,069,461	85,425,616	91,501,553	90,530,131	94,909,240	94,872,980	93,537,044	88,317,088	80,948,431	80,132,150	84,468,847	74,687,370	69,747,365
Colorado	6,291,390	6,105,130	6,334,861	6,513,704	6,403,127	5,912,545	5,683,332	5,621,254	5,187,797	4,860,577	4,666,350	4,295,239	3,909,362
Connecticut	4,908,546	4,614,954	4,485,808	4,846,870	4,316,376	4,193,874	3,802,923	3,727,280	3,534,857	3,313,737	3,030,485	3,734,962	3,252,917
Delaware	1,271,359	1,161,381	1,293,106	1,235,608	1,205,247	1,172,083	1,157,652	1,129,736	983,773	922,710	903,476	822,544	788,160
Florida	17,809,542	17,340,127	19,725,217	18,478,449	17,677,928	19,703,095	19,680,891	19,402,818	17,475,959	15,285,893	14,460,722	14,053,858	15,010,631
Georgia	10,361,359	10,223,211	10,600,099	10,747,620	10,816,572	10,415,395	10,515,856	9,991,603	9,548,675	9,331,174	9,016,458	8,644,827	8,383,261
Hawaii	220,844	194,791	207,988	177,624	159,452	137,771	138,054	157,863	147,201	134,452	125,434	130,387	124,448
Idaho	1,981,659	1,956,717	2,036,312	2,022,896	2,077,028	2,037,507	1,931,829	1,606,232	1,519,654	1,496,785	1,449,076	1,407,058	1,363,445
Illinois	15,549,167	15,866,914	15,711,057	15,530,746	15,034,787	14,585,898	14,079,487	13,946,155	14,212,820	13,303,609	13,369,662	13,090,976	12,770,065
Indiana	9,292,344	9,313,044	9,265,386	9,705,254	8,214,991	7,976,702	8,184,884	7,817,176	7,876,764	7,963,397	6,760,945	6,556,774	7,052,415
Iowa	4,753,646	4,804,976	5,151,627	4,528,319	4,660,802	4,142,960	3,892,136	3,881,967	3,642,335	3,529,971	3,442,552	3,326,499	3,284,057
Kansas	4,057,504	3,953,778	4,208,664	4,176,958	4,314,940	4,214,475	3,869,984	3,594,505	3,281,217	3,123,152	2,925,220	2,971,413	2,953,527
Kentucky	4,802,691	5,029,106	5,069,137	5,078,845	4,769,871	4,700,971	4,526,996	4,384,427	3,915,278	3,963,425	3,693,634	3,620,967	3,620,278
Louisiana	6,241,308	6,387,767	6,580,164	6,658,397	6,505,389	6,022,791	6,175,010	5,654,409	4,588,748	4,410,251	4,329,053	4,168,290	3,800,785
Maine	1,238,618	1,286,233	1,301,692	1,346,639	1,325,723	1,335,469	1,272,764	1,217,377	1,093,027	1,049,160	1,051,164	1,009,582	976,233
Maryland	8,641,281	8,380,215	8,124,451	8,592,779	8,654,935	8,509,003	7,568,283	6,916,136	5,679,626	5,632,520	5,358,342	5,235,506	5,003,670
Massachusetts	9,401,248	9,291,231	8,826,190	9,107,483	8,890,500	8,840,769	8,909,899	7,231,774	7,271,036	5,393,684	6,435,841	6,283,972	6,886,054
Michigan	19,249,754	19,021,267	19,878,322	19,410,018	19,656,877	19,519,271	19,395,333	19,409,591	19,307,932	19,035,055	19,851,778	19,067,058	18,145,167
Minnesota	12,975,915	10,833,320	11,102,449	10,427,657	11,199,230	11,188,797	10,686,237	10,867,738	10,108,813	9,638,153	9,618,471	8,271,462	8,196,532
Mississippi	5,053,070	5,138,081	5,253,307	5,272,442	5,156,650	5,111,703	5,086,220	4,826,721	4,005,786	3,880,446	3,665,580	3,456,588	3,354,226
Missouri	5,771,802	5,877,847	5,948,493	6,227,955	5,936,688	5,743,498	5,559,734	5,386,306	5,489,120	5,260,101	5,159,094	5,073,185	4,802,371
Montana	1,373,069	1,316,548	1,352,917	1,334,478	1,276,112	1,318,649	1,175,674	1,088,009	1,005,091	955,378	938,000	910,845	863,553
Nebraska	2,170,630	2,170,016	2,306,692	2,192,338	2,064,173	1,981,940	1,793,817	1,721,265	1,659,130	1,695,613	1,784,749	1,820,137	1,684,159
Nevada	4,214,581	4,120,103	3,905,016	3,703,574	3,864,223	3,860,236	3,826,539	3,667,299	3,272,860	2,948,274	2,648,660	2,495,552	2,271,654
New Hampshire	1,300,770	1,226,012	1,191,097	1,261,454	1,278,589	1,451,976	1,408,445	1,385,014	1,224,831	1,278,988	1,283,091	1,178,642	1,040,566
New Jersey	11,102,269	11,789,109	11,167,301	11,877,592	11,135,809	10,927,571	10,671,445	11,060,423	10,642,426	10,565,755	8,997,417	9,320,357	9,081,634
New Mexico	4,500,634	4,450,387	4,325,766	4,322,463	4,506,456	4,363,063	4,160,932	3,745,089	3,617,407	3,234,697	2,951,328	2,768,420	2,561,979
New York	56,236,537	57,406,012	59,697,916	54,318,363	55,107,082	52,820,634	50,527,547	45,615,561	43,731,212	44,112,115	40,874,514	38,982,253	34,712,602
North Carolina	13,172,640	13,514,695	13,633,379	13,429,946	13,562,079	13,152,908	12,499,778	11,721,637	11,637,674	10,226,422	10,356,152	9,450,766	9,309,537
North Dakota	1,632,316	1,643,402	1,300,989	1,245,686	933,974	805,351	741,535	735,705	701,125	613,513	606,096	585,521	569,034
Ohio	16,517,064	17,932,406	18,488,325	18,348,743	18,963,232	18,080,744	18,042,563	17,347,300	16,368,355	15,730,201	15,249,395	15,052,078	14,594,220
Oklahoma	4,213,211	4,230,427	4,477,819	4,546,446	4,506,207	4,391,106	4,014,883	3,871,117	3,711,117	3,669,052	3,395,494	3,377,045	3,486,043
Oregon	5,495,337	5,657,912	5,774,682	5,864,882	5,703,775	5,640,993	5,047,346	4,947,578	4,764,615	4,637,052	4,071,501	4,212,673	4,027,505
Pennsylvania	18,834,325	18,526,116	19,944,576	18,871,434	19,144,305	17,826,902	17,058,314	13,650,400	13,307,866	12,061,035	11,943,470	12,787,590	13,120,752
Rhode Island	1,170,440	1,143,486	1,074,302	1,193,060	1,002,915	1,067,689	1,076,589	998,505	908,479	865,956	828,198	749,034	711,439
South Carolina	5,454,008	5,312,018	5,585,665	5,369,519	5,520,979	5,719,235	4,870,680	4,699,299	4,245,394	4,159,942	4,155,920	4,241,010	4,168,449

See footnotes at end of table.

STATE INTERGOVERNMENTAL EXPENDITURES, BY STATE: 2001–2013—Continued
(In thousands of dollars)

State	2013	2012	2011	2010	2009	2008	2007	2006	2005	2004	2003	2002	2001
South Dakota	740,104	753,622	774,778	737,190	707,862	679,868	652,117	633,891	608,209	566,853	514,949	506,347	480,960
Tennessee	7,074,682	7,181,421	7,104,790	6,664,828	6,797,935	6,516,598	6,034,661	5,910,319	5,705,768	5,301,665	4,952,923	4,477,936	4,582,883
Texas	27,590,295	29,860,716	29,665,803	27,461,315	29,252,364	26,089,474	21,919,511	19,785,626	17,489,900	17,032,016	17,332,957	16,680,780	17,204,468
Utah	3,069,082	3,029,283	3,106,230	3,027,680	3,120,527	3,050,173	2,601,367	2,384,402	2,189,527	2,112,921	2,165,151	2,170,884	2,100,657
Vermont	1,501,657	1,636,024	1,552,853	1,518,129	1,532,766	1,340,755	1,415,922	1,357,660	1,266,715	981,307	938,085	918,858	919,865
Virginia	11,255,705	11,653,818	11,489,163	10,959,394	11,894,394	11,260,089	10,585,635	10,019,166	9,720,411	8,820,012	8,352,635	8,369,313	7,869,121
Washington	9,777,797	9,530,116	9,346,712	9,798,444	10,043,789	9,143,766	8,602,204	7,820,778	7,443,361	6,911,826	6,785,341	6,806,350	6,576,757
West Virginia	2,469,535	2,618,032	2,533,582	2,382,633	2,232,558	2,131,100	2,074,429	2,067,829	2,004,862	1,942,069	1,544,758	1,453,707	1,535,961
Wisconsin	9,637,247	9,741,343	10,428,954	10,253,124	10,199,520	9,881,119	9,620,506	9,560,976	9,200,766	9,285,137	9,478,166	9,523,191	8,895,941
Wyoming	1,681,018	1,702,814	1,653,068	1,760,946	1,919,231	1,769,009	1,568,884	1,301,223	1,337,226	1,207,193	952,705	974,608	818,841

Source: U.S. Census Bureau, Census of Governments: Finance (2002, 2007, and 2012), and Annual Survey of State Government Finances (remaining years). For information on sampling and nonsampling errors and definitions, see *http://www.census.gov/govs/state/how_data_collected.html.* Data users who create their own estimates from this table should cite the U.S. Census Bureau as the source of the original data only. Data in this table are based on information from public records and contain no confidential data. Although the data in this table come from a census of governmental units and are not subject to sampling error, the census results may contain nonsampling error. Additional information on nonsampling error, response rates, and definitions may be found within the survey methodology and technical documentation, *http://www2.census.gov/govs/state/13_methodology.pdf.*

Note: Includes payments to the federal government, primarily state reimbursements for the supplemental security income program. The statistics reflect state government fiscal years that end on June 30, except for four states with other ending dates: Alabama and Michigan (September 30), New York (March 31), and Texas (August 31).

Additional Note: Detail may not add to total due to rounding.

Table 2.3
STATE INTERGOVERNMENTAL EXPENDITURES, BY FUNCTION AND BY STATE: 2013
(In thousands of dollars)

State	Total	General local government support	Education	Public welfare	Highways	Health	Miscellaneous and combined
				Specified functions			
United States	$488,782,863	$28,412,169	$324,995,548	$55,565,254	$18,158,521	$20,242,808	$41,408,563
Alabama	6,476,073	206,798	4,786,505	112,719	207,478	41,229	1,121,344
Alaska	2,032,061	53,137	1,195,250	89,495	2,779	137,916	553,484
Arizona	8,209,708	2,011,941	4,875,144	278,934	710,416	87,688	245,585
Arkansas	4,937,560	277,404	4,260,638	0	178,732	952	219,834
California	95,069,461	2,376,481	49,676,956	28,188,143	4,095,287	7,215,873	3,516,721
Colorado	6,291,390	128,595	4,296,969	834,531	380,378	100,908	550,009
Connecticut	4,908,546	392,295	3,677,030	348,399	2,878	283,133	204,811
Delaware	1,271,359	0	1,113,944	9,883	5,741	19,933	121,858
Florida	17,809,542	1,770,457	13,917,786	79	586,460	63	1,534,697
Georgia	10,361,359	0	9,239,380	388,976	115,367	222,511	395,125
Hawaii	220,844	165,122	0	382	0	12,821	42,519
Idaho	1,981,659	214,682	1,577,707	0	124,622	3,684	60,964
Illinois	15,549,167	1,814,068	8,985,799	1,622,677	792,103	169,917	2,164,603
Indiana	9,292,344	673,655	7,638,130	45,234	800,244	29,131	105,950
Iowa	4,753,646	142,694	3,303,997	119,944	456,311	116,153	614,547
Kansas	4,057,504	149,485	3,511,730	1,822	205,305	49,563	139,599
Kentucky	4,802,691	0	4,042,320	117,689	187,793	134,554	320,335
Louisiana	6,241,308	195,942	4,418,515	141,231	55,495	0	1,430,125
Maine	1,238,618	119,936	1,011,583	17,221	23,633	100	66,145
Maryland	8,641,281	119,927	6,327,270	0	157,612	852,949	1,183,523
Massachusetts	9,401,248	955,227	6,819,860	285,033	206,756	16,625	1,117,747
Michigan	19,249,754	1,098,498	13,017,254	2,890,755	1,134,573	134,834	973,840
Minnesota	12,975,915	1,303,389	9,360,135	487,296	1,096,853	84,448	643,794
Mississippi	5,053,070	578,259	3,125,051	428,653	337,191	53,206	530,710
Missouri	5,771,802	199,438	5,137,864	1,764	184,907	1,623	246,206
Montana	1,373,069	145,613	915,953	36,917	17,683	14,446	242,457
Nebraska	2,170,630	482,439	1,451,769	43,167	8,119	52,895	132,241
Nevada	4,214,581	1,136,976	2,768,853	141,069	87,815	16,247	63,621
New Hampshire	1,300,770	58,805	1,042,021	142,280	34,897	2,342	20,425
New Jersey	11,102,269	1,249,362	7,704,621	980,027	191,983	27,472	948,804
New Mexico	4,500,634	1,301,539	2,997,241	0	43,854	7,642	150,358
New York	56,236,537	424,416	28,887,650	9,543,635	15,668	6,413,944	10,951,224
North Carolina	13,172,640	197,036	10,539,476	1,569,013	237,665	144,075	485,375
North Dakota	1,632,316	313,359	849,565	17,196	138,155	8,106	305,935
Ohio	16,517,064	1,461,936	10,923,197	1,536,390	794,746	544,559	1,256,236
Oklahoma	4,213,211	113,309	3,427,884	43,901	380,645	83,754	163,718
Oregon	5,495,337	190,526	3,657,321	635,121	443,229	157,121	412,019
Pennsylvania	18,834,325	234,928	12,164,335	1,990,320	694,614	1,116,494	2,633,634
Rhode Island	1,170,440	57,248	1,005,225	78,446	18,605	7	10,909
South Carolina	5,454,008	1,661,651	3,411,496	87,346	93,287	38,989	161,239
South Dakota	740,104	30,649	569,147	7,904	44,401	6,585	81,418
Tennessee	7,074,682	287,580	5,078,822	849,978	157,729	82,786	617,787
Texas	27,590,295	172,407	24,815,359	515,372	240,870	339,412	1,506,875
Utah	3,069,082	0	2,872,425	22,480	81,107	45,185	47,885
Vermont	1,501,657	0	1,473,024	0	52,640	0	-24,007
Virginia	11,255,705	1,001,724	6,805,350	584,083	535,328	392,596	1,936,624
Washington	9,777,797	118,744	7,546,421	7,128	657,272	627,462	820,770
West Virginia	2,469,535	108,276	2,018,529	39,353	13,038	58,498	231,841
Wisconsin	9,637,247	2,233,452	5,676,785	283,102	600,627	284,107	559,174
Wyoming	1,681,018	482,764	1,076,262	166	23,050	8,270	90,506

Source: U.S. Census Bureau, 2013 Annual Survey of State Government Finances.

Note: Data users who create their own estimates using these data should cite only the U.S. Census Bureau as the source of the original data. Data in this table are based on information from public records and contain no confidential data. Although the data in this table come from a census of governmental units and are not subject to sampling error, the census results may contain nonsampling error. Additional information on non-sampling error, response rates, and definitions may be found within the survey methodology *http://www2.census.gov/govs/state/13_methodology.pdf* and technical documentation.

Additional Note: Detail may not add to total due to rounding.

Table 2.4
STATE INTERGOVERNMENTAL EXPENDITURES, BY TYPE OF RECEIVING GOVERNMENT AND BY STATE: 2013
(In thousands of dollars)

State	Total intergovernmental expenditure	Federal	School districts	Other local governments
United States	$488,782,863	$3,392,576	$263,177,928	$222,212,359
Alabama.............................	6,476,073	0	4,772,486	1,703,587
Alaska................................	2,032,061	0	0	2,032,061
Arizona..............................	8,209,708	0	4,863,961	3,345,747
Arkansas............................	4,937,560	18	4,260,638	676,904
California	95,069,461	2,775,752	46,390,472	45,903,237
Colorado............................	6,291,390	3,005	4,272,693	2,015,692
Connecticut.......................	4,908,546	0	36,930	4,871,616
Delaware	1,271,359	956	1,107,792	162,611
Florida..............................	17,809,542	0	13,592,090	4,217,452
Georgia..............................	10,361,359	0	9,239,380	1,121,979
Hawaii...............................	220,844	0	0	220,844
Idaho.................................	1,981,659	382	1,577,707	403,570
Illinois...............................	15,549,167	0	8,926,732	6,622,435
Indiana..............................	9,292,344	8,950	7,638,105	1,645,289
Iowa	4,753,646	24,812	3,303,868	1,424,966
Kansas	4,057,504	0	3,511,730	545,774
Kentucky............................	4,802,691	1,751	4,042,320	758,620
Louisiana...........................	6,241,308	0	4,415,418	1,825,890
Maine.................................	1,238,618	0	0	1,238,618
Maryland............................	8,641,281	5,811	0	8,635,470
Massachusetts	9,401,248	0	1,142,934	8,258,314
Michigan............................	19,249,754	202,983	13,004,555	6,042,216
Minnesota..........................	12,975,915	13,613	9,338,113	3,624,189
Mississippi	5,053,070	0	3,103,894	1,949,176
Missouri.............................	5,771,802	0	5,137,864	633,938
Montana	1,373,069	68,036	915,828	389,205
Nebraska	2,170,630	303	1,451,769	718,558
Nevada...............................	4,214,581	43,057	2,768,851	1,402,673
New Hampshire	1,300,770	3,308	170,902	1,126,560
New Jersey	11,102,269	0	5,673,830	5,428,439
New Mexico	4,500,634	19,000	2,997,241	1,484,393
New York............................	56,236,537	0	15,547,705	40,688,832
North Carolina...................	13,172,640	0	0	13,172,640
North Dakota.....................	1,632,316	0	849,565	782,751
Ohio	16,517,064	0	10,923,197	5,593,867
Oklahoma...........................	4,213,211	9,929	3,417,884	785,398
Oregon...............................	5,495,337	54,786	3,655,869	1,784,682
Pennsylvania	18,834,325	0	11,567,331	7,266,994
Rhode Island......................	1,170,440	129,162	60,501	980,777
South Carolina...................	5,454,008	18,204	3,367,230	2,068,574
South Dakota.....................	740,104	0	569,147	170,957
Tennessee	7,074,682	0	303,949	6,770,733
Texas.................................	27,590,295	1,390	24,582,015	3,006,890
Utah..................................	3,069,082	0	2,870,958	198,124
Vermont.............................	1,501,657	0	1,473,024	28,633
Virginia..............................	11,255,705	0	24,392	11,231,313
Washington........................	9,777,797	1,312	7,546,300	2,230,185
West Virginia......................	2,469,535	4,404	2,007,711	457,420
Wisconsin	9,637,247	0	5,676,785	3,960,462
Wyoming............................	1,681,018	0	1,076,262	604,756

Source: U.S. Census Bureau, 2013 Annual Survey of State Government Finances.

Note: Data users who create their own estimates using these data should cite only the U.S. Census Bureau as the source of the original data. Data in this table are based on information from public records and contain no confidential data. Although the data in this table come from a census of governmental units and are not subject to sampling error, the census results may contain nonsampling error. Additional information on non-sampling error, response rates, and definitions may be found within the survey methodology *http://www2.census.gov/govs/state/13_methodology.pdf* and technical documentation *http://www2.census.gov/govs/state/statetechdoc2013.pdf*.

Additional Note: Detail may not add to total due to rounding.

Table 2.5
STATE INTERGOVERNMENTAL REVENUE FROM FEDERAL AND LOCAL GOVERNMENTS: 2013
(In thousands of dollars)

State	Total intergovernmental revenue	From federal government					From local governments				
		Total (a)	Education	Public welfare	Health & hospitals	Highways	Total (a)	Education	Public welfare	Health & hospitals	Highways
United States	$551,464,163	$513,478,951	$84,408,057	$307,610,126	$25,794,434	$41,431,014	$37,985,212	$3,266,668	$28,062,951	$1,185,097	$2,057,104
Alabama	8,338,033	8,226,967	1,617,012	4,773,253	248,645	789,850	111,066	11,187	0	35,205	46,168
Alaska	2,754,412	2,747,308	339,906	1,168,655	104,566	458,856	7,104	5,748	0	0	0
Arizona	10,580,523	10,166,478	1,711,418	6,687,404	326,336	831,892	414,045	11,255	304,888	65,319	6,456
Arkansas	5,724,598	5,689,390	801,886	3,297,154	126,098	584,654	35,208	34,629	0	404	0
California	58,096,373	54,827,525	10,277,690	35,518,804	2,268,814	3,277,021	3,268,848	237,947	1,356,873	8,291	741,014
Colorado	6,508,932	6,427,852	1,412,272	2,329,076	1,375,934	742,791	81,080	15,889	215	0	19,518
Connecticut	5,962,699	5,949,159	496,231	3,826,344	210,581	533,242	13,540	1,130	0	0	0
Delaware	1,996,011	1,929,185	237,438	1,143,896	99,474	211,245	66,826	62,910	0	0	0
Florida	23,880,229	23,506,254	4,406,907	13,359,266	1,900,559	2,090,984	373,975	10,130	0	279,942	0
Georgia	14,619,221	14,323,163	3,079,313	7,073,816	1,434,300	1,359,809	296,058	252,234	0	0	11,977
Hawaii	2,331,449	2,326,602	624,748	1,084,066	69,923	159,063	4,847	0	0	0	0
Idaho	2,541,438	2,522,766	379,866	1,310,994	229,954	306,062	18,672	345	13,236	0	5,043
Illinois	17,312,790	16,973,577	3,167,335	9,902,223	592,377	1,516,860	339,213	14,760	243,725	0	64,615
Indiana	11,267,810	11,192,452	1,712,086	7,039,516	278,939	1,110,281	75,358	9,815	22,824	2,994	38,578
Iowa	5,991,401	5,915,221	993,140	3,505,067	174,449	460,512	76,180	394	42,544	8,454	13,447
Kansas	3,845,073	3,788,962	790,747	1,880,823	284,174	415,551	56,111	19,878	78	983	32,320
Kentucky	8,083,482	8,047,093	1,307,298	4,900,886	293,812	694,374	36,389	20,170	0	0	0
Louisiana	10,660,261	10,592,657	1,378,099	5,539,233	347,567	861,383	67,604	20,390	0	2,905	2,271
Maine	2,830,353	2,821,145	273,128	1,852,027	80,768	231,265	9,208	0	0	50	6,305
Maryland	10,325,181	9,952,960	1,664,398	5,139,420	1,237,221	709,449	372,221	48,731	28,366	121,788	24,849
Massachusetts	13,706,498	13,233,244	1,573,978	7,815,079	690,661	669,273	473,254	12,977	67,583	45,316	4,838
Michigan	18,007,780	17,829,882	3,256,553	10,180,474	1,358,966	908,455	177,898	9,427	74,886	21	19,551
Minnesota	9,315,259	9,141,995	1,354,823	6,257,462	244,286	601,092	173,264	22,119	204	4	64,548
Mississippi	7,649,292	7,509,589	1,073,919	4,671,168	196,145	581,465	139,703	3,628	204	4	107,315
Missouri	10,497,449	10,188,272	1,281,738	5,734,532	1,395,472	954,875	309,177	1,335	227,827	14,051	42,066
Montana	2,161,997	2,158,227	289,552	957,523	126,650	463,116	3,770	9	646	0	1,614
Nebraska	3,212,304	3,154,670	220,738	2,236,135	59,625	363,498	57,634	33,217	347	98	20,596
Nevada	3,080,240	2,844,973	573,181	1,470,300	142,451	350,773	235,267	31,403	153,290	11,380	28,152
New Hampshire	1,883,424	1,659,853	239,779	769,128	28,895	153,145	223,571	4,310	179,004	0	29,554
New Jersey	14,471,986	13,755,548	2,017,443	6,996,729	453,955	848,794	716,438	272,480	0	85,012	211,304
New Mexico	5,416,068	5,228,141	740,798	3,486,139	180,584	433,818	187,927	59,341	0	128,586	0
New York	71,682,137	46,272,851	4,813,154	32,456,517	1,307,685	1,830,124	25,409,286	185,440	24,467,044	54,061	17,427
North Carolina	15,769,950	15,470,808	2,393,962	9,852,503	672,692	1,184,730	299,142	112,535	123,182	5,733	25,912
North Dakota	1,572,480	1,529,135	266,536	591,528	20,645	367,180	43,345	1	8,586	3,595	20,287
Ohio	21,113,847	20,482,575	2,705,082	14,310,434	433,821	1,593,734	631,272	25,119	344,242	64,775	59,696
Oklahoma	7,159,511	7,028,733	1,013,833	3,501,139	1,381,690	558,808	130,778	1,141	0	1,890	33,952
Oregon	8,003,252	7,987,139	1,255,941	5,138,896	468,597	384,064	16,113	11,591	0	0	0
Pennsylvania	21,412,638	21,219,116	3,272,854	14,276,610	472,266	1,758,508	193,522	170,779	0	798	13,935
Rhode Island	2,369,822	2,331,473	312,734	1,178,035	235,746	271,075	38,349	0	0	0	0
South Carolina	7,202,824	6,698,952	1,393,650	3,846,495	270,486	635,098	503,872	88,111	280,799	5,730	68,406

See footnotes at end of table.

STATE INTERGOVERNMENTAL REVENUE FROM FEDERAL AND LOCAL GOVERNMENTS: 2013 — Continued
(In thousands of dollars)

State	Total intergovernmental revenue	From federal government					From local governments				
		Total (a)	Education	Public welfare	Health & hospitals	Highways	Total (a)	Education	Public welfare	Health & hospitals	Highways
South Dakota	1,605,537	1,575,212	266,179	599,105	99,401	327,850	30,325	12,592	0	7,750	9,650
Tennessee	10,900,626	10,819,977	1,589,313	6,997,488	301,976	979,223	80,649	24,087	1,796	4,640	33,889
Texas	37,580,061	36,844,736	7,844,603	21,705,368	1,267,301	3,208,960	735,325	616,700	5,402	112,827	0
Utah	4,304,061	4,298,917	889,027	2,404,604	202,281	433,542	5,144	4,997	0	0	0
Vermont	1,872,013	1,869,831	270,364	1,060,200	58,112	264,720	2,182	0	0	0	2,036
Virginia	9,959,041	9,412,343	2,001,991	4,979,265	448,855	1,423,807	546,698	397,946	0	62,039	67,940
Washington	10,030,961	9,737,429	2,360,158	4,380,144	1,138,010	948,447	293,532	151,728	0	24,929	53,683
West Virginia	4,325,052	4,230,663	552,811	2,545,476	163,333	439,555	94,389	4,843	0	0	0
Wisconsin	9,228,907	8,952,020	1,489,040	5,492,779	245,373	783,832	276,887	14,407	114,853	23,242	95,940
Wyoming	2,318,877	2,085,931	423,405	386,948	43,953	364,309	232,946	216,863	0	2,285	12,252

Source: U.S. Census Bureau, 2013 Annual Survey of State Government Finances.
Note: Data users who create their own estimates using these data should cite only the U.S. Census Bureau as the source of the original data. Data in this table are based on information from public records and contain no confidential data. Although the data in this table come from a census of governmental units and are not subject to sampling error, the census results may contain nonsampling error. Additional information on nonsampling error, response rates, and definitions may be found within the survey methodology *http://www2.census.gov/govs/state/13_methodology.pdf* and technical documentation *http://www2.census.gov/govs/state/statetechdoc2013.pdf.*
Additional Note: Detail may not add to total due to rounding.
Key:
(a) Total includes other types of intergovernmental revenue not shown separately in this table.

Chapter Three

STATE LEGISLATIVE BRANCH

2015 State Elections

By Tim Storey and Dan Diorio

The handful of state elections in 2015 resulted in very little change to the state partisan landscape. Republicans maintained their historically strong hold on state governments.

State Partisan Landscape Mostly Unchanged after 2015 Odd-year Elections

The GOP remains the dominant party in control of state governments across the United States despite a couple of governor party control flips in the handful of 2015 state elections. Republicans control the most legislative chambers in the history of the party. Plus, they count 31 of the nation's 50 governors among their ranks. The state elections of 2015 were essentially a stalemate, leaving Democrats to hope for a rebound in 2016 from disappointing results over the past six years and Republicans wondering if they can pad their sizable advantage in state policymaking.

Only five states conducted regularly scheduled elections in 2015. Louisiana, Mississippi and Virginia voters decided on all legislative seats. New Jersey held elections for the Assembly only; the state's senators serve four-year terms and were all chosen in 2013. Three states held elections for governor: Kentucky, Louisiana and Mississippi.

None of the legislative elections led to a party control shift, and two of the governor's mansions switched party control. Kentucky went from a Democrat to a Republican and Louisiana went from a Republican to a Democrat, thus cancelling each other out with regard to the national tally. This led to only one minor update to the overall partisan control of states. Headed into 2015 elections, Republicans controlled all of state government (governor, house and senate) in 23 states. Democrats held seven, and in 19 states, partisan control was divided with neither party having the "trifecta."

In an open governor's race in Kentucky, voters handed the job from Democratic, term-limited incumbent Steve Beshear to Republican Matt Bevin. In the open gubernatorial race in Louisiana, Pelican State voters replaced term-limited Republican incumbent Bobby Jindal with Democrat John Bel Edwards. Kentucky remained a divided control state because the legislature is split control—the House is majority Democrat and the Senate is majority Republican. But in Louisiana, Republi-

cans lost full control of state government by losing the governor's seat, even though they retained control of both chambers of the Legislature.

With the lone party control shift in Louisiana, Republicans entered 2016 legislative sessions controlling all of state government in 22 states. Democrats held on to their seven, and the number of divided states ticked up to 20. Figure A shows the states where one party controls the legislature and governor's seat, and the states where that control is divided.

Legislative Seats Up

In total, 535 state legislative seats were up for grabs in 2015, representing slightly more than 7 percent of the 7,383 seats in the 50 states. The outcome of the elections did not change the overall legislative partisan control map—Louisiana and Virginia stayed red, Mississippi got redder and New Jersey got bluer. Going into, and emerging from, the 2015 races, Republicans controlled both houses of the legislature in 30 states, matching their highest point in history set back in 1920. Democrats held the majority in both chambers of the legislature in 11 states, and eight states were split. In terms of individual legislative bodies, Republicans control 68 of the 98 partisan legislative chambers in the country. Nebraska has a unicameral lawmaking body whose members are chosen in nonpartisan elections.

Including the slight changes in 2015, there are more than 4,125 Republican state legislators in the country representing 56.4 percent of all state legislative seats. Fewer legislators (a total of 3,163) are serving today under the Democratic banner than at any point since 1928. Only 43.3 percent of partisan seats are held by Democrats. Twenty-four lawmakers are independent or from the Progressive Party, and the balance of the seats are either temporarily vacant or belong to the 49 nonpartisan senators in Nebraska.

Heading into the 2015 campaign, the Virginia Senate, a 40-member chamber that has switched control three times in the past three years, appeared to be the most contested legislative chamber of the

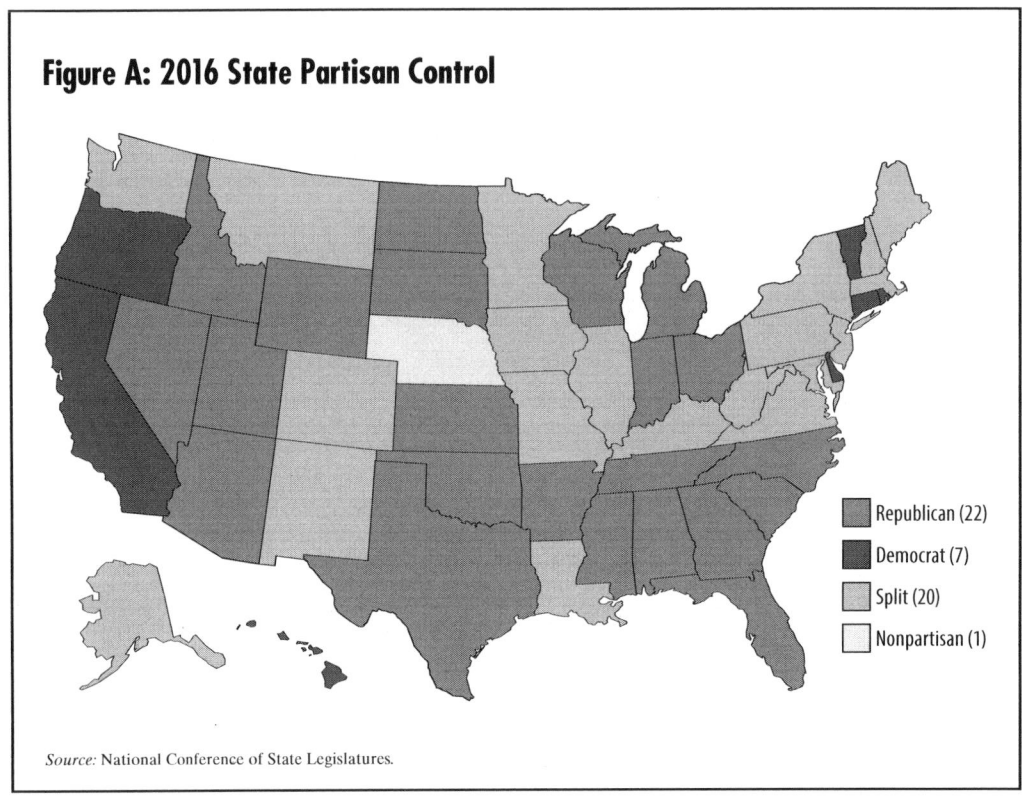

Figure A: 2016 State Partisan Control

Republican (22)

Democrat (7)

Split (20)

Nonpartisan (1)

Source: National Conference of State Legislatures.

seven that were up for grabs. Republicans held the Virginia Senate 21 to 19, meaning that Democrats only needed to gain one seat to regain control of the chamber if they could get it to a 20-20 tie, since Democratic Lt. Gov. Ralph Northam would be the tie-breaking vote. In the end, the numbers and partisan control did not change. Republicans maintained the 21-19 majority despite the fact that of the six open seats where incumbents retired, four were GOP and only two were Democrats.

While the bulk of the attention in the Old Dominion was on the Senate races in Virginia, every seat in the House of Delegates was also up for grabs. Republicans held a 67-33 majority in the 100-member chamber prior to Election Day and that didn't change much. Despite losing one seat, the GOP maintained its dominance in the House by a 66-34 margin.

In Mississippi, Republicans increased their numbers in the 122-member House of Representatives even knocking off House Democratic leader, Bobby Moak, in the process. But on Election Day, they fell short of the 74 seats needed to gain a key supermajority. Under Mississippi law, spending,

taxing and certain other measures require a three-fifths vote in the House and could only be enacted with Democratic support in the previous session. Shortly after the election, Democrat Rep. Jody Steverson announced that he was switching to the GOP, getting the party closer to a supermajority at 73-48 with one seat not determined because it had ended in a tie, each candidate receiving 4,589 votes.

Incumbent Rep. Bo Eaton, a Democrat, and Republican challenger Mark Tullos emerged from a recount with a rarity in elections—an honest-to-goodness tie. Mississippi law requires tied elections to be determined "by lot," so the candidates drew straws. Eaton won the drawing and was declared the winner. Tullos exercised his legal right to appeal the election results to the Republican-controlled House of Representatives. When the House convened in January 2016, it invalidated five votes for Eaton and voted to seat Tullos, giving Republicans a supermajority of 74-48. Republicans only gained the majority four years ago in 2011 when they captured the Mississippi House for the first time in 130 years. Republicans also maintained control of the Mississippi Senate by a 32-20 margin.

Louisiana held its "Cajun top-two primary" in October in which all candidates, Republicans, Democrats and others, run in the same primary. Under this system, if a candidate receives more than 50 percent of the votes in the primary, they win. If no one receives more than 50 percent, the top-two vote getters meet in the runoff election in late November. Although all 39 state Senate seats and 105 House seats were up for election, more than 50 percent of the seats were uncontested, leaving only 70 seats for the primary—18 Senate and 52 House. When all was said and done, Republicans maintained their majority in both the House (61-42-2) and the Senate (25-14).

In New Jersey, Democrats increased their majority in the Assembly by three to control the chamber 51-29. All Assembly districts in the Garden State are multimember where voters select two candidates. Democrats took over both seats in the formerly split District 1 and took out two GOP incumbents in District 11.

Governor Races Provided Some Excitement

Only three gubernatorial elections were decided in 2015—in Kentucky, Louisiana and Mississippi. The Louisiana governor's race proved to be the one to watch. A tight contest between Republican U.S. Sen. David Vitter and his Democratic challenger, state Rep. John Bel Edwards, went down to the wire on the Nov. 21 runoff. Bel Edwards pulled out a surprising upset over Vitter, replacing Republican Bobby Jindal who had held the post for the past eight years. Bel Edwards is one of three Democratic governors in the South along with West Virginia Gov. Earl Ray Tomblin and Virginia Gov. Terry McAuliffe.

The GOP gained a governor's seat in the South to offset the loss in Louisiana when Republican Matt Bevin defeated Democrat Jack Conway to replace term-limited Steve Beshear in Kentucky. The Bluegrass State remains in the split column because Democrats hold the majority in the state House of Representatives.

In Mississippi, incumbent Gov. Phil Bryant easily won re-election over Democratic challenger Robert Gray taking over 66 percent of the vote.

In 2016, the partisan affiliation of the governors stands at 31 Republicans and 18 Democrats. Alaska Gov. Bill Walker is the nation's lone independent governor.

Kentucky House Stands as Last Democratic Chamber in the South

The past six years have seen large Republican gains in state legislatures across the country, primarily due to a Republican takeover over of legislatures

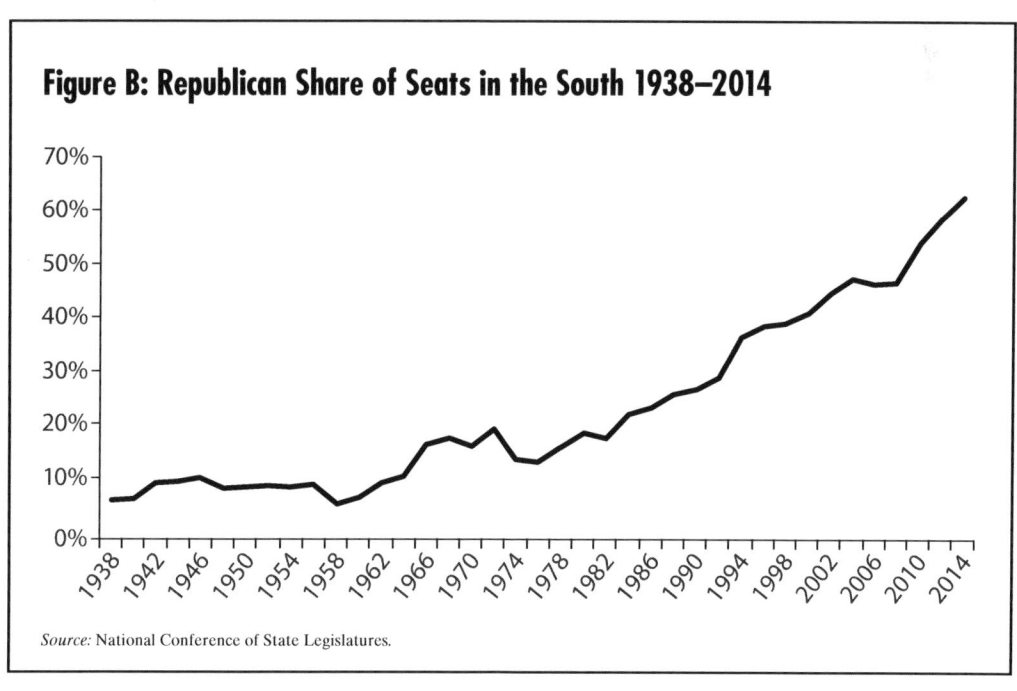

Figure B: Republican Share of Seats in the South 1938–2014

Source: National Conference of State Legislatures.

in the South. Chambers that had been held by Democrats for over a century in states like Louisiana and Mississippi are now solidly in Republican hands; in fact, Republicans control both legislative chambers in every Southern state, except for one — the Kentucky House of Representatives. Figure B shows the steady gains made by Republicans in Southern state legislatures. They now control over 62 percent of all Southern legislative seats. Only 24 years ago in 1992, Democrats held the majority in every Southern legislative chamber.

In late 2015, Democrats controlled the Kentucky House by a 54-46 margin. But by the end of December, two Democrats switched to the Republican Party, narrowing the Dems' majority to 52-48. To make matters worse for Kentucky Democratic leaders, two Democratic House members resigned to take positions in the new administration of Gov. Matt Bevin and two Republicans resigned after winning election to executive positions, putting control at 50-46 in favor of the Democrats. These four vacancies created the possibility that Republicans could take control of the Kentucky House in special elections in March 2016 and complete their takeover of Southern legislatures.

Democrats held on by winning three of the four special elections giving them a majority of 53-47. The Kentucky House will once again be a battleground in the 2016 elections.

2016 Elections

After the 2014 elections, Republicans hit record highs in control of state legislatures. 2016 may be a challenge for the party as they defend major gains accomplished during the Obama administration. And it is shaping up as an opportunity year for Democrats. Coattails will matter in 2016 with most voters focused on the race for the White House. The party of the winning presidential candidate typically fares better in presidential years and gains seats—only eight times in the past 116 years has the president's party lost state legislative seats in presidential election years. Voter turnout will increase in 2016 and that will undoubtedly have an impact in many legislative races, but especially in the battles to control the more than 20 legislative chambers that are easily in play for both parties in 2016.

Over 80 percent of legislative seats will be up for grabs in 2016 and there will be governors' races in 12 states. Six states do not have legislative elections in 2016: Alabama, Louisiana, Maryland, Mississippi, New Jersey and Virginia. In the other

44 states, there are 12 senates that would shift control if only three or fewer seats switched hands and eight state houses could shift if a net change of five seats occurs. The 2016 elections for legislatures could deliver a great deal of drama in terms of control of state policymaking, especially given that very few of the governors' races are likely to be competitive. And with Washington stuck in the mud, states are leading now more than ever when it comes to tackling problems and innovating new policies, so these elections matter.

About the Authors

Tim Storey is the director of state services of the Denver, Colorado, based National Conference of State Legislatures, or NCSL. He specializes in the areas of legislative leadership, elections and redistricting as well as legislative organization and management. He staffed NCSL's Redistricting and Elections Committee for more than 20 years and authored numerous articles on the topics of elections and redistricting. Every two years, he leads NCSL's StateVote project to track and analyze legislative election results. He graduated from Mars Hill College in North Carolina and received a master's degree from the University of Colorado's Graduate School of Public Affairs.

Dan Diorio is a policy specialist with the National Conference of State Legislatures. In this role he serves as editor of The Canvass, NCSL's monthly newsletter that summarizes complex election issues and trends. Diorio conducts research and analysis on election administration policy. Prior to joining NCSL, Dan worked in the Massachusetts Legislature, the United States Senate and for a private energy software company. and received a B.A. from Boston College.

Table 3.1
NAMES OF STATE LEGISLATIVE BODIES AND CONVENING PLACES

State or other jurisdiction	Both bodies	Upper house	Lower house	Convening place
Alabama	Legislature	Senate	House of Representatives	State House
Alaska	Legislature	Senate	House of Representatives	State Capitol
Arizona	Legislature	Senate	House of Representatives	State Capitol
Arkansas	General Assembly	Senate	House of Representatives	State Capitol
California	Legislature	Senate	Assembly	State Capitol
Colorado	General Assembly	Senate	House of Representatives	State Capitol
Connecticut	General Assembly	Senate	House of Representatives	State Capitol
Delaware	General Assembly	Senate	House of Representatives	Legislative Hall
Florida	Legislature	Senate	House of Representatives	The Capitol
Georgia	General Assembly	Senate	House of Representatives	State Capitol
Hawaii	Legislature	Senate	House of Representatives	State Capitol
Idaho	Legislature	Senate	House of Representatives	State Capitol
Illinois	General Assembly	Senate	House of Representatives	State House
Indiana	General Assembly	Senate	House of Representatives	State House
Iowa	General Assembly	Senate	House of Representatives	State Capitol
Kansas	Legislature	Senate	House of Representatives	State Capitol
Kentucky	General Assembly	Senate	House of Representatives	State Capitol
Louisiana	Legislature	Senate	House of Representatives	State Capitol
Maine	Legislature	Senate	House of Representatives	State House
Maryland	General Assembly	Senate	House of Delegates	State House
Massachusetts	General Court	Senate	House of Representatives	State House
Michigan	Legislature	Senate	House of Representatives	State Capitol
Minnesota	Legislature	Senate	House of Representatives	State Capitol
Mississippi	Legislature	Senate	House of Representatives	State Capitol
Missouri	General Assembly	Senate	House of Representatives	State Capitol
Montana	Legislature	Senate	House of Representatives	State Capitol
Nebraska	Legislature	(a)		State Capitol
Nevada	Legislature	Senate	Assembly	Legislative Building
New Hampshire	General Court	Senate	House of Representatives	State House
New Jersey	Legislature	Senate	General Assembly	State House
New Mexico	Legislature	Senate	House of Representatives	State Capitol
New York	Legislature	Senate	Assembly	State Capitol
North Carolina	General Assembly	Senate	House of Representatives	State Legislative Building
North Dakota	Legislative Assembly	Senate	House of Representatives	State Capitol
Ohio	General Assembly	Senate	House of Representatives	State House
Oklahoma	Legislature	Senate	House of Representatives	State Capitol
Oregon	Legislative Assembly	Senate	House of Representatives	State Capitol
Pennsylvania	General Assembly	Senate	House of Representatives	Main Capitol Building
Rhode Island	General Assembly	Senate	House of Representatives	State House
South Carolina	General Assembly	Senate	House of Representatives	State House
South Dakota	Legislature	Senate	House of Representatives	State Capitol
Tennessee	General Assembly	Senate	House of Representatives	State Capitol
Texas	Legislature	Senate	House of Representatives	State Capitol
Utah	Legislature	Senate	House of Representatives	State Capitol
Vermont	General Assembly	Senate	House of Representatives	State House
Virginia	General Assembly	Senate	House of Delegates	State Capitol
Washington	Legislature	Senate	House of Representatives	State Capitol
West Virginia	Legislature	Senate	House of Delegates	State Capitol
Wisconsin	Legislature	Senate	Assembly (b)	State Capitol
Wyoming	Legislature	Senate	House of Representatives	State Capitol
Dist. of Columbia	Council of the District of Columbia	(a)		Council Chamber
American Samoa	Legislature	Senate	House of Representatives	Maota Fono
Guam	Legislature	(a)		Congress Building
No. Mariana Islands	Legislature	Senate	House of Representatives	Civic Center Building
Puerto Rico	Legislative Assembly	Senate	House of Representatives	The Capitol
U.S. Virgin Islands	Legislature	(a)		Capitol Building

Source: The Council of State Governments, *Directory I—Elective Officials 2015.*
Key:
(a) Unicameral legislature. Except in the District of Columbia, members go by the title Senator.
(b) Members of the lower house go by the title Representative.

Table 3.2
LEGISLATIVE SESSIONS: LEGAL PROVISIONS

State or other jurisdiction	Regular sessions				Special sessions		
	Legislature convenes			Limitation on length of session (a)	Legislature may call	Legislature may determine subject	Limitation on length of session
	Year	Month	Day				
Alabama............	Annual	Jan. Mar. Feb.	2nd Tues. (b) 1st Tues. (c) 1st Tues. (d)(e)	30 L in 105 C	No	Yes (f)	12 L in 30 C
Alaska..............	Annual	Jan.	3rd Tues. (g)	121 C; 90 Statutory (g)	By petition, 2/3 members, each house	Yes	30 C
Arizona............	Annual	Jan.	2nd Mon.	(h)	By petition, 2/3 members, each house	Yes	None
Arkansas..........	Annual	Jan. Feb.	2nd Mon. 2nd Mon.	60 C (i) 30C (i)	No	No	None (j)
California.........	Biennium (k)	Jan.	1st Mon. (d)	None	No	No	None
Colorado..........	Annual	Jan.	No later than 2nd Wed.	120 C	By petition, 2/3 members, each house	Yes (l)	None
Connecticut......	Annual	Feb.	Wed. after 1st Mon. (odd years)	(m)	By petition, majority, each house (n)	Yes	None
Delaware..........	Biennium	Jan.	2nd Tues.	June 30	Joint call, presiding officers, both houses	Yes	None
Florida.............	Annual	Mar.	1st Tues. after 1st Mon. (o)	60 C (i)	Joint call, presiding officers, both houses or by petition	Yes	20 C (zz)
Georgia............	Annual	Jan.	2nd Mon.	40 L	By petition, 3/5 members, each house	No (p)	40 L
Hawaii.............	Annual	Jan.	3rd Wed.	60 L (i)	By petition, 2/3 members, each house (uu)	Yes	30 L (i)
Idaho..............	Annual	Jan.	Mon. on or nearest 9th day	None	No	No	20 C
Illinois............	Biennium	Jan.	2nd Wed.	None (q)	Joint call, presiding officers, both houses; Governor also may call	Yes	None
Indiana............	Annual	Jan.	2nd Mon. (r)	odd–61 C or Apr. 29; even–30 C or Mar. 14	No	Yes	30 L or 40 C
Iowa...............	Annual	Jan.	2nd Mon.	None (bbb)	By petition, 2/3 members, each house	Yes	None
Kansas............	Annual	Jan.	2nd Mon.	odd–None; even–90 C (i)	Petition to governor of 2/3 members, each house	Yes	None
Kentucky	Annual	Jan.	1st Tues. after 1st Mon.	even–60 L; odd–30 L (s)	No	No	None
Louisiana.........	Annual	Mar. (even years) Apr. (odd years)	second Mon. (even and odd years)	even–60 L in 85 C; odd–45 L in 60 C	By petition, majority, each house	Yes	30 C
Maine..............	(t)	Dec. (even years) Jan. (subsequent even year)	1st Wed. (quadrennial election year) Wed. after 1st Tues.	Calendar days set by statute (u)	Joint call, presiding officers of both houses with the consent of a majority of the members of each political party	Yes	None
Maryland	Annual	Jan.	2nd Wed.	90 C	By petition, majority, each house	Yes	30 C
Massachusetts	Biennium	Jan.	1st Wed.	(v)	By petition (w)	Yes	None
Michigan..........	Annual	Jan.	2nd Wed.	None	No	No	None
Minnesota.........	Biennium	Jan.	1st Tues. after 1st Mon. (odd years)	120 L	No (x)	Yes	None
Mississippi	Annual	Jan.	Tues. after 1st Mon.	125 C (y); 90 C (y)	No	No	None

See footnotes at end of table.

LEGISLATIVE SESSIONS: LEGAL PROVISIONS — Continued

State or other jurisdiction	Legislature convenes			Limitation on length of session (a)	Special sessions		
	Year	Month	Day		Legislature may call	Legislature may determine subject	Limitation on length of session
Missouri	Annual	Jan.	Wed. after 1st Mon.	May 30	By petition, 3/4 members, each house	Yes (l)	30 C (z)
Montana	Biennial–odd year	Jan.	1st Mon. (vv)	90 L	By petition, majority, each house (ww)	Yes	None
Nebraska	Annual	Jan.	Wed. after 1st Mon.	odd–90 L; even–60 L	By petition, 2/3 members, each house	Yes	None
Nevada	Biennial–odd year	Feb.	1st Mon.	120 C	By petition, 2/3 members, each house	Yes (aa)	20 C (aa)
New Hampshire	Annual	Jan.	Wed. after 1st Tues.	45 L	By petition (xx)	Yes	15 L (bb)
New Jersey	Biennium	Jan.	2nd Tues. of even year	None	By petition, majority, each house (cc)	Yes	None
New Mexico	Annual	Jan.	3rd Tues.	odd–60 C; even–30 C	By petition, 3/5 members, each house (l)	Yes (l)	30 C
New York	Annual	Jan. (dd)	Wed. after 1st Mon.	None	By petition, 2/3 members, each house	Yes (l)	None
North Carolina	(ee)	Jan.	3rd Wed. after 2nd Mon. (odd years)	None	By petition, 3/5 members, each house	Yes	None
North Dakota	Biennial–odd year	Jan.	First Tues. after the 3rd day in Jan.	80 L in the biennium	No	Yes	None
Ohio	Biennium	Jan.	1st Mon. (gg)	None	Joint call, presiding officers, both houses	Yes	None
Oklahoma	Annual	Feb.	1st Mon.	last Fri. in May	By petition, 2/3 members, each house	Yes	None
Oregon	Annual	Feb.	1st Mon.	(ff)	By petition, majority, each house	Yes	None
Pennsylvania	Biennium (hh)	Jan.	1st Tues.	None	Governor may call	No	None
Rhode Island	Annual	Jan.	1st Tues.	None	Joint call, presiding officers, both houses	Yes	None
South Carolina	Biennium	Jan.	2nd Tues.	(ii)	By vote, 2/3 members, each house	Yes	None
South Dakota	Annual	Jan.	2nd Tues.	odd–40 L; even–40 L	By petition, 2/3 members, each house	Yes (jj)	None
Tennessee	Biennium (kk)	Jan.	2nd Tues.	90 L (ll)	By petition, 2/3 members, each house	Yes	30 L (ll)
Texas	Biennial–odd year	Jan.	2nd Tues.	140 C	No	No	30 C
Utah	Annual	Jan.	4th Mon.	45 C	No	No	30 C
Vermont	Annual (yy)	Jan.	Wed. after 1st Mon. (yy)	None	No	Yes	None
Virginia	Annual	Jan.	2nd Wed.	odd–30 C (i); even–60 C (i)	(tt)	Yes	None (mm)
Washington	Annual	Jan.	2nd Mon.	odd–105 C; even–60 C	By vote, 2/3 members, each house	Yes	30 C
West Virginia	Annual	Jan	2nd Wed.	60 C (i)	By petition, 3/5 members, each house	Yes (l)	None
Wisconsin	Biennium	Jan.	1st Mon.	None	(nn)	No	None
Wyoming	Biennium	Jan. (odd years) / Feb. (even years)	2nd Tues (odd years) / 2nd Mon. (even years)	odd–40 L; even–20 L; biennium–60 L	By petition, majority members, each house	Yes	20 L (aaa)
Dist. of Columbia	(oo)	Jan.	2nd day	None	...	...	...
American Samoa	Annual	Jan. / July	2nd Mon. / 2nd Mon.	45 L / 45 L	No	No	None
Guam	(pp)	Jan.	2nd Mon.	None (pp)	Only the governor may call	No	None (pp)

See footnotes at end of table.

LEGISLATIVE SESSIONS: LEGAL PROVISIONS—Continued

State or other jurisdiction	Regular sessions				Special sessions		
	Legislature convenes			Limitation on length of session (a)	Legislature may call	Legislature may determine subject	Limitation on length of session
	Year	Month	Day				
		(rr)	(d)(rr)				
No. Mariana Islands	Annual	(rr)	(d)(rr)	90 L (qq)	Upon request of presiding officers, both houses	Yes (j)	10 C
Puerto Rico	Annual (rr)	Jan. / Aug.	2nd Mon. / 3rd Mon.	5 mo. / 4 mo.	No	No	20 C
U.S. Virgin Islands	Annual	Jan. (ss)	2nd Mon. (ss)	None	No, governor calls	No	None

Source: The Council of State Governments' survey November 2015 and state websites January 2016.

Key:
Annual—holds legislative sessions every year.
Biennial—odd year—holds legislative sessions every other year.
Biennium—holds legislative sessions in a two-year term of activity.
C—Calendar day
L—Legislative day (in some states called a session day or workday; definition may vary slightly, however, generally refers to any day on which either house of legislature is in session).
(a) Applies to each year unless otherwise indicated.
(b) General election year (quadrennial election year).
(c) In first year after quadrennial election.
(d) Legal provision for organizational session prior to stated convening date. Alabama—in the year after quadrennial election, second Tuesday in January for 10 C. California—in the even-numbered general election year, first Monday in December for an organizational session, recess until the first Monday in January of the odd-numbered year. No. Mariana Islands—in year after general election, second Monday in January.
(e) In second and third years of quadrennium.
(f) By 2/3 vote each house.
(g) Convening date is statutory. Length of session is 121 calendar days, 90 by statute.
(h) No constitutional or statutory provision; however, by legislative rule regular sessions shall be adjourned sine die no later than Saturday of the week during which the 100th day from the beginning of each regular session falls. The Speaker/President may by declaration authorize the extension of the session for a period not to exceed seven additional days. Thereafter the session can be extended only by a majority vote of the House/Senate.
(i) Session may be extended by vote of members in both houses. Arkansas—2/3 vote to extend up to 75 days; 3/4 vote to go beyond 75 days. Even year fiscal session may be extended one-time only by a 3/4 vote, with the extention no more than 15 C days. Florida—3/5 vote, session may be extended by vote of members in each house. Hawaii—petition of 2/3 membership for maximum 15-day extension. Kansas—2/3 vote. Virginia—2/3 vote for 30 C extension. West Virginia—may be extended by the governor.
(j) After governor's business has been disposed of, members may remain in session up to 15C days by a 2/3 vote of both houses.
(k) Regular sessions begin after general election, in December of even-numbered year. In California, in the even-numbered general election year, first Monday in December for an organizational session, recess until the first Monday in January of the odd-numbered year.
(l) Only if legislature convenes itself. In New York, special sessions may also be called by the governor. In New Mexico, special sessions may only be called by the governor and subjects are limited to issues included in governor's proclamation; extraordinary session may only be called by the legislature and have no limitations on subject.
(m) Odd-numbered years—not later than Wednesday after first Monday in June; even-numbered years—not later than Wednesday after first Monday in May.

(n) Adoption of a joint resolution by a majority of each house.
(o) A regular session of the legislature shall convene on the first Tuesday after the first Monday of each odd-numbered year, and on the first Tuesday after the first Monday in March, or such other date as may be fixed by law, of each even-numbered year.
(p) If three-fifths of the General Assembly certifies to governor that an emergency exists, governor must convene a special session for all purposes.
(q) Constitution encourages adjournment by May 31.
(r) Legislators may reconvene at any time after organizational meeting; however, second Monday in January is the final date by which regular session must be in process.
(s) During the odd-year session, the members convene for four days, then break until February.
(t) Regular session begins after general election in even-numbered years. Session which begins in December of general election year runs into the following year (odd-numbered); second session begins in next even-numbered year. The second session is limited to budgetary matters; legislation in the governor's call; emergency legislation; legislation referred to committee for study.
(u) Statutory adjournment for the First Regular Session (beginning in December of even-numbered years and continuing into the following odd-numbered year) is the third Wednesday of June; statutory adjournment for the Second Regular Session (beginning in January of the subsequent even-numbered year) is the third Wednesday in April. The statutes provide for up to two extensions of up to five legislative days each for each session.
(v) Legislative rules say formal business must be concluded by Nov. 15th of the 1st session in the biennium, or by July 31st of the 2nd session for the biennium.
(w) Joint rules provide for the submission of a written statement requesting special session by a specified number of members of each chamber.
(x) Special session is called by the governor.
(y) 90 C sessions every year, except the first year of a gubernatorial administration during which the legislative session runs for 125 C.
(z) 30 C if called by legislature; 60 C if called by governor.
(aa) Legislature may determine the subject if it calls itself into special session. Special sessions are limited to 20 calendar days except in cases of impeachment of state and judicial officers or expulsion of a member of the Legislature.
(bb) Limitation is on legislative pay and mileage.
(cc) Or by joint call, presiding officers, both houses.
(dd) Session officially begins on the first Wednesday following the first Monday of the new legislative term (commencing the first of the year), and lasts until the legislature completes its business and adjourns sine die. However, over the past several years, both houses have adopted the tactic of declaring a recess at the call of the leaders, in order to facilitate easy recall of the legislature to override vetoes, etc. Over time the custom has become to formally adjourn both houses just before the new session opens. This leads to the rather interesting convention that when the governor calls the legislature into session, it is considered "special" or "executive," even though the regular session is ongoing.

LEGISLATIVE SESSIONS: LEGAL PROVISIONS — Continued

(ee) Legal provision for session in odd-numbered year; however, legislature may divide, and in practice has divided, to meet in even-numbered years as well.

(ff) The Oregon Constitution establishes a maximum of 160 calendar days for an odd-year regular session and a maximum of 35 calendar days for an even-year regular session. Each regular session may be extended in five-day increments by the affirmative vote of two-thirds of the members of each house.

(gg) Unless Monday is a legal holiday; in second year, the General Assembly convenes on the same date.

(hh) Sessions are two years and begin on the 1st Tuesday of January of the odd-numbered year. Session ends on November 30 of the even-numbered year. Each calendar year receives its own legislative number.

(ii) The regular session ends the first Thursday in June; it can be extended with a two-thirds majority vote.

(jj) Legislators must address topic for which the special session was called.

(kk) Each General Assembly convenes for a First and Second Regular Session over a two-year period.

(ll) 90 legislative days over a two-year period. During special sessions members will be paid up to 30 legislative days; further days will be without pay or per diem.

(mm) No limitation, but the convening of the new General Assembly following an election would by operation end the special session.

(nn) The Legislature may call itself into Extraordinary Session on any subject by a majority vote of the organizing committees of each house, by joint resolution, or by a petition of a majority of each house. Only the governor may call a special session.

(oo) Each Council period begins on January 2 of each odd-numbered year and ends on January 1 of the following odd-numbered year.

(pp) Legislature meets on the first Monday of each month following its initial session in January. One legislative day or one special session day may become several calendar days. Special sessions may address only one subject.

(qq) 60 L before April 1 and 30 L after July 31.

(rr) Legislature meets twice a year. During general election years, the legislature only convenes on the January session.

(ss) The legislature convenes in January on the second Monday, March, June and September, the third Wednesday.

(tt) The Constitution provides that the governor must call a special session upon "application" of 2/3 of the members of each house.

(uu) Governor may call both houses of the legislature or the Senate alone into special session. Also, upon a 2/3 affirmative vote, the Senate may call itself into special session to consider judicial nominations.

(vv) If the first Monday falls on New Years Day, the Legislature convenes on the first Wednesday.

(ww) Majority of the total Legislature; i.e., 76 members of the combined 100-member House and 50-member Senate.

(xx) Petition filed with Secretary o State signed by not less than 50 members of House (not more than 10 from the same county) and not less than eight members of the Senate.

(yy) Constitutionally the sessions are convened biennially in the odd year. Since the late 1960s a second-year adjourned session has been held. Adjourned session date is legislatively set or a date during the first 10 days of January.

(zz) Session may be extended by 3/5 vote per s. 11.011, Florida Statutes, if 20 percent of the members of the Legislature certify in writing that conditions warrant convening a special session, the Department of State shall, within seven days after receiving the required number of certificates, poll the members. Upon affirmative vote of 3/5 of the members of both houses, the Department of State shall fix the day and hour for convening the special session.

(aaa) Twenty legislative days if Legislature calls themseleves. Unlimited if governor calls special session.

(bbb) No formal limitation, but legislator per diems are limited by statute to 110 calendar days during odd-year sessions and 100 calendar days during even-year sessions.

Table 3.3
THE LEGISLATORS: NUMBERS, TERMS, AND PARTY AFFILIATIONS: 2016

State or other jurisdiction	Senate Democrats	Republicans	Other	Vacancies	Total	Term	House/Assembly Democrats	Republicans	Other	Vacancies	Total	Term	Senate and House/ Assembly totals
State and territory totals	876	1,105	13	8	2,069*	...	2,363	3,061	38	20	5,505	...	7,571*
State totals....................	827	1,085	4	7	1,972*	...	2,335	3,031	25	20	5,414	...	7,383*
Alabama........................	8	26	1 (b)	...	35	4	33	70	...	2	105	4	140
Alaska...........................	6	14	...	...	20	4	16	23	1 (k)	...	40	2	60
Arizona.........................	12	18	...	...	30	2	24	36	...	...	60	2	90
Arkansas.......................	11	24	...	...	35	4	35	64	1 (b)	...	100	2	135
California	26	14	...	...	40	4	51	28	...	1	80	2	120
Colorado.......................	17	18	...	...	35	4	34	31	...	...	65	2	100
Connecticut...................	21	15	...	...	36	2	86	64	...	1	151	2	187
Delaware	12	9	...	...	21	4	25	16	...	...	41	2	62
Florida..........................	14	26	...	...	40	4	39	81	...	...	120	2	160
Georgia.........................	17	39	...	...	56	2	61	117	1 (b)	1	180	2	236
Hawaii...........................	24	1	...	...	25	4	44	7	...	...	51	2	76
Idaho.............................	7	28	...	...	35	2	14	56	...	...	70	2	105
Illinois..........................	39	20	...	...	59	(a)	71	47	...	...	118	2	177
Indiana..........................	10	40	...	...	50	4	29	71	...	...	100	2	150
Iowa	26	24	...	...	50	4	43	57	...	...	100	2	150
Kansas	8	32	...	...	40	4	28	97	...	...	125	2	165
Kentucky.......................	11	27	...	...	38	4	50	46	...	4	100	2	138
Louisiana......................	14	25	...	...	39	4	42	61	2 (b)	...	105	4	144
Maine............................	15	20	...	...	35	2	78	69	4 (c)	...	151	2	186
Maryland.......................	32	14	...	1	47	4	91	50	...	...	141	4	188
Massachusetts	34	5	...	1	40	2	123	34	...	3	160	2	200
Michigan.......................	11	27	...	...	38	4	46	61	...	3	110	2	148
Minnesota......................	39 (d)	28	...	...	67	4	61 (d)	72	...	1	134	2	201
Mississippi....................	20	32	...	...	52	4	48	74	...	...	122	4	174
Missouri........................	8	24	...	2	34	4	45	117	1 (b)	...	163	2	197
Montana	21	29	...	...	50	4	41	59	...	...	100	2	150
Nebraska	..Nonpartisan election..			...	49	4	...........................Unicameral						49
Nevada..........................	10	11	...	...	21	4	17	25	...	...	42	2	63
New Hampshire	14	10	...	...	24	2	160	239	1 (b)	...	400	2	424
New Jersey	24	16	...	...	40	4 (f)	52	28	...	...	80	2	120
New Mexico	25	17	...	...	42	4	33	37	...	...	70	2	112
New York.......................	31	32	...	...	63	2	104	43	...	3	150	2	213
North Carolina..............	16	34	...	...	50	2	45	74	1 (b)	...	120	2	170
North Dakota.................	15	32	...	...	47	4	23	71	...	...	94	4	141
Ohio..............................	10	23	...	...	33	4	34	65	...	...	99	2	132
Oklahoma......................	8	39	...	1	48	4	30	71	...	...	101	2	149
Oregon..........................	18	12	...	...	30	4	35	25	...	...	60	2	90
Pennsylvania	19	31	...	...	50	4	84	119	...	...	203	2	253
Rhode Island.................	32	4	1 (b)	1	38	2	63	11	1 (b)	...	75	2	113
South Carolina..............	17	28	...	1	46	4	46	78	...	...	124	2	170
South Dakota.................	8	27	...	...	35	2	12	58	...	...	70	2	105
Tennessee	5	28	...	...	33	4	26	73	...	...	99	2	132
Texas.............................	11	20	...	...	31	4	51	98	...	1	150	2	181
Utah..............................	5	24	...	...	29	4	12	63	...	...	75	2	104
Vermont.........................	19	9	2 (q)	...	30	2	85	53	12 (g)	...	150	2	180
Virginia.........................	19	21	...	...	40	4	34	66	...	...	100	2	140
Washington....................	24	25	...	...	49	4	50	48	...	...	98	2	147
West Virginia.................	16	18	...	...	34	4	36	64	...	...	100	2	134
Wisconsin	14	19	...	...	33 (h)	4	36	63	...	...	99 (h)	2	132
Wyoming	4	26	...	...	30	4	9	51	...	...	60	2	90
Dist. of Columbia (i)	11	0	2 (b)	...	13	4	...........................Unicameral..........................						13
American Samoa	.........Nonpartisan election..........				18 (j)	4	.........Nonpartisan election				20 (j)	2	38
Guam	9	6	...	...	15	2	...........................Unicameral						15
No. Mariana Islands	...	6	2 (b)	1	9	4	...	7	13 (b)	...	20	2	29
Puerto Rico	18 (m)	8 (n)	1 (l)	...	27 (p)	4	28 (m)	23 (n)	...	...	51 (p)	4	78
U.S. Virgin Islands	11	...	4 (o)	...	15	2	...........................Unicameral						15

See footnotes at end of table.

THE LEGISLATORS: NUMBERS, TERMS, AND PARTY AFFILIATIONS: 2016 — Continued

Source: The Council of State Governments, January 2016.

*Note: Senate and combined body (Senate and House/Assembly) totals include Unicameral legislatures.

Key:

... — Does not apply

(a) The entire Senate comes up for election in every year ending in "2" with districts based on the latest decennial Census. Senate districts are divided into three groups. One group elects senators for terms of four years, four years and two years; the second group for terms of four years, two years and four years; the third group for terms of two years, four years, and four years.

(b) Independent.

(c) Three Independent and one unenrolled.

(d) Democratic-Farmer-Labor.

(e) Independence Party.

(f) All 40 Senate terms are on a 10-year cycle which is made up of a two-year term, followed by two consecutive four-year terms, beginning after the decennial census.

(g) Independent (6); Progressive (6).

(h) All House seats contested in even-numbered years; In the Senate 17 seats contested in gubernatorial years; 16 seats contested in presidential years.

(i) Council of the District of Columbia.

(j) Senate: senators are not elected by popular vote, but by county council chiefs. House: 21 seats; 20 are elected by popular vote and one appointed, non-voting delegate from Swains Island.

(k) Non-affiliated.

(l) Puerto Rican Independence Party.

(m) Popular Democratic Party.

(n) New Progressive Party.

(o) Independent (3); Independent Citizens Movement (1).

(p) Constitutionally, the Senate consists of 27 seats and the House consists of 51 seats. However, extra at-large seats can be granted to the opposition to limit any party's control to 2/3.

(q) Progressive Party.

Table 3.4
MEMBERSHIP TURNOVER IN THE LEGISLATURES: 2015

State or other jurisdiction	Senate			House/Assembly		
	Total number of members	*Number of membership changes*	*Percentage change of total*	*Total number of members*	*Number of membership changes*	*Percentage change of total*
Alabama	35	0	0	105	0	0
Alaska	20	0	0	40	0	0
Arizona	30	2	7	60	1	2
Arkansas	35	0	0	100	0	0
California	40	2	5	80	0	0
Colorado	35	0	0	65	1	2
Connecticut	36	0	0	151	0	0
Delaware	21	0	0	41	1	2
Florida	40	1	3	120	0	0
Georgia	56	2	4	180	7	4
Hawaii	25	0	0	51	0	0
Idaho	35	1	3	70	0	0
Illinois	59	0	0	118	1	1
Indiana	50	1	2	100	1	1
Iowa	50	0	0	100	1	1
Kansas	40	0	0	125	1	1
Kentucky	38	0	0	100	4	4
Louisiana	39	11	28	105	29	28
Maine	35	0	0	151	2	1
Maryland	47	0	0	141	4	3
Massachusetts	40	0	0	160	1	1
Michigan	38	10	26	110	44	40
Minnesota	67	0	0	134	2	1
Mississippi	52	10	19	122	27	22
Missouri	34	0	0	163	2	1
Montana	50	0	0	100	0	0
Nebraska	49	1	2	.............Unicameral..............		
Nevada	21	0	0	42	0	0
New Hampshire	24	0	0	400	2	1
New Jersey	40	0	0	80	13	16
New Mexico	42	1	2	70	1	1
New York	63	2	3	150	4	3
North Carolina	50	0	0	120	3	3
North Dakota	47	0	0	94	0	0
Ohio	33	0	0	99	1	1
Oklahoma	48	1	2	101	2	2
Oregon	30	0	0	60	0	0
Pennsylvania	50	2	4	203	5	2
Rhode Island	38	0	0	75	1	1
South Carolina	46	1	2	124	2	2
South Dakota	35	0	0	70	0	0
Tennessee	33	0	0	99	1	1
Texas	31	0	0	150	1	1
Utah	29	0	0	75	1	1
Vermont	30	0	0	150	1	1
Virginia	40	7	18	100	12	12
Washington	49	1	2	98	3	3
West Virginia	34	1	3	100	1	1
Wisconsin	33	1	3	99	1	1
Wyoming	30	0	0	60	0	0
Dist. of Columbia	13	1	8	.............Unicameral..............		
American Samoa	18	N.A.	N.A.	20	0	0
Guam	15	0	0	.............Unicameral..............		
No. Mariana Islands	9	0	0	18	0	0
Puerto Rico	27	0	0	51	1	2
U.S. Virgin Islands	15	0	0	.............Unicameral..............		

Source: The Council of State Governments, January, 2016.

Table 3.5
THE LEGISLATORS: QUALIFICATIONS FOR ELECTION

State or other jurisdiction	House/Assembly					Senate				
	Minimum age	U.S. citizen (years) (a)	State resident (years) (b)	District resident (years)	Qualified voter (years)	Minimum age	U.S. citizen (years) (a)	State resident (years) (b)	District resident (years)	Qualified voter (years)
Alabama	21	…	3 (c)	1	…	25	…	3 (c)	1	…
Alaska	21	★	3	1	★	25	★	3	1	★
Arizona	25	★	3	1	…	25	★	3	1	…
Arkansas	21	★	2	1	★	25	★	2	1	★
California	18	3	3	1	★	18	3	3	1	★
Colorado	25	★	1	1	★	25	★	1	1	★
Connecticut	18	★	★	★	★	18	★	★	★	★
Delaware	24	★	3	1	★	27	★	3 (c)	★	★
Florida	21	…	2	★	★	21	★	2	★	★
Georgia	21	★	2 (c)	1	★	25	★	2 (c)	1	★
Hawaii	18	★	3	★	★	18	★	3	★	★
Idaho	21	★	1	1	★	21	★	1	1	★
Illinois	21	★	2	2 (d)	★	21	★	2	2 (d)	★
Indiana	21	★	2	1	…	25	2	2	1	…
Iowa	21	★	1	60 days	…	25	★	1	60 days	…
Kansas	18	★	★ (c)	1	★	18	★	★ (c)	★	★
Kentucky	24	★	2 (c)	1	★	30	★	6 (c)	1	★
Louisiana	18	★	2	1	★	18	★	2	1	★
Maine	21	5	1	3 mo.	…	25	5	1	3 mo.	…
Maryland	21	★	1 (c)	6 mo. (e)	2	25	★	1 (c)	6 mo. (e)	★
Massachusetts	18	…	…	1	★	18	…	5	5	★
Michigan	21	★	…	(f)	★	21	★	★	(f)	★
Minnesota	18	…	1	6 mo.	★	21	…	1	6 mo.	★
Mississippi	21	…	4 (c)	2	★	25	…	4 (c)	2	★
Missouri	24	★	★	1	2	30	★	★	1	3
Montana	18	…	1	6 mo. (g)	…	18	…	1	6 mo. (g)	…
Nebraska	U	U	U	U	U	21	★	★ (c)	1	★
Nevada	21	★	1 (c)	30 days (h)	★	21	★	1 (c)	30 days (h)	★
New Hampshire	18	…	2 (c)	1	★	30	…	7 (c)	1	★
New Jersey	21	★	2 (c)	1	★	30	★	2 (c)	1	★
New Mexico	21	★	★ (c)	★	★	25	★	5	1 (i)	★
New York	18	★	5	1	…	18	★	5	1	…
North Carolina	21	…	…	1 (i)	★	25	…	2	…	…
North Dakota	18	…	1	1	★	18	…	1	1	★
Ohio	18	★	1	30 days in precinct	★	18	★	30 days	1 (o)	★
Oklahoma	21	★	★ (c)	1 (o)	★	25	★	★ (c)	1	★
Oregon	21	★	…	…	★	21	★	★	…	★
Pennsylvania	21	…	4 (c)	1	…	25	★	4 (c)	1	…
Rhode Island	18	★	30 days	30 days	★	18	★	30 days	30 days	★
South Carolina	21	…	…	★ (j)	…	25	…	…	★ (j)	…

See footnotes at end of table.

THE LEGISLATORS: QUALIFICATIONS FOR ELECTION — Continued

State or other jurisdiction	House/Assembly					Senate				
	Minimum age	U.S. citizen (years) (a)	State resident (years) (b)	District resident (years)	Qualified voter (years)	Minimum age	U.S. citizen (years) (a)	State resident (years) (b)	District resident (years)	Qualified voter (years)
South Dakota	21	★	2	★	★	21	★	2	★	★
Tennessee	21	★	(c)	1	★	30	★	3	1	★
Texas	21	★	2	1	★	26	★	5	1	★
Utah	25	★	3 (c)	6 mo.	…	25	★	3 (c)	6 mo.	…
Vermont	18	★	2	1	…	18	★	2	1	…
Virginia	21	★	…	★	★	21	★	★	★	★
Washington	18	★	1	…	★	18	★	…	…	★
West Virginia	18	1	1 (c)	…	★ (k)	25	5	5 (c)	1	★
Wisconsin	18	★	1	★ (k)	★	25	★	1	★ (k)	★ (k)
Wyoming	21	★	★ (c)	1	★	25	★	★ (c)	1	★
Dist. of Columbia	U	U	U	U	U	18	…	1	★	★
American Samoa	25	★ (l)	5	1	U	30 (m)	★ (l)	5	1	…
Guam	U	U	U	U	U	25	★	5	…	★
No. Mariana Islands	21	…	3	(f)	★	25	…	5	(f)	★
Puerto Rico	25	★	2	1 (n)	U	30	★	2	1 (m)	…
U.S. Virgin Islands	U	U	U	U	U	21	…	3 (c)	3	★

Source: The Council of State Governments survey, November 2015 and state websites 2016.

Note: Many state constitutions have additional provisions disqualifying persons from holding office if they are convicted of a felony, bribery, perjury or other infamous crimes.

Key:
U — Unicameral legislature; members are called senators, except in District of Columbia.
★ — Formal provision; number of years not specified.
… — No formal provision.
(a) In some states candidate must be a U.S. citizen to be an elector, and must be an elector to run.
(b) In some states candidate must be a state resident to be an elector, and must be an elector to run.
(c) State citizenship requirement. In Tennessee — must be a citizen for three years.
(d) In the first election after a redistricting, a candidate may be elected from any district that contains a part of the district in which (s)he resided at the time of redistricting, and may be re-elected if a resident of the district (s)he represents for 18 months before re-election.

(e) If the district was established for less than six months, residency is length of establishment of district.
(f) Must be a qualified voter of the district; number of years not specified.
(g) Shall be a resident of the county if it contains one or more districts or if the district contains all or parts of more than one county.
(h) 30 days prior to close of filing for declaration of candidacy.
(i) After redistricting, candidate must have been a resident of the county in which the district is contained for one year immediately preceding election.
(j) At the time of filing.
(k) Twenty-eight days prior to election.
(l) Or U.S. national.
(m) Must be registered matai.
(n) The district legislator must live in the municipality he/she represents.
(o) One year unless absent from the district on the public business of the United States or Ohio.

Table 3.6
SENATE LEADERSHIP POSITIONS: METHODS OF SELECTION

State or other jurisdiction	President	President pro tem	Majority leader	Assistant majority leader	Majority floor leader	Assistant majority floor leader	Majority whip	Majority caucus chair	Minority leader	Assistant minority leader	Minority floor leader	Assistant minority floor leader	Minority whip	Minority caucus chair
Alabama (b)	(a)	ES	(b)	…	…	…	EC	…	(b)	…	…	…	EC	…
Alaska	ES	…	EC	…	…	…	EC	EC	EC	…	…	…	EC	EC
Arizona	ES	AP	EC	…	…	…	EC	…	EC	EC	…	…	EC	…
Arkansas	(a)	ES	EC	…	…	…	EC	EC	EC	…	…	…	EC	EC
California	(a)	ES	EC	…	…	…	EC	EC	EC	…	…	…	EC	EC
Colorado	ES	ES	EC	EC	…	…	EC	EC	EC	EC	…	…	EC	EC
Connecticut (c)	(a)	ES	AP	AP	AP	AP	AP	AP	EC	AL	…	AL	AL	AL
Delaware	ES	ES	EC	…	…	…	EC	…	EC	…	AL	…	AL	AL
Florida (mm)	EC/ES	ES	AP	AL	AP	AP	…	…	EC	EC	…	…	AL	AL
Georgia	(a)	ES	EC	AL	…	…	EC	EC	EC	…	…	…	EC	EC
Hawaii	(a)	ES (e)	EC	EC	EC	EC	EC	EC (f)	EC	EC	EC	…	…	…
Idaho	(a)	ES	EC	EC	…	…	…	EC	EC	AL	…	…	AL	EC
Illinois	ES	AP	AP	AP	…	…	AP	AP	EC	EC	…	…	(h)	AL
Indiana	(a)	ES	…	…	AT	…	AT	EC	EC	…	EC	(h)	EC	EC
Iowa	ES	ES	EC	EC	…	…	EC	EC	EC	EC	…	…	EC	EC
Kansas	ES	ES (e)	EC	EC	EC	…	EC	EC	EC	EC	…	…	EC	EC
Kentucky (i)	ES	ES	…	…	…	…	EC	EC	EC	EC	EC	…	EC	EC
Louisiana	ES	ES	…	…	EC	…	…	…	…	…	…	…	…	…
Maine (ll)	ES	ES	EC	EC	…	(j)	(k)	…	EC	…	(l)	(l)	(m)	(p)
Maryland	ES	ES	AP (n)	AP (n)	(n)	(n)	AP	…	EC (o)	EC	(o)	…	EC	EC
Massachusetts	EC	…	AP	AP	…	EC	…	…	EC	EC	…	…	…	…
Michigan (q)	(a)	ES	EC	EC	EC (j)	EC	EC	(p)	EC	EC	EC (l)	…	EC	EC
Minnesota	ES	ES	EC	EC	EC	EC	EC	EC	EC	EC	…	EC	EC	EC
Mississippi	(a)	ES	…	…	EC	…	EC	…	…	…	…	EC	…	…
Missouri (d)	ES	ES	…	…	…	…	…	…	…	…	…	…	…	…
Montana	ES	ES	EC	…	EC	…	EC	EC	EC	…	EC	…	EC	EC
Nebraska (U)(g)	(a)	ES (r)	EC	…	EC (t)	EC	…	…	EC (t)	…	EC (t)	…	…	…
Nevada (s)	ES	ES	…	…	AT (v)	EC	EC	EC	EC	…	EC	…	AL	EC
New Hampshire	AP	AP	AP	MA	MA	MA	MA	MA	EC	EC	…	…	MI	…
New Jersey	ES	ES	MA	MA	MA	MA	MA	MA	MA	MI	MI	MI	MI	MI
New Mexico	(a)	ES	EC (t)	EC	…	EC	AT	EC	EC (t)	…	EC (t)	…	EC	EC
New York (u)	(a)	ES	(v)	AT (v)	AT (v)	…	AT	AT (v)	EC (v)	AL (v)	AL (v)	AL (v)	AL (v)	AL (v)
North Carolina	(a)	ES	EC	EC	…	…	EC	EC	EC	EC	…	…	EC	EC
North Dakota	(a)	ES	EC	EC	EC	EC	EC	EC	EC	EC	EC	…	AL	EC
Ohio (w)(x)	ES (x)	ES	EC	AL	MA	…	ES	EC	ES (x)	ES	…	…	ES	…
Oklahoma	(a)	ES	EC	EC	EC	EC	EC	EC	EC	EC	EC	…	EC	EC
Oregon	ES	ES	EC	EC	…	…	EC	…	EC	EC	…	…	EC	EC
Pennsylvania	ES	ES	EC	EC	EC	EC	EC	EC	EC	EC	EC	…	EC	EC
Rhode Island (y)	ES	ES	EC	EC	…	…	EC	…	EC	EC	…	…	EC	EC
South Carolina	(a)	ES	EC	AL	…	…	AL	EC	EC	AL	…	…	AL	AL
South Dakota	ES	ES	EC	…	…	…	…	…	EC	…	…	…	…	EC
Tennessee	(a)	AP	EC	EC	EC	EC	EC	EC	EC	EC	EC	…	EC	EC
Texas	ES	ES	…	…	…	…	…	…	EC	…	…	…	…	…
Utah	(a)	AL (z)	EC	EC	EC	EC	EC	EC	EC	…	EC	EC (z)	EC	EC (z)
Vermont	(a)	ES	EC	EC	EC (aa)	EC (aa)	EC (aa)	EC (aa)	EC	EC	EC (aa)	EC (aa)	EC (aa)	EC (aa)

See footnotes at end of table.

SENATE LEADERSHIP POSITIONS: METHODS OF SELECTION—Continued

State or other jurisdiction	President	President pro tem	Majority leader	Assistant majority leader	Majority floor leader	Assistant majority floor leader	Majority whip	Majority caucus chair	Minority leader	Assistant minority leader	Minority floor leader	Assistant minority floor leader	Minority whip	Minority caucus chair
Virginia	(aa)	ES	EC(bb)	...	EC(bb)	...	EC	EC	EC	...	EC	EC	...	EC
Washington (cc)	(aa)	ES	EC	EC	EC	EC	AP	EC	EC	EC	EC	EC	EC	EC
West Virginia	ES	AP	AP	...	...	...	...	...	EC	EC	...	...	AL	...
Wisconsin	ES(dd)	EC	EC	EC	...	...	...	EC	EC	EC	EC	...	EC	EC
Wyoming	ES	ES(ee)	...	...	EC	...	...	...	...	...	EC	...	EC	EC
Dist. of Columbia (U)	(ee)	(ff)	...	...	...	...	...	...	...	...	...	...	...	...
American Samoa	ES	ES	EC	EC	EC	EC	EC	...	EC	EC	EC	EC	EC	...
Guam (U)(gg)	ES(rr)	ES(ee)	(hh)	...	ES(ii)	...	...	...	EC	...	EC	...	...	...
No. Mariana Islands	ES(hh)	...	EC	...	EC(jj)	...	...	(kk)	EC(pp)	...	EC(jj)	...	...	(pp)
Puerto Rico	ES(pp)	EC	...	...	...	...	...	...	...	...	...	...	...	...
U.S. Virgin Islands (U)	ES	...	ES	...	...	...	ES	ES	ES	...	...	...	...	ES

Source: The Council of State Governments' survey, November 2015 and state websites 2016.

Note: In some states, the leadership positions in the Senate are not empowered by the law or by the rules of the chamber, but rather by the party members themselves. Entry following slash indicates number of individuals holding specified position.

Key:
ES — Elected or confirmed by all members of the Senate.
EC — Elected by party caucus.
AP — Appointed by president.
AT — Appointed by president pro tempore.
AL — Appointed by party leader.
MA — Elected by majority party.
MI — Elected by minority party.
(U) — Unicameral legislative body.
... — Position does not exist or is not selected on a regular basis.

(aa) Lieutenant governor is president of the Senate by virtue of the office.
(bb) Majority leader elected by the members of the majority party. Minority leader elected by members of the minority party. Additional leadership positions: deputy president pro tempore – appointed by Committee on Assignments and Dean of Senate – appointed by Committee on Assignments.
(cc) Other position titles and methods of selection are as follows: chief deputy president pro tem (AT), deputy president pro tem (AT), assistant president pro tem (AT), Senate minority leader pro tem (AL), deputy Senate minority leader pro tem (AL), chief deputy minority leader (AL).
(dd) Additional positions of minority caucus secretary (EC) and majority caucus secretary (EC).
(ee) Official title is vice president. In Guam, vice speaker.
(ff) Official title is majority caucus leader.
(gg) Additional positions appointed by the majority leader: Senate Finance Committee chair, vice president pro tem, Majority Program Development Committee Chair, Majority Steering Committee chair, two assistant majority leaders, various deputies and assistants. Additional positions appointed by the minority leader: Senate Finance Committee ranking member, Minority Policy Committee chair, Minority Program Development chair, three additional minority leaders, various deputies and assistants.
(hh) Appointed by minority leader.
(ii) In each chamber, the membership elects chief clerk; assistant clerk; enrolling clerk; sergeant-at-arms; doorkeeper; janitor; cloakroom keeper; and pages.
(jj) Same position as majority leader.

(kk) Same position as assistant majority leader.
(ll) Same position as minority leader.
(mm) Same position as assistant minority leader.
(nn) Majority leader also serves as majority floor leader; deputy majority leader is official title and serves as assistant majority floor leader. There is also an assistant deputy majority leader, a majority whip, deputy majority whip, and two assistant majority whips.
(oo) Minority leader also serves as the minority floor leader.
(pp) President and minority floor leader are also caucus chairs. In Puerto Rico, president and minority leader. In Oregon, majority leader and minority leader.
(qq) Senate Rule 1.104 provides that the president pro tempore (ES), assistant president pro tempore (ES), and the associate president pro tempore (ES) are elected by a majority of the Senate.
(rr) Official title is speaker. In Guam the Speaker is elected on the Floor by majority and minority members on Inauguration Day.
(ss) Co-whips elected for 2015 session.
(tt) Majority leader also serves as majority floor leader. Minority leader also serves as minority floor leader.
(uu) Majority, appointed by president pro tem: Vice president pro tem. Assistant majority leader on conference operations, Deputy majority whip, Assistant Senate majority whip, Deputy majority leader for policy, et al. Minority, appointed by minority leader: Assistant democratic conference leader for conference operations, Vice chair of democratic conference, Deputy democratic conference whip, Assistant democratic conference whip, et al.
(vv) President pro tem is also majority leader. Assistant majority leader is called deputy majority leader for operations. Majority floor leader is called assistant majority leader for operations. Majority caucus chair called Senate majority caucus chair. Minority leader is called democratic conference leader, and independent democratic conference leader (i.e. two minority conferences); voting usually falls along conference lines. Assistant minority leader is called deputy democratic conference leader, and deputy independent democratic conference leader. Minority floor leader is called assistant democratic leader for floor operations. Assistant minority floor leader is called deputy democratic conference floor leader. Minority whip is called democratic conference whip, and independent democratic conference whip. Minority caucus chair is called chair of democratic conference.
(ww) While the entire membership actually votes on the election of leaders, selections generally have been made by the members of each party prior to the date of this formal election.
(xx) In Ohio president acts as majority leader and caucus chair; minority leader also acts as minority caucus chair; the fourth ranking minority leadership position is assistant minority whip (ES).

SENATE LEADERSHIP POSITIONS: METHODS OF SELECTION—Continued

(y) Additional positions include deputy president pro tempore.

(z) President pro tem appointed by party leader via Legislative Rules, SR1-3-103. Official title for majority floor leader is known as the assistant majority whip; the assistant minority floor leader is known as the assistant minority whip and the minority caucus chair is known as minority caucus manager.

(aa) Majority leader serves as majority floor leader and majority caucus chair. Assistant majority leader serves as assistant majority floor leader and majority whip. Minority leader serves as minority floor leader and minority caucus chair. Assistant minority leader serves as assistant minority floor leader and minority whip.

(bb) Majority party and Minority party in Senate elects caucus officers.

(cc) Washington Senate also has the leadership position of vice-president pro tem.

(dd) Caucus nominee elected by whole membership.

(ee) Chair of the Council, which is an elected position.

(ff) Appointed by the chair; official title is chair pro tem.

(gg) Additional positions include: Parliamentarian, elected by majority caucus and Senior Senator, elected by majority caucus.

(hh) Speaker also serves as majority leader.

(ii) Official title is floor leader.

(jj) Official title is alternate floor leader.

(kk) Official title is caucus chair.

(ll) Secretary of the Senate and Assistant Secretary of the Senate, both elected by the Senate membership.

(mm) All positions other than president, president pro tempore and majority leader are party caucus designations.

Table 3.7
HOUSE/ASSEMBLY LEADERSHIP POSITIONS: METHODS OF SELECTION

State or other jurisdiction	Speaker	Speaker pro tem	Majority leader	Assistant majority leader	Majority floor leader	Assistant majority floor leader	Majority whip	Majority caucus chair	Minority leader	Assistant minority leader	Minority floor leader	Assistant minority floor leader	Minority whip	Minority caucus chair
Alabama	EH	EH	EC						EC					
Alaska	EH	AS	EC				EC	EC	EC				EC	EC
Arizona	EH	AS	EC				EC	EC	EC	EC	EC	EC	EC	EC
Arkansas	EH	AS	EC		AS	AS	AS	EC	EC	AL	EC	EC	EC	EC
California	EH	AS			AS	AS	AS	EC	EC	AL	EC	EC	EC	EC
Colorado (a)	EH	AS	EC	EC			EC	EC	EC	EC	EC	EC	EC	EC
Connecticut (b)	EH	AS (b)	EC	EC (b)	AS	AS	AS	AS	EC	AL	AL	AL	AL	AL
Delaware	EH	EH	AS				EC		EC				EC	
Florida	EH	EH	AS	AS (ee)			AS (ee)		EC	EC (ee)	AL		AL (ee)	AL (ee)
Georgia	EH	EH	EC		EC		EC	EC	EC				EC	EC
Hawaii (c)	EH	EH (d)	EC	EC	EC	EC	EC	EC	EC	EC	EC	EC	EC	EC
Idaho	EH		EC	EC				EC	EC	EC	EC	EC	EC	EC
Illinois	EH	AL	AS	AS (e)	AL	AL	AL	AS (e)	EC	(e)	EC	AL	AL	AL (e)
Indiana	EH	AL	EC	AL	AL	AL	EC	AL	EC	EC	EC	AL	AL	AL
Iowa	EH	EH	EC	EC			EC	EC	EC	EC	EC	EC	EC	EC
Kansas (f)	EH	EH	EC	EC	EC		EC	EC	EC	EC	EC	EC	EC	EC
Kentucky (g)	EH	EH	EC (h)	EC (h)			EC	EC	EC (h)	EC (h)			EC	EC
Louisiana	EH	AS (h)	EC (l)	AS (j)	(h)	(h)	(h)		EC (l)	EC	(h)	(h)	(h)	
Maine (bb)	EH	EH (i)			(j)	AS	AS	(k)	EC	EC	EC (l)	EC (l)	EH	(k)
Maryland (cc)	EH	EH												
Massachusetts	EC	AS	AS	AS	AS	EC	EC	EC	EC	EC	EC	EC	EC	EC
Michigan (n)	EH	EH		EC	EC	EC	EC	EC	EC	AL	EC	EC	EC	EC
Minnesota	EH	AS	EC	EC			EC	EC		EC				
Mississippi	EH	EH			EC	EC	EC	EC		AL	EC	EC	EC	EC
Missouri (ff)	EH	EH			EC	EC	EC	EC	EC	EC	EC	EC	EC	EC
Montana							(o)							
Nebraska														
Nevada (gg)	EH	EH	AS	AS (dd)	EC	EC	EC	EC	EC	AL (dd)	EC	EC	EC	EC
New Hampshire	EH	AS (d)	MA	MA	MA	MA	MA	MA	AS	MI	MI	MI	MI	MI
New Jersey	EH	EH	MA	MA	MA	MA	MA	MA	MI	MI	MI	MI	MI	MI
New Mexico	EH		EC	AS	EC (m)		EC	EC	EC	EC	EC	EC	EC	EC
New York (p)	EH	AS	AS	AS			AS	AS (q)	EH	AL	MI	AL	AL	AL (q)
North Carolina	EH	EH	EC				AS	EC	EH	EC		EC	EC	EC
North Dakota	EH	EH	EC	EC	EC	EC	EC	EC	EC	EC	EC	EC	EC	EC
Ohio (r)	EH (k)	EH		EC	EH	EH	EH		EH (k)	EH			EH	(k)
Oklahoma	EH	EH	AS	AS	AS	AS	AS	EC	EC	AL	AL	AL	AL	EC
Oregon	EH	EH	EC	EC	EC	EC	EC	EC	EC	EC	EC	EC	EC	EC
Pennsylvania	EH	EH	EC	EC	EC	EC	EC	EC	EC	EC	EC	EC	EC	EC
Rhode Island	EH	EH	EC	AL	EC	EC	AL	EC	EC	AL	EC	EC	AL	AL
South Carolina	EH	EH	EC						EC					
South Dakota	EH	EH	EC	EC	EC		EC	EC	EC	EC	EC	EC	EC	EC
Tennessee	EH	EH	EC	EC	EC		EC	EC	EC	EC	EC	EC	EC	EC
Texas	EH	AS		EC (s)					EC	EC				
Utah	EH	AS		EC		EC (s)	EC		EC	EC	EC (s)	EC (s)	EC	EC (s)
Vermont	EH		EC	EC	(t)	(t)	(t)	(t)	EC	EC	(t)	(t)	(t)	(t)

See footnotes at end of table.

HOUSE/ASSEMBLY LEADERSHIP POSITIONS: METHODS OF SELECTION—Continued

State or other jurisdiction	Speaker	Speaker pro tem	Majority leader	Assistant majority leader	Majority floor leader	Assistant majority floor leader	Majority whip	Majority caucus chair	Minority leader	Assistant minority leader	Minority floor leader	Assistant minority floor leader	Minority whip	Minority caucus chair
Virginia (u)	EH	...	EC (v)	EC (v)	EC (v)	...	EC	EC	EC (w)	EC (w)	EC (w)	...	AL	EC
Washington	EH	EH	EC	EC	EC	EC	EC	EC	EC	EC	EC	EC	EC	EC
West Virginia	AS	AS	AS	AS	...	...	AS	AS	EC	EC	EC	...	...	...
Wisconsin	EH (x)	EH (x)	EC	EC	...	...	...	EC	EC	EC	...	...	EC	EC
Wyoming	EH	EH	EC	EC	EC	EC	EC	EC	EC	EC	EC	...	...	EC
Dist. of Columbia	...	...	...	...	...	...	...	(o)	...	...	...	...	...	...
American Samoa	EH	EH (d)	EH (d)	EC	...	...	...	...	...	...	...	...	...	...
Guam	...	...	...	...	...	...	...	(o)	...	...	...	...	...	...
No. Mariana Islands	EH (y)	...	(y)	...	EH (z)	...	...	...	EC	...	EC	...	...	...
Puerto Rico	EH (k)	EH (d)	EC	EC	EC (aa)	EC	...	EC (k)	EC (k)	EC	EC	...	EC	...
U.S. Virgin Islands	...	...	...	...	...	...	...	(o)	...	...	...	...	...	(k)

Source: The Council of State Governments' survey, November 2015 and state websites 2016.

Note: In some states, the leadership positions in the House are not empowered by the law or by the rules of the chamber, but rather by the party members themselves.

Key:
EH — Elected or confirmed by all members of the House.
EC — Elected by party caucus.
AS — Appointed by speaker.
AL — Appointed by party leader.
MA — Elected by majority party.
MI — Elected by minority party.
. . . — Position does not exist or is not selected on a regular basis.

(a) Additional positions include deputy majority whip (EC) and assistant majority caucus chair (EC).
(b) Official titles: speaker pro tem—deputy speaker, assistant majority leader—deputy majority leader.
(c) Other positions in Hawaii include speaker emeritus, majority policy leader (EC) and minority leader emeritus.
(d) Official title is deputy speaker. In Hawaii, American Samoa and Puerto Rico, vice speaker.
(e) The two deputy majority leaders appointed by the speaker are among eight assistant majority leaders; and the two deputy Republican (minority) leaders appointed by the Republican (minority) leader are among the eight assistant leaders.
(f) Additional positions include minority agenda chair (EC) and minority policy chair (EC).
(g) In each chamber, the membership elects chief clerk; assistant chief clerk; enrolling clerk; sergeant-at-arms; doorkeeper; janitor; cloakroom keeper; and pages.
(h) Speaker pro tem each occurrence. Majority leader also serves as majority floor leader; assistant majority leader also serves as assistant majority floor leader and majority whip; minority leader also serves as minority floor leader; assistant minority leader also serves as assistant minority floor leader and minority whip.
(i) There is also a deputy speaker pro tem.
(j) Majority leader also serves as majority floor leader. Official title of assistant majority leader is deputy majority leader. There are also an assistant majority floor leader, majority whip, chief deputy majority whips, and deputy majority whips.
(k) Speaker and minority leader are also caucus chairs.
(l) Minority leader also serves as the minority floor leader. There are also a minority whip, assistant minority leader, a chief deputy minority whip, an assistant minority whip, and several deputy minority whips.
(m) Majority leader also serves as majority floor leader; minority leader also serves as minority floor leader.
(n) Other positions include: two associate speakers pro tempore (EH); majority caucus chair (EC); assistant majority whip (EC); assistant associate minority floor leader (EC); minority assistant caucus chair (EC); assistant minority whip (EC).
(o) Unicameral legislature; see entries in Table 3.6, "Senate Leadership Positions—Methods of Selection."
(p) Additional majority positions appointed by the speaker: deputy speaker, assistant speaker, deputy majority leader, Ways and Means Committee chair, Democratic Program Committee chair, Democratic Steering Committee chair, various deputies and assistants. Additional minority positions appointed by the minority leader: deputy minority leader, Ways and Means Committee ranking member, Republican Steering Committee chair, Republican Program Committee chair, various deputies and assistants.
(q) Official titles: the majority caucus chair is majority conference chair; minority caucus chair is minority conference chair.
(r) While the entire membership actually votes on the election of leaders, selections generally have been made by the members of each party prior to the date of this formal election. Additional positions include assistant majority whip, the 6th ranking majority leadership position (EH) and assistant minority whip, the 4th ranking minority leadership position (EH).
(s) Assistant majority leader is known as majority assistant whip; assistant minority floor leader known as minority assistant whip; minority caucus chair known as minority caucus manager.
(t) Majority leader also serves as majority floor leader; assistant majority leader also serves as assistant majority floor leader and majority whip; minority leader also serves as minority floor leader; assistant minority leader also serves as assistant minority floor leader and minority whip.
(u) The majority caucus also has a secretary, who is appointed by the speaker; the minority caucus has 2 vice-chairs, 1 vice-chair/treasurer and an interim sergeant-at-arms.
(v) The title of majority leader is not used in Virginia; the title is majority floor leader.
(w) The title of minority leader is not used in Virginia; the title is minority floor leader.
(x) Caucus nominee elected by whole membership.
(y) Speaker also serves as majority leader.
(z) Official title is floor leader.
(aa) Official title is alternate floor leader.
(bb) Clerk of the House and Assistant Clerk of the House, both elected by the House leadership.
(cc) There is a parliamentarian for the majority appointed by the Speaker and a minority parliamentarian elected by the minority party caucus.
(dd) Assistant majority leader official title is deputy majority leader. Assistant minority leader official title is deputy minority leader. Additional position is deputy majority whip (AS).
(ee) The position of assistant majority leader is known as deputy majority leader. In addition to a majority whip, deputy whips are also appointed by the speaker. The position of assistant minority leader is known as minority leader pro tem. In addition to a minority whip, deputy whips are appointed by the minority party leader. There is no minority caucus chair—instead there is a policy chair.
(ff) Additional positions of minority and majority caucus secretaries (EC).
(gg) Co-assistant leaders elected for 2015 session and two assistant majority whips elected for the 2015 session.

Table 3.8
METHOD OF SETTING LEGISLATIVE COMPENSATION

State	Method
Alabama	Constitutional Amendment 57
Alaska	Compensation Commission; Alaska Stat. §24.10.100, §24.10.101; §39.23.200 thru 39.23.260
Arizona	Compensation Commission Send to a Public Vote Arizona Revised Statutes 41-1103 and 41-1904
Arkansas	Amendment 70, Ark. Stat. Ann. §10-2-212 et seq.
California	State Constitution—Art. III, §8, which establishes a compensation commission.
Colorado	Colorado Stat. 2-2-307 (1)
Connecticut	Conn. Gen. Stat. Ann. §2-9a; The General Assembly takes independent action pursuant to recommendations of a compensation commission.
Delaware	Del. Code Ann. Title 29, §710 et seq.; §§3301–3304; Are implemented automatically if not rejected by resolution.
Florida	Florida Statutes §11.13(1); statute provides members same percentage increase as state employees.
Georgia	Ga. Code Ann. §45-7-4 and §28-1-8
Hawaii	Hawaii State Constitution Article XVI §3.5; Legislative Salary Commission recommendations take effect unless rejected by concurrent resolution.
Idaho	Idaho Code 67-406a and 406b; Citizen's Committee on Legislative Compensation makes recommendations that the legislature can reduce or reject, but not increase.
Illinois	25 ILCS 120—Compensation Review Act and 25 ILCS 115—General Assembly Compensation Act
Indiana	IC 2-3-1-1: An amount equal to 18% of the annual salary of a judge under IC 33-38-5-6, as adjusted under IC 33-38-5-8.1.
Iowa	Iowa Code Ann. §2.10; Iowa Code Ann. §2A.1 thru 2A.5
Kansas	Kan. Stat. Ann. §46-137a et seq.; §75-3212
Kentucky	Kentucky Rev. Stat. Ann. §6.226-229. The Kentucky committee has not met since 1995; the most recent pay raise was initiated and passed by the General Assembly.
Louisiana	La. Rev. Stat. 24:31 & 31.1
Maine	Maine Constitution Article IV, part third, §7 and 3 MRSA, §2 and 2-A. Increase in compensation is presented to the legislature as legislation; the legislature must enact and the governor must sign into law. Takes effect only for subsequent legislatures.
Maryland	Article III, §15. Commission meets before each four-year term of office and presents recommendations to the General Assembly for action. Recommendations may be reduced or rejected.
Massachusetts	Massachusetts Gen. Laws Ann. ch. 3, §§9, 10. In 1998, the voters passed a legislative referendum that, starting with the 2001 session, members will receive an automatic increase or decrease according to the median household income for the commonwealth for the following two-year period.
Michigan	Article IV §12. Compensation Commission recommends legislature by majority vote; must approve or reduce for change to be effective for the session immediately following the next general election.
Minnesota	Minn. Stat. Ann §3.099 et seq.; §15A.082; The Council submits salary recommendations to the presiding officers by May 1 in odd numbered years.
Mississippi	Miss. Code Ann. 5-1-41
Missouri	Art. III, §§16, 34; Mo. Ann. Stat. §21.140; Recommendations are adjusted by legislature or governor if necessary.
Montana	Mont. Laws 5-2-301; Tied to executive broadband pay plan.
Nebraska	Neb. Const. Art. III, §7; Neb. Rev. Stat. 50-123.01
Nevada	§218.210–§218.225
New Hampshire	Art. XV, part second
New Jersey	Article IV Sec. IV 7, 8; NJSA 52:10A-1; NJSA 52:14-15.111–114
New Mexico	Art. IV. §10; 2-1-8 NMSA
New York	Constitution—Art. 3, §6; Consolidated Laws of NY—Legislative Law, Section 5
North Carolina	N.C.G.S. 120-3
North Dakota	NDCC 54-03-10 and 54-03-20
Ohio	Art. II, §31; Ohio Rev. Code Ann. title 1 ch. 101.27 thru 101.272
Oklahoma	Okla. Stat. Ann. title 74, §291 et seq.; Art V, §21; Title 74, §291.2 et seq.; Legislative Compensation Board
Oregon	Or. Rev. Stat. §171.072
Pennsylvania	Pa. Cons. Stat. Ann. 46 PS §5; 65 PS §366.1 et seq.; Legislators receive annual cost of living increase that is tied to the Consumer Price Index.
Rhode Island	Art. VI, §3

See footnotes at end of table.

METHOD OF SETTING LEGISLATIVE COMPENSATION — Continued

State	Method
South Carolina	S.C. Code Ann. 2-3-20 and the annual General Appropriations Act
South Dakota	Art. III, §6 and Art. XXI, §2; S.D. Codified Laws Ann. §20402 et seq.
Tennessee	Art. II, §23; Tenn. Code Ann. §3-1-106 et seq.
Texas	Art. III, §24; In 1991, a constitutional amendment was approved by voters to allow Ethics Commission to recommend the salaries of members. Any recommendations must be approved by voters to be effective. The provision has yet to be used.
Utah	Art. VI, §9; Utah Code Ann. §36-2-2, et seq.
Vermont	Vt. Stat. Ann. title 32, §1051 and §1052
Virginia	Art. IV, §5; Va. Code Ann. §30-19.11 thru §30-19.14
Washington	Article II §§23 and 43.03.060, Washington Rev. Code Ann. §43.03.028. The salary commission sets salaries of the legislature and other state officials based on market study and input from citizens.
West Virginia	Art. 6, §33; W. Va. Code §4-2A-1 et seq.; Submits by resolution and must be concurred by at least four members of the commission. The Legislature must enact the resolution into law and may reduce, but shall not increase, any item established in such resolution.
Wisconsin	Wisconsin Statutes §§20.923 and 230.12, created by Chapter 90, Laws of 1973, and amended by 1983 Wisconsin Acts 27 and 33. Generally, compensation is determined as part of the state compensation plan for non-represented employees and is approved by vote of the joint committee on employment relations.
Wyoming	Wyo. Stat. §28-5-101 thru §28-5-105

Source: National Conference of State Legislatures, 2015.

Table 3.9
LEGISLATIVE COMPENSATION AND LIVING EXPENSE ALLOWANCES DURING SESSIONS

State	Salaries — Regular sessions			Mileage cents per mile	Session per diem rate
	Per-diem salary	Limit on days	Annual salary		
Alabama	...	...	$42,830 (a)	54/mile.	(b)
Alaska	...	...	$50,400	54/mile.	$223 or $249/d (depending on the time of year). Tied to the federal rate. Legislators who reside in the capitol area receive 75% of the federal rate.
Arizona	...	...	$24,000	44.5/mile.	$35/d for the first 120 days of the regular session and for special sessions and $10/d thereafter; members residing outside Maricopa County receive an additional $25/d for the first 120 days of the regular session and for special sessions and an additional $10/d thereafter (V). Set by statute.
Arkansas	...	...	$39,400	54/mile.	$150/d plus mileage (V). Tied to the federal rate.
California	...	...	$100,113	53/mile.	$176/d for each day in session.
Colorado	...	...	$30,000	49/mile.	$99/d for members living outside Denver; $45/d for members who live 50 or fewer miles from the capitol (V). Set by the legislature.
Connecticut	...	...	$28,000	54/mile.	No per diem is paid.
Delaware	...	...	$44,541	40/mile.	No per diem is paid.
Florida	...	...	$29,697	44.5/mile.	$152/d based on the number of days in Tallahassee (V).
Georgia	...	...	$17,342	54/mile. Tied to federal rate.	$173/d (U). Set by the Legislative Services Committee.
Hawaii	...	...	$60,180	(c)	$175/d throughout session for members who do not reside on the island of Oahu; $10/d for members living on Oahu during the mandatory five-day recess only.
Idaho	...	...	$16,684	54/mile. One roundtrip per wk.	$129/d for members establishing a second residence in Boise; $49/d if no second residence is established and up to $25/d travel (V). Set by the compensation commission.
Illinois	...	...	$67,836	39/mile.	$111/session day.
Indiana	...	...	$24,671	54/mile. Tied to federal rate.	$161/d (U). Tied to federal rate.
Iowa	...	...	$25,000	39/mile.	$160/d; $120/d for Polk County legislators (U). Set by the legislature to coincide with the federal rate.
Kansas	$88.66/d (C)	...	...	54/mile.	$140/d.
Kentucky	$188.22/d	...	...	54/mile.	$154/d.
Louisiana	...	...	$16,800	54/mile. Tied to federal rate.	$157/d (U). Tied to federal rate.
Maine	...	...	$14,074/y first regular session; $9,982/y second regular session. (d)	44/mile.	$38/d lodging (or mileage and tolls up to $38/d in lieu of housing). $32/d meals. Set by statute.

See footnotes at end of table.

LEGISLATIVE COMPENSATION AND LIVING EXPENSE ALLOWANCES DURING SESSIONS — Continued

State	Salaries			Mileage cents per mile	Session per diem rate
	Regular sessions				
	Per-diem salary	Limit on days	Annual salary		
Maryland	...	...	$46,061	54/mile. (e)	$45/d meals. $101/d lodging.
Massachusetts	...	...	$60,032	(f)	(f)
Michigan	...	...	$71,685	54/mile.	$10,800/y expense allowance for session and interim (V). Set by the compensation commission.
Minnesota	...	...	$31,141	Tied to federal rate. (g)	$86/d for senators; $66/d for representatives.
Mississippi	...	...	$10,000	54/mile.	$140/d (U). Tied to federal rate.
Missouri	...	...	$35,915	37.5/mile	$112/d (U). Tied to federal rate.
Montana	$82.64 (L)	...	...	54/mile. Tied to federal rate.	$112.85/d (U).
Nebraska	...	...	$12,000	54/mile. Tied to federal rate.	$140/d for members residing 50 miles or more from the capitol; $51/d for members residing inside the 50-mile radius.
Nevada	$146.29/d (C)	Up to 60 days.	...	54/mile. Tied to federal rate.	$140/d.
New Hampshire	...	...	$200/2-y term	(h)	No per diem is paid.
New Jersey	...	...	$49,000	None	No per diem is paid.
New Mexico	...	...	...	54/mile. Tied to federal rate.	$163/d (V). Tied to federal rate.
New York	...	...	$79,500	54/mile. Tied to federal rate.	$174/d (including overnight) or $59/d (no overnight).
North Carolina	...	...	$13,951	29/mile. One roundtrip per wk.	$104/d (U). Set by statute.
North Dakota	$172/d (C)	...	...	54/mile. One roundtrip per wk. Tied to federal rate.	Up to $1,682/m lodging (V).
Ohio	...	...	$60,584	52/mile. (i)	No per diem is paid.
Oklahoma	...	...	$38,400	54/mile. Tied to federal rate.	$157/d (U). Tied to federal rate.
Oregon	...	...	$23,568	54/mile.	$140/d.
Pennsylvania	...	...	$85,339	54/mile. Tied to federal rate.	$175/d. Tied to federal rate.
Rhode Island	...	...	$15,414	57.5/mile.	No per diem is paid.
South Carolina	...	...	$10,400	54/mile. Tied to federal rate.	$140/d. Tied to federal rate.
South Dakota	...	...	$6,000/session	(j)	$140/d (L) (U).
Tennessee	...	...	$20,884	47/mile.	$204/d (L) (U). Tied to federal rate.

See footnotes at end of table.

LEGISLATIVE COMPENSATION AND LIVING EXPENSE ALLOWANCES DURING SESSIONS—Continued

State	Salaries — Regular sessions — Per-diem salary	Limit on days	Annual salary	Mileage cents per mile	Session per diem rate
Texas	...	...	$7,200	50/mile. $1.24/mile for single, twin and turbo engine airplanes. Set by general appropriations bill.	$190/d (U). Set by ethics commission.
Utah	$273/d (C)	...	...	56/mile.	Up to $100 plus tax/d (C) lodging; up to $39/d meals (V). Tied to in-state lodging and meal reimbursement rates.
Vermont	...	...	$693.74/w during session.	54/mile. Tied to federal rate.	$115/d lodging (including overnight) or $74/d (no overnight).
Virginia	...	...	$18,000/y Senate; $17,640/y House.	54/mile.	$185/d senators; $185/d delegates.
Washington	...	...	$45,474/y; increases to $46,839/y eff. 9/1/2016.	54/mile.	$120/d.
West Virginia	...	...	$20,000	48.5/mile.	$131/d (U). Set by compensation commission.
Wisconsin	...	...	$50,950	51/mile. One roundtrip per wk.	Senate—up to $88/d ($44/d legislators living in Dane County). Assembly—up to $138/d (including overnight) or up to $69/d (no overnight). The maximum number of days per year that per diem can be claimed is 80 days.
Wyoming	$150/d	...	...	54/mile.	$109/d (V). Set by legislature.

Source: National Conference of State Legislatures, 2016.

Key:
C — Calendar day
L — Legislative day
(U) — Unvouchered
(V) — Vouchered
... — Not applicable

(a) Alabama. The State Personnel Board met on Oct. 27, 2015, and set the median annual household income amount at $42,830.00. This current median annual household amount will begin on January 1, 2016 and will continue through December 31, 2016.

(b) Alabama. Legislators no longer receive a set per diem rate while in session. Legislators are reimbursed for in-state travel expenses which include mileage and per diem in accordance with rates and procedures applicable to state employees. All out-of-district reimbursable travel must be for official business and in the interests of the state or in the performance of official duties, as approved by the applicable presiding officer.

(c) Hawaii. Members may claim a mileage reimbursement for reasonable and necessary use of a personal automobile in the conduct of official legislative business and discharge of duties when meeting certain criteria.

(d) Maine. Annual cost of living adjustments apply. In addition, legislators receive a constituent service allowance ($2,000/year for Senators and $1,500/year for Representatives).

(e) Maryland. $750 annual allowance for in-district travel as taxable income; members may decline the allowance.

(f) Massachusetts. $10–$100/d depending on distance from State House (V). Set by the legislature.

(g) Minnesota. Senate: a reasonable allowance. House: range of $100–$1,650 per month for mileage reimbursement for travel in the Legislative district during interim. During session, House members can request up to one round trip per week if they live more than 50 miles from the Capitol.

(h) New Hampshire. Round trip home to the state House at 38/mile for the first 45 miles and 19/mile thereafter, or members will be reimbursed for actual expenses and mileage will be paid at the federal rate.

(i) Ohio. One roundtrip per wk from home to the state House for legislators outside Franklin County only.

(j) South Dakota. 42/mile for one roundtrip from capital to home each weekend. One trip is paid at 5/mile.

Table 3.10
LEGISLATIVE COMPENSATION: OTHER PAYMENTS AND BENEFITS

State	Legislator's compensation for office supplies, district offices and staffing	Phone allowance	Insurance benefits					
			Health	Dental	Vision	Disability insurance	Life insurance benefits
Alabama	None, although annual appropriation to certain positions may be so allocated.	Yes O.S.B.	S.A., O.P.	S.A., O.P.	S.A., O.P.	None.	None.
Alaska	$20,000/y Senators. $16,000/y Representatives for postage, stationery and other legislative expenses. Staffing allowance determined by rules and presiding officers, depending on time of year.	Yes O.S.B.	S.P.P.	S.P.P.	O.P., unless included in health insurance.	S.A. Optional; if selected is included in health insurance.	S.A. Small policy available. Additional is optional at legislator's expense.
Arizona	None.	(a)	S.A., S.P.P.	S.A., O.P.	S.A., O.P.	S.P.P.	S.P.P.
Arkansas	Up to $3,600/y additional reimbursement for committee chairs, vice chairs and standing subcommittee chairs.	No	S.P.P. (b)	O.P.	(b)	O.P.—supplemental.	The state pays for $30,000 as part of the health plan. Additional is optional at legislators' expense.
California	Senate member expenses are paid directly and maintained by the Senate Rules Committee. $263,000 Assembly members' base allowance.	No	S.P.P. (c)	(c)	(c)	Senators are covered by a long-term disability insurance policy; Assembly members do not have disability insurance coverage.	Senators are eligible for up to $250,000 term coverage: members pay 10% of the age-based premium plus the taxable value on coverage above $50,000. $250,000 term policy for the Assembly: members pay 18% of the premium plus the taxable value on coverage above $50,000.
Colorado	None.	Yes O.S.B.	S.P.P.—Amount differs according to plan selected.	S.P.P.—Amount differs according to plan selected.	None.	None.	S.A. State pays full amount for $12,000 policy. Additional is optional at legislator's expense.
Connecticut	$5,500 senators. $4,500 representatives.	No	S.P.P.	S.P.P.	Some health insurance plans include discounts on eyewear.	S.A., O.P.	S.A., O.P.
Delaware	$7,332/y expense allowance.	No	S.P.P. After 3/m state pays entire amount for basic plan.	O.P.	S.P.P. Only avail. through health ins. plan.	None	S.A., O.P.
Florida	$2,921/m Senate district office expenses. $2,482/m House district office expenses.	(d)	S.A. Legislators pay $50/m for individual coverage and $180/m for family coverage.	Dental coverage offered to state legislators and legislative employees.	O.P.	S.P.	S.A. Basic life insurance is provided for state legislators. Additional optional life insurance can be purchased.

See footnotes at end of table.

LEGISLATIVE COMPENSATION: OTHER PAYMENTS AND BENEFITS — Continued

State	Legislator's compensation for office supplies, district offices and staffing	Phone allowance	Insurance benefits				
			Health	Dental	Vision	Disability insurance	Life insurance benefits
Georgia............	$7,000/y reimbursable expense account for personal services, office equipment, rent, supplies, transportation, telecommunications, etc.	No	S.P.P.	S.P.P.	S.P.P.	S.A., S.P.P.	S.A., S.P.P.
Hawaii.............	$350–$500/d Senate staffing allowance. $5,000–$7,500/m House allocation for session staffing.	O.S.B.	S.P.P.	S.P.P.	S.P.P.	S.A., S.P.P.	S.A., S.P.P.
Idaho...............	$2,500/y for unvouchered constituent expense.	No	S.A., S.P.P.	S.A., S.P.P.	S.A., S.P.P.	S.A., S.P.P.	S.A., S.P.P.
Illinois.............	$83,063/y Senate office expenses, including district offices and staffing. $69,409/y House office expenses, including district offices and staffing.	No	S.P.P.	S.P.P.	S.P.P.	S.P.	S.A., S.P.P.
Indiana............	None.	No	S.A., S.P.P.	S.A., S.P.P.	S.A., S.P.P.	None.	S.A.
Iowa	$300/m district constituency postage, travel, telephone and other expenses.	No	S.P.P.	S.P.P.	S.A. Legislator pays entire premium.	S.A., S.P.	S.A. State pays first $20,000. Additional at legislator expense.
Kansas	$7,083/y. Staffing allowances vary for leadership.	Yes	S.A., S.P.P.	S.A., S.P. Legislator pays dependent portion.	S.A., O.P. Legislator pays dependent portion.	S.A., S.P.	S.A. 150% of annual salary if part of KPERS. Additional insurance is optional at legislator's expense.
Kentucky	$1,789/y district expenses during interim.	No	S.A.	O.P.	O.P.	S.A., O.P.	State pays $20,000. Additional is optional at legislator's expense.
Louisiana........	$500/m expenses in connection with holding office. $1,500/m supplemental allowance for vouchered office expenses, rent and travel mileage in district. $2,000–$3,000/m staff allowance.	Yes (e)	S.P.P.—State pays 50% and legislator pays 50%.	S.P.P.—State pays 50% and legislator pays 50%.	O.P.	S.A., O.P.	S.A., S.P.P.—State pays 50% and legislator pays 50%.
Maine.............	None. However, supplies for staff offices are provided and paid for out of general legislative account.	Yes (f)	S.A.—State pays up to 100% of legislator coverage and 50% of dependent coverage.	S.A., S.P.	O.P.	None	O.P.
Maryland	$18,965/y normal expenses of a district office with limits on staffing, postage, telephone and publications. $6,200–$15,500/y staff salaries and operating expenses. $16,325–$18,325/y in lieu of institutionally provided administrative assistant to House members.	No	S.A., S.P.P.—The state pays 85%, legislator pays 15% for HMO, legislator pays 17% for POS.	S.A., O.P.	Covered under the medical plan.	None	O.P.

See footnotes at end of table.

LEGISLATIVE COMPENSATION: OTHER PAYMENTS AND BENEFITS — Continued

State	Legislator's compensation for office supplies, district offices and staffing	Phone allowance	Insurance benefits				
			Health	Dental	Vision	Disability insurance	Life insurance benefits
Massachusetts	$7,200/y office expenses.	No	S.P.P. (State currently pays 80%)	S.P.P.	S.P.P.	S.A., O.P.	S.A. $5,000 policy provided. Additional up to 8 times salary at legislator's expense.
Michigan	Senate—$51,900/y office budget per senator. House—$102,000/y office allowance per maj. member. $99,000/y office allowance per min. member.	Yes O.S.B.	Health, vision, life, cancer, prescription, offered via cafeteria plan.			None.	Offered at different levels as part of cafeteria plan.
Minnesota	None.	Yes (g)	S.P.P. — The state pays 95% for single coverage and 88% of family coverage.	S.P.P. — The state pays 83% for single coverage and 61% for family coverage.	S.A.	S.A., O.P.	S.A. State pays first $35,000.
Mississippi	$1,500/m out of session.	No	S.P. — legislator only premiums.	O.P.	None.	None.	S.A., S.P.P. — State pays 50% and legislator pays 50%.
Missouri	Up to $700/m reasonable and necessary business expenses.	Yes (h)	S.A., S.P.P.	S.A., S.P.P.	S.A., S.P.P.	S.A., S.P.	S.A., S.P. — basic life insurance, 1x annual salary. Additional life insurance is optional at legislator's expense.
Montana	None.	Leaders only	S.A. S.P.P. — State pays almost full amount for individual	S.A., S.P.P. — State pays almost full amount for individual.	Included in health coverage.	None.	State pays $14,000 term policy. Additional at legislator's expense.
Nebraska	None.	Yes O.S.B.	O.P.	O.P.	O.P.	S.A., O.P.	S.A., O.P.
Nevada	Leaders: $900 each regular session and $64 each special session for postage, telephone tolls, and other communications charges for spkr., spkr. pro tem, maj. ldr., min. ldr. pres., pres. pro tem, maj. flr. ldr., min. flr. ldr. Senate and House Committee chairs: $900 each regular session and $64 each special session for postage, telephone tolls, and other communications charges. Any chair who would otherwise qualify for more than one allowance is entitled only to one allowance.	Yes (i)	S.A., O.P.	S.A., O.P.	S.A., O.P.	S.A., O.P.	S.A., O.P.
New Hampshire	None.	No	O.P.	O.P.	None.	None.	None.

See footnotes at end of table.

LEGISLATIVE COMPENSATION: OTHER PAYMENTS AND BENEFITS — Continued

State	Legislator's compensation for office supplies, district offices and staffing	Phone allowance	Insurance benefits Health	Dental	Vision	Disability insurance	Life insurance benefits
New Jersey	$1,250 office supplies. Equipment and furnishings supplied through a district office program. $110,000/y district office personnel. State provides stationery for each legislator and 10,000 postage stamps.	No	None.	S.A. – Members appointed or elected after 5/21/10 are not eligible for coverage.	S.A. – Members appointed or elected after 5/21/10 are not eligible for coverage.	Temporary disability insurance – none. Permanent disability – if enrolled in pension plan.	Members enrolled in the pension plan – up to three times annual salary. Members enrolled in defined contribution plan – one and a half times annual salary. Members not covered by either plan – no death benefit.
New Mexico	None.	No	None.	None.	None.	None.	None.
New York..............	Allowances are provided for in Senate Rule X, Sec. 8-10 and Assembly Rule V, Sec. 9.	No response.	No response.	No response.	No response.	No response.	No response.
North Carolina	Leaders: $16,956/y expense allowance each for pres, pro tem, spkr. $10,032/y expense allowance each for deputy pres, pro tem, spkr. pro tem. $7,992/y expense allowance each for maj. ldrs, min. ldrs. Non-leaders: $6,708/y any legislative expenses not otherwise provided. $2,275/y postage, stationery and telephone.	(j)	S.P. Family coverage optional at legislator's expense.	O.P.	O.P.	S.A., O.P.	S.A., O.P.
North Dakota........	None.	Yes (k)	S.P. – If legislator chooses state health plan.	O.P.	O.P.	S.A., O.P.	S.A. State pays for $3,500 term life policy.
Ohio....................	None.	Yes O.S.B.	S.P.P. – The state pays 85%, and legislators pay 15%.	S.P. (l)	S.P. (l)	None	S.P. – Once member has one year or more of continuous state service. Policy equal to the member's annual salary (rounded to the next higher multiple of $1,000). Supplemental and dependent life insurance is optional at legislator's expense.
Oklahoma..............	$1,500/y office expenses and electronic communications such as cell phone bills.	(m)	Up to $641/m allowance for all benefits for member and up to $1,678/m for member plus spouse and children.	Health, vision, life, cancer, prescription, offered via cafeteria plan.			S.A. State pays basic life for $20,000. Supplemental life is optional at legislator's expense.

See footnotes at end of table.

LEGISLATIVE COMPENSATION: OTHER PAYMENTS AND BENEFITS — Continued

State	Legislator's compensation for office supplies, district offices and staffing	Phone allowance	Insurance benefits				
			Health	Dental	Vision	Disability insurance	Life insurance benefits
Oregon	$69,952 per biennium for interim expenses. $37,662 session staffing. $2,736 session services and supplies. $450–750/m interim district allowance, depending on geographic size of district.	Yes O.S.B.	S.A., S.P.P.	S.A., S.P.P.	S.A., S.P.P.	S.A., O.P.	S.A., O.P.
Pennsylvania	Staffing is determined by leadership.	No	(n)	(n)	(n)	None.	Group life policy up to amount of salary.
Rhode Island	None.	No	S.A.	S.A.	S.A.	S.A., O.P.	S.A., O.P.
South Carolina	$1,000/m each member district expenses. $650/ interim committee chairs expense allowance. $3,400/y Senate postage, stationery and telephone. $1,800/y House telephone. $700/y House postage.	(o)	S.P.P.	S.P.P.	S.A., O.P.	S.A., S.P.P.	S.A., S.P.P.
South Dakota	None.	Yes (p)	None.	None.	None.	S.P.—accidental death/ dismemberment ins. only.	None.
Tennessee	$1,000/m expenses in district.	Yes (q)	S.P.P.—State pays 80%, legislator pays 20%.	O.P.	O.P.	None.	S.A. State pays first $20,000 of the basic life insurance; remainder paid by legislator.
Texas	Allowance for staff salaries, supplies, stationery, postage, district office rental, telephone expense, etc.	No	S.A., S.P.	O.P.	Included in health coverage.	S.A., O.P.	S.A., O.P.
Utah	None.	Yes (r)	S.P.P.	S.P.P.	Optional group discounts.	S.A., S.P.	S.A., S.P.—State pays full premium for $25,000 basic term life coverage.
Vermont	None.	Yes	None.	None.	None.	None.	None.
Virginia	Leaders: $76,377/y staffing allowance. $1,750/m office expense allowance. Legislators: $56,100/y staffing allowance. $1,250/m office expense allowance.	No	S.A., S.P.P.	S.A.	S.A.	None.	S.A., S.P.—The state pays for basic group life insurance. Optional Life Insurance (up to 4x salary) available at legislator's expense.
Washington	$7,800/y for legislative expenses, for which the legislator has not been otherwise entitled to reimbursement. No staffing allowance.	Yes O.S.B.	S.A.	S.A.	Included in medical.	S.A., S.P.P.	S.A., S.P.P.
West Virginia	None.	Yes	O.P.	O.P.	O.P.	None.	S.A., O.P.

See footnotes at end of table.

LEGISLATIVE COMPENSATION: OTHER PAYMENTS AND BENEFITS—Continued

State	Legislator's compensation for office supplies, district offices and staffing	Phone allowance	Insurance benefits				
			Health	Dental	Vision	Disability insurance	Life insurance benefits
Wisconsin	Senate: $214,950/2-y period staffing allowance. $55,955/2-y period office expenses. Assembly: $15,000/2-y session office expenses.	(s)	S.P.P.	(t)	(t)	S.P.P.—depending on legislator's accumulative sick leave balance.	S.P.P.—Group term life levels 1 and 2. Accidental death and dismemberment insurance (ADDI) are available at legislator's expense.
Wyoming	$750/quarter through constituent service allowance.	No	None.	None.	None.	None.	None.

Source: National Conference of State Legislatures, 2016.

Key:
(U) – Unvouchered.
(V) – Vouchered.
d – day.
m – month.
w – week.
y – year.
O.P. – Optional at legislator's expense.
O.S.B. – Official state or legislative business only.
S.A. – Same as state employees.
S.P. – State pays full amount.
S.P.P. – State pays portion and legislator pays portion.

(a) Arizona. Phone cards allowed for certain districts; none used at this time.
(b) Arkansas. Health: The state pays $410 monthly; legislators pay the balance depending on the plan chosen. Vision: Vision screening with co-pay, once/2-y with health plan; additional coverage optional at legislator's expense.
(c) California. Health: The state pays a portion (20% less than the contribution paid for state managerial employees); legislators pay a portion. Dental: Legislators pay 10% of the basic dental premium; enhanced coverage is available at an additional cost to the member. Vision: Legislators pay 10% of the basic vision premium; enhanced coverage is available at an additional cost to the member.
(d) Florida. May pay for phone service from district funds.

(e) Louisiana. District office line with one extension.
(f) Maine. Pre-paid phone cards issued and administered by the Senate and House.
(g) Minnesota. $200/m Senate communication reimbursement. $125/m House communications allowance.
(h) Missouri. Up to $50/month for data plan only.
(i) Nevada. $2,800/session allowance. $300/each special session.
(j) North Carolina. Included in office allowance.
(k) North Dakota. Legislative Council members or committee chairs only.
(l) Ohio. Vision and dental care coverage are available to a member and dependents after the member has completed one year of continuous state service.
(m) Oklahoma. Included in office allowance.
(n) Pennsylvania. Legislators pay 1% of salary toward medical/hospital, dental, vision and prescription benefits.
(o) South Carolina. Included in office allowance.
(p) South Dakota. Phone cards.
(q) Tennessee. In-state long distance only.
(r) Utah. State-paid mobile phone or reimbursement for personal phone at same rate as state-paid plan.
(s) Wisconsin. Included in office allowance.
(t) Wisconsin. Basic and diagnostic dental coverage is available; major dental coverage is available through supplemental plans, which is optional at legislator's expense. Diagnostic optical coverage is available; eye glass and contact lens coverage is available through supplemental vision plans, which is optional at legislator's expense.

Table 3.11
ADDITIONAL COMPENSATION FOR SENATE LEADERS

State	Presiding officer	Majority leader	Minority leader	Other leaders and committee chairs
Alabama	Lt. gov. holds this position.	None	None	None
Alaska	$500/y	None	None	None
Arizona	(a)	(a)	(a)	None
Arkansas	Lt. gov. holds this position.	None	None	$5,600/y pres. pro tem.
California	Lt. gov. holds this position.	$7,508/y maj. flr. ldr.	$15,061/y	$15,016/y pres. pro tem; $7,508/y second ranking min. ldr.
Colorado	(b)	(b)	(b)	(b)
Connecticut	Lt. gov. holds this position.	$8,835/y	$8,835/y	Leaders: $10,689/y pres. pro tem. $6,446/y each for dep. maj. ldrs., dep. min. ldrs. $4,241/y each for asst. maj. ldrs., asst. min. ldrs., maj. whips, min. whips. Committee chairs: $4,241/y.
Delaware	Lt. gov. holds this position.	$12,376/y	$12,376/y	Leaders: $19,983/y pres. pro tem. $7,794/y each for maj. whips, min. whips. Committee chairs: $11,459/y joint fin. chair. $4,578/y each for capital improvement chair and vice chair, sunset chair.
Florida	$11,484/year	None	None	None
Georgia	Lt. gov. holds this position.	$200/m	$200/m	Leaders: $400/m pres. pro tem. $200/m admin. floor leader. $100/m asst. admin. floor leader. Committee chairs: None.
Hawaii	$7,500/y	None	None	None
Idaho	Lt. gov. holds this position.	None	None	None
Illinois	$27,477/y	$20,650/y	$27,477/y	Leaders: $20,650/y each for asst. maj. ldrs., asst. min. ldrs., maj. caucus chairs, min. caucus chairs. Committee chairs: $10,326/y each for all chairs, min. cmte spokespersons.
Indiana	Lt. gov. holds this position.	$5,500/y for maj. flr. leader	$6,000/y min. flr. leader	Leaders: $7,000/y pres. pro tem. $5,500/y maj. caucus chair. $5,000/y each for min. caucus chair, asst. min. flr. ldr. $4,000/y maj. whip, $3,500/y asst maj. flr. leader. $3,000/y asst. pres. pro tem. $2,500/y maj. flr. ldr. emeritus. $2,000/y asst. maj. whip, min. whips. $1,500/y each for min. ldr. emeritus, asst. maj. caucus chairs $1,000/y each for asst. min. whip, asst. min. caucus chairs. (Ind. P.L. 213−2015). Committee chairs: $5,500/y each for app. chair, tax and fiscal policy chair. $2,000/y each for app. ranking maj. member, tax and fiscal policy ranking maj. member, app. ranking min. member, tax and fiscal policy ranking min. member. $1,000/y each for 21 other cmte. chairs. If an officer fills more than one leadership position, the officer shall be paid for the higher paid position. (Ind. P.L. 213−2015).
Iowa	$11,593/y	$11,593/y	$11,593/y	Leaders: $1,243/y pres. pro tem. Committee chairs: None.

See footnotes at end of table.

ADDITIONAL COMPENSATION FOR SENATE LEADERS — Continued

State	Presiding officer	Majority leader	Minority leader	Other leaders and committee chairs
Kansas	$14,039/y	$12,666/y	$12,666/y	Leaders: $7,165/y each for vice pres., asst. maj. ldrs., asst. min.ldrs. Committee chairs: $11,290/y w&m chair.
Kentucky	$47.35/d	$37.40/d	$37.40/d	Leaders: $28.66/d each for maj. caucus chairs, min. caucus chairs, maj. caucus whips, min. caucus whips. Committee chairs: $18.71/d for standing cmtes. only.
Louisiana	$15,200/y	None	None	Leaders: $7,700/y pres. pro tem. Committee chairs: $11,200/y each for joint budget chair and vice-chair.
Maine	50% of base salary/y	25% of base salary/y	12.5% of base salary/y	None
Maryland	$13,766/y	None	None	None
Massachusetts	$35,000/y	$22,500/y	$22,500/y	Leaders: $15,000/y each for pres. pro tem, asst. maj. ldrs., asst. min. ldrs. Committee leaders: $25,000/y w&m chair $7,500–$15,000/y each for other cmte chairs.
Michigan	Lt. gov. holds this position.	$23,400/y	$19,800/y	Leaders: $10,800/y maj. floor ldr., $9,000/y min. flr. ldr. $4,962/y pres. pro tem. Committee chairs: $6,300/y app. chairs.
Minnesota	None	$12,455/y	$12,455/y	Leaders: $4,151/y maj. whip. Committee chairs: $4,151/y each for tax chair, fin. chair.
Mississippi	Lt. gov. holds this position.	None	None	$5,000/y pres. pro tem
Missouri	Lt. gov. holds this position.	None	None	None
Montana	$5/d during session.	None	None	None
Nebraska	Lt. gov. holds this position.	None	None	None
Nevada	Lt. gov. holds this position.	None	None	None
New Hampshire	$50/2-y term	None	None	None
New Jersey	1/3 above annual base salary.	None	None	None
New Mexico	Lt. gov. holds this position.	None	None	None
New York	Lt. gov. holds this position.	(c)	$34,500/y	Leaders: $41,500/y pres. pro tem. $34,000/y each for vice pres. pro tem, dep. maj. ldr. $13,000–$27,500/y for 20 other leaders. Set in statute. Committee chairs: $9,000–$34,000/y each for chairs, ranking min. members. No member may receive more than one allowance for leaders or committee chairs and ranking minority members. Set in statute.
North Carolina	Lt. gov. holds this position.	$17,048/y	$17,048/y	Leaders: $38,151/year pres. pro tem. $21,739/year deputy pres. pro tem. Committee chairs: None

See footnotes at end of table.

ADDITIONAL COMPENSATION FOR SENATE LEADERS — Continued

State	Presiding officer	Majority leader	Minority leader	Other leaders and committee chairs
North Dakota..........	Lt. gov. holds this position.	$15/d during legis. sessions, plus $345/m during term of office.	$15/d during legis. sessions, plus $345/m during term of office.	Leaders: $10/d during session asst. ldrs. Committee chairs: $10/d all substantive standing cmtes.
Ohio..................	$33,853/y	$20,579/y maj. flr. ldr.	$25,581/y	Leaders: $25,581/y pres. pro tem. $18,084/y maj. whip. $2,797/y asst. min. whip. Committee chairs: $10,000/y fin. chair. $6,500/y each for fin. ranking min. member, fin. standing subcmte. chair, all other standing cmte. chairs. $5,500/y fin. vice chair. $5,000/y each for ranking min. member of fin. standing subcmte., vice-chairs, ranking min. members, standing subcmte. chairs. $2,500/y standing subcmte. ranking min. members.
Oklahoma..............	Lt. gov. holds this position.	$12,364/y	$12,364/y	Leaders: $17,932/y pres. pro tem. Committee chairs: $12,364 each for app. chair, budget chair.
Oregon................	$23,568/y	None	None	None
Pennsylvania	Lt. gov. holds this position.	$38,306/y	$38,306/y	Leaders: $47,880/y pres. pro tem. $29,071/y maj. whips, min. whips. $18,126/y each for maj. caucus chairs, min. caucus chairs. $11,971/y each for maj. caucus secretaries, min. caucus secretaries, maj. policy chairs, min. policy chairs, maj. caucus admin., min. caucus admin. Committee chairs: $29,071/y each for maj. app. chair, min. app. chair.
Rhode Island..........	$15,414/y	None	None	None
South Carolina........	Lt. gov. holds this position.	None	None	Leaders: $11,000/y pres. pro tem.
South Dakota..........	Lt. gov. holds this position.	None	None	None
Tennessee	$41,768/y	None	None	None
Texas.................	Lt. gov. holds this position.	None	None	None
Utah..................	$3,000/y	$2,000/y	$2,000/y	Leaders: $2,000/y each for maj. whips, min. whips, asst. maj. whips, asst. min. whips. Committee leaders: $2,000/y executive app. chair.
Vermont...............	Lt. gov. holds this position.	None	None	Leaders: $11,296/y, plus $730.66/w during session pres. pro tem. Committee chairs: None
Virginia..............	None	None	None	None
Washington............	Lt. gov. holds this position.	$8,640/y increases to $8,899/y eff. 9/1/2016.	$4,320/y increases to $4,449/y eff. 9/1/2016.	None
West Virginia.........	$150/d during session.	$50/d during session.	$50/d during session.	Leaders: $150/d (up to 30 days) for a maximum of six add'l persons named by presiding officer. Committee chairs: $150.00/d (up to 30 days) fin. and judiciary chairs.
Wisconsin	None	None	None	None
Wyoming	$3/day	None	None	None

Source: National Conference of State Legislatures, 2016.
Key:
d – day   m – month   w – week   y – year   app. – Appropriations
w&m – Ways and means   Lt. gov. – lieutenant governor who is not a member of the Senate

(a) Arizona. Generally approved for additional interim per diem.
(b) Colorado. All leaders receive $99/d salary during interim when in attendance at committee or leadership matters.
(c) New York. This position is combined with the position of pres. pro tem.

Table 3.12
ADDITIONAL COMPENSATION FOR HOUSE/ASSEMBLY LEADERS

State	Presiding officer	Majority leader	Minority leader	Other leaders and committee chairs
Alabama	$18,000/y	None	None	None
Alaska	$500/y	None	None	None
Arizona	(a)	(a)	(a)	None
Arkansas	$5,600/y	None	None	None
California	$15,016/y	$7,508/y	$15,016/y	Leaders: $7,508/y second ranking min. ldr. Committee chairs: None.
Colorado	(b)	(b)	(b)	(b)
Connecticut	$10,689/y	$8,835/y	$8,835/y	Leaders: $6,446/y each for dep. spkr., dep. maj. ldrs, min. ldrs., asst. maj. ldrs, asst. min. ldrs. $4,241/y each for maj. whips, min. whips. Committee chairs: $4,241/y.
Delaware	$19,893/y	$12,376/y	$12,376/y	Leaders: $7,794/y each for maj. whips, min. whips. Committee chairs: $11,459/y joint fin. chair. $4,578/y each for capital improvement chair and vice chair, sunset chair.
Florida	$11,484/y	None	None	None
Georgia	$6,811/m	$200/m	$200/m	Leaders: $400/m for spkr. pro tem. $200/m for gov's floor ldr. $100/m for asst. floor ldr. Committee chairs: None.
Hawaii	$7,500/y	None	None	None
Idaho	$4,000/y	None	None	None
Illinois	$27,477/y	$23,230/y	$18,067/y	Leaders: $19,792/y each for dep. maj. ldrs, dep. min. ldrs. $18,067/y each for asst. maj. ldrs, asst. min. ldrs. Committee chairs: $10,326/y each for chairs, min. cmte. spokespersons.
Indiana	$7,000/y	$5,500/y	$5,500/y	Leaders: $5,500/y maj. caucus chair. $5,000/y spkr. pro tem. $4,500/y each, min. floor ldr., min. caucus chair. $4,000/y maj. whip. $3,500/y asst. maj. fltr. ldrs. $3,000/y min. whip. $2,000/y each for dep. spkr. pro tem, asst. maj. caucus chairs, asst. maj. whips. $1,500/y each asst. min. ldr., asst. min. fltr. ldr., asst. min. caucus chair, asst. min. whip. (Ind. PL. 213–2015) Committee chairs: $5,500/y w&m chair. $4,000/y w&m vice chair. $3,500/y w&m cmte. ranking min. member. $3,000/y w&m budget subcmte. chair. $1,500/y each w&m K–12 subcmte. chair, w&m higher ed. subcmte. chair. $1,000/y each for 22 other cmte chairs. If an officer fills more than one (1) leadership position, the officer may be paid for each of the paid positions. (Ind. PL. 213–2015).
Iowa	$11,593/y	$11,593/y	$11,593/y	Leaders: $1,243/y spkr. pro tem. Committee chairs: None.
Kansas	$14,039/y	$12,665/y	$12,665/y	Leaders: $7,165/y each for spkr. pro tem, asst. maj. ldrs, asst. min. ldrs. Committee chairs: $11,290/y app. chair.

See footnotes at end of table.

ADDITIONAL COMPENSATION FOR HOUSE/ASSEMBLY LEADERS — Continued

State	Presiding officer	Majority leader	Minority leader	Other leaders and committee chairs
Kentucky	$47.35/d	$37.40/d	$37.40/d	Leaders: $28.66/d each for maj. caucus chairs & whips, min. caucus chairs & whips. Committee chairs: $18.71/d for standing cmtes. only.
Louisiana	$15,200/y	None	None	Leaders: $7,700/y spkr. pro tem. Committee chairs: None.
Maine	50% of base salary	25% of base salary	12.5% of base salary	None
Maryland	$13,766/y	None	None	None
Massachusetts	$35,000/y	$22,500/y	$22,500/y	Leaders: $15,000/y each for spkr. pro tem, asst. maj. ldrs, asst. min. ldrs. Committee chairs: $25,000/y w&m chairs. $7,500–$15,000/y other cmte. chairs.
Michigan	$27,000/y	Position does not exist.	$22,000/y	Leaders: $12,000/y maj. floor ldr. $10,000/y min. floor ldr. $5,513/y spkr. pro tem. Committee chairs: $6,300/y for app. chairs.
Minnesota	12,455/y	12,455/y	12,455/y	None
Mississippi	$50,000/y	None	None	Leaders: $5,000/y spkr. pro tem. Committee chairs: None.
Missouri	$208.34/m	$125/m	$125/m	None
Montana	$5/d during session	None	None	None
Nebraska	N/A — Unicameral legislature			N/A
Nevada	$2/d	None	None	None
New Hampshire	$50/2-y term	None	None	None
New Jersey	1/3 above annual base salary	None	None	None
New Mexico	None	None	None	None
New York	$41,500/y	$34,500/y	$34,500/y	Leaders: $9,000–$25,000/y for 31 ldrs. Set in statute. Committee chairs: $9,000–$34,000/y for chairs and ranking min. members of cmtes. No member may receive more than one allowance for ldrs or cmte. chairs and ranking min. members. Set in statute.
North Carolina	$24,200/y	$3,097/y	$3,097/y	Leaders: $7,788/y spkr. pro tem. Committee chairs: None.
North Dakota	$10/d during session	$15/d during session, plus $345/m during term of office.	$15/d during session, plus $345/m during term of office.	Leaders: $10/d for asst. ldrs during session. Committee chairs: $10/d for all substantive standing cmtes.
Ohio	$33,853/y	$20,579/y maj. flr. ldr.	$25,581/y	Leaders: $25,581/y spkr. pro tem. $18,084/y asst. maj. floor ldr. $10,589/y maj. whip. $5,591/y asst. maj. whip. $2,797/y asst. min. whip. Committee chairs: $10,000/y fin. chair. $6,500/y each for fin. ranking min. member, fin. cmte. standing subcmte. chair, all other standing cmte. chairs $5,500/y fin. vice chair. $5,000/y each for ranking min. member fin. standing subcmte. vice chairs, ranking min. members, standing subcmte. chairs. $2,500/y standing subcmte ranking min. members.

See footnotes at end of table.

ADDITIONAL COMPENSATION FOR HOUSE/ASSEMBLY LEADERS — Continued

State	Presiding officer	Majority leader	Minority leader	Other leaders and committee chairs
Oklahoma	$17,932/y	$12,364/y	$12,364/y	Leaders: $12,364/y spkr. pro tem. Committee chairs: $12,364/y each for app. chair, budget chair.
Oregon	$23,568/y	None	None	None
Pennsylvania	$47,880/y	$38,306/y	$38,306/y	Leaders: $29,071/y each for maj. whips, min. whips. $18,126/y each for maj. caucus chairs, min. caucus chairs. $11,971/y each for maj. caucus secretaries, min. caucus secretaries, maj. policy chairs, min. policy chairs, maj. caucus admin., min. caucus admin. Committee chairs: None
Rhode Island	$15,414/y	None	None	None
South Carolina	$11,000/y	None	None	Leaders: $3,600/y spkr. pro tem. Committee chairs: None.
South Dakota	None	None	None	None
Tennessee	$41,768/y	None	None	None
Texas	None	None	None	None
Utah	$5,000/y	$3,000/y	$3,000/y	Leaders: $3,000/y each for whips, asst. whips. Committee chairs: $2,000/y executive app. chair.
Vermont	$11,296/y; $730.66/w during session.	None	None	None
Virginia	$18,681/y	None	None	None
Washington	$8,640/y; increases to $8,899/y eff. 9/1/2016.	None	$4,320/y; increases to $4,449/y eff. 9/1/2016.	None
West Virginia	$150/d during session	$50/d during session	$50/d during session	Leaders: $150/d (up to 30 days) for a maximum of six add'l persons named by presiding officer. Committee chairs: $150.00/d (up to 30 days) fin. & judiciary chairs.
Wisconsin	$25/m	None	None	None
Wyoming	$3/d	None	None	None

(a) Arizona. Generally approved for additional interim per diem.
(b) Colorado. All leaders receive $99/d salary during interim when in attendance at committee or leadership matters.

Source: National Conference of State Legislatures, 2016.
Key:
d – day.
m – month.
w – week.
y – year.
app. – Appropriations
w&m – Ways and means

Table 3.13
STATE LEGISLATIVE RETIREMENT BENEFITS

State or other jurisdiction	Participation	Requirements for regular retirement	Employee contribution rate	Benefit formula
Alabama	None available.			
Alaska	Optional	Four tiers. Varies depending upon tier. Detailed information set forth in Public Employees' Retirement System (PERS) plan comparison chart.	Four tiers. Varies depending upon tier. Detailed information set forth in Public Employees' Retirement System (PERS) plan comparison chart.	Four tiers. Varies depending upon tier. Detailed information set forth in Public Employees' Retirement System (PERS) plan comparison chart.
Arizona	Mandatory except that officials subject to term limits may opt out for a term of office. AZ SB 1609 of 2011 — Contribution requirements affect all members; benefit and eligibility requirements affect those elected after January 1, 2012.	Age 65 with 5+ years of service; age 62 with 10+ years of service; or 20 years of service; earlier retirement with an actuarial reduction of benefits. Vesting at 5 years. AZ SB 1609 of 2011 — For those elected to office after 1/1/2012. Age 65 with 5+ years of service; age 62 with 10+ years of service. Vesting at 5 years. No provision for retirement after 20 years or for early retirement.	7% employee AZ SB 1609 of 2011 – 2011 legislation increases contribution rates in annual steps from the present 7% of gross salary to, in FY 2014, 13% or an actuarially based calculation, which can be revised. Affects all members. Newly elected officials as of 1/1/14 pay a rate of 8%.	4% x years of credited service x highest 3 yr. average in the past 10 years The benefit is capped at 80% of FAS. An elected official may purchase service credit in the plan for service earned in a non-elected position by buying it at an actuarially determined amount. AZ SB 1609 of 2011 — For those elected to office after 1/1/2012: 3% x years of credited service x highest 5 yr. average in the past 10 years The benefit is capped at 75% of FAS.
Arkansas	Optional. Those elected before 7/1/99 may have service covered as a regular state employee but must have 5 years of regular service to do so.	Age 65 with 10 years of service; 55/12; any age with 28 years of service; any age if serving in the General Assembly on 7/1/79; any age if in elected office on 7/1/79 with 17 and 1/2 years of service. As a regular employee, 65/5 or any age/28 years. Members of the contributory plan established in 2005 must have a minimum of 10 years legislative service if they have only legislative state employment.	Non-contributory plan in effect for those elected before 2006. For those elected then and thereafter, a contributory plan that requires 5% of salary.	For service that began after 7/1/99: 2.07% x FAS x years of service FAS based on three highest consecutive years of service. For service that began after July 1, 1991, $35 x years of service = monthly benefit. For contributory plan, 2% x FAS x years of service.
California	Legislators elected after 1990 are not eligible for retirement benefits for legislative service.			
Colorado	Mandatory	PERA: age 65 with 5 years of service; age 50 with 30 years of service; when age + service equals 80 or more (min. age of 55). State Defined Contribution Plan (DCP): no age requirement and immediate vesting.	Employee: 8%	PERA: 2.5% x FAS x years of service, capped at 100% of FAS. DCP benefit depends upon contributions and investment return.
Connecticut	Mandatory	Age 60 with 25 years credited service; age 62 with 10-25 years credited service; age 62 with 5 years actual state service. If elected after 2011—age 63 with 25 years of vesting service or age 65 with 10-25 years of vesting service. Reduced benefit available with earlier retirement ages.	Employee 2%	(1.33% x average annual salary) + (5% x average salary over "breakpoint") x credited service up to 35 years; 2003 — $36,400; 2004 — $38,600; 2005 — $40,900; 2006 — $43,400; 2007 — $46,000; 2008 — $48,800; 2009 — $51,700. After 2009 — increase breakpoint by 6% per year rounded to nearest $100.

See footnotes at end of table.

STATE LEGISLATIVE RETIREMENT BENEFITS—Continued

State or other jurisdiction	Participation	Requirements for regular retirement	Employee contribution rate	Benefit formula
Delaware	Mandatory. DE HB 81 of 2011—Mandatory for those elected after January 1, 2012.	Age 60 with 5 years of credited service; or 55 with 10 years of service. DE HB 81 of 2011—65 with 10 years of service; or 60 with 20 years of service. Vesting at 10 years.	3% of annual compensation in excess of $6,000. DE HB 81 of 2011—5% of annual compensation in excess of $6,000.	2% times FAS times years of service before 1997 + 1.85% times FAS times years of service from 1997 on. FAS = average of highest 3 years.
Florida	Optional. Elected officials may opt out or may choose between DB and DC plans. FL SB 2100 of 2011—SB 2100 affects those enrolled in the elected officers' class on or after July 1, 2011, except for a contribution requirement for all members.	Vesting in DB plan—6 years. Age 62 with 6 years; 30 years at any age. Changed in 2011 to age 62 without a service minimum. Vesting in DC plan—1 year, any age. FL SB 2100 of 2011—vesting in DB plan, 8 years. Retirement eligibility at age 65 or with 33 years of service at any age. No changes affecting the DC plan.	Employee contribution is 3%; employer contribution is 45.8%	DB plan—3% x years of creditable service x average final compensation (average of highest 5 years). DC plan—dependent upon investment experience. FL SB 2100 of 2011—Unchanged for the DB plan except that for those enrolled in the system after July 1, 2011, average final compensation will be based on the highest 8 years.
Georgia	Optional; choice when first elected.	Vested after 8 years. Age 62 with 8 years of service; age 60 with reduction for early retirement.	Employee: 3.75% + $7/m.	$36/month for each year of service. Post-retirement benefit increases are not available to any person who joins the system after July 1, 2009.
Hawaii	Mandatory. HI Act 163 of 2011—Act 163 affects For those who enter the plan after July 1, 2012.	Vesting at 5 years. Age 55 with 5 years of service, any age with 10 years of service. HI Act 163 of 2011—vesting at 10 years. Any age with 10 years of service.	Main plan is noncontributory: 7.8% for elected officials' plan for annuity. HI Act 163 of 2011—Contribution rate of 9.8%.	3.5% x years of service as elected official x highest average salary plus annuity based on contributions as an elected official. Highest average salary = average of 3 highest 12-month periods as elected official. Annual COLA of 2.5%. HI Act 163 of 2011—Multiplier for elected officials' reduced from 3.5% to 3.0%; COLA reduced from 2.5% annually to 1.5%.
Idaho	Mandatory; same plan as public employees (PERSI)	Age 65 with 5 years of service; reduced benefit at age 55 with 5 years of service.	6.79% paid by member, 11.32% paid by employer.	Average monthly salary for highest 42 consecutive months x 2% x months of credited service.
Illinois	Optional: not the same as the State Employees' Retirement System. Only state senators, representatives and statewide elected officials have the option to participate.	Tier 1—age 55 with 8 years of service or age 62 with 4 years of service. Tier 2—age 67 with 8 years of service or age 62 with 8 years of service reduced 1/2 of 1% for each month.	Tier 1—11.5% of salary (includes contributions for retirement annuity and survivors annuity) or 9.5% of salary as contributions for just retirement annuity (no survivor annuity). Tier 2—the same with the exception Tier 2 members only pay contributions on their salary up to the maximum salary for annuity purposes. In 2016 the maximum salary for annuity purposes is $115,480.89 (currently no legislators have salaries that exceed the maximum salary).	Tier 1—First 4 yrs x 3.0% = 12%; next 2 yrs x 3.5% = 7.0%; next 2 yrs x 4.0% = 8.0%; next 4 yrs x 4.5% = 18.0%; next 8 yrs x 5.0% = 40.0%. Tier 2—3% for each year of service.

See footnotes at end of table.

STATE LEGISLATIVE RETIREMENT BENEFITS—Continued

State or other jurisdiction	Participation	Requirements for regular retirement	Employee contribution rate	Benefit formula
Indiana	DB plan was mandatory for those serving before April 30, 1989, except that those serving on that day could opt to transfer to the DC plan. Defined contribution has been mandatory for those elected or appointed since 4/30/89.	DB plan—vesting at 10 years. Age 65 with 10 years of legislative service; or, if no longer in the legislature, these options apply: at least 10 years of service; no state salary; at age 55+ Rule of 85 applies; or age 60 with 15 years of service. Early retirement with reduced benefit. DC plan—immediate vesting.	DB plan—funded by employer and employee contributions. DC plan—5% employee, 20% state (of taxable income) through 2009. At present, the contribution is recalculated annually not to exceed the state contribution to the employee retirement plan.	DB plan—monthly benefit: Lesser of (a) $40 x years of General Assembly service completed before 11/8/89; or (b) 1/12 of the average of the three highest consecutive years of General Assembly service salary. DC plan—numerous options for withdrawing accumulations in accord with IRS regulations. Loans are available. A participant in both plans may receive a benefit from both plans.
Iowa	Optional	Age 65; age 62 with 20 years of service; Rule of 88; reduced benefit at 55 with at least 4 years of service.	5.95 % individual.	2% times FAS. x years of service for first 30 years, + 1% times FAS times years in excess of 30 but no more than 5 in excess of 30. FAS is average of 3 highest years.
Kansas	Optional for legislators and employees of the legislator leadership offices. Mandatory for all other regular, full time employees.	Age 65; age 62 with 5 years of service, or when age plus years of service equals 85.	6% (base may include salary, per diem, non-session allowance, session expenses; or various combinations at the legislator's option.)	3 highest years x 1.75% x years of service ÷ 12= monthly benefit.
Kentucky	Optional. Those who opt out are covered by the state employees' plan	Age 65 with 5 years of service; any age with 30 years of service, and intermediate provisions. Early retirement with reduced benefits.	5% of creditable compensation set by law at $27,500: not the same as actual salary. Revised to be payable on compensation reported on W-2 forms beginning in 2005. HB 1 of 2008 Special Session—raised the contribution level to 6% for legislators elected after 7/1/08.	2.75% of FAS (based on creditable compensation) x years of service. FAS is the average monthly earnings for the 60 months preceding retirement. HB 1 of 2008 Special Session—reduced the annual COLA for retired legislators from the CPI (capped at 5%) to 1.5% effective on July 1, 2008. This applies to current as well as to future retirees. The statutes reserve to the legislature the power to make such changes. The amount of the COLA may be increased by the legislature if the legislature prefunds the cost of the increase.
Louisiana	Legislative service for legislators elected after January 1, 1997, is ineligible for State Employee Retirement System benefits. (LSA-Const. Art. 10, § 29.1)			
Maine	Mandatory	Age 60 if 10 years of service on 7/1/93; age 62 if less than 10 years of service on 7/1/93. Reduced benefit available for earlier retirement.	7.65% legislators; employer contribution is actuarially determined.	2% of average final compensation (the average of the 3 high salary years) times years of service.
Maryland	Optional	Age 60 with 8 years; age 50 with 8+ years creditable service for early reduced retirement.	5% of annual salary.	3% of legislative salary for each year of service up to 22 years 3 months. Benefits are recalculated when legislative salaries are changed.
Massachusetts	Optional after each election or re-election to the General Court.	Vesting at 6 years with 6 years service: unreduced benefit at 65. Reduced benefits for retirement before age 65.	9%, although some legislators are grandfathered at lower rates.	2.5 times years of service times FAS. FAS = average of highest 36 months. Service credit is allowed for membership in other Massachusetts retirement plans.

See footnotes at end of table.

STATE LEGISLATIVE RETIREMENT BENEFITS — Continued

State or other jurisdiction	Participation	Requirements for regular retirement	Employee contribution rate	Benefit formula
Michigan	Optional	Age 55 with 5 years or when age plus years of service equal 70. Employee contributions are immediately vested. Employer contributions are vested as follows: Zero after one year; 50% after two years; 75% after three years; 100% after four years.	For legislators elected before 3/31/97 — 7-10% for (DB) plan. Elected after 3/31/97 — (DC) plan, the state contributes 4% of salary. Members may contribute up to 3% of salary. The state will match the member's contribution in addition to the state 4% contribution.	DB plans — various provisions, depending on when service started. DC plan — benefits depend upon contributions and earnings.
Minnesota	Mandatory	Legislators Retirement Plan (LRP) before 7/1/97 — 62 years with 6 years of service and fully vested. LRP members do not have Social Security coverage. Defined Contribution Plan (DCP) since 1997 — age 55 and immediate vesting. DCP members have Social Security coverage.	LRP — 9%. DCP — 5.5% from member, 6% from state.	2.7% x high 5 year average salary x years of service. DCP benefits depend upon contributions and investment return.
Mississippi	Mandatory	Age 60 with 4 or more years of service, or 25 years of service.	Regular — 15.75% state, 9.00% member. Supplemental Legislative Retirement Plan — 7.40% state, 3.00% member.	Legislators who qualify for regular state retirement benefits also automatically qualify for the legislators' supplemental benefits. Regular — 2% x average compensation x years of service up to and including 25 years of service + 2.5% x average compensation x service in excess of 25 years. Average compensation is calculated using the highest 4 years of compensation. Supplement — 1% x average compensation x years of legislative service through 25 years + 1.25% x average compensation x years of service in excess of 25.
Missouri	Mandatory. The retirement plan for Legislators is calculated differently from the plan for other state employees.	For those hired on or before 12/31/2010 — vesting at 6 years of service. Age 55; service in three full biennial assemblies (6 years) or Rule of 80. For those entering system after 1/1/2011 — vesting at 6 years of service. Age 62; service in three full biennial assemblies (6 years) or the Rule of 90 with a minimum age of 55.	For those hired on or before 12/31/2010 — non-contributory. For those entering system after 1/1/2011 — contribution of 4% of salary.	For those hired on or before 12/31/2010 — monthly pay divided by 24 x years of creditable service, capped at 100% of salary. Benefit is adjusted by the percentage increase in pay for an active legislator. For those entering system after 1/1/2011 — no change.
Montana	Optional	Hired before 7/1/11 — vesting at 5 years. Age 60 with at least 5 years service; age 65 regardless of years of service; or 30 years of service regardless of age. After 7/1/11 — vesting at 5 years. Age 65 with 5 years service, or age 70.	7.9% employee and 8.37% employer for DB and DC plan.	DB plan — Membership Service Factor (see below) x years of Service Credit x HAC. More than 5 years and less than 10 years of membership service — 1.5% Less than 30 years of membership service — 1.7857% 30 years or more of membership service — 2%

See footnotes at end of table.

STATE LEGISLATIVE RETIREMENT BENEFITS — Continued

State or other jurisdiction	Participation	Requirements for regular retirement	Employee contribution rate	Benefit formula
Nebraska	None available			
Nevada	Mandatory, but a legislator, within 30 days after he/she is first elected or appointed, may elect not to participate; a decision to terminate participation in the plan cannot be reversed. The legislators' retirement system is separate from the state employee retirement plan.	Must have at least 10 years of service, be age 60, and no longer be a legislator or in order to retire without benefit reduction. A legislator who is no longer serving, has at least 10 years of service, but is under the age of 60 can elect to wait to receive his/her benefit until the age of 60 or begin receiving a reduced benefit prior to the age of 60.	15% of session salary.	Number of years x $25 = monthly allowance.
New Hampshire	None available			
New Jersey	Mandatory	Vesting at 8 years. Age 60: no minimum service requirement. Early retirement with no benefit reduction with 25 years of service.	5% of salary	3% x FAS x years of service. FAS = higher of three highest years or three final years. Benefit is capped at 2/3 of FAS. Other formulas apply if a legislator also has other service covered by the Public Employee Retirement System.
New Mexico	Optional	Plans 1A and 1B — age 65 with 5 years of service; 64 with 8 years of service; 63 with 11 years of service; 60 with 12 years of service; or any age with 14 years of service. Plan 2 — age 65 with 5 years of service or at any age with 10 years of legislative service.	Plan 1A — $100 per year for service after 1959. Plan 1B — $200 per year (now closed to new enrollments). Plan 2 — $500 per year. Increased to $600 per year by 2012 legislation.	Plan 1A: $250 per year of service. Plan 1B: $500 per year of service after 1959. Plan 2: 11 percent of the IRS Legislative per diem rate in effect on December 31st of the year a legislator retires x 60 x the years of credited service. For a legislator who retired in 2111 the benefit would be $1,129 per year of credited service. Annual 3% COLA.
New York..............	Detailed information set forth in *Your Retirement Plan: Legislative and Executive Plan*, published by New York State Office of the State Comptroller.	Detailed information set forth in *Your Retirement Plan: Legislative and Executive Plan*, published by New York State Office of the State Comptroller.	Detailed information set forth in *Your Retirement Plan: Legislative and Executive Plan*, published by New York State Office of the State Comptroller.	Detailed information set forth in *Your Retirement Plan: Legislative and Executive Plan*, published by New York State Office of the State Comptroller.
North Carolina............	Mandatory	Age 65 with 5 years of service; reduced benefit available at earlier ages.	7%	Highest annual compensation x 4.02% x years of service.
North Dakota............	None available.			
Ohio..............	Optional. OPERS offers three plans for retirement — the traditional plan (a defined benefit plan); the member directed plan (a defined contribution plan); and the combined plan. Participation in the latter two plans is limited to new OPERS members and OPERS members who had less than 5 years of service on 12/31/2002.	Varies depending upon plan. Detailed information set forth in *Legislative Benefits, Privileges, and Restrictions of Office.*	Varies depending upon plan. Detailed information set forth in *Legislative Benefits, Privileges, and Restrictions of Office.*	Varies depending upon plan. Detailed information set forth in *Legislative Benefits, Privileges, and Restrictions of Office.*

See footnotes at end of table.

STATE LEGISLATIVE RETIREMENT BENEFITS — Continued

State or other jurisdiction	Participation	Requirements for regular retirement	Employee contribution rate	Benefit formula
Oklahoma............	Legislators may retain membership as regular public employees if they have that status when elected; one time option to join elected officials' plan. SB 794 of 2011—new provisions affect people elected to office after 11/1/2011.	Elected Officials' Plan—vesting at 6 years. Age 65, or age 60 with 6 years' service. SB 794 of 2011—vesting at 8 years. Age 65 or age 62 with 10 years of membership in the plan. Early retirement with reduced benefits at age 60 with 10 years of service.	Optional contribution levels—4.5%, 6%, 7.5%, 8.5%, 9% or 10%, of total compensation. SB 794 of 2011—schedule of options was repealed. Required contribution of 3.5% of total compensation.	Average participating salary x length of service x computation factor depending on optional contributions ranging from 1.9% for a 4.5% contribution to 4% for a 10% contribution. S.B. 1641 (Chapter 105, Laws of 2008)—people elected to office on or after 7/1/2008: formula described here can apply only to years of service as an elected official and can be based only on the higher year of salary received as an elected official (not on any subsequent salary from a non-elective post as was possible under the original provisions). Capped benefits at 100% of salary as a member of the OPERS (not clear whether this is highest salary as an elected official). S.B. 1889 (Chapter 435, Laws of 2010)—reduced the menu of options to the highest and lowest, which are shown above, for people elected to office after 11/1/2010. Those who fail to make a choice within 90 days of taking office default to the highest contribution and computation factor. SB 794 of 2011—2% of final average salary times years of service. SB 2322 of 2012—members may choose a benefit option of 2.5% of final average salary, for which members' contributions will be increased by an amount that will equal the actuarial cost of the increased benefit.
Oregon............	Optional	Normal retirement age for general service members is age 65 or age 58 with 30 years of retirement credit.	OPRSP DC component—employees contribute 6% of salary. DB component—non-contributory. 457 plans—members may contribute amounts to limits set by IRS.	OPRSP individual account component, or DC component—at retirement, employees may receive the IAP as a lump-sum payment or in equal installments over a 5, 10, 15 or 20-year period. DB component—benefit calculation is 1.5 percent x final average salary x years of service.
Pennsylvania............	Optional. Act 120 of 2010—applies to those who become state legislators on or after 12/1/2010.	Age 50 with 3 years of service; any age with 35 years of service; early retirement with reduced benefit. Act 120 of 2010—vesting at 10 years. Retirement age is 55 with 3 years of credited service or according to the Rule of 92 with a minimum of 35 years of service.	6.25%. Act 120 of 2010—6.25% or 9.3% (member's choice). Rate will vary with actuarial conditions; these are minimums.	3% x final average salary x credited years of service (x withdrawal factor if under 50), with a maximum benefit of 100% of FAS. Act 120 of 2010—new legislators may choose between plans with different contribution rates. The multiplier for the lower contribution will be 2% and for the higher contribution 2.5%. Cap on benefits is unchanged.
Rhode Island............	Legislators elected before January 1995—eligible for a pension of $600 a year for each year of legislative service, capped at an annual retirement benefit of $12,000. Legislators elected after January 1995—ineligible to earn credit for public retirement benefits. Different than state employee retirement plan.			

See footnotes at end of table.

STATE LEGISLATIVE RETIREMENT BENEFITS — Continued

State or other jurisdiction	Participation	Requirements for regular retirement	Employee contribution rate	Benefit formula
South Carolina............	Mandatory (but not available to any-one first elected to the General Assembly after November 2012). Act 278, Laws of 2012—mandatory choice for those elected in or after November 2012.	Age 60 with 8 years of service. 30 years of service regardless of age. Act 278, Laws of 2012—SCRS: vesting at 8 years; retirement benefits at age 65 with 8 years of service or in accord with the Rule of 90. Reduced benefits are available at age 60 with 8 years of service. ORP: immediate vesting in employer contributions.	10% 11% as of January 1, 2013. Act 278, Laws of 2012—SCRS: 7% as of July 1, 2012, rising to 8% on July 1, 2014. ORP: 7% + 5% employer contribution, immediately vested.	4.82% x earnable compensation x years of service. "Earnable compensation" means 40 x the daily rate of remuneration, plus $12,000, of a member of the General Assembly, as from time to time in effect. Act 278, Laws of 2012—SCRS: 2.25% x years of service x final average compensation, which is the average of the member's 5 highest years of earned compensation. ORP: upon retirement a member may annuitize the balance in the account or take a lump sum or partial distribution. Federal provisions apply.
South Dakota........	None available.			
Tennessee.................	Optional.	Age 55, 4 years of service.	Members hired before 7/1/14 participate in a non-contributory plan. Members hired after 7/1/14 participate in a contributory plan. State contributes 4% toward defined benefit, 5% into 401K Member contributes 5% toward defined benefit, 2% into 401K (can do more if so desired).	$85.21 per month x years of service with a cap 90% of final compensation. 2006 legislation provides for an annual adjustment in the base amount (not an annual COLA to recipients) and provides that a legislator may reject the increase in writing. $55.00 for those in the contributory plan.
Texas.................	Optional	Vesting at 8 years. Age 60 with 8 years of service; or age 50 with 12 years of service.	8%	2.3% x district judge's salary x length of service, with the monthly benefit capped at the level of a district judge's salary, and adjusted when such salaries are increased. Various annuity options are available. Military service credit may be purchased to add to elective class service membership. In September 2013, a district judge's salary was set at $140,000 a year.
Utah................	Mandatory	Age 62 with 10 years and an actuarial reduction; age 65 with 4 years of service for full benefits. 2010 legislation closed the Governors' and Legislators' Retirement Plan to legislators elected after 7/1/2011 and replaced it with the New Public Employees' Tier II Contributory Retirement Plan Defined Contribution Plan. The new DC plan will be a 401(k) with distribution of accumulations subject to federal rules.	Non-contributory. For the DC plan, employer will contribute 10% of compensation, which will vest after four years of service. Employees may, but are not required, to contribute.	$24.80/month (as of July 2004) x years of service; adjusted semi-annually according to consumer price index up to a maximum increase of 2%. For the DC plan, benefits will be based upon accumulations in the employee account.
Vermont.................	None available. Deferred compensation plan available.			

See footnotes at end of table.

STATE LEGISLATIVE RETIREMENT BENEFITS—Continued

State or other jurisdiction	Participation	Requirements for regular retirement	Employee contribution rate	Benefit formula
Virginia	Mandatory. Eligibility for various plans based on membership date. Same as state employees plan.	Plan 1—Age 50 with 30 years of service (unreduced); age 55 with 5 years of service; age 50 with 10 years (reduced). Plan 2—When age and service = 90; or normal Social Security retirement age with 5 years of service (unreduced); age 60 with 5 years of service (reduced). Hybrid plan—When age and service = 90; or normal Social Security retirement age with 5 years of service (unreduced); age 60 with 5 years of service (reduced).	Plan 1—members who qualify do not make an employee contribution. Plan 2—5% of creditable compensation. Hybrid plan—mandatory and voluntary contributions to defined benefit and defined contribution components.	Plan 1—1.7% of average final compensation x years of service (average over highest 36 consecutive months). Plan 2—1.65% of average final compensation x years of service (average over highest 60 consecutive months). Hybrid plan—1.65% of average final compensation x years of service (average over highest 60 consecutive months).
Washington	Optional. If before an election the legislator belonged to a state public retirement plan, he or she may continue in that plan by making contributions. Otherwise, new legislators may join PERS Plan 2 or Plan 3.	Plan 2—age 65 with 5 years of service credit. Plan 3—age 65 with 10 years of service credit for the DB side of the plan; immediate benefits (subject to federal restrictions) on the DC side of the plan. The member may choose various options for investment of contributions to the DC plan.	Plan 2—employee contribution of 2.43% for 2002. Estimated at 3.33% for 2005-2007. Plan 3—no required member contribution for the DB component. The member may contribute from 5% to 15% of salary to the DC component.	Plan 2—2% x years of service credit x average final compensation. Plan 3—DB is 1% x service credit years x average final compensation. DC benefit depends upon the value of accumulations.
West Virginia	Optional	Age 55, if years of service + age equal 80.	Before 10/1/87—7%. After 10/1/87—5%.	2% x final average salary x years of service. Final average salary is based on 3 highest years out of last 10 years.
Wisconsin	Wisconsin Retirement System (WRS)—mandatory. Deferred Compensation 457 Plan—optional.	Minimum retirement age is 55. Normal retirement age is 62. Normal retirement age with 30 years of WRS service is age 57.	2016 contribution rate is 6.6% of the legislator's salary. The employer matches this for a total contribution of 13.2%.	Retirement benefit is calculated under both "formula" and "money purchase" methods and will receive the higher of the two benefit calculations. Formula—if terminated prior to the year 2000, may not exceed 65% of the final average earnings (highest 3 years of salary), or 70% for 2000 or after. (2.165% x years of service x salary for service before 2000; 2% x years of service x salary for service 2000 and after). Money Purchase Calculation—based only on the dollar balance in WRS account and exact age (and therefore life expectancy) when annuity begins.
Wyoming	None available			

Source: National Conference of State Legislatures, March 2016.
Key:
COLA — Cost of living adjustment.
CPI — Consumer price index.
DB — Defined Benefit.
DC — Defined Contribution.
FAS — Final average salary.
None available — no retirement benefit provided.

OPERS — Ohio Public Employee's Retirement System.
OPERS — Oklahoma Public Employee's Retirement System.
OPSRP — Oregon Public Service Retirement System.
ORP — South Carolina State Optional Retirement Program.
PERA — Public employee retirement association.
PERS — Public Employee's Retirement System.
SCRS—South Carolina Retirement System.

Table 3.14
BILL PRE-FILING, REFERENCE AND CARRYOVER

State or other jurisdiction	Pre-filing of bills allowed (b)	Bills referred to committee by: Senate	Bills referred to committee by: House/ Assembly	Bill referral restricted by rule (a) Senate	Bill referral restricted by rule (a) House/ Assembly	Bill carryover allowed (c)
Alabama	★(d)	(e) (f)	Speaker (f)	L, M	L, M	...
Alaska	★	President	Speaker	L, M	L, M	★
Arizona	★	President	Speaker	L	L	...
Arkansas	★	President (g)	Speaker	L	L	...
California	★(h)	Rules Cmte.	Rules Cmte.	L	L	★(h)
Colorado	★	President	Speaker	(i)	(i)	...
Connecticut	★	Pres. Pro Tempore	Speaker	M	M	...
Delaware	★	Pres. Pro Tempore	Speaker	L	L	★
Florida	★	President	Speaker	M	...	...
Georgia	★	President (f)	Speaker	...	...	★
Hawaii	(j)	(j)	Speaker	...	...	★
Idaho	...	President (e)	Speaker	(qq)	(qq)	...
Illinois	★	Cmte. on Assignments	Rules Cmte.	(k)	(k)	★
Indiana	★(l)	Pres. Pro Tempore	Speaker	(m)	...	...
Iowa	★	President	Speaker	M	M	★
Kansas	★	President	Speaker	L (n)	L (n)	★
Kentucky	★	Cmte. on Cmtes.	Cmte. on Cmtes.	L, M	L, M	...
Louisiana	★	President (o)	Speaker (o)	L	L	...
Maine	★	Secy. of Senate	Clerk of House	(p)	(p)	★(rr)
Maryland	★	President (q)	Speaker (q)	L	L	...
Massachusetts	★	Clerk	Clerk	M	M	★
Michigan	...	Majority Ldr.	Speaker	(uu)	(uu)	★
Minnesota	★(r)	President	Speaker	L, M	L, M	★(r)
Mississippi	★	President (e)	Speaker	L	L	...
Missouri	★	Pres. Pro Tempore	Speaker	L	L	...
Montana	★	President	Speaker	L (tt)	L (tt)	...
Nebraska	★	Reference Cmte. (s)	U	L	U	★(t)
Nevada	★	President (u)	Speaker (u)	L (v)	...	...
New Hampshire	★	President	Speaker	M	M	★(ss)
New Jersey	★	President	Speaker	L, M	L, M	★
New Mexico	★	(w)	Speaker	L	L, M	...
New York	★	President pro tem in consultation with Independent democratic conference leader	Speaker	L, M	L, M	★
North Carolina	...	Rules Chair	Speaker	M	M	★
North Dakota	★	Majority Leader	Speaker	L	L	...
Ohio	★(y)	Reference Cmte.	Rules & Reference Cmte.	L (z)	L, M (aa)	★(bb)
Oklahoma	★	Majority Leader	Speaker	L	L	★(cc)
Oregon	★	President	Speaker	(dd)	(ee)	...
Pennsylvania	(x)	President Pro Tempore	Chief Clerk	M	M	...
Rhode Island	★	President	Speaker	M	M	★
South Carolina	★	President	Speaker	M	M	★(ff)
South Dakota	★	President Pro Tempore	Speaker	L	L	...
Tennessee	★	Speaker	Speaker	L, M	L, M	★(gg)
Texas	★	President	Speaker	L	L	...
Utah	★	President	Speaker	L	L	...
Vermont	(hh)	President	Speaker	L, M	L, M	★
Virginia	★	Clerk	Clerk (ii)	L, M (jj)	(kk)	★(ll)
Washington	★	(mm)	Speaker	L	L	★
West Virginia (nn)	★	President	Speaker	L, M	L, M	...
Wisconsin	...	President	Speaker	L, M	L, M	★(oo)
Wyoming	★	President	Speaker	L (vv)	L (vv)	...
American Samoa	...	...	...	...	...	...
Guam	★	Committee on Calendar Chairs	U	L, M (pp)	U	★
No. Mariana Islands	★	President	Speaker	L	L	...
Puerto Rico	...	President	Secretary	M	M	...
U.S. Virgin Islands	...	Senate President in Pro-Forma meeting	U	L	U	★

See footnotes at end of table.

BILL PRE-FILING, REFERENCE AND CARRYOVER — Continued

Sources: The Council of State Governments' survey, November 2015 and update from state websites 2016.

Key:

★ — Yes

. . . — No

L — Rules generally require all bills be referred to the appropriate committee of jurisdiction.

M — Rules require specific types of bills be referred to specific committees (e.g., appropriations, local bills).

U — Unicameral legislature.

(a) Legislative rules specify all or certain bills go to committees of jurisdiction.

(b) Unless otherwise indicated by footnote, bills may be introduced prior to convening each session of the legislature. In this column only: ★ — pre-filing is allowed in both chambers (or in the case of Nebraska, in the unicameral legislature); . . . — pre-filing is not allowed in either chamber.

(c) Bills carry over from the first year of the legislature to the second (does not apply in Alabama, Arkansas, Montana, Nevada, North Dakota, Oregon and Texas, where legislatures meet biennially). Bills generally do not carry over after an intervening legislative election.

(d) Except between the end of the last regular session of the legislature in any quadrennium and the organizational session following the general election and for special sessions.

(e) Lieutenant governor is the president of the Senate.

(f) Senate bills referred by president with concurrence of president pro tem. House bills referred by president pro tem with concurrence of president, if no concurrence, referred to majority leader.

(g) Senate chief counsel makes recommendations to the presiding officer.

(h) Bills may be drafted prior to session, but may not be introduced until the first day of session. Bills introduced in the first year of the regular session and passed by the house of origin on or before the January 31st constitutional deadline in the second year are carryover bills.

(i) In either house, state law requires any bill which affects the sentencing of criminal offenders and which would result in a net increase of imprisonment in state correctional facilities must be assigned to the appropriations committee of the house in which it was introduced. In the Senate, a bill must be referred to the Appropriations Committee if it contains an appropriation from the state treasury or the increase of any salary. Each bill which provides that any state revenue be devoted to any purpose other than that to which it is devoted under existing law must be referred to the Finance Committee.

(j) Prefiling allowed in the House by rule, seven calendar days before the commencement of the regular session, in even-numbered years. Senate allows prefiling of bills as determined on a year-to-year basis. Senate bills are referred to committee by the members of the majority leadership appointed by the President.

(k) In even-numbered years, the Committee on Assignments (Senate) or Rules Committee (House) is to refer to substantive committees only appropriation bills implementing the budget, and bills deemed by the Committee on Assignments (Senate) or Rules Committee (House) to be of an emergency nature or of substantial importance to the operation of government.

(l) Only in the Senate.

(m) At the discretion of President Pro Tempore.

(n) Appropriation bills are the only "specific type" mentioned in the rules to be referred to either House Appropriation Cmte. or Senate Ways and Means.

(o) Subject to approval or disapproval. Louisiana — majority members present.

(p) Maine Joint Rule 308 sections 1,2,3, "All bills and resolves must be referred to committee, except that this provision may be suspended by a majority vote in each chamber."

(q) The President and Speaker may refer bills to any of the standing committees or the Rules Committees, but usually bills are referred according to subject matter.

(r) Pre-filing of bills allowed prior to the convening of the 2nd year of the biennium. Bill carryover allowed if in second year of a two-year session.

(s) The Nebraska Legislature's Executive Board serves as the Reference Committee.

(t) Bills are carried over from the 90-day session beginning in the odd-numbered year to the 60-day session, which begins in even-numbered year. Bills that have not passed by the last day of the 60-day session are

all indefinitely postponed by motion on the last day of the session. The odd-numbered year shall be carried forward to the even-numbered year.

(u) In the Senate any member may make a motion for referral, but committee referrals are under the control of the Majority Floor Leader. In the House any member may make a motion for referral, and a chart is used to guide bill referrals based on statutory authority of committee, but committee referrals are under the control of the Majority Floor Leader.

(v) Rules do not require specific types of bills be referred to specific committees.

(w) Sponsor subject to approval of the body.

(x) Only in the Senate.

(y) Senate Rule 33: Between the general election and the time for the next convening session, a holdover member or member-elect may file bills for introduction in the next session with the Clerk's office. Those bills shall be treated as if they were bills introduced on the first day of the session. House Rule 61(d): Bills introduced prior to the convening of the session shall be treated as if they were bills introduced on the first day of the session. Between the general election and the time for the next convening session, a member-elect may file bills for introduction in the next session with the Clerk's office. The Clerk shall number such bills consecutively, in the order in which they are filed, beginning with the number "1."

(z) Rule 35. (Bills, Second Consideration and Committee on Reference, Public Hearing.) On the second reading of a bill, the Committee on Reference shall, if no motion or order be made to the contrary, refer the bill to the proper standing committee in regular order. Further, no bill shall be reported for a third reading and passage unless the same shall have been considered at a meeting of the committee to which the same has been referred. All Senate bills and resolutions referred by the Committee on Reference on or before the first day of April in an even-numbered year shall be scheduled by the chairperson of the committee to which the same has been referred for a minimum of one public hearing.

(aa) House Rule 37: (a) All House bills and resolutions introduced on or before the fifteenth day of May in an even-numbered year, and in compliance with the rules of the House, shall be referred to a standing, select, or special committee or standing subcommittee, and shall be scheduled by the chairman of the committee for a minimum of one public hearing. (b) The sponsor of a bill or resolution shall appear at least once before the committee that is considering the bill or resolution unless excused by the chairman of the committee or the Speaker. It is not in order for the committee to report the bill or resolution unless its sponsor has appeared or has been excused from appearing before the committee. Rule 65. (Bills carrying appropriations.) All bills carrying an appropriation shall be referred to the Finance Committee for consideration and report before being considered the third time.

(bb) Bills carry over between the first and second year of each regular annual session, but not to the next biennial 2-year General Assembly.

(cc) A legislature consists of two years. Bills from the first session can carry over to the second session only.

(dd) The President can refer bills to any standing or special committee and may also attach subsequent referrals to other committees following action by the first committee.

(ee) Rules specify bills shall be referred by the Speaker to any standing or special committee and may also attach subsequent referrals to other committees following action by the first committee.

(ff) Allowed during the first year of the two year session.

(gg) Bills and resolutions introduced in the First Regular Session may carry over to the Second Regular Session (odd-numbered year to even-numbered year) only.

(hh) Bills are drafted prior to session but released starting first day of session.

(ii) Under the direction of the speaker.

(jj) Jurisdiction of the committees by subject matter is listed in the Rules.

(kk) The House Rules establish jurisdictional committees. The Speaker refers legislation to those committees as he deems appropriate.

(ll) Even-numbered year session to odd-numbered year session.

(mm) By the floor leader.

(nn) Prefiling allowed only in the house in even-numbered years.

(oo) From odd-year to even-year, but not between biennial sessions.

(pp) Substantive resolutions referred to sponsor for public hearing.

(qq) Bills may be referred to any appropriate committee (Senate Rule 14). Bills may be referred to any standing committee (House Rule 43).

(rr) Allowed between session in a biennium, not to subsequent legislatures.

BILL PRE-FILING, REFERENCE AND CARRYOVER — Continued

(ss) Referred bills may be held in committee and acted on during second year session.

(tt) President and Speaker have broad discretion.

(uu) Senate Rule 3.203 a) The Senate Majority Leader shall refer all bills and joint resolutions to a standing committee no later than one (1) Senate legislative day after being submitted to the Secretary of the Senate. The presiding officer shall announce the reference of all bills and joint resolutions. ... c) The Senate Majority Leader may change the original referral of a bill or resolution by oral notice to the Senate or written communication submitted to the Secretary of the Senate before the end of session on the next Senate legislative day following the day of the original referral. Notices of the written communication shall be announced by the Secretary of the Senate during session and both oral and written notifications shall be printed in the Journal. House Rule 41: (4) The Speaker shall refer all bills and joint resolutions to a standing committee no later than one House legislative day after being submitted to the Clerk. (5) The Speaker may change the original referral of a bill or resolution by written communication submitted to the Clerk before the end of session on the next House legislative day following the day of the original referral. Notice of the referral shall be announced by the Clerk and printed in the Journal.

(vv) Bills containing an appropriation are rereferred to the Appropriations Committee.

Table 3.15
TIME LIMITS ON BILL INTRODUCTION

State or other jurisdiction	Time limit on introduction of bills	Procedures for granting exception to time limits
Alabama	House: no limit. Senate: 24th legislative day of regular session (a).	House: N.A. Senate: Unanimous vote to suspend rules.
Alaska	35th C day of 2nd regular session.	Introduction by committee or by suspension of operation of limiting rule.
Arizona	House: 29th day of regular session; 10th day of special session. Senate: 22nd day of regular session; 10th day of special session.	House: Permission of rules committee. Senate: Permission of rules committee.
Arkansas	55th day of regular session (50th day for appropriations bills). Retirement and health care legislation affecting licensures shall be introduced during the first 15 days.	2/3 vote of membership of each house for appropriations bills and all others except retirement and health care legislation affecting licensures which require 3/4 vote of the membership of each house.
California	Deadlines established by the Joint Rules Committee adpoted in each session.	Approval of Rules Committee and 3/4 vote of membership.
Colorado	House: 22nd C day of regular session. Senate: 17th C day of regular session.	Committees on delayed bills may extend deadline.
Connecticut	10 days into session in odd-numbered years, 3 days into session in even-numbered years (b).	2/3 vote of members present.
Delaware	House: no limit. Senate: no limit.	
Florida	House: noon of the first day of regular session (h). Senate: noon first day of regular session (h).	House: No exception as such; if need, one would be granted by waiving the rule by 2/3 vote on the floor. Senate: Existence of an emergency reasonably compelling consideration notwithstanding the deadline.
Georgia	Only for specific types of bills	
Hawaii	Actual dates established during session.	Majority vote of membership.
Idaho	House: 20th day of session for personal bills; 36th day of session for all committees; beyond that only privileged cmtes. Senate: 12th day of session for personal bills; 36th day of session for all committees; beyond that only privileged cmtes.	House and Senate: speaker/president pro tempore may designate any standing committee to serve as a privileged committee temporarily.
Illinois	House: determined by speaker. Senate: determined by senate president.	House: The speaker may set deadlines for any action on any category of legislative measure, including deadlines for introduction of bills. Senate: At any time, the president may set alternative deadlines for any legislative action with written notice filed with the secretary.
Indiana	House: Mid-January. Senate: Date specific—set in Rules, different for long and short session. Mid-January.	House: 2/3 vote. Senate: If date falls on weekend/Holiday—extended to next day. Sine die deadline set by statute, does not change.
Iowa	House: Drafting request received by Friday of 5th week of 1st regular session; or by Friday of 2nd week of 2nd regular session. Senate: Drafting request received by Friday of 5th week of 1st regular session; or by Friday of 2nd week of 2nd regular session.	House: Constitutional Majority. Senate: Constitutional majority.
Kansas	Actual dates established in the Joint Rules of the House and Senate every two years when the joint rules are adopted.	Resolution adopted by majority of members of either house may make specific exceptions to deadlines.
Kentucky	House: No introductions during the last 14 L days of odd-year session, during last 22 L days of even-year session. Senate: No introductions during the last 14 L days of odd-year session, during last 20 L days of even-year session.	None.
Louisiana	House: 10th C day of odd-year sessions and 23rd C day of even-year sessions. Senate: 10th C day of odd-year sessions and 23rd C day of even-year sessions.	None.
Maine	House: Cloture dates established by the Legislative Council. Senate: Cloture dates established by the Legislative Council.	House: Bills filed after cloture date must be approved by a majority of the Legislative Council. Senate: Appeals heard by Legislative Council. Six votes required to allow introduction of legislation.

See footnotes at end of table.

TIME LIMITS ON BILL INTRODUCTION — Continued

State or other jurisdiction	Time limit on introduction of bills	Procedures for granting exception to time limits
Maryland	House and Senate: No introductions during the last 35 days of regular session, unless 2/3 of the elected members of a chamber vote yes. Additional limitations involve committee action. Senate bills introduced after the 24th calendar day must be referred to the Senate Rules Committee and also Senate bills introduced after the 10th calendar day on behalf of the administration, i.e. the governor, must be referred to the Senate Rules Committee. House bills introduced during the last 59 calendar days (after the 31st day) are referred to the House Rules Committee. The Senate Rules and House Rules contain further provisions concerning the requirements for forcing legislation out of these committees.	House: 2/3 vote of elected members of each house.
Massachusetts	1st Wednesday in December even-numbered years. 1st Wednesday in November odd-numbered years.	2/3 vote of members present and voting.
Michigan	No limit.	
Minnesota	No limit.	
Mississippi	14th C day in 90-day session; 49th C day in 125-day session (e).	2/3 vote of members present and voting.
Missouri	House: 60th L day of regular session. Senate: March 1.	Majority vote of elected members each house; governor's request for consideration of bill by special message.
Montana	Introduction of bills & resolutions: 10th L day if requested prior to convening or 2 days after receipt of finished bill draft after session convenes, whichever is earlier. Requests for general bills and resolutions: 12th L day; revenue bills: 17th L day; committee bills and resolutions: 36th L day; appropriations bills: 45th L day; interim study resolutions: 60th L day; committee revenue bills and bill proposing referenda: 62nd L day; committee bills implementing provision of a general appropriation act: 67th L day; resolutions confirming governor appointees or bill amending/repealing administrative rule: no deadline.	2/3 vote of members.
Nebraska	10th L day of any session (f).	3/5 vote of elected membership.
Nevada	Actual dates established at start of session.	Waiver granted by majority leader of the Senate and speaker of the Assembly acting jointly.
New Hampshire	Determined by rules.	2/3 vote of members present.
New Jersey	No limit.	
New Mexico	House: 15 days in short session/even years, 30 days in long session/odd years. Senate: 15 days in short session/even years, 30 days in long session/odd years.	None. Statutory limit for legislators; governor not limited and can send bill with message.
New York	Assembly: For unlimited introduction of bills, the final day is the last Tuesday in May of the 2nd year of the legislative term. Senate: Determined by the Majority Conference leaders, but no earlier than 1st Tuesday in March; except introduction by agencies is March 1, for all other program bills it is 1st Tuesday in April.	Assembly: Introduction by Rules Cmte., by message from the Senate, or with consent of the speaker, by members elected at a special election who take office on or after the 1st Tues. in May. Senate: Introduction by Rules Committee after 2nd Friday in June, or by message from the Assembly.
North Carolina	Actual dates established during session.	Senate: 2/3 vote of membership present and voting shall be required.
North Dakota	House: 10th L day. Senate: 15th L day.	2/3 vote of the floor or by approval of Delayed Bills Committee.
Ohio	No limit.	
Oklahoma	Time limit set in rules.	2/3 vote of membership.

See footnotes at end of table.

TIME LIMITS ON BILL INTRODUCTION — Continued

State or other jurisdiction	Time limit on introduction of bills	Procedures for granting exception to time limits
Oregon	House: Set by House rules for odd-numbered year sessions. It was the 17th calendar day in 2015. All measures must be presession filed for even-year session. Senate: Set by Senate rules for odd-numbered year sessions. It was the 23rd calendar day in 2015. All measures must be presession filed for even-year session.	House: Bills approved by the Rules Committee; appropriation or fiscal measures sponsored by the Cmte. on Ways and Means; other committee bills approved by the Speaker; member priority requests (limited to 5 measures for odd-year session, none for even-year session). Senate: Measures approved by the Senate President; appropriations or fiscal measures sponsored by the Cmte. On Ways and Means; committee requests (limited to 4 measures in 2015); caucus leaders are limited to 2 measure requests after the deadlines; member priority requestes (limted to 5 measures for odd-year session, none for even-year session).
Pennsylvania	No limit.	
Rhode Island	Second week of February for Public Bills.	Sponsor must give one legislative day's notice.
South Carolina	House: Prior to April 15 of the 2nd yr. of a two-yr. legislative session; May 1 for bills first introduced in Senate. Rule 5.12. Senate: May 1 of regular session for bills originating in House. Rule 47.	House: 2/3 vote of members present and voting. Senate: 2/3 vote of members present and voting.
South Dakota	Individual bills: 40-day session: 15th L day; 35-day session: 10th L day. Committee bills: 40-day session: 16th L day; 35-day session: 11th L day. If a session calendar is adopted for a period of 36 days to 39 days, the legislative deadlines for the 35-day session shall be increased by the number of days by which the length of the session calendar exceeds 35 days.	2/3 approval of members-elect.
Tennessee	General bills, 10th L day of regular session (g).	Unanimous approval by Delayed Bills Committee.
Texas	60th C day of regular session, except for local bills, emergency appropriations and all emergency matters submitted by the governor in special message to the legislature.	4/5 vote of members present and voting.
Utah	12 p.m. on 11th day of session.	Motion for request must be approved by a constitutional majority vote.
Vermont	House: 1st session — last day of February; 2nd session — last day of January. Senate: 1st session — 70 day limit; 2nd session — 25 C days before start of session.	Approval by Rules Committee.
Virginia	Set by joint procedural resolution adopted at the beginning of the session (usually the second Friday of the session is the last day to introduce legislation that does not have any earlier deadline).	As provided in the joint procedural resolution (usually unanimous consent or at written request of the governor).
Washington	Until 10 days before the end of session unless 2/3 vote of elected members of each house.	2/3 vote of elected members of each house.
West Virginia	House: 42nd C day. Senate: 41st C day.	2/3 vote of members present.
Wisconsin	No limit.	
Wyoming	House: 15th L day of session in odd-numbered years. 5th L day in even-numbered years. Senate: 12th L day of session in odd-numbered years. 5th L day in even-numbered years	2/3 vote of elected members.
American Samoa	House: After the 25th L day of the fourth Regular Session. Senate: After the 15th L day.	
Guam	Public hearing on bill must be held no more than 120 days after date of bill introduction.	
No. Mariana Islands	No limit.	
Puerto Rico	1st session — within first 125 days; 2nd session — within first 60 days.	None.
U.S. Virgin Islands	No limit.	

See footnotes at end of table.

Sources: The Council of State Governments' survey, November 2015 and updates from state websites 2016.

Key:

C — Calendar

L — Legislative

(a) Not applicable to local bills, advertised or otherwise.

(b) Specific dates set in Joint Rules.

(c) Not applicable to appropriations bills.

(d) Not applicable to local bills and joint resolutions.

(e) Except Appropriation and Revenue bills (51st/86th C day) and Local & Private bills (83rd/118th C day).

(f) Except appropriations bills and bills introduced at the request of the governor, bills can be introduced during the first 10 legislative days of the session. Appropriation bills and bills introduced at the request of the governor can be introduced at any time during the session.

(g) Local bills have no cutoff.

(h) House: For Member-filed bills, noon of the first day of regular session. House Rule 5.2 sets a time limit for the introduction of bills, but this applies to Member-filed bills only. Proposed committee bills, local bills (dependent on completion of 30-day public notice period), and committee substitutes (treated by House Rules as new bills) are routinely filed after the first day of Session. Senate: Not applicable to appropriations bills, concurrent resolutions regarding certain subjects, local bills (which have no deadline), claim bills (deadline is August 1 of the year preceding consideration or within 62 days of a Senator's election), committee bills, trust fund bills, and public records exemptions linked to timely filed bills.

Table 3.16
ENACTING LEGISLATION: VETO, VETO OVERRIDE AND EFFECTIVE DATE

State or other jurisdiction	Governor may item veto appropriation bills		Days allowed governor to consider bill (a)			Votes required in each house to pass bills or items over veto (c)	Effective date of enacted legislation (d)
			During session	After session			
	Amount	Other (b)	Bill becomes law unless vetoed	Bill becomes law unless vetoed	Bill dies unless signed		
Alabama	★(e)	...	6 (f)	20P	10A	Majority of elected body	Date signed by governor, unless otherwise specified.
Alaska	★	...	15	10A		2/3 elected (g)	90 days after enactment or the specified effective date.
Arizona	★	★	5	10A		2/3 elected (h)	90 days after adjournment.
Arkansas	★	...	5	20A		Majority elected	91st day after adjournment.
California	★(i)	...	12 (j)	30A		2/3 elected (hhh)	(k)
Colorado	...	(l)	10P (ggg)	30A (m)		2/3 elected	90 days after adjournment. (n)
Connecticut	★	...	5	15P	(o)	2/3 elected	Oct. 1, unless otherwise specified.
Delaware	...	...	10P	10P	30A	3/5 elected	Immediately or enactment clause.
Florida	...	★	7 (ddd)	15P (m)		2/3 members present each house	60 days after adjournment since die or on specified date.
Georgia	★	★	6	40A		2/3 elected	Unless other date specified, July 1 for generals, date signed by governor for locals.
Hawaii (q)	★(r)	★	10 (s)	45A (s)(p)	10P (p)	2/3 elected	Immediately or on the prospective date stated in the legislation.
Idaho	★	★	5	10P		2/3 present	July 1
Illinois	★	...	60 (m)	60P (m)		3/5 elected (g)	Usually Jan. 1 of next year. (t)
Indiana	★	★	7	7P		Majority elected	(u)
Iowa	★	★	3		30A	2/3 elected	July 1, unless otherwise specified. Effective date for bills which become law on or after July 1, 45 days after approval, unless otherwise specified.
Kansas	★	★	10 (m)		10P	2/3 membership	Upon publication or specified date after publication.
Kentucky	★	...	10	90A		Majority elected	90 days after adjournment sine die. Unless the bill contains an emergency clause or special effective date.
Louisiana (q)	★	★	10 (m)	20P (m)		2/3 elected	Aug. 1
Maine	★(w)	...	10		(v)	2/3 elected	90 days after adjournment unless enacted as an emergency.
Maryland	★	★	6 (x)	30P (y)	(z)	3/5 elected (aa)	June 1 (bb)
Massachusetts	★	★	10	10P	10A	2/3 present	90 days after enactment.
Michigan	★	★	14 (m)		14P	2/3 elected and serving	Immediate effect if vote of 2/3 elected and serving. 90 days after adjournment, if immediate effect not given.
Minnesota	...	(i)	3P	14A, 3P	3A, 14P	2/3 elected—90 House; 45 Senate	Aug. 1 (cc)
Mississippi	★	...	5	15P (dd)		2/3 elected	July 1 unless specified otherwise.
Missouri	★	★	15	45A		2/3 elected	Aug. 28 (ee)
Montana (q)	★	★	10 (m)	25A (m)		2/3 present	Oct. 1 (cc)
Nebraska	★	...	5	5A, 5P	(ff)	3/5 elected	90 days following adjournment sine die. Unless bill contains an emergency clause.
Nevada	...	...	5 (gg)	10A (gg)		2/3 elected	Oct. 1, unless measure stipulates a different date.
New Hampshire	...	...	5	5P		2/3 elected	60 days after enactment, unless otherwise noted.
New Jersey	★	...	45			2/3 elected	Dates usually specified.
New Mexico	★	★	3 (hh)		20A	2/3 present	90 days after adjournment unless other date specified. General appropriations acts or emergency clauses passed by 2/3 present take effect immediately.
New York	★	...	10 (ii)	(ii)	30A	2/3 present	20 days after enactment.
North Carolina	...	...	10	30A		3/5 elected	60 days after enactment.
North Dakota	★	...	3	15A		2/3 elected	(jj)
Ohio	★	★	10	10P	10A	3/5 elected (kk)	91st day after filing with secretary of state. (ll)

See footnotes at end of table.

ENACTING LEGISLATION: VETO, VETO OVERRIDE AND EFFECTIVE DATE — Continued

State or other jurisdiction	Governor may item veto appropriation bills		Days allowed governor to consider bill (a)			Votes required in each house to pass bills or items over veto (c)	Effective date of enacted legislation (d)
	Amount	Other (b)	During session: Bill becomes law unless vetoed	After session: Bill becomes law unless vetoed	After session: Bill dies unless signed		
Oklahoma............	★	...	5 (mm)		15A (mm)	2/3 elected	90 days after adjournment unless specified in the bill.
Oregon..............	★	...	5	30A (s)		2/3 present	Jan. 1st of following year. (m)
Pennsylvania........	★	★	10	30A		2/3 majority	60 days after signed by governor.
Rhode Island........	...	...	6	10P (oo)	(oo)	3/5 present	Immediately (pp)
South Carolina......	...	★	5		(qq)	2/3 vote of the members present and voting	Date of signature.
South Dakota........	★	...	5 (rr)	15P (rr)		2/3 elected	July 1
Tennessee...........	★	...	10		(ss)	Constitutional majority	40 days after enactment unless otherwise specified.
Texas...............	★	...	10	20A		2/3 elected	90 days after adjournment unless otherwise specified.
Utah................	★	...	10P	20A		2/3 elected	60 days after adjournment of the session at which it passed.
Vermont.............	...	...	5	5A	(fff)	2/3 present	July 1 unless otherwise specified.
Virginia............	★	★ (tt)	7 (m)	30A (uu)		2/3 present (vv)	July 1 (ww)
Washington..........	★	★	5	20A		2/3 present	90 days after adjournment.
West Virginia.......	...	(i)	5	15A (xx)		Majority elected	90 days after enactment.
Wisconsin...........	★	★(eee)	6	6P		2/3 present	Day after publication date unless otherwise specified.
Wyoming.............	★	★	3	15A		2/3 elected	Specified in act.
American Samoa	★	★	10		30A	2/3 elected	60 days after adjournment. (yy)
Guam................	★	★	10	10P	30P (zz)	10 votes to override	Immediately (bbb)
No. Mariana Islands ...	★	...	40 (m)(aaa)			2/3 elected	Upon signing by the governor.
Puerto Rico.........	★	...	10		30P	2/3 elected	Specified in act.
U.S. Virgin Islands......	★(ccc)	★(ccc)	10	10P	30A	2/3 elected	Immediately

Sources: The Council of State Governments' survey, November 2015 and state websites January 2016.

Key:
★ — Yes
... — No
A — Days after adjournment of legislature.
P — Days after presentation to governor.
(a) Sundays excluded, unless otherwise indicated.
(b) Includes language in appropriations bill.
(c) Bill returned to house of origin with governor's objections.
(d) Effective date may be established by the law itself or may be otherwise changed by vote of the legislature. Special or emergency acts are usually effective immediately.
(e) The governor may line item distinct items or item veto amounts in appropriation bills, if returned prior to final adjournment.
(f) Except bills presented within five days of final adjournment. Sundays are included.
(g) Different number of votes required for revenue and appropriations bills. Alaska—3/4 elected. Illinois—Only the usual majority of members elected is required to restore a reduced item.
(h) Several specific requirements of 3/4 majority.
(i) Line item veto.
(j) For a bill to become law during session, if 12th day falls on a Saturday, Sunday, or holiday, the period is extended to the next day that is not a Saturday, Sunday, or holiday.
(k) For legislation enacted in regular sessions: January 1 of the following year. Urgency legislation: immediately upon chaptering by Secretary of State. Legislation enacted in special session: 91st day after adjournment of the special session at which the bill was passed.

(l) The governor may not line-item veto any portion of any bill (including appropriation clauses in bills) other than line items in the Long Appropriations Bill. The governor may line-item veto individual lines in the Long Appropriations Bill. In those instances, the governor must line-item veto the entire amount of any item; an item is an indivisible sum of money dedicated to a single purpose.
(m) Sundays included.
(n) An act takes effect on the date stated in the act, or if no date is stated in the act, then upon signature of the governor. If no safety clause on a bill, the bill takes effect 90 days after sine die if no referendum petition has been filed. The state constitution allows for a 90 day period following adjournment when petitions may be filed for bills that do not contain a safety clause.
(o) Bill enacted if not signed /vetoed within time frames.
(p) The governor must notify the legislature 10 days before the 45th day of his intent to veto a measure on that day. The legislature may convene at or before noon on the 45th day after adjournment to consider the vetoed measures. If the legislature fails to reconvene, the bill does not become law. If the legislature reconvenes, it may pass the measure over the governor's veto or it may amend the law to meet the governor's objections. If the law is amended, the governor must sign the bill within 10 days after it is presented to him in order for it to become law.
(q) Constitution withholds right to veto constitutional amendments proposed by the legislature.
(r) Governor can also reduce amounts in appropriations bills. In Hawaii, governor can reduce items in executive appropriations measures, but cannot reduce or item veto amounts appropriated for the judicial or legislative branches.
(s) Except Sundays and legal holidays. In Hawaii, except Saturdays, Sundays, holidays and any days in which the legislature is in recess prior to its adjournment. In Oregon, if the governor does not sign the bill within 30 days after adjournment, it becomes law without the governor's signature, Saturdays and Sundays are excluded.

ENACTING LEGISLATION: VETO, VETO OVERRIDE AND EFFECTIVE DATE—Continued

(t) Effective date for bills which become law on or after July 1: A bill passed after May 31 cannot take effect before June 1 of the following year unless it states an earlier effective date and is approved by 3/5 of the members elected to each house.

(u) Varies with date of the veto.

(v) "If the bill or resolution shall not be returned by the governor within 10 days (Sundays excepted) after it shall have been presented to the Governor, it shall have the same force and effect as if the Governor had signed it unless the Legislature by their adjournment prevent its return, in which case it shall have such force and effect, unless returned within 3 days after the next meeting of the same Legislature which enacted the bill or resolution; if there is no such next meeting of the Legislature which enacted the bill or resolution, the bill or resolution shall not be a law." (excerpted from Article IV, Part Third, Section 2 of the Constitution of Maine).

(w) The governor cannot veto the budget bill but may exercise a total veto or item veto on a supplementary appropriations bill. In practice this means the governor may strike items in the annual general capital loan bill. Occasionally the governor will also veto a bond bill or a portion of a bond bill.

(x) If a bill is presented to the governor in the first 83 days of session, the governor has only six days (not including Sunday) to act before the bill automatically becomes law.

(y) All bills passed at regular or special sessions must be presented to the governor no later than 20 days after adjournment. The governor has a limited time to sign or veto a bill after it is presented. If the governor does not act within that time, the bill becomes law automatically; there is no pocket veto. The time limit depends on when the presentment is made. Any bill presented in the last 7 days of the 90-day session or after adjournment must be acted on within 30 days after presentment. Bills vetoed after adjournment are returned to the legislature for reconsideration at the next meeting of the same General Assembly.

(z) The governor has a limited time to sign or veto a bill after it is presented. If the governor does not act within that time, the bill becomes law automatically; there is no pocket veto. The time limit depends on when the presentment is made.

(aa) Vetoed bills are returned to the house of origin immediately after that house has organized at the next regular or special session. When a new General Assembly is elected and sworn in, bills vetoed from the previous session are not returned. These vetoed bills are not subject to any further legislative action.

(bb) Unless otherwise provided, June 1 is the effective date for bond bills, July 1 for budget, tax and revenue bills. By custom October 1 is the usual effective date for other legislation. If the bill is an emergency measure, it may take effect immediately upon approval by the governor or at a specified date prior to June 1. For vetoed legislation, 30 days after the veto is overridden or on the date specified in the bill, whichever is later. An emergency bill passed over the governor's veto takes effect immediately.

(cc) Different date for fiscal legislation. Minnesota—July 1. Montana—Appropriations effective July 1 unless otherwise specified in bill; revenue bills effected July 1 unless otherwise specified in bill, often next Jan. 1.

(dd) Bills vetoed after adjournment are returned to the legislature for reconsideration. Mississippi—returned within three days after the beginning of the next session.

(ee) If bill has an emergency clause, it becomes effective upon governor's signature. If a bill is neither signed nor vetoed by a governor, it becomes law.

(ff) Bills are carried over from the 90-day session beginning in the odd-numbered year to the 60-day session, which begins in even-numbered years. Bills that have not passed by the last day of the 60-day session are all indefinitely postponed by motion on the last day of the session.

(gg) The day of delivery and Sundays are not counted for purposes of calculating these periods.

(hh) Except bills presented to the governor in the last three days of session, for which the governor has 20 days from adjournment.

(ii) If the legislature adjourns during the governor's consideration of a 10-day bill, the bill shall not become law without the governor's approval.

(jj) August 1 after filing with the secretary of state. Appropriations and tax bills July 1 after filing with secretary of state, or date set in legislation by Legislative Assembly, or by date established by emergency clause in a bill that passes each house by a vote of two-thirds of the members-elect of each house.

(kk) The exception covers such matters as emergency measures and court bills that originally required a 2/3 majority for passage. In those cases, the same extraordinary majority vote is required to override a veto.

(ll) Emergency, current appropriation, and tax legislation effective immediately. The General Assembly may also enact an uncodified section of law specifying a desired effective date that is after the constitutionally established effective date.

(mm) During session the governor has 5 days (except Sunday) to sign or veto a bill or it becomes law automatically. After Session a bill becomes a pocket veto if not signed 15 days after sine die.

(nn) Unless emergency declared or date specific in text of measure, which must be at least 90 days after adjournment sine die unless emergency is declared. Emergency cannot be declared in bills regulating taxation or exemption.

(oo) Bills become effective without signature if not signed or vetoed.

(pp) Date signed, date received by Secretary of State if effective without signature, date that veto is overridden, or other specified date.

(qq) Two days after the next meeting.

(rr) During a session, a bill becomes law if a governor signs it or does not act on it withing five days, not including Saturdays, Sundays or holidays. If the legislature has adjourned or recessed or is within five days of a recess or an adjournment, the governor has 15 days to act on the bill. If he does not act, the bill becomes law.

(ss) Adjournment of the legislature is irrelevant; the governor has 10 days to act on a bill after it is presented to him or it becomes law without his signature.

(tt) If part of the item.

(uu) The governor has thirty days after adjournment of the legislature to act on any bills. The Constitution of Virginia provides that : "If the governor does not act on any bill, it shall become law without his signature."

(vv) Must include majority of elected members.

(ww) Unless a different date is stated in the bill. Special sessions—first day of fourth month after adjournment.

(xx) Five days for supplemental appropriation bills.

(yy) Laws required to be approved only by the governor. An act required to be approved by the U.S. Secretary of the Interior only after it is vetoed by the governor and so approved takes effect 40 days after it is returned to the governor by the secretary.

(zz) After Legislature adjourns sine die at end of two-year term.

(aaa) Twenty days for appropriations bills.

(bbb) U.S. Congress may annul.

(ccc) May item veto language or amounts in a bill that contains two or more appropriations.

(ddd) The governor has seven days, Sundays included, to act on presented bills while the Legislature is in session. If the Legislature adjourns sine die during the seven-day period or takes a recess of more than 30 days, the governor has 15 consecutive days from the date of presentation to act on the bill(s).

(eee) Governor may partially veto words or numbers in the case of appropriation bills.

(fff) Three days subsequent to presentation following adjournment in even numbered years.

(ggg) Ten calendar days after receipt of bill. When the Governor receives bills within the last 10 days of session, the Governor has 30 days to act on the bills.

(hhh) Per Joint Rule 58.5, the Legislature may consider a Governor's veto for only 60 legislative days or until adjournment sine die of the session in which the bill subject to the veto was passed by the Legislature, whichever period is shorter.

Table 3.17
LEGISLATIVE APPROPRIATIONS PROCESS: BUDGET DOCUMENTS AND BILLS

State or other jurisdiction	Budget document submission							Budget bill introduction		
	Legal source of deadline		Submission date relative to convening					Same time as budget document	Another time	Not until committee review of budget document
	Constitutional	Statutory	Prior to session	Within one week	Within two weeks	Within one month	Over one month			
Alabama	★	★	(a)	...	...	...	...	★	...	...
Alaska	★	★	...	(a)	...	...	...	★	...	...
Arizona	...	★	★	...	...	...	...	...	...	★
Arkansas	...	★	★	...	...	...	...	...	...	★
California	★	...	...	...	...	(a)	...	★(b)	...	...
Colorado	...	★	★(a)	...	...	...	...	...	76th day by rule	...
Connecticut	...	★	...	...	...	(a)	...	★	...	...
Delaware	...	...	...	...	...	...	...	...	...	★
Florida	★	★	★	...	...	...	...	...	...	★
Georgia	★	...	...	(a)	...	...	...	★	...	...
Hawaii	...	★	30 days	...	...	...	...	...	★	...
Idaho	...	★	...	★	...	...	...	...	...	★
Illinois	...	★	...	...	...	...	★(a)	...	★(c)	...
Indiana	...	★	...	...	...	...	...	...	★	...
Iowa	...	★	...	...	...	(a)	...	...	...	★(d)
Kansas	...	★	...	...	★(e)	...	...	...	★	...
Kentucky	★	...	...	...	(a)	...	...	★	...	...
Louisiana	...	★	(f)	(f)	...	...	...	(g)	...	...
Maine	...	★	...	(a)	...	...	...	★	...	...
Maryland	★	...	★(e)	...	...	...	...	★(h)	...	...
Massachusetts	...	★	...	...	...	★	...	★	...	...
Michigan	...	★	...	...	...	★	...	★	...	...
Minnesota	...	★	...	...	...	(a)	...	...	...	★
Mississippi	...	★	★	...	...	...	...	...	★	...
Missouri	★	...	...	...	...	★	...	...	...	★
Montana	...	★	★	...	...	...	...	...	★	...
Nebraska	...	★	★	...	...	★	...	★(i)	...	...
Nevada	★	...	(a)	...	...	...	...	...	...	★
New Hampshire	...	★	...	...	...	...	(a)	...	★	...
New Jersey	...	★	...	...	...	...	...	...	...	★
New Mexico	...	★	...	...	...	(a)	...	...	★	...
New York	★	...	(a)	...	★(a)	...	...	...	★(j)	...
North Carolina	...	...	...	...	...	...	...	★	...	...
North Dakota	...	★	(k)	...	...	...	...	...	★(k)	...
Ohio	...	★	...	...	...	★(d)(e)	...	★(x)	...	...
Oklahoma	★	★	...	★	...	...	...	...	★	...
Oregon	...	★	★	...	...	...	★(l)	★(m)	...	★
Pennsylvania	★	...	...	...	...	...	★	...	...	★
Rhode Island	...	★	...	...	...	...	★	...	★	...
South Carolina	...	★	...	★	...	...	...	...	...	★
South Dakota	...	★	...	...	...	...	★(o)	...	★(p)	...
Tennessee	...	★	...	...	★(a)(e)	★(a)(e)	...	★	...	...
Texas	...	★	...	(n)	...	...	...	★(q)	...	...
Utah	...	★(t)	(a)	...	...	...	...	...	...	★
Vermont	...	★	(s)	...	...	...	...	...	...	★
Virginia	...	★	Dec. 20	...	...	...	...	★	...	...
Washington	★(t)	...	(u)	...	...	...	...	★	...	...
West Virginia	★	...	...	★	...	...	...	★	...	...
Wisconsin	...	★	...	...	...	★(v)	...	★	...	...
Wyoming	...	★	Dec. 1	...	...	...	...	...	...	★
American Samoa	...	★	★	...	...	...	...	★	...	...
Guam	...	★	...	...	...	★(w)	...	★	...	...
No. Mariana Islands	★	★	April 1	...	...	...	...	...	★	★
Puerto Rico	...	★	...	...	...	★	...	...	...	★
U.S. Virgin Islands	...	★	May 30	...	...	...	...	...	★	...

See footnotes at end of table.

LEGISLATIVE APPROPRIATIONS PROCESS: BUDGET DOCUMENTS AND BILLS — Continued

Sources: The Council of State Governments' survey, November 2015 and state websites, January 2016.

Key:

★ — Yes

. . . — No

(a) Specific time limitations: Alabama—within first five days of session; Alaska—December 15, 4th legislative day; California—January 10; Connecticut—not later than the first session day following the third day in February, in each odd-numbered year; Colorado—presented by November 1 to the Joint Budget Committee; Georgia—first five days of session; Illinois—Third Wednesday in February; Iowa—no later than February 1; Kentucky—10th legislative day; Maine—The governor shall transmit the budget document to the Legislature not later than the Friday following the first Monday in January of the first regular legislative session. ... A governor-elect elected to a first term of office shall transmit the budget document to the Legislature not later than the Friday following the first Monday in February of the first regular legislative session (Maine Revised Statutes, Title 5, Chapter 149, Section 1666); Minnesota—by the 4th Tuesday in January each odd-numbered year; Nevada—no later than 14 days before commencement of regular session; New Hampshire—by February 15; New Mexico—by January 1 each year; New York—The legislative budget must be submitted to the governor no later than December 1. The executive budget must be submitted by the governor to the Legislature by the 2nd Tuesday following the opening of session (or February 1 for the first session following a gubernatorial election); Tennessee—on or before February 1 for sitting governor; Utah—Must submit to the Legislature by the calendared floor time on the first day of the annual session.

(b) Budget and Budget Bill are annual—to be submitted within the first 10 days of each calendar year.

(c) Deadlines for introducing bills in general are set by Senate president and House speaker.

(d) Executive budget bill is introduced and used as a working tool for committee.

(e) Later for first session of a new governor; Kansas—21 days; Maryland—10 days after; New Jersey—February 15; Ohio—by March 15; Tennessee—March 1.

(f) The governor shall submit his executive budget to the Joint Legislative Committee on the budget no later than 45 days prior to each regular session; except that in the first year of each term, the executive budget shall be submitted no later than 30 days prior to the regular session. Copies shall be made available to the entire Legislature on the first day of each regular session.

(g) Bills appropriating monies for the general operating budget and ancillary appropriations, bills appropriating funds for the expenses of the Legislature and the judiciary must be submitted to the Legislature for introduction no later than 45 days prior to each regular session, except that in the first year of each term, such appropriation bills shall be submitted no later than 30 days prior to the regular session.

(h) Appropriations bill other than the budget bill (supplementary) may be introduced at any time. They must provide their own tax source and may not be enacted until the budget bill is enacted.

(i) Governor's budget bill is introduced and serves as a working document for the Appropriations Committee. The governor must submit the budget proposal by January 15 of each odd-numbered year. (Neb.Rev. Stat. sec.81-125). The statute extends this deadline to February 1 for a governor who is in his/her first year of office.

(j) Submission of the governor's budget bills to the Legislature occurs with submission of the executive budget.

(k) Legislative Council's Budget Section hears the executive budget recommendations during Legislature's December organizational session. Budget bill introduction one week after governor's budget message.

(l) By December 1 of even-numbered year unless new governor is elected; if new governor is elected, then February 1st of odd-numbered year.

(m) Legislature often introduces other budget bills during legislative session that are not part of the governor's recommended budget.

(n) The Legislative Budget Board is required to submit a copy of the budget of estimated appropriations to the governor and members of the Legislature not later than the fifth day after session convenes. The board is required to submit a copy of the general appropriations bill not later than the seventh day after session convenes.

(o) It is usually over a month. The budget must be delivered to the Legislature not later than the first Tuesday after the first Monday in December.

(p) It must be introduced no later than the 16th legislative day.

(q) State law does not specify a special deadline for filing the General Appropriations Act, but it is generally filed soon after the Legislative Budget Board submits the budget document.

(r) Legislative rules require budget bills to be introduced by the 43rd day of the session.

(s) Third Tuesday each year.

(t) And Rules.

(u) For fiscal period other than biennium, 20 days prior to first day of session.

(v) Last Tuesday in January. A later submission date may be requested by the governor.

(w) Usually January before end of current fiscal year.

(x) Bill may actually be officially introduced a few days later; it is usually not immediately introduced upon the presentation of the governor's budget.

Table 3.18
FISCAL NOTES: CONTENT AND DISTRIBUTION

State or other jurisdiction	Content						Distribution						
							Legislators						
							Available			Appropriations Committee			
	Intent or purpose of bill	Cost involved	Projected future cost	Proposed source of revenue	Fiscal impact on local government	Other	All	on request	Bill sponsor	Members	Chair only	Fiscal staff	Executive budget staff
Alabama	★	★	...	★	★	★(a)	...	★	★	...	...	...	...
Alaska	...	★	★	★	...	...	★	★	★	...	...	★	★
Arizona	★	★	★	★	★	★	★	★	★	★	...	★	★
Arkansas (b)	...	★	★	...	★	★	★	...	...	...	...	...	...
California	★	★	★	★	★	...	★	...	...	...	...	★	★
Colorado	★	★	★	★	★	...	★	...	...	...	...	...	...
Connecticut	★	★	★	★	★	...	(c)	...	...	...	...	...	...
Delaware	...	★	...	...	...	...	★	...	...	...	...	...	...
Florida	★	★	★	★	★	★	★	...	...	...	...	★	...
Georgia	...	★	★	...	★	...	★	★	...	...	...	...	...
Hawaii	...	...	...	...	...	★(hh)	★	...	...	...	...	...	...
Idaho	★	★	★	★	★	★(d)	★	...	...	...	...	(e)	(e)
Illinois	...	★	★	★	★	...	★(f)	★	★	...	...	...	...
Indiana	★	★	★	★	★	...	★	...	...	...	...	★	★
Iowa	★	★	★	★	★	...	............................(g)............................						
Kansas	★	★	★	★	★	...	★	★	★	...	★	★	★
Kentucky	★	★	★	★	★	★	...	★	★	★	...	★	...
Louisiana	...	★	★	...	★	...	★	★	...	★(h)	...	...	...
Maine	...	★	★	★	★	...	...	★(i)	★	...	...	★	★
Maryland	★	★	★	★	★	★(j)	...	...	★(k)	...	...	...	...
Massachusetts	...	★(l)	★	...	...	★	★	...	...	★	...	...	...
Michigan	★	★	★	★	★	★(m)	★(n)	...	...	...	...	...	...
Minnesota	★	★	★	★	★	...	...	...	★	...	★	★	★
Mississippi	...	★	★	★	...	...	...	...	★(o)	...	...	...	...
Missouri	★	★	★	★	...	...	...	★	★	...	...	...	★
Montana	...	★	★	...	★	★(p)	★	...	...	...	...	★	★
Nebraska	...	★	★	★	★	...	★	★	...	...	...	★	★
Nevada	...	★	★	★	★	...	★(kk)	...	...	...	...	...	...
New Hampshire (ii)	★	★	...	★	★	...	...	★	...	★	...	★	★
New Jersey	...	★	...	★	★	...	★	...	...	...	...	★	★
New Mexico	★	★	★	★	★	...	★	...	...	★	...	(q)	(q)
New York	★	★	★	...	★	★(r)	...	★	★	★	...	★	...
North Carolina	...	★	★	...	★	★	(s)	...	...	...	...	...	...
North Dakota	...	...	★	★	★	★(t)	(u)	★	...	...	...	★	★
Ohio	★	★	★	★	★	...	(v)	★	★	...	...	★	...
Oklahoma	★	★	★	★	...	...	...	★	★	...	★	★	...
Oregon	★	★	★	★	...	...	★	...	...	...	...	★	★
Pennsylvania	...	★	★	★	...	...	...	...	...	★	...	★	...
Rhode Island	★	★	★	★	★	...	...	★	...	★	...	★	★
South Carolina	★	★	★	★	★	...	★	...	...	(w)	...	★	★
South Dakota	...	★	★	★	★	...	★	...	...	...	...	...	...
Tennessee	★	★	★	...	★	...	★	★	★	...	...	...	...
Texas	...	★	★	★	★	★(x)	★	★	★	(jj)	...	...	...
Utah	...	★	★	...	★	★(y)	★	★	★	...	...	★	★
Vermont	............................(z)............................					...	...	★	...	★	...	...	...
Virginia	★	★	★	★	★	★(aa)	(bb)	...	★	...	★	★(cc)	...
Washington	...	★	★	★	★	★(dd)	★	★	★	★	★	★	...
West Virginia	...	★	★	★	★	...	...	...	...	★	...	...	...
Wisconsin	...	★	★	★	★	...	(ee)	...	...	...	...	(ee)	...
Wyoming	...	★	★	★	...	...	★	...	...	...	...	...	...
Guam	...	★	...	...	★	★(ff)	★	...	...	★	★	★	...
No. Mariana Islands	★	★	★	★	★	★	...	...	...	★	★	★	★
Puerto Rico	............................(gg)............................												
U.S. Virgin Islands	★	★	...	★	...	...	★	...	...	...	...	...	...

See footnotes at end of table.

FISCAL NOTES: CONTENT AND DISTRIBUTION — Continued

Source: The Council of State Governments' survey, November 2015.
Note: A fiscal note is a summary of the fiscal effects of a bill on government revenues, expenditures and liabilities.
Key:
★ — Yes
. . . — No

(a) Fiscal notes included on final passage calendar.

(b) Only retirement, corrections, revenue, tax and local government bills require fiscal notes. During the past session, fiscal notes were provided for education.

(c) The fiscal notes are printed with the bills favorably reported by the committees.

(d) Statement of purpose.

(e) Attached to bill, so available to both fiscal and executive budget staff.

(f) A summary of each fiscal note is attached to the summary of its bill in the printed Legislative Synopsis and Digest, and on the General Assembly's website. Fiscal notes are prepared for the sponsor and attached to the bill on file with the House Clerk or Senate Secretary.

(g) Fiscal notes are available to everyone.

(h) Prepared by the Legislative Fiscal Office when a state agency is involved and prepared by Legislative Auditor's office when a local board or commission is involved; copies sent to House and Senate staff offices respectively.

(i) Distributed to members of the committee of reference; also available on the Legislature's website.

(j) A fiscal note is now known as a fiscal and policy note to better reflect the contents. Fiscal and policy notes also identify any mandate on local government and include analyses of the economic impact on small businesses.

(k) In practice fiscal and policy notes are prepared on all bills and resolutions prior to a public hearing on the bills/resolutions. After initial hard copy distribution to sponsor and committee, the note is released to member computer system and thereafter to the legislative website.

(l) Fiscal notes are prepared only if cost exceeds $100,000 or matter has not been acted upon by the Joint Committee on Ways and Means.

(m) Other relevant data.

(n) At present, fiscal information is part of the bill analysis on the legislative website.

(o) And committee to which bill referred.

(p) Mechanical defects in bill.

(q) Fiscal impact statements prepared by Legislative Finance Committee staff are available to anyone on request and on the Legislature's website.

(r) Fiscal notes are required for retirement bills, bills enacting or amending tax expenditures, and all bills increasing or decreasing state revenues, or affecting appropriation or expenditure of state monies.

(s) Fiscal notes are posted on the Internet and available to all members.

(t) Notes required only if impact is $5,000 or more. Bills impacting workforce safety and insurance benefits or premiums have actuarial statements as do bills proposing changes in state and local retirement systems.

(u) Fiscal notes are available online to anyone from the legislative branch website.

(v) Fiscal notes are prepared for bills before being voted on in any standing committee or floor session. Fiscal notes for all introduced bills are posted on the Web. They are also distributed to the committees in which the bills are heard.

(w) Fiscal impact statements on proposed legislation are prepared by the Revenue and Fiscal Affairs Office and sent to the House or Senate standing committeee that requested the impact. All fiscal impacts are posted on the Revenue and Fiscal Affairs website.

(x) Some bills may also require the preparation of one or more of the following fiscal impact statements: an actuarial impact statement, a criminal justice policy impact statement, an equalized education funding impact statement, a higher education impact statement, an open government impact statement, an impact statement regarding the economic effect of tax changes, a tax/fee equity note, or a water development policy impact statement.

(y) Fiscal notes are to include cost and revenue estimates on all bills that anticipate direct impact on state government, local government, residents, and businesses.

(z) Fiscal notes are not mandatory and their content will vary.

(aa) Technical amendments, if needed. Fiscal notes do not provide statements or interpretations of legislative intent for legal purposes. A summary of the stated objective, effect, and impact may be included.

(bb) Fiscal impact statements are widely available because they are also posted on the Internet shortly after they are distributed. The Joint Legislative Audit Review Commission (JLARC) also prepares a review of the fiscal impact statement if requested by a standing committee chair. The review statement is also available on the Internet.

(cc) Legislative budget directors.

(dd) Impact on private sector.

(ee) The fiscal estimate is printed as an appendix to the bill; anyone that has a copy of the bill has a copy of the fiscal estimate.

(ff) Fiscal impact on local economy.

(gg) The Legislature of Puerto Rico does not prepare fiscal notes, but upon request the economics unit could prepare one. The Department of Treasury has the duty to analyze and prepare fiscal notes.

(hh) Hawaii does not require the submission of fiscal notes.

(ii) Whenver possible, fiscal notes appear at end of introduced version of bill.

(jj) After a bill has been set for hearing, the Legislative Budget Board distributes the fiscal note to the committee clerk and the sponsor of the bill. In the House, the fiscal note must be attached to the affected bill before a public hearing on the bill may be held, and Senate practice is for a copy of the fiscal note to be provided to the committee members before a final vote on a bill in committee is taken. If the bill is reported from committee, the fiscal note is attached to the bill as part of the committee report when it is printed and distributed to the legislators. Fiscal notes are publicly available online for bills that have been voted out of committee.

(kk) Fiscal notes are posted on the Legislature's website.

Table 3.19
BILL AND RESOLUTION INTRODUCTIONS AND ENACTMENTS:
2015 REGULAR SESSIONS

State	Duration of session**	Introductions		Enactments/Adoptions		Measures vetoed by governor (a)(b)	Length of session
		Bills	Resolutions*	Bills	Resolutions*		
Alabama	Mar. 3–Jun. 4, 2015	1,210	483	357	142	0	29L
Alaska	Jan. 20–Apr. 27, 2015	575	113	48	52	3	N.A.
Arizona	Jan. 12–Apr. 3, 2015	1,163	89	324	36	0	82C
Arkansas	Jan. 12–Apr. 22, 2015	2,062	137	1,289	N.A.	0	N.A.
California	Dec. 1, 2014–Sep. 11, 2015	2,370	326	807	274	133	127L
Colorado	Jan. 7–May 6, 2015	682	75	364	61	3	120C
Connecticut	Jan. 7–Jun. 3, 2015	3,202 (d)	232	261	124	4	152C
Delaware	Jan. 13–Jun. 30, 2015	370	123	194	3,202 (d)0	2	43L
Florida	Mar. 3–May 1, 2015 (j)	1,574	160	227	2	7	60C (j)
Georgia	Jan. 12–Apr. 2, 2015	955	1,610	312	1,439	301	N.A.
Hawaii	Jan. 21–May 7, 2015	2,894	753	252	190	8	60L
Idaho	Jan. 12–Apr. 11, 2015	523	72	382	48	4	89L
Illinois (k)	Jan. 14–Dec. 7, 2015	6,534	2,210	483	1,991	44	N.A.
Indiana	Jan. 6–Apr. 29, 2015	1,237	168	258	N.A.	0	N.A.
Iowa	Jan. 12–Jun. 5, 2015	1,851 (e)	118	143	53 (f)	1	145C
Kansas	Jan. 12–Jun. 26, 2015	746	108	105	8	1	114C
Kentucky	Jan. 6–Mar. 24, 2015	752	491	117	12	1	29L
Louisiana	Apr. 13–Jun. 11, 2015	1,106	832	469	250	9	36L
Maine	Dec. 3, 2014–Jul. 6, 2015	1,455	53 (f)0	442	53 (f)0	178	69L
Maryland	Jan. 14–Apr. 13, 2015	2,234	14	495	N.A.	193	90C
Massachusetts	Jan. 8–Jul. 31, 2014	6,988	4,546	704	N.A.	5	N.A.
Michigan	Jan. 14–Dec. 18, 2015	1,890	408	269	251	0	112L (i)
Minnesota	Jan. 6–May 18, 2015	4,605	N.A.	80	…	3	N.A.
Mississippi	Jan. 6–Apr. 2, 2015	2,620	304	347	253	5	90C
Missouri	Jan. 7–May 30, 2015	1,888	67	131	2	18	72L
Montana	Jan. 5–Apr. 28, 2015	1,187	103	457	80	52	87L
Nebraska (U)	Jan. 7–May 29, 2015	664	377	247	241	5	89L
Nevada	Feb. 2–June 1, 2015	1,013	62	556	41	7	120C
New Hampshire	Jan. 7–Sep. 16, 2015	902	33	276	1	10	19L
New Jersey	Jan. 14, 2014–Jan. 12, 2016	9,074	N.A.	381	16	62	728C
New Mexico	Jan. 20–Mar. 21, 2015	1,281	42	158	3	33	60C
New York	Jan. 7, 2015–Jan. 6, 2016	14,823	N.A.	589	3,734	125	365C
North Carolina	Jan. 14–Sep. 30, 2015	1,634	32	300	14	2	260C
North Dakota	Jan. 6–Apr. 29, 2015 (c)	854	87	484	53	1	79L
Ohio	Jan. 5–Dec. 30, 2015 (g)	678	53	45	14	0	125L (h)
Oklahoma	Jan. 6–May 22, 2015	2,112	182	398	72	17	64C
Oregon	Feb. 2–Jul. 6, 2015	2,641	158	848	74	0	154C
Pennsylvania	Jan. 6–Dec. 31, 2015	2,867	888	39	1	9	N.A.
Rhode Island	Jan. 6–Jun. 25, 2015	2,399	N.A.	423	439	0	176C
South Carolina	Jan. 13–Jun. 4, 2015	N.A.	259	138	143	2	143C
South Dakota	Jan. 13–Mar. 30, 2015	427	25	258	19	3	39L
Tennessee	Jan. 13–Apr. 22, 2015	N.A.	1,519	1,007	1,519	0	107C
Texas	Jan. 13–Jun. 1, 2015	6,276	374	1,323	107	42	140C
Utah	Jan. 26–Mar. 12, 2015	1,520	84	477	51	1	N.A.
Vermont	Jan. 7–May 16, 2015	666	267	64	251	0	130C
Virginia	Jan. 14–Feb. 27, 2015	1,919	857	774	713	17	45C
Washington	Jan. 12–Apr. 24, 2015	2,365	53	297	10	10	N.A.
West Virginia	Jan. 14–Mar. 14, 2015	1,607	256	262	143	19	60C
Wisconsin	Jan. 5–Dec 10, 2015	1,830	381	356	381	0	339C
Wyoming	Jan. 13–Mar. 6, 2015	391	17	204	6	3	37L

See footnotes at end of table.

BILL AND RESOLUTION INTRODUCTIONS AND ENACTMENTS:
2015 REGULAR SESSIONS — Continued

Source: The Council of State Governments' survey of legislative agencies and state Web sites, April 2016

* Includes Joint and Concurrent resolutions.

**Actual adjournment dates are listed regardless of constitutional or statutory limitations. For more information on provisions, see Table 3.2, "Legislative Sessions: Legal Provisions."

Key:

C—Calendar day.

L—Legislative day (in some states, called a session or workday; definition may vary slightly; however, it generally refers to any day on which either chamber of the legislature is in session).

U—Unicameral legislature

N.A.—Not available.

(a) Line item or partial vetoes: California—1; Illinois—1; Iowa—7; Kansas—1; Kentucky—1; Louisiana—5; Maine—152 (all over-ridden); Maryland—1; Michigan—1; New Mexico—3; New York—4; North Dakota—4; Ohio—2; Pennsylvania—1; Texas—23 line item vetoes in 2 bills; Virginia—68; Washington—9; Wyoming—2

(b) Number of vetoes overridden: Illinois—14; Kansas—1; Maine—126; Missouri—12; Nebraska—4; North Carolina—2; Oklahoma—1; South Dakota—1; West Virginia—1; Wyoming—1.

(c) Session also reconvened and adjourned on June 16, 2015.

(d) There is some redundancy in the numbers because committee bills are based on proposed bills, which are introduced by individual legislators at the beginning of the session. Governor's Bills are introduced on behalf of the governor by legislative leaders of the governor's party. They reflect initiatives of the governor, and not necessarily those of the introducing legislators. The total number, 3,202, breaks down as: 2,155 (Proposed Bills); 660 (Raised Bills); 350 (Committee Bills); 2 (Emergency Certified); 35 (Governor's Bills).

(e) Bill introductions total includes 551 filed study bills.

(f) Includes 42 simple resolution enactments.

(g) Senate only. House adjourned on 12/29.

(h) Senate only; 123 legislative days in House

(i) Senate only; 104 legislative days in House.

(j) Senate only. House adjourned on 4/28 and served 57 calendar days.

(k) Information and numbers as of Nov. 13, 2015.

Table 3.20
BILL AND RESOLUTION INTRODUCTIONS AND ENACTMENTS:
2015 SPECIAL SESSIONS

State or other jurisdiction	Duration of session**	Introductions		Enactments/adoptions		Measures vetoed by governor	Length of session
		Bills	Resolutions*	Bills	Resolutions*		
Alabama	Jul. 13–Aug. 11, 2015	118	39	27	8	0	8L
Alaska	Apr. 28–May 21, 2015	6	0	1	0	0	
	May 21–Jun. 11, 2015	3	3	1	2	0	
	Oct. 24–Nov. 5, 2015	3	3	1	3	0	
Arizona	Oct. 28–Oct. 30. 2015	4	2	2	1	0	3C
Arkansas	May 26–28, 2015	18	2	12	0	0	3C
California	Jun. 19, 2015 — (a)	39	2	0	2	0	(a)
	Jun. 19, 2015 - (d)	33	2	1	2	0	(d)
Colorado	No special session in 2015						
Connecticut	Jun. 29, 2015	6	5	6	5	0	1C
Delaware	Jul. 1, 2015	0	0	0	0	0	1L
	Oct. 28, 2015 (c)	0	0	0	0	0	1L
	Nov. 30, 2015 (c)	0	0	0	0	0	1L
Florida	June 1–19, 2015	37	4	12	0	(e)	19C
	Aug. 10–21, 2015	3	4	0	1	0	12C
	Oct. 19–Nov. 6, 2015	2	4	0	1	0	19C
Georgia	No special session in 2015						
Hawaii	Nov. 5–6, 2015 (b)	0	0	0	0	0	2L
Idaho	May 18, 2015	1	0	1	0	0	1C
Illinois	No special session in 2015						
Indiana	No special session in 2015						
Iowa	No special session in 2015						
Kansas	No special session in 2015						
Kentucky	No special session in 2015						
Louisiana	No special session in 2015						
Maine	No special session in 2015						
Maryland	No special session in 2015						
Massachusetts	No special session in 2015						
Michigan	No special session in 2015						
Minnesota	Jun. 12–13, 2015	30	N.A.		6	...	2C
Mississippi	No special session in 2015						
Missouri	No special session in 2015						
Montana	No special session in 2015						
Nebraska (U)	No special session in 2015						
Nevada	Dec. 16–19, 2015	4	7	4	7	0	4C
New Hampshire	Nov. 18, 2015	0	1	1	1	0	1L
New Jersey	No special session in 2015						
New Mexico	June 8, 2015	3	0	3	0	(f)	1C
New York	No special session in 2015						
North Carolina	No special session in 2015						
North Dakota	No special session in 2015						
Ohio	No special session in 2015						
Oklahoma	No special session in 2015						
Oregon	No special session in 2015						
Pennsylvania	No special session in 2015						
Rhode Island	No special session in 2015						
South Carolina	Jun. 16–18, 2015	25	33	23	31	N.A.	3C
South Dakota	No special session in 2015						
Tennessee	No special session in 2015						
Texas	No special session in 2015						
Utah	Aug. 19, 2015	4	2	4	1	0	1C
Vermont	No special session in 2015						
Virginia	Aug. 27, 2015	3	93	0	83	0	1C
Washington	Apr. 29–May 28, 2015	21	3	9	3	(f)	N.A.
	May 29–June 27, 2015	42	4	11	3	(f)	N.A.
	Jun. 28–Jul. 10, 2015	7	5	45	3	(g)	N.A.
West Virginia	No special session in 2015						
Wisconsin	No special session in 2015						
Wyoming	No special session in 2015						

See footnotes at end of table.

BILL AND RESOLUTION INTRODUCTIONS AND ENACTMENTS:
2015 SPECIAL SESSIONS — Continued

Source: The Council of State Governments' survey of state legislative agencies, November 2015 and state web sites March 2016.

* Includes Joint and Concurrrent resolutions.

** Actual adjournment dates are listed regardless of constitutional or statutory limitations. For more information on provisions, see Table 3.2, "Legislative Sessions: Legal Provisions."

Key:

N.A. — Not available

C — Calendar day.

L — Legislative day (in some states, called a session or workday; definition may vary slightly; however, it generally refers to any day on which either chamber of the legislature is in session).

U — Unicameral legislature.

(a) First Extraordinary Session has not yet adjourned; number of bill introductions includes constitutional amendments. Legislative days as of Nov. 2015: 26 (Senate) and 19 (Assembly).

(b) Only Senate convened in special session to confirm judicial nominations. No legislation other than administrative resolutions were introduced or adopted.

(c) Two executive sessions: Oct. 28, 2015 and Nov. 30, 2015 for confirmations of governor's nominees.

(d) Second Extraordinary Session has not yet adjourned. Legislative days as of Nov. 2015: 22 (Senate) and 21 (Assembly).

(e) One bill with 450 line item vetoes.

(f) One partial or line item veto.

(g) Four partial vetoes.

Table 3.21
STAFF FOR INDIVIDUAL LEGISLATORS

State or other jurisdiction	Senate Capitol Personal	Senate Capitol Shared	Senate District	House/Assembly Capitol Personal	House/Assembly Capitol Shared	House/Assembly District
Alabama	YR	YR/2	(a)	YR	YR/10	(a)
Alaska (b)	YR/SO	...	YR	YR/SO	...	YR
Arizona	YR (c)	...	...	...	YR (c)	...
Arkansas	...	YR	...	...	YR (d)	...
California	YR	...	YR	YR	...	YR
Colorado	SO (e)	YR (e)	...	YR (e)	YR (e)	...
Connecticut (f)	YR/36	...	...	...	YR/38	...
Delaware	.... (g)					
Florida	YR (h)	...	YR (h)	YR (h)	...	YR (h)
Georgia	...	YR/3, SO/68	...	...	YR/25, SO/113	...
Hawaii (nn)	YR/2+	...	...	YR/1+	...	...
Idaho	...	SO, YR (i)	...	...	SO, YR (i)	...
Illinois	YR (j)	YR (j)	YR (j)	YR (j)	YR (j)	YR (j)
Indiana	...	YR/2 (k)	...	...	YR	...
Iowa	SO/1 (oo)	...	(oo)	SO/1 (oo)	...	(oo)
Kansas	SO/1	...	...	(l)	SO/3	...
Kentucky	...	YR (m)	...	...	YR (m)	...
Louisiana	(n)	YR (o)	YR (n)	(n)	YR (o)	YR (n)
Maine	YR, SO (p)	YR/27, SO/7	YR	...	YR (q)	...
Maryland	YR, SO (r)	...	YR (r)	YR (r)	SO (r)	YR (r)
Massachusetts	YR	...	...	YR	...	...
Michigan	YR (s)	...	...	YR/2 (s)	...	...
Minnesota	YR (t)	Varies	...	YR/3	Varies	...
Mississippi	...	YR	...	...	YR	...
Missouri	YR	YR	...	YR	YR	...
Montana	...	SO	...	...	SO	...
Nebraska	YR (u)	...	...	.... Unicameral		
Nevada	SO (pp)	YR	...	SO (pp)	YR	...
New Hampshire	...	YR	...	...	YR	...
New Jersey	YR (h)	...	YR (h)	YR (h)	...	YR (h)
New Mexico	SO/1	...	...	...	SO/2	...
New York	YR (w)	...	YR (w)	YR (w)	...	YR (w)
North Carolina	YR (x)	YR	...	YR (x)	YR	...
North Dakota	...	SO (v)	...	...	SO (v)	...
Ohio	YR/2 (y)	...	(z)	YR/1 (aa)	...	(z)
Oklahoma	YR/1(bb)	YR (bb)	...	YR (bb)	YR/1 (bb)	...
Oregon	YR (cc)	YR	YR (dd)	YR (cc)	YR	YR (dd)
Pennsylvania	YR	...	YR	YR	...	YR
Rhode Island	...	YR (ee)	...	...	YR (ee)	...
South Carolina	...	YR/2	...	YR/4	...	...
South Dakota	(ff)	(ff)	...	(ff)	(ff)	...
Tennessee	YR/1	...	...	(gg)	YR/1	...
Texas	YR/6 (hh)	...	...	YR/3 (hh)	...	...
Utah	SO (ii)	YR /5-8(ii)	...	SO (ii)	...	...
Vermont	YR/1 (jj)	...	...	YR/1 (jj)	...	...
Virginia	SO/1 (kk)	...	(kk)	SO (kk)	SO/2	(kk)
Washington	YR/1	...	IO/1	YR/1	...	YR/1
West Virginia	SO	...	...	...	SO/17	...
Wisconsin	YR (ll)	YR	YR (ll)	YR (ll)	YR	YR (ll)
Wyoming	...	...	...	...	...	...
American Samoa	...	...	...	...	...	...
Guam	...	...	...	.... Unicameral		
No. Mariana Islands	YR (mm)	(mm)	...	YR (mm)	(mm)	(ll)
Puerto Rico	YR (mm)	...	...	YR (mm)	...	(ll)
U.S. Virgin Islands	YR (mm)	...	...	.... Unicameral		

See footnotes at end of table.

STAFF FOR INDIVIDUAL LEGISLATORS — Continued

Source: The Council of State Governments' survey, November 2015.

Note: For entries under column heading "Shared," figures after slash indicate approximate number of legislators per staff person, where available.

Key:

... — Staff not provided for individual legislators.

YR — Year-round.

SO — Session only.

IO — Interim only.

(a) Six counties have local delegation offices with shared staff.

(b) The number of staff per legislator varies depending on their position.

(c) Representatives share a secretary with another legislator; however, House leadership and committee chairs usually have their own secretarial staff. All legislators share professional research staff.

(d) The legislators share 21 staff people; 4.76 legislators per staff person.

(e) Senate: Personal — Each Senator is granted 570 aide hours and may employ up to two aides each fiscal year, with each aide working a maximum of 40 hours each week. Shared — 18 session-only employees are employed by the Senate: 2 each by the majority and the minority and 14 by the non-partisan staff. 17 year-round employees are employed by the Senate: 8 by the majority, 5 by the minority, and 4 by the non-partisan staff. There are also 4 session-only employees in the bill room who are jointly managed by the Colorado Senate and House House: Personal — Each Representative is allowed to hire up to 2 paid Legislative Aides who share a limit of 790 hours per fiscal year. Representatives may have an unlimited number of unpaid interns and volunteers. Shared — 65 House legislators share 17 full-time staff: 6 majority caucus staff, 5 minority caucus staff, 6 non-partisan staff. 65 Representatives share 28 session-only staff: 3 majority caucus staff, 2 minority caucus staff, 23 non-partisan staff.

(f) The numbers are for staff assigned to specific legislators. There is additional staff working in the leadership offices that also support the rank-and-file members.

(g) Staffers are a combination of full time, part time, shared, personal, etc. and their assignments change throughout the year.

(h) Personal and district staff are the same. In Florida, district employees may travel to the capitol for sessions (two district employees in the Senate and one district employee in the House).

(i) In the Senate, Idaho has one year-round full-time and two part-time year-round employees, with 60 additional employees during the session. The House has one full-time and one part-time person year round and 38 additional people during session.

(j) Each senator has one secretary and two House members share a secretary. Partisan staffers also help legislators with many issues as well as staffing committees. Most senators and representatives have one or two district office employees, paid from a separate allowance for that purpose.

(k) Leadership has one legislative assistant. During session, college interns are hired to provide additional staff — one for every two members. Leadership has one intern.

(l) One clerical staff person for three individual House members is the norm. Chairpersons are provided their own individual clerical staff person.

(m) The General Assembly is provided professional and clerical staff services by a centralized, non-partisan staff, with the exception of House and Senate leadership which employs partisan staff. No district staff provided.

(n) Each legislator may hire as many assistants as desired, but pay from public funds ranges from $2,000 to $3,000 per month per legislator. Assistant(s) generally work in the district office but may also work at the capitol during the session.

(o) The six caucuses are assigned one full-time position each (potentially 24 legislators per one staff person).

(p) President's office: six year round; Majority office: 7 year round, 1 session only; Secretary's office: nine year round, five session only.

(q) The 151 House members do not have individual staff. There are 21 people who work year round in the two partisan offices, 12 of whom are legislative aides who primarily work directly with legislators. Speaker's office: 8 year round. Clerk's office: 12 year round, 1 part-time, 10 session-only.

(r) Senators have one year round administrative aide and one session only secretary. Delegates have one part-time year round administrative aide and a shared session only secretary. Legislators may increase staff and also hire student interns if their district office funds are used.

(s) Senate — majority, 2–6 staff per legislator; minority, 2–3 staff per legislator. House — 2 staff per legislator.

(t) One to two staff persons per legislator.

(u) Two to five staff persons per legislator.

(v) Secretarial staff; in North Dakota, leadership only.

(w) Varies depending upon allowance allocated to each member. Members have considerable independence in hiring personal and committee staffs. Legislative employees can be annual, session, or temporary.

(x) Part time during interim.

(y) Some leadership offices have more.

(z) Some legislators maintain district offices at their own expense.

(aa) Some offices have more.

(bb) Senate: Pro Tem — 6 staff persons; Senate minority leader — 1 staff person. House: year round one to five, majority party only; minority party one staff person per legislator. Committee, fiscal and legal staffs are available to legislators on a year-round basis.

(cc) Two staff persons per legislator during session.

(dd) Senate — Equivalent of one full-time staff. House — 1 during interim.

(ee) The General Assembly has a total of 280 full-time positions, 267 full-time shared staff and additional 13 full-time positions for the House.

(ff) The non-partisan Legislative Research Council serves all members of both houses year round. Committee secretaries and legislative interns and pages provide support during the sessions.

(gg) Several House members have year-round personal staff. It depends on seniority, duties (such as committee chairs), and committee assignments.

(hh) Average staff numbers are from staff member totals from each chamber.

(ii) Most legislators are assigned one student intern during session who is temporarily employed by OLRGC. Some legislators provide their own personal intern (volunteer or financial arrangements are made between them). Senate shared staff: 5–8. In the fall of 2014, the Senate hired four full-time constituent services staff to take care of administrative matters and constituent inquiries year round. Three were hired for 24 majority members, one for five minority members.

(jj) No personal staff except one administrative assistant for the Speaker and one for the Senate Pro Tempore.

(kk) Senate — One administrative assistant (secretary) provided to the members during the session by the Clerk's offices. Members also receive a set dollar allowance to hire additional legislative assistants who may serve year round at the capitol and in the district. House — Members also receive a set dollar allowance to hire additional legislative assistants who may serve year round at the capitol and in the district.

(ll) Staffing levels vary according to majority/minority status and leadership or committee responsibilities. Members may assign staff to work in the district office.

(mm) Individual staffing and staff pool arrangements are at the discretion of the individual legislator.

(nn) Each senator has the authority to hire at least two full-time, year-round staff. Each representative has the authority to hire at least one full-time, year-round staff. Depending on leadership or committee chair assignment, additional staff positions may be authorized.

(oo) One clerk provided in capitol. District/Caucus — 11 staff persons for Republicans and 9 staff persons for Democrats.

(pp) Senate — Majority Leader, 3 staff; Minority Leader, 2 staff; Other Seantors, 1 staff per legislator. Secretarial staff. House- 1 staff per legislator. Secretarial staff; Leadership positions are assigned additional staff.

Table 3.22
STAFF FOR LEGISLATIVE STANDING COMMITTEES

State or other jurisdiction	Committee staff assistance				Source of staff services **							
	Senate		House/Assembly		Joint central agency (a)		Chamber agency (b)		Caucus or leadership		Committee or committee chair	
	Prof.	Cler.	Prof.	Cler.	Prof.	Cler.	Prof.	Cler.	Prof.	Cler.	Prof.	Cler.
Alabama	●	★	●	★	B	...	...	B	...	...	...	...
Alaska	★	★	★	★	B	B	...	...	...	...	B	B
Arizona	★	★	★	★	B	B	B	B	B	B	B	B
Arkansas	★	★	★	★	B	B	B	B	...	...	...	...
California	★	★	★	★	B	B	B	B	B	B	B	B
Colorado	★	...	★	...	B	...	B	B	B	B (c)	...	...
Connecticut	...	★	...	★	B	...	...	...	...	B	...	B
Delaware	...	★	...	★	B	...	B	...	B	...	...	B
Florida	★	★	★	★	B	B	B	B	B	B	B	B
Georgia	●	★	●	★	B	B	B	B	B	B	B	...
Hawaii	★	★	★	★	B	B	B	B	B	B	B	B
Idaho	...	★	...	★	B (d)	B (d)	B	B	...	B (e)	...	...
Illinois	★	★	★	★	...	...	B	B	B	B	...	...
Indiana	★	...	...	...	...	...	S	...	S	...	...	...
Iowa	★	★	★	★	B	...	B (f)	B	B	...	...	B
Kansas	★	★	★	★	B	B (g)	B	B	B	B	B	B
Kentucky	★	★	★	★	B	B	...	...	B (h)	B (h)	...	...
Louisiana	★(i)	★	★(i)	★	B	B	B	B	B	B	B (j)	B (j)
Maine	★(k)	★(k)	★(k)	★(k)	B	B	B	B	B	B	...	B
Maryland	★(l)	★ (l)	★(l)	★(l)	B	B	...	...	...	...	...	...
Massachusetts	★	★	★	★	...	...	...	...	...	...	...	...
Michigan	★	★	★	★	B	...	B	B	B	S	...	...
Minnesota	★	★	★	★	...	...	B	H	S	B	B	B
Mississippi	●	★	●	★	...	...	B	B	...	...	B	B
Missouri	★	...	★	...	B	...	B	...	S	S	B	...
Montana	★	★	★	★	B	...	...	B	...	...	...	...
Nebraska	★	★	U	U	(m)	...	(m)	...	(m)	...	S	S
Nevada	★	★	★	★	B	...	...	B	...	...	...	...
New Hampshire	★	★	★	★	B	B	B	B	...	S	...	S
New Jersey	★	★	★	★	B	B	B	B	...	...	...	...
New Mexico	★	★	★	★	...	...	B	B	...	...	...	...
New York	★	★	★	★	...	...	B	B	B	B	B	B
North Carolina	★	★(n)	★	★(n)	B	...	...	...	...	...	...	B (n)
North Dakota	●	★	●	★	B	B	...	...	...	...	...	...
Ohio	★	★	★	★	B	...	...	...	B	...	B	B
Oklahoma	★	★	★	★	...	...	B	B	S	...	B	B
Oregon	★	★	★	★	B	B	B	B	B	B	B	B
Pennsylvania	★	★	★	★	B	B	B	B	B	B	B	B
Rhode Island	●	★	●	★	B	B	...	B	...	...	B	...
South Carolina	★	★	★	★	B	B	B	B	B	B	B	...
South Dakota	★	★	★	★	B	...	...	(l)	...	(l)	...	(l)
Tennessee	★	★	★	★	B	...	B	B	...	...	...	B
Texas	★	★	★	★	B	B	B	B	...	...	B	B
Utah	★	★(r)	★	★(r)	B	B	...	B	B (s)	B	...	...
Vermont	★	●	★	●	B	B	...	...	...	...	...	...
Virginia	★	★	★	★	B	...	B	B	...	...	(o)	(o)
Washington	★	★	★	★	...	...	B	B	B	B	B	B
West Virginia	★	★	★	★	B	B	B	B	B	B	B	B
Wisconsin	★	★	★	★	B	...	...	...	...	...	(p)	B
Wyoming	...	★	...	★	B	...	...	B	...	...	...	...
American Samoa	●	★	●	★	B	B	B	B	...	...	B	...
Guam	★	★	U	U	...	...	S	S	...	...	...	...
No. Mariana Islands	★	★	★	★	B (q)	B (q)	B (q)	B (q)	B (q)	B (q)	B (q)	B (q)
Puerto Rico	★	★	★	★	B (q)	B (q)	B (q)	B (q)	B (q)	B (q)	B (q)	B (q)
U.S. Virgin Islands	★	★	U	U	S (q)	S (q)	S (q)	S (q)	S (q)	S (q)	S (q)	S (q)

See footnotes at end of table.

STAFF FOR LEGISLATIVE STANDING COMMITTEES — Continued

Source: The Council of State Governments' survey, November 2015.

**—Multiple entries reflect a combination of organizations and location of services.

Key:

★ — All committees
● — Some committees
... — Services not provided
B — Both chambers
H — House
S — Senate
U — Unicameral

(a) Includes legislative council or service agency or central management agency.

(b) Includes chamber management agency, office of clerk or secretary and House or Senate research office.

(c) Senate — there is secretarial staff for both majority and minority offices for the Senate in the Capitol. Most of the clerical work is done by caucus staff. House — the clerical and secretarial staff for the House is more centralized and is supervised by the Clerk of the House.

(d) Professional staff and clerical support is provided via the Legislative Services Office, a non-partisan office serving all members on a year round basis.

(e) Leadership in each party hire their respective support staff.

(f) The Senate secretary and House clerk maintain supervision of committee clerks.

(g) Senators and House chairpersons select their secretaries and notify the central administrative services agency; all administrative employee matters handled by the agency.

(h) Leadership employs partisan staff to provide professional and clerical services. However, all members, including leadership are also served by the centralized, non-partisan staff.

(i) House Appropriations and Senate Finance Committees have Legislative Fiscal Office staff at their hearings.

(j) Staff are assigned to each committee but work under the direction of the chair.

(k) Standing committees are joint House and Senate committees.

(l) The clerical support comes from employees who are hired to work only during the legislative sessions. They are employees of either the House or the Senate, and are not part of the central agency.

(m) Professional services are not provided, except that the staff of the Legislative Fiscal Office serves the Appropriations Committee. Individual senators are responsible for the process of hiring their own staff.

(n) Member's personal secretary serves as a clerk to the committee or subcommittee that the member chairs.

(o) The House Appropriations Committee and the Senate Finance Committees have their own staff. The staff members work under the direction of the chair.

(p) Standing committees are staffed by subject specialist from the Joint Legislative Council.

(q) In general, the legislative service agency provides legal and staff assistance for legislative meetings and provides associated materials. Individual legislators hire personal or committee staff as their budgets provide and at their own discretion.

(r) Clerical staff not assigned to Rules Cmtes.

(s) Refers only to Chief Deputy of the Senate and Chief of Staff in the House.

Table 3.23
STANDING COMMITTEES: APPOINTMENT AND NUMBER

State or other jurisdiction	Committee members appointed by: Senate	Committee members appointed by: House/Assembly	Committee chairpersons appointed by: Senate	Committee chairpersons appointed by: House/Assembly	Number of standing committees during regular 2016 session Senate	Number of standing committees during regular 2016 session House/Assembly	Number of standing committees during regular 2016 session Joint
Alabama	(v)	S	(v)	S	25	25	5
Alaska	CC	CC	CC	CC	10	10	11
Arizona	P	S	P	S	16	19	1
Arkansas	(a)	(b)	(a)	S	9	10	24
California	CR	S	CR	S	22	31	7
Colorado	MjL	S	MjL	S	10	11	3
Connecticut	CC	CC	CC	CC	22 (c)	22 (c)	22 (c)
Delaware	PT	S	PT	S	24	25	3
Florida	P	S	P	S	20	10	4
Georgia	CC	S	CC	S	30	38	1
Hawaii	P	S	P	(d)	16	19	...
Idaho	PT (f)	S	PT	S	10	14	3
Illinois	P, MnL (w)	S, MnL (w)	P, MnL (w)	S	22	36	...
Indiana	PT	S	PT	S	23	25	...
Iowa	MjL, MnL	S (x)	MjL	S	17	19	...
Kansas	(g)	S	P	S	15	23	19
Kentucky	CC	CC	CC	CC	15	19	15
Louisiana	P	S (h)	P	S	17	17	2
Maine	P	S	P	S	5	6	(i)
Maryland	P	S	P	S	5	7	19
Massachusetts	P	S	P	S	7	9	27
Michigan	MjL	S	MjL	S	22	24	...
Minnesota	CR	S	S	S	13	28	...
Mississippi	P	S	P	S	43	46	2
Missouri	PT (j)	S	PT	S	18	42	19
Montana	CC	S	CC	S	16	16	1
Nebraska	CC	U	E	U	14	U	U
Nevada	MjL (e)	S	MjL	S	10	10	...
New Hampshire	P (k)	S (k)	P (k)	S (k)	11	21	...
New Jersey	CC	CC	CC	CC	14	24	6
New Mexico	CC	S	CC	S	9 (l)	16 (l)	...
New York	PT	S	PT	S	37	37	...
North Carolina	PT	S	PT	S	18	28	...
North Dakota	CC	CC	CC	CC	11	11	...
Ohio	P (m)	S (m)	P (m)	S (m)	16	20	...
Oklahoma	PT (e)	S	PT	S	16	21	...
Oregon	P	S	P	S	13	15	14
Pennsylvania	PT	S	PT	S	22	27	...
Rhode Island	P	S	P	S	10	11	3
South Carolina	(n)	S	(o)	E	15	11	...
South Dakota	PT	S	PT	S	13	13	1
Tennessee	S	S	S	S	9	14	15
Texas	P	S (p)	P	S	14	38	1
Utah	P	S	P	S	11	14	0
Vermont	CC	S	CC	S	11	14	13
Virginia	E	S	(q)	S	11	14	...
Washington	CC	CC	CC (r)	CC (s)	15	23	7
West Virginia	P	S	P	S	19	18	...
Wisconsin	MjL	S	MjL	S	18	44	10
Wyoming	P	S	P	S	12	12	12
Dist. of Columbia	(t)	U	(t)	U	14	U	U
American Samoa	P	S	E	S	16	20	...
Guam	(u)	U	(u)	U	12	U	...
No. Mariana Islands	P	S	P	S	8	8	...
Puerto Rico	P	S	P	S	23	30	...
U.S. Virgin Islands	E	U	E	U	10	U	U

See footnotes at end of table.

STANDING COMMITTEES: APPOINTMENT AND NUMBER — Continued

Source: The Council of State Governments' survey, March 2016.

Key:
CC—Committee on Committees
CR—Committee on Rules
E—Election
MjL—Majority Leader
MnL—Minority Leader
P—President
PT—President pro tempore
S—Speaker
U—Unicameral Legislature
. . .—None reported.

(a) Selection process based on seniority.

(b) Members of the standing committees shall be selected by House District Caucuses with each caucus selecting five members for each "A" standing committee and five members for each "B" standing committee.

(c) Substantive standing committees are joint committees. There are also three joint statutory committees.

(d) By resolution with members of majority party designating the chair, vice-chairs and majority party members of committees, and members of minority party designating minority party members.

(e) Minority Leader selects minority members.

(f) Committee members appointed by the Senate leadership under the direction of the president pro tempore, by and with the Senate's consent.

(g) Committee on Organization, Calendar and Rules.

(h) Speaker appoints only 12 of the 19 members of the Committee on Appropriations.

(i) There are currently 16 Joint Standing Committees, two Joint Select Committees, and a joint Government Oversight Committee.

(j) Senate minority committee members chosen by minority caucus, but appointed by president pro tempore.

(k) Senate president and House speaker consult with minority leaders.

(l) Senate: includes eight substantive committees and one procedural committee. House: includes 12 substantive committees and three procedural committees.

(m) The minority leader may recommend for consideration minority party members for each committee.

(n) Appointment based on seniority (Senate Rule 19D).

(o) Appointed by seniority which is determined by tenure within the committee rather than tenure within the Senate. Also, chair is based on the majority party within the committee (Senate Rule 19E).

(p) For each standing substantive committee of the House, except for the appropriations committee, a maximum of one-half of the membership, exclusive of chair and vice-chair, is determined by seniority; the remaining membership of the committee is determined by the speaker.

(q) In the Virginia Senate, the chair is the committee member from the majority party who has the most seniority.

(r) Recommended by the Committee on Committees, approved by the president, then confirmed by the Senate.

(s) Recommended by the Committee on Committees, then confirmed by the House.

(t) Chair of the Council.

(u) Members are appointed by the Chairperson; Chairperson is elected during majority caucus prior to inauguration.

(v) Committee on Assignments.

(w) Senate: President and Minority Leader appoint committee members including chairperson and minority spokesperson. House: Speaker appoints chairperson and majority members; Minority Leader appoints minority members.

(x) Speaker confers with Minority Leader regarding minority member appointments.

Table 3.24
RULES ADOPTION AND STANDING COMMITTEES: PROCEDURE

State or other jurisdiction	Constitution permits each legislative body to determine its own rules	Committee meetings open to public*		Specific, advance notice provisions for committee meetings or hearings	Voting/roll call provisions to report a bill to floor
		Senate	House/Assembly		
Alabama	★	★	★	Senate: 4 hours, if possible. House: 24 hours, except Rules and Local Legislations Committee. Exceptions after 27th legislative day and special sessions.	Senate: final vote on a bill, except a local bill, is recorded. House: recorded vote if requested by member of committee and sustained by one additional committee member.
Alaska	...	★	★	For meetings, by 4:00 p.m. on the preceding Thurs.; for first hearings on bills, 5 days.	Roll call vote on any measure taken upon request by any member of either house.
Arizona	★	★	★	Senate: Written agenda for each regular and special meeting containing all bills, memorials and resolutions to be considered shall be distributed to each member of the committee and to the Secretary of the Senate at least five days prior to the committee meeting. House: The committee chair shall prepare an agenda and distribute copies to committee members, the Information Desk and the Chief Clerk's Office by 4 p.m. each Wednesday for all standing committees meeting on Monday of the following week and 4 p.m. each Thursday for all standing committees meeting on any day except Monday of the following week.	Senate: roll call vote. House: roll call vote.
Arkansas	★	★	★	Senate: 2 days (anytime with 2/3s vote of the committee). House: 18 hours (2 hours with 2/3s vote of the committee).	Senate: roll call votes are recorded. House: report of committee recommendation signed by committee chair.
California	★	★	★	Senate: advance notice provisions exist and are published in the agendas of each house. House: public notice is published in the agendas of each house. (h)	Senate: roll call. House: roll call.
Colorado	★	★	★	Senate: Final action on a measure is prohibited unless notice is posted one calendar day prior to its consideration. The prohibition does not apply if the action receives a majority vote of the committee. House: Meeting publicly announced while the House is in actual session as much in advance as possible.	Senate: final action by recorded roll call vote. House: final action by recorded roll call vote.
Connecticut	★	★	★	Senate: 1 day notice for meetings, 5 days notice for hearings. House: 1 day notice for meetings, 5 days notice for hearings.	Senate: roll call required. House: roll call required.
Delaware	★	★	★	Senate: agenda released 1 day before meetings. House: agenda released 4 days before meetings.	Senate: results of all committee reports are recorded. House: results of all committee reports are recorded.
Florida	★	★	★	Senate: during session—3 weekdays for first 40 days, 4 hours thereafter. House: 2 days for first 45 days, 1 day thereafter.	Senate: vote on final passage is recorded. House: vote on final passage is recorded.
Georgia	★	★	★	Senate: a list of committee meetings shall be posted by 10:00 a.m. the preceding Friday. House: none.	Senate: bills can be voted out by voice vote or roll call. House: bills can be voted out by voice vote or roll call.

See footnotes at end of table.

RULES ADOPTION AND STANDING COMMITTEES: PROCEDURE—Continued

State or other jurisdiction	Constitution permits each legislative body to determine its own rules	Committee meetings open to public*		Specific, advance notice provisions for committee meetings or hearings	Voting/roll call provisions to report a bill to floor
		Senate	House/ Assembly		
Hawaii	★	★(a)	★(a)	Senate: 72 hours before 1st referral committee meetings, 48 hours before subsequent referral committee. House: 48 hours.	Senate: a quorum of committee members must be present before voting. House: a quorum of committee members must be present before voting.
Idaho	★	★(a)	★(a)	Senate: none. House: per rule; chair provides notice of next meeting dates and times to clerk to be read prior to adjournment each day of session.	Senate: bills can be voted out by voice vote or roll call. House: bills can be voted out by voice vote or roll call.
Illinois	★	★(b)	★(b)	Senate: 6 days. House: 6 days.	Senate: votes on all legislative measures acted upon are recorded. House: votes on all legislative matters acted upon are recorded.
Indiana	★	★	★	Senate: 48 hours. House: prior to adjournment of the meeting day next preceding the meeting or announced during session.	Senate: committee reports—do pass; do pass amended, reported out without recommendation. House: majority of quorum; vote can be by roll call or consent.
Iowa	★	★	★	Senate: yes, but can be suspended. House: yes, but can be suspended.	Senate: final action by roll call. House: committee reports include roll call on final disposition.
Kansas	★	★	★	Senate: none. House: none.	Senate: vote recorded upon request of member. House: total for and against actions recorded.
Kentucky	★	★	★	Senate: none. House: none.	Senate: each member's vote recorded on each bill. House: each member's vote recorded on each bill.
Louisiana	★	★(a)	★(a)	Senate: no later than 1:00 p.m. the preceding day. House: no later than 4:00 p.m. the preceding day.	Senate: any motion to report an instrument is decided by a roll call vote. House: any motion to report an instrument is decided by a roll call vote.
Maine	★	★	★	Senate and House: must be advertised two weekends in advance.	Senate and House: recorded vote is required to report a bill out of committee.
Maryland	★	★	★	Senate: none. (c) House: none. (c)	Senate: the final vote on any bill is recorded. House: the final vote on any bill is recorded.
Massachusetts	★	★	★	Senate: 48 hours for public hearings. House: 48 hours for public hearings.	Senate: voice vote or recorded roll call vote at the request of two committee members. House: recorded vote upon request by a member.
Michigan	★	★	★	Senate and House: Notice shall be published in the journal in advance of a hearing. Notice of a special meeting shall be posted at least 18 hours before a meeting. Special provisions for conference committees.	Senate: committee reports include the vote of each member on any bill. House: the daily journal reports the roll call on all motions to report bills.
Minnesota	★	★	★	Senate: 3 days. House: 3 days.	Senate: not needed. House: not needed.

See footnotes at end of table.

RULES ADOPTION AND STANDING COMMITTEES: PROCEDURE — Continued

State or other jurisdiction	Constitution permits each legislative body to determine its own rules	Committee meetings open to public*		Specific, advance notice provisions for committee meetings or hearings	Voting/roll call provisions to report a bill to floor
		Senate	House/ Assembly		
Mississippi	★	★	★	Senate: none. House: none.	Senate: bills are reported out by voice vote or recorded roll call vote. House: bills are reported out by voice vote or recorded roll call vote.
Missouri	★	★	★	Senate: 24 hours. House: 24 hours.	Senate: bills are reported out by a recorded roll call vote. House: bills are reported out by a recorded roll call vote.
Montana	★	★	★	Senate: 3 legislative days or as circumstances require. House: 3 legislative days or as circumstances require.	Senate: every vote of each member is recorded and made public. House: every vote of each member is recorded and made public.
Nebraska	★	★	U	7 calendar days notice before hearing a bill.	In executive session, majority of the committee must vote in favor of the motion made.
Nevada	★	★	★	Senate: by rule—"adequate notice" shall be provided. (d) House: by rule—"adequate notice" shall be provided. (d)	Senate: recorded vote is taken upon final committee action on bills. House: recorded vote is taken upon final committee action on bills.
New Hampshire	★	★	★	Senate: 4 days. House: no less than 4 days.	Senate: committees report bills out by recorded roll call votes. House: committees report bills out by recorded roll call votes.
New Jersey	★	★	★	Senate: 5 state working days. House: 5 days.	Senate: the chair reports the vote of each member present on a motion to report a bill. House: the chair reports the vote of each member present on motions with respect to bills.
New Mexico	★	★	★	Senate: none. House: none.	Senate: vote on the final report of the committee taken by yeas and nays. Roll call vote upon request. House: vote on the final report of the committee taken by yeas and nays. Roll call vote upon request.
New York	★	★(a)	★(a)	Senate: 1 week for meetings. Rules require that notice be given for public hearings, but the rules are silent as to how long. House: 1 week for hearings, Thursday of prior week for meetings.	Senate: majority vote required. House: majority vote required.
North Carolina	(f)	★	★	Senate: none. (e) House: none. (e)	Senate: majority vote required. House: roll call vote taken on any question when requested by member and sustained by one-fifth of members present.
North Dakota	★	★	★	Senate: Printed and online hearing schedules, electronic signage, floor announcements, rss feeds, handheld device application. House: Printed and online hearing schedules, electronic signage, floor announcements, rss feeds, handheld device application.	Senate: recorded roll call vote of the committee members on each bill or resolution referred out of the committee and, in the case of divided reports, on each report. House: recorded roll call vote of the committee members on each bill or resolution referred out of the committee and, in the case of divided reports, on each report..

See footnotes at end of table.

RULES ADOPTION AND STANDING COMMITTEES: PROCEDURE — Continued

State or other jurisdiction	Constitution permits each legislative body to determine its own rules	Committee meetings open to public*		Specific, advance notice provisions for committee meetings or hearings	Voting/roll call provisions to report a bill to floor
		Senate	House/ Assembly		
Ohio...............	★	★	★	Senate: Rule 21 Each committee shall meet upon the call of its chairperson, and in case of the chairperson's absence, or refusal to call the committee together, a meeting may be called by a majority of the members of the committee. At least two days preceding the day bills or joint resolutions to propose a constitutional amendment are to be given a first hearing, the Clerk shall post in the Clerk's office the schedule of such bills and joint resolutions in each standing committee or subcommittee with the exception of the standing Committee on Rules. In a case of necessity, the notice of hearing may be given in a shorter period than two days by such reasonable method as shall be prescribed by the Committee on Rules. Where applicable, the rules of the Senate apply to the committee proceedings of the Senate. In addition, all committee meetings shall be governed by section 101.15 of the Revised Code. On any occasion when a majority or more of the members of a standing committee, select committee, or subcommittee of a standing or select committee of the Senate meet together for a prearranged discussion of the public business of the committee or subcommittee, the meeting shall be open to the public unless closed in accordance with Ohio Constitution, Article II, Section 13. House: Rule 36(a) The chair of a standing committee, subcommittee, select committee, or joint committee shall give due notice of a meeting of the committee, subcommittee, select committee, or joint committee not later than 24 hours before the meeting, in accordance with section 101.15 of the Revised Code, and shall attempt to give that notice not later than five days before the meeting. The notice shall identify the committee; identify the chair; state the date, time, and place at which the meeting will be held; and set forth an agenda showing each bill, resolution, or other matter that will be considered at the meeting. (b) It is not in order for a committee to meet at a date, time, or place, or to consider any bill, resolution, or other matter at a meeting, other than as stated in the notice of the meeting, unless otherwise ordered by the House or the committee. If, however, an emergency requires consideration of a matter at a meeting, and the matter has not been stated in the notice of the meeting, the chair may revise or supplement the notice at any time before or during the meeting to include the matter and the matter may then be considered as the emergency requires.	Senate: Rule 24 The affirmative votes of a majority of all members of a committee shall be necessary to report or to postpone further consideration of bills or resolutions. Every member present shall vote, unless excused by the chair. At discretion of chair the roll call may be continued for a vote by any member who was present at the prior meeting, but no later than 10:00 a.m. of next calendar day. House: Rule 40(b) The affirmative votes of a majority of all members constituting a committee shall be necessary to report a bill or resolution out of committee, and a record of every vote shall be kept by the committee. The affirmative vote of a majority of all the members constituting the committee shall be necessary to agree to any motion to recommend for passage or to postpone indefinitely further consideration of bills or resolutions, and a record of such vote shall be kept by the committee. Every member present shall vote unless excused by the committee. Rule 41(a) No proxy vote shall be valid. Nor shall any member vote except while sitting in committee in actual session, unless the member shall have first been present and recorded as such immediately before or during actual session before the vote is taken, and by motion the roll call on a motion to recommend a bill or resolution for passage is continued for a vote by any member who is temporarily absent from the meeting until the adjournment thereof, which shall be not later than 12:00 o'clock noon one day following the committee meeting. It is not in order for a member to vote on an amendment unless the member is actually present when the amendment is voted upon. (b) Three consecutive absences from regular committee meetings shall operate to suspend a member from such committee, unless excused by the chair of said committee.
Oklahoma.............	★	★	★	Senate: 48 hours notice. House: 3 days notice.	Senate: roll call vote. House: roll call vote.
Oregon.............	★	★	★	Senate: At least 48 hrs notice except at the end of session when President invokes 1-hour notice when adjournment sine die is imminent. House: First public hearing on a measure must have at least 72 hours notice, all other meetings at least 48 hours notice except in case of emergency.	Senate: affirmative roll call vote of majority of members of committee and recorded in committee minutes. House: affirmative roll call vote of majority of members of committee and recorded in committee minutes.

See footnotes at end of table.

RULES ADOPTION AND STANDING COMMITTEES: PROCEDURE—Continued

State or other jurisdiction	Constitution permits each legislative body to determine its own rules	Committee meetings open to public*		Specific, advance notice provisions for committee meetings or hearings	Voting/roll call provisions to report a bill to floor
		Senate	House/ Assembly		
Pennsylvania	★	★	★	Senate: written notice to members containing date, time, place and agenda. House: written notice to members containing date, time, place and agenda.	Senate: a majority vote of committee members. House: a majority vote of committee members.
Rhode Island...........	★	★	★	Senate: notice required. House: notice required.	Senate: majority vote of the members present. House: majority vote of the members present.
South Carolina........	★	★	★	Senate: 24 hours. House: 24 hours.	Senate: favorable report out of committee (majority of committee members voting in favor). House: favorable report out of committee (majority of committee members voting in favor).
South Dakota.........	★	★	★	Senate and House: at least one legislative day must intervene between the date of posting and the date of consideration in both houses.	Senate and House: a majority vote of the members-elect taken by roll call is needed for final disposition on a bill. This applies to both houses.
Tennessee	★	★	★	Senate: 6 days. House: 72 hours.	Senate: majority referral to Calendar and Rules Committee, majority of Calendar and Rules Committee referral to floor. House: majority referral to Calendar and Rules Committee, majority of Calendar and Rules Committee referral to floor.
Texas....................	★	★	★	Senate: 24 hours. House: The House requires five calendar days notice before a public hearing at which testimony will be taken, and two hours notice or an announcement from the floor before a formal meeting (testimony cannot be taken at a formal meeting). 24-hour advance notice is required during special session.	Senate: bills are reported by recorded roll call vote. House: committee reports include the record vote by which the report was adopted, including the vote of each member.
Utah......................	★	★	★	Senate: not less than 24 hours public notice. House: not less than 24 hours public notice.	Senate: voice vote accepting the recommendation of the committee. House: voice vote accepting the recommendation of the committee.
Vermont..................	★	★	★	Senate: none. House: none.	Senate: vote is recorded for each committee member for every bill considered. House: vote is recorded for each committee member for every bill considered.
Virginia..................	★	★(a)	★(a)	Senate: none. House: none.	Senate: recorded vote, except resolutions that do not have a specific vote requirement under the Rules. In these cases, a voice vote is sufficient. House: vote of each member is taken and recorded for each measure.
Washington............	★	★	★	Senate: 5 days. House: 5 days.	Senate: bills reported from a committee carry a majority report which must be signed by a majority of the committee. House: every vote to report a bill out of committee is by yeas and nays; the names of the members voting are recorded in the report.

See footnotes at end of table.

RULES ADOPTION AND STANDING COMMITTEES: PROCEDURE — Continued

State or other jurisdiction	Constitution permits each legislative body to determine its own rules	Committee meetings open to public*		Specific, advance notice provisions for committee meetings or hearings	Voting/roll call provisions to report a bill to floor
		Senate	House/ Assembly		
West Virginia.........	★	★	★	Senate: none. House: none.	Senate: majority of committee members voting. House: majority of committee members voting.
Wisconsin	★	★	★	Senate: Monday noon of the preceding week. House: Monday noon of the preceding week.	Senate: number of ayes and noes, and members absent or not voting are reported. House: number of ayes and noes are recorded.
Wyoming	★	★	★	Senate: by 3:00 p.m. of previous day. House: by 3:00 p.m. of previous day.	Senate: bills are reported out by recorded roll call vote. House: bills are reported out by recorded roll call vote.
American Samoa	★	★(g)	★(g)	Senate: at least 3 calendar days in advance. House: at least 3 calendar days in advance.	Senate/House: There are four methods of ascertaining the decision upon any matter: by raising of hands; by secret ballot, when authorized by law; by rising; and by call of the members and recorded by the Clerk of the vote of each.
Guam	★	★	U	5 days prior to public hearings.	Majority vote of committee members.
No. Mariana Islands...	★	★	★	Senate: 3 days. House: 1 day.	Senate and House: majority.
Puerto Rico.............	★	★	★	Senate: Must be notified every Thurs, one week in advance. House: 24 hours advanced notice, no later than 4:00 p.m. previous day.	Senate: bills reported from a committee carry a majority vote. House: bills reported from a committee carry a majority vote by referendum or in an ordinary meeting.
U.S. Virgin Islands	★	★	U	7 calendar days.	Bills must be reported to floor by Rules Committee.

Source: The Council of State Governments' survey, November 2015.

Key:

★ — Yes

U — Unicameral

* — Notice of committee meetings may also be subject to state open meetings laws; in some cases, listed times may be subject to suspension or enforceable only to the extent "feasible" or "whenever possible."

(a) Certain matters may be discussed in executive session. (Other states permit meetings to be closed for various reasons, but their rules do not specifically mention "executive session.")

(b) A session of a house or one of its committees can be closed to the public if two-thirds of the members elected to that house determine that the public interest so requires. A meeting of a joint committee or commission can be closed if two-thirds of the members of both houses so vote.

(c) General directive in the Senate and House rules to the Department of Legislative Services to compile a list of the meetings and to arrange for distribution which in practice is done on a regular basis.

(d) Senate: This rule may be suspended for emergencies by a two-thirds vote of appointed committee members. House: This rule may be suspended for emergencies by a majority vote of appointed committee members. In the Assembly this rule does not apply to committee meetings held on the floor during recess or conference committee meetings.

(e) If public hearing, five calendar days.

(f) Not referenced specifically, but each body publishes rules.

(g) Unless privileged information is being discussed with counsel or the security of the territory is involved.

(h) For bill hearings, the first committee of reference has a four-day notice and the second committee of reference has a two-day notice. Informational hearings have a four-day notice. No public notice is required for resolutions or special session bills.

Table 3.25
LEGISLATIVE REVIEW OF ADMINISTRATIVE REGULATIONS: STRUCTURES AND PROCEDURES

State or other jurisdiction	Type of reviewing committee	Rules reviewed	Time limits in review process
Alabama	Joint bipartisan, standing committee	P	If not approved or disapproved within 45 days of filing, rule is approved. If disapproved by committee, disapproval may be appealed to the lieutenant governor.
Alaska	Joint bipartisan, standing committee and Legislative Affairs Agency review of proposed regulations.	P, E	...
Arizona	Joint bipartisan	P, E	...
Arkansas	Joint bipartisan	P, E (k)	...
California	Standing committee	P, E	The Legislature may study and make recommendations regarding existing or proposed regulations. Comprehensive regulation review conducted by independent executive branch agency.
Colorado	Joint bipartisan	E	Rules continue unless the annual legislative Rule Reviews Bill discontinues a rule. The Rule Reviews Bill is effective upon the governor's signature, however, the Governor needs to sign the Rule Review Bill on or before midnight on May 15 or all of the rules and amendments to rules adopted during the year before will automatically expire pursuant to statute.
Connecticut	Joint bipartisan, standing committee	P	Submittal of proposed regulation shall be on the first Tuesday of month; after first submittal committee has 65 days after date of submission to review/take action on revised regulation. Second submittal: 35 days for committee to review/take action on revised regulation.
Delaware	Joint bipartisan, standing committee	P, E (j)	...
Florida	Joint bipartisan	P, E	...
Georgia	Standing committee	P	The agency notifies the Legislative Counsel 30 days prior to the effective dates of proposed rules.
Hawaii	Legislative agency	P, E	The legislative reference bureau assists agencies to comply with a uniform format of style. This does not affect the status of rules.
Idaho	Germane joint subcommittees	P	Germane joint subcommittees vote to object or not object to a rule. They cannot reject a proposed rule directly, only advise an agency which may choose to adopt a rule subject to review by the full legislature. The legislature as a whole reviews rules during the first three weeks of session to determine if they comport with state law. The Senate and House may reject rules via resolution adopted by both. Rules imposing fees must be approved or are deemed approved unless rejected. Temporary rules expire at the end of session unless extended by concurrent resolution.
Illinois	Joint bipartisan	P, E	An agency proposing non-emergency regulations must allow 45 days for public comment. At least five days after any public hearing on the proposal, the agency must give notice of the proposal to the Joint Committee on Administrative Rules, and allow it 45 days to approve or object to the proposed regulations.
Indiana			(a)
Iowa	Joint bipartisan	P, E	...
Kansas	Joint bipartisan	P	Agencies must give 60-day notice to the public and the Joint Committee of their intent to adopt or amend specific rules and regulations, a copy of which must be provided to the committee. Within the 60-day comment period, the Joint Committee must review and comment, if it feels necessary, on the proposals. Final rules and regulations which differ in subject matter or in any material respect from the rules and regulations originally proposed or which are not a logical outgrowth of the rules and regulations originally proposed must be resubmitted to the Joint Committee as part of new rulemaking.
Kentucky	Joint bipartisan statutory committee	P, E	45 days.

See footnotes at end of table.

LEGISLATIVE REVIEW OF ADMINISTRATIVE REGULATIONS: STRUCTURES AND PROCEDURES — Continued

State or other jurisdiction	Type of reviewing committee	Rules reviewed	Time limits in review process
Louisiana (b)	Standing committee	P	All proposed rules and fees are submitted to designated standing committees of the legislature. If a rule or fee is unacceptable, the committee sends a written report to the governor. The governor has 10 days to disapprove the committee report. If both Senate and House committees fail to find the rule unacceptable, or if the governor disapproves the action of a committee within 10 days, the agency may adopt the rule change. (d)
Maine	Joint bipartisan, standing committee	P (i)	One legislative session.
Maryland	Joint bipartisan	P, E	Proposed regulations are submitted for review at least 15 days before publication. Publication triggers 45 day review period which may be extended by the committee, but if agreement cannot be reached, the governor may instruct the agency to modify or withdraw the regulation, or may approve its adoption.
Massachusetts (b)	Public hearing by agency	P	In Massachusetts, the General Court (Legislature) may by statute authorize an administrative agency to promulgate regulations. The promulgation of such regulations are then governed by Chapter 30A of the Massachusetts General Laws. Chapter 30A requires 21 day notice to the public of a public hearing on a proposed regulation. After public hearing the proposed regulation is filed with the state secretary who approves it if it is in conformity with Chapter 30A. The state secretary maintains a register entitled "Massachusetts Register" and the regulation does not become effective until published in the register. The agency may promulgate amendments to the regulations following the same process.
Michigan	Joint bipartisan	P	Joint Committee on Administrative Rules (JCAR) has 15 session days in which to consider the rule and to object to the rule by filing a notice of objection. If no objection is made, the rules may be filed and go into effect. If JCAR does formally object, bills to block the rules are introduced in both houses of the legislature simultaneously by the committee chair and placed directly on the Senate and House calendars for action. If the bills are not enacted by the legislature and presented to the governor within 15 session days, the rules may be filed with the Secretary of state take effect. Between legislative sessions the committee can meet and suspend rules promulgated during the interim between sessions.
Minnesota	Joint bipartisan, standing committee	P, E	Minnesota Statute Sec. 3.842, subd. 4a
Mississippi	(a)	...	Administrative Regulations are not reviewed by the Mississippi Legislature.
Missouri	Joint bipartisan, statutory 536.037 RSMo.	P, E	The committee must disapprove a final order of rulemaking within 30 days upon receipt or the order of rulemaking is deemed approved.
Montana	Germane joint bipartisan committees	P	Prior to adoption.
Nebraska	Standing committee	P	If an agency proposes to repeal, adopt or amend a rule or regulation, it is required to provide the Executive Board Chair with the proposal at least 30 days prior to the public hearing, as required by law. The Executive Board Chair shall provide to the appropriate standing committee of the legislature, the agency proposal for comment.
Nevada	Ongoing statutory committee (Legislative Commission)	P	Proposed regulations are either reviewed at the Legislative Commission's next regularly scheduled meeting (if the regulation is received more than 10 working days before the meeting), or they are referred to the Commission's Subcommittee to Review Regulations. If there is no objection to the regulation, then the Commission will "promptly" file the approved regulation with the Secretary of State. If the Commission or its subcommittee objects to a regulation, then the Commission will "promptly" return the regulation to the agency for revision. Within 60 days of receiving the written notice of objection to the regulation, the agency must revise the regulation and return it to the Legislative Counsel. If the Commission or its subcommittee objects to the revised regulation, the agency shall continue to revise and resubmit it to the Commission or subcommittee within 30 days after receiving the written notice of objection to the revised regulation.

See footnotes at end of table.

LEGISLATIVE REVIEW OF ADMINISTRATIVE REGULATIONS: STRUCTURES AND PROCEDURES — Continued

State or other jurisdiction	Type of reviewing committee	Rules reviewed	Time limits in review process
New Hampshire	Joint bipartisan	P	Under APA, for regular rulemaking, the joint committee of administrative rules has 45 days to review a final proposed rule from an agency. Otherwise the rule is automatically approved. If JLCAR makes a preliminary or revised objection, the agency has 45 days to respond, and JLCAR has another 50 days to decide to vote to sponsor a joint resolution, which suspends the adoption process. JLCAR may also, or instead, make a final objection, which shifts the burden of proof in court to the agency. There is no time limit on making a final objection. If no JLCAR action in the 50 days to vote to sponsor a joint resolution, the agency may adopt the rule.
New Jersey	Joint bipartisan	P, E	The legislature must pass and transmit a concurrent resolution to the Gov. and head of the agency which promulgated or proposed the regulation. Agency has 30 days from receipt of concurrent resolution to amend or withdraw the regulation or proposed regulation. If the agency does not respond in a manner satisfactory to Legislature, the Legislature may, at least 20 calendar days after a transcrript of the legislative hearing concerning the regulation is placed on the desks of the members in open session, pass another concurrent resolution, this one invalidating the regulation.
New Mexico	....(g)..		
New York	Joint bipartisan commission	P, E	. . .
North Carolina	Rules Review Commission; Public membership appointed by legislature	P, E	The Rules Review Commission must review a permanent rule submitted to it on or before the 20th of the month by the last day of the next month. The commission must review a permanent rule submitted to it after the 20th of the month by the last day of the second subsequent month.
North Dakota	Interim committee	E	The Administrative Rules Committee meets in each calendar quarter to consider rules filed in previous 90 days.
Ohio	Joint bipartisan	P, E (h)	The committee's jurisdiction is 65 days from date of original filing plus an additional 30 days from date of re-filing. Rules filed with no changes, pursuant to the five-year review, are under a 90 day jurisdiction.
Oklahoma	Standing committee (c)	P, E	The legislature has 30 legislative days to review proposed rules. The legislature reviews all agency rules submitted prior to April 1st. Any rules submitted after April 1st are to be reviewed the next legislative session.
Oregon	Office of Legislative Counsel	E	Agencies must copy Legislative Counsel within 10 days of rule adoption.
Pennsylvania	Joint bipartisan, standing committee	P	Time limits decided by the president pro tempore and speaker of the House.
Rhode Island	....(a)..		
South Carolina	Standing committee (e)	P	General Assembly has 120 days to approve or disapprove. If not disapproved by joint resolution before 120 days, regulation is automatically approved. It can be approved during 120 day review period by joint resolution.
South Dakota	Joint bipartisan	P	Rules must be adopted within 75 days of the commencement of the public hearing; emergency rules must be adopted within 30 days of the date of the publication of the notice of intent. Many other deadlines exist; see SDCL 1-26-4 for further details.
Tennessee	Joint bipartisan	P	All permanent rules take effect 90 days after filing with the secretary of state. Emergency rules take effect upon filing with the secretary of state and may be effective for not longer than 180 days.
Texas	Standing committee	P, E	No time limit.
Utah	(f)	P, E	Except as provided in Subsection (2)(b), every agency rule that is in effect on February 28 of any calendar year expires May 1 of that year unless it has been reauthorized by the legislature. (UCA 63G-3-502)

See footnotes at end of table.

LEGISLATIVE REVIEW OF ADMINISTRATIVE REGULATIONS: STRUCTURES AND PROCEDURES — Continued

State or other jurisdiction	Type of reviewing committee	Rules reviewed	Time limits in review process
Vermont......................	Joint bipartisan	P	The Joint Legislative Committee on Rules must review a proposed rule within 30 days of submission to the committee.
Virginia......................	Joint bipartisan, standing committee	P	Standing committees and the Joint Commission on Administrative Rules may object to a proposed or final adopted rule before it becomes effective. This delays the process for 21 days and the agency must respond to the objection. In addition or as an alternative, standing committees and the Commission may suspend the effective date of all or a part of a final regulation until the end of the next regular session, with the concurrence of the Governor.
Washington................	Joint bipartisan	P, E	If the committee determines that a proposed rule does not comply with legislative intent, it notifies the agency, which must schedule a public hearing within 30 days of notification. The agency notifies the committee of its action within seven days after the hearing. If a hearing is not held or the agency does not amend the rule, the objection may be filed in the state register and referenced in the state code. The committee's powers, other than publication of its objections, are advisory.
West Virginia.............	Joint bipartisan	P, E	...
Wisconsin	Joint bipartisan, standing committee	P, E	The standing committee in each house has 30 days to conduct its review for a proposed rule. If either objects the Joint Committee for the Review of Administrative Rules has 30 days to introduce legislation in each house overturning the rules. After 40 days the bills are placed on the calendar. If either bill passes, the rules are overturned. If they fail to pass, the rules go into effect.
Wyoming	Joint bipartisan	P, E	An agency shall submit copies of adopted, amended or repealed rules to the legislative service office for review within five days after the date of the agency's final action adopting, amending or repealing those rules. The legislature makes its recommendations to the governor who within 15 days after receiving any recommendation, shall either order that the rule be amended or rescinded in accordance with the recommendation or file in writing his objections to the recommendation.
American Samoa	Standing committee	E	...
Guam	Standing committee	P	45 Calendar days
Puerto Rico...............	....(a)...		
U.S. Virgin Islands	....(a)...		

Source: The Council of State Governments' survey, November 2015.
Key:
P—Proposed rules
E—Existing rules
...—No formal time limits
(a) No formal rule review is performed by both legislative and executive branches.
(b) Review of rules is performed by both legislative and executive branches.
(c) House has a standing committee to which all rules are generally sent for review. In the Senate rules are sent to standing committee which deals with that specific agency.
(d) If the committees of both houses fail to find a fee unacceptable, it can be adopted. Committee action on proposed rules must be taken within 5 to 30 days after the agency reports to the committee on its public hearing (if any) and whether it is making changes on proposed rules.
(e) Submitted by General Assembly for approval.

(f) Created by statute (63G-3-501).
(g) No formal review is performed by legislature. Periodic review and report to legislative finance committee is required of certain agencies.
(h) The Committee reviews proposed new, amended, and rescinded rules. The Committee participates in a five -year review of every existing rule.
(i) Major substantive Rules (as designated by the Legislature) are subject to legislative review and approval; Routine Technical Rules are not subject to any formal legislative review and approval process.
(j) The chair of a standing committee can call a hearing to review the rule during the interim. The Joint Sunset Committee can order a review of an agency's rules furing regular session.
(k) Amendment 92 to the Arkansas Constitution, which passed in 2014, and laws enacted by Act 1258 of 2015 provided the General Assembly with the power of review and approval of all administrative rules and regulations.

Table 3.26
LEGISLATIVE REVIEW OF ADMINISTRATIVE RULES/REGULATIONS: POWERS

State or other jurisdiction	Reviewing committee's powers			Legislative powers
	Advisory powers only (a)	No objection constitutes approval of proposed rule	Committee may suspend rule	Method of legislative veto of rules
Alabama	...	★	★	If not approved or disapproved within 45 days of filing, rule is approved. If disapproved by committee, disapproval may be appealed to the lieutenant governor. If the lieutenant governor doesn't approve rule, it is disapproved. If lieutenant governor approves rule, rule is suspended until final adjournment, next regular session. Rule takes effect upon that final adjournment unless committee's isapproval is sustained by legislature. The committee may approve a rule.
Alaska	★	...	(b)	Constitution and Statute
Arizona	★	N.A.	N.A.	N.A.
Arkansas	(gg)	★	...	A motion may be made in the Legislative Council or its Administrative Rules and Regulations Subcommittee to not approve the rule. If such a motion is made, the legislator making the motion must state the basis for not approving the rule. The only two valid reasons for not approving the rule are that it is inconsistent with state or federal law or inconsistent with legislative intent.
California	★(cc)	...	...	Statute
Colorado	...	★	...	Rules that the General Assembly has determined should not be continued are listed as exceptions to the continuation.
Connecticut	...	★	...	Statute CGS 4-170 (d) and 4-171; (c)
Delaware	★(ff)	...	...	N.A.
Florida	★(ee)	...	...	Statute
Georgia	...	★	...	Resolution (d)
Hawaii	★	...	...	...
Idaho	...	★	...	Concurrent resolution. All rules are terminated one year after adoption unless the legislature reauthorizes the rule.
Illinois	...	(e)	★(f)	(f)
Indiana	...	...	...	(g)
Iowa	...	...	(h)	By constitutional majority vote of each house, by joint resolution, with approval of governor not required.
Kansas	★	...	...	Statute
Kentucky	(x)	(y)	(z)	Enacting legislation to void. (z)
Louisiana	...	★	(i)	Concurrent resolution to suspend, amend or repeal adopted rules or fees. Proposed rules and emergency rules exist (i).
Maine	★(aa)	★(bb)	...	(j)
Maryland	★(k)	...	...	...
Massachusetts	...	...	...	The legislature may pass a bill which would supersede a regulation if signed into law by the governor.
Michigan	...	...	(l)	Joint Committe on Rules has 15 session days to approve the filing of a notice of objection. The filing of the notice of objection starts another 15 day session period that stays the rules and causes committee members to introduce legislation in boht houses of the legislature for enactment and presentment to the governor. Any member of the legislature, pursuant to statute, can introduce a bill at a session, which in effect amends or rescinds a rule.
Minnesota	★	...	...	(m)
Mississippi			(n)	
Missouri	...	★	★	Concurrent resolution passed by both houses of the General Assembly.
Montana	...	...	★(o)	Statute
Nebraska	★	★	...	...

See footnotes at end of table.

LEGISLATIVE REVIEW OF ADMINISTRATIVE RULES/REGULATIONS: POWERS — Continued

State or other jurisdiction	Reviewing committee's powers			Legislative powers
	Advisory powers only (a)	No objection constitutes approval of proposed rule	Committee may suspend rule	Method of legislative veto of rules
Nevada.........................	N.A.	★	★	Proposed regulations are either reviewed at the Legislative Commission's next regularly scheduled meeting (if the regulation is received more than 10 working days before the meeting), or they are referred to the Commission's Subcommittee to Review Regulations. If there is no objection to the regulation, then the Commission will "promptly" file the approved regulation with the Secretary of State. If the Commission or its subcommittee objects to a regulation, then the Commission will "promptly" return the regulation to the agency for revision. Within 60 days of receiving the written notice of objection to the regulation, the agency must revise the regulation and return it to the Legislative Counsel. If the Commission or its subcommittee objects to the revised regulation, the agency shall continue to revise and resubmit it to the Commission or subcommittee within 30 days after receiving the written notice of objection to the revised regulation.
New Hampshire	★	(q)	. . .	(r)
New Jersey	★	. . .	. . .	(s)
New Mexico	N.A.	N.A.	N.A.	No formal mechanism exists for legislative review of administrative rules.
New York....................	(hh)	. . .	. . .	There is no legislative veto of administrative rules outside of bill process in New York.
North Carolina..........	★	★	★	. . .
North Dakota.............	. . .	★(t)	. . .	. . .
Ohio	★	. . .	. . .	Concurrent resolution. Committee recommends to the General Assembly that a rule be invalidated. The General Assembly invalidates a rule through adoption of concurrent resolution.
Oklahoma....................	★(p)	★(p)	★(p)	The legislature may disapprove (veto) proposed rules by concurrent or joint resolution. A concurrent resolution does not require the governor's signature. Existing rules may be disapproved by joint resolution. A committe may not disapprove; only the full legislature may do so. Failure of the legislature to disapprove constitutes approval. Pursuant to HB 2055 enacted in 2013, legislature shall adpot omnibus resolution approving all proposed permanent rules except those listed in resolution which are to be disapproved.
Oregon........................	★	★	(dd)	By passing statute that overrides terms of rule.
Pennsylvania	. . .	★	★	Upon vote of General Assembly
Rhode Island..............	. . . . (n)			
South Carolina..........	. . .	★	. . .	. . .
South Dakota.............	. . .	★	★	The Interim Rules Review Committee may, by statute, suspend rules that have not become effective yet by an affirmative vote of the majority of the committee.
Tennessee	. . .	. . .	★	The Government Operations committee of either house may stay a permanent rule for up to 60 days, and may request an agency to repeal, amend or withdraw. In accordance with statutorily-imposed termination dates, all permanent rules filed in one calendar year expire on June 30 of the subsequent year unless the general assemble enacts legislation to extend the rules to a date certain or indefinitely.
Texas..........................	★	. . .	. . .	N.A.
Utah	★	. . .	. . .	All rules must be reauthorized by the legislature annually. This is done by omnibus legislation, which also provides for the sunsetting of specific rules listed in the bill.
Vermont......................	. . . . (u)			Statute
Virginia......................	. . .	. . .	(v)	The General Assembly must pass a bill enacted into law to directly negate the administrative rule.
Washington................	★	★	★	N.A.
West Virginia.............	★	. . .	. . .	(w)

See footnotes at end of table.

LEGISLATIVE REVIEW OF ADMINISTRATIVE RULES/REGULATIONS: POWERS — Continued

State or other jurisdiction	Reviewing committee's powers			Legislative powers
	Advisory powers only (a)	No objection constitutes approval of proposed rule	Committee may suspend rule	Method of legislative veto of rules
Wisconsin	...	★	★	The standing committee in each house has 30 days to conduct its review for a proposed rule. If either objects the Joint Committee for the Review of Administrative Rules has 30 days to introduce legislation in each house overturning the rules. After 40 days the bills are placed on the calendar. If either bill passes, the rules are overturned. If they fail to pass, the rules go into effect.
Wyoming	★	★	...	Action must be taken by legislative order adopted by both houses before the end of the next succeeding legislative session to nullify a rule.
American Samoa				The enacting clause of all bills shall be: Be it by the Legislature of American Samoa, and no law shall be except by bill. Bills may originate in either house, and may be amended or rejected by the other. The Governor may submit proposed legislation to the Legislature for consideration by it. He may designate any such proposed legislation as urgent, if he so considers it.
Guam	N.A.	N.A.	N.A.	Legislation to disapprove rules and regulations.
No. Mariana Islands .	★	★	★	
U.S. Virgin Islands	....(n)...			

Source: The Council of State Governments' survey, November 2015.
Key:
★ — Yes
... — No
N.A. — Not applicable
(a) This column is defined by those legislatures or legislative committees that can only recommend changes to rules but have no power to enforce a change.
(b) Authorized, although constitutionally questionable.
(c) Disapproval of proposed regulations may be sustained, or reversed by action of the General Assembly in the ensuing session. The General Assembly may by resolution sustain or reverse a vote of disapproval.
(d) The reviewing committee must introduce a resolution to override a rule within the first 30 days of the next regular session of the General Assembly. If the resolution passes by less than a two-thirds majority of either house, the governor has final authority to affirm or veto the resolution.
(e) The Administrative Procedure Act is not clear on this point, but implies that the Joint Committee should either object or issue a statement of no objections.
(f) Joint Committee on Administrative Rules can send objections to issuing agency. If it does, the agency has 90 days from then to withdraw, change, or refuse to change the proposed regulations. If the Joint Committee determines that proposed regulations would seriously threaten the public good, it can block their adoption. Within 180 days the Joint Cmte., or both houses of the General Assembly, can "unblock" those regulations; if that does not happen, the regulations are dead.
(g) None — except by passing statute.
(h) Committee may delay or suspend object to rules, and has authority to approve emergency filed rules.
(i) If the committee determines that a proposed rule is unacceptable, it submits a report to the governor who then has 10 days to accept or reject the report. If the governor rejects the report, the rule change may be adopted by the agency. If the governor accepts the report, the agency may not adopt the rule. Emergency rules become effective upon adoption or up to 60 days after adoption as provided in the rule, but a standing committee or governor may void the rule by finding it unacceptable within 2 to 61 days after adoption and reporting such finding to agency within four days.
(j) No veto allowed. If Legislature wishes to stop a rule from being adopted, it must enact appropriate legislation prohibiting the agency from adopting the rule.
(k) Except for emergency regulations which require committee approval for adoption.
(l) Committee can suspend rules during interim.
(m) The Legislative Commission to Review Administrative Rules (LCRAR) ceased operating, effective July 1, 1996. The Legislative Coordinating Commission (LCC) may review a proposed or adopted rule. Contact the LCC for more information. See Minn. Stat. 3.842, subd. 4a.

(n) No formal mechanism for legislative review of administrative rules. In Virginia, legislative review is optional.
(o) A rule disapproved by the reviewing committee is reinstated at the end of the next session if a joint resolution in the legislature fails to sustain committee action.
(p) Pursuant to HB 2055 enacted in 2013, the legislature shall adopt omnibus resolution approving all proposed permanent rules except those listed in resolution which are to be disapproved. Full legislature may suspend rules.
(q) Failure to object or approve within 45 days of agency filing of final proposal constitutes approval.
(r) The legislature may permanently block rules through legislation. The vote to sponsor a joint resolution suspends the adoption of a proposed rule for a limited time so that the full legislature may act on the resolution, which would then be subject to governor's veto and override.
(s) Article V, Section IV, par. 6 of the NJ Constitution, as amended in 1992, says the legislature may review any rule or regulation to determine whether the rule or regulation is consistent with legislative intent. The legislature transmits its objections to existing or proposed rules or regulations to the governor and relevant agency via concurrent resolutions. The legislature may invalidate or prohibit an existing or proposed rule from taking effect by a majority vote of the authorized membership of each house, in compliance with constitutional provisions.
(t) Unless formal objections are made or the rule is declared void, rules are considered approved.
(u) JLCAR may recommend that an agency amend or withdraw a proposal. A vote opposing rule does not prohibit its adoption but assigns the burden of proof in any legal challenge to the agency.
(v) Standing committees and The Joint Commission on Administrative Rules may suspend the effective date of all or a part of a final regulation until the end of the next regular legislative session with the concurrence of the governor.
(w) State agencies have no power to promulgate rules without first submitting proposed rules to the legislature which must enact a statute authorizing the agency to promulgate the rule. If the legislature during a regular session disapproves all or part of any legislative rule, the agency may not issue the rule nor take action to implement all or part of the rule unless authorized to do so. However, the agency may resubmit the same or a similar proposed rule to the committee.
(x) The promulgating agency's proposed language may be amended upon agreement of the committee and the promulgating agency.
(y) The committee does not approve or disapprove administrative regulations. It reviews them and can propose amendments that will be made, if the promulgating agency agrees to the amendment.
(z) The committee may make a finding of deficiency. If that happens, a letter is sent to the Governor requesting the Governor's determination whether the administrative regulation should be withdrawn, withdrawn and amended, or put into effect notwithstanding the finding of deficiency. The finding itself does not stop the rule from going into effect. If the

LEGISLATIVE REVIEW OF ADMINISTRATIVE RULES/REGULATIONS: POWERS — Continued

Governor determines that the administrative regulation should go into effect notwithstanding the finding of deficiency, the General Assembly will usually address that issue in its next regular session, either by its own finding that the administrative regulation found deficient is null, void, and unenforceable, or by amending the authorizing statute to restrict the need for the administrative regulation.

(aa) Committee makes recommendations on Major Substantive Rules, but approval or disapproval is by the full Legislature (the instrument used is a resolve).

(bb) Under very specific circumstances the answer is yes with respect to Major Substantive Rules: if the rules are submitted in accordance with the timelines established by law, and the Legislature fails to act on them, the rules may be adopted as if the Legislature approved them.

(cc) Executive branch agency has more than advisory power.

(dd) Negative rule determinations are made public and remain on website until rule is modified to cmply with statutory authority, statute is modified to establish validity of rule or court case upholds validity of rule.

(ee) Joint Administrative Procedures Committee, with approval of the president and speaker, may seek judicial review of validity or invalidity of rules.

(ff) A standing committee can recommend a special session to consider committee's recommendations.

(gg) Amendment 92 to the Arkansas Constitution, which passed in 2014, and laws enacted by Act 1258 of 2015 provided the General Assembly with the power of review and approval of all administrative rules and regulations.

(hh) Commission may hold hearings, subpoena witnesses, administer oaths, take testimony, and compel the production of books, papers, documents and other evidence.

Table 3.27
SUMMARY OF SUNSET LEGISLATION

State	Scope	Preliminary evaluation conducted by	Other legislative review	Other oversight mechanisms in law	Phase-out period	Life of each agency (in years)	Other provisions
Alabama	C	Dept. of Examiners of Public Accounts	Standing Cmtes.	Perf. audit	No later than Oct. 1 of the year following the regular session or a time as may be specified in the Sunset bill.	(Usually 4)	Schedules of licensing boards and other enumerated agencies are repealed according to specified time tables.
Alaska	C	Budget & Audit Cmte.	...	...	1/y	...	...
Arizona	C	Legislative staff	Joint Cmte.	...	6/m	10	...
Arkansas	D	...	...	...	...	...	...
California	S	Jt. Legis. Sunset Review Cmte. (a)	...	Perf. eval.	...	Established by the Legislature	...
Colorado	R	Dept. of Regulatory Agencies	Legis. Cmtes. of Reference	Bills need adoption by the legislature.	1/y	Up to 15	State law provides certain criteria that are used to determine whether a public need exists for an entity or function to continue and that its regulation is the least restrictive regulation consistent with the public interest.
Connecticut	S	Committee of cognizance of program/entity being reviewed.	Further review conducted by Legis. Program Review and Investigations Cmte. upon request of cmte. of cogninzance.	Programs or entities must be affirmatively re-established by the legislature.	1/y (b)	10	(c)
Delaware	C	Agencies under review submit reports to Del. Sunset Comm. based on criteria for review and set forth in statute. Comm. staff conducts separate review.	...	Perf. audit	Dec. 31 of next succeeding calendar year	4	Yearly sunset review schedules must include at least four agencies.
Florida	S (f)	...	...	...	...	...	...
Georgia	R	Dept. of Audits	Standing Cmtes.	Perf. audit	...	...	A performance audit of each regulatory agency must be conducted upon the request of the Senate or House standing committee to which an agency has been assigned for oversight and review. (d)
Hawaii	R	Legis. Auditor	Standing Cmtes.	Perf. eval.	None	Established by the legislature	Schedules various professional and vocational licensing programs for repeal. Proposed new regulatory measures must be referred to the Auditor for sunrise analysis.

See footnotes at end of table.

SUMMARY OF SUNSET LEGISLATION — Continued

State	Scope	Preliminary evaluation conducted by	Other legislative review	Other oversight mechanisms in law	Phase-out period	Life of each agency (in years)	Other provisions
Idaho	S (e)	...	...	...	...	...	...
Illinois	R,S	Governor's Office of Mgmt. and Budget	Cmte. charged with re-enacting law	(g)	...	Usually 10	...
Indiana	S	Non-partisan staff units	Interim cmte. formed to review	...	...	...	Smaller program review process now in place after about a dozen years of formal sunset program.
Iowa					------- No Program -------			
Kansas	(h)	...	...	...	...	...	...
Kentucky	R	Administrative Regulation Review Subcommittee	Joint committee with subject matter jurisdiction.	Perf. Eval.	...	...	...
Louisiana	C	Standing cmtes. of the two houses with subject matter jurisdiction.	...	Perf. eval.	1/y	Up to 6	Act provides for termination of a department and all offices in a department. Also permits committees to select particular agencies or offices for more extensive evaluation. Provides for review by Jt. Legis. Cmte. on Budget of programs that were not funded during the prior fiscal year for possible repeal.
Maine	S (w)	Joint standing cmte. of jurisdiction.	Office of Program Evaluation and Government Accountability	...	...	Generally 10 years	...
Maryland	R	Dept. of Legislative Services	Standing Cmtes.	Perf. eval.	...	Varies (usually 10)	...
Massachusetts					------- No Program -------			
Michigan	(e)	...	...	...	...	...	...
Minnesota	S (y)	...	...	...	...	...	...
Mississippi	(i)	...	...	...	...	...	...
Missouri	R	Oversight Division of Cmte. on Legislative Research	...	...	...	6, not to exceed total of 12	Can be extended
Montana	(e)	...	...	...	...	...	...
Nebraska	D (e)/(j)	...	...	...	...	...	...

See footnotes at end of table.

SUMMARY OF SUNSET LEGISLATION—Continued

State	Scope	Preliminary evaluation conducted by	Other legislative review	Other oversight mechanisms in law	Phase-out period	Life of each agency (in years)	Other provisions
Nevada............	C (e)(x)	Sunset Subcommittee	Legislative Commission, Full Legislature	...	...	...	...
New Hampshire	(k)	...	...	...	...	...	...
New Jersey............	(e)	...	...	...	...	...	...
New Mexico	S	Legis. Finance Cmte.	...	Public hearing before termination	1/y	6	...
New York.............	(e)	...	...	...	...	...	...
North Carolina.......	(l)	...	...	...	...	...	...
North Dakota........			No Program				
Ohio..................	C (m)	Sunset Review Cmte.	...	Perf. eval.	(n)	6	...
Oklahoma...........	S, D	Senate: Standing Cmtes. with jurisdiction over sunset bills House: Joint Cmtes. with jurisdiction over sunset bills	Appropriations and Budget Cmte.	...	1/y	6	...
Oregon..............	D (o)	...	(o)	(o)	...	...	...
Pennsylvania	R	Leadership Cmte.	...	...	...	Varies	...
Rhode Island.........	(p)	...	No	...	...	...	...
South Carolina.......	(q)	...	...	Perf. eval.	1/y	...	...
South Dakota	(r)	...	...	...	...	...	...
Tennessee............	C	Office of the Comptroller	Government Operations Committees	...	1/y	Up to 6 years	...
Texas.................	S	Sunset Advisory Commission staff	...	...	1/y	12	...
Utah.................	S	Interim cmtes, then Legislative Mgmt. Cmte.	Standing cmtes. as amendments may be made to bill	...	(v)	(v)	...

See footnotes at end of table.

SUMMARY OF SUNSET LEGISLATION—Continued

State	Scope	Preliminary evaluation conducted by	Other legislative review	Other oversight mechanisms in law	Phase-out period	Life of each agency (in years)	Other provisions
Vermont................	(s)	Legis. Council staff	Senate and House Government Operations Cmtes.	...	...	...	...
Virginia................	S (e)	...	...	...	...	...	Sunset provisions vary in length. The only standard sunset required by law is on bills that create a new advisory board or commission in the executive branch of government. The legislation introduced for these boards and commissions must contain a sunset provision to expire the entity after three years.
Washington............	D	...	...	Perf. eval.	1/y	...	...
West Virginia..........	S	Jt. Cmte. on Govt. Operations	Performance Evaluation and Research Division	Perf. audit	1/y	6	Jt. Cmte. on Govt. Operations composed of five House members, five Senate members and five citizens appointed by governor. Agencies may be reviewed more frequently.
Wisconsin	(e)	...	...	...	...	...	...
Wyoming	D (t)	Program evaluation staff who work for Management Audit Cmte.	...	Perf. eval. (u)	...	...	...
No. Mariana Islands........		No	No	Perf. eval.	1/y	...	...

Source: The Council of State Governments' survey, November 2015.

Key:

C — Comprehensive—requires all statutory agencies to be subject to a sunset review once per review cycle.
R — Regulatory—review focus is on regulatory and licensing agencies and bureaus.
S — Selective—selective implementation and reviews are concentrated on entities such as occupational licensing and administrative agencies such as highway, health and education departments.
D — Discretionary—sunset review board has the ability to select which entities will face review.
d — day
m — month
y — year
... — Not applicable

(a) Jt. Legis. Sunset Review Cmte. — Review by the Jt. Legislative Sunset Review Cmte. of professional and vocational licensing boards, pursuant to Government Code 9147.7. Sunset clauses are included in other selected programs and legislation.
(b) Upon termination a program shall continue for one year to conclude its affairs.
(c) Process conducted in accordance with Chapter 28 of Connecticut General Statutes.
(d) The automatic sunsetting of an agency every six years was eliminated in 1992. The legislature must pass a bill in order to sunset a specific agency.
(e) While they have not enacted sunset legislation in the same sense as the other states with detailed

information in this table, the legislatures in Idaho, Michigan, Minnesota, Montana, Nebraska, Nevada, New Jersey, New York, Virginia and Wisconsin have included sunset clauses in selected programs or legislation.
(f) Comprehensive agency sunset review and repeal was repealed in 2011. Florida does have Open Government Sunset Review of public records and meetings exemptions with a 5-year review period.
(g) Governor is to read GOMB report and make recommendations to the General Assembly every even-numbered year.
(h) Sunset legislation terminated July 1992. Legislative oversight of designated state agencies, consisting of audit, review and evaluation, continues.
(i) Sunset Act terminated December 31, 1984. House and Senate Rules are available at *billstatus. ls.state.ms.us.* New Rules were adopted in January 2012.
(j) Sunset legislation is discretionary, meaning that senators are free to offer sunset legislation or attach termination dates to legislative proposals. There is no formal sunset commission. Nebraska. Revised Statutes section 50-1303 directs the Legislature's Government, Military and Veteran's Committee to conduct an evaluation of any board, commission, or similar state entity. The review must include, among other things, a recommendation as to whether the board, commission, or entity should be terminated, continued or modified.
(k) New Hampshire's Sunset Committee was repealed July 1, 1986.
(l) North Carolina's sunset law terminated on July 30, 1981. Successor vehicle, the Legislative Committee on Agency Review, operated until June 30, 1983.
(m) There are statutory exceptions.

SUMMARY OF SUNSET LEGISLATION — Continued

(n) Authority for latest review (SB 171 of the 129th General Assembly) expires December 31, 2016.

(o) Sunset legislation was repealed in 1993.No general law sunsetting rules or agencies. Oversight mechanisms, including auditing, reporting or performace measures, are discretionary but may be included in specific bills as determined by legislature.

(p) No standing sunset statutes or procedures at this time.

(q) Law repealed by 1998 Act 419, Part II, Sect. 35E.

(r) South Dakota suspended sunset legislation in 1979. A later law directing the Executive Board of the Legislative Research Council to establish one or more interim committees each year to review state agencies was repealed in 2012.

(s) Sunsets are at the legislature's discretion. Their structure will vary on an individual basis.

(t) Wyoming repealed sunset legislation in 1988.

(u) The program evaluation process evolved out of the sunset process, but Wyoming currently does not have a scheduled sunset of programs.

(v) Default is ten years, although years may be decreased by legislative decisions.

(w) Sometimes programs or agencies are subject to sunset provisions; this is entirely ad hoc as the Legislature determines appropriate. There is a general law, however, called State Government Evaluation Law that provides for regular reviews of agencies and boards by committee of jurisdiction; the committees can recommend termination (sunset) but, again, this is ad hoc.

(x) The 2011 Nevada Legislature created the Sunset Subcommittee of the Legislative Commission with the enactment of Senate Bill 251 (Chapter 480, Statutes of Nevada). The Subcommittee is to conduct reviews of all boards and commissions not provided for in the Nevada Constitution or created by Executive Order of the Governor, and is charged with determining whether those entities should be terminated, modified, consolidated, or continued. The Subcommittee must review each entity no less often than once every ten years. After making it's initial recommendations no later than June 30, 2012, the Subcommittee must submit all subsequent recommendations to the Legislative Commission on or before June 30 of each even numbered year. The Legislative Commission may accept or reject the recommendations in whole or part and may then request that legislation be drafted for consideration by the full Legislature.

(y) While they have not enacted sunset legislation in the same sense as the other states with detailed information in this table, the legislatures in Minnesota have included sunset clauses in selected programs or legislation.

Chapter Four

STATE EXECUTIVE BRANCH

The State of the State Addresses:
Governors in the Hot Seat[1]

By Katherine Willoughby

In this presidential election year, many state government chief executives found themselves in the proverbial "hot seat." Some had to deal with a precipitous drop in state revenues and so broached taboo topics in their state of state speeches, like painful cuts or new taxes. Others deflected criticisms related to religious liberty bills or defended themselves in the face of gross state mismanagement and ineptitude or even moral lapse. In light of a still sluggish economy and the caustic election climate, state chief executives, for the most part, keep their addresses short and focused. On average, governors addressed fewer issues than in the recent past. Also, the average number of topics addressed by at least two-thirds of governors dropped by half to two, from an average of four, evidenced over the last six years—that is, at least 66 percent of governors outlined their education and jobs agendas.

Still Red and Wary

Politically, U.S. state governments remain overwhelmingly under GOP executive control, with 31 Republican governors, 18 Democratic governors and one Independent (Alaska).[2] Like last year, control of state legislatures is overwhelmingly red, too. Republicans control both chambers in 30 legislatures compared to 11 Democratic legislatures. The number of states (22) controlled in both branches by the GOP reduced by just one with the 2015 elections —Democratic Gov. John Bel Edwards replaced his Republican predecessor, Bobby Jindal, in Louisiana. Only seven states are entirely blue—with a Democratic governor and legislature—the same as in 2015. Republicans have majorities in 33 state houses and 35 state senates, while Democrats have majorities in 16 houses and 14 senates.[3] Party control of the states in 2016 includes:

- Twenty-two with a Republican governor and Republican legislature;
- One with a Republican governor and a unicameral, nonpartisan legislature;
- Two with a Republican governor, Republican house and Democratic senate;
- Two with a Republican governor, Democratic house and Republican senate;
- Four with a Republican governor and a Democratic legislature;
- One with an Independent governor and a Republican legislature;
- Seven with a Democratic governor and a Republican legislature;

- Three with a Democratic governor, Democratic house and Republican senate;
- One with a Democratic governor, Republican house and Democratic senate; and
- Seven with a Democratic governor and Democratic legislature.[4]

Fiscally, 2015 ended pretty nicely for states with stable tax revenue growth. On the other hand, the forecast going forward is weak, with such growth expected to slow now and well into 2017.[5] Price dives of oil and coal have required painful introspection on the part of states heavily dependent upon these resources. That is, governors in oil- and mineral-dependent states including Alaska, Louisiana, New Mexico, Oklahoma, West Virginia and Wyoming could not hide the murky, undoubtedly uncomfortable road ahead when addressing their states' residents.[6] "Total tax revenues for these states [and including North Dakota and Texas] have declined by 3.2 percent, while the remaining 42 states have reported 6.5 percent growth in total tax revenues."[7]

Gubernatorial Agendas in 2016

Research pointed to in last year's assessment indicated that governors' words matter in their addresses and not only for successfully navigating budget and policy agendas through state legislatures.[8] The tone, focus, level of enthusiasm and truthfulness of these leaders' words has the power to energize citizens and spur investment. This year offers a mixed bag in terms of tone. Many governors offered upbeat talks,

Table A:
Issues Mentioned by Governors in State of the State Addresses, 2011–2016

Issue expressed by governors	2011 percentage of governors mentioning the issue (N=47)	2012 percentage of governors mentioning the issue (N=43)	2013 percentage of governors mentioning the issue (N=49)	2014 percentage of governors mentioning the issue (N=42)	2015 percentage of governors mentioning the issue (N=44)	2016 percentage of governors mentioning the issue (N=43)
Education	93.6%	95.3%	100.0%	95.2%	90.9%	88.4%
Economic development/jobs	87.2	90.7	77.6	83.3	81.8	72.1
Health care	72.3	55.8	79.6	73.8	59.1	65.1
Safety/corrections	38.3	55.8	67.3	73.8	63.6	62.8
Tax/revenue initiative	70.2	81.4	71.4	66.7	72.7	62.8
Natural resources/energy	44.7	65.1	57.1	59.5	61.4	53.5
Transportation/roads/bridges	46.8	48.8	46.9	50.0	68.2	48.8
Performance/accountability	83.0	55.8	30.6	33.3	56.8	39.5
Surplus/deficit/rainy day funds/reserves	34.0	60.5	32.7	54.8	36.4	32.6
Local government	17.0	25.6	14.3	26.2	36.4	30.2
Pensions/OPEBs	36.2	32.6	18.4	21.4	4.6	18.6
Transparency	2.1	25.6	12.2	26.2	11.4	9.3
Ethics reform	8.5	7.0	16.3	14.3	20.5	7.0
Debt reduction	8.5	7.0	6.1	16.7	6.8	7.0
Borders/illegal immigrants	8.5	11.6	8.2	7.1	6.8	4.7
Average # of Issues Mentioned by Governors	8	7	6	7	7	6
# Issues Mentioned by ≥66% of Governors	5	3	5	5	4	2

Sources: Content analysis of state of state addresses conducted by Byungwoo Cho, MPA candidate (2011); Megan Phillips, MPA candidate and Sarah Beth Gehl, Ph.D. candidate, Public Policy (2012); Sarah Beth Gehl, Ph.D. candidate, Public Policy (2013); Keegan Smith, MPA candidate (2014 and 2015), all students of the Andrew Young School of Policy Studies, Georgia State University, Atlanta, Georgia; Katherine Willoughby (2016).

praising state residents, their hard work and resilience, and committing themselves to values regarding high-quality public service, social justice and fiscal discipline. Others, however, were bombastic in tone, by calling for the courting of residents running from "poor performing" neighbor states, admonishing public pension protections for the "privileged few," articulating the consequences of impending "fiscal catastrophe," or lambasting the strategies of "socialist politicians" for hindering state progress.

Table A examines issues mentioned by chief executives in their state-of-state speeches for the last six years, indicating the proportion of governors discussing specific topics as relevant to their budget and policy agendas in the 2017 fiscal year and going forward. On average, governors addressed six of 15 issues, down from a mean of seven for the last six years. Governors in Kentucky and New York addressed nine issues each; those in Alaska and Pennsylvania considered just two apiece. At least 66 percent of governors lay out their education, economic development and jobs platforms in the 2016 speeches. That only two issues are harped on by two-thirds of governors drops the consideration of issues by half from an average of four in the last six years. Several things probably contributed to curt agendas. As noted earlier, some governors were in the spotlight (and often not in a good way) this year and had to spend the bulk of their address on one or two topics—be it declining revenues, a management disaster, pensions or the like—leaving little time for expanding upon their agendas. Also, a still sluggish economy and slow growth forecast has governors hesitant to over promise.

Education and economic development/jobs remain perennially important to state chief executives—considered consistently year to year by most governors. Another perennial issue is transportation that spiked in gubernatorial concern last year because of uncertainty surrounding federal highway funding, but settled back by 2016, realizing a dip in interest of 19 percent compared with 2015. Debt reduction exhibits the same characteristics as transportation as an agenda item, though of interest to relatively few governors; borders and illegal immigrants has been addressed consistently, too, in the past, again by few governors. Issues that display erratic interest among governors year to year, but seem to have settled into perennial status in 2016 include safety and corrections (almost two-thirds of governors mentioning) and natural resources and energy (over half of governors mentioning). Concerns related to local government have evidenced a cyclical pattern by governors in the past, but have been more consistently addressed in the last two years—30 percent of governors discussed their local government initiatives this year compared to 36 percent last year. Taxes and balance issues (surplus/deficit/rainy day fund/reserves) indicate waxing and waning interest by governors over the study period, following a business cycle model. The remaining issues—pensions,

performance/accountability, transparency and ethics—evidence eclectic patterns of interest on the part of governors across years. Pensions indicate the greatest spike in interest among governors this year, up 14 percent from 2015.

Education

Regarding education, governors centered their comments on enhancing the teaching profession, school choice, programming and access, and college affordability, curricula and degrees. Pay raises, career ladder opportunities, mentoring, and tax credits or funding to support out-of-pocket schools supplies, and college scholarships and loan repayment for students committed to teaching in state were all ideas provided by governors to advance teachers, teaching quality and the profession. Governors mentioned goals of universal pre-K and full-day kindergarten and related to K–12, revising education funding formulas, enriched reading programs and reformed student testing, increased local control of schools, enhanced school choice, lifting caps on charter school and specific educational programming for low-income children, distressed youth or special needs students. For higher education, chief executives called for a concentration on science, technology, engineering and math—or STEM—fields (Ohio Gov. John Kasich (R) suggested STEAM, including a focus on the arts along with science, technology, engineering and mathematics), advancing dual enrollment programs, university-technical/community college partnerships around curricula and degrees, college affordability, improving graduation rates, scholarships for part-time students, and sometimes massive building programs for schools and universities.

Some novel suggestions to enhance education by governors included Arizona Gov. Doug Ducey (R), who framed educational support with better foster care and going after deadbeat dads; Hawaii Gov. David Ige (D) talked of air-conditioning public school classrooms; Idaho Gov. Butch Otter (R) discussed moving toward "mastery-based" education that weighs individualized learning more heavily than "seat time" in the classroom; Maine Gov. Paul LePage (R) asked for tax credits to businesses that pay employees' student loans or credits directly to employees of non-profits; New Mexico Gov. Susana Martinez (R) suggested state government grant leave for employees to attend parent-teacher conferences to inspire parental involvement in their children's education; Gov. Kasich talked of investing in guidance counselors and improving pre-apprentice programs in high schools; South Carolina Gov. Nikki Haley (R) said voters should decide if the governor should appoint the superintendent of education—among other initiatives, she suggested that 1 percent of the state's bond capacity be permanently dedicated to K–12 education facilities. Vermont Gov. Peter Shumlin (D) supported funding college savings accounts and funding a semester of free courses and support services to help first-generation and low-income students get back in school. Wisconsin Gov. Scott Walker (R) said reforms to health insurance would provide savings that should be applied to support public education, and Wyoming Gov. Matthew Mead (R) talked of applying rainy day funds for capital investment in community colleges. Colorado Gov. John Hickenlooper (D) agonized about a $20 million cut to higher education with no increase for financial aid as "not the direction we want to be moving, but a direct result of conflicting budget mandates that are forcing painful choices like this one."

Economic Development and Jobs

Economic development and jobs-enhancing options mentioned by governors were heavily weighted to workforce development programming and the partnering of institutions of higher education with business to generate a pipeline of new talent. Capital investments were promoted, as was lobbying the federal government for funding to expand and build transportation and other commerce-related projects. For example, New York Gov. Andrew Cuomo (D) announced his Built to Lead program, a $100 billion investment in "transformative projects statewide." Other ideas included reforming workers' compensation systems, and eliminating and reforming labor regulations. The extension of broadband across states, making it easier to invest in start-ups and entrepreneurial ventures, continuing or rebooting marketing of state natural resources, parks and tourism, cutting business and property taxes, incentivizing those already in-state to stay and recruiting businesses and residents from other states were also on gubernatorial wish lists. For example, Arizona's governor suggested going after "businesses fleeing California and other states on the decline, and ensure job creators who are already here, stay and thrive."

Many governors talked of working locally to grow state economies from the ground up. Hickenlooper said his Colorado Blueprint 2.0 program's "tenacious, bottom-up approach is delivering exciting results" that would pump "Main Street" initiatives

and support emerging industries. This governor also mentioned support for a program "that helps fathers who owe child support to get jobs so they can contribute financially to their kids' well-being." Shumlin pushed a farm-to-plate, farm-to-glass, and farm-to-can revolution in Vermont to generate an "Agricultural Renaissance." Ige hawked community planning "the right way," with affordable housing, open space for recreation and commercial development to grow Hawaii's economy.

Louisiana Gov. John Bel Edwards (D) declared that "$7.25 per hour is simply not a living wage in 2016" and proposed an increase to the state's minimum wage, phased in over two years. He also said eliminating the wage gap between men and women would be a positive check for the state's economy. Washington Gov. Jay Inslee (D) in his address titled, "A State of Confidence," also supported development of a "true minimum wage and paid sick leave for hardworking Washingtonians. ... If you work 40 hours a week, you deserve a wage that puts a roof over your head and food on the table. ... You shouldn't have to give up a day's pay if you or your kids get sick." This governor suggested state influence "to reduce the widening pay gap between CEOs and their workers."

New Hampshire Gov. Maggie Hassan (D) asked to repurpose existing federal funds "to move people into jobs that pay sustainable wages, lessening their need for public assistance." She also suggested creating apprenticeship opportunities between community colleges and businesses to produce skilled workers, along with several reforms to state programs to keep people working and better prepare those entering the workforce for the first time. Similarly, Gov. Martinez talked about a Students Work internship portal as a shared website between business and universities to connect students to jobs. West Virginia Gov. Earl Ray Tomblin (D) recommended legislation to expand Learn and Earn that provides work-learn programs for students.

More unique notions related to economic development included that of LePage, who pressed for "lower electricity rates to keep and grow jobs." Missouri Gov. Jay Nixon (D) requested scholarships for the next generation dairy farmers, making child care more affordable for low income working families and expanding family-friendly policies like parental leave for state employees. Rhode Island Gov. Gina Raimondo (D) suggested competition to develop an "innovation campus" that would create jobs, a project modeled on South Carolina's BMW and Clemson University automotive research campus.

Health Care

Governors' thoughts about health care concentrated on increasing the supply of doctors, drug addiction programming and support, and Medicaid expansion. To generate a strong pipeline of doctors, governors mentioned adding more seats in medical schools, new residency programs, school loan forgiveness for doctors and other health care workers, and accepting out-of-state board certification. A few mentioned support for programs to steer doctors and health care professionals to rural service and for high-risk populations.

Some governors asked for more funding or facilities for preventive services, early intervention, mental and/or behavioral health programs and crisis clinics, while one or two focused on autism and developmental disabilities, specifically. Many who targeted drug addiction relayed ideas about prevention, care, costs and accountability, asking for better training of "prescribers," strengthened prescription drug monitoring, and expanded access to Narcan for recovery. New Jersey Gov. Chris Christie (R) announced expansion of a drug recovery program in which specialists leading interventions "are often in recovery themselves, and they're deployed to emergency rooms so they can provide guidance, support and referrals for treatment [given] the benefit of their own experiences on the path to recovery." Cuomo proposed $90 million for "the most aggressive breast cancer screening operation in this country."

Funding structures and changes were discussed by others. California Gov. Jerry Brown (D) cited increased costs to the state given health care obligations and asked legislators "to seriously consider the newly revised Managed Care Organization (MCO) financing reform. ... California should not shortchange itself. This is not a tax increase, no matter what anyone tells you. The arithmetic is simple: California comes out a clear winner." Iowa Gov. Terry Branstad (R) noted that because Medicaid "is stretching our budget too thin," the state must engage managed care; if managed care is not implemented, "the growth of Medicaid spending will consume virtually all of our revenue growth." Bel Edwards explained that expanding health care under the federal rubric will "stimulate economic activity and create thousands of new jobs....improve our workforce....save state dollars and greatly reduce uncompensated care, which will relieve a major financial burden on our hospitals." Governors in South Dakota, Virginia and Wyoming also broached Medicaid expansion.

South Dakota Gov. Dennis Daugaard (R) detailed his about-face on expansion:

"The federal healthcare law is about far more than Medicaid expansion, and we're already seeing how it has distorted the market for health insurance and led to higher costs. In my opinion the law needs to be repealed or significantly changed. But at the state level, we do not make federal policy. It's our responsibility to understand the federal programs as they exist and to make the best decisions for our state. That's why, although I opposed the federal health care reform law, my administration has spent three years discussing possible approaches to expansion with federal officials. The deal I am proposing makes sense for South Dakota; it is a very good deal. This plan will fix the longstanding Indian Health Service reimbursement issue, secure better health care for Native Americans, and cover 50,000 more South Dakotans at no cost to our state general fund. This change will benefit counties by relieving their indigent care costs and by reducing the health care costs for jail inmates. It will reduce the charity care expense that hospitals now pass on to patients like you. We all know that Native Americans in our state were promised health care by the federal government as a treaty obligation."

Virginia Gov. Terry McAuliffe (D) implored that "Each day that we do not close the coverage gap, we forfeit $6.6 million dollars in federal money," while Wyoming's governor relented that "We're out of timeouts, and we need to address Medicaid expansion this session." On the other hand, several governors held firm in rejecting expansion. Kansas Gov. Sam Brownback (R) emphasized that his state would not be part of federal health care expansion as did Nebraska Gov. Pete Ricketts (R), who stated that legislators have "wisely rejected Medicaid expansion. Obamacare is an example of government that does not work."

Safety and Corrections

In 2016, governors relayed their ideas for transforming, refurbishing, and repurposing correctional facilities; reforming juvenile justice programs; increasing judicial discretion in sentencing; reforming sentencing laws; enhancing rehabilitation programs; restructuring court funding; protecting against human trafficking and domestic violence; and training, hiring and equipping more troopers, police, probation/parole officers and correctional staff. Some also talked about targeted support for law enforcement to "hardest hit" and high-crime communities in their states. Some were very specific regarding their public safety initiatives. Kentucky Gov. Matt Bevin (R) discussed investment in reducing the backlog of rape cases. Florida Gov. Rick Scott (R) told of his budget allocation "to start the process of clearing rape backlogs," too, and developing a "community corrections center to provide tough love and on-site drug treatment and counseling" in the state's largest county. This governor is also going after deadbeat dads who evade responsibility "with no shame." In his words, "Effective immediately, the state is going to begin posting the photos, names and money owed by these losers to social media, with the hashtag 'deadbeat.'" Otter explained the need to fund changes to the state's public defense system, "to ensure all Idaho citizens can avail themselves of this fundamental constitutional right." Brownback delivered that his budget proposal supports arming and training additional personnel with security enhancements to National Guard facilities for safety and to "thwart every action the president takes to transfer terrorists to Kansas." On the other hand, Inslee talked about gun control in the State of Washington where, "my executive order would strengthen the background check system, collect information that will drive smart, data-driven solutions to gun violence and implement a statewide Suicide Prevention Plan."

Natural Resources and Transportation

In this year's speeches, governors outlined initiatives to preserve, protect and extend water, air and land resources, to explore sustainable and conservation opportunities (solar, wind and hydropower) and build up recreational natural resources. Brown outlined California's herculean task: "There is no magic bullet but a series of actions must be taken. We have to recharge our aquifers, manage the groundwater, recycle, capture storm water, build storage and reliable conveyance, improve efficiency everywhere, invest in new technologies—including desalination—and all the while recognize that there are some limits." Hickenlooper talked of funding to promote "a future where, within one generation, every Coloradan will live within a 10-minute walk of a park, trail or vibrant green space." This governor had to address the Gold King Mine wastewater spill of 2015 and subsequent contamination, claiming, "we are developing a statewide inventory of draining mines to prioritize for cleanup." Maryland

Gov. Larry Hogan (R) discussed restoration of the Chesapeake Bay while Michigan Gov. Rick Snyder (R), in accepting responsibility for cleaning up the Flint water disaster, talked about the need for lead testing for clean water and monitoring piping of energy sources. In Maine, LePage berated "Socialists [who] love to subsidize new wind and solar energy projects because they think it will save the earth, but that kind of expensive and inefficient energy benefits only a few wealthy investors and our electrical generation is already one of the cleanest in the country," and instead called for support of energy delivery through "our plentiful natural resource: wood."

Other governors addressed unique aspects of their state's natural resources and current circumstances. Tomblin discussed West Virginia's transitioning economy, given energy prices. He noted that possible federal funding has "the potential to help six counties in our southern coalfields adjust, adapt and advance their communities. If we're successful, these federal funds will help us rebuild aging infrastructure, promote land-use planning and hazard-reduction efforts and stimulate housing and economic development in areas outside of the region's floodplains." He also talked about finding new uses for old mining sites.

Otter discussed his state's problems requiring the protection and monitoring of natural habitats as well as wildfire prevention, suppression and amelioration. Inslee proposed using the state's Budget Stabilization Fund to cover costs related to battling dangerous wildfires, to help with recovery and to be better prepared for the next fire season.

Concerning transportation, many governors talked about deteriorating infrastructure, mostly roads, highways and bridges. Brown noted "no choice but to maintain our transportation infrastructure" and suggested new fees and taxes to do so. Georgia Gov. Nathan Deal (R) in his speech titled, "Ocean of Opportunity Lies Ahead for Georgia's Ship of State," proposed infrastructure maintenance using new user fees. Several governors discussed the need to modernize and add global gateways into their states. Ige spoke of the importance of easing travel into and around the state that would require a second international airport and upgrading the passport control system. Bevin asked for enhanced aviation funding: "Think about all the people that we want to come here to Kentucky, to bring their companies to Kentucky. How do they get here? They fly in on their corporate jets." Indiana Gov. Mike Pence (R) discussed building a fourth port in state. Nixon claimed future investment of "an additional $5 million to improve and expand our ports—so we can ship more Missouri goods around the world and create more jobs here at home." Cuomo mapped out an ambitious building plan that touched on roads, tollways and airports all over the state as well as mass transit and Penn Station. "Penn Station is grossly over capacity and underperforming. Penn is, in a word, miserable. Amtrak owns it. It is un-New York, it is unwelcoming and it is unacceptable." Along with investing in "shovel-ready projects," Hogan talked about transforming the transit system in Baltimore.

Other avenues to advance transportation suggested included that by Hassan to strengthen transportation infrastructure "through innovative public-private partnerships and the Ten-Year Transportation Plan that advances critical transportation goals while maintaining fiscal responsibility and living within our projected revenues." Haley emphasized an organizational first step: "I will not sign any piece of legislation that does not include real reform to the Department of Transportation, the days of horse-trading South Carolina roads have to end. …reform our flawed transportation system and invest in our roads." Also, Tennessee Gov. Bill Haslam (R) called for solving the state's transportations problems by repaying millions of dollars borrowed from the state's highway fund in the past. "Our current payment structure will not allow us to ensure the future safety of our road and bridges or, importantly, our ability to recruit the jobs we want in Tennessee."

Credit, Balance and Taxes

Governors referenced credit ratings, balance, debt reduction and long-term obligations to set the stage for their budget agenda choices. Regarding credit ratings, Utah Gov. Gary Herbert (R) is enthusiastic to be in the AAA club and reap its benefits. "Forty one other states have a tarnished bond rating. The United States of America recently had its own rating downgraded. … Don't think for a minute that this recognition does not matter. It saves the taxpayer money." Governors in Delaware, Indiana and Missouri made the same argument, with Gov. Nixon characterizing the AAA rating as "the gold standard. … It tells businesses around the globe that the Show-Me State is a smart place to invest." Daugaard said he was proud of his state's credit rating upgrade to AAA because of a structurally balanced budget, no unfunded

liabilities or deferred maintenance, reasonable regulations, low tax burden and "stellar" business climate. Governors in Wyoming and Nebraska acknowledged membership in the AAA club, but cautioned against loosening the state purse strings. Mead reminded lawmakers and constituents that it has been challenging, but the state has maintained its pristine rating, while Ricketts warned that "we cannot rest on our laurels as forecasts indicate a downward revenue trend by $154 million." Governors Ducey and Brown both hyped their credit rating upgrades as proof of good budget management in their states. Gov. Hassan emphasized that her hard work to date has been an effort to avert any negative impact New Hampshire's bond rating.

Two governors—those in Alaska and Pennsylvania—discussed the relevance of credit rating downgrades to their states' futures. Alaska Gov. Bill Walker (I) explained that the large structural budget deficit in the state's unrestricted general fund as reason for Standard & Poor's credit downgrade, emphasizing that living on reserves is unsustainable. Walker called for "Bold Steps" and "New Beginnings" to realize an "incredible future" for the state, "if we have the guts to take hold of the wheel with two strong hands (administration and legislature) and navigate through rough seas with some serious but necessary course corrections." This governor suggested a "family talk," prayer and pulling together to make corrections, in light of the tumble in oil prices even while touting progress made by ExxonMobile regarding oil production projects going forward. (Alternatively, Shumlin considered that his state "should not wait to rid ourselves of ExxonMobil stock. … Owning ExxonMobil stock is not a business Vermont should be in.") Walker discussed a $3.5 billion deficit, clarifying that "we are drawing down from our savings at a rate of $400,000 every hour." The governor's state of state hinges on protecting Alaska's Permanent Fund, generating new revenues through new taxes and increases to others, expenditure cuts, and mapping opportunities of growth including tourism, energy diversification, mining, shipping routes and carrots(!) in order to avoid a "terrible legacy to leave our children to build government funded primarily from one resource alone."

Pennsylvania Gov. Tom Wolf (D) discussed the fiscal catastrophe in his state by pointing to five credit downgrades in the last five years, "three times in the last two years alone." He explained that these downgrades are the result of "little tricks" the state has played to avoid hard decisions:

"Because of years of budgetary irresponsibility, the Commonwealth of Pennsylvania is considered to be among the least creditworthy states in America. This is embarrassing...because our credit has been downgraded so much, we are forced to pay a higher rate of interest on our $17 billion in debt. That costs us an extra $139 million a year...that doesn't go to improving our schools, or making our business environment more competitive, or lowering our taxes. It's a $139 million penalty that the people of Pennsylvania pay for Harrisburg's fiscal irresponsibility."

Referring to the state's $2 billion budget deficit as "simple math" and not a political fact, Wolf asked legislators to pass a compromise budget and not one "where the numbers simply don't add up." Somewhat similarly, in Kentucky, Bevin implored legislators to "stop digging. When you're in financial trouble, you're in debt, you stop digging. You don't borrow more money....I will not sign any bill or budget that encumbers future generations with debt that we refuse to take responsibility for today." Tomblin called for paying off workers' compensation debt and looking for new revenue sources, in light of changing energy prices and its negative impact on West Virginia's economy.

Some governors highlighted the role of reserves or rainy day funds related to budget health. Herbert characterized Utah's $528 million Rainy Day fund as "extraordinary" but still cautioned that his budget "calls for no new debt and no tax increases. … It pays off $350 million in existing debt, bringing the total debt paid off by the state over the last five years to over $1.4 billion." Likewise, Haslam in his address titled, "This is What We Do," talked fiscal conservatism and almost tripling Tennessee's rainy day fund by 2017 because, "it's always best to repair the roof when the sun is shining."

Minnesota Gov. Mark Dayton (D), while rejoicing in "building the budget reserve fund to an unprecedented level," stated his number one priority to be protecting the fiscal integrity of the state. Citing a projected national recession in 2018, he warned, "If Minnesota were to be caught in a national recession, the surplus for fiscal years 2018 and 2019 would quickly erode. I will never forget the experience of coming into office in January 2011 and being confronted with a projected $6 billion deficit for the upcoming biennium. I will not leave that kind of fiscal disaster to my successor or the people of Minnesota." Mead touted his state's robust rainy

day fund, too. "The Pew Institute has recognized our rainy day planning — Wyoming has the largest rainy day fund in the country in proportion to our overall budget. [This fund] is the third largest in terms of dollars." Still, especially in this mineral rich state, "reducing our budget is a reality we face." Massachusetts Gov. Charlie Baker (R) stated he would add money to the state's stabilization fund and not raise taxes or fees. Mississippi Gov. Phil Bryant's (R) budget "outlines a conservative and prudent spending plan that uses no one-time money for recurring expenses, replenishes the Rainy Day Fund to its statutory capacity and prioritizes core government functions...with most agencies level-funded at the revised state support amount, consistent with recent reductions, or are returned to pre-budget cut funding levels." Though additional funding goes to foster care as part settlement agreement, $51 million goes to the Rainy Day Fund, "which would boost the state's savings account to $428 million."

Other governors may not have mentioned credit ratings, but spent significant time and included much detail laying out fiscal sustainability plans for their states. Oklahoma Gov. Mary Fallin (R) used charts to display her strategy for addressing the state's poor budgetary outlook by "capturing" revenues, including those from a cigarette tax, from non-appropriated agency revenue sharing, by eliminating non-statutory, non-critical pass-through appropriations and automating reconciliation of some agency revolving funds, by reallocating apportionments to the General Revenue Fund "that currently go to noble but noncritical functions," and by modernizing state sales and use tax exemptions. Under her budget, most state agency budgets would be cut by 6 percent, with critical functions realizing just a 3 percent reduction (human welfare, public safety, public health, juvenile affairs and the state's School of Science and Mathematics). This governor is asking for sentencing reforms to help control prison costs and advance rehabilitation efforts. Spending for the state's prisons, foster care and education would increase, however, with the governor specifying in detail these efforts. She also called for funding to finish renovating Oklahoma's State Capitol.

Governors had lots of thoughts about state taxes and possible revenue generating or changing schemes. Ideas swirling around taxes included reform of state tax administration, vague "modernizing" of state tax codes, imposition or reform of various tax credits — for research and development, film, low-income housing, rural health care workers, bio-renewables, and child care — and considerations related to property, income, sales and cigarette taxes. Regarding property taxes, Illinois Gov. Bruce Rauner (R) talked about the need to reduce the property tax burden in his state. "We have the second highest property taxes in the country. They are crushing homeowners and small business owners." Brownback said he "would welcome legislation that strengthens the property tax lid by closing the existing loopholes." Ricketts crafted a proposal for property tax relief in Nebraska. In Pennsylvania, Wolf cautioned that, "If we don't have sustainable revenue sources in our budget, the result will be billions of dollars in new property tax hikes." Hogan called for tax relief on retirement income for all Maryland's retirees. In addition to asking for the acceleration of the Earned Income Tax Credit, this governor sought reduction or elimination of fees, elimination of the corporate tax and waiving "all state taxes on certain companies who commit to bringing jobs where unemployment is highest."

Washington Gov. Jay Inslee (D) called for paying for increased teacher pay by eliminating tax breaks "whose benefits simply do not outweigh our obligations to our students, to our teachers and to our schools." Nixon took fantasy sports to task. "Let's get real: this is gambling. If you're going to legalize it, we must regulate it and tax it just like we do casinos. This industry should follow the law, play by the rules and pay its fair share. This could mean millions of dollars a year for education." Tomblin talked about the serious need to "consider new revenue opportunities" via increasing West Virginia's tobacco tax, doing away with a sales tax exemption and bringing the "state's telecommunications tax in line with 41 other states across the country."

Tax cuts were brought up in speeches. Florida Gov. Rick Scott (R) extolled, "Let's keep cutting taxes! Floridians can spend their money better than government can." He called for cutting the tax on cell phones and TVs, permanently ending manufacturing equipment tax as well as the state sales tax on college textbooks. In New Jersey, Christie asked to abolish the Estate Tax because "14 states currently have estate taxes and six have inheritance taxes, but only New Jersey and Maryland have both." Cuomo proposed "a tax cut for small businesses because that is the engine that is driving the [New York] economy."

Commitments to no new taxes were evidenced as well. Massachusetts Gov. Charlie Baker (R) said his new budget "won't raise taxes or fees." Haley warned that she would "not sign any piece of legislation that raises taxes — not in year one, not in year five, not in year 10." She also sought state income tax cuts. Mead noted disagreement with any ideas for raising taxes in Wyoming, "I just don't think that is where we are today, because certainly we are at a point we're still spending on things we would not be spending on if we're at the point of considering more taxes."

Labor Costs and Unions

Four governors brought up unions and labor negotiations in their speeches this year. Connecticut Gov. Dan Malloy (D) discussed his state's fiscal problems, emphasizing he would "continue to negotiate with 13 state employee bargaining units" and that while he "strongly believes that working people who serve the public for decades deserve good benefits and a secure retirement… the obligation of maintaining this system cannot be solely supported by taxpayers. We should not wait until 2022 to have necessary discussions between labor and management." Rauner considered union compensation demands "out-of-touch with reality" and recognized Illinois' greatest costs are for compensating employees. He expressed that state employees "deserve to be well paid, and receive higher compensation in the future. But it should be based in part upon higher productivity and shared benefits in taxpayer savings, rather than just seniority." The union is asking for "$3 billion that should go into our schools and human services, not into government bureaucracy. Our state employees are paid almost 30 percent more than Illinois taxpayers are in their own jobs for the same work. That is not fair — and it's time we restore balance between taxpayers and state government. …We need to install common sense into our union contracts!" Christie admonished public unions in New Jersey, rallying against a proposed constitutional amendment to guarantee state pensions. Labeling state retirees as "the privileged few," he ranted that legislators not "soak every taxpayer" to pay pensions. Martinez was less strident regarding unions, suggesting that her state "end the practice of requiring New Mexicans to join a union or give money to one just to have a job."

Conclusion

The corrosive political environment in the United States, a dramatic drop in energy prices globally, and several ugly personal, policy or management gaffes by governors or those working for them has resulted in an interesting mix of speeches this year. While some governors provided highly detailed explanations of their budget problems and agendas, others discussed their views thematically, for example, regarding inequality and climate change. A few come off as belligerent—dismissive of other states, politicos in their own governments, or even specific members of society. On average, governors considered fewer of the issues expected to be addressed in these speeches. Also, there seemed to be a real hesitancy in making many promises past continuation budgets. There are a few outliers—one Democratic governor and one Republican governor considered nine issues each when laying out their budget and policy plans. In the end, what's important is what's mentioned. These chief executives understand what states do—primarily educate and push for economic prosperity. These issues remained at the forefront of governors' state of state speeches in 2016.

Notes

[1] U.S. state government chief executives report annually or biennially to their legislatures regarding their state's fiscal condition. They often use their address to lay out their policy and budget agendas for their upcoming or continuing administration. The 2016 state of the state addresses were accessed from Jan. 1–April 6, 2016, via *www.nga.org* or the state government's homepage. This research considers the 43 states with transcripts available at these sites as of April 6, 2016. Governors in Arkansas, Montana, Nevada, North Carolina, North Dakota, Oregon and Texas did not provide a speech in 2016. All quotes and data presented here are from the addresses accessed on these websites, unless otherwise noted. To conduct a content analysis of governors' state-of-state addresses, as in the past, topics were considered addressed if the chief executive specifically discussed them as relevant to state operations and the budget *going forward*. The governor needed to relay that the function, activity or issue is an important item in next year's—fiscal 2017—budget and policy direction. Just mentioning a state function or policy area like health care in a speech did not classify the issue as an agenda item addressed by a governor. Further, a review by a governor of his or her past accomplishments in any particular issue area did not count in this content analysis.

[2] National Governors Association. (2016). *Current Governors by State, Party Affiliation, and Terms in Office.* Accessed on March 1, 2016, via *http://www.nga.org/live/sites/NGA/files/pdf/GOVLIST.PDF.*

[3] National Conference of State Legislatures. (2016). *2016 State and Legislative Partisan Composition.* Accessed on March 1, 2016, via *http://www.ncsl.org/Portals/1/Documents/Elections/Legis_Control_2016_Mar17.pdf.*

[4] National Conference of State Legislatures, 2015.

[5] Dadayan, Lucy and Boyd, Donald J. (2016a). *Softening Third-Quarter Growth in State Taxes, Weak Forecasts for Fiscal 2016 and 2017,* March 7. Accessed March 1, 2016, via *http://www.rockinst.org/pdf/government_finance/state_revenue_report/2016-03-07-SRR_102.pdf.*

[6] Dadayan, Lucy and Boyd, Donald J. (2016b). *By the Numbers: Double, Double Oil and Trouble.* February 1. Accessed on March 1, 2016, via *http://www.rockinst.org/pdf/government_finance/2016-02-By_Numbers_Brief_No5.pdf.*

[7] Dadayan and Boyd, 2016b.

[8] See Crew, Jr., R.E. and Lewis, C. (2011). "Verbal Style, Gubernatorial Strategies, and Legislative Success." *Political Psychology.* August, 32(4), 623–642; Durney, A., Fauver, L. and Gupta, N. (2013). "Political Speech and Economic Outcomes: Running the Numbers." *ISB Insight,* October–December, 1(1), 8–14; and Smith, Keegan and Katherine Willoughby (2015). "The State of the State Addresses: More Comfortable, Still Cautious," in Audrey S. Wall, ed. *The Book of the States.* Vol. 46 (Lexington, KY: The Council of State Governments): 133–139.

About the Author

Katherine Willoughby is professor of public management and policy in the Andrew Young School of Policy Studies at Georgia State University in Atlanta. Her research concentrates on state and local government budgeting and financial management, public policy development and public organization theory. She has conducted extensive research in the area of state and local government budgeting, with a concentration on performance budgeting and management.

The Gubernatorial Elections of 2015: Hard-Fought Races for the Open Seats

By Jennifer M. Jensen and Thad Beyle

Only three governors were elected in 2015. Kentucky, Louisiana and Mississippi are the only states that hold their gubernatorial elections during the year prior to the presidential election. This means that these three states can be early indicators of any voter unrest that might unleash itself more broadly in the next year's congressional and presidential elections, and we saw some of this in the two races where candidates were vying for open seats. Mississippi Gov. Phil Bryant (R) was elected to a second term, running in a state that strongly favored his political party. Both Kentucky and Louisiana have elected Democrats and Republicans to the governorship in recent years, and each race was seen as up for grabs by many political pundits. In the end, each election resulted in the governorship turning over to the other political party.

Though Tea Party sentiments played a significant role in the primary elections in Kentucky and Louisiana, none of the general elections reflected the vigor that the Tea Party displayed in the 2014 gubernatorial elections. With only two open races and one safe incumbent on the ballot, the 2015 elections were generally not characterized as a major bellwether of the upcoming 2016 presidential election season. The Kentucky race, however, foreshadowed some of the turmoil that would play out as the presidential primary races geared up.

Kentucky

The Kentucky election was for an open seat as Gov. Steve Beshear (D) was term limited. Democrat Jack Conway, the sitting state attorney general, had an easy win in the Democratic primary over retired engineer and state employee Geoff Young, who had run previously for a U.S. House of Representatives seat and a statehouse seat.

The Republican primary election was hard fought, and in the end only 83 of the 214,193 total votes cast separated winner Matt Bevin and second-place finisher James Comer. Two other candidates, Hal Heiner and Will Scott, received a combined 73,316 votes compared to Bevin's 70,480 and Comer's 70,397, so Bevin won by a plurality, winning fewer than one-third of votes cast in the four-way race.

Bevin, a businessman and founder of several companies, including Integrity Asset Management and Veracity Funds, entered politics when he ran against U.S. Sen. Mitch McConnell (R-KY), a five-term incumbent and then Senate minority leader, in the 2014 Republican primary. Though ultimately

he lost badly to McConnell, he had name recognition when he entered the gubernatorial race as an anti-establishment candidate who ran an outsider's campaign against two Republicans who had held elected office. Bevin funded the vast majority of his primary spending himself, contributing more than $2.4 million to his own campaign. His anti-establishment message resonated at a time when Tea Party sentiments were running high, and it is likely that he was helped when a former girlfriend of primary candidate James Comer alleged that Comer abused her when they dated in college; Comer and Heiner subsequently got into a spat when Comer accused Heiner of orchestrating the allegation.[1]

In many ways, Bevin was not a strong candidate. With his history of mudslinging with McConnell in the U.S. Senate campaign, and his refusal to endorse McConnell in the general election, he was not loved by the party establishment. McConnell backers had framed Bevin as both untrustworthy and inconsistent in describing his own record and issue positions, charges that continued during the race for the governorship. For example, Bevin stated that he was opposed to gambling, yet his businesses had invested heavily in casino stocks.[2] He argued that he had opposed the Troubled Asset Relief Program, or TARP, bailout, but he had signed a letter to the Securities and Exchange Commission supporting TARP.[3] He backed away from his initial pledge to end the state's Medicaid expansion, which would have dropped hundreds of thousands of Kentucky residents from Medicaid eligibility.

Yet at a time when large segments of voters were disillusioned with politics as usual, Bevin's overall

Table A: Gubernatorial Elections: 1970–2015

		Democratic winner		Eligible to run		Actually ran		Won		Lost			
Year	Number of races	Number	Percent	Number	Percent	Number	Percent	Number	Percent	Number	Percent	In primary	In general election
1970	35	22	63%	29	83%	24	83%	16	64%	8	36%	1 (a)	7 (b)
1971	3	3	100	0	...	...	...	...	...	...	...	...	...
1972	18	11	61	15	83	11	73	7	64	4	36	2 (c)	2 (d)
1973	2	1	50	1	50	1	100	...	...	1	100	1 (e)	...
1974	35	27 (f)	77	29	83	22	76	17	77	5	24	1 (g)	4 (h)
1975	3	3	100	2	66	2	100	2	100	...	...	...	...
1976	14	9	64	12	86	8	67	5	63	3	33	1 (i)	2 (j)
1977	2	1	50	1	50	1	100	1	100	...	...	...	...
1978	36	21	58	29	81	23	79	16	73	7	30	2 (k)	5 (l)
1979	3	2	67	0	...	...	...	...	...	...	...	...	...
1980	13	6	46	12	92	12	100	7	58	5	42	2 (m)	3 (n)
1981	2	1	50	0	...	...	...	...	...	...	...	...	...
1982	36	27	75	33	92	25	76	19	76	6	24	1 (o)	5 (p)
1983	3	3	100	1	33	1	100	...	...	1	100	1 (q)	...
1984	13	5	38	9	69	6	67	4	67	2	33	...	2 (r)
1985	2	1	50	1	50	1	100	1	100	...	...	...	...
1986	36	19	53	24	67	18	75	15	83	3	18	1 (s)	2 (t)
1987	3	3	100	2	67	1	50	...	...	1	100	1 (u)	...
1988	12	5	42	9	75	9	100	8	89	1	11	...	1 (v)
1989	2	2	100	0	...	...	...	...	...	...	...	...	...
1990	36	19 (w)	53	33	92	23	70	17	74	6	26	...	6 (x)
1991	3	2	67	2	67	2	100	...	...	2	100	1 (y)	1 (z)
1992	12	8	67	9	75	4	44	4	100	...	...	...	...
1993	2	0	0	1	50	1	100	...	...	1	100	...	1 (aa)
1994	36	11 (bb)	31	30	83	23	77	17	74	6	26	2 (cc)	4 (dd)
1995	3	1	33	2	67	1	50	1	100	...	...	...	...
1996	11	7	64	9	82	7	78	7	100	...	...	...	...
1997	2	0	0	1	50	1	100	1	100	...	...	...	...
1998	36	11 (ee)	31	27	75	25	93	23	92	2	8	...	2 (ff)
1999	3	2	67	2	67	2	100	2	100	...	...	...	...
2000	11	8	73	7	88	6	86	5	83	1	17	...	1 (gg)
2001	2	2	100	0	...	...	...	...	...	...	...	...	...
2002	36	14	39	22	61	16	73	12	75	4	25	...	4 (hh)
2003	4 (ii)	1	25	2	50	2	100	...	...	2	100	...	2 (jj)
2004	11	6	55	11	100	8	73	4	50	4	50	2 (kk)	2 (ll)
2005	2	2	100	1	50	...	...	...	...	...	...	...	...
2006	36	20	56	31	86	27	87	25	93	2	7	1 (mm)	1 (nn)
2007	3	1	33	3	100	2	67	1	50	1	50	...	1 (oo)
2008	11	7	64	9	82	8	89	8	100	...	...	...	...
2009	2	0	0	1	50	1	100	...	...	1	100	...	1 (pp)
2010	37	13	35	22	60	14	64	11	79	3	21	1 (qq)	2 (rr)
2011	4	2	50	3	75	3	100	3	100	0	0	0	0
2012	12	7	58	8	67	7	88	7	100	...	...	...	...
2013	2	1	50	1	50	1	50	1	50	0	0	0	0
2014	36	13	36	31	86	29	81	26	72.2	3	8	1 (a)	2 (b)
2015	3	1	33	1	33	1	33	1	33	0	0	0	0
Totals:													
Number	629	331		478		379		294		85		22	63
Percent	100	52.6		76.0		79.3		77.6		22.4		25.9	74.1

Source: The Council of State Governments, *The Book of the States*, 2012, (Lexington, KY: The Council of State Governments, 2012), 204, updated.

Key:

(a) Albert Brewer, D-Alabama; Neil Abercrombie, D-Hawaii.

(b) Keith Miller, R-Alaska; Winthrop Rockefeller, R-Ark.; Claude Kirk, R-Fla.; Don Samuelson, R-Idaho; Norbert Tieman, R-Neb.; Dewey Bartlett, R-Okla.; Frank Farrar, R-S.D.; Sean Parnell, R-Alaska; Tom Corbett, R-Pennsylvania

(c) Walter Peterson, R-N.H.; Preston Smith, D-Texas.

(d) Russell Peterson, R-Del.; Richard Ogilvie, R-Ill.

(e) William Cahill, R-N.J.

(f) One independent candidate won: James Longley of Maine.

(g) David Hall, D-Okla.

(h) John Vanderhoof, R-Colo.; Francis Sargent, R-Mass.; Malcolm Wilson, R-N.Y.; John Gilligan, D-Ohio.

(i) Dan Walker, D-Ill.

(j) Sherman Tribbitt, D-Del.; Christopher 'Kit' Bond, R-Mo.

(k) Michael Dukakis, D-Mass., Dolph Briscoe, D-Texas.

(l) Robert F. Bennett, R-Kan.; Rudolph G. Perpich, D-Minn.; Meldrim Thompson, R-N.H.; Robert Straub, D-Oreg.; Martin J. Schreiber, D-Wis.

(m) Thomas L. Judge, D-Mont.; Dixy Lee Ray, D-Wash.

(n) Bill Clinton, D-Ark.; Joseph P. Teasdale, D-Mo.; Arthur A. Link, D-N.D.

Footnotes are continued on the next page.

Table A: Gubernatorial Elections: 1970–2015, Footnotes Continued

(o) Edward J. King, D-Mass.

(p) Frank D. White, R-Ark.; Charles Thone, R-Neb.; Robert F. List, R-Nev.; Hugh J. Gallen, D-N.H.; William P. Clements, R-Texas.

(q) David Treen, R-La.

(r) Allen I. Olson, R-N.D.; John D. Spellman, R-Wash.

(s) Bill Sheffield, D-Alaska

(t) Mark White, D-Texas; Anthony S. Earl, D-Wis.

(u) Edwin Edwards, D-La.

(v) Arch A. Moore, R-W. Va.

(w) Two Independent candidates won: Walter Hickel (Alaska) and Lowell Weiker (Conn.). Both were former statewide Republican office holders.

(x) Bob Martinez, R-Fla.; Mike Hayden, R-Kan.; James Blanchard, D-Mich.; Rudy Perpich, DFL-Minn.; Kay Orr, R-Neb.; Edward DiPrete, R-R.I.

(y) Buddy Roemer, R-La.

(z) Ray Mabus, D-Miss.

(aa) James Florio, D-N.J.

(bb) One Independent candidate won: Angus King of Maine.

(cc) Bruce Sundlun, D-R.I.; Walter Dean Miller, R-S.D.

(dd) James E. Folsom, Jr., D-Ala.; Bruce King, D-N.M.; Mario Cuomo, D-N.Y.; Ann Richards, D-Texas.

(ee) Two Independent candidates won: Angus King of Maine and Jesse Ventura of Minnesota.

(ff) Fob James, R-Ala.; David Beasley, R-S.C.

(gg) Cecil Underwood, R-W. Va.

(hh) Don Siegelman, D-Ala.; Roy Barnes, D-Ga., Jim Hodges, D-S.C.; and Scott McCallum, R-Wis.

(ii) The California recall election and replacement vote of 2003 is included in the 2003 election totals and as a general election for the last column.

(jj) Gray Davis, D-Calif., Ronnie Musgrove, D-Miss.

(kk) Bob Holden, D-Mo.; Olene Walker, R-Utah, lost in the pre-primary convention.

(ll) Joe Kernan, D-Ind.; Craig Benson, R-N.H.

(mm) Frank Murkowski, R-Alaska.

(nn) Robert Ehrlich, R-Md.

(oo) Ernie Fletcher, R-Ky.

(pp) Jon Corzine, D-N.J.

(qq) Jim Gibbons, R-Nev.

(rr) Chet Culver, D-Iowa; Ted Strickland, D-Ohio.

message resonated. Campaigning on a platform to improve the economy, roll back the Common Core curriculum in schools, pass right-to-work legislation to eliminate the requirement that employees must pay dues to unions, and fight the Obama White House on issues such as the Affordable Care Act, Bevin kept the general election race a tossup until the end.

The fact that Bevin could keep the election competitive speaks to the power of national political mood and the dissatisfaction with Obama that was widespread in Kentucky.[4] The same disillusioned Kentucky voters who would throw their support to Donald Trump in Kentucky's Republican presidential primary in March 2016 turned to Bevin in the governor's race. Bevin was likely helped by county clerk Kim Davis's refusal to certify gay marriages in her Kentucky county two months before the election. Davis's stand made national headlines and galvanized evangelical voters. Bevin visited her when she was jailed for contempt of court, saying that the state did not have the right to force a government official to act against religious beliefs. All this helped Bevin stay competitive in a state that had elected only two other Republican governors since the 1940s.

In the general election, Bevin's campaign was helped by sizeable contributions from others. As the campaign kicked into high gear in the summer, the Republican Governors Association ran television ads supporting Bevin. RGA support did not continue in the final weeks of the campaign, but it provided critical steam for Bevin.[5]

Kentucky voters were very familiar with Democratic Party nominee Jack Conway, who had served two terms as state attorney general, and who had run unsuccessfully for the U.S. Senate in 2010, losing to Rand Paul in the general election. Conway's issue positions were in line with those of the Democratic Party, including raising the minimum wage, maintaining the state expansion of Medicaid that would bring coverage to 10 percent of the state, maintaining the state's labor laws regarding union membership, and strengthening early childhood education.

Conway had deep support from the Democratic Party as he ran for governor, and he spent more than twice what Bevin spent in the general election campaign. The spending by the candidates is only one source of campaign funding in the race, however, as the political parties and other political groups made their own expenditures. The Republican Governors Association spent $5 million on the race, some of which came in the form of blistering attack ads about Conway in the crucial final weeks.[6] The Democratic Governors Association-funded superPAC Kentucky Family Values spent at least $3.5 million supporting Conway.[7] The race was widely acknowledged as an especially bitter one.

In an election year that favored outsiders, Conway had a difficult task: turning out Democratic voters in Louisville and Lexington without losing the more conservative vote in the rest of the state. A candidate who was considered by many to be a strong policymaker but by some a slightly stilted campaigner, he was unable to beat Bevin's outsider candidacy at a time that favored political

Table B: Total Cost of Gubernatorial Elections: 1977–2015 (in thousands of dollars)

Year	Number of races	Total campaign costs Actual $	Total campaign costs 2014$ (a)	Average cost per state (2014$)(b)
1977	2	$12,312	$47,336	$23,668
1978	36 (c)	102,342	365,638	10,157
1979	3	32,744	105,050	35,017
1980	13	35,634	100,746	7,750
1981	2	24,648	63,168	31,584
1982	36	181,832	438,890	12,191
1983	3	39,966	93,466	31,155
1984	13	47,156	105,731	8,133
1985	2	18,859	40,829	20,415
1986	36	270,605	575,143	15,976
1987	3	40,212	82,452	27,484
1988	12 (d)	52,208	102,812	8,568
1989	2	47,902	89,991	44,995
1990	36	345,493	615,742	17,104
1991	3	34,564	59,114	19,705
1992	12	60,278	100,080	8,340
1993	2	36,195	58,351	29,175
1994	36	417,873	656,826	18,245
1995	3	35,693	54,560	18,187
1996	11 (e)	68,610	101,871	9,261
1997	2	44,823	65,055	32,528
1998	36	470,326	672,182	18,672
1999	3	16,276	22,757	7,586
2000	11	97,098	131,125	11,920
2001	3	70,400	92,607	30,869
2002	36	841,427	1,089,649	30,268
2003	4 (f)	69,939	88,564	22,141
2004	11	112,625	138,889	12,626
2005	2	131,996	157,438	78,719
2006	36	727,552	840,712	23,353
2007	3	93,803	105,385	35,128
2008	11	118,912	128,651	11,696
2009	2	92,911	100,001	50,000
2010	37 (g)	920,735	983,586	26,583
2011	4 (h)	45,934	47,570	11,893
2012	12 (i)	144,044	146,149	12,179
2013	2	84,746	84,746	42,373
2014	36	704,300	704,300	19,564
2015 (j)	3	48,764	48,764	16,255

Sources: Thad Beyle, Jennifer Jensen and The Council of State Governments.

Key: -

(a) Developed from the table "Historic Consumer Price Index for All Urban Consumers (CPI-U)," created by the Bureau of Labor Statistics for the U.S. Department of Labor. Each year's expenditures are converted into the 2014$ value of the dollar by dividing those $ expenditures by the percent of that year's CPI-U value to control for the effect of inflation or recession over the period.

(b) Average cost per state is the result of dividing the 2014$ total campaign expenditures by the number of elections held that year.

(c) The expenditure data of 1978 are a particular problem as the two sources compiling data on this year's elections did so in differing ways that excluded some candidates. The result is that the numbers for 1978 under-represent the acutal costs of these elections by some unknown amount. The sources are: Rhodes Cook and Stacy West, "1978 Advantage," *CQ Weekly Report*, (1979): 1757–1758, and *The Great Louisiana Spendathon* (Baton Rouge: Public Affairs Research Council, March 1980).

(d) As of the 1986 election, Arkansas switched to a four-year term for the governor, hence the drop from 13 to 12 for this off-year.

(e) As of the 1994 election, Rhode Island switched to a four-year term for the governor, hence the drop from 12 to 11 for this off-year.

(f) In 2003, there was a special recall and replacement election held in California in which voters elected to recall incumbent Gov. Gray Davis (D) from office and replace him with Gov. Arnold Schwarzenegger (R), hence the fourth election in this off-year instead of the normal three.

(g) In 2010, Utah held a special election to elect Gov. Gary Herbert (R) to the position which he had been appointed in 2009. In 2009, then Lt. Gov. Herbert succeeded to the office of governor after Jon Hunstman (R) left to become U.S. ambassador to China. Under Utah law, voters must agree that a succeeding governor can hold the role until the next regularly scheduled election.

(h) In 2011, West Virginia held a special election to elect Gov. Earl Ray Tomblin (D) to the position he had been appointed to in 2010. Tomblin was appointed governor upon the resignation of Gov. Joe Manchin (D), who won a seat in the U.S. Senate. West Virginia law requires a special election must be held in the case of a gubernatorial succession.

(i) In 2012, Wisconsin held a special recall and replacement election focused on Gov. Scott Walker (R). Walker received 53 percent of the vote and was not recalled. In North Dakota, the law has been changed so that candidates no longer have to report the amount of $ expenditures made in the campaign.

(j) Amounts for 2015 gubernatorial elections are in 2015$.

outsiders. Conway also may have been hurt by his decision as state attorney general not to appeal a federal judge's decision to strike down part of the state's ban on gay marriage.[8] In the end, Bevin beat Conway 52.5 to 43.8 percent, winning 106 of 120 counties. His running mate for lieutenant governor, Jenean Hampton, became the first African-American elected to statewide office in Kentucky.

Louisiana

As the Kentucky governorship was changing hands from a Democrat to a Republican, the Louisiana governorship was changing hands from a Republican—the incumbent governor, Bobby Jindal, who was term limited—to a Democrat. In the end, state Rep. John Bel Edwards won the governorship with 56.11 percent of the vote in the general election.

Louisiana has a nonpartisan blanket primary for all candidates. In this so-called jungle primary, the top two vote-getters participate in a runoff election if there is no majority winner. Because the 2015 gubernatorial election would be before his U.S. Senate seat was up for reelection in 2016, U.S. Sen. David Vitter was able to throw his hat in the ring for governor while knowing that if he lost, he could still run for reelection in the Senate—and if he won, as governor he could appoint the replacement to complete his term in the Senate. (By the time of the general election, Vitter had announced that if he lost the race for governor, he would not run for reelection to the Senate.)

Vitter, the most conservative candidate in the race, remained the leading Republican in the race throughout the gubernatorial primary, though two other experienced Republican candidates maintained strong showings throughout the campaign. In the end, Vitter beat the next biggest vote-getter, former lieutenant governor and sitting public service commissioner Scott Angelle, by just over three points.

Longstanding personal issues dogged Vitter throughout the campaign. In 2007, three years into his Senate term, Vitter's phone number was linked to telephone records of a high-end escort service. Vitter stated that he had called the service, and he apologized for "a grave sin," but denied ever using prostitutes and claimed that he was the victim of a political smear campaign.[9] Considered extremely vulnerable at the start of his 2010 Senate reelection bid, he ran a strong campaign in a year when anti-Barack Obama sentiment was high in Louisiana, and ultimately won reelection with more than 56 percent of the vote. Yet the family values conservative was never able to shake concerns about his personal integrity. The prostitution allegations were raised by his opponents during both the primary and runoff elections. The three Republican candidates for governor—Vitter, Angelle and Lt. Gov. Jay Dardenne—engaged in bitter infighting that hurt Vitter's ability to run a strong campaign in the runoff. (Angelle did not endorse a candidate in the runoff election; Dardenne endorsed Vitter's opponent.)[10]

Most pundits gave the advantage to Vitter, and spring and summer polls showed him with more support than Democrat John Bel Edwards. Edwards did not garner much attention early in the race and ran a thinly staffed campaign. He was a strong candidate to challenge Vitter in the runoff, however, and as fall began and the primary campaign heated up, polls started showing that Edwards had a shot against Vitter in the runoff.[11]

Edwards, a West Point graduate, former U.S. Army Ranger and social conservative, took a strong anti-abortion stance during the campaign.[12] On bread-and-butter issues, he took more traditional Democratic stances on issues such as education funding. He advocated cutting both spending and tax breaks to address the state's enormous budget deficit and was the only major candidate to state early that he would accept Medicaid expansion funding from the federal government. As the race moved into summer, Edwards began to get more attention and more financial support.

The four major candidates spent nearly $30 million on their campaigns, and outside groups spent heavily in the race, particularly as the runoff heated up. Counting these expenses, approximately $50 million was spent on the race.

Mississippi

Mississippi's gubernatorial election was a foregone conclusion, with the most interesting activity in the primary elections rather than the general election. Incumbent governor and former lieutenant governor Phil Bryant ran for a second term, and he drew no strong competitors. With more than $2.4 million on hand at the end of 2014,[13] his financial resources were more than an order of magnitude greater than all other candidates combined.

That no other candidate in the race but Bryant had held or even run for office previously speaks to the strength of the Republican Party in statewide races. Since 1991, a Democrat has won the governorship only once—Ronnie Musgrove in 1999—and he won with a plurality of 49.6 percent of the vote against Republican Mike Parker's 48.5 percent. That race was ultimately decided by the Mississippi House of Representatives.[14] The three other most recent governors were all Republicans who were elected to two terms before being term-limited out of office.

Bryant was elected in the 2011 general election by 22 points over Democrat Johnny Dupree, former mayor of Hattiesburg. Bryant entered the 2015 election season with polling numbers that were strong enough to indicate that it would be very unlikely that a Democrat would win the governorship for the first time in 16 years. This is despite the fact that nearly three years into his first term in the office, Bryant was number one on the list of "most boring governors," as ranked by the percentage of respondents who responded in the "don't know/

Table C: Cost of Gubernatorial Campaigns, Most Recent Elections, 2012–2015

State	Year	Winner	Point margin	All candidates (2014$)	Cost per vote (2014$)	Winner Spent (2014$)	Winner Percent of all expenditures	Winner Vote percent
Alabama	2014	R★	+27.26	$7,990,363	6.77	$6,769,778	84.7%	63.6%
Alaska	2014	I★★★	+2.22	1,791,047	6.40	847,593	47.3	48.1
Arizona	2014	R#	+11.90	20,471,454	13.59	7,910,241	38.6	53.5
Arkansas	2014	R#	+12.96	15,950,408	18.79	5,883,158	38.9	55.5
California	2014	D★	+20.00	13,772,803	18.82	5,945,649	43.7	60.0
Colorado	2014	D★	+3.14	10,619,170	5.20	5,463,070	51.5	49.2
Connecticut	2014	D★	+2.82	16,892,137	15.46	6,735,418	39.9	51.4
Delaware	2012	D★	+40.64	1,958,861	4.92	1,656,189	96.5	69.3
Florida	2014	R★	+1.08	22,872,029	3.84	10,447,966	45.7	48.2
Georgia	2014	R★	+7.86	10,739,159	4.21	1,588,830	14.8	52.8
Hawaii	2014	D#	+12.30	9,173,312	25.04	2,029,646	22.1	49.0
Idaho	2014	R★	+15.35	6,595,929	6.70	2,143,926	32.5	54.9
Illinois	2014	R★	+3.92	102,434,649	28.16	65,426,075	63.9	50.3
Indiana	2012	R#	+2.89	20,535,517	7.97	13,085,571	65.7	49.5
Iowa	2014	R★	+21.80	10,516,834	9.31	8,577,632	81.6	59.0
Kansas	2014	R★	+3.70	7,121,660	8.19	2,268,612	31.9	49.8
Kentucky	2015	R#	+8.70	24,747,726 (b)	25.42 (b)	5,758,718 (b)	23.3	52.5
Louisiana	2015	D#	+12.20	19,618,604 (b)	17.02 (b)	8,679,334 (b)	44.2	56.1
Maine	2014	R★	+4.77	7,897,902	12.92	1,906,350	24.1	47.7
Maryland	2014	R#	+3.80	24,496,947	14.17	4,929,224	20.1	51.0
Massachusetts	2014	R#	+2.88	21,606,838	10.00	6,762,699	31.3	48.5
Michigan	2014	R★	+5.74	21,812,323	6.91	14,498,509	66.5	51.7
Minnesota	2014	D★	+5.56	5,451,188	2.76	3,039,926	55.8	50.1
Mississippi	2015	R★	+34.10	4,397,406 (b)	6.12 (b)	4,079,731 (b)	92.8	66.4
Missouri	2012	D★	+12.10	27,018,238	9.90	15,512,314	59.2	54.7
Montana	2012	D#	+1.56	4,656,165	9.53	1,708,031	36.7	48.9
Nebraska	2014	R#	+17.51	14,760,429	27.35	7,059,254	47.8	57.2
Nevada	2014	R★	+46.89	3,617,676	6.61	3,513,555	97.1	70.6
New Hampshire	2014	D★	+9.08	3,341,358	6.87	1,472,416	44.1	52.5
New Jersey	2013	R★	+22.10	27,040,070	12.75	19,820,437	75.6	60.3
New Mexico	2014	R★	+14.44	12,486,204	24.35	8,501,999	88.5	57.2
New York	2014	D★	+13.97	59,541,778	15.59	52,663,635	88.5	54.3
North Carolina	2012	R#	+11.49	17,398,973	3.90	11,161,800	66.2	54.7
North Dakota	2012	R★	+28.79	(a)	(a)	(a)	(a)	(a)
Ohio	2014	R★	+30.96	20,166,455	6.60	16,640,931	82.5	63.8
Oklahoma	2014	R★	+14.80	5,987,244	7.26	4,317,938	72.1	55.8
Oregon	2014	D★	+5.76	8,106,083	5.51	5,006,085	61.8	49.9
Pennsylvania	2014	D#	+9.86	75,887,787	21.70	31,364,073	41.3	54.9
Rhode Island	2014	D#	+4.50	13,488,998	41.62	6,284,440	46.6	40.7
South Carolina	2014	R★	+14.46	15,110,615	12.12	7,887,670	52.2	55.9
South Dakota	2014	R★	+45.04	1,857,606	6.70	1,506,034	81.1	70.5
Tennessee	2014	R★	+47.73	4,272,410	3.16	4,246,999	99.4	70.7
Texas	2014	R#	+20.32	78,983,336	16.74	49,460,752	67.6	59.2
Utah	2012	R★	+40.50	2,755,320	2.74	2,150,305	80.5	68.3
Vermont	2014	D★	+1.26	1,264,972	6.55	961,469	76.0	46.8
Virginia	2013	D#	+2.52	60,353,635	26.93	32,417,401	53.4	47.8
Washington	2012	D#	+3.40	24,559,984	8.00	11,484,573	48.2	51.5
West Virginia	2012	D★	+4.85	6,897,808	10.38	3,376,110	50.5	50.5
Wisconsin	2014	R★	+5.74	46,336,867	19.22	29,673,716	52.9	52.9
Wyoming	2014	R★	+31.52	4,118,264	24.53	626,707	49.2	52.5

Sources: Thad Beyle, Jennifer Jensen, Aaron Luedtke and The Council of State Governments.

Note: All dollar figures are in equivalent 2014$ except Kentucky, Louisiana and Mississippi, which are in 2015$.

Key:
D — Democrat   I — Independent   R — Republican
\# — Open seat
★ — Incumbent ran and won.
★★ — Incumbent ran and lost in party primary.
★★★ — Incumbent ran and lost in general election.

(a) Data unavailable due to a change in North Dakota's campaign contribution reporting requirements. They are no longer required to file the $ expenditures by candidates, but must file data on contributions of $200 or more received by candidates.

(b) Dollar figures for Kentucky, Louisiana and Mississippi are in 2015$ amounts.

Table D: Women Governors in the States

Governor	State	Year elected or succeeded to office	How woman became governor	Tenure of service	Previous offices held	Last elected position held before governorship
Phase I—From initial statehood to adoption of the 19th Amendment to U.S. Constitution (1920)						
No women elected or served as governor						
Phase II—Wives of former governors elected governor, 1924–1966						
Nellie Tayloe Ross (D)	Wyoming	1924	E	1/1925–1/1927	F	...
Miriam "Ma" Ferguson (D)	Texas	1924	E	1/1925–1/1927 1/1933–1/1935	F	...
Lurleen Wallace (D)	Alabama	1966	E	1/1967–5/1968	F	...
Phase III—Women who became governor on their own merit, 1970 to date						
Ella Grasso (D)	Connecticut	1974	E	1/1975–12/1980	SH, SOS, (a)	(a)
Dixy Lee Ray (D)	Washington	1976	E	1/1977–1/1981	(b)	...
Vesta M. Roy (R)	New Hampshire	1982	S (c)	12/1982–1/1983	(d)	(d)
Martha Layne Collins (D)	Kentucky	1983	E	12/1983–12/1987	(e), LG	LG
Madeleine M. Kunin (D)	Vermont	1984	E	1/1985–1/1991	SH, LG	LG
Kay A. Orr (R)	Nebraska	1986	E	1/1987–1/1991	T	T
Rose Mofford (D)	Arizona	1988	S (f)	4/1988–1/1991	SOS	SOS
Joan Finney (D)	Kansas	1990	E	1/1991–1/1995	T	T
Barbara Roberts (D)	Oregon	1990	E	1/1991–1/1995	(g), C, SH, SOS	SOS
Ann Richards (D)	Texas	1990	E	1/1991–1/1995	C, T	T
Christy Whitman (R)	New Jersey	1993	E	1/1994–1/2001	(h)	(h)
Jeanne Shaheen (D)	New Hampshire	1996	E	1/1997–1/2003	(d)	(d)
Jane Dee Hull (R)	Arizona	1997	S (i)	9/1997–1/2003	(j), SOS	SOS
Nancy P. Hollister (R)	Ohio	1998	S (k)	12/1998–1/1999	LG	LG
Ruth Ann Minner (D)	Delaware	2000	E	1/2001–1/2009	SH, SS, LG	LG
Judy Martz (R)	Montana	2000	E	1/2001–1/2005	LG	LG
Sila Calderón (Pop D)	Puerto Rico	2000	E	1/2001–1/2005	M	M
Jane Swift (R)	Massachusetts	2001	S (l)	4/2001–1/2003	SS, LG	LG
Janet Napolitano (D)	Arizona	2002	E	1/2003–1/2009	(m), AG	AG
Linda Lingle (R)	Hawaii	2002	E	12/2002–12/2010	C, M (n)	M
Kathleen Sebelius (D)	Kansas	2002	E	1/2003–4/2009	SH, (o)	(o)
Jennifer Granholm (D)	Michigan	2002	E	1/2003–1/2011	(p), AG	AG
Olene Walker (R)	Utah	2003	S (q)	11/2003–1/2005	SH, LG	LG
Kathleen Blanco (D)	Louisiana	2003	E	1/2004–1/2008	SH, LG	LG
M. Jodi Rell (R)	Connecticut	2004	S (r)	7/2004–1/2011	SH, LG	LG
Christine Gregoire (D)	Washington	2004	E	1/2005–1/2013	AG	AG
Sarah Palin (R)	Alaska	2006	E	1/2007–7/2009	M (s)	M
Beverly Perdue (D)	North Carolina	2008	E	1/2009–1/2013	SH, SS, LG	LG
Jan Brewer (R)	Arizona	2009	S (t)	1/2009–12/2014	C, SH, SS, SOS	SOS
Susana Martinez (R)	New Mexico	2010	E	1/2011–	(u)	(u)
Mary Fallin (R)	Oklahoma	2010	E	1/2011–	(a)	(a)
Nikki Haley (R)	South Carolina	2010	E	1/2011–	SH	SH
Maggie Wood Hassan (D)	New Hampshire	2012	E	1/2013–	SS	SS
Gina Raimondo (D)	Rhode Island	2014	E	1/2015–	ST	ST
Kate Brown (D)	Oregon	2015	S (v)	2/2015–	SH, SS, SOS	SOS

Sources: National Governors Association website, *www.nga.org,* and individual state government websites.

Key:
S — Succeeded to office upon death, resignation or removal of the incumbent governor.

AG — Attorney general	M — Mayor
C — City council or county commission	SH — State House member
E — Elected governor	SOS — Secretary of state
F — Former first lady	SS — State Senate member
LG — Lieutenant governor	T — State treasurer

(a) Congresswoman.
(b) Ray served on the U.S. Atomic Energy Commission from 1972 to 1975 and was chair of the AEC from 1973 to 1975.
(c) Roy as state Senate president succeeded to office upon the death of Gov. Hugh Gallen.
(d) State Senate president.
(e) State Supreme Court clerk.
(f) Mofford as secretary of state became acting governor in February 1988 and governor in April 1988 upon the impeachment and removal of Gov. Evan Mecham.
(g) Local school board member.
(h) Whitman was a former state utilities official.
(i) Hull as secretary of state became acting governor when Gov. Fife Symington resigned. Elected to full term in 1998.
(j) Speaker of the state House.

(k) Hollister as lieutenant governor became governor when Gov. George Voinovich stepped down to serve in the U.S. Senate.
(l) Swift as lieutenant governor succeeded Gov. Paul Celluci who resigned after being appointed ambassador to Canada. Was the first governor to give birth while serving in office.
(m) U.S. attorney.
(n) Lingle was mayor of Maui for two terms, elected in 1990 and 1996.
(o) Insurance commissioner.
(p) Federal prosecutor.
(q) Walker as lieutenant governor succeeded to the governorship upon the resignation of Gov. Mike Leavitt in 2003.
(r) Rell as lieutenant governor succeeded to the governorship upon the resignation of Gov. John Rowland in 2004.
(s) Palin was a two-term Mayor of Wasilla, Alaska, and had unsuccessfully sought the lieutenant governor's office in 2002. In 2008, Palin was nominated to be the vice presidential candidate on the Republican ticket with U.S. Sen. John McCain.
(t) Brewer as secretary of state succeeded to the governorship upon the resignation of Gov. Janet Napolitano in January 2009 after her confirmation as head of the U.S. Department of Homeland Security. Brewer then won a full term in the 2010 election.
(u) District Attorney—Dona Ana County, N.M.
(v) Kate Brown as secretary of state succeeded to the governorship upon the resignation of Gov. John Kitzhaber in February 2015 after allegations of criminal wrongdoing involving the role his fiancée, Cylvia Hayes, held in his office.

Table E: 2012–2015 Governors' Race Winners by Party and Margin

Democratic winners				*Republican winners*				*Independent winners*			
State	*Election Year*	*Percent of win*	*Point margin*	*State*	*Election Year*	*Percent of win*	*Point margin*	*State*	*Election Year*	*Percent of win*	*Point margin*
Delaware............	2012	69.3	+40.7	Nevada	2014	70.6	+46.7	Alaska	2014	48.1	+2.2
California............	2014	59.8	+19.6	South Dakota	2014	70.5	+45.0				
Vermont..............	2012	57.8	+22.2	Tennessee............	2014	70.3	+47.5				
Louisiana	2015	56.1	+12.2	Utah.....................	2012	68.4	+40.6				
Pennsylvania.......	2014	54.9	+9.9	Mississippi...........	2015	66.6	+34.5				
Missouri	2012	54.8	+12.3	Alabama	2014	64.0	+28.0				
New York	2014	54.3	+14.0	Ohio.....................	2014	63.6	+30.6				
New Hampshire...	2012	52.6	+12.1	North Dakota	2012	63.3	+28.8				
New Hampshire...	2014	52.5	+9.1	Wyoming..............	2014	62.6	+33.8				
Washington	2012	51.5	+3.0	New Jersey...........	2013	60.3	+22.1				
Connecticut	2014	51.0	+3.0	Texas....................	2014	59.2	+20.3				
West Virginia	2012	50.4	+4.7	Iowa.....................	2014	59.0	+21.8				
Minnesota	2014	49.8	+5.6	New Mexico.........	2014	57.2	+14.5				
Oregon	2014	49.8	+5.8	Nebraska..............	2014	57.2	+17.9				
Colorado	2014	49.2	+3.4	South Carolina	2014	55.9	+14.5				
Hawaii	2014	49.0	+12.3	Oklahoma	2014	55.8	+14.8				
Montana...............	2012	48.8	+1.6	Arkansas..............	2014	55.5	+13.0				
Virginia	2013	47.8	+2.5	North Carolina	2012	54.7	+11.5				
Vermont	2014	43.4	+1.3	Arizona	2014	53.5	+11.9				
Rhode Island	2014	40.7	+4.5	Idaho	2014	53.5	+14.9				
				Georgia	2014	53.0	+8.0				
				Kentucky..............	2015	52.5	+8.7				
				Wisconsin	2014	52.3	+5.7				
				Michigan	2014	52.2	+5.8				
				Maryland..............	2014	51.0	+3.8				
				Illinois..................	2014	50.3	+3.9				
				Kansas	2014	50.0	+4.0				
				Indiana	2012	49.7	+3.2				
				Massachusetts......	2014	48.5	+1.9				
				Florida..................	2014	48.1	+1.0				
				Maine	2014	48.0	+5.0				

Source: Thad Beyle.

Overall Results by Victory Point Margin: Party and Region

Point margin	*Number of states*	*Number of Republicans*	*Number of Democrats*	*Number of Independents*	*East*	*South*	*Midwest*	*West*
10+ points	28	20	8	0	5	10	5	8
5–10 points	9	5	4	0	3	2	3	1
0–5 points	15	6	8	1	5	3	3	4
Totals:	52	31	20	1	13	15	11	13

Source: Thad Beyle.

don't care/refuse to answer" categories of gubernatorial approval polls in 35 states. Rather than stating that they approved or disapproved of Gov. Bryant, 28 percent of Mississippians responded with ignorance or indifference when they were asked about their governor—more than in any of the states with polling data to analyze.[15]

As an incumbent governor, a strong conservative in a red state, and a well-funded candidate, Bryant never had viable competition during his reelection campaign, but he did draw a primary opponent. Bryant's opponent in the Republican primary, Mitch Young, was a U.S. Navy veteran who criticized Bryant for not adequately funding education and not doing enough to improve the economy.[16]

Though no Democrat had a serious chance to defeat Bryant, the Democratic primary was the most interesting part of the Mississippi gubernatorial

Table F: New Governors Elected Each 4-Year Period, 1970–2015 (a)

| Year | Number of gubernatorial elections | New Governors | | Incumbents Running | | | |
		Won	Percent	Number	Won	Lost	Percent Lost
1970	35	19	54	24	16	8	36
1971	3	3	100	…	…	…	…
1972	18	11	61	11	7	4	36
1973	2	2	100	1	…	1	100
1974	35	18	51	22	17	5	24
1975	3	1	33	2	2	…	…
1976	14	9	64	8	5	3	33
1977	2	1	50	1	1	…	…
1978	36	20	56	23	16	7	30
1979	3	3	100	…	…	…	…
1980	13	6	46	12	7	5	42
1981	2	2	100	…	…	…	…
1982	36	17	47	25	19	6	24
1983	3	3	100	1	…	1	100
1984	13	9	69	6	4	2	33
1985	2	1	50	1	1	…	…
1986	36	21	58	18	15	3	18
1987	3	3	100	1	…	1	100
1988	12	4	33	9	8	1	11
1989	2	2	100	…	…	…	…
1990	36	19	53	23	17	6	26
1991	3	3	100	2	…	2	100
1992	12	8	67	4	4	…	…
1993	2	1	50	1	…	1	100
1994	36	19	53	23	17	6	26
1995	3	2	67	1	1	…	…
1996	11	4	36	7	7	…	…
1997	2	1	50	1	1	…	…
1998	36	13	36	25	23	2	8
1999	3	1	33	2	2	…	…
2000	11	6	55	6	5	1	17
2001	2	2	100	…	…	…	…
2002	36	24	67	16	12	4	25
2003 (b)	4	4	100	2	…	2	100
2004	11	7	64	8	4	4	50
2005	2	2	100	…	…	…	…
2006	36	9	25	27	25	2	7
2007	3	2	67	2	1	1	50
2008	11	3	24	8	8	…	…
2009	2	2	100	1	…	1	100
2010	37	26	70	14	11	3	21
2011	4	1	25	3	3	…	…
2012 (c)	12	5	42	7	7	…	…
2013	2	1	50	1	1	…	…
2014	36	10	28	29	26	3	10
2015	3	2	67	1	1	…	…
Totals:	629	334	53	379	294	85	23

Source: Thad Beyle.
Key:
(a) Table A: Gubernatorial Elections: 1970–2010, *The Book of the States, 2011* (Lexington, KY: The Council of State Governments, 2011), 128.
(b) In 2003, there was a recall and replacement election vote in California in which the incumbent Gov. Gray Davis (D) was recalled and Republican Arnold Schwarzenegger was elected as his replacement.
(c) In June 2012, a recall and replacement election was held in Wisconsin. Gov. Scott Walker (R) won 53 percent of the votes cast and was not recalled.

election season. Two of the three candidates vying for the Democratic nomination were women, which was especially notable because they were the first women to run for governor of Mississippi since 1983.

Vicki Slater was considered the favorite in the Democratic primary. An attorney with no elective office experience, she previously had been president of the Mississippi Association for Justice, a trial lawyers organization.[17] During her campaign, Slater criticized Bryant for refusing to expand Medicaid coverage in Mississippi, as states are able to do under the Affordable Care Act. She also argued that the state lost jobs under Bryant and that Bryant did not adequately fund education. Slater was the best funded of the Democratic candidates, spending just over $260,000 on the primary election.

Dr. Valerie Short, an obstetrician-gynecologist and U.S. Air Force veteran, also campaigned for expanded Medicaid and more funding for public schools. If she had won, Short would have followed Johnny Dupree to become only the second African-American gubernatorial candidate to win the Democratic nomination for governor in Mississippi. She spent approximately $48,500 on her primary run.

The third Democratic candidate—long-haul truck driver and retired firefighter Robert Gray—was the least likely to win, and so it was particularly surprising when he won 79 of the 82 counties. He had neither raised nor spent any campaign funds before the August 4 primary. His mother did not know he was on the ballot before she voted for him, and he was too busy working on his truck to vote in the primary himself.[18] Despite a lack of a campaign, he won just shy of 51 percent of the vote compared to Slater's 30 percent and Short's nearly 19 percent. His win was widely attributed to two factors: being listed first on the primary ballot, and being the only man running against two women. No woman has ever received either party's nomination for governor.[19] As a candidate who was unknown to voters, he may have also benefitted from having a racially neutral name. Gray is African-American, but was far less visible during the campaign than either Slater or Short.

Gray spent less than $8,000 campaigning for general election.

Campaign Spending

The Mississippi race was the least expensive of the 2015 gubernatorial campaigns, both in aggregate and by the amount the campaigns spent per vote in the general election. At $6.12 per vote, the Mississippi gubernatorial election is one of the 20 states where total candidate spending was less than $10 per vote in the most recent gubernatorial election. Louisiana could be described as having moderate spending in its gubernatorial election, not considering spending by outside groups.

In the most recent gubernatorial campaigns nationwide, several saw candidate spending surpass $25 per general election vote. Kentucky fits into this category. No doubt some of Kentucky's high price tag stems from the fact that multimillionaire Bevin provided substantial self-funding, especially early in the race – spending that led to an arms race between candidates and outside groups in both the Republican primary and the general election as other candidates outspent Bevin.

Notes

[1] Gerth, Joseph. 2015. "College Girlfriend Says James Comer Abused Her." *Louisville Courier-Journal* online edition, May 5. *http://www.courier-journal.com/story/news/politics/elections/kentucky/2015/05/04/james-comer-domestic-violence/26901137/*. Accessed March 2, 2016; Sonka, Joe. 2015. "How Matt Bevin (Most Likely) Won a Thrilling GOP Primary." *Insider Louisville* May 20. *http://insiderlouisville.com/metro/matt-bevin-wins-primary-thriller-83-votes-likely-receive-gop-nomination-governor/*. Accessed November 15, 2015.

[2] Gerth, Joe. 2015. "Bevin's Gambling Stance, Investments at Odds." *Louisville Courier Journal* online edition, July 21. *http://www.courier-journal.com/story/news/politics/elections/2015/07/21/bevins-gambling-stance-investment-work-odds/30461831/*. Accessed November 3, 2015.

[3] McCormack, John. 2014. "Securities Law Expert on Matt Bevin's TARP Letter: 'There's an Argument That He Actually Violated the Law.'" *The Weekly Standard* February 13. *http://www.weeklystandard.com/securities-law-expert-on-matt-bevins-tarp-letter-theres-an-argument-that-he-actually-violated-the-law/article/781618*. Accessed March 1, 2016.

[4] Cizzilla, Chris. 2015. "Matt Bevin is the Next Governor of Kentucky. He has President Obama to Thank." *Washington Post Online*, The Fix blog, November 2. *https://www.washingtonpost.com/news/the-fix/wp/2015/11/03/matt-bevin-is-the-next-governor-of-kentucky-he-has-president-obama-to-thank/*. Accessed November 3, 2015.

[5] Barton, Ryland. 2015. "Republican Governors Association Stops Airing Bevin Ads." WFPL News (Louisville), September 29. *http://wfpl.org/republican-governors-association-stops-airing-bevin-ads/*. Accessed November 3, 2015.

[6] Gerth, Joseph. 2015. "Bevin Leads GOP Wave, Routs Conway." *Louisville Courier Journal* online edition, November 4. *http://www.courier-journal.com/story/news/politics/elections/kentucky/2015/11/03/jack-conway-matt-bevin-kentucky-governor-election/74327130/*. Accessed March 1, 2016.

[7] Loftus, Tom. 2015. "Conway Has Big Money Edge Over Bevin." *Louisville Courier Journal* online edition, October 8. *http://www.courier-journal.com/story/news/politics/elections/kentucky/2015/10/08/conway-has-big-money-edge-over-bevin/73568278/*. Accessed March 1, 2016.

[8] Gabriel, Trip. 2014. "Kentucky Law Official Will Not Defend Ban on Same-Sex Marriage." *New York Times* March 5, A17.

[9] Moller, Jan. 2010. "Sen. David Vitter Wins Re-Election in Remarkable Comeback." *Times-Picayune*, online edition, November 2. *http://www.nola.com/politics/index.ssf/2010/11/sen_david_vitter_wins_re-elect.html*. Accessed March 18, 2016.

[10] Robertson, Campbell. 2015. "A Red State, but Still an Uphill G.O.P. Bid." *New York Times* November 20, A18.

[11] See the Huffington Post Pollster blog for historical polling data from the Louisiana gubernatorial primary election. *http://elections.huffingtonpost.com/pollster/2015-louisiana-governor-primary*. Accessed March 18, 2016.

[12] Robertson, Campbell. 2015. "Louisiana Democrat Leapt Big Obstacles to Beat Vitter in Governor's Race." *New York Times* November 23, A9.

[13] Wyman, Hastings. 2015. "Mississippi Democrats Set for Another Shellacking." *Southern Political Report* March 10. *http://www.southernpoliticalreport.com/2015/03/10/mississippi-democrats-set-for-another-shellacking/*. Accessed March 12, 2016.

[14] Salter, Sid. 2015. "Looks Like Mississippi Will Have a 2015 Governor's Race." *Hattiesburg American* February 23. *http://www.hattiesburgamerican.com/story/opinion/columnists/2015/02/24/salter-mississippi-governor-race/23952805/*. Accessed March 12, 2016.

[15] Hickey, Walt and Harry Enten. 2014. "The Most Boring Governors in the United States." *FiveThirtyEight.com* article posted August 15, 2014. *https://fivethirtyeight.com/datalab/the-most-blah-governors-in-the-united-states/*. Accessed March 12, 2016.

[16] Pettus, Emily Wagster. 2015. "Five Seek Nominations for Mississippi Governors' Seat." *Hattiesburg American* August 2. *http://www.hattiesburgamerican.com/story/news/politics/elections/2015/08/02/mississippi-governor-race/31028549/*. Accessed March 12, 2016.

[17] Pettus, Emily Wagster. 2015. "Five Seek Nominations for Mississippi Governors' Seat." *Hattiesburg American* August 2. *http://www.hattiesburgamerican.com/story/news/politics/elections/2015/08/02/mississippi-governor-race/31028549/*. Accessed March 12, 2016.

[18] Robertson, Campbell. 2015. "Shy trucker emerges as Democrats' pick for Mississippi governor." *New York Times* September 8, A1, New York edition.

[19] Jackson Free Press Editorial Board. 2015. "Vicki Slater for Governor." *Jackson Free Press* July 31. *http://m.jacksonfreepress.com/news/2015/jul/31/vicki-slater-governor/*. Accessed April 18, 2016.

About the Authors

Thad Beyle is a professor emeritus of political science at the University of North Carolina at Chapel Hill. After completing his undergraduate and master's degrees at Syracuse University, he received his doctorate at the University of Illinois. He spent a year in the North Carolina governor's office in the mid-1960s, followed by two years with Terry Sanford's "A Study of American States" project at Duke University. He has also worked with the National Governors Association in several capacities on gubernatorial transitions.

Jennifer M. Jensen is deputy provost for academic affairs and associate professor of political science at Lehigh University. She earned her B.A. from the University of Michigan and her M.A. and Ph.D. from the University of North Carolina at Chapel Hill. She has worked in the U.S. House of Representatives and in governmental relations. She recently authored *The Governors' Lobbyists: Federal-State Relations Offices and Governors Associations in Washington* (University of Michigan Press, 2016).

Table 4.1
THE GOVERNORS, 2016

State or other jurisdiction	Name and party	Length of regular term in years	Date of first service	Present term ends	Number of previous terms	Term limits	Joint election of governor and lieutenant governor (a)	Official who succeeds governor	Birthdate	Birthplace
Alabama	Robert Bentley (R)	4	1/2011	1/2019	1	2-4	No	LG	2/3/1943	AL
Alaska	Bill Walker (I)	4	12/2014	12/2018	...	2-4	Yes	LG	4/16/1951	AK
Arizona	Doug Ducey (R)	4	1/2015	1/2019	...	2-4	(b)	SS	4/9/1964	OH
Arkansas	Asa Hutchinson (R)	4	1/2015	1/2019	...	2A	No	LG	12/3/1950	AR
California	Edmund Gerald "Jerry" Brown (D)	4	1/1975 (c)	1/2019	2 (c)	2A (c)	No	LG	4/7/1938	CA
Colorado	John Hickenlooper (D)	4	1/2011	1/2019	1	2-4	Yes	LG	2/7/1952	PA
Connecticut	Dan Malloy (D)	4	1/2011	1/2019	1	...	Yes	LG	7/21/1955	CT
Delaware	Jack Markell (D)	4	1/2009	1/2017	1	2A	No	LG	11/26/1960	DE
Florida	Rick Scott (R)	4	1/2011	1/2019	1	2-4	Yes	LG	12/2/1952	IL
Georgia	Nathan Deal (R)	4	1/2011	1/2019	1	2-4	No	LG	8/25/1942	GA
Hawaii	David Ige (D)	4	12/2014	12/2018	...	2-4	Yes	LG	6/26/1938	NY
Idaho	C.L. "Butch" Otter (R)	4	1/2007	1/2019	2	...	No	LG	5/3/1942	ID
Illinois	Bruce Rauner (R)	4	1/2015	1/2019	...	...	Yes	LG	12/16/1948	IL
Indiana	Mike Pence (R)	4	1/2013	1/2017	...	2-12	Yes	LG	6/7/1959	IN
Iowa	Terry Branstad (R)	4	1/1983 (d)	1/2019	5 (d)	...	Yes	LG	11/17/1946	IA
Kansas	Sam Brownback (R)	4	1/2011	1/2019	1	2-4	Yes	LG	9/12/1956	KS
Kentucky	Matt Bevin (R)	4	12/2015	12/2019	...	2-4	Yes	LG	1/9/1967	NH
Louisiana	John Bel Edwards (D)	4	1/2016	1/2020	...	2-4	No	LG	9/16/1966	LA
Maine	Paul LePage (R)	4	1/2011	1/2019	1	2-4	(b)	PS	10/9/1948	ME
Maryland	Larry Hogan (R)	4	1/2015	1/2019	...	2-4	Yes	LG	1/18/1963	MD
Massachusetts	Charlie Baker (R)	4	1/2015	1/2019	...	...	Yes	LG	7/31/1956	IL
Michigan	Rick Snyder (R)	4	1/2011	1/2019	1	2A	Yes	LG	8/19/1958	MI
Minnesota	Mark Dayton (D)	4	1/2011	1/2019	1	...	Yes	LG	1/26/1947	MN
Mississippi	Phil Bryant (R)	4	1/2012	1/2020	1	2A	Yes	LG	12/9/1954	MS
Missouri	Jay Nixon (D)	4	1/2009	1/2017	1	2A	No	LG	2/13/1956	MO
Montana	Steve Bullock (D)	4	1/2013	1/2017	...	2-16	Yes	LG	4/11/1966	MT
Nebraska	Pete Ricketts (R)	4	1/2015	1/2019	...	2-4	Yes	LG	5/12/1948	NE
Nevada	Brian Sandoval (R)	4	1/2011	1/2019	1	2A	No	LG	8/5/1963	CA
New Hampshire	Maggie Hassan (D)	2	1/2013	1/2017	1	...	(b)	PS	2/27/1958	MA
New Jersey	Chris Christie (R)	4	1/2010	1/2018	1	2-4	Yes	LG	9/6/1962	NJ
New Mexico	Susana Martinez (R)	4	1/2011	1/2019	1	2-4	Yes	LG	7/14/1959	TX
New York	Andrew Cuomo (D)	4	1/2011	1/2019	1	...	Yes	LG	12/6/1957	NY
North Carolina	Pat McCrory (R)	4	1/2013	1/2017	1	2-4	No	LG	10/17/1956	VA
North Dakota	Jack Dalrymple (R)	4	12/2010 (e)	12/2016	1	...	Yes	LG	10/16/1948	MN
Ohio	John Kasich (R)	4	1/2011	1/2019	1	2-4	Yes	LG	5/13/1952	PA
Oklahoma	Mary Fallin (R)	4	1/2011	1/2019	1	2-A	No	LG	12/9/1954	MO
Oregon	Kate Brown (D)	4	2/2015 (f)	1/2019	... (f)	2-12	(b)	SS	3/5/1947	MN
Pennsylvania	Tom Wolf (D)	4	1/2015	1/2019	...	2-4	Yes	LG	11/17/1948	PA
Rhode Island	Gina Raimondo (D)	4	1/2015	1/2019	...	2-4	No	LG	3/26/1953	RI
South Carolina	Nikki Haley (R)	4	1/2011	1/2019	1	2-4	No	LG	1/20/1972	SC

See footnotes at end of table.

THE GOVERNORS, 2016—Continued

State or other jurisdiction	Name and party	Length of regular term in years	Date of first service	Present term ends	Number of previous terms	Term limits	Joint election of governor and lieutenant governor (a)	Official who succeeds governor	Birthdate	Birthplace
South Dakota	Dennis Daugaard (R)	4	1/2011	1/2019	1	2-4	Yes	LG	6/11/1953	SD
Tennessee	Bill Haslam (R)	4	1/2011	1/2019	1	2-4	No	SpS (g)	8/23/1952	TN
Texas	Greg Abbott (R)	4	1/2015	1/2019	…	…	No	LG	3/4/1950	TX
Utah	Gary Herbert (R)	4	8/2009 (h)	1/2017	2	…	Yes	LG	5/7/1947	UT
Vermont	Peter Shumlin (D)	2	1/2011	1/2017	2	…	No	LG	3/24/1956	VT
Virginia	Terry McAuliffe (D)	4	1/2014	1/2018	…	1-4	No	LG	2/9/1957	NY
Washington	Jay Inslee (D)	4	1/2013	1/2017	…	…	No	LG	2/9/1951	WA
West Virginia	Earl Ray Tomblin (D)	4	11/2010 (i)	1/2017	1	2-4	(b)	PS (g)	3/15/1952	WV
Wisconsin	Scott Walker (R)	4	1/2011	1/2019	1	…	Yes	LG	11/2/1967	CO
Wyoming	Matt Mead (R)	4	1/2011	1/2019	1	2-16	(b)	SS	3/11/1962	WY
American Samoa	Lolo Matalasi Moliga (I)	4	1/2013	1/2017	1	2-4	Yes	LG	1949	AS
Guam	Eddie Calvo (R)	4	1/2011	1/2019	1	2-4	Yes	LG	8/29/1961	Guam
No. Mariana Islands	Eloy Inos (C)	4	2/2013 (j)	1/2019	1	2A	Yes	LG	11/27/1945	CNMI
Puerto Rico	Alejandro García Padilla (PDP)	4	1/2013	1/2017	…	(b)	(b)	SS	8/3/1971	PR
U.S. Virgin Islands	Kenneth Mapp (I)	4	1/2015	1/2019	…	2-4	Yes	LG	11/13/1957	USVI

Source: The Council of State Governments, November 2015.

Key:
C – Covenant
D – Democrat
I – Independent
PDP – Popular Democratic Party
R – Republican
LG – Lieutenant Governor
SS – Secretary of State
PS – President of the Senate
SpS – Speaker of the Senate
… – Not applicable
2A – Two terms, absolute.
2-4 – Two terms, re-eligible after four yrs.
2-12 – Two terms, eligible for eight out of 12 yrs.
2-16 – Two terms, eligible for eight out of 16 yrs.
1-4 – One term, re-eligible after four years.
(a) The following also choose candidates for governor and lieutenant governor through a joint nomination process: Florida, Kansas, Maryland, Minnesota, Montana, North Dakota, Ohio, Utah, American Samoa, Guam, No. Mariana Islands and U.S. Virgin Islands.
(b) No lieutenant governor.
(c) Gov. Brown previously served two terms as governor of California from 1975 to 1983. He was elected again in November 2010 and in November 2014 and is now serving his fourth and final term. California instituted absolute term-limits of two four-year terms for the office of governor in 1990. Those who served as governor prior to that date are eligible for re-election. Gov. Brown is now limited to completing his current term.

(d) Gov. Branstad was first elected in 1983 and served for four terms until 1999. He was elected to a fifth term in November of 2010 and sixth, and final, in 2014.
(e) Lt. Gov. Dalrymple was sworn in on December 21, 2010 to complete Gov. Hoeven's term as governor of North Dakota after Hoeven was elected to the Senate.
(f) Oregon Secretary of State Kate Brown became governor on February 18, 2015, following Gov. John Kitzhaber's resignation. A special gubernatorial election will be held in November 2016 to fill the position for the final two years of Gov. Kitzhaber's term.
(g) Official bears the additional title of "lieutenant governor."
(h) Lt. Gov. Gary Herbert was sworn in as governor on August 10, 2009 after Gov. Huntsman resigned to accept President Obama's appointment as Ambassador to China. Utah law states that a replacement governor elevated in a term's first year will face a special election at the next regularly scheduled general election, November 2010, instead of serving the remainder of the term. Gov. Herbert was elected to serve a full term in Nov. 2012.
(i) Senate President Earl Ray Tomblin was sworn in as governor on November 15, 2010 after Gov. Manchin was elected in the November election to fill Sen. Robert Byrd's seat. He was elected to a full term in November 2012.
(j) Northern Mariana Islands Lt. Gov. Eloy S. Inos became governor on Feb. 20, 2013, completing the unexpired term of Gov. Benigno Fitial following his resignation. Gov. Fitial was serving a five-year second term in office as governor instead of the normal four-year term. This was due to Senate Legislative Initiative 16-11, which changed future general elections to even-numbered years. Gov. Inos was elected in 2014 to a regular 4-year term.

Table 4.2
THE GOVERNORS: QUALIFICATIONS FOR OFFICE

State or other jurisdiction	Minimum age	State citizen (years)	U.S. citizen (years) (a)	State resident (years) (b)	Qualified voter (years)
Alabama	30	7	10	7	★
Alaska	30	★	7	7	★
Arizona	25	5	10	. . .	. . .
Arkansas	30	★	★	7	★
California	18	. . .	5	5	★
Colorado	30	. . .	★	2	. . .
Connecticut	30	6 months	★	★	★
Delaware	30	. . .	12	6	. . .
Florida	30	★	. . .	7	7
Georgia	30	. . .	15	6	. . .
Hawaii	30	. . .	5	5	★
Idaho	30	2	★	2	★
Illinois	25	3	★	3	★
Indiana	30	. . .	5	5	★
Iowa	30	2	2	2	★
Kansas	. . .	. . .	. . .	. . .	. . .
Kentucky	30	6	. . .	6	. . .
Louisiana	25	5	5	5	★
Maine	30	. . .	15	5	. . .
Maryland	30	. . .	(c)	5	5
Massachusetts	. . .	. . .	. . .	7	. . .
Michigan	30	. . .	★	★	4
Minnesota	25	. . .	★	1	★
Mississippi	30	★	20	5	★
Missouri	30	. . .	15	10	. . .
Montana	25	★	★	2	★
Nebraska	30	5	5	5	. . .
Nevada	25	2	. . .	2	★
New Hampshire	30	. . .	. . .	7	. . .
New Jersey	30	. . .	20	7	. . .
New Mexico	30	. . .	★	5	★
New York	30	. . .	★	5	. . .
North Carolina	30	. . .	5	2	★
North Dakota	30	. . .	★	5	★
Ohio	18	. . .	★	★	★
Oklahoma	31	. . .	10	10	(d)
Oregon	30	. . .	★	3	. . .
Pennsylvania	30	★	★	7	★
Rhode Island	18	30 days	30 days	30 days	30 days
South Carolina	30	5	5	5	. . .
South Dakota	18	★	★	★	★
Tennessee	30	7	★	. . .	. . .
Texas	30	. . .	★	5	. . .
Utah	30	5	3	5	★
Vermont	. . .	. . .	. . .	4	. . .
Virginia	30	★	★	★	5
Washington	18	. . .	★	★	★
West Virginia	30	5	★	★	★
Wisconsin	18	★	★	★	★
Wyoming	30	★	★	5	★
American Samoa	35	. . .	★	5	. . .
Guam	30	. . .	5	5	★
No. Mariana Islands	35	. . .	★	10	★
Puerto Rico	35	5	5	5	. . .
U.S. Virgin Islands	30	. . .	5	5	★

Source: The Council of State Governments' survey of governors' offices, November 2015.

Key:

★ — Formal provision; number of years not specified.

. . . — No formal provision.

(a) In some states you must be a U.S. citizen to be an elector, and must be an elector to run.

(b) In some states you must be a state resident to be an elector, and must be an elector to run.

(c) *Crosse v. Board of Supervisors of Elections* 243 Md. 555, 221 A.2d 431 (1966) — opinion rendered indicated that U.S. citizenship was, by necessity, a requirement for office.

(d) In order to file as a candidate for nomination by a political party to any state or county office, a person must have been a registered voter of that party for the six-month period preceding the first day of the filing period (26 O.S.§. 5 - 105A - A).

Table 4.3
THE GOVERNORS: COMPENSATION, STAFF, TRAVEL AND RESIDENCE

State or other jurisdiction	Salary	Governor's office staff (a)	Access to state transportation			Receives travel allowance	Reimbursed for travel expenses	Official residence
			Automobile	Airplane	Helicopter			
Alabama	(c)	40	★	★	★	...	★(b)	★
Alaska	145,000	71	★	★	...	...	★(b)	★
Arizona	95,000	29 (f)	★	★	...	...	★(b)	...
Arkansas	141,000	55	★	★	...	...	★	★
California	182,789	81	★	...	...	...	(d)	...
Colorado	90,000	50	★	★	...	★	★	(e)
Connecticut	150,000	27	★	...	...	...	...	(e)
Delaware	171,000	32	★	...	...	...	...	★
Florida	130,273	256 (f)	★	★(j)	...	(b)	(b)	★
Georgia	139,339	56 (f)	★	★	★	...	...	★
Hawaii	149,556	51	★	...	...	★	★	★
Idaho	122,597	18	★	★	...	...	★	...
Illinois	177,412	99	★	★	★	★	(d)	★
Indiana	111,688	34	★	★	★	★(b)	★(b)	★
Iowa	130,000	17	★	...	...	...	★	★
Kansas	99,636	24	★	★	★	...	★	★
Kentucky	140,070	45	★	★	★	...	★(b)	★
Louisiana	130,000	93 (f)	★	★	★	...	★	★
Maine	70,000	21	★	...	...	★	★	★
Maryland	170,000	85 (f)	★	★	★	(b)	(b)	★
Massachusetts	151,800	approx. 60	★	...	★	★(b)	★(b)	...
Michigan	159,300 (c)	73	★	★	★	(b)	(b)	★
Minnesota	127,150	35	★	★	★	...	★	★
Mississippi	122,160	29	★	★(k)	...	...	★	★
Missouri	133,821	21	★	★	...	(b)	(d)	★
Montana	111,569	58 (f)	★	★	★	...	★	★
Nebraska	105,000	9	★	★	...	★	★	★
Nevada	149,573	18 (f)	★	★	...	(b)	★(b)	★
New Hampshire	127,443	19	★	...	...	(b)	(d)	(e)
New Jersey	175,000	128	★	...	★	★	★(b)	★
New Mexico	110,000	33	★	★	★	...	★	★
New York	179,000 (c)	180	★	★	★	...	★	★
North Carolina	142,265	68	★	★	...	★	★	★
North Dakota	129,096	17	★	★	...	...	★	★
Ohio	148,304	60	★	★	★	(b)	(d)	(e)
Oklahoma	147,000	34	★	★	...	...(b)	★(b)	★
Oregon	98,600	65 (f)	★	...	...	★(b)	★(b)	★
Pennsylvania	190,823	68	★	★	...	...	★(b)	★
Rhode Island	132,710	38	★	...	★	...	(b)	...
South Carolina	106,078	16	★	★	...	...	★	★
South Dakota	109,264	18.75	★	★	...	...	★	★
Tennessee	187,500 (c)	36	★	★	★	★(b)	(d)	★
Texas	153,750	277	★	★	★	...	★	★
Utah	109,900	23	★	★	★	...	★	★
Vermont	145,538	14	★	★	...	★	...	...
Virginia	175,000	36	★	★	★	...	★	★
Washington	171,898	36	★	★	...	(b)	(d)	★
West Virginia	150,000	56	★	★	★	(b)	...	★
Wisconsin	147,328	25	★	★	...	...	(d)	★
Wyoming	105,000	29	★	★	...	...	★(b)	★
American Samoa	90,000	23	★	...	...	(b)	...	★
Guam	130,000	42	★	...	...	$218/day	...	★
No. Mariana Islands	70,000	16	★	...	...	(b)	...	★
Puerto Rico	70,000	28	★	(g)	(g)	...	★	★
U.S. Virgin Islands	150,000	84	★	...	...	...	★	★

See footnotes at end of table.

THE GOVERNORS: COMPENSATION, STAFF, TRAVEL AND RESIDENCE—Continued

Source: The Council of State Governments survey of governors' offices, October 2015 and March 2016.

Key:

★ — Yes

. . . — No

N.A. — Not available.

(a) Definitions of "governor's office staff" vary across the states–from general office support to staffing for various operations within the executive office.

(b) Travel expenses.

Alabama — According to state policy.

Alaska — $42/day per diem plus actual lodging expenses.

American Samoa — $105,000. Amount includes travel allowance for entire staff.

Arizona — Receives up to $59/day for meals based on location; receives per diem for lodging out of state; default $34/day for meals and $60/day lodging in state.

Florida — The Executive Office of the Governor allocates an annual budget for the governor's travel expenses. Gov. Scott is not reimbursed for personally incurred travel expenses. The Executive Office of the Governor pays the governor's travel expenses directly (hotel accommodations, meals, etc.) out of funds allocated for travel.

Guam — The amount varies based on destination but averages $218/per day.

Indiana — Statute allows $12,000 but due to budget cuts the amount has been reduced to $9,800 and reimbursed for actual expenses for travel/lodging.

Kentucky — Mileage at same rate as other state officials.

Maryland — Travel allowance included in office budget.

Massachusetts — As necessary.

Michigan — The Governor is provided a $54,000 annual expense allowance, as determined by the State Officers Compensation Commission in 2010. "Expense allowance" is for normal, reimbursable personal expenses such as food, lodging, and travel costs incurred by an individual in carrying out the responsibilities of state office.

Missouri — Amount includes travel allowance for entire staff. Amount not available.

Nevada — Amount includes travel allowance for entire staff. The following figures include travel expenses for governor and staff, $28,982 in state; $12,767 out of state. Reimbursed for travel expenses per GSA/Conus rate.

New Hampshire — Travel allowance included in office budget.

New Jersey — Reimbursement may be provided for necessary expenses.

Northern Mariana Islands — Travel allowance included in office budget. Governor has a "contingency account" that can be used for travel expenses and expenses in other departments or other projects.

Ohio — Set administratively.

Oklahoma — Reimbursed for actual and necessary expenses.

Oregon — $1,000 a month for expenses, not specific to travel. Reimbursed for actual travel expenses.

Pennsylvania — Reimbursed for reasonable expenses.

Rhode Island — The majority of travel expenses are not reimbursed since the State has centralized direct pay agreements with the various airlines/hotels for approved travel for state employees. If necessary, the governor is subject to the same per diem allowance for personal meals as other state employees, which is a maximum of $35 per day.

Tennessee — Travel allowance included in office budget.

Washington — Travel allowance included in office budget.

West Virginia — Included in general expense account.

Wyoming — Actual lodging and transportation/federal M&IE rates.

(c) Governor's salary:

Alabama — Gov. Robert Bentley is not accepting his salary, until the unemployment rate in Alabama drops.

Michigan — The Governor returns all but $1 of his salary.

New York Gov. Andrew Cuomo has reduced his salary by 5 percent.

Tennessee — Gov. Haslam returns his salary to the state.

(d) Information not provided.

(e) Governor's residence: Many governors are choosing to live in their own residences even when an official residence is provided .

Colorado — The governor chooses to live in his private home and allow cabinet members who live farther away to occupy the governor's mansion.

Connecticut — Provided by the Department of Administrative Services.

New Hampshire — The current governor does not occupy the official residence.

Ohio — The governor chooses not to live in the state provided housing.

(f) Governor's staff:

Arizona — There are 29 members of the governor's executive staff, not including administrative staff.

Florida — There are 256 full-time employees. Those are broken into the following areas: Executive Direction and Support Services — 104 positions; Systems Development and Design — 48 positions; Office of Policy and Budget — 104 positions.

Georgia — Full-time employees — 56 and 2 part-time employees.

Louisiana — Full-time employees — 93, part-time (non-student) — 21, students — 25.

Maryland — Full-time employees — 85 and 1 part-time employee.

Montana — Including 16 employees in the Office of Budget and Program Planning.

Nevada — Currently 18. Maximum permitted is 23.

Oregon — Of this total, 45 are true Governor's staff and 20 are on loan for agency staff.

Vermont — Voluntary 5 percent salary reduction.

(g) The Governor's office pays for access to an airplane or helicopter with a corporate credit card and requests a refund of those expenses with the corresponding documentation to the Dept. of Treasury.

(h) Provided for security reasons as determined by the state police.

(i) When not in use by other state agencies.

(j) Gov. Scott does not utilize a state-owned airplane, but instead uses his personal aircraft.

(k) Only for official business.

Table 4.4
THE GOVERNORS: POWERS

State or other jurisdiction	Budget making power		Item veto power					Authorization for reorganization through executive order (a)
	Full responsibility	Shares responsibility	Governor has item veto power on all bills	Governor has item veto power on appropriations only	Governor has no item veto power	Item veto — 2/3 legislators present or 3/5 elected to override	Item veto — majority legislators elected to override	
Alabama	★(b)	...	★	...	...	...	★	★
Alaska	★	...	...	★	...	★	...	★
Arizona	★(b)	★	...	★	...	...	(c)	★
Arkansas	...	...	...	★	...	...	★	...
California	★(b)	...	★	★	...	★	...	★(d)
Colorado	...	★	...	★	...	★	...	...
Connecticut	...	★	★	...	...	★	...	★(e)
Delaware	★(b)	★	★	★	...	★	...	★
Florida	...	★	...	★	...	★	...	★
Georgia	★	...	...	★	...	(c)	...	★
Hawaii	...	★	★	★	...	★	...	★
Idaho	...	★	...	★	...	★	...	...
Illinois	...	★	★	★	...	★	...	★
Indiana	...	★	★	★	...	...	...	★
Iowa	...	★	...	★	★	...	...	★
Kansas	★	...	...	★	...	★	...	★
Kentucky	★(b)	...	...	★	...	★	★(g)	★
Louisiana	...	★	...	★	...	★	★	★(h)
Maine	...	★	...	★	...	...	...	★
Maryland	★	...	★	★	...	★	...	★
Massachusetts	★(i)	...	★	★(j)	...	...	★(g)	...
Michigan	...	...	★	★	...	★(g)	★(g)	★
Minnesota	...	★	★	★	...	★	...	★(d)
Mississippi	...	★(k)	...	★	...	...	...	★(l)
Missouri	★(b)	...	...	★	...	★	...	★
Montana	★	...	...	★	...	★(g)	★(g)	★(m)
Nebraska	★	...	★	★	...	★(n)	...	...
Nevada	★(b)	...	...	...	★	...	...	★(o)
New Hampshire	★(b)	...	...	★	...	★	...	...
New Jersey	★(b)	...	...	★	...	★	★(g)	★(p)
New Mexico	...	...	★	★	...	★	...	...
New York	★	...	...	★	...	★	...	...
North Carolina	...	★	...	★	...	★	...	★(q)
North Dakota	★	★	...	★	...	★	...	★
Ohio	★	...	...	★	...	★	...	...
Oklahoma	...	...	...	★	...	...	★(g)	...
Oregon	...	★	...	★	★	...	...	★(q)
Pennsylvania	★	...	...	★	...	★	...	★(r)
Rhode Island	...	★	...	...	★	...	...	★
South Carolina	...	★	...	★	...	★	...	...

See footnotes at end of table.

THE GOVERNORS: POWERS—Continued

State or other jurisdiction	Budget making power — Full responsibility	Budget making power — Shares responsibility	Governor has item veto power on all bills	Governor has item veto power on appropriations only	Item veto power — Governor has no item veto power	Item veto — 2/3 legislators present or 3/5 elected to override	Item veto — majority legislators elected to override	Authorization for reorganization through executive order (a)
South Dakota	★	…	…	★	…	★(s)	…	★
Tennessee	…	★	…	★	…	…	★	★
Texas	…	★	…	★	…	★	…	★
Utah	★	…	…	★	…	★	…	★
Vermont	★	…	…	…	★	…	…	…
Virginia	★	…	…	★	…	★	…	★
Washington	★	…	★(t)	…	…	★	…	…
West Virginia	★	…	…	★(u)	…	★	…	…
Wisconsin	★(b)	…	…	★(u)	…	★(s)	…	…
Wyoming	…	★	…	★	…	★	…	…
American Samoa	★	…	…	…	…	…	…	★
Guam	★	…	★	…	…	★	…	★
No. Mariana Islands	…	★	…	★	…	★	…	★
Puerto Rico	…	★	…	★	…	★	…	★(f)
U.S. Virgin Islands	★	…	…	★	…	★	…	…

Source: The Council of State Governments' survey of governors' offices, October 2015.

Key:

★ — Yes; provision for.

… — No; not applicable.

(a) For additional information on executive orders, see Table 4.5.

(b) Full responsibility to propose; legislature adopts or revises and governor signs or vetoes.

(c) 2/3 of members to which each house is entitled are required to override veto.

(d) Authorization for reorganization provided for in state constitution.

(e) Governor cannot create a budgeted agency but may "direct such action by the several budgeted agencies as will, in his judgment, effect efficiency and economy in the conduct of the affairs of the state government."

(f) Only if it is not prohibited by law.

(g) 2/3 of elected legislators of each house to override.

(h) Only for agencies and offices within the Governor's Office.

(i) Governor has sole authority to propose annual budget. No money may be paid out of state treasury except in pursuance of appropriations made by law and passed by the legislature.

(j) Governor may veto any distinct item or items appropriating money in any appropriations bill.

(k) Governor has the responsibility of presenting a balanced budget. The budget is based on revenue estimated by the Governor's office and the Legislative Budget Committee.

(l) Statute provides for reorganization by the Commissioner of Administration with the approval of the governor.

(m) The office of the governor shall continuously study and evaluate the organizational structure, management practices, and functions of the executive branch and of each agency. The governor shall, by executive order or other means within the authority granted to him, take action to improve the manageability of the executive branch.

(n) 3/5 majority required to override line item veto.

(o) Only as to commissions, boards and councils.

(p) Executive reorganization plans can be disapproved by majority vote in both houses of the legislature.

(q) Executive Order must be approved by the legislature if changes affect existing law.

(t) The governor has the authority, through statute, to enact executive orders that: create agencies, boards and commissions; and reassigns agencies, boards and commissions to different cabinet secretaries. However, in order for the continued operation of any agency created by executive order, the state legislature must approve legislation that allows the agency to continue to operate; if not, the agency cannot continue operation beyond sine die adjournment of the legislature for the session.

(s) Requires 2/3 of legislators elected to override.

(u) In Wisconsin, governor has "partial" veto over appropriation bills. The partial veto is broader than item veto.

Table 4.5
GUBERNATORIAL EXECUTIVE ORDERS: AUTHORIZATION, PROVISIONS, PROCEDURES

State or other jurisdiction	Authorization for executive orders	Provisions								Procedures		
		Civil defense emergencies, public disasters	Energy emergencies and conservation	Other emergencies	Executive branch reorganization plans and agency creation	Create advisory, coordinating, study or investigative committees/commissions	Respond to federal programs and requirements	State personnel administration	Other administration	Filing and publication procedures	Subject to administrative procedure act	Subject to legislative review
Alabama	S,I, Case Law	★	★	★	★	★	…	…	…	★★	…	★
Alaska	C	★(a)	…	…	★(a)	…	…	…	…	★★	…	★
Arizona	I	★(a)	★(a)	★(a)	★(a)	★(a)	★(a)	★(a)	★(a)	★(b)	…	…
Arkansas	S,I, Common Law	★	★	★	★	★	★	★	★	★	★	…
California	I (q)	★	★	★	★	★	★	★	★	★	★	…
Colorado	C	★	★	★	★	★	★	★	★	★	…	…
Connecticut	C,S	★	★	★	★	★	★	★	…	(b)	★	…
Delaware	C	★	★	★	★	★	★	★	…	★	★	…
Florida	C,S	★	★	★	★	★	★	★	★	★	★	★
Georgia	S,I (d)	★	★	★	★	★	★	★	★	★	★	★
Hawaii	C,S, Common Practice	★	★	★	★	★	★	★	(g)	★	★	…
Idaho	S	★	★	★	…	★	★	★	…	★	★	★
Illinois	C,S	★	★	★	★	★	★	★	…	★	★	★
Indiana	C,S, Case Law	★	★	★	★(limited)	★	★	★	★	★	★	★
Iowa	(f)	★	★	…	…	★	★	★	…	★	…	★
Kansas	C,S	★	★	★(i)	★	★	★	★	…	★	…	…
Kentucky	C,S	★	★	★	★	★	★	★	★(j)(k)(l)	★(b)	…	(h)★
Louisiana	C,S (m)	★	★	★	★	★	★	★	…	★	…	…
Maine	I	★	★	★	★	★	★	★	…	★	…	…
Maryland	C,S	★	★	★	★	★	★	★	★(n)	★	★	…
Massachusetts	C,S	★	★	★	★	★	★	★	…	★	…	★(o)
Michigan	C	★	★	★	★(p)	★	★	★	…	★(p)	…	★(o)
Minnesota	S	★	★	★	★	★	★	★	…	★(b)	…	…
Mississippi	C,S	★	★	★	★	★	★	★	(bb)(r)	(s)	(s)	★(o)
Missouri	C,S, Common Law	★	★	★	★	★	★	★	★	★(o)	★	★(o)(t)
Montana	S,I, Common Law	★	★	★	…	★	★	…	…	★	…	…
Nebraska	C,S	★	★	★	…	★	★	…	★(k)	★(c)	…	★(o)
Nevada	S,I	★	★	★	★	★	★	★	★(u)	★	…	…
New Hampshire	S	★	★(a)	★	★	★	★	★	…	★	…	…
New Jersey	C,S,I	★	★	★	★	★	★	★	…	★	…	…
New Mexico	C,S	★	★	★	…	★	★	★	…	…	…	…
New York	C,S	★	★	★	…	★	★	★	…	…	…	…
North Carolina	C,S	★	★	★	…	★	★	★	…	…	…	…
North Dakota	S,I	★	★	★	★	★	★	★	(l)(r)(u)(w)(x)(y)	★	…	★(v)
Ohio	S,I (z)	★	★	(bb)(cc)(dd)(n)	(aa)	★	★	★	…	★	…	…
Oklahoma	C	★	★	★	…	★	★	★	…	★	…	…
Oregon	I	★	★	★	★	★	★	★★	★(dd)	★(b)(bb)	★	★
Pennsylvania	C,S	★	★	★	★	★	★	★	★	★	…	…
Rhode Island	S,I, Case Law	★	★	★	…	★	★	★	…	★	…	…
South Carolina	S	★	★	★	★	★	★	★	★	★	…	…

See footnotes at end of table.

GUBERNATORIAL EXECUTIVE ORDERS: AUTHORIZATION, PROVISIONS, PROCEDURES—Continued

State or other jurisdiction	Authorization for executive orders	Provisions — Civil defense disasters, public emergencies	Energy emergencies and conservation	Other emergencies	Executive branch reorganization plans and agency creation	Create advisory, coordinating, study or investigative committees/commissions	Respond to federal programs and requirements	State personnel administration	Other administration	Procedures — Filing and publication procedures	Subject to administrative procedure act	Subject to legislative review
South Dakota	C	★	★	★	★	★	★	★	★	★	…	★
Tennessee	S	★	★	★	★	★	★	★	★	★(b)	…	…
Texas	C,S,I	★	★	★	…	★	★	★	★	…	…	…
Utah	S,I	★	★	…	…	★	★	…	…	…	…	…
Vermont	S,I	★	★	★	★(ee)	…	★	★	…	…	…	★(ff)
Virginia	S	★	…	…	…	★	★	★	★	…	★	…
Washington	S	★	…	★	…	★	…	…	…	…	…	…
West Virginia	C,S	★	★	★	…	★	★	…	…	★	…	…
Wisconsin	C,S	★	★	…	…	★	…	…	…	…	…	…
Wyoming	(gg)	…	…	…	…	…	…	…	…	…	…	…
American Samoa	C,S	★	★	…	★	★	★	★	★	★(hh)	★(hh)	…
Guam	C	★	…	…	(ii)	★	★	★	★	…	…	…
No. Mariana Islands	C	★	…	★	★	★	★	★	★	…	…	…
Puerto Rico	C,S,I, Case Law	★	★	★	★	★	★	★	★	(jj)	…	…
U.S. Virgin Islands	S	★	★	★	★	★	★	★	★	…	…	…

Source: The Council of State Governments' survey of governors' offices, October 2015.

Key:
C — Constitutional
S — Statutory
I — Implied
★ — Formal provision.
… — No formal provision.

(a) Broad interpretation of gubernatorial authority. In Arizona, the governor is authorized to make executive orders in all of these areas and situations so long as there is not a conflicting statute in place.
(b) Executive orders must be filed with secretary of state or other designated officer.
(c) In addition to filing and publication procedures, Executive Orders are countersigned by and filed with the secretary of state and published.
(d) Implied from Constitution.
(e) Some implied.
(f) Constitution, statute, implied, case law, common law.
(g) Executive clemency.
(h) Only for EROs. When an ERO is submitted the legislature has 30 days to veto the ERO or it becomes law.
(i) To give immediate effect to state regulation in emergencies.
(j) To control administration of state contracts and procedures.
(k) To impound or freeze certain state matching funds.
(l) To reduce state expenditures in revenue shortfall.
(m) Inherent.
(n) To control procedures for dealing with public.
(o) Reorganization plans and agency creation.
(p) Executive reorganizations not effective if rejected by both houses of legislature within 60 calendar days. Executive orders reducing appropriations not effective unless approved by appropriations committees of both houses of legislature.

(q) Authorization implied from constitution and statute as recognized by 63 ops. Cal. Atty. Gen. 583.
(r) To assign duties to lieutenant governor; issue writ of special election.
(s) Governor is exempt from the Administrative Procedures Act and filing and administrative procedures Miss. Code Ann. § 25-43-102 (1972).
(t) Reorganization plans and agency creation and for meeting federal program requirements. To administer and govern the armed forces of the state.
(u) To administer and govern the armed forces of the state.
(v) Must submit to the secretary of state who must compile, index and publish Executive Orders. Copies must also be sent to President of the Senate, Speaker of House and Principal Clerk of each chamber.
(w) To suspend certain officials and/or other civil actions.
(x) To designate game and wildlife areas or other public areas.
(y) Appointive powers.
(z) Executive authority implied except for emergencies which are established by statute.
(aa) The governor has the authority, through state statute, to enact executive orders that: create agencies, boards and commissions; and reassigns agencies, boards and commissions to different cabinet secretaries. However, in order for the continued operation of any agency created by executive order, the state legislature must approve legislation that allows the agency to continue to operate; if not, the agency cannot continue operation beyond sine die adjournment of the legislature for the session.
(bb) Filing.
(cc) For fire emergencies.
(dd) To transfer funds in an emergency.
(ee) Subject to legislative approval when inconsistent with statute.
(ff) Only if reorganization order filed with the legislature.
(gg) No specific authorization granted, general authority only.
(hh) If executive order fits definition of rule.
(ii) Can reorganize, but not create.
(jj) Executive Orders are filed in the Department of State.

Table 4.6
STATE CABINET SYSTEMS

State or other jurisdiction	Authorization for cabinet system				Criteria for membership			Number of members in cabinet (including governor)	Frequency of cabinet meetings	Open cabinet meetings
	State statute	State constitution	Governor created	Tradition in state	Appointed to specific office (a)	Elected to specified office (a)	Gubernatorial appointment regardless of office			
Alabama	★	★	★	★	★	...	...	23	Quarterly	...
Alaska	...	...	★	...	★	...	★	19	Gov.'s discretion	★ (b)
Arizona	...	...	★	...	★	...	★	36	Monthly	...
Arkansas	...	...	★	...	★	...	...	44	Monthly	...
California	...	★	★	...	★	...	★	11	Every two weeks	...
Colorado	★	...	★	...	...	...	★	21	Monthly	...
Connecticut	★(k)	...	...	...	...	...	★	14	Gov.'s discretion	...
Delaware	★	...	...	...	★	...	★	19	Gov.'s discretion	...
Florida	★	★	...	...	...	★	...	4	Bi-weekly	★
Georgia							(d)			
Hawaii	★	★	...	...	★	...	★	20	Bi-monthly	...
Idaho	★	★	...	...	...	...	★	39	Gov.'s discretion	...
Illinois	★	★	...	...	...	...	★	18	N.A.	...
Indiana	...	...	★	...	...	...	★	16	Bi-monthly	...
Iowa	★	★	★	★	★	...	...	30	Monthly	...
Kansas	...	★	...	...	...	...	★	14	Bi-weekly	...
Kentucky	...	★	★	...	...	...	★	13	Quarterly	...
Louisiana	★	...	★	★	★	...	...	16	Monthly	...
Maine	...	...	...	★	...	...	★	16	Monthly	...
Maryland	★	...	...	...	★	...	...	25	Every other week	...
Massachusetts	...	★	...	...	★	...	...	10	Bi-weekly	...
Michigan	★	★	★	...	★	★	(e)	22	Gov.'s discretion	...
Minnesota	...	...	★	...	★	...	...	25	Quarterly	...
Mississippi							(d)			
Missouri	★	...	...	★	★	...	...	17	Gov.'s discretion	...
Montana	★	★	...	...	★	...	...	19	Monthly	★
Nebraska	...	...	★	★	★	...	★	30	Monthly	...
Nevada			(d)					21	At call of the governor	...
New Hampshire							(d)			
New Jersey	★	★	...	...	★	...	...	23	Gov.'s discretion	...
New Mexico	★	★	...	★	...	...	...	29	Gov.'s discretion	...
New York	...	...	...	★	...	...	★	75	Gov.'s discretion	...
North Carolina (f)			★	...	...	...	★	9	Weekly	(n)
North Dakota	...	...	★	...	...	...	★	18	Monthly	★
Ohio	★	...	...	...	★	...	...	24	Gov.'s discretion	★
Oklahoma	...	★	...	...	...	...	★	16 (h)	Monthly	...
Oregon							(d)			
Pennsylvania	★	★	★	...	★(i)	...	★	28	Gov.'s discretion	★
Rhode Island	...	...	★	★	...	...	★(l)	27	Gov.'s discretion	★(m)
South Carolina	★	★	...	...	★(i)	...	...	15	Monthly	★
South Dakota	★	★	...	...	★	...	...	19	Monthly	...
Tennessee	★	...	...	...	★	...	...	29	Monthly	...
Texas							(d)			
Utah	...	★	★	...	★	...	★	24	Monthly, weekly during legislative session	...
Vermont	★	★	...	...	★	...	...	12	Gov.'s discretion	...
Virginia	★	...	★	★	★	...	★(j)	15	Weekly	...
Washington	...	...	★	...	★	...	...	25	Monthly	...
West Virginia	...	...	★	★	★	...	...	10	Weekly	...
Wisconsin	...	★	...	...	★	...	...	16	Gov.'s discretion	★
Wyoming	...	...	★	...	...	...	★	48	Quarterly	...
American Samoa	★	★	...	...	★	...	★	16	Gov.'s discretion	★
Guam	...	...	★	...	★	...	...	55	Bi-monthly	...
No. Mariana Islands	...	★	...	...	★	...	...	17	Gov.'s discretion	★
Puerto Rico	★	★	...	...	...	...	★	10 (c)	Every 6 weeks	...
U.S. Virgin Islands	★	...	...	...	★	...	...	21	Monthly	★

See footnotes at end of table.

STATE CABINET SYSTEMS — Continued

Source: The Council of State Governments survey of governors' offices, November 2015.

Key:

★ — Yes

... — No

N.A. — Not available

(a) Individual is a member by virtue of election or appointment to a cabinet-level position.

(b) Except when in executive session.

(c) The Constitutional Cabinet has 10 members including the governor. There are other members of the Cabinet provided by statute.

(d) No formal cabinet system. In Nevada, the cabinet is traditionally comprised of Directors, Chairpersons and leaders of Nevada's top agencies, departments, institutions and the National Guard, in addition to the Lt. Governor.

(e) Membership determined by governor. Some officers formally designated as cabinet member by executive order.

(f) The Governor's Cabinet consists of eight department heads who have responsibility for the majority of the executive banch. They are appointed by the Governor and report to the Governor.

The Council of State exists as a separate body and is composed independently elected statewide officials who oversee certain areas of the executive branch. While the Council of State is provided for in the Constitution and state statutes, the Cabinet is created by the Govenor.

(g) Frequency of meetings may fluctuate with Governor's schedule.

(h) State statute allows for 15 cabinet members. With the Governor included there are 16 members.

(i) With the consent of the senate.

(j) Appointed by the governor and confirmed by each house.

(k) Governor's cabinet is specified in statute, but no longer in use. Governor directs department heads through commissioners' meetings and subject matter groups called clusters.

(l) At the discretion of the governor.

(m) Varies by meeting.

(n) Council of State, but not cabinent meetings, are open to the public.

Table 4.7
THE GOVERNORS: PROVISIONS AND PROCEDURES FOR TRANSITION

State or other jurisdiction	Legislation pertaining to gubernatorial transition	Appropriation available to gov-elect ($)	Gov-elect's participation in state budget for coming fiscal year	Gov-elect to hire staff to assist during transition	State personnel to be made available to assist gov-elect	Office space in buildings to be made available to gov-elect	Acquainting gov-elect staff with office procedures and routine office functions	Transfer of information (files, records, etc.)
Alabama	...	...	★	●	●	●	●	●
Alaska	●	●	...	●	●	●	●	★
Arizona	...	...	★	...	●	●	●	●
Arkansas	●	10,000	...	...	...	...	...	...
California	★	450,000	★	★	★	★	●	●
Colorado	★	10,000	★	★	★	★	●	★
Connecticut	★	★	★	★	★	★	★	★
Delaware	★	15,000	●	★	●	●	●	●
Florida	★	(b)	●	★	●	★	●	●
Georgia	★	50,000	●	★	★	★	●	★
Hawaii	★	50,000	★	★	●	★	●	●
Idaho	★	15,000	★	●	★	★	★	★
Illinois	...	...	...	★	...	★	★	★
Indiana	★	40,000	...	...	...	★	★	★
Iowa	●	100,000	★	●	●	●	●	★
Kansas	★	150,000 (c)	★	★	★	★	★	★
Kentucky	★	220,000	★	★	★	★	★	●
Louisiana	★	● 65,000	★	★	...	★	...	●
Maine	●	5,000	★	●	●	●	●	●
Maryland	★	●	...	★	★	★	●	★
Massachusetts	●	●	●	...	●	●	●	●
Michigan	●	$1.5 million ● (t)	...	●	●	●	●	●
Minnesota	★	(e)	★	★	★	★	●	★
Mississippi	●	★(f)	★	★	★	★	★	★
Missouri	★	100,000	★	★	●	★	●	●(g)
Montana	★	★	★	★	★	★	★	★
Nebraska	★	85,288	★	...	★	★	★	★
Nevada	★	Reasonable amount	★	★	...	★	...	★
New Hampshire	★	75,000	★	★	★	★	★	...
New Jersey	★	★(j)	●	★	★	★	●	★
New Mexico	★	(k)	★	★	★	★	★	★
New York	...	...	...	...	★	★	★	★
North Carolina	★	★(l)	...	★	●	★	★	★
North Dakota	●	10,000	(m)	(n)	●	...	●	★
Ohio	★	Unspecified (o)	●	★	●	...	●	★
Oklahoma	●	●	★	●	●	★	●	●
Oregon	★	★	★	★	★	★	★	★
Pennsylvania	★	...	...	★	●	●	●	...
Rhode Island	★	(s)	●	★	★	★	●	●
South Carolina	...	●	●	●	●	●	●	●
South Dakota	★	...	...	...	...	...	...	...
Tennessee	★	★	●	★	★	★	●	●
Texas	●	●	●	●	●	●	●	●
Utah	★	★(p)	★	★	★	★	★	★
Vermont	●	★(q)	★	...	★	...	...	...
Virginia	★	★(h)	★	★	★	★	★	★
Washington	★	★	●	★	●	★	●	●
West Virginia	...	●	...	●	...	●	●	●
Wisconsin	★	Unspecified	★	★	★	★	★	★
Wyoming	●	...	●	●	●	●	●	●
American Samoa	...	Unspecified	★(i)	★	●	●	★	●
Guam	★	(r)	...	...	★	★	★	★
No. Mariana Islands	★	Unspecified	...	★	★	★	★	★
Puerto Rico	★	...	★	★	★	★	★	★
U.S. Virgin Islands	★	100,000	...	★	★	★	★	★

See footnotes at end of table.

THE GOVERNORS: PROVISIONS AND PROCEDURES FOR TRANSITION — Continued

Source: The Council of State Governments' survey of governors' offices, November 2015.

Key:

... — No provisions or procedures.

★ — Formal provisions or procedures.

● — No formal provisions, occurs informally.

N.A. — Not applicable.

(a) Varies.

(b) Section 14.057, Florida Statute provides: Governor-elect; establishment of operating fund. — (1) There is established an operating fund for the use of the Governor-elect during the period dating from the certification of his or her election by the Elections Canvassing Commission to his or her inauguration as Governor. The Governor-elect during this period may allocate the fund to travel, expenses, his or her salary, and the salaries of the Governor-elect's staff as he or she determines. Such staff may include, but not be limited to, a chief administrative assistant, a legal adviser, a fiscal expert, and a public relations and information adviser. The salary of the Governor-elect and each member of the Governor-elect's staff during this period shall be determined by the Governor-elect, except that the total expenditures chargeable to the state under this section, including salaries, shall not exceed the amount appropriated to the operating fund. The Executive Office of the Governor shall supply to the Governor-elect suitable forms to provide for the expenditure of the fund and suitable forms to provide for the reporting of all expenditures therefrom. The Chief Financial Officer shall release moneys from this fund upon the request of the Governor-elect properly filed.

(c) Transition funds are used by both the incoming and outgoing administrations.

(d) Amount to be determined.

(e) 1.5% of amount appropriated for the fiscal year to the Governor's office.

(f) Miss. Code Ann. § 7-1-101 provides as follows: the governor's office of general services shall provide a governor-elect with office space and office equipment for the period between the election and inauguration. A special appropriation to the governor's office of general services is hereby authorized to defray the expenses of providing necessary staff employees and for the operation of the office of governor-elect during the period between the election and inauguration. The department of finance and administration shall make available to a governor-elect and his designated representatives information on the following: (a) all information and reports used in the preparation of the budget report; and (b) all information and reports on projected income and revenue estimates for the state.

(g) Activity is traditional and routine, although there is no specific statutory provision.

(h) Determined every 4 years.

(i) Can submit reprogramming or supplemental appropriation measure for current fiscal year.

(j) No specific amount — necessary services and facilities.

(k) Legislature required to make appropriation; no dollar amount stated in legislation.

(l) Governor receives $80,000 and lieutenant governor receives $10,000.

(m) Responsible for submitting budget for coming biennium.

(n) Governor usually hires several incoming key staff during transition.

(o) Determined in budget.

(p) Appropriated by legislature at the time of transition.

(q) Governor-elect entitled to 70% of Governor's salary.

(r) Appropriations given upon the request of governor-elect.

(s) The governor's transition team was authorized $130,000 for transition costs during the 2014–2015 transition. Approximately $120,000 was spent.

(t) Typically the appropriation is included in the budget but may fluctuate in size.

Table 4.8
IMPEACHMENT PROVISIONS IN THE STATES

State or other jurisdiction	Governor and other state executive and judicial officers subject to impeachment	Legislative body which holds power of impeachment	Vote required for impeachment	Legislative body which conducts impeachment trial	Chief justice presides at impeachment trial (a)	Vote required for conviction	Official who serves as acting governor if governor impeached (b)	Legislature may call special session for impeachment
Alabama	★	H	maj. mbrs.	S		majority of elected mbrs.	LG	★
Alaska	★	S	2/3 mbrs.	H	(c)	2/3 mbrs.	LG	★★
Arizona	★(d)	H	maj. mbrs.	S	★(e)	2/3 mbrs.	SS	★★
Arkansas	★	H	maj. mbrs.	S	...	2/3 mbrs.	LG	...
California	★	S	...	S	...	2/3 mbrs.	LG	...
Colorado	★	H	maj. mbrs.	S		2/3 mbrs.	LG	...
Connecticut	★	H	maj. mbrs.	S	★(f)	2/3 mbrs. must be present	LG	★
Delaware	★	H	2/3 mbrs.	S	★	2/3 mbrs.	LG	...
Florida	★	H	2/3 mbrs.	S	★(g)	2/3 mbrs. present (h)	LG (i)	...
Georgia	★	H	...	S	★(e)	2/3 mbrs.	...	★(j)
Hawaii	★	H	2/3 mbrs.	S	...	2/3 mbrs.	LG	★
Idaho	★	H	2/3 mbrs. (k)	S	★	2/3 mbrs.	LG	...
Illinois	★(l)	H	2/3 mbrs.	S	★	2/3 mbrs.	LG	★
Indiana	★	H	2/3 mbrs.	S	...	2/3 mbrs.	LG	...
Iowa	★	H	maj. mbrs.	S	...	majority of elected mbrs.	LG	★
Kansas	★	H	(m)	S	...	2/3 mbrs.	LG	...
Kentucky	★	H	(n)	S	★	2/3 mbrs. present	LG	...
Louisiana	★	H	maj. mbrs.	S	...	(n)	LG	...
Maine	★	H	maj. mbrs.	S	...	2/3 mbrs. present	PS	★★
Maryland	★	H	2/3 mbrs. present	S	...	2/3 mbrs.	LG	...
Massachusetts	★	H	maj. mbrs.	S	...	2/3 mbrs. present	LG	★
Michigan	★	H	maj. mbrs.	S	★		LG	...
Minnesota	★	H	maj. mbrs.	S	...	2/3 mbrs. present	PS	...
Mississippi	★	H	2/3 mbrs.	S	★(r)	2/3 mbrs.	LG	...
Missouri	★	H	2/3 mbrs. present	(t)	★(t)	2/3 mbrs. present (s)	LG	(u)
Montana	★	H	2/3 mbrs.	S	★	2/3 mbrs.	LG	★
Nebraska	★(d)	S (v)	maj. mbrs.	(w)	(w)	(w)	LG	...
Nevada	★(d)	H	maj. mbrs.	S	★	2/3 mbrs.	LG	...
New Hampshire	★	H	...	S	★	...	PS	...
New Jersey	★	H	maj. mbrs.	S	★	2/3 mbrs.	LG	★(aa)
New Mexico	★	H	maj. mbrs.	S	★(p)	2/3 mbrs. present	LG	★
New York	★	H	maj. mbrs.	S	★	2/3 mbrs. present	LG	★★
North Carolina	★(d)	H	2/3 mbrs.	S	★(x)	2/3 mbrs. present	LG	★★
North Dakota	★(d)	H	maj. mbrs.	S	...	2/3 mbrs.	LG	...
Ohio	★	H	maj. mbrs.	S	...	2/3 mbrs. present	LG	...
Oklahoma	★	S	maj. mbrs.	S	★	2/3 mbrs. present	LG	★
Oregon	.... (y)			H & S				
Pennsylvania	★	H	2/3 maj. mbrs.	S	★	2/3 maj. mbrs.	LG	★
Rhode Island	★	H	maj. mbrs.	S	...	2/3 maj. mbrs.	LG	★★
South Carolina	★	H	2/3 mbrs.	S	★	2/3 mbrs.	LG	...

See footnotes at end of table.

IMPEACHMENT PROVISIONS IN THE STATES—Continued

State or other jurisdiction	Governor and other state executive and judicial officers subject to impeachment	Legislative body which holds power of impeachment	Vote required for impeachment	Legislative body which conducts impeachment trial	Chief justice presides at impeachment trial (a)	Vote required for conviction	Official who serves as acting governor if governor impeached (b)	Legislature may call special session for impeachment
South Dakota	★	H	maj. mbrs.	S	★	2/3 mbrs.	LG	★
Tennessee	★	H	maj. mbrs.	S	...	2/3 mbrs. (z)	PS	★
Texas	★	H (o)	maj. mbrs.	S	...	2/3 mbrs. present	LG	...
Utah	★	H	2/3 mbrs.	S	★(f)	2/3 mbrs.	LG	★
Vermont	★	H	2/3 mbrs.	S	...	2/3 mbrs.	LG	...
Virginia	★	H	maj. mbrs.	S	...	2/3 mbrs. present	LG	★
Washington	★(d)	H	maj. mbrs.	S	★	2/3 mbrs.	LG	...
West Virginia	★	H	...	S	★	2/3 mbrs.	PS	★
Wisconsin	★	H	maj. mbrs.	S	...	2/3 mbrs.	LG	...
Wyoming	★	H	maj. mbrs.	S	★	2/3 mbrs.	SS	★
Dist. of Columbia				(p)				...
American Samoa	(q)	H	2/3 mbrs.	S	★	2/3 mbrs.	...	...
Guam	...			(p)				...
No. Mariana Islands	★	H	2/3 mbrs.	S	...	2/3 mbrs.	-LG	...
Puerto Rico	★	H	2/3 mbrs.	S	★	3/4 mbrs.	SS	★
U.S. Virgin Islands				(p)				

Source: The Council of State Governments survey of governors' offices, November 2015.

Key:
★ – Yes, provision for.
... – Not specified, or no provision for.
H – House or Assembly (lower chamber).
S – Senate.
LG – Lieutenant Governor.
PS – President or Speaker of the Senate.
SS – Secretary of State.

(a) Presiding justice of state court of last resort. In many states, provision indicates that chief justice presides only on occasion of impeachment of governor.
(b) For provisions on official next in line of succession if governor is convicted and removed from office, refer to Chapter 4, "The Governors."
(c) An appointed Supreme Court justice presides.
(d) With exception of certain judicial officers. In Arizona and Washington—justices of courts not of record. In Nevada—justices of the peace, justices of the peace, and police magistrates.
(e) Should the Chief Justice be on trial, or otherwise disqualified, the Senate shall elect a judge of the Supreme Court to preside.
(f) Only if governor is on trial.
(g) Except in a trial of the chief justice, in which case the governor shall preside.
(h) An officer impeached by the House of Representatives shall be disqualified from performing any official duties until acquitted by the Senate, and, unless impeached, the governor may by appointment fill the office until completion of the trial.
(i) Governor may appoint someone to serve until the impeachment procedures are final.
(j) Special sessions of the General Assembly shall be limited to a period of 40 days unless extended by 3/5 vote of each house and approved by the governor or unless at the expiration of such period an impeachment trial of some officer of state government is pending, in which event the House shall adjourn and the Senate shall remain in session until such trial is completed.

(k) No person shall be convicted without the concurrence of two-thirds of the senators elected. When the governor is impeached, the chief justice shall preside.
(l) Judges not included.
(m) No statute, simple majority is the assumption.
(n) Concurrence of 2/3 of the elected senators.
(o) House votes on articles of impeachment; Senate presides over impeachment trial to remove official.
(p) Removal of elected officials by recall procedure only.
(q) Governor, lieutenant governor.
(r) When the governor is tried; if Chief Justice is unable to preside, the next longest serving justice shall preside.
(s) No person shall be convicted without concurrence of 2/3 of all senators present. Miss Const. 1890 Art. IV § 52.
(t) All impeachments are tried before the state Supreme Court, except that the governor or a member of the Supreme Court is tried by a special commission of seven eminent jurists to be elected by the Senate. A vote of 5/7 of the court of special commission is necessary to convict.
(u) It is implied but not addressed directly in Miss Const. 1890 Art. IV §§ 49–53.
(v) Unicameral legislature; members use the title "senator."
(w) Court of impeachment is composed of chief justice and supreme court. A vote of 2/3 present of the court is necessary to convict.
(x) Chief Justice presides if it is the governor or lieutenant governor; otherwise, the president of the Senate presides.
(y) No provision for impeachment. Public officers may be tried for incompetence, corruption, malfeasance, or delinquency in office in same manner as criminal offenses.
(z) Vote of 2/3 of members sworn to try the officer impeached.
(aa) In the event of simultaneous vacancies in both the offices of governor and lieutenant governor resulting from any cause, the president of the Senate shall become governor until a new governor or lieutenant governor is elected and qualifies.

Table 4.9
CONSTITUTIONAL AND STATUTORY PROVISIONS FOR
NUMBER OF CONSECUTIVE TERMS OF ELECTED STATE OFFICIALS
(All terms are four years unless otherwise noted)

State or other jurisdiction	Governor	Lt. Governor	Secretary of state	Attorney general	Treasurer	Auditor	Comptroller	Education	Agriculture	Labor	Insurance
Alabama	2 C	2 C	2 C	2 C	2 C	2 C	...	2 C	2 C	...	...
Alaska	2 C	2	(a)	...	(b)	...	...	...	...	...	...
Arizona	2 C	(c)	2	2	2	...	...	2	...	...	...
Arkansas	2 T	2 T	2 T	2 T	2 T	2 T	...	...	...	...	...
California	2 T	2 T	2 T	2 T	2 T	...	2 T	2 T	...	...	2 T
Colorado	2 C	2 C	2 C	2 C	2 C	...	...	...	...	...	...
Connecticut	N	N	N	N	N	...	N	...	...	...	...
Delaware	2 T	2 T	...	N	N	N	...	...	...	...	N
Florida	2 C	2 C	N	2 C	2 C (d)	...	2 C (d)	N	2 C	...	2 C (d)
Georgia	2 C	N	N	N	...	...	...	N	N	N	N
Hawaii	2 C	2 C	(a)	...	...	...	...	...	...	...	...
Idaho	N	N	N	N	N	...	2 C	N	...	...	...
Illinois	N	N	N	N	N	...	N	...	...	...	...
Indiana	2 (e)	2C	2 (e)	...	2 (e)	2 (e)	(f)	...	...	...	...
Iowa	N	N	N	N	N	N	...	...	N	...	...
Kansas	2 C	2 C	N	N	N	...	...	...	...	...	N
Kentucky	2 C	2 C	2 C	2 C	2 C	2 C	...	...	2 C	2 C	...
Louisiana	2 C	N	N	N	N	...	...	N	N	...	N
Maine	2 C	(g)	...	...	...	...	...	...	...	...	...
Maryland	2 C	N	...	N	...	...	N	...	...	...	...
Massachusetts	N	N	N	N	N	N	...	...	...	...	...
Michigan	2 T	2 T	2 T	2 T	...	...	...	...	...	...	...
Minnesota	N	N	N	N	...	N	...	...	...	...	(h)
Mississippi	2 T	2 T	N	N	N	N	...	...	...	...	...
Missouri	2 T	N	N	N	2 T	N	...	...	...	...	...
Montana	2 (i)	2 (i)	2 (i)	2 (i)	...	2 (i)	...	2 (i)	...	...	...
Nebraska	2 C	2 C	N	N	2 C	N	...	...	...	...	...
Nevada	2 T	2 T	2 T	2 T	2 T	...	2 T	...	...	...	...
New Hampshire	N (j)	...	...	...	...	...	...	...	...	...	...
New Jersey	2 C	2 C	...	...	...	...	...	...	...	...	...
New Mexico	2 C	2 C	2 C	2 C	2 C	2 C	...	...	...	...	...
New York	N	N	...	N	...	N (k)	N	...	...	...	...
North Carolina	2 C	2 C	N	N	N	N	...	N	N	N	N
North Dakota	N	N	N	N	N	N	...	N	N	N	N
Ohio	2 C	2 C	2 C	2 C	2 C	2 C	...	...	...	...	...
Oklahoma	2 (l)	N	...	N	N	N	...	N	...	N	N
Oregon	2 (e)	(m)	2 (e)	N	2 (e)	...	...	...	...	...	...
Pennsylvania	2 C	2 C	...	2 C	2 C (n)	2 C	...	...	...	...	...
Rhode Island	2 C	2 C	2 C	2 C	2 C	...	...	...	...	...	...
South Carolina	2 C	2 C	N	N	N	...	N	N	N	...	...
South Dakota	2 C	2 C	2 C	2 C	2 C	2 C	...	2 C	...	...	...
Tennessee	2 C	(f)	...	(o)	...	...	...	...	N	...	...
Texas	N	N	...	N	(k)	...	...	N	...	...	...
Utah	N	N	(a)	N	N	N	...	...	...	...	...
Vermont	N (j)	N (j)	N (j)	N (j)	N (j)	N (j)	...	...	...	...	...
Virginia	1 C	N	...	N	...	...	...	...	...	...	...
Washington	N	N	N	N	N	N	...	N	...	...	...
West Virginia	2 C	N (g)	N	N	N	...	N	...	N	...	...
Wisconsin	N	N	N	N	N	...	...	N	...	...	...
Wyoming	2 (i)	(m)	N	...	N	N	...	N	...	...	...
Dist. of Columbia	N (p)	...	...	...	...	...	...	...	...	...	...
American Samoa	2 C	2 C	(a)	...	...	...	(q)	...	...	...	...
Guam	2 C	2 C	(a)	2 C	...	2 C	(r)	...	...	...	...
No. Mariana Islands	2 T	2 T	...	...	...	2 T	(q)	...	...	...	(h)
Puerto Rico	N	(m)	...	...	...	...	...	...	...	...	...
U.S. Virgin Islands	2 C	2 C	(k)	...	(c)	...	(c)	...	...	...	(a)

See footnotes at end of table.

CONSTITUTIONAL AND STATUTORY PROVISIONS FOR
NUMBER OF CONSECUTIVE TERMS OF ELECTED STATE OFFICIALS — Continued
(All terms are four years unless otherwise noted)

Source: The Council of State Governments, November 2015.

Note: All terms last four years unless otherwise noted. Footnotes specify if a position's functions are performed by an official under a different title.

Key:

N — No provision specifying number of terms allowed.

C — Consecutive Terms

T — Total Terms

. . . — Position is appointed or elected by governmental entity (not chosen by the electorate).

(a) Lieutenant Governor performs this function.

(b) Deputy Commissioner of Department of Revenue performs function.

(c) Finance Administrator performs function.

(d) Chief Financial Officer performs this function as of January 2003.

(e) Eligible for eight years out of any period of twelve years.

(f) State auditor performs this function.

(g) President or Speaker of the Senate is next in line of succession to the governorship. In Tennessee and West Virginia, Speaker of the Senate has the statutory title " Lieutenant Governor".

(h) Commerce administrator performs this function.

(i) Eligible for eight out of sixteen years.

(j) Two-year term.

(k) Comptroller performs this function.

(l) Limited to 8 years per office during a lifetime.

(m) Secretary of State is next in line to the governorship.

(n) Treasurer must wait four years before being eligible for the office of auditor general.

(o) Term is 8 years; attorney general is appointed by the state Supreme Court.

(p) Mayor.

(q) State treasurer performs this function.

(r) General services administrator performs function.

Table 4.10
SELECTED STATE ADMINISTRATIVE OFFICIALS: METHODS OF SELECTION

State or other jurisdiction	Governor	Lieutenant governor	Secretary of state	Attorney general	Treasurer	Adjutant general	Administration	Agriculture	Auditor	Banking
Alabama	CE	CE	CE	CE	CE	G	G	SE	CE	GS
Alaska	CE	CE	(a-1)	GB	AG	GB	GB	AG	L	AG
Arizona	CE	(a-2)	CE	CE	CE	GS	GS	GS	L	GS
Arkansas	CE	CE	CE	CE	CE	G	G	BG	CE	GS
California	CE	CE	CE	CE	CE	GS	...	G	GB	GS
Colorado	CE	CE	CE	CE	CE	GS	GS	GS	L	A
Connecticut	CE	CE	CE	CE	CE	GE	GE	GE	(b)	GE
Delaware	CE	CE	GS	CE	CE	GS	(c)	GS	CE	GS
Florida	CE	CE	GS	CE	CE	GS	GS	CE	L	CE
Georgia	CE	CE	CE	CE	G	G	G	CE	CL	G
Hawaii	CE	CE	N.O.	GS	GS	GS	N.O.	GS	CL	AG
Idaho	CE	CE	CE	CE	CE	GS	GS	GS	N.O.	(a-24)
Illinois	CE	CE	CE	CE	CE	GS	GS	GS	CL	GS
Indiana	CE	CE	CE	SE	CE	G	G	LG	CE	G
Iowa	CE	CE	CE	CE	CE	GS	GS	CE	CE	GS
Kansas	CE	CE	CE	CE	CE	GS	GS	GS	N.A.	GS
Kentucky	CE	CE	CE	CE	CE	G	N.O.	CE	CE	G
Louisiana	CE	CE	CE	CE	CE	GS	GS	CE	GS	GS
Maine	CE	N.O.	CL	CL	CL	GLS	GLS	GLS	L	GLS
Maryland	CE	CE	GS	CE	CL	G	GS	GS	N.A.	AG
Massachusetts	CE	CE	CE	CE	CE	G	G	CG	CE	G
Michigan	CE	CE	CE	CE	GS	GS	GS	GS	CL	GS
Minnesota	CE	CE	CE	CE	(a-24)	GS	GS	GS	CE	A
Mississippi	CE	CE	CE	CE	CE	GE	GS	SE	CE	GS
Missouri	CE	CE	CE	CE	CE	GS	GS	GS	CE	GS
Montana	CE	CE	CE	CE	GS	GS	GS	GS	CE	A
Nebraska	CE	CE	CE	CE	CE	GS	GS	BG	CE	GS
Nevada	CE	CE	CE	CE	CE	G	G	BG	N.O.	A
New Hampshire	CE	(e)	CL	CL	GC	GC	GC	GC	...	GC
New Jersey	CE	CE	(a-1)	GS	GS	GS	N.O.	BG	(g)	GS
New Mexico	CE	CE	CE	CE	CE	G	(a-26)	A	CE	N.A.
New York	CE	CE	GS	CE	GS	G	G	GS	CE	GS
North Carolina	CE	CE	CE	CE	CE	A	G	CE	CE	G
North Dakota	CE	CE	CE	CE	CE	G	N.O.	CE	CE	GS
Ohio	CE	CE	CE	CE	CE	G	GS	GS	CE	A
Oklahoma	CE	CE	GS	CE	CE	GS	GS	GS	CE	GS
Oregon	CE	(a-2)	CE	SE	CE	G	GS	GS	SS	N.O.
Pennsylvania	CE	CE	GS	CE	CE	GS	G	GS	CE	GS
Rhode Island	SE	SE	CE	SE	SE	GS	GS	GS	LS	GS
South Carolina	CE	CE	CE	CE	CE	CE	B	CE	B	A
South Dakota	CE	CE	CE	CE	CE	GS	GS	GS	L	AB
Tennessee	CE	CL (e)	CL	CT	CL	G	G	G	(a-14)	G
Texas	CE	CE	G	CE	(a-14)	G	A	SE	L	B
Utah	CE	CE	(a-1)	CE	CE	GS	GS	GS	CE	GS
Vermont	CE	CE	CE	SE	CE	SL	GS	GS	CE	GS
Virginia	CE	CE	GB	CE	GB	GB	GB	GB	SL	B
Washington	CE	CE	CE	CE	CE	G	G	G	CE	G
West Virginia	CE	(e)	CE	CE	CE	GS	GS	CE	CE	GS
Wisconsin	CE	CE	CE	CE	CE	G	GS	GS	LS	A
Wyoming	CE	(a-2)	CE	GS	CE	G	GS	GS	CE	AG
American Samoa	CE	CE	(a-1)	GB	GB	N.A.	GB	GB	N.A.	N.A.
Guam	CE	CE	...	CE	CS	GS	GS	GS	CE	GS
No. Mariana Islands	CE	CE	...	GS	CS	...	G	...	GB	C
Puerto Rico	CE	...	GS	GS	GS	GS	...	GS	GS	GS
U.S. Virgin Islands	SE	SE	(a-1)	GS	GS	GS	GS	GS	GS	LG

Source: The Council of State Governments' survey of state personnel agencies and state websites, April 2016.

Key:
N.A. — Not available.
N.O. — No office.
... — No specific chief administrative official or agency in charge of function.
CE — Constitutional, elected by public.
CL — Constitutional, elected by legislature.
SE — Statutory, elected by public.
SL — Statutory, elected by legislature.
L — Selected by legislature or one of its organs.
CT — Constitutional, elected by state court of last resort.
CP — Competitve process.

Appointed by:
G — Governor
GS — Governor .... Senate (in Neb., unicameral legislature)
GB — Governor .... Both houses
GE — Governor .... Either house
GC — Governor .... Council
GD — Governor .... Departmental board
GLS — Governor .... Appropriate legislative committee and Senate

Approved by:
GOC — Governor and
        Council or cabinet
LG — Lieut. Governor
LGS — Lieut. Governor...... Senate
AT — Attorney General
ATS — Attorney General ...Senate
SS — Secretary of State

SELECTED STATE ADMINISTRATIVE OFFICIALS: METHODS OF SELECTION — Continued

State or other jurisdiction	Budget	Civil rights	Commerce	Community affairs	Comptroller	Consumer affairs	Corrections	Economic development	Education	Election admin.
Alabama	CS	N.O.	G	G	CS	CS	G	(a-12)	B	CS
Alaska	G	GB	GB	(a-12)	AG	(a-12)	GB	(a-12)	BG	LG
Arizona	G	N.A.	B	N.A.	A	N.A.	GS	B	CE	(a-2)
Arkansas	AG	N.O.	N.O.	N.A.	N.O.	N.O.	B	GS	BG	B
California	(a-24)	...	...	GS	CE	G	GS	...	CE	G
Colorado	G	A	N.O.	A	A	AT	GS	G	AB	CS
Connecticut	CS	GE	GE	GE	CE	GE	GE	GE	GE	CS
Delaware	GS	CG	(a-2)	N.O.	CG	AT	GS	GS	GS	GS
Florida	G	A	N.A.	A	CE	A	GS	GS	B	A
Georgia	G	G	B	GD	N.O.	BG	GD	G	CE	A
Hawaii	GS	B	GS	N.O.	GS	A	GS	GS	B	B
Idaho	GS	B	GS	N.O.	CE	(a-3)	B	(a-12)	CE	(a-2)
Illinois	G	GS	GS	(a-12)	CE	(a-3)	GS	(a-12)	B	B
Indiana	G	G	G	G	(a-8)	AT	G	G	CE	(b)
Iowa	GS	GS	N.O.	A	N.O.	AT	GS	GS	GS	SS
Kansas	G	B	GS	C	C	AT	GS	C	B	CE
Kentucky	G	B	G	G	CG	AT	G	GC	B	B
Louisiana	CS	B	GS	G	GS	A	GS	GS	BG	A
Maine	A	B	(a-17)	(a-17)	A	GLS	GLS	GLS	GLS	SS
Maryland	GS	G	GS	N.O.	CE	A	GS	GS	B	B
Massachusetts	C	G	G	G	G	G	CG	G	B	CE
Michigan	GS	B	GS	N.O.	CS	N.O.	GS	(l)	B	(b)
Minnesota	(a-24)	GS	GS	(a-17)	(a-24)	A	GS	GS	GS	(a-2)
Mississippi	(a-6)	N.O.	SE	A	(a-6)	A	GS	GS	BS	A
Missouri	AGS	B	GS	A	A	CE	GS	GS	B	SS
Montana	G	CP	GS	CP	CP	CP	GS	G	CE	SS
Nebraska	A	B	GS	A	A	CE	GS	GS	B	A
Nevada	(a-5)	G	G	N.O.	CE	A	G	G	G	(b)
New Hampshire	GC	CS	GC	N.O.	AGC	AGC	GC	AGC	B	CL
New Jersey	GS	A	(a-17)	GS	GS	A	GS	G	GS	A
New Mexico	G	N.A.	(a-17)	N.A.	N.A.	AT	GS	GS	GS	CE
New York	G	GS	GS	GS	CE	GS	GS	GS	B	(b)
North Carolina	(a-24)	A	G	A	G	(i)	G	A	CE	G
North Dakota	A	G	G	N.O.	A	AT	G	N.A.	CE	SS
Ohio	GS	B	GS	A	GS	A	GS	GS	B	CE
Oklahoma	A	B	GS	(i)	A	B	B	GS	CE	L
Oregon	A	A	GS	G	A	GS	GS	GS	SE	A
Pennsylvania	G	B	G	G	G	AT	GS	GS	GS	AG
Rhode Island	A	B	GS	N.O.	A	SE	GS	GS (j)	B	B
South Carolina	A	B	GS	N.A.	CE	B	GS	GS	CE	B
South Dakota	CP	CP	(a-44)	(a-48)	(a-40)	AT	GS	GS	GS	SS
Tennessee	A	G	G	G	SL	A	G	G	G	A
Texas	G	B	G	G	CE	(i)	B	G	B	(b)
Utah	G	A	GS	GS	AG	GS	GS	A	B	A
Vermont	CG	AT	GS	CG	CG	AT	CG	CG	GS	CE
Virginia	GB	AT	GB	GB	GB	A	GB	B	GB	GB
Washington	(a-14)	I	G	(a-12)	G	(a-3)	G	(a-12)	CE	(a-2)
West Virginia	CS	GS	GS	B	(a-8)	(a-13)	GS	(a-13)	B	(a-2)
Wisconsin	A	A	GS	A	A	A	GS	CS	CE	B
Wyoming	AG	CS	GS	N.A.	(a-8)	SS	GS	(a-13)	CE	A
American Samoa	GB	N.A.	GB	(a-12)	(a-4)	(a-3)	A	(a-12)	GB	G
Guam	GS	...	GS	...	CS	CS	GS	B	B	GS
No. Mariana Islands	G	A	GS	GS	C	GS	C	C	B	B
Puerto Rico	G	N.A.	GS	N.A.	GB	GS	GS	GS	GS	N.A.
U.S. Virgin Islands	GS	GS	GS	GS	(a-24)	GS	GS	GS	GS	B

Appointed by:
C — Cabinet Secretary
CG — Cabinet Secretary.........Governor
A — Agency head
AB — Agency head................Board
AG — Agency head................Governor
AGC — Agency head.............Governor and Council
AGS — Agency head.............Senate
ALS — Agency head..............Appropriate legislative committee
ASH — Agency head.............Senate president and House speaker
B — Board or commission
BG — Board ....Governor
BGS — Board ....Governor and Senate
BS — Board or commission ....Senate
BA — Board or commission ... Agency head
CS — Civil Service
LS — Legislative Committee ..Senate

Approved by:

(a) Chief administrative official or agency in charge of function:
(a-1) Lieutenant governor.
(a-2) Secretary of state.
(a-3) Attorney general.
(a-4) Treasurer.
(a-5) Adjutant general.
(a-6) Administration.
(a-7) Agriculture.
(a-8) Auditor.
(a-9) Banking.
(a-10) Budget.
(a-11) Civil rights.
(a-12) Commerce.
(a-13) Community affairs.
(a-14) Comptroller.
(a-15) Consumer affairs.
(a-16) Corrections.

SELECTED STATE ADMINISTRATIVE OFFICIALS: METHODS OF SELECTION — Continued

State or other jurisdiction	Emergency management	Employment services	Energy	Environmental protection	Finance	Fish & wildlife	General services	Health	Higher education	Highways
Alabama	G	CS	CS	B	G	CS	CS	B	B	G
Alaska	AG	AG	(k)	GB	AG	GB	AG	GB	B	AG
Arizona	G	A	A	GS	(a-14)	B	A	GS	B	A
Arkansas	GS	G	N.O.	BG/BS	G	B	GS	BG	BG	BS
California	GS	GS	G	GS	G	G	GS	GS (b)	B (b)	(a-49)
Colorado	A	A	G	A	A	A	A	GS	GS	GS
Connecticut	GE	GE	GE	GE	GE	(b)	GE	GE	BG	GE
Delaware	CG	CG	CG	(a-35)	GS	CG	CG	CG	B	(a-49)
Florida	G	GS	A	GS	CE	B	GS	GS	B	GOC
Georgia	AG	A	CE	BG	G	A	N.O.	A	B	AG
Hawaii	A	CS	CS	CS	(b)	CS	GS	GS	B	CS
Idaho	A	GS	AGS	GS	GS	B	N.O.	GS	B	(a-49)
Illinois	GS	GS	(a-42)	GS	(a-10)	(a-35)	(a-6)	GS	B	(a-49)
Indiana	G	G	LG	G	G	A	(a-6)	G	G	(a-49)
Iowa	GS	GS	GS	A	A	A	A	GS	N.O.	A
Kansas	(b)	GS	B	C	N.A.	CS	GS	GS	B	GS
Kentucky	AG	AG	AG	G	G	G	N.O.	CG	B	CG
Louisiana	GS	A	CS	GS	GS	GS	GS	GS	B	GS
Maine	A	(a-32)	(a-38)	GLS	(a-6)	GLS	A	GLS	N.A.	(a-49)
Maryland	AG	A	G	GS	GS	GS	(a-6)	GS	G	AG
Massachusetts	G	CG	CG	CG	G	CG	G	CG	B	G
Michigan	GS	CS	CS	GS	(a-10)	(b)	N.O.	GS	N.O.	(a-49)
Minnesota	GS	N.O.	A	GS	GS	A	(a-6)	GS	B	GS
Mississippi	GS	GS	A	GS	(a-6)	GS	N.O.	BS	BS	B
Missouri	A	A	G	A	AGS	(b)	A	GS	B	B
Montana	CP	CP	CP	GS	CP	GS	CP	GS	CP	(a-49)
Nebraska	GS	A	GS	GS	(b)	A	A	GS	B	GS
Nevada	A	A	G	A	(a-14)	GD	N.O.	(b)	B	(a-49)
New Hampshire	G	GC	G	GC	(a-6)	BGS	GC	AGC	B	(a-49)
New Jersey	GS	A	A	GS	GS	B	(b)	GS	B	A
New Mexico	GS	(a-32)	GS	GS	GS	A	GS	GS	GS	A
New York	GS	GS	B	GS	CE	GS	G	GS	B	GS
North Carolina	G	G	A	G	G	G	G	G	B	A
North Dakota	A	G	A	A	A	G	G	G	B	(a-49)
Ohio	AG	GS	GS	GS	A (b)	A	A	GS	B	GS
Oklahoma	GS	B	GS	B	GS	B	GS	B	B	B
Oregon	AG	GS	G	B	(a-4)	B	(a-6)	A	B	A
Pennsylvania	G	AG	AG	GS	G	(b)	GS	GS	AG	AG
Rhode Island	G	GS	A	GS	GS	GS	GS	GS	B (b)	GS
South Carolina	A	B	A	(b)	B	B	A	GS	B	B
South Dakota	A	A	(a-42)	(a-35)	GS	GS	(a-6)	GS	B	A
Tennessee	A	G	A	G	G	B	G	G	B	(a-49)
Texas	A	B	N.O.	B	(a-14)	B	B	BG	B	(a-49)
Utah	A	GS	A	GS	AG	A	A	GS	B	(a-49)
Vermont	AG	GS	GS	CG	CG	CG	CG	CG	N.O.	CG
Virginia	GB	GB	A	GB	GB	B	GB	GB	B	GB
Washington	(a-5)	GS	G	(a-22)	(a-14)	?	(a-6)	G	N.A.	(a-49)
West Virginia	GS	GS	GS	GS	(a-6)	CS	C	GS	B	GS
Wisconsin	A	GS	A	A	A	A	GS	A	N.A.	A
Wyoming	G	GS	G	GS	N.A.	GD	AG	GS	GB	GS
American Samoa	G	A	GB	GB	(a-4)	GB	G	GB	(a-18)	(a-49)
Guam	GS	GS	G	GS	GS	GS	CS	GS	B	GS
No. Mariana Islands	G	C	C	G	GS	C	GS	GS	B	C
Puerto Rico	N.A.	GS	N.A.	N.A.	G	N.A.	GS	GS	N.A.	GS
U.S. Virgin Islands	GS	GS	GS	GS	GS	GS	GS	GS	GS	GS

(a-17) Economic development.
(a-18) Education (chief state school officer).
(a-19) Election administration.
(a-20) Emergency management.
(a-21) Employment Services.
(a-22) Energy.
(a-23) Environmental protection.
(a-24) Finance.
(a-25) Fish and wildlife.
(a-26) General services.
(a-27) Health.
(a-28) Higher education.
(a-29) Highways.
(a-30) Information systems.
(a-31) Insurance.
(a-32) Labor.
(a-33) Licensing.

(a-34) Mental health.
(a-35) Natural resources.
(a-36) Parks and recreation.
(a-37) Personnel.
(a-38) Planning.
(a-39) Post audit.
(a-40) Pre-audit.
(a-41) Public library development.
(a-42) Public utility regulation.
(a-43) Purchasing.
(a-44) Revenue.
(a-45) Social services.
(a-46) Solid waste management.
(a-47) State police.
(a-48) Tourism.
(a-49) Transportation.
(a-50) Welfare.

SELECTED STATE ADMINISTRATIVE OFFICIALS: METHODS OF SELECTION—Continued

State or other jurisdiction	Information systems	Insurance	Labor	Licensing	Mental health & retardation	Natural resources	Parks & recreation	Personnel	Planning	Post audit
Alabama	CS	G	G	N.O.	G	G	CS	B	(a-12)	LS
Alaska	AG	AG	GB	AG	B	GB	AG	AG	N.O.	(a-8)
Arizona	A	GS	BS	N.O.	B	GS	GS	A	(a-10)	N.O.
Arkansas	GS	GS	GS	N.O.	A	G	GS	AG	N.O.	L
California	G	CE	AG	G	(b)	GS	GS	GS	...	...
Colorado	G	BA	GS	A	A	GS	A	A	G	(a-8)
Connecticut	GE	GE	GE	CS	(b)	CS	CS	CS	A	(a-8)
Delaware	GS	CE	GS	CG	(b)	GS	CG	CG	CG	(a-8)
Florida	GS	GOC	GS	.	N.A.	GS	A	A	A	CE
Georgia	GD	CE	CE	A	BG	BG	A	A	(a-10)	(a-8)
Hawaii	CS	AG	GS	CS	G	GS	CS	GS	CS	CS
Idaho	(a-6)	GS	GS	GS	N.O.	B	B	GS	N.O.	(a-14)
Illinois	(a-6)	GS	GS	(a-9)	(a-45)	GS	(a-35)	(a-6)	N.O.	(a-8)
Indiana	G	G	G	G	A	G	A	G	N.O.	G
Iowa	GS	GS	GS	N.O.	A	GS	A	A	N.O.	N.O.
Kansas	G	SE	GS	B	C	GS	CS	C	N.A.	L
Kentucky	G	G	G	N.O.	CG	G	CG	G	G	CE
Louisiana	A	CE	GS	N.O.	GS	GS	LGS	B	CS	CL
Maine	A	GLS	GLS	A	(a-45)	GLS	(a-35)	A	N.A.	N.A.
Maryland	A	GS	GS	A	(b)	GS	A	A	GS	A
Massachusetts	C	G	G	G	(b)	CG	CG	CG	G	CE
Michigan	GS	(a-9)	GS	(a-32)	CS	GS	CS	CS	N.O.	CL
Minnesota	GS	A	GS	A	GS	GS	A	(a-24)	N.A.	(a-8)
Mississippi	BS	SE	N.O.	N.O.	B	GS	GS	B	A	CE
Missouri	A	GS	GS	A	BS	GS	A	G	AGS	CE
Montana	A	CE	GS	CP	CP	GS	CP	CP	G	L
Nebraska	GS	GS	GS	A	GS	GS	B	A	GS	CE
Nevada	G	A	A	N.O.	(b)	G	A	GS	N.O.	N.O.
New Hampshire	GC	GC	GC	GC	AGC	GC	AGC	AGC	...	(a-14)
New Jersey	A	GS	GS	N.O.	A (b)	A	A	GS	A	N.O.
New Mexico	GS	G	GS	G	N.O.	GS	N.A.	GD	N.A.	(a-8)
New York	G	GS	GS	(b)	(b)	GS	GS	GS	GS	CE
North Carolina	G	CE	CE	N.O.	A	G	A	G	N.A.	(a-8)
North Dakota	G	CE	G	N.O.	A	N.O.	G	A	N.O.	A
Ohio	G	GS	A	N.O.	GS (b)	GS	A	A	GS	CE
Oklahoma	A	CE	CE	N.O.	B	(a-48)	(a-48)	GS	N.O.	N.O.
Oregon	A	GS	SE	N.O.	A	N.O.	B	A	N.O.	SS
Pennsylvania	G	GS	GS	AG	G	GS	A	G	G	(a-8)
Rhode Island	A	GS	GS	(i)	GS	GS	GS	A	A	N.O.
South Carolina	A	GS	GS	GS	(b)	B	GS	A	AB	B
South Dakota	GS	A	GS	N.O.	GS	GS	A	GS	N.O.	(a-8)
Tennessee	A	G	G	A	G	G	A	G	A	SL
Texas	B	G	B	B	B	B	B	N.O.	G	L
Utah	GS	GS	GS	AG	AB	GS	AG	GS	G	(a-8)
Vermont	CG	GS	GS	SS	CG	GS	CG	CG	N.O.	(a-8)
Virginia	B	B	GB	GB	GB	GB	GB	GB	(a-10)	(a-8)
Washington	GS	SE	G	G	(a-45)	CE	I	(a-14)	(a-14)	N.A.
West Virginia	C	GS	GS	N.O.	(a-27)	(a-25)	(a-25)	C	(a-17)	LS
Wisconsin	A	GS	GS	GS	A	GS	A	GS	N.O.	(a-31)
Wyoming	GS	GS	AG	CS	AG	G	GS	AG	G	AG
American Samoa	(a-49)	G	N.A.	N.A.	(a-45)	AG	GB	A	(a-12)	G
Guam	GS	GS	GS	GS	GS	GS	GS	GS	GS	CE
No. Mariana Islands	C	CS	C	B	C	GS	C	GS	G	GS
Puerto Rico	N.A.	N.A.	GS	N.A.	N.A.	GS	GS	GS	GS	N.A.
U.S. Virgin Islands	G	SE	GS	GS	GS	GS	GS	GS	G	L

(b)
California—Health—Responsibilities shared between Director of Health Care Services and Director of Public Health, both (GS).

California—Higher Education—Responsibilities shared between Chancellor of California Community Colleges (B) and California Postsecondary Education Commission (B).

California—Mental Health and Retardation—Responsibilities shared between Director of Mental Health (GS) and Director of Developmental Services (GS).

Connecticut—Responsibilities shared between Robert M. Ward and John C. Geragosian. Positions are selected by the legislature.

Connecticut—Fish and Wildlife—Responsibilities shared between Director of Wildlife (CS), Director of Inland Fisheries (CS) and Director of Marine Fisheries (CS).

Connecticut—Mental Health and Retardation—Responsibilities shared between Commissioner of Mental Health (GE) and Commissioner of Retardation (GE).

Delaware—Mental Health and Retardation—Responsibilities shared between Director, Division of Substance Abuse and Mental Health (CG); and Director, Division of Developmental Disabilities Services, same department (CG).

Delaware—Social Services—Responsibilities shared between Secretary of Health and Social Services (GS); and Acting Secretary, Department of Services of Children, Youth and their Families (GS).

Hawaii—Finance—Responsibilities shared between Director of Budget and Finance (GS) and the Comptroller (GS).

Indiana—Election Administration—Responsibilities shared between Co-Directors.

Kansas—Emergency Management—Responsibilities shared between Adjutant General (GS) and Deputy Director (C).

Maryland—Mental Health and Retardation—Responsibilities shared between Executive Director, Mental Hygiene Administration (A); and Secretary, Department of Disabilities (A).

SELECTED STATE ADMINISTRATIVE OFFICIALS: METHODS OF SELECTION — Continued

State or other jurisdiction	Pre-audit	Public library development	Public utility regulation	Purchasing	Revenue	Social services	Solid waste mgmt.	State police	Tourism	Transportation	Welfare
Alabama	(a-14)	B	SE	CS	G	B	CS	G	G	(a-29)	(a-45)
Alaska	N.O.	AG	GB	AG	GB	GB	AG	GB	AG	GB	AG
Arizona	(a-14)	SS	B	A	GS	GS	A	GS	GS	GS	(a-45)
Arkansas	N.A.	B	GS	AG	AG	GS	N.A.	BG	AG	BS	GS
California	(a-14)	...	GS	(a-26)	BS	GS	G	GS	...	GS	AG
Colorado	(a-14)	BA	CS	CS	GS	GS	CS	A	CS	GS	GS
Connecticut	CE	B	GB	CS	GE	GE	CS	GE	GE	GE	GE
Delaware	(a-8)	CG	CG	(a-26)	G	(b)	B	CG	CG	GS	CG
Florida	CE	A	B	A	GOC	GS	A	GOC	N.O.	GS	A
Georgia	(a-8)	N.A.	CE	A	G	G	A	BG	A	G	AG
Hawaii	CS	(i)	GS	GS	GS	GS	CS	N.O.	B	GS	CS
Idaho	(a-14)	B	GS	(a-6)	GS	(a-27)	N.O.	GS	GS	B	A
Illinois	(a-14)	SS	GS	(a-6)	GS	GS	(a-23)	GS	(a-12)	GS	GS
Indiana	CE	G	G	A	G	G	A	G	LG	G	(a-45)
Iowa	A	B	GS	A	GS	GS	A	GS	A	GS	A
Kansas	CS	GS	B	C	GS	GS	C	GS	C	GS	C
Kentucky	N.O.	G	G	G	G	G	AG	G	G	G	(a-45)
Louisiana	A	BGS	BS	A	GS	GS	GS	GS	LGS	GS	GS
Maine	(a-14)	B	G	CS	A	GLS	CS	A/GLS	(a-17)	GLS	(a-45)
Maryland	A	A	GS	A	A	GS	A	GS	A	GS	(a-45)
Massachusetts	CE	B	G	CG	CG	CG	CG	CG	G	G	CG
Michigan	N.O.	N.O.	GS	CS	CS	GS	CS	GS	N.O.	GS	GS
Minnesota	(a-8)	N.A.	(b)	A	GS	(a-34)	GS	A	A	GS	(a-34)
Mississippi	CE	B	GS	A	GS	GS	A	GS	A	B	GS
Missouri	A	B	GS	A	GS	GS	A	GS	A	B	A
Montana	(a-39)	CP	CE	CP	GS	GS	GS	CP	CP	GS	GS
Nebraska	A	B	B	A	GS	GS	A	GS	B	GS	GS
Nevada	N.O.	(b)	G	A	G	G	(a-23)	G	GD	B	(b)
New Hampshire	(a-14)	AGC	GC	CS	GC	GC	AGC	AGC	AGC	GC	AGC
New Jersey	N.O.	N.O.	GS	GS	A	(b)	A	GS	A	GS	A
New Mexico	N.A.	N.A.	G	N.A.	GS	N.A.	N.A.	GS	GS	GS	N.A.
New York	CE	B	GS	G	GS	GS	GS	GS	GS	GS	GS
North Carolina	(a-8)	A	G	A	G	A	A	G	A	G	A
North Dakota	N.O.	N.O.	CE	A	CE	G	A	G	G	G	G
Ohio	GS	B	BG	A	GS	(b)	A	GS	LG	A	GS
Oklahoma	(a-14)	B	(b)	A	GS	GS	A	A	B	B	GS
Oregon	(a-10)	B	GS	A	GS	GS	N.O.	GS	N.O.	GS	GS
Pennsylvania	(a-4)	G	GS	AG	GS	GS	AG	GS	A	GS	GS
Rhode Island	(a-14)	A	GS	A	GS	GS (b)	(h)	G	(a-17)	GS	GS
South Carolina	(a-14)	B	B	A	GS	GS	BS	B	GS	GS	(a-45)
South Dakota	CE	A	CE	A	GS	GS	A	A	GS	GS	(a-45)
Tennessee	A	A	SE	A	G	G	A	G	G	G	G
Texas	(a-14)	A	B	A	(a-14)	(i)	N.O.	B	A	B	BG
Utah	AG	A	A	A	BS	GS	A	A	A	GS	GS
Vermont	(a-24)	CG	BGS	CG	CG	CG	CG	GS	CG	GS	CG
Virginia	(a-14)	B	(b)	A	GB	GB	GB	GB	G	GB	GB
Washington	(a-4)	(a-2)	GS	(a-6)	G	G	G	G	N.A.	(a-29)	(a-45)
West Virginia	(a-8)	B	GS	CS	GS	(a-27)	B	GS	GS	(a-29)	(a-27)
Wisconsin	A	A	GS	A	GS	A	A	A	GS	GS	(a-45)
Wyoming	(a-8)	AG	GS	CS	GS	GS	AG	AG	AG	(a-29)	(a-45)
American Samoa	(a-4)	(a-18)	N.A.	A	(a-4)	GB	GB	GB	(a-12)	(a-29)	N.A.
Guam	GS	(i)	GS	GS	GS	GS	GS	GS	B	...	GS
No. Mariana Islands	G	B	B	C	C	C	A	GS	GB	CS	A
Puerto Rico	N.A.	N.A.	GS	GS	GS	N.A.	N.A.	GS	GS	GS	N.A.
U.S. Virgin Islands	GS	GS	G	GS	GS	G	GS	GS	GS	GS	GS

Massachusetts—Mental Health and Retardation—Responsibilities shared between Commissioner, Department of Developmental Disabilities (CG); and Commissioner, Department of Mental Health, Executive Office of Human Services (CG).

Michigan—Fish and Wildlife—Responsibilities shared between Director (GS), Chief of Fisheries (CS) and Chief of Wildlife (CS).

Michigan—Election Administration—Responsibilities shared between Secretary of State (CE); and Director, Bureau of Elections (CS).

Minnesota—Human/Social Services, Mental Health and Retardation and Welfare are under the Commissioner of Human Services (GS).

Minnesota—Public Utility Regulation—Responsibilities shared between the five Public Utility Commissioners (G).

Missouri—Fish and Wildlife—Responsibilities shared between Administrator, Division of Fisheries, Department of Conservation; Administrator, Division of Wildlife, same department (AB).

Nebraska—Finance—Responsibilities shared between State Tax Commissioner, Department of Revenue (GS); Administrator, Budget Division (A) and the Auditor of Public Accounts (CE).

Nevada—Election Administration—Responsibilities shared between Secretary of State (CE), Deputy Secretary of State (SS), Chief Deputy, Secretary of State (A).

Nevada—Health—Responsibilities shared between Director of Health and Human Services (G) and Division Administrator, Health (AG).

Nevada—Mental Health and Retardation—Responsibilities shared between Director of Health and Human Services (G) and Division Administrator, MHDS (G).

Nevada—Public Library—Responsibilities shared between Director, Dept. of Tourism and Cultural Affairs (G) and Division Administrator of Library and Archives (A).

SELECTED STATE ADMINISTRATIVE OFFICIALS: METHODS OF SELECTION—Continued

Nevada—Welfare—Responsibilities shared between Director of Health and Human Services (G) and Division Administrator, Welfare and Support Services (AG).

New Jersey—General Services—Responsibilities shared between Director, Division of Purchase and Property, Dept. of Treasury (GS), and Director, Division of Property Management and Construction, Dept. of the Treasury (A).

New Jersey—Mental Health and Retardation—Responsibilities shared between Director, Division of Mental Health Services, Dept. of Human Services (A) and Director, Division of Developmental Disabilities, Dept. of Human Services (A).

New Jersey—Commissioner, Dept. of Human Services (GS) and Commissioner, Dept. of Children and Families (GS).

New York—Responsibilities shared between Board of Election members. Two co-chairs and two commissioners (B).

New York—Licensing—Responsibilities shared between Secretary of State (GS) and Commissioner of State Education Department (B).

New York—Mental Health and Retardation—Responsibilities shared between Commissioner, Office of Mental Health, and Commissioner, Office for People with Developmental Disabilities, both (GS).

Ohio—Finance—Responsibilities shared between Assistant Director, Office of Budget and Management (A) and Deputy Director, same office (A).

Ohio—Mental Health and Retardation—Responsibilities shared between Director, Dept. of Developmental Disabilities (GS) and Director, Department of Mental Health and Addiction Services. (GS).

Ohio—Social Services—Responsibilities shared between Director, OH Dept. of Job and Family Services (GS), Superintendent of Public Instruction, Dept. of Education (B), Executive Director of Opportunities for Ohioans with Disabilities (B), Director of Dept. of Aging (GS).

Oklahoma—Public Utility Regulation—Responsibilities shared between General Administrator, Public Utility Division, Corporation Commission (B); and 3 Commissioners, Corporation Commission (SE).

Pennsylvania—Shared between Executive Director (Fish) (B) and Executive Director (Game) (B).

Rhode Island—Higher Education—This employee serves in a dual role as Commissioner of Higher Education and as the President of the Community College of Rhode Island.

Rhode Island—Social Services—This position is filled by two employees; one, Stephen Costantino, is the Commissioner, Office of Health and Human Services; Sandra Powell serves as the Director of Human Services and reports to the Commissioner, Office of Health and Human Services.

South Carolina—Environmental Protection—Responsibilities shared between two Commissioners. One selected by (BS) and the other by (B).

South Carolina—Mental Health and Retardation—Responsibilities shared between Director of Disabilities and Special Needs (B) and Director of Mental Health (B).

Texas—Election Administration—Responsibilities shared between Secretary of State (G); and Division Director of Elections, Elections Division, Secretary of State (A).

Virginia—Public Utility Regulation—No single position. Functions are shared between Communication, Energy Regulation and Utility and Railroad Safety, all (B).

(c) Department abolished July 1, 2005; responsibilities transferred to office of Management and Budget, General Services and Department of State.

(d) Appointed by the House and approved by the Senate.

(e) In Maine, New Hampshire, Tennessee and West Virginia, the Presidents (or Speakers) of the Senate are next in line of succession to the Governorship. In Tennessee and West Virginia, the Speaker of the Senate bears the statutory title of Lieutenant Governor.

(f) The Governor has assigned the role of Secretary of State (GS) to the Lieutenant Governor, with no additional salary.

(g) The New Jersey State constitution states: "The State Auditor shall be appointed by the Senate and General Assembly in joint meeting for a term of five years and until his successor shall be appointed and qualify." So it is a Constitutional Officer, but is appointed, not elected by the legislature.

(h) Solid waste is managed by the Rhode Island Resource Recovery Corporation (RIRRC). Although not a department of the state government, RIRRC is a public corporation and a component of the State of Rhode Island for financial reporting purposes. To be financially self-sufficient, the agency earns revenue through the sale of recyclable products, methane gas royalties and fees for its services.

(i) Method not specified.

(j) The Rhode Island Economic Development Corporation is a quasi-public agency.

(k) The authority is a public corporation of the state and a body corporate and politic constituting a political subdivision within the Department of Commerce, Community, and Economic Development, but with separate and independent legal existence.

(l) Economic Development is considered corporate and state does not control method of selection or wages for this position.

Table 4.11
SELECTED STATE ADMINISTRATIVE OFFICIALS: ANNUAL SALARIES

State or other jurisdiction	Governor	Lieutenant governor	Secretary of state	Attorney general	Treasurer	Adjutant general	Admin.	Agriculture	Auditor	Banking
Alabama	$0(d)	$60,830	$85,248	$168,002	$85,248	$91,014	N.A.	$84,655	$85,248	$157,380
Alaska	145,000	115,000	(a-1)	141,156	154,824	141,156	141,156	102,972	148,920	122,988
Arizona	95,000	(a-2)	70,000	90,000	70,000	146,000	215,250	132,000	141,986	93,775
Arkansas	141,000	42,315	90,000	130,000	85,000	118,680	157,182	101,969	85,000	140,552
California	182,791	137,093	137,093	158,775	146,232	182,001	N.O.	188,451	188,451	156,951
Colorado	90,000	158,016	68,500	80,000	68,500	151,945	154,968	154,968	165,360	135,564
Connecticut	150,000	110,000	110,000	110,000	110,000	182,132	175,000	132,160	(c)	142,500
Delaware	171,000	79,053	128,090	145,707	113,874	122,321	(c)	119,540	109,032	111,916
Florida	130,273	124,851	141,000	128,972	(a-24)	170,352	141,000	128,972	140,004	(a-24)
Georgia	139,339	91,609	123,637	139,169	165,000	163,768	153,000	121,557	152,160	148,358
Hawaii	149,556	145,884	N.O.	145,884	145,884	221,672	(c)	138,936	136,212	138,936
Idaho	122,597	42,909	104,207	124,000	104,207	145,121	95,201	130,936	N.O.	(a-24)
Illinois	177,412	135,669	156,541	156,541	135,669	115,613	142,339	133,273	157,212	135,081
Indiana	111,688	90,490	78,584	94,538	78,584	131,840	135,200	144,457	78,584	120,000
Iowa	130,000	103,212	103,212	123,669	103,212	175,106	142,938	103,212	103,212	117,832
Kansas	99,636	54,000	86,003	98,901	86,003	106,392	120,000	110,000	N.A.	105,000
Kentucky	140,070	119,080	119,080	119,080	119,080	130,476	N.O.	119,080	119,080	128,533
Louisiana	130,000	115,000	115,000	115,000	115,000	192,566	237,500	115,000	132,620	145,000
Maine	70,000	(e)	83,032	111,134	79,419	127,878	127,878	127,878	97,780	105,498
Maryland	170,000	141,500	99,500	141,500	141,500	141,277(b)	146,743(b)	140,674(b)	N.O.	101,463(b)
Massachusetts	151,800	122,058	130,916	130,582	127,917	172,062	161,522	136,000	134,952	141,254
Michigan	159,300(d)	111,510	112,410	112,410	174,204	135,340	169,125	155,000	166,464	145,000
Minnesota	127,150	82,638	95,347	120,786	(a-24)	171,413	144,435	144,435	108,077	125,112
Mississippi	122,160	60,000	90,000	108,960	90,000	124,443	140,174	90,000	90,000	140,898
Missouri	133,821	86,484	107,746	116,437	107,746	91,524	125,712	121,705	107,746	102,243
Montana	111,569	86,362	92,236	123,499	108,650(q)	119,150	108,650	108,650	92,236	108,650
Nebraska	105,000	75,000	85,000	95,000	85,000	106,173	115,000	113,965	85,000	102,251
Nevada	149,573	63,648	102,898	141,086	102,898	118,200	128,998	118,200	N.O.	98,880
New Hampshire	127,443	(e)	105,930	117,913	105,930	105,930	117,913	100,171	N.O.	105,929
New Jersey	175,000	141,000	(a-1)	140,000	141,000	141,000	N.O.	141,000	144,629	141,000
New Mexico	110,000	85,000	85,000	95,000	85,000	193,787	126,250	125,000	85,000	90,900
New York	179,000(d)	151,500	120,800	151,500	127,000	120,800	179,451	120,800	151,500	127,000
North Carolina	142,265	125,676	125,676	125,676	125,676	105,901	N.A.	125,676	125,676	N.A.
North Dakota	129,096	100,224	102,689	152,436	96,972	196,236	N.A.	105,491	102,688	120,888
Ohio	148,304	150,404	109,553	109,553	109,553	125,278	133,868	125,278	109,553	103,001
Oklahoma	147,000	114,713	140,000	132,825	114,713	172,062	100,000	87,005	114,713	187,354
Oregon	98,600	(a-2)	77,000	82,220	77,000	151,236	180,540	148,572	161,342	N.O.
Pennsylvania	190,823	160,289	137,392	158,764	158,764	137,057	152,666	137,392	158,764	137,392
Rhode Island (g)	132,710	117,637	117,637	124,991	117,637	141,259	136,510	(a-23)	159,248	135,000
South Carolina	106,078	46,545	92,007	92,007	92,007	92,007	192,937	92,007	141,396	125,000
South Dakota	109,264	(h)	87,341	109,149	87,341	113,687	97,666	107,064	87,341	106,439
Tennessee	187,500(d)	62,652(e)	190,260	158,764	190,260	158,556	190,260	158,556	190,260	158,556
Texas	153,750	9,612(i)	132,924	153,750	(a-14)	167,923	N.O.	137,500	181,128	242,925(j)
Utah	109,900	104,405	(a-1)	104,405	104,405	107,037	119,891	115,586	104,405	119,288
Vermont	145,538	61,776	99,944	118,581	96,949	106,600	128,690	128,690	99,944	111,966
Virginia	175,000	36,321	158,966	150,000	167,408	135,548	159,762	165,552	173,530	165,853
Washington	171,898	100,880	120,459	156,270	133,750	172,062	151,428	125,400	120,459	129,168
West Virginia	150,000	20,000(e)	95,000	95,000	95,000	125,000	115,000	95,000	95,000	75,000
Wisconsin	147,328	77,795	69,936	142,966	69,936	130,000	128,546	121,950	117,354	N.A.
Wyoming	105,000	(a-2)	92,000	175,000	92,000	133,139	165,000	124,378	92,000	107,184
Guam	130,000	85,000	N.O.	105,286	52,492	68,152	88,915	60,850	100,000	88,915
No. Mariana Islands	70,000	65,000	N.O.	80,000	40,800(b)	N.O.	54,000	40,800(b)	80,000	40,800(b)
Puerto Rico	70,000	N.O.	125,000	N.A.	N.A.	N.A.	N.A.	N.A.	N.A.	N.A.
U.S. Virgin Islands	150,000	75,000	(a-1)	76,500	76,500	85,000	76,500	76,500	76,500	75,000

Sources: The Council of State Governments' survey of state personnel agencies and state websites, March 2016.

Note: Alabama, Idaho and New Hampshire did not respond to inquiries for salary updates. Figures presented are from state websites, April 2016.

Key:

N.A. — Not available.

N.O. — No specific chief administrative official or agency in charge of function.

(a) Chief administrative official or agency in charge of function:
(a-1) Lieutenant governor.
(a-2) Secretary of state.
(a-3) Attorney general.
(a-4) Treasurer.
(a-5) Adjutant general.
(a-6) Administration.

(a-7) Agriculture.
(a-8) Auditor.
(a-9) Banking.
(a-10) Budget.
(a-11) Civil rights.
(a-12) Commerce.
(a-13) Community affairs.
(a-14) Comptroller.
(a-15) Consumer affairs.
(a-16) Corrections.
(a-17) Economic development.
(a-18) Education (chief state school officer).
(a-19) Election administration.
(a-20) Emergency administration.
(a-21) Employment Services.

SELECTED STATE ADMINISTRATIVE OFFICIALS: ANNUAL SALARIES — Continued

State or other jurisdiction	Budget	Civil rights	Commerce	Community affairs	Comptroller	Consumer affairs	Corrections	Economic development	Education	Election admin.
Alabama	$177,266	N.O.	$162,232	$164,419	$138,305	$72,686	$71,712	(a-12)	$250,000	$72,686
Alaska	194,760	165,096	141,156	(a-12)	133,332	(a-12)	141,156	(a-12)	141,156	124,452
Arizona	162,000	N.A.	250,000	N.A.	123,587	N.A.	168,000	(a-12)	85,000	70,000
Arkansas	101,077	N.O.	N.O.	N.A.	N.O.	N.O.	150,507	121,038	233,488	73,152
California	(a-24)	N.O.	N.O.	142,488	146,232	152,557	243,360	N.O.	158,775	128,520
Colorado	164,380	131,676	N.O.	94,200	126,540	151,152	131,688	159,180	245,688	110,400
Connecticut	161,922	129,780	190,400	(a-12)	110,000	142,800	167,500	190,400	192,500	116,537
Delaware	147,870	79,754	(a-2)	N.O	147,870	122,268	147,870	128,090	160,645	81,628
Florida	145,000	99,500	N.A.	110,000	128,972	100,000	160,000	141,000	276,000	97,250
Georgia	175,615	105,202	125,000	160,000	N.A.	131,301	160,000	169,500	123,270	72,427
Hawaii	145,884	105,252	138,936	N.O.	138,936	111,924	138,936	138,936	200,000	90,000
Idaho	122,990	67,787	130,000	N.O.	104,207	(a-3)	139,984	(a-12)	104,207	(a-2)
Illinois	150,000	115,613	142,339	(a-12)	135,669	(a-3)	150,228	(a-12)	225,000	130,008
Indiana	138,432	110,000	(a-17)	113,299	(a-8)	101,631	136,578	200,850	94,538	(c)
Iowa	141,960	87,000	N.O.	98,592	N.O.	128,890	142,500	154,300	140,000	106,309
Kansas	130,000	76,476	125,000	N.A.	115,000	95,000	125,000	108,529	175,000	(a-2)
Kentucky	130,476	126,200	130,476	109,524	107,214	82,800	118,000	250,000	240,000	78,513
Louisiana	136,261	N.A.	237,500	159,016	237,500	106,080	136,719	237,500	275,000	121,909
Maine	108,826	75,837	(a-17)	(a-17)	108,826	112,195	127,878	127,878	123,698	94,058
Maryland	174,417(b)	114,865(b)	172,021(b)	N.O.	141,500	134,749(b)	159,072(b)	172,021(b)	153,532(b)	130,059(b)
Massachusetts	132,600	137,382	161,522	145,000	176,624	145,000	150,000	161,522	161,522	130,916
Michigan	155,000	145,000	(a-32)	N.O.	141,760	N.O.	155,000	(s)	204,000	(c)
Minnesota	(a-24)	144,435	144,435	(a-17)	(a-24)	113,173	149,427	149,427	149,427	(a-2)
Mississippi	(a-6)	N.O.	90,000	130,000	(a-6)	91,000	132,761	183,000	300,000	80,000
Missouri	77,667	81,305	121,200	104,838	96,746	116,437	121,705	121,200	187,776	91,044
Montana	112,040	80,517	108,650	71,338	105,644	76,168	108,650	103,783	104,635	96,590
Nebraska	156,515	88,510	127,812	88,035	95,002	95,000	179,999	145,000	220,725	91,394
Nevada	(a-6)	88,651	128,998	N.O.	102,898	75,111	128,998	N.A.	128,998	(c)
New Hampshire	105,930	80,971	114,554	N.O.	106,575	100,171	117,913	87,423	114,553	(a-2)
New Jersey	132,000	120,000	(a-17)	141,000	141,000	136,000	141,000	225,000	141,000	125,000
New Mexico	95,950	N.O.	123,725	N.O.	118,000	83,891	123,725	123,725	126,250	85,000
New York	184,350	109,800	120,800	120,800	151,500	127,000	175,267	1(d)	250,000	(k)
North Carolina	(a-24)	99,446	136,000	N.O.	156,159	N.A.	N.A.	N.A.	125,676	106,000
North Dakota	131,136	100,260	157,284	N.A.	131,136	137,268	132,588	128,928	116,903	52,080
Ohio	165,734	98,820	131,268	135,033	165,734	80,600	133,764	135,033	192,504	109,553
Oklahoma	100,000	N.A.	126,508	N.A.	120,000	125,000	165,000	N.A.	124,373	115,386
Oregon	155,851	109,416	155,940	152,583	127,884	163,776	171,965	163,762	225,300	153,632
Pennsylvania	165,008	135,609	155,365	N.A.	144,861	122,362	152,657	145,025	152,657	120,001
Rhode Island (g)	185,739	86,342	205,706	N.A.	140,645	(a-3)	145,644	185,000(l)	212,106	145,993
South Carolina	130,000	104,070	172,529	N.A.	92,007	111,075	161,137	(a-12)	92,007	90,281
South Dakota	71,871	48,711	(a-44)	(a-48)	(a-40)	55,313	118,234	131,877	117,666	72,471
Tennessee	148,668	116,964	180,000	180,000	190,260	N.A.	158,556	180,000	200,004	123,996
Texas	159,131	117,875	N.O.	(a-8)	172,997	153,750	141,484	266,500	N.A.	220,375	(c)
Utah	141,835	100,630	136,635	67,475	(a-24)	(a-12)	125,091	132,974	230,069	109,013
Vermont	119,870	101,670	128,440	92,310	119,870	101,670	114,171	92,310	128,690	99,944
Virginia	167,669	90,800	166,915	133,297	167,541	102,102	156,060	195,000	206,467	108,202
Washington	(a-14)	107,628	156,252	(a-12)	167,952	(a-3)	167,952	(a-12)	132,883	(a-2)
West Virginia	99,120	55,000	95,000	106,280	(a-8)	(a-3)	90,504	(a-13)	230,000	(a-2)
Wisconsin	125,757	97,573	N.O.	N.O.	N.A.	99,590	127,026	N.O.	121,307	106,704
Wyoming	134,358	81,322	142,943	N.A.	(a-8)	134,260	148,628	(a-12)	92,000	98,134
Guam	88,915	N.O.	88,915	N.O.	83,400	55,341	67,150	82,025	82,025	61,939
No. Mariana Islands	54,000	49,000	52,000	52,000	40,800(b)	52,000	40,800(b)	45,000	80,000	53,000
Puerto Rico	N.A.	N.A.	N.A.	N.A.	N.A.	N.A.	N.A.	N.A.	N.A.	N.A.
U.S. Virgin Islands	76,500	60,000	76,500	(c)	76,500	76,500	76,500	85,000	76,500	135,000

(a-22) Energy.
(a-23) Environmental protection.
(a-24) Finance.
(a-25) Fish and wildlife.
(a-26) General services.
(a-27) Health.
(a-28) Higher education.
(a-29) Highways.
(a-30) Information systems.
(a-31) Insurance.
(a-32) Labor.
(a-33) Licensing.
(a-34) Mental health.
(a-35) Natural resources.
(a-36) Parks and recreation.

(a-37) Personnel.
(a-38) Planning.
(a-39) Post audit.
(a-40) Pre-audit.
(a-41) Public library development.
(a-42) Public utility regulation.
(a-43) Purchasing.
(a-44) Revenue.
(a-45) Social services.
(a-46) Solid waste management.
(a-47) State police.
(a-48) Tourism.
(a-49) Transportation.
(a-50) Welfare.

SELECTED STATE ADMINISTRATIVE OFFICIALS: ANNUAL SALARIES — Continued

State or other jurisdiction	Emergency mgmt.	Employment services	Energy	Environ. protection	Finance	Fish & wildlife	General services	Health	Higher education	Highways
Alabama	$124,200	$88,543	$97,766	$152,618	$177,266	$113,479	$97,766	$282,446	$206,184	$169,000
Alaska	137,352	122,988	175,000	141,156	139,008	141,156	(a-43)	141,156	313,151	132,036
Arizona	102,355	115,850	N.A.	175,000	(a-14)	160,000	120,000	205,505	320,000	159,814
Arkansas	98,327	147,460	N.O.	130,250	(a-6)	134,056	133,797	219,779	168,810	183,924
California	188,451	156,942	143,520	188,451	188,451	161,650	171,545	(c)	(c)	(a-49)
Colorado	119,292	127,716	146,568	155,400	135,216	151,464	141,600	142,812	148,056	138,000
Connecticut	183,340	157,000	139,050	139,050	209,439	(c)	175,000	190,000	335,000	190,749
Delaware	91,215	96,566	98,570	(a-35)	147,870	99,040	108,671	170,483	109,801	(a-49)
Florida	141,000	141,000	91,960	150,000	128,972	140,737	141,000	N.A.	200,000	150,000
Georgia	167,821	84,427	116,452	175,000	155,400	118,718	N.A.	175,000	497,000	120,000
Hawaii	120,864	96,588(b)	96,588(b)	96,588(b)	(c)	N.A.	(a-14)	138,936	375,000	124,812
Idaho	122,532	126,152	86,174	115,960	106,890	136,572	N.O.	157,185	126,048	(a-49)
Illinois	128,920	142,339	(a-42)	133,273	(a-10)	(a-35)	(a-6)	150,228	200,004	(a-49)
Indiana	132,870	154,500	78,795	127,063	141,110	85,541	(a-6)	170,465	171,249	(a-49)
Iowa	112,070	135,000	(a-17)	134,472	140,629	102,690	118,019	135,387	N.O.	163,634
Kansas	(c)	108,000	71,600	105,019	115,000	73,320	114,000	190,000	200,000	(a-49)
Kentucky	84,349	N.A.	130,476	104,969	130,476	125,000	N.O.	N.A.	360,000	N.A.
Louisiana	130,000	108,621	121,909	137,197	237,500	123,614	237,500	236,001	364,000	176,000
Maine	83,533	(a-32)	(a-38)	127,878	(a-6)	127,878	98,717	127,878	N.A.	(a-49)
Maryland	150,000(b)	161,975(b)	138,631(b)	104,235(b)	174,417(b)	116,185(b)	(a-6)	170,997(b)	157,558(b)	160,742
Massachusetts	143,000	161,522	135,000	139,050	161,522	129,000	138,338	140,000	217,500	151,267
Michigan	(a-47)	135,252	143,000	155,000	(a-10)	(c)	N.O.	175,000	N.O.	(a-49)
Minnesota	154,398	N.O.	125,112	149,427	154,398	125,112	(a-6)	149,427	390,000	154,398
Mississippi	107,868	135,315	140,000	129,347	(a-6)	126,668	N.O.	230,000	300,000	139,700
Missouri	98,483	99,504	96,504	104,011	77,667	(c)	96,746	121,709	172,205	174,000
Montana	90,370	102,695	110,817	108,650	105,644	108,650	94,826	108,650(r)	309,206	(a-49)
Nebraska	95,001	107,879	102,250	120,000	(c)	107,912	112,620	200,000	180,983	145,001
Nevada	118,200	128,998	107,973	125,021	(a-14)	118,200	N.O.	(c)	N.A.	(a-49)
New Hampshire	105,930	105,930	80,971	114,554	(a-10)	100,171	(a-6)	100,171	79,664	(a-49)
New Jersey	132,300	N.A.	100,000	141,000	133,507	105,783	(c)	141,000	141,000	123,500
New Mexico	125,000	113,827	106,050	113,827	126,250	103,000	106,050	123,725	126,250	105,000
New York	136,000	N.A.	120,800	159,181	151,500	159,181	136,000	136,000	250,000	136,000
North Carolina	98,352	121,000	99,817	127,385	145,000	139,293	N.A.	144,499	775,000	162,080
North Dakota	107,820	118,452	157,284	123,564	131,136	125,628	190,428	200,196	372,000	(a-49)
Ohio	103,417	137,113	135,033	134,388	(c)	110,344	90,646	133,744	163,488	137,113
Oklahoma	95,000	115,110	114,000	123,013	171,833	135,644	100,000	194,244	394,983	(a-49)
Oregon	114,768	163,776	148,572	148,572	(a-4)	148,572	(a-6)	180,540	150,244	161,343
Pennsylvania	140,010	135,512	127,942	152,657	165,008	(c)	145,025	152,657	130,094	145,272
Rhode Island (g)	136,489	135,000	140,513	135,000	(a-44)	(a-23)	(a-6)	134,975	265,000(c)	(a-49)
South Carolina	98,940	158,340	110,033	(c)	166,073	129,877	118,320	159,130	N.A.	162,313
South Dakota	85,405	61,964	(a-42)	(a-35)	136,424	118,234	(a-6)	122,163	367,096	100,247
Tennessee	N.A.	152,256	156,504	168,708	190,260	168,708	159,996	176,868	176,652	158,556
Texas	198,164	179,500	N.O.	210,695	(a-14)	195,749	170,824	242,353	205,160	(a-49)
Utah	92,310	140,379	117,000	115,586	133,266	118,269	119,558	191,470	N.A.	(a-49)
Vermont	81,994	105,498	111,966	104,000	119,870	91,541	106,018	126,131	N.O.	109,491
Virginia	122,791	156,970	96,523	184,649	170,854	140,208	162,344	196,139	193,669	202,419
Washington	(a-5)	156,252	149,352	(a-22)	(a-14)	150,000	(a-6)	148,656	N.A.	167,952
West Virginia	65,000	75,000	82,404	95,000	(a-6)	75,000	80,508	85,512	N.A.	120,000
Wisconsin	104,832	111,800	94,910	127,026	125,757	127,026	127,546	125,133	525,000	127,026
Wyoming	100,147	155,913	121,000	130,577	N.O.	148,593	116,552	202,952	168,600	156,000
Guam	68,152	73,020	55,303	60,850	88,915	60,850	60,528	74,096	195,000	88,915
No. Mariana Islands	45,000	40,800(b)	45,000	58,000	54,000	40,800(b)	54,000	80,000	80,000	40,800(b)
Puerto Rico	N.A.	N.A.	N.A.	N.A.	N.A.	N.A.	N.A.	N.A.	N.A.	N.A.
U.S. Virgin Islands	71,250	76,500	69,350	76,500	76,500	76,500	76,500	76,500	76,500	65,000

(b) Salary ranges, top figure in ranges follow:

Hawaii: Employment Services, $160,776; Energy, $160,776; Environmental Protection, $160,776; Information Systems, $160,776; Licensing, $153,096; Parks and Recreation, $160,776; Pre-Audit, $160,776; Solid Waste Management, $153,096; Welfare, $175,680.

Maryland: For these positions the salary in the chart is the actual salary and the following are the salary ranges: Adjutant General, $114,874–$153,532; Administration, $114,874–$153,532; Agriculture, $114,874–$153,532; Banking, $73,612–$118,197; Budget, $133,069–$177,977; Civil Rights, $92,333–$123,236; Commerce, $133,069–$177,977; Consumer Affairs, $83,836–$134,749; Corrections, $133,069–$177,977; Economic Development, $133,069–$177,977; Education, $114,784–$153,532; Elections Administration, $99,275–$132,569; Emergency Management, $114,784–$153,532; Workforce Development, $123,618–$165,281; Energy, $106,773–$142,646; Environmental Protection,

$78,595–126,1865; Finance, $133,069–177,977; Fish and Wildlife, $92,333–$123,236; Health, $133,069–$177,977; Higher Education, $123,618–$165,281; Information Services, $133,069–$177,977; Insurance, $133,069–$177,977; Labor, $123,618–$165,281; Licensing, $92,333–$123,236; Mental Health shared duties, $154,064–$254,576 (vacant at press time) and $114,874–$153,532 (actual, $137,770); Natural Resources, $123,618–$165,281; Parks and Recreation, $68,292–$124,989; Personnel, $106,773–$142,646; Planning, $114,874–$153,532; Post-Audit, $53,193–$85,401; Pre-Audit, $99,275–$132,569; Public Library, $92,333–$123,236; Public Utility Regulation, $153,027–$256,866; Purchasing, $85,902–$114,600 (vacant at press time); Revenue, $99,275–$132,569; Social Services, $133,069–$177,977; Solid Waste Management, $106,773–$142,646; State Police, $133,069–$177,977; Tourism, $73,612–$118,197; Transportation, $133,069–$177,977; Welfare, $92,333–$123,236.

SELECTED STATE ADMINISTRATIVE OFFICIALS: ANNUAL SALARIES — Continued

State or other jurisdiction	Info. systems	Insurance	Labor	Licensing	Mental health	Natural resources	Parks & recreation	Personnel	Planning	Post audit
Alabama	$177,266	$164,419	$139,859	N.O.	$152,618	$141,000	$100,198	$168,622	(a-12)	$241,695
Alaska	122,988	122,988	141,156	124,452	101,280	141,156	127,596	129,132	N.O.	(a-8)
Arizona	180,000	120,000	140,000	N.O.	120,058	175,000	159,952	121,800	(a-10)	N.O.
Arkansas	137,360	132,128	130,138	N.O.	135,567	112,756	130,000	106,549	N.O.	185,439
California	188,451	146,232	188,451	156,825	(c)	188,451	161,650	171,179	N.O.	N.O.
Colorado	160,704	135,564	158,064	138,840	142,812	158,076	153,000	151,476	138,000	(a-8)
Connecticut	176,960	160,000	157,000	118,362	(c)	155,767	155,767	140,000	158,592	(a-8)
Delaware	160,645	109,032	119,540	106,500	(c)	128,090	99,039	118,252	95,658	(a-8)
Florida	130,000	134,158	141,000	71,400	N.A.	150,000	114,000	111,000	100,000	(a-24)
Georgia	160,000	120,394	122,786	86,709	183,618	175,000	116,390	135,000	(a-10)	(a-8)
Hawaii	96,588(b)	115,008	138,936	91,992(b)	127,812	138,936	96,588(b)	138,936	N.A.	N.A.
Idaho	(a-6)	102,273	(a-21)	83,116	N.O.	129,771	91,561	99,548	N.O.	(a-14)
Illinois	(a-6)	135,081	124,090	(a-9)	(a-45)	133,273	(a-35)	(a-6)	N.O.	(a-8)
Indiana	126,299	110,313	110,313	105,060	113,454	120,819	88,718	121,992	N.O.	109,262
Iowa	140,400	128,890	112,070	N.O	128,066	128,890	(a-25)	127,317	N.O.	N.O.
Kansas	185,000	86,003	108,000	65,153	75,000	111,490	111,490	95,000	N.O.	115,296
Kentucky	N.A.	105,000	130,476	N.O.	N.A.	95,238	108,000	130,476	130,476	119,080
Louisiana	150,000	115,000	137,000	N.O.	219,128	129,210	120,016	140,046	113,277	N.A.
Maine	125,689	105,498	127,878	127,878	(a-45)	127,878	(a-35)	102,690	N.A.	N.A.
Maryland	167,433(b)	157,386(b)	161,975(b)	105,000(b)	(b)(c)	159,312(b)	116,053(b)	141,365(b)	135,048(b)	73,361(b)
Massachusetts	145,297	130,000	117,300	105,000	(c)	161,522	130,000	157,678	161,522	(a-8)
Michigan	169,125	(a-9)	155,000	(a-32)	141,758	148,500	128,080	160,414	N.O.	(a-8)
Minnesota	149,427	N.A.	144,435	108,618	(a-45)	154,398	125,112	(a-24)	N.A.	(a-8)
Mississippi	173,209	90,000	N.O.	N.O.	170,180	129,347	126,668	119,657	97,128	(a-8)
Missouri	93,000	121,705	121,705	110,000	125,000	121,705	111,605	96,746	77,667	107,746
Montana	124,910	92,236	108,650	98,446	99,881	108,650	105,439	99,662	103,783	130,165
Nebraska	170,000	124,132	127,812	77,468	135,000	145,003	132,771	100,000	130,000	85,000
Nevada	118,200	118,200	98,880	N.O.	(c)	128,998	108,540	108,540	N.O.	N.O.
New Hampshire	117,913	105,930	105,930	105,930	105,930	114,554	91,965	88,933	N.O.	(a-14)
New Jersey	140,000	130,000	141,000	N.O.	(c)	125,000	110,000	141,000	95,000	N.O.
New Mexico	113,827	114,000	113,827	101,000	N.O.	106,050	91,001	105,000	76,198	85,000
New York	176,868	127,000	N.O.	(c)	(c)	159,181	127,000	N.A.	1	151,500
North Carolina	164,000	125,676	125,676	N.O.	135,000	129,000	118,815	140,000	N.A.	(a-8)
North Dakota	165,252	102,687	100,260	N.O.	99,540	N.O.	110,268	111,780	N.O.	113,100
Ohio	127,878	150,404	82,326	(m)	(c)	137,113	101,275	106,600	135,033	(a-8)
Oklahoma	160,000	126,713	105,053	N.O.	173,318	126,508	126,508	120,000	N.O.	N.O.
Oregon	205,339	166,922	77,000	N.A.	150,276	N.A.	148,572	146,603	N.O.	161,352
Pennsylvania	150,006	137,392	152,657	109,008	139,248	145,025	108,773	154,661	105,018	(a-8)
Rhode Island (g)	205,706	(a-9)	(a-21)	(n)	135,000	(a-23)	(a-23)	146,994	102,860	N.A.
South Carolina	163,200	137,904	124,973	124,973	(c)	129,877	127,698	120,000	N.A.	101,361
South Dakota	125,056	90,128	107,161	N.O.	108,002	113,687	94,354	113,687	N.A.	(a-8)
Tennessee	171,468	158,556	152,256	119,916	158,556	168,708	92,592	158,556	N.A.	(a-14)
Texas	184,792	202,383	179,500	179,375	241,273	210,695	195,749	N.O.	159,131	(a-8)
Utah	125,008	114,670	107,037	119,850	124,758	132,974	119,600	119,891	(a-10)	(a-8)
Vermont	118,810	111,969	105,498	89,669	114,171	128,939	99,466	106,517	N.O.	(a-8)
Virginia	175,000	164,643	126,710	137,700	175,000	158,966	147,162	145,628	167,669	(a-8)
Washington	156,252	121,628	152,952	145,800	(a-45)	130,253	127,956	(a-14)	(a-14)	N.A.
West Virginia	133,428	92,500	70,504	N.O.	(a-27)	(a-25)	(a-25)	70,000	(a-17)	N.A.
Wisconsin	121,950	119,413	101,130	112,300	112,300	127,026	108,618	111,800	N.O.	(a-8)
Wyoming	153,326	122,900	94,824	69,783	(c)	123,257	108,433	112,000	175,000	106,966
Guam	88,915	88,915	73,020	88,915	75,208	60,850	60,850	88,915	88,915	100,000
No. Mariana Islands	45,000	40,800(b)	45,000	45,360	40,800(b)	52,000	40,800(b)	60,000	45,000	80,000
Puerto Rico	N.A.	N.A.	N.A.	N.A.	N.A.	N.A.	N.A.	N.A.	N.A.	N.A.
U.S. Virgin Islands	71,250	75,000	76,500	76,500	70,000	76,500	76,500	76,500	76,500	55,000

Northern Mariana Islands: $49,266 top of range applies to the following positions: Treasurer, Banking, Comptroller, Corrections, Employment Services, Fish and Wildlife, Highways, Insurance, Mental Health and Retardation, Parks and Recreation, Purchasing, Social/Human Services, Transportation.

(c) Responsibilities shared between:

California—Health—Responsibilities shared between Director of Health Care Services, $186,572 and Director Department of Public Health $239,064.

California—Higher Education—Responsibilities shared between Chancellor of California Community Colleges, $213,756 and California Post Secondary Education Commission Director, $139,992.

California—Mental Health—Responsibilities shared between Director of Mental Health, $177,683 and Director of Developmental Services, $177,683.

California—Welfare is now part of Social Services.

Connecticut—Auditor—Responsibilities shared between John C. Geragosian, $173,389 and Robert M. Ward, $178,928.

Connecticut—Fish and Wildlife—Responsibilities shared between Director of Wildlife, $144,021, Director of Inland Fisheries, $128,962, and Director of Marine Fisheries, $144,021.

Connecticut—Mental Health—Responsibilities shared between Commissioner, Mental Health, $160,000 and Commissioner, Retardation, $168,000.

Delaware—The Dept. of Administration was abolished in 2005. Responsibilities are now shared between the Office of Management and Budget, General Services and Dept. of State.

Delaware—Mental Health—Responsibilities shared between Director, Division of Substance Abuse and Mental Health, Department of Health and Social Services, $143,713 and Director, Division of Developmental Disabilities Service, same department, $115,419.

SELECTED STATE ADMINISTRATIVE OFFICIALS: ANNUAL SALARIES — Continued

State or other jurisdiction	Pre-audit	Public library dvpmt.	Public utility reg.	Purchasing	Revenue	Social services	Solid waste mgmt.	State police	Tourism	Transportation	Welfare
Alabama	(a-14)	$95,000	$103,490	$95,359	$164,419	$140,000	$105,403	$149,000	$91,014	(a-29)	(a-45)
Alaska	N.O.	138,334	129,132	108,120	141,156	(a-27)	126,984	141,156	108,120	141,156	129,132
Arizona	(a-14)	68,000	154,320	150,000	175,000	215,250	115,000	175,000	175,000	136,500	(a-45)
Arkansas	N.A.	110,812	126,748	102,088	139,919	162,648	N.A.	118,786	105,000	(a-29)	(a-45)
California	(a-14)	N.O.	142,411	(a-26)	180,000	219,267	153,960	239,282	N.O.	177,683	(a-45)(c)
Colorado	(a-14)	122,556	122,712	104,556	158,100	162,396	146,568	106,740	127,356	161,112	162,348
Connecticut	(a-14)	151,000	145,948	149,423	190,400	190,400	144,021	183,340	155,000	190,750	190,400
Delaware	(a-8)	84,307	104,500	(a-26)	125,103	(c)	163,000	170,598	93,223	138,945	115,522
Florida	(a-24)	83,000	131,036	110,000	150,000	140,000	113,000	140,100	N.O.	141,000	N.A.
Georgia	(a-8)	N.A.	116,452	139,008	158,000	150,000	85,000	140,000	130,000	185,000	162,000
Hawaii	96,588(b)	120,000	120,876	120,864	138,936	138,936	91,992(b)	N.O.	270,000	138,936	105,576(b)
Idaho	(a-14)	96,636	95,899	(a-6)	88,908	(a-27)	N.O.	117,707	(a-12)	184,849	125,195
Illinois	(a-14)	102,252	130,008	(a-6)	142,339	150,228	(a-23)	132,566	(a-12)	150,228	142,339
Indiana	78,584	N.A.	120,716	86,528	129,980	173,349	102,884	138,628	110,000	147,457	(a-45)
Iowa	111,259	117,832	128,890	110,302	154,300	154,300	(a-23)	110,240	102,066	147,014	128,066
Kansas	80,460	85,000	99,292	88,000	107,990	105,000	86,965	110,000	84,000	110,000	N.O.
Kentucky	N.O.	79,976	113,121	86,205	111,681	106,981	81,342	119,048	103,000	130,476	(a-45)
Louisiana	124,384	111,280	137,904	118,726	250,000	129,995	N.A.	134,351	111,280	176,900	110,411
Maine	(a-14)	84,032	126,901	78,062	108,826	127,878	78,062	110,593	(a-17)	127,878	(a-45)
Maryland	114,752(b)	123,236(b)	165,565	(b)	132,569(b)	167,488(b)	140,489(b)	167,661(b)	113,763(b)	174,419(b)	(a-45)
Massachusetts	(a-8)	119,351	129,000	138,338	(p)	140,000	139,050	231,253	110,000	161,522	150,000
Michigan	N.O.	N.O.	140,000	141,758	128,223	175,000	122,204	155,000	N.O.	155,000	175,000
Minnesota	(a-8)	N.A.	(c)	120,786	154,398	154,398	149,427	125,112	125,112	154,398	(a-34)
Mississippi	(a-8)	90,000	108,850	71,991	142,296	130,000	81,909	138,115	85,748	139,700	130,000
Missouri	96,746	85,344	106,625	96,746	121,705	121,704	73,225	118,800	85,000	174,000	104,838
Montana	(a-39)	97,340	101,772	94,826	108,650	108,650(r)	108,650	105,830	92,768	108,650	108,650(r)
Nebraska	95,002	103,884	150,000	100,000	160,000	200,000	74,947	90,002	86,364	145,001	200,000
Nevada	N.O.	(c)	125,021	98,880	128,998	128,998	(a-23)	128,998	118,200	128,998	(c)
New Hampshire	(a-14)	91,965	111,687	75,410	117,913	121,896	100,171	105,930	91,965	117,913	100,171
New Jersey	N.O.	N.O.	125,301	130,000	128,000	(c)	108,128	132,300	92,490	141,000	127,200
New Mexico	90,228	N.A.	90,000	91,910	106,050	126,250	87,929	125,000	106,050	113,827	123,725
New York	151,500	250,000	127,000	136,000	127,000	136,000	159,181	136,000	1(a-38)	136,000	136,000
North Carolina	(a-8)	109,068	139,849	N.A.	129,000	123,861	107,000	123,409	80,853	136,000	N.A.
North Dakota	N.A.	N.A.	105,490	101,244	111,447	179,040	102,840	118,260	123,768	167,784	179,040
Ohio	(a-10)	102,416	132,496	90,646	137,113	(c)	90,688	136,572	102,523	84,988	137,113
Oklahoma	(a-14)	85,850	(c)	95,700	123,126	185,000	112,057	136,471	126,508	156,128	185,000
Oregon	(a-10)	122,316	153,029	104,244	141,446	176,568	N.A.	163,776	N.A.	180,154	176,568
Pennsylvania	(a-4)	N.A.	147,525	130,015	145,025	152,657	127,942	145,025	129,605	152,657	152,657
Rhode Island (g)	(a-14)	113,146	117,412	125,874	130,100	(c)	(o)	148,937	(a-17)	135,000	(a-45)
South Carolina	(a-14)	95,780	189,500	118,690	160,650	159,130	189,000	162,313	127,698	180,000	(a-45)
South Dakota	74,676	80,284	101,861	59,749	108,002	118,234	100,085	104,297	107,038	118,234	(c)
Tennessee	139,440	129,372	158,352	147,900	158,556	158,556	125,460	188,148	159,996	158,556	158,556
Texas	(a-14)	143,500	158,075	174,803	(a-14)	230,523	N.O.	214,672	159,131	299,812	266,500
Utah	(a-24)	116,376	95,680	(a-26)	80,766	126,194	118,144	116,355	N.A.	160,222	(a-45)
Vermont	119,870	94,744	139,818	106,018	104,250	128,690	104,000	119,600	91,707	128,690	114,171
Virginia	(a-14)	149,112	(c)	123,570	159,855	150,915	184,649	179,325	168,826	166,915	150,915
Washington	(a-4)	(a-2)	132,000	(a-6)	149,352	167,952	(a-22)	156,252	N.A.	(a-29)	(a-45)
West Virginia	(a-8)	72,000	90,000	105,648	95,000	(a-27)	79,700	85,000	93,504	120,000	(a-27)
Wisconsin	(a-8)	115,981	118,000	109,158	122,470	123,989	108,618	107,411	109,762	127,026	101,629
Wyoming	(a-8)	86,526	130,591	74,764	126,994	142,064	115,620	124,152	139,000	(a-29)	(a-45)
Guam	88,915	55,303	1,200	88,915	88,915	74,096	88,915	74,096	88,591	N.O.	74,096
No. Mariana Islands	54,000	45,000	80,000	40,800(b)	45,000	40,800(b)	54,000	54,000	70,000	40,800(b)	52,000
Puerto Rico	N.A.	N.A.	N.A.	N.A.	N.A.	N.A.	N.A.	108,000	N.A.	N.A.	N.A.
U.S. Virgin Islands	76,500	53,350	54,500	76,500	76,500	76,500	76,500	76,500	76,500	65,000	76,500

Delaware—Social Services—Function split between two cabinet positions: Secretary, Dept. of Health and Social Services, $147,870 and Secretary, Dept. of Svcs. for Children, Youth and their Families, $133,241.

Hawaii—Administration—There is no single agency for Administration. The functions are divided among the Director of Budget and Finance, Director of Human Resources Development and the Comptroller.

Hawaii—Finance—Responsibilities shared between Director of Budget and Finance, $145,884 and Comptroller, $138,936.

Indiana—Elections Administration—Responsibilities shared between Co-Directors Brad King, $79,129 and Angela Nussmeyer, $78,555.

Kansas—Emergency Management—Responsibilities shared between Adjutant General, $106,392 and deputy director, $72,000.

Maryland—Mental Health—Responsibilities shared between Executive Director of Mental Hygiene Administration, salary range $154,064–$254,576 (position vacant at press time) and Director of Developmental Disabilities Administration, $137,770.

Massachusetts—Mental Health—Responsibilities shared between Commissioners Joan Mikula, $157,982 and Elin M. Howe, $153,511.

Michigan—Elections Administration—Responsibilities shared between Secretary of State Ruth Johnson, $112,410 and Bureau Director Christopher Thomas, $131,738.

Michigan—Fish and Wildlife—Responsibilities shared between Chief of Fisheries, Jim Dexter, $120,954 and Chief of Wildlife, James Russ Mason, $119,539.

Minnesota—Public Utility Regulation—Responsibilities shared between five commissioner's with salaries of $139,464 for each.

SELECTED STATE ADMINISTRATIVE OFFICIALS: ANNUAL SALARIES — Continued

Missouri—Fish and Wildlife—Responsibilities shared between Larry Yamnitz, Administrator, Division of Fisheries, Department of Conservation, $101,352; Jason Sumners, Administrator, Division of Wildlife, same department, $71,268.

Nebraska—Finance—Responsibilities shared between Auditor of Public Accounts—$85,000; Director of Administration—$156,515 and State Tax Commissioner—$160,000.

Nevada—Elections Administration—Responsibilities shared between Secretary of State, $102,898; Deputy Secretary of State for Elections, $108,540 and Chief Deputy Secretary of State, $118,200.

Nevada—Health and Welfare—Responsibilities shared between Richard Whitley, Director, Health and Human Services, $128,998 and Steve Fisher, Division Administrator, Welfare and Support Services, $118,200.

Nevada—Mental Health—Responsibilities shared between Director, Health and Human Services, $128,998 and Division Administrator, $125,021.

Nevada—Public Library Development—Responsibilities shared between Director, Department of Tourism and Cultural Affairs, $118,200 and Division Administrator, Library and Archives, $98,880.

New Jersey—General Services—Responsibilities shared between Jignasa Desai Director, Division of Purchase and Property, Dept. of the Treasury, $130,000 and Steven Sutkin, Division of Property Management and Construction, Dept. of the Treasury, $130,000.

New Jersey—Mental Health—Responsibilities shared between Assistant Commissioner Lynn Kovich, Division of Mental Health Services, Dept. of Human Services, $128,000 and position of Assistant Commissioner Elizabeth Shea, Division of Developmental Disabilities, Dept. of Human Services, $128,000.

New Jersey—Social Services—Responsibilities shared between Jennifer Velez, Commissioner, Department of Human Services, $141,000 and Allison Blake, Commissioner, Department of Children and Families, $141,000.

New York—Licensing—Responsibilities shared between Commissioner, State Education Department, $250,000; Secretary of State, Department of State, $120,800.

New York—Mental Health—Responsibilities shared between Commissioner of Office for People with Developmental Disabilities, $166,903 and Commissioner of Office of Mental Health, $136,000.

Ohio—Finance—Responsibilities shared between Kurt Kauffman, Interim Assistant Director of Budget and Management, $117,124 and Fred Church, Deputy Director, Office of Budget and Management, $115,356.

Ohio—Mental Health—Responsibilities shared between John L. Martin, Director of Dept. of Mental Health, $135,720 and Tracy J. Plouck, Director, Dept. of Mental Health and Addiction Services, $125,278.

Ohio—Social Services—Responsibilities shared between Director, Dept. of Job and Family Services, $137,113; Superintendent of Dept. of Education, $192,504; Executive Director Opportunites for Ohioans with Disabilities, $111,716 and Director of Dept. of Aging, $128,939.

Oklahoma—Public Utility Regulation—Responsibilities shared between three Commissioners, Commissioner Bob Anthony, $116,713, Commissioner Dana Murphy, $114,713 and Commissioner Jimmie Hiett, $114,713 and Timothy Rhodes, Director of Administration Div., $125,000.

Pennsylvania—Fish and Wildlife—Responsibilities shared between Executive Director (Fish), $135,609 and Executive Director (Game), $135,609.

Rhode Island—Higher Education—Serves a dual role as Commissioner of Higher Education and as the President of the Community College of Rhode Island.

Rhode Island—Social Services—Responsibilities shared between Commissioner, Office of Health and Human Services, $141,828 and

Director of the Dept. Human Service, $135,000, and reports to the Commissioner, Office of Health and Human Services.

South Carolina—Environmental Protection—Responsibilities shared between Commissioner Catherine Heigel $189,000 (BS) and Director Alvin Taylor $129,877 (B).

South Carolina—Mental Health—Responsibilities shared between Director for Disabilities and Special Needs, Beverly Bucemei $158,010 and Director of Mental Health, John Magill $191,695.

Texas—Elections Administration—Responsibilities shared between Secretary of State, $132,924; and Division Director, $125,447.

U.S. Virgin Islands—Community Affairs—Responsibilities for St. Thomas, $74,400; St. Croix, $76,500; St. John, $74,400.

Virginia—Public Utility Regulation—Functions shared between Communications, William Irby, $165,933; Energy Regulation, William F. Stephens, $165,853; Utility and Railroad Safety, Massoud Tahamtani, $162,826.

Wyoming—Mental Health—Responsibilities shared between State Hospital, William Sexton, $150,000 and Life Resource Center, Richard Dunkley, $120,000.

(d) These individuals have voluntarily taken no salary or a reduced salary:

Alabama—Gov. Robert Bentley is not accepting his salary, $120,395, until the unemployment rate in Alabama drops.

Michigan—Gov. Rick Snyder returns all but $1.00 of his salary.

New York—Governor Andrew Cuomo has reduced his salary by 5 percent.

Tennessee—Governor Haslam returns his salary to the state.

(e) In Maine, New Hampshire, Tennessee and West Virginia, the presidents (or speakers) of the Senate are next in line of succession to the governorship. In Tennessee and West Virginia, the speaker of the Senate bears the statutory title of lieutenant governor.

(g) A number of the employees receive a stipend for their length of service to the State (known as a longevity payment). This amount can vary significantly among employees and, depending on state turnover, can show dramatic changes in actual salaries from year to year.

(h) $66,874 part time.

(i) Lieutenant Governor receives additional pay when serving as acting governor.

(j) This agency is now a self-directed state agency.

(k) The statutory salary for each of the four members of the Board of Elections is $25,000, including the two co-chairs, Douglas A. Kellner and Peter S. Kosinski.

(l) The Rhode Island Economic Development Corporation is a quasi-public agency. The salary shown is for the previous director.

(m) Numerous licensing boards, too many to list.

(n) Varies by department.

(o) Solid waste is managed by the Rhode Island Resource Recovery Corporation (RIRRC). Although not a department of the state government, RIRRC is a public corporation and a component of the State of Rhode Island for financial reporting purposes. To be financially self-sufficient, the agency earns revenue through the sale of recyclable products, methane gas royalties and fees for it services.

(p) Commissioner Mark Nunnelly waives his salary. The last reported salary for this position was $155,318.

(q) Montana does not have a treasurer per se. The Director of the Dept. of Administration is responsible for these duties.

(r) Montana has combined health, social services and welfare into one agency.

(s) Economic development is considered "Corporate" and wages are not set by the state.

Table 4.12
THE LIEUTENANT GOVERNORS, 2016

State or other jurisdiction	Name and party	Method of selection	Length of regular term in years	Date of first service	Present term ends	Number of previous terms	Joint election of governor and lieutenant governor (a)
Alabama	Kay Ivey (R)	CE	4	1/2011	1/2019	1	No
Alaska	Byron Mallott (I)	CE	4	12/2014	12/2018	. . .	Yes
Arizona	. . . . (b)						
Arkansas	Tim Griffin (R)	CE	4	1/2015	1/2019	. . .	No
California	Gavin Newsom (D)	CE	4	1/2011	1/2019	1	No
Colorado	Joseph Garcia (D)	CE	4	1/2011	1/2019	1	Yes
Connecticut	Nancy Wyman (D)	CE	4	1/2011	1/2019	1	Yes
Delaware	Vacant (d)	CE	4	. . .	. . .	. . .	No
Florida	Carlos Lopez-Cantera (R)	CE	4	2/2014 (k)	1/2019	(k)	Yes
Georgia	Casey Cagle (R)	CE	4	1/2007	1/2019	2	No
Hawaii	Shan Tsutsui (D)	CE	4	1/2013 (e)	12/2018	(e)	Yes
Idaho	Brad Little (R)	CE	4	1/2009 (c)	1/2019	(c)	Yes
Illinois	Evelyn Sanguinetti (R)	CE	4	1/2015	1/2019	. . .	Yes
Indiana	Sue Ellspermann (R)	CE	4	1/2013	1/2017	. . .	Yes
Iowa	Kim Reynolds (R)	CE	4	1/2011	1/2019	1	Yes
Kansas	Jeff Colyer (R)	CE	4	1/2011	1/2019	1	Yes
Kentucky	Jenean Hampton (R)	CE	4	12/2015	12/2019	. . .	Yes
Louisiana	Billy Nungesser (R)	CE	4	1/2016	1/2020	. . .	No
Maine	. . . . (b)						
Maryland	Boyd Rutherford (R)	CE	4	1/2015	1/2019	. . .	Yes
Massachusetts	Karyn Polito (R)	CE	4	1/2015	1/2019	. . .	Yes
Michigan	Brian Calley (R)	CE	4	1/2011	1/2019	1	Yes
Minnesota	Tina Smith (D)	CE	4	1/2015	1/2019	. . .	Yes
Mississippi	Tate Reeves (R)	CE	4	1/2012	1/2020	1	No
Missouri	Peter Kinder (R)	CE	4	1/2005	1/2017	2	No
Montana	Angela McLean (D)	CE	4	2/2014 (j)	1/2017	. . .	Yes
Nebraska	Mike Foley (R)	CE	4	1/2015	1/2019	. . .	Yes
Nevada	Mark Hutchison (R)	CE	4	1/2015	1/2019	. . .	No
New Hampshire	. . . . (b)						
New Jersey	Kim Guadagno (R)	CE	4	1/2010	1/2018	1	Yes
New Mexico	John Sanchez (R)	CE	4	1/2011	1/2019	1	Yes
New York	Kathy Hochul (D)	CE	4	1/2015	1/2019	. . .	Yes
North Carolina	Dan Forest (R)	CE	4	1/2013	1/2017	. . .	No
North Dakota	Drew Wrigley (R)	CE	4	12/2010 (f)	12/2018	1	Yes
Ohio	Mary Taylor (R)	SE	4	1/2011	1/2019	1	Yes
Oklahoma	Todd Lamb (R)	CE	4	1/2011	1/2019	1	No
Oregon	. . . . (b)						
Pennsylvania	Mike Stack (D)	CE	4	1/2015	1/2019	. . .	Yes
Rhode Island	Dan McKee (D)	SE	4	1/2015	1/2019	. . .	No
South Carolina	Henry McMaster (R)	CE	4	1/2015	1/2019	. . .	No
South Dakota	Matt Michels (R)	CE	4	1/2011	1/2019	1	Yes
Tennessee	Ron Ramsey (R)	(g)	2	1/2007	1/2017	4 (g)	No
Texas	Dan Patrick (R)	CE	4	1/2015	1/2019	. . .	No
Utah	Spencer J. Cox (R)	CE	4	10/2013 (h)	1/2017	. . .	Yes
Vermont	Phil Scott (R)	CE	2	1/2011	1/2017	2	No
Virginia	Ralph Northam (D)	CE	4	1/2014	1/2018	. . .	No
Washington	Brad Owen (D)	CE	4	1/1997	1/2017	4	No
West Virginia	Bill Cole (R)	(i)	2	1/2015	1/2017	. . .	No
Wisconsin	Rebecca Kleefisch (R)	CE	4	1/2011	1/2019	1	Yes (l)
Wyoming	. . . . (b)						
American Samoa	Lemanu Peleti Mauga (D)	CE	4	1/2013	1/2017	. . .	Yes
Guam	Ray Tenorio (R)	CE	4	1/2011	1/2019	1	Yes
No. Mariana Islands	Ralph Torres (R)	CE	4	1/2015	1/2019	. . .	Yes
Puerto Rico	. . . . (b)						
U.S. Virgin Islands	Osbert Potter (I)	SE	4	1/2015	1/2019	. . .	Yes

See footnotes at end of table.

THE LIEUTENANT GOVERNORS, 2016—Continued

Source: The Council of State Governments, November 2015.

Key:

CE — Constitutional, elected by public.

SE — Statutory, elected by public.

. . . — Not applicable.

(a) The following also choose candidates for governor and lieutenant governor through a joint nomination process: Florida, Kansas, Maryland, Minnesota, Montana, North Dakota, Ohio, Utah, American Samoa, Guam, No. Mariana Islands, and U.S. Virgin Islands. For additional information see The National Lieutenant Governors Association website at *http://www.nlga.us.*

(b) No lieutenant governor.

(c) Brad Little was appointed by Gov. Otter and confirmed by the state Senate after Lt. Gov. Ritsch won the U.S. Senate seat.

(d) Lt. Gov. Matthew Denn resigned Jan. 6, 2015, upon taking the oath of office to serve as Delaware's attorney general, a position he was elected to during the Nov. 4, 2014 general election. The office of lieutenant governor will remain vacant until the 2016 elections after the General Assembly's failed attempt to pass legislation providing a method to choose a new lt. governor in the event of a vacancy. The current successor is Secretary of State Jeffrey Bullock.

(e) Senate President Shan Tsutsui was sworn in as Hawaii's lieutenant governor on January 3, 2013. Gov. Abercrombie named Lt. Gov. Schatz as the replacement for U.S. Sen. Daniel Inouye who died on Dec. 17, 2012. Under Hawaii law, the Senate president has the choice as to whether to become lieutenant governor.

(f) Lt. Gov. Drew Wrigley was appointed by Gov. Jack Dalrymple, who moved from the office of lieutenant governor to governor when Gov. John Hoeven resigned to become a U.S. senator.

(g) In Tennessee, the president of the Senate and the lieutenant governor are one in the same. The legislature provided in statute the title of lieutenant governor upon the Senate president. The Senate president serves two-year terms, elected by the Senate on the first day of the first session of each two-year legislative term.

(h) Lt. Gov. Spencer J. Cox was appointed to the office of lieutenant governor in Oct. 2013 after Lt. Gov. Greg Bell resigned to return to the private sector.

(i) In West Virginia, the president of the Senate and the lieutenant governor are one in the same. The legislature provided in statute the title of lieutenant governor upon the Senate president. The Senate president serves two-year terms, elected by the Senate on the first day of the first session of each two-year legislative term.

(j) Angela McLean was sworn in on Feb. 17, 2014 after Lt. Gov. John Walsh was appointed to fill a vacant U.S. Senate seat.

(k) Carlos Lopez-Cantera was appointed lt. governor on Feb. 3, 2014 after Lt. Gov. Jennifer Carroll resigned Mar. 12, 2013 amid charges of misconduct.

(l) The governor and lt. governor are elected on a joint ticket at the November general election. However, they run on separate party primary ballots in the August primary election.

Table 4.13
LIEUTENANT GOVERNORS: QUALIFICATIONS AND TERMS

State or other jurisdiction	Minimum age	State citizen (years)	U.S. citizen (years) (a)	State resident (years) (b)	Qualified voter (years)	Length of term (years)	Maximum consecutive terms allowed
Alabama	30	7	10	7	...	4	2
Alaska	30	7	7	7	★	4	2
Arizona				...(c)			
Arkansas	30	7	★	7	...	4	2
California	18	★	★	5	★	4	2
Colorado	30	...	★	2	...	4	2
Connecticut	30	★	★	★	★	4	...
Delaware	30	★	12	6	★	4	2
Florida	30	★	★	7	★	4	2
Georgia	30	★	15	6	★	4	...
Hawaii	30	5	★	5	★	4	2
Idaho	30	...	★	2	...	4	...
Illinois	25	...	★	3	...	4	...
Indiana	30	★	★	★	★	4	2
Iowa	30	...	2	2	...	4	...
Kansas	...	...	...	...	...	4	2
Kentucky	30	6	★	★	★	4	2
Louisiana	25	5	5	5	...	4	...
Maine				...(c)			
Maryland	30	★	★	★	★	4	2
Massachusetts	...	★	★	★	★	4	...
Michigan	30	★	★	4	4	4	2 (d)
Minnesota	25	...	★	1	...	4	...
Mississippi	30	...	20	5	★	4	2
Missouri	30	10	15	10	...	4	...
Montana	25	2	★	2	...	4	2 (e)
Nebraska	30	5	★	5	★	4	2
Nevada	25	2	★	2	★	4	2
New Hampshire				...(c)			
New Jersey	30	...	20	7	...	4	2
New Mexico	30	★	★	5	★	4	2
New York	30	★	★	5	★	4	...
North Carolina	30	...	5	2	...	4	2
North Dakota	30	5	...	...	...	4	...
Ohio	18	...	★	★	★	4	2
Oklahoma	31	10	★	★	★	4	...
Oregon				...(c)			
Pennsylvania	30	★	★	7	★	4	2
Rhode Island	18	★	★	★	★	4	2
South Carolina	30	5	5	5	★	4	2
South Dakota	21	2	★	2	★	4	2
Tennessee (f)	30	★	★	3	1	2	...
Texas	30	...	★	5	...	4	...
Utah	30	★	★	★	★	4	...
Vermont	18	4	★	4	★	2	...
Virginia	30	...	★	5	5	4	...
Washington	18	★	★	★	★	4	...
West Virginia (g)	25	5	...	1	★	2	...
Wisconsin	18	★	★	★	★	4	...
Wyoming				...(c)			
American Samoa	35	(h)	★	5	★	4	2
Guam	30	...	5	5	★	4	2
No. Mariana Islands	35	★	★	★	★	4	2
Puerto Rico				...(c)			
U.S. Virgin Islands	30	...	5	5	5	4	2

Source: The Council of State Government's survey of lieutenant governors' offices, November 2015.

Note: This table includes constitutional and statutory qualifications.

Key:

★ — Formal provision; number of years not specified.

... — No formal provision.

(a) In some states you must be a U.S. citizen to be an elector, and must be an elector to run.

(b) In some states you must be a state resident to be an elector, and must be an elector to run.

(c) No lieutenant governor.

(d) In 1993 a constitutional limit of two lifetime terms in the office was enacted.

(e) Eligible for eight out of 16 years.

(f) In Tennessee, the speaker of the senate, elected from Senate membership, has statutory title of "lieutenant governor."

(g) In West Virginia, the president of the senate and the lieutenant governor are one in the same. The legislature provided in statute the title of lieutenant governor upon the senate president. The senate president serves two-year terms, elected by the Senate on the first day of the first session of each two year legislative term.

(h) Must be a U.S. national.

Table 4.14
LIEUTENANT GOVERNORS: POWERS AND DUTIES

State or other jurisdiction	Presides over Senate	Appoints committees	Breaks roll-call ties	Assigns bills	Authority for governor to assign duties	Member of governor's cabinet or advisory body	Serves as acting governor when governor out of state	Other duties (a)
Alabama	★	...	★	★	...	...	★(b)	...
Alaska	...	...	...	...	★	★	★	(c)
Arizona	.... (d)							
Arkansas	★	...	★	...	...	...	★	...
California	★	...	★	...	★	...	★	(c)
Colorado	...	...	...	...	★	★	★	(c)
Connecticut	★	...	★	...	★	★	★	...
Delaware	★	...	★	...	...	★	...	(c)
Florida	...	...	...	...	★	...	★	...
Georgia	★	★	...	★	★	★	...	(c)
Hawaii	...	...	...	...	★	...	★	(c)
Idaho	★	...	★	...	★	...	★	...
Illinois	...	...	...	...	★	★	...	(c)
Indiana	★	...	★	...	...	...	...	(c)
Iowa	...	(e)	...	...	★	(f)	(g)	...
Kansas	...	...	...	...	...	★	...	...
Kentucky	...	...	...	...	★	...	(h)	(c)
Louisiana	...	...	...	...	★	★	★	...
Maine	.... (i)							
Maryland	...	...	...	...	★	★	...	...
Massachusetts	...	★	...	...	★	★	★	(c)
Michigan	★	...	★	...	★	★	★(j)	(c)
Minnesota	...	...	...	...	★	...	★	(c)
Mississippi	★	★	★	★	...	...	★	(c)
Missouri	★	...	★	...	★	...	★	(c)
Montana	...	...	...	...	★	★	★	...
Nebraska	★(k)	...	...	...	...	★	★	...
Nevada	★	...	★(l)	...	...	★	★	...
New Hampshire	.... (i)							
New Jersey	...	...	...	...	★	★	★	(c)
New Mexico	★	...	★	...	...	★	★	...
New York	★	...	★(m)	...	★	★	★	...
North Carolina	★	...	★	...	★	...	★	(c)
North Dakota	★	...	...	...	★	★	...	...
Ohio	...	...	...	...	★	★	...	...
Oklahoma	★(n)	...	★	...	...	...	★	(c)
Oregon	.... (d)							
Pennsylvania	★	...	★	...	...	...	...	(c)
Rhode Island	...	...	...	...	...	...	...	(c)
South Carolina	★	★	★	★	...	★	★	(c)
South Dakota	★	...	★	...	★	★	★	(c)
Tennessee	★	★	★	★	...	...	...	...
Texas	★	★	★	★	...	...	★	...
Utah	...	...	...	...	...	★	...	(c)
Vermont	★	★(o)	★	★(o)	...	...	★	...
Virginia	★	...	★	...	...	★	...	...
Washington	★	★	★	...	...	...	★	...
West Virginia	★	★	...	★	...	...	...	(c)
Wisconsin	...	...	...	...	★	★	★	...
Wyoming	.... (d)							
American Samoa	...	...	...	...	...	...	★	...
Guam	(k)	...	...	...	★	★	★	...
No. Mariana Islands	...	...	...	...	...	★	★	(c)
Puerto Rico	.... (d)							
U.S. Virgin Islands	...	...	...	...	★(f)	★	★	...

See footnotes at end of table.

LIEUTENANT GOVERNORS: POWERS AND DUTIES — Continued

Sources: The Council of State Governments survey of lieutenant governors' offices, November 2015.

Key:

★ — Provision for responsibility.

... — No provision for responsibility.

(a) Lieutenant governors may obtain duties through gubernatorial appointment, statute, the Constitution, direct democracy action, or personal initiative. Hence, an exhaustive list of duties is not maintained, but this chart provides examples which are not all inclusive.

(b) The lieutenant governor performs the duties of the governor in the event of the governor's death, impeachment, disability, or absence from the state for more than 20 days.

(c) Alaska — The lieutenant governor bears these additional responsibilities: Alaska Historical Commission Chair; Alaska Workforce Investment Board; supervise the Division of Elections: supervise the certification process for citizen ballot initiative and referenda; provide constituent care and communications; lend support to governor's legislative and administrative initiatives; sign and file regulations; publish the Alaska Administrative Code and the OnlinePublic Notice System; commission notaries public; regulate commercial and advtertising use of State Seal, co-chair Alaska Criminal Justice Working Group; member of Clemency Advisory Cmte.; represent Alaska on the Aerospace States Association (ASA), the National Association of Secretaries of State and the National Lieutenant Governors' Association; Arctic Winter Games.

California — Lieutenant governor is an ex-officio regent, University of California Board of Regents; ex-officio regent, California State University Board of Trustees; chair, California Commission for Economic Development; member and current chair, California State Lands Commission (chair rotates annually between Lt. Governor and State Controller); member, California Ocean Protection Council (membership rotates with chair of State Lands Commission); and ex-officio commissioner of the California Coastal Commission (membership rotates with chair of State Lands Commission);

Colorado — Additional responsibilities include: director of the Colorado Department of Higher Education and chair of the Colorado Commission of Indian Affairs (by statute).

Delaware — Serves as President of the Board of Pardons.

Georgia — The lieutenant governor, by statute, is responsible for board, commission and committee appointments. In addition the lieutenant governor appoints conference committees, rules on germaneness, and must sign all acts of the General Assembly.

Hawaii — Also serves as Secretary of State.

Illinois — The lt. governor serves on or chairs several bodies according to statute and executive order including the: Illinois River Coordinating Council, Mississippi River Coordinating Council, Wabash and Ohio River Coordinating Council, Interagency Military Base Support & Economic Development Committee, Illinois Discharged Service Member Task Force, Governor's Rural Affairs Council, IL Farmers Market Task Force, Illinois Local Food, Farms, & Jobs Council, Commission to End Hunger, Illinois Main Street, Housing Task Force, Commission to Eliminate Poverty, Illinois Broadband Deployment Council, ISBE/ROE Service Evaluation Committee, Charitable Trust Stabilization Committee.

Indiana — Serves as Secretary of Agriculture and Rural Development. Oversees six state agencies: Department of Agriculture, Office of Community and Rural Affairs, Office of Defense Development, Office of Tourism Development, Indianan Small Business Development Center and the Indiana Housing and Community Development Authority.

Kentucky — In addition to the duties set forth by the Kentucky Constitution, state law also gives the lieutenant governor the responsibility to act as chair, or serve as a member, on various boards and commissions. Some of these include: the State Property and Buildings Commission, Kentucky Turnpike Authority, Kentucky Council on Agriculture, Board of the Kentucky Housing Corporation and the Appalachian Development Council. The governor also has the power to give the lieutenant governor other specific job duties.

Massachusetts — The lieutenant governor is a member of, and presides over, the Governor's Council, an elected body of 8 members which approves all judicial nominations.

Michigan — The lieutenant governor serves as a member of the State Administrative Board; and represents the governor and the state at selected local, state, and national meetings. In addition the governor may delegate additional responsibilities.

Minnesota — Serves as the Chair of the Capitol Area Architectural and Planning Board Committee.

Mississippi — The lieutenant governor also appoints chairs of standing committees, appoints conferees to committees and is a member of the Legislative Budget Committee, chair of this committee every other year.

Missouri — Other duties of the lieutenant governor include: Official Senior Advocate for State of Missouri and Advisor to Department of Elementary and Secondary Education on early childhood education and

Parents-as-Teachers program. The lieutenant governor also serves on the following boards and commissions: Board of Fund Commissioners; Board of Public Buildings; Governor's Advisory Council for Veteran's (chair); Missouri Community Service Commission; Missouri Development Finance Board; Missouri Housing Development Commission; Missouri Rural Economic Development Council; Missouri Rural Economic Development Council; Missouri Senior Rx Program (chair); Missouri Tourism Commission (vice-chair); Personal Independence Commission (co-chair); Second State Capitol Commission; Statewide Safety Steering Committee; Veteran's Benefits Awareness Task Force (chair); Special Health, Psychological, and Social Needs of Minority Older Individuals Commission; Mental Health Task Force (chair); Missouri Energy Task Force.

New Jersey — The Lieutenant Governor will serve as the head of a principal department or other executive or administrative agency or delegate duties of the office of governor or both. (Lt. Gov. Guadagno is currently appointed as secretary of state.

North Carolina — Serves as a voting member on the State Board of Education. Serves on the State Board of Economic Development. Serves on the State Community College Board. Serves as Chairman of the Energy Policy Counil. Serves on the Military Affairs Commission. Serves as Chair of the eLearning Commission.

Oklahoma — Lieutenant Governor also serves on 10 boards and commissions: Tourism and Recreation Commission, Indian Cultural and Educational Authority, State Board of Equalization, School Land Commission, the Oklahoma Capitol Improvement Authority, the Oklahoma Archives and Records Commission, the Oklahoma Film and Music Advisory Commission, CompSource Oklahoma Board of Managers, the Commissioners of the Land Office, and the Oklahoma Linked Deposit Review Board.

Pennsylvania — Chairs the Board of Pardons (Constitutional); chairs the Pa. Emergency Management Council (appointed by Gov.); chairs the Pa. Military Community Enhancement Commission (member by statute, elected chair by members); chairs Local Government Advisory Commission (statute.)

Rhode Island — Serves as Chair of a number of Advisory Councils including issues related to Emergency Management, Long Term Care and Small Business. Each year submits a legislative package to the General Assembly.

South Carolina — The lieutenant governor heads the State Office on Aging; appoints members and chairs the South Carolina Affordable Housing Commission.

South Dakota — The lieutenant governor also serves as the Chair of the Workers Compensation Advisory Commission and as a member of the Constitutional Revision Commission.

Utah — The lieutenant governor serves as Chief Election Officer (statutory); Chair of the Lieutenant Governor's Commission on Volunteers (statutory); Chair of the Lieutenant Governor's Commission on Civic and Character Education (statutory); Chair of the Utah Capitol Preservation Board (statutory);

West Virginia — The President of the Senate and the Lieutenant Governor are one in the same. The legislature provided in statute the title of Lieutenant Governor upon the Senate President. The West Virginia Constitution requires that, in case of the death, conviction or impeachment, failure to qualify, resignation, or other disability of the governor, the President of the Senate shall act as governor until the vacancy is filled, or the disability removed.

Northern Mariana Islands — The Lieutenant Governor is charged with overseeing administrative functions.

(d) No lieutenant governor; secretary of state is next in line of succession to governorship.

(e) Appoints all standing committees. Iowa — appoints some special committees.

(f) Presides over cabinet meetings in absence of governor.

(g) Only in emergency situations.

(h) The Kentucky Constitution specifically gives the lieutenant governor the power to act as governor, in the event the governor is unable to fulfill the duties of office.

(i) No lieutenant governor; senate president or speaker is next in line of succession to governorship.

(j) As defined in the state constitution, the lieutenant governor performs gubernatorial functions in the governor's absence. In the event of a vacancy in the office of governor, the lieutenant governor is first in line to succeed to the position.

(k) Unicameral legislative body. In Guam, that body elects own presiding officer.

(l) Except on final passage of bills and joint resolutions.

(m) With respect to procedural matters, not legislation.

(n) May preside over the Senate when desired.

(o) Appoints committees with the Pres. Pro Tem and one Senator on Committee on Committees. Committee on Committees assigns bills.

(p) In the event of a vacancy in the office of Governor resulting from the death, resignation or removal of a Governor in office, or the death of a Governor-elect, or from any other cause the Lieutenant Governor shall become Governor, until a new Governor is elected and qualifies.

From Innovation to Disruption: State Voter Registration Practices Hit a Digital Turning Point for Election 2016

By Kay Stimson

As states harness technology to modernize their election systems, no area of policymaking has more momentum than voter registration. Online registration, automatic voter registration and Election Day registration are increasingly popular options, with election officials predicting unprecedented levels of eligible voter enrollment and government cost-savings in 2016. Yet as states move away from inefficient paper forms to embrace digital processes, new questions are emerging about verifying, sharing and securing voter registration data.

With the 2016 presidential election cycle being called the "Year of Disruption," one need only look at state voter registration practices for an issue that is going anywhere but in the direction of conventional, middle-of-the-road solutions. From challenging the notion that citizens must proactively take the initiative to register themselves, to pushing back against a historical overreliance on the use of paper forms for registration, times are quickly changing.

Thanks to the Help America Vote Act of 2002, today's statewide electronic databases are the launching pad for a host of voter registration innovations—most notably online voter registration. The November 2016 elections will mark the first time that well over half of the eligible voting population in the U.S. will be able to register to vote via the internet. Thirty-one states plus the District of Columbia currently offer such services, with more states expected to come online before Nov. 8.

"Make no mistake about it, this is the last clipboard election," said Louisiana Secretary of State Tom Schedler, who heads the National Association of Secretaries of State. "The era of voter registration drives with volunteers carrying around reams of forms, and election clerks manually processing those stacks of paper, are going the way of the dinosaur. With online registration spreading around the country, there will be a much greater reliance on more accurate and efficient electronic processes in the future."

Replacing antiquated, paper-based voter registration drives with online registration reduces delays and handwriting errors or omissions, ensuring that people who sign up ultimately get placed on the voter rolls. It also prevents the systemic overwhelm that can occur when large numbers of

voter registration applications are submitted to local election offices at the last minute.

"Online voter registration is the new norm," remarked Pennsylvania Secretary of State Pedro A. Cortés, whose state online system—launched in August 2015—registered more than 100,000 eligible voters in less than six months' time. "The data is too convincing to ignore, both in terms of potential increases in voter participation and the cost savings to governments at all levels."

In addition to driving more voter registration activity online, Cortés points to Pennsylvania's system as a platform for enhancing multilingual services and accessibility options for voters with disabilities. It's also optimized for use by younger voters, who tend to rely on mobile devices for carrying out everyday business.

Challenging the Status Quo

Automatic voter registration, or AVR, may be the most disruptive idea this year, shifting the traditionally passive process of having citizens register to vote onto the government. All eyes are on Oregon, which became the first state to launch AVR on Jan. 1, 2016. Eligible voters are automatically registered to vote when they renew or apply for a driver's license. The Oregon Motor Voter Act also requires automatic registration for eligible voters who have conducted business with the Department of Motor Vehicles since 2013. Registered voters receive a mailing from the secretary of state's office advising them to choose a political party, opt out, or do nothing (to be listed as non-affiliated voters). California passed a similar law, but it has yet to go into effect.[1]

In February, Oregon Secretary of State Jeanne Atkins reported a smooth rollout of automatic voter registration. She noted that more than 4,000 new voters were registered in the first six days, compared to an average of 2,000 new registrations per month under the old system. Roughly 7 percent of eligible citizens had opted out of registration altogether.

Atkins added that her office discovered a few surprises with the new system. First, the secretary of state's office didn't receive a high volume of calls or emails from people who were upset about being automatically added to the voter rolls, as some had anticipated. Second, the AVR system made it possible for Oregon officials to quickly update 17,000 existing voter registrations to reflect changes of address.

"Under our old system, it could take weeks, months—or even years—to update someone's voter registration information after they moved within the state," said Atkins. "Now, we have a much more efficient way to address a huge administrative issue for us, especially as a state that conducts its elections entirely by mail."

While more than 15 states are expected to consider automatic voter registration proposals for 2016, including Connecticut, Illinois and Maryland, the biggest challenge may be finding a way to adapt the concept beyond blue-leaning states.

Washington Secretary of State Kim Wyman, a Republican, introduced bipartisan legislation that would bring automatic voter registration to her state. Washington doesn't check for proof of citizenship in order to get a regular driver's license, so under her proposal, those with commercial or enhanced licenses who have undergone citizenship checks and meet other voting requirements—as well as those receiving social services that verify citizenship, or those who are getting health insurance through the state health exchange—would be automatically registered to vote.[2] Like Oregon, citizens would also have the choice of opting out.

Wyman estimated that if the bill becomes law, the number of new voters could range from the tens of thousands to as high as 500,000.

"We are looking at ways to find that very important middle ground in election administration—balancing access with security," said Wyman. "It's the result of compromise that both major political parties should be able to accept."

Another innovation whose adoption is often split along partisan lines is Election Day registration, which allows eligible voters to register and vote same-day at a polling site or at county/town offices. Once a practice in just a handful of places, it has now been adopted in 15 states (although California and Hawaii have not yet implemented the practice).

Utah is currently running a three-year pilot program to determine whether same-day registration increases voter participation. So far, at least five counties have reported significant improvements in turnout, particularly among voters between the ages of 18 and 24 years old.

Proponents say Election Day registration provides convenience and reduces the need for provisional ballots. Opponents say it can create longer lines and waiting times at the polls, and open up a potential avenue for fraud.

Protecting Digital Voter Registration Lists

With so many states looking at new ways to get people added to their voter rolls, questions have also recently emerged about the best ways to collect, share and secure voter registration files.

In December 2015, the voter registration data of 191 million Americans was discovered on the internet by security experts who found what was apparently a misconfigured server owned by an unidentified data aggregator. Although it is all publicly available information, many Americans consider details like their political party affiliation or home address to be private data. New issues are being raised about what states can and should be doing to protect and manage the data involved.

For example, what kinds of safeguards should be in place when it comes to personal information contained in publicly available voter registration files? Should there be state notification laws when voter registration data is found to be improperly accessed or exposed, much like medical or financial data? Should firms that purchase or obtain public data on voter registration for political purposes be held accountable for providing access to clients or campaigns that leave personal information unsecured and available on the internet?

"We need to do more in educating voters up front that state voter files are public information," said California Secretary of State Alex Padilla. "California data file rules are pretty specific about sharing or selling data. However, we may need to look at establishing better protocols on what recipients of the data are doing with it."

Padilla also is overseeing an effort to allow for third-party integration with California's new online voter registration system, allowing voter outreach groups to build registration into their own online platforms and track users who are registering with their tools. West Virginia and Pennsylvania have been conducting similar pilots. Washington, one of the first states to offer online registration in 2008, has taken it a step beyond and integrated its process with social media platform Facebook.

All of these changes leave no doubt that in the course of just 15 years, the process of voter registration and how people interact with government for electoral engagement have fundamentally shifted toward the digital age. Modernization is bringing high risk and high reward for those who embrace change. Policy makers considering voter registration advances will need to understand all of the new technological and legal issues involving online registration, automatic registration and Election Day registration, and they should prepare to adopt data policies that guide digital voter registration practices.

"We are in a cycle of relentless innovation for election officials and voters alike," observed Washington's Wyman, who has worked in election administration for more than 20 years. "If you're not thinking about revolution, you should at least understand the technological evolution and all of the state changes that are driving the trends."

Notes

[1] New Jersey Governor Chris Christie vetoed automatic voter registration legislation passed by the New Jersey State Legislature.

[2] Unlike California and Oregon, Washington does not require proof of U.S. citizenship or legal presence in order to get a driver's license, which is why proponents are not seeking automatic voter registration for everyone.

About the Author

Kay Stimson is director of communications and special projects for the National Association of Secretaries of State in Washington, D.C. A former television news reporter who covered the state legislatures in Maryland and South Carolina, she enjoys writing about state and federal policy issues facing lawmakers.

Table 4.15
THE SECRETARIES OF STATE, 2016

State or other jurisdiction	Name and party	Method of selection	Length of regular term in years	Date of first service	Present term ends	Number of previous terms	Maximum consecutive terms allowed by constitution
Alabama	John Merrill (R)	E	4	1/2015	1/2019	...	2
Alaska	......................(a)......................						
Arizona	Michele Reagan (R)	E	4	1/2015	1/2019	...	2
Arkansas	Mark Martin (R)	E	4	1/2011	1/2019	1	2
California	Alex Padilla (D)	E	4	1/2015	1/2019	...	2
Colorado	Wayne Williams (R)	E	4	1/2015	1/2019	...	2
Connecticut	Denise Merrill (D)	E	4	1/2011	1/2019	1	...
Delaware	Jeffrey Bullock (D)	A (c)	4	1/2009	...	...	...
Florida	Kenneth Detzner (R) (e)	A	4	2/2012	...	(e)	2
Georgia	Brian Kemp (R)	E (d)	4	1/2010 (d)	1/2019	(d)	...
Hawaii	......................(a)......................						
Idaho	Lawerence Denney (R)	E	4	1/2015	1/2019	...	...
Illinois	Jesse White (D)	E	4	1/1999	1/2019	4	...
Indiana	Connie Lawson (R) (f)	E	4	3/2012 (f)	1/2019	(f)	2
Iowa	Paul Pate (R)	E	4	12/2014	12/2018	...	...
Kansas	Kris Kobach (R)	E	4	1/2011	1/2019	1	...
Kentucky	Alison Lundergan Grimes (D)	E	4	12/2011	12/2019	1	2
Louisiana	Tom Schedler (R)	E (g)	4	11/2010	1/2020	1	...
Maine	Matt Dunlap (D)	L	2	1/2005 (m)	1/2017	(m)	4 (h)
Maryland	John Wobensmith (R)	A	...	1/2015	...	...	...
Massachusetts	William Francis Galvin (D)	E	4	1/1995	1/2019	5	...
Michigan	Ruth Johnson (R)	E	4	1/2011	1/2019	1	2
Minnesota	Steve Simon (DFL)	E	4	1/2015	1/2019	...	...
Mississippi	C. Delbert Hosemann Jr.(R)	E	4	1/2008	1/2020	2	...
Missouri	Jason Kander (D)	E	4	1/2013	1/2017	...	...
Montana	Linda McCulloch (D)	E	4	1/2009	1/2017	1	(i)
Nebraska	John Gale (R)	E	4	12/2000 (j)	1/2019	(j)	...
Nevada	Barbara Cegavske (R)	E	4	1/2015	1/2019	...	2
New Hampshire	William Gardner (D)	L	2	12/1976	12/2018	20	...
New Jersey	......................(a)(k)......................						
New Mexico	Dianna Duran (R)	E	4	12/2010	12/2018	1	2
New York	Cesar Perales (D)	A	...	5/2011	...	...	...
North Carolina	Elaine Marshall (D)	E	4	1/1997	1/2017	4	...
North Dakota	Alvin A. Jaeger (R)	E	4	1/1993	12/2018	5	...
Ohio	Jon Husted (R)	E	4	1/2011	1/2019	1	2
Oklahoma	Chris Benge (R) (n)	A	4	11/2013 (n)	1/2019	(n)	...
Oregon	Jeanne Atkins (D)	E	4	3/2015	1/2017	...	2
Pennsylvania	Pedro Cortes (D)	A	...	1/2003 (b)	...	(b)	...
Rhode Island	Nellie Gorbea (D)	E	4	1/2015	1/2019	...	2
South Carolina	Mark Hammond (R)	E	4	1/2003	1/2019	3	...
South Dakota	Shantel Krebs (R)	E	4	1/2015	1/2019	...	2
Tennessee	Tre Hargett (R)	L	4	1/2009	1/2017	1	...
Texas	Nandita Berry (R)	A	...	1/2014	...	...	...
Utah	......................(a)......................						
Vermont	Jim Condos (D)	E	2	1/2011	1/2017	2	...
Virginia	Kelly Thomasson (D)	A	...	4/2016	...	...	...
Washington	Kim Wyman (R)	E	4	1/2013	1/2017	...	...
West Virginia	Natalie Tennant (D)	E	4	1/2009	1/2017	1	...
Wisconsin	Douglas LaFollette (D)	E	4	1/1/1974 (l)	1/2019	10 (l)	...
Wyoming	Ed Murray (R)	E	4	1/2015	1/2019	...	...
American Samoa	......................(a)......................						
Guam	......................(a)......................						
No. Mariana Islands	......................(a)......................						
Puerto Rico	Javier Gonzalez (PDP)	A	...	10/2016 (o)	1/2017	...	...
U.S. Virgin Islands	......................(a)......................						

See footnotes at end of table.

THE SECRETARIES OF STATE, 2016—Continued

Source: The Council of State Governments, November 2015.
Key:
E — Elected by voters.
A — Appointed by governor.
L — Elected by legislature.
. . . — No provision for.

(a) No secretary of state; lieutenant govenor performs functions of this office. See Tables 4.12 through 4.14.

(b) Cortes served as secretary of the commonwealth from 2003 to 2010. He was appointed as secretary by Gov. Tom Wolf in January 2015.

(c) Appointed by the governor and confirmed by the Senate.

(d) Gov. Perdue appointed Brian Kemp on January 8, 2010 to replace Karen Handel after she resigned to run for the office of governor. Kemp was elected to a full term in the 2010 general election and re-elected in 2014.

(e) Detzner was appointed in February 2012. He served previously in 2003 as the office transitioned from an elected position to an appointed one.

(f) Lawson was appointed March 16, 2012 to fill the position left vacant when Charlie White was dismissed Feb. 4, 2012 after his conviction on felony charges. She was elected to a full term in 2014.

(g) Schedler was appointed and sworn in as secretary of state on Nov. 22, 2010 after Jay Dardenne was elected to serve as lieutenant governor.

(h) Statutory term limit of four consecutive two-year terms.

(i) Eligible for eight out of 16 years.

(j) Gale was appointed by Gov. Mike Johanns in December 2000 upon the resignation of Scott Moore. He was elected to full four-year terms in November 2002, 2006, 2010 and again in 2014.

(k) The secretary of state of New Jersey is an appointed position. Gov. Christie appointed Lt. Gov. Kim Guadagno to serve as secretary of state for this term of office.

(l) LaFollette was first elected in 1974 and served a four-year term. He was elected again in 1982 and has been re-elected since. The present term ends in 2019.

(m) Secretary Matthew Dunlap previously served as secretary of state from 2005 to 2010. He was elected by the Legislature to serve again in January 2013 and re-elected in January 2015.

(n) Benge was appointed by Gov. Mary Fallin on November 8, 2013.

(o) Gonzalez began serving as acting secretary of state upon the Oct. 26, 2015 resignation of Secretary David Bernier.

(p) Appointed by Gov. Terry McAuliffe after the resignation of Levar Stoney.

Table 4.16
SECRETARIES OF STATE: QUALIFICATIONS FOR OFFICE

State or other jurisdiction	Minimum age	U.S. citizen (years) (a)	State resident (years) (b)	Qualified voter (years)	Method of selection to office
Alabama	25	7	5	★	E
Alaska	....(c)..				
Arizona	25	10	5	...	E
Arkansas	18	★	★	★	E
California	18	★	★	★	E
Colorado	25	★	2	...	E
Connecticut	18	★	★	★	E
Delaware	...	...	...	...	A
Florida	....(d)..				A
Georgia	25	10	4	★	E
Hawaii	....(c)..				
Idaho	25	★	2	★	E
Illinois	25	★	3	...	E
Indiana	...	★	★	★	E
Iowa	18	★	...	...	E
Kansas	...	...	...	...	E
Kentucky	30	★	★	★	E
Louisiana	25	5	5	★	E
Maine	...	...	...	...	(e)
Maryland	...	...	...	...	A
Massachusetts	18	★	5	★	E
Michigan	18	★	★	★	E
Minnesota	21	★	1	★	E
Mississippi	25	★	5	★	E
Missouri	...	★	★	2	E
Montana	25	★	2	★	E
Nebraska	★	★	★	★	E
Nevada	25	2	2	...	E
New Hampshire	18	★	★	★	(e)
New Jersey	18	★	★	★	A
New Mexico	30	★	5	★	E
New York	18	★	★	...	A
North Carolina	21	★	★	★	E
North Dakota	25	★	5	5	E
Ohio	18	★	★	★	E
Oklahoma	31	★	★	10	A
Oregon	18	★	★	★	E
Pennsylvania	...	...	...	...	A
Rhode Island	18	★	30 days	★	E
South Carolina	...	★	★	★	E
South Dakota	...	...	...	...	E
Tennessee	...	...	...	...	(e)
Texas	18	★	...	...	A
Utah	....(c)..				
Vermont	18	★	★	★	E
Virginia	...	...	...	...	A
Washington	18	★	★	★	E
West Virginia	...	★	★	★	E
Wisconsin	18	★	★	★	E
Wyoming	25	★	1	★	E
American Samoa	....(c)..				
Guam	....(c)..				
No. Mariana Islands	....(c)..				
Puerto Rico	...	5	5	...	A
U.S. Virgin Islands	....(c)..				

Source: The Council of State Governments survey of secretaries of state offices, November 2015.

Key:
★—Formal provision; number of years not specified.
...—No formal provision.
A—Appointed by governor.
E—Elected by voters.
(a) In some states you must be a U.S. citizen to be an elector, and must be an elector to run.

(b) In some states you must be a state resident to be an elector, and must be an elector to run.
(c) No secretary of state.
(d) As of January 1, 2003, the office of Secretary of State shall be an appointed position (appointed by the governor). It will no longer be a cabinet position, but an agency head and the Department of State shall be an agency under the governor's office.
(e) Chosen by joint ballot of state senators and representatives. In Maine and New Hampshire, every two years. In Tennessee, every four years.

Table 4.17
SECRETARIES OF STATE: ELECTION AND REGISTRATION DUTIES

State or other jurisdiction	Chief election officer	Determines ballot eligibility of political parties	Receives initiative and/or referendum petition	Files certificate of nomination or election	Supplies election ballots or materials to local officials	Files candidates' expense papers	Files other campaign reports	Conducts voter education programs	Registers charitable organizations	Registers corporations (a)	Processes and/or commissions notaries public	Registers securities	Registers trade names/marks
Alabama	★	★	...	★	★	★	★	★	★	★	★	...	★
Alaska (b)	★	★	★	★	★	...	...	★	...	...	★	...	...
Arizona	★	★	★	★	...	★	★	★	★	...	★	...	★
Arkansas	★	★	★	★	...	★	★	★	...	★	★	...	★
California	★(c)	★	...	★	★	★	★	★	(d)	★	★	...	★
Colorado	★	★	★	★	...	★	★	★	★	★	★	...	★
Connecticut	★	★	...	★	★	...	...	★	★	★	★	...	★
Delaware	...	...	...	(e)	...	(f)	...		★(g)	★	★	...	★
Florida (v)	★	★	★	★	...	★	★	...	...	★	★	...	★
Georgia	★	★	...	★	★	★	★	★	★	★	...	★	★
Hawaii (b)	...	...	...	...	...	...	...	...	...	★	★	...	★
Idaho	★	★	★	★	★	★	★	★	...	★	★	...	★
Illinois	...	...	★	(h)	...	...	...	...	★	★	★	★	★
Indiana (i)	★	★	...	★	★	★	★	★	★	★	★	...	★
Iowa	★	★	...	★	...	...	...	★	★	★	★	...	★
Kansas	★	★	...	★	★	★	...	★	★	★	★	...	★
Kentucky	★	★	...	★	...	...	...	★	★	★	★	...	★
Louisiana	★	...	...	★	★	...	...	★	★	★	★	...	★
Maine	★	★	★	★	★	...	...	★	(y)	★	★	...	★
Maryland	...	...	...	...	...	...	...	...	★	...	★	...	★
Massachusetts	★	★	★	★	★	(f)	(f)	★	...	★	★	★	★
Michigan	★	★	★	★	...	★	★	★	...	★	★	...	...
Minnesota (z)	★	★	...	★	★	...	...	★	★	★	★	...	★
Mississippi	★	★	★	★	★	★	★	★	★	★	★	...	★
Missouri	★	★	★	★	...	...	...	★	★	★	★	★	★
Montana	★	★	★	★	★	...	...	★	★	★	★	...	★
Nebraska	★	★	★	★	★	...	...	★	★	★	★	...	★
Nevada (j)	★	★	★	★	★	★	★	★	...	★	★	★	★
New Hampshire	★	★	...	★	★	★	★	...	★	★	★	★	★
New Jersey	★	★	★	★	★	★	★	★	★	★	★	...	★
New Mexico	★	★	...	...	★	★	★	★	★	★	★	...	★
New York	...	...	...	...	...	...	...	...	★	★	★	...	★
North Carolina (k)	...	...	...	...	...	...	...	...	★	★	★	...	★
North Dakota	★	★	★	★	★	★	★	★	★	★	★	...	★
Ohio (l)	★	★	★	★(m)	★	★	★	★	...	★	★	★	★
Oklahoma	...	...	★	...	...	...	...	...	★	★(n)	★	...	★
Oregon	★	★	★	★	★	★	★	★	★	★	★	...	★
Pennsylvania	★	★	...	★	...	...	★	★	★	★	★	...	★
Rhode Island (o)	★	★	...	★	★	...	...	★	...	★	★	...	★
South Carolina	...	...	...	...	...	...	...	...	★	★(p)	★	...	★
South Dakota	★	★	★	★	...	★	★	★	...	★	★	...	★
Tennessee (q)	★	★	...	★	★	...	...	★	★	★	★	...	★
Texas	★	★	...	★	★	...	★	★	...	★	★	...	★
Utah (b)	★	★	★	★	★	★	★	★	★	★	...	...	★
Vermont (r)	★	...	...	★	★	★	...	★	★	★	★	...	★
Virginia (x)	...	...	...	...	...	...	...	...	★	★	...	★	...
Washington (w)	★	...	★	★	...	...	...	...	★	★	★	★	★
West Virginia	★	★	...	★	...	★	★	...	★	★	★	...	★
Wisconsin (s)	...	...	...	...	...	...	...	...	...	...	★	...	★
Wyoming	★	★	★	★	(t)	★	★	★	★	★	★	★	★
American Samoa (b)	...	...	...	★	...	★	★	★	★	★	★	...	...
Guam (b)	...	...	...	...	...	...	...	...	★	★	★	...	★
Puerto Rico	...	...	...	...	...	...	...	...	★	★	★	★	★
U.S. Virgin Islands (b)	...	...	...	...	...	...	...	...	★	★(u)	★	...	★

See footnotes at end of table.

SECRETARIES OF STATE: ELECTION AND REGISTRATION DUTIES — Continued

Source: The Council of State Governments' survey of secretaries of state offices, November 2015.

Key:

★ — Responsible for activity.

... — Not responsible for activity.

(a) Unless otherwise indicated, office registers domestic, foreign and non-profit corporations.

(b) No secretary of state. Duties indicated are performed by lieutenant governor. In Hawaii, election related responsibilities have been transferred to an independent Chief Election Officer. In U. S. Virgin Islands election duties are performed by Supervisor of Elections.

(c) Other election duties include: tallying votes from all 58 counties, testing and certifying voting systems for use by local elections officials, maintaining statewide voter registration database, publishing state Voter Information Guide/State Ballot Pamphlet and qualifing statewide ballot initiatives and referenda.

(d) This office does not register charitable trusts, but does register charitable organizations as nonprofit corporations; also limited partnerships, limited liability corporations, and domestic partners, Advanced Health care Directives, and administers the Safe at Home mail forwarding program.

(e) Files certificates of election for publication purposes only; does not file certificates of nomination.

(f) Federal candidates only.

(g) Incorporated organizations only.

(h) Office issues document, but does not receive it.

(i) Additional election duties include: statewide voter registration system administrator. Additional registration duties include securities enforcement and auto dealer registration and enforcement.

(j) Additional registration duties include:Issues annual State Business License, registers Domestic Partnerships, register advanced directives for health care.

(k) Other election duties: administers the Electoral College. Other registration duties: Maintains secure online registry of advance health care directives.

(l) Supplies poll worker training materials to county boards of elections: certifies official form of the ballot to county board of elections.

(m) Issues certificate of nomination or election to all statewide candidates and U.S. Representatives.

(n) Certifies U.S. Congressional election results to Washington D.C. Also registers partnerships, limited liability companies, limited liability partnerships, limited liability companies and limited liability partnerships.

(o) Additional registration duties include: Non-resident landlord appointment of agent for service and Uniform Commercial Code.

(p) Also registers the Cable Franchise Authority.

(q) Appoints the Coordinator of Elections who performs the election duties indicated above, and also prepares the elections manjual and elections handbook for use by state officials. Also registers athlete agents, as well as individuals and entities seeking exemption from Tennessee's workers' compensation requitements.

(r) Additional registration duties include: registers temporary officiants for civil marriages.

(s) Additional registration duties include: Issues authentications and apostilles.

(t) Materials not ballots.

(u) Both domestic and foreign profit; but only domestic non-profit.

(v) Additional registration duties include: registers fictitious names and other types of business entities.

(w) Additional registration duties include: registers domestic partnerships and registers international student exchange programs.

(x) Additional registration duties include: registering organizations' mottos; registering logos and insignias; authentications.

(y) Registers nonprofit entities.

(z) Additional registration duties include: registers LLCs, limited partnerships.

Table 4.18
SECRETARIES OF STATE: CUSTODIAL, PUBLICATION AND LEGISLATIVE DUTIES

State or other jurisdiction	Archives state records and regulations	Files state agency rules and regulations	Administers uniform commercial code provisions	Files other corporate documents	State manual or directory	Session laws	State constitution	Statutes	Administrative rules and regulations	Opens legislative sessions (a)	Enrolls or engrosses bills	Retains copies of bills	Registers lobbyists
	Custodial				*Publication*					*Legislative*			
Alabama	...	...	★	★	...	★	★	★	...	...	★	★	...
Alaska (b)	...	★	...	...	...	...	★	...	★	★	...	★	...
Arizona	★	★	★	...	...	...	★	...	★	...	...	★	★
Arkansas (c)	★	★	★	★	...	★	...	...	★	...	...	★	★
California	★	★	★	★	★	...	...	...	...	...	(d)	...	★
Colorado	...	★	★	★	...	...	★	...	★	...	...	★	★
Connecticut	★(e)	★	★	★	★	...	...	...	★(v)	S	...	★	★
Delaware	★	★	★	★	...	...	...	...	...	...	...	...	...
Florida (u)	★	★	★	★	...	★	★	★	★	...	...	...	...
Georgia	★	★	...	...	★	...	★	...	★	...	...	...	...
Hawaii (b)	...	★	...	...	...	★	...	★	...	...	...	★	...
Idaho	...	...	★	★	★	★	★	...	...	...	...	★	★
Illinois	★	★	★	★	★	★	★	...	★	H	...	★	★
Indiana	(n)	...	★	★	...	...	...	...	...	H	...	(n)	...
Iowa	★	...	★	★	...	★	★	...	...	...	★	★	...
Kansas (s)	...	★	★	★	★	★	...	(o)	★	★	...	★	★
Kentucky	★	...	★	★	...	★	...	...	...	...	★	★	...
Louisiana	★	...	★	★	★	...	...	★	★	...	★	★	(f)
Maine	★	★	★	★	...	...	★	...	★	...	...	...	...
Maryland	...	★	...	...	...	★	...	...	...	...	★	★	...
Massachusetts	★	★	★	★	★	★	★	★	★	...	★	★	★
Michigan	★	★	★	...	★	★	★	★	★	...	...	...	★
Minnesota	★	★	★	★	★	...	...	...	...	H	...	★	...
Mississippi	★	★	★	★	★	★	★	...	★	H	...	(p)	★
Missouri	★(h)	★	★	★	★	...	★	...	★	H	...	★	...
Montana	★	★	★	★	...	...	★	...	★	H	★	★	...
Nebraska	★	★	★	★	...	...	★	...	★	...	...	★	...
Nevada	★	★	★	★	...	...	★	...	★	...	...	★	...
New Hampshire	★	...	★	★	★	...	★	...	...	...	★	★	★
New Jersey	★	...	...	...	...	...	★	...	...	...	...	★	...
New Mexico	...	★	★	★	★	★	★	★	★	H	...	★	★
New York	...	★	★	...	★	...	★	...	★	...	...	...	...
North Carolina (t)	★	★	★	...	★	...	★	...	...	...	★	★	★
North Dakota	...	★	★	★	...	...	...	...	...	...	...	★	★
Ohio (i)	...	★	★	★	★	★	★	...	...	...	...	★	...
Oklahoma (j)	...	★	...	★	...	...	...	...	★	...	...	★	...
Oregon	★	★	★	★	★	...	★	...	★	...	...	★	★
Pennsylvania	...	...	★	★	...	...	★	...	★	...	★	★	...
Rhode Island (k)	★	★	★	★	★	...	★	...	★	...	...	★	★
South Carolina	...	...	★	★	...	...	...	...	...	...	...	★	...
South Dakota	★	★	★	★	★	★	...	★	★	H	...	★	★
Tennessee	★(q)	★	★	★	★(l)	★	...	★	★	H	...	...	...
Texas	...	★	★	★	...	★	...	...	...	H	...	★	...
Utah (b)	...	...	...	...	...	...	...	...	...	...	...	★	★
Vermont (m)	★	★	★	★	★	★	★	...	...	H	...	★	★
Virginia (g)	...	...	...	...	★	...	...	...	...	...	...	...	...
Washington (w)	★	...	...	★	★	...	★	...	...	...	★	★	...
West Virginia	★	★	★	★	...	...	...	...	★	...	...	★	...
Wisconsin	★	...	...	...	...	...	...	...	...	...	...	...	...
Wyoming	★	★	★	★	★	...	★	...	...	H	...	★	★
American Samoa (b)	...	★	...	★	...	★	★	...	★	...	...	...	...
Guam (b)	...	...	★	...	...	...	...	★	...	...	...	...	...
Puerto Rico	...	★	★	★	...	★	★	★	★	...	...	...	...
U.S. Virgin Islands (b)	...	★	★	★	...	...	...	...	...	...	★	★	...

See footnotes at end of table.

SECRETARIES OF STATE: CUSTODIAL, PUBLICATION AND LEGISLATIVE DUTIES — Continued

Sources: The Council of State Governments' survey of secretaries of state offices, November 2015.

Key:

★ — Responsible for activity.

. . . — Not responsible for activity.

(a) In this column only: ★–Both houses; H–House; S–Senate.

(b) No secretary of state. Duties indicated are performed by lieutenant governor.

(c) Additional custodial duties for the Arkansas Secretary of State include serving as the caretaker for the Arkansas State Capitol Building and Grounds, including all custodial duties, HVAC system, building maintenance, historic preservation and conducting tours.

(d) Office does not enroll or engross bills but does chapter bills that are signed into law and retains final chaptered copies.

(e) The secretary of state is keeper of public records, but the state archives is a department of the Connecticut State Library.

(f) Only registers political pollsters.

(g) Other custodial duties include: restoration of civil rights; liasion to Virginia Indians; gubernatorial appointments. Other publication duties include: state organization charts. Other registration duties include: Pardons; Service of Process

(h) Also responsible for the State Library.

(i) Additional publication duties include: elections statistics, official roser of federal, state, and county officers and official roster of township and municipal officers. Additional legislative duties include: Distributing laws to specified state and local government agencies.

(j) Other custodial duties include: Effective Financing Statements identifying farm products that are subject to a security interest, UCC and mortgage documents pertaining to transmitting utilities and also railroads and files open meeting notices.

(k) Additional duties include administering oaths of office to general officers and legislators.

(l) The Division of Publications of the Office of the Secretary of State also publishes the following: The Tennessee Blue Book, Board and Commission vacancies, and Executive Orders and Proclamations.

(m) Additional custodial duties include: records management, and certifying vital records.

(n) The Secretary of State's office receives and authenticates Bills and Enrolled Acts, but does not keep or maintain them. Post-session legislative materials are mantained by the Indiana Public Records Commission.

(o) Responsible for distribution only.

(p) Chapters and indexes all signed bill and chamber and concurrent resolutions.

(q) The Division of Records Management of the Office of the Secretary of State assists state agencies in the appropriate utilization, disposition, retention and destruction of state records.

(s) Additionally, the secretary of state publishes the Kansas Register and opens legislative reorganization meetings.

(t) Other publication duties include: Publishes state board and commission meeting notices online. Other legislative duties include: The Secretary of State is responsible for the certification of election results before legislators take the the oath of office at the opening of each session of the General Assembly.

(u) Files other types of business entity and cable franchis documents, records federal tax liens and judgement liens and issues Apostilles

(v) The regulations function is being developed and will be fully implemented in 2015.

(w) Legislative duties also include: chapters bills.

The Authority of State Attorneys General and Their Efforts on 21st Century Policing

By Emily Myers and Ayeisha Cox

Several situations in 2015 and 2016 challenged the attorney general's role as representative of the state in litigation and his or her ability to determine when to seek judicial review, particularly in connection with policy issues that are being hotly debated. Additionally, attorneys general have the vital task of cooperatively enforcing state laws and promoting sound law enforcement policies. To that end, the second half of this article covers police body-worn cameras as part of a national AG initiative on 21st century policing.

The Authority of State Attorneys General to Control State Litigation

The attorney general of a state is its chief law officer, with authority to represent, defend and enforce the legal interests of the state government and the public. Litigation on behalf of the state is one of the attorney general's primary duties. The attorney general is typically authorized, in either state statutes or the state constitution, to "appear for the state in all causes in the supreme and federal court wherein the state is directly interested, also in all civil cases of like nature in all other courts of the state whenever, in his opinion, the interests of the state require it."[1]

In addition to this explicit authority to control the legal business of the state, in most states the attorney general has common law powers not specified by statute but long recognized by the courts. Although common law powers are defined differently in the states, they generally include "the right to institute, conduct and maintain all suits necessary for the enforcement of the laws of the State, preservation of order and the protection of public rights."[2]

Several recent situations have challenged the attorney general's role as representative of the state in litigation and his or her ability to determine when to seek judicial review. These issues have arisen in connection with policy issues that are being hotly debated throughout the country. In some cases, the governor or the legislature disagreed with the attorney general's decision to file suit in a particular case. In other cases, the governor or legislature wanted the attorney general to file suit and the attorney general declined to do so. In each of these circumstances, the question of who represents the state was raised, and in each case, the attorney general's authority was confirmed.

In the most recent instance, Colorado Attorney General Cynthia Coffman filed three federal lawsuits against the federal government that the governor did not support, challenging rules promulgated by the U.S. Department of the Interior and the Environmental Protection Agency. The governor filed a petition in the Colorado Supreme Court, seeking a ruling on the authority of the attorney general to sue the federal government without the consent of the governor. Colorado statutes state that the attorney general "shall appear for the state and prosecute and defend all actions and proceedings, civil and criminal, in which the state is a party or is interested when required to do so by the governor." Gov. John Hickenlooper argued that the governor is the supreme executive of the state and that his decision is therefore binding on the attorney general; that the language of the statute limited the attorney general's authority to sue to situations in which the governor requested her to do so; and that by undertaking these lawsuits against his wishes, the attorney general created a conflict of interest that prevents her from advising the governor on issues involved in the cases.

The attorney general argued that an earlier decision by the Colorado Supreme Court, involving a similar situation, had already established that the executive power of Colorado is intentionally diffused, rather than hierarchical, as the governor argued; that the Colorado attorney general, in addition to powers conferred by statute, has common law powers which have not been specifically repealed by any statute; and that, "the Attorney General must consider the broader institutional concerns of the state even though these concerns are not shared by an individual agency or officer." The attorney general noted that in prior cases where the governor had disagreed with the attorney general, he had filed an amicus brief expressing his views as governor.

Although it did not address any of these arguments specifically, the court, citing its prior decision, held that the governor had an "adequate alternative remedy" and denied the governor's petition.[3]

Other state officials also have tested the authority of an attorney general to decline to challenge legislation. In Indiana, several parties challenged the constitutionality of an Indiana statute addressing enforcement of immigration laws. The attorney general represented the state and the case had already begun when the U.S. Supreme Court issued a decision striking down an Arizona statutory provision identical to one in the Indiana litigation. The attorney general acknowledged that the Indiana statutory provision was unconstitutional, and stated that the provision "will not be defended and a ruling by this Court to that effect will be accepted." Although the attorney general continued to defend other provisions of the state law, three state senators sought to intervene in the case to defend the statutory provision that the attorney general declined to defend.

The court cited longstanding Indiana case law under which the attorney general "has exclusive power and right in most instances to represent the State, its agencies and officers, and the agencies and officers may not hire outside counsel unless the Attorney General has consented in writing." The court declined to allow the intervention, because "allowing the three individual legislators to intervene here in their official capacities as State Senators not only would conflict with this well-settled state law, but would provide the legislators a trump card with respect to the Attorney General's statutorily derived discretion in this context."[4]

In another case involving the decision of an attorney general not to challenge a statute, the New Hampshire Senate enacted HB 89, a bill which "requir[ed] the Attorney General to join the lawsuit challenging the Patient Protection and Affordable Care Act." The state Supreme Court held that HB 89 was unconstitutional because it violated the separation of powers doctrine in the New Hampshire Constitution, which provides, "In the government of this state, the three essential powers thereof, to wit, the legislative, executive and judicial, ought to be kept as separate from, and independent of, each other as the nature of free government will admit." Citing previous decisions, the court held that "the New Hampshire Separation of Powers clause is violated when one branch usurps an essential power of another." Reviewing the history of the state's constitution, the court concluded that

the constitution gives "the executive the exclusive power to enforce the law" and made the executive responsible for "initiating civil actions on behalf of the State ... The executive branch alone has the power to decide the State's interest in litigation." The court did not agree with the legislature that this statute was an exercise of the legislature's power "to set forth the several duties, powers and limits, of the several civil and military officers of this state...." Rather, the court stated, "In mandating this action—to join a specific lawsuit on a particular side—the legislature would exceed its authority to prescribe the duties of the attorney general. In so doing, it would deprive the executive of its essential power to determine the State's interest in civil litigation." The court also dismissed the legislature's argument that the filing of this case was a political, rather than a legal, decision. The court stated, "It is the executive, not the legislative branch, in which the constitution vests the power to determine the State's interest in any litigation."[5]

The attorney general's authority to control litigation filed on behalf of the state will undoubtedly be tested and affirmed around the country as new public policy debates arise.

The Pros and Cons of Police Body-Worn Cameras

"To Protect and Serve with 21st Century Policing" is the National Association of Attorneys General 2015–16 presidential initiative. Its goal is to offer the latest approaches, processes and possible solutions in such areas as community protection and involvement, officer-involved shootings and campus sexual assaults. This section focuses on police body-worn cameras, or BWCs.

Police body-worn cameras have gained public interest in recent years in response to demands for more transparency in allegations of police brutality.[6] As a result, states and municipalities have begun integrating BWCs into law enforcement policies.[7] A 2014 Accenture survey found that 8 out of 10 Americans believed the "expanded use of new and advanced digital tools would improve police services."[8] Use of BWCs has support from organizations such as the American Civil Liberties Union, known as the ACLU. The ACLU supports BWC policies that ensure the public privacy of citizens, while at the same time maintain public confidence in the integrity of those privacy protections.[9]

The implementation of BWCs will provide for more accountability and transparency. However, BWCs are not a panacea. The sustainability and long-term utility of BWCs is uncertain. This article explores the benefits and negative effects of implementing BWCs, and addresses actions that federal government and state attorneys general have taken to implement BWC programs.

Implementing Policies

Police departments have discretion in implementing their own BWC policies. A successful BWC program will take into consideration the benefits and negatives of BWCs, with the overall goal of reducing police use-of-force incidents and false police brutality complaints. The following are issues to consider when implementing BWC policies.

Police departments may or may not be required to release videos. Because of the enormous volume of data compiled by jurisdictions using BWCs, this is posing a special problem for those states who would otherwise release the videos. A number of states are in the process of considering legislative responses to dealing with this problem of having to balance compliance with existing laws with the extraordinarily huge administrative burden of cataloging and archiving hundreds of thousands of hours of videos. Additionally, many states' open record laws are subject to the "ongoing investigation" exemption. This exemption has been used on numerous occasions to withhold BWC videos of high public interest.

Benefits of Body-Worn Camera Programs

Overall, studies show law enforcement has been more accountable and professional from the use of BWCs.[10] Offices that have been experimenting with BWCs for the past five years have reported significant reductions in officer complaints.[11] The most obvious benefit of BWCs is the reduction of police brutality and abuse of power. A Rialto study examined BWCs from February 2012 to July 2013 in Rialto, Calif.[12] It revealed that shifts where officers were not equipped with BWCs had twice as many incidents of force as shifts where officers were equipped.[13] A separate experiment in Mesa, Ariz., revealed similar results, with a 12 percent decline in use-of-force incidents and a 23 percent decline in citizen complaints against officers.[14]

Not only have police officers' behavior improved when using BWCs, but research also suggests members of the community who interact with law enforcement have exhibited better behavior when a camera is present.[15] Police officers are deterred from using inappropriate, aggressive conduct and civilians are also deterred from inappropriate behavior.

Footage from BWCs will provide concrete, solid evidence, which is crucial for prosecutors.[16] They will be helpful in resolving factual disputes between police officers and members of the community.[17] Footage also can be used to train young officers on tactical mistakes and how to improve responses.[18]

Negative Effects of Body-Worn Camera Programs

One major concern for law enforcement is the cost of BWCs. Prices range depending on the capability to meet law enforcement's needs and can cost up to $1,000 per camera.[19] Costs include the initial purchase of cameras and costs of implementation. For law enforcement offices that struggle with low budgets, the initial costs may be easily absorbed. However, the costs to implement the cameras and store data may become a significant burden.[20] Policies must include a plan to store data for a certain amount of time, which can be difficult to assess.[21]

Creating policies for when to start and stop recording will be challenging. There are costs involved in reviewing footage. Law enforcement must spend hours reviewing, or hiring personnel to review, hours of footage from each officer patrolling each day.[22] Video recordings present additional concerns for prosecutors. Prosecutors have ethical requirements to turn evidence over to the defense. This puts pressure on prosecutors to timely review the video recordings, which can come from different law enforcement agencies that may use different equipment and methods.[23] Prosecutors may need to redact and cut information from the recordings and have discretion to consider what is useful.[24]

Privacy issues are also a concern. Anonymity is a useful tool for law enforcement to investigate various crimes.[25] Tips and leads come from informants and witnesses who wish to remain anonymous for protection, and the use of cameras may deter citizens from reporting crimes and helping during investigations.[26] There is an expectation of privacy in certain settings and the use of BWCs has the potential to violate that privacy.[27]

BWCs are not a panacea for accountability of police officers. Recordings are beneficial, but they do not amount to the high effectiveness of the human eye.[28] Footage will not be captured at all times and from the officer's peripheral vision.[29] BWCs may also result in community members having high expectations in the accountability of law enforcement officers. Jurors may expect footage to be used in trial, and may cause jurors to be impartial if footage is not available.

Federal Government Action

In September 2015, U.S. Attorney General Loretta Lynch announced that the U.S. Justice Department would award $23 million to help local agencies fund 50,000 BWCs and study their impact.[30] Agencies awarded grants will be responsible for purchasing equipment and developing policies to improve transparency and accountability. Policies must implement a plan for long-term storage of data. The pilot program will allocate $19.3 million to purchase body-worn cameras, $2 million for training and technical assistance, and $1.9 million to study the impact of the use of body-worn cameras.

The Bureau of Justice Assistance's Smart Policing Initiative also awarded grants to law enforcement in Miami, Milwaukee and Phoenix to study the impact of BWCs.[31] To assist local police departments, the Bureau launched an online toolkit to help police departments implement successful practices and policies for BWCs.[32]

State Actions

Attorney general offices in Maine and Ohio started BWC program discussions and drafting model policies. Washington Attorney General Bob Ferguson issued an opinion in 2014 addressing some of the issues surrounding BWCs.[33]

Delaware

In September 2015, Delaware Gov. Jack Markell launched a 30–45 day pilot program to deploy body cameras to various law enforcement agencies across the state.[34]

Missouri

In 2014, Missouri Attorney General Chris Koster recommended statutory changes to the law at the Roundtable on Representative Policing. One of the recommendations was to implement body-worn police cameras on law enforcement officers while on active patrol duty.[35]

New Jersey

New Jersey recently provided state funding for police BWCs. New Jersey Acting Attorney General John Hoffman issued a directive to law enforcement personnel in July 2015.[36] The directive served as guidance for New Jersey law enforcement personnel on the use of BWCs. The directive instructed law enforcement agencies to have policies that 1) require BWCs be activated only while on performance of duties, 2) require footage be retained for no less than 90 days with extension of retaining records for certain investigations and complaints, and 3) state the circumstances under which requests for footage can be denied.[37]

Conclusion

BWCs are largely beneficial in establishing better relations and trust between law enforcement and local communities. However, BWCs are not a panacea and policies should reflect the limitations of implementing BWC programs.

Notes

[1] Minn. Stat. §8.01.

[2] *Hood ex rel. Mississippi v. AstraZeneca Pharms. L.P.*, 744 F. Supp. 2d 390, 395, N.D. Miss. 2010).

[3] In re: *Hickenlooper v. Coffman*, No. 2015SA296 (Colo. Dec. 3, 2015).

[4] *Buquer v. City of Indianapolis*, 2013 WL 1332137 (S.D. Ind. Mar. 28, 2013).

[5] *Opinion of the Justices (Requiring Attorney General to Join Suit)*, No. 2011-319 (N.H., June 15, 2011).

[6] Maciag, Mike. *What We Can Learn From the Police That Pioneered Body Cameras. Governing the States and Localities*, April 13, 2015. Available at *http://www.governing.com/topics/public-justice-safety/gov-body-cameras-chesapeake-virginia.html*.

[7] For example, the District of Columbia recently passed legislation to allow officers to review footage before writing a police report. Stein, Perry. *Should Officers Be Able to Review Body Camera Footage Before Writing Police Reports?*, available at *https://www.washingtonpost.com/news/local/wp/2015/12/17/should-officers-be-able-to-review-body-camera-footage-before-writing-police-reports/?hpid=hp_no-name_hp-in-the-news%3Apage%2Fin-the-news* (last visited Feb. 5, 2016).

[8] *Eight out of 10 Citizens Believe More Digital Tools Can Improve Police Services, According to New Research by Accenture. http://newsroom.accenture.com/news/eight-out-of-10-citizens-believe-more-digital-tools-can-improve-police-services-according-to-new-research-by-accenture.htm* (last visited Feb. 2, 2016).

[9] *https://www.aclu.org/police-body-mounted-cameras-right-policies-place-win-all*.

[10] Feeney, Matthew. *Watching the Watchmen. Best Practices for Police Body Cameras*, Oct. 27, 2015. Available at *http://www.cato.org/publications/policy-analysis/watching-watchmen-best-practices-police-body-cameras*.

[11] *Id.*

[12] Simmons, Kami. *Body-Mounted Police Cameras: A Primer on Police Accountability vs. Privacy.* 58 HOWARD L.J. 881, 885 (2015).

[13] *Id.*

[14] *Id.* at 886.

[15] *Supra* n. 5.

[16] *Body-Worn Cameras by Police Officers–A Prosecutor's Perspective: Hearing Before the Subcomm. on Crime and Terrorism of the Sen. Comm, on the Judiciary*, 114th Cong. (2015) (testimony of Peter A. Weir, Dist. Atty.).

17 *Id.*

18 Harris, Meena. See "Looking at Police-Community Relations Through the Lens of Body-Worn Cameras." *The National Law Review*, Dec. 19, 2014. Available at *http://www.natlawreview.com/article/looking-police-community-relations-through-lens-body-worn-cameras.*

19 Merzon, Antonia. *The Colorado Best Practices Committee for Prosecutors Presents Body Worn Cameras: A Report for Law Enforcement*, p.5. (2015). Prices range from $119.95 to $1,000 per camera.

20 Sallee, Vern, *Outsourcing the Evidence Room: Moving Digital Evidence to the Cloud. http://www.policechiefmagazine.org/magazine/index.cfm?fuseaction=display_arch&article_id=3319&issue_id=42014* (last visited Jan. 21, 2016).

21 *Id.*

22 Jackson, Jodie, *Police Body Camera Footage Increases Workload, Prosecutor Says*, Oct. 28, 2014. Available at *http://www.columbiatribune.com/news/local/police-body-camera-footage-increases-workload-prosecutor-says/article_d8c948c9-ec63-58cf-a148-5717c65015fd.html* (last visited Jan. 5, 2016).

23 Cohen, Kay. *The Impact of Body-Worn Cameras on a Prosecutor. https://www.bjatraining.org/media/blog/impact-body-worn-cameras-prosecutor* (last visited Jan. 21, 2016).

24 Prosecutors will have to review recordings marked by police officers and decide what is most useful for their case. *Id.*

25 Letourneau, Dru. Note, *Police Body Cameras: Implementation with Caution, Forethought, and Policy*. 50 U. RICH. L. Rev. 469, 456 (2015).

26 *Id.* Cameras may have a chilling effect on witness and informants.

27 *Id.* at 453.

28 Finnemore, Melody. *High-Tech: Electronic Evidence from a Broadening Array of Sources is Creating a Sea Change for Police, Prosecutors and Defense Attorneys*. 76 OR. ST. B. BULL. 26, 28. (2015). Challenges such as poor lighting or jumble during physical activity affect quality of the footage.

29 Circumstances may occur where it is difficult for an officer to turn the camera on. *Id.*

30 *Justice Department Awards over $23 Million in Funding for Body-Worn Camera Pilot Program to Support Law Enforcement Agencies in 32 States*, Sept., 21, 2015. Available at *http://www.justice.gov/opa/pr/justice-department-awards-over-23-million-funding-body-worn-camera-pilot-program-support-law.*

31 *Id.*

32 *Id.* Toolkit is available at *https://www.bja.gov/bwc/.*

33 Video and Audio Recording of Communications Between Citizens and Law Enforcement Officers Using Body Cameras Attached to Police Uniforms, WA AGO 2014 No. 8.

34 *State Announcing Pilot Program for Police Body Cameras. Available at http://news.delaware.gov/2015/09/23/state-announces-pilot-program-for-police-body-cameras/.* (last visited Jan. 5, 2016).

35 *Attorney General Koster's Roundtable on Representative Policing.* Recommendation No. 1, p.2, Oct. 1, 2014. Available at *https://ago.mo.gov/docs/default-source/press-releases/2015/agkoster-roundtablerepresentativepolicingreport.pdf?sfvrsn=4.*

36 *Law Enforcement Directive Regarding Police Body Worn Cameras (BWCs) and Stored BWC Recordings*, July 28, 2015. Directive No. 2015-1.

37 *Id.*

About the Authors and the National Association of Attorneys General

Emily Myers is the antitrust and powers and duties chief counsel of the National Association of Attorneys General, or NAAG.

Ayeisha Cox served until February 2016 as visiting counsel for the National Attorneys General Training and Research Institute, or NAGTRI, an NAAG branch.

NAAG, *www.naag.org*, was founded in 1907 to help attorneys general fulfill the responsibilities of their office to the states and territorial jurisdictions. Its members are the attorneys general of the 50 states and Washington, D.C., and the chief legal officers of the commonwealths of Puerto Rico (secretary of justice) and the Northern Mariana Islands, and the territories of American Samoa, Guam and the U.S. Virgin Islands.

Table 4.19
THE ATTORNEYS GENERAL, 2016

State or other jurisdiction	Name and party	Method of selection	Length of regular term in years	Date of first service	Present term ends	Number of previous terms	Maximum consecutive terms allowed
Alabama	Luther Strange (R)	E	4	1/2011	1/2019	1	2
Alaska	Craig W. Richards (R)	A	...	12/2014	...	0	...
Arizona	Mark Brnovich (R)	E	4	1/2015	1/2019	0	2
Arkansas	Leslie Rutledge (R)	E	4	1/2015	1/2019	0	2
California	Kamala Harris (D)	E	4	1/2011	1/2019	1	2
Colorado	Cynthia Coffman (R)	E	4	1/2015	1/2019	0	2
Connecticut	George Jepsen (D)	E	4	1/2011	1/2019	1	★
Delaware	Matthew Denn (D)	E	4	1/2015	1/2019	0	★
Florida	Pam Bondi (R)	E	4	1/2011	1/2019	1	2
Georgia	Sam Olens (R)	E	4	1/2011	1/2019	1	★
Hawaii	Doug Chin (D)	A	4 (a)	1/2015	1/2019	0	...
Idaho	Lawrence Wasden (R)	E	4	1/2003	1/2019	3	★
Illinois	Lisa Madigan (D)	E	4	1/2003	1/2019	3	★
Indiana	Greg Zoeller (R)	E	4	1/2009	1/2017	1	★
Iowa	Tom Miller (D)	E	4	1/1979 (b)	1/2019	8 (b)	★
Kansas	Derek Schmidt (R)	E	4	1/2011	1/2019	1	★
Kentucky	Andy Beshear (D)	E	4	12/2016	12/2020	0	2
Louisiana	Jeff Landry (R)	E	4	1/2016	1/2020	0	★
Maine	Janet T. Mills (D)	L (c)	2	1/2011	...	1 (d)	4
Maryland	Brian Frosh (D)	E	4	1/2015	1/2019	0	★
Massachusetts	Maura Healey (D)	E	4	1/2015	1/2019	0	...
Michigan	Bill Schuette (R)	E	4	1/2011	1/2019	1	2
Minnesota	Lori Swanson (D)	E	4	1/2007	1/2019	2	★
Mississippi	Jim Hood (D)	E	4	1/2004	1/2020	3	★
Missouri	Chris Koster (D)	E	4	1/2009	1/2017	1	★
Montana	Tim Fox (R)	E	4	1/2013	1/2017	0	2
Nebraska	Doug Peterson (R)	E	4	1/2015	1/2019	0	★
Nevada	Adam Laxalt (R)	E	4	1/2015	1/2019	0	2
New Hampshire	Joseph A. Foster (D)	A	4	5/2013	1/2017	0	...
New Jersey	John Jay Hoffman (R) (e)	A	4	6/2013 (e)	(e)	0	...
New Mexico	Hector Balderas (D)	E	4	1/2015	1/2019	0	2 (f)
New York	Eric Schneiderman (D)	E	4	1/2011	1/2019	1	★
North Carolina	Roy Cooper (D)	E	4	1/2001	1/2017	3	★
North Dakota	Wayne Stenehjem (R)	E	4 (g)	1/2001	12/2019	3 (g)	★
Ohio	Mike DeWine (R)	E	4	1/2011	1/2019	1	2
Oklahoma	Scott Pruitt (R)	E	4	1/2011	1/2019	1	★
Oregon	Ellen F. Rosenblum (D)	E	4	6/2012 (i)	1/2017	0	★
Pennsylvania	Kathleen Kane (D) (h)	E	4	5/2011(h)	1/2017	0	2
Rhode Island	Peter Kilmartin (D)	E	4	1/2011	1/2019	1	2
South Carolina	Alan Wilson (R)	E	4	1/2011	1/2019	1	★
South Dakota	Martin J. Jackley (R)	E	4	9/2009 (j)	1/2019	2	2 (f)
Tennessee	Herbert Slatery (R)	(k)	8	10/2014	8/2022	0	...
Texas	Ken Paxton (R)	E	4	1/2015	1/2019	0	★
Utah	Sean Reyes (R)	E	4	12/2013	1/2017	0	★
Vermont	William H. Sorrell (D)	E	2	5/1997 (l)	1/2017	7 (l)	★
Virginia	Mark Herring (D)	E	4	1/2014	1/2018	0	(m)
Washington	Bob Ferguson (D)	E	4	1/2013	1/2017	0	★
West Virginia	Patrick Morrisey (R)	E	4	1/2013	1/2017	0	★
Wisconsin	Brad Schimel (R)	E	4	1/2015	1/2019	0	★
Wyoming	Peter Michael (R)	A	...	7/2013	...	0	...
Dist. of Columbia	Karl Racine (D)	A	...	1/2015	1/2019	0	...
American Samoa	Talauega Eleasalo V. Ale (D)	A	4	1/2014	...	...	...
Guam	Elizabeth Barrett-Anderson (R)	E	4	1/2015	1/2019	0	...
No. Mariana Islands	Edward Manibusan (I)	A	4	11/2015	...	0	...
Puerto Rico	Cesar Miranda Rodriguez (PPD/D)	A	4	1/2014	...	0	...
U.S. Virgin Islands	Claude Walker (Acting)	A	4	8/2015	...	0	...

See footnotes at end of table.

THE ATTORNEYS GENERAL, 2016—Continued

Source: The Council of State Governments, December 2015.

Key:

★ — No provision specifying number of terms allowed.

. . . — No formal provision, position is appointed or elected by governmental entity (not chosen by the electorate).

A — Appointed by the governor.

E — Elected by the voters.

L — Elected by the legislature.

N.A. — Not available.

(a) Term runs concurrently with the governor.

(b) Attorney General Miller was elected in 1978, 1982, 1986, 1994, 1998, 2002, 2006, 2010 and 2014.

(c) Chosen biennially by joint ballot of state senators and representatives.

(d) Janet Mills previously served as attorney general from Jan. 2001 through Jan. 2011.

(e) On June 6, 2013 Gov. Christie appointed Attorney General Jeff Chiesa to fill the Senate seat left vacant by Sen. Frank Lautenberg's death. Currently John Jay Hoffman, former Executive Assistant Attorney General is serving as Acting Attorney General. Hoffman has served as Acting AG since May 2013.

(f) After two consecutive terms, must wait four years and/or one full term before being eligible again.

(g) The term of the office of the elected official is four years, except that in 2004 the attorney general was elected for a term of two years.

(h) Appointed to fill Tom Corbett's unexpired term after he was elected to PA governor's office in May 2011.

(i) Rosenblum was appointed by Gov. Kitzhaber on June 29, 2012 to fill the term left vacant when AG John Kroger resigned to become President of Reed College. She was elected in Nov. 2012 to a full term.

(j) Appointed September 4, 2009 to fill Larry Long's unexpired term. AG Long resigned to accept a state judgeship.

(k) Appointed by judges of state Supreme Court.

(l) Appointed to fill unexpired term in May 1997. He was elected in 1998 to his first full term.

(m) Provision specifying individual may hold office for an unlimited number of terms.

(n) Must be confirmed by the Senate.

Table 4.20
ATTORNEYS GENERAL: QUALIFICATIONS FOR OFFICE

State or other jurisdiction	Minimum age	U.S. citizen (years) (a)	State resident (years) (b)	Qualified voter (years)	Licensed attorney (years)	Membership in the state bar (years)	Method of selection to office
Alabama	25	7	5	★	...	...	E
Alaska	18	★	...	...	★	★	A
Arizona	25	10	5	★	5	...	E
Arkansas	...	...	★	★	...	...	E
California	18	★	★	★	★	5	E
Colorado	27	★	2	★	★	...	E
Connecticut	18	★	★	★	10	10	E
Delaware	...	...	...	...	...	...	E
Florida	30	★	7	★	★	5	E
Georgia	25	10	4	★	7	7	E
Hawaii	...	1	1	...	★	(d)	A
Idaho	30	★	2	...	★	★	E
Illinois	25	★	3	★	★	★	E
Indiana	...	2	2	★	5	...	E
Iowa	18	★	★	...	...	...	E
Kansas	...	...	...	...	...	...	E
Kentucky	30	...	2 (e)	...	8	2	E
Louisiana	25	★	5	★	★	★	E
Maine	...	...	...	...	★	★	(f)
Maryland	...	★(g)	★	★	★	10	E
Massachusetts	18	...	5	★	...	★	E
Michigan	18	★	★	...	★	★	E
Minnesota	21	★	30 days	★	...	...	E
Mississippi	26	★	5	★	5	★	E
Missouri	...	★	1	...	...	...	E
Montana	25	★	2	...	5	...	E
Nebraska	...	...	★	...	...	...	E
Nevada	25	★	2	★	...	...	E
New Hampshire	...	★	★	...	★	★	A (h)
New Jersey	18	...	★	...	...	...	A
New Mexico	30	★	5	★	★	...	E
New York	30	★	5	...	(i)	...	E
North Carolina	21	★	★	★	★	(i)	E
North Dakota	25	★	5	★	★	★	E
Ohio	18	★	★	★	...	...	E
Oklahoma	31	★	★	10	...	...	E
Oregon	18	★	★	★	...	...	E
Pennsylvania	30	★	...	...	★	...	E
Rhode Island	18	...	...	...	★	★	E
South Carolina	...	★	30 days	★	...	...	E
South Dakota	18	★	★	★	(i)	(i)	E
Tennessee	...	...	...	...	...	...	(j)
Texas	...	...	...	...	(i)	(i)	E
Utah	25	★	5 (e)	★	★	★	E
Vermont	18	★	★	★	...	...	E
Virginia	30	★	1 (k)	★	...	5 (k)	E
Washington	18	★	★	★	★	★	E
West Virginia	25	...	5	★	...	...	E
Wisconsin	...	★	★	...	...	...	E
Wyoming	...	★	★	★	4	4	A (l)
Dist. of Columbia	...	...	★	...	★	★	A
American Samoa	...	...	(c)	...	(i)	(i)	A
Guam	...	...	...	...	...	...	A
No. Mariana Islands	...	...	3	...	5	...	A
Puerto Rico	...	★	...	...	★	★	A
U.S. Virgin Islands	...	...	★	★	★	★	A

Sources: The Council of State Governments' survey of attorneys general, state constitutions and statutes, November 2015.

Key:
★ — Formal provision; number of years not specified.
... — No formal provision.
A — Appointed by governor.
E — Elected by voters.
(a) In some states you must be a U.S. citizen to be an elector, and must be an elector to run.
(b) In some states you must be a state resident to be an elector, and must be an elector to run.
(c) No statute specifically requires this, but the State Bar Act can be interpreted as making this a qualification.

(d) No period specified, all licensed attorneys are members of the state bar.
(e) State citizenship requirement.
(f) Chosen biennially by joint ballot of state senators and representatives.
(g) *Crosse v. Board of Supervisors of Elections* 243 Md. 555, 221 A.2d 431 (1966) — opinion rendered indicated that U.S. citizenship was, by necessity, a requirement for office.
(h) Appointed by the governor and confirmed by the governor and the executive council.
(i) Implied.
(j) Appointed by state supreme court.
(k) Same as qualifications of a judge of a court of record.
(l) Must be confirmed by the Senate.

Table 4.21
ATTORNEYS GENERAL: PROSECUTORIAL AND ADVISORY DUTIES

State or other jurisdiction	Authority in local prosecutions:				Issues advisory opinions (a):				Reviews legislation (b):	
	Authority to initiate local prosecutions	May intervene in local prosecutions	May assist local prosecutor	May supersede local prosecutor	To state executive officials	To legislators	To local prosecutors	On the constitutionality of bills or ordinances	Prior to passage	Before signing
Alabama	A	A,D	A,D	A	★	★	★	...	★	...
Alaska	(c)	(c)	(c)	(c)	★	★	...	★	★	★
Arizona	A	A	A,B	A,F	★	★	★	★	(u)	(u)
Arkansas	...	...	D	...	★	★	★	★	...	...
California	A,B,C,D,E,F	A,B,C,D,E,F	A,B,C,D,E,F	A,B,C,D,E,F,G	★	★	★	★	(v)	(v)
Colorado	A,F	A	D,F	A	★	★	★	★	★	★
Connecticut	...	...	...	...	★	(d)	...	★	(e)	(e)
Delaware	A (f)	(f)	(f)	(f)	★	★	...	★	(g)	(g)
Florida	F	...	D	...	★	★	★	...	...	...
Georgia	B,D,F,G	...	A,D	...	★	★	★	...	...	...
Hawaii	A,B,C,D,E	A,B,C,D,E	A,B,C,D,E	A,B,C,D,E	★	★	...	★(h)	★	★
Idaho	B,D,F	D, F	D	...	★	★	★	★	★	★
Illinois	D,F	D,G	D	G	★	★	★	...	(i)	(i)
Indiana	F	...	D	...	★	★	★	★	...	...
Iowa	D,F	D,F	D,F	D,E,F	★	★	★	...	(j)	(j)
Kansas	B,C,D,F	B,C,D,F,G	D	B,C,D,F,G	★	★	★	...	...	...
Kentucky	D,F,G	B,D,G	D	B	★	★	★	★	...	...
Louisiana	D,E,G	D,E,G	D,E,G	E,G	★	★	★	...	★	★
Maine	A	A	A	A	★	★	...	...	...	...
Maryland	B,F	D	D	...	★	★	★	★	★	★
Massachusetts	A	A	A,D	A	★	★(k)	★	★	(l)	(l)
Michigan	A	A	A	A	★	★	★	★	...	...
Minnesota	B,F	B,D,G	A,B,D,G	B	★	★(k)	★	...	...	(l)
Mississippi	A,D,F	D,F	A,D,F	D,F	★	★	★	...	...	...
Missouri	B,F,G	F	B,F	G	★	★	★	...	(l)	(l)
Montana	D	E	E	E	★	★(m)	★	★	...	...
Nebraska	A,D	A,D	A,D,E,F	...	★	★	★	★	...	...
Nevada	D,F,G	D	...	...	★	...	★	★	...	...
New Hampshire	A,E,F	A,E,F	A,D,E,F	A,E,F	★	★	★	...	(n)	(n)
New Jersey	A,B,C,D	A,B,C,D	A,B,C,D	A,B,C,D	★	...	★	★	★	★
New Mexico	B,D,E,F	D,E,F	A,B,D,E,F	D,E,F,G	★	★	★	★	★	★
New York	B,F	B,D,F	D	B	★	★(k)	★	★	★	★
North Carolina	...	D	D	...	★	★	★	★	★	...
North Dakota	A,D,E,F,G	A,D,E,G	A,B,D,E,F,G	A,D,E,G	★	★	★	★	...	...
Ohio	D, F	D	D	F	★	(m)	★	...	...	...
Oklahoma	A,B,C,D,E,F,G	A,B,C,D,E,F,G	A,B,C,D,E,F,G	A,B,C,D,E,F,G	★	★	★	★	★	★
Oregon	B,D,F	B,D	B,D	B	★	★	★	...	...	★
Pennsylvania	A,D,F	D,F	D,F	...	★	...	...	...	...	...
Rhode Island	A	A	A	A	★	★	...	...	...	...
South Carolina	A,D,E,F	A,B,C,D,E,F	A,D,E	A,E	★	(q)	★	★	★(w)	★(w)
South Dakota	A,B,D,E,F (p)	D,G	A,B,D,E	D,F	★	★	★	★	★	...
Tennessee	D,F,G	D,G	D,F	F,G	★	★	★	★	...	...
Texas	D,F	F	D,F	D,F	★	★	★	★	...	...
Utah	A,B,D,E,F,G	E,G	D,E	E	★	★(q)	★	★	★(l)	★(l)
Vermont	A	A	A	G	★	★	★	★	★	★
Virginia	B,F	B,D,F	B,D,F	B	★	★	★	★	★	★
Washington	B,D,G	B,D,G	B,D,G	B,D,G	★	★	★	...	(o)	(o)
West Virginia	(r)	...	...	...	★	★	★	...	...	...
Wisconsin	B,C,D,F	B,C,D	D	B	★	★	★	★	(e)	(e)
Wyoming	B,D,F	B,D	B,D	G	★	★	★	★(h)	★	★
Dist. of Columbia	F	D	D	F	★	★	(s)	★	★	★
American Samoa	A (t)	(t)	(t)	(t)	★	...	(t)	(e)	(l)	(l)
Guam	A	A	A	A	★	★	★	★	(l)	B
No. Mariana Islands	A (t)	(t)	(t)	(t)	★	★	...	★	...	...
Puerto Rico	A	(t)	(t)	(t)	★	★	...	...	★	★
U.S. Virgin Islands	A (t)	(t)	(t)	(t)	★	...	...	★	★	★

See footnotes at end of table.

ATTORNEYS GENERAL: PROSECUTORIAL AND ADVISORY DUTIES — Continued

Sources: The Council of State Governments' survey of attorneys general, state constitutions and statutes, November 2015.

Key:

A — On own initiative.
B — On request of governor.
C — On request of legislature.
D — On request of local prosecutor.
E — When in state's interest.
F — Under certain statutes for specific crimes.
G — On authorization of court or other body.
★ — Has authority in area.
... — Does not have authority in area.

(a) Also issues advisory opinions to: Alabama—Designated heads of state departments, agencies, boards, and commissions; local public officials; and political subdivisions. Hawaii—Judges/judiciary as requested. Kansas—to counsel for local units of government. Montana—county and city attorneys, city commissioners. Wisconsin—corporation counsel.

(b) Also reviews legislation: Alabama—when requested by the governor. Alaska—after passage. Arizona—at the request of the legislature. Kansas—upon request of Legislator, no formal authority.

(c) The attorney general functions as the local prosecutor.

(d) To legislative leadership.

(e) Informally reviews bills or does so upon request.

(f) The attorney general prosecutes all criminal offenses in Delaware.

(g) At the request of agency or legislature.

(h) Bills, not ordinances.

(i) Review and track legislation that relates to the Office of Attorney General and the office mission.

(j) No requirements for review.

(k) To legislature as a whole not individual legislators.

(l) Only when requested by governor or legislature.

(m) To either house of legislature, not individual legislators; To law directors of limited home rule townships; To agencies, boards, commissions, and departments of state government (not to individual members).

(n) Provides information when requested by the Legislature. Testifies for or against bills on the Attorney General's own initiative.

(o) May review legislation at request of clients or legislature.

(p) Certain statutes provide for concurrent jurisdiction with local prosecutors.

(q) Only when requested by legislature.

(r) Can be involved in local at request of local prosecutors. If requested by local authority, can participate in criminal prosecutions.

(s) The office of attorney general prosecutes local crimes to an extent. The office's Legal Counsel Division may issue legal advice to the office's prosecutorial arm. Otherwise, the office does not usually advise the OUSA, the district's other local prosecutor.

(t) The attorney general functions as the local prosecutor.

(u) Reviews enacted legislation only when there is a compelling need.

(v) May review legislation at any time but does not have a de jure role in approval of bills as to form or constitutionality; California has a separate Legislative Counsel to advise the legislature on bills.

(w)

Table 4.22
ATTORNEYS GENERAL: CONSUMER PROTECTION ACTIVITIES, SUBPOENA POWERS AND ANTITRUST DUTIES

State or other jurisdiction	May commence civil proceedings	May commence criminal proceedings	Represents the state before regulatory agencies (a)	Administers consumer protection programs	Handles consumer complaints	Subpoena powers (b)	Antitrust duties
Alabama	★	★	★	★	★	●	A,B,C
Alaska	★	...	★	★	★	★	A,B,C,D
Arizona	★	...	...	★(c)	★	★	A,B,C,D
Arkansas	★	...	★	★	★	●	A,B
California	★	★	★	★	★	★	A,B,C,D
Colorado	★	★	★	★	★	●	A,C,D
Connecticut	★	(d)	★	★	★	●	A,B,D
Delaware	★	★	★	★	★	★	A,B,D
Florida	★	...	...	★	★	★	A,B,D
Georgia	★	★	★	★	★	●	...
Hawaii	★	★	★	...	★	★	A,B,C,D
Idaho	★	...	★	★	★	●	A,B,D
Illinois	★	...	★	★	★	●	A,B,C
Indiana	★	...	★	★	★	★	A,B
Iowa	★	★	★	★	★	★	B,C
Kansas	★	★	...	★	★	★	A,B,D
Kentucky	★	★	★	★	★	★	A,B,C,D
Louisiana	★	★	★	★	★	★	A,B,C
Maine	★	★	★	★	★	★	A,B,C
Maryland	★	★(e)	★	★	★	★	B,C,D
Massachusetts	★	★	★	★	★	★	A,B,C,D
Michigan	★	★	★	★	★	★	A,B,C,D
Minnesota	★	...	★	★	★	●	A,B,C
Mississippi	★	★	...	★	★	★	A,B,C,D
Missouri	★	★	★	★	★	★	A,B,C,D
Montana	★	★	...	★	★	...	A,B
Nebraska	★	★	★	★	★	★	A,B,C,D
Nevada	★	★	★	★	★	●	A,B,C,D
New Hampshire	★	★	★	★	★	★	A,B,C,D
New Jersey	★	★	★	★	★	★	A,B,C,D
New Mexico	★	★	★	★	★	★	A,B,C (g)
New York	★	★	★	★	★	★	A,B,C,D
North Carolina	★	★(f)	★	★	★	★	A,B,C,D
North Dakota	★	...	★	★	★	★	A,B,D
Ohio (n)	★	...	...	★	☆	★	A,B,C,D
Oklahoma	★	★	★	★	★	★	A,B,C,D
Oregon	★	★(f)	★	★	★	●	A,B,C,D
Pennsylvania	★	★	★	★	★	★	A,B
Rhode Island	★	★	...	★	★	★	A,B,C
South Carolina	★(a)	★(h)	★	...	(i)	●	A,B,C,D
South Dakota	★	★	★	★	★	★	A,B,C
Tennessee	★	(e)(f)	(f)	★	...	★	B,C,D
Texas	★	...	...	★	★	●	A,B,D
Utah	★(j)	★	★(j)	...	★(k)	●	A (l),B,C,D (l)
Vermont	★	★	★	★	★	★	A,B,C
Virginia	★	(f)	★	★(k)	★(k)	●	A,B,C,D
Washington	★	...	★	★	★	★	A,B,D
West Virginia	★	...	★	★	★	★	A,B,D
Wisconsin	★	★	★	★	★	●	A,B,C (g)
Wyoming	★	...	★	★	★	●	A,B
Dist. of Columbia	★	★(m)	★	★	★	★	A,B,C,D
American Samoa	★	★	★	★	★	...	...
Guam	★	★	★	★	★	●	A,B,C,D
No. Mariana Islands	★	★	★	★	★	★	A,B
Puerto Rico	★	★	...	...	...	★	A,B,C,D
U.S. Virgin Islands	★	★	★	★	★	●	A

See footnotes at end of table.

ATTORNEYS GENERAL: CONSUMER PROTECTION ACTIVITIES, SUBPOENA POWERS AND ANTITRUST DUTIES — Continued

Sources: The Council of State Governments' survey of attorneys general, state constitutions and statutes, November 2015.

Key:

A — Has parens patriae authority to commence suits on behalf of consumers in state antitrust damage actions in state courts.

B — May initiate damage actions on behalf of state in state courts.

C — May commence criminal proceedings.

D — May represent cities, counties and other governmental entities in recovering civil damages under federal or state law.

★ — Has authority in area.

... — Does not have authority in area.

(a) May represent state on behalf of: the "people" of the state; an agency of the state; or the state before a federal regulatory agency.

(b) In this column only: ★ broad powers and ● limited powers.

(c) The 49th Legislature, first regular session, established a statutory scheme that provided for a mortgage recovery fund to pay those harmed by dishonest loan originators. The attorney general is now authorized to try to recover from the dishonest loan originators the money that the fund paid out (See ARS 6-991.15).

(d) In certain cases only.

(e) May commence criminal proceedings with local district attorney.

(f) To a limited extent.

(g) May represent other governmental entities in recovering civil damages under federal or state law.

(h) When permitted to intervene.

(i) On a limited basis because the state has a separate consumer affairs department.

(j) Attorney general has exclusive authority.

(k) Attorney general handles legal matters only with no administrative handling of complaints.

(l) Opinion only, since there are no controlling precedents.

(m) In antitrust, not criminal proceedings.

(n) Also provides investigative and prosecutorial assistance to local law enforcement upon request; provides service to cosnumers through the Identity Theft Unit, administration of Ohio's Title Defect Rescission Fund, and the registration of non-charitable telephone solicitors.

Table 4.23
ATTORNEYS GENERAL: DUTIES TO ADMINISTRATIVE AGENCIES AND OTHER RESPONSIBILITIES

State or other jurisdiction	Serves as counsel for state	Appears for state in criminal appeals	Issues official advice	Interprets statutes or regulations	Conducts litigation: On behalf of agency	Conducts litigation: Against agency	Prepares or reviews legal documents	Represents the public before the agency	Involved in rule-making	Reviews rules for legality
Alabama	A,B,C (a)	★ (a)	★	★	★	★	(b)	(b)	★	★
Alaska	A,B,C	★	★	★	★	★	★	★	★	★
Arizona	A,B,C	★	★	★	★	★	★	...	★	★
Arkansas	A,B,C	★	★	★	★	★	★	★	...	...
California	A,B,C	★	★	★	★	...	★	...	★	★
Colorado	A,B,C	★	★	★	★	★	★	★	★	★
Connecticut	A,B,C	(b)	★	★	★	★	★	★	★	★
Delaware	A,B,C	★(d)	★	★	★	★	★	★	★	★
Florida	A,B,C	★	★	★	★	★	...	★	...	...
Georgia	A,B,C	★	★	★	★	...	★	...	...	★
Hawaii	A,B,C	★	★	★	★	★	★	★	★	★
Idaho	A,B,C	★ (a)	★	★	★	★	★	★	★	★
Illinois	A,B,C	★	...	★	★	★	★	...	...	...
Indiana	A,B,C	★	★	★	★	...	★	...	★	★
Iowa	A,B,C	★	★	★	★	★	★	★	★	★
Kansas	A,B,C	★	★	★	★	★	★	...	★	★
Kentucky	A,B,C	★	★	★	★	...	...	★	...	...
Louisiana	A,B,C	...	★	★	★	...	★	★	★	★
Maine	A,B,C	★	★	★	★	...	★	...	...	★
Maryland	A,B,C	★	★	★	★	(b)	★	★	★	★
Massachusetts	A,B,C	(b)(c)(d)	★	★	★	★	★	★	★	★
Michigan	A,B,C	★	★	★	★	★	★	★	★	★
Minnesota	A,B,C	(c)(d)	★	★	(a)	★	★	★	★	★
Mississippi	A,B,C	...	★	★	★	...	★	...	...	★
Missouri	A,B,C	★	★	★	★	...	★	...	★	...
Montana (f)	A,B	...	★	★	★	...	★	...	...	...
Nebraska	A,B,C	★	★	★	★	★	★	...	...	★
Nevada	A,B,C	★	★	★	★	...	★	...	★	★
New Hampshire	A,B,C	★	★	★	★	...	★	★	★	...
New Jersey	A,B,C	★	★	★	★	...	★	...	★	★
New Mexico	A,B,C	★	★	★	★	★	★	★	★	★
New York	A,B,C	(b)	...	★	★	(b)	★	(b)	...	...
North Carolina	A,B,C	★	★	★	★	★	★	(b)	★	★
North Dakota	A,B,C	★	★	★	★	★	★	...	★	★
Ohio	A,B,C	★	★	...	★	...	★	...	...	...
Oklahoma	A,B,C	★	★	★	★	★	★	★	★	★
Oregon	A,B	★	★	★	★	...	★	...	★	★
Pennsylvania	A,B	...	...	...	★	...	★	...	...	★
Rhode Island	A,B,C	★	★	★	★	★	★	...	...	...
South Carolina	A,B,C	★ (d)	(a)	★	★	(b)	★	...	★	★
South Dakota	A,B,C	★	★	★	★	★	★	★	...	...
Tennessee	A,B,C	★	★	★	★	...	★	(e)	(e)	★
Texas (g)	A,B,C	★	★	★	★	★	★	★(k)	★	...
Utah	A,B,C	★ (a)	★	★	★	★	★	(b)	★	★
Vermont	A,B,C	★	★	★	★	★	★	★	★	★
Virginia	A,B,C	★	★	★	★	★	★	★	★	★
Washington	A,B,C	★ (i)	★	★	★	★	★	★	★	★
West Virginia	A,B,C	★	★	★	★	★	★	...	(j)	(j)
Wisconsin	A,B,C	★	★	★	★	(b)	(b)	(b)	(b)	(b)
Wyoming	A,B,C	★	★	★	★	★	★	...	★	★
Dist. of Columbia	A,B	★ (h)	★	★	★	...	★	...	★	★
American Samoa	A,B,C	★ (a)	★	★	★	...	★	...	★	★
Guam	A,B,C	★	★	★	(d)	★	★	(b)	★	★
No. Mariana Islands	A,B,C	★	★	★	★	★	★	...	★	★
Puerto Rico	A,B,C	★	★	★	★	...	★	★	★	★
U.S. Virgin Islands	A,B	★	★	★	★	★	★	★	...	★

See footnotes at end of table.

ATTORNEYS GENERAL: DUTIES TO ADMINISTRATIVE AGENCIES AND OTHER RESPONSIBILITIES — Continued

Sources: The Council of State Governments' survey of attorneys general, state constitutions and statutes, November 2015.

Key:

A—Defend state law when challenged on federal constitutional grounds.

B—Conduct litigation on behalf of state in federal and other states' courts.

C—Prosecute actions against another state in U.S. Supreme Court.

★—Has authority in area.

...—Does not have authority in area.

(a) Attorney general has exclusive jurisdiction.

(b) In certain cases only to prepare or review legal documents and represent the public before the agency.

(c) When assisting local prosecutor in the appeal.

(d) Can appear on own discretion.

(e) Consumer Advocate Division represents the public in utility rate making hearings and rule making proceedings.

(f) Most state agencies are represented by agency counsel who do not answer to the attorney general. The attorney general does provide representation for agencies in conflict situations and where the agency requires additional or specialized assistance.

(g) Other administrative duties include representing one state agency before another state agency.

(h) However, OUSA handles felony cases and most major misdemeanors.

(i) Limited to certain collateral challenges to state criminal convictions.

(j) On request of agency. Office acts as legal counsel to any state agency on request and that can include reviewing legislation and drafting rules and regulations.

(k) Represents the public before an agency only in energy rate cases.

Table 4.24
THE TREASURERS, 2016

State or other jurisdiction	Name and party	Method of selection	Length of regular term in years	Date of first service	Present term ends	Maximum consecutive terms allowed by constitution
Alabama	Young Boozer (R)	E	4	1/2015	1/2019	2
Alaska	Pamela Leary	A	Governor's Discretion	1/2018	...	...
Arizona	Jeff DeWit (R)	E	4	1/2019	1/2023	2
Arkansas	Dennis Milligan (R)	A	4	1/2019	1/2023	2
California	John Chiang (D)	E	4	1/2019	1/2023	2
Colorado	Walker Stapleton (R)	E	4	1/2015	1/2023	2
Connecticut	Denise L. Nappier (D)	E	4	1/1999	1/2023	★
Delaware	Ken Simpler (R)	E	4	1/2019	1/2023	★
Florida (a)	Jeff Atwater (R)	E	4	1/2015	1/2023	2
Georgia	Steve McCoy	A	Pleasure of the Board	11/2015	...	...
Hawaii (b)	Wesley Machida (D)	A	Governor's Discretion	3/2019		...
Idaho	Ron G. Crane (R)	E	4	1/2003	1/2023	★
Illinois	Mike Frerichs (D)	E	4	1/2019	1/2023	★
Indiana	Kelly Mitchell (R)	E	4	1/2019	1/2023	(d)(c)
Iowa	Michael L. Fitzgerald (D)	E	4	1/1987	1/2023	★
Kansas	Ron Estes (R)	E	4	1/2015	1/2023	★
Kentucky	Alison Ball (R)	E	4	1/2020	12/2023	2
Louisiana	John N. Kennedy (R)	E	4	1/2000	1/2024	★
Maine	Terry Hayes (I)	L	2	1/2019	1/2021	4
Maryland	Nancy K. Kopp (D)	L	4	2/2006	2/2023	★
Massachusetts	Deb Goldberg (D)	E	4	1/2019	1/2023	★
Michigan	Nick Khouri	A	Governor's Discretion	4/2019	...	...
Minnesota (d)	Myron Frans	A	Governor's Discretion	2/2019	...	...
Mississippi	Lynn Fitch (R)	E	4	1/2016	1/2024	★
Missouri	Clint Zweifel (D)	E	4	1/2013	1/2021	2
Montana	Sheila Hogan	A	Governor's Discretion	12/2016	...	...
Nebraska	Don Stenberg (R)	E	4	1/2015	1/2023	2
Nevada	Dan Schwartz (R)	E	4	1/2019	1/2023	2
New Hampshire	William Dwyer	L	2	12/2018	12/2020	★
New Jersey	Ford Scudder	A	Governor's Discretion	11/2019	...	...
New Mexico	Tim Eichenberg (D)	E	4	1/2019	1/2023	2
New York	Eric Mostert	A	Governor's Discretion	N.A.	...	...
North Carolina	Janet Cowell (D)	E	4	1/2013	1/2021	★
North Dakota	Kelly L. Schmidt (R)	E	4	1/2009	1/2021	★
Ohio	Josh Mandel (R)	E	4	1/2015	1/2023	2
Oklahoma	Ken Miller (R)	E	4	1/2015	1/2023	★
Oregon	Ted Wheeler (D)(e)	E	4	3/2014	1/2021	2
Pennsylvania	Tim Reese (f)	E	4	6/2015(f)	1/2021	2
Rhode Island	Seth Magaziner (D)	E	4	1/2019	1/2023	2
South Carolina	Curtis Loftis (R)	E	4	1/2015	1/2023	★
South Dakota	Richard Sattgast (R)	E	4	1/2015	1/2023	2
Tennessee	David H. Lillard Jr.	L	2	1/2013	1/2021	...
Texas (g)	Glenn Hegar (R)	E	4	1/2019	1/2023	★
Utah	David Damschen	E	4	12/2019	1/2021	★
Vermont	Elizabeth Pearce (D)	E	2	1/2015	1/2021	★
Virginia	Manju Ganeriwala	A	Governor's Discretion	1/2013	...	...
Washington	James L. McIntire (D)	E	4	1/2013	1/2021	★
West Virginia	John D. Perdue (D)	E	4	1/2001	1/2021	★
Wisconsin	Mattt Adamczyk (R)	E	4	1/2019	1/2023	★
Wyoming	Mark Gordon (R)	E	4	10/2012 (h)	1/2023	★
American Samoa	Falema'o Pili	A	4	1/2013	...	...
Dist. of Columbia	Jeffrey Barnette	A	Pleasure of CFO	7/2016	N.A.	...
Guam	Rosita Fejeran	CS	...	N.A.	...	...
No. Mariana Islands...	Antoinette S. Calvo	A	4	N.A.	N.A.	...
Puerto Rico	Melba Acosta (PPD/D)	A	4	1/17	N.A.	...
U.S. Virgin Islands	Valdamier Collens	A	4	N.A.	N.A.	...

Source: The National Association of State Treasurers, 2016

Key:

★ — No provision specifying number of terms allowed.

... — No formal provision, position is appointed or elected by governmental entity (not chosen by the electorate).

A — Appointed by the governor. (In the District of Columbia, the Treasurer is appointed by the Chief Financial Officer. In Georgia, position is appointed by the State Depository Board.)

E — Elected by the voters.

L — Elected by the legislature.

CS — Civil Service

N.A. — Not available.

(a) The official title of the office of state treasurer is Chief Financial Officer.

(b) The Director of Finance performs this function.

(c) Eligible for eight out of any period of twelve years.

(d) The Commissioner of Management and Budget performs this function.

(e) Wheeler was appointed as state treasurer in March 2010 and served as an interim designee. He was elected by Oregon voters in November 2010 and again in November 2012 to a full four-year term.

(f) Tim Reese was appointed Treasurer by Gov. Tom Wolf and confirmed by the Senate.

(g) The Comptroller of Public Accounts performs this function.

(h) Gordon was appointed as state treasurer in October 2012 after the death of Joseph Meyer.

Table 4.25
TREASURERS: QUALIFICATIONS FOR OFFICE

State or other jurisdiction	Minimum age	U.S. citizen (years)	State resident (years)	Qualified voter (years)
Alabama	25	7	5	...
Alaska	...	...	...	...
Arizona	25	10	5	★
Arkansas	21	★	★	...
California	18	★	★	★
Colorado	25	★	2	★
Connecticut	18	★	★	★
Delaware	18	★	★	★
Florida	30	★	7	★
Georgia	...	★	★	...
Hawaii	...	★	1	...
Idaho	25	2	2	...
Illinois	25	★	3	...
Indiana	...	★	★	★
Iowa	18	...	★	★
Kansas	...	...	...	...
Kentucky	30	2	2	★
Louisiana	25	5	5	★
Maine	...	★	★	...
Maryland	...	...	...	...
Massachusetts	...	...	...	...
Michigan	...	...	...	...
Minnesota	...	...	...	...
Mississippi	25	★	★	★
Missouri	30	15	10	★
Montana	...	...	...	...
Nebraska	...	★	★	★
Nevada	25	2	2	★
New Hampshire	...	...	...	...
New Jersey	...	...	★	...
New Mexico	30	★	5	★
New York	...	...	...	...
North Carolina	21	★	1	...
North Dakota	25	★	★	★
Ohio	18	★	★	★
Oklahoma	31	10	10	★
Oregon	18	...	★	...
Pennsylvania	...	...	...	...
Rhode Island	18	★	★	★
South Carolina	...	★	★	★
South Dakota	...	...	...	...
Tennessee	...	...	...	...
Texas	18	★	★	...
Utah	25	...	5	★
Vermont	...	★	★	...
Virginia	...	...	...	...
Washington	18	★	...	★
West Virginia	18	★	★	★
Wisconsin	18	★	★	★
Wyoming	25	★	★	★
Dist. of Columbia	...	★	...	...

Source: National Association of State Treasurers, January 2016.
Key:
★—Formal provision; number of years not specified.
... —No formal provision.
N.A.—Not applicable.
(a) Five years immediately preceding the date of qualification for office.

Table 4.26
RESPONSIBILITIES OF THE TREASURER'S OFFICE

State or other jurisdiction	Cash management	Banking services	Investment of retirement funds	Investment of trust funds	Deferred compensation	Management of bonded debt	Bond issuance	Debt service	Arbitrage	Unclaimed property	Archives for disbursement of documents	College savings	Collateral programs	Local government investment pool	Other
Alabama	★	★	...	...	...	★	...	★	...	★	...	★	★	...	...
Alaska	★	★	★	★	...	...	★	★	★	★	...	...	...	...	...
Arizona	★	★	...	★	...	...	...	...	...	...	...	...	...	★	...
Arkansas	★	★	★	...	...	...	...	...	...	...	★	...	...	★	...
California	★	★	...	★	...	★	★	★	★	...	...	★	★	★	...
Colorado	★	★	...	...	...	...	★	★	...	★	...	...	...	...	...
Connecticut	★	★	★	★	...	★	★	★	★	★	...	★	...	★	(a)
Delaware	★	★	...	...	★	...	★	★	★	...	...	...	★	★	(b)
Florida	★	★	...	★	★	...	...	...	...	★	...	...	★	...	(c)
Georgia	★	★	...	★	...	...	...	★	...	...	...	...	★	★	(d)
Hawaii	★	★	...	...	...	★	...	★	...	★	...	★	...	★	...
Idaho	★	★	...	...	...	...	★	...	...	★	...	★	...	★	...
Illinois	★	★	...	★	...	...	...	★	★	★	...	★	...	★	...
Indiana	★	★	...	★	...	★	...	...	...	...	★	★	...	★	...
Iowa	★	★	★	★	...	★	★	★	...	★	...	★	★	...	...
Kansas	★	★	...	...	...	...	...	...	...	★	...	★	...	...	(e)
Kentucky	★	★	...	...	...	...	...	...	...	★	★	...	...	...	(f)
Louisiana	★	★	...	★	...	★	★	★	★	★	...	★	...	...	...
Maine	★	★	...	...	...	★	...	★	★	★	...	★	...	...	(g)
Maryland	★	★	...	...	...	★	★	★	★	...	...	...	★	★	...
Massachusetts	★	★	★	★	★	...	★	★	...	★	...	★	...	...	...
Michigan	★	★	★	★	...	★	★	★	★	★	...	★	...	...	...
Minnesota	★	★	...	...	...	...	★	★	...	★	...	...	...	...	...
Mississippi	★	★	★	★	...	★	★	...	★	★	...	★	★	★	...
Missouri	★	★	...	...	...	...	...	★	...	★	...	★	...	...	(h)
Montana	★	★	...	...	...	★	★	★	★	...	...	...	...	...	...
Nebraska	★	★	...	...	...	...	...	...	...	★	...	★	...	...	(i)
Nevada	★	★	...	★	...	★	★	★	...	★	...	★	★	★	...
New Hampshire	★	★	...	★	...	★	★	★	★	★	...	...	...	...	...
New Jersey	★	★	★	★	★	★	★	★	...	...	...	...	...	★	...
New Mexico	★	★	...	...	...	★	...	★	...	...	★	...	...	★	...
New York	★	★	★	★	...	...	...	...	...	★	...	...	...	★	...
North Carolina	★	★	★	★	...	★	★	★	★	★	...	★	...	★	...
North Dakota	★	...	...	★	...	...	...	...	...	★	...	...	...	★	(j)
Ohio	★	★	...	★	...	★	★	★	...	★	...	...	★	★	...
Oklahoma	★	★	...	★	...	...	...	...	...	★	...	★	...	★	...
Oregon	★	★	★	★	★	★	★	★	★	★	...	★	...	★	...
Pennsylvania	★	★	★	★	...	...	...	★	...	★	...	★	...	★	...
Rhode Island	★	★	...	★	...	...	★	★	★	★	...	★	...	★	...
South Carolina	★	★	...	★	...	★	★	★	★	★	...	★	★	★	...
South Dakota	★	★	★	★	...	...	...	...	...	★	...	...	★	...	(k)
Tennessee	★	★	★	...	★	...	...	...	...	★	...	★	★	★	...
Texas	★	★	...	★	...	...	★	...	...	★	...	★	★	★	(l)
Utah	★	★	...	★	...	★	★	★	★	★	...	...	...	★	...
Vermont	★	★	★	★	★	★	★	...	★	★	...	...	...	...	...
Virginia	★	★	...	★	...	★	★	★	★	★	...	...	★	★	(m)
Washington	★	★	...	★	...	★	★	★	★	...	...	★	★	★	...
West Virginia	★	★	...	★	★	...	...	...	...	★	...	★	★	★	...
Wisconsin	...	...	...	...	...	...	...	...	...	★	...	...	...	★	...
Wyoming	★	★	...	★	...	★	★	★	★	★	...	...	★	★	(n)
Dist. of Columbia	★	★	★	★	★	★	★	★	★	★	...	★	★	...	...

Source: The National Association of State Treasurer's, Jan. 2016.
Key:
★ —Responsible for activity.
... —Not responsible for activity.
N.A. —Data not available.
(a) Second Injury Fund.
(b) General Fund account reconcilement; Disbursements—2004.
(c) State Accounting Disbursement, Fire Marshall, Insurance and Banking Consumer Services, Insurance Rehabilitation.
(d) Merchant Card Services.
(e) Municipal bond servicing.
(f) Social Security for Section 218 Agreements—2004.
(g) Municipal Revenue Sharing.
(h) Investment of all State funds.
(i) Nebraska Child Support Payment Center, Long-Term Care Savings Plan.
(j) Financial Literacy.
(k) Treasurer is a member of the trust and retirement investment programs—2004.
(l) Tax Administration/Collection/Estimating.
(m) Risk Management.
(n) Several other legislatively designated programs.

Continuing Municipal Disclosures: Are You in Compliance?

By R. Kinney Poynter

The U.S. Securities and Exchange Commission, or SEC, launched an initiative in 2014 to encourage issuers and underwriters of municipal securities to self-report certain violations of the federal securities laws rather than wait for their violations to be detected. The Municipalities Continuing Disclosure Cooperation, or MCDC, Initiative is intended to address widespread violations of the federal securities laws by municipal issuers and underwriters in connection with certain representations about continuing disclosures in bond offering documents. The SEC began issuing fines and penalties against underwriters in July 2015, and is now turning its attention to issuers.

On March 10, 2014, the U.S. Securities and Exchange Commission's, or SEC, Enforcement Division announced the Municipalities Continuing Disclosure Cooperation, or MCDC, Initiative to provide issuers and underwriters the opportunity to self-report instances of material misstatements in bond offering documents regarding the issuer's prior compliance with its continuing disclosure obligations.

According to the SEC,

"continuing disclosures are a critical source of information for investors in municipal securities, and offering documents should accurately disclose issuers' prior compliance with their disclosure obligations. This initiative is designed to promote improved compliance by encouraging responsible behavior by market participants who have failed to meet their obligations in the past."[1]

Under the MCDC initiative, the SEC indicated that it would recommend standardized, favorable settlement terms to municipal issuers and underwriters who self-report that they made inaccurate statements in bond offerings about their compliance with continuing disclosure obligations specified in Rule 15c2-12 9, or the Rule, under the Securities Exchange Act of 1934, or Exchange Act.

The SEC established two deadlines for self-reporting under the MCDC initiative:

- September 10, 2014, for underwriters, and
- December 1, 2014, for issuers.

As part of the initiative, the SEC did not define the term "material," but it did indicate that a determination of materiality would be made on a case-by-case basis depending on the overall facts and circumstances of the situation. Accordingly,

municipal market participants—underwriters and issuers—are watching very closely since enforcement actions will provide some insight on what the SEC determines to be material.

In response to the MCDC Initiative, the underwriter community conducted internal compliance investigations by reviewing the official statements for all bonds underwritten since 2009 and associated continuing disclosure filing data to confirm whether the official statements accurately described the issuer's prior compliance with continuing disclosure undertakings.

In most cases, underwriters compiled a list of bond issues that contained a misstatement regarding continuing disclosure compliance. These lists were compiled using continuing disclosure filings since 2009 made through the Electronic Municipal Market Access, or EMMA, platform of the Municipal Securities Rulemaking Board, or MSRB.

Although underwriters were encouraged to contact issuers with the results of their review to discuss any potential misstatements, they were not required to do so, and in some cases did not have time to contact all issuers because of the unreasonably short deadline for the MCDC Initiative—September 10, 2014. The difference between the reporting dates for underwriters and issuers caused confusion and even some discrepancies between noncompliance reported by the underwriter and noncompliance reported by the issuer.

The Requirements

The Rule generally prohibits an underwriter from purchasing or selling municipal securities unless an issuer has committed to provide annually financial information and operating data specified in a written Continuing Disclosure Agreement, or CDA. Additionally, the Rule requires underwriters to obtain and review a final official statement that discloses when the issuer has failed to file information required by the CDA during the previous five years.[2] As such, the underwriter and the issuer have primary responsibility for continuing disclosure compliance.

While the Rule only applies to underwriters, and the SEC is prohibited from directly regulating issuers under the 1975 Tower Amendment to the Exchange Act, the SEC has demonstrated through recent enforcement actions that making false statements in official statements about compliance with continuing disclosure obligations will be construed as securities law violations under Section 17(a) of the Securities Act of 1933 and/or Section 10(b) of the Exchange Act.[3]

Because of the Rule, issuers of most municipal security offerings provide certain disclosures when issuing securities (primary market disclosures) as well as certain times thereafter (continuing disclosures). Continuing disclosure consists of important information about a municipal bond that arises after the initial issuance. This information generally reflects the financial health or operating condition of the state or local government as it changes over time or the occurrence of specific events that can have an impact on key features of the bonds.

Continuing disclosure agreements normally require the following:[4]

Annual Financial Information

- Financial information and operating data provided by state or local governments or other obligated persons.
- Audited financial statements for state or local governments or other obligated persons, if available.

Event Notices

- Principal and interest payment delinquencies.
- Non-payment related defaults.
- Unscheduled draws on debt service reserves reflecting financial difficulties.
- Unscheduled draws on credit enhancements reflecting financial difficulties.
- Substitution of credit or liquidity providers, or their failure to perform.
- Adverse tax opinions or events affecting the tax-exempt status of the security.
- Modifications to rights of security holders.

- Bond calls and tender offers.
- Defeasances.
- Release, substitution or sale of property securing repayment of the securities.
- Rating changes.
- Bankruptcy, insolvency or receivership.
- Merger, acquisition or sale of all issuer assets.
- Appointment of successor trustee.

MCDC Results

On February 2, 2016, the SEC announced its third, and final, round of fines and penalties against underwriters. In total, 72 underwriters were charged $18 million under the voluntary self-reporting program targeting material misstatements and omissions in municipal bond offering documents. According to the SEC, "As part of the settlements, 72 underwriting firms–comprising approximately 96% of the market share for municipal underwritings–have agreed to improve their due diligence procedures and we expect that investors will benefit from those improvements."[5]

Now, the SEC is turning its attention to **issuers**. At this time, only one announcement has been made regarding issuers; however, it is anticipated that the SEC will be releasing the names of several more issuers soon. It is unclear what penalties might be assessed against the issuers, but it is certain that no government wants the negative publicity that will accompany an SEC finding of noncompliance. After all, government employees are entrusted with public funds, and with that high level of fiduciary responsibility comes an obligation to comply with laws and regulations, including continuing disclosures.

Ensuring Compliance: Do Auditors Have a Potential Role?

For several years, many municipal market groups—including the Government Finance Officers Association; National Association of Bond Lawyers; National Association of State Auditors, Comptrollers and Treasurers; National Association of State Treasurers; and the Securities Industry and Financial Markets Association—have strived to improve continuing municipal disclosures.

First, the organizations have worked to identify the major causes of noncompliance. Overall, it seems that a lack of knowledge and education is the primary culprit. For example, a small government issuer that goes to the market infrequently is not likely to have a system in place to remind key personnel of the disclosure requirement. Staff turnover is also likely—the finance manager or treasurer that issues the bonds may not be there five years down the road. Therefore, the continuing disclosure compliance requirements get overlooked. Similar issues can occur for underwriters, particularly small, infrequent issuers.

While great strides have been made, including a "tickler" in the EMMA system that reminds issuers of their continuing disclosure obligations, the MCDC Initiative has shown that compliance problems still exist.

In October 2015, the stakeholder groups reconvened in an effort to identify new ways to increase compliance in this area. While a number of ideas and suggestions were made, there was much discussion about the role of the independent auditor. In government audits, independent auditors test for compliance with applicable laws and regulations as part of their routine audit work.

Can the independent financial auditor be a key part of increasing compliance? Yes and no. The problem lies with the fact that the independent financial auditor is focused primarily on noncompliance with laws, regulations, contracts and grants that have a *direct* and *material* effect on the financial statements. Rarely, would noncompliance with continuing disclosure requirements rise to this level. Accordingly, most auditors would not specifically test compliance for continuing disclosures unless the government had a long history of problems in this area or similar extenuating circumstances.

Government Auditing Standards does provide that auditors should communicate "instances of fraud and noncompliance with provisions of law or regulations that have a material effect on the audit **and** any other instances that warrant the attention of those charged with governance."[6] (Emphasis added.) Accordingly, the professional audit standards do provide auditors some flexibility in this area.

The National Association of State Auditors, Comptrollers and Treasurers conducted a survey in January 2016 to learn not only what testing state auditors are doing in this area, but also what communication and educational materials are issued by state comptrollers and treasurers to improve compliance. Survey results varied significantly. For example, Louisiana passed a statute in 2014 that required (1) all public entity issuers of securities to be in compliance and (2) auditors to test for compliance.[7] On the opposite end of the spectrum were states that do not currently test compliance with continuing disclosures at all—due to the materiality issue discussed above—and do not provide educational materials to local government issuers.

There were a few states that have started *inquiring* of the government's management about compliance and are considering adding this compliance item to the standard management representation letter. This would be a positive step, and especially important for small governments, since it would at least raise the issue with management each year.

Conclusion

The MCDC Initiative has demonstrated that improvements in continuing disclosure compliance are needed. It is equally clear that a one-size-fits-all regulatory regime will not work—there are simply too many different types of issuers in the municipal market ranging from very large states to small local governments or utilities.

Success requires a concerted effort by many different parties, primarily the underwriter and management of the issuing government. The issuing government should ask for assistance from bond counsel and the bond agent where appropriate. The independent auditor may also have a role to play as part of annual compliance testing as discussed above.

One thing is clear. The SEC continues to increase its focus on the municipal market. It is incumbent on issuers to comply with the terms of its continuing disclosure agreement. Now more than ever, it is critical to inquire about internal controls pertaining to compliance with continuing disclosures and make sure agencies are taking the necessary steps to comply.

Don't be caught off-guard!

Notes

[1] "SEC Launches Enforcement Cooperation Initiative for Municipal Issuers and Underwriters," March 10, 2014, U.S. Securities and Exchange Commission, press release 2014-46, *https://www.sec.gov/News/PressRelease/Detail/PressRelease/1370541090828.*

[2] "Municipalities Continuing Disclosure Cooperation Initiative," Modified November 13, 2014, U.S. Securities and Exchange Commission, *www.sec.gov/divisions/enforce/municipalities-continuing-disclosure-cooperation-initiative.shtml.*

[3] Government Finance Officers Association, "GFOA Alert: The SEC MCDC Initiative and Issuers," July 7, 2014. *www.gfoa.org/gfoa-alert-sec-mcdc-initiative-and-issuers.*

[4] Municipal Securities Rulemaking Board, "SEC Rule 15c2-12: Continuing Disclosure," January 1, 2013, *www.msrb.org/msrb1/pdfs/SECRule15c2-12.pdf.*

[5] U.S. Securities and Exchange Commission, "SEC Completes Muni-Underwriter Enforcement Sweep," February 2, 2016, press release 2016–18, *www.sec.gov/news/pressrelease/2016-18.html.*

[6] U.S. Government Accountability Office, paragraph 4.23, *Government Auditing Standards 2011 Revision*, December 2011.

[7] Act 463, Louisiana Legislature, July 2014, *www.legis.la.gov/legis/ViewDocument.aspx?d=913479&n=SB384%20Act.*

About the Author

Robert M. "Kinney" Poynter is the executive director of the National Association of State Auditors, Comptrollers, and Treasurers. NASACT is a professional organization whose mission is to assist state leaders to enhance and promote effective and efficient management of governmental resources. Kinney has B.S. and M.S. degrees in accounting from the University of Kentucky. He is a certified public accountant and a member of the American Institute of Certified Public Accountants. He previously served as a member of the AICPA Council.

Table 4.27
THE STATE AUDITORS, 2016

State or other jurisdiction	State agency	Agency head	Title	Legal basis for office	Method of selection	Term of office	U.S. citizen	State resident	Maximum consecutive terms allowed
Alabama	Department of Examiners of Public Accounts	Ronald L. Jones	Chief Examiner	S	LC	7 yrs.	★		None
Alaska	Division of Legislative Audit	Kris Curtis	Legislative Auditor	C,S	L	(a)			None
Arizona	Office of the Auditor General	Debra K. Davenport	Auditor General	S	LC	5 yrs.			None
Arkansas	Division of Legislative Audit	Roger A. Norman	Legislative Auditor	S	LC	Indefinite	★	★	None
California	Bureau of State Audits	Elaine M. Howle	State Auditor	S	G	4 yrs.	★		None
Colorado	Office of the State Auditor	Dianne E. Ray	State Auditor	C,S	LC	5 yrs.			None
Connecticut	Office of the Auditors of Public Accounts	John C. Geragosian and Robert M. Ward	State Auditors	S	L	4 yrs.			None
Delaware	Office of the Auditor of Accounts	R. Thomas Wagner, Jr.	Auditor of Accounts	C,S	E	4 yrs.	★	★	None
Florida	Office of the Auditor General	Sherrill F. Norman	Auditor General	C,S	L	(a)			None
Georgia	Department of Audits and Accounts	Greg S. Griffin	State Auditor	S	L	Indefinite			None
Hawaii	Office of the Auditor	Jan K. Yamane	State Auditor	C	L	8 yrs.		★	None
Idaho	Legislative Services Office—Legislative Audits	April J. Renfro	Division Manager	S	LC	(b)	★	★	None
Illinois	Office of the Auditor General	Frank Mautino	Auditor General	C,S	L	10 yrs.			None
Indiana	State Board of Accounts	Paul D. Joyce	State Examiner	S	GLC	4 yrs.			None
Iowa	Office of the Auditor of State	Mary Mosiman	Auditor of State	C,S	E	4 yrs.	★	★	None
Kansas	Legislative Division of Post Audit	Scott E. Frank	Legislative Post Auditor	S	LC	(b)			None
Kentucky	Office of the Auditor of Public Accounts	Mike Harmon	Auditor of Public Accounts	C,S	E	4 yrs.	★	★	2
Louisiana	Office of the Legislative Auditor	Daryl G. Purpera	Legislative Auditor	C,S	L	(a)	★	★	None
Maine	Department of Audit	Pola A. Buckley	State Auditor	S	L	4 yrs.			2
Maryland	Office of Legislative Audits	Thomas J. Barnickel III	Legislative Auditor	S	ED	Indefinite			None
Massachusetts	Office of the Auditor of the Commonwealth	Suzanne M. Bump	Auditor of the Commonwealth	C,S	E	4 yrs.	★	★	None
Michigan	Office of the Auditor General	Doug Ringler	Auditor General	C	L	8 yrs.			None
Minnesota	Office of the Legislative Auditor	James R. Nobles	Legislative Auditor	S	LC	6 yrs. (a)			None
Minnesota	Office of the State Auditor	Rebecca Otto	State Auditor	C	E	4 yrs.	★	★	None
Mississippi	Office of the State Auditor	Stacey E. Pickering	State Auditor	C	E	4 yrs.	★	★	None
Missouri	Office of the State Auditor	Nicole Galloway	State Auditor	C,S	E	4 yrs.	★	★	None
Montana	Legislative Audit Division	Tori Hunthausen	Legislative Auditor	C,S	LC	2 yrs.			None
Nebraska	Office of the Auditor of Public Accounts	Charlie Janssen	Auditor of Public Accounts	C	E	4 yrs.	★	★	None
Nevada	Legislative Counsel Bureau, Audit Division	Rocky Cooper	Legislative Auditor	S	LC	Indefinite			None
New Hampshire	Office of the Legislative Budget Assistant	Michael W. Kane	Legislative Budget Assistant	S	LC	2 yrs. (b)			None
New Jersey	Office of the State Auditor	Stephen M. Eells	State Auditor	C,S	L	5 yr. term and until successor is appointed	★	★	None
	Office of the State Comptroller	Philip Degnan	State Comptroller	S	G	6 yrs.			2
New Mexico	Office of the State Auditor	Tim Keller	State Auditor	C,S	E	4 yrs.	★	★	2
New York	Office of the State Comptroller, State Audit Bureau	Thomas P. DiNapoli	State Comptroller	C,S	E	4 yrs.	★	★	None
North Carolina	Office of the State Auditor	Beth A. Wood	State Auditor	C	E	4 yrs.	★	★	None
North Dakota	Office of the State Auditor	Robert R. Peterson	State Auditor	C,S	E	Indefinite	★	★	None
Ohio	Office of the Auditor of State	Dave Yost	Auditor of State	C,S	E	4 yrs.			2

See footnotes at end of table.

THE STATE AUDITORS, 2016—Continued

State or other jurisdiction	State agency	Agency head	Title	Legal basis for office	Method of selection	Term of office	U.S. citizen	State resident	Maximum consecutive terms allowed
Oklahoma	Office of the State Auditor and Inspector	Gary Jones	State Auditor and Inspector	C,S	E	4 yrs.	★	★	None
Oregon	Division of Audits	Mary Wenger	Interim Director	C,S	SS	Indefinite	…	…	None
Pennsylvania	Department of the Auditor General	Eugene DePasquale	Auditor General	C,S	E	4 yrs.	…	…	2
Rhode Island	Office of the Auditor General	Dennis E. Hoyle	Auditor General	S	LC	(b)	…	…	None
South Carolina	Legislative Audit Council	Earle Powell	Director	S	LC	4 yrs.	…	…	None
South Carolina	Office of the State Auditor	George Kennedy	State Auditor	S	SB	Indefinite (c)	…	…	None
South Dakota	Department of Legislative Audit	Martin L. Guindon	Auditor General	S	L	8 yrs. (a)	…	…	None
Tennessee	Comptroller of the Treasury, Dept. of Audit	Justin P. Wilson	Comptroller of the Treasury	C,S	L	2 yrs.	…	…	None
Texas	Office of the State Auditor	Lisa Collier	Interim State Auditor	S	LC	(b)	…	…	None
Utah	Office of the State Auditor	John Dougall	State Auditor	C,S	E	4 yrs.	★	★	None
Vermont	Office of the State Auditor	Douglas R. Hoffer	State Auditor	C,S	E	2 yrs.	…	★	None
Virginia	Office of the Auditor of Public Accounts	Martha S. Mavredes	Auditor of Public Accounts	C,S	L	4 yrs.	…	…	None
Washington	Office of the State Auditor	Troy Kelley	State Auditor	C,S	E	4 yrs.	★	★	None
West Virginia	Legislative Auditor's Office	Aaron Allred	Legislative Auditor	S	L	(a)	…	…	None
Wisconsin	Legislative Audit Bureau	Joe Chrisman	State Auditor	S	LC	Indefinite (b)	…	…	None
Wyoming	Department of Audit	Jeffrey C. Vogel	Director	S	GC	6 yrs.	★	★	None
Dist. Of Columbia	Office of the D.C. Auditor	Kathleen Patterson	District of Columbia Auditor						
American Samoa	AS Territorial Auditor Office	Liua Fatuesi	Territorial Auditor						
Guam	Office of the Public Auditor	Doris Flores Brooks	Public Auditor	S	E	4 yrs.	★	★	None
No. Mariana Islands	Office of the Public Auditor	Michael Pai	Public Auditor	C,S.	GL	6 yrs.	N.A.	N.A.	2
Puerto Rico	Office of the Comptroller	Yesmin M. Valdivieso-Galib	Comptroller	C,S.	GL	10 yrs.	N.A.	★	1

Source: Auditing in the States: A Summary, 2015 edition, The National Association of State Auditors, Comptrollers and Treasurers.

Key:
★—Provision for.
…—No provision for.
E—Elected by the public.
L—Appointed by the legislature.
G—Appointed by the governor.
SS—Appointed by the secretary of state.
LC—selected by legislative committee, commission or council.
ED—appointed by the executive director of legislative services

GC—Appointed by governor, secretary of state and treasurer.
GL—Appointed by the governor and confirmed by both chambers of the legislature
GLC—Appointed by the governor and confirmed by legislative council
SB—Appointed by state budget and control board.
C—Constitutional
S—Statutory
N.A.—Not applicable.
(a) Serves at the pleasure of the legislature.
(b) Serves at the pleasure of a legislative committee.
(c) The term is indefinite, but the state auditor serves at the pleasure of the five-member board.

Table 4.28
STATE AUDITORS: SCOPE OF AGENCY AUTHORITY

State or other jurisdiction	Authority to audit all state agencies	Authority to audit local governments	Authority to obtain information	Authority to issue subpoenas	Authority to specify accounting principles for local governments	Investigations Agency investigates fraud, waste, abuse, and/or illegal acts	Agency operates a hotline
Alabama	★	...	★	★	★(a)	★	...
Alaska	★	...	★	★	...	★	...
Arizona	★	...	★	...	...	★	...
Arkansas	★	★	★	★	...	★	...
California	★	★	★	★	...	★	★
Colorado	★	...	★	★	★	★	★
Connecticut	★	...	★	...	...	★	★
Delaware	★	★(l)	★	★	...	★	★
Florida	(b)	★	★	...	...	★	...
Georgia	★	(m)	★	★	★	★	...
Hawaii	★	★	★	★	...	★	...
Idaho	★	(n)	★	...	...	★	...
Illinois	★	(c)	★	★	...	★	★
Indiana	★	★	★	★	★	★	...
Iowa	★	★	★	★	...	★	...
Kansas	★	★	★	...	...	...	...
Kentucky	★	★	★	★	...	★	★
Louisiana	★	★(o)	★	★	★	★	★
Maine	★	★	★	...	★	★	★
Maryland	★(b)	(d)	★	★	★	★	★
Massachusetts	★	★	★	★	...	★	★
Michigan	★	...	★	★	...	★	...
Minnesota							
Legislative Auditor	★	★	★	★	...	★	...
State Auditor	(e)	★	★	★	★	★	...
Mississippi	★	(p)	★	★	★	★	★
Missouri	★	(q)	★	★	...	★	★
Montana	★	...	★	...	...	★	★
Nebraska	★	★	★	...	★	★	★
Nevada	★	★	★	...	...	★	...
New Hampshire	(j)	...	★	...	...	★	...
New Jersey							
State Auditor	★	(r)	★	...	...	...	...
State Comptroller	★	★	★	★	...	★	★
New Mexico	★	★	★	★	★	★	★
New York	★	★	★	★	★	★	★
North Carolina	★	...	★	★	...	★	★
North Dakota	(f)	(s)	★	...	...	★	...
Ohio	★	★	★	★	★	★	★
Oklahoma	★	(t)	★	★	(k)	★	★
Oregon	★	...	★	★	★	★	★
Pennsylvania	(g)	★(u)	★	...	...	★	★
Rhode Island	★	(v)	★	★	★	★	...
South Carolina							
Legislative Audit Council	★	...	★	...	...	★	...
State Auditor	(h)	...	★	...	...	★	...
South Dakota	★	★	★	★	...	★	...
Tennessee	★	★	★	★	★	★	★
Texas	★	(i)	★	...	...	★	★
Utah	★	★	★	★	★	★	★
Vermont	★	★(w)	★	★	...	★	★
Virginia	★	(x)	★	★	★	★	...
Washington	★	★	★	★	★	★	★
West Virginia	★	...	★	...	...	★	...
Wisconsin	★	(y)	★	★	...	★	★
Wyoming	★	★	★	★	...	★	...
Guam	★	★	★	★	★	★	★
No. Mariana Islands	★	N.A.	★	★	★	★	N.A.
Puerto Rico	★	★	★	★	...	★	★

See footnotes at end of table.

STATE AUDITORS: SCOPE OF AGENCY AUTHORITY — Continued

Source: Auditing in the States, 2015 Edition, The National Association of State Auditors, Comptrollers and Treasurers.

Key:

★ — Provision for responsibility.

. . . — No provision for responsibility.

N.A. — Not available.

(a) Municipalities not covered.

(b) The legislature or legislative branch is excluded from audit authority.

(c) Audits of local governments conducted as directed by the General Assembly.

(d) Authority to audit local school systems only.

(e) State agencies are audited by the Office of Legislative Auditor.

(f) The Bank of North Dakota is excluded.

(g) The legislative and judicial branches are excluded from audit authority.

(h) The state auditor's office is responsible for auditing all state agencies with the exception the state's public colleges and universities and a few agencies. The state auditor's office is charged with approving the selection of the auditors for the public colleges and universities.

(i) The state auditor can conduct an audit or investigation of any entity receiving funds from the stated; also, certain political subdivisions of the state.

(j) Entities excluded are the University System of New Hampshire, Community College System of New Hampshire, and the New Hampshire Retirement System,

all of which are component units of the state that hire their own auditors in accordance with statute.

(k) Only county government is included, all others are not covered.

(l) Municipalities that receive state funds are excluded.

(m) The department has the authority to aduit all local boards of education. They do not have the authority to conduct the audits of local governments. However, they review the financial audit to ensure it was done in accordance with standards.

(n) They are not prohibited from performing audits on local governments, but they are also not required to perform the audit. They're generally performed by CPA firms.

(o) Generally independent CPA firms perform local government audits.

(p) Audits of municipalities are currently excluded from the state auditor's office authority to audit.

(q) SAO has audit authority for counties that do not elect a county auditor, transportation development districts, school districts or charter schools, other political subdivisions upon petition by the voters of those subdivision, and any local government as requested by the governor.

(r) Those which do not receive state aid or grants are excluded. Also, they would only be auditing the state funds.

(s) Local governments have the option of having their audits done by a CPA firm.

(t) Cities and towns, only by request of district attorney or by petition request are excluded.

(u) Local government excluded to the textent they receive state money, or federal money flowing through the state treasury.

(v) None are specifically excluded, but the agency goes in on orders from the Joint Committee on Legislative Services.

(w) If the local government received monies disbursed from the commissioner of finance and management or the state treasurer, the nthe auditor has the authority to audit.

(x) Oversight over the audits of local government, but CPA firms do the audits.

(y) By statute, the Legislative Audit Bureau has the authority to conduct audits of local units of government only when directed to do so by the Joint Legislative Audit Committee.

Only three such audits may be authorized by the committee in any given year. The bureau can, however, audit any funds made through state appropriations that local governments receive.

Table 4.29
STATE AUDITORS: TYPES OF AUDITS

State or other jurisdiction	Financial statement	Single audit	Attestation engagements	Compliance only	Economy and efficiency	Program	Sunset	Performance measures	IT	Accounting and review services	Other audits
Alabama	★	★									
Alaska	★	★	★	★	★	★	★	★	★		
Arizona	★	★	★	★	★	★	★		★	★	(a)
Arkansas	★	★	★	★		★			★	★	
California	★	★		★	★	★		★	★	★	(b)
Colorado	★	★	★			★		★	★		
Connecticut	★	★		★	★	★		★	★		(c)
Delaware	★		★	★	★	★		★	★		
Florida	★	★	★	★	★	★			★		
Georgia	★	★	★	★	★				★	★	(e)
Hawaii	★	★	★	★	★	★	★	★	★		
Idaho	★	★		★		★	★	★	★		
Illinois	★	★	★	★	★				★	★	(c)
Indiana	★	★	★	★	★	★		★	★	★	
Iowa	★	★	★	★	★	★		★	★		
Kansas	★	★	★	★	★	★			★		
Kentucky	★	★	★	★	★	★		★	★		
Louisiana	★	★	★	★	★	★		★	★		
Maine	★	★		★	★		★	★	★	★	(f)
Maryland			★	★	★	★			★		
Massachusetts		★	★	★	★	★		★	★	★	(g)
Michigan	★	★	★	★	★	★			★		(h)
Minnesota											
Legislative Auditor	★	★	★		★	★		★	★		
State Auditor	★	★		★				★			(c)
Mississippi	★	★	★	★	★	★		★	★		
Missouri	★			★	★	★		★	★		
Montana	★	★	★	★	★	★		★	★		
Nebraska	★	★	★	★	★	★			★		
Nevada	★				★	★		★	★		
New Hampshire	★	★	★		★	★		★	★		(i)
New Jersey											
State Auditor	★	★			★	★			★		
State Comptroller								★	★		(j)
New Mexico	★	★	★	★	★	★		★	★		
New York	★	★	★		★	★			★	★	
North Carolina	★	★		★	★	★			★		
North Dakota	★	★		★	★	★		★	★		(k)
Ohio	★	★	★	★	★	★		★	★	★	

See footnotes at end of table.

STATE AUDITORS: TYPES OF AUDITS—Continued

State or other jurisdiction	Financial statement	Single audit	Attestation engagements	Compliance only	Economy and efficiency	Program	Sunset	Performance measures	IT	Accounting and review services	Other audits
Oklahoma	★	★	★		★	★			★		(l)
Oregon	★	★	★		★	★			★	★	
Pennsylvania	★	★	★	★	★	★			★		
Rhode Island	★	★	★	★					★		
South Carolina											
Legislative Audit Council					★	★				★	
State Auditor	★	★	★								
South Dakota	★	★	★	★	★	★		★		★	
Tennessee	★	★	★	★	★	★	★	★	★	★	
Texas	★	★	★	★	★	★		★	★		(m)
Utah	★	★		★	★	★		★	★	★	
Vermont	★	★		★	★	★		★	★	★	
Virginia	★	★	★	★		★		★	★	★	(n)
Washington	★	★	★	★	★	★		★	★	★	
West Virginia											
Performance Evaluation Research Division					★	★		★			
Post Audit Division					★	★	★	★			
Wisconsin	★	★			★	★		★			
Wyoming				★	★			★			
Guam	★	★	★	★	★	★					(d)
No. Mariana Islands	★	★	★		★	★				★	
Puerto Rico				★				★	★		

Sources: Auditing in the States: A Summary, 2015 edition. The National Association of State Auditors, Comptrollers and Treasurers and state constitutions and statutes.

Key:
★ – Provision for responsibility.
. . . – No provision for responsibility.
N.A. – Not available.

(a) Internal control and compliance reviews; financial compliance reports; special reports; investigative reports.
(b) Investigations, assessments related to high risk.
(c) Agreed-upon procedures.
(d) Performance audits.

(e) Desk reviews.
(f) Investigative or forensic audits.
(g) Privatization audits.
(h) Internal control and compliance audits.
(i) Internal control reviews.
(j) School district forensic audits.
(k) Internal control reviews; studies.
(l) Investigations (reviews).
(m) Special projects, feasibility studies.
(n) Cash receipts audits at local courts.

Table 4.30
THE STATE COMPTROLLERS, 2016

State	Agency or office	Name	Title	Legal basis for office	Method of selection	Approval or confirmation, if necessary	Length of term	Elected comptroller's maximum consecutive terms	Civil service or merit system employee
Alabama	Office of the State Comptroller	Thomas L. White, Jr.	State Comptroller	S	(c)	AG	(b)	...	★
Alaska	Division of Finance	Scot Arehart	Division Director	S	(d)	AG	(a)	...	★
Arizona	General Accounting Office	D. Clark Partridge	State Comptroller	S	(d)	AG	(b)	...	...
Arkansas	Dept. of Finance and Administration	Larry Walther	Chief Fiscal Officer, Director	S	G		(a)	...	...
	Office of the State Auditor	Andrea Lea	State Auditor	C	E		4 yrs.	2 terms	...
California	Office of the State Controller	Betty Yee (D)	State Controller	C	E		4 yrs.	2 terms	...
	Department of Finance	Todd Jerue	Chief Operating Officer	S	(d)	AG	(g)	...	...
Colorado	Department of Personnel and Administration	Bob Jaros	State Controller	S	(d)	AG	(g)	...	★
Connecticut	Office of the Comptroller	Kevin P. Lembo (D)	Comptroller	C	E		4 yrs.	unlimited	...
Delaware	Dept. of Finance	Kristopher Knight	Director, Division of Accounting	S	G	AS	(a)	...	...
Florida	Dept. of Financial Services	Jeff Atwater	Chief Financial Officer	C,S	E		4 yrs.	2 terms	...
Georgia	State Accounting Office	Alan Skelton	State Accounting Officer	S	G		(a)	...	...
Hawaii	Dept. of Accounting and General Services	Douglas Murdock	State Comptroller	S	G	AS	4 yrs.	...	★
Idaho	Office of State Controller	Brandon Woolf	State Controller	C	E		4 yrs.	2 terms	...
Illinois	Office of the State Comptroller	Leslie Munger (R)	State Comptroller	C	E		4 yrs.	unlimited	...
Indiana	Office of the Auditor of State	Suzanne Crouch	Auditor of State	C	E		4 yrs.	2 terms	...
Iowa	State Accounting Enterprise	Calvin McKelvogue	Chief Operating Officer	S	(g)	AS	(a)	...	...
Kansas	Office of Management, Analysis and Standards	DeAnn Hill	Director	S	(d)		(b)	...	★
Kentucky	Office of the Controller	Edgar C. Ross	Controller	S	(f)	AG	(i)	...	...
Louisiana	Division of Administration	John McLean	Director	S	G		(a)	...	...
Maine	Office of the State Controller	Douglas Cotnoir	State Controller	S	(f)	AG	(i)	...	...
Maryland	Office of the Comptroller of the Treasury	Peter Franchot (D)	State Comptroller	C	E		4 yrs.	unlimited	...
Massachusetts	Office of the Comptroller	Thomas Shack, III	Comptroller	S	G	SBD	4 yrs.	...	...
Michigan	Office of Financial Management	Michael J. Moody	Director	S	SBD		(k)	...	★
Minnesota	Department of Finance	Myron Frans	Commissioner	S	G	AS	(a)	...	...
Mississippi	Department of Finance and Administration	Mark Valentine	Director, Office of Fiscal Management	C,S	G		(a)	...	...
Missouri	Division of Accounting	Stacy Neal	Director of Accounting	S	(d)		(g)	...	...
Montana	State Accounting Division	Cody Pearce	Administrator	S	(m)		(b)	...	...
Nebraska	Accounting Division	Jerry Broz	State Accounting Administrator	S	(d)		(b)	...	★
Nevada	Office of the State Controller	Ron Knecht (R)	State Controller	C,S	E		4 yrs.	2 terms	...
New Hampshire	Department of Administration	Gerard Murphy	State Comptroller	S	G		4 yrs.	...	...
New Jersey	Office of Management and Budget	Philip Degnan	State Comptroller	S	G	AS	(a)	...	★

See footnotes at end of table.

THE STATE COMPTROLLERS, 2016—Continued

State	Agency or office	Name	Title	Legal basis for office	Method of selection	Approval or confirmation, if necessary	Length of term	Elected comptroller's maximum consecutive terms	Civil service or merit system employee
New Mexico	Department of Finance and Administration, Financial Control Division	Ronald Spilman	State Controller	S	G	...	(a)	...	★
New York	Office of the State Comptroller	Thomas P. DiNapoli	State Comptroller	C,S	E	...	4 yrs.	unlimited	...
North Carolina	Office of the State Controller	Linda Combs	State Controller	S	G	GA	7 yrs.	unlimited	...
North Dakota	Office of Management and Budget	Pam Sharp	Director	S	G	AS	(a)	unlimited	...
Ohio	Office of Budget and Management	Timothy S. Keen	Director	S	G	AS	(a)	...	...
Oklahoma	Office of State Finance	Lynne Bajema	State Comptroller	S	(e)	...	(h)	...	...
Oregon	Chief Financial Office	Robert Hamilton	Manager, Statewide Accounting and Reporting	S	(d)	AG	(g)	...	...
Pennsylvania	Office of the Budget/Comptroller Operations	Anna Maria Kiehl	Chief Accounting Officer	S	SBD	AG	(a)	...	...
Rhode Island	Office of Accounts and Control	Marc Leonetti	State Controller	S	(d)	...	(b)	...	...
South Carolina	Office of the Comptroller General	Richard Eckstrom (R)	Comptroller General	C,S	E	...	4 yrs.	unlimited	★
South Dakota	Office of the State Auditor	Steve Barnett (R)	State Auditor	C	E	...	4 yrs.	2 terms	...
Tennessee	Division of Accounts	Mike Corricelli	Chief of Accounts	S	(f)	...	(b)	...	...
Texas	Office of the Comptroller of Public Accounts	Glenn Hegar (R)	Comptroller of Public Accounts	C,S	E	...	4 yrs.	unlimited	...
Utah	Division of Finance	John C. Reidhead	Director	S	(d)	AG	(g)	...	...
Vermont	Department of Finance and Management	Andy Pallito	Commissioner	S	G	AS	(a)	...	...
Virginia	Department of Accounts	David A. Von Moll	State Comptroller	S	G	GA	(a)	...	...
Washington	Office of Financial Management	David Schumacher	Director	C	G	...	(a)	...	...
West Virginia	Office of the State Auditor	Glen B. Gainier III (D)	State Auditor	C	E	...	4 yrs.	unlimited	...
Finance Division	Finance Division, Office of the State Comptroller	Dave Mullins	State Comptroller and Finance Director	S	(d)	AG	AG	unlimited	...
Wisconsin	State Controller's Office	Jeffrey Anderson	State Controller	S	CS	...	(b)	...	★
Wyoming	Office of the State Auditor	Cynthia Cloud	State Auditor	C	E	...	4 yrs.	2 terms	...

Sources: Comptrollers: Technical Activities and Functions, 2012 edition, National Association of State Auditors, Comptrollers and Treasurers and The Council of State Governments, April 2016.

Key:
★ —Yes, provision for.
... —No provision for.
C—Constitutional
S—Statutory
N.A.—Not applicable.
E—Elected by the public.
G—Appointed by the Governor.
CS—Civil Service.
AG—Approved by the governor.
AS—Approved/confirmed by the Senate.
SBD—Approved by State Budget Director.
GA—Confirmed by the General Assembly.
SDB—Confirmed by State Depository Board.

(a) Serves at the pleasure of the governor.
(b) Indefinite.
(c) Appointed by the Director of the Dept. of Finance (merit system position).
(d) Appointed by the head of the department of administration or administrative services.
(e) Appointed by the head of finance. department or agency.
(f) Appointed by the head of financial and administrative services.
(g) Serves at the pleasure of the head of the department of administration or administrative services.
(h) Serves at the pleasure of the head of the finance department or agency.
(i) Serves at the pleasure of the head of the financial and administrative services.
(j) Appointed by the governor for a term coterminous with the governor.
(k) Two-year renewable contractual term; classified executive service.
(l) As of July 1, 2005, the responsibility for accounting and financial reporting in Georgia was transferred to the newly-created State Accounting Office.
(m) Classified position.

Table 4.31
STATE COMPTROLLERS: QUALIFICATIONS FOR OFFICE

State	Minimum age	U.S. citizen (years)	State resident (years) (a)	Education years or degree	Professional experience and years	Professional certification and years	Other qualifications	No specific qualifications for office
Alabama	★	★	★	★, B.S.	★, 10 yrs.	(b)	...	...
Alaska	...	...	...	...	...	...	...	★
Arizona	...	★, 1 yr.	★, 1 yr.	★, B.S.	★, 7-10 yrs.	★(c)	...	...
Arkansas	30	...	...	...	★	...	...	...
California	★	...	...	...	...	...	...	...
Colorado	...	...	...	★(d)	★6,yrs.	★, CPA	...	...
Connecticut	...	...	★	...	...	...	...	...
Delaware	...	...	...	...	...	...	...	★
Florida	30	...	★, 7 yrs.	...	...	...	...	...
Georgia	...	...	...	...	...	...	...	★
Hawaii	...	...	30 days	...	...	...	...	★
Idaho	25	(e)	★, 2 yrs.	...	...	...	...	...
Illinois	25	★	★, 3 yrs.	...	...	...	...	...
Indiana	...	...	★(e)	...	...	...	...	...
Iowa	...	...	...	...	...	...	...	★
Kansas	...	...	...	...	...	...	...	★
Kentucky	...	...	...	...	...	...	(f)	★
Louisiana	...	...	...	...	...	...	...	★
Maine	...	...	...	...	...	...	(g)	★
Maryland	18	★	★	...	...	...	...	★
Massachusetts	...	...	...	★(h)	★, 7 yrs.	...	...	...
Michigan	...	...	...	★(i)	★, 2 yrs.	(i)	(i)	...
Minnesota	...	...	...	...	...	...	...	★
Mississippi	...	...	...	★(h)	★, 10 yrs.	★, CPA	(j)	...
Missouri	...	...	...	...	...	...	...	★
Montana	...	...	...	★(k)	★, 10 yrs.	★, CPA	...	★
Nebraska	...	...	...	★(l)	★(m)	★, CPA	...	...
Nevada	25	★	★, 2 yrs.	...	...	...	...	...
New Hampshire	...	...	...	...	...	...	(n)	★
New Jersey	...	...	...	...	...	...	...	★
New Mexico	30	★	5	N.A.	N.A.	N.A.	N.A.	N.A.
New York	30	★	★, (o)	...	...	...	...	...
North Carolina	...	...	...	★(p)	★	...	★(p)	...
North Dakota	...	...	...	...	...	...	...	★
Ohio	...	...	...	...	...	...	...	★
Oklahoma	...	★	★	★	★, 5 yrs.	...	...	★
Oregon	...	...	...	...	...	...	...	★
Pennsylvania	...	...	...	...	...	...	...	★
Rhode Island	...	★	★	★(q)	...	★, CPA	...	...
South Carolina	18	★	...	...	...	...	...	...
South Dakota	★	★	★, 1 yr.	...	...	...	...	...
Tennessee	...	...	...	★	★, 7 yrs.	★, CPA	...	...
Texas	18	★(e)	★, 1 yr.	★	★, 6 yrs.	★, CPA	...	...
Utah	...	★	...	★	★, 6 yrs.	★, CPA	...	...
Vermont	...	...	...	...	...	...	...	★
Virginia	...	...	...	...	...	...	...	★
Washington	★	★, Whole life	★	★	★	★	...	...
West Virginia-								
Office of State Auditor	25	★	★	...	...	...	...	...
Division of Finance, Office of State Comptroller	...	★	★	★, B.S.B.A.	★, 4 yrs.	...	...	...
Wisconsin	...	...	...	★B.S.	...	★, CPA	...	...
Wyoming	★	★	★	...	...	...	...	...

Sources: The National Association of State Auditors, Comptrollers and Treasurers. January 2014 and The Council of State Governments, April 2016.

Key:

★—Formal provision.

. . .—No formal provision.

N.A.—Not applicable.

(a) 18 yrs. At time of election or appointment and a citizen of the state.

(b) One of the following CPA, CIA, CPM, CGFM or CGFO.

(c) Any of those mentioned or CFE, CPM, etc.

(d) 5 yrs. or college degree.

(e) Years not specified.

(f) The Kentucky Revised Statutes state that "The state controller shall be a person qualified by education and experience for the position and held in high esteem in the accounting community."

(g) There are no educational or professional mandates, yet the appointed official is generally qualified by a combination of experience and education.

(h) Master's degree. For Massachusetts amd advanced degree in accounting, auditing, financial management, business administration or public administration (M.G.L.C. 7A, S.1)

(i) Bachelor's degree no professional certification required, but CPA certification is considered desirable. Financial management experience, knowledge of GAAP and good communication skills are other qualifications.

(j) The executive director (a) shall be a certified public accountant; or (b) shall possess a master's degree in busioness, public administration or a related field; or (c) shall have at least 10 yrs. experience in management in the private or public sector and a minimum of 5 yrs. experience in high level management with a documented record of management.

(k) Bachelor's degree in accounting.

(l) 4 yr. degree with concentration in accounting.

(m) 3 yrs. directing the work of others.

(n) Education and relevant experience.

(o) Five preceding elections.

(p) Qualified by education and experience for the position.

(q) Master's degree in accounting or business administration.

Table 4.32
STATE COMPTROLLERS: DUTIES, RESPONSIBILITIES AND FUNCTIONS

State	Disbursements	Payroll	Pre-audit	Post-audit	Operating the financial management system	Financial reporting	Debt management
Alabama	★	★	★	...	★	★	...
Alaska	★	★	...	...	★	★	...
Arizona	N.A.	N.A.	N.A.	N.A.	N.A.	N.A.	N.A.
Arkansas	N.A.	N.A.	N.A.	N.A.	N.A.	N.A.	N.A.
California	N.A.	N.A.	N.A.	N.A.	N.A.	N.A.	N.A.
Colorado	★	★	★	...	★	★	★
Connecticut	N.A.	N.A.	N.A.	N.A.	N.A.	N.A.	N.A.
Delaware	★	...	★	★	★	★	...
Florida	★	★	★	★	★	★	...
Georgia	...	...	...	...	...	★	...
Hawaii	★	★	★	★	★	★	...
Idaho	★	★	...	...	★	★	...
Illinois	★	★	★	★	★	★	...
Indiana	★	★	★	...	★	★	...
Iowa	★	★	★	★	★	★	...
Kansas	★	...	★	...	...	★	...
Kentucky	★	...	★	...	★	★	★
Louisiana	★	★	...	...	★	★	...
Maine	★	★	★	★	★	★	...
Maryland	★	★	★	★	★	★	...
Massachusetts	★	★	★	★	★	★	★
Michigan	...	★	...	...	★	★	...
Minnesota	N.A.	N.A.	N.A.	N.A.	N.A.	N.A.	N.A.
Mississippi	★	★	★	★	★	★	★
Missouri	★	★	★	...	★	★	★
Montana	★	...	...	...	★	★	...
Nebraska	★	★	★	...	★	★	★
Nevada	★	...	...	...	★	★	...
New Hampshire	N.A.	N.A.	N.A.	N.A.	N.A.	N.A.	N.A.
New Jersey	★	★	...	★	★	★	...
New Mexico	N.A.	N.A.	N.A.	N.A.	N.A.	N.A.	N.A.
New York	★	★	★	★	★	★	★
North Carolina	★	★	...	...	★	★	...
North Dakota	★	★	...	...	★	★	...
Ohio	★	...	★	★	★	★	★
Oklahoma	★	★	★	★	★	★	...
Oregon	...	★	...	...	★	★	...
Pennsylvania	...	★	★	★	★	★	...
Rhode Island	★	★	★	★	★	★	...
South Carolina	★	★	★	...	★	★	...
South Dakota	...	...	...	★	★	★	...
Tennessee	★	★	★	★	...	★	...
Texas	★	★	★	★	★	★	...
Utah	★	★	...	★	★	★	★
Vermont	★	★	...	...	★	★	...
Virginia	★	★	★	★	★	★	...
Washington	...	...	...	...	...	★	...
West Virginia	★	★	★	★	★	★	...
Wisconsin	★	★	★	...	★	★	...
Wyoming	★	★	★	...	★	★	...

Source: State Comptrollers: Technical Activities and Functions, 2014 edition, National Association of State Auditors, Comptrollers and Treasurers.

Key:
★ — Formal provision.
... — No formal provision.
N.A. — Not available.
(a) Enterprise travel office and one-card program.
(b) Some of the functions are shared with the Office of Information Technology.
(c) Payroll compliance (not processing).
(d) State treasury — deposit security and funds management, risk management, and unclaimed property.
(e) Shared services, accounting policies and state travel office.

(f) Income offsets, CMIA & SWCAP and 1099 reporting.
(g) Planning and budgeting, and facility planning and control (capital outlay)
(h) Tax collection, tax compliance, and revenue estimates.
(i) State Social Security administrator.
(j) Treasury — deposits and recons, local government audit and reporting, and Social Security administrator.
(k) Purchasing card administration.
(l) Budget, accounting and shared services.
(m) Employee travel planning and reimbursement, policy/planning, payable service center, contract review and internal audits.
(n) Policy development, technical accounting training, CMIA and certain banking relationships.

STATE COMPTROLLERS: DUTIES, RESPONSIBILITIES AND FUNCTIONS — Continued

State	Investment management	Internal control oversight	Transparency	Quality assurance	Enterprise Resource Planning System responsibility	Data Warehouse	Other
Alabama	...	...	★	...	...		...
Alaska	...	...	★	...	...		(a)
Arizona	N.A.	N.A.	N.A.	N.A.	N.A.	N.A.	N.A.
Arkansas	N.A.	N.A.	N.A.	N.A.	N.A.	N.A.	N.A.
California	N.A.	N.A.	N.A.	N.A.	N.A.	N.A.	N.A.
Colorado	...	★	★	★	★	...	(b)
Connecticut	N.A.	N.A.	N.A.	N.A.	N.A.	N.A.	N.A.
Delaware	...	★	★	★	★	...	(c)
Florida	★	...	★	...	...	...	(d)
Georgia	...	★	...	...	★		(e)
Hawaii	...	★	...	...	★	★	(q)
Idaho	...	...	★	...	★	★	(r)
Illinois	...	...	★	★	...	...	...
Indiana	...	...	★	...	★	★	(s)
Iowa	...	...	...	...	★		(f)
Kansas	...	...	★	...	...	...	(t)
Kentucky	★	...	★	...	★	★	(u)
Louisiana	...	...	★	...	★	★	(g)
Maine	...	★	★	★	★	★	...
Maryland	...	...	★	★	...	...	(h)
Massachusetts	...	★	★	★	...	...	...
Michigan	...	...	★	...	...	...	...
Minnesota	N.A.	N.A.	N.A.	N.A.	N.A.	N.A.	N.A.
Mississippi	...	★	★	★	★	★	...
Missouri	..	★	★	...	★		(i)
Montana	...	...	...	★	★	★	(j)
Nebraska	...	★	★	★	★	...	...
Nevada	...	...	★	...	★	★	...
New Hampshire	N.A.	N.A.	N.A.	N.A.	N.A.	N.A.	N.A.
New Jersey	...	...	★	★	★	...	...
New Mexico	N.A.	N.A.	N.A.	N.A.	N.A.	N.A.	N.A.
New York	★	...	...	...	...	...	...
North Carolina	...	★	★	★	★	...	...
North Dakota	...	...	★	...	★	★	(k)
Ohio	...	★	...	...	★	...	(l)
Oklahoma	...	...	★	★	★	...	...
Oregon	...	...	★	★	...	...	(v)
Pennsylvania	...	★	★	★	★	★(w)	(m)
Rhode Island	...	...	★	...	...	...	...
South Carolina	...	★	★	★	★	★	(x)
South Dakota	...	★	★	...	...	...	...
Tennessee	...	...	★	★	...	...	(n)
Texas	★	...	★	...	★	...	...
Utah	...	★	★	...	★	★	(o)
Vermont	...	★	...	...	...	...	(y)
Virginia	...	★	★	★	★	...	...
Washington	...	...	...	...	...	...	(p)
West Virginia	...	...	...	...	...	...	...
Wisconsin	...	★	★	★	★	...	(z)
Wyoming	...	...	...	...	...	...	...

(o) Loan servicing, central budget and accounting debt collection.

(p) Developing statewide budget, & HR policies/Labor Relations Office, setting statewdie admin. policies & procedures, forecasting statewide population and Office of the Chief Information Officer.

(q) Archives, records management, risk management, land, public works, office leasing, repairs, custodial, motor pool and parking.

(r) Data center.

(s) Distributions to local governments.

(t) Municipals statewide, audit of agencies—three-year cycle, internal control/systems monitoring.

(u) State risk pools (fire and auto).

(v) Statewide financial management services and DataMart.

(w) The comptroller maintains reporting hierarchies for the CAFR in the data warehouse.

(x) P-card administration (with state procurement) and state employee unemployment insurance program.

(y) Budgeting.

(z) Treasury management, capital accounting and federal cash draws.

Chapter Five

STATE JUDICIAL BRANCH

Tailoring Innovation for Today's State Courts

By Kathryn Holt and Shelley Spacek Miller

State courts adopted unprecedented cost-saving strategies and innovations during the Great Recession. Today, courts continue to embrace this legacy of innovation to maintain, and even improve, the administration of justice. The projects featured in this article highlight the large gains and potential for future innovation in the state courts.

The Court Innovation Context

A departure from the traditional approach to judicial system administration, the state courts increasingly require agility, stakeholder collaboration and creativity to meet the changing needs and expectations of their constituents. While budget cuts have subsided in recent years,[1] demands on tight resources continue. Changing population dynamics (e.g., influx of unaccompanied minors and increases in geriatric populations) also bring new challenges to the courts[2] along with increased expectations around technology and desire to use technology in the courts. In a 2014 international survey by Accenture, 82 percent of respondents said that they would interact with justice system using a digital interface either instead of or in addition to traditional means.[3] Additionally, 56 percent of U.S. respondents believed digital technology can reduce the public cost of the justice system. Simply put, it is a new world for courts. This new environment presents opportunities for courts, often staid institutions, to rise to the occasion of incorporating and tailoring innovation into the delivery of justice while still safeguarding constitutional protections.

A 21st Century Response

While innovation is often synonymous with new technologies, and this chapter explores these types of innovations exclusively, it is important to note that innovation does not have to be technology-based. Taken alone, new strategies around triaging legal cases and unbundling legal services have the potential to transform legal service delivery. Add technology, and that impact can increase exponentially. However, technology is not a panacea. Applying or overlaying technology to a bad underlying process still results in a bad process—and may even magnify it. Efforts to innovate should be well thought out, possess a good governance structure and meaningfully measure impacts to the extent possible.

Despite the gains in and changing attitudes toward innovation, courts still lag behind other industries and face systemic challenges when incorporating technology and other innovative solutions. Lack of funds often prohibits courts from hiring and retaining top technology staff and keeping up with the pace of technological advancements and improvements. As a result, courts often find themselves with out-of-date legacy systems, dependent on expensive outside contractors to update or improve the system. Traditionally siloed court systems and insufficient governance structures can also make adopting these changes in a systematic and meaningful way very difficult.

Even faced with this environment, courts still recognize the potential for technology to open access for constituents and gain efficiencies in administration. In 2015, technology was the most referenced topic in state of judiciary addresses, increasing 6 percent since addresses in 2010.[4] Whether introducing an entirely new concept, or applying a past concept in a new context or situation, courts are tailoring modern technology to fit their needs and rethinking past processes to improve upon inefficiencies and antiquated methodology. The projects highlighted in this article provide a limited sample of these innovation efforts and demonstrate how innovative ideas, enabled by technology, can have a broad positive impact and improve the way courts do business without sacrificing traditional constitutional safeguards.

Minnesota's Conservatorship Account Auditing Program

Conservatorship cases increasingly capture media attention. When high-profile individuals fall victim to financial exploitation, or cases of embezzlement from protected persons' accounts are uncovered, the spotlight focuses on an often the overlooked work of the courts–conservatorship cases. However, it is not just the extreme cases that deserve attention. An estimated $1.5 billion in estates of vulnerable persons (e.g., those with dementia or traumatic brain injury) are under court oversight and require regular monitoring.[5] This dollar value is a rough estimate based on limited data and will only grow as the population ages and relies on the state courts to ensure protection of their finances and assets. State courts are often statutorily required to regularly audit and hold hearings on accounts associated with these cases, yet the high volume of accounting information and lack of training and resources often keep judges and court staff from fulfilling their responsibility in a meaningful way.

Minnesota is taking affirmative steps to remedy this problem. Through a unique combination of statewide online accounting submission software and a central auditing program, Minnesota is the first state to electronically collect data on conservatorship cases and establish a systematic statewide, web-based approach to this process.

Prior to 2011, conservators in Minnesota submitted annual paper accountings of the protected person's assets to the court. The content and detail in these reports, as well as the level of scrutiny with which they were reviewed, varied widely. Judges and court staff with little to no training on accounting practices were required to sort through boxes of documentation and attempt to make sense of the accounts. This process was time consuming and ineffective, resulting in accounts that were rarely audited in the truest sense.

Between 2010 and 2012 the Minnesota Judicial Council mandated that conservators submit standard accountings online and established the Conservatorship Account Auditing Program, or CAAP. The CAAP is a central office of trained auditors in the Minnesota Judicial Branch. The CAAP reviews annual accountings of both private and public conservators submitted through MyMNConservator, or MMC, software. Within the software, auditors can view specific transactions and a list of the protected person's assets, to ensure balances are as expected and document any suspicious activity (e.g., car payments when the protected person doesn't own a vehicle).

To assist in this review process, the MMC software is automatically programmed to generate red flags to alert auditors of potentially suspicious or odd transactions. The auditors are then able to review the case and follow up on flagged items by asking for supporting documentation or explanations from the conservator. Ultimately, after the review, auditors categorize account audit reports

into four levels based on issues or problems. Level 1 audits are cases with no concerns. Levels 2 and 3 have varying degrees of accounting errors that need to be corrected (e.g., transactions were not listed or balances were not correct). Level 4 audits are those where there is a concern of loss or misuse of funds. These finding levels and supporting information are electronically submitted to the court via the MMC software. With the information from the audits, the judge has discretion to call hearings, inquire further about the loss, order repayment of lost funds, or petition criminal charges in extreme cases.

In 2015 the CAAP received four awards for their innovation.[6] Having now amassed close to two years of data in MMC, Minnesota is currently in the process of refining and calibrating the red flags using predictive analytics to better assist in identifying cases that require court review or intervention. The goal is that data on past loss and misuse of funds will predict future issues. With early intervention from the courts, financial exploitation of vulnerable persons will be stopped before it happens.

Alamance County, N.C., Electronic Protective Order System

Obtaining a protective order can be a complicated and lengthy process, one that must be navigated at a time when every minute counts. Considerations around child care, lost work time/wages and threats to safety can all prevent victims in danger and in need of a protective order from seeking assistance. Prior to 2013, domestic violence victims in Alamance County, N.C., had to interact with four entities—the Family Justice Center, or FJC; Clerk's Office; District Court; and Sheriff's Department—at four different locations to secure a protective order.[7] The process usually took 12 hours and as a result about 12 percent of orders were not being completed by victims.[8] Victims also were not getting needed service referrals from the Family Justice Center, as they were spending too much time trying to navigate the system to serve the protective order.

Alamance County's Electronic Protective Order System, or EPOS, streamlined this process, cutting down the time to six hours and the lack of follow through to six percent. Victims now only need to visit the Family Justice Center, where all the steps can be completed. From the center, victims fill out a complaint and submit this to a FJC advocate who enters this information into the

EPOS that is then electronically submitted to the Clerk of Court. The clerk processes the complaint, and electronic documents are sent to the judge to alert of the pending protective order. The hearing between the judge and victim is held via video-conference, with the victim still at the center. This hearing is now a private conversation between the judge and the victim, rather than taking place in a public courtroom. If granted, the order is sent to the center for the advocate to print a copy for the victim. The Sheriff's Department also immediately gets an electronic version for the deputies to print and serve as well as to have an electronic version on file. Via text message or email the victim is alerted when the order has been served to the defendant and informed of the next steps to take. Not only is the process now faster, victims spend this time at the Family Justice Center where they can get referrals to counseling and legal aid. Since implementation, referrals have more than doubled.

This project was developed in collaboration between the North Carolina Administrative Office of the Courts, the Alamance County Management Information Systems and an outside IT vendor, as well as representatives from the four agencies involved in processing protective orders and the District Court Chief Judge. By converting the paper/physical process into an electronic one, all stakeholders realized benefits. Victims do not have to leave the safety of the FJC to file the petition and, while there, can be referred for additional services. Court clerks have less data entry with the electronic transfer of information into the court's case management system. Judges benefit from timely hearings when the petitioner is ready and more able to candidly address their issues. Sheriffs and deputies have immediate and easy access to protective orders, giving them confidence when serving and enforcing orders knowing supporting documentation is easily available.

Michigan Online Dispute Resolution

Low-level criminal offenses such as traffic cases make up a majority of state court caseloads. In 2013, traffic and infraction related cases alone comprised approximately 54 percent of the total incoming state courts' caseload.[9] Often faced with judicial staffing shortages, this leads to over-crowded and time-pressed dockets for courts, legal professionals and litigants. In addition, citizens face costs (e.g., time off work, childcare) just to come to court. A new online platform for resolution of traffic and other low-level criminal cases

addresses these and other real barriers to effective and efficient justice.

Several Michigan judicial districts are coordinating with an outside vendor, Court Innovations, to pilot an online dispute resolution platform for warrants and low-level traffic offenses. Through the platform, defendants are able to look up their case, determine if it is eligible for online resolution and register their position in the case. Prosecutors then review the defendant's offer, provide their own input and pass it along to the district's judicial officer to determine if the resolution is acceptable.[10] If a resolution is unacceptable or if the defendant ever chooses, they may always revert to the traditional court processes at the courthouse.

With these jurisdictions' online case resolution platforms, a defendant can resolve their case without ever needing to take off work, arrange childcare and transportation, and sit through an extended docket to resolve their case. This effort also highlights the gains courts can achieve through a private-public technology partnership. This program required buy-in from multiple stakeholders to be successful. Court leaders collaborated with law enforcement, court technology staff, citizens, the private partner (Court Innovations) and others to ensure program buy-in from the outset, with both the courts and stakeholders seeing benefits.

Police officers are no longer required to spend as much time in court waiting for their cases to be called while prosecutors can easily review outcomes for consistency and fairness, which is often challenging with numerous dockets. Finally, the judge still has control over the resolution of the case and can review cases whenever they are free to do so. Perhaps the most concrete benefits of this platform are the time and savings gains. Preliminary data show that, depending on the court, cases can be resolved in an average of seven to nine days instead of months. Additionally, nearly 40 percent of system users resolve their case with a mobile device.[11] Efforts to evaluate and expand the program are ongoing.

On the Horizon

The innovations described above provide only a glimpse into innovative efforts underway in state courts today. It should be noted that innovation also is occurring jurisdiction by jurisdiction, with many making a dedicated effort to document and share these efforts within and outside their state to spur further development. Court leaders are paying more attention to innovation and recognizing the potential lessons learned from other industries. Entire conferences and summits are dedicated to rethinking the work of the courts. Efforts including the continued revolution of "e-everything," judicial dashboards, remote interpreting and litigant self-help portals are evidence that courts continue to strive to deliver more with fewer resources to achieve increased court responsiveness and access to justice. Recently such efforts culminated in the first ever 2016 CourtHack where technology and content experts gathered for two days to work to find creative solutions to everyday problems facing the courts. While there is still much work to be done, the innovative mindset is here to stay as courts, and court users, look to the future of the legal system.

Notes

[1] Carol Flango, Deborah Smith, Charles Campbell, Elizabeth Maddox, and Neal Kauder. *Trends in State Courts 2015* (Williamsburg, Va.: National Center for State Courts, 2015), 6.

[2] These might result in increased case filings for certain case types or increased demands on coordination between multiple stakeholders. *See* Slayton, David, "How the Unaccompanied Minor Crisis is Affecting the State Courts," *Trends in State Courts*, 2014, *http://www.ncsc.org/sitecore/content/microsites/trends/home/Monthly-Trends-Articles/2014/Unaccompanied-Minors-in-State-Courts.aspx.*

[3] Accenture, "Accenture Citizen Survey on Justice 2014: How Can Justice Agencies Better Meet Citizen's Expectations?" *Accenture*, 5, *https://www.accenture.com/us-en/~/media/Accenture/Conversion-Assets/DotCom/Documents/Global/PDF/Dualpub_9/Accenture-How-Can-Justice-Agencies-Better-Meet-Citizens-Expectation.*

[4] Carol Flango, Deborah Smith, Charles Campbell, Elizabeth Maddox, and Neal Kauder. *Trends in State Courts 2015* (Williamsburg, Va.: National Center for State Courts, 2015), 6.

[5] Brenda Uekert and Richard Van Duizend, "Adult Guardianships: A 'Best Guess' National Estimate and the Momentum for Reform," *Future Trends in State Courts 2011* (2011): 109.

[6] Minnesota Judicial Branch, "Report to the Community: the 2015 Annual Report of the Minnesota Judicial Branch" *http://www.mncourts.gov/mncourtsgov/media/assets/documents/reports/2015AnnualReport.pdf.*

[7] Stephanie Satkowiak, "eCourts: Civil Domestic Violence System" (presentation, 2015 Workshop for State Court VAW Points of Contact: Assessing and Using the STOP set-aside for Courts, Williamsburg, Va., October 27-28, 2015).

[8] Stephanie Kanowitz, "County speed protective orders for victims of domestic violence," *GCN*, September 26, 2014, *gnc.com/Articles/2014/09/26/GCN-Award-Alamance-County.aspx?Page=1.*

[9] Robert LaFountain, Shauna Strickland, Richard Schauffler, Kathryn Holt and Kathryn Lewis, *Examining the Work of State Courts: An Overview of 2013 State Court Caseloads.* (Williamsburg, Va.: National Center for State Courts, 2015), 7.

[10] Judge Dawn Kildea, "Courts are Reinventing for the 21st Century" *National Center for State Courts: Court Technology Bulletin*, September 14, 2015, *http://courttech-bulletin.blogspot.com/2015/09/courts-are-reinventing-for-21st-century.html.*

[11] Michigan Courts News Release, "Online Ticket Review Helps Make Courts More Accessible and Efficient" June 8, 2015, *http://courts.mi.gov/News-Events/press_releases/Documents/Online%20Ticket%20Review%20news%20release.pdf.*

About the Authors

Kathryn Holt is a Senior Court Research Analyst at the National Center for State Courts in Williamsburg, Va. She works on multiple national data collection projects including the Court Statistics Project and State Court Organization.

Shelley Spacek Miller is a Senior Court Research Analyst at the National Center for State Courts in Williamsburg, Va. Her areas of interest include civil justice reform, access to justice and caseflow management.

Judicial Birthdays and Benefits

By Jarret W. Hann and William E. Raftery

A detailed look at two issues impacting judges: The unsuccessful push by judges to increase or repeal mandatory judicial retirement ages, and the ongoing struggle judges have maintaining established judicial benefits.

There has been growing interest in increasing or repealing mandatory judicial retirement ages in the states. Voters, however, have not been keen on such measures.

With the average life expectancy of the U.S. population increasing and modern medicine allowing people to remain vital and active longer, many of the old concepts related to retirement have been brushed aside in recent years. This wave of change has not always, however, found its way into state judiciaries, which continue to contend, in many instances, with mandatory judicial retirement ages. Moreover, while state legislators have proven willing to consider increasing the ages or repealing them outright, voters have tended to reject such efforts at the ballot box.

The idea of a mandatory judicial retirement age dates back to at least the time of the American Revolution. Early state constitutions included such provisions; in 1789, Alexander Hamilton in Federalist #79 noted that New York had a mandatory judicial retirement age of 60 and argued against the practice for both the federal and state judiciaries. Today, they take on three different formulations.

1. Mandatory loss or vacancy of office: A judge's birthday party doubles as a retirement party. A few states offer some extensions (end of the month, end of the year or end of the term), but most do not.

2. Loss of retirement benefits: A judge is not automatically forced from office, but if they fail to leave some or all of their retirement benefits are forfeit.

3. Electoral disqualifier: A person may serve out the term they are in, but their age makes them ineligible for reelection or reappointment.

Overall, 32 states plus the District of Columbia have a retirement age for appellate or general-jurisdiction court judges; most use 70 as the threshold, and the remaining states use either 72, 74, 75, or in the case of Vermont, 90. Regarding limited-jurisdiction court judges, most state constitutions and statutes leave those ages up to the local appointing bodies or are simply silent on the matter. The states are divided on the legislature's ability to alter these ages, with some set by state constitution and others left to the legislature. Those states that have constitutional provisions regarding ages have found efforts to increase them much more difficult due, in large part, to the need to obtain voters' approval.

Of all the proposals debated in the last two decades, most have focused on increasing rather than eliminating the ages—for example, moving from 70 to 72 or 75. Proponents argue four key points.

1. Life expectancies and vitality are increasing, and the ages currently in place were set as many as two centuries ago.

2. Officials of the other two branches are not similarly subject to mandatory retirement.

3. The ages were often put in place to contend with judges who had aged into, as Alexander Hamilton put it, "inability." Judicial conduct and disciplinary commissions in existence today can act to remove judges who are unable to carry out their duties.

4. Even if such ages should be kept, 70 is far too low, and the age should be increased.

Opponents often focus on three areas.

1. There is no evidence that mandatory judicial retirement harms the judiciary.

2. Mandatory retirement ages help the judiciary by injecting new ideas and new judges into the mix.

3. Legislators are disinclined to extend the existing terms for particular judges. As a result, many of these proposals have been amended to apply only to future judges. For example, in New Jersey a plan to increase the mandatory retirement age for judges was derailed when the measure included the Supreme Court. When the age increase was amended to apply only to lower-court judges, it moved out of committee.

Those changes to mandatory judicial retirement ages that have occurred recently have been in states with statute-based provisions, such as Virginia (2015) and Indiana (2011, trial courts only). Those efforts that required constitutional amendments, and therefore public approval, have appeared on ballots 11 times in nine states since 1995 and almost all have failed: Arizona (2012), Hawaii (2006 and 2014), Louisiana (1995 and 2014), New York (2013) and Ohio (2011). Additionally, Hawaii voters in 2012 rejected an effort to permit judges forced out due to mandatory retirement to be recalled into service. The 2012 Arizona proposal is notable for its linkage to other topics. Often, legislators recognizing judges want to have an increase in retirement age will attach it to other provisions, which the judiciary may or may not favor. In the case of Arizona, the 2012 proposition also included giving the governor more control over the state's merit-selection commissions.

Of the states that have seen fruitful efforts, success has been limited. Aside from Vermont (2002), the only time such efforts have succeeded has been in off-year elections and then not to increase or repeal the ages but to let judges serve out their terms (Louisiana in 2003 and Texas in 2007) or until the end of the year (Pennsylvania in 2001). In 2016, this trend may change; in November voters in Pennsylvania will vote on a plan to increase that state's retirement age from the end of the year in which a judge reaches 75, up from end of the year in which a judge reaches 70. Oregon voters will decide November 2016 on an outright repeal of that state's retirement age.

Salary is often cited as an important factor in attracting and keeping well-qualified judges. But there are challenges over how to determine judicial compensation in the face of budget cuts and constitutional questions.

Several authors have attempted to analyze whether judges are compensated adequately.[1] It proves to be a difficult task, often illustrating the wide salary gulf between sitting judges and lawyers in private law firms. Predictably, such comparisons create great debate fodder. Advocates for comparable pay cite warnings about the developing constitutional crisis[2] surrounding inadequate judicial salaries, while advocates of the status quo cite judicial benefits, job security (for federal and select state judges), prestige and power as the sort of compensation that keep the scales of justice in balance.

Stagnant Salaries, Increased Contributions

Since the 1970s, the National Center for State Courts, or NCSC, has tracked the salaries of state court judges. Over the years, judges' salaries have changed to keep pace with inflation and the cost of living; however, these increases are often not without significant battles between the legislative and judicial branches. Examples are numerous: New York state court judges finally received an increase in 2011 after not having seen any change in their salaries in 12 years,[3] while Michigan judges currently hold the record for the longest period without an increase, dating back to 2002. In recent years, a new compensation battle looms as judges have seen an erosion of their judicial benefits, namely their retirement benefits, and the overall shift toward defined contributions.

In the spring of 2013, researchers at NCSC collected and analyzed data on state employee retirement systems to inform the work of the Conference of Chief Justices' Task Force on Politics and Judicial Selection/Compensation. Changes to contribution rates were rare between 1999 and 2007, but 22 states increased judges' contribution rates between 2008 and 2012. Given that state court judges' salaries are in large part protected by the judicial clause of their state constitutions, some state legislatures have taken the position that an increase in the required contribution by judges to their retirement funds does not violate the state constitutional clause, regardless of the fact that it reduces overall compensation.

Figure A: Average Judges' Retirement Contribution Rate for All States

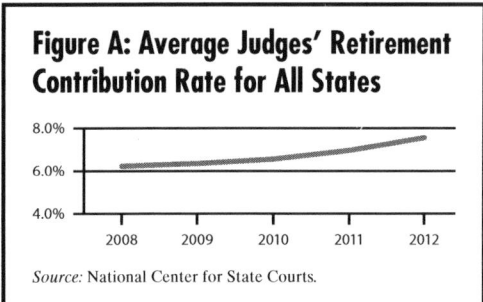

Source: National Center for State Courts.

Difficulty Making a Winning Case for Judges

Part of the difficulty of determining whether judicial benefits—salary, retirement, leave, etc.—are adequate involves assessing the overall quality of a given judge. Judicial caseloads vary greatly from court to court in both volume and variety. How can you rate a judge for an adequate criminal sentencing, or for a trial's duration taking the optimal amount of time? In 2009, a paper published in the *Journal of Legal Analysis* went to great lengths quantifying different variables to assess whether judges were adequately compensated. The authors expressed the difficulty of accurately measuring a judge's quality, given the vast number of intangible variables. However, they also said:

Comparisons of the salaries of judges and law firm associates are for this reason likely to be misleading. Finally, when high-quality people become judges, they must leave the private sector, vacating jobs where they may have a relatively high value compared with their value as judges. Judges should be paid their social value, and not more, but no one knows whether their social value is higher or lower than their current salary.[4]

Every judge faces a unique set of circumstances, from the resources—law clerks, technology, staff—they have at their disposal, to the types of cases before them. Without simple and easily digestible facts, as private-practice attorneys have with hours billed, states where legislatures control judicial salaries are able to make cuts, often with public support, that can reduce a judge's aggregate compensation.

Does It Change the Face of the Judiciary?

While the defense of inadequate judicial pay and benefits may be difficult to measure on a purely academic basis, there is some evidence from judges who left the bench citing compensation as the primary reason. Former Texas Chief Justice Wallace Jefferson, while clearly stating he was not "complaining about the level of pay for judges," said that having one child in college and two more in high school, while living in the costly urban environment of Austin, put significant financial pressures on his family, and that as a result he was returning to private practice.[5] Likewise, former federal judge Stephen Larson stepped down to return to private practice, saying:

The costs associated with raising our family are increasing significantly, while our salary remains stagnant and, in terms of its purchasing power, is actually declining. I must place my family's interest, particularly the future of my children, ahead of my own fervent desire to remain a federal judge.[6]

Conclusions

An increase in retirement contribution rates without a corresponding increase in salary effectively decreases judges' aggregate compensation. The challenge posed by reducing judicial compensation is that it may reduce the attractiveness of pursuing a judgeship. We can expect to see continued challenges and proposed cuts in judicial compensation. Further, until an adequate measure of societal cost can be made to the public, judges may continue to find themselves on the losing side of the argument when matters are decided by state legislatures or a public vote.

State judges will always represent a collection of talented jurists, no matter their background. However, unless judicial compensation keeps pace with inflation through cost-of-living adjustments and periodic reviews, and maintains parity with benchmark groups, the judicial pool risks losing diversity in legal experience. More specifically, the bench may have a more difficult time attracting lawyers who have significant mass tort litigation or other complex civil experience typically handled by larger, higher-paying private law firms. This could leave the bench with a larger proportion of former prosecutors and solo and small-firm attorneys who, while talented and skilled in many areas, may not bring the requisite experience needed to balance the demands of a typical state court docket. This will potentially impact the experience litigants have with the courts and jeopardize the trust and confidence that the public has in our nation's state judiciaries.

Notes

[1] For example, see A. Liptak, "How Much Should Judges Make?" *New York Times*, January 19, 2009; also see Texas Office of Court Administration, "Report on Judicial Salaries and Turnover for Fiscal Years 2010 and 2011," December 2011.

[2] See L. Greenhouse, "Chief Justice Advocates Higher Pay for Judiciary" *New York Times*, January 1, 2007.

[3] See S. Kavanaugh, "State's Top Judges Finally Get a Raise," *Crain's New York Business*, August 26, 2011.

[4] See S. J. Choi, G. M. Gulati, and E. A. Posner, "Are Judges Overpaid? A Skeptical Response to the Judicial Salary Debate," *Journal of Legal Analysis*. Winter 2009; Volume 1, Number 1. p. 102.

[5] See P. Hart, "Jefferson Retiring from State Supreme Court" *San Antonio Express-News*. September 3, 2013.

[6] See "U.S. Federal Judge Quits; Cites Flat pay, 7 Children" Reuters, New York. September 17, 2009.

About the Authors

William E. Raftery, PhD is a Knowledge and Information Services analyst with the National Center for State Courts in Williamsburg, Va. His current work includes research on legislative-judicial relations, judicial selection, judicial conduct, and court security. He is the editor of Gavel to Gavel, a review of state legislation affecting the courts.

Jarret W. Hann joined the National Center in June 2012. He is responsible for providing technical assistance to constituents, creating Web content, and participating in a variety of other projects. He came to the Center having practiced law for several years both in private practice and as a federal prosecutor. He is a founding member of the BIL Organization at the University of Calgary.

Table 5.1
STATE COURTS OF LAST RESORT

State or other jurisdiction	Name of court	Justices chosen (a) — At large	Justices chosen (a) — By district	No. of judges (b)	Term (in years) (c)	Chief justice — Method of selection	Chief justice — Term of office for chief justice
Alabama	S.C.	★		9	6	Partisan election	6 years
Alaska	S.C.	★		5	10	By court	3 years
Arizona	S.C.	★		7	6	By court	6 years
Arkansas	S.C.	★		7	8	Non-partisan popular election	8 years
California	S.C.	★		7	12	Gubernatorial appointment with consent of Commission on Judicial Appointments	12 years
Colorado	S.C.	★		7	10	By court	10 years
Connecticut	S.C.	★		7	8	Gubernatorial appointment with consent of the Legislature	8 years
Delaware	S.C.	★		5	12	Gubernatorial appointment from judicial nominating commission with consent of the Legislature	12 years
Florida	S.C.	★(d)	★(d)	7	6	By court	2 years
Georgia	S.C.	★		7	6	By court	6 years
Hawaii	S.C.	★		5	10	Gubernatorial appointment from judicial nominating commission with consent of the Senate	10 years
Idaho	S.C.	★		5	6	By court	4 years
Illinois	S.C.	★(e)	★(e)	7	10	By court	3 years
Indiana	S.C.	★	★	5	10	Judicial nominating commission	2 years
Iowa	S.C.	★		7	8	By court	8 years
Kansas	S.C.	★		7	6	Rotation by seniority	Duration of service
Kentucky	S.C.		★	7	8	By court	4 years
Louisiana	S.C.		★	7	10	By seniority of service	Duration of service
Maine	S.J.C.	★		7	7	Appointed by governor with consent of the Legislature	7 years
Maryland	C.A.		★	7	10	Appointed by governor	To age 70
Massachusetts	S.J.C.	★		7	To age 70	Gubernatorial appointment with approval of elected executive council	To age 70
Michigan	S.C.	★		7	8	By court	8 years
Minnesota	S.C.	★		7	6	Non-partisan popular election	Duration of service
Mississippi	S.C.		★(g)	9	8	By seniority of service	Duration of service
Missouri	S.C.	★		7	12	By court	2 years
Montana	S.C.	★		7	8	Non-partisan popular election	8 years
Nebraska	S.C.	★(h)	★(h)	7	6	Gubernatorial appointment from judicial nominating commission	Duration of service
Nevada	S.C.	★		7	6	Rotation by seniority	(i)
New Hampshire	S.C.	★		5	To age 70	Gubernatorial appointment with approval of elected executive council	To age 70
New Jersey	S.C.	★		7	7 / To age 70 (j)	Gubernatorial appointment with consent of the Senate	7 years, plus tenure, to age 70
New Mexico	S.C.	★		5	8	By court	2 years
New York	C.A.	★		7	14	Gubernatorial appointment from judicial nominating commission with consent of the Senate	14 years
North Carolina	S.C.	★		7	8	Non-partisan popular election	8 years
North Dakota	S.C.	★		5	10	By Supreme and District Court judges	5 years
Ohio	S.C.	★		7	6	Popular election (k)	6 years

See footnotes at end of table.

STATE COURTS OF LAST RESORT — Continued

State or other jurisdiction	Name of court	Justices chosen (a) — At large	Justices chosen (a) — By district	No. of judges (b)	Term (in years) (c)	Chief justice — Method of selection	Chief justice — Term of office for chief justice
Oklahoma	S.C.		★	9	6	By court	2 years
	C.C.A.		★	5	6	By court	1 year
Oregon	S.C.	★		7	6	By court	6 years
Pennsylvania	S.C.	★		7	10	By court	6 years
Rhode Island	S.C.	★		5	Life	Seniority	To age 70
South Carolina	S.C.	★		5	10	Gubernatorial appointment from judicial nominating commission with consent of the Legislature	Hold office during good behavior
South Dakota	S.C.	★(l)		5	8	Legislative appointment	10 years
Tennessee	S.C.	★		5	8	By court	4 years
Texas	S.C.	★		9	6	By court	2 years
	C.C.A.	★		9	6	Partisan election	6 years
Utah	S.C.	★		5	10	Partisan election	6 years
Vermont	S.C.	★		5	6	By court	4 years
Virginia	S.C.	★		7	12	Gubernatorial appointment from judicial nominating commission with consent of the Legislature	6 years
Washington	S.C.	★		9	6	By court	4 years
West Virginia	S.C.A.	★		5	12	By court	To age 75
Wisconsin	S.C.	★		7	10	By court	1 year
Wyoming	S.C.	★		5	8	By court	2 years
Dist. of Columbia	C.A.	★		9	15	By court	4 years
Puerto Rico	S.C.	★		9	To age 70	Judicial nominating commission appointment	4 years
						Gubernatorial appointment with consent of the Legislature	To age 70

Sources: S. Strickland, R. Schauffler, R. LaFountain and K. Holt, eds. State Court Organization. Last updated April 8, 2016. National Center for State Courts. www.ncsc.org/sco.

Key:
★ — Yes
S.C. — Supreme Court
S.C.A. — Supreme Court of Appeals
S.J.C. — Supreme Judicial Court
C.A. — Court of Appeals
C.C.A. — Court of Criminal Appeals
(a) See Table 5.6, entitled "Selection and Retention of Appellate Court Judges," for more detail.
(b) Number includes chief justice.
(c) The initial term may be shorter. See Table 5.6, entitled "Selection and Retention of Appellate Court Judges," for more detail.

(d) Elected statewide, but each of 5 regional appellate districts entitled to at least one justice.
(e) Three justices chosen from First District (Cook County), rest from other districts.
(g) Three justices chosen from each of three districts.
(h) Chief justice chosen statewide; associate judges chosen by district.
(i) The senior justice in commission is the Chief Justice, and in case the commissions of two or more of the justices bear the same date, the justices shall determine by lot who is the Chief Justice.
(j) All judges are subject to gubernatorial reappointment and consent by the Senate after an initial seven-year term; thereafter, they may serve until mandatory retirement at age 70.
(k) Party affiliation is not included on the ballot in the general election, but candidates are chosen through partisan primary nominations.
(l) Initially chosen by district; retention determined statewide.

Table 5.2
STATE INTERMEDIATE APPELLATE COURTS AND GENERAL TRIAL COURTS: NUMBER OF JUDGES AND TERMS

State or other jurisdiction	Intermediate appellate court			General trial court		
	Name of court	2015 No. of judges	Term (years)	Name of court	2015 No. of judges	Term (years)
Alabama	Court of Criminal Appeals	5	6	Circuit Court	144	6
	Court of Civil Appeals	5	6			
Alaska	Court of Appeals	3	8	Superior Court	42	6
Arizona	Court of Appeals	22	6	Superior Court	174	4 (a)
				Tax Court	1	
Arkansas	Court of Appeals	12	8	Circuit Court	121	6
California	Courts of Appeal	96	12	Superior Court	1,695	6
Colorado	Court of Appeals	22	8	District Court	168 (b)	6
				Denver Juvenile Court	3	6
				Denver Probate Court	1	6
Connecticut	Appellate Court	9	8	Superior Court	165	8
Delaware	...	...	...	Superior Court	21	12
				Court of Chancery	5	12
Florida	District Courts of Appeals	61	6	Circuit Court	599	6
Georgia	Court of Appeals	12	6	Superior Court	209	4
Hawaii	Intermediate Court of Appeals	6	10	Circuit Court	31	10
Idaho	Court of Appeals	4	6	District Court	45	4
Illinois	Appellate Court	54	10	Circuit Court	916 (c)	6
Indiana	Court of Appeals	15	10	Superior Court, Probate Court and Circuit Court	315	6
	Tax Court	1	10			
Iowa	Court of Appeals	9	6	District Court	337 (d)	6
Kansas	Court of Appeals	14	4	District Court	248 (e)	4
Kentucky	Court of Appeals	14	8	Circuit Court	94	8
				Family Court	51	8
Louisiana	Courts of Appeal	53	10	District Court	218	6
				Juvenile & Family Court	18	6
Maine	...	...	...	Superior Court	17	7
				District Court	36	7
Maryland	Court of Special Appeals	12	10	Circuit Court	157	15
Massachusetts	Appeals Court	28	To age 70	Superior Court	80	To age 70
Michigan	Court of Appeals	28	6	Circuit Court	218	6
				Court of Claims	4	6
Minnesota	Court of Appeals	19	6	District Court	280	6
Mississippi	Court of Appeals	10	8	Circuit Court	53	4
Missouri	Court of Appeals	32	12	Circuit Court	334 (f)	6 (g)
Montana	...	...	...	District Court	46 (h)	6
				Water Court	5	4
				Workers' Compensation Court	1	6
Nebraska	Court of Appeals	6	6	District Court	55	6
Nevada	Court of Appeals	3	6	District Court	82	6
New Hampshire	...	...	...	Superior Court	22	To age 70
New Jersey	Appellate Division of Superior Court	33	7 / To age 70 (i)	Superior Court	409	7 / To age 70 (i)

See footnotes at end of table.

STATE INTERMEDIATE APPELLATE COURTS AND GENERAL TRIAL COURTS: NUMBER OF JUDGES AND TERMS — Continued

State or other jurisdiction	Intermediate appellate court			General trial court		
	Name of court	2015 No. of judges	Term (years)	Name of court	2015 No. of judges	Term (years)
New Mexico	Court of Appeals	10	8	District Court	75	6
New York	Appellate Division of Supreme Court	55	5 (j)	Supreme Court	269	14
	Appellate Terms of Supreme Court	11	Duration of term	County Court	127	10
North Carolina	Court of Appeals	15	8	Superior Court	112 (k)	8 (l)
North Dakota	Temporary Court of Appeals	3	1 (m)	District Court	44	6
Ohio	Courts of Appeals	69	6	Court of Common Pleas	384	6
Oklahoma	Court of Civil Appeals	12	6	District Court	241 (n)	4 (o)
Oregon	Court of Appeals	13	6	Circuit Court	173	6
				Tax Court	1	6
Pennsylvania	Superior Court	23	10	Court of Common Pleas	449 (p)	10
	Commonwealth Court	9	10			
Rhode Island	. . .	. . .	. . .	Superior Court	25 (q)	Life
South Carolina	Court of Appeals	9	6	Circuit Court	47	6
South Dakota	. . .	. . .	. . .	Circuit Court	41	8
Tennessee	Court of Appeals	12	8	Chancery Court	34	8
	Court of Criminal Appeals	12	8	Circuit Court	83	8
				Criminal Court	33	8
				Probate Court	2	8
Texas	Courts of Appeals	80	6	District Court	458	4
Utah	Court of Appeals	7	6	District Court	75	6
Vermont	. . .	. . .	. . .	Superior Court	32	6
Virginia	Court of Appeals	11	8	Circuit Court	158	8
Washington	Courts of Appeal	22	6	Superior Court	189	4
West Virginia	. . .	. . .	. . .	Circuit Court	70	8
Wisconsin	Court of Appeals	16	6	Circuit Court	249	6
Wyoming	. . .	. . .	. . .	District Court	23	6
Dist. of Columbia	. . .	. . .	. . .	Superior Court	62	15
Puerto Rico	Court of Appeals	39	16	Court of First Instance	338 (r)	12 (s)

Sources: S. Strickland, R. Schauffler, R. LaFountain and K. Holt, eds. *State Court Organization.* Last updated April 8, 2016. National Center for State Courts, *www.ncsc.org/sco.*

Key:

. . . — Court does not exist in jurisdiction or not applicable.
(a) Unless rotated to a different court by the presiding judge.
(b) Judges also serve Water Court.
(c) 514 Circuit Court Judges and 378 Associate Judges.
(d) 146 of these are part-time judicial magistrates.
(e) Includes both district judges and district magistrate judges.
(f) The number of Circuit Court judges includes associate judges.
(g) Associate Circuit judges serve a term of four years.
(h) Three of those judges serve the Water Court.
(i) Followed by tenure. All judges are subject to gubernatorial reappointment and consent by the Senate after an initial seven-year term; thereafter, they may serve until mandatory retirement at age 70.

(j) Or duration.
(k) The number of Superior Court judges includes special judges.
(l) Special judges serve a term of four years.
(m) Assignments are for a specified time, not to exceed one year or the completion of one or more cases on the docket of the supreme court.
(n) The number of District Court judges includes associate judges and special judges.
(o) District and associate judges serve four-year terms; special judges serve at pleasure.
(p) Includes both active and senior judges.
(q) The number of judges includes magistrates.
(r) The number of Court of First Instance judges includes Municipal Division judges.
(s) Municipal judges serve a term of eight years.

Table 5.3
QUALIFICATIONS OF JUDGES OF STATE APPELLATE COURTS AND GENERAL TRIAL COURTS

State or other jurisdiction	Residency requirement State		Local		Minimum age		Legal credentials	
	A	T	A	T	A	T	A	T
Alabama	1 yr.	1 yr.	...	1 yr.	...	18	10 years state bar	5 years state bar
Alaska	5 yrs.	5 yrs.	...	...	...	...	8 years practice	5 years practice
Arizona	5/10 yrs. (a)	5 yrs.	(b)	1 yr.	30	30	(c)	(d)
Arkansas	...	...	★	...	...	...	8 years practice	6 years licensed in state
California	★	...	...	...	...	...	10 years state bar	10 years state bar
Colorado	★	★	...	★	...	...	5 years state bar	5 years state bar
Connecticut	★	★	...	...	...	...	Licensed attorney	Member of the bar
Delaware	★	★	...	★	...	...	"Learned in law"	"Learned in law"
Florida	★	★	★(f)	★(g)	...	...	10 years state bar	5 years state bar
Georgia	★	3 yrs.	...	must reside within court circuit	...	30	7 years state bar	7 years state bar
Hawaii	★	★	...	...	...	30	10 years state bar	10 years state bar
Idaho	2 yrs.	1 yr.	...	...	30	...	10 years state bar	10 years state bar
Illinois	★	★	★	★	...	...	Licensed attorney	Law degree
Indiana	★	1 yr.	...	★	...	...	10 years state bar (h)	Licensed attorney
Iowa	★	★	...	★	...	...	Licensed attorney	Admitted to state bar
Kansas	...	5 yrs.	...	...	30	30	10 years active and continuous practice (i)	5 years state bar
Kentucky	2 yrs.	2 yrs.	2 yrs.	2 yrs.	...	...	8 years state bar and licensed attorney	8 years state bar
Louisiana	1 yrs.	1 yrs.	1 yrs.	1 yrs.	...	...	10 years state bar	8 years state bar
Maine	...	...	...	...	...	...	"Learned in law"	1 year state bar
Maryland	5 yrs.	5 yrs.	6 mos.	6 mos.	30	30	State bar member	State bar member
Massachusetts	...	...	...	...	...	...	...	State bar member
Michigan	★	★	...	...	...	...	State bar member and 5 years practice	State bar member
Minnesota	30 days	30 days	...	30 days	...	...	Licensed attorney	Licensed attorney
Mississippi	5 yrs.	5 yrs.	★(j)	...	30	26	5 years state bar	5 years practice
Missouri	9 yrs. (k)	3 yrs. (k)	...	1 yr. (k)	30	30	State bar member	State bar member
Montana	2 yrs.	2 yrs.	...	...	...	...	5 years state bar	5 years state bar
Nebraska	3 yrs.	★	★	★	30	30	5 years practice	5 years practice
Nevada	2 yrs.	2 yrs.	...	...	25	25	State bar member (l)	2 years state bar member and 10 years practice
New Hampshire	...	...	...	...	...	...	10 years practice	State bar member
New Jersey	★	(m)	...	(m)	...	...	Admitted to practice in state for at least 10 years	10 years practice of law
New Mexico	3 yrs.	3 yrs.	...	★	35	35	10 years practice	6 years active practice
New York	★	★	...	...	...	18	10 years state bar	10 years state bar
North Carolina	...	★	...	(n)	...	...	State bar member	State bar member
North Dakota	★	★	...	★	...	...	License to practice law	State bar member
Ohio	★	★	...	★	...	...	6 years practice	6 years practice
Oklahoma	★	(o)	1 yr.	★	30	...	5 years state bar	(p)
Oregon	3 yrs.	3 yrs.	...	1 yr.	...	...	State bar member	State bar member
Pennsylvania	1 yr.	★	...	1 yr.	...	21	State bar member	State bar member
Rhode Island	...	...	...	...	21	...	License to practice law	State bar member
South Carolina	5 yrs.	5 yrs.	...	(q)	32	32	8 years state bar	8 years state bar
South Dakota	★	★	★	★	...	...	State bar member	State bar member
Tennessee	5 yrs.	5 yrs.	★(r)	1 yr.	35/30 (s)	30	License to practice law	License to practice law
Texas	★	...	...	2 yrs.	35	25	(t)	(u)
Utah	5 yrs.	3 yrs.	...	★	30	25	State bar member	State bar member
Vermont	...	...	...	...	...	...	5 years state bar	5 years state bar
Virginia	...	★	...	★	...	...	5 years state bar	5 years state bar
Washington	1 yr.	1 yr.	1 yr.	1 yr.	...	...	State bar member	State bar member
West Virginia	5 yrs.	★	...	★	30	30	10 years state bar	5 years state bar
Wisconsin	28 days	28 days	28 days	28 days	...	18	5 years state bar	5 years state bar
Wyoming	3 yrs.	2 yrs.	...	...	30	28	9 years practice	Law degree
Dist. of Columbia	N.A.	N.A.	90 days	90 days	...	...	5 years practice	5 years state bar (v)
Puerto Rico	5 yrs.	...	...	...	...	...	10 years practice	7 years state bar

See footnotes at end of table.

QUALIFICATIONS OF JUDGES OF STATE APPELLATE COURTS
AND GENERAL TRIAL COURTS — Continued

Sources: S. Strickland, R. Schauffler, R. LaFountain, & K. Holt, eds. *State Court Organization.* National Center for State Courts. April 8, 2016. *www.ncsc.org/sco.*

Key:

A—Judges of courts of last resort and intermediate appellate courts.

T—Judges of general trial courts.

★—Provision; length of time not specified.

...—No specific provision.

N.A.—Not applicable

(a) For court of appeals, five years.

(b) No local residency requirement stated for Supreme Court. Local residency of 3 years required for Court of Appeals.

(c) Supreme Court—ten years state bar, Court of Appeals—five years state bar.

(d) Admitted to the practice of law in Arizona for five years.

(e) Court of Appeals minimum age is 30.

(f) The candidate must be a resident of the district at the time of the original appointment.

(g) Circuit court judge must reside within the territorial jurisdiction of the court.

(h) In the Supreme Court and the Court of Appeals, five years service as a general jurisdiction judge may be substituted.

(i) Relevant legal experience, such as being a member of a law faculty or sitting as a judge, may qualify under the 10 year requirement.

(j) Must reside within the district.

(k) At the appellate level must have been a state voter for nine years. At the general trial court level must have been a state voter for three years and resident of the circuit for 1 year.

(l) Minimum of two years state bar member and at least 15 years of legal practice.

(m) Restricted Superior court judgeships require residence within the particular county of assignment at time of appointment and reappointment.

(n) Resident judges of the Superior Court are required to have local residency, but special judges are not.

(o) District and associate judges must be state residents for six months if elected, and associate judges must be county residents.

(p) District Court: judges must be a state bar member for four years or a judge of court record. Associate judges must be a state bar member for two years or a judge of a court of record.

(q) Circuit judges must be county electors and residents of the circuit.

(r) Supreme Court: One justice from each of three divisions and two seats at large; no more than two may be from any grand division. Court of Appeals and Court of Criminal Appeals: Must reside in the grand division served.

(s) 35 for Supreme Court, 30 for Court of Appeals & Court of Criminal Appeals

(t) Ten years practicing law or a lawyer and judge of a court of record at least 10 years.

(u) District Court: judges must have been a practicing lawyer or a judge of a court in this state, or both combined, for four years.

(v) Superior Court: Judge must also be an active member of the unified District of Columbia bar and have been engaged, during the five years immediately preceding the judicial nomination, in the active practice of law as an attorney in the District, been on the faculty of a law school in the District, or been employed by either the by the United States or District of Columbia government.

Table 5.4
COMPENSATION OF JUDGES OF APPELLATE COURTS AND GENERAL TRIAL COURTS

State or other jurisdiction	Appellate courts				Judges salaries	General trial courts	Salary
	Court of last resort	Chief Justice salaries	Associate Justice salaries	Intermediate appellate court			
Alabama	Supreme Court	(a)	(b)	Court of Criminal Appeals	(d)	Circuit courts	(e)
Alaska	Supreme Court	$200,760	$200,172	Court of Appeals	$189,108	Superior courts	$185,088
Arizona	Supreme Court	160,000	155,000	Court of Appeals	150,000	Superior courts	145,000
Arkansas	Supreme Court	166,500	166,500	Court of Appeals	161,500	Chancery courts	160,000
California	Supreme Court	241,978	230,750	Court of Appeals	216,330	Superior court	189,041
Colorado	Supreme Court	176,799	173,024	Court of Appeals	166,170	District courts	159,320
Connecticut	Supreme Court	200,599	185,610	Appellate Court	174,323	Superior courts	167,634
Delaware	Supreme Court	201,131	192,360		…	Superior courts	180,733
Florida	Supreme Court	162,200	162,200	District Court of Appeals	154,140	Circuit courts	146,080
Georgia	Supreme Court	167,210	167,210	Court of Appeals	166,186	Superior courts	156,252
Hawaii	Supreme Court	222,480	214,524	Intermediate Court	198,624	Circuit courts	193,248
Idaho	Supreme Court	137,000	135,000	Court of Appeals	130,000	District courts	124,000
Illinois	Supreme Court	220,873	220,873	Court of Appeals	207,882	Circuit courts	190,758
Indiana	Supreme Court	165,078	165,078	Court of Appeals	160,468	Circuit courts	137,062
Iowa	Supreme Court	178,538	170,544	Court of Appeals	154,556	District courts	143,897
Kansas	Supreme Court	139,310	135,905	Court of Appeals	131,518	District courts	120,037
Kentucky	Supreme Court	140,504	135,504	Court of Appeals	130,044	Circuit courts	124,620
Louisiana	Supreme Court	172,819	164,589	Court of Appeals	154,059	District courts	148,108
Maine	Supreme Judicial Court	149,864	129,625			Superior courts	121,472
Maryland	Court of Appeals	195,433	176,433	Court of Special Appeals	163,633	Circuit courts	154,433
Massachusetts	Supreme Judicial Court	181,239	175,984	Appellate Court	165,087	Superior courts	159,694
Michigan	Supreme Court	164,610	164,610	Court of Appeals	151,441	Circuit courts	139,919
Minnesota	Supreme Court	178,892	162,630	Court of Appeals	153,240	District courts	143,851
Mississippi	Supreme Court	148,097	142,320	Court of Appeals	134,883	Chancery courts	128,042
Missouri	Supreme Court	178,089	170,292	Court of Appeals	155,709	Circuit courts	146,803
Montana	Supreme Court	137,571	136,177			District courts	126,131
Nebraska	Supreme Court	166,159	166,169	Court of Appeals	157,851	District courts	153,697
Nevada	Supreme Court	170,000	170,000			District courts	160,000
New Hampshire	Supreme Court	160,746	155,907			Superior courts	146,236
New Jersey	Supreme Court	192,795	185,482	Appellate division of	175,534	Superior courts	165,000
New Mexico	Supreme Court	133,174	131,174	Court of Appeals	124,616	District courts	118,385
New York	Court of Appeals	198,600	192,500	Appellate divisions of	177,900	Supreme courts	174,000
North Carolina	Supreme Court	143,623	139,896	Court of Appeals	134,109	Superior courts	126,875
North Dakota	Supreme Court	156,813	152,486			District courts	139,679
Ohio	Supreme Court	150,850	141,600	Court of Appeals	132,000	Courts of common pleas	121,350
Oklahoma	Supreme Court	147,000	137,655	Court of Appeals	130,410	District courts	131,835
Oregon	Supreme Court	138,556	135,688	Court of Appeals	132,820	Circuit courts	124,468
Pennsylvania	Supreme Court	209,329	203,409	Superior Court	191,926	Courts of common pleas	176,572
Rhode Island	Supreme Court	189,665	172,422			Superior courts	155,235
South Carolina	Supreme Court	151,317	144,111	Court of Appeals	140,508	Circuit courts	136,905

See footnotes at end of table.

COMPENSATION OF JUDGES OF APPELLATE COURTS AND GENERAL TRIAL COURTS—Continued

State or other jurisdiction	Appellate courts					General trial courts	
	Court of last resort	Chief Justice salaries	Associate Justice salaries	Intermediate appellate court	Judges salaries	trial courts	Salary
South Dakota............	Supreme Court	133,713	131,713	...	...	Circuit courts	123,024
Tennessee.............	Supreme Court	187,500	182,508	Court of Appeals	173,436	Chancery courts	170,352
Texas.................	Supreme Court	170,500	168,000	Court of Appeals	(g)	District courts	(h)
Utah..................	Supreme Court	170,150	168,150	Court of Appeals	160,500	District courts	152,850
Vermont..............	Supreme Court	154,124	147,095	...	...	Superior/District/Family	139,837
Virginia...............	Supreme Court (i)	200,552	188,949	Court of Appeals (j)	173,177	Circuit courts	162,878
Washington..........	Supreme Court	172,531	172,531	Court of Appeals	164,238	Superior courts	156,363
West Virginia........	Supreme Court	136,000	136,000	...	...	Circuit courts	126,000
Wisconsin............	Supreme Court	155,403	147,403	Court of Appeals	139,059	Circuit courts	131,187
Wyoming.............	Supreme Court	165,000	165,000	...	...	District courts	150,000

Source: National Center for State Courts, July 1, 2015.

Note: Compensation is shown rounded to the nearest thousand, and is reported according to most recent legislation, even though laws may not yet have taken effect. There are other non-salary forms of judicial compensation that can be a significant part of a judge's compensation package. It should be noted that many of these can be important to judges or attorneys who might be interested in becoming judges or justices. These include retirement, disability, and death benefits, expense accounts, vacation, holiday, and sick leave and various forms of insurance coverage.

Key:
(a) Salary range is between $161,002-$201,252.
(b) Salary range is between $160,003-$200,007.
(c) Salary range is between $159,503-$199,378.
(d) Salary range is between $159,003-$198,753.
(e) Salary range is between $119,949-$149,936.
(g) Salary range is between $154,000-$163,000.
(h) Salary range is between $140,000-$158,000.
(i) Plus $13,500 in lieu of travel, lodging, and other expenses.
(j) Plus $6,500 in lieu of travel, lodging, and other expenses.

Table 5.5
SELECTED DATA ON COURT ADMINISTRATIVE OFFICES

State or other jurisdiction	Title	Established	Appointed by (a)	Salary
Alabama	Administrative Director of Courts	1971	CJ (b)	(g)
Alaska	Administrative Director	1959	CJ (b)	198,172
Arizona	Administrative Director of Courts	1960	SC	(h)
Arkansas	Director, Administrative Office of the Courts	1965	CJ (c)	114,866
California	Administrative Director of the Courts	1960	JC	245,640
Colorado	State Court Administrator	1959	SC	169,977
Connecticut	Chief Court Administrator (d)	1965	CJ	192,763
Delaware	Director, Administrative Office of the Courts	1971	CJ	135,078
Florida	State Courts Administrator	1972	SC	135,999
Georgia	Director, Administrative Office of the Courts	1973	JC	132,000
Hawaii	Administrative Director of the Courts	1959	CJ (b)	145,844
Idaho	Administrative Director of the Courts	1967	SC	130,000
Illinois	Administrative Director of the Courts	1959	SC	207,882
Indiana	Executive Director, Division of State Court Administration	1975	CJ	129,794
Iowa	Court Administrator	1971	SC	154,000
Kansas	Judicial Administrator	1965	CJ	120,037
Kentucky	Administrative Director of the Courts	1976	CJ	127,100
Louisiana	Judicial Administrator	1954	SC	154,059
Maine	Court Administrator	1975	CJ	121,472
Maryland	State Court Administrator	1955	CJ (b)	146,881
Massachusetts	Chief Justice for Administration & Management	1978	SC	170,358
Michigan	State Court Administrator	1952	SC	157,452
Minnesota	State Court Administrator	1963	SC	171,404
Mississippi	Court Administrator	1974	SC	92,960
Missouri	State Courts Administrator	1970	SC	124,472
Montana	State Court Administrator	1975	SC	111,570
Nebraska	State Court Administrator	1972	CJ	135,844
Nevada	Director, Office of Court Administration	1971	SC	123,788
New Hampshire	Director of the Administrative Office of the Court	1980	SC	125,092
New Jersey	Administrative Director of the Courts	1948	CJ	175,534
New Mexico	Director, Administrative Office of the Courts	1959	SC	131,165
New York	Chief Administrator of the Courts	1978	CJ	180,400
North Carolina	Director, Administrative Office of the Courts	1965	CJ	129,259
North Dakota	Court Administrator (h)	1971	CJ	138,768
Ohio	Administrative Director of the Courts	1955	SC	(l)
Oklahoma	Administrative Director of the Courts	1967	SC	130,410
Oregon	Court Administrator	1971	SC	(m)
Pennsylvania	Court Administrator	1968	SC	191,926
Rhode Island	State Court Administrator	1969	CJ	(n)
South Carolina	Director of Court Administration	1973	CJ	132,292
South Dakota	State Court Administrator	1974	SC	112,478
Tennessee	Director	1963	SC	170,352
Texas	Administrative Director of the Courts (i)	1977	SC	157,920
Utah	Court Administrator	1973	SC	152,850
Vermont	Court Administrator	1967	SC	139,837
Virginia	Executive Secretary to the Supreme Court	1952	SC	173,177
Washington	Administrator for the Courts	1957	SC (e)	142,800
West Virginia	Administrative Director of the Supreme Court of Appeals	1975	SC	145,000
Wisconsin	Director of State Courts	1978	SC	139,059
Wyoming	Court Coordinator	1974	SC	118,000
Dist. of Columbia	Executive Officer, Courts of D.C.	1971	(f)	201,100
American Samoa	Administrator/Comptroller	N.A	N.A.	N.A.
Guam	Administrative Director of Superior Court	N.A.	CJ	N.A.
No. Mariana Islands	Director of Courts	N.A.	N.A.	N.A.
Puerto Rico	Administrative Director of the Courts	1952	CJ	N.A.
U.S. Virgin Islands	Court/Administrative Clerk	N.A.	N.A.	N.A.

Source: National Center for State Courts, July 1, 2015.

Note: Compensation shown is rounded to the nearest thousand, and is reported according to most recent legislation, even though laws may not yet have taken effect. Other information from State Court Administrator web sites.

Key:
SC—State court of last resort.
CJ—Chief justice or chief judge of court of last resort.
JC—Judicial council.
N.A.—Not available.

(a) Term of office for all court administrators is at pleasure of appointing authority.
(b) With approval of Supreme Court.
(c) With approval of Judicial Council.
(d) Administrator is an associate judge of the Supreme Court.
(e) Appointed from list of five submitted by governor.
(f) Joint Committee on Judicial Administration.
(g) Salary range is between $100,197 and $152,618.
(h) Salary range is between $109,000 and $197,000.
(j) Salary range is between $109,704 and $148,123.
(l) Salary range is between $125,000 and $145,000.
(m) Salary range is between $103,056 and 167,784.
(n) Salary range is between $129,132 and $143,163.

Table 5.6
SELECTION AND RETENTION OF APPELLATE COURT JUDGES

State or other jurisdiction	Name of court	Type of court	Method of selection		Method of retention	Geographic basis for selection
			Unexpired term	Full term		
Alabama	Supreme Court	SC	GU	PE	PE	SW
	Court of Civil Appeals	IA	GU	PE	PE	SW
	Court of Criminal Appeals	IA	GU	PE	PE	SW
Alaska	Supreme Court	SC	GN	GN	RE (a)	SW
	Court of Appeals	IA	GN	GN	RE (a)	SW
Arizona	Supreme Court	SC	GN	GN	RE	SW
	Court of Appeals	IA	GN	GN	RE	DS
Arkansas	Supreme Court	SC	GU	NP	NP	SW
	Court of Appeals	IA	GU	NP	NP	DS
California	Supreme Court	SC	GU	GU	RE	SW
	Courts of Appeal	IA	GU	GU	RE	DS
Colorado	Supreme Court	SC	GN	GN	RE	SW
	Court of Appeals	IA	GN	GN	RE	SW
Connecticut	Supreme Court	SC	GNL	GNL	GNL	SW
	Appellate Court	IA	GNL	GNL	GNL	SW
Delaware	Supreme Court	SC	GNL	GNL	GNL	SW
Florida	Supreme Court	SC	GN	GN	RE	DS and SW (b)
	District Courts of Appeal	IA	GN	GN	RE	DS
Georgia	Supreme Court	SC	GN	NP	NP	SW
	Court of Appeals	IA	GN	NP	NP	SW
Hawaii	Supreme Court	SC	GNL	GNL	JN	SW
	Intermediate Court of Appeals	IA	GNL	GNL	JN	SW
Idaho	Supreme Court	SC	GN	NP	NP	SW
	Court of Appeals	IA	GN	NP	NP	SW
Illinois	Supreme Court	SC	CS	PE	RE	DS
	Appellate Court	IA	SC	PE	RE	DS
Indiana	Supreme Court	SC	GN	GN	RE	SW
	Court of Appeals	IA	GN	GN	RE	DS
	Tax Court	IA	GN	GN	RE	SW
Iowa	Supreme Court	SC	GN	GN	RE	SW
	Court of Appeals	IA	GN	GN	RE	SW
Kansas	Supreme Court	SC	GN	GN	RE	SW
	Court of Appeals	IA	GL	GL	RE	SW
Kentucky	Supreme Court	SC	GN	NP	NP	DS
	Court of Appeals	IA	GN	NP	NP	DS
Louisiana	Supreme Court	SC	CS (c)	PE (d)	PE (d)	DS
	Courts of Appeal	IA	SC (c)	PE (d)	PE (d)	DS
Maine	Supreme Judicial Court	SC	GL	GL	GL	SW
Maryland	Court of Appeals	SC	GNL	GNL	RE	DS
	Court of Special Appeals	IA	GNL	GNL	RE	DS
Massachusetts	Supreme Judicial Court	SC	(e)	GNE (f)	(g)	SW
	Appeals Court	IA	(e)	GNE (f)	(g)	SW
Michigan	Supreme Court	SC	GU	PE (h)	PE (h)	SW
	Court of Appeals	IA	GU	PE (h)	PE (h)	DS
Minnesota	Supreme Court	SC	GU	NP	NP	SW
	Court of Appeals	IA	GU	NP	NP	SW
Mississippi	Supreme Court	SC	GU	NP	NP	DS
	Court of Appeals	IA	GU	NP	NP	DS
Missouri	Supreme Court	SC	GN	GN	RE	SW
	Court of Appeals	IA	GN	GN	RE	DS
Montana	Supreme Court	SC	GNL	NP	NP (i)	SW
Nebraska	Supreme Court	SC	GN	GN	RE	SW and DS (j)
	Court of Appeals	IA	GN	GN	RE	DS
Nevada	Supreme Court	SC	GN	NP	NP	SW
	Court of Appeals	IA	GN	NP	NP	SW

See footnotes at end of table.

SELECTION AND RETENTION OF APPELLATE COURT JUDGES — Continued

State or other jurisdiction	Name of court	Type of court	Method of selection		Method of retention	Geographic basis for selection
			Unexpired term	Full term		
New Hampshire	Supreme Court	SC	GE	GE	(k)	SW
New Jersey	Supreme Court	SC	GL	GL	GL	SW
	Superior Court, Appellate Div.	IA	GL	GL (l)	GL (l)	SW
New Mexico	Supreme Court	SC	GN	PE	RE	SW
	Court of Appeals	IA	GN	PE	RE	SW
New York	Court of Appeals	SC	GNL	GNL	GNL	SW
	Supreme Ct., Appellate Div.	IA	GN	GN	GN	SW (m)
North Carolina	Supreme Court	SC	GU	NP	RE	SW
	Court of Appeals	IA	GU	PE	PE	SW
North Dakota	Supreme Court	SC	GN (n)	NP	NP	SW
	Temporary Court of Appeals	IA	(o)	SC (p)	(o)	SW
Ohio	Supreme Court	SC	GU	PE (q)	PE (q)	SW
	Courts of Appeals	IA	GU	PE (q)	PE (q)	DS
Oklahoma	Supreme Court	SC	GN	GN	RE	DS
	Court of Criminal Appeals	SC	GN	GN	RE	DS
	Court of Civil Appeals	IA	GN	GN	RE	DS
Oregon	Supreme Court	SC	GU	NP	NP	SW
	Court of Appeals	IA	GU	NP	NP	SW
Pennsylvania	Supreme Court	SC	GL	PE	RE	SW
	Superior Court	IA	GL	PE	RE	SW
	Commonwealth Court	IA	GL	PE	RE	SW
Rhode Island	Supreme Court	SC	GN	GN	(r)	SW
South Carolina	Supreme Court	SC	LA	LA	LA	SW
	Court of Appeals	IA	LA	LA	LA	SW
South Dakota	Supreme Court	SC	GN	GN	RE	DS and SW (s)
Tennessee	Supreme Court	SC	GL	GL	RE	SW
	Court of Appeals	SC	GL	GL	RE	SW
	Court of Criminal Appeals	IA	GL	GL	RE	SW
Texas	Supreme Court	SC	GU	PE	PE	SW
	Court of Criminal Appeals	SC	GU	PE	PE	SW
	Courts of Appeals	IA	GU	PE	PE	DS
Utah	Supreme Court	SC	GNL	GNL	RE	SW
	Court of Appeals	IA	GNL	GNL	RE	SW
Vermont	Supreme Court	SC	GNL	GNL	LA	SW
Virginia	Supreme Court	SC	GU (t)	LA	LA	SW
	Court of Appeals	IA	GU (t)	LA	LA	SW
Washington	Supreme Court	SC	GU	NP	NP	SW
	Courts of Appeals	IA	GU	NP	NP	DS
West Virginia	Supreme Court of Appeals	SC	GU (u)	NP	NP	SW
Wisconsin	Supreme Court	SC	GU	NP	NP	SW
	Court of Appeals	IA	GU	NP	NP	DS
Wyoming	Supreme Court	SC	GN	GN	RE	SW
District of Columbia	Court of Appeals	SC	(v)	(t)	(t)	SW (w)
Puerto Rico	Supreme Court	SC	GL	GL	(x)	SW
	Court of Appeals	IA	GL	GL	GL	SW

See footnotes at end of table.

SELECTION AND RETENTION OF APPELLATE COURT JUDGES — Continued

Sources: S. Strickland, R. Schauffler, R. LaFountain & K. Holt, eds. State Court Organization. Last updated 8 April 2016. National Center for State Courts. *www.ncsc.org/sco.*

Key:
SC—Court of last resort
IA—Intermediate appellate court
N/S—Not stated
N.A.—Not applicable
AP—At pleasure
CS—Court selection
DS—District
DU—Duration of service
GE—Gubernatorial appointment with approval of elected executive council
GL—Gubernatorial appointment with consent of the legislature
GN—Gubernatorial appointment from judicial nominating commission
GNE—Gubernatorial appointment from judicial nominating commission with approval of elected executive council
GNL—Gubernatorial appointment from judicial nominating commission with consent of the legislature
GU—Gubernatorial appointment
ID—Indefinite
JN—Judicial nominating commission appoints
LA—Legislative appointment
NP—Non-partisan election
PE—Partisan election
RE—Retention election
SC—Court of last resort appoints
SCJ—Chief justice/judge of the court of last resort appoints
SN—Seniority
SW—Statewide

(a) A judge must run for a retention election at the next election, immediately following the third year from the time of initial appointment.

(b) Five justices are selected by region (based on the District Courts of Appeal) and two justices are selected statewide.

(c) The person selected by the Supreme Court is prohibited from running for that judgeship; an election is held within one year to serve the remainder of the term.

(d) Louisiana uses a blanket primary, in which all candidates appear with party labels on the primary ballot. The two top vote getters compete in the general election.

(e) There are no expired judicial terms. A judicial term expires upon the death, resignation, retirement, or removal of an incumbent.

(f) The Executive (Governor's) Council is made up of nine people elected by geographical area and presided over by the Lieutenant Governor.

(g) There is no retention process. Judges serve during good behavior to age 70.

(h) Candidates may be nominated by political parties and are elected on a nonpartisan ballot.

(i) If the justice/judge is unopposed, a retention election is held.

(j) Chief Justices are selected statewide while Associate Justices are selected by district.

(k) There is no retention process. Judges serve during good behavior to age 70.

(l) All Superior Court judges, including Appellate Division judges, are subject to gubernatorial reappointment and consent by the Senate after an initial seven-year term. Among all the judges, the Chief Justice designates the judges of the Appellate Division.

(m) The Presiding Judge of each Appellate Division must be a resident of the department.

(n) The Governor may appoint from a list of names or call a special election at his discretion.

(o) The supreme court may provide for the assignment of active or retired district court judges, retired justices of the supreme court, and lawyers, to serve on three-judge panels.

(p) There is neither a retention process nor unexpired terms. Assignments are for a specified time, not to exceed one year or the completion of one or more cases on the docket of the supreme court.

(q) Party affiliation is not included on the ballot in the general election, but candidates are chosen through partisan primary nominations.

(r) There is no retention process. Judges serve during good behavior for a life tenure.

(s) Initial selection is by district, but retention selection is statewide.

(t) Gubernatorial appointment is for interim appointments.

(u) Appointment is effective only until the next election year; the appointee may run for election to any remaining portion of the unexpired term.

(v) Initial appointment is made by the President of the United States and confirmed by the Senate. Six months prior to the expiration of the term of office, the judge's performance is reviewed by the tenure commission. Those found "well qualified" are automatically reappointed. If a judge is found to be "qualified" the President may nominate the judge for an additional term (subject to Senate confirmation). If the President does not wish to reappoint the judge, the District of Columbia Nomination Commission compiles a new list of candidates.

(w) The geographic basis of selection is the District of Columbia.

(x) There is no retention process. Judges serve during good behavior to age 70.

Table 5.7
SELECTION AND RETENTION OF TRIAL COURT JUDGES

State or other jurisdiction	Name of Court	Types of court	Method of selection		Method of retention	Geographic basis for selection
			Unexpired term	Full term		
Alabama	Circuit	GJ	GU (a)	PE	PE	Circuit
	District	LJ	GU (a)	PE	PE	County
	Municipal	LJ	MU	MU	RA	Municipality
	Probate	LJ	GU	PE	PE	County
Alaska	Superior	GJ	GN	GN	RE (b)	State (c)
	District	LJ	GN	GN	RE (d)	District
	Magistrate's Division	N.A.	PJ	PJ	PJ	District
Arizona	Superior	GJ	GN (e)	GN or NP (f)	NP or RE (f)	County
	Justice of the Peace	LJ	CO	PE	PE	Precinct
	Municipal	LJ	CC (g)	CC (g)	CC (g)	Municipality
Arkansas	Circuit	GJ	GU (h)	NP	NP	Circuit
	District	LJ	GU	NP	NP	District
	City	LJ	LD	LD	LD	City
California	Superior	GJ	GU	NP	NP (i)	County
Colorado	District	GJ	GN	GN	RE	District
	Denver Probate	GJ	GN	GN	RE	District
	Denver Juvenile	GJ	GN	GN	RE	District
	Water	GJ	SC (j)	SC (j)	RE	District
	County	LJ	GN	GN (k)	RE	County
	Municipal	LJ	MU	MU	RA	Municipality
Connecticut	Superior	GJ	GNL	GNL	GNL	State
	Probate	LJ	PE	PE	PE	District
Delaware	Superior	GJ	GNL	GNL	GNL	State
	Chancery	LJ	GNL	GNL	GNL	State
	Justice of the Peace	LJ	GNL (l)	GNL (l)	GU	County
	Family	LJ	GNL	GNL	GNL	County
	Common Pleas	LJ	GNL	GNL	GNL	County
	Alderman's	LJ	LD	CC	LD	Town
Florida	Circuit	GJ	GN	NP	NP	Circuit
	County	LJ	GN	NP	NP	County
Georgia	Superior	GJ	GN	NP	NP	Circuit
	Juvenile	LJ	CS (m)	CS (m)	CS (m)	County/Circuit
	Civil	LJ	GU	PE	PE	County
	State	LJ	GU	NP	NP	County
	Probate	LJ	GU	PE (n)	PE (n)	County
	Magistrate	LJ	LD	LD (o)	LD (o)	County
	Municipal/of Columbus	LJ	MA	Elected	Elected	Municipality
	County Recorder's	LJ	LD	LD	LD	County
	Municipal/City of Atlanta	LJ	MU	MU	LD	Municipality
Hawaii	Circuit	GJ	GNL	GNL	JN	State
	District	LJ	SCJ (p)	SCJ (p)	JN	Circuit
Idaho	District	GJ	GN	NP	NP	District
	Magistrate's Division	LJ	JN (q)	JN (q)	RE	County
Illinois	Circuit	GJ	SC	PE	RE	Circuit/County (r)
	Associate Division	N.A.	SC	PE	RE	Circuit/County (r)
Indiana	Superior	GJ	GU	PE (s)	PE (s)	County
	Circuit	GJ	GU	PE (t)	PE (t)	County
	Probate	GJ	GU	PE	PE	County
	County	LJ	GU	PE	PE	County
	City	LJ	GU	PE	PE	Municipality
	Town	LJ	GU	PE	PE	Municipality
	Small Claims/Marion County	LJ	GU	PE	PE	Township
Iowa	District	GJ	GN (u)	GN (u)	RE (u)	District
Kansas	District	GJ	GN and PE (v)	GN and PE (v)	RE and PE (v)	District
	Municipal	LJ	MU	MU	MU	City
Kentucky	Circuit	GJ	GN	NP	NP	Circuit
	District	LJ	GN	NP	NP	District
Louisiana	District	GJ	SC (w)	PE	PE	District
	Juvenile & Family	GJ	SC (w)	PE	PE	District
	Justice of the Peace	LJ	SC (w)	PE (x)	PE	Ward
	Mayor's	LJ	MA	LD	LD	City
	City & Parish	LJ	SC (w)	PE	PE	Ward

See footnotes at end of table.

SELECTION AND RETENTION OF TRIAL COURT JUDGES — Continued

State or other jurisdiction	Name of Court	Types of court	Method of selection — Unexpired term	Method of selection — Full term	Method of retention	Geographic basis for selection
Maine	Superior	GJ	GL	GL	GL	State
	District	GJ	GL	GL	GL	State and District (y)
	Probate	LJ	GU	PE	PE	County
Maryland	Circuit	GJ	GNL	GNL	NP	County
	District	LJ	GNL	GNL	RA	District
	Orphan's	LJ	GU	PE (z)	PE (z)	County
Massachusetts	Superior	GJ	(aa)	GNE (bb)	(cc)	State
	District	LJ	(aa)	GNE (bb)	(cc)	State
	Probate & Family	LJ	(aa)	GNE (bb)	(cc)	State
	Juvenile	LJ	(aa)	GNE (bb)	(cc)	State
	Housing	LJ	(aa)	GNE (bb)	(cc)	State
	Boston Municipal	LJ	(aa)	GNE (bb)	(cc)	State
	Land	LJ	(aa)	GNE (bb)	(cc)	State
Michigan	Circuit	GJ	GU	NP	NP	Circuit
	Claims	GJ	GU	NP	NP	Circuit
	District	LJ	GU	NP	NP	District
	Probate	LJ	GU	NP	NP	District and Circuit
	Municipal	LJ	LD	NP	NP	City
Minnesota	District	GJ	GN	NP	NP	District
Mississippi	Circuit	GJ	GU	NP	NP	District
	Chancery	LJ	GU	NP	NP	District
	County	LJ	GU	NP	NP	County
	Municipal	LJ	LD	LD	LD	Municipality
	Justice	LJ	LD	PE	PE	District in County
Missouri	Circuit	GJ	GU and GN (dd)	PE and GN (ee)	PE and RE (ff)	Circuit/County (gg)
	Municipal	LJ	LD	LD	LD	City
Montana	District	GJ	GN	NP	NP	District
	Workers' Compensation	GJ	GN	GN	RA	State
	Water	GJ	SCJ (hh)	SCJ (hh)	SCJ (ii)	State
	Justice of the Peace	LJ	CO	NP	NP	County
	Municipal	LJ	MU	NP	NP	City
	City	LJ	CC	NP	NP	City
Nebraska	District	GJ	GN	GN	RE	District
	Separate Juvenile	LJ	GN	GN	RE	District
	County	LJ	GN	GN	RE	District
	Workers' Compensation	LJ	GN	GN	RE	District
Nevada	District	GJ	GN	NP	NP	District
	Justice	LJ	CO	NP	NP	Township
	Municipal	LJ	CC	NP	NP	City
New Hampshire	Superior	GJ	GE	GE	(jj)	State
	District	LJ	GE	GE	(jj)	District
	Probate	LJ	GE	GE	(jj)	County
New Jersey	Superior	GJ	GL	GL	GL	County
	Tax	LJ	GL	GL	GL	State
	Municipal	LJ	MA or MU (kk)	MA or MU (kk)	MU	Municipality
New Mexico	District	GJ	GN	PE	RE	District
	Magistrate	LJ	GU	PE	PE	County
	Metropolitan/Bernalillo County	LJ	GN	PE	RE	County
	Municipal	LJ	MU	PE	PE	City
	Probate	LJ	CO	PE	PE	County
New York	Supreme	GJ	GL	PE	PE	District
	County	GJ	GL	PE	PE	County
	Claims	GJ	GNL	GNL	GU	State
	Surrogates'	LJ	GNL	PE	PE	County
	Family	LJ	GNL and MU (ll)	PE and MU (ll)	PE and MU (ll)	County and NYC
	District	LJ	(mm)	PE	PE	District
	City	LJ	Elected	Elected	LD	City
	NYC Civil	LJ	MA (nn)	PE	PE	City
	NYC Criminal	LJ	MA	MA	MA	City
	Town & Village Justice	LJ	LD	LD	LD	Town or Village
North Carolina	Superior	GJ	GU	NP	NP	District
	District	LJ	GU	NP	NP	District

See footnotes at end of table.

SELECTION AND RETENTION OF TRIAL COURT JUDGES — Continued

State or other jurisdiction	Name of Court	Types of court	Method of selection		Method of retention	Geographic basis for selection
			Unexpired term	Full term		
North Dakota	District	GJ	GN	NP	NP	District
	Municipal	LJ	MA	NP	NP	City
Ohio............................	Common Pleas	GJ	GU	PE (oo)	PE (oo)	County
	Municipal	LJ	GU	PE (oo)	PE (oo)	County/City
	County	LJ	GU	PE (oo)	PE (oo)	County
	Claims	LJ	SCJ	SCJ	SCJ	N.A.
	Mayor's	LJ	Elected	PE	PE	City/Village
Oklahoma	District	GJ	GN (pp)	NP (pp)	NP (pp)	District
	Municipal Not of Record	LJ	MM	MM	MM	Municipality
	Municipal of Record	LJ	MU	MU	MU	Municipality
	Workers' Compensation	LJ	GN	GN	GN	State
	Tax Review	LJ	SCJ	SCJ	SCJ	District
Oregon	Circuit	GJ	GU	NP	NP	District
	Tax	GJ	GU	NP	NP	State
	County	LJ	CO	NP	NP	County
	Justice	LJ	GU	NP	NP	County
	Municipal	LJ	CC	CC/Elected	CC/Elected	(qq)
Pennsylvania...............	Common Pleas	GJ	GL	PE	RE	District
	Philadelphia Municipal	LJ	GL	PE	RE	City/County
	Magisterial District Judges	LJ	GL	PE	PE	District
	Philadelphia Traffic	LJ	GL	PE	RE	City/County
Rhode Island	Superior	GJ	GN	GN	(rr)	State
	Workers' Compensation	LJ	GN	GN	(rr)	State
	District	LJ	GN	GN	(rr)	State
	Family	LJ	GN	GN	(rr)	State
	Probate	LJ	CC	CC or MA	RA	Town
	Municipal	LJ	CC	CC or MA	CC or MA	Town
	Traffic Tribunal	LJ	GN	GN	(rr)	State
South Carolina	Circuit	GJ	LA and GN (ss)(tt)	LA and GN (tt)	LA and GL (tt)	Circuit and State (tt)
	Family	LJ	LA	LA	LA	Circuit
	Magistrate	LJ	GL	GL	GL	County
	Probate	LJ	GU	PE	PE	County
	Municipal	LJ	CC	CC	CC	District
South Dakota	Circuit	GJ	GN	NP	NP	Circuit
	Magistrate	LJ	PJS	PJS	PJS	Circuit
Tennessee....................	Circuit	GJ	GU	PE (uu)	PE	District
	Chancery	GJ	GU	PE (uu)	PE	District
	Criminal	GJ	GU	PE (uu)	PE	District
	Probate	GJ	(vv)	PE (uu)	PE	District
	Juvenile	LJ	(vv)	PE (uu)	PE	County
	Municipal	LJ	LD	LD (uu)	LD	Municipality
	General Sessions	LJ	MU	PE (uu)	PE	County
Texas............................	District	GJ	GL	PE	PE	District
	Constitutional County	LJ	CO	PE	PE	County
	Probate	LJ	CO	PE	PE	County
	County at Law	LJ	CO	PE	PE	County
	Justice of the Peace	LJ	CO	PE	PE	Precinct
	Municipal	LJ	CC	LD	LD	Municipality
Utah............................	District	GJ	(ww)	GNL	RE	District
	Justice	LJ	MM (xx)	MM (xx)	RE and RA (yy)	County/Municipality
	Juvenile	LJ	(ww)	GNL	RE	District
Vermont	Superior (zz)	GJ	GNL	GNL	LA	State
	Judicial Bureau	LJ	PJ	PJ	AP	State
Virginia	Circuit	GJ	GU	LA	LA	Circuit
	District	LJ	CS (aaa)	LA	LA	District
Washington.................	Superior	GJ	GU	NP	NP	County
	District	LJ	CO	NP	NP	District
	Municipal	LJ	CC	MA/CC	MA/CC (bbb)	Municipality
West Virginia	Circuit	GJ	GU	NP	NP	Circuit
	Magistrate	LJ	PJ	NP	NP	County
	Municipal	LJ	LD	LD	LD	Municipality
	Family	LJ	GU	NP	NP	Circuit

See footnotes at end of table.

SELECTION AND RETENTION OF TRIAL COURT JUDGES — Continued

State or other jurisdiction	Name of Court	Types of court	Method of selection		Method of retention	Geographic basis for selection
			Unexpired term	Full term		
Wisconsin	Circuit	GJ	GU	NP	NP	District
	Municipal	LJ	MU (ccc)	NP	NP	Municipality
Wyoming	District	GJ	GN	GN	RE	District
	Circuit	LJ	GN	GN	RE	Circuit
	Municipal	LJ	MA	MA	LD	Municipality
Dist. of Columbia	Superior	GJ	(ddd)	(ddd)	(ddd)	State (eee)
Puerto Rico	First Instance	GJ	GL	GL	GL	State

Sources: S. Strickland, R. Schauffler, R. LaFountain and K. Holt, eds. *State Court Organization.* Last updated April 8, 2016. National Center for State Courts. *www.ncsc.org/sco.*

Key:
GJ — General jurisdiction court
LJ — Limited jurisdiction court
N/S — Not stated
N.A. — Not applicable
AP — At pleasure
CA — Court administrator appointment
CC — City or town council/commission appointment
CO — County board/commission appointment
CS — Court selection
DU — Duration of service
GE — Gubernatorial appointment with approval of elected executive council
GL — Gubernatorial appointment with consent of the legislature
GN — Gubernatorial appointment from judicial nominating commission
GNE — Gubernatorial appointment from judicial nominating commission with approval of elected executive council
GNL — Gubernatorial appointment from judicial nominating commission with consent of the legislature
GU — Gubernatorial appointment
JN — Judicial nominating commission appoints
LA — Legislative appointment
LD — Locally determined
MA — Mayoral appointment
MC — Mayoral appointment with consent of city council
MM — Mayoral appointment with consent of governing municipal body
MU — Governing municipal body appointment
NP — Non-partisan election
PE — Partisan election
PJ — Presiding judge of the general jurisdiction court appoints
PJS — Presiding judge of the general jurisdiction court appoints with approval of the court of last resort
RA — Reappointment
RE — Retention election
SC — Court of last resort appoints
SCJ — Chief justice/judge of the court of last resort appoints
(a) The counties of Baldwin, Jefferson, Lauderdale, Madison, Mobile, Shelby, Talladega, and Tuscaloosa use gubernatorial appointment from the recommendations of the Judicial Nominating Commission.
(b) A judge must run for retention at the next election immediately following the third year from the time of the initial appointment.
(c) Judges are selected on a statewide basis, but run for retention on a district-wide basis.
(d) Judges must run for retention at the first general election held more than one year after appointment.
(e) Maricopa and Pima counties use the gubernatorial appointment from the Judicial Nominating Commission process. The method for submitting names for the other 13 counties varies.
(f) Maricopa and Pima counties use the gubernatorial appointment from the Judicial Nominating Commission process. The other 13 counties hold non-partisan elections.
(g) Municipal court judges are usually appointed by the city or town council except in Yuma, where judges are elected.
(h) The office can be held until December 31 following the next general election and then the judge must run in a non-partisan election for the remainder of the term.
(i) If unopposed for reelection, incumbent's name does not appear on the ballot unless a petition was filed not less than 83 days before the election date indicating that a write-in campaign will be conducted for the office.

An unopposed incumbent is not declared elected until the election date. This is for the general election; different timing may apply for the primary election (see Elec. Code §8203).
(j) Judges are chosen by the Supreme Court from among District Court judges.
(k) The mayor appoints Denver County Court judges.
(l) The Magistrate Screening Commission recommends candidates.
(m) Juvenile Court judges are appointed by Superior Court judges in all but one county, in which juvenile judges are elected. Associate judges (formerly referees) must be a member of the state bar or law school graduates. They serve at the pleasure of the judge(s).
(n) Probate judges are selected in non-partisan elections in 66 of 159 counties.
(o) Magistrate judges are selected in nonpartisan elections in 41 of 159 counties.
(p) Selection occurs by means of Chief Justice appointment from the Judicial Nominating Commission with consent of the Senate.
(q) The Magistrate Commission consists of the administrative judge, three mayors and two electors appointed by the governor, and two attorneys (nominated by the district bar and appointed by the state bar). There is one commission in each district.
(r) There exists a unit less than county in Cook County.
(s) Non-partisan elections are used in the Superior Courts in Allen and Vanderburgh counties. Nominating commissions are used in St. Joseph County and in some courts in Lake County. In those courts that use the nominating commission process for selection; retention elections are used as the method of retention.
(t) Non-partisan elections are used in the Circuit Courts in Vanderburgh County.
(u) This applies to district judges only. Associate judges are selected by the district judges and retention is by a retention election. Magistrates are selected and retained by appointment from the County Judicial Magistrate Nominating Commission. The County Judicial Magistrate Nominating Commission consists of three members appointed by the county board and two elected by the county bar, presided over by a District Court judge.
(v) Seventeen districts use gubernatorial appointment from the Judicial Nominating Commission for selection and retention elections for retention. Fourteen districts use partisan elections for selection and retention.
(w) Depending on the amount of time remaining, selection may be by election following a Supreme Court appointment.
(x) Louisiana uses a blanket primary in which all candidates appear with party labels on the primary ballot. The top two vote getters compete in the general election.
(y) At least one judge who is a resident of the county in which the district lies must be appointed from each of the 13 districts.
(z) Two exceptions are Hartford and Montgomery counties where Circuit Court judges are assigned.
(aa) There are no expired judicial terms. A judicial term expires upon the death, resignation, retirement, or removal of an incumbent.
(bb) The Executive (Governor's) Council is made up of eight people elected by geographical area and presided over by the lieutenant governor.
(cc) There is no retention process. Judges serve during good behavior to age 70.
(dd) Gubernatorial appointment occurs in partisan circuits; gubernatorial appointment from Judicial Nominating Commission takes place in non-partisan circuits.
(ee) Partisan elections occur in some circuits; gubernatorial appointment from the Judicial Nominating Commission with a non-partisan election takes place in others.
(ff) Partisan elections take place in some circuits; retention elections occur in other circuits.
(gg) Associate circuit judges are selected on a county basis.

SELECTION AND RETENTION OF TRIAL COURT JUDGES — Continued

(hh) Selection occurs through Chief Justice appointment from Judicial Nominating Commission.

(ii) Other judges are designated by the District Court judges.

(jj) There is no retention process. Judges serve during good behavior to age 70.

(kk) In multi-municipality, joint, or countywide municipal courts, selection is by gubernatorial appointment with consent of the senate.

(ll) Mayoral appointment occurs in New York City.

(mm) The appointment is made by the County Chief Executive Officer with confirmation by District Board of Supervisors.

(nn) Housing judges are appointed by the Chief Administrator of the courts.

(oo) Party affiliation is not included on the ballot in the general election, but candidates are chosen through partisan primary nominations.

(pp) This applies to district and associate judges; special judges are selected by the district judges.

(qq) The geographic basis for selection is the municipality for those judges that are elected. Judges that are either appointed or are under contract may be from other cities.

(rr) There is no retention process. Judges serve during good behavior for a life tenure.

(ss) The governor may appoint a candidate if the unexpired term is less than one year.

(tt) In addition to Circuit Court judges, the Circuit Court has masters-in-equity whose jurisdiction is in matters referred to them in the Circuit Court. Masters-in-equity are selected by gubernatorial appointment from the Judicial Merit Selection Commission, retained by gubernatorial appointment with the consent of the senate, and the geographic basis for selection is the state.

(uu) Each county legislative body has the discretion to require elections to be non-partisan.

(vv) The selection method used to fill an unexpired term is established by a special legislative act.

(ww) There are no expired terms; each new judge begins a new term.

(xx) Appointment is by the local government executive with confirmation by the local government legislative body (may be either county or municipal government).

(yy) County judges are retained by retention election; municipal judges are reappointed by the city executive.

(zz) Effective 2011, the Family, District, Environmental and Probate Courts were combined into the Superior Court.

(aaa) Circuit Court judges appoint.

(bbb) Full-time municipal judges must stand for non-partisan election.

(ccc) A permanent vacancy in the office of municipal judge may be filled by temporary appointment of the municipal governing body or jointly by the governing bodies of all municipalities served by the judge.

(ddd) The Judicial Nomination Commission nominates for Presidential appointment and Senate confirmation. Not less than six months prior to the expiration of the term of office, the judge's performance is reviewed by the Commission on Judicial Disabilities and Tenure. A judge found "well qualified" is automatically reappointed for a new term of 15 years; a judge found "qualified" may be renominated by the President (and subject to Senate confirmation). A judge found "unqualified" is ineligible for reappointment or if the President does not wish to reappoint a judge, the Nomination Commission compiles a new list of candidates.

(eee) The geographic basis for selection is the District of Columbia.

Table 5.8
JUDICIAL DISCIPLINE: INVESTIGATING AND ADJUDICATING BODIES

State or other jurisdiction	Investigating body	Adjudicating body	Appeals from adjudication are filed with:	Final disciplining body	Point at which reprimands are made public
Alabama	Judicial Inquiry Committee	Court of the Judiciary	Court of Last Resort	Court of the Judiciary	Filing of the complaint with the Court of the Judiciary
Alaska	Committee on Judicial Conduct	Supreme Court	Court of Last Resort	Supreme Court	Filing of recommendation with Supreme Court
Arizona	Commission on Judicial Conduct	Commission on Judicial Conduct	Court of Last Resort	Supreme Court	Within 15 days of formal charges being brought, unless a motion for reconsideration is filed
Arkansas	Judicial Discipline and Disability Committees	Commission	Court of Last Resort	Supreme Court	At disposition of case
California	Commission on Judicial Performance	Commission on Judicial Performance	Court of Last Resort	Commission on Judicial Performance	Upon commission determination (a)
Colorado	Commission on Judicial Discipline	Commission on Judicial Discipline	No appeal	Supreme Court	Adjudication
Connecticut	Judicial Review Council	Judicial Review Council; Supreme Court (b)	Court of Last Resort	Supreme Court	Public censure is issued at between 10 and 30 days after notice to the judge, provided that if the judge appeals there is an automatic stay of disclosure
Delaware	Preliminary Committee of the Court on the Judiciary	Court on the Judiciary	No appeal	Court on the Judiciary	Upon issuance of opinion and imposition of sanction
Florida	Judicial Qualifications Commission	Judicial Qualifications Commission (b)	No appeal	Supreme Court	Filing of formal charges by Committee with Supreme Court Clerk
Georgia	Judicial Qualifications Commission	Supreme Court	No appeal	Supreme Court	Formal Hearing
Hawaii	Commission on Judicial Conduct	Commission on Judicial Conduct	No appeal	Supreme Court	Imposition of public discipline by Supreme Court
Idaho	Judicial Council	Supreme Court	Court of Last Resort	Supreme Court	Filing with the Supreme Court
Illinois	Judicial Inquiry Board	Courts Commission	No appeal	Courts Commission	Filing of decision by Courts Commission
Indiana	Commission on Judicial Qualifications	Supreme Court	Court of Last Resort	Supreme Court	After disciplinary charges are filed and case is tried or agreed resolution is accepted by Supreme Court
Iowa	Judicial Qualifications Commission	Judicial Qualifications Commission	Court of Last Resort	Supreme Court	Referral by the commission to the Supreme Court recommending formal sanction
Kansas	Commission on Judicial Qualifications	Supreme Court	Court of Last Resort	Supreme Court	Reprimand is published if approved by Supreme Court
Kentucky	Judicial Conduct Commission	Judicial Conduct Commission	Court of Last Resort	Judicial Conduct Commission	Once the judge has responded to the formal charges
Louisiana	Judiciary Commission	Supreme Court	No appeal	Supreme Court	The lodging of the record of proceedings and a recommendation by the Judiciary Commission to the Supreme Court
Maine	Committee on Judicial Responsibility and Disability	Supreme Judicial Court	No appeal	Supreme Court	Filing of report to Supreme Judicial Court
Maryland	Commission on Judicial Disabilities	Commission on Judicial Disabilities	Court of Last Resort	Court of Appeals	Unless confidential, upon filing of a response (or expiration of the time for filing a response) with the Commission
Massachusetts	Commission on Judicial Conduct	Supreme Judicial Court	No appeal	Supreme Judicial Court	Supreme Judicial Court

See footnotes at end of table.

JUDICIAL DISCIPLINE: INVESTIGATING AND ADJUDICATING BODIES—Continued

State or other jurisdiction	Investigating body	Adjudicating body	Appeals from adjudication are filed with:	Final disciplining body	Point at which reprimands are made public
Michigan	Judicial Tenure Commission	Supreme Court	Court of Last Resort	Supreme Court	Filing of formal complaint by commission with Supreme Court or upon filing in the Supreme Court a consent resolution to a matter
Minnesota	Board on Judicial Standards	Supreme Court	No appeal	Supreme Court	Filing of formal charges by committee with Supreme Court
Mississippi	Commission on Judicial Performance	Supreme Court	No appeal	Supreme Court	Recommendation of Commission to Supreme Court
Missouri	Commission on Retirement, Removal and Discipline	Commission on Retirement, Removal and Discipline	Court of Last Resort	Supreme Court	Filing of recommendation by Committee to Supreme Court
Montana	Judicial Standards Commission	Supreme Court	No appeal	Supreme Court	Filing of record by Committee with Supreme Court
Nebraska	Commission on Judicial Qualification	Supreme Court	No appeal	Supreme Court	Commission may issue a public reprimand
Nevada	Commission on Judicial Discipline	Commission on Judicial Discipline	Court of Last Resort	Commission on Judicial Discipline	Discretion of the Commission, upon filing of report by Committee and service upon judge
New Hampshire	Supreme Court Committee on Judicial Conduct	Supreme Court	No appeal	Supreme Court	On issuance of reprimand
New Jersey	Advisory Committee on Judicial Conduct	Supreme Court	No appeal	Supreme Court	When reprimand is filed by Supreme Court
New Mexico	Judicial Standards Commission	Supreme Court	No appeal	Supreme Court	Upon recommendation of Commission to Supreme Court
New York	Commission on Judicial Conduct	Commission on Judicial Conduct	Court of Last Resort	Commission on Judicial Conduct and Court of Appeals	After a hearing at which a judge is admonished, censured, removed or retired, and after the judge is served
North Carolina	Judicial Standards Commission	Supreme Court	No appeal	Supreme Court	Public imposition of disciplinary action by the Supreme Court
North Dakota	Commission on Judicial Conduct	Supreme Court	No appeal	Supreme Court	At formal hearing
Ohio	Office of Disciplinary Counsel	Board of Commissioners on Grievance and Discipline	Court of Last Resort	Supreme Court	Adjudication
Oklahoma	Court on the Judiciary Trial Division Council	Court on the Judiciary Trial Division; Council on Judicial Complaints	Court on the Judiciary Division: no appeal from Council on Judicial Complaints	Court on the Judiciary Appellate Division	Filing with clerk of the appellate court
Oregon	Commission on Judicial Fitness and Disability	Supreme Court	No appeal	Supreme Court	Allegations become public when the commission issues a notice of public hearing
Pennsylvania	Judicial Conduct Board	Court of Judicial Discipline	Court of Last Resort	Supreme Court	Once a final decision has been made
Rhode Island	Commission on Judicial Tenure and Discipline	Supreme Court	No appeal	Supreme Court	Unless private, after the commission files its recommendation with the Chief Justice
South Carolina	Commission on Judicial Conduct	Supreme Court	No appeal	Supreme Court	Adjudication
South Dakota	Judicial Qualifications Commission	Supreme Court	No appeal	Supreme Court	Filing with the Supreme Court
Tennessee	Board of Judicial Conduct	Board of Judicial Conduct	Court of Last Resort	General Assembly	Filing formal charges with Board of Judicial Conduct
Texas	State Commission on Judicial Conduct	State Commission on Judicial Conduct (d)	Court of Last Resort	Special Court of Review	When issued by the Commission

See footnotes at end of table.

JUDICIAL DISCIPLINE: INVESTIGATING AND ADJUDICATING BODIES — Continued

State or other jurisdiction	Investigating body	Adjudicating body	Appeals from adjudication are filed with:	Final disciplining body	Point at which reprimands are made public
Utah..................	Judicial Conduct Commission	Judicial Conduct Commission (e)	Court of Last Resort	Supreme Court	10 days after filing appeal
Vermont	Judicial Conduct Board	Supreme Court	Court of Last Resort	Supreme Court	Supreme Court
Virginia	Judicial Inquiry and Review Commission	Supreme Court	Court of Last Resort	Supreme Court	Filing of formal complaint by Commission with Supreme Court
Washington............	Commission on Judicial Conduct	Commission on Judicial Conduct	Supreme Court	Supreme Court	At termination of proceeding in CJC
West Virginia	Judicial Investigation Commission	Judicial Hearing Board	Court of Last Resort	Supreme Court of Appeals	Upon decision by Supreme Court of Appeals
Wisconsin	Judicial Commission	Supreme Court	No appeal	Supreme Court	Filing of formal complaint with Supreme Court
Wyoming	Commission on Judicial Conduct and Ethics	Supreme Court	No appeal	Supreme Court or Special Supreme Court	Upon the recommendation of the Conduct and Ethics Commission and Order of the Supreme Court
Dist. of Columbia.......	Commission on Judicial Disabilities and Tenure	Commission on Judicial Disabilities and Tenure	Chief Justice of U.S. Supreme Court	Commission on Judicial Disabilities and Tenure	Public reprimands are issued with the judge's consent; orders of involuntary removal become public upon filing with the D.C. Court of Appeals
Puerto Rico	Judicial Discipline Commission	Supreme Court	No appeal	Supreme Court	Filing of formal complaint to the Judicial Discipline Commission

Sources: S. Strickland, R. Schauffler, R. LaFountain and K. Holt, eds. *State Court Organization.* Last updated April 4, 2016. National Center for State Courts. *www.ncsc.org/sco.*

Key:

N.A. — Not applicable

(a) Public admonishments or public censures are sent to the judge describing the improper conduct and stating the findings made by the commission; these notices are made available to the press and the general public.

(b) For suspensions in excess of 1 year or removal from office, the Judicial Review Council makes a recommendation and the Supreme Court makes the decision.

(c) The Judicial Qualifications Commission investigates and makes recommendations to the Supreme Court for discipline or removal. The Commission has the authority to issue sanctions, but recommendations of removal must be brought before the Supreme Court.

(d) Decision by the conduct commission cannot be implemented until reviewed and approved by the Supreme Court.

Chapter Six

ELECTIONS

How America's Diversity Explosion Is Changing the Political Landscape

By William H. Frey

The sweeping diversity explosion now underway in the U.S. will continue to impact the political landscape as the racial profiles of the electorate and voters continue to change.[1] Testament to this is the election of the nation's first black president, Barack Obama, which can be attributed, in large part, to a growing minority electorate both nationally and in previously Republican-leaning Sun Belt states. This article reviews the nation's new racial demographic shifts with an eye to how it has changed the electorate and outcomes of the past three presidential elections, and suggesting what it may mean for the future.

Rising Racial Diversity Among the U.S. Population and Voters

The increased growth of new minorities—Hispanics and Asians and persons of two or more races—has begun to make its mark on the nation's electorate by reducing the white portion of total voters. As recently as the 1980 presidential election, racial minorities comprised less than 10 percent of voters, compared with fully 26 percent in 2012. Yet the minority share of voters was still lower than its share of the total U.S. population, which was 37 percent.

The reason for this discrepancy between the racial makeup of voters and the population might be termed a "voter representation gap." A large part

of this gap for Hispanics and Asians is attributable to two factors. First, compared with whites, more Hispanics in America are under 18 years of age and are, therefore, too young to vote. Second, even among those Hispanics and Asians who are old enough to vote, a smaller share have become citizens, even if they reside in the United States legally.

As a consequence, the portion of all Hispanics and Asians who are eligible to vote—citizens age 18 and above—constituted only about one-half or less of their total populations. (See Figure A.) This contrasts with blacks and whites, of whom 69 percent and 79 percent of their respective populations were eligible to vote.

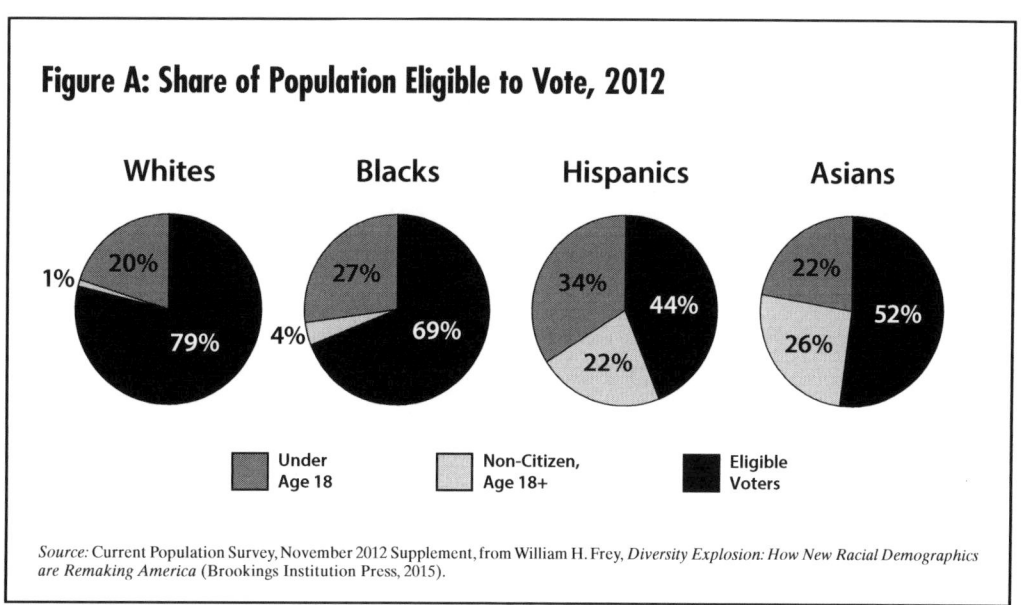

Figure A: Share of Population Eligible to Vote, 2012

Whites — 1%, 20%, 79%
Blacks — 27%, 4%, 69%
Hispanics — 34%, 22%, 44%
Asians — 22%, 26%, 52%

Legend: Under Age 18 | Non-Citizen, Age 18+ | Eligible Voters

Source: Current Population Survey, November 2012 Supplement, from William H. Frey, *Diversity Explosion: How New Racial Demographics are Remaking America* (Brookings Institution Press, 2015).

Figure B: U.S. Total and Eligible Voter Population by Race-Ethnicity, 2004–2012

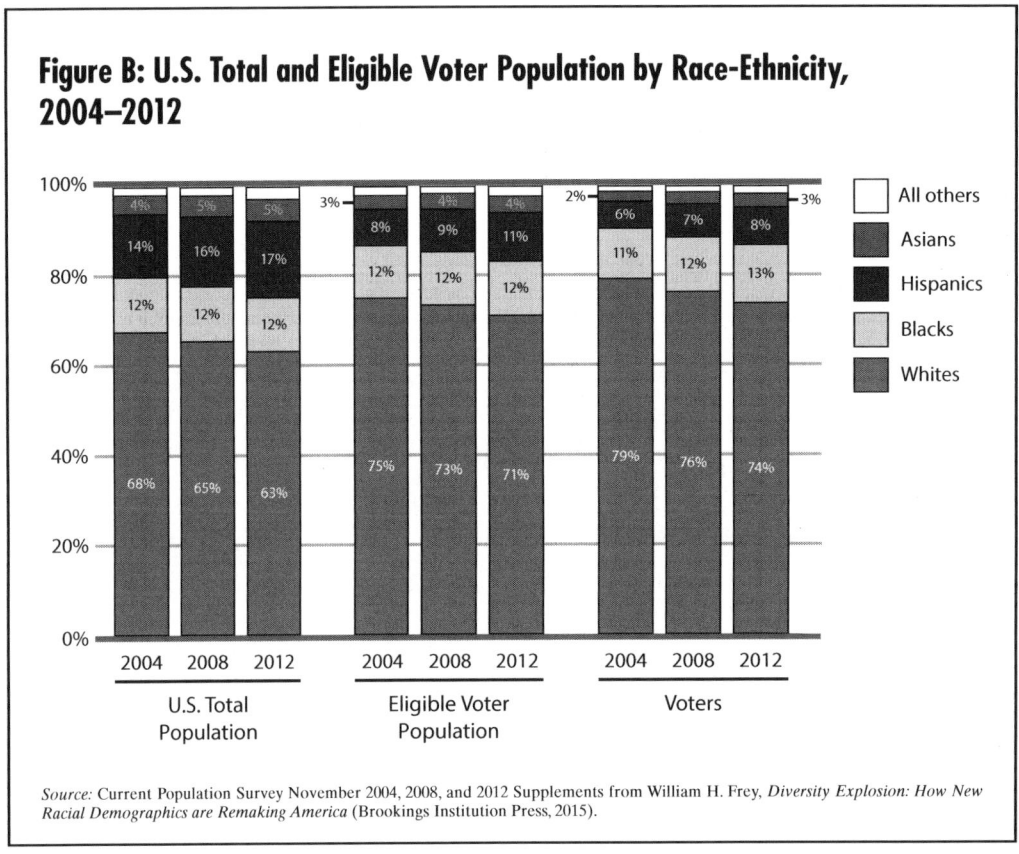

Source: Current Population Survey November 2004, 2008, and 2012 Supplements from William H. Frey, *Diversity Explosion: How New Racial Demographics are Remaking America* (Brookings Institution Press, 2015).

Figure B illustrates the lag in translating the Hispanic and Asian representation in the total population (left panel) to the population that is eligible to vote (middle panel). For example, the Hispanic portion of the total population increased from 14 to 17 percent between the 2004 and 2012 elections. Yet, its portion of eligible voters increased from just 8 to 11 percent, respectively. In contrast, whites are more highly represented among eligible voters compared with the total population (71 percent versus 63 percent in 2012).

The representation gap for Hispanics and Asians that existed between the total population and eligible voters is even further widened among *actual* voters (Figure B, third panel). This is because, compared with whites and blacks, fewer Hispanics and Asians who are eligible to vote actually show up at the polls. Because of their recent residence status or lack of information, Hispanics and Asians are less likely to register to vote and to cast ballots. Thus, Hispanics represented only 8 percent of voters in the 2012 presidential election despite constituting more than twice that share of the population. Whites, on the other hand, are far more highly represented among voters than in the population as a whole.

Higher Minority Turnout Impacted the 2008 and 2012 Popular Vote

Although the nation's electorate still lags behind its population with respect to its racial makeup, the minority population made the difference in electing Barack Obama in the 2008 and 2012 presidential elections. A key reason for this was the improved turnout of racial minorities, which magnified their clout among voters.

Minority turnout is important for Democrats in presidential elections. Since the mid-1960s, minorities (as a whole) favored Democrats and whites favored Republicans for president in the national popular vote. The black population has shown the most consistent voting patterns, favoring Democratic presidential candidates since the 1936 second-term election of Franklin D. Roosevelt. While not as

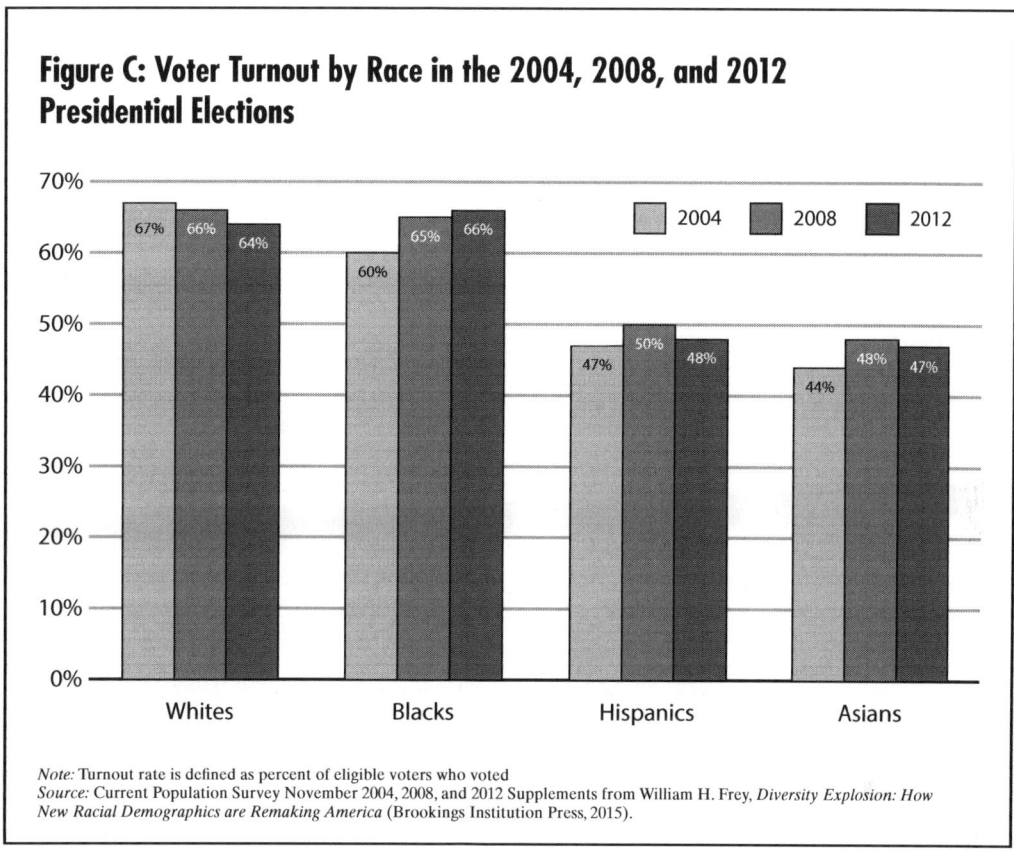

Figure C: Voter Turnout by Race in the 2004, 2008, and 2012 Presidential Elections

Legend: 2004, 2008, 2012

Whites: 67%, 66%, 64%
Blacks: 60%, 65%, 66%
Hispanics: 47%, 50%, 48%
Asians: 44%, 48%, 47%

Note: Turnout rate is defined as percent of eligible voters who voted
Source: Current Population Survey November 2004, 2008, and 2012 Supplements from William H. Frey, *Diversity Explosion: How New Racial Demographics are Remaking America* (Brookings Institution Press, 2015).

strongly favoring Democrats as blacks, Hispanics and Asians also have voted primarily for Democratic candidates in recent elections.

The higher voter turnout of minorities in 2008 and 2012 is shown in Figure C. Black voter turnout increased to a point where nearly two-thirds of black eligible voters cast ballots in 2008 and 2012. Along with the decline in white voter turnout, the 2012 black voter turnout exceeded white voter turnout for the first time since such statistics have been recorded. Although lower than voter turnout for blacks, Hispanic and Asian turnouts were higher in both Obama elections than in 2004. This higher turnout among all three groups enlarged the size and effect of these voters on the final election outcome.

Obama's two victories followed the 2004 election in which Republican George W. Bush was reelected by 3 million votes—gaining a net of 16 million white votes and losing 13 million minorities. In the subsequent two elections, Obama versus John McCain in 2008 and Obama versus Mitt Romney in 2012,

the sizes of minority gains rose to 21 million, and then 23 million votes, respectively. Meanwhile, Republicans showed a decline in white gains, down to just 12 million in 2008, before registering an insufficient gain of 18 million votes in 2012.

Obama's continued gains in the minority vote were attributable, in part, to the rise in the portion of eligible voters who were minorities (shown in Figure B). But it was also attributable to higher turnout rates for minorities—increasing their share of all voters—as well as the stronger tendency for these minorities to vote Democratic.[2]

Race and the Nation's Battleground States

The increased minority influence on the popular vote outcomes of the 2008 and 2012 elections were magnified in the Electoral College vote outcomes as the nation's racial demographic shifts dispersed across regions and states. In particular, the Sun Belt region is becoming part of an enlarged battleground of states as minorities become increasingly represented there.

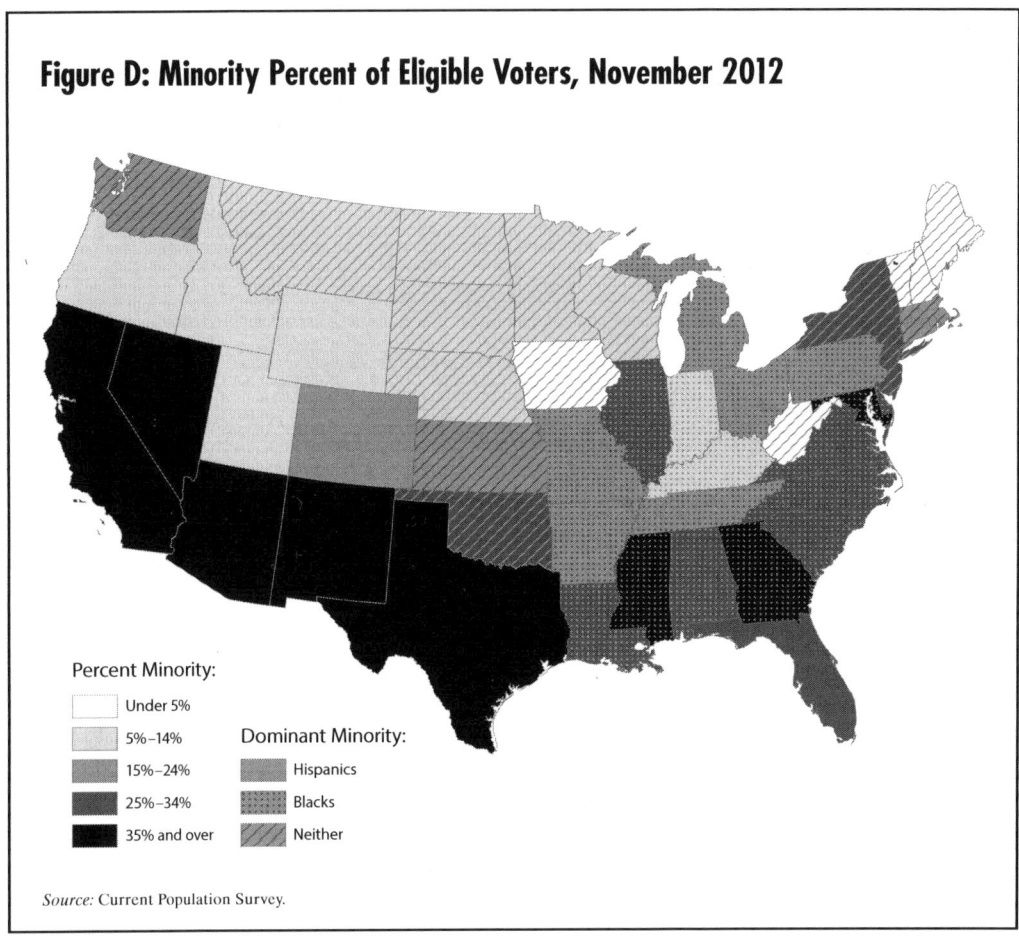

Figure D: Minority Percent of Eligible Voters, November 2012

Percent Minority:

- Under 5%
- 5%–14%
- 15%–24%
- 25%–34%
- 35% and over

Dominant Minority:

- Hispanics
- Blacks
- Neither

Source: Current Population Survey.

Figure D portrays the racial makeup of eligible voters by state at the time of the 2012 election. Clearly, racial minorities make up a sizable presence in many states including those not in traditional coastal settlement areas. Minorities constitute nearly one-half or more of the electorates in Hawaii, New Mexico, California, Texas and D.C., and at least one-third or more in a swath of additional states in the South and interior West. (See Table C.)

Hispanics embody substantial and increasing portions of the electorates in many Western states as well as Connecticut, Florida, New Jersey, New York and Texas. The Hispanic population may soon approach the black population in electoral clout. Minorities constitute more than one-quarter of the electorate in most Southern states and blacks are the largest group except in Florida, Oklahoma and Texas. Blacks still dominate the small minority populations in whiter heartland states such as

Michigan, Ohio and Pennsylvania, though their much smaller Hispanic populations are rising as in other parts of that region.

Although the nation's electorate is still divided somewhat between whiter heartland states and heavily minority coastal states, states in the Sun Belt stand in the forefront of racial electorate change. These include fast-growing Western interior states that are receiving Hispanics and other minorities, and prosperous Southern states that are attracting blacks along with Hispanics from other regions.

The geographic dispersion of new minorities and southward migration of blacks advantage the Democrats by enlarging the number of available battleground states. This allowed Democrats to cut into a new electoral turf that Republicans held steadily for a long period, and these trends should pave the way for new state battlegrounds in the future.

Figure E: States Won by Democratic and Republican Candidates, 2004, 2008, 2012

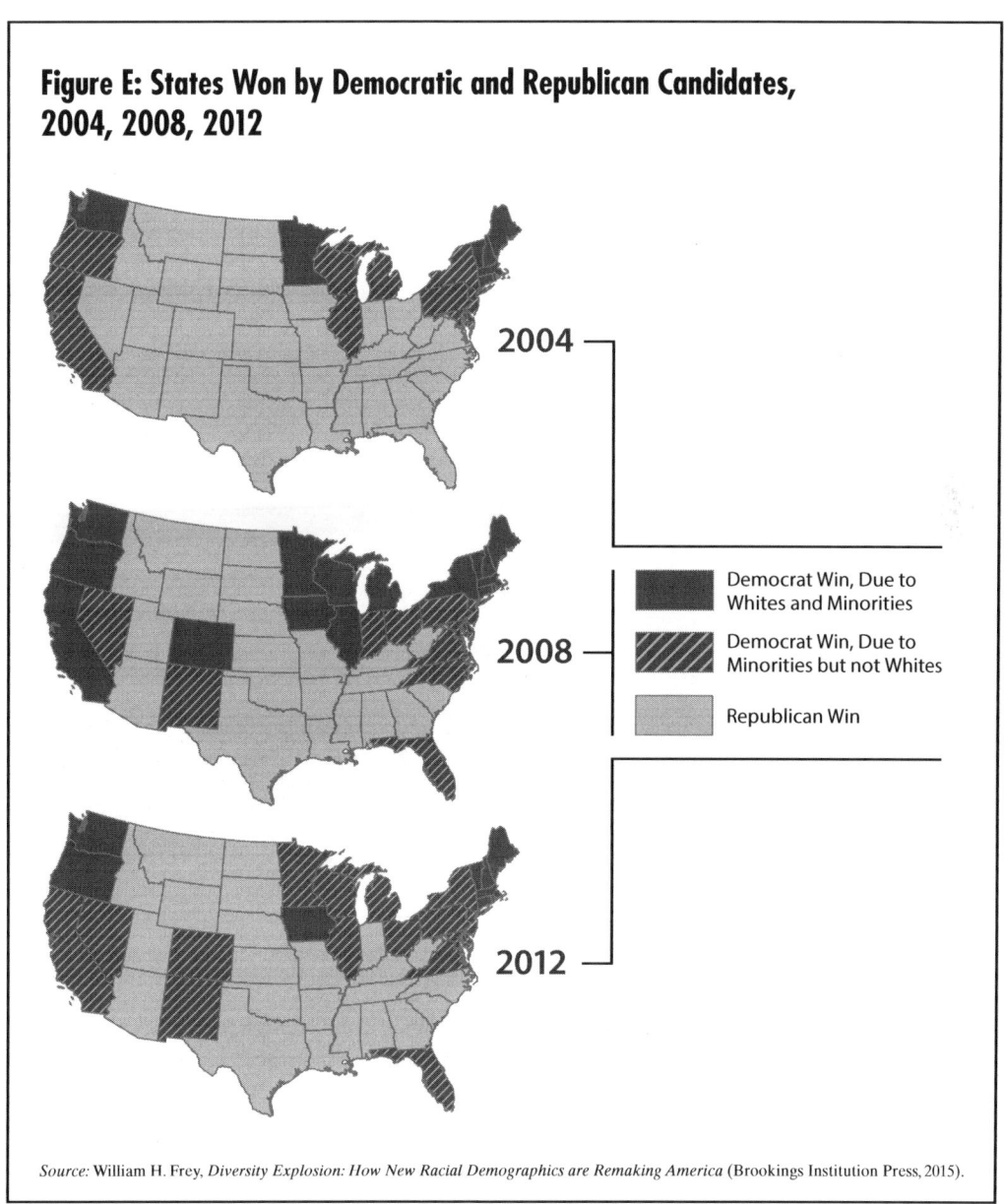

Source: William H. Frey, *Diversity Explosion: How New Racial Demographics are Remaking America* (Brookings Institution Press, 2015).

In the 2004 election, as in the election four years earlier, George W. Bush won by taking a nearly clean sweep of the interior West and South, along with Great Plains and several Northern states—most notably Ohio—that were then dubbed battlegrounds (See Figure E). This Sun Belt sweep was not new to Republicans. Although they lost some Sun Belt states when Southerner Bill Clinton ran in the three-way elections of 1992 and 1996, and when Southerner Jimmy Carter ran in 1976 and 1980, Republicans held fairly firm control of the South since the Civil Rights years when white Southerners started voting in large numbers for Republican candidates. With very few exceptions, the mostly white conservative-leaning interior West states voted for Republicans continuously from 1968 to 2004, aside from the three-way elections of the 1990s.

Table A: States with Largest Voter Representation Gaps, November 2012

	Minority percent of		
State	Population	Voters	Difference
Arizona.....................	48	28	-20
California	60	43	-17
Texas.........................	58	41	-17
New Mexico	58	43	-15
Nevada.....................	47	33	-14

*Difference between Racial Minority Percent of Voters and Racial Minority Percent of Population in November 2012.

Source: U.S. Census Current Population Survey, November Supplement 2012 (compiled from Public Use Microfile).

The Democratic strongholds for the two elections prior to 2008 consisted of urbanized, racially diverse coastal states such as California and New York and a swath of New England, Northeastern, and Midwestern states with industrial or farming histories. Although these states held constituencies reflecting both new and old strengths of the party—minorities, union workers, progressive professionals and women—they did not represent the most rapidly growing parts of the country.

This geographic map changed with both the 2008 and 2012 elections owing to the changing racial demographics of a number of New Sun Belt states. This can be seen in Figure E, which shows that, in contrast to 2004, Obama won new West and South battleground states of Colorado, Florida, Nevada, New Mexico, Virginia and, in 2008, North Carolina.

The effect of the changing demography along with the heightened minority enthusiasm for Obama is illustrated in Nevada. In 2004, Nevada's voters were 80 percent white, 8 percent Hispanic, 6 percent black, and 6 percent Asian or another race. Nevada's white share dropped to 73 percent in 2008 and to 67 percent in 2012 such that, in the latter year, the voters included 15 percent Hispanics, 9 percent blacks, and 9 percent Asians or another race. Aside from demographics alone, the Democratic voting margins (percent voting Democrat minus percent voting Republican) continued to increase particularly for Hispanics from 21 in 2004 to 54 in 2008 and 47 in 2012.

Shifts in this direction were evident in most of the other Sun Belt states that Obama won in 2008, where a rise in the minority Democratic vote overcame the Republican white vote. (See Table B) For most of these South and West battleground states (North Carolina is the exception), Obama's minority support was strong enough to overcome an increased white Republican margin in 2012. This was especially crucial in Florida, where the white Republican margin increased from 14 to 24 between 2008 and 2012. But due to a larger minority turnout and increased Democratic margins, Obama won this key battleground state again.

Racial minorities were responsible for winning five Southern and Western states designated as "battlegrounds" in 2008 (Florida, Nevada, New Mexico, North Carolina and Virginia) and a similar number in 2012 (excluding North Carolina but including Colorado)—besting the white Republican advantages for these states. This means that the growth of Hispanics, Asians and other new minorities as well as the southward migration of blacks was opening the door to greater future Democratic prospects in the Sun Belt.

Among such states are Arizona and Texas, which are among the five states with the highest minority voter representation gaps, (See Table A) due largely to their substantial and younger Hispanic populations. While both states have voted solidly Republican in past elections, this could change if current race-related Republican and Democratic voting proclivities continue. In these and other states, this representation gap should eventually close—albeit gradually. The "too young to vote" share of the Hispanic population is projected to decrease over time and, as more in the population turn 18, it has been estimated that they will add up to one million new voting-age Hispanic citizens annually for the foreseeable future.[3]

Moreover, the ceiling for greater "new minority" voter participation will increase for two reasons. First, there will be higher rates of naturalization among Hispanic and Asian permanent residents who are eligible to become citizens. Naturalized citizenship rates have increased in recent years, though there is room for further growth. Second, voter turnout rates among Hispanics and Asians, discussed below, will increase as members of these communities become more familiar with registration and voting practices with the help of local government and civic organizations.

It is highly likely that the continued dispersion of minorities to many of the interior Sun Belt states will continue into the future. This would make the longstanding "solid Republican" South and much of the Mountain West become more open to gains by Democrats.[4]

Table B: State Minority Percentages of Total Population, Eligible Voters and Voters, 2004, 2008 and 2012

State or other jurisdiction	Total population			Eligible voters			Voters		
	2004	2008	2012	2004	2008	2012	2004	2008	2012
Alabama	30	30	34	27	27	29	26	27	29
Alaska	28	31	35	23	27	29	18	19	22
Arizona	43	42	48	27	30	35	19	22	28
Arkansas	24	23	28	19	18	21	16	15	17
California	56	58	60	43	45	49	35	40	43
Colorado	29	28	29	19	19	21	13	15	16
Connecticut	22	27	29	16	20	23	13	14	19
Delaware	29	32	35	24	25	27	19	22	24
Florida	37	38	43	28	31	34	24	29	33
Georgia	39	42	45	32	36	38	30	36	38
Hawaii	82	81	82	79	77	77	72	72	70
Idaho	18	17	19	11	12	10	5	8	7
Illinois	31	34	35	24	25	27	22	22	27
Indiana	15	16	16	12	11	12	11	10	12
Iowa	9	13	14	5	7	8	4	6	6
Kansas	20	21	24	12	15	16	9	12	11
Kentucky	11	12	13	9	9	10	9	9	9
Louisiana	37	39	38	32	34	34	31	32	35
Maine	4	6	6	4	5	4	4	4	3
Maryland	39	43	46	33	36	37	30	37	37
Massachusetts	19	22	27	13	15	19	9	11	16
Michigan	22	22	24	18	18	20	17	18	18
Minnesota	13	15	16	9	9	10	8	7	9
Mississippi	41	40	43	37	37	38	39	38	40
Missouri	18	18	19	15	14	15	15	15	15
Montana	11	10	13	7	8	10	5	7	8
Nebraska	18	16	18	11	10	11	7	7	8
Nevada	35	41	47	24	30	35	20	27	33
New Hampshire	6	6	10	4	5	6	3	4	5
New Jersey	34	41	41	25	32	32	23	29	30
New Mexico	56	60	58	50	52	50	44	45	43
New York	38	39	43	30	31	34	24	27	33
North Carolina	33	33	36	26	26	28	25	25	31
North Dakota	7	14	16	6	11	12	4	10	9
Ohio	17	19	19	14	15	15	14	15	17
Oklahoma	28	31	36	23	24	30	19	22	25
Oregon	16	21	22	10	13	14	7	10	11
Pennsylvania	16	18	21	13	14	16	11	13	15
Rhode Island	19	19	25	11	13	16	8	11	15
South Carolina	33	33	34	29	29	30	27	31	31
South Dakota	10	12	17	6	8	13	4	5	9
Tennessee	22	24	24	17	19	20	16	19	21
Texas	52	56	58	42	45	48	34	37	41
Utah	13	15	21	7	10	14	4	5	8
Vermont	5	5	7	4	3	5	3	3	5
Virginia	31	33	34	25	26	27	19	26	26
Washington	25	24	28	17	19	21	14	14	18
West Virginia	6	5	6	5	4	4	4	4	4
Wisconsin	15	17	17	10	11	12	9	9	11
Wyoming	10	11	14	8	8	11	6	6	6
Dist. of Columbia	69	68	63	64	64	57	59	60	57

Source: U.S. Census Current Population Survey, November Supplement, 2004, 2008, 2012 (compiled from Public Use Microfiles).

Table C: State Racial Compositions of Total Population, Eligible Voters and Voters, November 2012 (Percentages)

State or other jurisdiction	Total population				Eligible voters				Voters			
	White	Black	Hispanic	Other	White	Black	Hispanic	Other	White	Black	Hispanic	Other
Alabama	66	26	4	4	71	26	1	3	71	26	0	3
Alaska	65	3	6	26	71	4	4	21	78	2	2	18
Arizona	52	3	35	10	65	4	23	9	72	4	17	7
Arkansas	72	15	8	5	79	15	3	3	83	14	1	2
California	40	5	40	15	51	7	28	15	57	7	23	13
Colorado	71	4	21	5	79	3	14	4	84	2	10	3
Connecticut	71	10	12	7	77	9	9	5	81	9	7	3
Delaware	65	21	10	5	73	20	4	3	76	19	2	2
Florida	57	15	24	4	66	14	17	4	67	13	17	3
Georgia	55	31	8	6	62	30	4	4	62	32	3	3
Hawaii	18	2	11	69	23	2	8	68	30	2	5	62
Idaho	81	1	14	4	90	0	6	3	93	0	4	3
Illinois	65	14	14	7	73	14	9	4	73	17	5	4
Indiana	84	9	4	3	88	8	3	1	88	9	2	1
Iowa	86	3	7	5	92	2	3	3	94	2	2	2
Kansas	76	6	11	8	84	5	5	5	89	4	3	4
Kentucky	87	7	3	3	90	6	1	2	91	7	1	2
Louisiana	62	31	4	3	66	30	2	2	65	31	2	2
Maine	94	1	1	4	96	1	1	3	97	1	1	2
Maryland	54	28	9	9	63	28	4	5	63	29	4	4
Massachusetts	73	6	11	9	81	6	7	6	84	6	6	5
Michigan	76	13	5	6	80	13	3	3	82	13	3	2
Minnesota	84	5	4	7	90	3	2	4	91	3	2	4
Mississippi	57	37	2	4	62	35	1	2	60	39	0	1
Missouri	81	12	4	3	85	11	2	2	85	11	2	2
Montana	87	1	2	10	90	0	2	8	92	0	1	6
Nebraska	82	4	9	4	89	3	5	3	92	4	3	2
Nevada	53	8	28	11	65	9	17	10	67	9	15	9
New Hampshire	90	1	4	4	94	1	2	2	95	1	2	2
New Jersey	59	12	19	10	68	12	13	7	70	14	11	6
New Mexico	42	2	43	13	50	3	38	9	57	3	35	5
New York	57	15	18	11	66	15	12	7	67	17	11	5
North Carolina	64	21	10	5	72	22	3	4	69	26	2	3
North Dakota	84	1	3	12	88	1	3	8	91	1	2	7
Ohio	81	12	3	4	85	11	2	2	83	13	2	2
Oklahoma	64	7	8	20	70	7	5	18	75	7	3	15
Oregon	78	2	10	10	86	1	4	9	89	1	3	7
Pennsylvania	79	10	6	4	84	10	4	2	85	10	3	2
Rhode Island	75	6	14	5	84	5	8	3	85	6	7	2
South Carolina	66	27	4	3	70	27	1	2	69	29	1	2
South Dakota	83	1	3	13	87	1	2	10	91	0	1	8
Tennessee	76	15	6	4	80	15	3	2	79	16	3	2
Texas	42	12	41	6	52	13	30	5	59	15	22	4
Utah	79	1	14	5	86	1	8	4	92	1	5	2
Vermont	93	1	2	5	95	1	1	3	95	1	1	3
Virginia	66	19	7	8	73	19	3	6	74	19	3	5
Washington	72	3	11	14	79	3	6	12	82	2	4	11
West Virginia	94	3	1	2	96	2	1	1	96	3	1	1
Wisconsin	83	6	6	5	88	5	4	3	89	6	2	3
Wyoming	86	1	9	4	89	1	6	4	94	1	3	2
Dist. of Columbia	37	48	11	5	43	49	4	4	43	49	4	3

Source: U.S. Census Current Population Survey, November Supplement, 2012 (compiled from Public Use Microfiles).

Still, this longer-term prognostication makes some strong assumptions. First, that longstanding white, Republican preferences and minority, Democratic preferences continue into the future. Second, that many of the nation's industrial Midwest states, which will continue to remain "whiter" than the rest of the country, shall remain Democratic.

At least in the short term, the latter assumption may not hold, given that recent Democratic wins were fairly small in Ohio and Pennsylvania, and that Republicans could also be competitive in Iowa and Wisconsin and perhaps Michigan. This is because largely white Republican-leaning baby boomers and seniors could turnout heavily for a popular candidate in these states and could, at least in the short run, counter the growing Democratic-leaning minority populations in the Sun Belt. Still, in the long run, both parties will come to recognize that the larger minority shares of the electorate will not only continue but also need to be reckoned with by adjusting their messages and policy agendas appropriately.

Notes

[1] William H. Frey, *Diversity Explosion: How New Racial Demographics are Remaking America* (Brookings Institution Press, 2015).

[2] William H. Frey, "Minority Turnout Determined the 2012 Election" (Washington DC: Brookings Institution, May 10, 2013). *http://www.brookings.edu/research/papers/2013/05/10-election-2012-minority-voter-turnout-frey.*

[3] Pew Research Center, "An Awakened Giant: The Hispanic Electorate is Likely to Double by 2030." (Washington DC: Pew Hispanic Center, November 14, 2012), p. 7. *http://www.pewhispanic.org/files/2012/11/hispanic_vote_likely_to_double_by_2030_11-14-12.pdf.*

[4] See William H. Frey, Ruy Teixeira and Robert Griffin, "America's Electoral Future: How Changing Demographics Could Impact Presidential Elections from 2016 to 2032" (Washington DC: Center for American Progress, American Enterprise Institute, Brookings Institution, February 2016). *http://www.brookings.edu/~/media/Research/Files/Reports/2016/02/25-states-of-change-frey/SOC2016report.pdf?la=en.*

About the author

William H. Frey is a senior fellow with the Brookings Institution and research professor in population studies at the University of Michigan. An expert on U.S. demographics and American political demographics, he is author of *Diversity Explosion: How New Racial Demographics are Remaking America* (Brookings Institution Press, 2015).

Voters are Marketplace Consumers

By Matt Boehmer

The American public expects customer service in their everyday activities and voters are no exception. The election community has an opportunity to improve the absentee voting process for military and overseas citizens by communicating to them at each stage of progression toward a counted ballot. Adopting this practice can help empower a set of voters who may otherwise have serious doubts about their votes being counted.

In today's world, Americans expect excellent customer service during their everyday experiences. They expect to find the product or information they need quickly, to be provided simple instructions on completing a task and receive confirmation of its completion. This includes the voting process—particularly for military and overseas voters.

Most people do not think of the Department of Defense, or DoD, when discussing the topic of voting. It may not even occur to some service members that DOD's Federal Voting Assistance Program, or FVAP, exists to provide voting assistance to military personnel, their eligible family members and overseas citizens. FVAP works to ensure that they are aware of their right to vote and have the tools and resources to successfully do so from anywhere in the world.

Unique Challenges

What is particular about this set of voters and the assistance they require? Military and overseas voters face unique challenges, namely: mobility, time and complexity.

Military families are highly mobile. They might move every two or three years, and submitting a new registration and ballot request may not top their list of priorities. FVAP has inserted address-update reminders into the automated change-of-duty-station process and is working continually to improve education and outreach efforts informing these citizens of the importance of keeping their contact information current with election officials. FVAP also has created videos aimed at younger voters to educate them on the importance of updating their address regularly.

While the 2009 amendments to the Uniformed and Overseas Citizens Absentee Voting Act, or UOCAVA, largely addressed the time issue by requiring states to offer electronic blank ballot delivery—cutting the round-trip transit time of mailed ballot delivery in half—complexity remains an obstacle.

The process is relatively simple for an individual voter, but can be complex when considering the absentee voting system as a whole. Every state and territory has different requirements and deadlines regarding the treatment and processing of applications and ballots. That is why it is important FVAP continues its work with election officials. A successfully cast ballot is a transaction between the voter and his or her local or state government—and focusing on one without the other does not make sense. FVAP maintains current state information and policies on its website, *FVAP.gov*.

Absentee Ballots Don't Count?

FVAP conducts surveys of active duty military members following each regularly scheduled general election. The 2014 data indicate that 67 percent of military personnel were not confident that their ballot would be counted during the election, and 35 percent thought the voting process was too hard or did not know how to get their ballot.[1] FVAP's qualitative research efforts also validate that key finding: many voters believe that either their ballot will not count once it arrives, or that it will not actually make it to its destination. This perception is exaggerated among overseas voters who feel more disconnected from the U.S. and find it hard to believe that their ballot will make it all the way back home and will actually be counted.[2] FVAP and the election community must do more to dispel myths surrounding absentee voting.

Take a Lesson from Online Retail

The American public expects customer service, especially online. It is not even something that consumers consider to be extraordinary; it is simply an expectation. Americans expect to find the product or information they need quickly, to be provided simple instructions on completing their order, and receive status updates and confirmation of its completion. Military and overseas voters are accustomed

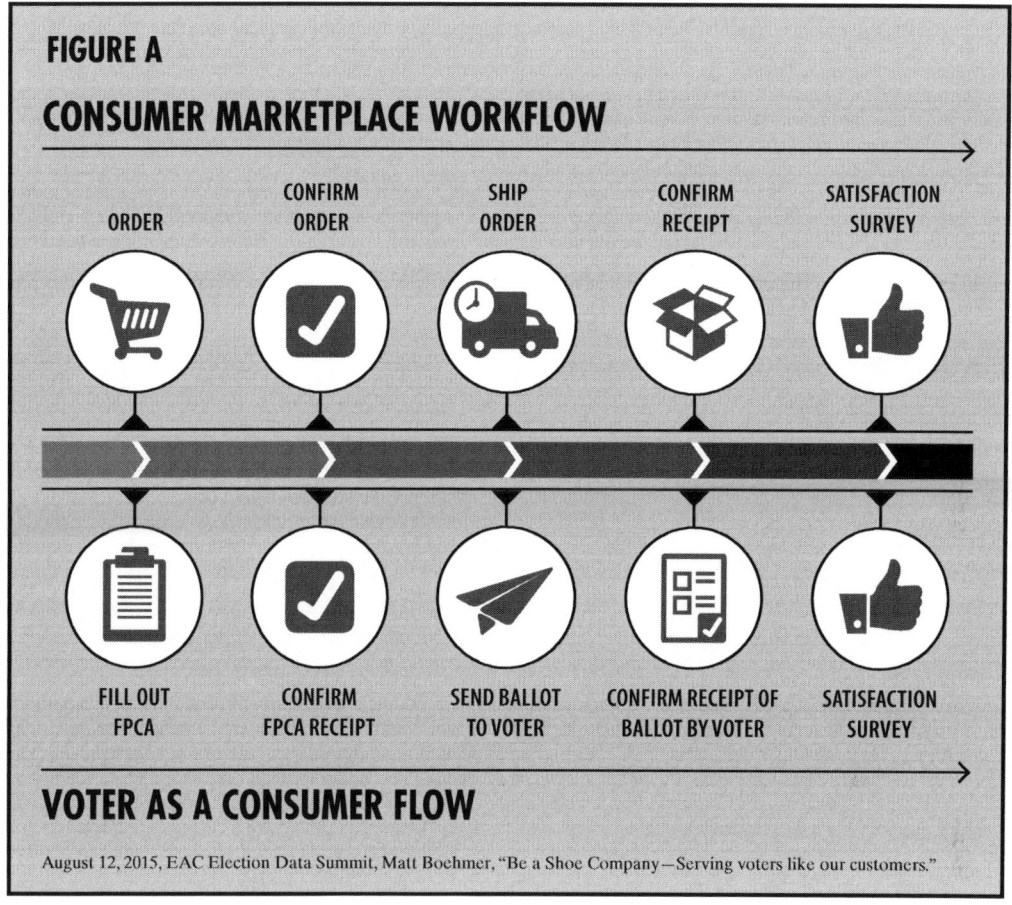

FIGURE A

CONSUMER MARKETPLACE WORKFLOW

| ORDER | CONFIRM ORDER | SHIP ORDER | CONFIRM RECEIPT | SATISFACTION SURVEY |

| FILL OUT FPCA | CONFIRM FPCA RECEIPT | SEND BALLOT TO VOTER | CONFIRM RECEIPT OF BALLOT BY VOTER | SATISFACTION SURVEY |

VOTER AS A CONSUMER FLOW

August 12, 2015, EAC Election Data Summit, Matt Boehmer, "Be a Shoe Company—Serving voters like our customers."

to this level of service as well and can become frustrated when states and localities do not communicate throughout the absentee voting process.

Zappos, an online shoe retailer, provides exceptional customer service. Tony Hsieh, CEO of Zappos, created the "WOW" philosophy—providing excellent customer service to everyone, every time, so they know exactly what to expect.[3] Communicating to customers is one aspect of this strategy. When customers order a pair of shoes, they receive status confirmations throughout the process: receipt of the order, when the order is shipped and when the shoes have been delivered.

What if the election community applied this notion of voters-as-consumers to its own business rules and processes? The data show that military and overseas voters have serious doubts about their ability to successfully participate in the country's electoral process. Why should they bother with the seemingly challenging steps if they do not believe their vote will

ultimately count? The lack of confirmation within the absentee voting process itself perpetuates this misconception; however, through a little extra effort, the election community has a real opportunity to dispel this myth and increase voter confidence.

Communication is the Key

Could simply providing updates on voters' progress during the absentee voting process assuage doubts? Would that in turn increase motivation to participate?

There are several opportunities to communicate —and instill confidence—to military and overseas voters:

- At the start of an election cycle;
- When the election office has received the Federal Post Card Application, or FPCA;
- When the election office has processed the FPCA;

- When the voter can expect to receive the blank ballot;
- When the election office has mailed/sent the blank ballot;
- When election office receives voted ballot; and
- When the vote has been counted.

The principles of consumer behavior need to be incorporated beyond the state level, and FVAP has renewed its own focus on customer service. Historically, FVAP has leveraged DoD's network of voting assistance officers. FVAP continues to work closely with the military services to train and inform voting assistance officers but it also is attempting to bridge a wide gap by communicating directly with individual voters. Rather than relying solely on the services to reach voters, FVAP created a suite of marketing and outreach materials, conducts communication campaigns and operates an internal call center. Following the 2014 election, FVAP conducted a systematic review of its materials to identify potential challenges with the language, design and organization of content. The majority of the military population is under the age of 30. To reach and communicate more effectively with this demographic, FVAP created new content tailored specifically for a generation that primarily interacts through digital and social media platforms.

Collaborating to Find Real Solutions

While FVAP has made great strides in improving its education and outreach efforts to date, it relies on collaboration with its many stakeholders to identify solutions to improve the absentee voting process. FVAP entered into a cooperative agreement in September 2013 with The Council of State Governments, or CSG, in an effort to identify ways to improve the absentee voting process and build state election administrators' and policymakers' awareness and understanding of their UOCAVA responsibilities as well as DoD's voting assistance mission. The CSG Overseas Voting Initiative was formed through the agreement and is charged with developing targeted and actionable improvements to the voting process for military and overseas citizen voters.

The CSG Overseas Voting Initiative, or OVI, created two primary working groups consisting of state and local election officials:

1. As a starting point to identify improvements, **the OVI Policy Working Group** examined the Presidential Commission on Election Adminis-

tration's military and overseas voter recommendations. Through the leadership, cooperation and dedication of the participating election officials, this effort resulted in actionable items that states can easily implement either through administrative or legislative action.

2. **The OVI Technology Working Group** is exploring the areas of performance metrics, data standardization, best practices with processing of UOCAVA ballots and the possibility for acceptance of electronic signatures from the DoD Common Access Card during the registration process. FVAP anticipates recommendations and best practices from this group following the completion of pilots and research done during the 2016 election.

When adopted by states and localities, these recommendations will have a hugely positive impact on the absentee voting process for military members, their families and overseas citizens.

One of the recommendations is directly aligned with providing customer service to voters by seizing real and immediate opportunities to improve voter communication, such as:

- Using plain language—clear, concise and accessible written and verbal communications targeting military and overseas voters at every step of the voting process;
- Using election websites and social media effectively to reach and educate these unique voters on the opportunity to vote;
- Using simple instructions on how to assemble a voted ballot package, delivered to the voter online, for return by mail to the election official. These origami-type return envelope instructions can be confusing, especially for first-time voters.
- Communicating to voters about when the ballot application is received and accepted goes a long way to easing voter concerns about their status in the process.

Better Data Equals Better Elections

Retailers like Zappos collect customer service data. Following the completion of the transaction, a consumer will receive a customer satisfaction survey that says, "Tell me about your experience as a customer. Did we deliver? Did the product meet expectation? And did we, as a company and as a brand, meet those expectations to you?"

Those in the election community are no strangers to data. Election practitioners and researchers may have different viewpoints on how to interpret data, how to collect it and the various methods for improving its quality, but everyone shares the ultimate goal: using sound data to improve elections.

Pulling together information in response to the Election Assistance Commission's Election Administration and Voting Survey, or EAVS, may initially prove challenging, but there is no question it is a critically important tool for collecting transactional data. These data need to be accurate, with emphasis placed on a common data format and data standardization. To address this, CSG has created an additional working group of election officials, the EAC and FVAP to explore content and process improvements specifically for the EAVS UOCAVA data section. Given this, however, the election community's survey repertoire is missing a key data set–attitudinal data. Knowing the quality of voters' experiences is crucial to improving them. Collecting this data provides an exciting opportunity—the coupling of transactional and attitudinal data to tell the full story that the elections community needs to hear in order to make improvements that are meaningful to voters.

At its core, the incorporation of customer service into systems also has the potential to improve the process. If customer service management systems enable the election official to understand, communicate and pull data, then they can understand the problems faced by consumers and address them in real time instead of waiting until the next election cycle to incorporate change.

We Can Do More

The election community is doing great things to reach military and overseas voters, but there is always more we can do and challenges to overcome. The election community has three distinct opportunities:

1. Educate—show the voters how to complete their absentee vote, in simple steps, delivered right to them.

2. Collect customer service data to understand the voter's experience.

3. Include customer service touchpoints during the creation of systems so that information is pushed out to the voter as much as possible during the absentee voting process.

In the consumer product brand market, if people are unsatisfied with one brand, they have the ability to simply switch to another. In the case of military and overseas voting, there is no opportunity to switch providers. If these citizens do not receive an

acceptable level of assistance, the probable outcome is that they will say it is too difficult and not vote at all. The men and women who protect and serve our country—which allows the American public to enjoy their freedoms—deserve the WOW experience, and the election community has the ability to instill confidence within the democratic process these brave citizens fight proudly to defend. We simply need to treat them like the valued customers they are.

Notes

[1] Federal Voting Assistance Program, 2014 Post-Election Voting Survey of the Active Duty Military, *https://www.fvap.gov/uploads/FVAP/Surveys/PEV51401_TabVolume.pdf*.

[2] Federal Voting Assistance Program, Uniformed and Overseas Citizens Absentee Voting Act Voting: Successes and Challenges, *https://www.fvap.gov/uploads/FVAP/Reports/FVAP_QualitativeResearch_20150731_final.pdf*.

[3] Barry Glassman, "What Zappos Taught Us about Creating the Ultimate Client Experience," *Forbes*, accessed January 29, 2016. *http://www.forbes.com/sites/advisor/2013/05/13/what-zappos-taught-us-about-creating-the-ultimate-client-experience/#1838297e6c69*.

About the Author

Matt Boehmer is director of the Department of Defense's Federal Voting Assistance Program. He administers the federal responsibilities of the Uniformed and Overseas Citizens Absentee Voting Act for the secretary of defense. With a focus on marketing communications and outreach, he works to ensure that military personnel, their families and overseas citizens are aware of their right to vote and have the tools to successfully do so—from anywhere in the world.

Modern Elections: Are We There Yet?

By Christy McCormick

The 2000 Election debacle led to the creation of the Help America Vote Act (HAVA). This article discusses whether the promise of HAVA, to modernize American elections, has been met, and reviews the current trends and innovations happening in elections across the country. The emerging technologies are making this an exciting time, but elections remain a people-driven and people-serving process, and we need to continue to encourage people to get involved as election specialists and poll workers.

Fifteen years ago, America was still reeling from the events of the 2000 presidential election: butterfly ballots, punch cards, hand recounts, magnifying glasses, hanging chads, fat chads, dimpled chads, pregnant chads, undervotes, overvotes, court battles —it was a national mess. A year later, in 2002, it resulted in Congress passing the Help America Vote Act, or HAVA, in an effort to improve voting processes and modernize election administration. HAVA came with billions of dollars, which many states used to purchase new voting systems. HAVA also created the U.S. Election Assistance Commission, or EAC, and established minimum standards for states and units of local government responsible for administering federal elections. Has it made a difference? Are U.S. elections actually any better?

The answers to these questions are yes and yes. While some immediate actions taken post-HAVA were perhaps premature, for example, the purchase of new voting systems prior to the development of the Federal Voluntary Voting Systems Guidelines, or VVSG, overall we've seen great strides. Almost all states have computerized statewide voter registration lists, the vast majority of punch card and lever machines have been replaced, voting systems allow voters to correct errors and have audit capabilities, no voter is automatically turned away from the polls and may fill out a provisional ballot, and the EAC is, after some years in the wilderness, back to assisting the states in improving the conduct of elections. But has the promise of HAVA been fulfilled? Are America's elections modernized?

To those questions, the answers are, unfortunately, no and no. While some progress has been made, voting systems are still not fully accessible for individuals with disabilities, in that they do not provide the same opportunity for access and participation as for other voters. Military and overseas citizens continue to be disenfranchised at a high rate because of logistical problems in transmitting ballots. States and the EAC have robust voting system testing and certification programs, but huge leaps in technology have occurred and the definition of what constitutes a voting system is rapidly changing. Most systems are tested under guidelines that were enacted in 2005, two years before the first Apple iPhone was released. After complaints of long lines in 2012, President Barack Obama formed the Presidential Commission on Election Administration, PCEA, which among other things reported that there is an "impending crisis in voting technology."[1] Many of the voting systems being used right now are at the end of their life cycles and no more federal money will be coming to buy the next round of machines. Voter registration and list maintenance look quite different, certainly since the National Voter Registration Act, or NVRA, was passed in 1993, but also since the passage of HAVA. Paper registration forms are getting close to being passé, and in some places, registration by the voter is going away. Bad data from motor vehicle agencies continues to be a problem. Expectations of voters have changed over the past 14 years. They expect to vote like they live the rest of their lives; they demand that the voting experience be customer-oriented (more like Amazon and Zappos), efficient, convenient and fast. And much more work has to be done to guarantee privacy and security before online voting becomes acceptable: one of the questions election officials hear most is, "When will I be able to vote on my phone?"

The good news is that interest in election administration issues has not waned since 2000. And, the phrase that Justice Louis Brandeis popularized in 1932, that a "state may, if its citizens choose, serve as a laboratory; and try novel social and economic experiments without risk to the rest of the country,"[2] is still true in the elections arena. Innovation is happening across the country and much is changing quickly, and partnerships between the states and the federal election assistance agencies are helping to spread the best ideas. It is an interesting time in the history of voting and elections.

Voting Systems Developments

Election administrators across the country saddled with old or "legacy" voting systems are working hard to sustain and maintain their machines and are taking whatever steps necessary to prevent a crisis while they wait for the opportunity to purchase new systems.[3] Fourteen years is a long lifespan for a computer; most people have replaced their personal computers several times in that time period. Some jurisdictions are purchasing new systems now; some are waiting on funding to replace systems, while others want to see what options will soon be in the market.

When the 2005 VVSG was enacted, voting systems were stand-alone machines that captured and tabulated votes, but with emerging technology, the lines of what constitutes a voting system are blurring. Los Angeles County, Calif., and Travis County, Texas, are developing their own voting systems, and while they have each approached the issue in their own way (Los Angeles County concentrating on the "voter experience" and Travis County on "vote verification"), both counties are helping to drive the conversation and development of innovative solutions in voting technology. Both those jurisdictions and many others are investing in commercial off-the-shelf, or COTS, technology as part of their voting systems. Elections administrators want to be able to add or subtract components as they need them. While the central voting and tabulating machine is still at the center of the traditional voting system, innovation is happening around that system by leaps and bounds.

Some states are employing election technology committees to explore options in voting technology.[4] Colorado's committee recently evaluated a number of voting systems piloted in several counties that allowed Colorado Secretary of State Wayne Williams to select a new system to replace its current patchwork of voting systems.[5] The selected system integrates a commercially available tablet, commercially available printer and uses regular paper. Other trends in this area include ballot-on-demand (allowing timely access to any ballot style for a given election) and ballot-marking devices (allowing components such that a voter can direct the marking of a paper ballot, have the system interpret and com-municate the selections back to the voter, and print a ballot for the voter to review and verify). While there is still a long way to go, there have been significant developments in assistive technology, including large visual display, voice input selection, improved audio options, tactile input devices and, importantly, use of the voter's own assistive technology. Prime III, an open-source, software-based assistive technology with a multimodal user interface was rolled out in New Hampshire under the name One4all for the 2016 primary.[6]

Funding new voting technology is a hot topic of discussion. Some jurisdictions, like Maryland, are leasing their equipment. Others are budgeting over time or making capital appropriation requests. Open-source software is a potential cost-saving consideration, as are non-dedicated use of COTS products and equipment sharing between jurisdictions. Without new federal funding, election administrators are putting on their creative funding hats and investigating all available options.

The EAC is providing assistance to election administrators to manage election technology. It has recently published new guides on selecting a new voting system, managing aging voting systems and considerations for implementing voting systems with COTS products.[7] The EAC also is collecting and posting requests for proposals, or RFPs, and information on e-pollbooks, so those who are in the process of purchasing new technology can see what other jurisdictions have done. In an effort to save states time and money and create efficiencies, the EAC is continuing to map state certification requirements to the federal VVSG. Last year the EAC enacted an update to the 2005 guidelines, VVSG 1.1, along with some program and laboratory manuals, opening up the standards to innovation. A long overdue new iteration of the VVSG is already underway, but it will be a challenge to craft new standards that adhere to the scope of HAVA (which was formulated before the surge in technology) continue to encourage and not deter innovation, and support ideas such as a common data format to integrate voting system components.

Pre-Election Trends

Online voter registration, or OVR, a bipartisan effort, is the hottest new development in elections. Currently, at least 30 states use OVR and at least five more are considering it in 2016.[8] Because elections officials can process online registrations in a matter of seconds, time and cost savings are a huge benefit. Errors are reduced and cleaner voting rolls result, as the voter is entering his or her most up-to-date information. Applicants find it easy because they can do it online, perhaps even on their phones, so it matches their lifestyle. Everyone wins with this trend.

Automatic voter registration, or AVR, is another development so far implemented only in Oregon. AVR is a process by which a state, utilizing data collected on its residents from DMVs or other agencies, registers persons without requiring an application. Subsequently, the state mails a notice that requires persons to opt out within a short period of time, and unless a person affirmatively declines, he or she is permanently registered. California has passed AVR legislation, but it will not fully go into effect until the state completes its statewide voter registration system. In New Jersey, a bill including AVR was vetoed by Gov. Chris Christie in late 2015.[9] AVR legislation has been proposed in a number of mostly "blue" states, and does not appear to be a bipartisan effort or based on any particular data. Whether AVR is successful and withstands scrutiny is yet to be seen.

Early voting is another trend across the nation. More than two-third of states allow voters to cast a ballot before Election Day without an excuse or justification, and of those that do allow it, periods range from four to 45 days.[10] Thirteen states only allow absentee voting if the voter can provide an acceptable excuse.[11]

Of course, every state is required to mail ballots to military and overseas citizens at least 45 days before an election according to the Uniformed and Overseas Citizens Absentee Voting Act, known as UOCAVA, and the Military and Overseas Voter Empowerment, or MOVE, Act. While online voting is still quite problematic, electronic ballot transmission for these voters (and some others) is already occurring. Several states have introduced legislation to allow it and some are conducting pilots. Alaska allows it for all voters and Hawaii is considering the same. Currently five states allow some or all ballot transmission through an online website; 22 (including Washington, D.C.) allow ballots to be transmitted by email or facsimile, six allow by facsimile, and 18 allow transmittal only by mail.

Another pre-Election Day trend is the growth of interstate data matching for list maintenance and integrity purposes. The two interstate data matching programs, the Electronic Registration Information Center, or ERIC,[12] and the Interstate Voter Registration Crosscheck Program, known as Crosscheck, are not identical, but both allow participating states to share voter registration and voter history data, upload that information to a database and compare states' data, match records, and report back so states can take action. Fifteen states are members of ERIC, 30 states utilize Crosscheck and six states are members of both programs.

Table A: Ballot Transmission Methods

Online Website	Email/Facsimile	Facsimile	Mail only
Alabama	Colorado	California	Arkansas
Alaska	Delaware	Florida	Connecticut
Arizona	Idaho	Hawaii	Georgia
Missouri	Indiana	Louisiana	Illinois
North Dakota	Iowa	Rhode Island	Kentucky
	Kansas	Texas	Maryland
	Maine	Oregon	Michigan
	Massachusetts	South Carolina	Minnesota
	Mississippi	Utah	New Hampshire
	Montana	Washington	New York
	Nebraska	Washington, DC	Ohio
	Nevada	West Virginia	Pennsylvania
	New Jersey		South Dakota
	New Mexico		Tennessee
	North Carolina		Vermont
	Oklahoma		Virginia
			Wisconsin
			Wyoming

Election Day Trends

The use of electronic or e-pollbooks tops the trends for Election Day. Traditionally, checking into a polling place required a voter to approach an election official who would look up the voter's name and address in a paper poll book before issuing a ballot. That process often caused bottlenecks and lines at polling places. E-pollbooks, which consist of a laptop or tablet fitted with a card swiper, use driver's licenses to quickly pull up a voter's information and allows the sign-in process to be completed electronically. The e-pollbook verifies whether the voter is eligible and in his or her precinct, and if not, will provide the voter's correct polling location. Some e-pollbooks will even produce a map with directions. E-pollbooks can also show whether a voter has already voted and, if networked, can provide real-time updates on whether the voter has voted at another location.

Three states are now utilizing mail-in ballots for all of their voters: Colorado, Oregon and Washington. Voters are automatically mailed a ballot to the address on the voter registration list. Voters may return the ballot by mail or use an official ballot drop-off location, which are available 24 hours a day and monitored by camera. Ballots delivered to the elections office are sent through a machine that removes a flap from the return envelope to reveal the voter's signature. Signatures are scanned and electronically sent to signature verification teams who compare them to other signatures of the voter on file in order to verify authenticity before the ballot envelope is opened and the ballot is counted. States using mail-in ballots have seen some increases in turnout.

Another growing trend is the use of vote centers, which permit a voter to cast a ballot outside of a traditional precinct/polling place. A number of states have passed legislation to permit the use of vote centers as these centers may reduce cost as well as increase convenience for voters. Some have authorized pilot programs (for example, San Diego, Calif.), to determine whether a larger roll-out is warranted. Colorado is utilizing vote centers for those voters who don't want to vote by mail but still want to vote in person. Vote centers may reduce costs as well as increase convenience for voters. A downside is the loss of traditional civic interaction and possible voter confusion without a robust voter education program.

Same-day voter registration is also on the rise. It allows a voter to show up at a polling location, provide proof of residency and some form of acceptable ID, and then proceed to cast a ballot. Thirteen states and territories have same-day registration: Colorado, Connecticut, Idaho, Illinois, Iowa, Maine, Minnesota, Montana, New Hampshire, Vermont, Wisconsin, Wyoming and Washington D.C. California has passed legislation allowing for same-day registration, which will take effect once the state has a functioning statewide voter registration database, and Hawaii will implement it in 2018.

Voters are now also able to use a variety of apps to facilitate the voting process. Various apps furnish voters with their polling location,[13] compare candidates and tell the voter what is on the ballot,[14] get results,[15] and even track ballots so the voter knows exactly where his or her ballot is at all times.[16] An app to track wait times is also under construction.[17]

Voter ID is also trending upward. Thirty-three states have some form of voter identification in place this year, while three states have seen their voter ID laws struck down: Arkansas, Missouri and Pennsylvania.[18] In 2015, a federal court decided that part of Texas' voter ID law is unenforceable, but it appears ID will still be required to vote. North Carolina's law is still in litigation and the outcome is uncertain. States are also starting to consider biometric identification, which could be an interesting development.

Post-Election Day Trends

Post-Election Day developments include audits, election night reporting and ballot adjudication. More than half of states require post-election audits. Last year, Connecticut and New York authorized automatic audits. Some states also are considering risk-limiting audits, which use statistical evidence to determine whether a reported outcome, rather than the tabulation, is accurate. If the outcome is questionable, a hand recount may be required to correct a possibly incorrect outcome.

Election night reporting software has improved and now allows jurisdictions to use electronic interfaces to provide real-time updates and reports in graphic formats. Interactive maps immediately illustrate voter turnout, voting trends, vote totals by type, and individual polling place results. Web-based applications let jurisdictions display results automatically for the media outlets, candidates and the public.

The ballot adjudication process also is changing due to emerging technology. Traditionally, marked ballots are scanned through high-speed ballot scanners to read the voter's marks and pass the results to a tabulation computer. If the scanner rejects an unreadable ballot, it must be manually reviewed, usually by a bipartisan team. If the team determines that the ballot is capable of adjudication, the ballot is examined to determine a voter's intent and a duplicate is created by hand marking a blank ballot so it can be scanned and counted. Ballots often have stray marks, contain over/under votes, and sometimes the intent of the voter is unclear by the way the voter marks the ballot (for example, by circling the candidate's name and writing it in). Just touching a ballot can create additional marks or tears, so the rejected ballots need to be handled carefully. Some jurisdictions, such as Denver, Colo., are using technology that allows the rejected ballot to be digitally scanned or photographed, allowing an adjudication team to bring a rejected ballot up on a screen, zoom in, identify the cause of the rejection and fix discrepancies to reflect the voter's intent without even touching a ballot. The adjudication team can digitally duplicate the ballot so that it can be scanned and tabulated and a log of the team's decisions remains attached to the ballot in case of further questions. Digital adjudication speeds up the process, creates a trackable record and better preserves the original ballot in case it is needed for comparison.

A Call to Action

There is much more innovation happening than can be outlined here. Elections are getting better and are well on their way to meeting the promise of HAVA and being the up-to-date modern elections that voters expect. The changes occurring in the various states and jurisdictions are being shared and duplicated throughout the nation. The emerging technologies are making this an exciting time in elections.

Still, elections remain a people-driven and people-serving process. There is an urgent need for an elections workforce. We need to continue to encourage people to get involved as election specialists and poll workers. Even with all the new and emerging technology, voting can only happen if we have trained personnel to work at the polls, bilingual speakers to help minority language speakers, truck drivers to deliver equipment or pick up ballots from drop-boxes, warehouse crews to manage storage, IT experts to test and maintain voting equipment and systems, and staff to serve at election offices and on adjudication teams. Technology is great and it is helping us improve elections, but our focus still needs to remain on people and the voters, which is what elections are all about.

Notes

[1] Presidential Commission on Election Administration, "The American Voting Experience: Report and Recommendations of the Presidential Commission on Election Administration," p.4 (January 2014), accessed on February 18, 2016 at *https://www.supportthevoter.gov/files/2014/01/Amer-Voting-Exper-final-draft-01-09-14-508.pdf*.

[2] *New State Ice Co. v. Liebmann*, 285 U.S. 262 (1932), Brandeis, J. dissenting.

[3] Norden, Lawrence, and Famhigetti, Chris, "America's Voting Machines at Risk," Brennan Center for Justice (September 15, 2015), accessed on February 18, 2016 at *https://www.brennancenter.org/sites/default/files/publications/Americas_Voting_Machines_At_Risk.pdf*.

[4] For example, see Nebraska One Hundred Fourth Legislature, Second Session, Legislative Resolution 403 (January 12, 2016), accessed on February 18, 2016 at *http://nebraskalegislature.gov/FloorDocs/Current/PDF/Intro/LR403.pdf*.

[5] Colorado Secretary of State's Office, News Release (December 22, 2015), accessed on February 18, 2016 at *http://www.sos.state.co.us/pubs/newsRoom/pressReleases/2015/PR20151222Dominion.html*; also see Lovato, Jerome, "State of Colorado, UVS Pilot Project, " 2015 State Certification of Testing Voting Systems National Conference (May 19, 2015), accessed on February 18, 2016 at *http://bowencenterforpublicaffairs.org/wp-content/uploads/2015/05/Colorado-UVS-Pilot-Project-Presentation.pdf*.

[6] Ganley, Rick, and Brindley, Michael, "Tablet-Based Ballot for Blind Voters to Debut During N.H. Primary," NHPR (February 8, 2016), accessed on February 18, 2016 at *http://nhpr.org/post/tablet-based-ballot-system-blind-voters-debut-during-nh-primary*.

[7] U.S. Election Assistance Commission, "Managing Election Technology" (Silver Spring, MD, 2016), accessed on February 18, 2016 at *http://www.eac.gov/testing_and_certification/managing_election_technology.aspx*.

[8] National Conference of State Legislatures, "Online Voter Registration" (February 2, 2016); accessed on February 18, 2016 at *http://www.ncsl.org/research/elections-and-campaigns/electronic-or-online-voter-registration.aspx*.

[9] Underhill, Wendy, February 18, 2016 (3:34 p.m.), "Automatic Voter Registration Hits Speed Bump in New Jersey, *NCSL Blog*, November 12, 1015, National Conference of State Legislatures, *http://www.ncsl.org/blog/2015/11/12/automatic-motor-voter-registration-hits-speed-bump-in-new-jersey.aspx*.

[10] National Conference of State Legislatures, "Absentee and Early Voting" (February 2, 2016); accessed on February 18, 2016 at *http://www.ncsl.org/research/elections-and-campaigns/absentee-and-early-voting.aspx*.

[11] Id.

[12] The Electronic Registration Information Center, homepage, accessed on February 18, 2106 at *http://www.ericstates.org*.

[13] TurboVote, accessed on February 18, 2016 at *https://turbovote.org/register*.

[14] Think Voting, accessed on February 18, 2016 at *http://thinkvoting.com/the-voting-app/*.

[15] My Vote, accessed on February 18, 2016 at *https://www.myvote.io*; see also, Interknowlgy, accessed on February 18, 2016 at *http://www.interknowlogy.com/projects/#iowa-caucus*.

[16] Denver Elections Division, "What is Ballot Trace?", accessed on February 18, 2016 at *https://www.denvergov.org/content/denvergov/en/denver-elections-divison/voter-election-information/ballot-trace.html*.

[17] Ms. Voting Matters, February 18, 2016 (3:56 p.m.), "Siri, How Busy Is My Polling Place?" *Oset Foundation Blog*, (October 10, 2014), Oset Foundation, *http://www.osetfoundation.org/blog/2014/9/3/siri-how-busy-is-my-polling-place*.

[18] National Conference of State Legislatures, "Voter Identification Update/Voter ID Laws" (January 4, 2016); accessed on February 18, 2016 at *http://www.ncsl.org/research/elections-and-campaigns/voter-id.aspx*.

About the author

Christy McCormick was appointed to the U.S. Election Assistance Commission in January 2015. From 2006–2015, she was a Senior Trial Attorney in the Voting Section of the U.S. Department of Justice, where she prosecuted federal voting statutes, including UOCAVA and the MOVE Act. From 2009–2010, she was detailed to Baghdad, Iraq, to work on the Iraq elections and rule of law matters. Prior to D.O.J., Ms. McCormick worked in several capacities in Virginia government.

Table 6.1
STATE EXECUTIVE BRANCH OFFICIALS TO BE ELECTED: 2016–2020

State or other jurisdiction	2016	2017	2018	2019	2020
Alabama	...	...	G,LG,AG,AR,A,SS,T (a)	...	(a)
Alaska	...	...	G,LG	...	...
Arizona	(b)	...	G,AG,SS,SP,T (b)	...	(b)
Arkansas	...	...	G,LG,AG,A,SS,T (c)	...	...
California	...	...	G,LG,AG,C,CI,SS,SP,T (d)	...	...
Colorado	(e)	...	G,LG,AG,SS,T (e)	...	(e)
Connecticut	...	...	G,LG,AG,C,SS,T	...	...
Delaware	G,LG,CI	...	AG,A,T	...	G,LG,CI
Florida	...	...	G,LG,AG,AR,CFO	...	...
Georgia	(f)	...	G,LG,AG,AR,CI,SS,SP (f)	...	(f)
Hawaii	...	...	G,LG	...	...
Idaho	...	...	G,LG,AG,C,SS,SP,T	...	...
Illinois	C (g)	...	G,LG,AG,C,SS,T	...	...
Indiana	G,LG,AG,SP	...	A,SS,T	...	G,LG,AG,SP
Iowa	...	...	G,LG,AG,AR,A,SS,T	...	...
Kansas	...	...	G,LG,AG,CI,SS,T	...	...
Kentucky	...	...	...	G,LG,AG,AR,A,SS,T	...
Louisiana	(h)	...	(h)	G,LG,AG,AR,CI,SS,T	(h)
Maine (i)	...	...	G	...	...
Maryland	...	...	G,LG,AG,C	...	...
Massachusetts	...	...	G,LG,AG,A,SS,T	...	...
Michigan	(j)	...	G,LG,AG,SS (j)	...	(j)
Minnesota	...	...	G,LG,AG,A,SS	...	...
Mississippi	...	...	...	G,LG,AG,AR,A,CI,SS,T	...
Missouri	G,LG,AG,SS,T	...	A	...	G,LG,AG,SS,T
Montana	G,LG,AG,A,SS,SP (k)	...	...	...	G,LG,AG,A,SS,SP (k)
Nebraska	(l)	...	G,LG,AG,A,SS,T (l)	...	(l)
Nevada	...	...	G,LG,AG,C,SS,T	...	...
New Hampshire	G	...	G	...	G
New Jersey	...	G,LG	...	...	...
New Mexico	SS (m)	...	G,LG,AG,A,SS,T (m)	...	(m)
New York	...	...	G,LG,AG,C	...	...
North Carolina	G,LG,AG,AR,A,CI,SS,SP,T (n)	...	...	...	G,LG,AG,AR,A,CI,SS,SP,T (n)
North Dakota	G,LG,A,CI,SP,T (o)	...	AG,AR,SS (o)	...	G,LG,A,CI,SP,T (o)
Ohio	...	...	G,LG,AG,A,SS,T	...	...
Oklahoma	...	...	G,LG,AG,A,CI,SP,T (p)	...	(p)
Oregon	G,AG,SS,T (q)	...	G (r)	...	AG,SS,T
Pennsylvania	AG,A,T	...	G,LG	...	AG,A,T
Rhode Island	...	...	G,LG,AG,SS,T	...	...
South Carolina	...	...	G,LG,AG,AR,C,SS,SP,T (s)	...	...
South Dakota	(t)	...	G,LG,AG,A,SS,SP,T (t)	...	(t)
Tennessee	...	...	G	...	...
Texas	(u)	...	G,LG,AG,AR,C (u)	...	(u)
Utah	G,LG,AG,A,T	...	...	...	G,LG,AG,A,T
Vermont	G,LG,AG,A,SS,T	...	G,LG,AG,A,SS,T	...	G,LG,AG,A,SS,T

See footnotes at end of table.

STATE EXECUTIVE BRANCH OFFICIALS TO BE ELECTED: 2016–2020—Continued

State or other jurisdiction	2016	2017	2018	2019	2020
Virginia	...	G,LG,AG	...	...	...
Washington	G,LG,AG,A,CI,SS,SP,T (v)	...	...	...	G,LG,AG,A,CI,SS,SP,T (v)
West Virginia	G,AG,AR,A,SS,T	...	...	...	G,AG,AR,A,SS,T
Wisconsin	...	SP	G,LG,AG,SS,T	...	...
Wyoming	...	...	G,A,SS,SP,T	...	...
American Samoa	G,LG	...	...	...	G,LG
Guam	A	...	G,LG,AG	...	A
No. Mariana Islands	...	...	G,LG	...	G
Puerto Rico	G	...	...	...	G
U.S. Virgin Islands	...	...	G,LG	...	...
Totals for year					
Governor	14		39	3	13
Lieutenant Governor	10	2	33	3	10
Attorney General	10	1	31	3	10
Agriculture	2	0	7	3	2
Auditor	9	0	15	2	9
Chief Financial Officer	0	0	1	0	0
Comptroller	0	0	9	0	0
Comm. of Insurance	4	0	4	2	4
Secretary of State	8	0	26	3	7
Supt. of Public Inst. or Comm. of Education	5	1	8	0	5
Treasurer	9	0	24	3	9

Sources: The Council of State Governments' survey and state election administration offices and websites, March 2016.

Note: This table shows the executive branch officials up for election in a given year. Footnotes indicate other offices (e.g. commissioners of labor, public service, etc.) also up for election in a given year. The data contained in this table reflect information available at press time.

Key:

... — No regularly scheduled elections of state executive officials.
G — Governor
LG — Lieutenant Governor
AG — Attorney General
AR — Agriculture
A — Auditor
C — Comptroller/Controller
CFO — Chief Financial Officer
CI — Commissioner of Insurance
SS — Secretary of State
SP — Superintendent of Public Instruction or Commissioner of Education
T — Treasurer

(a) Public Service Commissioner (3)—4-year terms, 2016—1 seat (president), 2018—2 seats (associate commissioners), 2020—1 seat (president).
(b) Corporation Commissioner (5)—4-year terms, 2016—3 seats, 2018—2 seats; State Mine Inspector—4-year term, 2018.
(c) Commissioner of State Lands—4-year term, 2018.
(d) Four (4) Board of Equalization members are elected to serve 4-year concurrent terms. The State Controller is the 5th member of the Board.

(e) University of Colorado Board of Regents (9, one elected from each of the state's congressional districts and two at-large members)—6-year terms, 2016—1 statewide, 2 districts, 2018—1 statewide, 2 districts, 2020—3 districts.
(f) Commissioner of Labor—4-year term, 2018; Public Service Commissioner (5)—6-year terms, 2016—1, 2018—2, 2020—2.
(g) Illinois is holding a special election for the office of Comptroller. Judy Baar Topinka, the previous comptroller, died on December 8, 2014, just weeks after winning reelection. Governor Bruce Rauner appointed Leslie Munger to fill the vacancy, and he wanted her to complete Topinka's full 4-year term. However, the General Assembly set a special two-year election for 2016. The winner of the special election will serve for 2 years.
(h) Public Commissioner (5)—6-year terms, 2016—2, 2018—1, 2020—2.
(i) The Maine legislature elects constitutional officers (AG,SS,T) for 2-year terms; the auditor was elected by the legislature in 2012 and serves a 4-year term.
(j) Michigan State University trustees (8)—8-year terms, 2016—2, 2018—2, 2020—2, 2022—2; University of Michigan regents (8)—8-year terms, 2016—2, 2018—2, 2020—2, 2022—2; Wayne State University governors (8)—8-year terms, 2016—2, 2018—2, 2020—2, 2022—2; State Board of Education (8)—8-year terms, 2016—2, 2018—2, 2020—2, 2022—2.
(k) Public Service Commissioner (5)—4-year terms, 2016—3, 2018—2.
(l) Public Service Commissioner (5)—6-year terms, 2016—2, 2018—2, 2020—2.
(m) There will be a special election to fill the vacant office of Secretary of State, following the October 2015 resignation of Dianna Duran, who was later convicted of embezzlement and other charges. Commissioner of Public Lands—4-year term, 2018; Public Education Commission (10)—4-year terms, 2016—5, 2018—5, 2020—5; Public Regulation Commissioner (5)—4-year terms, 2016—2, 2018—1, 2020—2.
(n) Commissioner of Labor—4-year term, 2016, 2020.
(o) Tax Commissioner—4-year term, 2018; Public Service Commissioner (3)—6-year terms, 2016—1, 2018—1, 2020—1.

STATE EXECUTIVE BRANCH OFFICIALS TO BE ELECTED: 2016–2020—Continued

(p) Commissioner of Labor—4-year term, 2018; Corporation Commissioner (3)—6-year terms, 2016–1, 2018–1, 2020–1.

(q) In 2016 there will be a special election to fill the remaining two years in Gov. John Kitzhaber's term. He was re-elected in 2014 and resigned in February 2015. Incumbent Governor Kate Brown succeeded to the governor's office as Secretary of State.

(r) Commissioner of the Bureau of Labor and Industries. 4-year term, 2018.

(s) Adjutant General—4-year term, 2018.

(t) The title is Commissioner of Schools and Public Lands; Public Utility Commissioner (3)—6-year terms, 2016–1, 2018–1, 2020–1.

(u) Commissioner of General Land Office—4-year term, 2018; railroad commissioners (3)—6-year terms, 2016–1, 2018–1, 2020–1.

(v) Commissioner of Public Lands—4-year term, 2016, 2020.

Table 6.2
STATE LEGISLATURE MEMBERS TO BE ELECTED: 2016–2020

State or other jurisdiction	Total legislators Senate	Total legislators House/Assembly	2016 Senate	2016 House/Assembly	2017 Senate	2017 House/Assembly	2018 Senate	2018 House/Assembly	2019 Senate	2019 House/Assembly	2020 Senate	2020 House/Assembly
Alabama	35	105	...	...	...	...	35	105	...	...	...	...
Alaska	20	40	10	40	...	...	10	40	...	...	10	40
Arizona	30	60	30	60	...	...	30	60	...	...	30	60
Arkansas	35	100	17	100	...	...	18	100	...	...	17	100
California	40	80	20 (a)	80	...	...	20 (b)	80	...	...	20 (a)	80
Colorado	35	65	18	65	...	...	17	65	...	...	18	65
Connecticut	36	151	36	151	...	...	36	151	...	...	36	151
Delaware	21	41	11	41	...	...	10	41	...	...	11	41
Florida	40	120	40 (c)	120	...	...	20 (b)	120	...	...	20 (a)	120
Georgia	56	180	56	180	...	...	56	180	...	...	56	180
Hawaii	25	51	14 (d)	51	...	...	12	51	...	...	13	51
Idaho	35	70	35	70	...	...	35	70	...	...	35	70
Illinois	59	118	40 (e)	118	...	...	39 (f)	118	...	...	20 (e)	118
Indiana	50	100	25	100	...	...	25	100	...	...	25	100
Iowa	50	100	25 (b)	100	...	...	25 (a)	100	...	...	25 (b)	100
Kansas	40	125	40	125	...	...	...	125	...	...	40	125
Kentucky	38	100	19 (a)	100	...	...	19 (b)	100	...	...	19 (a)	100
Louisiana	39	105	...	...	...	...	...	...	39	105	...	...
Maine	35	151 (f)	35	151	...	...	35	151	...	...	35	151
Maryland	47	141	...	...	...	...	47	141	...	...	...	...
Massachusetts	40	160	40	160	...	...	40	160	...	...	40	160
Michigan	38	110	...	110	...	...	38	110	...	...	...	110
Minnesota	67	134	67	134	...	...	...	134	...	...	67	134
Mississippi	52	122	...	...	...	...	...	...	52	122	...	...
Missouri	34	163	17 (a)	163	...	...	17 (b)	163	...	...	17 (a)	163
Montana	50	100	25	100	...	...	25	100	...	...	25	100
Nebraska	49	U	25 (a)	U	...	...	24 (b)	U	...	...	25 (a)	U
Nevada	21	42	11 (g)	42	...	...	11	42	...	...	10	42
New Hampshire	24	400	24	400	...	...	24	400	...	...	24	400
New Jersey	40	80	...	...	40	80	...	...	...	80	...	...
New Mexico	42	70	42	70	...	...	...	70	...	...	42	70
New York	63	150	63	150	...	...	63	150	...	...	63	150
North Carolina	50	120	50	120	...	...	50	120	...	...	50	120
North Dakota	47	94	23 (b)	46 (b)	...	...	24 (a)	48 (a)	...	...	23 (b)	46 (b)
Ohio	33	99	16 (b)	99	...	...	17 (a)	99	...	...	16 (b)	99
Oklahoma	48	101	25 (a)(h)	101	...	...	24 (b)	101	...	...	24 (a)	101
Oregon	30	60	15	60	...	...	15	60	...	...	15	60
Pennsylvania	50	203	25 (a)	203	...	...	25 (b)	203	...	...	25 (a)	203
Rhode Island	38	75	38	75	...	...	38	75	...	...	38	75
South Carolina	46	124	46	124	...	...	...	124	...	...	46	124

See footnotes at end of table.

STATE LEGISLATURE MEMBERS TO BE ELECTED: 2016–2020—Continued

State or other jurisdiction	Total legislators		2016		2017		2018		2019		2020	
	Senate	House/Assembly	Senate	House/Assembly	Senate	House/Assembly	Senate	House/Assembly	Senate	House/Assembly	Senate	House/Assembly
South Dakota	35	70	35	70	…	…	35	70	…	…	35	70
Tennessee	33	99	16 (b)	99	…	…	17 (a)	99	…	…	16 (b)	99
Texas	31	150	16	150	…	…	15	150	…	…	16	150
Utah	29	75	15	75	…	…	14	75	…	…	15	75
Vermont	30	150	30	150	…	…	30	150	…	…	30	150
Virginia	40	100	40	100	100				40	100		
Washington	49	98	26 (i)	98	…	…	24	98	…	…	25	98
West Virginia	34	100	18 (j)	100	…	…	17	100	…	…	17	100
Wisconsin	33	99	16 (b)	99	…	…	17 (a)	99	…	…	16 (b)	99
Wyoming	30	60	15 (b)	60	…	…	15 (a)	60	…	…	15 (b)	60
Dist. of Columbia	13	U	6	U	…	…	7	U	…	…	6	U
American Samoa	18 (k)	20 (k)	18 (k)	20 (k)	…	…	18 (k)	20 (k)	…	…	18 (k)	20 (k)
Guam	15	U	15	U	…	…	15		…	…	15	
No. Marianas Islands (l)	9	20	3	20	…	…	6	20	…	…	3	20
Puerto Rico (m)	27	51	27	51	…	…			27	51	27	51
U.S. Virgin Islands	15	U	15	U	…	…	15	U	…	…	15	U
State Totals	1,972	5,411	1,210	4,710	40	180	1,108	4,958	131	407	1,165	4,710
Totals	2,069	5,502	1,294	4,801	40	180	1,169	4,998	131	407	1,249	4,801

Source: The Council of State Governments, March 2016.

Note: This table shows the number of elections in a given year. The data compiles in this table reflect information available at press time. See Chapter 3.3 table entitled, "The Legislators: Numbers, Terms, and Party Affiliations," for specific information on legislative terms.

Key:

. . .—No regularly scheduled elections

U—Unicameral legislature

(a) Odd-numbered Senate districts.

(b) Even-numbered Senate districts.

(c) On December 30, 2015, a state judge ruled that the Senate district boundaries were drawn unconstitutionally and instituted a new map drawn by a coalition of voters groups. Typically, half of the Senate seats (odd-numbered in 2016) are up for election every two years. However, when districts are redrawn, every seat must be decided by a new election.

(d) Typically 13 seats. The election for Senate District 1 is to fill the remainder of the term expiring in 2018.

(e) The Illinois Senate operates on a ten-year election cycle. All 59 senators are elected in each year ending with a "2" (following redistricting following the decennial census). Senate districts are then divided into three groups. Each group of senators is elected to one of the following schedules: terms of four years, four years and two years; terms of two years, four years and four years; and terms of four years, two years and four years. Depending on the year, roughly 1/3, 2/3 or all of the senate seats will be up for election.

(f) In addition, there are three nonvoting members representing the Penobscot Nation, the Passamaquoddy Tribe and the Houlton Band of Maliseet Indians.

(g) Typically 10 seats. The election for District 13 is to fill the remainder of the term expiring in 2018, following the death of Sen. Debbie Smith in February 2016.

(h) Typically 24 seats. The election for District 12 is to fill the remainder of the term expiring in 2018. Term limits prevent Sen. Brian Bingman from completing the full term of his office.

(i) Typically 25 seats. The election for District 36 is to fill the remainder of the term expiring in 2018, following the resignation of Sen. Jeanne Kohl-Welles who was elected to the King County Council.

(j) Typically 17 seats. The election for District 3 is to fill the remainder of the term expiring in 2018, following the resignation of Sen. Dave Nohe, who accepted a position on the state Parole Board.

(k) In American Samoa, Senators are not elected by popular vote. They are selected by the county council of chiefs. House: 21 seats; 20 are elected by popular vote and one appointed, non-voting delegate from Swains Island.

(l) In 2009, voters approved a constitutional amendment (Senate Legislative Initiative 16-1) that changed future general elections from odd to even-numbered years.

(m) Constitutionally, the Senate consists of 27 seats and the House 51 seats. However, extra at-large seats can be granted to the opposition to limit any party's control to two thirds.

Table 6.3
METHODS OF NOMINATING CANDIDATES FOR STATE OFFICES

State or other jurisdiction	Methods of nominating candidates
Alabama	Primary election; however, the state executive committee or other governing body of any political party may choose instead to hold a state convention for the purpose of nominating candidates. Submitting a petition to run as an independent or third-party candidate or an independent nominating procedure.
Alaska	Primary election. Petition for no-party candidates.
Arizona	Candidates who are members of a recognized party are nominated by an open primary election. Candidates who are not members of a recognized political party may file petitions to appear on the general election ballot. A write-in option is also available.
Arkansas	Primary election, convention and petition.
California	Primary election or independent nomination procedure.
Colorado	Primary election, convention or by petition.
Connecticut	Convention/primary election. Major political parties hold state conventions (convening not earlier than the 68th day and closing not later than the 50th day before the date of the primary) for the purpose of endorsing candidates. If no one challenges the endorsed candidate, no primary election is held. However, if anyone (who received at least 15 percent of the delegate vote on any roll call at the convention) challenges the endorsed candidate, a primary election is held to determine the party nominee for the general election.
Delaware	Primary election for Democrats and primary election and convention for Republicans.
Florida	Primary election. Minor parties may nominate their candidate in any manner they deem proper.
Georgia	Primary election.
Hawaii	Primary election.
Idaho	Primary election and convention. New political parties hold a convention to nominate candidates to be placed on a general election ballot.
Illinois	Primary election. The primary election nominates established party candidates. New political parties and independent candidates go directly to the general election file based on a petition process.
Indiana	Primary election, convention and petition. The governor is chosen by a primary. All other state officers are chosen at a state convention, unless the candidate is an independent. Any party that obtains between 2 percent and 8 percent of the vote for secretary of state may hold a convention to select a candidate.
Iowa	Primary election, convention and petition.
Kansas	Candidates for the two major parties are nominated by primary election. Candidates for minor parties are nominated for the general election at state party conventions. Independent candidates are nominated for the general election by petition.
Kentucky	Primary election. A slate of candidates for governor and lieutenant governor that receives the highest number of its party's votes but which number is less than 40 percent of the votes cast for all slates of candidates of that party, shall be required to participate in a runoff primary with the slate of candidates of the same party receiving the second highest number of votes.
Louisiana	Candidates may qualify for any office they wish, regardless of party affiliation, by completing the qualifying document and paying the appropriate qualifying fee; or a candidate may file a nominating petition.
Maine	Primary election or non-party petition.
Maryland	Primary election, convention and petition. Unaffiliated candidates or candidates affiliated with non-recognized political parties may run for elective office by collecting the requisite number of signatures on a petition. The required number equals 1 percent of the number of registered voters eligible to vote for office. Only recognized non-principal political parties may nominate its candidate by a convention in accordance with its bylaws (at this time, Maryland has four non-principal parties: Libertarian, Green, Constitution and Populist.)
Massachusetts	Primary election.
Michigan	Governor, state house, state senate use primary election. Lieutenant governor runs as the running mate to gubernatorial candidate, not separately, and is selected through the convention process. Secretary of state and attorney general candidates are chosen at convention. Nominees for State Board of Education, University of Michigan Regents, Michigan State University Trustees and Wayne State University Governors are nominated by convention. Minor parties nominate candidates to all partisan offices by convention.
Minnesota	Primary election. Candidates for minor parties or independent candidates are by petition. They must have the signatures of 2,000 people who will be eligible to vote in the next general election.
Mississippi	Primary election, petition (for independent candidates), independent nominating procedures (third-party candidate).
Missouri	Primary election.
Montana	Primary election and independent nominating procedure.
Nebraska	Primary election.
Nevada	Primary election. Independent candidates are nominated by petition for the general election. Minor parties nominated by petition or by party.
New Hampshire	Primary election. Minor parties by petition.

See footnotes at end of table.

METHODS OF NOMINATING CANDIDATES FOR STATE OFFICES — Continued

State or other jurisdiction	Methods of nominating candidates
New Jersey	Primary election. Independent candidates are nominated by petition for the general election.
New Mexico	Statewide candidates petition to go to convention and are nominated in a primary election. District and legislative candidate petition for primary ballot access.
New York	Primary election/petition.
North Carolina	Primary election. Newly recognized parties just granted access submit their first nominees by convention. All established parties use primaries.
North Dakota	Convention/primary election. Political parties hold state conventions for the purpose of endorsing candidates. Endorsed candidates are automatically placed on the primary election ballot, but other candidates may also petition their name on the ballot.
Ohio	Primary election, petition and by declaration of intent to be a write-in candidate.
Oklahoma	Primary election.
Oregon	Primary election. Minor parties hold conventions.
Pennsylvania	Primary election, and petition. Nomination petitions filed by major party candidates to access primary ballot. Nomination papers filed by minor party and independent candidates to access November ballot.
Rhode Island	Primary election.
South Carolina	Primary election for Republicans and Democrats; party conventions held for minor parties. Candidates can have name on ballot via petition.
South Dakota	Convention, petition and independent nominating procedure.
Tennessee	Primary election/petition.
Texas	Primary election/convention. Minor parties without ballot access nominate candidates for the general election after qualifying for ballot access by petition.
Utah	Convention, primary election and petition.
Vermont	Primary election. Major parties by primary, minor parties by convention, independents by petition.
Virginia	Primary election, convention and petition.
Washington	Primary election.
West Virginia	Primary election, convention, petition and independent nominating procedure.
Wisconsin	Primary election/petition. Candidates must file nomination papers (petitions) containing the minimum number of signatures required by law. Candidates appear on the primary ballot for the party they represent. The candidate receiving the most votes in each party primary goes on to the November election.
Wyoming	Primary election.
Dist. of Columbia	Primary election. Independent and minor party candidates file by nominating petition.
American Samoa	Individual files petition for candidacy with the chief election officer. Petition must be signed by statutorily mandated number of qualified voters.
Guam	Individual files petition for candidacy with the chief election officer. Petition must be signed by statutorily mandated number of qualified voters.
No. Mariana Islands	Candidates are all nominated by petition. Candidates seeking the endorsement of recognized political parties must also include in their submitted petition submission a document signed by the recognized political parties' chairperson/president and secretary attesting to such nomination. Recognized political parties may, or may not, depending on their bylaws and party rules conduct primaries separate from any state election agency participation.
Puerto Rico	Primary election and convention.
U.S. Virgin Islands	Primary election.

Source: The Council of State Governments' survey of state websites, March 2016.
Note: The nominating methods described here are for state offices; procedures may vary for local candidates. Also, independent candidates may have to petition for nomination.

Table 6.4
ELECTION DATES FOR NATIONAL AND STATE ELECTIONS
(Formulas and dates of state elections)

State or other jurisdiction	National (a) Primary	National (a) General	State (b) Primary	State (b) Runoff	State (b) General	Type of primary (c)
Alabama	March, 1st T March 1, 2016	Nov.,★ Nov. 8, 2016	March, 1st T March 1, 2016	6th T AP April 17, 2018	Nov.,★ Nov. 6, 2018	Open
Alaska	(d) Rep: March 1, 2016 Dem: March 26, 2016	Nov.,★ Nov. 8, 2016	Aug., 3rd T Aug. 16, 2016	…	Nov.,★ Nov. 8, 2016	(e)
Arizona	T following March 15 March 22, 2016	Nov.,★ Nov. 8, 2016	10th T Prior Aug. 30, 2016	…	Nov.,★ Nov. 8, 2016	Partially Closed
Arkansas	March, 1st T March 1, 2016	Nov.,★ Nov. 8, 2016	T 3 wks. prior to runoff March 1, 2016 (f)	March, 4th T March 22, 2016 (f)	Nov.,★ Nov. 8, 2016	Open
California	June,★ June 7, 2016	Nov.,★ Nov. 8, 2016	June,★ June 7, 2016	…	Nov.,★ Nov. 8, 2016	Top Two
Colorado	(d)(g) March 1, 2016	Nov.,★ Nov. 8, 2016	June, last T June 28, 2016	…	Nov.,★ Nov. 8, 2016	Partially Closed
Connecticut	April, Last T April 26, 2016	Nov.,★ Nov. 8, 2016	Aug., 2nd T Aug. 9, 2016	…	Nov.,★ Nov. 8, 2016	Closed
Delaware	April, 4th T April 26, 2016	Nov.,★ Nov. 8, 2016	Sept., 2nd T after 1st M Sept. 13, 2016	…	Nov.,★ Nov. 8, 2016	Closed
Florida	March, 3rd T March 15, 2016	Nov.,★ Nov. 8, 2016	10th T prior to General Aug. 30, 2016	…	Nov.,★ Nov. 8, 2016	Closed
Georgia	(h) March 1, 2016	Nov.,★ Nov. 8, 2016	24th T prior to General May 24, 2016	9th T after Primary July 26, 2016	Nov.,★ Nov. 8, 2016	Open
Hawaii	(d) Rep: March 8, 2016 Dem: March 26, 2016	Nov.,★ Nov. 8, 2016	Aug., 2nd S Aug. 13, 2016	…	Nov.,★ Nov. 8, 2016	Open
Idaho	(d) Rep: March 8, 2016 Dem: March 22, 2016	Nov.,★ Nov. 8, 2016	May, 3rd T May 17, 2016	…	Nov.,★ Nov. 8, 2016	Rep: Closed (i) Dem: Partially Closed
Illinois	March, 3rd T March 15, 2016	Nov.,★ Nov. 8, 2016	March, 3rd T March 15, 2016	…	Nov.,★ Nov. 8, 2016	Partially Open
Indiana	May,★ May 3, 2016	Nov.,★ Nov. 8, 2016	May,★ May 3, 2016	…	Nov.,★ Nov. 8, 2016	Partially Open
Iowa	(d) Feb. 1, 2016	Nov.,★ Nov. 8, 2016	June,★ June 7, 2016	…	Nov.,★ Nov. 8, 2016	Partially Open
Kansas	(d)(j) March 5, 2016	Nov.,★ Nov. 8, 2016	Aug., 1st T Aug. 2, 2016	…	Nov.,★ Nov. 8, 2016	Closed (k)
Kentucky	(d) Rep: March 5, 2016 (l) Dem: May 17, 2016	Nov.,★ Nov. 8, 2016	May, 1st T after 3rd M May 17, 2016	…	Nov.,★ Nov. 8, 2016	Closed
Louisiana	March, 1st S March 5, 2016	Nov.,★ Nov. 8, 2016	Oct., 2nd to last S (m) Oct. 19, 2019	…	Nov., 4th S AP (m) Nov. 16, 2019	Top Two
Maine	(d) Rep: March 5, 2016 Dem: March 6, 2016	Nov.,★ Nov. 8, 2016	June, 2nd T June 14, 2016	…	Nov.,★ Nov. 8, 2016	Closed (n)

See footnotes at end of table.

ELECTION DATES FOR NATIONAL AND STATE ELECTIONS
(Formulas and dates of state elections)

State or other jurisdiction	National (a)		State (b)			Type of primary (c)
	Primary	General	Primary	Runoff	General	
Maryland..............	April, 4th T (o) April 26, 2016	Nov.★ Nov. 8, 2016	April, 4th T (o) April 24, 2018	...	Nov.★ Nov. 6, 2018	Closed (p)
Massachusetts	March, 1st T March 1, 2016	Nov.★ Nov. 8, 2016	Sept. 8, 2016 (q)	...	Nov.★ Nov. 8, 2016	Partially Closed
Michigan..............	March, 2nd T March 8, 2016	Nov.★ Nov. 8, 2016	Aug.★ Aug. 2, 2016	...	Nov.★ Nov. 8, 2016	Open
Minnesota..............	(d)(r) March 1, 2016	Nov.★ Nov. 8, 2016	Aug., 2nd T Aug. 9, 2016	...	Nov.★ Nov. 8, 2016	Open
Mississippi	March, 2nd T March 8, 2016	Nov.★ Nov. 8, 2016	Aug.★ Aug. 6, 2019	3rd T AP Aug. 27, 2019	Nov.★ Nov. 5, 2019	(s)
Missouri	March, 2nd T after 1st M March 15, 2016	Nov.★ Nov. 8, 2016	Aug.★ Aug. 2, 2016	...	Nov.★ Nov. 8, 2016	Open
Montana	June★ June 7, 2016	Nov.★ Nov. 8, 2016	June★ June 7, 2016	...	Nov.★ Nov. 8, 2016	Open
Nebraska	May, 1st T after 2nd M May 10, 2016	Nov.★ Nov. 8, 2016	May, 1st T after 2nd M May 10, 2016	...	Nov.★ Nov. 8, 2016	Top Two
Nevada..............	(d) Rep: Feb. 23, 2016 Dem: Feb. 20, 2016	Nov.★ Nov. 8, 2016	June, 2nd T June 14, 2016	...	Nov.★ Nov. 8, 2016	Closed
New Hampshire	(t) Feb. 9, 2016	Nov.★ Nov. 8, 2016	Sept., 2nd T Sept. 13, 2016	...	Nov.★ Nov. 8, 2016	Partially Closed (u)
New Jersey	June★ June 7, 2016	Nov.★ Nov. 8, 2016	June★ June 6, 2017	...	Nov.★ Nov. 7, 2017	Closed
New Mexico	June★ June 7, 2016	Nov.★ Nov. 8, 2016	June★ June 7, 2016	...	Nov.★ Nov. 8, 2016	Closed
New York..............	April 19, 2016 (v)	Nov.★ Nov. 8, 2016	Sept., 1st T after 2nd M Sept. 13, 2016 (v)	...	Nov.★ Nov. 8, 2016	Closed
North Carolina..............	March 15, 2016 (w)	Nov.★ Nov. 8, 2016	March 15, 2016 (w)	(w)	Nov.★ Nov. 8, 2016	Partially Closed
North Dakota..............	(d)(x) Dem: June 7, 2016	Nov.★ Nov. 8, 2016	June, 2nd T June 14, 2016	...	Nov.★ Nov. 8, 2016	Open
Ohio..............	March, 2nd T after 1st M March 15, 2016 (y)	Nov.★ Nov. 8, 2016	March, 2nd T after 1st M March 15, 2016 (y)	...	Nov.★ Nov. 8, 2016	Partially Open
Oklahoma..............	March, 1st T March 1, 2016	Nov.★ Nov. 8, 2016	June, last T June 28, 2016	Aug., 4th T Aug. 23, 2016	Nov.★ Nov. 8, 2016	Dem: Partially Closed Rep: Closed (z)
Oregon..............	May, 3rd T May 17, 2016	Nov.★ Nov. 8, 2016	May, 3rd T May 17, 2016	...	Nov.★ Nov. 8, 2016	Closed

See footnotes at end of table.

ELECTION DATES FOR NATIONAL AND STATE ELECTIONS
(Formulas and dates of state elections)

State or other jurisdiction	National (a) Primary	National (a) General	State (b) Primary	State (b) Runoff	State (b) General	Type of primary (c)
Pennsylvania	April, 4th T April 26, 2016	Nov., ★ Nov. 8, 2016	April, 4th T April 26, 2016	...	Nov., ★ Nov. 8, 2016	Closed
Rhode Island	April, 4th T April 26, 2016	Nov., ★ Nov. 8, 2016	Sept., 2nd T after 1st M Sept. 13, 2016	...	Nov., ★ Nov. 8, 2016	Partially Open
South Carolina	(d) Rep: Feb. 20, 2016 Dem: Feb. 27, 2016	Nov., ★ Nov. 8, 2016	June, 2nd T June 14, 2016	2nd T AP June 28, 2016	Nov., ★ Nov. 8, 2016	Open
South Dakota	June, ★ June 7, 2016	Nov., ★ Nov. 8, 2016	June, ★ June 7, 2016	10th T AP (aa) Aug. 16, 2016	Nov., ★ Nov. 8, 2016	Rep: Closed Dem: Partially Closed
Tennessee	March, 1st T March 1, 2016	Nov., ★ Nov. 8, 2016	Aug., 1st TH Aug. 4, 2016	...	Nov., ★ Nov. 8, 2016	Open
Texas	March, 1st T March 1, 2016	Nov., ★ Nov. 8, 2016	March, 1st T March 1, 2016	May, 4th T May 24, 2016	Nov., ★ Nov. 8, 2016	Open
Utah	(bb) March 22, 2016	Nov., ★ Nov. 8, 2016	June, 4th T June 28, 2016	...	Nov., ★ Nov. 8, 2016	Rep: Closed (cc) Dem: Open
Vermont	March, 1st T March 1, 2016	Nov., ★ Nov. 8, 2016	Aug., 2nd T Aug. 9, 2016	...	Nov., ★ Nov. 8, 2016	Open
Virginia	March, 1st T March 1, 2016	Nov., ★ Nov. 8, 2016	June, 2nd T June 13, 2017	...	Nov., ★ Nov. 7, 2017	Open
Washington	May, 4th T May 24, 2016	Nov., ★ Nov. 8, 2016	Aug., 1st T Aug. 2, 2016	...	Nov., ★ Nov. 8, 2016	Top Two
West Virginia	May, 2nd T May 10, 2016	Nov., ★ Nov. 8, 2016	May, 2nd T May 10, 2016	...	Nov., ★ Nov. 8, 2016	Partially Closed
Wisconsin	April, 1st T April 5, 2016	Nov., ★ Nov. 8, 2016	Aug., 2nd T Aug. 9, 2016	...	Nov., ★ Nov. 8, 2016	Open
Wyoming	(d) Rep: March 1, 2016 Dem: April 9, 2016	Nov., ★ Nov. 8, 2016	Aug., 1st T after 3rd M Aug. 16, 2016	...	Nov., ★ Nov. 8, 2016	Closed
Dist. of Columbia	Rep: March 12, 2016 (dd) Dem: June 14, 2016 (dd)	Nov., ★ Nov. 8, 2016	June, 2nd T (dd) June 14, 2016	...	Nov., ★ Nov. 8, 2016	Closed
American Samoa	(d) Rep: March 22, 2016 Dem: March 1, 2016	(ee)	(ff)	...	(ee)	(ff)
Guam	(d) Rep: March 12, 2016 Dem: May 7, 2016	(ee)	Aug., last S Aug. 27, 2016	...	(ee)	Open
No. Marianas Islands	(d) Rep: March 17, 2016 Dem: March 15, 2016	(ee)	(ff)	...	(ee)	(ff)
Puerto Rico	Rep: March 6, 2016 Dem: June 5, 2016	Nov., ★ Nov. 8, 2016	June 5, 2016	...	Nov., ★ Nov. 8, 2016	Open
U.S. Virgin Islands	(d) Rep: March 10, 2016 Dem: June 4, 2016	(ee)	Aug., 1st S Aug. 6, 2016	...	(ee)	Closed

See footnotes at end of table.

ELECTION DATES FOR NATIONAL AND STATE ELECTIONS
(Formulas and dates of state elections)

Source: The Council of State Governments, March 2016.

Note: This table describes the basic formulas for determining when national and state elections will be held. For specific information on a particular state, the reader is advised to contact the state election administration office. All dates provided are based on the state election formula and dates are subject to change.

Key:

★ — First Tuesday after first Monday.

. . . — No provision.

M — Monday.

T — Tuesday.

TH — Thursday.

S — Saturday.

SN — Sunday.

Prior — Prior to general election.

AP — After primary.

(a) National refers to presidential elections.

(b) State refers to election in which a state executive official or legislator is to be elected. See Table 6.1, State Executive Branch Officials to Be Elected, and Table 6.2, State Legislature Members to be Elected.

(c) Open: Voters can privately select which party's ballot to vote, regardless of party affiliation. Partially Open: Voters must be a registered member of the party to vote in their party's primary ballot. Partially Open: Voters can choose in which primary to vote but that choice is not private. In certain states, a voter's primary ballot selection may be regarded as a form of registration with the corresponding party. Partially Closed: Unaffiliated voters may participate in any party's primary. Members of a political party are not allowed to cross over and vote in a different political party's primary. Top Two primaries: All voters in California and Washington receive one ballot with candidates from all parties listed together. The top two finishers face each other at the general election. Louisiana has a similar election type but its primary is held in October with a runoff election in November if no candidate garners 50 percent or more of the vote. Nebraska uses a single primary ballot to elect lawmakers to its nonpartisan legislature.

(d) The dates for presidential caucuses are set by the political parties.

(e) Alaska law allows a political party to select who may participate in their party's primary. Parties may expand or limit who may participate in their Primary Election by submitting a written notice with a copy of their pre-cleared bylaws to the Director of Elections no later than September 1 of the year prior to the year in which a Primary Election is to be held.

(f) In 2015, the Arkansas General Assembly passed a bill (SB 8) to move the primary to March 1, 2016 and the runoff to March 22, 2016. The measure applies only to the 2016 elections.

(g) The state parties have the option of choosing either the first Tuesday in March (March 1, 2016) date called for in the statute or moving up to the first Tuesday in February (Feb. 2, 2016).

(h) The Secretary of State has the authority to set the date of the presidential primary election. Currently held in March, the presidential primary could be held as late as June 14.

(i) In 2011, the Idaho Legislature passed HB 351, implementing a closed primary system. However, the law gives political parties the option of opening their primary elections to unaffiliated voters and members of other political parties. The party chairman must notify the Secretary of State 6 months prior to the primary if the party intends to open its primary election to those outside of the party. The Republican Party currently allows only voters registered with its party to vote (closed), while the Democratic Party allows unaffiliated voters to vote in its primary (partially closed).

(j) In 2015, the Kansas legislature passed a bill (HB 2104) that repealed the statute calling for a presidential preference primary election. It replaces it with a requirement that each recognized political party select a presidential nominee in accordance with party procedures, for every presidential election beginning with the 2016 election.

(k) Unaffiliated voters may register with a party on primary day to vote in that party's primary.

(l) In 2015, the central committee of the Kentucky Republican Party voted to adopt a March 5 caucus for the 2016 presidential nomination process. The switch from a May 17 primary to a caucus allowed Sen. Rand Paul to run for the Republican presidential nomination and the U.S. Senate, because state law prohibits a candidate from running for more than one office on a ballot.

(m) Louisiana has an open primary which requires all candidates, regardless of party affiliation, to appear on a single ballot. If a candidate receives over 50 percent of the vote in the primary, that candidate is elected to the office. If no candidate receives a majority vote, then a single election is held between the two candidates receiving the most votes. For national elections, the first vote is held on the first Saturday in October of even-numbered years with the general election held on the first Tuesday after the first Monday in November. For state elections, the election is held on the second to last Saturday in October with the runoff being held on the fourth Saturday after first election.

(n) Voters who have already registered but have not enrolled in a party may enroll in a party at the polls on Election Day. Any voter who wishes to change party enrollment must do so at least 15 days before the vote.

(o) In 2015, Maryland lawmakers passed a bill (SB 204) to move the primary back three weeks, shifting the election further from the Easter holiday, which would have coincided with the first day of early voting in 2016.

(p) Under Maryland law, parties may allow unaffiliated voters to cast ballots in their primaries by notifying the election board six months in advance. However, both major parties currently hold closed primaries.

(q) Massachusetts lawmakers set the 2016 primary date for Thursday, September 8 as part of a supplemental appropriations bill (HB 3829). This date was selected to avoid having the primary on the Tuesday after Labor Day, as many cities and towns would accrue additional costs since they would have to pay workers overtime to set up polling places.

(r) Parties must notify the Secretary of State's Office in writing prior to Dec. 1st the year preceding the date of the election of their intentions to hold a preference primary election. Unless the chairs of the two major political parties jointly propose a different date, the caucuses are held on the first Tuesday in February.

(s) Mississippi voters do not have to register with a party, but state law requires they must intend to support the party nominee if they vote in that party's primary election. Since voter intent is difficult to dispute in court, some characterize Mississippi's system an open partisan primary.

(t) The Secretary of State selects a date for the primary, which must be 7 days or more immediately preceding the date on which any other state holds a similar election.

(u) An unaffiliated voter may choose one party's ballot, which makes them a registered member of that party. However, temporary affiliation is possible, as voters can fill out a card at the polling place to return to undeclared status after the vote is cast.

(v) In 2015, the New York Legislature passed legislation (SB 5958) that sets the state's presidential primary date for 2016 to April 19, 2016. At press time, the Legislature was considering legislation (AB 9108) that would combine the state's primary with the federal primary on June 28, 2016, to bring the state into compliance with the federal Military and Overseas Voter Empowerment (MOVE) Act, which ensures military and overseas voters are able to participate in the electoral process.

(w) In 2015, the North Carolina Legislature passed a bill (HB 373) that sets the presidential and state primary date as March 15 for 2016 only. The presidential primary is set in statute for the Tuesday after the South Carolina primary, while the state primary is the second Tuesday in June. Per HB 2 passed in the 2016 extra session, there will be no runoff elections in 2016; all 2016 elections will be determined by a plurality.

(x) The Republican Party will not vote at its caucus, allowing its 28 delegates to remain unpledged to a specific candidate.

(y) In 2015, Ohio lawmakers passed a bill (HB 153) that moves the date of the primary back one week to the second Tuesday after the first Monday in March. In non-presidential election years, the primary is held on the first Tuesday after the first Monday in May. The move to a later week allows Republicans to allocate delegates in a winner-take-all fashion.

ELECTION DATES FOR NATIONAL AND STATE ELECTIONS
(Formulas and dates of state elections)

(z) In November of each odd-numbered year, recognized political parties declare whether or not they will permit Independents to vote in their primary elections during the following two calendar years. For 2016 and 2017, the Democratic Party granted permission for Independents to vote in its primaries and runoff primaries. Independents cannot vote in Republican primaries.

(aa) South Dakota only holds runoffs for the offices of U.S. Senator, U.S. Representative and governor.

(bb) In 2015, the Utah legislature failed to pass a bill (HB 329) to allocate $3 million to move the presidential primary from June to March. As a result, the presidential primary is scheduled for the same date as the June state primary date. However, it is too late under both Republican and Democratic party rules, making the state "out of compliance," resulting in penalties from the national parties. Both parties are instead holding a caucus.

(cc) In November, 2015, a federal judge ruled that the state cannot force political parties to open their primaries to unaffiliated voters, invalidating a provision in a 2014 law (SB 54). This decision allows the Utah Republican Party to continue to hold closed primaries.

(dd) In 2014, the Council of the District of Columbia passed a bill (B20-0265) to move the presidential primary from the 1st Tuesday in April to the 2nd Tuesday in June. Because the national Republican convention will be held in mid-July, the June 14 primary date violates Republican National Committee rules. As a result, D.C. Republicans will hold a convention on March 16.

(ee) Residents of U.S. territories may vote in presidential primaries, but the Electoral College system does not permit them to vote in presidential elections.

(ff) American Samoa and the Northern Marianas Islands do not conduct primary elections. Instead, the law provides for a runoff when none of the candidates receives more than 50% of the vote.

Table 6.5
POLLING HOURS: GENERAL ELECTIONS

State or other jurisdiction	Polls open	Polls close	Notes on hours (a)
Alabama	7 a.m.	7 p.m.	Polling places located in the Eastern Time Zone may be open from 7 a.m. to 7 p.m. ET.
Alaska	7 a.m.	8 p.m.	
Arizona	6 a.m.	7 p.m.	
Arkansas	7:30 a.m.	7:30 p.m.	
California	7 a.m.	8 p.m.	
Colorado	7 a.m.	7 p.m.	
Connecticut	6 a.m.	8 p.m.	
Delaware	7 a.m.	8 p.m.	
Florida	7 a.m.	7 p.m.	
Georgia	7 a.m.	7 p.m.	
Hawaii	7 a.m.	6 p.m.	
Idaho	8 a.m.	8 p.m.	Clerk has the option of opening all polls at 7 a.m. Idaho is in two time zones—MT and PT.
Illinois	6 a.m.	7 p.m.	
Indiana	6 a.m.	6 p.m.	For those counties on Central time, polling places will observe these times in Central time.
Iowa	7 a.m.	9 p.m.	
Kansas	7 a.m.	7 p.m.	Counties may open the polls earlier and close them later. Several western counties are in the Mountain Time Zone.
Kentucky	6 a.m.	6 p.m.	Counties may be either in Eastern or Central Time Zones.
Louisiana	6 a.m.	8 p.m.	
Maine	Between 6 and 10 a.m.	8 p.m.	Applicable opening time depends on variables related to the size of the precinct.
Maryland	7 a.m.	8 p.m.	
Massachusetts	7 a.m.	8 p.m.	Some municipalities may open their polls as early as 5:45 a.m.
Michigan	7 a.m.	8 p.m.	Eastern Time Zone and Central Time Zone
Minnesota	7 a.m.	8 p.m.	A few polling places in small townships located outside the eleven-county metropolitan area may open as late as 10 a.m.
Mississippi	7 a.m.	7 p.m.	
Missouri	6 a.m.	7 p.m.	
Montana	7 a.m.	8 p.m.	A polling place having fewer than 400 registered electors must be open from at least noon to 8 p.m. or until all registered electors in any precinct have voted, at which time that precinct in the polling place must be closed immediately.
Nebraska	7 a.m MT/8 a.m. CT	7 p.m. MT/8 p.m. CT	
Nevada	7 a.m.	7 p.m.	
New Hampshire	No later than 11 a.m.	No earlier than 7 p.m.	Polling hours vary from town to town.
New Jersey	6 a.m.	8 p.m.	
New Mexico	7 a.m.	7 p.m.	
New York	6 a.m.	9 p.m.	
North Carolina	6:30 a.m.	7:30 p.m.	
North Dakota	Between 7 and 9 a.m.	Between 7 and 9 p.m.	Polling locations cannot open earlier than 7 a.m. and must be open by 9 a.m., with the exception of those precincts in which fewer than 75 votes were cast in the last General Election, which must open no later than noon. All polling locations must remain open until 7 p.m. and close no later than 9 p.m.
Ohio	6:30 a.m.	7:30 p.m.	
Oklahoma	7 a.m.	7 p.m.	

See footnotes at end of table.

POLLING HOURS: GENERAL ELECTIONS — Continued

State or other jurisdiction	Polls open	Polls close	Notes on hours (a)
Oregon	7 a.m.	8 p.m.	Official dropsites open 8 hours or more and until 8 p.m. for depositing cast ballots. County Clerks office open 7 a.m.–8 p.m. for issuing and depositing ballots
Pennsylvania	7 a.m.	8 p.m.	
Rhode Island	Between 7 and 9 a.m	8 p.m.	Polls open at 9 a.m. in special elections.
South Carolina	7 a.m.	7 p.m.	
South Dakota	7 a.m.	7 p.m.	
Tennessee	8 a.m. (may be earlier)	7 p.m. CT/ 8 p.m. ET	Polling places must be open a minimum of ten continuous hours, but no more than 13 hours. In any county having a population of not less than 120,000, all polling places must open by 8 a.m., but nothing prevents an earlier opening time at the discretion of the county election commission.
Texas	7 a.m.	7 p.m.	
Utah	7 a.m.	8 p.m.	
Vermont	Between 5 and 10 a.m.	7 p.m.	The opening time for polls is set by local boards of civil authority.
Virginia	6 a.m.	7 p.m.	
Washington	NA	NA	Washington votes by mail. The ballot must be postmarked no later than Election Day; or returned to a designated ballot drop box by 8 p.m. on Election Day; or returned in person to the county elections department by 8 p.m. on Election Day.
West Virginia	6:30 a.m.	7:30 p.m.	
Wisconsin	7 a.m.	8 p.m.	
Wyoming	7 a.m.	7 p.m.	
Dist. of Columbia	7 a.m.	8 p.m.	
American Samoa	6 a.m	6 p.m.	
Guam	7 a.m.	8 p.m.	
No. Mariana Islands	7 a.m.	7 p.m.	
Puerto Rico	9 a.m.	5 p.m.	
U.S. Virgin Islands	7 a.m.	7 p.m.	

Sources: The Council of State Governments and state websites, September 2014.

Note: Hours for primary, municipal and special elections may differ from those noted.

(a) In all states, voters standing in line when the polls close are allowed to vote; however, provisions for handling those voters vary across jurisdictions.

Table 6.6
VOTER REGISTRATION INFORMATION

State or other jurisdiction	Closing date for registration before general election (days)	Same-day registration	Online registration	Automatic registration (a)	Residency requirements (b)	Registration in other places prohibited (c)	Provision regarding mental competency
Alabama	14	…	★	…	S	★	★
Alaska	30	(d)	★	…	S, D, 30	★	★
Arizona	29	…	★	…	S, C, 29	★	★
Arkansas	30	…	…	…	S, 30	★	★
California	15	★(e)	★	★	S	…	★
Colorado	22 days through voter registration drive, 8 online or by mail, Election Day in person	★	★	…	S, 22	…	…
Connecticut	14 by mail, 7 in person, Election Day	★	★	…	S, T	★	★
Delaware	24	…	★(f)	…	S	★	★
Florida	29	…	★(f)	…	S	…	★
Georgia	28	…	★	…	S, C	…	★
Hawaii	30	★(g)	★(f)	…	S	★	★
Idaho	25 or Election Day	★	★(f)	…	S, C, 30	★	★
Illinois	27 (h)	★	★	…	S, P, 30	★	★
Indiana	29	…	★	…	S, P, 30	★	★
Iowa	10 or Election Day	★	★	…	S	…	★
Kansas	21	…	★	…	S	★	★
Kentucky	29	…	★	…	S, P, 28	★	★
Louisiana	30	…	★	…	S, Parish, 30	★	★
Maine	21 by mail, up to Election Day in person	★	★	…	S, M	★	★
Maryland	21 by mail, early voting period in person	★(i)	★	…	S, 21	★	★
Massachusetts	20	★	★	…	S	…	★
Michigan	30	…	(j)	…	S, M, 30	★	★
Minnesota	21 or Election Day	★	★	…	S, 20	…	★
Mississippi	30	…	(k)	…	S, T, 30	★	★
Missouri	28	…	★	…	S	…	★
Montana	30 by mail or up to Election Day in person	★	…	…	S, 30	★	★
Nebraska	17 by mail, 10 in person	…	★	…	S	★	★
Nevada	31 by mail, 21 in person or online	…	★	…	S, C, 30; P, 10	★	★
New Hampshire	10 or Election Day	★	…	…	S	★	★
New Jersey	21	…	…	…	S, C, 30	★	★
New Mexico	28	…	(k)	…	S	…	★
New York	25	…	★	★	S, P, 30	★	★
North Carolina	25 (l)	(l)	…	…	S, C, 30	★	★
North Dakota	(m)	(m)	(m)	…	S, P, 30	(m)	★
Ohio	30 (n)	(n)	(k)	…	S, 30	★	★
Oklahoma	24	…	★(f)	…	S	…	★
Oregon	21	…	★	★	S	…	★
Pennsylvania	30	…	★	…	S, D, 30	★	★
Rhode Island	30	★(d)	★(f)	…	S, T	★	★
South Carolina	30	…	★	…	S, C, P	★	★

See footnotes at end of table.

VOTER REGISTRATION INFORMATION—Continued

State or other jurisdiction	Closing date for registration before general election (days)	Same-day registration	Online registration	Automatic registration (a)	Residency requirements (b)	Registration in other places prohibited (c)	Provision regarding mental competency
South Dakota	15	…	…		S	★	★
Tennessee	30	…	★(f)		S	★	★
Texas	30	…	★		S, C	…	★
Utah	30 by mail, 7 in person or online (o)	…	★		S, 30	★	★
Vermont	6	★(p)	…	★	S, T	…	…
Virginia	22	…	★		S	★	★
Washington	30 by mail, 8 in person	…	★		S, 30	★	★
West Virginia	21	…	★(f)		S, T, 30	★	★
Wisconsin	20 by mail, 4 in person, or Election Day	★	…		S, P, 28	…	★
Wyoming	14 or Election Day	★	…	★	S, P	★	★
Dist. of Columbia	30 by mail, Election Day in person	★	★		D, 30	★	★
American Samoa	30	…	…		D	★	…
Guam	10	…	…		Territory	★	★
No. Mariana Islands	60	…	…		Territory, 120	★	★
Puerto Rico	50	…	…		Territory (q)	★	★
U.S. Virgin Islands	30	…	…		Territory, P, 90	…	★

Source: The Council of State Governments survey of state election websites, May 2016.

Key:

★ — Provision exists.

… — No state provision.

(a) Eligible citizens who interact with government agencies are automatically registered to vote unless they decline.

(b) Key for residency requirements: S — State; C — County; D — District; M — Municipality; P — Precinct; T — Town. Numbers represent the number of days before an election for which one must be a resident.

(c) State provision prohibiting registration or claiming the right to vote in another state or jurisdiction.

(d) Election-day registration is available in presidential election years, but voters who do so can vote only for the offices of President and Vice President, not in state or local races.

(e) California's same-day registration will take effect on January 1 of the year following the year in which the Secretary of State certifies that the state has a statewide voter registration database that complies with the requirements of the federal Help America Vote Act of 2002.

(f) Not yet implemented: Florida, passed in 2015 and must be implemented by October 2017; Idaho, passed in 2016 and effective January 1, 2017; Oklahoma, passed in 2015; Rhode Island, passed in 2016 and Secretary of State Nellie Gorbea indicates it will be in place before the November elections; Tennessee, passed in 2016 and effective July 1, 2017; and Wisconsin, passed in 2016 and must be in place before the Spring 2017 primary.

(g) In 2014 Hawaii lawmakers passed legislation (HB 2590) to allow voters to register at early voting sites beginning in 2016 or at their assigned polling places on Election Day starting in 2018.

(h) Registration closes 27 days before a general election. Illinois also has a "grace period" registration that extends registration from the normal close of registration up through the 3rd day before the elec-

tion. Once registered, this voter may cast a ballot during this "Grace Period" at the election authority's office or at a location specifically designated for this purpose by the election authority, or by mail, at the discretion of the election authority.

(i) As of January 1, 2016, Maryland voters are able to register and vote on the same day at early voting locations, but not on Election Day.

(j) An online system allows voters to change their address for both their drivers license and voter registration at the same time. Michigan law requires that the same address be on record for both.

(k) In Mississippi, New Mexico, and Ohio, a registered voter can update an existing registration record online, but new applications must still be made on paper.

(l) In 2014, the North Carolina legislature eliminated voters' ability to register and vote on the same day at early voting locations. Registered voters may still update their name and address on their voter registration at an Early Voting site.

(m) No voter registration.

(n) In 2014, the Ohio Legislature passed a bill that eliminated the ability of voters to register during the six early voting days referred to as "Golden Week," when people could both register to vote and cast an in-person absentee ballot.

(o) Must be postmarked 30 days before an election. Voters can register in-person or online up to 7 days before the election. However, these voters will not be eligible to participate in early voting, and must vote on election day.

(p) The Vermont Legislature passed a bill (SB 29) in 2015 to allow for same-day voter registration, effective January 1, 2017.

(q) Voters must have a permanent residence in Puerto Rico to be a qualified elector.

Table 6.6a
VOTER INFORMATION

State or other jurisdiction	Vote by mail or Online (a)	Early voting allowed (b)	Voter ID required (c)	Photo ID required	Persons eligible for absentee voting (d)	Permanent absentee status available (e)	Absentee votes signed by witness or notary (f)	Voting rights revoked	Method/ process or provision for restoration (g)
Alabama	No	Yes	Yes (h)	Excuse required	...	N or 2 W	★	B
Alaska	★(i)	Yes	Yes (j)	No	No excuse required	...	N or 1 W	★	C
Arizona		Yes	Yes	No	No excuse required	★	...	★	B
Arkansas		Yes	Yes	No (k)	Excuse required	...	...	★	C
California		Yes	No	No	No excuse required	★	...	★	C
Colorado	★(l)	Yes	Yes	No	N/A	N/A	...	★	C
Connecticut		No	No	No	Excuse required	...	...	★	C
Delaware		No	Yes	No	Excuse required	...	...	★	B
Florida		Yes	Yes	Yes	No excuse required	...	...	★	A
Georgia		Yes	Yes	Yes	No excuse required	...	...	★	C
Hawaii		Yes	Yes	No	No excuse required	★	...	★	C
Idaho		Yes (m)	Yes	Yes (n)	No excuse required	...	...	★	C
Illinois		Yes	No	No	No excuse required	...	...	★	C
Indiana		Yes (m)	Yes	Yes	Excuse required	...	...	★	C
Iowa		Yes (m)	No	No	No excuse required	...	...	★	A
Kansas		Yes	Yes	Yes	No excuse required	...	...	★	C
Kentucky		No	Yes	No	Excuse required	...	...	★	A
Louisiana		Yes	Yes	Yes	Excuse required	...	N or W	★	C
Maine		Yes (m)	No	No	No excuse required	...	...	...	N/A
Maryland		Yes	No	No	No excuse required	...	...	★	C
Massachusetts		Yes (o)	No	No	Excuse required	...	...	★	C
Michigan		No	Yes	Yes	Excuse required	...	...	★	C
Minnesota		Yes (m)	No	No	No excuse required	...	N or W (p)	★	C
Mississippi		No	Yes	Yes	Excuse required	...	N (q)	★	B
Missouri		No	Yes	No	Excuse required	...	N (r)	★	C
Montana		Yes (m)	Yes	No	No excuse required	★	...	★	C
Nebraska		Yes	No	No	No excuse required	...	...	★	C
Nevada		Yes	No	No	No excuse required	...	...	★	B
New Hampshire		No	Yes	Yes	Excuse required	...	...	★	C
New Jersey		Yes (m)	No	No	No excuse required	★	...	★	C
New Mexico		Yes	No	No	No excuse required	...	...	★	C
New York		No	No	No	Excuse required	...	...	★	C
North Carolina		Yes	Yes	No (s)	No excuse required	...	N or 2 W	★	C
North Dakota		Yes	Yes	Yes	No excuse required	...	...	★	C
Ohio		Yes (m)	Yes	No	No excuse required	...	...	★	C
Oklahoma		Yes (m)	Yes	No (t)	No excuse required	...	N (u)	★	C
Oregon	★(v)	N/A	No	No	N/A	N/A	...	★	C
Pennsylvania		No	No (w)	No (w)	Excuse required	...	...	★	C
Rhode Island		No	Yes	Yes	Excuse required	...	N or 2W (x)	★	C
South Carolina		No	Yes	No (y)	Excuse required	...	W (z)	★	C
South Dakota		Yes (m)	Yes	Yes	No excuse required	...	(aa)	★	C
Tennessee		Yes	Yes	Yes	Excuse required	...	...	★	B
Texas		Yes	Yes	Yes	Excuse required	...	...	★	C
Utah		Yes	Yes	No	No excuse required	★	...	★	C
Vermont		Yes (m)	No	No	No excuse required	...	...	...	N/A
Virginia		No	Yes	Yes	Excuse required	...	W	★	C (bb)
Washington	★(cc)	N/A	No	No	N/A	N/A	...	★	C
West Virginia		Yes	No (dd)	No (dd)	Excuse required	...	...	★	C
Wisconsin		Yes (m)	Yes	Yes	No excuse required	...	W	★	C
Wyoming		Yes (m)	No	No	No excuse required	...	...	★	B
Dist. of Columbia		Yes	No	No	No excuse required	★	...	★	C
American Samoa		No	No	No	Excuse required	...	...	★	C
Guam		No	No	No	Excuse required	...	N	★	C
No. Mariana Islands		No	No	No	Excuse required	...	N	★	C
Puerto Rico		Yes	Yes	No	Excuse required	...	(ee)	...	N/A
U.S. Virgin Islands		No	Yes	No	Excuse required	...	Affidavit	★	C

See footnotes at end of table.

VOTER INFORMATION — Continued

Sources: The Council of State Governments survey of state websites, May 2016.

Key:

★ — Provision exists.

. . . — No state provision.

N/A — Not Applicable.

(a) Three states—Colorado, Oregon, and Washington—conduct elections by mail. All registered voters are automatically mailed a ballot in advance of Election Day. Alaska is the first state to allow all voters—not just those covered by the federal Uniformed and Overseas Citizens Absentee Voting Act (UOCAVA)—to submit an absentee ballot electronically. Civilian voters must apply for an electronic ballot beginning 15 days before the election.

(b) Early voting is usually done in person on the same equipment as that used on Election Day. An excuse is not required.

(c) Voter identification laws include both photo or non-photo identification requirements.

(d) Typical excuses include some or all of the following: absent on business; senior citizen; disabled persons; not absent, but prevented by employment from voting; out of state on Election Day; out of precinct on Election Day; absent for religious reasons; students; temporarily out of jurisdiction.

(e) State allows voters to be added to the permanent absentee voter list, in which an absentee ballot will be automatically sent for each election. No excuse is required. This does not include states that allow certain voters to be added to the list, including permanently disabled or ill voters, the elderly, uniformed service members and their families, or people who live outside the United States.

(f) Absentee votes must be signed by, N—Notary or W—Witness. Numbers indicated the number of signatures required.

(g) A—permanent disenfranchisement for all offenders; states that permanently disenfranchise all or some felons may allow felons to apply, on an individual basis, to the state for an exemption that will restore their voting rights.

B—permanent disenfranchisement for some offenders; in these states, felons who commit certain felonies are permanently disenfranchised.

C—voting rights restored after completion of some or all of sentence; 20 states (Alaska, Ark., Ga., Idaho, Kans., La., Minn., Mo., Nebr., N.J., N.M., N.C., Okla., S.C., S.D., Texas, Va., Wash., W. Va., Wis.) restore rights after completion of entire sentence, including parole and probation; 14 states (Hawaii, Ill., Ind., Md., Mass., Mich., Mont., N.H., N.D., Ohio, Ore., Pa., R.I., Utah) plus the District of Columbia restore rights after completion of prison sentence, allowing parolees and probationers to vote; 4 states (Calif., Colo., Conn., N.Y.) restore rights after completion of prison time and parole, allowing probationers to vote.

(h) Photo identification is not required if two election officials can sign sworn statements saying they know the voter.

(i) Alaska is the first state to allow all voters—not just those covered by the federal Uniformed and Overseas Citizens Absentee Voting Act (UOCAVA)—to submit an absentee ballot electronically. Civilian voters must apply for an electronic ballot beginning 15 days before the election.

(j) An election officer may waive the identification requirement if the election officials knows the identity of the voter.

(k) In October 2014, the Arkansas Supreme Court struck down a state law that requires voters to show photo identification before casting a ballot, ruling the requirement unconstitutional.

(l) While all registered voters are automatically mailed a ballot prior to the election, the state also operates in-person voting sites.

(m) Functional early voting, as the state permits in-person absentee voting, in which voters, within a certain period of time before the election, can apply in person for an absentee ballot (no excuse required) and cast a ballot in the election office.

(n) A registered voter must either present a photo ID or sign a Personal Identification Affidavit. After signing the Affidavit, the voter will be issued a ballot to be tabulated with all other ballots.

(o) Beginning in 2016, Massachusetts will have early voting only during even-year November elections. There are no early voting periods for primaries or municipal elections.

(p) Unless the witness is a notary, the witness must also be a registered Minnesota voter.

(q) Disabled voters do not need to have an absentee ballot notarized, but it must be witnessed.

(r) All absentee ballots must be notarized with the exception of the following: Missouri residents outside the U.S., including military on active duty and their immediate family members; permanently disabled voters and those voting absentee due to illness or physical disability; and caregivers.

(s) Photo identification will be required starting in 2016. However, voters who are unable to obtain an acceptable photo ID due to a reasonable impediment may still vote a provisional ballot at the polls. Examples of a reasonable impediment include but are not limited to the lack of proper documents, family obligations, transportation problems, work schedule, illness or disability, among other reasonable impediments faced by the voter. Voters must also sign a declaration describing their impediment; and provide their date of birth and last four digits of their Social Security number, or present their current voter registration card or a copy of an acceptable document bearing their name and address. (Acceptable documents include a current utility bill, bank statement, government check, paycheck, or other government-issued document.) The provisional ballot will be counted when the information on the declaration is verified and all other eligibility requirements are met.

(t) A Voter Identification Card issued by the County Election Board is the only valid proof of identity that does not include a photograph.

(u) All absentee ballots must notarized with the following exceptions: Physically incapacitated voters and voters who care for physically incapacitated persons (ballot affidavit must be witnessed by two people); voters in a nursing home; overseas voters.

(v) State conducts election by mail. All registered voters are automatically mailed a ballot in advance of Election Day.

(w) In 2012, the legislature enacted a law requiring voters to show photo identification. However, in 2014 a state judge struck down the law.

(x) All absentee ballots must be notarized or signed by two witnesses with the following exceptions: military and overseas voters.

(y) If a voter has a reasonable impediment to obtaining photo identification, he or she may vote a provisional ballot after showing a non-photo voter registration card. State law defines a reasonable impediment as any valid reason, beyond a person's control, that creates an obstacle to obtaining Photo ID. Some examples include: religious objection to being photographed; disability or illness; work schedule; lack of transportation; lack of birth certificate; family responsibilities; election within short time frame of implementation of photo ID law (January 1, 2013); and any other obstacle a person finds reasonable.

(z) All absentee ballots must be notarized or signed by one witness, with the exception of qualified voters under the Uniformed and Overseas Citizens Absentee Voters Act.

(aa) Absentee ballot applications (not absentee ballots) are required to be notarized unless a copy of the voter's photo identification is also submitted.

(bb) On Apr. 22, 2016, Virginia Gov. Terry McAuliffe signed an order restoring the vote to all felons in Virginia, regardless of their charge, who had completed their term of incarceration and their term of probation or parole. The governor's action will not apply to felons released in the future, but aides say the governor plans to issue similar orders on a monthly basis to cover people as they are released.

(cc) State conducts election by mail. All registered voters are automatically mailed a ballot in advance of Election Day. Only Pierce County offers in-person voting.

(dd) In 2016, the West Virginia Legislature approved a bill that will require voters to show some form of identification before casting a ballot. Approved forms of identification include any government-issued ID or permit, with or without a photo, including a voter registration card; any college or high school issued ID; a health insurance card; a utility bill; a bank card or bank statement; or verification of identification by another adult who has known the voter for at least 6 months, including a poll worker. It is effective January 1, 2018.

(ee) Absentee ballot applications (not absentee ballots) are required to be certified by various officials, depending on the reason for voting absentee, such as a college registrar, employer, or medical official.

Table 6.7
VOTING STATISTICS FOR GUBERNATORIAL ELECTIONS

State or other jurisdiction	Date of last election	Primary election					General election								
		Republican	Democrat	3rd Party	Independent	Total votes	Republican	Percent	Democrat	Percent	3rd Party	Percent	Independent and Write-in	Percent	Total votes
Alabama	2014	434,525	180,658	0	0	615,183	750,231	63.6	427,787	36.2	0	0.0	2,395	0.2	1,180,413
Alaska	2014	106,648	46,427 (a)	0	0	153,075	128,435	45.9	8,985 (b)	3.2	6,987	2.5	135,551 (b)	48.4	279,958
Arizona	2014	539,690	271,276 (c)	4,739	0	815,705	805,062	53.4	626,921	41.6	72,769	4.8	1,664	0.1	1,506,416
Arkansas	2014	179,225	153,343	0	0	332,568	470,429	55.4	352,115	41.5	26,408	3.1	0	0.0	848,952
California (d)	2014	1,729,985	2,391,810	119,579	91,654	4,333,028	2,929,213	40.0	4,388,368	60.0	0	0.0	0	0.0	7,317,581
Colorado	2014	384,749	214,403 (c)	0	0	599,152	938,195	46.0	1,006,433	49.3	96,946	4.7	0	0.0	2,041,574
Connecticut	2014	79,426	(c)	0	0	79,426	526,295 (e)	48.2	554,314 (e)	50.7	0	0.0	12,164	1.1	1,092,773
Delaware	2012	(c)	(c)	0	0	0	113,793	28.6	275,993	69.3	8,369	2.1	0	0.0	398,155
Florida	2014	949,144	837,796	0	0	1,786,940	2,865,343	48.1	2,801,198	47.1	223,356	3.8	61,664	1.0	5,951,561
Georgia	2014	596,218	304,243 (c)	0	0	900,461	1,345,237	52.7	1,144,794	44.9	60,185	2.4	432	0.0	2,550,648
Hawaii	2014	43,052	233,179	2,526	0	278,757	135,775	37.1	181,106	49.5	49,329	13.5	0	0.0	366,210
Idaho	2014	155,310	25,638	0	0	180,948	235,378	53.2	169,595	38.3	25,627	5.8	11,668	2.6	442,268
Illinois	2014	819,710	447,318	0	0	1,267,028	1,833,627	50.4	1,681,343	46.2	121,534	3.3	1,186	0.0	3,637,690
Indiana	2012	554,412 (c)	207,365 (c)	0	0	761,777	1,275,424	49.5	1,200,016	46.6	101,868	4.0	21	0.0	2,577,329
Iowa	2014	162,589	72,382	0	0	234,971	666,023	59.0	420,778	37.3	41,140	3.6	1,093	0.1	1,129,034
Kansas	2014	263,594	66,357 (c)	0	0	329,951	433,196	49.8	401,100	46.1	35,206	4.0	0	0.0	869,502
Kentucky	2015	214,193	178,541	0	0	392,734	511,374	52.5	426,620	43.8	0	0.0	35,698	3.7	973,692
Louisiana (f)	2015	637,938	463,700	0	12,698	1,114,336	505,940	43.9	646,924	56.1	0	0.0	0	0.0	1,152,864
Maine	2014	50,856 (c)	56,286 (c)	0	0	107,142	294,519	48.2	265,114	43.4	51,515	8.4	79	0.0	611,227
Maryland	2014	214,935	485,093	0	0	700,028	884,400	51.2	818,890	47.4	25,382	1.5	303	0.0	1,728,975
Massachusetts	2014	156,580	540,733	0	0	697,313	1,044,573	48.4	1,004,408	46.5	71,814	3.3	37,531	1.7	2,158,326
Michigan	2014	617,720 (c)	513,263 (c)	5,822	0	1,130,983	1,607,399	50.9	1,479,057	46.9	70,025	2.2	50	0.0	3,156,531
Minnesota	2014	184,110	191,259	0	0	381,191	879,257	44.5	989,113	50.1	106,241	5.4	795	0.0	1,975,406
Mississippi	2015	274,407	299,368	0	0	573,775	476,697	66.4	231,643	32.3	9,845	1.3	0	0.0	718,185
Missouri	2012	557,406	314,158	2,500	0	874,064	1,160,265	42.5	1,494,056	54.8	73,509	2.7	53	0.0	2,727,883
Montana	2012	88,561	136,060	0	0	224,621	228,879	47.3	236,450	48.9	18,160	3.8	0	0.0	483,489
Nebraska	2014	221,020	65,620 (c)	402 (c)	0	287,042	308,751	57.2	211,905	39.3	19,001	3.5	0	0.0	539,657
Nevada	2014	117,510 (g)	72,521 (g)	0	0	190,031	386,340	70.6	130,722	23.9	14,536	2.7	15,751 (g)	2.9	547,349
New Hampshire	2014	41,976	113,273	0	0	155,249	230,610	47.4	254,666	52.4	0	0.0	907	0.2	486,183
New Jersey	2013	223,761	197,171	0	0	420,932	1,278,932	60.3	809,978	38.2	29,172	1.4	2,784	0.1	2,120,866
New Mexico	2014	64,413 (c)	125,371	0	0	189,784	293,443	57.2	219,362	42.8	0	0.0	0	0.0	512,805
New York	2014	(c)	574,350	0	0	574,350	1,536,879 (h)	40.2	2,069,480 (h)	54.2	206,349	5.4	6,719	0.2	3,819,427
North Carolina	2012	897,137	934,287	0	0	1,831,424	2,440,707	54.6	1,931,580	43.2	94,652	2.1	1,356	0.0	4,468,295
North Dakota	2012	95,483 (c)	52,238 (c)	664	0	148,385	200,525	63.1	109,048	34.3	7,974	2.5	267	0.1	317,814
Ohio	2014	559,671 (c)	440,253	674	0	1,000,598	1,944,848	63.6	1,009,359	33.0	101,706	3.3	0	0.0	3,055,913
Oklahoma	2014	264,894	(c)	0	0	264,894	460,298	55.8	338,239	41.0	0	0.0	26,294	3.2	824,831
Oregon	2014	248,552	301,875	0	0	550,427	648,542	44.1	733,230	49.9	81,298	5.5	6,654	0.5	1,469,724
Pennsylvania	2014	(c)	1,920,355	0	0	1,920,355	1,575,511	45.1	1,920,355	54.9	0	0.0	0	0.0	3,495,866
Rhode Island	2014	31,929	128,095	0	0	160,024	117,428	36.2	131,899	40.7	69,278	21.4	5,450	1.7	324,055
South Carolina	2014	(c)	(c)	0	0	0	696,645	55.9	516,166	41.4	21,060	1.7	12,432	1.0	1,246,303

See footnotes at end of table.

VOTING STATISTICS FOR GUBERNATORIAL ELECTIONS—Continued

State or other jurisdiction	Date of last election	Primary election Republican	Democrat	3rd Party	Independent	Total votes	General election Republican	Percent	Democrat	Percent	3rd Party	Percent	Independent and Write-in	Percent	Total votes
South Dakota...........	2014	74,213	27,594	0	0	101,807	195,477	70.5	70,549	25.4	0	0.0	11,377	4.1	277,403
Tennessee	2014	651,247	228,025	0	0	879,272	951,796	70.3	309,237	22.8	45,150	3.3	47,545	3.5	1,353,728
Texas.................	2014	1,337,875	554,014	0	0	1,891,889	2,796,547	59.3	1,835,596	38.9	85,063	1.8	1,062	0.0	4,718,268
Utah..................	2012	(i)	(i)	3,333	0	3,333	688,592	68.4	277,622	27.6	40,307	4.0	3	0.0	1,006,524
Vermont...............	2014	16,010	19,828	263	0	36,101	87,075	45.1	89,509	46.4	10,101	5.2	6,402	3.3	193,087
Virginia...............	2013	(i)	(c)	(i)	0	0	1,013,354	45.2	1,069,789	47.8	146,084	6.5	11,087	0.5	2,240,314
Washington............	2012	665,925	709,987	23,498	10,457	1,409,867	1,488,245	48.5	1,582,802	51.5	0	0.0	0	0.0	3,071,047
West Virginia..........	2012	104,090	202,068	0	0	306,158	303,291	45.6	335,468	50.5	25,696	3.9	0	0.0	664,455
Wisconsin	2014	240,102(c)	312,106	141	0	552,349	1,259,706	52.3	1,122,913	46.6	0	0.0	27,695	1.1	2,410,314
Wyoming	2014	97,884	15,799(c)	0	0	113,684	99,700	59.4	45,752	27.3	4,040	2.4	18,385	11.0	167,877
American Samoa	2012	(i)	(i)	(i)	(i)	(i)	2,521	19.3	4,315(j)	33.1	0	0.0	6,217(j)	47.6	13,053
Guam	2014	11,034(c)	7,330(c)	0	0	18,364	22,512	63.9	12,712	36.1	0	0.0	0	0.0	35,224
No. Mariana Islands ...	2014	(k)	(k)	(k)	(k)	(k)	541	3.9	6,342	46.0	0	0.0	6,915	50.1	13,798
Puerto Rico	2012	(c)	(c)	0	0	0	884,775	47.1	896,060	47.7	82,834	4.4	13,510	0.7	1,877,179
U.S. Virgin Islands.....	2014	N/A	9,962	0	0	9,962	0	0.0	10,173(l)	39.2	0	0.0	15,802(l)	60.8	25,975

Source: The Council of State Governments' survey of state elections websites, January 2016.

Key:

N/A — Not Applicable

(a) In 2014, the Democratic Primary featured candidates from the Democratic Party and the Libertarian Party.

(b) In a move endorsed by the Alaska Democratic Party, independent gubernatorial candidate Bill Walker and Democratic candidate Byron Mallot joined forces in a self-proclaimed "unity" ticket to challenge — and ultimately defeat — incumbent Republican Gov. Sean Parnell. Walker, a Republican who petitioned on to the ballot as an independent, headed the ticket, while the Democratic candidate Mallot ran as the lieutenant governor. This move required Hollis French, the Democratic lieutenant governor candidate, and Craig Fleener, Walker's former running mate, to resign from their respective ballots. As a result, there were no Democratic candidates for governor for the first time in state history. The unity ticket received 134,658 votes. Write-in votes totaled 893.

(c) Candidate ran unopposed.

(d) California became an open primary state after passage of Proposition 14 in the June 2010 election. The top two vote-getters in primary races for congressional, state legislative and statewide offices, regardless of political party, will be in a face-off in the general election.

(e) Republican vote total includes 22,297 votes from the Independent party. Democratic vote total includes 24,762 from the Working Families Party.

(f) Louisiana has an open primary which requires all candidates, regardless of party affiliation, to appear on a single ballot. If a candidate receives over 50 percent of the vote in the primary, he is elected to the office. If no candidate receives a majority vote, then a single election is held between the two candidates receiving the most votes.

(g) Nevada voters have the option to select "None of These Candidates." If the "None of These Candidates" option receives the most votes in an election, the actual candidate who receives the most votes wins the election. In the Democratic primary, the "None of These Candidates" option received the most votes (21,725 or 30%). The winner of the primary — Robert Goodman — received 17,691 votes (25%). In the Republican primary, 3,509 voters selected that option. The "None of These Candidates" option received 15,751 votes in the general election.

(h) Democratic vote includes 73,266 from the Independence Party, 51,052 from the Women's Equality Party, and 120,446 from the Working Families Party. The Republican vote includes 239,266 from the Conservative Party and 50,242 from the Stop Common Core Party.

(i) Candidate nominated by convention.

(j) There are no primaries. Instead, the law provides for a runoff when none of the candidates receives more than 50% of the vote. In the general election, a runoff was held. The vote total in the runoff election was 12,553, with the Independent candidate Lolo Letalu Matalasi Moliga defeating the Democratic candidate, winning with 52.9% of the vote.

(k) There are no primaries. Instead, the law provides for a runoff when none of the candidates receives more than 50% of the vote.

(l) In the general election in the U.S. Virgin Islands, a runoff was held because no candidate received more than 50% of the vote. The vote total in the runoff election was 25,396, with the Independent candidate Kenneth Mapp winning with 62.7% of the vote.

Table 6.8
VOTER TURNOUT FOR PRESIDENTIAL ELECTIONS BY REGION: 2004, 2008 AND 2012
(In thousands)

State or other jurisdiction	2012 Voting age population (a)	2012 Number registered	2012 Number voting (b)	2008 Voting age population (a)	2008 Number registered	2008 Number voting (b)	2004 Voting age population (a)	2004 Number registered	2004 Number voting (b)
U.S. Total..................	234,564	153,161	129,140	227,719	189,391	128,628	208,247	170,937	122,501
Alabama........................	3,647	2,556	2,074	3,504	2,841	2,100	3,252	2,597	1,883
Alaska...........................	523	361	300	501	496	326	460	472	313
Arizona	4,763	2,812	2,299	4,668	2,987	2,321	3,800	2,643	2,038
Arkansas	2,204	1,376	1,069	2,134	1,686	1,087	1,951	1,686	1,055
California......................	27,959	15,356	13,039	27,169	23,209	13,214	22,075	16,557	12,589
Colorado	3,804	2,635	2,570	3,668	3,209	2,401	3,246	2,890	2,130
Connecticut..................	2,757	1,760	1,558	2,682	2,210	1,645	2,574	1,823	1,579
Delaware.......................	692	470	414	659	602	391	594	554	376
Florida..........................	14,799	9,102	8,474	14,207	11,248	8,358	12,539	10,301	7,610
Georgia.........................	7,196	4,767	3,898	7,013	5,266	3,924	6,080	4,249	3,285
Hawaii..........................	1,056	547	437	997	691	454	873	647	429
Idaho............................	1,139	745	652	1,091	862	655	996	798	613
Illinois	9,701	6,425	5,242	9,653	7,790	5,578	9,519	7,499	5,274
Indiana.........................	4,876	3,270	2,625	4,758	4,515	2,751	4,420	4,163	2,468
Iowa.............................	2,318	1,745	1,582	2,276	2,076	1,537	2,212	2,107	1,522
Kansas	2,126	1,467	1,160	2,079	1,750	1,751	2,038	1,694	1,188
Kentucky.......................	3,316	2,303	1,797	3,237	2,907	1,827	3,012	2,819	1,796
Louisiana......................	3,415	2,498	1,994	3,213	2,945	1,961	3,249	2,923	1,957
Maine............................	1,054	787	725	1,037	1,000	731	1,042	957	741
Maryland.......................	4,421	2,888	2,707	4,259	3,429	2,632	3,922	3,070	2,396
Massachusetts..............	5,129	3,759	3,184	5,016	4,220	3,103	4,931	3,973	2,927
Michigan.......................	7,540	5,620	4,731	7,624	7,471	5,044	7,541	7,164	4,839
Minnesota.....................	4,020	3,085	2,937	3,937	3,200	2,910	3,823	2,977	2,828
Mississippi....................	2,212	1,794	1,286	2,150	1,873	1,290	2,014	1,865	1,140
Missouri........................	4,563	3,384	2,757	4,453	4,181	2,925	4,297	4,194	2,731
Montana........................	766	553	484	738	668	490	680	596	450
Nebraska.......................	1,367	901	794	1,328	1,157	801	1,257	1,160	778
Nevada..........................	2,036	1,176	1,015	1,905	1,208	968	1,580	1,094	830
New Hampshire.............	1,029	752	711	1,017	864	708	991	856	684
New Jersey....................	6,727	4,326	3,638	6,622	5,379	3,868	6,669	5,009	3,612
New Mexico...................	1,541	978	784	1,469	1,193	830	1,318	1,105	756
New York	15,053	8,887	7,117	14,884	12,031	7,675	14,206	11,837	7,448
North Carolina..............	7,254	5,295	4,505	6,843	6,226	4,311	6,453	5,527	3,501
North Dakota................	523	383 (c)	323	496	(c)	317	487	(c)	316
Ohio.............................	8,806	6,076	5,581	8,715	8,163	5,698	8,604	7,973	5,426
Oklahoma	2,822	1,806	1,335	2,717	2,184	1,463	2,515	2,143	1,464
Oregon..........................	2,965	2,086	1,789	2,884	2,154	1,828	2,665	2,120	1,837
Pennsylvania.................	9,910	6,795	5,742	9,646	8,730	5,995	9,404	8,367	5,770
Rhode Island.................	829	552	446	824	701	470	803	709	437
South Carolina..............	3,545	2,479	1,964	3,347	2,554	1,921	3,214	2,315	1,618
South Dakota	611	454	364	599	508	382	573	502	395
Tennessee......................	4,850	3,210	2,459	4,685	3,978	2,600	4,284	3,532	2,437
Texas............................	18,280	10,749	7,994	17,281	13,575	8,077	16,071	13,098	7,411
Utah..............................	1,893	1,138	1,017	1,828	1,433	905	1,522	1,278	928
Vermont........................	497	357	299	489	454	325	490	445	312
Virginia........................	6,147	4,210	3,854	5,885	5,044	3,724	5,194	4,528	3,195
Washington...................	5,143	3,533	3,126	4,932	3,630	3,037	4,596	3,508	2,883
West Virginia................	1,466	982	670	1,424	1,212	713	1,406	1,169	744
Wisconsin......................	4,347	3,318	3,071	4,280	3,405	2,983	4,119	2,957 (c)	2,997
Wyoming.......................	428	268	251	397	276	255	370	246	244
Dist. of Columbia..........	501	385	294	475	427	267	435	384	228

Sources: U.S. Congress, Clerk of the House, Statistics of the Presidential and Congressional Election, 2004, 2008, 2012. U.S. Census Bureau, Resident Population of Voting Age and Percent Casting Votes—States, as of July 1, 2010. U.S. Census Bureau, Table 4a: Reported Voting and Registration of the Citizen Voting-Age Population, for States: November 2012. U.S. Census Bureau, Current Population Survey, December 2008. The Council of State Governments' survey of election officials, January 2009, January 2005.

Key:
(a) Estimated population, 18 years old and over. Includes armed forces in each state, aliens, and institutional population.
(b) Number voting is number of ballots cast in presidential race.
(c) No statewide registration required.

2015 Ballot Propositions

By John G. Matsusaka

Voters decided only 28 state-level ballot propositions in 2015, as direct democracy activity continued to cool in the 21st century. High profile issues included rejection of marijuana legalization in Ohio, selection of the chief justice in Wisconsin, and sales tax changes in Michigan and Washington.

Overview

Ballot proposition activity was muted in 2015, at least at the state level. The number of propositions is always lower in odd-numbered than even-numbered years, but 2015's total of 28 state-level propositions was the lowest in the 21st century. Considered together with the 158 propositions in 2014, which was the lowest total for an even-numbered year in the 21st century, the use of direct democracy continues to decline as the new century progresses. The 67 percent passage rate in 2015 was similar to historical rates, meaning that the overall appeal of the propositions on the ballot has not changed.

The 28 propositions in 2015 were distributed across nine states. Texas had the most, with seven, all of which passed. All of Texas' propositions were *legislative measures*, placed on the ballot by the legislature. Legislative measures are by far the most common type of proposition; two-thirds of the propositions in 2015 were legislative measures, exactly the historical average for the 21st century. Five propositions were *citizen initiatives*, new laws placed on the ballot by citizen petition. There were also four advisory propositions in Washington state that were required by the state constitution.

See Table A for a summary of propositions by state and type in 2015, Table B for a year-by-year breakdown of ballot proposition activity since 2000, and Table C for a complete list of propositions decided in 2015.

Initiative Trends

In most years, initiatives are the most visible and controversial propositions on the ballot, and they attract the lion's share of funding. Initiative proponents view the process as an important supplement to representative democracy that allows citizens to counteract the influence of special interests in the legislature; while opponents view the process as increasing the influence of wealthy and organized interest groups that can fund petition drives

and the election campaigns. The initiative and referendum system emerged in the United States during the Progressive Era; South Dakota was the first state to adopt the process in 1898, followed by Utah in 1900 and Oregon in 1902. By 1918, 19 states had adopted the process, and adoption has continued at the rate of about one state every 20 years. Mississippi was the most recent state to adopt the initiative process in 1992, bringing the total number of states that allow initiatives to 24.[1] The initiative process is widely available in states west of the Mississippi River, but it is not a purely Western phenomenon; there are initiative states in the Northeast (Maine and Massachusetts), South (Arkansas and Florida), and Midwest (Michigan and Ohio).

The total count of five initiatives in 2015 was typical for an odd-numbered year. The approval rate of 40 percent was equal to the long-run historical average. Initiative use overall appears to be waning from its peak in the mid-1990s. Figure A shows the number of initiatives by decade, beginning in 1904 when the first initiatives appeared on the ballot in Oregon. Initiatives were common in the first four decades of the 20th century, particularly in the Progressive Era that preceded the Great Depression. Many initiatives during this period were fueled by tensions between the new urban majorities in many states and the rural interests that still controlled state legislatures, because district lines were not regularly redrawn to accommodate population changes. Initiative activity tailed off in the middle decades of the 20th century, with a trough of only 89 measures from 1961 to 1970. Beginning in the late 1970s, initiative use picked up again, following California's Proposition 13 in 1978 that set off a national tax revolt. Each successive decade after Proposition 13 set a new record for the number of initiatives, peaking with 394 from 1991 to 2000. Voters have decided 101 initiatives so far in the current

Table A: State-by-State Totals for 2015

State	Initiatives	Legislative measures	Advisory	Total	Issues
Colorado..................	...	1 (1)	...	1 (1)	Use of marijuana tax revenue
Louisiana (a)...........	...	4 (2)	...	4 (2)	Transportation projects; state infrastructure bank
Maine......................	1 (1)	2 (2)	...	3 (3)	Public fundings of campaigns; $100 million in bonds
Michigan (b)............	...	1 (0)	...	1 (0)	Increase sales tax from 6% to 7%
Mississippi	1 (0)	1 (0)	...	2 (0)	State support for public schools
Ohio.........................	1 (0)	2 (2)	...	3 (1)	Marijuana legalization; bipartisan redistricting
Texas.......................	...	7 (7)	...	7 (7)	Property tax exemptions; right to hunt and fish
Washington..............	2 (2)	...	4 (2)	6 (4)	Reduce sales tax from 6.5% to 5.5%; animal trafficking
Wisconsin (c)..........	...	1 (1)	...	1 (1)	Selection of chief justice of the supreme court
Total........................	5 (2)	19 (15)	4 (2)	28 (19)	

Source: Initiative & Referendum Institute (*www.iandrinstitute.org*).
Note: The table reports the total number of propositions during 2015. Except as noted below, all propositions appeared on the ballot on Nov. 3. The main entry is the number of propositions appearing; the number approved is in parentheses. For advisory measures in Washington, the proposition is classifed as "approved" if the recommendation was to maintain the existing law.

Key:
(a) All Louisiana amendments were on the Oct. 24 ballot.
(b) The Michigan proposal was decided in a May 5 special election.
(c) The Wisconsin amendment was on the April 7 special election ballot.

decade, well below the pace in the preceding two decades. Halfway through the decade, initiative use is on target to fall to the level of the 1970s.

In terms of individual states, Oregon is the overall leader, having voted on 367 initiatives since adopting the process in 1902. California is a close second with 357 initiatives since adopting the process in 1911. Rounding out the top five are Colorado with 225, North Dakota with 192 and Washington with 176. Initiative activity is particularly high in the western half of the country. East of the Mississippi River, Arkansas has voted on the most initiatives with 123. In the 21st century, California leads with 88 initiatives, followed by 64 in Oregon, 50 in Colorado and 48 in Washington. Citizen lawmaking has become a central feature of the political process on the West Coast, particularly the Pacific states.

High Profile Issues

Despite the modest overall level of activity, individual propositions in several states garnered significant attention in 2015.

Ohio: Marijuana Legalization

One of the highest profile issues was Ohio's Issue 3, an initiative that would have legalized recreational use of marijuana. Public opinion has been shifting rapidly on marijuana—according to survey data from the General Social Survey, for the first time ever a majority of Americans now support legal-

ization—and four states recently decriminalized its recreational use through ballot measures (Alaska, Colorado, Oregon and Washington, as well as the District of Columbia).

Issue 3 went beyond the marijuana initiatives in other states by establishing monopolies across regions of the state for commercial growing of marijuana—and going so far as to identify the specific parcels of land that would have the monopolies. The parcels of land were owned by the initiative's sponsors. In response to this part of the initiative, the legislature placed Issue 2 on the ballot that would invalidate the granting of monopolies in Issue 3. Proponents of Issue 3 spent $21.5 million to persuade voters, a huge imbalance compared to the $2.2 million spent by opponents of the measure, but in the end appear to have overreached, as voters decisively rejected Issue 3 by a margin of 36 percent to 64 percent. Voters approved the legislature's amendment that would prohibit earmarked monopolies in the future. Proponents have announced their intention to return to the ballot with a better proposal in 2016.

Mississippi: Education Funding

Another interesting contest concerned Mississippi's Initiative Measure 42, a constitutional amendment that would have required the state to provide an "adequate and efficient system of free public schools." Constitutional provisions that commit a

Table B: Number of Ballot Propositions by Year Since 2000

Year	All	Initiatives	Referendums	Legislative	Other
2000	239	76	6	151	6
2001	39	4	0	35	0
2002	224	51	5	164	4
2003	68	7	0	61	0
2004	176	64	3	108	1
2005	45	18	1	26	0
2006	226	79	4	142	1
2007	43	2	2	39	0
2008	168	68	6	90	4
2009	32	5	3	24	0
2010	184	46	4	130	4
2011	34	10	2	22	0
2012	187	48	14	122	3
2013	31	3	0	23	5
2014	158	35	5	111	7
2015	28	5	0	19	4
2000–2015	1,882	521	55	1,267	39

Source: Initiative & Referendum Institute (www.iandrinstitute.org).
Note: "Other" includes propositions placed on the ballot by commissions, constitutions, or statutes.

state to provide support for education are not unusual, although the language in Measure 42 was unusually vague. One of the most controversial features of the initiative was its explicit assignment of enforcement power to the judiciary. In response, the legislature placed a competing measure on the ballot, Alternative Measure 42A, that was the same in all respects except that it assigned enforcement to the legislature.

The election for Measures 42 and 42A also was notable for the convoluted way the choices were presented on the ballot. Standard practice would be to ask voters to register a "yes" or "no" opinion on each measure, with the measure receiving the largest majority of "yes" opinions (if any) being approved. In contrast, Mississippi asked voters first to indicate whether they favored approval of "either" 42 or 42A, or "neither" of them. Then voters were asked to indicate which of the two they preferred, assuming one of the two would go into effect. In any event, neither proposal passed the first hurdle;

by a 48 percent to 52 percent margin voters rejected both measures in the first step of the ballot.

Washington: Sales Tax

Washington's I-1366 incorporated an interesting new direction in initiative strategy. In Washington, initiatives may only be used to pass statutes; they are not permitted to amend the constitution. The only way to amend the constitution is for the state legislature to propose an amendment, and for the voters to approve the amendment. Anti-tax advocates in the state have long wanted to restrict the ability of the legislature to raise taxes, but statutory initiatives that cut taxes can and are repealed by the legislature and attempts to change legislative structure are difficult without amending the constitution. Voters previously approved initiatives to require a supermajority vote for tax increases, but the state Supreme Court ruled that such laws were unconstitutional.

Sponsored by initiative activist Tim Eyman, I-1366 proposed a statutory cut in the state sales tax from 6.5 percent to 5.5 percent. However, the cuts would not go into effect if the legislature was to propose a constitutional amendment requiring a two-thirds legislative vote or approval by the people for future tax increases. Voters narrowly approved the initiative 52 percent to 48 percent. After the election, opponents of the initiative, led by Democratic lawmakers, filed suit in state court to block the initiative on the grounds that it violated the single-subject rule. A court ruling had not been issued at the time of writing.

Wisconsin: Chief Justice

In April, Wisconsin voters approved Question 1, a constitutional amendment that changed the method for selecting the state supreme court's chief justice. The Wisconsin Supreme Court has been a lightning rod for controversy for several years, with some elections for its members attracting significant attention and funding from outside the state. Under existing law, the chief justice position was assigned automatically to the most senior justice, which since 1996 had been Shirley Abrahamson, a

Figure A: Number of Initiatives by Decade

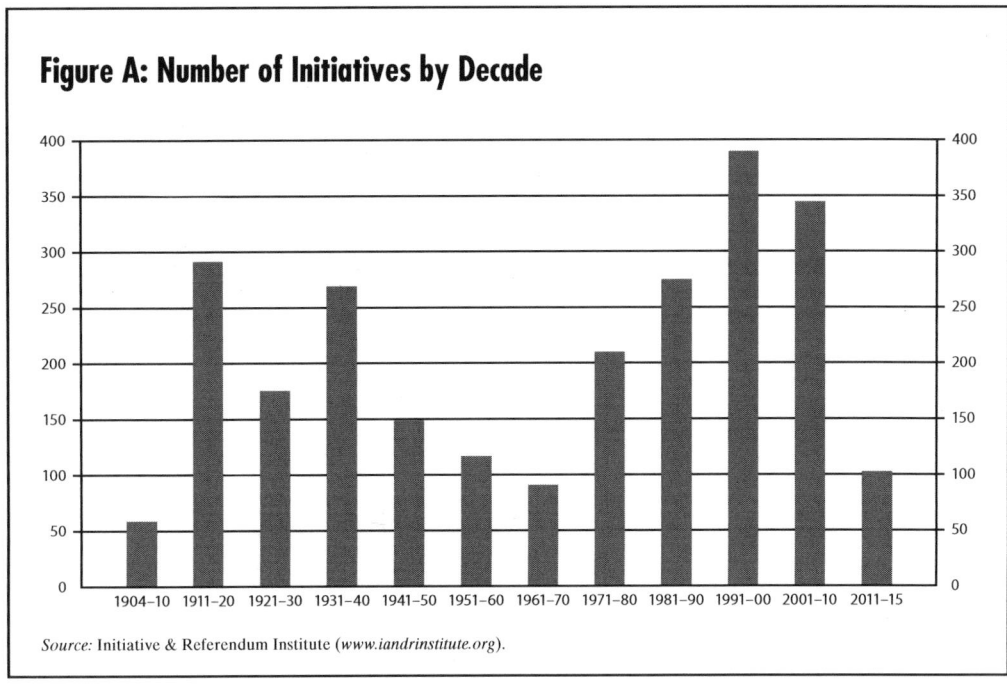

Source: Initiative & Referendum Institute (*www.iandrinstitute.org*).

member of the court's liberal minority. Question 1 allowed the justices to select their own chief justice.

Following the election, the conservative majority selected one of their members, Patience Roggensack, as the new chief justice. The ousted chief justice filed suit against the voters, claiming that her due process and equal protection rights were violated by being removed from her position; the courts rejected her claims.

Local Issues

The overall number of local ballot propositions is not tracked by any organization, but greatly exceeds the number of state-level propositions. In 2015, a number of controversial issues came before local voters. Some of the more interesting issues included:

San Francisco Prop F: Anti-Airbnb

San Francisco voters rejected a proposal to restrict the use of homes for vacation rentals. The initiative was promoted by housing activists, landlords and the hotel workers union. Airbnb poured in $8 million against the initiative, vastly more than the $500,000 spent by proponents.

Seattle: Campaign Contribution Vouchers

Seattle voters overwhelmingly approved I-122, a radically new approach to campaign finance. The

initiative created a public financing system in which each city resident will receive four $25 vouchers that can be given to any local candidate for office. The idea behind the initiative was to reduce the influence of large donors by enabling campaigns to raise large sums of money by collecting vouchers from numerous "ordinary" residents. The funding for the program, expected to be about $3 million per year, was not specified in the initiative.

Houston: Gay Rights

Another measure that attracted national attention was Houston's referendum on its Equal Rights Ordinance. The original law, approved by the City Council in May 2014, banned discrimination based on gender identity and sexual orientation. Conservative Christian activists challenged the law by collecting signatures to place it on the ballot, labeling it the "bathroom ordinance," based on the idea that the law would have allowed male sexual predators to enter women's bathrooms. The ordinance was repealed with more than 60 percent voting in favor of repeal.

Various: Marijuana Legalization

The battle for legalization of marijuana was fought at the local level across the country in 2015. In terms of legalization, voters in Toledo, Ohio; East Lansing

Table C: List of State Propositions, 2015

State	Type	Result	Short description
Colorado			
Prop BB	L/ST	Approved 69-31	Permits state to spend marijuana tax revenue.
Louisiana			
Amendment 1	L/CA	Failed 47-53	Creates transportation project fund.
Amendment 2	L/CA	Approved 53-47	Creates state infrastructure bank.
Amendment 3	L/CA	Failed 46-54	Legislature can consider revenue bills in certain sessions.
Amendment 4	L/CA	Approved 51-49	Local governments can tax property of other state governments.
Maine			
Question 1	I/ST	Approved 55-45	Public funding of political campaigns.
Question 2	L/ST	Approved 69-31	$15 million bond issue for senior homes.
Question 3	L/ST	Approved 73-27	$85 million bond issue for transportation projects.
Michigan			
Proposal 15-1	L/CA	Failed 20-80	Increase sales tax from 6% to 7%.
Mississippi			
Initiative Measure 42	I/CA	Failed (b)	Education funding law, empowers courts to enforce.
Initiative Measure 42 A	L/CA	Failed (b)	Education funding law, empowers legislature to enforce.
Ohio			
Issue 1	L/CA	Approved 71-29	Creates bipartisan redistricting commission.
Issue 2	L/CA	Approved 51-49	Prohibits initiatives that benefit specific individuals.
Issue 3	L/CA	Failed 36-64	Legalizes marijuana, grants production monopolies.
Texas			
Prop 1	L/CA	Approved 86-14	Increases exemption from school property taxes.
Prop 2	L/CA	Approved 91-9	Property tax exemption for spouse of deceased veteran.
Prop 3	L/CA	Approved 66-34	Allows legislators to reside outside state capital.
Prop 4	L/CA	Approved 69-31	Allows professional sports team charitable raffles.
Prop 5	L/CA	Approved 83-17	Authorizes small counties to construct private roads.
Prop 6	L/CA	Approved 81-19	Recognizes right to hunt and fish.
Prop 7	L/CA	Approved 83-17	Dedicates certain sales tax revenue to roads.
Washington			
I-1366	I/ST	Approved 52-48	Decreases sales tax from 6.5% to 5.5%.
I-1401	I/ST	Approved 70-30	Prohibits trafficking in parts of threatened animals.
Advisory Vote 10 (a)	Adv/ST	Maintained 51-49	Maintain or repeal tax on oil products carried by railroads.
Advisory Vote 11 (a)	Adv/ST	Maintained 59-41	Maintain or repeal tax on medical marijuana.
Advisory Vote 12 (a)	Adv/ST	Repealed 36-64	Maintain or repeal tax on gas.
Advisory Vote 13 (a)	Adv/ST	Repealed 37-63	Maintain or repeal business tax.
Wisconsin			
Question 1	L/CA	Approved 53-47	Allow supreme court justices to select chief justice.

Source: Initiative & Referendum Institute, Jan. 2016.
Note: An advisory vote is classified as "maintained" if the majority recommendation is to maintain the existing law.
Key:
I — initiative   ST — statute
L — legislative measure   Adv — advisory
CA — constitutional amendment

(a) Washington requires advisory votes on legislative tax increases.
(b) Mississippi determined the fate of the two propositions based on two questions: the vote was 48-52 for approval of "either" 42 or 42A, and 41-59 for 42 versus 42A.

and Portage, Mich.; and Wichita, Kan., voted to decriminalize marijuana or substantially reduce penalties, while voters in Montrose, Mich., rejected legalization. In Alaska, voters in Palmer voted to ban marijuana while voters in Houston rejected a ban. Proposals to allow marijuana distribution facilities in the city limits were rejected by voters in Brownsville, Ore., and Riverside and Yucca Valley, Calif.

Ohio Counties: Fracking

Three Ohio counties were set to vote on whether to amend their charters to ban hydraulic fracturing, or *fracking*, in their limits, but the state's secretary of state disallowed the votes. The Ohio Supreme Court has ruled that local governments do not have the authority to ban drilling that has been approved by the state legislature.

Notes

[1] For detailed information on initiative adoption and provisions and a discussion of pros and cons about the process, see John G. Matsusaka, *For the Many or the Few: The Initiative, Public Policy, and American Democracy* (University of Chicago Press, 2004) and M. Dane Waters, *Initiative and Referendum Almanac* (Carolina Academic Press, 2003).

About the author

John G. Matsusaka is the Charles F. Sexton Chair in American Enterprise in the Marshall School of Business, Gould School of Law and Department of Political Science, and executive director of the Initiative & Referendum Institute, all at the University of Southern California. He is the author of *For the Many or the Few: The Initiative, Public Policy, and American Democracy* (University of Chicago Press, 2004).

Table 6.9
STATEWIDE INITIATIVE AND REFERENDUM

State or other jurisdiction	Changes to constitution			Changes to statutes			
	Initiative		Referendum	Initiative		Referendum	
	Direct (a)	Indirect (a)	Legislative (b)	Direct (c)	Indirect (c)	Legislative	Citizen petition (d)
Alabama	...	...	★	...	...	...	...
Alaska	...	...	★	...	★	...	★
Arizona	★	...	★	★	...	★	★
Arkansas	★	...	★	★	...	★	★
California	★	...	★	★	...	★	★
Colorado	★	...	★	★	...	★	★
Connecticut	...	...	★	...	...	...	...
Delaware	...	...	...	...	...	★	...
Florida	★	...	★	...	...	...	...
Georgia	...	...	★	...	...	...	...
Hawaii	...	...	★	...	...	...	...
Idaho	...	...	★	★	...	★	★
Illinois	★	...	★	...	...	★	...
Indiana	...	...	★	...	...	...	...
Iowa	...	...	★	...	...	...	...
Kansas	...	...	★	...	...	...	...
Kentucky	...	...	★	...	...	★	...
Louisiana	...	...	★	...	...	...	...
Maine	...	...	★	...	★	★	★
Maryland	...	...	★	...	...	★	★
Massachusetts	...	★	★	...	★	★	★
Michigan	★	...	★	...	★	★	★
Minnesota	...	...	★	...	...	...	...
Mississippi	...	★	★	...	...	...	...
Missouri	★	...	★	★	...	★	★
Montana	★	...	★	★	...	★	★
Nebraska	★	...	★	★	...	★	★
Nevada	★	...	★	...	★	★	★
New Hampshire	...	...	★	...	...	...	...
New Jersey	...	...	★	...	...	...	...
New Mexico	...	...	★	...	...	★	...
New York	...	...	★	...	...	...	...
North Carolina	...	...	★(e)	...	...	...	...
North Dakota	★	...	★	★	...	★	★
Ohio	★	...	★	...	★	★	★
Oklahoma	★	...	★	★	...	★	★
Oregon	★	...	★	★	...	★	★
Pennsylvania	...	...	★	...	...	...	...
Rhode Island	...	...	★	...	...	...	...
South Carolina	...	...	★	...	...	...	...
South Dakota	★	...	★	★	...	★	★
Tennessee	...	...	★	...	...	...	...
Texas	...	...	★	...	...	...	...
Utah	...	...	★	★	★	★	★
Vermont	...	...	★	...	...	...	...
Virginia	...	...	★	...	...	...	...
Washington	...	...	★	★	★	★	★
West Virginia	...	...	★	...	...	...	...
Wisconsin	...	...	★	...	...	...	...
Wyoming	...	...	★	...	★	...	★
American Samoa	...	...	★	...	...	...	...
No. Mariana Islands	★	★	★	★	★	★	★
Puerto Rico	...	...	★	...	...	★	...
U.S. Virgin Islands	★	...	★	...	...	★	...

See footnotes at end of table.

STATEWIDE INITIATIVE AND REFERENDUM — Continued

Sources: The Council of State Governments' survey of state election website, Initiative & Referendum Institute website and Ballotpedia website, February 2016.

Note: This table summarizes state provisions for initiatives and referenda. Initiatives may propose constitutional amendments or develop state legislation and may be formed either directly or indirectly. The direct initiative allows a proposed measure to be placed on the ballot after a specific number of signatures have been secured on a citizen petition. The indirect initiative must be submitted to the legislature for a decision after the required number of signatures has been secured on a petition and prior to placing the proposed measure on the ballot.

Referendum refers to the process whereby a state law or constitutional amendment passed by the legislature may be referred to the voters before it goes into effect.

Three forms of referenda exist: (1) citizen petition, whereby the people may petition for a referendum on legislation which has been considered by the legislature; (2) submission by the legislature (designated in table as "Legislative"), whereby the legislature may voluntarily submit laws to the voters for their approval; and (3) constitutional requirement, whereby the state constitution may require that certain questions be submitted to the voters.

Key:

★— State Provision.

... — No state provision.

(a) See Table 1.3, "Constitutional Amendment Procedure: By Initiative," for more detail.

(b) See Table 1.2, "Constitutional Amendment Procedure: By the Legislature," for more detail.

(c) See Chapter 6 tables on State Initiatives, for more detail.

(d) See Chapter 6 tables on State Referendums, for more detail.

(e) Only the legislature can make statutory changes while in session. Proposed constitutional changes must be passed by the legislature and then are submitted to the citizens to be voted on.

Table 6.10
STATE INITIATIVES: REQUESTING PERMISSION TO CIRCULATE A PETITION

State or other jurisdiction	Applied to (a) Const. amdt.	Statute	Signatures required to request a petition (b) Const. amdt.	Statute	Request submitted to	Request form furnished by (c)	Restricted subject matter (d)	Individual responsible for petition Title	Summary	Financial contributions reported (e)	Deposits required (f)
Alabama											
Alaska		I		100	LG	(p)	Y	LG	LG	Y	$100
Arizona	D	D			SS	SS	N	P,SP	P,SP	Y	N
Arkansas	D	D			AG	SP	N	AG	AG	Y	N
California	D	D	25 (g)	25 (g)	AG	SP	Y	AG	AG	Y	$200
Colorado	D	D			SS	SS	N	(i)	(i)	Y	N
Connecticut	D				SS	SS				Y	
Delaware											
Florida	D				SS	SP	N	SP	SP	Y	
Georgia										Y	N (q)
Hawaii											
Idaho	D			20	SS	SP	N	AG	AG	Y	N
Illinois	D						Y			Y	N
Indiana											
Iowa											
Kansas											
Kentucky											
Louisiana											
Maine		I	6 (j)	(k)	SS	SS	Y	P		Y	N
Maryland					SS (l)	SBE	Y		SS	Y	N
Massachusetts	I	I		10	AG	SS	Y	AG	AG	Y	N
Michigan	D	I		10	SS		Y	SP	SP	Y	N
Minnesota											
Mississippi	D	D			SS	SS	Y	AG	AG	Y	$500
Missouri	D	D			SS	SP	Y	SS,AG	SS,AG	Y	N
Montana	D	D			SS (o)	SP	Y	AG	AG	Y	N
Nebraska	D	D			SS	SP	Y	SP	SP	Y	N
Nevada	D	I			SS	SS	Y	P,SP	P,SP	Y	N
New Hampshire											
New Jersey											
New Mexico											
New York											
North Carolina											
North Dakota	D	I	25	25	SS	SP	N	SS,AG	SS	Y (e)	N
Ohio	D	I		1,000	AG	(m)	Y	(m)	(m)	Y	N
Oklahoma	D	D			SS,AG	O	N	P	P	Y	N
Oregon	D	D	1,000	1,000	SS	SS	N	AG	AG	Y	N
Pennsylvania											
Rhode Island											
South Carolina											

See footnotes at end of table.

STATE INITIATIVES: REQUESTING PERMISSION TO CIRCULATE A PETITION—Continued

State or other jurisdiction	Applied to (a)		Signatures required to request a petition (b)		Request submitted to	Request form furnished by (c)	Restricted subject matter (d)	Individual responsible for petition		Financial contributions reported (e)	Deposits required (f)
	Const. amdt.	Statute	Const. amdt.	Statute				Title	Summary		
South Dakota	D	D	...	...	SS	SS	Y	AG	AG	Y	N
Tennessee	...	...	...	...	...	...	...	...	...	...	...
Texas	...	...	...	...	...	...	...	...	...	...	...
Utah	...	D,I	...	5 SP	LG	LG	N	SP	SP	Y	N
Vermont	...	...	...	...	...	...	...	...	...	...	...
Virginia	...	...	...	...	...	...	...	...	...	...	...
Washington	...	D,I	...	...	SS	SP	N	AG	AG	Y	$5
West Virginia	...	...	...	...	...	...	...	...	...	...	...
Wisconsin	...	I	...	...	...	...	...	...	...	...	...
Wyoming	...	...	...	100	SS	SS	Y	SS	SS	Y	$500
American Samoa	D	I	...	...	AG	AG	Y	SP	SP	Y	N
No. Mariana Islands	...	...	...	...	SBE	(n)	N	(n)	(n)	Y	...
Puerto Rico	...	D	...	...	SBE	...	...	...	...	Y	$500
U.S. Virgin Islands	D	...	...	...	SBE	SBE	Y	SBE	SBE	Y	N

Sources: The Council of State Governments' survey of state election websites, Initiative & Referendum Institute website and Ballotpedia website, February 2016.

Key:
... – Not applicable
D – Direct initiative
I – Indirect initiative
EV – Eligible voters
LG – Lieutenant Governor
SS – Secretary of State
SBE –State Board of Elections

(a) An initiative may provide a constitutional amendment or develop a new statute, and may be formed either directly or indirectly. The direct initiative allows a proposed measure to be placed on the ballot after a specific number of signatures have been secured on a petition. The indirect initiative must first be submitted to the legislature for decision after the required number of signatures have been secured on a petition, prior to placing the proposed measure on the ballot.

(b) Prior to circulating a statewide petition, a request for permission to do so must first be submitted to a specified state officer.

(c) The form on which the request for petition is submitted may be the responsibility of the sponsor or may be furnished by the state.

(d) Restrictions may exist regarding the subject matter to which an initiative may be applied. The majority of these restrictions pertain to the dedication of state revenues and appropriations, and laws that maintain the preservation of public peace, safety, and health. In Illinois, amendments are restricted to "structural and procedural subjects contained in" the legislative article.

(e) In some states, a list of financial contributors and the amount of their contributions must be submitted to the specified state officer with whom the petition is filed. In North Dakota, must report any contributions and/or expenditures in excess of $100. Must also report the gross total of all contributions received and gross totals of all expenditures made. Must give total cash on hand in the filer's account at the start and close of a reporting period.

(f) A deposit may be required after permission to circulate a petition has been granted. This amount is refunded when the completed petition has been filed correctly.

(g) Signatures required to seek asssistance of Office of Legislative Counsel in drafting measure before filing with the Attorney General's office.

(h) The secretary of state charges a 10 cent fee per signature that must be verfied for ballot consideration.

(i) Title Setting Board–secretary of state, attorney general, director of legislative legal services.

(j) The signature of six voters.

(k) Three percent of the total qualified voters from the last gubernatorial election.

(l) Secretary of state accepts and turns over to State Board of Elections.

(m) Petitioners. Petitioners must prepare the summary and submit it to the Ohio Attorney General, who then must certify whether the summary fully and accurately describes the proposal.

(n) Office of the Supervisor of Elections Titling Board.

(o) After submitted, the secretary of state tranfers it over to the Legislative Services Division.

(p) Division of Elections.

Table 6.11
STATE INITIATIVES: CIRCULATING THE PETITION

State or other jurisdiction	Basis for signatures (see key below) Const. amdt.	Statute	Maximum time period allowed for petition circulation (a)	Can signatures be removed from petition? (b)	Completed petition filed with	Days prior to election Const. amdt.	Statute
Alabama	…	…	…	…	…	…	…
Alaska	…	10% TV from 3/4 SLD (c)	1 yr.	Y	LG	…	…
Arizona	15% VG	10% VG	2 yr.	Y	SS	4 mos.	4 mos.
Arkansas	10% VG (d)	8% VG (d)	150 days	N	SS	120 days	120 days
California	8% VG	5% VG	6 mos. (3 mos. prior to election)	Y	SS (e)	131 days	131 days
Colorado	5% VSS	5% VSS	…	Y	SS	90 days	90 days
Connecticut	…	…	…	…	…	…	…
Delaware	…	…	2 yr.	…	…	…	…
Florida	8% VEP, 8% from 1/2 CD	…	2 yr.	N	SS	Feb. 1 (f)	…
Georgia	…	…	…	…	…	…	…
Hawaii	…	…	…	…	…	…	…
Idaho	…	6% EV (cc)	(g)	Y	SS	…	4 mos.
Illinois	8% VG	…	18 mos. prior to election	Y	SBE	6 mos.	…
Indiana	…	…	…	…	…	…	…
Iowa	…	…	…	…	…	…	…
Kansas	…	…	…	…	…	…	…
Kentucky	…	…	…	…	…	…	…
Louisiana	…	…	…	…	…	…	…
Maine	…	10% VG	1 yr.	…	SS	…	(h)
Maryland	…	…	…	…	…	…	…
Massachusetts	3% VG, no more than 25% from 1 county	3% VG, no more than 25% from 1 county (i)	From 3rd Wed. in Sept. to 1st Wed. in Dec. (k)	Y (j)	SS (k)	(i)	(l)
Michigan	10% VG	8% VG	180 days	N (m)	SS	120 days	160 days
Minnesota	…	…	…	…	…	…	…
Mississippi	12% VG (n)	…	1 yr.	Y	SS (e)	90 days prior to LS	…
Missouri	8% VG, 8% each from 2/3 CD	5% VG, 5% each from 2/3 CD	Approx. 18 mos.	Y	SS (e)	6 mos.	6 mos.
Montana	10% VG and 10% in 40 of the SLD	5% VG and 5% in 34 of the SLD	(o)	Y	SS	4 mos.	4 mos.
Nebraska	10% EV	7% EV	…	Y	SS	4 mos.	4 mos.
Nevada	10% TV (p)	10% TV (p)	(q)	Y	SS	90 days	30 days prior to LS
New Hampshire	…	…	…	…	…	…	…
New Jersey	…	…	…	…	…	…	…
New Mexico	…	…	…	…	…	…	…
New York	…	…	…	…	…	…	…
North Carolina	…	…	…	…	…	…	…
North Dakota	4% resident population (r)	2% resident population (r)	1 yr.	N	SS	120 days	…
Ohio	10% VG, 5% each from 1/2 counties	3% VG, 1.5% each from 1/2 counties	…	Y	SS	90 days	(s)
Oklahoma	15% VG (t)	8% VG (t)	90 days	Y	SS	60 days	60 days
Oregon	8% VG	6% VG	…	Y (u)	SS	4 mos.	4 mos.
Pennsylvania	…	…	…	…	…	…	…
Rhode Island	…	…	…	…	…	…	…
South Carolina	…	…	…	…	…	…	…

See footnotes at end of table.

STATE INITIATIVES: CIRCULATING THE PETITION—Continued

State or other jurisdiction	Basis for signatures (see key below)		Maximum time period allowed for petition circulation (a)	Can signatures be removed from petition? (b)	Completed petition filed with	Days prior to election	
	Const. amdt.	Statute				Const. amdt.	Statute
South Dakota	10% VG	5% VG	(v)	N	SS	...	...
Tennessee	...	...	...	...	...	...	...
Texas	...	...	...	...	...	...	June 1
Utah	...	10% VEP, 10% each from 26 of 29 senate districts (w)	316 days	Y	LG	...	...
Vermont	...	...	...	...	...	...	...
Virginia	...	8% VG	6 to 9 mos. (x)	N	SS	...	...
Washington	...	...	...	...	...	...	...
West Virginia	...	...	...	...	...	...	(y)
Wisconsin	...	15% TV, from 2/3 counties	18 mos.	Y	SS	...	...
Wyoming	...	...	...	...	...	...	120 days
American Samoa	...	20%	...	Y	...	...	...
No. Mariana Islands	50% (z)	(bb)	(aa)	Y	...	...	...
Puerto Rico	...	...	...	...	...	...	...
U.S. Virgin Islands	...	10 % ED	180 days	Y	SS	...	6 mos.

Sources: The Council of State Governments' survey of state election websites, Initiative & Referendum Institute website and Ballotpedia website, February 2016.

Key:

... — Not applicable.

VG — Total votes cast for the position of governor in the last election.

EV — Eligible voters.

VH — Total votes cast for the office receiving the highest number of votes in last election.

TV — Total voters in last election.

VSS — Total votes cast for all candidates for the office of secretary of state at the previous general election.

VEP — Total votes cast in the state as a whole in the last presidential election.

ED — Election district.

CD — Congressional district.

SBE — State Board of Elections.

SLD — State legislative district for House.

LG — Lieutenant Governor.

SS — Secretary of State.

LS — Legislative session.

Y — Yes.

N — No.

T — Tuesday.

(a) The petition circulation period begins when petition forms have been approved and provided to sponsors. Sponsors are those individuals granted permission to circulate a petition, and are therefore responsible for the validity of each signature on a given petition.

(b) Should an individual wish to remove his/her name from a petition, a request to do so must be submitted in writing to the state officer with whom the petition is filed.

(c) Petition signatures must be from residents of at least three-quarters of house districts and who, in each of the house districts, are equal in number to at least seven percent of those voting in the last general election.

(d) Distributed across at least 15 counties.

(e) County elections officials.

(f) February 1 of the general election year.

(g) Eighteen months from receipt of ballot title or April 30 of year of election on initiative, whichever occurs first.

(h) To be placed on November ballot, petitions must be submitted to SS by 5:00 p.m. on 50th day after convening of Legislature in 1st regular session, or by 5:00 p.m. on 25th day in 2nd regular session.

(i) First Wednesday in December.

(j) Should an individual wish to remove his/her name from a petition, a request to do so must be submitted in writing to the local election official before the petition is submitted for certification of signatures.

(k) Petitions first must be submitted to local municipal clerks for signature certification.

(l) After legislative inaction, petitions must be filed no later than the 1st Wednesday in July, signed by not less than 1/2 of 1 percent of the last vote cast for governor.

(m) Not after petition has been filed.

(n) The signatures must be distributed among the state's Congressional districts. If less than the minimum in any one district, the entire petition will be ruled invalid.

(o) There is a maximum of one year to circulate petitions and receive certification from county election officials. The county officials must submit each verified petition to the secretary of state by the final filing deadline, which is the third Friday of the fourth month prior to the election. Proponents must submit their petitions to county officials no sooner than nine months and no later than four weeks prior to the final filing deadline.

(p) In each "petition district" (per SB 212, effective 2009) which are set the same as Congressional districts.

(q) Each have different deadlines and circulation periods. Amendments: Initial filing cannot be made before Sept. 1 of the year preceding the election year and the petition must be filed with the county officials by the third Tuesday in June of an even-numbered year. Statues: Initial filing cannot be made before Jan. 1 of the year preceding the next regular legislative session and the petition must be filed with county officials by the second Tuesday in November of an even-numbered year.

(r) Percentage of resident population of the state at the last federal decennial census.

(s) Ten days prior to commencement of General Assembly session for initial filing; second petition must be filed within 90 days after General Assembly takes no action, fails to enact or passes amended form; the petition is filed with the secretary of state.

(t) In 2012, voters approved a constitutional amendment placed on the ballot by the legislature that changed the signature requirement from percentage of votes cast for the office receiving the highest number of votes in last general election to percentage of votes cast for position of governor in the last election.

(u) Only by the chief petitioners before submitting signatures for verification. Signatures may not be removed once the signatures have been submitted to the secretary of state.

(v) No more than 24 months preceding the election date specified on the petition, however petition is submitted 12 months before the election.

(w) Five percent in both categories for indirect.

(x) Six months for direct initiative and nine months for indirect initiative. Signatures for indirect initiatives are due at least four months prior to the general election. Signatures for indirect initiatives are due at least 10 days prior to the beginning of the session.

(y) Initiatives to the legislature must be turned in 10 days before the legislature convenes. If the legislature does not act, the initiative goes to the next General Election ballot.

(z) At least 25 percent in each senate district.

(aa) Until 120 days before the date of the election.

(bb) Ten percent district and 41 percent territorial.

(cc) Geographic distribution shall be as follows: 6% of the qualified electors at the time of the last general election in each of at least 18 legislative districts; provided however, the total number of signatures shall be equal to or greater than 6% of the qualified electors in the state at the time of the last general election.

Table 6.12
STATE INITIATIVES: PREPARING THE INITIATIVE TO BE PLACED ON THE BALLOT

State or other jurisdiction	Signatures verified by: (a)	Within how many days after filing	Number of days to amend/appeal a petition that is: Incomplete (b)	Not accepted (c)	Penalty for falsifying petition (denotes fine, jail term)	Petition certified by: (d)
Alabama	…	…	…	…	…	…
Alaska	Division of Elections	60 days	…	…	Class B misdemeanor	LG
Arizona	County recorder	(e)	…	…	Class 1 misdemeanor	SS
Arkansas	SS	30 days	30 days	…	Class A misdemeanor	SS
California	County clerk	30 days	…	30 days	Felony or misdemeanor (depending on severity)	SS
Colorado	SS	30 days	10 days	…	(f)	…
Connecticut	…	…	…	…	…	…
Delaware	…	…	…	…	…	…
Florida	Supervisor of elections	N.A.	N.A.	N.A.	First degree misdemeanor	SS
Georgia	…	…	…	…	…	…
Hawaii	…	…	…	…	…	…
Idaho	County clerk	60 days	(h)	10 days	$5,000, 2 yrs.	SS
Illinois	SBE (g)	…	(h)	(h)	Class 3 felony	SBE
Indiana	…	…	…	…	…	…
Iowa	…	…	…	…	…	…
Kansas	…	…	…	…	…	…
Kentucky	…	…	…	…	…	…
Louisiana	…	…	…	…	…	…
Maine	Registrar of voters	…	…	…	…	SS
Maryland	…	…	…	…	…	…
Massachusetts	Local board of registrar	2 weeks	…	…	$1,000, 1 yr.	SS
Michigan	SS	Approx. 60 days	…	…	$500, 90 days	BSC
Minnesota	…	…	…	…	…	…
Mississippi	Circuit clerk	…	10 days	10 days	$1,000, 1 yr.	CC
Missouri	County clerk	63 days	…	10 days	Class A misdemeanor	SS
Montana	County election administrators	4 weeks	10 days	10 days	$500, 6 mos.	SS
Nebraska	County clerk	40 days	10 days	…	…	SS
Nevada	County clerk	(i)	5 days (j)	…	…	SS
New Hampshire	…	…	…	…	…	…
New Jersey	…	…	…	…	…	…
New Mexico	…	…	…	…	…	…
New York	…	…	…	…	…	…
North Carolina	SS	…	…	…	…	…
North Dakota	SS	…	…	…	(k)	…
Ohio	County board of elections	35 days	10 days	…	5th degree felony	SS
Oklahoma	SS	10 days	10 days	…	$1,000, 1 yr.	SS
Oregon	County clerk	30 days	(l)	…	(m)	SS
Pennsylvania	…	…	…	…	…	…
Rhode Island	…	…	…	…	…	…
South Carolina	…	…	…	…	…	SS

See footnotes at end of table.

STATE INITIATIVES: PREPARING THE INITIATIVE TO BE PLACED ON THE BALLOT—Continued

State or other jurisdiction	Signatures verified by: (a)	Within how many days after filing	Number of days to amend/appeal a petition that is:		Penalty for falsifying petition (denotes fine, jail term)	Petition certified by: (d)
			Incomplete (b)	Not accepted (c)		
South Dakota	SS	...	...	...	Class 1 misdemeanor	SBE
Tennessee	...	...	...	...	...	...
Texas	...	...	...	...	...	...
Utah	County clerk	30 days	...	14 days	Class A misdemeanor	LG
Vermont	...	...	...	...	...	...
Virginia	...	...	...	...	...	...
Washington	SS	...	5 days	5	Fine or imprisonment	SS
West Virginia	...	...	...	...	...	...
Wisconsin	SS	60 days	30 days	30 days	$1,000, 1 yr.	SS
Wyoming	...	...	...	...	...	...
American Samoa	Election Commission	(n)	30 days (o)	119 days	(p)	AG
No. Mariana Islands	Office of the Supervisor of Elections	15 days	3 days	...	...	SBE
Puerto Rico	Office of the Supervisor of Elections	15 days	7 days	...	...	Office of the Supervisor of Elections
U.S. Virgin Islands						

Sources: The Council of State Governments' survey of state election websites, Initiative & Referendum Institute website and Ballotpedia website, February 2016 .

Key:

... —Not applicable.
CC—Circuit Clerk.
SS—Secretary of State.
LG—Lieutenant Governor.
BSC—Board of State Canvassers.
SBE—State Board of Elections.

(a) The validity of the signatures, as well as the correct number of required signatures must be verified before the initiative is allowed on the ballot.

(b) If an insufficient number of signatures is submitted, sponsors may amend the original petition by filing additional signatures within a given number of days after filing. If the necessary number of signatures has not been submitted by this date, the petition is declared void.

(c) In some cases, the state officer will not accept a valid petition. In such a case, sponsors may appeal this decision to the Supreme Court, where the sufficiency of the petition will be determined. If the petition is determined to be sufficient, the initiative is required to be placed on the ballot.

(d) A petition is certified for the ballot when the required number of signatures has been submitted by the filing deadline, and are determined to be valid.

(e) Removal of petition and ineligible signatures by Secretary of State's office 20 days, certification by County Recorder 15 days after receipt from secretary of State's office.

(f) Secretary conducts hearing, then turns over to the attorney general for investigation/possible criminal prosecution.

(g) State Board of Elections and County Clerks or Municipal Boards of Election Commissioners. Individual petition sheets must be from a single jurisdiction. The SBE verifies that all signatures are from a single jurisdiction and the County Clerks or Municipal Boards verify the signatures against their registration files.

(h) Amendments are not permitted. Judicial review must be sought within ten days after determination be State Board of Elections.

(i) 1. Within four days county clerk totals the number of signatures and forwards to the secretary of state. 2. The secretary of state immediately notifies county clerks if they are to proceed or not proceed with the signature verification. 3. If ordered by the secretary of state, the county clerks verify signatures within nine days (excluding weekends and holidays).

(j) In Nevada, appeal must be within 5 working days after SS determines the petition is not sufficient.

(k) Any violations discovered will be reported to the attorney general for investigation and prosecution.

(l) Additional signatures may be submitted if signatures were turned in prior to deadline for submitting signatures.

(m) Whether a penalty is assessed would be based upon what information on the petition was falsified.

(n) Within 90 days before the date of election.

(o) 30 days if submitted 150 days before the date of the election. No amendment/appeal if submitted 120 days before the date of election.

(p) Subject to statute governing fraud and perjury.

Table 6.13
STATE INITIATIVES: VOTING ON THE INITIATIVE

State or other jurisdiction	Ballot (a)		Election where initiative voted on	Effective date of approved initiative (b)		Days to contest election results (c)	Can an approved initiative be:			Can a defeated initiative be refiled?
	Title by:	Summary by:		Const. amdt.	Statute		Amended?	Vetoed?	Repealed?	
Alabama										
Alaska	LG	LG	GE,PR or SP		90 days (d)	10	Y	N	Y (e)	N
Arizona	SS,AG	SS,AG	GE		IM (f)	5	(g)	N	N	Y
Arkansas	AG	AG	GE	30 days	30 days	20	Y	N	Y	Y
California	AG	AG	GE	1 day (h)	1 day (h)	5 (d)	Y (i)	N	Y (i)	Y
Colorado	TB (j)	TB (j)	GE, Odd year	30 days	30 days	10	N (k)	N (k)	N (k)	
Connecticut										
Delaware										
Florida	SP	SP	GE	(m)		10	Y (n)	N	Y (n)	Y
Georgia										
Hawaii										
Idaho	AG	AG	GE		IM	20	Y	N	Y	Y
Illinois		SS (o)	GE		30 days	30	(p)			Y
Indiana										
Iowa										
Kansas										
Kentucky										
Louisiana										
Maine	Sponsor, SS	SS	REG or SP		30 days (f)	5	Y	N	Y	after 2 biennial elections
Maryland										
Massachusetts	AG	AG	GE	30 days	30 days	10	Y	Y	Y	Y
Michigan	BSC	BSC	GE	45 days	10 days	2 (r)	Y	N	Y	Y
Minnesota										
Mississippi	AG	AG	GE	30 days			Y (s)	Y (s)	N	after 2 yrs.
Missouri	SS,AG	SS,AG	GE	30 days	IM	30 (r)	Y	N	Y	Y
Montana	AG	AG	GE	Jul. 1	Oct. 1	1 yr.	Y	N	Y	Y
Nebraska	AG	AG	GE	10 days	10 days	40	Y	N	Y	Y
Nevada	SS,AG	SS,AG	GE	(u)	(u)	14	(v)	(v)	(v)	N (t)
New Hampshire										
New Jersey										
New Mexico										
New York										
North Carolina										
North Dakota	SS,AG	SS	PR or GE	30 days	30 days (w)	14	(x)	N	(x)	Y
Ohio	Ohio Ballot Board	P (y)	GE	30 days	30 days	15	(z)	N	N	Y
Oklahoma	AG	AG	GE or SP	IM	IM		Y	Y	Y	after 3 yrs. (aa)
Oregon	AG	AG	GE	30 days	30 days	40	Y	Y	Y	Y
Pennsylvania										
Rhode Island										
South Carolina										

See footnotes at end of table.

STATE INITIATIVES: VOTING ON THE INITIATIVE—Continued

State or other jurisdiction	Ballot (a)		Election where initiative voted on	Effective date of approved initiative (b)		Days to contest election results (c)	Can an approved initiative be:			Can a defeated initiative be refiled?
	Title by:	Summary by:		Const. amdt.	Statute		Amended?	Vetoed?	Repealed?	
South Dakota	AG	AG	GE	(bb)	(bb)	...	Y	N	N	Y
Tennessee	...	...	...	...	...	...	...	...	...	...
Texas	...	...	...	...	...	...	...	...	...	...
Utah	LLS	LLS	GE	...	5 days (cc)	40	Y	N	N	after 2 yrs.
Vermont	...	...	...	...	...	...	...	...	...	...
Virginia	...	...	...	...	...	...	...	...	...	...
Washington	AG	AG	GE	...	30 days	10 days	Y (l)	...	Y (l)	Y
West Virginia	...	...	...	...	...	...	...	...	...	...
Wisconsin	...	...	...	...	...	...	...	...	...	...
Wyoming	SS	SS,AG	GE 120 days after LS	...	90 days	15 after Canvass	Y	N	after 2 yrs.	after 5 yrs.
American Samoa	...	AG	GE	(q)	IM	30	...	...	...	Y
No. Mariana Islands	LC	AG,LLS	GE	...	...	...	...	...	...	Y
Puerto Rico	...	...	...	...	...	...	...	...	...	...
U.S. Virgin Islands	Office of Supervisor of Elections	Office of Supervisor of Elections	Any election	IM	IM	7	Y (v)	N	(v)	Y

Sources: The Council of State Governments' survey of state election websites, Initiative & Referendum Institute website and Ballotpedia website, February 2016.

Key:
PR – Primary election.
... – Not applicable.
LG – Lieutenant Governor.
SS – Secretary of State.
AG – Attorney General.
P – Proponent.
LC – Legislative Council.
LLS – Legislative Legal Services.
BSC – Board of State Canvassers.
SBE – State Board of Elections.
GE – General election.
REG – Regular election.
SP – Special election.
IM – Immediately.
LS – Legislative session.
TB – Title Board.
Y – Yes.
N – No.
w/i – Within.

(a) In some states, the ballot title and summary will differ from that on the petition.
(b) A majority of the popular vote is required to enact a measure. In Massachusetts and Nebraska, 30% and 35% of the total votes cast in favor, respectively. An initiative approved by the voters may be put into effect immediately after the approving votes have been canvassed. In California and Nebraska, the measure may specify an enacting date. In Colorado, measures take effect from the date of proclamation by governor, but no later than 30 days after votes have been canvassed and certified by secretary of state. In Nebraska, 10 days after completion of canvass by the State Board of Canvassers.
(c) Individuals may contest the results of a vote on an initiative within a certain number of days after the election including the measure proposed.
(d) After certification of election.
(e) May not be repealed within 2 years of its effective date.
(f) Upon governor's proclamation.
(g) Initiative can be amended by three-fourths of the members of each house of the legislature (AZ Constitution Article 4, Part 1, Section14).
(h) Unless the measure requires otherwise.
(i) Changes must be submitted to voters unless the measure provided for legislative amendment or repeal.
(j) Ballot title: Drafted by Legislative Council of the General Assembly, then finalized by three board members called the Title Board. Summary by: Legislative Council of the General Assembly.
(k) If it is statutory it can be changed by the legislature.
(l) No initiated statute can be amended or repealed within 2 years without a 2/3s super majority in both chambers. Any initiated law so amended is not subject to veto referendum.

(m) It is effective the first Tuesday after the first Monday in January following election unless specified in the amendment.
(n) Amendments or repeal must be voted on by the voters.
(o) Subject to approval of the Attorney General.
(p) Changing a constitutional amendment would require another constitutional amendment.
(q) Effective upon approval by voters and certification of election result by Election Commission: usually 15 days after date of election or later if there is an election contest.
(r) After election is certified.
(s) The approved initiative to amend the Constitution can be adopted, amended or rejected by the legislature or no action can be taken. In all cases, the initiative and alternative adopted are placed on the next statewide general election ballot.
(t) Not on next ballot.
(u) Constitutional amendment—after passed twice by the voters it becomes effective upon the completion of the canvass of votes by the Supreme Court on the fourth Tuesday of November following the election. Statute—effective on the date approved by the governor or the canvass of the vote by the Supreme Court.
(v) It cannot be amended or repealed within three years from the date it takes effect.
(w) An initiative to repeal a statute is effective immediately following the election.
(x) A measure approved by the electors may not be amended or repealed by the legislative assembly for seven years from its effective date, except by a two-thirds vote of the members elected to each house; majority vote thereafter.
(y) No summary, but the Ohio Ballot Board prescribes the ballot language. Also explanations and arguments for and against the proposal may be prepared by the petitioner and the person(s) appointed by the governor or, if appropriate, the General Assembly. The Ohio Ballot Board must prepare any missing explanation or argument.
(z) Initiated constitutional amendment proposed by petition cannot be vetoed; cannot be amended or repealed except by another constitutional amendment. Initiated statute cannot be vetoed by the governor, but may be amended or repealed after its effective date via legislation or another initiative.
(aa) Three-year waiting period unless proponents can gather signatures equal to 25 percent of total vote cast in last governor's election.
(bb) Upon completion of official canvass of votes.
(cc) If an indirect initiative is adopted by the legislature, it takes effect 60 days after the adjournment of the legislative session in which it is passed. Unless otherwise specified in the measure, direct initiatives take effect five days after the governor proclaims the official election results.

Table 6.14
STATE REFERENDUMS: REQUESTING PERMISSION TO CIRCULATE A CITIZEN PETITION

State or other jurisdiction	Citizen petition (a)	Signatures required to request a petition (b)	Request submitted to:	Request forms furnished by: (c)	Restricted subject matter (d)	Individual responsible for petition		Financial contributions reported (e)	Deposit required (f)
						Title	Summary		
Alabama	...	...	...	...	...	...	...	...	...
Alaska	Y	100	LG	DV	Y	LG	LG	Y	$100
Arizona	Y	5% VG	SS	SS	Y	P	P	Y	N
Arkansas	Y	8% VG initiative; 6% referendum VG	AG	SP	N	AG	AG	Y	N
California	Y	25	AG	LC	Y	AG	AG	N	$200
Colorado	Y	At least 2 people representing issue	LS,SS	LS	Y	SP	LS	Y	N
Connecticut	...	...	...	...	...	...	...	...	...
Delaware	...	...	...	...	...	...	...	...	...
Florida	Y	8% of vote in last presidential election & 1/2 of congressional districts	SS	SS	N (g)	SP	SP	Y	N (h)
Georgia	...	...	...	...	...	...	...	...	...
Hawaii	...	...	...	...	...	...	...	...	...
Idaho	Y	20	SS	SP	N	AG	AG	Y	N
Illinois	Y	...	...	...	Y	P	...	Y, for $3,000 or more	...
Indiana	(i)	Varies	SS	SS	Y	Varies	...	...	...
Iowa	...	...	...	...	...	...	...	...	...
Kansas	...	...	...	...	...	...	...	...	...
Kentucky	...	...	...	...	...	...	...	...	...
Louisiana	...	...	...	...	...	...	...	...	...
Maine	Y	5	SS	SS	Y	SP,SS	SS (j)	Y	...
Maryland	Y	(k)	SS	SBE	Y	SP	AG	Y	N
Massachusetts	Y	10	AG	SS	Y	AG	AG	Y	N
Michigan	Y	8% VG, initiative; 5% VG, referendum VG	SS	SS	Y	Board of State Canvassers	Board of State Canvassers	Y	N
Minnesota	...	...	...	...	...	...	...	...	...
Mississippi	Y	Any "qualified elector" may file	SS	SS	Y	AG	AG	Y	$500
Missouri	Y	...	SS	DV	Y	SS,AG	SS,AG	Y	N
Montana	Y	(l)	LS,SS,AG	SP	Y	AG	AG	Y	N
Nebraska	Y	...	SS	...	Y	SP	SP	Y	N
Nevada	Y	...	SS	SS	Y	P,SP	P,SP	Y	N
New Hampshire	...	...	...	...	...	...	...	...	...
New Jersey	...	...	...	...	...	...	...	...	...
New Mexico	...	...	...	...	...	...	...	...	...
New York	...	...	...	...	...	...	...	...	...
North Carolina	...	...	...	...	...	...	...	...	...
North Dakota	Y	25 "qualified voters"	SS	SP	N	SS,AG	SS	Y	N
Ohio	Y	1,000 "qualified electors"	SS,AG	PE	Y	PE	PE (m)	Y	$25
Oklahoma	Y	(n)	SS	SS	N	P	P	Y	N
Oregon	Y	4% of VG	LC,SS (o)	SS	Y	AG	AG	Y	N
Pennsylvania	...	...	...	...	...	...	...	...	...
Rhode Island	...	...	...	...	...	...	...	...	...
South Carolina	...	...	...	...	...	...	...	...	...
South Dakota	Y	5% of VG	LS	SP	Y	AG	AG	Y	N
Tennessee	...	...	...	...	...	...	...	...	...
Texas	...	...	...	...	...	...	...	...	...
Utah	Y	5 SP	LG	LG	Y (p)	SP	SP	Y	...
Vermont	...	...	...	...	...	...	...	...	...
Virginia	...	...	...	...	...	...	...	...	...
Washington	Y	8% VG, initiative; 4% VG, referendum VG	SS	SS	Y (q)	AG	AG	Y	$5
West Virginia	N	...	...	...	...	...	...	...	...
Wisconsin	...	...	...	...	...	...	...	...	...
Wyoming	Y	100	SS	SS	Y	SS	SS	Y	$500
American Samoa	...	...	...	...	...	...	...	...	...
No. Mariana Islands	Y	...	...	...	Y	SP	AG	Y	...
Puerto Rico	Y	10% district/ 41% territorial	Other	SBE	N	SP	Other	Y	N
U.S. Virgin Islands	...	...	L	L	N	L	L	N	N

See footnotes at end of table.

STATE REFERENDUMS: REQUESTING PERMISSION TO CIRCULATE A CITIZEN PETITION — Continued

Source: The Council of State Governments' survey of state election administration offices, April 2014.

Key:

... — Not applicable.

EV — Eligible voters.

VG — Total votes cast for the position of governor in the last election.

LG — Lieutenant Governor.

LS — Legislative services.

L — Legislature.

LC — Office of Legislative Counsel.

SS — Secretary of State.

SBE — State Board of Elections.

DV — Division of Elections.

AG — Attorney General.

P — Proponent.

PE — Petitioner.

ST — State.

SP — Sponsor.

Y — Yes.

N — No.

(a) Three forms of referenda exist: citizen petition, submission by the legislature, and constitutional requirement. This table outlines the steps necessary to enact a citizen's petition.

(b) Prior to circulating a statewide petition, a request for permission to do so must first be submitted to a specified state officer. Some states require such signatures to only be those of eligible voters.

(c) The form on which the request for petition is submitted may be the responsibility of the sponsor or may be furnished by the state.

(d) Restrictions may exist regarding the subject matter to which a referendum may be applied. The majority of these restrictions pertain to the dedication of state revenues and appropriations, and laws that maintain the preservation of public peace, safety and health. In Kentucky, referenda are only permitted for the establishment of soil and water and watershed conservation districts.

(e) In some states, a list of individuals who contribute financially to the referendum campaign must be submitted to the specified state officer with whom the petition is filed.

(f) A deposit may be required after permission to circulate a petition has been granted. This amount is refunded when the completed petition has been filed correctly.

(g) New fees/taxes requires 2/3 majority vote.

(h) The secretary of state charges a 10 cent fee per signature that must be verfied for ballot consideration.

(i) A referendum can only be placed on the ballot if authorized by a state law. As a result, a county or town election board cannot print any referendum on the ballot unless the legislature has already passed a law to permit the referendum. Therefore, each statute is different.

(j) Petition sponsor may submit proposed petition summary for approval to State Administrator of Elections but a formal request to circulate a petition is not required.

(k) No specific requirement to request a petition. Legislative Services receives the request and reviews it, and then the sponsor submits it to the Secretary of State and Attorney General for petition format review and legal and constitutional sufficiency review.

(l) State auditor writes the fiscal note.

(m) Petitioners must prepare the summary, and submit it to the Ohio Attorney General, who then must certify whether the summary fully and accurately describes the proposal.

(n) Five percent of legal voters based upon the total number of votes cast at the last general election for the state office receiving the highest number of votes.

(o) LC must also reasonably expect the measure to be put to a vote w/ verified # of signatures (4% for referendum of VG, stautory/const. amdts. different).

(p) May not challenge laws passed by two-thirds of each house of the legislature; any measure prohibiting/limiting wildlife hunting/management takes two-thirds vote in support.

(q) No bills with an emergency clause.

Table 6.15
STATE REFERENDUMS: CIRCULATING THE CITIZEN PETITION

State or other jurisdiction	Basis for signatures	Maximum time period allowed for petition circulation (a)	Can signatures be removed from petition? (b)	Completed petition filed: With	Completed petition filed: Days after legislative session
Alabama	...	...	...	...	...
Alaska	10% TV, from 3/4 ED	w/i 90 days of LS	Y	LG	90 days
Arizona	5% VG	24 months prior to GE	Y	SS	90 days
Arkansas	8% for initiated act; 6% for referenda VG	...	N	SS	90 days
California	5% VG	90 days; 131 days for initiatives prior to GE	Y	(c)	...
Colorado	5% of votes cast for prior SS election	6 months	Y	SS	...
Connecticut	...	...	...	...	...
Delaware	...	...	...	...	...
Florida	8% of TV in prior Presidential election	Up to 2 years (d)	.....	CES	...
Georgia	...	...	...	...	...
Hawaii	...	...	...	...	...
Idaho	6% EV	w/i 60 days after LS	Y	SS	60 days
Illinois	8% VG (e)	24 months prior to GE	Y	SBE	...
Indiana	...	...	...	...	...
Iowa	...	...	...	...	...
Kansas	...	...	...	...	...
Kentucky	...	...	...	...	...
Louisiana	...	...	...	...	...
Maine	10% VG	18 months	...	SS	50 days for 1st session; 25 days for 2nd session
Maryland	3 % VG	(f)	Y	SS	...
Massachusetts	1.5% VG for emergency 2% or immediate suspension	First state election 60 or more days after filing certified petition	Y (g)	SS	90 days after signed by governor
Michigan	5% VG	90 days after LS	N	SS	90 days after enactment
Minnesota	...	...	...	...	...
Mississippi	...	...	...	...	...
Missouri	5% VG, from 2/3 ED	w/i 90 days after LS	Y	SS	90 days
Montana	5% EV and 5% from 34 of 100 ED	(h)	Y	SS	6 mos.
Nebraska	5% EV	...	Y	SS	90 days
Nevada	10% EV last GE	(i)	Y	CC, SS	120 prior to next GE
New Hampshire	...	...	...	...	...
New Jersey	...	...	...	...	...
New Mexico	...	...	...	...	...
New York	...	...	...	...	...
North Carolina	...	...	...	...	...
North Dakota	2% total population	90 days	N	SS	(j)
Ohio	6% VG, 3% each from 1/2 counties	90 days	Y	SS	90 days
Oklahoma	5% VH	w/i 90 days of LS	Y	SS	90 days
Oregon	4% VG	w/i 90 days of LS	Y (k)	SS	90 days
Pennsylvania	...	...	...	...	...
Rhode Island	...	...	...	...	...
South Carolina	...	...	...	...	...
South Dakota	5% VG	24 months prior to GE	N	SS	90 days
Tennessee	...	...	...	...	...
Texas	...	...	...	...	...
Utah	10% VG	40 days after LS	Y	CC	40 days
Vermont	...	...	...	...	...
Virginia	...	...	...	...	...
Washington	4% VG	Approx. 90 days	N	SS	90 days
West Virginia	...	...	...	...	...
Wisconsin	...	...	...	...	...
Wyoming	15% TV, from 2/3 county	18 months	N	SS	90 days
American Samoa	...	...	...	...	...
No. Mariana Islands	...	Up to 120 days before election	Y	AG	...
Puerto Rico	...	...	...	...	...
U.S. Virgin Islands	No. of registered voters	180 days	...	...	...

See footnotes at end of table.

STATE REFERENDUMS: CIRCULATING THE CITIZEN PETITION — Continued

Sources: The Council of State Governments' survey of state election websites, Initiative & Referendum Institute website and Ballotpedia website, February 2016 .

Key:

. . . — Not applicable.

VG — Total votes cast for the position of governor in the last election.

EV — Eligible voters.

TV — Total voters in the last general election.

VH — Total votes cast for the office receiving the highest number of votes in last general election.

VSS — Total votes cast for all candidates for the office of secretary of state at the previous general election.

ED — Election district.

GE — General election.

LS — Legislative session.

LG — Lieutenant governor.

SBE — State Board of Elections.

SS — Secretary of state.

AG — Attorney General.

CC — County clerk.

CES — County election supervisor.

Y — Yes

N — No

w/i — Within

(a) The petition circulation period begins when petition forms have been approved and provided to or by the sponsors. Sponsors are those individuals granted permission to circulate a petition, and are therefore responsible for the validity of each signature on a given petition.

(b) Should an individual wish to remove his/her name from a petition, a request to do so must first be submitted in writing to the state officer with whom the petition is filed.

(c) County elections office.

(d) Signatures must be verified by Feb 1 in year of election.

(e) Referenda are advisory only.

(f) No signature may be collected until the final action of the General Assembly. Session ends the second Monday in April. One third of the signatures must be submitted not later than May 31. The remaining signatures are due no later than June 30th.

(g) Should an individual wish to remove his/her name from a petition, a request to do so must first be submitted in writing to the local election official prior to the petition being submitted for certification of signatures.

(h) No specific beginning date for circulation of petitions, so there is no maximum time period. There is an ending deadline of 6 months after legislative session.

(i) Not later than the third Tuesday in May of even-numbered years.

(j) Within 90 days after the legislation is filed in the Secretary of State's office.

(k) Only by the chief petitioners before submitting signatures before verification. Signatures may not be removed once the signatures have been submitted to the secretary of state for verification.

Table 6.16
STATE REFERENDUMS: PREPARING THE CITIZEN PETITION REFERENDUM TO BE PLACED ON BALLOT

State or other jurisdiction	Signatures verified by: (a)	Within how many days after filing?	No. of days to amend/ appeal petition that is: Incomplete (b)	No. of days to amend/ appeal petition that is: Not accepted (c)	Penalty for falsifying petition (denotes fine, jail term)	Petition certified by: (d)
Alabama	...	...	...	...	...	...
Alaska	Division of elections	60	10	10	Class B misdemeanor	LG
Arizona	County recorder	(e)	...	...	Class 1 misdemeanor	SS
Arkansas	SS	30	...	30	Class D felony	SS
California	County clerk	8 (f)	...	...	Felony or misdemeanor (depending on severity)	SS
Colorado	SS	(g)	15	3 months and 3 weeks before election	Fines up to $1,000 and forgery is a Class 5 felony	SS
Connecticut	...	...	...	...	...	...
Delaware	...	...	...	...	...	...
Florida	Supervisor of Elections	30	...	...	1st degree misdemeanor	SS
Georgia	...	...	...	...	...	...
Hawaii	...	...	...	...	...	...
Idaho	County clerk	...	...	...	$5,000, 2 yrs.	SS
Illinois	State Board of Elections	varies	...	...	Class 3 felony	SBE
Indiana	County clerk	...	...	...	...	...
Iowa	...	...	...	...	...	...
Kansas	...	...	...	...	...	...
Kentucky	...	...	...	...	...	...
Louisiana	...	...	...	...	...	...
Maine	Registrars of voters	30	...	...	Class E crime	SS
Maryland	Local Board of Elections	20	...	...	Misdemeanor (h)	SS, SBE
Massachusetts	Local boards of registrars	14	...	...	$1,000, 1 year	SS
Michigan	SS	Approx. 60	...	...	$500, 90 days	BSC
Minnesota	...	...	...	...	...	...
Mississippi	...	...	...	...	...	...
Missouri	County clerk	(i)	..,	10	Class A misdemeanor	SS
Montana	County election administrators	28	10	10	$500, 6 mos.	SS
Nebraska	County clerk	40	...	...	Penalty up to $1,000 and 1 year in prison	SS
Nevada	County clerk	(j)	5	...	...	SS
New Hampshire	...	...	...	...	...	...
New Jersey	...	...	...	...	...	...
New Mexico	...	...	...	...	...	...
New York	...	...	...	...	...	...
North Carolina	...	...	...	...	...	...
North Dakota	SS	35	...	20	(k)	SS
Ohio	SS	no later than 105 days before election	10	...	5th degree felony	SS
Oklahoma	SS	...	10	...	$1,000, 1 year	SS, State Supreme Court
Oregon	SS, county clerk	30	...	...	(l)	SS
Pennsylvania	...	...	...	...	...	...
Rhode Island	...	...	...	...	...	...
South Carolina	...	...	...	...	...	...
South Dakota	SS	...	...	...	Class 1 misdemeanor	SS
Tennessee	...	...	...	...	...	...
Texas	...	...	...	...	...	...
Utah	County clerks	55 (m)	...	10	Class A misdemeanor	LG
Vermont	...	...	...	...	...	...
Virginia	...	...	...	...	...	...
Washington	SS	(n)	...	10	Class C felony (possible)	SS
West Virginia	...	...	...	...	...	...
Wisconsin	...	...	...	...	...	...
Wyoming	SS	60	60	60	$1,000, 1 yr.	SS
American Samoa	...	...	...	...	...	...
No. Mariana Islands	AG	...	(o)	(o)	(p)	AG
Puerto Rico	...	...	...	...	...	...
U.S. Virgin Islands	Supervisor of Elections	15	...	...	...	Supervisor of Elections.

See footnotes at end of table.

STATE REFERENDUMS: PREPARING THE CITIZEN PETITION REFERENDUM
TO BE PLACED ON BALLOT — Continued

Sources: The Council of State Governments' survey of state election websites, Initiative & Referendum Institute website and Ballotpedia website, February 2016 .

Key:

. . . — Not applicable.

SS—Secretary of State.

LG—Lieutenant Governor.

BSC—Board of State Canvassers.

SBE—State Board of Elections.

(a) The validity of the signatures, as well as the correct number of required signatures must be verified before the referendum is allowed on the ballot.

(b) If an insufficient number of signatures are submitted, sponsors may amend the original petition by filing additional signatures within a given number of days after filing. If the necessary number of signatures have not been submitted by this date, the petition is declared void.

(c) In some cases, the state officer will not accept a valid petition. In such cases, sponsors may appeal this decision to the Supreme Court, where the sufficiency of the petition will be determined. If the petition is determined to be sufficient, the referendum is required to be placed on the ballot.

(d) A petition is certified for the ballot when the required number of signatures have been submitted by the filing deadline, and are determined to be valid.

(e) In Arizona, the secretary of state has 20 days to count signatures and to complete random sample; the county recorder then has 15 days to verify signatures.

(f) Clerk has 8 days to report raw totals of signatures and 30 days for random sampling to verify signatures

(g) At least 30 days for internal review process to conduct random sampling; must verify at least 90% are valid.

(h) Misdemeanor, punishable by a $10-$250 fine or 30 days - six months in jail, or both.

(i) In Missouri, must be certified as sufficient or insufficient by the 13th Tuesday prior to the general election.

(j) 1. Within four days county clerks count total number of signatures and forward to the secretary of state. 2. The secretary of state immediately notifies county clerks if they are to proceed or not proceed with the signature verification. 3. If ordered by the secretary of state, the county clerks verify signatures within nine days (excluding weekends and holidays).

(k) Any violations discovered will be reported to the attorney general for investigation and prosecution.

(l) Whether a penalty is assessed would be based upon what information on the petition was falsified.

(m) After the end of the legislative session.

(n) Not later than the third Tuesday following the primary election.

(o) Incomplete: 30 or more days if submitted 150 days before date of the election; none if submitted 120 days before date of election. Not accepted: If submitted 119 days or less before the election.

(p) Subject to statute governing fraud or perjury.

Table 6.17
STATE REFERENDUMS: VOTING ON THE CITIZEN PETITION REFERENDUM

State or other jurisdiction	Ballot (a) Title by:	Ballot (a) Summary by:	Election where referendum voted on	Effective date of approved referendum (b)	Days to contest election results (c)
Alabama	...	...	...	...	...
Alaska	LG	LG	1st statewide election 180 days after LS	30 days	10
Arizona	SS, AG	LC	GE	(d)	5
Arkansas	AG	...	GE	...	20
California	AG	AG	GE or PR	1 day	5 (e)
Colorado	..	...	...	...	...
Connecticut	...	...	...	...	...
Delaware	...	...	...	...	...
Florida	...	...	...	...	...
Georgia	...	...	...	...	...
Hawaii	...	...	...	...	...
Idaho	AG	AG	GE	30 days	20 (e)
Illinois	...	...	GE	Advisory only	30
Indiana	...	...	...	...	...
Iowa	...	...	...	...	...
Kansas	...	...	...	...	...
Kentucky	...	...	GE or SP	IM	...
Louisiana	...	...	...	...	...
Maine	SS	...	GE or statewide election more than 60 days after filing	30 days	5
Maryland	SS	LSS	GE	(f)	...
Massachusetts	SS, AG	AG	GE more than 60 days after filing	30 days	10
Michigan	BSC	BSC	GE	10 days	2 (e)
Minnesota	...	...	...	...	...
Mississippi	...	...	...	...	...
Missouri	SS, AG	SS	GE	IM	30
Montana	AG	AG	GE	(g)	1 yr.
Nebraska	AG	AG	GE	...	...
Nevada	SS, AG	SS, AG	GE	Nov., 4th Tues.	14
New Hampshire	...	...	...	...	...
New Jersey	...	...	...	...	...
New Mexico	...	...	...	...	...
New York	...	...	...	...	...
North Carolina	...	...	...	...	...
North Dakota	SS, AG	SS	PR	30 days	14 (e)
Ohio	...	...	GE more than 60 days after filing.	IM	15 (h)
Oklahoma	LLS, AG	LLS	GE or SP	...	...
Oregon	AG	AG	GE (i)	30 days	40
Pennsylvania	...	...	...	...	...
Rhode Island	...	...	...	...	...
South Carolina	...	...	...	...	...
South Dakota	AG	AG	GE	1 day	...
Tennessee	...	...	...	...	...
Texas	...	...	...	...	...
Utah	LLS	LLS	GE	5 days	40
Vermont	...	...	...	...	...
Virginia	...	...	...	...	...
Washington	AG	AG	GE	30 days	10
West Virginia	...	...	...	...	...
Wisconsin	...	...	...	...	...
Wyoming	SS	SS, AG	GE more than 120 days after LS	90 days	15
American Samoa	...	...	...	...	...
No. Mariana Islands	AG	AG	GE or special election if specified	(j)	30 days
Puerto Rico	...	...	...	...	...
U.S. Virgin Islands	...	...	...	...	...

See footnotes at end of table.

STATE REFERENDUMS: VOTING ON THE CITIZEN PETITION REFERENDUM — Continued

Sources: The Council of State Governments' survey of state election websites, Initiative & Referendum Institute website and Ballotpedia website, February 2016.

Key:

... — Not applicable.

LG — Lieutenant Governor.

AG — Attorney General.

SS — Secretary of State.

BSC — Board of State Canvassers.

LC — Legislative Counsel.

LSS — Legislative Legal Services.

SBE — State Board of Elections.

(a) In some states, the ballot title and summary will differ from that on the petition.

(b) A majority of the popular vote is required to enact a measure in every state. In Arizona, a referendum approved by the voters becomes effective upon the governor's proclamation. In Nebraska, a referendum may be put into effect immediately after the approving votes have been canvassed by the Board of State Canvassers and upon the governor's proclamation. In Massachusetts the measure must also receive at lease 30 percent of the total ballots cast in the last election. In Oklahoma, put into effect upon certification of election results by state election board. In Utah, after proclamation by governor and upon date specified in petition.

(c) Individuals may contest the results of a vote on a referendum within a certain number of days after the election including this matter. In Alaska, five days to request recount with appeal to the court within five days after recount.

(d) Upon proclamation of the governor after the canvas. (AZ Const. Article 4, Part 1, Section 13).

(e) After election is certified.

(f) After the certification of election results. Sepends on date Board of State Canvassers meets. They must meet within 35 days after General Election.

(g) Unless specifically provided by the legislature in an act referred by it to the people or until suspended by a petition signed by at least 15% of the qualified electors in a majority of the legislative representative districts, an act referred to the people is in effect as provided by law until it is approved or rejected at the election. An act that is rejected is repealed effective the date the result of the canvass is filed by the secretary of state under 13-27-503. An act referred to the people that was in effect at the time of the election and is approved by the people remains in effect. An act that was suspended by a petition and is approved by the people is effective the date the result of the canvass is filed by the secretary of state under 13-27-503. An act referred by the legislature that contains an effective date following the election becomes effective on that date if approved by the people. An act that provides no effective date and whose substantive provisions were delayed by the legislature pending approval at an election and that is approved is effective October 1 following the election.

(h) After election is certified or if recount conducted, 10 days after recount.

(i) Special election can be held at the request of the Legislative Assembly.

(j) Upon approval by voters and certification of election results by Election Commission, usually 15 days after date of election if no contest.

Table 6.18
STATE RECALL PROVISIONS

State or other jurisdiction	Provision for recall	Officials subject to recall	Constitutional and statutory citations for recall of state officials	Constitutional or statutory language
Alabama	No			
Alaska	Yes	All (a)	Const. Art., 11 § 8; AS § 15.45.470 et seq.	All elected public officials in the State, except judicial officers, are subject to recall by the voters of the State or political subdivision from which elected.
Arizona	Yes	All	Const. Art. 8, § 1-6; ARS § 19-201–19-234	Every public officer in the state of Arizona, holding an elective office, either by election or appointment, is subject to recall from such office by the qualified electors of the electoral district from which candidates are elected to such office.
Arkansas	No			
California	Yes	All	Const. Art. 2, § 13-19; CA Election Code § 11000–11386	Recall is the power of the electors to remove an elective officer. Recall of a state officer is initiated by delivering to the Secretary of State a petition alleging reason for recall. Sufficiency of reason is not reviewable.
Colorado	Yes	All	Const. Art. 21, § 1; CRS § 1-12-101–1-12-122, 23-17-120.5, 31-4-501-505	Every elective public officer of the state of Colorado may be recalled from office at any time by the registered electors entitled to vote for a successor of such incumbent through the procedure and in the manner herein provided for, which procedure shall be known as the recall, and shall be in addition to and without excluding any other method of removal by law.
Connecticut	No			
Delaware	No			
Florida	No			
Georgia	Yes	All	Const. Art. 2, § 2.4; GA Code § 21-4-1 et seq.	The General Assembly is hereby authorized to provide by general law for the recall of public officials who hold elective office. The procedures, grounds, and all other matters relative to such recall shall be provided for in such law.
Hawaii	No			
Idaho	Yes	All (a)	Const. Art 6, § 6; ID Code § 34-1701–34-1715	Every public officer in the state of Idaho, excepting the judicial officers, is subject to recall by the legal voters of the state or of the electoral district from which he is elected. The legislature shall pass the necessary laws to carry this provision into effect.
Illinois (b)	Yes	(b)	Const. Art 3, § 7	The recall of the Governor may be proposed by a petition signed by a number of electors equal in number to at least 15% of the total votes cast for Governor in the preceding gubernatorial election, with at least 100 signatures from each of at least 25 separate counties. A petition shall have been signed by the petitioning electors not more than 150 days after an affidavit has been filed with the State Board of Elections providing notice of intent to circulate a petition to recall the Governor. The affidavit may be filed no sooner than 6 months after the beginning of the Governor's term of office. The affidavit shall have been signed by the proponent of the recall petition, at least 20 members of the House of Representatives, and at least 10 members of the Senate, with no more than half of the signatures of members of each chamber from the same established political party.
Indiana	No			

See footnotes at end of table.

STATE RECALL PROVISIONS — Continued

State or other jurisdiction	Provision for recall	Officials subject to recall	Constitutional and statutory citations for recall of state officials	Constitutional or statutory language
Iowa	No			
Kansas	Yes	All (a)	Const. Art. 4, § 3; KSA § 25-4301–25-4331	All elected public officials in the State, except judicial officers, shall be subject to recall by voters of the state or political subdivision from which elected. Procedures and grounds for recall shall be prescribed by law.
Kentucky	No			
Louisiana	Yes	All (a)	Const. Art. 10, § 26; LRS § 18:1300.1–18:1300.17	The legislature shall provide by general law for the recall by election of any state, district, parochial, ward, or municipal officer except judges of the courts of record. The sole issue at a recall election shall be whether the official shall be recalled.
Maine	No			
Maryland	No			
Massachusetts	No			
Michigan	Yes	All (a)	Const. Art. 2, § 8; MCL § 168.951–168.975	Laws shall be enacted to provide for the recall of all elective officers except judges of courts of record upon petition of electors equal in number to 25 percent of the number of persons voting in the last preceding election for the office of governor in the electoral district of the officer sought to be recalled. The sufficiency of any statement of reasons or grounds procedurally required shall be a political rather than a judicial question.
Minnesota	Yes	(c)	Const. Art. 8, § 6; MS § 211C.01 et. seq.	A state officer other than a judge may be subject to recall for serious malfeasance or nonfeasance during the term of office in the performance of the duties of the office or conviction during the term of office for a serious crime.
Mississippi	No			
Missouri	No			
Montana	Yes	All	Mont. Code § 2-16-601–2-16-635	Every person holding a public office of the state or any of its political subdivisions, either by election or appointment, is subject to recall from such office.
Nebraska	No			
Nevada	Yes	All	Const. Art. 2, § 9; NRS § 294A.006, Chapter 306	Every public officer in the State of Nevada is subject, as herein provided, to recall from office by the registered voters of the state, or of the county, district, or municipality which he represents.
New Hampshire	No			
New Jersey	Yes	All	Const. Art. 1, § 2; NJRS § 19:27A-1–19:27A-18	The people reserve unto themselves the power to recall, after at least one year of service, any elected official in this State or representing this State in the United States Congress.
New Mexico	No			
New York	No			
North Carolina	No			
North Dakota	Yes	All (d)	Const. Art. 3, § 1 and 10; ND Century Code § 16.1-01-09.1	Any elected official of the state, of any county or of any legislative or county commissioner district shall be subject to recall by petition of electors equal in number to twenty-five percent of those who voted at the preceding general election for the office of governor in the state, county, or district in which the official is to be recalled.

See footnotes at end of table.

STATE RECALL PROVISIONS — Continued

State or other jurisdiction	Provision for recall	Officials subject to recall	Constitutional and statutory citations for recall of state officials	Constitutional or statutory language
Ohio	No			
Oklahoma	No			
Oregon	Yes	All (d)	Const. Art. 2, § 18; ORS § 249.865–249.880	Every public official in Oregon is subject, as herein provided, to recall by the electors of the state or of the electoral district from which the public official is elected.
Pennsylvania	No			
Rhode Island	Yes	(e)	Const. Art. 4, § 1	Recall is authorized in the case of a general officer who has been indicted or informed against for a felony, convicted of a misdemeanor, or against whom a finding of probable cause of violation of the code of ethics has been made by the ethics commission.
South Carolina	No			
South Dakota	No			
Tennessee	No			
Texas	No			
Utah	No			
Vermont	No			
Virginia	No (f)			
Washington	Yes	All (a)	Const. Art. 1, Sec. 33–34; WRC § 29.82-010–29.82.220	Every elective public officer of the state of Washington except judges of courts of record is subject to recall and discharge by the legal voters of the state, or of the political subdivision of the state, from which he was elected whenever a petition demanding his recall, . . . is filed with the officer with whom a petition for nomination, or certificate for nomination, to such office must be filed under the laws of this state, and the same officer shall call a special election as provided by the general election laws of this state and the result determined as therein provided.
West Virginia	No			
Wisconsin	Yes	All	Const. Art. 13, § 12; Wisc. Stat. § 9.10	The qualified electors of the state, of any congressional, judicial or legislative district or of any county may petition for the recall of any incumbent elective officer after the first year of the term for which the incumbent was elected, by filing a petition with the filing officer with whom the nomination petition is filed, demanding the recall of the incumbent.
Wyoming	No			
No. Marianas Islands	Yes	All	N.A.	N.A.
Puerto Rico	Yes	All	N.A.	N.A.
U.S. Virgin Islands	Yes	All	Constitutional and statutory citations exist	N.A.

Sources: The Council of State Governments, state constitutions and statutes, March 2016.
Note: This table refers only to officials elected to statewide office. Many local governments allow recall of elected officials.

Key:
N.A. — Not available
(a) Except judicial.
(b) Illinois allows for recall of the governor.
(c) State executive officers, legislators, and judicial officers.
(d) Except for U.S. Congress.
(e) Governor, lieutenant governor, secretary of state, treasurer, and attorney general.
(f) Virginia permits a recall trial, not a recall election.

Table 6.19
STATE RECALL PROVISIONS: APPLICABILITY TO STATE OFFICIALS AND PETITION CIRCULATION

State or other jurisdiction	Officers to whom recall is applicable (a)	No. of times recall can be attempted	Recall may be initiated after official has been in office	Recall may not be initiated with days remaining in term	Basis for signatures (b) (see key below)		Maximum time allowed for petition circulation (c)
					Statewide officers	Others	
Alabama		…	…	…	…	…	…
Alaska	All but judicial officers	…	120 days	180	25% VO	25% VO	…
Arizona	All elected officials	1 (d)	6 mos./5 days legislators	…	25% VO (e)	25% VO (e)	120 days
Arkansas		…	…	…	…	…	…
California	All elected officials	(f)	90 days	6 mos.	12% VO, 1% from 5 counties	20% VO	160 days
Colorado	All elected officials	(g)	6 mos.	6 mos.	25% VO	25% VO	60 days
Connecticut		…	…	…	…	…	…
Delaware		…	…	…	…	…	…
Florida		…	…	…	…	…	…
Georgia	All state level officials, county and city elected officials	…	180 days	180	15% EV (h), 1/15 from each congressional district	30% EV (h)	(i)
Hawaii		…	…	…	…	…	…
Idaho	All but judicial officers	(d)	90 days	…	20% EVg	50% VO	60 days
Illinois	Governor	…	…	…	15% VO from 25 counties	20 state Rep. and 10 state Sen.	150 days
Indiana		…	…	…	…	…	…
Iowa		…	…	…	…	…	…
Kansas	All but judicial officers	1	120 days	180	40% VO	40% VO	90 days
Kentucky		…	…	…	…	…	…
Louisiana	All but judicial officers	(j)	1 day	6 mos.	33 1/3% EV (k)	40% EV (k)	180 days
Maine		…	…	…	…	…	…
Maryland		…	…	…	…	…	…
Massachusetts		…	…	…	…	…	…
Michigan	All but judicial officers	No limit	1 year	1 year	25% VG in district	25% VG in district	60 days
Minnesota	All state level officials	No limit	6 mos.	6 mos.	25% VO	25% VO	90 days
Mississippi		…	…	…	…	…	…
Missouri		…	…	…	…	…	…
Montana	All state level officers & elected officials	(l)	2 mos.	…	10% EV	(m)	3 mos.
Nebraska	Elected officials from political subdivisions	(n)	6 mos.	…	…	35–45% VO	…
Nevada	All officers	(d)	6 mos. (o)	6 mos.	25% VO in given jurisdiction	25% VO in given jurisdiction	90 days
New Hampshire		…	…	…	…	…	…
New Jersey	All elected officials	(p)	(q)	(r)	25% EV in given jurisdiction	25% EV in given jurisdiction	(s)
New Mexico		…	…	…	…	…	…
New York		…	…	…	…	…	…
North Carolina		…	…	…	…	…	…
North Dakota	All elected state officials	1	…	190	25% EVg	25% EV	90 days
Ohio		…	…	…	…	…	…
Oklahoma		…	…	…	…	…	…
Oregon	All elected state officials	No limit	180 days (t)	…	15% (u)	15% (u)	90 days
Pennsylvania		…	…	…	…	…	…
Rhode Island	Gov., lt. gov., atty. gen., sec. of state, treasurer	…	6 mos.	…	15% VO	25% VO	90 days
South Carolina		…	…	…	…	…	…

See footnotes at end of table.

RECALL

STATE RECALL PROVISIONS: APPLICABILITY TO STATE OFFICIALS AND PETITION CIRCULATION — Continued

State or other jurisdiction	Officers to whom recall is applicable (a)	No. of times recall can be attempted	Recall may be initiated after official has been in office	Recall may not be initiated with days remaining in term	Basis for signatures (b) (see key below)		Maximum time allowed for petition circulation (c)
					Statewide officers	Others	
South Dakota	...	...	...	...	...	...	...
Tennessee	...	...	...	...	...	...	...
Texas	...	...	...	...	...	...	...
Utah	...	...	...	...	...	...	...
Vermont	...	...	...	...	...	...	...
Virginia	...	...	...	...	...	...	...
Washington	All but judges of courts of records	...	IM	180	25% VO	35% VO	(v)
West Virginia	...	...	...	...	...	...	...
Wisconsin	All elected officials	1	1 yr.	...	25% VG (w)	25% VG (w)	60 days
Wyoming	...	...	...	...	...	...	...
American Samoa	...	...	...	...	...	...	...
No. Mariana Island.	All elected officials	(x)	180 days	...	40% EV (y)	...	(z)
Puerto Rico	...	...	...	...	...	...	...
U.S. Virgin Islands	All elected officials	Unlimited	1 year	365	...	Registered electors	180 days

Sources: The Council of State Governments, Mar. 2016.

Key:
... — Not applicable.
All — All elective officials.
VO — Number of votes cast in the last election for the office or official being recalled.
EVg — Number of eligible voters in the last general election for governor.
EV — Eligible voters.
VG — Total votes cast for the position of governor in the last election.
VP — Total votes cast for position of president in last presidential election.
IM — Immediately.

(a) An elective official may be recalled by qualified voters entitled to vote for the recalled official's successor. An appointed official may be recalled by qualified voters entitled to vote for the successor(s) of the elective officer(s) authorized to appoint an individual to the position.

(b) Signature requirements for recall of those other than state elective officials are based on votes in the jurisdiction to which the said official has been elected.

(c) The petition circulation period begins when petition forms have been approved and provided to sponsors. Sponsors are those individuals granted permission to circulate a petition, and are therefore responsible for the validity of each signature on a given petition.

(d) Additional recall attempts can be made provided that the state treasury is reimbursed the cost of the previous recall attempt(s). The specific reason for recalling on one petition cannot be the basis for a second recall petition during the current term of office.

(e) 25% of the number of votes cast at the preceding general election for all candidates for the office held by the officer, even if the officer was not elected at that election, divided by the number of offices that were being filled at that election. (A.R.S.§ 19-201.)

(f) Open ended.

(g) One attempt unless a second petition is circulated and valid signatures gathered are at least 50% of votes cast for all candidates in last election.

(h) Eligible voters for office at last general election to fill office.

(i) For any statewide office, 90 days. Any officer holding an office other than statewide office and for whom no less than 5,000 signatures are required for the recall petition, 45 days. Any officer holding an office other than statewide office and for whom less than 5,000 are required, 30 days.

(j) Unlimited. Once every 18 months.

(k) Basis for signatures 33 1/3 percent if over 1,000 eligible voters; 40 percent if under 1,000 eligible voters.

(l) No recall petition may be filed against an officer for whom a recall election has been held for a period of 2 years during his term of office unless the state or political subdivisions financing such recall election is first reimbursed for all expenses of the preceding election.

(m) 15 percent of eligible for district offices.

(n) If voted on, no recall for one year.

(o) For legislators, anytime after 10 days from the beginning of the first legislative session after their election.

(p) An elected official sought to be recalled who is not recalled as the result of a recall election shall not again be subject to recall until after having served one year of a term calculated from the date of the recall election.

(q) The recall drive may not commence before the 50th day preceding the completion of the elected official's first year of the current term.

(r) No election to recall an elected official shall be held after the date occurring six months prior to the general election or regular election for that office, as appropriate, in the final year of the officials term.

(s) The maximum time allowed for petition circulation is 320 days for a governor or U.S. Senator or 160 days for other elected officials.

(t) Unless it is a state senator or representative and then it is anytime after fifth day form the beginning of legislative sessionor after election of legislator.

(u) 15 percent of the total number of votes cast in the public officer's electoral district for all candidates for governor at the last election at which a candidate for governor was elected to a full term.

(v) Statewide officials 270 days; others 180 days.

(w) At least 25 percent of the vote case for the office of governor at the last election within the same district or territory as that of the officeholder being recalled.

(x) Not more than once a year or not during the first six months in office.

(y) Grounds for recall must be stated and must be signed by 40% of voters represented by the elected official.

(z) Until 120 days before the election.

Table 6.20
STATE RECALL PROVISIONS: PETITION REVIEW, APPEAL AND ELECTION

State or other jurisdiction	Signatures verified (a) by:	Days to amend/appeal a petition that is: Incomplete (b)	Not accepted (c)	Penalty for falsifying petition (denotes fines, jail time)	Days allowed for petition to be certified (d)	Days to step down after certification (e)	Voting on the recall (f): Election held	Election type	Days to contest election results (g)
Alabama	Division of Elections	20	20	Class B misdemeanor	30	…	60-90 days after cert.	GE,PR,SP	10
Alaska	County recorder	…	…	Class 1 misdemeanor	70	1	(h)	(i)	5
Arizona	…	…	…	…	…	5	…	…	5
Arkansas	…	…	…	…	…	…	…	…	…
California	County clerk/registrar of voters	10	10	…	10	(j)	60-80 days after cert.	GE	5
Colorado	SS	…	15 (k)	…	10	5	45-75 days after cert.	SP or GE	10
Connecticut	…	…	…	…	…	…	…	…	…
Delaware	…	…	…	…	…	…	…	…	…
Florida	Registrar of voters	…	…	…	…	…	…	…	…
Georgia	…	…	…	Misdemeanor	30-45	…	30-45 days after cert.	SP	5
Hawaii	…	…	…	…	…	…	…	…	…
Idaho	County clerk	30	…	$5,000, 2 yrs.	10	5	45+ days after cert. (l)	SP , PR, GE (l)	20 (m)
Illinois	SBE	…	…	…	…	…	100 days after cert.	SP	…
Indiana	…	…	…	…	…	…	…	…	…
Iowa	…	…	…	…	…	…	…	…	…
Kansas	County clerk	…	…	Class B misdemeanor; up to $1,000, up to one year or both.	30	Next day	60-90 days after cert.	SP	5 (m)
Kentucky	…	…	…	…	…	…	…	…	…
Louisiana	Registrar of voters	(n)	(n)	…	15-20 days	(o)	(p)	SP	(q)
Maine	…	…	…	…	…	…	…	…	…
Maryland	…	…	…	…	…	…	…	…	…
Massachusetts	…	…	…	…	…	…	…	…	…
Michigan	SS, local election officials (r)	…	…	$500, 90 days	35	…	(s)	SP	2 (m)
Minnesota	SS	90	…	Felony	10	…	(t)	GE	7
Mississippi	…	…	…	…	…	…	…	…	…
Missouri	…	…	…	…	…	…	…	…	…
Montana	County election administrators	10	10	$500 or six months in county jail, or both.	(u)	5	(v)	SP or GE (dd) (v)	12 mos.
Nebraska	County clerk	…	…	…	15	5	30-45 days after cert.	SP	40
Nevada	County clerk, registrar of voters	5	…	Misdemeanor	(w)	5	(x)	SP	(y)
New Hampshire	…	…	…	…	…	…	…	…	…
New Jersey	Recall elections official	…	…	Crime of the 4th degree	10	5	(z)	SP or GE	(aa)
New Mexico	…	…	…	…	…	…	…	…	…
New York	…	…	…	…	…	…	…	…	…
North Carolina	…	…	…	…	…	…	…	…	…
North Dakota	SS	…	…	…	30	10	50-60	SP	14 (bb)
Ohio	…	…	…	…	…	…	…	…	…
Oklahoma	…	…	…	…	…	…	…	…	…
Oregon	County clerk	(cc)	…	(dd)	10	5	w/i 35 days after resignation period	SP	40
Pennsylvania	…	…	…	…	…	…	…	…	…
Rhode Island	SBE	w/i 90 days	…	Misdemeanor and/or felony	90	…	…	SP	…
South Carolina	…	…	…	…	…	…	…	…	…

See footnotes at end of table.

STATE RECALL PROVISIONS: PETITION REVIEW, APPEAL AND ELECTION — Continued

State or other jurisdiction	Signatures verified (a) by:	Days to amend/appeal a petition that is:		Penalty for falsifying petition (denotes fines, jail time) (c)	Days allowed for petition to be certified (d)	Days to step down after certification (e)	Voting on the recall (f)		Days to contest election results (g)
		Incomplete (b)	Not accepted (c)				Election held	Election type	
South Dakota	...	...	...	...	...	...	...	...	...
Tennessee	...	...	...	...	...	...	...	...	...
Texas	...	...	...	...	...	...	...	...	...
Utah	...	...	...	...	...	...	...	...	...
Vermont	...	...	...	...	...	...	...	...	...
Virginia	...	...	...	...	...	...	...	...	...
Washington	SS	30	...	Class B felony or misdemeanor	not specified	...	45-60 days after cert. (ee)	SP	3
West Virginia	...	...	...	...	...	...	...	...	...
Wisconsin	SBE	...	...	Class 1 felony - $10,000, 3 yrs. prison or both.	31	10	6 weeks after cert.	GE or PR	3 (ff)
Wyoming	...	...	...	...	...	...	...	...	...
American Samoa	...	...	...	...	...	...	...	...	...
No. Mariana Islands...	AG	150 days	...	Statute governs fraud or perjury.	15 days	...	(gg)	GE, SP	30
Puerto Rico	...	...	...	...	...	...	...	...	...
U.S. Virgin Islands	Office of the Supervisor of Elections	...	...	...	10	IM	...	GE	5

Sources: The Council of State Governments Mar. 2016.

Key:

... —Not applicable.
SBE—State Board of Elections.
SS—Secretary of State.
SP—Special election.
GE—General election.
PR—Primary election.
IM—Immediate and automatic removal from office.
w/i—Within
N.A.—Information not available.

(a) The validity of the signatures, as well as the correct number of required signatures must be verified before the recall is allowed on the ballot.

(b) If an insufficient number of signatures are submitted, sponsors may amend the original petition by filing additional signatures within a given number of days. If the necessary number of signatures have not been submitted by this date, the petition is declared void.

(c) In some cases, the state officer will not accept a valid petition. In such a case, sponsors may appeal this decision to the Supreme Court, where the sufficiency of the petition will be determined. When this is declared, the recall is required to be placed on the ballot.

(d) A petition is certified for the ballot when the required number of signatures has been submitted by the filing deadline, and are determined to be valid.

(e) The official to whom a recall is proposed has a certain number of days to step down from his position before a recall election is initiated, if the desires to do so.

(f) A majority of the popular vote is required to recall an official in each state.

(g) Individuals may contest the results of a vote on a recall within a certain number of days after the results are certified. In Alaska, an appeal to courts must be filed within five days of the recount.

(h) The election order is issued within 15 days if the officer does not resign within five days after certification.

(i) To be held on the next consolidated election date pursuant to § 16-204 that is 90 days or more after the order calling the election (A.R.S. § 19-209(A)).

(j) Prior to election being called.

(k) After determination of sufficiency.

(l) In Idaho, the dates on which elections may be conducted are the first Tuesday in February, the fourth Tuesday in May, the first Tuesday in August, or the Tuesday following the first Monday in November. In addition, an emergency election may be called upon motion of the governing board of a political subdivision. Recall elections conducted by any political subdivision shall be held on the nearest of these dates which falls more than 45 days after the clerk of the political subdivision orders that the recall election shall be held.

(m) After election is certified. In Michigan, if a petition is filed against a local officer, a recount can be requested up to 6 days after certification of recall election.

(n) The Registrar of Voters shall honor the written request of any voter who either desires to have his handwritten signature stricken from or added to the petition at any time prior to certification of the petition, or within five days after receipt of such signed petition, whichever is earlier.

(o) (y) Election returns are certified on the fifth day after the election, and the office is immediately vacant.

(p) The local registrar of voters sends the original certified recall petition to the governor, who issues, within 15 days, a proclamation calling a special election, placing the special election on the next regularly scheduled election date.

(q) Not later than 4:30 p.m. of the 30th day after the official promulgation of the results of the election. Promulgation is on or before the 12th day after the election.

(r) Secretary of state if filed on the state level; county or local clerks if filed on county level.

(s) Under Michigan's consolidated elections, the recall election is held on the next fixed election date that falls at least 95 days after the recall petition is filed.

(t) An election will not be held in the last 6 mos. of a term after certification.

(u) County election administrators have 30 days; sponsor has three mos. to submit the petition from the date of certification.

(v) A special election is called unless the filing is within 90 days of a general election.

(w) Within four days, county clerks count signature totals and forward to the Secretary of State. The Secretary of State immediately notifies the clerks if they are to proceed with signature verification.

STATE RECALL PROVISIONS: PETITION REVIEW, APPEAL AND ELECTION — Continued

(x) In Nevada, a recall election is held 10–20 days after the Secretary of State completes notification of the petition sufficiency unless a complaint is filed, the clerk shall issue a call for the election which is to be held within 30 days after the issuance of the call.

(y) Five days after recount is completed or 14 days after the election if no recount is demanded.

(z) New Jersey Permanent Statutes,19:27A-13, In the case of an office which is ordinarily filled at the general election, a recall election shall be held at the next general election occurring at least 55 days following the fifth business day after service of certification, unless it was indicated in the notice of intention to recall that the recall election shall be held at a special election in which case the recall election official shall order and fix the date for holding the recall election to be the next Tuesday occurring during the period beginning with the 55th day and ending on the 61st day following the fifth business day after service of the certification of the petition.

(aa) New Jersey Permanent Statutes, 19:27A-16.

(bb) Fourteen days after the canvas board has certified the results.

(cc) Chief petitioners may submit additional signatures if the deadline for submitting signatures has not passed.

(dd) Whether a penalty is assessd would depend on what information on the petition was falsified.

(ee) If possible to be held on a regularly scheduled election; cannot be held between the primary and general.

(ff) Business days.

(gg) The election is held at the next regular general election or at a special election set forth int he recall petition.

Chapter Seven

STATE FINANCE

State Budgets in 2015 and 2016:
Most States Show Continued Growth,
Some Face Significant Challenges

By Brian Sigritz

Overall, state fiscal conditions showed modest improvements in fiscal year 2015. Revenue growth accelerated, mostly due to strong income tax collections, while total state spending from all fund sources increased at its fastest rate since 1992 due to additional federal funds from the Affordable Care Act. In addition, the number of states making mid-year budget cuts remained low, and states' total balances reached an all-time high in actual dollar terms. In fiscal 2016, states expect both revenue and spending to grow slowly. However, some states are facing significant budgetary challenges associated with the decline in oil prices. It is likely that budget proposals for fiscal 2017 and beyond will remain mostly cautious with limited spending growth.

By most measures, state finances moderately improved in fiscal year 2015. Revenue growth accelerated in fiscal 2015, growing 4.8 percent compared to 1.9 percent growth in fiscal 2014.[1] The increase in tax collections was mainly attributable to an increase in income tax collections, partly from the strong stock market performance in calendar year 2014. While the vast majority of states experienced at least moderate revenue growth in fiscal 2015, some states heavily reliant on oil and natural gas tax collections experienced significant declines. Total state spending, including general funds, other state funds, bonds and federal funds, also increased in fiscal 2015. The year-over-year percentage growth rate of 7.8 percent was the highest rate since fiscal 1992. The rise in total state spending resulted from a combination of a rapid increase in federal funds to states due to additional Medicaid dollars from the Affordable Care Act for those states that expanded Medicaid, and modest growth in states' own fund sources.[2] Looking only at states' general fund spending, elementary and secondary education and higher education saw the largest spending growth in fiscal 2015.[3] Other indicators of the improvement in state fiscal conditions include that mid-year budget cuts totaled approximately $1 billion in fiscal 2015, compared to more than $31 billion during the peak of the economic downturn,[4] and that total balances, including both ending balances and rainy day funds, reached an all-time high in actual dollars in fiscal 2015.[5]

In fiscal 2016, it is projected that both state general fund spending and revenue will increase for the sixth consecutive year, although the growth is expected to be modest. Revenue collections are projected to increase at a slower growth rate than in fiscal 2015. Total state general fund revenues are projected to grow 2.5 percent in fiscal 2016, less than fiscal 2015's growth rate of 4.8 percent, and less than the 38-year historical average revenue growth rate of 5.6 percent.[6] According to appropriated budgets, general fund expenditures are expected to increase by 4.1 percent in fiscal 2016. However, general fund spending growth is projected to be slower than fiscal 2015 and also once again remain below the historical average spending growth rate of 5.5 percent.[7] In examining other indicators of state fiscal health for fiscal 2016, states enacted an aggregate net increase of $545 million in tax and fee changes following two consecutive years of net reductions,[8] total balances are projected to slightly decrease resulting from an anticipated decline in ending balances,[9] and it is likely that the number of states making mid-year budget cuts will remain well below the level experienced during the past economic downturn. While most states are anticipating at least moderate growth in spending and revenue for fiscal 2016, some states are facing negative budgetary impacts associated with the declining price of oil. Additionally, a number of states continue to experience budget challenges associated with slow economic growth, the rising cost of health care, pent-up demand for infrastructure, the underfunding of pensions and retiree health care, and federal spending cuts.

The Current State Fiscal Condition

Revenues in Fiscal 2015

Revenue growth accelerated in fiscal 2015, growing 4.8 percent compared to 1.9 percent growth in fiscal 2014.[10] Part of the reason for the more robust growth was the fact that most states experienced a positive "April surprise" in fiscal 2015, in contrast to fiscal 2014. April surprises often occur in states after taxpayers pay both their federal and state income taxes. The positive April surprise in fiscal 2015 is mainly attributable to an increase in income tax collections, partly from the strong stock market performance in calendar year 2014, and is viewed as a one-time occurrence. Both corporate income taxes and personal income taxes posted strong gains in fiscal 2015, growing 8.7 percent and 8.0 percent respectively, while sales tax revenues increased 5.2 percent.[11] Revenue growth in fiscal 2015 was widespread, with 45 states experiencing nominal revenue increases compared to fiscal 2014.[12] In addition, 39 states saw revenues come in above final projections, three states had revenues come in on target, and in seven states revenues came in below projections (one state was not able to report data).[13] While the vast majority of states experienced at least moderate revenue gains in fiscal 2015, some states heavily reliant on oil and natural gas tax collections experienced significant declines. Alaska, the state with revenues most significantly affected by the declining price of oil, saw revenue collections decline from $5.4 billion in fiscal 2014 to $2.2 billion in fiscal 2015. Overall, state general fund revenue collections totaled $765.4 billion in fiscal 2015, up from $730.3 billion in fiscal 2014.[14]

Revenues in Fiscal 2016

Revenue growth is projected to increase in fiscal 2016 for the sixth consecutive year but remain slow and below the historical average. In addition, revenue collections are projected to increase at a significantly slower growth rate than fiscal 2015. Total state general fund revenues are projected to grow 2.5 percent in fiscal 2016, less than fiscal 2015's growth rate of 4.8 percent. Since 1979, general fund revenues have increased on average 5.6 percent, according to NASBO's Fiscal Survey of States.[15] Overall, general fund revenues are projected to grow by $19.2 billion in fiscal 2016 from $765.4 billion to $784.7 billion, with sales taxes increasing by $8.8 billion (3.9 percent), personal income taxes growing by $10 billion (3.3 percent),

and corporate income taxes declining by $227 million (-0.5 percent).[16]

Through the first part of fiscal 2016, revenue growth has been near or slightly above projections for most states. According to the Rockefeller Institute of Government, preliminary figures show state revenues growing 4.3 percent during the first quarter of fiscal 2016 (July–September 2015).[17] Additionally, according to NASBO data collected in the fall of 2015, 20 states were seeing revenues coming in on target for fiscal 2016, with 16 higher and six lower (not all states were able to report data).[18] While most states have seen stable revenue growth so far in fiscal 2016, some have experienced significant revenue difficulties—most notably states heavily reliant on severance taxes generated from resources such as oil, natural gas and coal. In addition, income tax collections in fiscal 2016 may be impacted by the poor stock market performance in calendar year 2015.

Tax and Fee Changes in Fiscal 2016

Twenty-two states enacted net tax and fee increases in fiscal 2016, while 18 states passed net decreases in fiscal 2016, resulting in an aggregate net increase of $545 million. Fiscal 2016 contrasts with the previous two fiscal years when states enacted net revenue decreases. States with the largest increases in taxes and fees in fiscal 2016 include Connecticut and Louisiana, both of which modified certain provisions and reduced tax breaks across a number of revenue categories; Georgia, which increased taxes and fees to fund transportation projects; and Nevada, which enacted various tax increases to enhance funding for K-12 education. Texas enacted the largest net tax decrease with its property tax relief and reduction in the business franchise tax rate, followed by Ohio's personal income tax cuts.[19] It should be noted that while states enacted more than $500 million in net tax and fee increases in fiscal 2016, the overall net increase only represents 0.07 percent of total general fund revenue.

In fiscal 2016, personal income taxes saw the largest enacted decrease, reduced by $1.3 billion; much of the decline in personal income taxes came from actions taken by Ohio, California and North Carolina. The second largest decline was in "other taxes" at $239 million, with much of it attributed to decreases enacted by Texas and Florida. Additional revenue sources that experienced a net decrease include fees (-$19 million) and alcohol (-$9 million). A number of revenue sources saw similar-sized moderate net increases including corporate income taxes ($576 million), cigarette and tobacco taxes ($535 million), sales taxes ($494 million) and motor fuel taxes ($472 million).[20]

State Spending in 2015

Total state spending[21] sharply increased in fiscal 2015 with the year-over-year percentage growth rate of 7.8 percent—the highest rate since fiscal 1992. The rise in total state spending resulted from a combination of a rapid increase in federal funds to states, and modest growth in states' own fund sources. The acceleration of federal funds to states in fiscal 2015 was almost solely due to states receiving significantly more federal Medicaid dollars as part of the first full year of Medicaid expansion under the Affordable Care Act, or ACA.

Over the past several years, spending from states' own fund sources has moderately grown as states' revenues have slowly rebounded from the most recent recession and the national economy has gradually improved. Spending from state funds—including general funds and other state funds, but not federal funds or bonds—increased 4.6 percent in fiscal 2011, 3.8 percent in fiscal 2012, 2.6 percent in fiscal 2013, 4.0 percent in fiscal 2014 and an estimated 5.9 percent in fiscal 2015. In fiscal 2015, spending from state funds was partly bolstered by strong growth in personal income tax collections.

While the level of spending growth from state funds has been relatively stable in recent years, the level of growth in federal funds to states has fluctuated. Due to the wind-down of funds from the American Recovery and Reinvestment Act of 2009, also known as the Recovery Act or stimulus, federal funds to states only grew 1 percent in fiscal 2011, declined 9.8 percent in fiscal 2012 and decreased an additional 2.6 percent in fiscal 2013. However, federal funds rose by 4.7 percent in fiscal 2014 as some states began to receive additional Medicaid funds through the ACA in January 2014. In fiscal 2015, it is estimated that federal funds to states rose 12.2 percent during the first full year of the optional Medicaid expansion under the ACA. It should also be noted that while federal funds to states rose sharply in fiscal 2015, the increase was almost solely due to increased Medicaid dollars. Federal Medicaid funds to states increased 22.5 percent in fiscal 2015, while all other federal funds to states only grew 2 percent.[22]

Looking in greater detail at fiscal 2015, total state expenditures—general funds, federal funds, other state funds and bonds combined—grew from $1.74 trillion to $1.87 trillion.[23] Medicaid remained the largest category of total state spending in fiscal 2015, representing 27.4 percent. Other categories of total state expenditures include elementary and secondary education (19.3 percent), higher education (10.3 percent), transportation (7.7 percent), corrections (3.1 percent), public assistance (1.3 percent) and "all other" (30.9 percent).[24] All areas of total state spending experienced increases in fiscal 2015 with the exception of public assistance, which declined 7.3 percent; public assistance figures only include cash assistance and not other forms of public assistance such as child care, housing or employment programs. Medicaid experienced the largest gains at 15.1 percent, followed by all other (6.2 percent), higher education (6 percent), elementary and secondary education (5.1 percent), transportation (4.4 percent) and corrections (4 percent).[25]

General fund spending is estimated to be $748.7 billion in fiscal 2015, a 4.9 percent increase from fiscal 2014. General funds typically receive their revenue from broad-based state taxes such as sales and personal income taxes. As with total state spending, all program areas saw at least some general fund spending growth in fiscal 2015 with the exception of public assistance, which declined 6.6 percent. Higher education grew fastest at 7.7 percent, followed by K-12 (5.6 percent), Medicaid (5.1 percent), corrections (3.9 percent), all other (3.9 percent) and transportation (3.1 percent).[26] Elementary and secondary education remained the largest category of general fund expenditures in fiscal 2015, accounting for 35.2 percent. Medicaid represented 19.3 percent and higher education accounted for 10 percent. Combined, education (both K-12 and higher education) and Medicaid comprised nearly two-thirds of general fund spending. Other categories of general fund spending included corrections (6.8 percent), public assistance (1.2 percent), transportation (0.7 percent)[27] and all other (26.7 percent).[28]

State Spending in 2016

According to appropriated budgets, general fund expenditures are expected to increase by 4.1 percent in fiscal 2016, the sixth consecutive year of modest general fund spending growth following back-to-back declines in fiscal 2009 and fiscal 2010. Despite increases in fiscal 2016, general fund spending growth is projected to be slower than fiscal 2015 and also once again remain below the 38-year historical average of 5.5 percent.[29] In total, general fund expenditures are estimated to be $790.3 billion in fiscal 2016, a $30.9 billion increase from the prior year. Forty-three states enacted a fiscal 2016 budget with general fund spending levels above fiscal 2015, with 30 states reporting general fund expenditure growth between 0.1 and 4.9 percent, and 13 states reporting growth greater than 5 percent.[30] Although the vast majority of states enacted fiscal 2016 budgets with general fund spending growth, in eight states general fund spending levels remain below fiscal 2008, with several of these states facing negative budgetary impacts associated with the declining price in oil.[31]

Budget Cuts

A clear indicator of the current improvement in state fiscal conditions is that the amount of mid-year budget cuts has sharply declined since the most recent national recession. During the midst of the economic downturn, 41 states made net mid-year cuts in fiscal 2009 totaling $31.3 billion, and 39 states made mid-year cuts in fiscal 2010 totaling $18.3 billion, demonstrating the widespread impact of the recession. Similar to the past several years, mid-year budget reduction amounts were minimal in fiscal 2015, with 14 states making net mid-year budget cuts totaling $999 million. While the number of states with net mid-year budget cuts in fiscal 2015 is a bit higher than has been observed in recent years, most of these reductions were relatively small in value. Also, these reductions do not always reflect fiscal stress or even true spending cuts, but sometimes are the result of technical or accounting changes. The largest program areas of net mid-year cuts in fiscal 2015 include K-12 (17 states), Medicaid (14 states), corrections (13 states) and higher education (13 states).[32]

Through December 2015, two states had made net mid-year budget cuts in fiscal 2016 totaling $62.5 million. This figure is expected to rise as fiscal 2016 progresses, although the total will likely once again remain much lower than what was seen during and immediately after the last economic downturn.[33]

Balances

Total balances include both ending balances as well as the amounts in states' budget stabilization, or rainy day, funds. Combined, these reserves reflect the funds states may use to respond to budget gaps or unforeseen circumstances. Forty-eight states have either a budget stabilization fund or a rainy day fund, with about three-fifths of the states having limits on the size of these funds.[34]

Total balances reached a recent low in fiscal 2010 due to the severe decline in revenues and rise in expenditure demands tied to the recession. Since that time, states have made significant progress rebuilding budget reserves. In fiscal 2015, total balances amounted to $73.3 billion, representing an all-time high in actual dollars, and 9.6 percent of general fund expenditures. Total balances are projected to decrease in fiscal 2016 to $61 billion, or 8.8 percent of expenditures, resulting from an anticipated decline in ending balances. In addition, the fiscal 2016 figure excludes five states for which data are not available. While total balances are expected to moderately decline in fiscal 2016, rainy day funds, which tend to fluctuate less year-to-year than ending balances, are projected to slightly increase. Rainy day funds were $40.8 billion, or 6.2 percent of general fund expenditures, in fiscal 2015 and are expected to rise to $43.5 billion, or 6.3 percent of expenditures, in fiscal 2016.[35]

Looking Ahead

In many ways, the state fiscal environment has shown measurable improvements since the end of the most recent national recession. States have enacted spending increases in many areas, most notably in education. State spending on Medicaid is currently growing more slowly. Both budget gaps and mid-year budget cuts have significantly decreased. Revenues have grown and remain on target or above projections in most states. Finally, total balances reached an all-time high in fiscal 2015 in actual dollars. However, states face major challenges to their budgets in fiscal 2016 and beyond. Both spending and revenue have yet to surpass pre-recession highs after accounting for inflation. There remains a pent-up demand to increase infrastructure spending. States must continue to address the underfunding of pensions and retiree health care. Health care spending is expected to grow faster than state revenues. And states continue to be concerned about future national economic growth levels and uncertainty at the federal level. In addition, some states continue to face very significant budgetary difficulties associated with the decline of oil and natural gas prices, while other states have been particularly challenged by issues associated with slow economic growth, revenue volatility, tax changes, federal cuts and long-term liabilities. Looking forward, it is likely that budget proposals will remain mostly cautious with limited spending growth and an emphasis on ensuring that budgets are structurally balanced and sustainable in the future

Notes

[1] National Association of State Budget Officers, *The Fiscal Survey of States* (December 2015), 51.

[2] National Association of State Budget Officers, *Summary: NASBO State Expenditure Report*, (November 19, 2015), 1-2.

[3] National Association of State Budget Officers, *The State Expenditure Report* (November 2015), 7.

[4] *The Fiscal Survey of States* (December 2015), 10.

[5] *The Fiscal Survey of States* (December 2015), 67.

[6] See note 1 above.

[7] *The Fiscal Survey of States* (December 2015), 3.

[8] *The Fiscal Survey of States* (December 2015), 58.

[9] See note 5 above.

[10] See note 1 above.

[11] *The Fiscal Survey of States* (December 2015), 55.

[12] *The Fiscal Survey of States* (December 2015), 49.

[13] *The Fiscal Survey of States* (December 2015), 52.

[14] *The Fiscal Survey of States* (December 2015), 6-7.

[15] See note 1 above.

[16] *The Fiscal Survey of States* (December 2015), 54-55.

[17] Nelson A. Rockefeller Institute of Government, *State Revenue Report*, (November 2015), 1.

[18] See note 13 above.

[19] National Association of State Budget Officers, *Summary: Fall 2015 Fiscal Survey of States*, (December 15), 4.

[20] *The Fiscal Survey of States* (December 2015), 60.

[21] Total state spending consists of general funds, other state funds, bonds and federal funds combined.

[22] *Summary: NASBO State Expenditure Report*, (November 19, 2015), 1-2.

[23] *State Expenditure Report* (November 2015), 8.

[24] *State Expenditure Report* (November 2015), 10-11.

[25] *State Expenditure Report* (November 2015), 4.

[26] *State Expenditure Report* (November 2015), 7-8.

[27] Transportation spending mostly comes from "other state funds" and federal funds, while general funds only comprise 3.9 percent of total state transportation expenditures.

[28] *State Expenditure Report* (November 2015), 11.

[29] See note 7 above.

[30] *The Fiscal Survey of States* (December 2015), 5.

[31] *The Fiscal Survey of States* (December 2015), 2.

[32] *The Fiscal Survey of States* (December 2015), 11-12.

[33] *The Fiscal Survey of States* (December 2015), 17.

[34] National Association of State Budget Officers, *Budget Processes in the States*, (Spring 2015), 75-79.

[35] *The Fiscal Survey of States* (December 2015), 71-72.

About the Author

Brian Sigritz is the director of state fiscal studies at the National Association of State Budget Officers, or NASBO. He received an M.P.A. from the George Washington University and a B.A. from St. Bonaventure University. Prior to working at NASBO, Sigritz worked for the Ohio Senate and the Ohio House of Representatives.

Table 7.1
FISCAL 2014 STATE GENERAL FUND, ACTUAL
(In millions of dollars)

State	Beginning balance	Revenues	Adjustments	Total resources	Expenditures	Adjustments	Ending balance	Budget stabilization fund
Total.............................	$37,425	$730,280		$767,235	$725,666		$35,032	$47,719
Alabama* (a)	304	7,353	204	7,862	7,479	330	52	11
Alaska* (b)	0	5,390	35	5,425	7,323	-184	-1,714	15,574
Arizona* (c)	896	8,329	154	9,378	8,801	0	577	455
Arkansas......................	0	4,944	0	4,944	4,944	0	0	0
California* (d)	2,528	103,375	-977	104,925	100,005	-670	5,590	4,619
Colorado* (e)	373	8,978	14	9,365	8,764	-50	651	411
Connecticut (f)	0	17,608	-408	17,200	16,980	-29	249	519
Delaware*	636	3,573	0	4,209	3,794	0	414	202
Florida	2,892	26,604	0	29,495	26,914	0	2,581	925
Georgia* (g)	900	19,168	95	20,163	19,109	0	1,055	863
Hawaii..........................	844	6,096	0	6,940	6,275	0	665	83
Idaho (h)	80	2,815	-67	2,828	2,781	3	44	162
Illinois (i)	154	34,646	2,142	36,912	31,479	5,359	74	276
Indiana (j)	1,428	14,660	22	16,110	14,553	520	1,036	969
Iowa	0	6,489	679	7,168	6,462	0	707	670
Kansas (l)	709	5,653	0	6,363	5,983	0	380	0
Kentucky (m)	123	9,621	302	10,046	9,864	102	80	77
Louisiana (n)	0	8,217	545	8,762	8,583	0	179	445
Maine (o)	8	3,114	91	3,212	3,149	51	12	93
Maryland (p)	502	15,106	78	15,686	15,659	-120	148	764
Massachusetts* (q)	1,874	35,473	0	37,347	35,897	0	1,450	1,243
Michigan (r)	1,187	9,788	-1,687	9,287	8,981	0	306	386
Minnesota* (s)	1,712	19,522	0	21,234	19,348	0	1,886	661
Mississippi	54	5,403	0	5,457	5,416	0	41	110
Missouri (t)	447	8,003	124	8,574	8,385	0	189	277
Montana (u)	538	2,077	-2	2,613	2,188	1	424	0
Nebraska (v)	815	4,106	-456	4,465	3,791	0	674	719
Nevada..........................	300	3,067	142	3,509	3,291	34	184	28
New Hampshire* (w) ...	82	1,322	0	1,404	1,251	122	31	9
New Jersey (x)	310	31,072	1,721	33,103	32,807	0	296	0
New Mexico* (y)..........	671	6,097	0	6,769	5,991	140	638	638
New York* (z)	1,610	61,868	0	63,478	61,243	0	2,235	1,481
North Carolina	351	20,988	0	21,339	20,930	139	269	651
North Dakota (aa)	1,396	2,586	342	4,324	3,237	0	1,087	584
Ohio (bb)......................	2,639	29,233	0	31,872	30,172	0	1,700	1,478
Oklahoma (cc)	133	6,330	37	6,500	6,500	0	0	535
Oregon (dd)	470	7,634	-164	7,940	7,693	0	247	153
Pennsylvania (ee)	541	28,607	-672	28,476	28,395	0	81	0
Rhode Island (ff)	104	3,430	-99	3,436	3,337	31	68	177
South Carolina* (gg) ...	1,046	6,552	0	7,599	6,329	106	1,163	408
South Dakota (hh).......	24	1,354	98	1,476	1,442	24	10	139
Tennessee (ii)	800	12,052	154	13,006	12,136	486	384	456
Texas (jj)	5,505	51,640	-3,413	53,732	46,764	0	6,968	6,703
Utah (kk)......................	122	5,420	0	5,542	5,402	0	140	432
Vermont (ll)	0	1,388	12	1,400	1,386	14	0	71
Virginia.........................	880	17,304	0	18,184	17,705	0	479	688
Washington (mm)	168	16,383	-98	16,453	16,079	0	373	415
West Virginia (nn)	512	4,106	8	4,626	4,208	6	412	956
Wisconsin (oo)	759	13,948	606	15,313	14,674	122	517	280
Wyoming (pp)	0	1,787	0	1,787	1,787	0	0	926

See footnotes at end of table.

FISCAL 2014 STATE GENERAL FUND, ACTUAL — Continued
(In millions of dollars)

Source: National Association of State Budget Officers. December 2015.

Note: NA Indicates data not available.

Key:

* — In these states, the ending balance includes the balance in the budget stabilization fund.

... — Not applicable

(a) Revenue adjustments include one-time revenues of $145.8 million, tobacco settlement funds of $46.4 million and an insurance settlement of $12.0 million. Expenditure adjustments include Rainy Day Account repayments of $330.4.

(b) Revenues: Spring 2015 Revenue Source Book (Total Revenue) Revenue Adjustments: SLA 2014 Fiscal Summary (Revenue Carryforward) Expenditures: SLA 2014 Fiscal Summary (Pre-Transfer Authorization) Ending Balance: SLA 2014 Fiscal Summary (Transfer to SBR) Day Balance: FY 2014 Comprehensive Annual Financial Report (CAFR).

(c) Adjustments to revenue include revenues from budget transfers.

(d) Represents adjustments to the Beginning Fund Balance. This consists primarily of adjustments made to major taxes and K–12 spending.

(e) Of the ending balance of $650.9M, $215.0M is transferred, leaving $25.0M to add to the statutory reserve of $410.9M, for a total of $435.9M. For more information, please see page 61, of the OSPB June 2015 forecast.

(f) FY 2014: Revenue adjustments include release of reserved fund balance of $190.8 million, $598.5 million for GAAP conversion bonds, and $0.5 million reserved for future fiscal years. Expenditure adjustments include $2.2 million in miscellaneous adjustments, and $26.5 million in net adjustments due to carry-forward of appropriations. The reported rainy day fund balance includes the ending balance.

(g) Beginning and ending balances reflect the total Revenue Shortfall Reserve balance as reported in the Budgetary Compliance Report. Adjustments to Revenues include surplus from state agencies and other funds collected by the State Treasury. Final Rainy Day Fund Balance reflects the ending balance less the 1% mid-term adjustment for K–12 enrollment appropriated during FY 2015.

(h) Transfers to included: Budget Stabilization Fund—$26,375,800, Business Job Development Fund—$3,000,000, Water Resources Boards—$15,000,000, Permanent Building Fund—$10,000,000, Public Education Stabilization Fund—$10,000,000, Higher Education Stabilization Fund—$2,000,000, Deficiency Warrant Fund—$11,875,000. Transfers in include $6,430,800 from the Catastrophic Health Care Fund, and $4,413,700 in miscellaneous adjustments. Expenditure adjustments include $10,463,500 for supplementals, $8,178,700 in reversions/rescissions, and $234,600 in miscellaneous receipts.

(i) Revenue adjustments include transfers in to the general fund. Expenditure adjustments include transfers out of the general fund and the change in accounts payable.

(j) Revenue adjustments include PTRC and homestead credit adjustments HEA 1072-2011 loan repayments, and a transfer from the Mine Subsidence Fund. Expenditure adjustments include reversions from distributions, capital, and reconciliations; the cost of a 13th check for pension recipients; transfer to the Major Moves 2020 trust fund; transfer to the tuition reserve fund; and state agency and university line-item capital projects.

(l) Kansas does not have a "Rainy Day" fund. However, the balanced budget provision of the constitution requires revenues to finance the approved budget.

(m) Revenue includes $159.4 million in Tobacco Settlement funds. Adjustment for Revenues includes $156.4 million that represents appropriation balances carried over from the prior fiscal year, and $145.7 million from fund transfers into the General Fund. Adjustment to Expenditures represents appropriation balances forwarded to the next fiscal year.

(n) Revenues adjustments—Includes transfer of $198.7 from various funds and $345.8 million in undesignated General Fund Cash Balance from prior years.

(o) Revenue and Expenditure adjustments reflect legislatively authorized transfers. Previous surveys included only the Budget Stabilization Fund. This survey reflects the total of all General Fund reserves.

(p) May differ from prior submissions, as pensions are now treated as budgetary expense; added to revenue and expenditures.

(q) Fiscal 2014 revenue adjustments include the impact of federal and state law changes (-$769.1 million); revenue sharing payments to local government units (-$396.6 million); deposits from restricted funds ($120.0 million); deposit to the rainy day fund (-$75.0 million); deposit

to the Roads and Risks Reserve Fund (-$230.0 million); and general fund revenue dedicated for roads (-$336.6 million). Fiscal 2014 expenditures include $515.7 million in one-time spending financed from one-time revenue, excluding deposits to the rainy day fund, the Roads and Risks Reserve Fund, and funds earmarked for transportation.

(r) Ending balance includes cash flow account of $350 million, budget reserve account of $660.9 million, and stadium reserve of $39.7 million.

(s) Revenue adjustments include transfers from other funds into the general revenue fund.

(t) Adjustments to revenues included prior year revenue activity. Adjustments to expenditures include adjustments to fund balance made as part of the state's final CAFR.

(u) Revenue adjustments are transfers between the General Fund and other funds. Per Nebraska law, includes a transfer of $285.3 million to the Cash Reserve Fund (Rainy Day Fund) of the amount the prior year's net General Fund receipts exceeded the official forecast and an additional $49.4 million transferred from the General Fund to the Cash Reserve Fund to set aside additional funds as a result of increasing General Fund revenues. Among others, also includes a $113 million transfer from the General Fund to the Property Tax Credit Cash Fund.

(v) Revenue adjustments are restricted revenue, reversions and Rainy Day transfers. Expenditure adjustments are restricted transfers.

(w) Expenditure Adjustments: $102 million moved to the Education Trust Fund and $.7 million moved to the Fish and Game Fund at year end (Adjustments also included $18.9 million of GAAP and Other).

(x) Budget vs GAAP entries; lapses and transfers to other funds.

(y) $30 million contingent liability for cash reconciliation from FY 13 audit, $36 million contingent liability for PED Maintenance of Effort, $73.7 million for contingent liability for Medicaid receivables.

(z) The ending balance includes approximately $1.5 billion in rainy day reserve funds, $88 million reserved to cover costs of potential retroactive labor settlements with certain unions, $87 million in a community projects fund, $500 million reserved for debt reduction, $21 million reserved for litigation risks, and $58 million from a monetary settlement with J.P. Morgan.

(aa) Revenue adjustments are a $341.8 million transfer from the property tax relief fund into the general fund.

(bb) FY 2014 expenditures include expenditures against prior year encumbrances as well as $1,270.2 million in transfers out of the GRF.

(cc) Revenue adjustment represents the difference in cash flow. There was no expenditure adjustment, since no deposit was made into the Rainy Day Fund.

(dd) Revenue adjustments include: prior biennium transfer adjustment; transfer 2011–13 biennium ending GF balance to Rainy Day Fund (up to 1% of total biennial budget appropriation minus GF reversions); cost of Tax Anticipation Notes; statutory dedication of some corp. taxes to RDF; and, a statutory transfer to local governments for local property tax relief. As in previous reports, the Rainy Day Fund balance is a combined total of RDF (primarily GF) and Education Stability Fund (primarily Lottery Fund).

(ee) Revenue Adjustments for $1.1M in refunds, $427M in prior year lapses and $6M adjustment to beginning balance.

(ff) Adjustments to revenues reflect a transfer of $106.0 million to the Budget Reserve Fund plus a reappropriation of $7.1 million from FY 2013. Total expenditure adjustments of $31.2 million reflect transfers to the Accelerated Depreciation Fund of $10.0 million, anticipated transfer of surplus revenues to the State Retirement Fund of $13.8 million, and reappropriations of $7.4 million to FY 2015.

(gg) Ending Balance = 5% General Reserve ($292.9) + 2% Capital Reserve ($114.9) + Surplus Contingency Reserve ($265.6) + Agency Appropriation Balances Carried Forward to Next FY ($489.9); Expenditure Adjustments include FY 12–13 Capital Reserve Funds transferred to state agencies.

(hh) The beginning balance of $24.2 million and adjustment to expenditures reflects the prior year's ending balance that is transferred to the rainy day fund. Adjustments to revenue of $98.2 million are from one-time receipts. The ending balance of $9.9 million is cash that is obligated to the Budget Reserve fund the following fiscal year. This $9.9 million is not included in the total rainy day fund balance of $139.3 million.

(ii) Revenue Adjustments include $83.5 million transfer from debt service fund unexpended appropriations; -$100.0 million transfer to Rainy Day Fund; $315.9 million transfer from reserves to closing; and a -145.3 million transfer to dedicated revenue reserves. Expenditure Adjustments include $215.9 million transfer to capital outlay projects

FISCAL 2014 STATE GENERAL FUND, ACTUAL — Continued
(In millions of dollars)

fund; $170.8 million transfer to state office buildings and support facilities fund; $3.8 million transfer to debt service fund; $3.6 million transfer to Systems Development Fund; $91.9 million transfer to reserves for unexpended appropriations. Ending Balance includes $272.5 million reserve for appropriations 2014–2015 and $111.3 million unappropriated budget surplus at June 30, 2014.

(jj) Adjustments are net of set aside for transfer to Rainy Day Fund (-$1,383.5 million) and the State Highway Fund 6 (-$1,383.4 million). In addition, the Comptroller adjustment to general fund dedicated account balances (-$646.1 million).

(kk) Adjustments include transfers from previous year balance, to/from Rainy Day Fund, and special revenue funds.

(ll) Adjustments = net transfer effect in/out of the General Fund.

(mm) Adjustments include fund transfers between General Fund and other accounts, and changes made by the 2014 Legislature.

(nn) Fiscal Year 2014 Beginning balance includes $456.2 million in Reappropriations, Unappropriated Surplus Balance of $11.8 million, and FY 2013 13th month expenditures of $44.1 million. Expenditures include Regular, Surplus and Reappropriated funds and $44.1 million of 31 day prior year expenditures. Revenue adjustments are prior year redeposits and special revenue expirations. Expenditure adjustment represents the amount transferred to the Rainy Day Fund. The ending balance is mostly the historically carried forward reappropriation amounts that will remain and be reappropriated to the next fiscal year, the 13th month expenditures and unappropriated surplus balance.

(oo) Revenue adjustments include Designated Balance, $18.8 million and Other Revenue, $587.1 million. Expenditure adjustments include Designation for Continuing Balances, $122.4 million.

(pp) Wyoming budgets on a biennial basis. To arrive at annual figures certain assumptions and estimates were required.

Table 7.2
FISCAL 2015 STATE GENERAL FUND, PRELIMINARY ACTUAL
(In millions of dollars)

State	Beginning balance	Revenues	Adjustments	Resources	Expenditures	Adjustments	Ending balance	Budget stabilization fund
Total.................	$35,335	$765,446	...	$800,313	$759,396	...	$37,764	$43,995
Alabama (a).................	52	7,815	85	7,952	7,702	35	215	412
Alaska (b)...................	0	2,216	71	2,287	6,014	-1,008	-2,719	10,084
Arizona (c)..................	577	8,933	67	9,578	9,287	0	291	457
Arkansas....................	0	5,059	0	5,059	5,059	0	0	0
California (d)...............	5,590	111,307	0	116,896	114,473	0	2,423	3,058
Colorado* (e)...............	436	9,816	66	10,318	9,706	0	612	577
Connecticut (f).............	0	17,314	0	17,314	17,405	-21	-71	448
Delaware*..................	414	3,955	0	4,370	3,833	0	537	213
Florida	2,581	27,959	0	30,541	28,189	0	2,352	1,139
Georgia* (g)................	1,055	20,435	9	21,498	20,047	0	1,451	1,246
Hawaii......................	665	6,577	0	7,242	6,413	0	828	90
Idaho (h)	44	2,965	-51	2,958	2,936	-20	42	190
Illinois (i)..................	74	32,333	1,736	34,143	31,110	2,959	74	276
Indiana (j)	1,036	15,145	15	16,196	14,935	374	887	1,254
Iowa (k)	0	6,767	642	7,410	6,982	64	364	696
Kansas (l)	380	5,947	0	6,327	6,251	0	76	0
Kentucky (m)	81	10,029	324	10,433	10,108	104	221	77
Louisiana (n)...............	0	8,508	201	8,709	8,715	-6	0	470
Maine (o)...................	13	3,329	-100	3,242	3,166	51	26	128
Maryland (p)...............	148	15,923	161	16,231	15,995	-84	320	766
Massachusetts* (q)	1,450	38,181	0	39,631	38,146	0	1,485	1,179
Michigan (r)	306	10,480	-1,227	9,559	9,389	0	170	498
Minnesota* (s).............	1,886	19,916	0	21,802	20,381	0	1,421	994
Mississippi (t)..............	41	5,537	0	5,578	5,511	1	66	395
Missouri (u).................	189	8,709	124	9,022	8,744	0	278	270
Montana (v).................	424	2,200	1	2,625	2,168	2	455	0
Nebraska (w)................	674	4,306	-217	4,763	4,030	0	732	728
Nevada (x)...................	184	3,222	149	3,555	3,398	11	146	0
New Hampshire* (y)......	31	1,404	0	1,435	1,259	94	83	9
New Jersey (z).............	296	32,768	330	33,394	32,767	0	627	0
New Mexico*...............	638	6,309	0	6,946	6,313	0	634	634
New York* (aa)............	2,235	67,921	0	70,156	62,856	0	7,300	1,798
North Carolina.............	269	22,331	0	22,600	21,538	198	864	652
North Dakota (bb)	1,087	2,354	520	3,961	3,231	0	730	573
Ohio (cc)	1,700	31,473	0	33,173	31,462	0	1,712	1,478
Oklahoma (dd)	0	6,465	-13	6,452	6,403	0	49	385
Oregon (ee).................	247	8,499	-44	8,703	8,226	0	477	391
Pennsylvania (ff).........	81	30,177	-1,198	29,060	29,048	3	9	0
Rhode Island (gg)........	68	3,641	-80	3,628	3,455	7	166	185
South Carolina* hh)	1,163	6,960	0	8,124	6,815	127	1,182	447
South Dakota (ii).........	10	1,381	27	1,418	1,386	10	22	149
Tennessee (jj)	384	13,020	66	13,469	12,509	142	819	492
Texas (kk)...................	6,933	52,580	-2,774	56,739	48,401	0	8,338	7,500
Utah (ll)	113	6,040	0	6,153	5,749	0	404	491
Vermont (mm)	0	1,444	5	1,449	1,429	20	0	76
Virginia.....................	479	18,009	0	18,487	18,240	0	247	468
Washington (nn)	373	17,270	-72	17,572	16,706	0	866	513
West Virginia (oo)	412	4,204	37	4,653	4,234	0	420	869
Wisconsin (pp)............	517	14,541	672	15,730	15,504	91	136	280
Wyoming (qq).............	0	1,774	0	1,774	1,774	0	0	960

See footnotes at end of table.

FISCAL 2015 STATE GENERAL FUND, PRELIMINARY ACTUAL — Continued
(In millions of dollars)

Source: National Association of State Budget Officers. December 2015.

*In these states, the ending balance includes the balance in the budget stabilization fund.

Key:

... — Not applicable.

(a) Revenue adjustments include one-time revenues of $145.8 million, a transfer of $20.0 million, a -$23.6 million transfer repayment to the Prepaid Affordable College Tuition Program and a -$57.5 million transfer repayment to the Rainy Day Account. Expenditure adjustments include a Rainy Day Account Repayment of $35.1 million.

(b) Revenues: SLA 2015 Fiscal Summary (Total Revenue) Revenue Adjustments: SLA 2015 Fiscal Summary (Revenue Carryforward) Expenditures: SLA 2015 Fiscal Summary (Pre-Transfer Authorization) Ending Balance: SLA 2015 Fiscal Summary (Transfer to SBR/CBR) Rainy Day Balance: OMB Spring Fiscal Model.

(c) Adjustments to revenue include revenues from budget transfers. No transfer from the RDF was required.

(d) Ending balance excludes $1,606.4 million that was transferred to the Budget Stabilization Account for "rainy day" purposes. The Rainy Day Fund balance consists of the Special Fund for Economic Uncertainties (which is the General Fund Ending Balance less specific reserves) and the Budget Stabilization Account; however, withdrawals from the BSA are subject to provisions of Proposition 2, 2014. The Ending Balance is only the General Fund balance and excludes the Budget Stabilization Account (a rainy day reserve held in a separate fund). The excluded amount is $1,606.4 million in FY 2015. The "Total Balance" that includes the ending balance and all rainy day funds, including the Budget Stabilization Account amounts, would be $4,029.6 million in FY 2015.

(e) Ending reserve requirement is $576.5M; ending balance of $612.1M is $35.6M higher than the statutory reserve requirement.

(f) FY 2015: $20.8 million adjustment in FY 2015 due to continuing appropriations. The reported rainy day fund balance includes the ending balance.

(g) Figures are preliminary and are subject to change pending final audit. Rainy Day Fund balance reflects preliminary balance less the required 1% FY 2016 midterm appropriation for K–12 enrollment. Final Rainy Day Fund balance will be higher pending the lapse of current year surplus for state agencies.

(h) Transfers to include: Wolf Control Fund—$400,000, Permanent Building Fund—$101,200, Time Sensitive Fund Health and Welfare—$225,800, Constitutional Defense Fund—$1,000,000, Permanent Building Fund—$1,050,000, Budget Stabilization Fund—$28,154,300, and Deficiency Warrant Fund—$17,981,900. Miscellaneous Adjustments include: $9,142,100 Health and Welfare reversion. Expenditure adjustments include $12,758,800 in negative supplementals and $7,421,900 in early rescissions.

(i) Revenue adjustments include transfers in to the general fund. Expenditure adjustments include transfers out of the general fund and the change in accounts payable.

(j) Revenue adjustments include funds from the S&P Settlement. Expenditure adjustments include reversions from distributions, capital, and reconciliations; the cost of a 13th check for pension recipients; transfer to the Major Moves 2020 trust fund; transfer to the tuition reserve fund; and state agency and university line-item capital projects.

(k) Revenue adjustments include an estimated $642.2 million of residual funds transferred to the General Fund after the Reserve Funds are filled to their statutorily set maximum amounts. The Ending balance of the General Fund is transferred in the current fiscal year to the Reserve Funds in the subsequent fiscal year. After the Reserve Funds are at their statutorily set maximum amounts, the remainder of the funds are transferred back to the General Fund in that subsequent fiscal year. FY 2015 Revenues are based upon the March 2015 Revenue Estimating Conference estimates. Also included is $53.0 million in supplemental appropriations and $7.8 million in changes in estimates for standing unlimited appropriations.

(l) Kansas does not have a "Rainy Day" fund. However, the balanced budget provision of the constitution requires revenues to finance the approved budget appropriations and $7.8 million in changes in estimates for standing unlimited appropriations.

(m) Revenue includes $61.9 million in Tobacco Settlement funds. Adjustment for Revenues includes $101.8 million that represents appropriation balances carried over from the prior fiscal year, and $222.6 million from fund transfers into the General Fund. Adjustment to Expenditures represents appropriation balances forwarded to the next fiscal year.

(n) Revenues adjustments—Includes $11.2 million from carryforwards and $189.8 million from various funds. Expenditure adjustments—Includes the remaining $6.5 million state general fund reduction as authorized by Act 15 of the 2014 legislative session.

(o) Revenue and Expenditure adjustments reflect legislatively authorized transfers. Previous surveys included only the Budget Stabilization Fund. This survey reflects the total of all General Fund reserves.

(p) Revenue adjustments include $17.6 million in transfers from tax credit reserves and $143.4 million in transfers from other funds. Expenditure adjustments include -$0.3 million in identified reversions and -$83.7 million in reversions to the unappropriated General Fund balance.

(q) May differ from prior submissions, as pensions are now treated as budgetary expense: added to revenue and expenditures. Include -$0.3 million in identified reversions and -$83.7 million in reversions to the unappropriated General Fund balance.

(r) Fiscal 2015 revenue adjustments include the impact of federal and state law changes (-$754.6 million); revenue sharing payments to local government units (-$468.0 million); deposits from restricted funds ($374.8 million); deposit to the rainy day fund (-$94.0 million); and general fund revenue dedicated for roads (-$285.0 million).

(s) Ending balance includes cash flow account of $350 million, budget reserve account of $994.3 million, and stadium reserve of $29.9 million.

(t) The Expenditure Adjustment of $750,000 provides aid to municipalities.

(u) Revenue adjustments include transfers from other funds into the general revenue fund. The enacted revenue estimate was insufficient to cover budget expenses. The above expenditures include expenditure restrictions.

(v) Adjustments to revenues included prior year revenue activity. Adjustments to expenditures include adjustments to fund balance made as part of the state's final CAFR.

(w) Revenue adjustments are transfers between the General Fund and other funds. Per Nebraska law, includes a transfer of $96.7 million to the Cash Reserve Fund (Rainy Day Fund) of the amount the prior year's net General Fund receipts exceeded the official forecast. Among others, also includes a $138 million transfer from the General Fund to the Property Tax Credit Cash Fund.

(x) Revenue adjustments are restricted revenue, reversions, Rainy Day transfers and reserve transfers. Expenditure adjustments are restricted transfers.

(y) Expenditure Adjustments: $77.2 million to be moved to the Education Trust Fund and $0.7 million moved to the Fish and Game Funds at year end (Adjustments also include $15.6 million of GAAP and Other).

(z) Balances targeted to be lapsed; transfers to other funds.

(aa) The ending balance includes approximately $1.8 billion in rainy day reserve funds, $50 million reserved to cover costs of potential retroactive labor settlements with certain unions, $74 million in a community projects fund, $500 million reserved for debt reduction, $21 million reserved for litigation risks, $190 million in undesignated fund balance to be used for gap-closing purposes in FY 2016, and approximately $4.7 billion in proceeds from monetary settlements.

(bb) Revenue adjustments are a $520.0 million transfer from the strategic investment and improvements fund to the general fund.

(cc) FY 2015 expenditures include expenditures against prior year encumbrances as well as $629.9 million transfers out of the GRF.

(dd) Revenue amounts are based upon reconciled, but yet uncertified, FY 2015 collections; Revenue adjustment represents the difference in cash flow. There was no expenditure adjustment, since no deposit was made into the Rainy Day Fund.

(ee) Revenue adjustment is a statutory transfer to local governments for local property tax relief.

(ff) Revenue Adjustments for $1.287M in refunds and $90M in prior year lapses. Expense Adjustments for transfer to Budget Stabilization Reserve Fund.

(gg) Adjustments to revenues reflect a transfer of $111.3 million to the Budget Reserve Fund plus a reappropriation of $7.4 million from FY 2014, a transfer of $10.0 million from the Accelerated Deprecation Fund, and a repeal of the prior year transfer to the RI Employees Retirement System of $13.8 million. Total expenditure adjustments include reappropriations of $6.9 million to FY 2016.

(hh) Ending Balance = 5% General Reserve (-$319.5 million) + 2% Capital Reserve ($127.8 million) + Surplus Contingency Reserve ($136.7 million) + Agency Appropriation Balances Carried Forward to Next FY ($415.1 million); Expenditure Adjustments include FY 13–14 Capital

FISCAL 2015 STATE GENERAL FUND, PRELIMINARY ACTUAL—Continued
(In millions of dollars)

Reserve Funds transferred to State agencies and $12.0 million loan to a State-funded university.

(ii) The beginning balance of $9.9 million and adjustment to expenditures reflects the prior year's ending balance that is transferred to the rainy day fund. Adjustments to revenue of $26.5 million are from one-time receipts. The ending balance of $21.5 million is cash that is obligated to the Budget Reserve fund the following fiscal year. This $21.5 million is not included in the total rainy day fund balance of $149.2 million.

(jj) Revenue Adjustments include $72.0 million transfer from debt service fund unexpended appropriations; $18.5 million transfer from TennCare Reserve Fund; $7.0 million transfer from Purchasing Reserve; $3.8 million transfer from Severance Carryforward; and -$35.5 million transfer to Rainy Day Fund. Expenditure Adjustments include $123.6 million transfer to capital outlay projects fund; $13.1 million transfer to state office buildings and support facilities fund; $3.8 million transfer to debt service fund; and $1.0 million transfer to reserves for dedicated revenue appropriations. Ending Balance includes $819.2 million unappropriated budget surplus at June 30, 2015.

(kk) Revenue adjustment to Dedicated Account Balances (-$341m); Also, adjustment for transfers to the Economic Stabilization and State Highway Funds (-$2,433m).

(ll) Includes transfers from previous year balance, to/from Rainy Day Fund, and special revenue funds.

(mm) Adjustments = net transfer effect in/out of the General Fund.

(nn) Adjustments include fund transfers between General Fund and other accounts, and changes made by the 2015 Legislature.

(oo) Fiscal Year 2015 beginning balance includes $378.2 million in reappropriations, unappropriated surplus balance of $18.3 million, and FY 2014 13th month expenditures of $15.9 million. Expenditures include Regular, Surplus and Reappropriated funds and $15.9 million of 31 day prior year expenditures and special revenue expirations. Expenditure adjustment represents the amount anticipated to be transferred to the Rainy Day Fund. The ending balance is mostly the historically carried forward reappropriation amounts that will remain and be reappropriated to the next fiscal year, the 13th month expenditures and any unappropriated surplus balance.

(pp) Revenue adjustments include Tribal Gaming, $48.9 million; Other Revenue, $501 million; and Prior Year Designated Balance, $122.4 million. Expenditure adjustments include Designation for Continuing Balances, $91.3 million.

(qq) Wyoming budgets on a biennial basis. To arrive at annual figures certain assumptions and estimates were required.

Table 7.3
FISCAL 2016 STATE GENERAL FUND, APPROPRIATED
(In millions of dollars)

State or other jurisdiction	Beginning balance	Revenues	Adjustments	Resources	Expenditures	Adjustments	Ending balance	Rainy day fund balance
Total **	$38,471	$784,661	...	$820,788	$790,344	...	$24,120	$44,744
Alabama (a)	215	7,936	(31)	8,120	7,801	-	318	412
Alaska (b)	-	2,206	-	2,206	5,180	(226)	(2,748)	7,287
Arizona (c)	12	8,852	235	9,099	9,134	-	(35)	313
Arkansas....................	-	5,186	-	5,186	5,186	-	-	-
California (d)	2,423	115,033	-	117,456	115,370	-	2,086	4,576
Colorado* (e)..............	612	10,254	16	10,882	10,340	-	542	542
Connecticut (f)............	-	18,187	(25)	18,162	18,162	-	1	449
Delaware* (g)	537	3,939	-	4,476	3,933	-	543	215
Florida	2,352	28,694	-	31,045	29,336	-	1,709	1,354
Georgia (h)..................	1,449	20,709	-	22,158	20,709	-	N/A	N/A
Hawaii..........................	828	6,800	-	7,628	6,876	-	752	108
Idaho (i)	42	3,128	(89)	3,081	3,072	-	9	219
Illinois (j)	N/A	N/A	N/A	N/A	N/A	N/A	N/A	N/A
Indiana (k)	887	15,195	(42)	16,040	15,099	198	743	1,316
Iowa (l)	-	7,176	341	7,517	7,168	-	349	719
Kansas (m)	76	6,334	-	6,410	6,322	-	88	-
Kentucky (n)	221	10,140	187	10,548	10,369	179	-	209
Louisiana (o)...............	-	8,596	292	8,888	9,008	(122)	1	515
Maine (p)......................	26	3,311	3	3,340	3,335	3	2	128
Maryland (q)	320	16,323	56	16,700	16,434	(30)	295	794
Massachusetts* (r).......	1,485	40,540	-	42,025	40,877	-	1,148	1,184
Michigan (s)	170	10,831	(1,504)	9,497	9,474	-	23	611
Minnesota* (t)	1,421	20,893	-	22,314	20,500	-	1,814	994
Mississippi	89	5,655	-	5,744	5,744	-	-	395
Missouri (u)..................	278	8,675	93	9,046	8,950	-	96	291
Montana (v)	455	2,263	-	2,718	2,359	-	359	-
Nebraska (w)................	732	4,474	(302)	4,904	4,272	369	263	729
Nevada (x)....................	146	3,602	49	3,797	3,521	9	268	-
New Hampshire* (y) ...	73	1,431	-	1,504	1,367	80	57	24
New Jersey	627	33,663	-	34,290	33,526	-	764	-
New Mexico* (z).........	634	6,305	-	6,939	6,325	-	614	614
New York* (aa)............	7,300	68,285	-	75,585	72,090	-	3,495	1,798
North Carolina............	265	21,653	-	21,917	21,735	-	183	852
North Dakota (bb)	730	2,477	657	3,864	3,013	-	851	573
Ohio (cc)	1,712	34,807	-	36,519	35,622	-	896	2,005
Oklahoma (dd)	49	6,475	-	6,524	6,307	-	217	N/A
Oregon (ee)..................	477	9,093	(583)	8,987	8,515	-	473	652
Pennsylvania (ff).........	N/A	N/A	N/A	N/A	N/A	N/A	N/A	N/A
Rhode Island (gg)........	119	3,544	(110)	3,553	3,552	-	1	183
South Carolina* (hh)...	1,182	7,045	77	8,304	7,166	128	1,010	459
South Dakota (ii)........	22	1,433	-	1,455	1,433	22	-	171
Tennessee (jj)	819	12,862	(70)	13,611	12,946	316	348	568
Texas (kk).....................	7,533	53,778	(2,395)	58,916	53,814	-	5,102	9,900
Utah (ll).......................	404	5,884	-	6,288	6,282	-	6	491
Vermont (mm)	-	1,470	-	1,470	1,470	(0)	0	71
Virginia........................	247	18,522	-	18,769	18,764	-	5	237
Washington (nn)	866	17,989	(16)	18,839	18,211	-	628	695
West Virginia (oo)	420	4,306	-	4,725	4,342	6	377	853
Wisconsin (pp)	136	15,208	540	15,883	15,886	(301)	297	N/A
Wyoming (qq)..............	1	1,773	-	1,774	1,774	-	-	960

See footnotes at end of table.

FISCAL 2016 STATE GENERAL FUND, APPROPRIATED—Continued
(In millions of dollars)

Source: National Association of State Budget Officers, December 2015.

Key:

* In these states, the ending balance includes the balance in the budget stabilization fund.

**Totals include the fiscal 2016 general fund amounts for Illinois and Pennsylvania reported in NASBO's Spring 2015 Fiscal Survey of States, which were based on governors' recommended budgets. These are being used as placeholders in order to calculate 50-state total figures that are comparable to prior fiscal years for the purposes of this report.

NA—Indicates data are not available.

... — Not applicable

(a) Revenue adjustments include $2.9 million in expedited ad valorem on automobiles and a ($34.0 million) transfer payment to the Prepaid Affordable College Tuition Program.

(b) Revenues: SLA2016 Fiscal Summary (Total Revenue) Revenue Adjustments: SLA2016 Fiscal Summary (Revenue Carryforward) Expenditures: SLA2016 Fiscal Summary (Pre-Transfer Authorization) Ending Balance: SLA2016 Fiscal Summary (Transfer to SBR/CBR) Rainy Day Balance: OMB Spring Fiscal Model.

(c) Adjustments to revenue include revenues from budget transfers. Beginning balance includes a transfer of $144.3M from the RDF. The enacted budget was passed in March of 2015. Revenues through the end of the fiscal year came in above the estimates used for the enacted budget.

(d) Ending balance excludes projected $1,854 million transfer to the Budget Stabilization Account for "rainy day" purposes. The Rainy Day Fund balance consists of the Special Fund for Economic Uncertainties (which is the General Fund Ending Balance less specific reserves) and the Budget Stabilization Account (BSA); however, withdrawals from the BSA are subject to provisions of Proposition 2, 2014. The Ending Balance is only the General Fund balance and excludes the Budget Stabilization Account (a rainy day reserve held in a separate fund). The excluded amounts are $1,606.4 million in FY 2015 and an additional $1,854 million added in FY 2016. Adding these amounts to the FY 2016 Ending Balance, the projected "Total Balance" is $5,546.7 million in FY 2016.

(e) Ending balance of $542.3M is $69.0M short of the $611.32M GF reserve requirement for a 6.5% reserve. (The $542.3M equates to a 5.8% reserve.)

(f) FY 2016: Revenue adjustments include a $25.0 million transfer of FY 2016 Resources to FY 2017. The reported rainy day fund balance includes the ending balance.

(g) Figures based on enacted FY 2016 General Fund appropriations and revenue estimates contained in HJR 9 of the 148th General Assembly. Revenue adjustments from the June 2015 DEFAC Fiscal Year 2016 revenue forecast include a $20 million increase to the General Fund by funding the annual Farmland Preservation and Open Space programs funding through special funds, an additional $5.0 million increase to the General Fund by directing the Energy Efficiency Investment Fund annual funding be deposited to the General Fund, and an increase of $40 million by waiving the earmark of Abandoned Property funds to the Transportation Trust Fund.

(h) Georgia does not project future Rainy Day fund balances, but expects the reserve to continue to grow in future years.

(i) Transfer to include: Budget Stabilization Fund—$29,535,200, Commerce Opportunity Grant—$1,750,000, Wolf Control Fund—$400,000, Economic Recovery Reserve Fund for FY 2017—27th payroll cost—$20,000,000, $500,000 Water Board for aquifer recharge, and $27,000,000 to Fire Suppression fund for anticipated cost for the 2015 fire season. Transfers in include $780,000 from the Consolidated Election Fund. Other adjustments include $10,933,500 for legislation with a fiscal impact.

(j) As of November 12, 2015, Illinois had not yet enacted a budget for fiscal 2016.

(k) Revenue adjustments include the SGO tax credit cap increase, teacher tax credit, income tax credit for certain hospitals, SOS paper business filing fees, outside acts, and a transfer from the Political Subdivision Risk Management Fund. Expenditure adjustments include reversions from distributions, capital, and reconciliations; the cost of a 13th check for pension recipients; transfer to the Major Moves 2020 trust fund; transfer to the tuition reserve fund; and state agency and university line item capital projects.

(l) Revenue adjustments include an estimated $330.0 million of residual funds transferred to the General Fund after the Reserve Funds are filled to their statutorily set maximum amounts. The Ending balance of the General Fund is transferred in the current fiscal year to the Reserve Funds in the subsequent fiscal year. After the Reserve Funds are at their statutorily set maximum amounts, the remainder of the funds are transferred back to the General Fund in that subsequent fiscal year. Also included in revenue adjustments is an $11.2 million adjustment for the legislative changes approved by the Legislature and signed by the Governor. FY2016 Revenues are based upon the March 2015 Revenue Estimating Conference estimates.

(m) Kansas does not have a "Rainy Day" fund. However, the balanced budget provision of the constitution requires revenues to finance the approved budget.

(n) Revenue includes $72.4 million in Tobacco Settlement funds. Adjustment for Revenues includes $109.8 million that represents appropriation balances carried over from the prior fiscal year, and $77.4 million from fund transfers into the General Fund. Adjustment to Expenditures represents appropriation balances forwarded to the next fiscal year.

(o) Revenues adjustments—Includes $261.3 from Tax Credit Suspension and $30.3 from various funds. Expenditure adjustments—Includes $18.8 Preamble reduction and a $102.9 MOF substitution per Act 16 of the 2015 legislative session. Rainy Day Fund Balance—One-third of the fund balance may be used during the fiscal year.

(p) Revenue and Expenditure adjustments reflect legislatively authorized transfers. Previous surveys included only the Budget Stabilization Fund. This survey reflects the total of all General Fund reserves.

(q) Revenue adjustments include $17.4 million in transfers from tax credit reserves and $4.5 million in transfers from other funds. There is an additional transfer of $34.0 million from the Rainy Day Fund, which are funds in excess of the State's goal of maintaining a Rainy Day Fund of 5% of the State's annual General Fund revenue. Expenditure adjustments include -$30 million in unidentified estimated reversions to the unappropriated General Fund balance.

(r) May differ from prior submissions, as pensions are now treated as budgetary expense: added to revenue and expenditures.

(s) Fiscal 2016 revenue adjustments include the impact of federal and state law changes (-$949.4 million); revenue sharing payments to local government units (-$468.5 million); deposits from restricted funds ($408.7 million); deposit to the rainy day fund (-$95.0 million); and general fund revenue dedicated for roads (-$400.0 million). Fiscal 2016 expenditures include $98.5 million in one-time spending financed from one-time revenue, excluding deposit to the rainy day fund, and funds earmarked for transportation.

(t) Ending balance includes cash flow account of $350 million, budget reserve account of $994.3 million, and stadium reserve of $13.8 million.

(u) Revenue adjustments include transfers from other funds into the general revenue fund. The above expenditures assume expenditure restrictions.

(v) FY 16 expenditures include the actual transfer made to the state's fire fund due to revenues exceeding the official estimate in FY 2015 and reversions in excess of 0.5%.

(w) Revenue adjustments are transfers between the General Fund and other funds. Per Nebraska law, includes an estimated transfer of $61.5 million to the Cash Reserve Fund (Rainy Day Fund) of the amount the prior year's net General Fund receipts are estimated to exceed the official forecast. Among others, also includes a $202 million transfer (a $64 million increase) from the General Fund to the Property Tax Credit Cash Fund. Expenditure adjustments represent $5 million reserved for potential deficit appropriations and a net $354 million reserved for authorized reappropriations and carryover obligations from FY 2015.

(x) Revenue adjustments are restricted revenue and estimated reversions. Expenditure adjustments are restricted transfers.

(y) Expenditure Adjustments: The enacted FY 2016 budget anticipates moving $79.4 million to the Education Trust Fund and moving $.7 million to the Fish and Game Fund at year end.

(z) FY16 expenditure amounts reflect the FY16 budget approp-riation as passed during the 2015 Legislative Session. Revenue Amounts reflect the August 2015 estimate.

(aa) The ending balance includes approximately $1.8 billion in rainy day reserve funds, $60 million reserved to cover costs of potential retroactive labor settlements with certain unions, $74 million in a community projects fund, $500 million reserved for debt reduction, $21 million reserved for litigation risks, and approximately $1 billion in proceeds from monetary settlements.

FISCAL 2016 STATE GENERAL FUND, APPROPRIATED — Continued
(In millions of dollars)

(bb) Revenue adjustments are a $657.0 million transfer from the tax relief fund into the general fund.

(cc) Estimated FY 2016 include expenditures against prior year encumbrances as well as $810.9 million in transfers out of the GRF. $526.6 million of the $810.9 million in transfers out will go to the Budget Stabilization (Rainy Day) Fund. Medicaid expansion was not funded through the General Revenue Fund (GRF) in fiscal 2015, but it is in fiscal 2016. This change is responsible for the majority of the fiscal 2016 growth. In addition, federal reimbursements for Medicaid expenditures funded from the GRF are deposited into the GRF. This will tend to make Ohio's GRF expenditures look higher relative to most states that don't follow this practice.

(dd) Revenue and expenditure adjustments cannot be calculated at this time; nor can we calculate the final balance of the Rainy Day Fund at year-end.

(ee) Revenue adjustments include: transfer 2013-15 biennium ending GF balance to Rainy Day Fund (up to 1% of total biennial budget appropriation); cost of Tax Anticipation Notes; a statutory transfer to local governments for local property tax relief; and, refund of personal income tax collections/revenues that exceeded the 2015 "close of session" forecast (aka "kicker"). Expenditures represent 48% of the 2015–17 (Biennium) Legislatively Adopted Budget.

(ff) As of November 12, 2015, Pennsylvania had not yet enacted a budget for fiscal 2016.

(gg) Adjustments to revenues reflect a transfer of $109.9 million to the Budget Reserve Fund.

(hh) Revenue Adjustments: Includes $77.3 in nonrecurring revenues from a legal settlements and a transfer of excess cash from the State's Unclaimed Property Fund. Expenditure Adjustments include FY14–15 Capital Reserve Funds transferred to State agencies.

(ii) The beginning balance of $21.5 million and adjustment to expenditures reflect the prior year's ending balance which is transferred to the rainy day fund.

(jj) Revenue Adjustments include -$76.5 million transfer to Rainy Day Fund and $6.1 million transfer from TennCare Reserve Fund.

Expenditure Adjustments include $135.4 million transfer to capital outlay projects fund; $176.1 million transfer to state office buildings and support facilities fund; $3.8 million transfer to debt service fund; and $1.0 million transfer to reserves for dedicated revenue appropriations. Ending Balance includes $348.2 million undesignated balance.

(kk) Revenue adjustment for transfers to the Economic Stabilization and State Highway Funds (-$2,395m). Enacted general fund spending amount for FY 2016 comes from Conference Committee Report for H.B. No. 1. Texas is projected to have an $11.1 billion balance in its Economic Stabilization Fund at the end of fiscal 2017. The $9.9 billion figure is an estimate for fiscal 2016 based on this biennial projection and expected transfers to the ESF.

(ll) Includes transfers from previous year balance, to/from Rainy Day Fund, and special revenue funds.

(mm) Adjustments = net transfer effect in/out of the General Fund

(nn) Adjustments include fund transfers between General Fund and other accounts, and changes made by the 2015 Legislature.

(oo) Fiscal Year 2016 Beginning balance includes $368.2 million in Reappropriations, Unappropriated Surplus Balance of $12.8 million, $0.2 million of cash balance adjustments, and FY 2015 13th month expenditures of $38.4 million. Expenditures include Regular funds and surplus funds and $38.4 million of 31 day prior year expenditures. Revenue adjustments are prior year redeposits and special revenue expirations. Expenditure adjustment represents the amount to be transferred to the Rainy Day Fund. The ending balance is mostly the historically carried forward reappropriation amounts that will remain and be reappropriated to the next fiscal year, the 13th month expenditures & any unappropriated surplus balance.

(pp) Revenue adjustments include Tribal Gaming, $23.4 million and Other Revenue, $516.1 million. Expenditure adjustments include Transfers to Transportation fund $38.0 million; Lapses, −$349.2 million; and Compensation Reserves, $10.7 million.

(qq) Wyoming budgets on a biennial basis. To arrive at annual figures certain assumptions and estimates were required.

Table 7.4
FISCAL 2015 STATE TAX COLLECTIONS COMPARED WITH PROJECTIONS
USED IN ADOPTING FISCAL 2015 BUDGETS**
(In millions of dollars)

State or other jurisdiction	Sales tax Original estimate	Sales tax Current estimate	Personal income tax Original estimate	Personal income tax Current estimate	Corporate income tax Original estimate	Corporate income tax Current estimate
Total (a)........................	$222,658	$223,987	$298,557	$306,896	$42,010	$44,778
Alabama	2,120	2,143	3,397	3,332	387	492
Alaska...........................	N/A	N/A	N/A	N/A	591	320
Arizona.........................	4,208	4,190	3,697	3,761	671	663
Arkansas.......................	2,208	2,198	3,173	3,189	450	493
California	23,823	23,684	70,238	75,384	8,910	9,809
Colorado.......................	2,413	2,588	6,113	6,368	775	708
Connecticut..................	4,167	4,211	9,265	9,154	704	812
Delaware	N/A	N/A	1,226	1,252	212	269
Florida..........................	21,012	21,063	N/A	N/A	2,185	2,236
Georgia.........................	5,340	5,390	9,364	9,679	955	1,001
Hawaii...........................	2,882	2,993	1,820	1,988	65	52
Idaho.............................	1,204	1,219	1,413	1,471	200	215
Illinois..........................	7,847	N/A	14,845	N/A	3,071	N/A
Indiana..........................	7,442	7,195	5,419	5,233	869	1,094
Iowa	2,770	2,761	4,272	4,162	564	550
Kansas	2,505	2,485	2,280	2,278	425	417
Kentucky	3,150	3,267	3,977	4,070	463	528
Louisiana......................	2,696	2,730	2,932	2,863	351	385
Maine	1,147	1,244	1,438	1,522	214	169
Maryland	4,335	4,351	8,168	8,346	768	777
Massachusetts	5,820	5,774	14,021	14,448	2,000	2,172
Michigan (b)..................	7,549	7,504	8,506	8,691	468	259
Minnesota.....................	5,145	5,163	9,860	10,415	1,372	1,441
Mississippi	2,073	2,034	1,749	1,743	691	714
Missouri........................	2,034	1,988	5,991	5,948	442	436
Montana	65	64	1,143	1,176	154	173
Nebraska	1,560	1,535	2,190	2,206	345	347
Nevada (c)....................	1,023	1,034	N/A	N/A	N/A	N/A
New Hampshire	N/A	N/A	N/A	N/A	356	352
New Jersey	9,332	9,039	12,627	13,403	2,820	2,870
New Mexico	2,665	2,695	1,280	1,340	289	255
New York.......................	12,114	12,137	43,735	43,710	5,438	6,265
North Carolina.............	6,244	6,252	10,885	11,079	1,095	1,328
North Dakota................	1,324	1,266	415	536	193	196
Ohio	9,914	9,960	8,717	8,507	833	854
Oklahoma......................	2,034	2,020	2,129	2,161	375	304
Oregon..........................	N/A	N/A	7,068	7,330	524	622
Pennsylvania	9,477	N/A	12,033	N/A	2,501	N/A
Rhode Island................	954	964	1,227	1,228	143	148
South Carolina.............	2,590	2,657	3,013	3,159	304	327
South Dakota................	851	837	N/A	N/A	N/A	N/A
Tennessee	7,515	7,724	264	303	1,904	2,204
Texas.............................	28,219	28,957	N/A	N/A	N/A	N/A
Utah..............................	1,730	1,712	3,034	3,173	372	373
Vermont........................	366	365	702	706	103	122
Virginia.........................	3,271	3,235	12,252	12,329	830	832
Washington...................	8,405	8,620	N/A	N/A	N/A	N/A
West Virginia................	1,314	1,289	1,905	1,932	206	190
Wisconsin	4,607	4,892	7,651	7,326	994	1,005
Wyoming	521	561	N/A	N/A	N/A	N/A

See footnotes at end of table.

FISCAL 2015 STATE TAX COLLECTIONS COMPARED WITH PROJECTIONS USED IN ADOPTING FISCAL 2015 BUDGETS** — Continued
(In millions of dollars)

Source: National Association of State Budget Officers, December 2015.

Note: Unless otherwise noted, original estimates reflect the figures used when the fiscal 2015 budget was adopted, and current estimates reflect preliminary actual tax collections.

Key:

N/A — Indicates data are not available because, in most cases, these states do not have that type of tax.

(a) Totals include only those states with data for both fiscal 2015 projections and actual collections.

(b) Corporate Income Tax Collections include net revenue from the Corporate Income Tax, the Michigan Business Tax, and the Single Business Tax. Preliminary Actuals for FY 2015 are based on May 2015 revenue estimates for the fiscal year ending September 30, 2015.

(c) Sales tax collections for preliminary actual for FY 2015 are missing June collection. Data not released until end of August.

Table 7.5
COMPARISON OF TAX COLLECTIONS IN FISCAL 2014, FISCAL 2015, AND ENACTED FISCAL 2016
(In millions of dollars)

State or other jurisdiction	Sales tax Fiscal 2014	Fiscal 2015	Fiscal 2016	Personal income tax Fiscal 2014	Fiscal 2015	Fiscal 2016	Corporate income tax Fiscal 2014	Fiscal 2015	Fiscal 2016
Total (a)	$212,895	$223,987	$232,749	$284,242	$306,896	$316,877	$41,180	$44,778	$44,551
Alabama	2,075	2,143	2,191	3,202	3,332	3,419	378	492	393
Alaska	N/A	N/A	N/A	N/A	N/A	N/A	408	320	275
Arizona	3,986	4,190	4,276	3,462	3,761	3,671	575	663	623
Arkansas	2,173	2,198	2,273	3,111	3,189	3,092	440	493	476
California	22,263	23,684	25,240	67,025	75,384	77,700	9,093	9,809	10,342
Colorado	2,416	2,588	2,722	5,696	6,368	6,611	721	708	785
Connecticut	4,101	4,211	4,121	8,719	9,154	9,834	782.2	812.0	902.2
Delaware	N/A	N/A	N/A	1,188	1,252	1,297	102	269	154
Florida	19,708	21,063	21,957	N/A	N/A	N/A	2,043	2,236	2,350
Georgia	5,126	5,390	5,594	8,966	9,679	9,884	944	1,001	996
Hawaii (b)	2,825	2,993	3,181	1,745	1,988	1,915	87	52	100
Idaho	1,146	1,219	1,270	1,329	1,471	1,489	188	215	213
Illinois	7,676	N/A	N/A	16,642	N/A	N/A	3,164	N/A	N/A
Indiana	6,926	7,195	7,505	4,899	5,233	5,122	1,054	1,094	985
Iowa	2,642	2,761	2,891	3,975	4,162	4,494	550	550	560
Kansas	2,446	2,485	2,786	2,218	2,278	2,462	399	417	445
Kentucky	3,131	3,267	3,216	3,749	4,070	4,130	475	528	434
Louisiana	2,620	2,730	2,935	2,751	2,863	3,013	330	385	790
Maine	1,156	1,244	1,179	1,406	1,522	1,549	183	169	150
Maryland	4,143	4,351	4,530	7,774	8,346	8,629	761	777	822
Massachusetts	5,496	5,774	6,008	13,202	14,448	14,789	2,049	2,172	2,226
Michigan (c)	7,355	7,504	7,822	8,014	8,691	8,940	138	259	161
Minnesota (d)	5,043	5,163	5,328	9,660	10,415	10,736	1,278	1,441	1,299
Mississippi	1,955	2,034	2,135	1,667	1,743	1,814	677	714	693
Missouri	1,925	1,988	2,032	5,404	5,948	6,023	396	436	340
Montana	63	64	66	1,063	1,176	1,230	148	173	180
Nebraska	1,525	1,535	1,614	2,061	2,206	2,299	307	347	329
Nevada (e)	968	1,034	1,098	N/A	N/A	N/A	N/A	N/A	N/A
New Hampshire	N/A	N/A	N/A	N/A	N/A	N/A	345	352	354
New Jersey	8,849	9,039	9,253	12,312	13,403	13,930	2,299	2,870	2,862
New Mexico	2,514	2,695	2,807	1,255	1,340	1,360	197	255	225
New York	11,786	12,137	12,649	42,961	43,710	47,075	6,046	6,265	5,897
North Carolina	5,567	6,252	6,289	10,272	11,079	10,961	1,357	1,328	1,093
North Dakota	1,213	1,266	1,378	514	536	371	239	196	186
Ohio (f)	9,166	9,960	10,373	8,065	8,507	8,093	794	854	1,282
Oklahoma	1,959	2,020	2,134	2,028	2,161	2,076	307	304	250
Oregon	N/A	N/A	N/A	6,628	7,330	7,660	495	622	540
Pennsylvania	9,130	N/A	N/A	11,437	N/A	N/A	2,502	N/A	N/A
Rhode Island	916	964	970	1,116	1,228	1,216	114	148	136
South Carolina	2,517	2,657	2,714	2,921	3,159	3,251	288	327	308
South Dakota	823	837	869	N/A	N/A	N/A	N/A	N/A	N/A
Tennessee (g)	7,286	7,724	7,878	239	303	269	1,859	2,204	1,938
Texas (h)	27,400	28,957	29,680	N/A	N/A	N/A	N/A	N/A	N/A
Utah	1,657	1,712	1,800	2,890	3,173	3,163	314	373	381
Vermont	354	365	378	671	706	740	95	122	82
Virginia	3,067	3,235	3,401	11,253	12,329	12,759	758	832	827
Wisconsin	8,237	8,620	9,287	N/A	N/A	N/A	N/A	N/A	N/A
West Virginia	1,222	1,289	1,321	1,770	1,932	1,956	204	190	178
Washington	4,628	4,892	5,054	7,061	7,326	7,859	967	1,005	994
Wyoming	521	561	546	N/A	N/A	N/A	N/A	N/A	N/A

See footnotes at end of table.

COMPARISON OF TAX COLLECTIONS IN FISCAL 2014, FISCAL 2015, AND ENACTED FISCAL 2016—Continued
(In millions of dollars)

Source: National Association of State Budget Officers. December 2015.

Note: Unless otherwise noted, fiscal 2014 figures reflect actual tax collections, fiscal 2015 figures reflect preliminary actual tax collections estimates, and fiscal 2016 figures reflect the estimates used in enacted budgets.

Key:

N.A. — Indicates data are not available because, in most cases, these states do not have that type of tax.

(a) Totals include only those states with data for all years.

(b) All numbers reflect appropriation.

(c) Corporate Income Tax Collections include net revenue from the Corporate Income Tax, the Michigan Business Tax, and the Single Business Tax. Preliminary Actuals for FY 2015 are based on May 2015 revenue estimates for the fiscal year ending September 30, 2015. Reported collections for fiscal 2014 and fiscal 2015 are from REC May 2014.

(d) Sources: Actual FY 2014—2015 EOS FBA; Estimates for FY 2015 Budget—2014 EOS FBA; Preliminary Actual FY 2015—Economic Update; Estimates for FY 2016 Budget—2015 EOS FBA.

(e) Sales tax collections for preliminary actual for FY 2015 are missing June collection. Data not released until end of August.

(f) Ohio doesn't have a corporate income tax and instead has a commercial activities tax (CAT). The large increase in fiscal 2016 is the result of allocating a higher percentage of the CAT revenue to the general fund and a lower percentage to property tax replacement funds.

(g) Sales tax, personal income tax, and corporate income tax are shared with local governments. Corporate income tax includes franchise tax.

(h) Texas does not have a corporate income tax, but it does have a franchise tax, a privilege tax imposed on each taxable entity chartered/organized in Texas or doing business in Texas. Franchise tax collections totaled $4,700 million in fiscal 2014, $2,874 million in fiscal 2015, and are projected to total $2,800 million in fiscal 2016.

Table 7.6
TOTAL STATE EXPENDITURES: CAPITAL INCLUSIVE
(In millions of dollars)

State	Actual fiscal 2013					Actual fiscal 2014					Estimated fiscal 2015				
	General fund	Federal funds	Other state funds	Bonds	Total	General fund	Federal funds	Other state funds	Bonds	Total	General fund	Federal funds	Other state funds	Bonds	Total
Total	$682,934	$496,394	$445,842	$36,460	$1,661,630	$710,580	$519,937	$464,555	$33,849	$1,728,921	$745,422	$583,376	$498,008	$36,725	$1,863,531
Alabama (a)	7,124	9,488	7,699	224	24,535	7,819	9,360	7,398	386	24,963	7,836	9,556	7,154	608	25,154
Alaska	7,690	2,589	1,258	485	12,022	7,226	2,705	1,466	0	11,397	6,013	3,134	4,620	173	13,940
Arizona	8,414	12,008	6,946	192	27,560	8,848	12,837	7,220	198	29,103	9,335	13,152	8,695	150	31,332
Arkansas	4,744	6,068	10,433	203	21,448	4,909	6,504	11,196	156	22,765	5,063	7,131	11,439	171	23,804
California	96,562	70,431	37,724	6,715	211,432	100,005	72,583	38,311	4,494	215,393	114,473	93,554	44,523	6,089	258,639
Colorado	9,024	7,423	13,664	0	30,111	9,048	7,859	14,439	0	31,346	9,539	8,716	14,746	0	33,001
Connecticut	19,026	2,595	3,764	2,384	27,769	16,980	5,409	3,904	2,900	29,193	17,405	5,980	4,336	2,976	30,697
Delaware	3,659	1,783	3,281	439	9,162	3,794	1,903	3,459	452	9,608	3,832	2,063	3,523	351	9,769
Florida	24,490	24,160	13,439	1,882	63,971	26,315	24,354	15,801	1,563	68,033	27,914	25,492	22,089	1,578	77,073
Georgia	18,019	13,046	10,571	808	42,444	18,843	13,184	10,567	850	43,444	20,021	12,901	10,572	878	44,372
Hawaii	5,666	1,912	3,271	735	11,584	6,275	2,166	3,337	825	12,603	6,416	2,250	3,434	769	12,869
Idaho	2,691	2,647	1,342	10	6,690	2,767	2,614	1,456	28	6,865	2,915	2,837	1,861	21	7,634
Illinois	26,901	12,918	16,383	1,970	58,172	28,381	13,562	16,698	2,398	61,039	28,853	17,904	22,653	2,100	71,510
Indiana	14,189	10,357	3,625	0	28,171	14,553	9,978	2,729	0	27,260	15,346	10,305	3,691	0	29,342
Iowa	6,299	5,727	7,398	107	19,531	6,564	5,928	7,747	107	20,346	6,994	6,335	8,435	25	21,789
Kansas	6,146	3,890	3,518	415	13,969	5,983	3,900	4,474	366	14,723	6,255	3,882	4,906	402	15,445
Kentucky	9,426	8,001	8,246	0	25,673	9,706	9,597	9,638	0	28,941	9,705	11,830	9,807	0	31,342
Louisiana	8,347	9,520	9,838	378	28,083	8,565	8,993	9,220	501	27,279	8,715	10,149	10,865	607	30,336
Maine	3,041	2,563	2,059	16	7,679	3,149	2,696	2,180	63	8,088	3,164	2,422	2,025	115	7,726
Maryland	15,127	9,184	10,809	1,167	36,287	15,603	10,514	10,773	1,146	38,036	15,998	12,053	12,285	1,217	41,553
Massachusetts	27,326	8,079	17,077	2,154	54,636	28,534	8,681	16,500	2,535	56,250	30,330	9,435	15,205	2,335	57,305
Michigan	8,882	17,423	20,766	326	47,397	9,485	18,152	21,689	330	49,656	9,702	22,633	21,530	355	54,220
Minnesota	18,739	8,345	3,627	810	31,521	19,348	8,900	3,646	779	32,673	20,381	10,601	4,232	767	35,981
Mississippi	4,699	8,141	5,595	760	19,195	5,023	7,562	5,723	250	18,558	5,504	8,953	5,977	765	21,199
Missouri	8,022	7,209	7,711	0	22,942	8,349	7,201	7,622	0	23,172	8,773	7,495	7,853	1	24,122
Montana	1,947	2,115	1,978	0	6,040	2,041	2,149	1,998	0	6,188	2,138	2,189	2,056	0	6,383
Nebraska	3,589	3,014	3,559	0	10,162	3,792	2,911	3,839	0	10,542	4,031	2,908	4,043	0	10,982
Nevada	3,185	2,796	2,629	41	8,651	3,125	2,859	3,405	20	9,409	3,369	3,897	3,560	28	10,854
New Hampshire	1,266	1,604	2,060	87	5,017	1,249	1,701	2,131	63	5,144	1,259	1,944	2,185	58	5,446
New Jersey	31,195	12,041	6,194	1,374	50,804	31,103	13,372	7,255	1,373	53,103	32,174	15,142	7,286	1,225	55,827
New Mexico	5,651	5,799	3,246	0	14,696	5,910	6,108	4,180	0	16,198	6,151	6,581	4,359	0	17,091
New York	58,960	38,574	32,305	3,258	133,097	61,243	41,171	31,672	3,440	137,526	62,856	45,743	31,768	3,524	143,891
North Carolina	20,202	12,638	9,788	231	42,859	20,234	13,512	9,860	187	43,793	20,666	13,950	9,760	101	44,457
North Dakota	2,220	1,536	1,950	6	5,712	3,237	1,523	1,816	16	6,592	3,224	1,674	2,850	14	7,762
Ohio	27,439	12,647	15,996	2,186	58,268	28,902	13,046	17,141	2,133	61,222	30,831	13,994	17,762	2,509	65,096
Oklahoma	6,630	6,653	7,764	383	21,430	6,859	7,404	7,851	267	22,381	6,909	7,268	7,873	338	22,388
Oregon	5,957	7,451	12,263	132	25,803	7,930	8,102	16,191	160	32,383	7,959	11,302	14,132	132	33,525
Pennsylvania	27,716	24,614	15,392	1,379	69,101	28,394	23,894	15,726	800	68,814	29,106	25,921	17,794	1,265	74,086
Rhode Island	3,223	2,522	2,468	158	8,371	3,336	2,676	2,790	142	8,944	3,402	2,820	2,595	103	8,920
South Carolina	6,200	7,800	8,208	0	22,208	6,329	7,542	8,116	53	22,040	6,851	7,631	8,075	98	22,655

See footnotes at end of table.

TOTAL STATE EXPENDITURES: CAPITAL INCLUSIVE—Continued
(In millions of dollars)

State	Actual fiscal 2013					Actual fiscal 2014					Estimated fiscal 2015				
	General fund	Federal funds	Other state funds	Bonds	Total	General fund	Federal funds	Other state funds	Bonds	Total	General fund	Federal funds	Other state funds	Bonds	Total
South Dakota..........	1,291	1,494	1,312	35	4,132	1,427	1,403	1,248	21	4,099	1,378	1,347	1,164	60	3,949
Tennessee (b	12,093	12,552	5,565	301	30,491	12,837	12,200	5,480	185	30,702	13,198	13,156	5,608	84	32,046
Texas	40,830	37,364	20,974	1,760	100,928	46,764	41,348	20,412	1,622	110,146	48,406	43,430	20,746	1,997	114,579
Utah	5,098	3,462	3,529	0	12,089	5,383	3,497	3,304	0	12,184	5,749	3,642	3,561	0	12,952
Vermont	1,352	1,695	1,845	73	4,965	1,392	1,760	2,003	116	5,271	1,413	1,919	1,999	98	5,429
Virginia.............	18,833	9,546	16,191	1,167	45,737	18,052	9,568	17,071	1,167	45,858	17,744	9,706	18,513	1,089	47,052
Washington.............	15,479	8,100	8,785	1,632	33,996	16,079	9,631	9,478	1,679	36,867	16,560	10,975	10,110	1,472	39,117
West Virginia.............	4,283	4,075	13,885	77	22,320	4,256	4,412	15,142	78	23,888	4,259	4,372	14,785	77	23,493
Wisconsin	14,042	10,815	17,912	0	42,769	14,634	11,006	19,253	0	44,893	15,307	11,122	18,968	0	45,397
Wyoming (c).............	3,709	2,354	3,069	0	9,132	3,011	2,082	2,532	0	7,625	3,297	2,298	3,242	0	8,837

Source: National Association of State Budget Officers, State Expenditure Report (Fiscal 2013–2015).
Note: "State funds" refers to general funds plus other state fund spending. State spending from bonds is excluded. "Total funds" refers to funding from all sources-general fund, federal funds, other state funds and bonds. Small dollar amounts, when rounded, cause an aberration in the percentage increase. In these instances, the actual dollar amounts should be consulted to determine the exact percentage increase.

Key:
(a) Amounts shown in fiscal years 2013 and 2014 are based on actual expenditures during these years, regardless of the year appropriated. Fiscal 2015 amounts shown are equal to actual expenditures through 9 months and then annualized for the year.

(b) Tennessee collects personal income tax on income from dividends on stocks and interest on certain bonds. Tax revenue estimates do not include federal funds and other departmental revenues. However, federal funds and other departmental revenues are included in the budget as funding sources for the general fund, along with state tax revenues.

(c) Part of Wyoming's yearly variation in expenditure totals is due to the fact that the state budgets on a two year cycle.

Table 7.7
ELEMENTARY AND SECONDARY EDUCATION EXPENDITURES, BY STATE
(In millions of dollars)

State	Actual fiscal 2013					Actual fiscal 2014					Estimated fiscal 2015				
	General fund	Federal funds	Other state funds	Bonds	Total	General fund	Federal funds	Other state funds	Bonds	Total	General fund	Federal funds	Other state funds	Bonds	Total
Total..............	$187,206	$42,388	$34,584	$1,513	$265,691	$196,044	$42,661	$35,145	$1,431	$275,281	$202,702	$43,197	$36,586	$1,578	$284,063
Alabama (a)..............	3,773	967	273	0	5,013	4,017	919	181	0	5,117	4,109	1,396	187	0	5,692
Alaska..............	1,364	209	32	0	1,605	1,359	210	33	0	1,602	1,500	228	31	0	1,759
Arizona..............	3,465	1,119	544	0	5,128	3,662	1,075	592	0	5,329	3,835	1,082	633	0	5,550
Arkansas..............	2,056	519	767	0	3,342	2,103	520	816	0	3,439	2,181	534	761	0	3,476
California (b)..............	37,979	6,307	127	872	45,285	39,221	6,198	74	407	45,900	45,878	7,061	72	37	53,048
Colorado (c)..............	3,015	614	3,918	0	7,547	3,199	594	4,169	0	7,962	3,358	585	4,513	0	8,456
Connecticut..............	$2,880	$484	$3	$563	$3,930	$3,039	$475	$2	$628	$4,144	$3,265	$489	$2	$528	$4,284
Delaware..............	1,194	211	681	141	2,227	1,243	208	700	168	2,319	1,278	209	747	98	2,332
Florida..............	9,106	1,893	1,004	0	12,003	10,020	1,950	1,116	0	13,086	10,174	1,730	1,317	0	13,221
Georgia..............	7,380	2,353	334	167	10,234	7,597	2,385	349	239	10,570	8,139	2,411	360	273	11,183
Hawaii..............	1,444	287	63	0	1,794	1,537	303	49	0	1,889	1,582	241	68	0	1,891
Idaho..............	1,299	243	80	0	1,622	1,327	232	86	0	1,645	1,398	286	96	0	1,780
Illinois..............	6,539	2,128	34	0	8,701	6,681	2,217	41	0	8,939	6,555	2,977	268	0	9,800
Indiana..............	7,452	1,057	171	0	8,680	7,625	980	120	0	8,725	7,705	968	142	0	8,815
Iowa..............	2,731	444	31	0	3,206	2,864	439	67	0	3,370	3,006	460	77	0	3,543
Kansas (d)..............	3,092	479	171	0	3,742	2,963	470	376	0	3,809	3,172	478	928	0	4,578
Kentucky..............	4,141	846	34	0	5,021	4,202	797	35	0	5,034	4,390	802	35	0	5,227
Louisiana..............	3,370	1,042	847	0	5,259	3,514	1,049	601	0	5,164	3,520	1,086	725	0	5,331
Maine (e)..............	1,087	202	8	0	1,297	1,150	194	30	0	1,374	1,137	192	30	0	1,359
Maryland..............	5,552	969	437	0	6,958	5,690	1,044	406	0	7,140	5,864	1,101	406	0	7,371
Massachusetts..............	4,742	1,072	687	0	6,501	4,919	1,086	733	0	6,738	4,992	934	698	0	6,624
Michigan (f)..............	313	1,743	10,841	0	12,897	185	1,900	11,288	0	13,373	73	1,911	11,848	0	13,832
Minnesota..............	8,865	745	38	1	9,649	8,430	737	40	3	9,210	8,188	835	46	0	9,069
Mississippi..............	2,011	705	324	0	3,040	2,059	639	324	0	3,022	2,154	798	370	0	3,322
Missouri..............	2,914	957	1,358	0	5,229	2,922	943	1,426	0	5,291	3,141	958	1,405	0	5,504
Montana..............	697	162	77	0	936	721	163	86	0	970	758	167	82	0	1,007
Nebraska..............	1,088	328	72	0	1,488	1,142	303	77	0	1,522	1,209	322	79	0	1,610
Nevada..............	1,214	384	382	0	1,980	1,298	257	291	0	1,846	1,371	289	293	0	1,953
New Hampshire..............	0	199	959	14	1,172	0	186	954	1	1,141	0	179	946	1	1,126
New Jersey..............	11,754	856	20	0	12,630	11,713	782	19	0	12,514	12,047	852	16	0	12,915
New Mexico..............	2,455	414	1	0	2,870	2,556	414	2	0	2,972	2,715	414	5	0	3,134
New York..............	19,070	3,407	3,164	16	25,657	19,297	3,927	3,310	17	26,533	20,534	3,433	3,344	15	27,326
North Carolina (g)..............	7,740	2,040	24	0	9,804	7,768	2,035	23	0	9,826	8,047	2,174	24	0	10,245
North Dakota..............	660	141	57	0	858	841	127	74	0	1,042	880	115	69	0	1,064
Ohio (h)..............	6,831	2,000	751	312	9,894	7,128	1,912	1,045	201	10,286	7,617	1,871	1,098	378	10,964
Oklahoma..............	2,007	616	851	0	3,474	2,046	628	817	0	3,491	2,104	638	857	0	3,599
Oregon..............	2,527	560	593	0	3,680	3,356	593	1,852	0	5,801	3,408	648	399	0	4,455
Pennsylvania..............	9,705	2,423	618	0	12,746	9,847	2,386	614	0	12,847	10,287	2,541	847	0	13,675
Rhode Island..............	928	214	29	1	1,172	960	204	34	2	1,200	995	171	29	7	1,202
South Carolina..............	2,264	890	749	0	3,903	2,416	901	735	0	4,052	2,538	852	754	0	4,144

See footnotes at end of table.

ELEMENTARY AND SECONDARY EDUCATION EXPENDITURES, BY STATE—Continued
(In millions of dollars)

State	Actual fiscal 2013					Actual fiscal 2014					Estimated fiscal 2015				
	General fund	Federal funds	Other state funds	Bonds	Total	General fund	Federal funds	Other state funds	Bonds	Total	General fund	Federal funds	Other state funds	Bonds	Total
South Dakota............	402	173	3	0	578	401	168	5	0	574	405	169	6	0	580
Tennessee	4,160	1,165	89	0	5,414	4,327	1,207	70	0	5,604	4,354	1,094	105	0	5,553
Texas......................	14,826	4,961	5,900	3	25,690	18,683	4,784	4,056	3	27,526	19,221	4,948	4,219	0	28,388
Utah........................	2,534	433	26	0	2,993	2,654	419	60	0	3,133	2,756	482	124	0	3,362
Vermont...................	357	121	1,103	8	1,589	370	116	1,176	7	1,669	387	117	1,212	10	1,726
Virginia...................	5,254	1,029	645	0	6,928	5,302	967	678	0	6,947	5,471	906	939	0	7,316
Washington (i)	6,735	856	109	264	7,964	7,219	916	348	139	8,622	7,612	767	366	245	8,990
West Virginia..........	1,969	346	14	23	2,352	1,970	340	14	23	2,347	1,975	340	15	23	2,353
Wisconsin................	5,915	782	238	0	6,935	6,080	875	253	0	7,208	6,277	842	257	0	7,376
Wyoming.................	2	28	964	0	994	0	3	763	0	766	0	0	933	0	934

Source: National Association of State Budget Officers, *State Expenditure Report* (Fiscal 2013–2015).
Note: Small dollar amounts, when rounded, cause an aberration in the percentage increase. In these instances, the actual dollar amounts should be consulted to determine the exact percentage increase.

Key:
(a) Federal funds received directly by local school systems are not reported at the state budget level.
(b) State funding for schools and community colleges is determined largely by a constitutional formula, enacted by Proposition 98 in 1988. The Proposition 98 funding level increased significantly in 2015 primarily due to increases in General Fund revenues.
(c) School personnel are paid at the school district level—state costs for employer contributions to employee pensions and health benefits only reflect Colorado Dept. of Education personnel. Funds library-related programs across the state.
(d) Beginning in fiscal 2015, revenues generated from the state's 20-mill local property tax levy are deposited in the state treasury and distributed to school districts as state aid. Prior to fiscal 2015, these funds were collected and remitted by county treasurers and were not part of the state's budget. For fiscal 2015, from the 20-mill tax levy totaled $579.0 million.

(e) The Elementary and Secondary Education expenditure category includes capital expenditures in amounts less than $200,000 each fiscal year.
(f) Figures reflect K-12 education, the Michigan Department of Education, adult education and pre-school. Employer contributions to current employees' pensions and health benefits are reported for Department of Education employees and partially excluded for employees of K-12 schools. Effective for fiscal 2013, state funds partially offset employer-paid retirement obligations for employees of K-12 schools.
(g) Community college funding is now included in the higher education section, whereas in last year's edition of the State Expenditure Report it was included in the elementary and secondary education section.
(h) Employer contributions to current employees' pensions are not directly appropriated, or fully funded, by the state; however, some of the unrestricted support provided to localities for elementary and secondary education is used to help cover these costs. There are no direct appropriations for employer contributions to health benefits, though it can be assumed that some of the unrestricted support provided for elementary and secondary education is used for these costs.
(i) Figures for Elementary and Secondary Education include Capital expenditures.

Table 7.8
MEDICAID EXPENDITURES BY STATE
(In millions of dollars)

State	Actual fiscal 2013				Actual fiscal 2014				Estimated fiscal 2015			
	General fund	Federal funds	Other state funds	Total	General fund	Federal funds	Other state funds	Total	General fund	Federal funds	Other state funds	Total
Total....................	$132,294	$228,262	$45,812	$406,368	$137,885	$258,987	$48,117	$444,989	$144,859	$317,302	$50,154	$512,315
Alabama (a)............	595	3,820	1,171	5,586	625	3,920	1,266	5,811	685	4,155	1,192	6,032
Alaska (b)	568	817	3	1,388	445	816	1	1,262	694	951	5	1,650
Arizona.................	2,069	5,756	606	8,431	2,125	6,332	557	9,014	2,279	8,040	602	10,921
Arkansas...............	736	3,180	595	4,511	818	3,802	404	5,024	898	4,568	593	6,059
California (c)...........	14,473	25,715	6,211	46,399	15,711	30,983	5,687	52,381	16,599	52,658	5,699	74,956
Colorado (d)	1,844	2,805	1,736	6,385	2,091	3,489	1,636	7,216	2,312	4,557	735	7,604
Connecticut (e).........	6,202	0	0	6,202	3,779	2,992	0	6,771	3,496	3,483	0	6,979
Delaware	707	870	0	1,577	662	1,001	0	1,663	668	1,193	14	1,875
Florida..................	4,721	11,823	3,789	20,333	5,015	12,716	4,056	21,787	5,294	13,799	4,487	23,580
Georgia.................	2,755	5,914	363	9,032	2,769	6,236	370	9,375	3,052	5,943	329	9,324
Hawaii..................	796	877	0	1,673	844	1,112	0	1,956	888	1,160	0	2,048
Idaho...................	467	1,241	168	1,876	469	1,262	189	1,920	475	1,304	250	2,029
Illinois.................	4,811	7,464	3,098	15,373	4,354	8,135	3,452	15,941	4,445	9,921	3,235	17,601
Indiana.................	1,883	5,950	956	8,789	1,815	6,225	679	8,719	2,009	6,476	677	9,162
Iowa....................	987	2,140	749	3,876	1,171	2,390	690	4,251	1,268	2,846	691	4,805
Kansas..................	1,100	1,425	58	2,583	1,176	1,583	544	3,303	1,281	1,689	578	3,548
Kentucky	1,267	3,923	436	5,626	1,443	5,042	449	6,934	1,501	7,517	504	9,522
Louisiana	1,425	4,721	704	6,850	1,725	4,668	916	7,309	1,610	4,588	1,216	7,414
Maine (f)	737	1,517	256	2,510	746	1,767	267	2,780	753	1,510	270	2,553
Maryland (g)...........	2,758	3,893	974	7,625	2,893	4,807	860	8,560	2,922	5,688	951	9,561
Massachusetts	5,916	4,884	316	11,116	6,359	5,542	143	12,044	7,120	6,704	171	13,995
Michigan (h)...........	2,330	8,194	1,990	12,514	2,428	9,287	1,995	13,710	2,797	12,494	2,029	17,320
Minnesota..............	4,127	4,293	131	8,551	4,453	5,143	154	9,750	4,533	6,187	164	10,884
Mississippi.............	316	3,627	891	4,834	475	3,312	781	4,568	640	3,633	635	4,908
Missouri (i)............	1,636	4,112	2,289	8,037	1,804	4,246	2,254	8,304	1,778	4,511	2,419	8,708
Montana	235	736	110	1,081	255	714	86	1,055	271	748	91	1,110
Nebraska	784	1,003	35	1,822	817	1,006	34	1,857	850	968	37	1,855
Nevada	549	1,043	181	1,773	521	1,363	142	2,026	564	2,225	114	2,903
New Hampshire	511	605	169	1,285	546	660	175	1,381	548	917	166	1,631
New Jersey (j)	3,718	5,546	1,092	10,356	3,961	6,920	1,043	11,924	3,869	8,912	1,068	13,849
New Mexico	868	2,560	250	3,678	874	3,063	235	4,172	862	4,036	238	5,136
New York	10,602	23,421	4,769	38,792	10,981	24,237	4,754	39,972	11,161	29,393	5,114	45,668
North Carolina (k)......	3,518	7,720	1,406	12,644	3,404	8,433	1,467	13,304	3,594	8,752	1,435	13,781
North Dakota...........	355	421	6	782	388	455	6	849	441	697	7	1,145
Ohio (l)................	12,030	4,102	878	17,010	13,571	6,317	2,053	21,941	14,861	7,541	1,925	24,327
Oklahoma..............	1,343	2,931	646	4,920	1,412	3,079	692	5,183	1,417	2,930	717	5,064
Oregon.................	923	3,476	1,111	5,510	1,342	4,623	791	6,756	728	6,683	1,260	8,671
Pennsylvania...........	7,620	12,245	2,364	22,229	7,945	12,371	2,632	22,948	8,298	12,996	2,849	24,143
Rhode Island (m).......	939	1,007	28	1,974	998	1,190	31	2,219	1,067	1,482	30	2,579
South Carolina.........	688	3,519	683	4,890	746	3,909	773	5,428	1,023	4,359	640	6,022

See footnotes at end of table.

MEDICAID EXPENDITURES BY STATE—Continued
(In millions of dollars)

State	Actual fiscal 2013				Actual fiscal 2014				Estimated fiscal 2015			
	General fund	Federal funds	Other state funds	Total	General fund	Federal funds	Other state funds	Total	General fund	Federal funds	Other state funds	Total
South Dakota............	316	500	0	816	335	498	0	833	364	484	0	848
Tennessee (n).............	2,787	6,121	491	9,399	3,071	5,869	452	9,392	3,316	6,673	370	10,359
Texas........................	10,190	17,483	1,845	29,518	10,724	19,674	2,807	33,205	11,381	22,197	3,983	37,561
Utah (o)....................	380	1,435	369	2,184	364	1,593	424	2,381	400	1,614	467	2,481
Vermont (p)...............	295	775	334	1,404	282	797	332	1,411	283	824	335	1,442
Virginia....................	3,862	3,772	0	7,634	3,934	3,961	0	7,895	4,114	4,123	0	8,237
Washington................	1,764	1,993	280	4,037	2,023	3,712	366	6,101	2,008	5,285	180	7,473
West Virginia.............	375	2,143	490	3,008	518	2,612	404	3,534	520	2,610	400	3,530
Wisconsin..................	2,144	4,435	762	7,341	2,411	4,806	1,044	8,261	2,650	4,969	1,259	8,878
Wyoming (q)..............	272	309	23	604	267	317	24	608	272	309	23	604

Source: National Association of State Budget Officers, State Expenditure Report (Fiscal 2013–2015).

Notes: States were asked to report Medicaid expenditures as follows: General Funds: all general funds appropriated to the Medicaid agency and any other agency which are used for direct Medicaid matching purposes under Title XIX. Other state funds: other funds and revenue sources used as Medicaid match, such as local funds and provider taxes, fees, donations, assessments (as defined by the Centers for Medicare and Medicaid Services). Federal Funds: all federal matching funds provided pursuant to Title XIX.

(1) The states were asked to separately detail the amount of provider taxes, fees, donations, assessments and local funds reported as Other State Funds.

(2) Small dollar amounts, when rounded, cause an aberration in the percentage determining the exact percentage increase. In these instances, the actual dollar amounts should be consulted to determine the exact percentage increase.

(3) "State funds" refers to general funds plus other state fund spending. State spending from bonds is excluded.

(4) "Total funds" refers to funding from all sources—general fund, federal funds, other state funds, and bonds.

(5) All States: Medicaid reflects provider taxes, fees, assessments, donations, and local funds in Other State Funds.

Key:

(a) Fiscal 2013 through fiscal 2015 Other State Funds includes provider taxes in the amounts of $356M, $374M, and $370M, respectively. Amounts shown in fiscal years 2013 and 2014 are based on actual expenditures during these years, regardless of the year appropriated. Fiscal 2015 amounts shown are equal to actual expenditures through 9 months and then annualized for the year.

(b) Due to a one-time accounting item, $132 million of state general fund expenditures were moved from prior year (fiscal 2014) to current year (fiscal 2015). This does not reflect a change in Medicaid spending for the fiscal year, rather, this is a technical audit adjustment regarding the issuance of advanced payments to providers following the rollout of a new information system. General Funds include Unrestricted General Funds only. Designated general funds are reported in the other state funds category. Additionally, a $3 billion transfer to the state retirement systems (PERS and TRS) was made at the beginning of fiscal 2015 from the Constitutional Budget Reserve fund in order to pay down a $12 billion unfunded pension liability, and is included in fiscal 2015 other state funds for the "all other" category.

(c) Changes in Medicaid program costs in fiscal 2015 reflect, among other things, increased costs associated with the Affordable Care Act's Medicaid expansion.

(d) In fiscal 2015, there was a policy change to split and charge expenses directly to cash funds rather than as transfers out from the cash funds to the General Fund from which the payment was made. In the past the cash funds data included both the transfer and the real expenses; this is a permanent change going forward. CHIP is included in "Medicaid" expenditures, all part of the Department of Health Care Policy and Financing.

(e) "In fiscal 2013, Medicaid was "gross funded" with federal funds deposited directly to the General Fund. Beginning in fiscal 2014, the Medicaid appropriation in the Department of Social Services (DSS) is "net funded" while other Medicaid expenditures remain gross funded. With the exception of an enhanced reimbursement rate for certain populations and services, Connecticut's FMAP is 50%. Includes Medicaid expenditures for administrative services organizations and fiscal intermediaries in DSS. Excludes state portion of Qualified Decrease in General Fund expenditures and increase in Federal Funds expenditures from Fiscal 2013 to 2014 due to net budgeting of Medicaid. Medicare Beneficiaries and School-Based Child Health as those expenditures are netted out of federal Medicaid reimbursement. Also excludes provider taxes, which are deposited directly to the General Fund.

(f) Medicaid Other State Funds provider taxes are: fiscal 2013, $153.3 million; fiscal 2014, $168.1 million; and fiscal 2015, $171.7 million.

(g) For Medicaid and CHIP fiscal 2015 estimate: Used actual data for the first three quarters of the year and projected the fourth quarter using the average of the first three. Fourth quarter data will be updated when available.

(h) Increased spending in fiscal 2014 and fiscal 2015 is primarily due to Medicaid expansion under the federal Affordable Care Act (ACA) known as the Healthy Michigan Plan. Other state funds include local funds of $99.0 million and provider taxes of $973.6 million for fiscal 2013; local funds of $86.0 million and provider taxes of $977.4 million for fiscal 2014; and local funds of $76.3 million and provider taxes of $1.04 billion for fiscal 2015. Public health and community and institutional care for mentally and developmentally disabled persons are partially reported in the Medicaid totals.

(i) Total Medicaid expenditures were incorrectly reported in the 2013 survey. The amount reported in 2013 included CHIP funding. The amounts reported on the 2014 survey are correct. The fiscal 2015 amounts reported are actual expenditures. Total expenditure amounts do not include employee benefits by each expenditure category; those are included in the "All Other" state expenditures.

(j) Medicaid Other State Funds: FY13/FY14/FY15 (in millions): Nursing Home Provider Tax $134/126/127; Other Assessments/Taxes/Fees $570/571/584. Beginning in federal fiscal year 2014, CHIP parents were moved to Medicaid (Title XIX).

(k) Fiscal 2013 and fiscal 2014 in this edition of the State Expenditure Report have been adjusted from last year's edition.

(l) Federal reimbursements for Medicaid expenditures funded from the General Revenue Fund

MEDICAID EXPENDITURES BY STATE — Continued
(In millions of dollars)

(GRF) are deposited into the GRF. Federal reimbursements for Medicaid expenditures from non-GRF sources are deposited into the appropriate federal fund. Expenditures of federal funds are contained in the General Fund number to be consistent with Ohio accounting practices and with other portrayals of Ohio's general fund. This amounts to $9,353.6 million in fiscal 2015. This will tend to make Ohio's GRF expenditures look higher and conversely make Ohio's federal expenditures look lower relative to most other states that don't follow this practice. Also, inherent in Ohio's budgetary accounting environment are significant overstatements of total state spending due to two phenomena. First, fiduciary fund expenditures represent the distribution of funds collected by the state on behalf of other entities. These are not operating, program, or subsidy expenditures of the state. Examples of this would be the collection and distribution of county and local permissive sales taxes or motor vehicle registration taxes. Fiduciary fund group expenditures totaled $6,476.9 million in fiscal 2015. Second, "double counting" of revenue and expenditures related to intrastate transactions overstates overall state expenditure activity. Intrastate transactions totaled $710.8 million in fiscal 2015. These accounting practices will tend to make Ohio's "All-Other" expenditures look higher, on a dollar and percentage basis, and conversely make Ohio's other categories look lower, on a percentage basis, relative to other states that don't follow similar practices.

(m) Fiscal 2013 expenditures are revised to more accurately reflect actual expenditures, primarily in Medicaid, Corrections, Transportation, and "All Other State Expenditures."

(n) Regarding premium revenue: fiscal 2013 totals $302 million, fiscal 2014 totals $322 million, and fiscal 2015 totals $323 million. Certified Public Expenditures—Local Fund from Hospitals: fiscal 2013 totals $378 million, fiscal 2014 totals $120 million, and fiscal 2015 totals $124 million. Nursing Home Tax:

fiscal 2013 totals $83 million, fiscal 2014 totals $84 million, and fiscal 2015 totals $107 million. ICF/MR 6 percent Gross Receipts Tax: fiscal 2013 totals $14 million, fiscal 2014 totals $12 million, and fiscal 2015 totals $11 million. Intergovernmental Transfers: fiscal 2013 totals $70 million, fiscal 2014 totals $100 million, and fiscal 2015 totals $100 million. Tennessee collects personal income tax on income from dividends on stocks and interest on certain bonds. Tax revenue estimates do not include federal funds and other departmental revenues. However, federal funds and other departmental revenues are included in the budget as funding sources for the general fund, along with state tax revenues.

(o) Expenditures of operating and capital budgets include expendable revenue funds and accounts, but do not include any expenditures of local property tax revenue.

(p) The breakdown of local funds, etc. included in Other State Funds is as follows for fiscal 2013: provider tax $148,638,656; employee assessment $11,886,600; local match provided by schools $17,758,156; tobacco litigation settlement funds $31,343,693; other $124,012,725. The breakdown is as follows for fiscal 2014: provider tax $140,255,562; employee assessment $12,995,400; local match provided by schools $19,206,889; tobacco litigation settlement funds $35,975,693, other $123,177,964. The breakdown is as follows for estimated fiscal 2015: provider tax $143,454,419; employee assessment $15,640,000; local match provided by schools $20,649,819; tobacco litigation settlement funds $33,031,032, other $122,650,110.

(q) Part of Wyoming's yearly variation in expenditure totals is due to the fact that the state budget is on a two-year cycle.

State and Local Governments Reshape Their Finances

By Don Boyd and Lucy Dadayan

State and local governments have been reshaping their finances since the Great Recession. They have been struggling with three major sources of fiscal stress: slow tax revenue growth, growth in pension contributions that has been heavily concentrated in a few states, and Medicaid spending growth driven by recession-related enrollment. In 37 states, pension contributions plus state-funded Medicaid grew by more than state and local government tax revenue between 2007 and 2014, in real per-capita terms. In response to these strains, state and local governments have cut infrastructure investment, slashed support for higher education, cut spending on K–12 education, cut spending on social benefits other than Medicaid, reduced administrative staff and reduced most other areas of the budget.

Introduction

State and local governments have been remaking their finances since the Great Recession, doing less of many traditional activities so that they can do more of what they must do. They have been struggling with three major sources of fiscal stress: slow tax revenue growth, growth in pension contributions that has been heavily concentrated in a few states, and Medicaid spending growth driven by recession-related enrollment. Some states have been unscathed by one or more of these forces, but in combination their effect has been substantial for most. In 37 states, pension contributions plus state-funded Medicaid

grew by more than state and local government tax revenue between 2007 and 2014, in real per-capita terms. In response to these strains, state and local governments have cut infrastructure investment, slashed support for higher education, cut social benefits other than Medicaid, cut spending on K–12 education, reduced administrative staff and reduced most other areas of the budget.

The near-term outlook is dour. Tax revenue is likely to grow slowly, pension contributions almost certainly will increase substantially and forecasters anticipate that the state share of Medicaid will

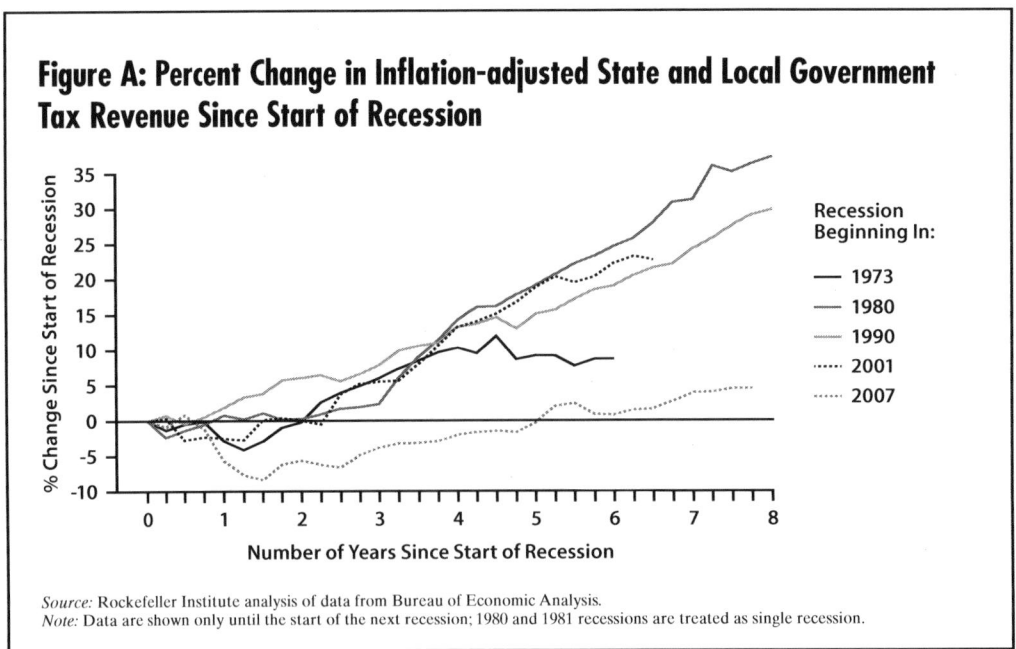

Figure A: Percent Change in Inflation-adjusted State and Local Government Tax Revenue Since Start of Recession

Recession Beginning In:
— 1973
— 1980
— 1990
······ 2001
······ 2007

Source: Rockefeller Institute analysis of data from Bureau of Economic Analysis.
Note: Data are shown only until the start of the next recession; 1980 and 1981 recessions are treated as single recession.

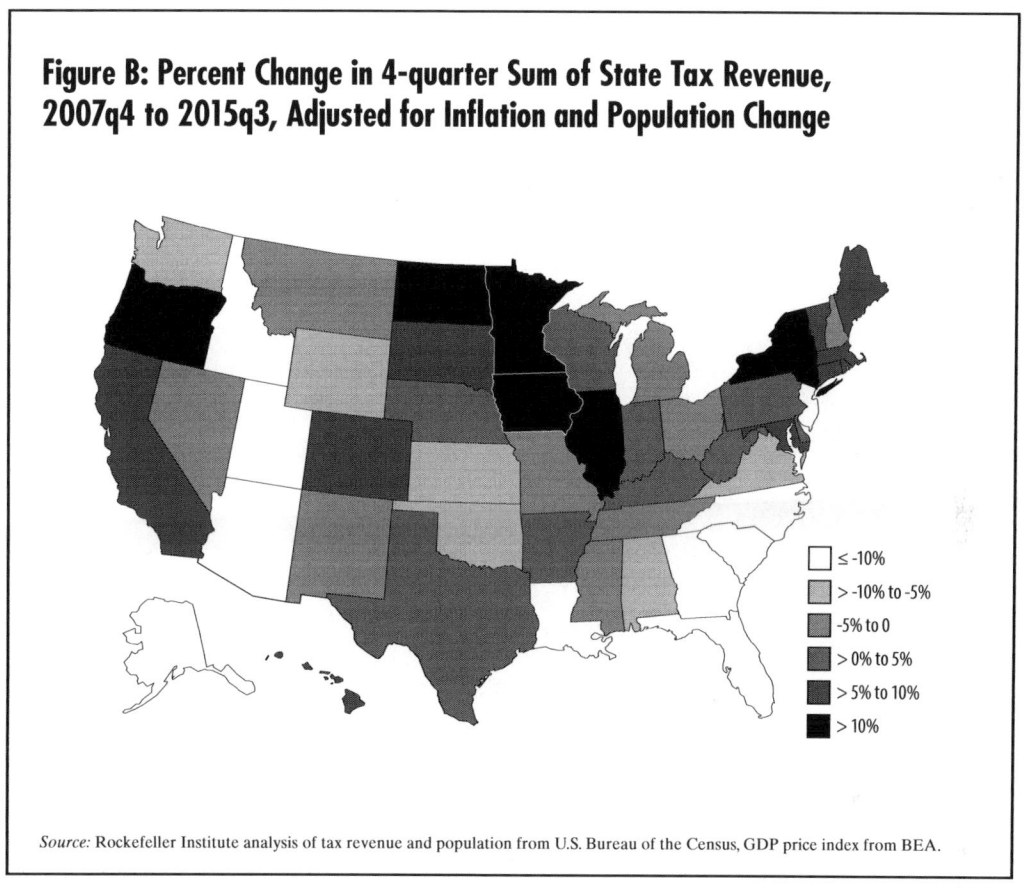

Figure B: Percent Change in 4-quarter Sum of State Tax Revenue, 2007q4 to 2015q3, Adjusted for Inflation and Population Change

Legend:
- ≤ -10%
- > -10% to -5%
- -5% to 0
- > 0% to 5%
- > 5% to 10%
- > 10%

Source: Rockefeller Institute analysis of tax revenue and population from U.S. Bureau of the Census, GDP price index from BEA.

continue to grow faster than the economy. This suggests that many states will struggle to fund desired programs. As always, conditions vary greatly across states. Oil-patch states are suffering devastating revenue declines and several states face extreme pension problems, but some states are relatively unstressed.

Three Major Sources of Stress: Taxes, Pensions and Medicaid

State and local government tax revenue has grown far more slowly than it has following prior recessions. Nearly eight years after the start of the recession, inflation-adjusted tax revenue is only 4.5 percent above the pre-recession level, compared to about 37 percent after the 1980 recession, 30 percent after the 1990 recession and 23 percent after the 2001 recession.[1] (See Figure A.)

The main reasons for weak tax revenue relative to past recessions are (1) the drop in revenue at the start of this recession was much larger than

previous declines, (2) the economic recovery has been slow and (3) states have had little appetite for tax increases. We have discussed these issues in depth elsewhere.[2]

State government tax revenue has been hit harder than local government revenue because many states rely especially heavily on economically sensitive personal income and sales taxes. The extent of weakness varies greatly. In 25 states, inflation-adjusted per capita state government tax revenue remains below its level at the start of the recession, particularly in the Southeast and the Southwest—many of these states suffered greatly from the real estate bust and also have been reluctant to raise taxes. Revenue is up more than 10 percent in six states, and more than 5 percent in 15 states; revenue growth has been strongest among states where the economic recovery has been strong and among states willing to increase taxes (Figure B). Real per capita state tax revenue rose by more than $100 in only 16 states.

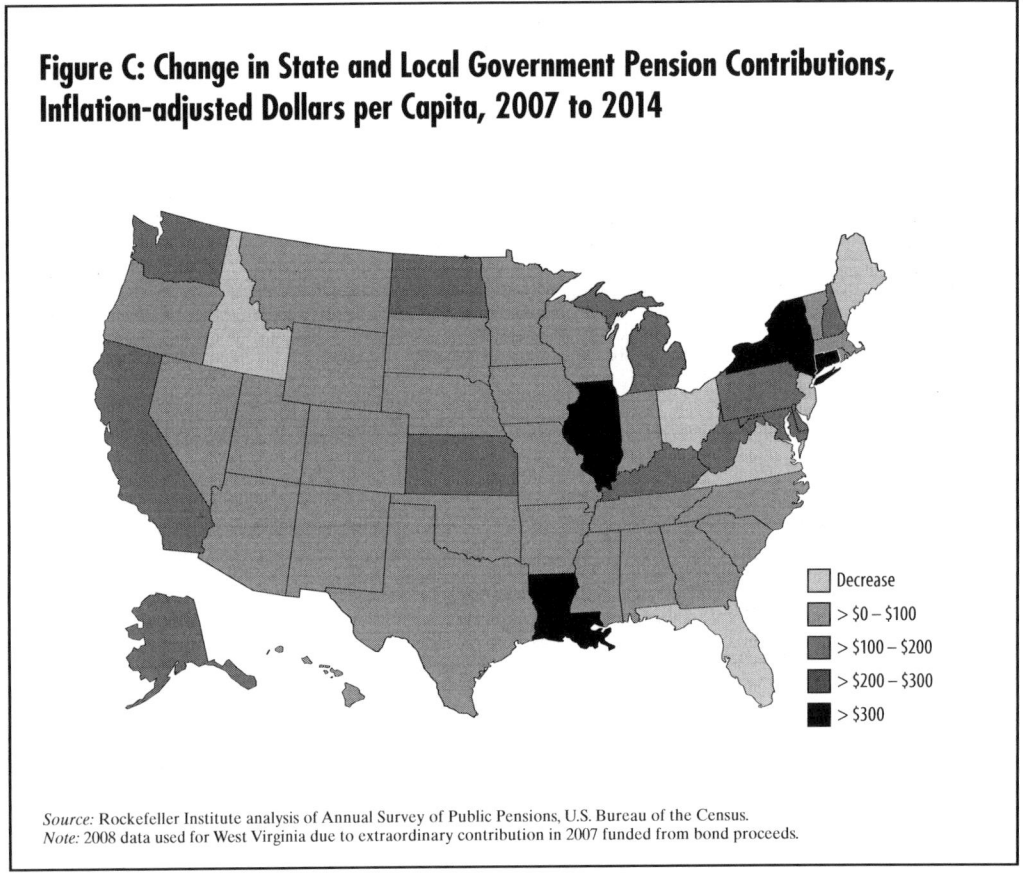

Figure C: Change in State and Local Government Pension Contributions, Inflation-adjusted Dollars per Capita, 2007 to 2014

Decrease
\> $0 – $100
\> $100 – $200
\> $200 – $300
\> $300

Source: Rockefeller Institute analysis of Annual Survey of Public Pensions, U.S. Bureau of the Census.
Note: 2008 data used for West Virginia due to extraordinary contribution in 2007 funded from bond proceeds.

Extraordinary Growth in Pension Contributions in Some States

Pension contributions historically have been a relatively small share of state budgets and until recently had not been a major source of fiscal stress. In 2007, contributions were 5.8 percent of state and local government tax revenue and were only 3.3 percent of total general expenditures. Pension contributions are essentially "must do" expenditures: Most public pensions have strong legal protections and if pension funds become underfunded, state and local governments must eventually make up the shortfalls. These catch-up contributions are particularly painful because they purchase no new services—they are needed to pay for services delivered years in the past.

Pension contributions for the United States as a whole have been driven up dramatically since the recession, primarily because of pension fund investment shortfalls. Between fiscal years 2007 and 2014, inflation-adjusted state and local government annual pension contributions increased by $39 billion, or 46.9 percent. This amounted to 92 percent of the growth in state and local government inflation-adjusted tax revenue over this period.

Pension contribution increases have been very uneven. Real per capita expenditures rose by more than $300 in four states (Connecticut, Illinois, Louisiana and New York), accounting for nearly half of the national contribution increase. Contributions rose by $100 to $200 in 12 states (no states were between $200 and $300), and increased by less than $100 in 35 states (including declines in six states) (Figure C). Thus, the extent to which pension contributions have caused fiscal stress varies greatly.

Higher Medicaid Spending Driven by Recession-related Enrollment Growth

State-financed Medicaid expenditures have risen by $37 billion, or 23 percent, since 2008 after adjusting for inflation. Most of this increase was driven by recession-related rises in enrollment that have not been reversed. Between 2008 and 2011 enrollment rose by 18.5 percent, compared to an increase of only 2.9 percent over the prior three-year period. While states can choose how generous their Medicaid programs will be, both in terms of populations and services covered, within those parameters Medicaid is essentially an entitlement, and the costs of enrollment increases must be funded unless policies are changed.

Table A: Medicaid Expenditures and Enrollment Before, During and After the Great Recession

Federal fiscal years	Enrollment (millions)	Expenditures: billions of 2015$		
		Total	Federal	State
2005	46.3	$357.6	$204.7	$152.9
2008	47.7	368.5	210.3	158.3
2011	56.5	431.8	275.2	156.6
2013	58.9	442.6	254.3	188.3
2015	70.1	524.5	329.3	195.2
		% change		
2005 to 2008	2.9%	3.1%	2.7%	3.5%
2008 to 2011	18.5	17.2	30.9	-1.1
2011 to 2013	4.3	2.5	-7.6	20.3
2013 to 2015	19.0	18.5	29.5	3.7
Post recession: 2008 to 2015	47.1	42.3	56.6	23.4
		% change		
2005 to 2008	1.3	$10.9	$5.6	$5.4
2008 to 2011	8.8	63.2	64.9	(1.7)
2011 to 2013	2.4	10.8	(20.9)	31.7
2013 to 2015	11.2	81.9	75.0	6.9
Post recession: 2008 to 2015	22.4	156.0	119.0	37.0

Sources: Centers for Medicare and Medicaid Services (exependitures), MACPAC (enrollment), Bureau of Economic Analysis (GDP price index).

Note: Enrollment is average monthly enrollment for the federal fiscal year. Enrollment for 2015 estimated by authors.

States were protected initially from the costs of recession-related enrollment increases by the federal stimulus program, the American Recovery and Reinvestment Act, or ARRA. However, ARRA provided only temporary support to states, and as that support was removed, states had to replace lost federal funds. Although enrollment rose by only 4.3 percent between 2011 and 2013, state

inflation-adjusted expenditures rose by 20.3 percent while federal expenditures declined by 7.6 percent. (See Table A.)

After 2013, enrollment began to rise in large part because of newly eligible enrollees in states opting into Medicaid expansion under the Affordable Care Act, or ACA. Enrollment rose by an estimated 19 percent between 2013 and 2015.[3] These enrollment increases had little impact on state finances because the federal government picked up new costs in expansion states. Thus, between 2013 and 2015, state-financed Medicaid spending increased by only 3.7 percent even though federal spending increased by 29.5 percent (adjusted for inflation). In fact, inflation-adjusted state-financed Medicaid spending was up only 1.3 percent in expansion states, and was up 10.3 percent in non-expansion states.

Figure D maps the change in Medicaid spending per capita, adjusted for inflation, between 2008, before recession-related enrollment increases were substantial, and 2015.[4] Spending increased in 45 states and was up by $73 per capita in the median state, but the range was great. Two of the nation's most populous states had large increases. California's increase in Medicaid spending of $234 per capita requires taxpayers to pay $9 billion more than in 2008, given the state's population of approximately 39 million.[5] Texas' increase of $142 per capita amounts to almost $3.9 billion more annually given the state's population of 27.5 million. By contrast, Medicaid spending increased by less than $50 per capita in 21 states, presumably causing relatively little fiscal stress in those states.

Net effect: Tax Revenue Growth has not Kept up with Pension Contribution and Medicaid Increases

These three sources of stress have cramped the ability of state and local governments to finance other services. State and local governments' inflation-adjusted spending on pension contributions and state-funded Medicaid increased by a combined $73 billion between 2007 and 2014, while state and local government tax revenue increased by only $42 billion[6] (Table B). These difficult-to-avoid spending increases were nearly twice as great as tax revenue increases, leading state and local governments to cut elsewhere in their budgets.

Figure E shows the net impact by state. Because state tax revenue data were available for 2014 but local revenue data were not, we estimated local government tax revenue to obtain state and local tax revenue for each state.[7, 8] Different states have

Figure D: Change in Per-capita State-funded Medicaid Expenditures, 2008 to 2015, Adjusted for Inflation, in 2015 Dollars

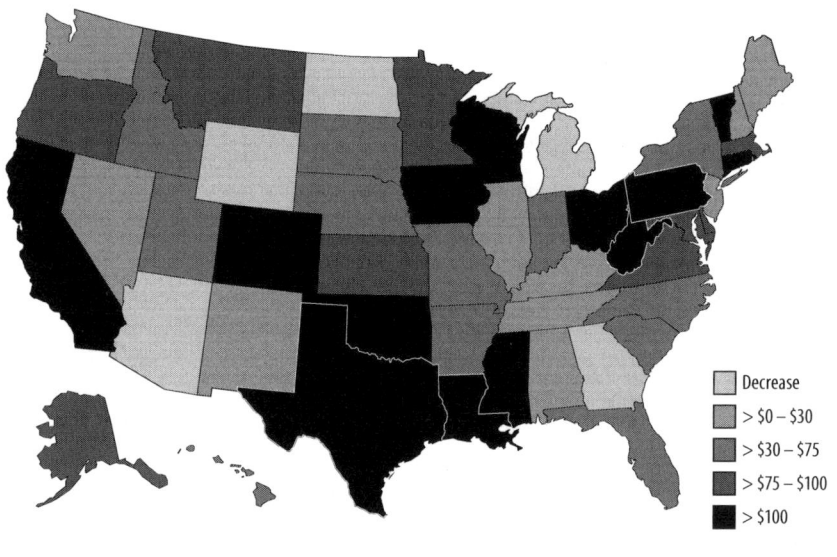

Decrease
> $0 – $30
> $30 – $75
> $75 – $100
> $100

Source: Rockefeller Institute analysis of data from CMS (Medicaid). Census (population), and BEA (GDP price index).

been affected in different ways. For example, 15 states had inflation-adjusted per capita pension contribution increases of more than $100, 20 states had state-funded Medicaid increases of more than $100, and 24 states had declines in state and local tax revenue of $100 or more. In combination, the effect has been widespread and substantial. In 37 states pension contributions plus state-funded Medicaid have grown by more than state and local government tax revenue (Figure E).

Table B: Pension Contributions, Medicaid and Taxes: Before and After the Recession (Billions of 2014$)

	2007	2014	$ change	% change	$ change as % of change in taxes
Pension contributions—state and local	$82.4	$121.1	$36.6	46.9%	91.8%
Medicaid state share (mostly paid by states)	151.2	185.4	34.2	22.6%	81.3%
Pensions plus Medicaid	233.6	306.4	72.9	31.2%	173.1%
Taxes—state and local	$1,475.4	$1,517.5	$42.1	2.9%	

Notes and Sources: Pension contributions: data are for pension fund fiscal year; source is Census Bureau Annual Survey of Public Pensions. Medicaid state-share: data are for federal fiscal year; source is Centers for Medicare and Medicaid Services. Taxes state and local: data are for calendar year; source is Bureau of Economic Analysis, NIPA Table 3.3. All values are adjusted to 2014 dollars using the gross domestic price index from BEA.

Figure E: Change in Real Per-capita State-local Taxes from 2007 to 2014 Minus Change in Pension Contributions Plus State-financed Medicaid, in 2014 Dollars

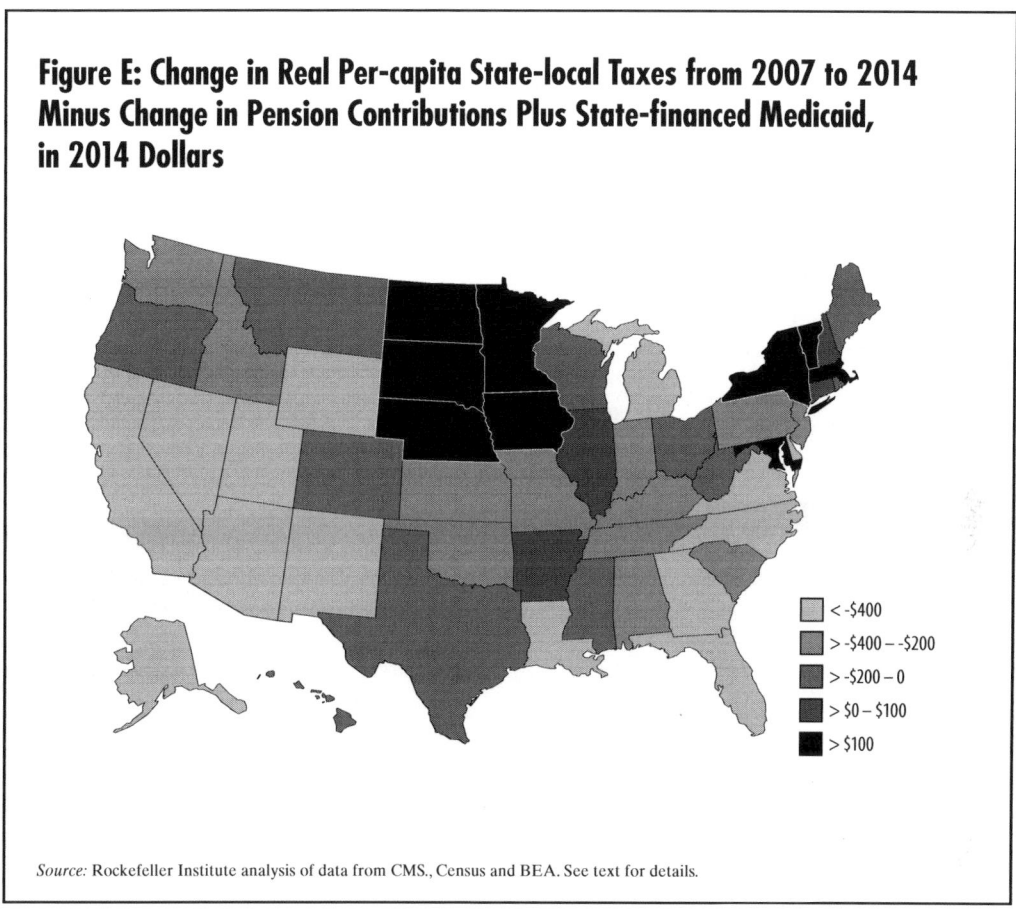

Legend:
- < -$400
- > -$400 – -$200
- > -$200 – 0
- > $0 – $100
- > $100

Source: Rockefeller Institute analysis of data from CMS., Census and BEA. See text for details.

States Face Different Stresses

Louisiana faced difficulty in all three areas; pension contributions and state-funded Medicaid both increased by more than twice the United States average, while tax revenue declined by more than $500 per capita. Alaska, too, faced difficulty in all three areas.

By contrast, in Florida pension contributions did not increase and Medicaid spending increases were far below the U.S. average; however, tax revenue is below pre-recession levels (as Figure B showed for state government taxes). As a result, pension contributions plus Medicaid spending increased by more than taxes in that state. Although Florida governments in aggregate have less inflation-adjusted revenue per capita than before the recession, this may be exactly what political leaders want. It does not necessarily mean that the state is stressed, but it does mean that cuts in spending have been needed to keep spending within available resources.

In Illinois, tax revenue growth outstripped growth in pension contributions plus Medicaid because the state enacted very large tax increases. Tax revenue grew by more than pensions plus Medicaid in New York even though New York had the second-highest pension contribution increase in the nation (after Illinois), because Medicaid growth was slow and tax revenue was strong.

Some states have not experienced stress by these measures, particularly the oil patch states, because the tax data do not reflect their tax revenue declines. Unfortunately, their situation is worsening.

How Governments have Responded— The Reshaping of State and Local Government Finance

State and local governments have responded to sharply constrained resources not by raising taxes (with some exceptions), but by slashing capital spending and cutting many other areas sharply. The

Bureau of Economic Analysis develops estimates of annual state and local government expenditures. These expenditures include amounts spent from state and local governments' own funds as well as amounts spent from federal funds or financed by bonds. We have arranged these expenditures into four broad categories:

- Consumption expenditures, which include spending on critical current activities such as education, public safety, public health, income security, and parks and recreation.[9]

- Social benefit spending, which includes Medicaid spending (including spending from federal funds) and other social program spending.

- Net investment spending, which includes gross investment (actual outlays) on capital projects such as highway and water infrastructure, school buildings and power projects, reduced by an estimate of the amount of capital that was consumed or used up by wear and tear, economic obsolescence, and other factors. (Consumption of capital is a non-cash expenditure.) In concept, net investment spending is the amount actually added to state and local government capital stock above and beyond what is needed to make up for wear and tear and obsolescence.

- All other expenditures, amounting to less than 10 percent of the total. This includes interest payments among other things.

In the tables that follow, we examine how inflation-adjusted state and local government spending changed between 2009 and 2014. We begin with 2009 because that was the peak recession-related year—it takes time for elected officials to change policies in response to a shock such as the Great Recession, and policy responses play out over several years. We end with 2014 because that is the latest year available. We convert all numbers to 2014 dollars using the gross domestic product price index so that they are on the same basis as most other data in this chapter.[10]

Table C shows that total state and local government expenditures, as measured by the Bureau of Economic Analysis, were down by 2.9 percent between 2009 and 2014. Medicaid expenditures were up 21.5 percent, and capital used up or "consumed" (a non-cash expenditure) also increased, but all other major categories decreased. Gross investment—that is, the amount actually spent on capital— was down 16 percent. And because gross investment in 2014 was only slightly more than the capital that was used up, state and local governments added 49 percent less to their capital stock in 2014 than they did in 2009.

We examine several of these areas in more detail below.

Cuts in Infrastructure Spending

State and local government net investment fell as a share of the gross domestic product from the late 1960s through the early 1980s after the buildout of the national highway system, then was relatively stable for about 20 years before falling after the 2001 recession and plunging after the Great Recession. It is now at its lowest point in more than 50 years (Figure F).

The available data do not allow us to examine changes in *net* investment by category, but they do allow us to examine *gross* investment. Table D shows that every major category of investment was down between 2009 and 2014. The largest dollar decline was in education, reflecting reductions in construction of education buildings. Spending

Table C: State and Local Government Inflation-adjusted Total Expenditures (Billions of 2014$)

	2009	2014	Change	% change
Total expenditures	$2,563.3	$2,487.8	($75.5)	-2.9%
Consumption expenditures	1,639.5	1,601.0	(38.5)	-2.4
Medicaid (including federal share)	401.3	487.4	86.1	21.5
Other social benefit spending	134.1	122.5	(11.6)	-8.7
Net investment	168.3	85.2	(83.1)	-49.4
Gross investment in infrastructure, buildings, other capital	394.6	331.3	(63.3)	-16.0
Less: Consumption of fixed capital	226.3	246.1	19.8	8.7
All other expenditures	220.1	191.7	(28.4)	-12.9

Source: U.S. Bureau of Economic Analysis.
Note: All items adjusted by gross domestic product price index, not expenditure-specific indexes.

Figure F: State and Local Government Net Investment as Percent of Gross Domestic Product

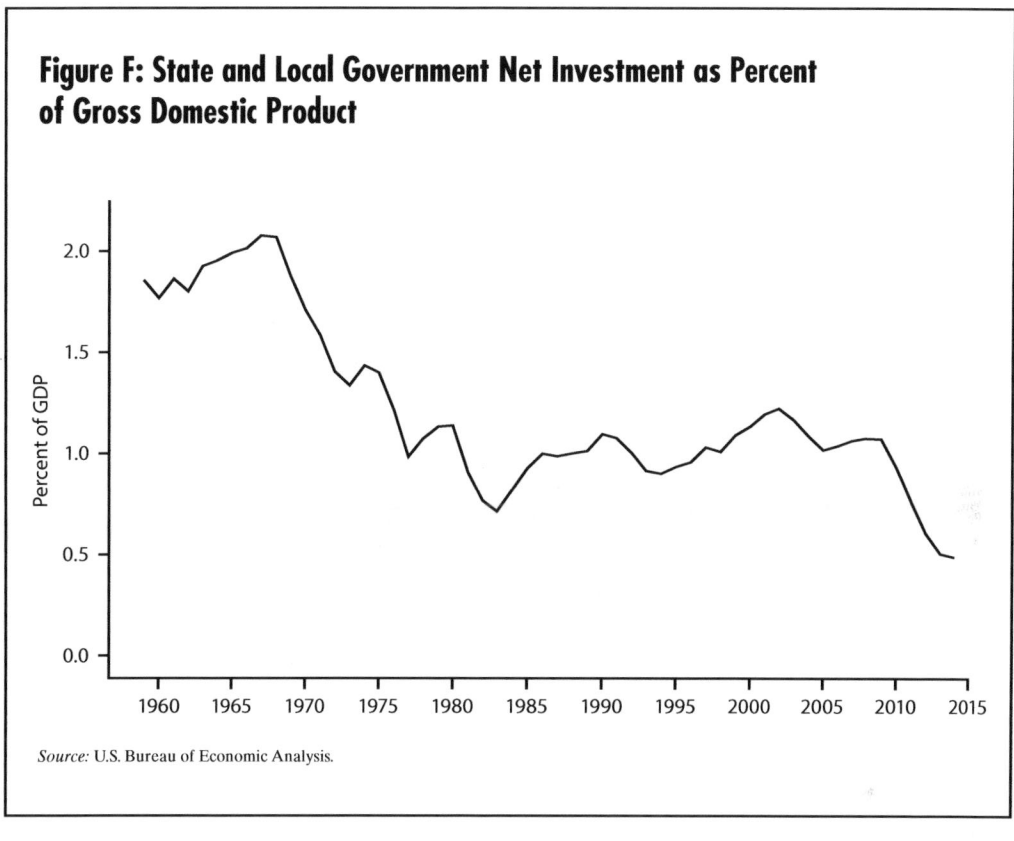

Percent of GDP

Source: U.S. Bureau of Economic Analysis.

on water and sewer systems, public safety, and most other categories was down by double-digit percentages. The most notable exception was transportation investment spending, which was down by 4.1 percent, much less than most categories.

The U.S. Census Bureau collects capital expenditure data for each state; the most recent year for these data is 2013, making it possible to determine which states have cut total capital expenditures the most. As Figure G shows, capital expenditure cuts have been widespread and real per capita spending is down in 43 states. Spending was down by more than $100 per capita in 33 states. It is not possible to know from these data the extent to which individual states have cut spending on traditional infrastructure, such as highways, transit, and water and sewer systems, versus spending on school buildings, office buildings and other purposes that are not traditional inventory assets.

Table D: State and Local Government Inflation-adjusted Gross Investment (Billions of 2014$)

	2009	2014	Change	% change
Gross investment	$394.6	$331.3	($63.3)	-16.0%
Education	90.0	61.0	(29.0)	-32.2
Water & sewer systems	41.2	33.6	(7.6)	-18.4
Office	23.2	17.7	(5.5)	-23.5
Transportation total	110.7	106.1	(4.6)	-4.1
Highways and streets	87.4	83.5	(3.9)	-4.5
Other transportation	23.3	22.6	(0.7)	-2.8
Public safety	5.1	3.3	(1.8)	-35.4
Health care	6.6	5.6		-15.5
Amusement and recreation	8.4	5.3	(3.1)	-36.7
Power	12.2	9.7	(2.5)	-20.3
Equipment, intellectual property	87.1	80.3	(6.8)	-7.8
All other	10.2	8.7	(1.5)	-14.8

Source: U.S. Bureau of Economic Analysis.
Note: All items adjusted by gross domestic product price index, not expenditure-specific indexes.

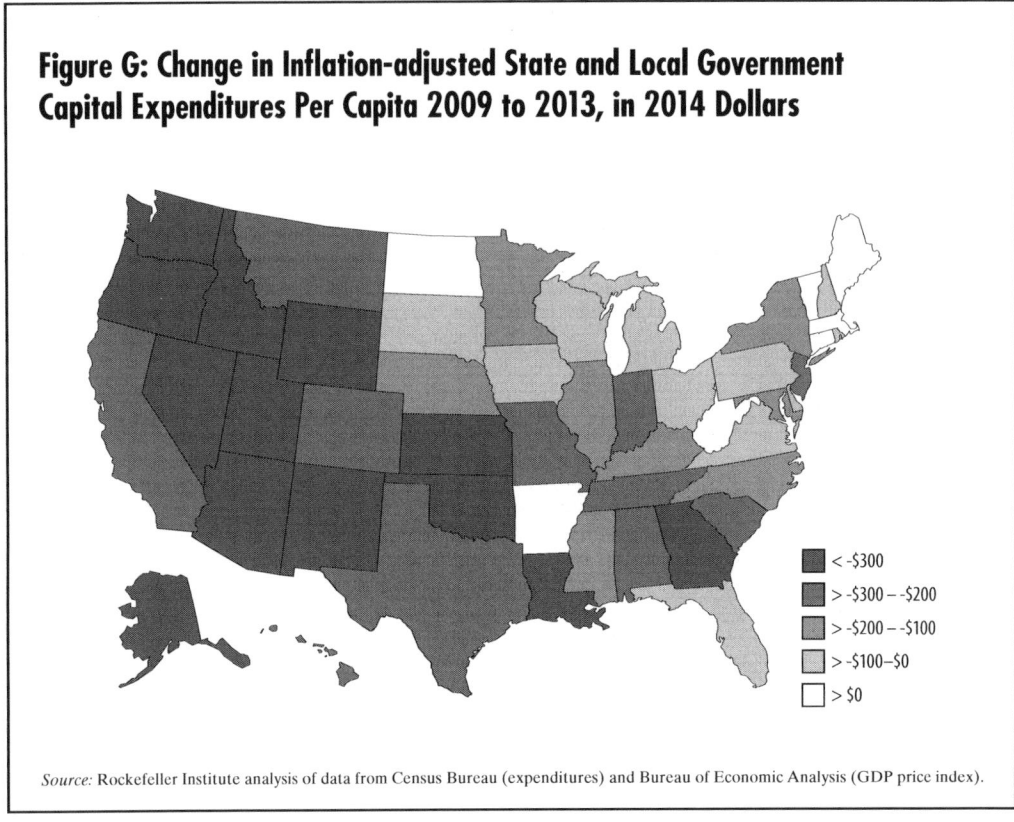

Figure G: Change in Inflation-adjusted State and Local Government Capital Expenditures Per Capita 2009 to 2013, in 2014 Dollars

Legend:
- < -$300
- > -$300 – -$200
- > -$200 – -$100
- > -$100–$0
- > $0

Source: Rockefeller Institute analysis of data from Census Bureau (expenditures) and Bureau of Economic Analysis (GDP price index).

Cuts in Consumption and Social Benefit Spending

States have cut consumption spending, although not by as much as capital spending. Table E shows that the largest cuts in dollar terms have been in education. However, several of the largest cuts in percentage terms have been in categories that tend to include assistance for the needy, such as income security and housing and community service.

Cuts in Higher Education Support

Higher education is often called the "balance wheel" of state budgets—when times are bad, states cut support substantially and when times are good,

Table E: State and Local Government Inflation-adjusted Consumption Expenditures (Billions of 2014$)

	2009	2014	Change	% change
State & local government consumption expenditures, total	$1,639.5	$1,601.0	($38.5)	-2.4%
Education	768.8	754.9	(13.9)	-1.8
Public safety	306.1	301.9	(4.2)	-1.4
Economic affairs	183.3	182.9	(0.4)	-0.2
General public service	189.8	181.9	(7.9)	-4.2
Income security	81.7	76.8	(4.9)	-6.0
Net health expenditures; excludes Medicaid	67.9	63.6	(4.3)	-6.4
Recreation & culture	32.0	29.7	(2.3)	-7.1
Housing and community service	10.0	9.3	(0.7)	-7.0

Source: U.S. Bureau of Economic Analysis.
Note: All items adjusted by gross domestic product price index, not expenditure-specific indexes.

Figure H: Trends in Non-mortgage Balances, Debt Balance Composition

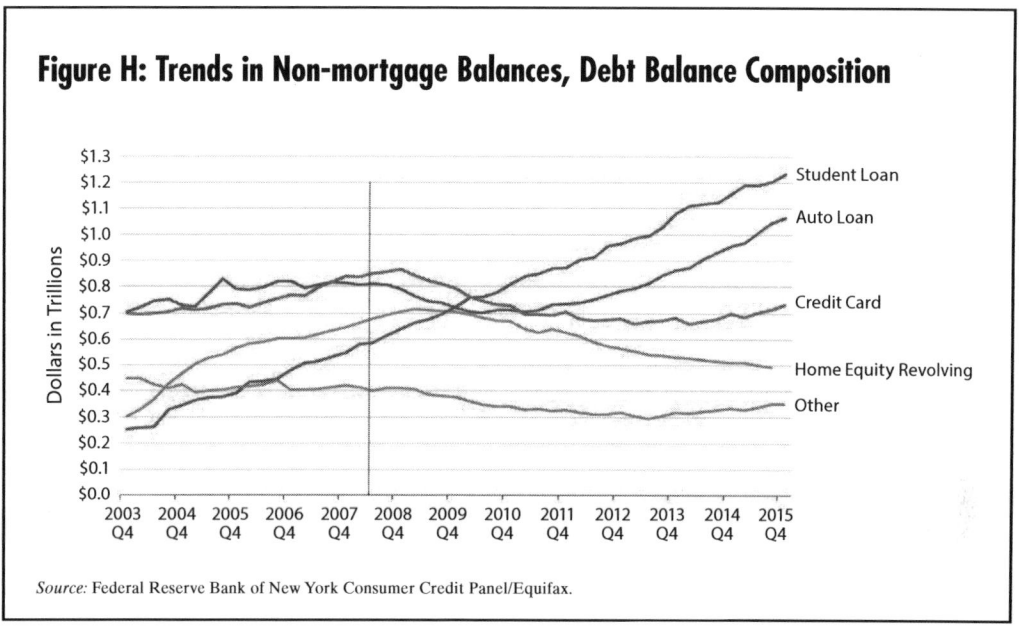

Source: Federal Reserve Bank of New York Consumer Credit Panel/Equifax.

they increase support. States do this in part because there is another major source of revenue—tuition—that institutions or states can raise in response.[11] Because enrollment has been rising over most of the last two decades, cuts per full-time enrolled student, or FTE, have been large, while restorations per FTE have been muted.

In response to the Great Recession, almost every state substantially cut funding for higher education.

For the United States as a whole, inflation-adjusted state appropriations per FTE declined by 17.6 percent between the peak year of 2008 and 2014 (see Table F, which also provides data for periods before the recession). These cuts were widespread and deep. Of the 47 states that cut inflation-adjusted appropriations per FTE, 40 cut funding by more than 10 percent, 32 cut by more than 20 percent, and eight states cut by more than 30 percent[12] (Table G).

Table F: Higher Education Enrollment and Inflation-adjusted Per-FTE Revenues Before, During and After the Great Recession

| State FY | FTE enrollment (millions) | 2014$ per FTE | | | Net tuition as % of total education revenues |
		Educational appropriations	Net tuition	Total educational revenues	
2000	8.605	$8,000	$3,309	$11,308	29.3%
2005	9.896	7,145	4,047	11,154	36.3
2008	10.254	7,956	4,413	12,328	35.8
2011	11.644	6,708	4,941	11,597	42.6
2014	11.138	6,552	5,777	12,266	47.1
		% change			Change in %
2000 to 2005	15.0	(10.7)	22.3	(1.4)	7.0
2005 to 2008	3.6	11.4	9.0	10.5	(0.5)
2008 to 2011	13.6	(15.7)	12.0	(5.9)	6.8
2011 to 2014	(4.4)	(2.3)	16.9	5.8	4.5
Post-recession:					
2008 to 2014	8.6	(17.6)	30.9	(0.5)	11.3

Source: State Higher Education Executive Officers.
Note: Adjusted for inflation using gross domestic product price index.

Higher education institutions and states responded by raising tuition. For the United States as a whole, inflation adjusted net tuition per student increased from $4,413 in 2008 to $5,777 in 2014, or 30.9 percent. Of the 47 states that increased inflation-adjusted tuition per FTE, 44 increased tuition by more than 10 percent, 37 increased it by more than 20 percent and 25 states increased tuition by more than 30 percent.

Appropriation cuts and tuition increases have shifted costs from states to students; between 2008 and 2014, the tuition share of education revenue increased from 35.8 percent to 47.1 percent (Table F). This was part of a longer term trend—back in 2000, the tuition share of education revenue was only 29.3 percent. Tuition increases have made higher education more difficult to afford and potentially have reduced access. In addition, tuition increases have not kept up fully with appropriation cuts. Total education revenue is down slightly since 2008, potentially jeopardizing education quality. In fact, costs of higher education have been increasing more rapidly than overall prices in the economy, so institutions are able to buy less with a dollar now than they could previously.[13] Public higher education institutions in many states cut full-time faculty positions, eliminated course offerings, and reduced library and computer lab services, among other service reductions. These cuts diminish the quality of education and the potential quality of the workforce, which in return can have a negative impact on longer-term economic growth.

Tuition increases also have contributed to increases in student loans, which nearly doubled between 2008 and 2014, from about $600 billion to nearly $1.2 trillion, and student loans outstanding now surpass all other types of non-mortgage debt (See Figure H).

Cuts in K–12 Education Spending

A majority of states have cut K–12 spending in response to the Great Recession. For the United States as a whole, inflation-adjusted per pupil K–12 spending from state, local and federal sources combined declined by 6.2 percent between 2008 and 2013, in contrast to more than 20 percent growth between 2000 and 2008 before the Great Recession (Table H). Overall, 33 states cut inflation-adjusted per pupil spending between 2008 and 2013, 10 of which cut funding by more than 10 percent (Table I). Most of the states that cut per pupil K–12 spending are in the South or the West.

Table G: Percent Change in Enrollment and Inflation-adjusted Per-FTE Revenue Sources, 2008 to 2014

State	FTE enrllmt.	Educ. approps.	Net tuition	Total education revenues
United States	8.6	(17.6)	30.9	(0.5)
Florida	12.5	(30.7)	29.8	(17.2)
Louisiana	1.3	(39.6)	53.9	(16.9)
Mississippi	11.5	(22.5)	(3.2)	(15.7)
Massachusetts	16.4	(21.9)	(6.1)	(15.6)
Nevada	1.9	(29.7)	37.4	(14.6)
Idaho....................	27.8	(32.4)	71.0	(12.3)
Missouri	19.9	(26.7)	11.6	(11.1)
Hawaii..................	14.0	(23.6)	42.0	(9.4)
North Carolina......	12.5	(20.5)	33.3	(8.0)
South Carolina	14.4	(35.5)	29.2	(6.8)
Texas	23.6	(13.4)	6.1	(6.7)
Kentucky	8.7	(23.3)	22.0	(6.6)
Connecticut	15.0	(25.2)	24.0	(5.8)
Utah	15.8	(24.5)	32.7	(5.4)
Arizona................	15.7	(34.7)	50.1	(4.9)
California	0.3	(13.6)	49.0	(4.9)
Oklahoma.............	10.8	(20.1)	31.2	(3.9)
Wyoming	8.4	(3.8)	(2.7)	(3.8)
Pennsylvania	4.6	(36.4)	20.9	(3.7)
New Jersey	15.2	(27.2)	25.7	(3.0)
Ohio.....................	6.9	(22.3)	14.1	(2.7)
Oregon.................	27.7	(28.3)	26.4	(2.6)
Tennessee	9.7	(21.7)	40.2	(1.5)
Maryland	12.3	(11.1)	10.7	(1.3)
West Virginia........	3.6	(24.7)	31.6	(1.1)
Kansas	8.8	(17.2)	22.2	(0.9)
Alabama	4.6	(37.9)	59.4	0.5
Georgia................	11.9	(21.9)	92.4	0.9
Wisconsin	2.2	(16.9)	31.7	1.2
Minnesota.............	4.1	(22.8)	32.2	1.3
Virginia................	12.8	(25.0)	33.2	2.2
New Mexico	15.8	(22.6)	223.0	2.2
Arkansas..............	11.3	(4.3)	21.0	2.4
Washington...........	10.7	(24.0)	64.5	2.4
Montana	11.0	(3.6)	9.3	2.8
Vermont................	5.8	(9.6)	7.6	3.2
New Hampshire ...	12.1	(32.2)	18.2	3.3
Maine...................	2.9	(11.4)	19.4	4.0
Iowa	10.8	(19.6)	31.2	4.9
New York..............	7.5	(3.2)	27.3	6.0
Rhode Island........	3.9	(22.8)	27.0	6.4
Nebraska	5.6	(4.1)	34.4	8.6
Alaska..................	9.4	7.4	13.4	8.9
Indiana................	8.1	(2.9)	20.8	9.6
Michigan..............	1.2	(21.7)	35.5	11.0
South Dakota	13.8	(17.9)	45.5	11.2
Delaware	12.8	(23.2)	37.3	13.5
Colorado..............	12.3	(26.4)	49.1	16.6
North Dakota.......	5.6	39.7	12.2	25.5
Illinois.................	(16.6)	52.5	92.3	60.7

Source: State Higher Education Executive Officers (SHEEO).

Figure I: Percent Change in State and Local Government Employment, Fiscal Years 2009 to 2015

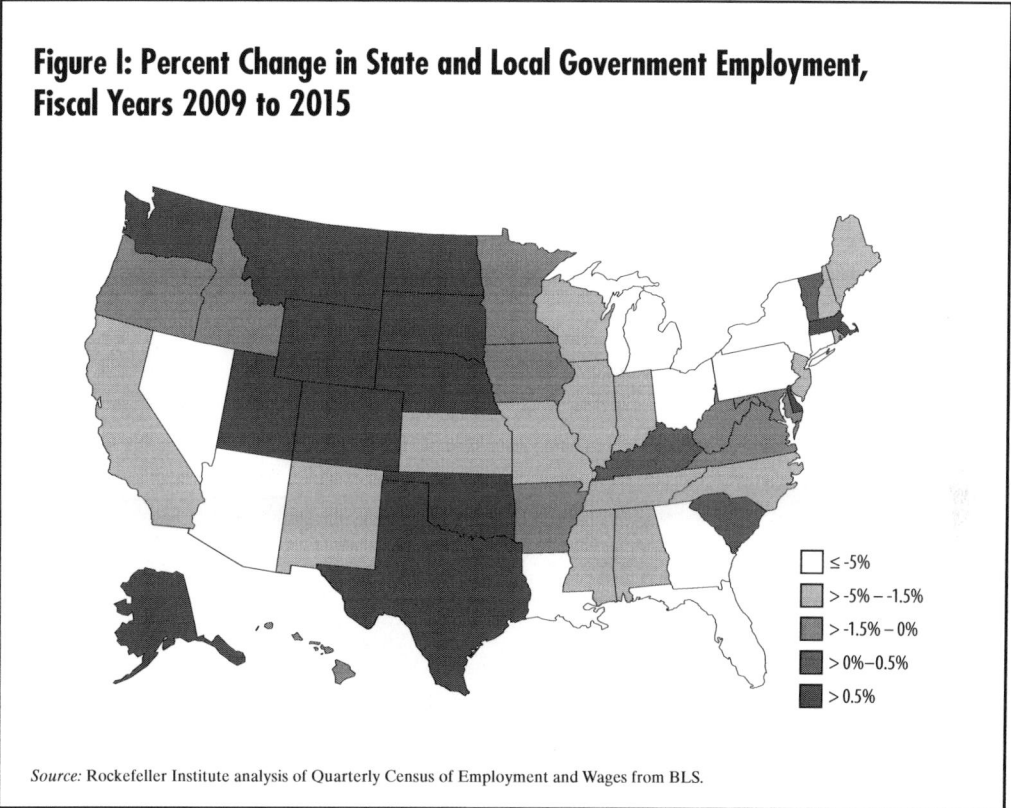

☐	≤ -5%
▨	> -5% – -1.5%
▨	> -1.5% – 0%
▨	> 0% – 0.5%
■	> 0.5%

Source: Rockefeller Institute analysis of Quarterly Census of Employment and Wages from BLS.

Despite post-recession economic growth, many states have continued to cut funding for K–12 education.[14] States' cuts in K–12 funding have been driven by factors including state efforts to close budget shortfalls, rising costs, reduction in federal education aid and other state policy choices.[15] The cuts in K–12 education spending have resulted in layoffs of more recently hired teachers, larger class sizes, cuts in instructional and non-instructional services, cuts in professional development for teachers and staff, among other service reductions. While the cuts may help states to close the budget shortfalls, they could result in diminished educational outcomes and a less qualified workforce for the future.

Workforce Changes

As we have discussed elsewhere, state and local governments cut employment considerably in response to the Great Recession, unlike most prior recessions when employ-

Table H: K–12 Enrollment and Inflation-adjusted Expenditures Before, During and After the Great Recession

		2013$	
School year	Fall enrollment (millions)	K–12 expenditures ($ billions)	K–12 per pupil expenditures
2000	46.857	$498.60	$10,714
2005	48.795	580.8	11,965
2008	49.291	643.8	13,054
2011	49.484	625.4	12,670
2013	49.77	606.5	12,247
		% change	
2000 to 2005	4.1	16.5	11.7
2005 to 2008	1	10.8	9.1
2008 to 2011	0.4	-2.9	-2.9
2011 to 2013	0.6	-3	-3.3
Post-recession: 2008 to 2013	1	-5.8	-6.2

Source: National Center for Education Statistics.

Table I: Percent Change in Enrollment and Inflation-adjusted Per-pupil K–12 Spending, 2008 to 2013

State	K–12 enrollment			K–12 per-pupil real spending		
	Fall 2008	Fall 2013	% change, 2008–13	2008	2013	% change, 2008–13
United States	49,290,559	49,769,818	1.0%	$13,054	$12,247	-6.2%
Florida	2,666,811	2,692,162	1.0	12,716	9,692	(23.8)
Nevada.................	429,362	445,707	3.8	11,362	9,170	(19.3)
Idaho....................	272,119	284,834	4.7	9,369	7,605	(18.8)
Arizona................	1,087,447	1,089,384	0.2	10,633	8,663	(18.5)
Georgia................	1,649,589	1,703,332	3.3	12,575	10,346	(17.7)
Colorado..............	801,867	863,561	7.7	12,118	10,281	(15.2)
California	6,343,471	6,299,451	(0.7)	12,427	10,755	(13.4)
Texas....................	4,674,832	5,077,659	8.6	11,679	10,142	(13.2)
Alabama...............	742,919	744,637	0.2	11,462	9,990	(12.8)
Utah	576,244	613,279	6.4	9,413	8,239	(12.5)
North Carolina.....	1,489,492	1,518,465	1.9	9,985	8,848	(11.4)
Oregon.................	565,586	587,564	3.9	12,129	10,772	(11.2)
New Mexico	329,040	338,220	2.8	11,678	10,449	(10.5)
Wisconsin	874,633	872,436	(0.3)	13,489	12,309	(8.7)
Hawaii.................	179,897	184,760	2.7	13,970	12,759	(8.7)
Virginia................	1,230,857	1,265,419	2.8	13,146	12,093	(8.0)
South Carolina.....	712,317	735,998	3.3	12,183	11,320	(7.1)
Mississippi	494,122	493,650	(0.1)	9,304	8,745	(6.0)
Missouri...............	917,188	917,900	0.1	11,820	11,224	(5.0)
Washington..........	1,030,247	1,051,694	2.1	12,173	11,561	(5.0)
Louisiana	681,038	710,903	4.4	12,393	11,838	(4.5)
Maine...................	196,245	185,739	(5.4)	13,982	13,385	(4.3)
Michigan	1,692,739	1,555,370	(8.1)	12,344	11,862	(3.9)
Maryland	845,700	859,638	1.6	16,147	15,554	(3.7)
Wyoming	86,422	90,993	5.3	19,120	18,461	(3.4)
New Jersey	1,382,348	1,372,203	(0.7)	20,548	19,976	(2.8)
Delaware	122,574	129,026	5.3	15,830	15,458	(2.3)
Indiana.................	1,046,764	1,041,369	(0.5)	10,963	10,752	(1.9)
Oklahoma.............	642,065	673,483	4.9	9,103	8,948	(1.7)
Ohio.....................	1,827,184	1,729,916	(5.3)	13,122	13,029	(0.7)
Kansas	468,295	489,043	4.4	11,864	11,782	(0.7)
South Dakota.......	121,606	130,471	7.3	10,504	10,469	(0.3)
Tennessee	964,259	993,496	3.0	9,358	9,355	0.0
Minnesota............	837,578	845,404	0.9	13,351	13,355	0.0
Montana	142,823	142,908	0.1	11,676	11,700	0.2
Kentucky	666,225	685,167	2.8	10,733	10,778	0.4
Arkansas..............	479,016	486,157	1.5	10,860	11,037	1.6
Nebraska	291,244	303,505	4.2	12,957	13,170	1.6
Rhode Island........	147,629	142,481	(3.5)	16,011	16,416	2.5
Massachusetts	962,958	954,773	(0.8)	16,071	16,572	3.1
West Virginia.......	282,535	283,044	0.2	11,323	11,705	3.4
Pennsylvania	1,801,971	1,763,677	(2.1)	14,600	15,188	4.0
Iowa	485,115	499,825	3.0	11,794	12,272	4.0
New Hampshire ...	200,772	188,974	(5.9)	13,862	14,474	4.4
Connecticut..........	570,626	550,954	(3.4)	17,948	18,941	5.5
New York.............	2,765,435	2,710,703	(2.0)	19,944	21,537	8.0
Illinois.................	2,112,805	2,072,120	(1.9)	12,846	13,884	8.1
Vermont...............	94,038	89,624	(4.7)	16,527	18,122	9.6
Alaska..................	131,029	131,489	0.4	18,488	20,536	11.1
Dist. of Columbia	78,422	76,140	(2.9)	23,517	27,855	18.4
North Dakota.......	95,059	101,111	6.4	11,078	14,564	31.5

Source: National Center for Education Statistics (NCES).

Table J: State and Local Government Employment Most Recent Year Compared to Peak Following Start of Great Recession

| | Year ending June: | | | |
	2009 emplymt. in thousands	2015 emplymt. in thousands	Change	% change
Total state and local government employment	**18,888**	**18,372**	**(516)**	**-2.7%**
Education	**9,752**	**9,556**	**(197)**	**-2.0**
Elementary and secondary education	7,400	7,123	(277)	-3.7
Colleges, universities and junior colleges	2,290	2,371	81	3.5
Business, trade and other instructional schools	46	37	(9)	-20.5
Education consultants, guidance counselors, testing and other support	17	25	9	52.9
Justice, public order and safety activities	**1,674**	**1,618**	**(56)**	**-3.4**
Fire protection	188	198	10	5.4
Police protection	512	509	(3)	-0.5
Correctional institutions, parole and probation	548	505	(43)	-7.9
Courts, legal counsel and prosecution	269	261	(8)	-3.0
Other justice and safety activities	157	144	(13)	-8.0
Health care	**1,323**	**1,284**	**(39)**	**-3.0**
Hospitals other that psychiatric and substance abuse	867	863	(5)	-0.5
Physicians, medical & diagnostic laboratories & other ambulatory health care	91	100	9	10.0
Nursing, community care and other residential facilities	99	97	(3)	-2.9
Psychiatric and substance abuse hospitals and residential mental health facilities	263	223	(40)	-15.3
Social assistance services for children, youth, elderly, disabled	**235**	**237**	**2**	**0.9**
General administration	**4,312**	**4,117**	**(195)**	**-4.5**
Executive and legislative offices, legislative bodies, commissions	2,982	2,843	(139)	-4.7
Administration of programs	1,330	1,274	(56)	-4.2
All other	**1,591**	**1,560**	**(31)**	**-2.0**

Source: Quarterly Census of Employment and Wages, U.S. Bureau of Labor Statistics.

ment growth generally slowed but did not decline.[16] State and local governments cut employment repeatedly between the peak in state fiscal year 2009 and state fiscal year 2013, before employment stabilized and began to rise slightly. As of state fiscal year 2015, state and local government employment was down by over half a million jobs.

Table J shows the change in employment by major activity of government, based on the Quarterly Census of Employment and Wages from the Bureau of Labor Statistics. K–12 education accounts for more than half of the decline in employment, followed by general administration, including cuts to executive and legislative bodies and boards and commissions, as well as administrators of major governmental programs.

States and localities in 35 states cut government employment between 2009 and 2015, as Figure I shows, with the deepest cuts in the eastern and southwestern states. Employment generally grew in oil-dependent states, which boomed during much of this period, but that may change given the plunge in oil prices and cuts in oil production.

Table K: Most Recent Revenue Forecasts from States

	FY 2015	FY 2016	FY 2017	Change from 2015 to 2016	Change from 2016 to 2017
Personal income tax					
Median forecast	7.80%	4.60%	4.40%	-3.20%	-0.20%
Number of states expecting >5% growth	29	12	12	-17	0
Sales tax					
Median forecast	4.70%	3.80%	3.90%	-0.90%	0.10%
Number of states expecting >5% growth	17	9	10	-8	1

*Reflects 36 states with income tax forecasts and 38 states with sales tax forecasts.

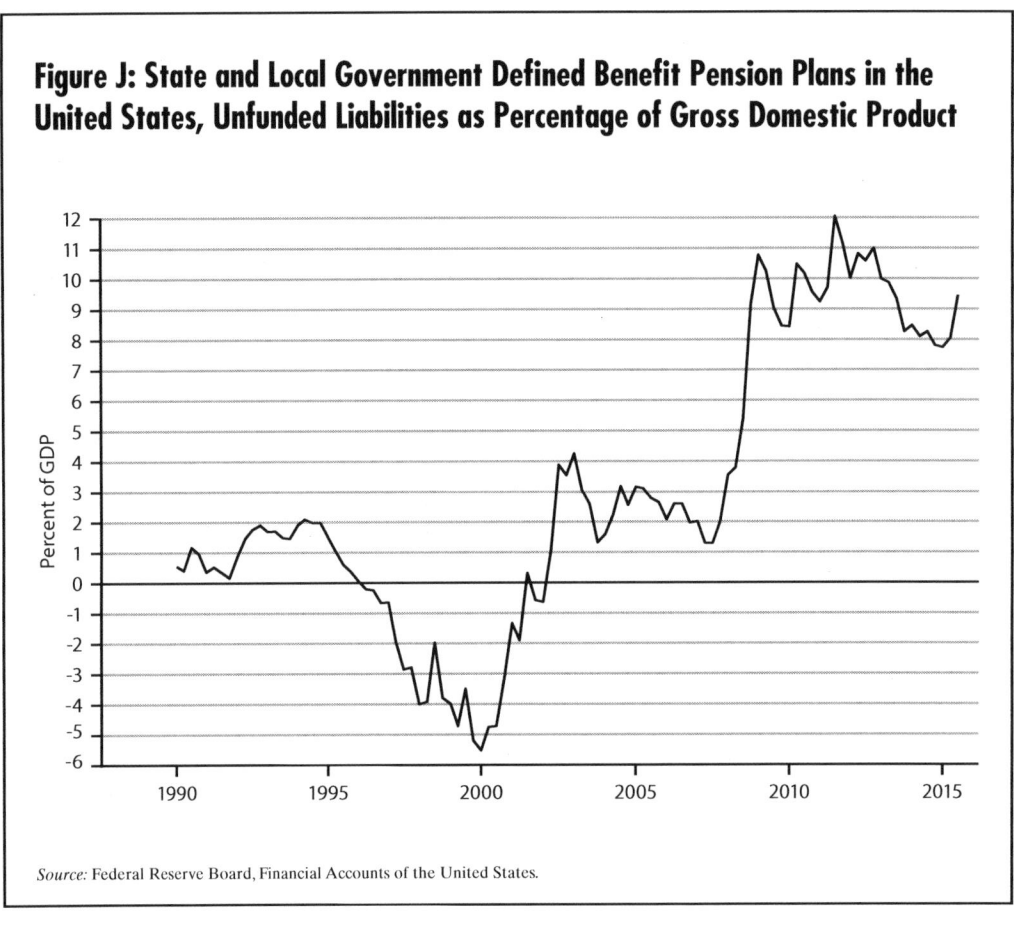

Figure J: State and Local Government Defined Benefit Pension Plans in the United States, Unfunded Liabilities as Percentage of Gross Domestic Product

Source: Federal Reserve Board, Financial Accounts of the United States.

The Outlook

Tax revenue growth is likely to continue to be slow

The current economic environment is not likely to support strong tax revenue growth for state and local governments. Economic growth has accelerated slightly, as has inflation, but both remain low by historical standards. In its latest economic forecast, the Congressional Budget Office anticipated real gross domestic product growth of 2.5 percent in 2016, consumer price inflation of 1.3 percent and growth in nominal GDP of 4.1 percent.[17] This is broadly consistent with the consensus of private forecasters.[18] Moderate economic growth and low inflation is likely to lead to relatively slow tax revenue growth. All else equal, sales taxes tend to be higher when prices are higher, and higher prices often work their way into wages and other forms of income, boosting income taxes. Lower inflation tends to restrain state and local tax revenue growth.

One factor that can make income tax revenue grow faster or slower than the economy is the stock market. A strong stock market often leads to significantly higher capital gains income, and a declining stock market can lead to sharp decreases. The 2015 stock market will affect tax returns filed in April 2016, shortly after this writing. The stock market declined by about 0.7 percent in 2015, so states seem unlikely to get a boost from this source, and might even get an unpleasant surprise. And as of this writing, the stock market is down about 8 percent thus far in 2016.[19] Based on other work of the Rockefeller Institute, the states that have the most to gain or lose from large shifts in capital gains, in order, are New York, California, Oregon, Connecticut and Massachusetts, followed by Minnesota, Montana and New Jersey. Most other states are much less affected by swings in capital gains.

State revenue forecasters are aware of these trends and risks, and generally are forecasting slower tax revenue growth in the 2017 fiscal year than in 2016.[20] In the next section we examine current state forecasts and in the following section we summarize the troubles of oil and coal states, discussed more fully in a recent Rockefeller Institute brief.[21]

States forecast slow tax revenue growth in fiscal years 2016 and 2017

States expect tax revenue growth to be slower in fiscal years 2016 and 2017. Table K summarizes states' most recent forecasts for income and sales taxes—the two largest taxes—for 41 states for which we were able to collect forecast data for fiscal years 2016 and 2017. (See Table L for individual states' forecasts.) The median state forecast for personal income tax growth is 4.6 percent in 2016 and 4.4 percent in 2017, both of which are down from state-estimated growth of 7.8 percent in 2015. Similarly, the median sales tax forecast slows from 4.7 percent in 2015 to 3.8 percent in 2016 and 3.9 percent in 2017. Fewer states are forecasting growth of more than 5 percent in both 2016 and 2017 than in 2015, for both the income tax and the sales tax. Overall, 19 of 36 states with income tax forecasts are forecasting slower income tax growth in 2017 than in 2016, and 18 of 38 states are forecasting slower sales tax growth.

States benefited from the strong stock market in 2014, which led to strong income tax collections in fiscal 2015. The subsequent weakening of the stock market likely is contributing to states' forecasts of slower income tax growth in 2016 and 2017.

Table L shows the forecasts for the individual states. It also shows the forecast month and year. Forecasts vary significantly from state to state, reflecting many factors including reliance on capital gains, state overall economic conditions, oil supplies and oil prices, financial and real estate market developments, state specific policy changes, and others. Most states anticipate considerable downward pressure over the long-term revenue forecast horizon. The overall picture is of continued but sluggish growth in fiscal years 2016 and 2017 and continued fiscal challenges and uncertainties for the states.

Oil and coal states face special difficulties

Oil prices dropped from an average of $99 per barrel in 2014 to $52 in 2015, and fell below $30 in January 2016, the lowest level in the last 12 years. The steep declines in oil prices throughout 2015 and early 2016 had a negative economic and fiscal impact on oil- and mineral-dependent states. Oil, natural gas and mining account for about 10 percent

or more of gross domestic product in eight states: Alaska, Louisiana, New Mexico, North Dakota, Oklahoma, Texas, West Virginia and Wyoming. As a group, these states rely on severance taxes for 16 percent of their tax revenue, far more than the 0.2 percent for the rest of the country. They accounted for nearly 90 percent of the $18 billion in severance tax revenue raised nationally in 2014. This revenue fell by 35.5 percent in the 12 months ending in September 2015, with declines that ranged from 15.8 percent in West Virginia to 87.9 percent in Alaska. (See Table M).

The steep price declines are leading to cuts in production and employment, weakening mineral-state economies and likely leading to slower growth in revenue from other tax sources. At the end of 2015, total employment was lower in six of the eight states than it was in January 2015. Revenue from non-severance taxes, such as income and sales taxes, grew nearly 2 percentage points more slowly in these eight states than in the other 42 states, primarily reflecting a decline in Alaska. Total tax revenues in the eight states declined by 3.2 percent. The remaining 42 states reported 6.5 percent growth in total tax revenues.

As a result, the oil- and mineral-dependent states are all facing fiscal challenges and budget shortfalls, particularly Alaska, North Dakota and Wyoming, where severance taxes are a significant share of total taxes.[22]

Pension contributions are poised to rise further

Despite large contribution increases discussed earlier and widespread benefit cuts, public pensions in aggregate remain woefully underfunded. At the end of September 2015, unfunded liability as measured by the Bureau of Economic Analysis and the Federal Reserve Board was $1.7 trillion, or 9.5 percent of gross domestic product. This was little better than the situation shortly after the worst of the recession-related stock market declines, even though we are seven years past the declines of 2008 (Figure J). (Note that the Federal Reserve Board estimates of unfunded liabilities are greater than those of actuaries.[23])

Pension contributions now are generally being made on the basis of actuarial valuations developed in 2014 and 2015, and recognize very little if any of the investment shortfalls that have occurred since then. In fiscal year 2015, the median public pension fund earned about 3.4 percent despite assuming that it would earn approximately 7.5 percent.[24] Fiscal year 2016, so far, is off to a bad

Table L: State Personal Income and Sales Tax Revenue Forecasts for FY 2016 and FY 2017

		Personal Income Tax ($ in Millions)					Sales Tax ($ in Millions)				
State	Forecast month	FY 2015 actual	FY 2016 forecast	FY 2017 forecast	% change 2015– 2016	% change 2016– 2017	FY 2015 actual	FY 2016 forecast	FY 2017 forecast	% change 2015– 2016	% change 2016– 2017
Arizona............	Jan. 16	3,761.30	3,940.60	4,147.10	4.8	5.2	4,190.50	4,330.60	4,502.50	3.3	4.0
Arkansas............	Feb. 16	2,664.20	2,699.40	2,741.10	1.3	1.5	2,197.80	2,305.40	2,396.00	4.9	3.9
California	Jan. 16	75,384.00	77,700.00	81,652.00	3.1	5.1	23,684.00	25,240.00	25,761.00	6.6	2.1
Colorado.............	Dec. 15	6,350.10	6,477.50	6,973.90	2.0	7.7	2,879.40	2,966.50	3,139.50	3.0	5.8
Connecticut........	Jan. 16	9,151.00	9,570.00	9,829.10	4.6	2.7	4,205.10	4,230.30	4,092.20	0.6	(3.3)
Delaware	Dec. 15	1,251.90	1,306.80	1,360.80	4.4	4.1	N/A	N/A	N/A	N/A	N/A
Florida	Jan. 16	N/A	N/A	N/A	N/A	N/A	21,062.70	22,086.10	23,242.90	4.9	5.2
Georgia................	Jan. 16	9,678.50	10,084.30	10,715.60	4.2	6.3	5,390.40	5,432.90	5,658.90	0.8	4.2
Hawaii.................	Jan. 16	1,987.80	2,085.50	2,190.10	4.9	5.0	2,992.70	3,197.60	3,373.70	6.8	5.5
Idaho....................	Jan. 16	1,470.80	1,523.90	1,606.20	3.6	5.4	1,218.80	1,279.00	1,345.10	4.9	5.2
Indiana.................	Dec. 15	5,233.00	5,250.10	5,372.10	0.3	2.3	7,194.80	7,345.60	7,665.30	2.1	4.4
Iowa.....................	Dec. 15	4,207.30	4,502.10	4,707.70	7.0	4.6	2,753.00	2,838.80	2,914.50	3.1	2.7
Kansas	Nov. 15	2,277.50	2,450.00	2,485.00	7.6	1.4	2,485.00	2,675.00	2,775.00	7.6	3.7
Kentucky	Feb. 16	4,069.50	4,233.50	4,411.10	4.0	4.2	3,267.30	3,420.50	3,539.80	4.7	3.5
Louisiana.............	Nov. 15	2,886.10	3,054.80	3,221.50	5.8	5.5	2,700.80	2,872.20	2,840.60	6.3	(1.1)
Maine...................	May 15	1,521.80	1,548.80	1,640.40	1.8	5.9	1,195.00	1,127.50	1,180.60	(5.7)	4.7
Maryland	Dec. 15	8,346.10	8,779.10	9,273.20	5.2	5.6	4,350.70	4,515.70	4,662.30	3.8	3.2
Massachusetts	Jan. 16	14,449.00	14,940.00	15,543.00	3.4	4.0	5,774.00	6,090.00	6,436.00	5.5	5.7
Michigan..............	Jan. 16	8,979.50	9,031.90	9,345.80	0.6	3.5	7,819.00	8,045.80	8,059.20	2.9	0.2
Minnesota............	Nov. 15	10,403.00	10,678.00	11,278.00	2.6	5.6	5,131.00	5,368.00	5,663.00	4.6	5.5
Mississippi	Oct. 15	1,743.40	1,830.00	1,903.20	5.0	4.0	2,260.80	2,326.70	2,415.10	2.9	3.8
Missouri................	Jan. 16	6,890.80	7,221.10	7,566.10	4.8	4.8	2,014.40	2,073.30	2,137.10	2.9	3.1
Montana	Nov. 15	1,175.70	1,243.00	1,313.00	5.7	5.6	N/A	N/A	N/A	N/A	N/A
Nebraska	Oct. 15	2,205.50	2,300.00	2,415.00	4.3	5.0	1,535.40	1,565.00	1,620.00	1.9	3.5
New Mexico	Jan. 16	1,339.70	1,401.00	1,455.00	4.6	3.9	2,167.00	2,144.40	2,280.10		6.3
New York..............	Aug. 15	43,709.00	47,075.00	49,701.00	7.7	5.6	12,991.00	13,532.00	14,067.00	4.2	4.0
Oklahoma.............	Feb. 16	2,160.80	1,970.80	1,751.90	(8.8)	(11.1)	2,224.00	2,037.60	2,069.50	(8.4)	1.6
Oregon..................	Feb. 16	7,330.30	7,716.00	7,976.10	5.3	3.4	N/A	N/A	N/A	N/A	N/A
Pennsylvania	Dec. 15	12,107.00	12,687.00	13,180.00	4.8	3.9	9,493.00	9,840.00	10,188.00	3.7	3.5
Rhode Island........	Nov. 15	1,227.60	1,214.90	1,265.40		4.2	963.4	981	1,015.00	1.8	3.5
South Carolina......	Nov. 15	3,661.20	3,888.10	4,066.70	6.2	4.6	2,643.70	2,785.50	2,925.80	5.4	5.0
South Dakota.......	Dec. 15	N/A	N/A	N/A	N/A	N/A	836.6	872.6	904.9	4.3	3.7
Tennessee	Nov. 15	303.4	325.6	341	7.3	4.7	7,706.10	8,140.90	8,575.70	5.6	5.3
Texas.....................	Oct. 15	N/A	N/A	N/A	N/A	N/A	28,787.40	29,143.70	30,546.20	1.2	4.8
Utah......................	Nov. 15	3,157.70	3,320.90	3,466.60	5.2	4.4	1,715.00	1,780.30	1,852.40	3.8	4.0
Vermont.................	Jul. 15	705.9	763.8	797.8	8.2	4.5	364.6	382.2	394.3	4.8	3.2
Virginia.................	Dec. 15	12,328.70	12,778.00	13,162.40	3.6	3.0	3,235.40	3,397.70	3,528.90	5.0	3.9
Washington...........	Nov. 15	N/A	N/A	N/A	N/A	N/A	8,793.20	9,427.90	9,811.60	7.2	4.1
West Virginia........	Jan. 16	1,840.10	1,861.00	1,935.00	1.1	4.0	1,228.20	1,270.00	1,379.00	3.4	8.6
Wisconsin	Jan. 16	7,325.80	7,810.00	8,050.00	6.6	3.1	4,892.10	5,050.90	5,217.50	3.2	3.3
Wyoming	Jan. 16	N/A	N/A	N/A	N/A	N/A	544	466.8	470.5	(14.2)	0.8
US Median		$276,859	$288,622	$301,951	4.6	4.4	$198,499	$205,950	$213,748	3.7	3.8

Source: Individual state data, analysis by the Rockefeller Institute.
Notes: Data are missing for seven states: AL, IL, NC, ND, NJ, NV and OH. In addition, no data is reported for AK and NH as both states don't have either personal income or sales tax.

start; The typical pension fund still assumes it will earn about 7.5 percent on its portfolio, generally suggesting that it needs to earn considerably more on the equities portion of its portfolio (and less on the fixed income portion). But between the July 1, 2015, start of the typical pension fund year and mid-February 2016, the stock market is down more than 8 percent. With more than $3.5 trillion of assets under investment, the shortfalls for the 2015 and 2016 fiscal years are likely to be substantial.

Although pension funds are slow to reflect these shortfalls in actuarially determined contributions, over the next several years requested contributions are likely to rise substantially. In what may

Table M: Economy, Employment and Taxes in Oil- and Mineral-dependent States

| State | Mining industries as share of state GDP, 2013 | | | Percent change, 4 quarters ending September 2015 vs. year earlier | | | | |
	Oil & gax extraction	All other mining activities	Total mining	Emplymt. change Dec. 2015 vs. Jan. 2015	Severance taxes as % of total taxes (FY 2014)	Severance taxes	Other taxes	Total taxes
Alaska....................	22.1%	6.4%	28.4%	-0.3%	72.4%	-87.9%	-17.6%	-67.2%
Louisiana	7.5	2.6	10.1	-0.5	8.9	-22.9	2.5	-3.2
New Mexico	6.1	3.5	9.6	0.2	18.5	-25.4	6.8	-0.3
North Dakota.......	6.4	8.3	14.6	-4.3	53.8	-31.9	6.8	-15.8
Oklahoma..............	11.4	2.9	14.3	-0.7	7.5	-33.7	5.4	-0.3
Texas.....................	11.6	2.1	13.8	1.3	10.9	-33.4	4.9	-0.1
West Virginia........	2.0	11.4	13.4	-1.8	12.7	-15.8	3.5	1.4
Wyoming	14.9	18.2	33.1	-2.4	39.0	0.1	6.7	3.9
Oil & coal states ...	10.9	3.1	14.0	0.5	16.4	-35.5	4.6	-3.2
Other states..........	0.4	0.5	0.9	1.7	0.2	-19.8	6.4	6.5
United States	1.8	0.9	2.7	1.6	2.1	-33.7	6.2	5.4

Source: Rockefeller Institute analysis of data from BEA (GDP, BLS (employment)) and Census Bureau (taxes).

seem like an unfair twist, these increases often will be largest for governments with the best funded plans, because those are the plans with the most assets and therefore the most to lose.

Over the longer term, public pensions will be a major risk for state and local governments. Public pension funds keep contributions low by assuming that they will earn about 7.5 percent annually through investments in diversified portfolios of stocks, bonds, real estate, hedge funds and many other assets. This may or may not be attainable, but the risk is sizeable. For example, annual contributions would have to be $130 billion to $200 billion higher than they are now to fund public pensions without taking investment risk, based on our analysis of estimates by the Bureau of Economic Analysis.[25] Governments certainly don't want to pay the higher contributions that would be needed to avoid this risk; instead, they (and their taxpayers) will be exposed to the risk of loss.

In some states pensions are not just a longer term risk—they are a near and present danger. In particular, Connecticut, Illinois, Kentucky, New Jersey and Pennsylvania all face pension crises that will play out over the next several years. In California, contributions were slated to rise substantially even before the latest stock market declines; legislation finally requires governments to contribute actuarially-based payments to CalSTRS, and so contributions will rise. In addition, CalPERS has announced that it intends to mitigate risk by slowly lowering its earnings assumption, which in turn will raise contributions for the state

and local governments. These actions will help make these funds and their beneficiaries more secure than they otherwise would be—and they may not even go far enough—but they will squeeze their governments and taxpayers.

Pension fund stress is going to be a continuing issue for state and local governments for many years.

Medicaid still expected to grow faster than the economy

Medicaid has been a long-term source of fiscal pressure for state and local governments, although not as much as in past years and decades. According to the Centers for Medicare and Medicaid Services, between 1990 and 2007 total Medicaid expenditures grew at an average annual rate of 9.7 percent, while the economy (gross domestic product) grew at an annual rate of 5.4 percent—a difference of 4.3 percentage points, far outstripping growth in tax bases.[26] As discussed earlier, after the Great Recession federal spending on Medicaid grew rapidly as a result of recession-related enrollment increases, and states absorbed some of those costs after the federal stimulus program waned.

Looking forward, CMS researchers expect that state-funded Medicaid will grow at an average annual rate of 6.1 percent between 2015 and 2018 while the economy grows at a 5.1 percent rate—a gap of 1 percentage point. Between 2018 and 2024, CMS forecasts state-funded Medicaid will grow at a 6.7 percent rate, 1.9 percentage points faster than anticipated GDP growth.[27] CMS forecasts that growth in spending per enrollee will accelerate as dually eligible beneficiaries (eligible for both Medicare and Medicaid) age into the program and as the aging of the population leads to higher costs, particularly for nursing home care. Thus, Medicaid is likely to be a continuing source of pressure on state budgets, albeit not as great as in the 1990s and early 2000s.

Conclusion

State and local governments play a crucial role in the nation's economy. They are responsible for three-quarters of the nation's transportation and water infrastructure, they finance 90 percent of the nation's public elementary and secondary schools, they provide a majority of the nation's higher education in degree-granting institutions, and they implement much of the nation's social safety net. They have scaled many of these activities back in response to slow growth in taxes, rapid growth in pension contributions and enrollment-driven Medicaid growth. The outlook is for more of the same over the next several years, suggesting that states will continue to struggle to provide these crucial services.

Notes

[1] Percentage change in taxes after the start of a recession are calculated only until the start of the next recession, consistent with Figure A.

[2] Donald J. Boyd and Lucy Dadayan, "The Economy Recovers While State Finances Lag," The Blinken Report, Nelson A. Rockefeller Institute of Government, June 2015. http://www.rockinst.org/pdf/government_finance/2015-06-23-Blinken_Report_Two.pdf. Also see the Institute's quarterly State Revenue Reports.

[3] We estimated federal fiscal year 2015 average monthly enrollment assuming growth of 8.2 percent, which is the growth rate for average monthly enrollment reported in the December 2015 "CMS Fast Facts," Centers for Medicare & Medicaid Services, December 2015. https://www.cms.gov/Research-Statistics-Data-and-Systems/Statistics-Trends-and-Reports/CMS-Fast-Facts/index.html. It is faster than the 6.3 percent growth rate implied in an earlier CMS publication, "2015 CMS Statistics," Centers for Medicare & Medicaid Services, n.d. https://www.cms.gov/Research-Statistics-Data-and-Systems/Statistics-Trends-and-Reports/CMS-Statistics-Reference-Booklet/Downloads/2015CMS Statistics.pdf. Table I.16, was based on the president's budget from early 2015. It appears to be broadly consistent with the 13.8 percent June-to-June growth estimated in Robin Rudowitz, Laura Snyder, and Vernon K. Smith, "Medicaid Enrollment & Spending Growth: FY 2015 & 2016," Issue Brief, Kaiser Commission on Medicaid and the Uninsured, October 2015, based on our examination

of the past relationship between fiscal year growth and June-to-June growth.

[4] Per capita spending means spending per person in the state, not per Medicaid enrollee.

[5] States do have other resources besides taxes with which to pay pensions and other expenditures—fees, for example—but as a practical matter, higher pension contributions generally will require higher taxes or cuts in other spending.

[6] We use 2007 through 2014 to have a consistent set of years for all three sources of stress, even though our earlier Medicaid analysis began with 2008 terminated in 2015. State-financed Medicaid trends between 2007 and 2014 were very similar to those between 2008 and 2015, so this choice has very little impact on the results. It is not possible to make perfect comparisons because available measures for these sources of stress come from different data sources and are for slightly different annual periods.

[7] For each state, we estimated 2014 local government taxes by adding the average annual growth rate in local government taxes from 2010 to 2013 to 2013 local tax revenue. We then added this estimate of 2014 local government taxes to reported 2014 state government taxes. All tax data were from U.S. Census Bureau surveys.

[8] As in the earlier pension contributions analysis, we used 2008 pension contributions for West Virginia.

[9] Consumption expenditures include, within each category, what the Bureau of Economic Analysis calls "consumption of fixed capital"—the estimated amount of state and local government capital stock, such as roads and bridges, that is used up by wear and tear, economic obsolescence, and other causes. It is similar in concept to depreciation. It is not a cash expenditure.

[10] Explain why we use GDPPI for everything.

[11] For research and pragmatic underpinnings, see Donald Boyd, "Public Research Universities: Changes in State Funding," The Lincoln Project, October 2015.

[12] Forty-eight states cut funding for educational services when we include Illinois, where the reported funding increase supported underfunded university pensions rather than current students. Ibid.

[13] In this analysis, we adjust education revenue using the GDP price index, so that they are comparable to other inflation-adjusted numbers in this report. In essence, the result is a measure of effort by governments rather than a measure of how much may be bought of each governmental good or service. However, according to estimates by the State Higher Education Executive Officers, or SHEEO, the cost of "producing" education has risen more rapidly than prices in the overall economy. Between 2008 and 2014, SHEEO's higher education cost index rose by 11.3 percent, compared to 9.6 percent for the GDP price index; between 2000 and 2014, the higher education cost index increased by 44.6 percent compared to 32.7 percent for the GDP price index.

[14] Michael Leachman et. al, "Most States Have Cut School Funding, and Some Continue Cutting," Center on Budget and Policy Priorities, Jan. 25, 2016. http://www.cbpp.org/research/state-budget-and-tax/most-states-have-cut-school-funding-and-some-continue-cutting.

[15] Ibid.

[16] Lucy Dadayan and Robert B. Ward, "Data Alert: State and Local Government Employment Shows Broad, Continuing Declines," July 22, 2011. *http://archive.constantcontact.com/fs091/1104610489644/archive/1106689721430.html.*; Donald J. Boyd and Lucy Dadayan, "The Economy Recovers While State Finances Lag."

[17] "The Budget and Economic Outlook: 2016 to 2026," Congressional Budget Office, January 2016. *https://www.cbo.gov/publication/51129.*

[18] "Economic Forecasting Survey," accessed Feb. 15, 2016. *http://projects.wsj.com/econforecast/#ind=gdp&r=20.*

[19] Based on S&P 500 adjusted close at end of 2014, 2015 and Feb. 12, 2016, as obtained from the Yahoo API using the R package quantmod.

[20] Lucy Dadayan and Donald J. Boyd, "By The Numbers: States Forecast Slower Tax Growth Through 2017 and Beyond," Rockefeller Institute of Government, Dec. 23, 2015. *http://www.rockinst.org/pdf/government_finance/2015-12-By_Numbers_Brief_2_Page.pdf.*

[21] Lucy Dadayan and Donald J. Boyd, "By The Numbers: Double, Double, Oil and Trouble," Rockefeller Institute of Government, Feb. 1, 2016. *http://www.rockinst.org/pdf/government_finance/2016-02-By_Numbers_Brief_No5.pdf.*

[22] Ibid.

[23] Discussed in Donald J. Boyd and Yimeng Yin, "By The Numbers: State and Local Government Unfunded Pension Liabilities Rise by $268 Billion in the Third Quarter of 2015," Rockefeller Institute of Government, Jan. 30, 2016. *http://www.rockinst.org/pdf/government_finance/2016-01-20_By_the_Numbers_Brief_No4.pdf.*

[24] Wilshire Trust Universe Comparison Service calculated the median return of public plans with more than $5 billion in assets at 3.4%, and Callan Associates Inc. calculated an average investment return of 3.2% for 265 public plans with assets of more than $1 billion. *http://www.pionline.com/article/20150810/PRINT/308109985/high-return-era-ends-for-many-big-public-pension-funds.*

[25] According to NIPA table 7.24 published on Aug. 26, 2015, employer contributions in 2014 were $71 billion below what was needed to fund annual benefits earned without taking investment risk (Imputed employer contributions, Line 6). In addition, unfunded liabilities were accruing interest of $63 billion (Line 13). Thus, to avoid taking investment risk, governments would have needed to pay an additional $134 billion ($71 billion + $63 billion) just to keep unfunded liabilities from rising. Amortizing the existing unfunded liabilities would take another $70 billion or more in annual contributions, depending on the amortization method chosen.

[26] Exhibit 3, S.P. Keehan et al., "National Health Expenditure Projections, 2014-24: Spending Growth Faster Than Recent Trends," *Health Affairs* 34, no. 8 (Aug. 1, 2015): 1407–17, doi:10.1377/hlthaff.2015.0600.

[27] Ibid.

About the Authors

Donald J. Boyd is director of fiscal studies at the Rockefeller Institute of Government. Boyd has over three decades of experience analyzing state and local government fiscal issues, and has written or co-authored many of the Rockefeller Institute's reports on the fiscal climate in the 50 states. Boyd currently is principal investigator for the Institute's Pension Simulation Project, which is examining risks associated with public pension plans. His previous positions include executive director of the State Budget Crisis Task Force created by former Federal Reserve Board Chairman Paul Volcker and former New York Lieutenant Governor Richard Ravitch; director of the economic and revenue staff for the New York State Division of the Budget; and director of the tax staff for the New York State Assembly Ways and Means Committee. Boyd holds a Ph.D. in managerial economics from Rensselaer Polytechnic Institute.

Lucy Dadayan is a senior policy analyst at the Rockefeller Institute of Government. She has conducted research and coauthored reports on state and local government fiscal policy issues; state spending on public policy programs and the effects of state fiscal capacity and economic changes; among other topics. Dadayan holds a Ph.D. in Informatics from the State University of New York.

Table 7.9
STATE TAX AMNESTY PROGRAMS, 1982–Present

State or other jurisdiction	Amnesty period	Legislative authorization	Major taxes covered	Accounts receivable included	Collections ($ millions) (a)	Installment arrangements permitted (b)
Alabama	1/20/84–4/1/84	No (c)	All	No	3.2	No
	2/1/09–5/15/09	Yes	Ind. Income, Corp. Income, Business, Sales and Use	N.A.	8.1	N.A.
	6/30/16–8/30/16	Yes	All	No	N.A.	No
Arizona	11/22/82–1/20/83	No (c)	All	No	6.0	Yes
	1/1/02–2/28/02	Yes	Individual income	No	N.A.	No
	9/1/03–10/31/03	Yes	All (t)	N.A.	73.0	Yes
	5/1/09– 6/1/09	N.A.	All	N.A.	32.0	N.A.
	9/1/15–10/31/15	Yes	All	Yes	55.5	No
Arkansas	9/1/87–11/30/87	Yes	All	No	1.7	Yes
	7/1/04–12/31/04	Yes	All	N.A.	N.A.	No
California	12/10/84–3/15/85	Yes	Individual income	Yes	154.0	Yes
		Yes	Sales	No	43.0	Yes
	2/1/05–3/31/05	Yes	Income, Franchise, Sales	N.A.	N.A.	Yes
Colorado	9/16/85–11/15/85	Yes	All	No	6.4	Yes
	6/1/03–6/30/03	N.A.	All	N.A.	18.4	Yes
	10/1/11–11/15/11	Yes	All	No	N.A.	No
Connecticut	9/1/90–11/30/90	Yes	All	Yes	54.0	Yes
	9/1/95–11/30/95	Yes	All	Yes	46.2	Yes
	9/1/02–12/2/02	N.A.	All	N.A.	109.0	N.A.
	5/1/09–6/25/09	Yes	All	No	40.0	No
	9/16/13–11/15/13	Yes	All	Yes	193.5	No
Delaware	9/1/09–10/30/09	Yes	All	Yes	N.A.	Yes
Florida	1/1/87–6/30/87	Yes	Intangibles	No	13.0	No
	1/1/88–6/30/88	Yes (d)	All	No	8.4 (d)	No
	7/1/03–10/31/03	Yes	All	N.A.	80.0	N.A.
	7/1/10–9/30/10	Yes	All	Yes	N.A.	Yes
Georgia	10/1/92–12/5/92	Yes	All	Yes	51.3	No
Hawaii	5/27/09–6/26/09	N.A.	All	No	14.0	No
Idaho	5/20/83–8/30/83	No (c)	Individual income	No	0.3	No
Illinois	10/1/84–11/30/84	Yes	All (u)	Yes	160.5	No
	10/1/03–11/17/03	Yes	All	N.A.	532.0	N.A.
	10/1/10–11/8/10	Yes	All	Yes	314 (y)	No
Indiana	9/15/05–11/15/05	Yes	All	Yes	244.0	Yes
Iowa	9/2/86–10/31/86	Yes	All	Yes	35.1	N.A.
	9/4/07–10/31/07	Yes	All	Yes	N.A.	N.A.
Kansas	7/1/84–9/30/84	Yes	All	No	0.6	No
	10/1/03–11/30/03	Yes	All	Yes	53.7	N.A.
	9/1/10–10/15/10	Yes	All	Yes	N.A.	No
	9/1/15–10/15/15	Yes	All	Yes	N.A.	No
Kentucky	9/15/88–9/30/88	Yes (c)	All	No	100.0	No
	8/1/02–9/30/02	Yes (c)	All	No	100.0	No
	10/1/12–11/30/12	Yes	All	Yes	N.A.	No
Louisiana	10/1/85–12/31/85	Yes	All	No	1.2	Yes (f)
	10/1/87–12/15/87	Yes	All	No	0.3	Yes (f)
	10/1/98–12/31/98	Yes	All	No (q)	1.3	No
	9/1/01–10/30/01	Yes	All	Yes	192.9	No
	9/1/09–10/31/09	Yes	All	N.A.	303.7	N.A.
	9/23/13–11/22/13	Yes	All	Yes	435.0	No
	10/15/14–11/14/14	Yes	All	Yes	N.A.	Yes
	11/16/15–12/15/15	Yes	All	Yes		Yes
Maine	11/1/90–12/31/90	Yes	All	Yes	29.0	Yes
	9/1/03–11/30/03	Yes	All	N.A.	37.6	N.A.
	9/1/09–11/30/09	Yes	All	Yes	16.2	No
Maryland	9/1/87–11/2/87	Yes	All	Yes	34.6 (g)	No
	9/1/01–10/31/01	Yes	All	Yes	39.2	No
	9/1/09–10/31/09	Yes	Income, Withholding, Sales and Use	Yes	9.6	Yes
	9/1/15–10/30/15	Yes	All	Yes		Yes

See footnotes at end of table.

STATE TAX AMNESTY PROGRAMS, 1982–Present—Continued

State or other jurisdiction	Amnesty period	Legislative authorization	Major taxes covered	Accounts receivable included	Collections ($ millions) (a)	Installment arrangements permitted (b)
Massachusetts	10/17/83–1/17/84	Yes	All	Yes	86.5	Yes (h)
	10/1/02–11/30/02	Yes	All	Yes	96.1	Yes
	1/1/03–2/28/03	Yes	All	Yes	11.2	N.A.
	4/1/10–6/1/10	Yes	All	Yes	32.6	No
	9/2/14–10/31/14	Yes	All	Yes	N.A.	No
	3/16/15–5/15/15	Yes	Corporate	Yes	18.6	No
	4/1/16–5/31/16	Yes	All	No	N.A.	No
Michigan	5/12/86–6/30/86	Yes	All	Yes	109.8	No
	5/15/02–6/30/02	Yes	All	Yes	N.A.	N.A.
	5/15/11–6/30/11	Yes	All	Yes	76.0	No
Minnesota	8/1/84–10/31/84	Yes	All	Yes	12.1	No
Mississippi	9/1/86–11/30/86	Yes	All	No	1.0	No
	9/1/04–12/31/04	Yes	All	No	7.9	No
Missouri	9/1/83–10/31/83	No (c)	All	No	0.9	No
	8/1/02–10/31/02	Yes	All	Yes	76.4	N.A.
	8/1/03–10/31/03	Yes	All	Yes	20.0	N.A.
	9/1/15–11/30/15	Yes	All	Yes		No
Nebraska	8/1/04–10/31/04	Yes	All	No	7.5	No
Nevada	2/1/02–6/30/02	N.A.	All	N.A.	7.3	N.A.
	7/1/08–10/28/08	No	Sales, Business, License	Yes	N.A.	No
	7/1/10–10/1/10	Yes	All	Yes	N.A.	No
New Hampshire	12/1/97–2/17/98	Yes	All	Yes	13.5	No
	12/1/01–2/15/02	Yes	All	Yes	13.5	N.A.
	12/1/15–2/15/16	Yes	All	Yes	18.9	No
New Jersey	9/10/87–12/8/87	Yes	All	Yes	186.5	Yes
	3/15/96–6/1/96	Yes	All	Yes	359.0	No
	4/15/02–6/10/02	Yes	All	Yes	276.9	N.A.
	5/4/09–6/15/09	Yes	All	N.A.	725.0	N.A.
	10/1/14–11/17/14	N.A.	All	Yes	N.A.	No
New Mexico	8/15/85–11/13/85	Yes	All (i)	No	13.6	Yes
	8/16/99–11/12/99	Yes	All	Yes	45.0	Yes
	6/7/10–9/30/10	Yes	All	No	N.A.	Yes
New York	11/1/85–1/31/86	Yes	All (j)	Yes	401.3	Yes
	11/1/96–1/31/97	Yes	All	Yes	253.4	Yes (o)
	11/18/02–1/31/03	Yes	All	Yes	582.7	Yes (s)
	10/1/05–3/1/06	N.A.	Income, Corporate	N.A.	349.0	N.A.
	1/15/10–3/15/10	Yes	All	Yes	56.5	No
New York City	10/20/03–1/23/04	Yes	All (v)	Yes (w)	N.A.	No
North Carolina	9/1/89–12/1/89	Yes	All (k)	Yes	37.6	No
North Dakota	9/1/83–11/30/83	No (c)	All	No	0.2	Yes
	10/1/03–1/31/04	Yes	N.A.	N.A.	6.9	N.A.
Ohio	10/15/01–1/15/02	Yes	All	No	48.5	No
	1/1/06–2/15/06	Yes	All	No	63.0	No
Oklahoma	7/1/84–12/31/84	Yes	Income, Sales	Yes	13.9	No (l)
	8/15/02–11/15/02	N.A.	All (r)	Yes	N.A.	N.A.
	9/15/08–11/14/08	Yes	All	Yes	81.0	Yes
	9/14/15–11/13/15	Yes	All	Yes	N.A.	Yes
Oregon	10/1/09–11/19/09	Yes	Personal, Corporate, Inheritance	No	N.A.	No
Pennsylvania	10/13/95–1/10/96	Yes	All	Yes	N.A.	No
	4/26/10–6/18/10	Yes	All	Yes	261.0	No
Rhode Island	10/15/86–1/12/87	Yes	All	No	0.7	Yes
	4/15/96–6/28/96	Yes	All	Yes	7.9	Yes
	7/15/06–9/30/06	N.A.	All	Yes	6.5	Yes
	9/2/12–11/15/12	Yes	All	Yes	22.3	Yes
South Carolina	9/1/85–11/30/85	Yes	All	Yes	7.1	Yes
	10/15/02–12/2/02	Yes	All	Yes	66.2	N.A.
South Dakota	4/1/99–5/15/99	Yes	All	Yes	0.5	N.A.

See footnotes at end of table.

STATE TAX AMNESTY PROGRAMS, 1982–Present — Continued

State or other jurisdiction	Amnesty period	Legislative authorization	Major taxes covered	Accounts receivable included	Collections ($ millions) (a)	Installment arrangements permitted (b)
Texas................................	2/1/84–2/29/84	No (c)	All (m)	No	0.5	No
	3/11/04–3/31/04	No (c)	All (m)	No	N.A.	No
	6/15/07–8/15/07	No (c)	All (m)	No	100	No
	6/12/12–8/17/12	No (c)	All (m)	No	100	No
Vermont........................	5/15/90–6/25/90	Yes	All	Yes	1 (e)	No
	7/20/09–8/31/09	Yes	All	N.A.	2.2	N.A.
Virginia..........................	2/1/90–3/31/90	Yes	All	Yes	32.2	No
	9/2/03–11/3/03	Yes	All	Yes	98.3	N.A.
	10/7/09–12/5/09	Yes	All	Yes	102.1	No
Washington....................	2/1/11–4/30/11	Yes	All	Yes	346.0	No
West Virginia................	10/1/86–12/31/86	Yes	All	Yes	15.9	Yes
	9/1/04–10/31/04	Yes	All	N.A.	10.4	Yes
Wisconsin	9/15/85–11/22/85	Yes	All	Yes (n)	27.3	Yes
	6/15/98–8/14/98	Yes	All	Yes	30.9	N.A.
Dist. of Columbia	7/1/87–9/30/87	Yes	All	Yes	24.3	Yes
	7/10/95–8/31/95	Yes	All (p)	Yes	19.5	Yes (p)
	8/2/10–9/30/10	Yes	All (p)	Yes	N.A.	No
No. Mariana Islands	9/30/05–3/30/06	Yes	All	N.A.	N.A.	N.A.

Source: The Federation of Tax Administrators, April 2016.
Key:
N.A. — Not available.

(a) Where applicable, figure includes local portions of certain taxes collected under the state tax amnesty program.

(b) "No" indicates requirement of full payment by the expiration of the amnesty period. "Yes" indicates allowance of full payment after the expiration of the amnesty period.

(c) Authority for amnesty derived from pre-existing statutory powers permitting the waiver of tax penalties.

(d) Does not include intangibles tax and drug taxes. Gross collections totaled $22.1 million, with $13.7 million in penalties withdrawn.

(e) Preliminary figure.

(f) Amnesty taxpayers were billed for the interest owed, with payment due within 30 days of notification.

(g) Figure includes $1.1 million for the separate program conducted by the Department of Natural Resources for the boat excise tax.

(h) The amnesty statute was construed to extend the amnesty to those who applied to the department before the end of the amnesty period, and permitted them to file overdue returns and pay back taxes and interest at a later date.

(i) The severance taxes, including the six oil and gas severance taxes, the resources excise tax, the corporate franchise tax, and the special fuels tax were not subject to amnesty.

(j) Availability of amnesty for the corporation tax, the oil company taxes, the transporation and transmissions companies tax, the gross receipts oil tax and the unincorporated business tax restricted to entities with 500 or fewer employees in the United States on the date of application. In addition, a taxpayer principally engaged in aviation, or a utility subject to the supervision of the State Department of Public Service was also ineligible.

(k) Local taxes and real property taxes were not included.

(l) Full payment of tax liability required before the end of the amnesty period to avoid civil penalties.

(m) Texas does not impose a corporate or individual income tax. In practical effect, the amnesty was limited to the sales tax and other excises.

(n) Waiver terms varied depending upon the date the tax liability was assessed.

(o) Installment arrangements were permitted if applicant demonstrated that payment would present a severe financial hardship.

(p) Does not include real property taxes. All interest was waived on tax payments made before July 31, 1995. After this date, only 50% of the interest was waived.

(q) Exception for individuals who owed $500 or less.

(r) Except for property and motor fuel taxes.

(s) Multiple payments could be made so long as the required balance was paid in full no later than March 15, 2003.

(t) All taxes except property, estate and unclaimed property.

(u) Does not include the motor fuel use tax.

(v) All NYC taxes administered by the NYC Dept. of Finance are covered except for Real Estate Tax. NYC Sales & Use Tax & NYC Resident Personal Income Tax also are not covered because they are administered by the NYS Dept. of Taxation & Finance.

(w) Taxpayers under audit as of 3/10/03 are ineligible; Taxpayers with an existing installment agreement are ineligible; Taxpayers under criminal investigation are ineligible; Taxpayers party to an administrative or court porceding must withdraw as a condition.

(x) The Massachusetts Department of Revenue was required to hold an amnesty to end before June 30, 2010.

(y) In Illinois, the 2010 Amnesty called collected a total of $717 million, $314 for the state GF and the rest for local governments

Table 7.10a
STATE EXCISE TAX RATES
(As of January 1, 2016)

State or other jurisdiction	General sales and gross receipts tax (percent)	Cigarettes (cents per pack of 20)	Distilled spirits	
			Excise tax rate ($ per gallon)	Sales taxes applied
Alabama	4.0	67.5 (e)	(j)	Yes
Alaska	(a)	200	12.8 (l)	...
Arizona	5.6	200	3	Yes
Arkansas	6.5	115	2.5 (l)	Yes
California	7.5 (b)	87	3.3 (l)	Yes
Colorado	2.9	84	2.28	Yes
Connecticut	6.35	365 (n)	5.4 (l)	Yes
Delaware	(a)	160	3.75 (l)	...
Florida	6.0	133.9 (f)	6.5 (l)	Yes
Georgia	4.0	37	3.79 (l)	Yes
Hawaii	4.0	320	5.98	Yes
Idaho	6.0	57	(j)	Yes
Illinois	6.25	198 (e)	8.55 (l)	Yes
Indiana	7.0	99.5	2.68 (l)	Yes
Iowa	6.0	136	(j)	Yes
Kansas	6.50	129	2.5 (l)	...
Kentucky	6.0	60 (g)	1.92 (l)	Yes
Louisiana	4.0	86	2.50	Yes
Maine	5.5	200	(j)	Yes
Maryland	6.0	200	1.5 (l)	Yes
Massachusetts	6.25	351	4.05 (l)	...
Michigan	6.0	200	(j)	Yes
Minnesota	6.875	300 (h)	5.03 (l)	...
Mississippi	7.0	68	(j)	Yes
Missouri	4.225	17 (e)	2	Yes
Montana	(a)	170	(j)	...
Nebraska	5.5	64	3.75	Yes
Nevada	6.85	180	3.6 (l)	Yes
New Hampshire	(a)	178	(j)	...
New Jersey	7.0	270	5.5	Yes
New Mexico	5.125	166	6.06	Yes
New York	4.0	435 (e)	6.44 (l)	Yes
North Carolina	4.75	45	(j)	Yes (k)
North Dakota	5.0	44	2.5 (l)	...
Ohio	5.75	160	(j)	Yes
Oklahoma	4.5	103	5.56 (l)	Yes
Oregon	(a)	132	(j)	...
Pennsylvania	6.0	160	(j)	Yes
Rhode Island	7.0	375	5.40	Yes
South Carolina	6.0	57	2.72 (l)	Yes
South Dakota	4.0	153	3.93 (l)	Yes
Tennessee	7.0	62 (e)(g)	4.4 (l)	Yes
Texas	6.25	141	2.4 (l)	Yes
Utah	5.95 (c)	170	(j)	Yes
Vermont	6.0	308	(j) (l)	...
Virginia	5.3 (d)	30 (e)	(j)	Yes
Washington	6.5	302.5	14.27 (l)(m)	...
West Virginia	6.0	55	(j)	Yes
Wisconsin	5.0	252	3.25 (l)	Yes
Wyoming	4.0	60	(j)	Yes
Dist. of Columbia	5.75	250 (i)	1.5 (l)	...

See footnotes at end of table.

STATE EXCISE TAX RATES—Continued
(As of January 1, 2016)

Source: Compiled by The Federation of Tax Administrators from various sources, January 2016.

Key:

... —Tax is not applicable.

(a) These states do not have a general sales and gross receipts tax.

(b) The tax rate may be adjusted annually according to a formula based on balances in the unappropriated general fund and the school foundation fund. Rate is scheduled to decrease jto 7,25% in Jan. 1, 2017.

(c) Includes statewide tax of 1.25 percent levied by local governments in Utah.

(d) Includes statewide 1.0% tax levied by local governments in Virginia.

(e) Counties and cities may impose an additional tax on a pack of cigarettes: in Alabama, 1¢ to 25¢; Illinois, 10¢ to $4.18; Missouri, 4¢ to 7¢; New York City, $1.50; Tennessee, 1¢; and Virginia, 2¢ to 15¢.

(f) Florida's rate includes a surcharge of $1 per pack.

(g) Dealers pay an additional enforcement and administrative fee of 0.05¢ in Tennessee.

(h) In addition, Minnesota imposes an in lieu cigarette sales tax determined annually by the Department.

The current rate is 54.3¢ through Dec. 31, 2016.

(i) In addition, District of Columbia imposes an in lieu cigarette sales tax calculated every March 31. The curent rate is 41¢.

(j) In 17 states, the government directly controls the sales of distilled spirits. Revenue in these states is generated from various taxes, fees, price mark-ups, and net liquor profits.

(k) General sales tax applies to on-premise sales only.

(l) Other taxes in addition to excise taxes for the following states: Alaska, under 21%—$2.50/gallon; Arkansas, under 5%—$0.50/gallon, under 21%—$1.00/gallon; $0.20/case; 3% off—14% on-premise retail taxes; California, over 50%—6.6./gallon; Connecticut, under 7%—$2.46/gallon; Delaware. 25% or less—$2.30/gallon; Florida, under 17.259%—$2.25/gallon, over 55.780%—$9.53/gallon; Georgia, $0.83/gallon local tax; Illinois, under 20%—$1.39/gallon; $2.68/gallon in Chicago and $2.50/gallon in Cook County; Indiana, under 15%—$0.47/gallon; Kansas, 8% off- and 10% on-premise retail tax; Kentucky, under 6%—$0.25/gallon; $0.05/case and 10.75% wholesale tax; Maryland, 9% sales tax; Massachusetts, under 15%—$1.10/gallon, over 50% alcohol—$4.05/proof; gallon; 0.57% on private club sales; Minnesota, $0.01/bottle (except miniatures) and 9% sales tax; Nevada, 5% to 14%—$0.70/gallon, 15% to 22%—$1.30/gallon; New York, under 24%—$2.54/gal.; additional $1.00/gal. in New York City; North Dakota, 7% state sales tax; Oklahoma, 13.5% on-premise; South Carolina, $5.36/case and 9% surtax; additional 5% on-premise tax; South Dakota, under 14%—$0.93/gallon; 2% wholesale tax; Tennessee, 15% on-premise; under 7%—$1.10/gallon.; Texas, 6.7% on-premise and $0.05/drink on airline sales; Vermont, 10% on-premise sales tax; Washington, $9.24/gal. on-premise; 20.5% retail sales tax to on-premise; Wisconsin, $0.03/gallon administrative fee; Dist. of Columbia, 9% off- and on-premise sales tax;

(m) Washington privatized liquor sales effective June 1, 2012.

(n) Connecticut's tax rate is schedued to increase to $3.90 a pack on July 1, 2016.

Table 7.10b
STATE EXCISE TAX RATES
(As of January 1, 2016)

State or other jurisdiction	Gasoline			Diesel fuel			Gasohol		
	Excise	Fee/Tax	Total	Excise	Fee/Tax	Total	Excise	Fee/Tax	Total
Federal (g)(k)....................	18.3	0.1	18.4	24.3	0.1	24.4	13.0	0.1	13.1
Alabama (a)(j)(l)...............	16.0	2.0	18.0	19.0		19.0	16.0	2.0	18.0
Alaska (m)	8.0	0.95	8.95	8.0	0.95	8.95	8.0	0.95	8.95
Arizona (i)(k)	18.0	1.0	19.0	26.0	1.0	27.0	18.0	1.0	19.0
Arkansas (n)	21.5	0.3	21.8	22.5	0.3	22.8	21.5	0.3	21.8
California (h)(p)	30.0	5.0	35.0	13.0	22.5	35.5	30.0	5.0	35.0
Colorado.............................	22.0		22.0	20.5		20.5	20.0		20.0
Connecticut (p)...................	25.0		25.0	50.3		50.3	25.0		25.0
Delaware (p).......................	23.0		23.0	22.0		22.0	23.0		23.0
Florida (b)(p).....................	4.0	24.4	28.4	4.0	27.7	31.7	4.0	24.4	28.4
Georgia (e)(p).....................	26.0		26.0	29.0		29.0	26.0		26.0
Hawaii (a)(p)	17.0		17.0	17.0		17.0	17.0		17.0
Idaho (g)(p).......................	32.0	1	33.0	32.0	1	33.0	32.0	1	33.0
Illinois (a)(c)(p)................	19.0	1.1	20.1	21.5	1.1	22.6	19.0	1.1	20.1
Indiana (c)(p).....................	18.0		18.0	16.0		16.0	18.0		18.0
Iowa (n).............................	30.8	1.0	31.8	32.5	1.0	33.5	29.3	1.0	30.3
Kansas (l)(n)......................	24.0	1.03	25.03	26.0	1.03	27.030	24.0	1.03	25.03
Kentucky (c)(d)(n)	24.6	1.4	26.0	21.6	1.4	23.0	24.6	1.4	26.0
Louisiana (l).......................	20.0	0.125	20.125	20.0	0.125	20.125	20.0	0.125	20.125
Maine	30.0		30.0	31.2		31.2	30.0		30.0
Maryland (e)	32.6		32.6	33.35		33.35	32.6		32.6
Massachusetts	24.0		24.0	24.0		24.0	24.0		24.0
Michigan (p)........................	19.0		19.0	15.0		15.0	19.0		19.0
Minnesota (l)	28.5	0.1	28.6	28.5	0.1	28.6	28.5	0.1	28.6
Mississippi (n)	18.0	0.4	18.4	18.0	0.4	18.4	18.0	0.4	18.4
Missouri (p)........................	17.0	0.3	17.3	17.0	0.3	17.3	17.0	0.3	17.3
Montana	27.0		27.0	27.75		27.75	27.0		27.0
Nebraska (p)	26.8	0.9	27.7	26.8	0.3	27.1	26.8	0.9	27.7
Nevada (a)(p)......................	23.0	0.805	23.805	27.0	0.75	27.75	23.0	0.805	23.805
New Hampshire (p)...........	22.2	1.625	23.825	22.2	1.625	23.825	22.2	1.625	23.825
New Jersey(p)	10.5	4.0	14.50	13.5	4.0	17.50	10.5	4.0	14.50
New Mexico (p)	17.0	1.875	18.875	21.0	1.875	22.875	17.0	1.875	18.875
New York (p)	8.0	17.0	25.0	8.0	15.25	23.25	8.0	17.0	25.0
North Carolina (e)(j)(o) ...	35.0	0.25	35.25	35.0	0.25	35.25	35.0	0.25	35.25
North Dakota......................	23.0		23.0	23.0		23.0	23.0		23.0
Ohio	28.0		28.0	28.0		28.0	28.0		28.0
Oklahoma (n)......................	16.0	1.0	17.0	13.0	1.0	14.0	16.0	1.0	17.0
Oregon (a)..........................	30.0		30.0	30.0		30.0	30.0		30.0
Pennsylvania (p)	50.3		50.3	64.0		64.0	50.3		50.3
Rhode Island (k)................	33.0	1	34.0	33.0	1	34.0	33.0	1	34.0
South Carolina (k)(l)........	16.0	0.75	16.75	16.0	0.75	16.75	16.0	0.75	16.75
South Dakota (a)(l)..........	28.0	2	30.0	28.0	2	30.0	28.0	2	30.0
Tennessee (a)(p).................	20.0	1.4	21.4	17.0	1.4	18.4	20.0	1.4	21.4
Texas.................................	20.0		20.0	20.0		20.0	20.0		20.0
Utah	29.4		29.4	29.4		29.4	29.4		29.4
Vermont (e)(p)	12.1	18.36	30.46	28.0	4.0	32.0	12.1	18.36	30.46
Virginia (a)(f)	16.2		16.2	20.2		20.2	16.2		16.2
Washington (j)(p)	44.5		44.5	44.5		44.5	44.5		44.5
West Virginia (p)	20.5	12.7	33.2	20.5	12.7	33.2	20.5	12.7	33.2
Wisconsin (p)......................	30.9	2.0	32.9	30.9	2.0	32.9	30.9	2.0	32.9
Wyoming (p)	23.0	1	24.0	23.0	1	24.0	23.0	1	24.0
Dist. of Columbia	23.5		23.5	23.5		23.5	23.5		23.5

See footnotes at end of table.

STATE EXCISE TAX RATES — Continued
(As of January 1, 2016)

Source: Compiled by The Federation of Tax Administrators from various sources, January 2016.

Key:

. . . — Tax is not applicable.

Note: The tax rates listed are fuel excise taxes collected by distributor/supplier/retailers in each state. Additional taxes may apply to motor carriers. Carrier taxes are coordinated by the International Fuel Tax Association.

(a) Tax rates do not include local option taxes. In AL, 1 to 3 cents; HI, 8.8 to 18.0 cents; IL, 5 cents in Chicago and 6 cents in Cook county (gasoline only); NV, 4.0 to 9.0 cents; OR, 1 to 5 cents; SD and TN, one cent; and VA, 2.1%.

(b) Local taxes for gasoline and gasohol vary from 11.1 cents to 19.1 cents. Includes Inspection Fee, SCETS, and Additional Local Tax.

(c) Carriers pay an additional surcharge equal to IL—19.3 cents (g) 20.1 cents (d), IN—11 cents, KY—2% (g) 4.7% (d).

(d) Tax rate is based on the average wholesale price and is adjusted annually. The actual rates are: KY, 9%; and UT, 12%.

(e) Portion of the rate is adjustable based on maintenance costs, sales volume, cost of fuel to state government, or inflation.

(f) Large trucks pay an additional (d) 3.5 cents (g) 12.6 cents. Actual rates (g) 5.1%, (d) 6%.

(g) Tax rate is reduced by the percentage of ethanol used in blending (reported rate assumes the max. 10% ethanol).

(h) Califonia Gasoline subject to 2.25% sales tax. Diesel subject to a 9.25% sales tax.

(i) Diesel rate specified is the fuel use tax rate on large trucks. Small vehicles are subject to 18 cent tax rate.

(j) Tax rates scheduled to increase to 49.4 cents in WA, 7/1/16, 18 cents in AL (g), 10/1/16. Decrease to 34 cents in NC, 7/1/15.

(k) LUST tax.

(l) Inspection fee.

(m) Refining surcharge.

(n) Environmental fee.

(o) Inspection tax.

(p)

California—Includes prepaid sales tax

Connecticut—Plus a 8.1% Petroleum tax (gas)

Delaware—Plus 0.9% GRT

Florida—Sales tax added to excise

Georgia—Local sales tax additional

Hawaii—Sales tax additional

Idaho—Clean water tax

Illinois—Sales tax add., env. and LUST fee

Indiana—Sales tax additional

Michigan—Sales tax additional

Missouri—Inspection and Load fees

Nebraska—Petroleum fee

Nevada—Inspection and cleanup fee

New Hampshire—Oil discharge cleanup fee

New Jersey—Petroleum fee

New Mexico—Petroleum loading fee

New York—Petroleum tax, Sales tax additional

Pennsylvania—Oil franchise tax only

Tennessee—Petroleum tax and Envir. fee

Vermont—Cleanup Fee and Trans. Fee

Washington—0.5% privilege tax

West Virginia—Sales tax added to excise

Wisconsin—Petroleum inspection fee

Wyoming—License tax

Table 7.11
STATE SALES TAX RATES AND FOOD AND DRUG EXEMPTIONS
(As of January 1, 2016)

State or other jurisdiction	Tax rate (percentage)	Exemptions		
		Food (a)	Prescription drugs	Nonprescription drugs
Alabama	4.0	...	★	...
Alaska	none	...	...	...
Arizona	5.6	★	★	...
Arkansas	6.5	1.5% (f)	★	...
California	7.5 (b)	★	★	...
Colorado	2.9	★	★	...
Connecticut	6.35	★	★	★
Delaware	none	...	...	...
Florida	6.0	★	★	★
Georgia	4.0	★ (f)	★	...
Hawaii	4.0	...	★	...
Idaho	6.0	...	★	...
Illinois	6.25	1%	1%	1%
Indiana	7.0	★	★	...
Iowa	6.0	★	★	...
Kansas	6.5	...	★	...
Kentucky	6.0	★	★	...
Louisiana	4.0	★ (f)	★	...
Maine	5.5	★	★	...
Maryland	6.0	★	★	★
Massachusetts	6.25	★	★	...
Michigan	6.0	★	★	...
Minnesota	6.875	★	★	★
Mississippi	7.0	...	★	...
Missouri	4.225	1.225%	★	...
Montana	none	...	...	...
Nebraska	5.5	★	★	...
Nevada	6.85	★	★	...
New Hampshire	none	...	...	...
New Jersey	7.0	★	★	★
New Mexico	5.125	★	★	...
New York	4.0	★	★	★
North Carolina	4.75	★ (f)	★	...
North Dakota	5.0	★	★	...
Ohio	5.75	★	★	...
Oklahoma	4.5	...	★	...
Oregon	none	...	...	...
Pennsylvania	6.0	★	★	★
Rhode Island	7.0	★	★	...
South Carolina	6.0	★	★	...
South Dakota	4.0	...	★	...
Tennessee	7.0	5.0%	★	...
Texas	6.25	★	★	★
Utah	5.95 (c)	3.0% (c)	★	...
Vermont	6.0	★	★	★
Virginia	5.3 (d)	2.5% (d)	★	★
Washington	6.5 (e)	★	★	...
West Virginia	6.0	★	★	...
Wisconsin	5.0	★	★	...
Wyoming	4.0	★	★	...
Dist. of Columbia	5.75	★	★	★

Source: Compiled by FTA from various sources. January 2016.
Key:
★ — Indicates exempt from tax.
... — Indicates subject to general sales tax rate.
(a) Some states tax food, but allow a rebate or income tax credit to compensate poor households. They are: Hawaii, Idaho, Kansas, Oklahoma and South Dakota.
(b) Tax rate may be adjusted annually according to a formula based on balances in the unappropriated general fund and the school foundation fund. Rate is scheduled to decrease to 7.25% on 1/1/17.

(c) Includes statewide tax of 1.25 percent levied by local governments in Utah. Food sales subject to local taxes.
(d) Includes statewide 1.0% tax levied by local governments in Virginia.
(e) Washington tax rate may fall to 5.5% on 4/15/16, if state legislature does not act on Initiative 1366.
(f) Food sales subject to local taxes.
(g) Includes a statewide 1.25% tax levied by local governments in Utah.

Table 7.12
STATE INDIVIDUAL INCOME TAXES
(Tax rates for tax year 2016—as of January 1, 2016)

State or other jurisdiction	Tax rate range (in percents)		Number of brackets	Income brackets		Personal exemptions			Federal income tax deductible
	Low	High		Lowest	Highest	Single	Married	Dependents	
Alabama	2.0	- 5.0	3	500 (b)	- 3,001 (b)	1,500	3,000	500 (e)	★
Alaska..........................				— (No state income tax) —					...
Arizona........................	2.59	- 4.54	5	10,163 (b)	- 152,434 (b)	2,100	4,200	2,300	...
Arkansas (a)...............	0.9	- 6.9	6	4,299	- 35,100	26 (c)	52 (c)	26 (c)	...
California (a)	1.0	12.3 (f)	9	7,850 (b)	- 526,443(b)	109 (c)	218 (c)	337 (c)	...
Colorado......................	4.63		1	——Flat rate——		4,050 (d)	8,100 (d)	4,050 (d)	...
Connecticut.................	3.0	- 7.0	7	10,000 (b)	- 500,000 (b)	14,500 (g)	24,000 (g)	0	...
Delaware	0.0	- 6.6	7	2,000	- 60,001	110 (c)	220 (c)	110 (c)	...
Florida				— (No state income tax) —					...
Georgia........................	1.0	- 6.0	6	750 (h)	- 7,001 (h)	2,700	5,400	3,000	...
Hawaii..........................	1.4	- 8.25	9	2,400 (b)	- 48,000 (b)	1,144	2,288	1,144	...
Idaho (a)......................	1.6	- 7.4	7	1,452 (b)	- 10,890 (b)	4,050 (d)	8,100 (d)	4,050 (d)	...
Illinois........................	3.75		1	——Flat rate——		2,000	4,000	2,000	...
Indiana........................	3.3		1	——Flat rate——		1,000	2,000	2,500 (i)	...
Iowa (a)	0.36	- 8.98	9	1,554	- 69,930	40 (c)	80 (c)	40 (c)	★
Kansas	2.7	- 4.6	2	15,000 (b)		2,250	4,500	2,250	...
Kentucky	2.0	- 6.0	6	3,000	- 75,001	20 (c)	40 (c)	20 (c)	...
Louisiana....................	2.0	- 6.0	3	12,500 (b)	- 50,001 (b)	4,500 (j)	9,000 (j)	1,000	★
Maine (a).....................	5.8	- 7.15	3	21,050(b)	- 37,500 (b)	4,050 (d)	8,100 (d)	4,050 (d)	...
Maryland.....................	2.0	- 5.75	8	1,000 (k)	- 250,000 (k)	3,200	6,400	3,200	...
Massachusetts	5.10		1	——Flat rate——		4,400	8,800	1,000	...
Michigan (a)...............	4.25		1	——Flat rate——		3,950	7,900	3,950	...
Minnesota (a).............	5.35	- 9.85	4	25,180 (l)	- 155,651 (l)	4,050 (d)	8,100 (d)	4,050 (d)	...
Mississippi	3.0	- 5.0	3	5,000	- 10,001	6,000	12,000	1,500	...
Missouri......................	1.5	- 6.0	10	1,000	- 9,001	2,100	4,200	1,200	★(m)
Montana (a)	1.0	- 6.9	7	2,300	- 17,100	2,330	4,660	2,330	★(m)
Nebraska (a)	2.46	- 6.84	4	3,050 (b)	- 29,640 (b)	131 (c)	262 (c)	131 (c)	...
Nevada.........................				— (No state income tax) —					...
New Hampshire				—(State income tax of 5% on dividends and interest income only.)—					...
New Jersey	1.4	- 8.97	6	20,000 (n)	- 500,000 (n)	1,000	2,000	1,500	...
New Mexico	1.7	- 4.9	4	5,500 (o)	- 16,001 (o)	4,050 (d)	8,100 (d)	4,050 (d)	...
New York (a)...............	4.0	- 8.82	8	8,450 (b)	- 1,070,350 (b)	0	0	1,000	...
North Carolina...........	5.75		1	——Flat rate——		— None —			...
North Dakota (a).......	1.10	- 2.90	5	37,650 (p)	- 413,350 (p)	4,050 (d)	8,100 (d)	4,050 (d)	...
Ohio (a)......................	0.495	4.997	9	5,200	- 208,500	2,200 (q)	4,400 (q)	1,700 (q)	...
Oklahoma....................	0.5	- 5.00	6	1,000 (r)	- 7,200 (r)	1,000	2,000	1,000	...
Oregon (a)..................	5.0	- 9.9	4	3,350 (b)	- 125,000 (b)	194 (c)	390 (c)	195 (c)	★(m)
Pennsylvania	3.07		1	——Flat rate——		— None —			...
Rhode Island (a)........	3.75	- 5.99	3	60,850	- 138,300	3,900	7,800	3,900	...
South Carolina (a).....	0.0	- 7.0	6	2,920	- 14,600	4,050 (d)	8,100 (d)	4,050 (d)	...
South Dakota				— (No state income tax) —					...
Tennessee				–(State income tax 6% on dividends and interest income only.)–		1,250	2,500	0	...
Texas...........................				— (No state income tax) —					...
Utah.............................	5.0		1	——Flat rate——		(s)	(s)	(s)	...
Vermont (a).................	3.55	- 8.95	5	37,450 (t)	- 411,500 (t)	4,050 (d)	8,100 (d)	4,050 (d)	...
Virginia.......................	2.0	- 5.75	4	3,000	- 17,001	930	1,860	930	...
Washington.................				— (No state income tax) —					...
West Virginia..............	3.0	- 6.5	5	10,000	- 60,000	2,000	4,000	2,000	...
Wisconsin (a)	4.0	- 7.65	4	11,090 (u)	- 244,270 (u)	700	1,400	700	...
Wyoming.....................				— (No state income tax) —					...
Dist. of Columbia	4.0	- 8.95	4	10,000	- 350,000	1,675	3,350	1,675	...

See footnotes at end of table.

STATE INDIVIDUAL INCOME TAXES—Continued
(Tax rates for tax year 2016—as of January 1, 2016)

Source: The Federation of Tax Administrators from various sources, January 2016.

Key:

★ — Yes

. . . — No

(a) Eighteen states have statutory provision for automatically adjusting to the rate of inflation the dollar values of the income tax brackets, standard deductions, and/or personal exemptions. Massachusetts, Michigan, and Nebraska index the personal exemption only. Oregon does not index the income brackets for $125,000 and over. Maine has suspended indexing for 2014 and 2015.

(b) For joint returns, taxes are twice the tax on half the couple's income.

(c) The personal exemption takes the form of a tax credit instead of a deduction.

(d) These states use the personal exemption amounts provided in the federal Internal Revenue Code.

(e) In Alabama, the per-dependent exemption is $1,000 for taxpayers with state AGI of $20,000 or less, $500 with AGI from $20,001 to $100,000, and $300 with AGI over $100,000.

(f) California imposes an additional 1% tax on taxable income over $1 million, making the maximum rate 13.3% over $1 million.

(g) Connecticut's personal exemption incorporates a standard deduction. An additional tax credit is allowed ranging from 75% to 0% based on state adjusted gross income. Exemption amounts are phased out for higher income taxpayers until they are eliminated for households earning over $71,000.

(h) The Georgia income brackets reported are for single individuals. For married couples filing jointly, the same tax rates apply to income brackets ranging from $1,000, to $10,000.

(i) In Indiana, includes an additional exemption of $1,500 for each dependent child.

(j) The amounts reported for Louisiana are a combined personal exemption-standard deduction.

(k) The income brackets reported for Maryland are for single individuals. For married couples filing jointly, the same tax rates apply to income brackets ranging from $1,000, to $300,000.

(l) The income brackets reported for Minnesota are for single individuals. For married couples filing jointly, the same tax rates apply to income brackets ranging from $36,820 to $259,421.

(m) The deduction for federal income tax is limited to $5,000 for individuals and $10,000 for joint returns in Missouri and Montana, and to $6,350 for all filers in Oregon.

(n) The New Jersey rates reported are for single individuals. For married couples filing jointly, the tax rates also range from 1.4% to 8.97%, with seven brackets and the same high and low income ranges.

(o) The income brackets reported for New Mexico are for single individuals. For married couples filing jointly, the same tax rates apply to income brackets ranging from $8,000 to $24,000.

(p) The income brackets reported for North Dakota are for single individuals. For married couples filing jointly, the same tax rates apply to income brackets ranging from $62,600 to $413,350.

(q) Ohio provides an additional tax credit of $20 per exemption.

(r) The income brackets reported for Oklahoma are for single persons. For married persons filing jointly, the same tax rates apply to income brackets ranging from $2,000, to $12,200.

(s) Utah provides a tax credit equal to 6% of the federal personal exemption amounts (an applicable standard deduction).

(t) Vermont's income brackets reported are for single individuals. For married taxpayers filing jointly, the same tax rates apply to income brackets ranging from $62,600 to $411,500.

(u) The Wisconsin income brackets reported are for single individuals. For married taxpayers filing jointly, the same tax rates apply income brackets ranging from $14,820 to $326,330.

Table 7.13
STATE PERSONAL INCOME TAXES: FEDERAL STARTING POINTS
(As of January 1, 2016)

State or other jurisdiction	Relation to Internal Revenue Code	Federal tax base used as a starting point to calculate state taxable income
Alabama	...	...
Alaska	————————————No state income tax ————————	
Arizona	1/1/2015	Adjusted gross income
Arkansas	...	...
California	1/1/2015	Adjusted gross income
Colorado	Current	Taxable income
Connecticut	Current	Adjusted gross income
Delaware	Current	Adjusted gross income
Florida	————————————No state income tax ————————	
Georgia	1/1/2015	Adjusted gross income
Hawaii	12/31/2014	Adjusted gross income
Idaho	1/1/2015	Taxable income
Illinois	Current	Adjusted gross income
Indiana	1/1/2015	Adjusted gross income
Iowa	1/1/2015	Adjusted gross income
Kansas	Current	Adjusted gross income
Kentucky	12/31/2013	Adjusted gross income
Louisiana	Current	Adjusted gross income
Maine	12/31/2014	Adjusted gross income
Maryland	Current	Adjusted gross income
Massachusetts	1/1/2005	Adjusted gross income
Michigan	Current (a)	Adjusted gross income
Minnesota	12/31/2014	Taxable income
Mississippi	...	...
Missouri	Current	Adjusted gross income
Montana	Current	Adjusted gross income
Nebraska	Current	Adjusted gross income
Nevada	————————————No state income tax ————————	
New Hampshire	———————— On interest and dividends only————————	
New Jersey	...	...
New Mexico	Current	Adjusted gross income
New York	Current	Adjusted gross income
North Carolina	1/1/2015	Adjusted gross income
North Dakota	Current	Taxable income
Ohio	3/22/2013	Adjusted gross income
Oklahoma	Current	Adjusted gross income
Oregon	1/3/2013	Taxable income
Pennsylvania	...	...
Rhode Island	Current	Adjusted gross income
South Carolina	12/31/2014	Taxable income
South Dakota	————————————No state income tax ————————	
Tennessee	———————— On interest and dividends only————————	
Texas	————————————No state income tax ————————	
Utah	Current	Adjusted gross income
Vermont	1/1/2014	Taxable income
Virginia	1/2/2013	Adjusted gross income
Washington	————————————No state income tax ————————	
West Virginia	12/31/2014	Adjusted gross income
Wisconsin	12/31/2013	Adjusted gross income
Wyoming	————————————No state income tax ————————	
Dist. of Columbia	Current	Adjusted gross income

Source: Compiled by the Federation of Tax Administrators from various sources. January 2016.

Key:
... — State does not employ a federal starting point.
Current — Indicates state has adopted the Internal Revenue Code as currently in effect. Dates indicate state has adopted IRC as amended to that date.
(a) Michigan's taxpayers can choose to use either current or 1/1/1996 federal law.

Table 7.14
RANGE OF STATE CORPORATE INCOME TAX RATES
(For tax year 2016, as of January 1, 2016)

State or other jurisdiction	Tax rate (percent)	Tax brackets		Number of brackets	Financial institution tax rates (percent) (a)	Federal income tax deductible
		Lowest	Highest			
Alabama	6.5	--------- Flat Rate ---------		1	6.5	★
Alaska	0 - 9.4	25,000	222,000	10		...
Arizona	5.5 (b)	--------- Flat Rate ---------		1		...
Arkansas	1.0 - 6.5	3,000	100,001	6		...
California	8.84 (c)	--------- Flat Rate ---------		1	10.84 (c)	...
Colorado	4.63	--------- Flat Rate ---------		1	4.63	...
Connecticut	7.5 (d)	--------- Flat Rate ---------		1		...
Delaware	8.7	--------- Flat Rate ---------		1	8.7 - 1.7 (e)	...
Florida	5.5 (f)	--------- Flat Rate ---------		1		...
Georgia	6.0	--------- Flat Rate ---------		1	6.0	...
Hawaii	4.4 - 6.4 (g)	25,000	100,001	3	7.92 (g)	...
Idaho	7.4 (h)	--------- Flat Rate ---------		1		...
Illinois	7.75 (i)	--------- Flat Rate ---------		1		...
Indiana	6.5 (j)	--------- Flat Rate ---------		1	8.5 (j)	...
Iowa	6.0 - 12.0	25,000	250,001	4	5.0	★(k)
Kansas	4.0 (l)	--------- Flat Rate ---------		1	2.25 (l)	...
Kentucky	4.0 - 6.0	50,000	100,001	3	--- (a)	...
Louisiana	4.0 - 8.0	25,000	200,001	5	4.0 - 8.0	★
Maine	3.5 - 8.93	25,000	250,000	4	1.0 (m)	...
Maryland	8.25	--------- Flat Rate ---------		1	8.25	...
Massachusetts	8.0 (n)	--------- Flat Rate ---------		1	9.0 (n)	...
Michigan	6.0	--------- Flat Rate ---------		1	--- (a)	...
Minnesota	9.8 (o)	--------- Flat Rate ---------		1		...
Mississippi	3.0 - 5.0	5,000	10,001	3		...
Missouri	6.25	--------- Flat Rate ---------		1	7.0	★(k)
Montana	6.75 (p)	--------- Flat Rate ---------		1		...
Nebraska	5.58 - 7.81	1,000		2	--- (a)	...
Nevada	--------------------------------------- No corporate income tax ---------------------------------------					
New Hampshire	8.5 (q)	--------- Flat Rate ---------		1		...
New Jersey	9.0 (r)	--------- Flat Rate ---------		1		...
New Mexico	4.8 - 6.6 (s)	500,000	1 million	3		...
New York	6.5 (t)	--------- Flat Rate ---------		1	6.5 (t)	...
North Carolina	4.0 (u)	--------- Flat Rate ---------		1	6.0 (u)	...
North Dakota	1.41 - 4.31(z)	25,000	50,001	3	7.0 (b)	★
Ohio	-- (v) --					...
Oklahoma	6.0	--------- Flat Rate ---------		1	6.0	...
Oregon	6.6 - 7.6 (w)	1 million		2		...
Pennsylvania	9.99	--------- Flat Rate ---------		1	--- (a)	...
Rhode Island	7.0 (c)	--------- Flat Rate ---------		1		...
South Carolina	5.0	--------- Flat Rate ---------		1	4.5 (x)	...
South Dakota	---------------------- No corporate income tax ----------------------				6.0 - 0.25 (b)	...
Tennessee	6.5	--------- Flat Rate ---------		1	6.5	...
Texas	-- (y) --					...
Utah	5.0 (c)					...
Vermont	6.0 - 8.5 (c)	10,000	25,000	3	--- (a)	...
Virginia	6.0	--------- Flat Rate ---------		1	6.0	...
Washington	No corporate income tax					
West Virginia	6.5	--------- Flat Rate ---------		1	6.5	...
Wisconsin	7.9	--------- Flat Rate ---------		1	7.9	...
Wyoming	--------------------------------------- No corporate income tax ---------------------------------------					
Dist. of Columbia	9.4 (c)	--------- Flat Rate ---------		1		...

See footnotes at end of table.

RANGE OF STATE CORPORATE INCOME TAX RATES — Continued
(For tax year 2016, as of January 1, 2016)

Source: Compiled by the Federation of Tax Administrators from various sources, January 2016.

Key:

★ — Yes

... — No

(a) Rates listed are the corporate income tax rate applied to financial institutions or excise taxes based on income. Some states have other taxes based upon the value of deposits or shares.

(b) Arizona minimum tax is $100. Tax rate is scheduled to decrease to 4.9% in tax years 2017.

(c) Minimum tax is $800 in California, $100 in District of Columbia, $50 in North Dakota (banks), $500 in Rhode Island, $200 per location in South Dakota (banks), $100 in Utah, $250 in Vermont.

(d) Connecticut's tax is the greater of the 7.5% tax on net income, a 0.31% tax on capital stock and surplus (maximum tax of $1 million), or $250 (the minimum tax). Plus, an additional 20% surtax applies for tax years 2012 and 2016.

(e) The Delaware Bank marginal rate decreases over 4 brackets ranging from $20 to $650 million in taxable income. Building and loan associations are taxed at a flat 8.7%.

(f) An exemption of $50,000 is allowed. Florida's Alternative Minimum Tax rate is 3.3%.

(g) Hawaii taxes capital gains at 4%. Financial institutions pay a franchise tax of 7.92% of taxable income (in lieu of the corporate income tax and general excise taxes).

(h) Idaho's minimum tax on a corporation is $20. The $10 Permanent Building Fund Tax must be paid by each corporation in a unitary group filing a combined return. Taxpayers with gross sales in Idaho under $100,000, and with no property or payroll in Idaho, may elect to pay 1% on such sales (instead of the tax on net income).

(i) The Illinois rate of 7.75% is the sum of a corporate income tax rate of 5.25% plus a replacement tax of 2.5%.

(j) The Indiana tax rate is scheduled to decrease to 6.25% on July 1, 2016.

(k) 50% of the federal income tax is deductible.

(l) In addition to the flat 4% corporate income tax, Kansas levies a 3.0% surtax on taxable income over $50,000. Banks pay a privilege tax of 2.25% of net income, plus a surtax of 2.125% (2.25% for savings and loans, trust companies, and federally chartered savings banks) on net income in excess of $25,000.

(m) The state franchise tax on financial institutions is either (1) the sum of 1% of the Maine net income of the financial institution for the taxable year, plus 8¢ per $1,000 of the institution's Maine assets as of the end of its taxable year, or (2) 39¢ per $1,000 of the institution's Maine assets as of the end of its taxable year.

(n) Business and manufacturing corporations pay an additional tax of $2.60 per $1,000 on either taxable Massachusetts tangible property or taxable net worth allocable to the state (for intangible property corporations). The minimum tax for both corporations and financial institutions is $456.

(o) In addition, Minnesota levies a 5.8% tentative minimum tax on Alternative Minimum Taxable Income.

(p) Montana levies a 7% tax on taxpayers using water's edge combination. The minimum tax per corporation is $50; the $50 minimum applies to each corporation included on a combined tax return. Taxpayers with gross sales in Montana of $100,000 or less may pay an alternative tax of 0.5% on such sales, instead of the net income tax.

(q) New Hampshire's 8.5% Business Profits Tax is imposed on both corporations and unincorporated associations with gross income over $50,000. In addition, New Hampshire levies a Business Enterprise Tax of 0.75% on the enterprise base (total compensation, interest and dividends paid) for businesses with gross income over $150,000 or base over $75,000. The Business Profits Tax is scheduled to decrease to 8.2% for tax years beginning on or after 2017.

(r) In New Jersey small businesses with annual entire net income under $100,000 pay a tax rate of 7.5%; businesses with income under $50,000 pay 6.5%. The minimum Corporation Business Tax is based on New Jersey gross receipts. It ranges from $500 for a corporation with gross receipts less than $100,000, to $2,000 for a corporation with gross receipts of $1 million or more.

(s) New Mexico tax rates are scheduled to decrease for tax year 2017.

(t) New York's General business corporate rate shown. Corporations may also be subject to a capital stocks tax, which is being phased out through 2021. A minimum tax ranges from $25 to $200,000, depending on receipts ($250 minimum for banks). Certain qualified New York manufacturers pay 0%.

(u) In North Carolina financial institutions are also subject to a tax equal to $30 per one million in assets. Tax rate is scheduled to decrease to 3% in tax year 2017, if certain revenue targets are met.

(v) Ohio no longer levies a tax based on income (except for a particular subset of corporations), but instead imposes a Commercial Activity Tax (CAT) equal to $150 for gross receipts sitused to Ohio of between $150,000 and $1 million, plus 0.26% of gross receipts over $1 million. Banks continue to pay a franchise tax of 1.3% of net worth. For those few corporations for whom the franchise tax on net worth or net income still applies, a litter tax also applies.

(w) Oregon's minimum tax for C corporations depends on the Oregon sales of the filing group. The minimum tax ranges from $150 for corporations with sales under $500,000, up to $100,000 for companies with sales of $100 million or above.

(x) South Carolina taxes savings and loans at a 6% rate.

(y) Texas imposes a Franchise Tax, otherwise known as margin tax, imposed on entities with more than $1,110,000 total revenues at rate of 0.75%, or 0.375% for entities primarily engaged in retail or wholesale trade, on lesser of 70% of total revenues or 100% of gross receipts after deductions for either compensation or cost of goods sold.

(z) North Dakota imposes a 3.5% surtax for filers electing to use the water's edge method to apportion income.

State Revenues from Gambling Shrinking

By Lucy Dadayan

States expanded allowable gambling options significantly in the past two decades, particularly in the wake of the Great Recession when more than a dozen states authorized new options in an effort to generate more revenues. Despite these expansions, state and local government gambling revenues have softened significantly in recent years. History shows that in the long run growth in state revenues from gambling activities slows or even reverses and declines. Therefore, states considering further expansions of gambling should take into consideration market competition within the state and among neighboring states.

Gambling has become very popular as a way for states to raise revenue. Many states have been authorizing and expanding additional forms of gambling and finding ways to raise revenues from those activities. States are particularly likely to expand gambling in the aftermath of recessions and subsequent economic downturns in the hopes of raising more revenues.

In the short run, states indeed raise additional revenues due to expansion of gambling activities and facilities. However, history shows that in the long run the growth in state revenues from gambling activities eventually slows, or even reverses and declines. In short, the revenue returns deteriorate — and often quickly. This pattern of deterioration may be due to competition with other states for a limited market (saturation), competition between different forms of gambling (substitution) or other factors. Despite the deterioration, the dynamic often continues, as states find new forms of gambling to authorize, open new facilities and impose higher taxes on gambling. The results are short-run yields and longer-run deterioration.

In addition to the weak long-run growth of gambling revenues, the expansion of highly taxed gambling activities also raises equity issues, since the revenues come largely from low and moderate income households, whose incomes have declined — or not grown — in real terms along with their spending. A related equity issue is the competitive pressure that expansion of state-sanctioned commercial casinos creates for Native American casinos, which may see a reduction in their revenue yields. This can have negative effects on low-income communities that found a source of income in casinos after they were first authorized in 1988.

Why Do States Legalize and Expand Gambling?

Desperate fiscal times often lead to overeager legislative measures, including legalization and expansion of gambling without considering the long-term effects. However, fiscal stress is not the only motivation for gambling adoption.

Many researchers have examined factors leading to the legalization and adoption of gambling activities. The most compelling factors for gambling legalization are state fiscal conditions, economic development, political alignments and interstate competition.[1]

States often legalize and expand gambling activities during or after fiscal crises to generate new streams of tax revenues without increasing tax rates on income or sales. When state finances are depressed, legislators turn to gambling to attract tourism and keep gambling residents in state.[2]

State voters and legislators may also turn to casinos and racinos — hybrids of casinos and racetracks — in the hope of stimulating economic development and revitalizing distressed economies. However, there is no consensus on whether the operation of casinos and racinos leads to economic development.[3]

Politics and interest group lobbying are also contributing factors to gambling adoption and expansion. The gambling industry is a significant contributor to politicians and political parties and plays a crucial role in the political process. Some researchers have argued that the interests of the casino industry, state politicians and legislators are often aligned.[4]

The rapid expansion and geographic proliferation of gambling activities in the past decade has led to increased interstate competition for the gambling market.[5] State politicians and legislators often legalize gambling activities in response to

Table A: State Lottery Net Revenue, FYs 2008–2015

| | $ millions, adjusted to inflation | | | | | | | | % chg. | CAGR | % chg. | $ chg. |
State	FY 2008	FY 2009	FY 2010	FY 2011	FY 2012	FY 2013	FY 2014	FY 2015	FY 2014–15	FY 2008–15	FY 2008–15	FY 2008–15
United States	$18,181.7	$17,539.1	$17,854.4	$17,409.8	$18,375.7	$18,557.1	$18,337.5	$18,213.1	-0.7%	0.0%	0.2%	$31.4
Arizona................	160.7	141.2	154.4	156.3	172.6	183.0	177.9	176.0	(1.0)	1.3	9.5	15.3
Arkansas..............	N/A	N/A	90.3	79.5	102.4	93.1	82.7	72.8	(12.0)	NM	NM	NM
California	1,217.5	1,147.3	1,185.7	1,205.7	1,383.6	1,322.2	1,366.8	1,391.7	1.8	1.9	14.3	174.2
Colorado..............	136.0	130.9	122.9	121.1	129.1	139.6	131.8	128.0	(2.9)	(0.9)	(5.9)	(8.0)
Connecticut..........	314.7	309.6	310.6	309.1	324.8	321.3	323.6	319.7	(1.2)	0.2	1.6	5.0
Delaware	43.9	40.9	40.1	40.8	42.1	44.6	44.9	39.4	(12.3)	(1.5)	(10.2)	(4.5)
Florida................	1,427.1	1,409.0	1,356.6	1,273.2	1,384.5	1,466.2	1,514.5	1,496.4	(1.2)	0.7	4.9	69.3
Georgia................	964.8	954.1	961.7	903.9	944.2	954.8	957.1	980.5	2.4	0.2	1.6	15.7
Idaho..................	39.3	38.6	39.9	39.6	43.6	49.7	49.7	45.1	(9.3)	2.0	14.7	5.8
Illinois................	721.1	694.4	709.6	714.1	794.3	843.5	787.3	690.3	(12.3)	(0.6)	(4.3)	(30.7)
Indiana................	241.4	195.8	206.4	201.1	215.0	231.7	254.3	242.7	(4.6)	0.1	0.5	1.3
Iowa	62.9	66.2	63.0	72.6	82.5	87.4	74.9	74.5	(0.5)	2.5	18.5	11.6
Kansas................	77.9	74.6	75.1	74.8	75.4	76.7	75.2	75.0	(0.3)	(0.5)	(3.7)	(2.9)
Kentucky	213.6	223.6	233.1	226.8	226.7	230.4	229.0	236.1	3.1	1.4	10.5	22.5
Louisiana..............	146.6	148.7	145.5	145.7	164.4	164.9	172.8	184.8	6.9	3.4	26.0	38.1
Maine..................	55.0	54.5	56.8	52.9	56.3	54.5	52.6	54.0	2.8	(0.3)	(1.9)	(1.0)
Maryland..............	588.7	539.6	555.6	554.9	582.7	561.3	527.7	526.5	(0.2)	(1.6)	(10.6)	(62.2)
Massachusetts	1,141.9	988.1	1,032.3	948.6	1,030.6	983.9	941.7	959.0	1.8	(2.5)	(16.0)	(182.9)
Michigan..............	836.6	806.6	776.5	788.1	824.4	761.6	756.3	799.4	5.7	(0.6)	(4.5)	(37.2)
Minnesota............	129.3	129.4	133.0	130.2	129.7	139.1	128.6	133.4	3.7	0.4	3.2	4.1
Missouri..............	296.5	280.4	282.5	273.3	286.6	288.2	281.1	271.3	(3.5)	(1.3)	(8.5)	(25.3)
Montana	12.3	11.1	11.5	11.6	13.7	13.6	12.4	12.4	0.1	0.1	0.8	0.1
Nebraska	34.5	33.1	34.8	34.2	37.8	41.2	38.5	37.1	(3.6)	1.1	7.6	2.6
New Hampshire ...	84.1	74.8	72.1	66.5	69.9	76.5	73.3	74.3	1.4	(1.7)	(11.6)	(9.8)
New Jersey	980.8	970.7	1,005.4	993.5	995.3	1,116.9	977.3	960.0	(1.8)	(0.3)	(2.1)	(20.8)
New Mexico	45.4	44.7	47.4	44.1	43.3	45.0	41.5	41.1	(0.8)	(1.4)	(9.4)	(4.3)
New York.............	2,354.0	2,277.5	2,410.3	2,252.3	2,249.5	2,267.9	2,263.5	2,220.0	(1.9)	(0.8)	(5.7)	(134.0)
North Carolina.....	387.3	452.9	470.3	466.0	481.3	492.6	509.5	526.4	3.3	4.5	35.9	139.1
North Dakota.......	6.6	7.0	6.2	6.3	8.0	8.2	7.9	6.7	(15.1)	0.3	2.1	0.1
Ohio	747.4	768.4	792.8	789.3	807.7	774.6	774.6	739.9	(4.5)	(0.1)	(1.0)	(7.5)
Oklahoma.............	78.9	75.6	76.2	74.3	73.5	72.3	68.2	60.6	(11.1)	(3.7)	(23.2)	(18.3)
Oregon................	722.5	650.2	588.7	585.9	550.1	564.6	515.4	547.8	6.3	(3.9)	(24.2)	(174.6)
Pennsylvania	1,032.0	996.1	996.4	1,026.2	1,111.4	1,098.8	1,095.3	1,060.9	(3.1)	0.4	2.8	28.9
Rhode Island.......	66.1	64.8	60.4	57.5	59.7	65.3	58.9	56.9	(3.4)	(2.1)	(13.9)	(9.2)
South Carolina.....	295.0	286.1	296.5	289.9	314.4	314.2	330.7	343.5	3.9	2.2	16.4	48.5
South Dakota.......	137.1	131.2	130.3	115.4	108.6	110.9	107.6	112.1	4.2	(2.8)	(18.3)	(25.0)
Tennessee	318.2	306.5	314.3	313.5	338.8	349.7	341.6	347.8	1.8	1.3	9.3	29.6
Texas..................	1,150.8	1,162.1	1,156.7	1,093.7	1,210.5	1,249.8	1,236.3	1,242.7	0.5	1.1	8.0	91.9
Vermont...............	25.3	23.1	23.5	22.9	23.4	23.6	22.8	22.8	(0.4)	(1.5)	(9.9)	(2.5)
Virginia................	506.2	480.4	468.1	474.6	510.2	500.8	545.4	533.8	(2.1)	0.8	5.4	27.5
Washington...........	144.9	131.7	155.0	160.4	144.6	143.3	149.6	141.3	(5.6)	(0.4)	(2.5)	(3.6)
West Virginia.......	73.0	71.7	66.4	63.9	70.3	68.3	65.1	61.1	(6.1)	(2.5)	(16.3)	(11.9)
Wisconsin	164.0	145.9	139.4	155.4	158.1	161.4	171.5	167.5	(2.4)	0.3	2.1	3.4

Source: Rockefeller Institute review of state lottery financial reports.
Notes: VLT revenues are excluded for Delaware, Maryland, New York, Ohio, Rhode Island and West Virginia. Those revenues are reported under racinos or casinos. NM = not meaningful. N/A = Not applicable.

interstate competition and in the hopes of keeping residents and gambling taxes within the state.

Gambling and State-Local Government Revenues

State-sanctioned legalized gambling has expanded gradually and continuously over the last four decades. All states except Hawaii and Utah collect revenue from one or more forms of gambling such as lotteries, commercial casinos, racinos, pari-mutuel wagering, Native American casinos and some less common types of gambling activities. Currently, 44 states operate lotteries, 24 states have legalized commercial casino or racino operations, and more than 40 states allow pari-mutuel wagering. In addition, Native American casinos are legal in 29 states.

States derive the bulk of gambling-related revenues from three major sources—lotteries, commercial

Table B: Commercial Casino/Racino Legalization and Opening Dates, Distribution and Format

State	Casino legalization date	First casino opening date	Racino legalization date	First racino opening date	Number of operating casinos/racinos, FY 2015	Casino/racino format
Colorado............	1990	1991			36	Land-based
Delaware			1994	1995	3	VLTs / Table games
Florida			2006	2006	7	Slot machines
Illinois..................	1990	1991			10	Riverboat
Indiana................	1993	1995	2007	2008	13	Riverboat (10), Land-based (1), Racino (2)
Iowa.....................	1989	1991	1994	1995	18	Riverboat (4), Land-based (11), Racino (3)
Kansas	2007	2009			3	Land-based
Louisiana.............	1991	1993	1997	2002	20	Riverboat (15), Land-based (1), Racino (4)
Maine (a).............	2010	2012	2004	2005	2	Land-based
Maryland	2008	2010	2008	2011	5	Land-based (4), Racino (1)
Massachusetts (b)	2011	2015			0	Land-based
Michigan..............	1996	1999			3	Land-based
Mississippi	1990	1992			28	Dockside, Land-based
Missouri...............	1993	1994			13	Riverboat
Nevada.................	1931	1931			271	Land-based
New Jersey	1976	1978			8	Land-based
New Mexico			1997	1999	5	Slot machines
New York (c)........	2014		2001	2004	9	VLTs
Ohio.....................	2009	2012	2009	2012	11	Land-based (4), Racino (7)
Oklahoma.............			2004	2005	2	Slot machines
Pennsylvania	2004	2007	2004	2006	12	Land-based (6), Racino (6)
Rhode Island (c)..			1992	1992	2	VLTs / Table games
South Dakota.......	1989	1989			17	Land-based
West Virginia........	2009	2010	1994	1994	5	Land-based (1), Racino (4)

Source: Rockefeller Institute review of state gaming regulatory agency information.
Note: Shaded rows indicate casino legalization dates during or after the Great Recession period.

Key:
(a) Maine converted its only racino into a casino in March 2012.
(b) Massachusetts legalized casino operations in 2011 and opened the first casino on June 24, 2015.
(c) In addition to racino operations, New York also legalized casino operations in 2014 and expects to open four destination casinos.

casinos and racinos. While commercial casinos experienced dramatic growth during the 1990s, that trend shifted downward over the past decade. In recent years, much of the growth has shifted to racinos as more states have approved such facilities.

In this report, we provide detailed analysis of government tax and fee revenue from lottery and commercial casino/racino operations. We define gambling revenues as revenues from various taxes and fees transferred to state and local governments.

Lotteries

While casinos and racinos are the focus in many states, lotteries remain the primary source of gambling revenue to governments and represent about two-thirds of all gambling revenues.

Table A shows state-by-state inflation-adjusted revenue collections from lottery operations for fiscal years 2008–2015. In fiscal year 2015, states took in about $18.2 billion from lotteries. Inflation-adjusted revenues declined in 27 states while 16 states reported growth compared to fiscal year 2014.

Table A also shows compound annual growth rates between 2008 and 2015. For the nation as a whole, the compound annual growth rate was less than 0.1 percent between fiscal years 2008 and 2015.

Finally, Table A shows the growth between 2008 and 2015, both in percentage and dollar terms. Inflation-adjusted revenue collections from lottery operations for fiscal years 2008–2015. Inflation-adjusted state revenues from lotteries grew by $31.2 million, or 0.2 percent, between fiscal year 2008 and 2015. Twenty-one states saw declines in real lottery revenues between 2008 and 2015, with nine states seeing double-digit declines. Another five states reported declines of over 5 percent.

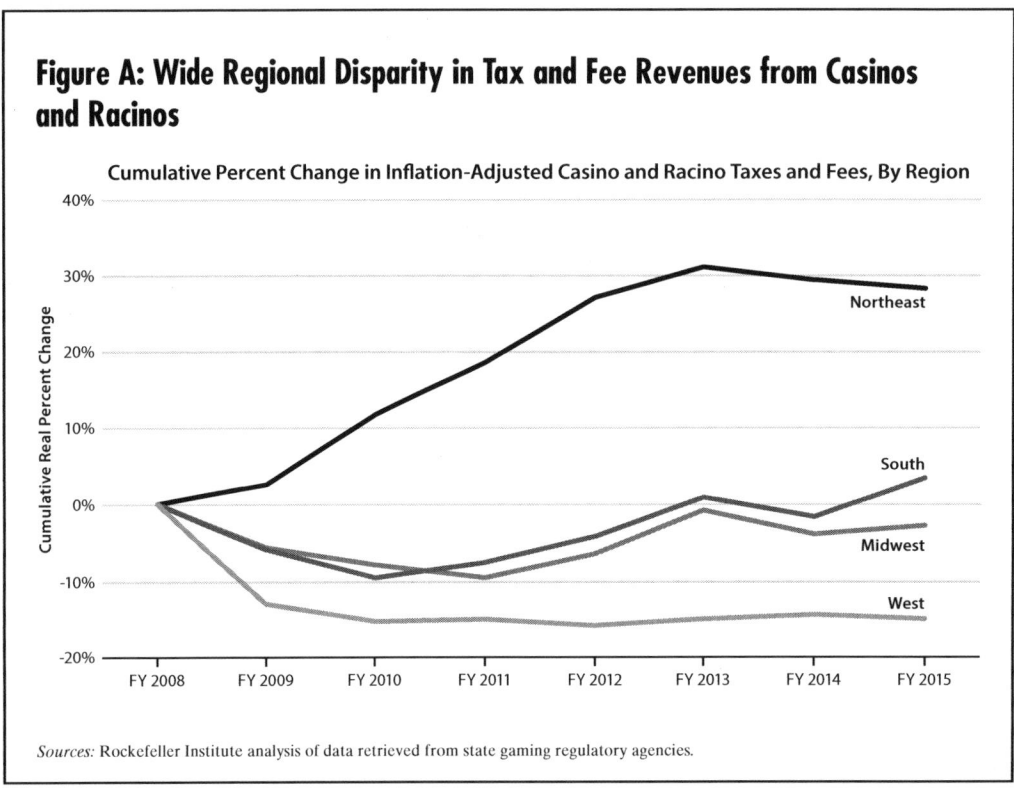

Figure A: Wide Regional Disparity in Tax and Fee Revenues from Casinos and Racinos

Cumulative Percent Change in Inflation-Adjusted Casino and Racino Taxes and Fees, By Region

Sources: Rockefeller Institute analysis of data retrieved from state gaming regulatory agencies.

Commercial Casinos and Racinos

Commercial casinos and racinos are operated by businesses and taxed by the states. Commercial casinos and racinos have been on the rise in the last decade. Before 1991, there were very few commercial casinos across the country outside of Nevada. About 50 percent of all casinos and racinos outside of Nevada were opened after 2001. In most states, casino and racino facilities are located near state border lines with other states to take advantage of cross-border consumers.

Currently, 24 states have legalized commercial casino and racino operations. Seven states legalized casino operations and three states legalized racino operations during or after the Great Recession (see Table B). In addition, a number of states introduced table games at their casino/racino facilities in the hopes of raising more revenues.

Figure A shows cumulative percent change since the Great Recession in inflation-adjusted tax and fee revenues for all commercial casinos and racinos by region. Tax and fee revenues from commercial casinos and racinos are still below the pre-recession levels in the Midwest and West regions and only

slightly above the pre-recession level in the South. The modest growth in the South is mostly attributable to a single state, Maryland, which legalized casino and racino operations only in 2008. The Northeast experienced steep growth in revenues from casinos and racinos since the start of the Great Recession, although the growth has softened in the last two fiscal years. The large growth in casino and racino revenues in the Northeast region is almost exclusively attributable to a single state, Pennsylvania, and to a single racino located in New York City. Pennsylvania legalized casino and racino operations in 2004 and opened five racinos in fiscal year 2007. Pennsylvania opened an additional racino and six casinos since fiscal year 2008. While racinos in New York have been operational since fiscal year 2004, the facility located in New York City was opened more recently, in fiscal year 2012.

Table C shows state-by-state inflation-adjusted revenue collections from casinos and racinos for fiscal years 2008–2015. The states are divided into two groups: the older casino/racino states and the newer casino/racino states. The older states include

Table C: Casino and Racino Tax and Fee Revenues to State-Local Governments, FYs 2008–2015

$ millions, adjusted to inflation

State	FY 2008	FY 2009	FY 2010	FY 2011	FY 2012	FY 2013	FY 2014	FY 2015	% chg. FY 2014–15	CAGR FY 2008–15	% chg. FY 2008–15	$ chg. FY 2008–15
United States	$8,248.5	$7,878.1	$7,919.6	$8,068.3	$8,405.8	$8,761.0	$8,592.0	$8,686.4	1.1%	0.7%	5.3%	$437.9
"Older" casino/ racino states	$7,255.3	$6,709.0	$6,467.8	$6,401.1	$6,535.8	$6,417.0	$6,144.7	$6,073.0	-1.2%	-2.5%	-16.3%	($1,182.3)
Colorado.............	120.3	103.8	117.1	112.0	107.0	107.2	106.2	110.1	3.6	(1.3)	(8.5)	(10.2)
Delaware.............	236.9	230.5	258.0	263.5	237.5	194.8	166.0	151.0	(9.1)	(6.2)	(36.3)	(85.9)
Illinois.................	776.4	582.3	525.6	488.6	574.4	574.4	523.2	498.3	(4.8)	(6.1)	(35.8)	(278.1)
Indiana	910.7	958.1	949.5	923.5	868.5	774.5	662.3	617.9	(6.7)	(5.4)	(32.1)	(292.8)
Iowa	339.4	328.1	322.0	312.9	327.3	318.7	303.3	305.0	0.6	(1.5)	(10.1)	(34.4)
Louisiana.............	596.5	572.7	527.4	522.6	513.5	507.7	506.0	534.9	5.7	(1.5)	(10.3)	(61.5)
Maine..................	22.7	28.9	30.7	29.5	31.7	52.0	51.5	51.7	0.5	12.5	127.9	29.0
Michigan (a)........	332.2	307.9	287.7	300.8	299.4	281.3	267.3	273.5	2.3	(2.7)	(17.7)	(58.6)
Mississippi...........	383.2	341.5	312.3	293.3	294.9	271.5	251.0	250.2	(0.3)	(5.9)	(34.7)	(133.0)
Missouri...............	476.6	499.7	516.5	521.2	503.3	477.8	444.4	440.9	(0.8)	(1.1)	(7.5)	(35.7)
Nevada	1,089.8	938.7	902.3	911.8	905.8	918.3	924.0	909.9	(1.5)	(2.5)	(16.5)	(179.9)
New Jersey	523.5	440.9	373.1	330.0	292.4	258.0	260.9	241.2	(7.6)	(10.5)	(53.9)	(282.3)
New Mexico	74.6	75.7	70.8	69.8	68.5	65.2	67.8	70.6	4.1	(0.8)	(5.4)	(4.0)
New York (b)	545.7	505.8	535.8	562.6	714.2	896.6	949.6	943.7	(0.6)	8.1	72.9	398.0
Oklahoma.............	12.0	15.3	15.1	18.6	19.9	21.3	20.9	20.6	(1.2)	8.1	72.3	8.7
Rhode Island.......	327.0	309.7	312.4	321.9	338.2	327.3	324.4	327.2	0.9	0.0	0.1	0.2
South Dakota........	17.7	17.4	18.5	17.7	17.9	17.6	16.4	16.1	(2.0)	(1.4)	(9.3)	(1.6)
West Virginia........	470.2	452.2	392.8	401.1	421.6	352.7	299.6	310.2	3.5	(5.8)	(34.0)	(160.0)
"New" casino/ racino states	$993.2	$1,169.1	$1,451.8	$1,667.1	$1,870.0	$2,344.1	$2,447.2	$2,613.4	6.8%	14.8%	163.1%	$1,620.2
Florida	134.1	113.7	150.3	133.6	150.8	157.0	176.2	182.6	3.6	4.5	36.2	48.5
Kansas			6.1	11.6	55.8	100.3	96.8	98.6	1.8			98.6
Maryland.............				63.3	117.2	344.5	383.7	445.5	16.1			445.5
Ohio.....................					24.6	289.2	426.8	527.5	23.6			527.5
Pennsylvania	859.1	1,055.5	1,295.4	1,458.6	1,521.6	1,453.1	1,363.7	1,359.2	(0.3)	6.8	58.2	500.1

Sources: Rockefeller Institute review of state gaming regulatory agencies' financial reports.
Note: States that opened the first casino/racino facilities in 2006 or later are classified as "new" casino/racino states. Shaded rows indicate casino legalization dates during or after the Great Recession period.

Key:
(a) Michigan's state fiscal year is from Oct. 1 to Sept. 30.
(b) New York's state fiscal year is from Apr. 1 to Mar. 31.

those states that had casino or racino operations in place before 2006, while the newer states include states that opened casino or racino facilities in 2006 or beyond.

In fiscal year 2015, states took in just about $8.7 billion from commercial casinos and racinos. Inflation-adjusted revenues declined in 11 of 23 states with casino or racino operations compared to fiscal year 2014. The largest growth was in Ohio and Maryland at 23.6 and 16.1 percent, respectively. In both states the strong growth is attributable to the opening of new facilities in fiscal 2015.

Table C also shows compound annual growth rates between 2008 and 2015. For the nation as a whole, the compound annual growth rate was 0.7 percent between fiscal years 2008 and 2015, which is slower compared to the growth rates in overall state tax collections. Moreover, the compound annual growth rate was negative 2.5 in the older casino/racino states.

Finally, Table C shows the growth between 2008 and 2015, both in percentage and dollar terms. Between 2008 and 2015, inflation-adjusted tax and fee revenues from casino/racino operations grew by $5.3 percent or $438 million nationally—with growth of more than $1.6 billion in newer casino/racino states and a decline of $1.2 billion in older casino/racino states. Declines were reported in 14 of the 18 older casino/racino states, indicating that casinos in older casino/racino states either reached saturation or have been cannibalized by newer casino/racino states.

The regional competition for casino tax dollars is at its height, particularly for the states in the Northeastern region. For example, when Pennsylvania legalized and opened the doors to casino and racino operations in mid-2000s, casino revenues in New Jersey saw declines and officials in New Jersey put the blame on the new competition in its neighboring state. Pennsylvania enjoyed the boom of tax revenue growth from casino and racino operations for the next few years, until the neighboring states Ohio and Maryland legalized and opened their own casinos and racinos. Moreover, the opening of a new racino in New York City also had a negative impact on casino/racino revenues in Pennsylvania.

While the expansion of casino and racino operations leads to some growth in total revenues, much of the growth appears to come at the expense of already established operations. The growth in gambling revenues is not sustainable and the empirical studies indicate that Americans are spending much less on gambling than they used to. The Great Recession and its anemic recovery had a big impact on consumer discretionary spending behavior, including spending on gambling activities. Moreover, baby boomers have far less retirement savings after the 2008 stock market crash and millennials and Generation Xers simply don't gamble as much as the baby boomers do.

The bottom line is that the trends talk for themselves: Gambling is not a reliable and sustainable source of revenue for the states.

Conclusions

Revenue from legally sanctioned gambling plays a small, but politically important, role in states' budgets. States are most likely to expand gambling operations when tax revenues are depressed by a weak economy, or to pay for new spending programs. Many states expanded and encouraged gambling during and after the Great Recession in response to historic declines in tax revenues. Still, the growth in revenue collections from gambling is not nearly as strong as it used to be.

The softening in the growth in gambling revenues is partially due to the impact of the Great Recession and due to changing consumer behavior in most recent years. In the wake of the Great Recession, many consumers became more conservative in their spending behavior, particularly when it came to discretionary spending. Since spending money on gambling activities is discretionary, consumers are less likely to spend significantly more on gambling despite the expansion of gambling activities. The recent geographic expansion of gambling created stiff competition, particularly in certain regions of the nation where states and facilities are competing for the same pool of consumers. Therefore, the weakening of the growth in gambling revenues is also attributable to market saturation and industry cannibalization.

If history offers any lesson, it is that gambling is only a short-term solution to state budget gaps. Gambling legalization and expansion lead to some revenue gains. However, such gains are short-lived and create longer-term fiscal challenges for the states as revenue growth slows or declines. In addition, gambling is associated with social and economic costs which often are hard to quantify and measure.

Notes

[1] See Edward J. Furlong, "A Logistic Regression Model Explaining Recent State Casino Gaming Adoptions," *Policy Studies Journal* 26, 3 (1998): 371–83; Peter T. Calcagno, Douglas M. Walker, and John D. Jackson, "Determinants of the Probability and Timing of Commercial Casino Legalization in the United States." *Public Choice* 142 (2010): 69–90.

[2] Ibid.

[3] Ernest H. Wohlenberg, "Recent U.S. Gambling Legalization: A Case Study of Lotteries," *Social Science Journal* 29, 2 (1992): 167–83; Steven D. Gold, *Gambling Is No Panacea for Ailing State Budgets, State Fiscal Brief* (Albany: Rockefeller Institute of Government, October 1993); Calcagno, Walker, and Jackson, "Determinants of the Probability and Timing of Commercial Casino Legalization in the United States."

[4] Earl J. Grinols, "The Impact of Casino Gambling on Income and Jobs," *Casino Development: How Would Casinos Affect New England's Economy?* (Boston: Federal Reserve Bank of Boston, October 1996): 3–17; Jamisen Etzel, "The House of Cards Is Falling: Why States Should Cooperate on Legal Gambling" *New York University Journal of Legislation & Public Policy* 15, 1 (2012) 199–246; Douglas M. Walker and Peter T. Calcagno, "Casinos and Political Corruption in the United States: A Granger Causality Analysis," *Applied Economics* 45, 34 (2013): 4781–95.

[5] Furlong, "A Logistic Regression Model Explaining Recent State Casino Gaming Adoptions;" Calcagno, Walker, and Jackson, "Determinants of the Probability and Timing of Commercial Casino Legalization in the United States;" Etzel, "The House of Cards Is Falling."

[6] William R. Eadington, "After the Great Recession: The Future of Casino Gaming in America and Europe," *Economic Affairs* 31, 1 (March 2011): 27–33.

About the Author

Lucy Dadayan is a senior policy analyst at the Rockefeller Institute of Government. She has conducted research and coauthored reports on state and local government fiscal policy issues; state spending on public policy programs and the effects of state fiscal capacity and economic changes; among other topics. Dadayan holds a Ph.D. in Informatics from the State University of New York.

Table 7.15
STATE SEVERANCE TAXES: 2016

State	Title and application of tax (a)	Rate
Alabama	Iron Ore Mining Tax	$.03/ton.
	Forest Products Severance Tax	Varies by species and ultimate use.
	Oil and Gas Conservation & Regulation of Production Tax	2% of gross value at point of production, of all oil and gas produced. 1% of the gross value (for a 5-year period from the date production begins) for well, for which the initial permit issued by the Oil and Gas Board is dated on or after July 1, 1996 and before July 1, 2002, except a replacement well for which the initial permit was dated before July 1, 1996; 1.66% gross proceeds from offshore production greater than 8,000 ft. below sea level.
	Oil and Gas Privilege Tax on Production	8% of gross value at point of production; 4% of gross value at point of incremental production resulting from a qualified enhanced recovery project; 4% if wells produce 25 bbl. or less oil per day or 200,000 cu. ft. or less gas per day; 6% of gross value at point of production for certain on-shore and off-shore wells. A 50% rate reduction for wells permitted by the oil and gas board on or after July 1, 1996, and before July 1, 2002, for 5 years from initial production, except for replacement wells for which the initial permit was dated before July 1, 1996; 3.65% gross proceeds from offshore production greater than 8,000 ft. below sea level;
	Coal and Lignite Severance Tax	$.20/ton in addition to coal severance tax. In 2012, state legislature extended through 2021.
	Local Solid Minerals Tax	Varies by county for sand, clay, gravel, granite, shale, and other products.
Alaska	Uniform Natural Minerals Tax	$.10/ton.
	Cost Recovery Fisheries Assessment (b)	Elective; currently no assessments in place.
	Dive Fishery Management Assessment (b)	Elective; currently 7% of value for select dive fishery species in select management regions.
	Fisheries Business Tax	Tax based on unprocessed value of fishery resources processed in or exported from the state. 1% of value for shore-based processing in developing fisheries; 3% of value for floating processing in developing fisheries or shore-based processing in established fisheries; 4.5% of value for salmon cannery processing in established fisheries; 5% of value for floating processing in established fisheries.
	Fishery Resource Landing Tax	Tax based on unprocessed value of fishery resources processed outside and first landed in the state. 1% of value for developing fisheries; 3% of value for established fisheries.
	Mining License Tax	Up to 7% of net income and royalties received in connection with mining properties and activities in Alaska. New mining operations other than sand and gravel exempt for 3 ½ years after production begins.
	Alaska Oil Production Tax	Alaska will impose a base rate of 35 percent on oil companies' net profits in the state, replacing a 25 percent base rate that increased by 0.4 percentage points for every $1 above a net wellhead price of $30.
	Salmon Enhancement Tax (b)	Elective; 2% or 3% of value for salmon sold in or exported from select aquaculture regions.
	Seafood Development Tax (b)	Elective; currently 1% of value for select commercial fish species in select seafood development regions.
	Seafood Marketing Assessment (b)	Elective; currently 0.5% of value for all commercial fish species exported from, landed or processed in-state.
Arizona	Severance Tax	2.5% of net severance base for mining (metalliferous minerals); $1.51/1,000 board ft. ($2.13 for ponderosa pine) for timbering. 3.125% for oil and gas production and nonmetal mining.
Arkansas	Natural Resources Severance Tax	Separate rate for each substance. Timber $0.178/ton (pine), all other $0.125/ton.
	Oil and Gas Conservation Tax	Natural gas 1.25%, 1.5%, and 5% depending on well classification; crude oil 4% to 5% depending on production levels.
	Oil and Gas Conservation Assessment	Maximum 43 mills/bbl. of oil and 9 mills per MCF produced of gas.
California	Oil and Gas Production Assessment	Rate determined annually by Department of Conservation to fund agency operations; no state severance tax. The assessment rate for fiscal year 2015/16 is $0.3243123.
	Lumber Tax	The Lumber Tax was enacted in Sept. 2012. Retailers are required to impose a 1% tax on lumber sold in California.
Colorado	Severance Tax (c)	Taxable years commencing prior to July 1, 1999, 2.25% of gross income exceeding $11 million for metallic minerals and taxable years commencing after July 1,1999, 2.25% of gross income exceeding $19 million for metallic minerals; on or after July 1,1999, $.05/ton for each ton exceeding 625,000 tons each quarter for molybdenum ore; 2% to 5% based on gross income for oil, gas, CO_2, and coalbed methane; after July 1,1999, $.36/ton adjusted by the producers' prices index for each ton exceeding 300,000 tons each quarter for coal; and 4% of gross proceeds on production exceeding 15,000 tons per day for oil shale.
	Oil and Gas Conservation Levy (d)	0.07% charge on all oil, natural gas, and CO_2 produced.

See footnotes at end of table.

STATE SEVERANCE TAXES: 2016—Continued

State	Title and application of tax (a)	Rate
Florida	Oil, Gas and Sulfur Production Tax	5% of gross value for small well oil, and 8% of gross value for all other, and an additional 12.5% for escaped oil; tiered formula for tertiary oil; the gas base rate ($0.171) times the gas base adjustment rate each fiscal year for gas; and the sulfur base rate ($2.43) times the sulfur base rate adjustment each fiscal year for sulfur.
	Solid Minerals Tax (e)	8% of the value of the minerals severed; heavy minerals (rate computed annually at $1.34/ton plus times the surcharge rate currently at 2.57) and phosphate rock (rate computed annually at a base rate of $1.80/ton plus $1.38 surcharge adjustment).
Idaho	Mine License Tax	1% of net value.
	Oil and Gas Production Tax	Maximum of 5 mills/bbl. of oil and 5 mills/50,000 cu. ft. of gas. Current conservation rate is 5 mills (.005).
	Additional Oil and Gas Production Tax	2.5% of market value at site of production.
Illinois	Oil and Gas Production Assessment (f)	0.1% fee per well of gross revenue for oil and natural gas.
	Timber Fee	4% of purchase price. (g)
Indiana	Petroleum Severance Tax (h)	1% of value or $.24 per barrel for oil or $.03 per 1,000 cu. ft. of gas, whichever is greater.
Kansas	Severance Tax (i)	8% of gross value of oil and gas, less property tax credit of 3.67%; $1/ton of coal.
	Oil Inspection Fee/barrel (i)	$0.015/barrel.
	Oil and Gas Conservation Tax	91.00 mills/bbl. crude oil or petroleum marketed or used each month; 12.9 mills/1,000 cu. ft. of gas sold or marketed each month.
	Mined-Land Conservation & Reclamation Tax	$50, plus per ton fee of between $.03 and $.10.
Kentucky	Oil Production Tax	4.5% of market value.
	Coal Severance Tax	4.5% of gross value, less transportation expenses; $0.50/ton minimum for extraction and processing.
	Natural Resource Severance Tax	4.5% of gross value, less transportation expenses.
Louisiana	Natural Gas Severance Tax (j)	The natural gas severance tax rate effective July 1, 2015 through June 30, 2016 has been set at 15.8 cents per thousand cubic feet (MCF) measured at a base pressure of 15.025 pounds per square inch absolute and at the temperature base of 60 degrees Fahrenheit. This tax rate is set each year by multiplying the natural gas severance tax base rate of 7 cents per MCF by the "gas base rate adjustment" determined by the Secretary of the Department of Natural Resources in accordance with R.S. 47:633(9)(d)(i). The "gas base rate adjustment" is a fraction, of which the numerator is the average of the New York Mercantile Exchange (NYMEX) Henry Hub settled price on the last trading day for the month, as reported in *The Wall Street Journal* for the previous 12-month period ending on March 31, and the denominator is the average of the monthly average spot market prices of gas fuels delivered into the pipelines in Louisiana as reported by the Natural Gas Clearing House for the 12-month period ending March 31, 1990 (1.7446 $/MMBTU). Based on this computation, the Secretary of the Department of Natural Resources has determined the natural gas severance "gas base rate adjustment" for July 1, 2015, through June 30, 2016, to be 225.01 percent. Applying this gas base rate adjustment to the base tax rate of 7 cents per MCF produces a tax rate of 15.8 cents per MCF effective July 1, 2015, through June 30, 2016. The reduced natural gas severance tax rates provided for in R.S. 47:633(9)(b) and (c) remain the same.
	Oil/Condensate Severance Tax (j)	Value on a per barrel basis (42 gallons) the rates are: full-rate, 12.5%; incapable oil rate, 6.25%; stripper oil rate, 3.125%; reclaimed oil, 3.125%; produced water full-rate, 10%; produced water incapable oil rate, 5.0%; produced water stripper oil rate, 2.5%.
	Timber Severance Tax (j)	Louisiana Revised Statute 47:633 imposes a severance tax on timber and pulpwood based on the trees and timber 2.25% of current stumpage value determined by state commission; pulpwood 5% of current stumpage value; current average stumpage market value determined annually on the second Monday of December by the Louisiana Forestry Commission Effective for 2015, the timber values to be used to determine the severance tax on timber are as follows: Pine Sawtimber, Value Per Ton $31.68, Tax Rate 2.25%, Tax Per Ton $0.71; Hardwood Sawtimber, Value Per Ton $35, Tax Rate 2.25%, Tax Per Ton $0.79; Pine Chip-n-Saw, Value Per Ton $16.50, Tax Rate 2.25%, Tax Per Ton $0.37; Pulpwood Pine, Value Per Ton $8.76, Tax Rate 5.00%, Tax Per Ton $0.44; Pulpwood Hardwood, Value Per Ton $10.50, Tax Rate 5.00%, Tax Per Ton $0.53.
	Mineral Severance Tax (j)	Various fees on a per ton basis for products like sulphur, salt, marble, stone, sand, lignit, and others.
	Oil Field Site Restoration Fee	Rate varies according to type of well and production.
	Freshwater Mussel Tax	5% of revenues from the sale of whole freshwater mussels, at the point of first sale.

See footnotes at end of table.

STATE SEVERANCE TAXES: 2016—Continued

State	Title and application of tax (a)	Rate
Maine	Mining Excise Tax	The greater of a tax on facilities and equipment or a tax on gross proceeds.
Maryland	Mine Reclamation Surcharge	$.15/ton of coal removed by open-pit, strip or deep mine methods. Of the $.15, $.06 is remitted to the county from which the coal was removed.
Michigan	Gas and Oil Severance Tax	5% (gas), 6.6% (oil) and 4% (oil from stripper wells and marginal properties) of gross cash market value of the total production. Maximum additional fee of 1% of gross cash market value on all oil and gas (2016 fee).
Minnesota	Taconite and Iron Sulfides	$2.56 per ton of concentrates or pellets (rate indexed to inflation by law).
	Direct Reduced Iron (k)	$2.56 per ton of concentrates plus an additional $.03 per ton for each 1% that the iron content exceeds 72%.
Mississippi	Oil and Gas Severance Tax	6% of value at point of gas production; 3% of gross value of occluded natural gas from coal seams at point of production for well's first five years; also, maximum 35 mills/bbl. oil or 4 mills/1,000 cu. ft. gas (Oil and Gas Board maintenance tax). 6% of value at point of oil production; 3% of value at production when enhanced oil recovery method used.
	Timber Severance Tax	Varies depending on type of wood and ultimate use.
	Salt Severance Tax	3% of value of entire production in state.
Montana	Coal Severance Tax	Varies from 3% to 15% depending on quality of coal and type of mine.
	Metalliferous Mines License Tax (l)	Progressive rate, taxed on amounts in excess of $250,000. For concentrate shipped to smelter, mill or reduction work, 1.81%. Gold, silver or any platinum group metal shipped to refinery, 1.6%.
	Oil or Gas Conservation Tax	Maximum 0.3% on the market value of each barrel of crude petroleum oil or 10,000 cu. ft. of natural gas produced, saved and marketed or stored within or exported from the state. (m)
	Oil and Natural Gas Production Tax	Varies from 0.5% to 14.8% according to the type of well and type of production.
	Miscellaneous Minerals License Tax	$.05/ton.
	Cement License Tax (n)	$.22/ton of cement, $.05/ton of cement, plaster, gypsum or gypsum products.
	Resource Indemnity Trust Tax	$25 plus 0.5% of gross value greater than $5,000. For talc, $25 plus 4% of gross value greater than $625. For coal, $25 plus 0.40% of gross value greater than $6,250. For vermiculite, $25 plus 2% of gross value greater than $1,250. For limestone, $25 plus 10% of gross value greater than $250. For industrial garnets, $25 plus 1% of gross value greater than $2,500.00.
Nebraska	Oil and Gas Severance Tax	3% of value of nonstripper oil and natural gas; 2% of value of stripper oil.
	Oil and Gas Conservation Tax	Two percent of value of stripper oil. Maximum 15 mills/$1 of value at wellhead, as of January 1, 2000. (f)
	Uranium Tax	2% of gross value over $5 million. The value of the uranium severed subject to tax is the gross value less transportation and processing costs.
Nevada	Minerals Extraction Tax	Between 2% and 5% of net proceeds of each geographically separate extractive operation, based on ratio of net proceeds to gross proceeds of whole operation.
	Oil and Gas Conservation Tax	$50/mills/bbl. of oil and 50 mills/50,000 cu. ft. of gas.
New Hampshire	Refined Petroleum Products Tax	0.1% of fair market value.
	Excavation Tax	$.02 per cubic yard of earth excavated.
	Timber Tax	10% of stumpage value at the time of cutting. Not assessed under the general property tax but rather is taxed by municipalities.
New Mexico	Resources Excise Tax (o)	Potash .5%, molybdenum .125%, all others .75% of value.
	Severance Tax (o)	Copper .5%, timber .125% of value. Pumice, gypsum, sand, gravel, clay, fluorspar and other non-metallic minerals, .125% of value. Gold, silver .20%; Lead, zinc, thorium, molybdenum, manganese, rare earth and other .125% of value.
	Oil and Gas Severance Tax	3.75% of value of oil, other liquid hydrocarbons, natural gas and carbon dioxide.
	Oil and Gas Emergency School Tax	3.15% of value of oil, other liquid hydrocarbons and carbon dioxide. 4% of value of natural gas.
	Natural Gas Processor's Tax	$0.0220/Mmbtu tax on volume.
	Oil and Gas Ad Valorem Production Tax	Varies, based on property tax in district of production.
	Oil and Gas Conservation Tax (p)	0.19% of value.
North Carolina	Oil and Gas Conservation Tax	Maximum 5 mills/barrel of oil and 0.5 mill/1,000 cu. ft. of gas.
	Primary Forest Product Assessment Tax	$.50/1,000 board ft. for softwood sawtimber, $.40/1,000 board ft. for hardwood sawtimber, $.20/cord for softwood pulpwood, $.12/cord hardwood pulpwood.
	Extracted Energy Minerals Tax	Oil and condensates: 2% of gross price paid. Gas: 0.9% of the market value as determined in N.C. Gen. Stat. § 105-187.78.

See footnotes at end of table.

STATE SEVERANCE TAXES: 2016—Continued

State	Title and application of tax (a)	Rate
North Dakota	Oil Gross Production Tax	5% of gross value at well.
	Gas Gross Production Tax	$.04/1,000 cu.ft. of gas produced (the rate is subject to a gas rate adjustment each fiscal year). Through June 30, 2016, the rate is cents $.1106 per mcf.
	Coal Severance Tax	$.375/ton plus $.02/ton. (q)
	Oil Extraction Tax	5% of gross value at well (with exceptions due to production volumes and and production incentives for enhanced recovery projects).
Ohio	Resource Severance Tax	$.10/bbl. of oil; $.025/1,000 cu. ft. of natural gas; $.04/ton of salt; $.02/ ton of sand, gravel, limestone and dolomite; $.10/ton of coal; and $0.01/ ton of clay, sandstone or conglomerate, shale, gypsum or quartzite.
Oklahoma	Oil, Gas and Mineral Gross Production Tax and Petroleum Excise Tax (r)	Rate: 0.75% levied on asphalt and metals. 7% (if greater than $2.10 mcf) 4% (if greater than $1.75 mcf, but less than $2.10 mcf) 1% (if less than $1.75 mcf) casinghead gas and natural gas as well as 0.95% being levied on crude oil, casinghead gas and natural gas. Oil Gross Production Tax is now a variable rate tax, beginning with January 1999 production, at the following rates based on the average price of Oklahoma oil: a) If the average price equals or exceeds $17/bbl, the tax shall be 7%; b) If the average price is less than $17/bbl, but is equal to or exceeds $14/bbl, the tax shall be 4%; c) If the average price is less than $14/bbl, the tax shall be 1%.
Oregon	Forest Products Harvest Tax	$3.7287/1,000 board ft. harvested from public and private land—through Dec. 31, 2016.
	Oil and Gas Production Tax	6% of gross value at well.
	STF Severance Tax— Eastern Oregon Forestland Option	$4.15/1,000 board ft. harvested from land under the Small Tract Forestland Option—through Dec. 31, 2015.
	STF Severance Tax— Western Oregon Forestland Option	$5.33/1,000 board ft. harvested from land under the Small Tract Forestland Option—through Dec. 31, 2015.
Pennsylvania	Natural Gas Severance Tax	Annual $50,000 per-well fee. Local fees and taxes determined by county.
South Carolina	Forest Renewal Tax	Softwood products: 50 cents per 1,000 board feet or 20 cents per cord. Hardwood products: 25 cents per 1,000 board feet or 7 cents per cord.
South Dakota	Precious Metals Severance Tax	$4 per ounce of gold severed plus additional tax depending on price of gold; 10% on net profits or royalties from sale of precious metals, and 8% of royalty value.
	Energy Minerals Severance Tax (s)	4.5% of taxable value of any energy minerals.
	Conservation Tax	2.4 mills of taxable value of any energy minerals.
Tennessee	Oil and Gas Severance Tax	3% of sales price.
	Coal Severance Tax (t)	$1.00/ton (effective 7/17/13).
	Mineral Tax	Up to $0.15 per ton, rate set by county legislative body.
Texas	Natural Gas Production Tax	7.5% of market value of gas. Condensate Production Tax: 4.6% of market value of gas.
	Crude Oil Production Tax	4.6% of market value or $.046/bbl.
	Sulphur Production Tax	$1.03/long ton or fraction thereof.
	Cement Production Tax	$0.55 per ton or $.0275/100 lbs. or fraction of 100 pounds of taxable cement.
	Oil-Field Cleanup Regulatory Fees	5/8 of $.01/barrel; 1/15 of $.01/1,000 cubic feet of gas. (u)
	Oyster Sales Fee	$1 per 300 lb. barrel of oysters taken from Texas waters.
Utah	Mining Severance Tax	2.6% of taxable value for metals or metalliferous minerals sold or otherwise disposed of.
	Oil and Gas Severance Tax	3% of value for the first $13 per barrel of oil, 5% from $13.01 and above; 3% of value for first $1.50/mcf, 5% from $1.51 and above; and 4% of taxable value of natural gas liquids.
	Oil and Gas Conservation Fee	.002% of market value at wellhead.
Virginia	Forest Products Tax	$1.15 per 1,000 feet B.M. of pine lumber and 1,000 board feet of pine logs. $0.475 collected per cord of pine pulpwood.
	Coal Surface Mining Reclamation Tax	Varies depending on balance of Coal Surface Mining Reclamation Fund.
Washington	Uranium and Thorium Milling Tax (tax reported as inactive)	$0.05/per pound.
	Enhanced Food Fish Tax	0.09% to 5.62% of value (depending on species) at point of landing.
	Timber Excise Tax	5% of stumpage value for harvests on public and private lands.

See footnotes at end of table.

STATE SEVERANCE TAXES: 2016—Continued

State	Title and application of tax (a)	Rate
West Virginia...............	Natural Resource Severance Taxes	Coal: State rate is greater of 5% or $.75 per ton (4.65% for state purposes and .35% for distribution to local governments). Special state rates for coal from new low seam mines. For seams between 37" and 45" the rate is greater of 2% or $.75/ton (1.65% for state purposes and .35% for distribution to local governments). For seams less than 37" the rate is greater of 1% or $.75/ton (.65% for state purposes and .35% for distribution to local governments). For coal from gob, refuse piles, or other sources of waste coal, the rate is 2.5% (distributed to local governments). Additional tax for workers' compensation debt reduction is $.56/ton. Two special reclamation taxes at $.07/clean ton and $.02/clean ton. Limestone or sandstone, quarried or mined, and other natural resources: 5% of gross value. Natural gas: 5% of gross value (10% of net tax distributed to local governments), additional tax for workers' compensation debt reduction is $.047/mcf of natural gas produced. Oil: 5% of gross value (10% of net tax distributed to local governments). Sand, gravel or other mineral products not quarried or mined: 5% of gross value. Timber: 1.22%, additional tax for workers' compensation debt reduction is 2.78%.
Wisconsin	Mining Net Proceeds Tax	Progressive net proceeds tax ranging from 3% to 15% is imposed on the net proceeds from mining metalliferous minerals. The tax brackets are annually adjusted for inflation based on the change in the GNP deflator.
	Oil and Gas Severance Tax	7% of market value of oil or gas at the mouth of the well.
	Forest Crop Law Severance Tax	10% of stumpage.
	Managed Forest Law Yield Tax	5% yield tax. This tax will be waived for the first five years of most MFL land.
Wyoming	Severance Taxes	Severance Tax is defined as an excise tax imposed on the present and continuing privilege of removing, extracting, severing or producing any mineral in this state. Except as otherwise provided by W.S. 39-14-205. The total Severance Tax on crude oil, lease condensate or natural gas shall be six percent (6%). Stripper oil is taxed at four percent (4%). Surface coal is taxed at seven percent (7%). Underground coal is taxed at three and three-fourths percent (3.75%). Trona is taxed at four percent (4%). Bentonite, sand and gravel, and all other minerals are taxed at two percent (2%). Tertiary Oil (4%). Natural Gas (6%). Uranium (4%).

Source: The Council of State Governments, 2016.

Note: Severance tax collection totals may be found in the Chapter 7 table entitled "State Government Revenue, By Type of Tax."

Key:

(a) Application of tax is same as that of title unless otherwise indicated by a footnote.

(b) Tax rates and applicability for these severance taxes determined by a vote of the appropriate association within the seafood industry, by the Alaska Seafood Marketing Institute, or by the Department of Revenue. Proceeds from these elective assessments are customarily appropriated for benefit of the seafood industry.

(c) Metallic minerals, molybdenum ore, coal, oil shale, oil, gas, CO_2, and coalbed methane. Petroleum Profits Tax (PPT) was changed in 2007.

(d) As of July 1, 2007, set at .0007 mill/$1.

(e) Clay, gravel, phosphate rock, lime, shells, stone, sand, heavy minerals and rare earths.

(f) Fee sunsets in 2018 under state law.

(g) Buyer deducts amount from payment to grower; amount forwarded to Department of Natural Resources.

(h) Petroleum, oil, gas and other hydrocarbons. Oil inspection fee rate based Dept. of Revenue factsheet.

(i) Coal, oil and gas, based on Department of Revenue information.

(j) Oil inspection fee rate based Dept. of Revenue factsheet.

(k) Coal, oil and gas, based on Department of Revenue information.

(l) Production is considered commercial when it exceeds 50,000 tons annually. There is a six-year phase-in of the tax. In years one and two, the rate is zero. In year three, it is 25% of the statutory rate and 50% and 75% in years four and five respectively. An Aggregate Materials Tax is imposed by resolution of of county boards. It is not required that any county impose the tax, which is $.10/cubic yard or $.07/ton on materials produced in the county.

(m) Metals, precious and semi-precious stones and gems.

(n) The maximum rate of 0.3% is split between the Oil or Gas Conservation Tax and the Oil, Gas and Coal Natural Resource Account Fund. Currently the Oil or Gas Conservation Tax is .18% and the Oil, Gas and Coal Natural Resource Account fund tax rate is .08%.

(o) Cement and gypsum or allied products.

(p) Natural resources except oil, natural gas, liquid hydrocarbons or carbon dioxide.

(q) Oil, coal, gas, liquid hydrocarbons, geothermal energy, carbon dioxide and uranium.

(r) Rate reduced by 50 percent if burned in cogeneration facility using renewable resources as fuel to generate at least 10 percent of its energy output. Coal shipped out of state is subject to the $.02/ton tax and 30% of the $.375/ton tax. The coal may be subject to up to the $.375/ton tax at the option of the county in which the coal is mined.

(s) Asphalt and ores bearing lead, zinc, jack, gold, silver, copper or petroleum or other crude oil or other mineral oil, natural gas or casing-head gas and uranium ore.

(t) Any mineral fuel used in the production of energy, including coal, lignite, petroleum, oil, natural gas, uranium and thorium.

(u) Counties and municipalities also authorized to levy severance taxes on sand, gravel, sandstone, chert and limestone at a rate up to $.15/ton.

(v) Fees will not be collected when Oil-Field Cleanup Fund reaches $20 million, but will again be collected when fund falls below $10 million.

Table 7.16
STATE GOVERNMENT TAX REVENUE, BY SELECTED TYPES OF TAX: 2013
(In thousands of dollars)

State	Total taxes	Sales and gross receipts	Licenses	Individual income	Corporation net income	Severance	Property taxes	Death and gift	Documentary and stock transfer	Other
United States	$847,077,345	$393,764,504	$55,460,732	$309,524,489	$45,015,768	$16,493,397	$13,053,517	$4,882,887	$6,376,472	$2,505,579
Alabama	9,267,567	4,708,518	490,430	3,202,520	382,202	119,424	322,300	18	42,155	0
Alaska	5,132,811	249,586	135,720	0	630,941	4,016,966	99,598	0	0	0
Arizona	13,471,690	8,206,708	412,769	3,397,707	662,026	29,829	762,651	0	0	0
Arkansas	8,586,407	4,019,203	356,920	2,649,577	402,874	80,862	1,022,066	92	30,190	24,623
California	133,184,246	48,074,580	8,743,748	66,809,000	7,462,000	37,732	1,982,208	*	0	74,978
Colorado	11,245,662	4,279,544	637,707	5,528,485	652,180	147,732	0	14		3,059
Connecticut	16,189,525	6,776,058	453,112	7,811,949	572,628	30	0	421,065	151,624	1,173
Delaware	3,346,316	487,202	1,259,277	1,130,501	309,644	0	0	20,161	138,358	0
Florida	35,377,566	29,315,741	1,993,965	0	2,071,710	47,050	360	290	1,948,450	0
Georgia	17,794,152	7,408,422	744,401	8,772,227	797,255	0	61,052	0	10,795	0
Hawaii	6,092,893	3,932,220	230,189	1,735,718	123,661	0	0	14,886	56,219	0
Idaho	3,579,093	1,773,270	306,627	1,292,562	200,340	6,224	0	70		0
Illinois	38,729,322	14,719,741	2,583,108	16,538,662	4,462,627	0	61,806	309,376	54,002	0
Indiana	16,930,731	10,298,491	699,373	4,976,375	781,585	2,421	7,008	165,478		0
Iowa	8,374,376	3,608,991	798,137	3,436,758	428,554	0	0	86,785	15,151	0
Kansas	7,620,282	3,742,916	382,944	2,956,588	384,553	73,806	79,475	0		0
Kentucky	10,815,954	5,110,456	462,726	3,722,964	646,875	269,786	558,377	41,326	3,444	0
Louisiana	9,223,829	4,974,642	369,930	2,739,083	252,430	834,116	52,686	42	0	0
Maine	3,884,450	1,779,873	260,918	1,531,504	171,987	0	38,636	79,083	22,449	0
Maryland	18,118,191	7,347,048	805,292	7,693,324	952,092	0	750,927	234,552	145,753	189,203
Massachusetts	23,901,047	7,455,326	945,922	12,876,192	1,888,449	0	4,795	313,395	219,465	197,503
Michigan	24,936,087	12,298,069	1,464,607	8,126,352	895,183	70,236	1,879,024	293	202,323	0
Minnesota	21,031,809	8,289,780	1,184,465	8,950,755	1,363,128	54,343	821,799	159,115	208,424	0
Mississippi	7,402,725	4,571,294	530,010	1,755,424	415,980	104,692	24,122	21	0	1,182
Missouri	11,139,394	4,791,043	549,473	5,380,651	377,258	8	29,896	175	10,815	75
Montana	2,644,610	558,961	320,858	1,045,500	170,999	282,356	262,313	0	0	3,623
Nebraska	4,718,944	2,197,988	130,762	2,101,694	275,563	4,064	148	0	8,725	0
Nevada	7,026,626	5,468,363	586,801	0	0	290,448	235,143	0	59,261	386,610
New Hampshire	2,349,693	945,290	252,442	99,027	553,197	0	400,369	0	99,368	0
New Jersey	29,076,881	12,198,133	1,516,432	12,108,615	2,282,055	0	4,620	623,840	343,186	0
New Mexico	5,201,576	2,651,625	255,968	1,240,945	267,457	713,998	71,583	0	0	0
New York	73,667,171	23,217,491	1,952,367	40,230,379	4,920,605	0	0	1,014,862	877,859	1,453,608
North Carolina	23,768,578	9,714,217	1,543,201	11,068,166	1,285,907	1,656	0	112,364	43,067	0
North Dakota	5,298,770	1,763,437	207,482	641,766	225,719	2,457,530	2,808	28	0	0
Ohio	27,516,947	13,822,045	3,445,620	9,869,545	262,226	12,308	0	105,203	0	0
Oklahoma	8,892,503	3,848,451	1,010,430	2,916,615	585,146	515,981	0	874	15,006	0
Oregon	9,160,887	1,369,266	923,123	6,260,161	459,744	23,305	19,893	101,831	3,564	0
Pennsylvania	33,965,626	17,106,300	2,585,202	10,777,334	2,208,163	0	55,537	812,350	395,176	25,564
Rhode Island	2,940,433	1,516,423	138,518	1,088,992	144,310	0	2,331	31,156	18,703	0
South Carolina	8,721,305	4,476,982	439,843	3,357,518	386,669	0	8,549	0	51,744	0

See footnotes at end of table.

STATE GOVERNMENT TAX REVENUE, BY SELECTED TYPES OF TAX: 2013
(In thousands of dollars) — Continued

State	Total taxes	Sales and gross receipts	Licenses	Individual income	Corporation net income	Severance	Property taxes	Death and gift	Documentary and stock transfer	Other
South Dakota.........	1,533,663	1,228,262	257,220	0	37,172	10,816	0	0	193	0
Tennessee..............	12,366,891	9,128,175	1,421,174	262,842	1,256,173	2,502	0	114,191	161,183	20,651
Texas....................	51,714,295	39,277,583	7,788,864	0	0	4,647,848	0	0	0	0
Utah.....................	6,325,126	2,739,916	290,388	2,852,088	330,684	112,050	0	0	0	4,681
Vermont................	2,878,930	983,226	106,509	663,027	105,635	0	971,718	15,387	28,747	4,681
Virginia................	19,186,853	6,192,666	806,572	10,900,860	772,001	2,117	33,188	0	376,892	102,557
Washington...........	18,667,044	14,647,173	1,359,685	0	0	38,656	1,939,883	104,258	577,389	0
West Virginia........	5,378,122	2,579,011	137,437	1,795,947	242,429	608,371	6,149	2	8,776	0
Wisconsin	16,513,692	7,088,411	1,026,823	7,227,690	955,752	6,201	148,600	304	48,016	11,895
Wyoming	2,186,054	826,387	155,241	0	0	867,933	331,899	0	0	4,594

Source: U.S. Census Bureau, 2013 Annual Survey of State Government Finances.

Note: Data users who create their own estimates using these data should cite only the U.S. Census Bureau as the source of the original data. Data in this table are based on information from public records and contain no confidential data. Although the data in this table come from a census of governmental units and are not subject to sampling error, the census results may contain nonsampling error. Addi-tional information on nonsampling error, response rates, and definitions may be found within the survey methodology, *http://www2.census.gov/govs/state/13_methodology.pdf,* and technical documentation, *http://www2.census.gov/govs/state/statetechdoc2013.pdf.*

Note: Detail may not add to total due to rounding.

Table 7.17
STATE GOVERNMENT SALES AND GROSS RECEIPTS TAX REVENUE: 2013
(In thousands of dollars)

State	Total	General sales or gross receipts	Total	Motor fuels	Insurance premiums	Public utilities	Tobacco products	Alcoholic beverages	Amusements	Pari-mutuels	Other
						Selective sales taxes					
United States	$393,764,504	$254,792,055	$138,972,449	$40,089,067	$17,427,572	$14,356,400	$17,858,789	$6,058,633	$6,861,882	$129,610	$36,190,496
Alabama	4,708,518	2,331,676	2,376,842	530,244	297,958	737,619	120,110	174,395	93	1,557	514,866
Alaska	249,586	0	249,586	41,608	60,236	4,295	69,175	39,194	8,427	0	26,651
Arizona	8,206,708	6,472,777	1,733,931	781,426	424,369	21,013	315,428	68,684	531	234	122,246
Arkansas	4,019,203	2,837,788	1,181,415	455,914	162,962	0	237,328	50,656	36,109	3,113	235,333
California	48,074,580	33,915,885	14,158,695	5,492,850	2,242,379	676,997	868,703	357,000	0	14,088	4,506,678
Colorado	4,279,544	2,416,731	1,862,813	626,619	211,320	11,528	197,026	39,217	94,699	610	681,794
Connecticut	6,776,058	3,855,861	2,920,197	483,881	242,448	340,920	399,885	60,416	382,390	6,876	1,003,381
Delaware	487,202	0	487,202	112,616	87,512	58,866	115,191	18,412	0	79	94,526
Florida	29,315,741	20,785,507	8,530,234	2,332,191	657,710	3,045,930	1,172,500	486,278	165,804	9,150	660,671
Georgia	7,408,422	5,277,211	2,131,211	1,000,626	329,237	0	211,618	180,786	0	0	408,944
Hawaii	3,932,220	2,944,487	987,733	92,516	136,542	163,930	112,104	48,962	0	0	433,679
Idaho	1,773,270	1,324,182	449,088	244,738	72,251	1,920	49,324	8,588	0	1,195	71,072
Illinois	14,719,741	8,159,003	6,560,738	1,259,834	359,578	1,638,578	857,110	279,928	598,897	5,881	1,560,932
Indiana	10,298,491	6,793,923	3,504,568	803,376	207,800	224,212	461,637	45,053	754,248	2,543	1,005,699
Iowa	3,608,991	2,520,072	1,088,919	440,365	104,885	0	226,300	13,865	270,659	3,996	28,849
Kansas	3,742,916	2,897,033	845,883	415,352	174,531	321	98,985	119,462	391	0	36,841
Kentucky	5,110,456	3,021,794	2,088,662	838,344	139,471	67,197	260,358	121,753	184	4,843	656,512
Louisiana	4,974,642	2,825,752	2,148,890	583,025	399,551	9,680	123,497	56,879	675,249	4,660	296,349
Maine	1,779,873	1,071,886	707,987	237,675	99,693	29,599	137,952	17,518	51,162	2,068	132,320
Maryland	7,347,048	4,114,296	3,232,752	740,556	429,410	123,431	415,922	30,867	25,281	1,203	1,466,082
Massachusetts	7,455,326	5,184,312	2,271,014	651,375	403,757	23,738	558,297	77,357	2,670	1,830	551,990
Michigan	12,298,069	8,465,895	3,832,174	956,173	301,883	35,653	958,961	138,900	110,668	4,599	1,325,337
Minnesota	8,289,780	5,009,508	3,280,272	860,833	400,974	50	392,552	80,153	37,253	544	1,507,913
Mississippi	4,571,294	3,191,683	1,379,611	412,966	212,493	6,191	150,277	41,787	139,630	0	416,267
Missouri	4,791,043	3,154,531	1,636,512	701,078	274,089	0	103,734	36,119	379,828	0	141,664
Montana	558,961	0	558,961	216,155	74,667	47,861	87,935	31,743	57,295	11	43,294
Nebraska	2,197,988	1,669,380	528,608	297,483	69,248	53,887	66,049	28,936	4,229	237	8,539
Nevada	5,468,363	3,637,356	1,831,007	297,387	249,390	21,993	104,766	40,903	921,872	0	194,696
New Hampshire	945,290	0	945,290	143,132	83,547	73,141	209,555	9,682	454	677	425,102
New Jersey	12,198,133	8,454,788	3,743,345	524,557	568,484	959,009	753,562	136,066	214,859	0	586,808
New Mexico	2,651,625	1,968,571	683,054	235,375	125,836	22,334	71,420	40,980	55,281	942	130,886
New York	23,217,491	12,117,579	11,099,912	1,634,932	1,435,166	1,027,932	1,543,018	247,303	1,030	22,270	5,188,261
North Carolina	9,714,217	5,592,560	4,121,657	1,893,576	542,551	396,056	281,097	332,656	14,703	0	661,018
North Dakota	1,763,437	1,268,695	494,742	211,700	47,867	39,807	28,743	9,154	5,521	742	151,208
Ohio	13,822,045	8,626,426	5,195,619	1,704,594	504,075	1,111,197	828,703	98,279	225,439	6,246	717,086
Oklahoma	3,848,451	2,518,598	1,329,853	434,719	268,121	41,207	283,902	111,001	20,767	1,191	168,945
Oregon	1,369,266	0	1,369,266	498,778	101,569	84,131	269,344	16,294	0	2,138	397,012
Pennsylvania	17,106,300	9,243,355	7,862,945	2,046,738	790,975	1,312,254	1,074,092	336,400	1,447,200	13,149	842,137
Rhode Island	1,516,423	881,458	634,965	94,191	94,915	101,502	131,974	12,717	0	1,184	198,482
South Carolina	4,476,982	3,199,752	1,277,230	520,501	150,213	26,831	27,677	156,759	39,172	0	356,077

See footnotes at end of table.

STATE GOVERNMENT SALES AND GROSS RECEIPTS TAX REVENUE: 2013—Continued
(In thousands of dollars)

State	Total	General sales or gross receipts	Selective sales taxes								
			Total	Motor fuels	Insurance premiums	Public utilities	Tobacco products	Alcoholic beverages	Amusements	Pari-mutuels	Other
South Dakota............	1,228,262	853,570	374,692	142,364	71,989	3,558	60,969	16,027	9,325	534	69,926
Tennessee	9,128,175	6,629,923	2,498,252	834,999	686,280	9,461	274,471	140,068	0	0	552,973
Texas......................	39,277,583	26,127,421	13,150,162	3,228,437	1,788,471	636,274	1,534,004	984,423	39,979	7,169	4,931,405
Utah........................	2,739,916	1,884,170	855,746	373,242	108,872	24,484	120,472	48,228	0	0	180,448
Vermont..................	983,226	347,273	635,953	106,840	57,517	17,272	74,270	23,159	0	0	356,895
Virginia	6,192,666	3,708,389	2,484,277	910,038	392,397	128,780	187,943	204,049	81	0	660,989
Washington	14,647,173	11,122,868	3,524,305	1,194,910	436,118	462,736	465,148	364,795	0	1,594	599,004
West Virginia	2,579,011	1,255,377	1,323,634	408,914	151,136	160,762	107,022	17,690	70,259	2,312	405,539
Wisconsin	7,088,411	4,410,130	2,678,281	968,338	176,710	368,708	632,174	57,290	243	0	474,818
Wyoming	826,387	702,623	123,764	70,986	18,419	3,555	26,505	1,802	0	145	2,352

Source: U.S. Census Bureau, 2013 Annual Survey of State Government Finances.
Note: Data users who create their own estimates using these data should cite only the U.S. Census Bureau as the source of the original data. Data in this table are based on information from public records and contain no confidential data. Although the data in this table come from a census of governmental units and are not subject to sampling error, the census results may contain nonsampling error. Additional information on nonsampling error, response rates, and definitions may be found within the survey methodology, *http://www2.census.gov/govs/state/13_methodology.pdf,* and technical documentation, *http://www2.census.gov/govs/state/statetechdoc2013.pdf.*
Note: Detail may not add to total due to rounding.

Table 7.18
STATE GOVERNMENT LICENSE TAX REVENUE: 2013
(In thousands of dollars)

State	Total license tax revenue	Motor vehicle license revenue	Occupation and business license, NEC	Corporation license	Motor vehicle operator's license	Hunting and fishing license	Public utility license	Alcoholic beverage license	Amusement license	Other license taxes
United States	$55,460,732	$2,509,665	$13,390,705	$11,414,552	$23,213,282	$1,554,995	$945,119	$692,086	$596,089	$1,144,239
Alabama	490,430	21,031	87,908	136,786	204,960	21,470	14,086	4,185	0	4
Alaska	135,720	0	40,522		58,822	25,569	514	1,788	1	8,504
Arizona	412,769	29,620	126,846	10,357	193,816	29,246	15,747	5,164	0	1,973
Arkansas	356,920	17,486	121,868	27,376	149,982	23,760	9,917	4,424	458	1,649
California	8,743,748	311,239	4,202,960	59,998	3,579,253	102,073	416,056	53,008	15,134	4,027
Colorado	637,707	30,945	39,378	13,175	462,676	71,096	12,140	6,734	629	934
Connecticut	453,112	42,607	155,506	27,828	209,745	5,713	686	8,803	209	2,015
Delaware	1,259,277	5,712	379,809	812,596	51,237	2,728	0	1,943	328	4,924
Florida	1,993,965	203,842	212,184	284,117	1,227,158	15,392	25,096	8,332	16,000	1,844
Georgia	744,401	49,334	133,903	39,243	457,490	23,502	0	3,512	797	36,620
Hawaii	230,189	389	30,866	1,606	175,341	488	20,111	0	0	1,388
Idaho	306,627	11,403	69,984	2,077	133,204	32,868	51,453	1,727	294	3,617
Illinois	2,583,108	103,140	430,765	345,961	1,584,922	38,472	18,262	12,289	17,658	31,639
Indiana	699,373	218,479	31,739	7,421	336,161	18,493	0	9,954	8,452	68,674
Iowa	798,137	14,237	112,333	43,938	540,619	28,719	12,033	14,564	23,997	7,697
Kansas	382,944	21,256	55,457	0	205,760	89,900	5,685	3,282	15	1,589
Kentucky	462,726	16,050	124,506	98,774	184,760	26,535	0	6,281	264	5,556
Louisiana	369,930	12,178	106,332	105,789	105,963	28,488	7,066	0	0	4,114
Maine	260,918	10,728	102,584	8,980	107,906	16,148	0	5,377	700	8,495
Maryland	805,292	34,569	208,228	92,984	450,618	15,770	0	1,266	30	1,827
Massachusetts	945,922	107,398	265,590	25,624	381,189	5,302	0	3,067	231	157,521
Michigan	1,464,607	56,672	160,987	22,736	943,486	49,326	30,696	16,118	0	184,586
Minnesota	1,184,465	44,130	321,197	8,491	668,947	55,580	752	1,966	3,141	80,261
Mississippi	530,010	37,793	96,020	149,321	151,627	17,341	14,717	2,927	17,410	42,854
Missouri	549,473	17,039	131,276	54,666	266,955	31,614	19,998	5,035	1,762	21,128
Montana	320,858	9,067	96,145	3,230	149,104	46,590	6	2,079	4,489	10,008
Nebraska	130,762	6,200	10,805	3,055	95,343	13,681	0	1,068	610	0
Nevada	586,801	21,729	230,099	65,070	162,250	10,121	0	0	92,967	4,565
New Hampshire	252,442	12,603	84,265	38,129	92,324	10,036	9,606	4,321	233	925
New Jersey	1,516,432	53,515	509,584	253,561	615,425	13,150	6,797	3,960	58,402	2,038
New Mexico	255,968	3,528	25,909	30,624	168,125	24,668	536	2,216	362	0
New York	1,952,367	145,008	226,912	60,319	1,377,900	56,643	22,842	61,225	59	1,459
North Carolina	1,543,201	112,726	232,570	575,862	581,590	16,619	0	15,915	0	7,919
North Dakota	207,482	5,135	73,437	0	113,651	14,087	3	347	822	0
Ohio	3,445,620	82,767	753,465	1,649,423	714,947	38,069	31,094	40,844	118,919	16,092
Oklahoma	1,010,430	15,517	115,344	44,580	649,232	19,683	5	1,224	152,863	11,982
Oregon	923,123	39,447	266,125	29,474	512,729	50,246	13,063	4,421	825	6,793
Pennsylvania	2,585,202	61,907	987,918	488,427	837,215	72,852	72,092	16,740	29,968	18,083
Rhode Island	138,518	4,991	54,000	4,719	66,202	1,668	0	73	169	6,696
South Carolina	439,843	9,449	98,299	74,208	210,000	17,346	0	12,394	1,718	16,429

See footnotes at end of table.

STATE GOVERNMENT LICENSE TAX REVENUE: 2013—Continued
(In thousands of dollars)

State	Total license tax revenue	Motor vehicle license revenue	Occupation and business license, NEC	Corporation license	Motor vehicle operator's license	Hunting and fishing license	Public utility license	Alcoholic beverage license	Amusement license	Other license taxes
South Dakota	257,220	3,739	126,781	4,504	66,660	28,140	0	785	7,628	18,983
Tennessee	1,421,174	46,945	298,207	758,051	270,469	31,380	5,995	1,320	314	8,493
Texas	7,788,864	132,626	509,681	4,824,007	1,934,422	103,912	21,659	66,463	8,069	188,025
Utah	290,388	15,244	47,700	490	195,363	28,726	0	1,936	0	929
Vermont	106,509	7,410	18,144	1,945	69,563	7,253	0	376	38	1,780
Virginia	806,572	62,311	185,964	57,191	452,626	29,503	0	12,284	102	6,591
Washington	1,359,685	91,739	280,384	30,836	509,854	43,289	18,762	257,601	6,045	121,175
West Virginia	137,437	105,877	11,887	4,858	2,456	113	304	1,392	3,483	7,067
Wisconsin	1,026,823	40,610	372,894	19,649	452,850	66,863	67,340	1,356	494	4,767
Wyoming	155,241	2,298	25,298	12,496	80,385	34,764	0	0	0	0

Source: U.S. Census Bureau, 2013 Annual Survey of State Government Finances.
Note: Data users who create their own estimates using these data should cite only the U.S. Census Bureau as the source of the original data. Data in this table are based on information from public records and contain no confidential data. Although the data in this table come from a census of governmental units and are not subject to sampling error, the census results may contain nonsampling error. Additional information on nonsampling error, response rates, and definitions may be found within the survey methodology, *http://www2.census.gov/govs/state/13_methodology.pdf*, and technical documentation, *http://www2.census.gov/govs/state/statetechdoc2013.pdf.*
Note: Detail may not add to total due to rounding.

Table 7.19
SUMMARY OF FINANCIAL AGGREGATES, BY STATE: 2013
(In millions of dollars)

State	Revenue Total	Revenue General	Utilities & liquor store	Insurance trust (a)	Expenditure Total	Expenditure General	Utilities & liquor store	Insurance trust	Total debt outstanding at end of fiscal year	Total cash and security holdings at end of fiscal year
United States	$2,216,076	$1,709,786	$21,055	$485,235	$2,005,912	$1,683,170	$30,294	$292,448	$1,137,364	$3,837,747
Alabama	29,093	22,760	278	6,055	28,204	24,602	267	3,335	9,055	41,204
Alaska.....................	14,018	12,280	17	1,721	12,215	10,707	209	1,298	6,218	80,064
Arizona...................	36,948	29,176	33	7,739	31,968	27,751	35	4,183	13,723	52,507
Arkansas.................	21,542	17,310	0	4,232	19,522	17,560	0	1,963	3,947	27,942
California	315,359	219,693	1,021	94,645	283,572	233,454	870	49,248	152,186	559,096
Colorado.................	30,987	23,129	0	7,857	28,744	23,189	16	5,539	16,309	68,213
Connecticut	31,851	25,446	37	6,368	29,303	23,719	752	4,832	32,357	42,600
Delaware	8,908	7,794	17	1,097	8,648	7,783	135	731	5,755	13,396
Florida	95,694	74,726	24	20,944	80,436	71,098	142	9,196	37,892	196,509
Georgia...................	53,487	38,392	7	15,088	45,484	38,702	37	6,744	13,293	86,023
Hawaii....................	12,945	10,825	0	2,120	11,478	10,098	6	1,374	8,318	16,243
Idaho......................	9,391	7,340	137	1,914	8,531	7,378	104	1,049	3,648	20,044
Illinois....................	84,493	65,562	0	18,932	75,325	61,222	0	14,103	63,660	128,341
Indiana...................	38,142	33,499	0	4,643	36,794	33,450	0	3,344	22,564	59,309
Iowa	23,103	18,534	259	4,310	20,518	17,902	176	2,441	6,648	40,606
Kansas....................	18,013	15,246	0	2,767	16,437	14,516	0	1,921	6,825	19,908
Kentucky	28,637	22,927	0	5,711	28,888	24,458	26	4,404	14,984	38,513
Louisiana................	31,238	25,255	7	5,976	32,038	27,800	5	4,233	18,589	56,742
Maine.....................	9,571	7,991	9	1,571	8,950	7,877	24	1,050	5,375	17,672
Maryland	41,802	34,779	138	6,885	39,557	34,171	932	4,454	26,067	61,078
Massachusetts	55,438	46,180	784	8,474	56,773	46,360	2,289	8,123	76,161	86,423
Michigan.................	66,401	54,343	912	11,146	62,945	53,550	883	8,513	30,377	70,535
Minnesota...............	45,594	34,651	0	10,942	39,943	35,059	9	4,876	13,573	66,051
Mississippi	21,865	17,511	282	4,073	20,102	17,387	227	2,488	7,113	28,227
Missouri..................	37,529	26,662	0	10,867	30,451	26,039	0	4,412	19,308	62,864
Montana	7,982	5,768	82	2,132	7,075	6,061	83	932	3,558	17,770
Nebraska	11,484	9,819	0	1,665	9,881	9,184	0	696	1,847	15,789
Nevada....................	17,041	11,402	79	5,559	13,274	10,639	84	2,551	3,610	31,311
New Hampshire	8,164	6,132	589	1,443	7,420	6,207	469	744	8,763	13,889
New Jersey	67,918	53,864	989	13,065	67,363	50,052	2,777	14,533	64,264	113,531
New Mexico	17,808	14,295	0	3,513	17,200	15,015	0	2,185	7,233	46,721
New York................	212,859	165,201	7,900	39,758	184,040	147,156	12,795	24,089	136,014	318,156
North Carolina........	60,004	47,575	0	12,430	53,626	46,103	72	7,451	19,055	101,336
North Dakota..........	8,830	8,060	0	771	6,410	5,786	0	624	1,834	20,326
Ohio.......................	90,344	60,946	929	28,469	76,292	59,502	356	16,434	33,133	220,915
Oklahoma...............	26,345	20,800	602	4,943	22,920	19,579	814	2,527	9,514	40,244
Oregon....................	32,915	22,833	498	9,584	26,850	21,465	271	5,114	13,598	69,419
Pennsylvania	87,911	69,756	1,731	16,424	87,533	72,244	1,586	13,702	47,021	124,835
Rhode Island...........	8,682	6,933	33	1,715	8,189	6,563	155	1,472	9,568	15,100
South Carolina........	29,639	22,161	1,875	5,603	28,246	22,331	2,227	3,688	14,724	41,025
South Dakota	5,759	4,036	0	1,724	4,477	4,011	0	466	3,425	14,202
Tennessee	32,356	27,402	0	4,955	30,586	27,831	0	2,755	6,192	47,293
Texas......................	136,487	112,936	0	23,551	124,930	108,025	0	16,905	39,625	303,266
Utah.......................	18,442	14,811	291	3,341	16,823	14,956	206	1,660	7,050	29,361
Vermont..................	6,296	5,635	51	610	6,018	5,608	52	358	3,330	7,476
Virginia..................	50,852	41,140	637	9,075	47,614	42,530	514	4,570	28,023	76,703
Washington.............	47,862	35,670	612	11,581	45,726	37,865	516	7,345	30,474	92,193
West Virginia..........	14,581	12,391	93	2,098	13,234	11,709	79	1,446	7,356	21,396
Wisconsin	45,892	32,281	0	13,611	37,525	31,878	8	5,638	23,188	87,571
Wyoming	7,574	5,929	102	1,543	5,835	5,037	88	711	1,021	27,812

See footnotes at end of table.

SUMMARY OF FINANCIAL AGGREGATES, BY STATE: 2013 — Continued
(In millions of dollars)

Source: U.S. Census Bureau, 2013 Annual Survey of State Government Finances.

Note: Data users who create their own estimates using these data should cite only the U.S. Census Bureau as the source of the original data. Data in this table are based on information from public records and contain no confidential data. Although the data in this table come from a census of governmental units and are not subject to sampling error, the census results may contain nonsampling error. Additional information on nonsampling error, response rates, and definitions may be found within the survey methodology, *http://www2.census.gov/govs/ state/13_methodology.pdf*, and technical documentation, *http://www2. census.gov/govs/state/statetechdoc2013.pdf*.

Note: Detail may not add to total due to rounding. Data presented are statistical in nature and do not represent an accounting statement. Therefore, a difference between an individual government's total revenue and expenditure does not necessarily indicate a budget surplus or deficit.

Key:

(a) Within insurance trust revenue, net earnings of state0administered pension systems is a calculated statistic (the item code in the data file is X08), and thus can be positive or negative. Net earnings is the sum of earnings on investments plus gains on investments minus losses on investments. The change made in 2002 for asset valuation from book to market value in accordance with Statement 34 of the Governmental Accounting Standards Board is reflected in the calculated statistics. The statistics reflect state government fiscal years that end on June 30, except for four states with other ending dates: Alabama and Michigan (September 30), New York (March 31), and Texas (August 31).

Table 7.20
NATIONAL TOTALS OF STATE GOVERNMENT FINANCES FOR SELECTED YEARS: 2005–2013 (In thousands of dollars)

Item	2013	2012	2011	2010	2009	2008	2007	2006	2005
Revenue total	$2,216,076,231	$1,905,807,119	$2,266,850,424	$2,039,926,569	$1,133,446,448	$1,579,327,215	$1,995,259,199	$1,774,648,692	$1,642,468,017
General revenue	1,709,786,388	1,629,267,996	1,658,377,770	1,567,206,839	1,493,989,614	1,509,888,971	1,451,775,306	1,391,133,672	1,286,899,373
Taxes	847,077,345	798,586,949	762,378,532	705,929,253	713,474,529	779,716,635	757,467,232	715,973,170	650,611,855
Intergovernmental revenue	551,464,163	533,655,081	595,028,792	575,371,668	494,782,446	441,972,830	426,590,487	419,640,660	407,791,786
From Federal Government	513,478,951	514,139,109	575,788,668	555,592,308	475,661,252	419,965,984	407,263,017	398,200,459	386,313,543
Public welfare	307,610,126	296,964,692	332,256,781	315,808,952	280,281,988	240,299,037	230,623,974	224,406,166	223,248,268
Education	84,408,057	90,264,309	104,711,082	105,511,630	82,447,792	74,307,867	73,422,139	72,376,901	68,882,228
Highways	41,431,014	43,199,512	44,245,077	42,969,373	36,518,798	35,722,224	35,200,889	34,187,690	32,676,739
Employment security administration	4,647,159	4,771,326	5,174,051	4,888,356	4,455,882	3,952,385	3,932,896	4,380,567	4,412,445
Other	70,770,258	74,371,641	84,933,214	82,442,778	68,492,747	65,684,471	60,639,547	62,849,135	53,823,548
From local government	37,985,212	19,515,972	19,240,124	19,779,360	19,121,194	22,006,846	19,327,470	21,440,201	21,478,243
Charges and miscellaneous revenue	311,244,880	297,025,966	300,970,446	285,905,918	285,732,639	288,199,506	267,717,587	255,519,842	228,495,732
Liquor stores revenue	7,480,124	7,114,248	6,739,028	6,494,993	6,376,562	6,128,282	5,799,273	5,475,273	5,118,462
Utility revenue	13,574,604	13,626,445	14,991,180	15,121,578	16,471,341	16,521,947	16,735,684	15,816,555	14,628,425
Insurance trust revenue (a)	485,235,115	255,798,430	586,742,446	451,103,159	-383,391,069	46,788,015	520,948,936	362,223,228	335,821,757
Employee retirement	388,424,920	152,590,817	476,654,285	353,373,854	-449,271,197	-11,549,775	457,687,157	295,602,816	269,617,472
Unemployment compensation	74,232,787	80,109,746	87,410,032	75,037,579	41,976,470	34,359,648	34,063,242	36,863,504	35,242,919
Worker compensation	15,295,670	15,526,364	15,032,589	15,311,140	16,618,791	18,574,527	19,785,182	21,906,234	23,352,729
Other	7,281,258	7,571,503	7,645,540	7,380,586	5,403,615	5,405,615	9,413,355	7,850,674	7,608,637
Expenditure and debt redemption	2,140,494,012	2,105,861,811	2,112,703,375	2,052,749,013	1,937,658,906	1,816,831,616	1,713,047,679	1,631,438,503	1,556,924,635
Debt redemption	134,582,345	124,664,050	106,755,419	109,226,381	105,062,105	77,528,415	75,083,761	76,905,629	84,382,231
Expenditure total	2,005,911,667	1,981,197,761	2,005,947,956	1,943,522,632	1,832,596,801	1,739,303,201	1,637,963,918	1,554,532,874	1,472,542,404
General expenditure	1,683,170,060	1,648,195,648	1,654,428,735	1,593,693,957	1,560,046,263	1,508,097,761	1,426,195,280	1,349,968,143	1,278,433,682
Education	599,151,748	588,340,483	592,863,150	571,147,157	567,674,062	547,511,580	514,588,891	483,476,753	454,348,376
Intergovernmental expenditure	324,995,548	317,839,562	330,482,270	317,389,500	324,374,036	315,424,647	301,062,065	280,090,982	263,625,820
State institutions of higher education	232,678,490	230,296,706	222,760,979	214,010,622	207,010,341	197,886,661	180,960,143	169,883,923	160,884,249
Other education	41,477,710	40,204,215	39,619,901	39,747,035	36,289,685	34,200,272	32,566,683	33,501,848	29,838,307
Public welfare	519,178,293	489,162,351	494,828,803	462,430,908	438,744,629	411,662,728	393,323,467	376,675,058	368,764,661
Intergovernmental expenditure	28,086,238	29,222,998	28,128,920	29,280,893	28,045,391	28,083,853	30,343,357	30,310,961	32,738,159
Cash assistance, categorical program	6,508,047	6,401,260	6,582,490	6,164,123	6,290,097	5,730,497	4,823,199	4,516,397	2,717,631
Cash assistance, other									
Other public welfare	484,584,008	453,538,093	460,117,393	426,985,892	404,409,141	377,848,378	358,156,911	341,847,700	333,308,871
Highways	112,174,050	115,296,570	109,397,936	111,169,808	107,286,437	107,584,368	103,511,290	100,841,813	92,816,461
Intergovernmental expenditure		17,787,581	17,243,590	18,043,061	16,492,780	16,549,366	14,881,789	15,495,306	14,500,232
Regular state highway facilities	104,088,029	105,496,969	101,913,730	102,742,620	98,889,122	99,047,331	95,954,560	93,964,195	86,571,074
State toll highways/facilities	8,086,021	9,799,601	7,484,206	8,427,188	8,397,315	8,537,037	7,556,730	6,877,618	6,245,387
Health and hospitals	130,680,311	130,621,569	126,020,387	122,754,039	120,594,797	115,742,953	107,236,896	96,663,369	92,256,859
Hospitals	67,433,480	69,265,569	65,985,505	64,509,024	58,041,020	54,733,920	49,798,760	45,960,293	43,623,308
Health	63,246,831	61,356,000	60,034,882	58,245,015	62,553,777	61,009,033	57,438,136	50,703,076	48,633,551
Natural resources	21,345,804	22,051,093	21,989,895	21,514,767	22,605,445	22,538,841	22,053,343	20,036,460	18,822,456
Corrections	48,407,786	48,439,991	49,166,999	48,549,551	50,382,439	49,880,748	46,485,220	42,793,514	40,562,217
Financial administration	23,136,739	21,771,566	22,334,533	22,610,662	22,979,925	23,457,406	22,574,672	21,676,940	21,224,584
Employment security administration	4,846,304	5,065,317	5,214,711	5,108,615	4,520,197	4,037,994	3,975,130	4,551,037	4,259,347
Police protection	15,106,964	14,275,634	14,248,537	13,828,055	13,676,971	13,617,829	12,879,814	12,220,732	11,395,489
Interest on general debt	46,138,932	47,273,956	46,653,282	45,259,591	45,281,069	44,838,072	41,694,648	38,231,722	34,242,019
Veterans' services	523,718	470,153	515,414	476,593	423,542	399,051	375,475	992,146	294,264
Utility expenditure	24,661,698	23,724,473	25,548,643	23,864,159	26,295,576	24,578,412	24,280,280	24,922,440	21,827,440
Insurance trust expenditure	292,447,534	303,669,929	320,563,723	320,720,833	241,080,311	201,682,378	182,824,248	175,304,033	168,199,527
Employee retirement	203,454,835	190,622,956	180,712,886	166,956,051	156,708,757	148,157,101	136,241,863	127,501,115	118,332,771
Unemployment compensation	71,181,425	95,317,383	121,384,316	134,908,383	65,974,092	35,470,883	28,854,007	28,008,860	29,776,222
Other	17,811,274	17,729,143	18,466,521	18,856,399	18,397,462	18,054,394	17,728,378	19,794,058	20,090,534

See footnotes at end of table.

NATIONAL TOTALS OF STATE GOVERNMENT FINANCES FOR SELECTED YEARS: 2005–2013—Continued
(In thousands of dollars)

Item	2013	2012	2011	2010	2009	2008	2007	2006	2005
Total expenditure by character and object	2,005,911,667	1,981,197,761	2,005,947,956	1,943,522,632	1,832,596,801	1,739,303,201	1,637,963,918	1,554,532,874	1,472,542,404
Direct expenditure	1,517,128,804	1,499,314,531	1,509,115,520	1,457,965,445	1,341,709,410	1,260,772,627	1,178,221,623	1,122,267,668	1,066,617,117
Current operation	1,020,376,950	986,062,966	984,180,683	934,321,563	901,310,643	866,901,215	810,478,208	774,002,589	738,885,771
Capital outlay	114,980,312	119,668,339	115,570,769	118,010,630	116,989,763	112,695,425	110,483,120	103,253,138	95,155,295
Construction	97,778,294	102,756,659	98,061,234	100,962,250	97,929,543	92,779,391	91,190,839	85,712,794	78,049,253
Other capital outlay	17,202,018	16,911,680	17,509,535	17,048,380	19,060,220	19,916,034	19,292,281	17,540,344	17,106,042
Assistance and subsidies	40,795,280	40,078,288	39,762,087	37,561,512	35,005,215	32,657,676	30,750,791	29,564,773	28,403,006
Interest on debt	48,528,728	49,835,009	49,038,258	47,350,907	47,323,478	46,835,933	43,685,256	40,143,135	35,973,518
Insurance benefits and repayments	292,447,534	303,669,929	320,563,723	320,720,833	241,080,311	201,682,378	182,824,248	175,304,033	168,199,527
Intergovernmental expenditure	488,782,863	481,883,230	496,832,436	485,557,187	490,887,391	478,530,574	459,742,295	432,265,206	405,925,287
Cash and security holdings at end of fiscal year	3,837,746,513	3,667,671,249	3,672,783,154	3,323,047,498	3,082,511,650	3,758,006,530	3,862,584,916	3,443,236,625	3,153,795,074
Insurance trust	1,572,694,369	1,523,149,081	2,518,525,924	2,214,651,546	2,020,928,749	2,656,071,709	2,814,408,903	2,495,133,155	2,306,208,483
Unemployment fund balance	3,723,399	-11,838,923	-18,830,490	-17,632,312	9,820,731	38,489,823	39,795,912	35,053,864	27,595,746
Debt offsets	458,510,770	485,559,643	500,220,858	500,337,284	491,111,560	461,876,851	429,725,192	390,865,042	363,955,939

Source: U.S. Census Bureau, Census of Governments: Finance (2007 and 2012) and Annual Survey of State Government Finances (remaining years).

Notes: Data users who create their own estimates using these data should cite only the U.S. Census Bureau as the source of the original data. Data in this table are based on information from public records and contain no confidential data. Although the data in this table come from a census of governmental units and are not subject to sampling error, the census results may contain nonsampling error. Additional information on nonsampling error, response rates, and definitions may be found within the survey methodology and technical documentation. The statistics reflect state government fiscal years that end on June 30, except for four states with other ending dates: Alabama and Michigan (September 30), New York (March 31), and Texas (August 31). Data are released on a flow basis and will be replaced when updated data are available. For more information, see the Federal, State, and Local Governments release schedule.

Key:

(a) Within insurance trust revenue, net earnings of state-administered pension systems is a calculated statistic (the item code in the data file is X08), and thus can be positive or negative. Net earnings is the sum of earnings on investments plus gains on investments minus losses on investments. The change made in 2002 for asset valuation from book to market value in accordance with Statement 34 of the Governmental Accounting Standards Board is reflected in the calculated statistics.

Table 7.21
STATE GENERAL REVENUE, BY SOURCE AND BY STATE: 2013 (In thousands of dollars)

State	Total general revenue (a)	Taxes Total (b)	Sales and gross receipts Total (b)	Sales and gross receipts General	Sales and gross receipts Motor fuels	Licenses Total (b)	Licenses Motor vehicle	Individual income	Corporation net income	Intergovernmental revenue	Charges and miscellaneous general revenue
United States	$1,709,786,388	$847,077,345	$393,764,504	$254,792,055	$40,089,067	$55,460,732	$23,213,282	$309,524,489	$45,015,768	$551,464,163	$311,244,880
Alabama...............	22,759,645	9,267,567	4,708,518	2,331,676	530,244	490,430	204,960	3,202,520	382,202	8,338,033	5,154,045
Alaska.................	12,280,315	5,132,811	249,586	0	41,608	135,720	58,822	0	630,941	2,754,412	4,393,092
Arizona...............	29,176,274	13,471,690	8,206,708	6,472,777	781,426	412,769	193,816	3,397,707	662,026	10,580,523	5,124,061
Arkansas..............	17,310,068	8,586,407	4,019,203	2,837,788	455,914	356,920	149,982	2,649,577	402,874	5,724,598	2,999,063
California.............	219,692,720	133,184,246	48,074,580	33,915,885	5,492,850	8,743,748	3,579,253	66,809,000	7,462,000	58,096,373	28,412,101
Colorado..............	23,129,280	11,245,662	4,279,544	2,416,731	626,619	637,707	462,676	5,528,485	652,180	6,508,932	5,374,686
Connecticut...........	25,446,414	16,189,525	6,776,058	3,855,861	483,881	453,112	209,745	7,811,949	572,628	5,962,699	3,294,190
Delaware..............	7,793,920	3,346,316	487,202	0	112,616	1,259,277	51,237	1,130,501	309,644	1,996,011	2,451,593
Florida................	74,725,923	35,377,566	29,315,741	20,785,507	2,332,191	1,993,965	1,227,158	0	2,071,710	23,880,229	15,468,128
Georgia................	38,391,794	17,794,152	7,408,422	5,277,211	1,000,626	744,401	457,490	8,772,227	797,255	14,619,221	5,978,421
Hawaii................	10,825,114	6,092,893	3,932,220	2,944,487	92,516	230,189	175,341	1,735,718	123,661	2,331,449	2,400,772
Idaho.................	7,340,263	3,579,093	1,773,270	1,324,182	244,738	306,627	133,204	1,292,562	200,340	2,541,438	1,219,732
Illinois...............	65,561,519	38,729,322	14,719,741	8,159,003	1,259,834	2,583,108	1,584,922	16,538,662	4,462,627	17,312,790	9,519,407
Indiana...............	33,499,152	16,930,731	10,298,491	6,793,923	803,376	699,373	336,161	4,976,375	781,585	11,267,810	5,300,611
Iowa..................	18,533,679	8,374,376	3,608,991	2,520,072	440,365	798,137	540,619	3,436,758	428,554	5,991,401	4,167,902
Kansas	15,245,978	7,620,282	3,742,916	2,897,033	415,352	382,944	205,760	2,956,588	384,553	3,845,073	3,780,623
Kentucky	22,926,606	10,815,954	5,110,456	3,021,794	838,344	462,726	184,760	3,722,964	646,875	8,083,482	4,027,170
Louisiana..............	25,255,359	9,223,829	4,974,642	2,825,752	583,025	369,930	105,963	2,739,983	252,430	10,660,261	5,371,269
Maine.................	7,990,979	3,884,450	1,779,873	1,071,886	237,675	260,918	107,906	1,531,504	171,987	2,830,353	1,276,176
Maryland..............	34,779,321	18,118,191	7,347,048	4,114,296	740,556	805,292	450,618	7,693,324	952,092	10,325,181	6,335,949
Massachusetts	46,180,318	23,901,047	7,455,326	5,184,312	651,375	945,922	381,189	12,876,192	1,888,449	13,706,498	8,572,773
Michigan	54,343,294	24,936,087	12,298,069	8,465,895	956,173	1,464,607	943,486	8,126,352	895,183	18,007,780	11,399,427
Minnesota.............	34,651,478	21,031,809	8,289,780	5,009,508	860,833	1,184,465	668,947	8,950,755	1,363,128	9,315,259	4,304,410
Mississippi............	17,510,532	7,402,725	4,571,294	3,191,683	412,966	530,010	151,627	1,755,424	415,980	7,649,292	2,458,515
Missouri...............	26,662,036	11,139,394	4,791,043	3,154,531	701,078	549,473	266,955	5,380,651	377,258	10,497,449	5,025,193
Montana	5,767,554	2,644,610	558,961	0	216,155	320,858	149,104	1,045,500	170,999	2,161,997	960,947
Nebraska	9,819,327	4,718,944	2,197,988	1,669,380	297,483	130,762	95,343	2,101,694	275,563	3,212,304	1,888,079
Nevada	11,402,396	7,026,626	5,468,363	3,637,356	297,387	586,801	162,250	0	0	3,080,240	1,295,530
New Hampshire	6,132,439	2,349,693	945,290	0	143,132	252,442	92,324	99,027	553,197	1,883,424	1,899,322
New Jersey	53,863,834	29,076,881	12,198,133	8,454,788	524,557	1,516,432	615,425	12,108,615	2,282,055	14,471,986	10,314,967
New Mexico	14,295,361	5,201,576	2,651,625	1,968,571	235,375	255,968	168,125	1,240,945	267,457	5,416,068	3,677,717
New York..............	165,200,561	73,667,171	23,217,491	12,117,579	1,634,932	1,952,367	1,377,900	40,230,379	4,920,605	71,682,137	19,851,253
North Carolina.........	47,574,530	23,768,578	9,714,217	5,592,560	1,893,576	1,543,201	581,590	11,068,166	1,285,907	15,769,950	8,036,002
North Dakota..........	8,059,929	5,298,770	1,763,437	1,268,695	211,700	207,482	113,651	641,766	225,719	1,572,480	1,188,679
Ohio..................	60,945,518	27,516,947	13,822,045	8,626,426	1,704,594	3,445,620	714,947	9,869,545	262,226	21,113,847	12,314,724
Oklahoma.............	20,799,702	8,892,503	3,848,451	2,518,598	434,719	1,010,430	649,232	2,916,615	585,146	7,159,511	4,747,688
Oregon................	22,833,016	9,160,887	1,369,266	0	498,778	923,123	512,729	6,260,161	459,744	8,003,252	5,668,877
Pennsylvania..........	69,755,731	33,965,626	17,106,300	9,243,355	2,046,738	2,585,202	837,215	10,777,334	2,208,163	21,412,638	14,377,467
Rhode Island..........	6,933,496	2,940,433	1,516,423	881,458	94,191	138,518	66,202	1,088,992	144,310	2,369,822	1,623,241
South Carolina.........	22,160,859	8,721,305	4,476,982	3,199,752	520,501	439,843	210,000	3,357,518	386,669	7,202,824	6,236,730

See footnotes at end of table.

STATE GENERAL REVENUE, BY SOURCE AND BY STATE: 2013 (In thousands of dollars) — Continued

State	Total general revenue (a)	Taxes Total (b)	Sales and gross receipts Total (b)	General	Motor fuels	Licenses Total (b)	Motor vehicle	Individual income	Corporation net income	Intergovernmental revenue	Charges and miscellaneous general revenue
South Dakota	4,035,680	1,533,663	1,228,262	853,570	142,364	257,220	66,660	0	37,172	1,605,537	896,480
Tennessee	27,401,810	12,366,891	9,128,175	6,629,923	834,999	1,421,174	270,469	262,842	1,256,173	10,900,626	4,134,293
Texas	112,935,910	51,714,295	39,277,583	26,127,421	3,228,437	7,788,864	1,934,422	0	0	37,580,061	23,641,554
Utah	14,810,655	6,325,126	2,739,916	1,884,170	373,242	290,388	195,363	2,852,088	330,684	4,304,061	4,181,468
Vermont	5,635,209	2,878,930	983,226	347,273	106,840	106,509	69,563	663,027	105,635	1,872,013	884,266
Virginia	41,140,409	19,186,853	6,192,666	3,708,389	910,038	806,572	452,626	10,900,860	772,001	9,959,041	11,994,515
Washington	35,669,826	18,667,044	14,647,173	11,122,868	1,194,910	1,359,685	509,854	0	0	10,030,961	6,971,821
West Virginia	12,390,766	5,378,122	2,579,011	1,255,377	408,914	137,437	2,456	1,795,947	242,429	4,325,052	2,687,592
Wisconsin	32,280,837	16,513,692	7,088,411	4,410,130	968,338	1,026,823	452,850	7,227,690	955,752	9,228,907	6,538,238
Wyoming	5,929,052	2,186,054	826,387	702,623	70,986	155,241	80,385	0	0	2,318,877	1,424,121

Source: U.S. Census Bureau, 2013 Annual Survey of State Government Finances.
Note: Data users who create their own estimates using these data should cite only the U.S. Census Bureau as the source of the original data. Data in this table are based on information from public records and contain no confidential data. Although the data in this table come from a census of governmental units and are not subject to sampling error, the census results may contain nonsampling error. Additional information on nonsampling error, response rates, and definitions may be found within the survey methodology, http://www2.census.gov/govs/state/13_methodology.pdf, and technical documentation, http://www2.census.gov/govs/state/statetechdoc2013.pdf.

Note: Detail may not add to total due to rounding.
Key:
(a) Total general revenue equals total taxes plus intergovernmental revenue plus charges and miscellaneous revenue.
(b) Total includes other taxes not shown separately in this table.

Table 7.22
STATE EXPENDITURE, BY CHARACTER AND OBJECT AND BY STATE: 2013 (In thousands of dollars)

State	Intergovernmental expenditures	Direct expenditures Total	Current operation	Capital outlay Total	Construction	Other	Assistance and subsidies	Interest on debt	Insurance benefits and repayments	Exhibit: Total salaries and wages
United States	$488,782,863	$1,517,128,804	$1,020,376,950	$114,980,312	$97,778,294	$17,202,018	$40,795,280	$48,528,728	$292,447,534	$259,634,720
Alabama	6,476,073	21,727,685	15,061,164	2,358,894	1,757,651	601,243	617,154	355,035	3,335,438	4,511,760
Alaska	2,032,061	10,182,537	6,962,794	1,460,784	1,209,809	250,975	192,835	267,684	1,298,440	1,886,305
Arizona	8,209,708	23,758,373	16,816,013	1,568,048	1,230,675	337,373	691,319	500,034	4,182,959	3,283,193
Arkansas	4,937,560	14,584,692	10,892,041	1,073,644	963,990	109,654	518,755	137,746	1,962,506	2,981,327
California	95,069,461	188,503,030	118,110,030	9,367,080	8,171,192	1,195,888	4,285,537	7,492,325	49,248,058	28,083,907
Colorado	6,291,390	22,452,523	14,204,199	1,485,834	1,260,385	225,449	362,907	860,563	5,539,020	4,034,587
Connecticut	4,908,546	24,394,169	15,752,174	1,827,444	1,491,095	336,349	547,167	1,435,495	4,831,889	4,272,596
Delaware	1,271,359	7,376,891	5,254,757	780,520	657,534	122,986	257,805	353,163	730,646	2,473,124
Florida	17,809,542	62,626,494	44,962,402	5,190,234	4,600,075	590,159	1,963,673	1,313,796	9,196,389	8,926,358
Georgia	10,361,359	35,122,420	24,073,754	2,659,934	2,362,882	297,052	979,446	665,293	6,743,993	5,931,608
Hawaii	220,844	11,256,867	8,491,719	897,975	712,640	185,335	144,068	349,062	1,374,043	2,310,366
Idaho	1,981,659	6,549,199	4,653,245	551,740	441,930	109,810	133,844	161,777	1,048,593	1,090,045
Illinois	15,549,167	59,775,553	36,944,818	3,962,519	3,599,768	362,751	1,262,268	3,503,179	14,102,769	8,904,708
Indiana	9,292,344	27,501,295	19,786,809	2,427,613	2,005,994	421,619	981,692	961,664	3,343,517	4,314,917
Iowa	4,753,646	15,764,288	10,900,406	1,619,526	1,402,346	217,180	557,861	245,725	2,440,770	2,682,143
Kansas	4,057,504	12,379,202	8,991,368	1,089,440	910,880	178,560	162,307	215,245	1,920,842	3,644,550
Kentucky	4,802,691	24,085,092	16,123,500	1,968,741	1,698,449	270,292	896,380	692,650	4,403,821	3,969,946
Louisiana	6,241,308	25,796,270	18,265,363	1,998,074	1,721,187	276,887	451,268	849,059	4,232,506	4,050,956
Maine	1,238,618	7,711,789	5,852,116	433,151	364,216	68,935	143,592	233,066	1,049,864	756,435
Maryland	8,641,281	30,915,712	20,952,583	2,493,037	2,039,893	453,144	1,914,736	1,101,621	4,453,735	4,857,463
Massachusetts	9,401,248	47,371,526	31,853,811	3,290,261	3,068,603	221,658	840,410	3,263,912	8,123,132	6,268,290
Michigan	19,249,754	43,695,740	30,360,266	2,148,561	1,663,829	484,732	1,233,603	1,440,019	8,513,291	7,727,625
Minnesota	12,975,915	26,967,577	18,908,308	1,581,068	1,281,852	299,216	1,120,702	481,576	4,875,923	5,209,914
Mississippi	5,053,070	15,048,856	10,814,367	1,190,761	1,011,876	178,885	280,220	275,259	2,488,249	2,518,296
Missouri	5,771,802	24,679,576	17,463,592	1,457,994	1,236,785	221,209	554,905	790,713	4,412,372	3,794,857
Montana	1,373,069	5,702,348	3,883,434	630,469	553,929	76,540	115,506	140,943	931,996	1,026,453
Nebraska	2,170,630	7,710,207	5,891,144	879,194	801,046	78,148	173,474	70,011	696,384	2,372,694
Nevada	4,214,581	9,059,226	5,368,958	632,219	553,757	78,462	315,805	191,517	2,550,727	1,563,233
New Hampshire	1,300,770	6,119,650	4,385,046	484,826	406,241	78,585	148,436	357,212	744,130	900,538
New Jersey	11,102,269	56,260,341	34,168,935	4,102,039	3,592,902	509,137	1,292,133	2,164,380	14,532,854	10,349,020
New Mexico	4,500,634	12,699,840	9,093,983	872,853	810,827	62,026	259,745	288,029	2,185,230	2,662,738
New York	56,236,537	127,803,663	86,853,934	9,493,079	7,548,281	1,944,798	1,636,851	5,730,909	24,088,890	22,974,180
North Carolina	13,172,640	40,453,222	28,260,807	3,466,699	2,726,764	739,935	655,108	619,671	7,450,937	9,281,523
North Dakota	1,632,316	4,777,845	3,055,372	841,567	776,951	64,616	159,841	97,306	623,759	1,108,571
Ohio	16,517,064	59,774,607	35,493,425	4,611,905	4,215,143	396,762	2,003,369	1,231,811	16,434,097	9,396,073

See footnotes at end of table.

STATE EXPENDITURE, BY CHARACTER AND OBJECT AND BY STATE: 2013 (In thousands of dollars) — Continued

State	Intergovernmental expenditures	Direct expenditures					Assistance and subsidies	Interest on debt	Insurance benefits and repayments	Exhibit: Total salaries and wages
		Total	Current operation	Capital outlay						
				Total	Construction	Other				
Oklahoma	4,213,211	18,707,163	13,302,644	1,883,892	1,567,708	316,184	453,666	539,565	2,527,396	3,162,736
Oregon	5,495,337	21,354,747	14,100,769	1,138,779	882,046	256,733	577,064	424,175	5,113,960	4,797,424
Pennsylvania	18,834,325	68,698,329	44,347,538	7,054,683	6,353,219	701,464	2,147,773	1,446,132	13,702,203	8,090,451
Rhode Island	1,170,440	7,018,575	4,518,481	404,000	352,174	51,826	150,354	474,116	1,471,624	1,176,761
South Carolina	5,454,008	22,791,696	15,772,341	1,663,802	1,542,292	121,510	1,017,174	650,863	3,687,516	3,596,657
South Dakota	740,104	3,736,621	2,433,676	639,183	591,828	47,355	83,929	114,194	465,639	956,329
Tennessee	7,074,682	23,511,638	17,700,839	1,618,748	1,424,748	194,000	1,172,474	264,464	2,755,113	3,766,072
Texas	27,590,295	97,339,243	68,361,537	8,045,756	6,255,591	1,790,165	2,297,935	1,729,403	16,904,612	16,384,939
Utah	3,069,082	13,753,420	9,766,636	1,324,378	1,093,409	230,969	731,866	270,687	1,659,853	2,925,621
Vermont	1,501,657	4,516,590	3,710,721	204,307	172,888	31,419	149,104	94,202	358,256	789,408
Virginia	11,255,705	36,358,360	25,953,846	3,059,704	2,545,039	514,665	1,615,558	1,159,003	4,570,249	6,777,430
Washington	9,777,797	35,948,066	22,335,778	3,380,742	2,890,088	490,654	1,597,316	1,289,645	7,344,585	10,114,009
West Virginia	2,469,535	10,764,620	7,755,238	1,074,774	916,095	158,679	234,604	253,663	1,446,341	1,868,736
Wisconsin	9,637,247	27,887,557	18,591,474	2,086,899	1,868,764	218,135	641,349	929,923	5,637,912	4,369,544
Wyoming	1,681,018	4,153,874	2,818,795	502,938	471,028	31,910	70,392	51,243	710,506	738,304

Source: U.S. Census Bureau, 2013 Annual Survey of State Government Finances.

Note: Data users who create their own estimates using these data should cite only the U.S. Census Bureau as the source of the original data. Data in this table are based on information from public records and contain no confidential data. Although the data in this table come from a census of governmental units and are not subject to sampling error, the census results may contain nonsampling error. Additional information on nonsampling error, response rates, and definitions may be found within the survey methodology, *http://www2.census.gov/govs/state/13_methodology.pdf*, and technical documentation, *http://www2.census.gov/govs/state/statetechdoc2013.pdf*.

Note: Detail may not add to total due to rounding.

Table 7.23
STATE GENERAL EXPENDITURE, BY FUNCTION AND BY STATE: 2013 (In thousands of dollars)

State	Total general expenditures (a)	Education	Public welfare	Highways	Hospitals	Natural Resources	Health	Corrections	Financial administration	Employment security administration	Police
United States	$1,683,170,060	$599,151,748	$519,178,293	$112,174,050	$67,433,480	$21,345,804	$63,246,831	$48,407,786	$23,136,739	$4,846,304	$15,106,964
Alabama	24,601,701	10,616,535	6,386,764	1,753,303	2,132,163	276,034	558,857	533,083	248,400	97,936	160,779
Alaska	10,707,194	2,806,879	2,084,000	1,152,768	79,817	331,740	348,730	335,234	233,899	48,632	166,917
Arizona	27,750,523	9,423,140	8,494,905	1,971,558	683,817	263,092	1,924,080	829,019	300,229	96,683	232,360
Arkansas	17,559,746	7,518,389	5,139,921	1,219,251	936,138	248,511	297,457	403,821	414,188	96,127	109,098
California	233,454,218	80,195,847	80,014,405	13,193,489	9,107,869	4,102,500	8,785,009	7,844,627	3,299,564	517,095	1,600,910
Colorado	23,189,078	9,478,848	5,840,287	1,448,635	710,618	321,265	1,055,306	975,698	302,682	75,354	172,792
Connecticut	23,719,309	7,019,066	7,318,979	1,056,211	1,288,711	164,033	950,351	669,700	360,713	98,246	232,639
Delaware	7,782,971	2,745,343	1,971,064	595,377	47,575	73,337	449,699	282,015	198,775	18,282	126,436
Florida	71,097,679	23,904,253	22,528,115	5,869,267	820,601	1,100,119	3,763,817	2,145,818	571,434	358,667	514,377
Georgia	38,702,490	17,337,702	11,518,235	2,170,602	948,316	454,830	1,204,357	1,487,452	487,975	63,052	319,687
Hawaii	10,098,104	3,404,040	2,098,924	409,269	799,790	113,135	494,927	200,984	109,106	5,750	34,307
Idaho	7,378,235	2,658,667	2,190,795	691,516	52,453	217,916	178,448	251,160	213,786	48,114	54,577
Illinois	61,221,951	17,272,058	20,424,637	4,969,276	1,345,563	237,443	2,240,614	1,327,176	705,952	125,536	467,598
Indiana	33,450,122	14,613,475	10,748,417	2,530,006	160,643	335,053	495,892	688,283	291,830	113,760	237,564
Iowa	17,901,551	6,469,134	5,265,106	1,658,218	1,519,773	295,335	256,786	334,893	211,928	46,577	96,322
Kansas	14,515,864	6,057,156	3,386,863	1,181,586	1,556,542	231,678	356,630	347,040	184,930	20,511	105,054
Kentucky	24,457,976	9,453,475	7,083,731	2,365,583	1,132,362	333,797	691,179	532,134	273,401	90,298	197,374
Louisiana	27,799,897	8,881,174	7,165,251	1,716,072	1,930,770	801,023	523,905	701,296	408,892	111,845	356,701
Maine	7,876,981	2,019,094	2,892,491	614,592	111,922	171,924	484,261	136,811	139,977	19,694	75,602
Maryland	34,170,869	11,398,463	10,044,675	1,949,117	517,097	447,136	2,149,504	1,396,307	934,704	57,276	550,989
Massachusetts	46,360,151	13,010,482	15,560,077	2,005,325	489,640	343,750	1,151,865	1,095,858	562,992	67,307	829,770
Michigan	53,549,642	22,972,166	14,985,940	2,419,026	3,080,402	318,918	1,329,434	1,857,508	464,546	191,770	401,026
Minnesota	35,058,976	15,026,229	11,323,904	2,464,343	265,135	607,961	431,809	514,959	354,857	91,989	382,588
Mississippi	17,386,707	5,456,159	5,816,559	1,376,640	1,131,700	291,359	403,671	376,455	175,333	80,982	112,169
Missouri	26,039,006	8,952,460	7,988,161	1,595,271	1,683,129	339,286	1,585,857	736,445	213,122	29,526	214,524
Montana	6,060,601	1,856,783	1,421,146	683,224	49,673	322,807	175,007	191,150	183,610	24,055	51,138
Nebraska	9,184,453	3,367,219	2,517,272	754,226	261,809	251,065	476,668	246,519	94,011	42,792	85,623
Nevada	10,639,400	4,365,150	2,400,389	721,780	265,446	116,153	275,542	283,918	111,986	87,305	101,604
New Hampshire	6,207,431	2,068,121	1,682,499	557,978	49,410	76,860	140,321	112,422	76,680	40,634	56,132
New Jersey	50,052,284	16,426,314	14,701,447	3,192,396	2,106,102	581,243	1,260,358	1,436,484	672,255	191,609	818,347
New Mexico	15,015,244	5,406,138	3,946,347	756,210	953,684	182,694	491,298	400,947	229,196	10,247	134,511
New York	147,156,113	41,151,716	58,009,518	4,238,973	4,750,662	423,976	9,215,195	3,438,227	2,386,723	283,741	995,306
North Carolina	46,102,728	19,250,605	12,977,012	3,688,451	2,020,269	511,455	1,368,833	1,210,318	507,385	58,332	703,083
North Dakota	5,786,402	1,931,216	943,371	1,051,899	53,709	329,500	161,118	96,683	61,813	10,586	35,210
Ohio	59,501,507	21,606,929	19,186,691	3,678,390	3,125,123	390,327	2,493,472	1,543,631	1,261,016	385,494	318,780

See footnotes at end of table.

STATE GENERAL EXPENDITURE, BY FUNCTION AND BY STATE: 2013 (In thousands of dollars) —Continued

State	Total general expenditures (a)	Education	Public welfare	Highways	Hospitals	Natural Resources	Health	Corrections	Financial administration	Employment security administration	Police
Oklahoma...............	19,579,099	7,321,724	6,258,083	1,802,547	258,175	231,332	861,552	569,140	407,392	52,785	233,623
Oregon..................	21,465,429	7,172,341	6,575,475	1,312,821	1,548,755	449,716	792,133	730,873	570,068	65,984	183,495
Pennsylvania............	72,244,141	22,628,667	23,078,652	7,601,344	3,789,791	642,051	3,080,531	2,119,602	1,318,587	99,390	911,672
Rhode Island............	6,562,768	1,986,630	2,394,541	318,630	66,449	59,205	158,767	182,888	131,144	20,998	71,704
South Carolina..........	22,331,442	8,352,080	6,050,877	923,605	1,444,046	196,531	1,011,767	490,627	366,655	71,703	183,055
South Dakota...........	4,011,086	1,266,106	971,649	653,007	21,930	178,255	178,414	116,535	94,118	23,154	38,321
Tennessee..............	27,831,207	9,810,510	10,959,849	1,752,119	404,978	291,223	672,883	889,870	302,528	90,721	232,868
Texas..................	108,024,926	47,479,191	30,780,705	7,536,463	5,237,650	1,040,736	2,774,086	3,701,789	833,467	206,143	799,712
Utah...................	14,956,224	6,874,554	3,017,968	961,772	1,180,848	172,571	390,835	310,560	245,280	13,770	143,594
Vermont................	5,607,879	2,407,364	1,629,482	455,461	287	81,883	235,775	135,127	76,114	14,018	91,112
Virginia................	42,529,852	15,214,402	9,855,058	3,912,825	3,598,411	248,919	1,343,432	1,706,864	538,886	137,156	559,409
Washington.............	37,864,966	15,582,462	8,389,040	3,183,817	2,160,922	861,649	2,185,121	954,986	414,185	203,385	356,847
West Virginia...........	11,708,850	4,333,893	3,526,796	1,102,651	126,185	225,833	345,537	300,693	184,365	28,088	75,101
Wisconsin..............	31,878,459	10,877,543	8,849,077	2,409,285	1,422,217	664,438	771,081	1,090,920	300,364	99,154	122,600
Wyoming...............	5,036,628	1,723,856	783,143	547,875	4,403	394,207	274,660	143,237	105,696	14,051	50,957

Source: U.S. Census Bureau, 2013 Annual Survey of State Government Finances.
Note: Data users who create their own estimates using these data should cite only the U.S. Census Bureau as the source of the original data. Data in this table are based on information from public records and contain no confidential data. Although the data in this table come from a census of governmental units and are not subject to sampling error, the census results may contain nonsampling error. Additional information on nonsampling error, response rates, and definitions may be found within the survey methodology, *http://www2.census.gov/govs/state/13_methodology.pdf,* and technical documentation, *http://www2.census.gov/govs/state/statetechdoc2013.pdf.*
Note: Detail may not add to total due to rounding.
Key:
(a) Total includes other expenditures not shown separately in this table.

Table 7.24
STATE DEBT OUTSTANDING AT END OF FISCAL YEAR, BY STATE: 2013
(In thousands of dollars)

State	Total	Long-term total	Short-term	Net long-term total (a)
United States	$1,137,363,585	$1,131,695,556	$5,668,029	$673,184,786
Alabama	9,055,227	9,022,866	32,361	7,205,340
Alaska	6,218,363	6,039,975	178,388	2,381,602
Arizona	13,723,166	13,674,685	48,481	9,649,947
Arkansas	3,947,169	3,947,169	0	2,400,990
California	152,186,012	152,186,012	0	120,765,605
Colorado	16,309,217	16,289,471	19,746	4,213,322
Connecticut	32,356,807	32,355,800	1,007	17,864,967
Delaware	5,754,587	5,754,587	0	3,313,777
Florida	37,892,165	37,858,479	0	30,634,276
Georgia	13,292,965	13,173,035	33,686	9,959,599
Hawaii	8,318,403	8,318,403	119,930	7,519,815
Idaho	3,647,841	3,636,772	0	719,176
Illinois	63,660,340	63,648,354	11,069	33,460,534
Indiana	22,564,017	22,362,681	11,986	2,710,889
Iowa	6,647,699	6,647,699	201,336	1,074,694
Kansas	6,825,293	6,765,478	0	3,697,606
Kentucky	14,983,712	14,943,682	59,815	9,064,992
Louisiana	18,589,438	18,586,813	40,030	10,445,065
Maine	5,374,528	5,374,528	2,625	1,248,448
Maryland	26,066,617	25,993,895	0	13,848,190
Massachusetts	76,160,503	75,929,609	72,722	42,797,116
Michigan	30,377,220	30,094,468	230,894	14,961,706
Minnesota	13,572,769	13,566,980	282,752	7,496,166
Mississippi	7,112,560	7,090,975	5,789	5,603,193
Missouri	19,307,770	19,247,522	21,585	5,224,768
Montana	3,558,343	3,558,105	60,248	264,988
Nebraska	1,846,583	1,845,318	238	393,202
Nevada	3,609,752	3,609,752	1,265	2,495,628
New Hampshire	8,763,339	8,713,495	0	2,890,268
New Jersey	64,264,050	64,203,722	49,844	42,754,931
New Mexico	7,232,938	7,200,981	60,328	4,153,974
New York	136,014,460	135,379,542	31,957	93,627,253
North Carolina	19,054,585	19,023,785	634,918	8,033,114
North Dakota	1,834,319	1,823,782	30,800	743,278
Ohio	33,132,906	32,548,652	10,537	13,341,595
Oklahoma	9,514,281	9,500,592	584,254	5,962,964
Oregon	13,598,468	13,466,596	13,689	8,967,771
Pennsylvania	47,020,552	46,739,081	131,872	24,342,530
Rhode Island	9,568,297	9,496,920	281,471	2,688,126
South Carolina	14,723,546	14,394,263	71,377	10,293,755
South Dakota	3,425,424	3,424,634	329,283	846,820
Tennessee	6,191,955	5,723,281	790	1,643,059
Texas	39,624,672	38,452,696	468,674	29,565,812
Utah	7,049,552	7,001,324	1,171,976	4,256,379
Vermont	3,330,238	3,195,300	48,228	988,749
Virginia	28,022,656	27,845,516	134,938	13,514,926
Washington	30,474,333	30,474,333	177,140	20,981,521
West Virginia	7,355,630	7,355,630	0	3,155,400
Wisconsin	23,187,772	23,187,772	0	8,879,389
Wyoming	1,020,546	1,020,546	0	137,571

Source: U.S. Census Bureau, 2013 Annual Survey of State Government Finances.

Note: Data users who create their own estimates using these data should cite only the U.S. Census Bureau as the source of the original data. Data in this table are based on information from public records and contain no confidential data. Although the data in this table come from a census of governmental units and are not subject to sampling error, the census results may contain nonsampling error. Additional information on nonsampling error, response rates, and definitions may be found within the survey methodology, *http://www2.census.gov/govs/state/13_methodology.pdf*, and technical documentation, *http://www2.census.gov/govs/state/statetechdoc2013.pdf*.

Note: Detail may not add to total due to rounding.

Key:

(a) Long-term debt outstanding minus long-term debt offsets.

Table 7.25
MEMBERSHIP OF STATE PUBLIC-EMPLOYEE PENSION SYSTEMS
BY STATE: FISCAL YEAR 2014 (a)

State	Membership			Total beneficiaries receiving periodic benefit payments
	Total	Active members	Inactive members	
United States........................	17,699,320	12,603,149	5,096,171	8,181,463
Alabama.............................	248,148	220,750	27,398	127,035
Alaska................................	40,280	29,400	10,880	43,853
Arizona	460,506	241,510	218,996	145,380
Arkansas	165,169	133,564	31,605	78,179
California...........................	1,928,754	1,315,324	613,430	936,841
Colorado	416,338	207,650	208,688	110,148
Connecticut	125,681	110,415	15,266	87,160
Delaware............................	46,958	43,956	3,002	26,180
Florida...............................	616,375	512,364	104,011	361,775
Georgia	617,567	355,076	262,491	189,225
Hawaii	75,109	67,555	7,554	41,944
Idaho	77,784	66,277	11,507	40,862
Illinois...............................	790,422	466,962	323,460	347,485
Indiana	266,290	223,594	42,696	134,829
Iowa	243,252	170,606	72,646	112,875
Kansas	200,286	155,446	44,840	90,314
Kentucky............................	344,788	221,968	122,820	143,501
Louisiana	282,962	188,031	94,931	162,160
Maine	60,438	50,782	9,656	41,135
Maryland............................	254,659	200,857	53,802	144,690
Massachusetts.....................	249,565	210,898	38,667	138,521
Michigan	292,195	262,521	29,674	300,084
Minnesota	525,789	286,872	238,917	195,469
Mississippi.........................	294,711	162,044	132,667	96,301
Missouri.............................	297,877	232,470	65,407	155,796
Montana.............................	78,564	52,293	26,271	38,198
Nebraska............................	87,449	59,757	27,692	22,902
Nevada...............................	115,227	100,562	14,665	55,287
New Hampshire	57,761	48,362	9,399	31,109
New Jersey.........................	555,280	462,791	92,489	299,464
New Mexico........................	165,376	118,132	47,244	76,927
New York............................	913,698	786,749	126,949	578,336
North Carolina	664,229	482,408	181,821	262,605
North Dakota......................	39,100	32,567	6,533	17,102
Ohio...................................	1,286,902	662,567	624,335	439,986
Oklahoma	170,996	152,290	18,706	102,377
Oregon	208,620	164,974	43,646	131,217
Pennsylvania......................	531,210	377,228	153,982	333,774
Rhode Island	37,966	32,221	5,745	21,926
South Carolina	381,134	212,311	168,823	143,877
South Dakota	54,943	38,951	15,992	24,563
Tennessee...........................	253,207	214,060	39,147	127,918
Texas..................................	1,632,295	1,357,996	274,299	561,046
Utah...................................	143,597	102,256	41,341	53,433
Vermont	32,205	24,941	7,264	16,425
Virginia	467,742	341,499	126,243	177,126
Washington........................	322,889	267,760	55,129	152,080
West Virginia......................	95,028	74,518	20,510	56,473
Wisconsin...........................	414,549	256,788	157,761	180,056
Wyoming............................	67,450	42,276	25,174	25,514

Source: U.S. Census Bureau, 2014 Annual Survey of Public Pensions: State-Administered Defined Benefit Data.

Note: Effective with the 2012 survey cycle, the Annual Survey of Public Pensions: State-Administered Defined Benefit Data revised the survey form to implement changes in asset classification. These changes apply to the categories designated as corporate stocks, corporate bonds, federal government securities, state and local government securities, and other securities. Federally-sponsored agency securities are classified under federal government securities instead of corporate bonds. Private equity, venture capital, and leverage buyouts are classified under: corporate stocks instead of other securities. Due to these changes in asset classification, there are shifts in the distribution of assets from corporate bonds to federal government securities and from other securities to corporate stocks. However, since investment decisions guide the distribution of assets, we cannot calculate the exact impact that the changes in classification had on the asset distribution for 2012. As such, for the above mentioned asset categories, any data comparisons between data from 2012 to the present, and data prior to 2012 should be exercised with caution.

Note: Data users who create their own estimates using these data should cite the U.S. Census Bureau as the source of the original data only. The data in this table are based on information from public records and contain no confidential data. The data in this table come from a sample of governmental units and are thus subject to both sampling and non-sampling error. Additional information on nonsampling error, response rates, and definitions may be found within the survey methodology http://www2.census.gov/govs/retire/2014 survey methodology.pdf.

Note: Detail may not add to total due to rounding.

Note: Pension obligations and Covered payroll for defined benefit pension systems are only collected at the state level.

Key:

(a)There are exceptions to the fiscal year rule for the state pension systems in Alabama, Michigan, and Texas. For systems in these states, the fiscal year moves beyond the June 30 cutoff. The data for the survey year 2014 covers the fiscal year ending August 31, 2014 for Texas and September 30, 2014 for Alabama and Michigan. These exceptions are made to better align the data with the Survey of State Government Finances.

Table 7.26
FINANCES OF STATE PUBLIC-EMPLOYEE PENSION SYSTEMS, BY STATE: FISCAL YEAR 2014*
(In thousands of dollars)

State and level of government	Total receipts	Employee contributions	Government contributions Total	From state government	From local government	Earnings on investments (b)	Total payments	Benefits	Withdrawals	Other payments
United States.........	569,556,939	38,182,057	92,278,074	51,881,368	40,396,706	439,096,808	223,754,432	208,377,743	4,940,765	10,435,928
Alabama (a)	5,560,719	708,216	1,148,534	898,186	250,348	3,703,969	3,071,679	2,928,387	102,832	40,460
Alaska	2,671,946	155,070	639,063	519,415	119,648	1,877,813	1,087,886	1,049,321	13,786	24,779
Arizona	9,518,820	1,218,137	1,496,087	313,155	1,182,932	6,804,596	4,006,687	3,373,283	291,200	342,204
Arkansas	5,213,032	195,757	790,272	320,665	469,607	4,227,003	1,583,507	1,453,894	31,436	98,177
California	106,615,920	6,641,367	14,262,852	6,962,459	7,300,393	85,711,701	33,815,771	32,477,634	453,577	884,560
Colorado	8,644,419	681,295	1,236,639	408,245	828,394	6,726,485	4,337,822	3,960,949	188,443	188,430
Connecticut	6,334,292	371,054	2,384,992	2,235,205	149,787	3,578,246	3,479,421	3,479,401	20	0
Delaware	1,718,900	63,019	255,067	242,735	12,332	1,400,814	583,676	549,723	3,980	29,973
Florida	26,036,948	839,720	2,417,733	531,895	1,885,838	22,779,495	7,695,295	7,159,236	6,994	529,065
Georgia	15,360,772	694,229	1,882,002	1,147,946	734,056	12,784,541	5,536,067	5,335,793	99,923	100,352
Hawaii	3,829,855	191,036	599,983	450,117	149,866	3,038,836	1,138,441	1,079,351	7,538	51,552
Idaho	2,583,069	204,398	311,579	80,080	231,499	2,067,092	788,836	734,853	0	53,983
Illinois...................	27,497,680	1,838,063	7,836,249	6,746,945	1,089,304	17,823,368	11,472,251	10,785,298	231,046	455,907
Indiana	5,748,909	341,430	1,741,840	1,149,273	592,567	3,665,639	2,566,703	2,249,634	85,754	231,315
Iowa	5,631,979	474,572	736,129	135,547	600,582	4,421,278	2,092,115	1,941,109	49,314	101,692
Kansas	3,703,568	338,499	759,572	500,507	259,065	2,605,497	1,537,226	1,418,516	56,971	61,739
Kentucky................	5,973,824	602,142	1,353,808	894,601	459,207	4,017,874	3,567,223	3,397,170	53,902	116,151
Louisiana	9,365,127	723,353	3,328,079	2,019,534	1,308,545	5,313,695	4,066,487	3,725,983	156,265	184,239
Maine	2,338,315	155,006	339,533	197,230	142,303	1,843,776	876,191	795,296	29,193	51,702
Maryland................	8,144,017	736,713	1,706,896	1,011,978	694,918	5,700,408	3,335,653	2,991,513	38,894	305,246
Massachusetts........	14,475,355	1,388,068	1,884,192	1,736,148	148,044	11,203,095	4,735,491	4,424,792	123,927	186,773
Michigan	12,318,060	565,333	2,780,271	903,986	1,876,285	8,972,456	6,481,048	6,370,489	39,111	71,448
Minnesota	11,537,381	882,237	1,090,490	244,792	845,698	9,564,654	4,202,326	4,041,317	67,154	93,855
Mississippi..............	5,630,213	551,777	1,004,893	373,763	631,130	4,073,543	2,386,870	2,164,293	121,599	100,978
Missouri.................	11,803,862	851,177	1,595,124	660,142	934,982	9,357,561	4,517,739	3,612,880	83,605	821,245
Montana.................	2,645,087	199,801	229,726	143,387	86,339	2,215,560	705,590	651,047	18,829	35,715
Nebraska................	2,282,134	209,790	273,425	83,960	189,465	1,798,919	573,628	495,490	73,776	4,362
Nevada	6,592,283	109,683	1,405,220	206,291	1,198,929	5,077,380	1,896,045	1,817,228	23,049	55,768
New Hampshire	1,655,541	199,675	332,295	75,116	257,179	1,123,571	662,988	604,770	26,120	32,098
New Jersey.............	6,862,652	1,964,317	2,489,493	2,489,493	0	2,408,842	9,498,966	9,270,793	182,425	45,748
New Mexico...........	4,830,832	509,140	668,811	257,033	411,778	3,652,881	1,979,833	1,821,097	86,367	72,370
New York	46,905,604	402,428	8,432,752	4,493,998	3,938,754	38,070,424	17,085,651	16,098,252	18,991	968,408
North Carolina........	13,700,302	1,182,129	1,638,519	1,206,042	432,477	10,879,654	5,309,955	4,980,605	178,149	151,201
North Dakota........	783,241	115,280	192,495	62,193	130,302	475,466	301,339	271,651	10,495	19,193
Ohio......................	31,065,614	2,834,125	3,730,164	1,915,073	1,815,091	24,501,325	14,795,893	13,547,926	719,398	528,569
Oklahoma	6,253,467	422,810	1,176,239	659,485	516,754	4,654,418	2,144,448	2,003,787	46,651	94,010
Oregon	11,268,234	15,319	915,237	233,409	681,828	10,337,678	4,350,189	3,837,871	25,560	486,758
Pennsylvania...........	15,971,091	1,341,310	2,826,701	1,904,389	922,312	11,803,080	9,710,685	8,931,702	43,788	735,195
Rhode Island	1,600,521	80,013	395,337	254,841	140,496	1,125,171	937,125	902,780	12,529	21,816
South Carolina	6,445,503	751,413	1,132,128	430,146	701,982	4,561,962	3,610,842	3,023,148	106,434	481,260
South Dakota..........	1,954,895	106,176	112,551	42,188	70,363	1,736,168	488,002	425,824	24,667	37,511
Tennessee...............	4,687,353	270,551	1,034,694	348,475	686,219	3,382,108	1,971,439	1,923,743	39,518	8,178
Texas (a).................	37,270,746	3,508,876	5,358,267	2,632,780	2,725,487	28,403,603	12,940,034	11,858,162	715,362	366,510
Utah......................	4,261,673	40,167	902,264	755,159	147,105	3,319,242	1,315,629	1,242,156	4,949	68,524
Vermont	695,682	77,539	121,729	121,729	0	496,414	312,803	287,694	6,005	19,104
Virginia	11,431,061	702,089	1,830,381	605,161	1,225,220	8,898,591	4,188,874	3,711,208	98,049	379,617
Washington	14,082,270	645,368	1,573,143	1,573,143	0	11,863,759	3,782,595	3,433,703	56,046	292,846
West Virginia	3,019,749	169,056	760,681	363,127	397,554	2,090,012	1,108,602	1,066,392	31,862	10,348
Wisconsin	13,921,478	773,500	1,006,066	285,006	721,060	12,141,912	4,645,068	4,224,701	33,271	387,096
Wyoming................	1,112,944	139,834	157,877	55,195	102,682	815,233	475,798	445,889	22,011	7,898

See footnotes at end of table.

FINANCES OF STATE PUBLIC-EMPLOYEE PENSION SYSTEMS, BY STATE: FISCAL YEAR 2014*
(In thousands of dollars) — Continued

Source: 2014 Annual Survey of Public Pensions: State- and Locally-Administered Defined Benefit Data. Data users who create their own estimates using data from this report should cite the U.S. Census Bureau as the source of the original data only. The data in this table are based on information from public records and contain no confidential data. Although the data in this table come from a census of pension systems and are not subject to sampling error, the census results do contain nonsampling error. Additional information on nonsampling error, and response rates may be found at <http://www.census.gov/govs/retire/how_data_collected.html>.

*Effective with the 2012 survey cycle, the Annual Survey of Public Pensions: State-Administered Defined Benefit Data revised the survey form to implement changes in asset classification. These changes apply to the categories designated as corporate stocks, corporate bonds, federal government securities, state and local government securities, and other securities. Federally-sponsored agency securities are classified under federal government securities instead of corporate bonds. Private equity, venture capital, and leverage buyouts are classified under corporate stocks instead of other securities. Due to these changes in asset classification, there are shifts in the distribution of assets from corporate bonds to federal government securities and from other securities to corporate stocks. However, since investment decisions guide the distribution of assets, we cannot calculate the exact impact that the changes in classification had on the asset distribution for 2012. As such, for the above mentioned asset categories, any data comparisons between data from 2012 to the present, and data prior to 2012 should be exercised with caution.

Notes: Pension obligations and Covered payroll for defined benefit pension systems are only collected at the state level. Data users who create their own estimates using these data should cite the U.S. Census Bureau as the source of the original data only. The data in this table are based on information from public records and contain no confidential data. Although the data in this table come from a census of pension systems and are not subject to sampling error, the census results do contain nonsampling error. Additional information on nonsampling error, response rates, and definitions may be found within the survey methodology <http://www2.census.gov/govs/retire/2013surveymeth.pdf>. Detail may not add to total due to rounding.

Key:

(a) There are exceptions to the fiscal year rule for the state pension systems in Alabama, Michigan, and Texas. For systems in these states, the fiscal year moves beyond the June 30 cutoff. The data for the survey year 2014 covers the fiscal year ending August 31, 2014 for Texas and September 30, 2014 for Alabama and Michigan.

These exceptions are made to better align the data with the Survey of State Government Finances.

(b) The total of ""net earnings"" is a calculated statistic and thus can be positive or negative. Net earnings is the sum of earnings on investments plus gains on investments minus losses on investments. The change made in 2002 for asset valuation from book to market value in accordance with Statement 34 of the Governmental Accounting Standards Board is reflected in the calculated statistics.

Table 7.27
NATIONAL SUMMARY OF STATE-ADMINISTERED DEFINED BENEFIT PENSION SYSTEM FINANCES: FISCAL YEARS, 2012–2014*

	Amount (in thousands of dollars)			Percentage distribution		
	2014	2013	2012	2014	2013	2012
Total contributions	$130,460,131	$119,413,342	$110,502,765	100.0%	100.0%	100.0%
Employee contributions	38,182,057	37,195,712	35,922,274	29.3	31.1	32.5
Government contributions	92,278,074	82,217,630	74,580,491	70.7	68.9	67.5
State government contributions	51,881,368	46,331,424	42,567,232	39.8	38.8	38.5
Local government contributions	40,396,706	35,886,206	32,013,259	31.0	30.1	29.0
Earnings on investments (a)	439,096,808	315,289,602	79,491,686	100.0	100.0	100.0
Total Payments	223,754,432	212,293,495	196,881,290	100.0	100.0	100.0
Benefits	208,377,743	197,857,574	183,811,738	93.1	93.2	93.4
Withdrawals	4,940,765	4,682,239	4,348,826	2.2	2.2	2.2
Other payments	10,435,928	9,753,682	8,720,726	4.7	4.6	4.4
Total cash and investment holdings	3,068,060,000	2,724,750,000	2,529,180,000	100.0	100.0	100.0
Cash and short-term investments	95,693,793	88,522,762	83,393,715	3.1	3.2	3.3
Total securities	2,547,250,000	2,241,520,000	2,029,330,000	83.0	82.3	80.2
Government securities	261,524,084	247,083,765	254,772,544	8.5	9.1	10.1
Federal government	260,006,539	245,751,621	254,035,123	8.5	9.0	10.0
United States Treasury	162,268,329	155,153,570	159,080,230	5.3	5.7	6.3
Federal agency	97,738,210	90,598,051	94,954,893	3.2	3.3	3.8
State and local government	1,517,546	1,332,144	737,421	0.0	0.0	0.0
Nongovernmental securities	2,285,730,000	1,994,440,000	1,774,560,000	74.5	73.2	70.2
Corporate bonds	359,272,327	310,488,641	316,898,602	11.7	11.4	12.5
Corporate stocks	1,117,680,000	993,612,260	929,406,850	36.4	36.5	36.7
Mortgages	8,783,146	8,310,181	9,613,974	0.3	0.3	0.4
Funds held in trust	57,667,807	53,472,922	35,131,534	1.9	2.0	1.4
Foreign and international	628,907,459	540,262,506	452,978,219	20.5	19.8	17.9
Other nongovernmental securities	113,413,653	88,291,313	30,531,108	3.2	3.2	1.2
Other investments	425,118,529	394,703,710	416,455,951	13.9	14.5	16.5
Real property	141,031,785	110,485,764	105,991,152	4.6	4.1	4.2
Miscellaneous investments	284,086,744	284,217,946	310,464,799	9.3	10.4	12.3

Sources: The 2013–2014 Annual Surveys of Public Pensions: State- and Locally-Defined Benefits Data and the 2012 Census of Governments: Finance – Survey of Public Pensions: State- and Locally-Defined Benefit Data. Data users who create their own estimates using data from this report should cite the U.S. Census Bureau as the source of the original data only. The data in this table are based on information from public records and contain no confidential data. Although the data in this table come from a census of pension systems and are not subject to sampling error, the census results do contain nonsampling error. Additional information on nonsampling error, and response rates may be found at *http://www.census.gov/govs/retire/how_data_collected.html.*

*Effective with the 2012 survey cycle, the Annual Survey of Public Pensions: State-Administered Defined Benefit Data revised the survey form to implement changes in asset classification. These changes apply to the categories designated as corporate stocks, corporate bonds, federal government securities, state and local government securities and other securities. Federally-sponsored agency securities are classified under federal government securities instead of corporate bonds. Private equity, venture capital, and leverage buyouts are classified under corporate stocks instead of other securities. Due to these changes in asset classification, there are shifts in the distribution of assets from corporate bonds to federal government securities and from other securities to corporate stocks. However, since investment decisions guide the distribution of assets, we cannot calculate the exact impact that the changes in classification had on the asset distribution for 2012. As such, for the above mentioned asset categories, any data comparisons between data from 2012 to the present, and data prior to 2012 should be exercised with caution.

Notes: Detail may not add to total due to rounding. Total Receipts are the sum of earnings on investments and total contributions.

Key:
(a) The total of "net earnings" is a calculated statistic (the item code in the data file is X08), and thus can be positive or negative. Net earnings is the sum of earnings on investments plus gains on investments minus losses on investments in 2002 for asset valuation from book to market value in accordance with Statement 34 of the Governmental Accounting Standards Board is reflected in the calculated statistics.

Chapter Eight

STATE MANAGEMENT, ADMINISTRATION AND DEMOGRAPHICS

The New World of Big-Data-Informed Performance Management

By CSG Senior Fellows Katherine Barrett and Richard Greene

How much will the increasing capacity of states to gather and manipulate large quantities of data help improve the use of performance measurement to make decisions? The possibilities are exciting and just begin with: an increased capacity to disaggregate performance measures, which helps attract public attention; better validation of performance measures and the capacity to make more use of information about the value-added aspects of programs.

Performance-informed management has been around for many decades. There was a rebirth of interest around 25 years ago, but this was only the beginning of public sector excitement about its possibilities. States that had never considered making an effort to replace the private sector profit-and-loss statement with their own measures of success were just beginning to explore the value of such efforts and the process necessary to make first steps. It wasn't until 2007 that all 50 states had bought into the notion that performance management—and its primary tool, measurement of progress within programs—was a worthwhile effort statewide.[1]

Just a couple of decades ago, in fact, the possibility of measuring the results of government programs was often spoken of in the future tense. The big topic of the day was Total Quality Management, an effort underway in about 36 states to help ideas percolate from the bottom, carefully determine what citizens really want and measure the progress made.[2] But though interest was high, for many states Total Quality Management eventually wound up on a list of forgotten management initiatives.

What's more, for those states that were beginning to issue performance measurement reports back in the 1990s, there was a huge gap between what governments wanted to measure and what they could measure. Performance measurement documents were riddled with NAs—for "Not Available"—when it came to actually showing data that supported the measurements. There were plenty of state officials who were still dubious about the whole process, arguing that performance measurement would steal far too much time and resources away from actually providing direct services to the public. As one state budget officer told the authors of this essay in 1992, "I think that the people who want to see more performance measurement are dying off—one zealot at a time."[3]

Back then, the focus of the effort, even for many enthusiasts, was on "performance reporting in a static fashion," according to Donald Moynihan, a professor at the La Follette School of Public Affairs at the University of Wisconsin. You made it available to interested parties, "and your job was done."[4]

Of course, that kind of thinking changed as time passed. Just publishing reports, particularly ones with lots of missing data, did not produce a strong impact. As Moynihan recalls, the more people thought about performance measurement, the more they came to the conclusion that it had to be utilized in a fashion that would actually permit it to affect decision making.[5]

As years passed, pressure began to accumulate to move from measuring simple outputs—like the total number of people served in a drug rehabilitation program—to outcomes, like the percentage of those people who were still off drugs after three or five years. By 2008, the vast majority of the states had agencies that were involved in just this kind of work. As the Pew Charitable Trusts' Government Performance Project stated in early 2008, "A growing number of (governors) are now personally involved in improving the way information is used to manage their states."[6]

As published in *Governing* magazine, the report offered some specific examples. During his term, Ohio Gov. Ted Strickland began the "Turn Around Ohio" plan that includes flexible performance agreements with his agency heads. Similarly, Maryland's former Gov. Martin O'Malley built StateStat, a comprehensive means for making decisions based on data, similar to his CitiStat effort in Baltimore. He described it as a system "that actually sets goals and has the guts to measure progress towards achieving those goals."[7]

Though the researchers for the Government Performance Project couldn't have known it at the time, the emphasis on heightened use of so-called "big data" has become the new Holy Grail in many states' efforts to measure—and manage—performance. The term "big data" means different things to different people. But for the purposes of this essay, the authors will use the term simply to mean the technologically infused capacity of states to gather and analyze huge amounts of concrete measurable information—across agency silos, wherever possible—to help guide their actions. "Big data has reduced the barriers to useful performance management," said Dustin Brown, deputy assistant director for personnel and performance management at the U.S. Office of Management and Budget.[8]

The arrival of big data on the public sector stage has generated a kind of electricity in the air that is similar to that felt a couple of decades ago about performance measurement generally. As John Kamensky, senior fellow for the IBM Center for the Business of Government said, "The biggest thing in the whole performance measurement world is the introduction of data analytics. The use of analytics with performance measures can actually change the performance on the ground."[9]

Better data analysis will cause the states to think about how they were going to get to their objectives. "I'm just thrilled when governments use any kind of data and start to play with it," said Jeff Tryens, a performance measurement authority whose experience includes stints in South Australia, Oregon and New York City.[10]

Paul Epstein, principal with New York-based consulting firm Epstein and Fass, emphasizes that he hasn't seen examples where this marriage has been fully consummated. Before big data can help improve performance measurement, "a government organization needs a functioning performance management system that agency managers are comfortable working with in a performance improvement mode, not in a defensive mode where they try to get away with conservative targets," he said.[11]

The degree to which big data will change the performance management world won't be known for some time. But there's room for optimism. For one thing, public—and state employee—familiarity with the potential for data use has grown enormously. "They know they can Google anything," said Philip Kase, performance management chief at the Oregon Department of Transportation.[12]

Nathalie Molliet-Ribet, senior associate director of Virginia's Joint Legislative Audit and Review Commission agreed. "The expectations have gotten really high that folks should have access to everything we know about what's happening," she said.[13]

Benefits of Big-data-informed Performance Measurement

There are many ways in which performance measurement can benefit from the use of big data, not the least of which is the credibility that validated information brings to any kind of work. Legislators are far more inclined to pay attention to the information that they find on their desks if it's backed with careful analysis of great quantities of data—even if, realistically, they don't actually look at the data itself.

There also has been a growing emphasis in legislative circles on considering policies that have roots in actual evidence; successful experiences from other states or other agencies within their state. This underlines the importance of standardized data, which enables states and the federal government to compare and analyze the success of programs.

"Many states have started to embrace the technological changes that would make it possible to electronically track performance. It comes down to common data formats," said Hudson Hollister, executive director of the Data Coalition. "If the information is searchable across all of the different agencies and offices of the states, then it can be used to automatically track whatever the subject matter is. But if the information is not searchable and there is not a common format, then complicated translations and analytics are necessary."[14]

Another area for which growing integration of data and performance measurement is important is in the use of social impact bonds, sometimes called social benefit bonds. These bonds are agreements between investors and the public sector to invest in programs that will result eventually in better outcomes and savings. The savings are then to be used to pay back the investors with interest. While the use of such instruments isn't common yet, they are being considered by many states, and it's clear that their success will come only if the public has faith that the savings will be added up using sophisticated data-based techniques coupled with measures of performance.

Of course, one of the most obvious performance management uses for big data comes with the ability it provides to compare entities across state government and invest tax dollars wisely. This is the kind of thing that simply is not possible if statewide systems don't exist to gather and validate parallel information from counties, cities, towns and so on. Similarly, big data can help provide states with the ability to work with and aid local governments in comparing themselves to others and uncover the cities or counties that can serve as models.

There are other benefits to be found at the juncture of big data and performance measurement. A few of these:

- It offers new abilities to communicate with citizens—particularly given the potential to disaggregate information—so that it is meaningful to individuals, who can see the impact of programs on their own lives. Data analysis can shift the measures of government performance away from a technocratic world and turn them into information that the average taxpayer can understand and use.

- Simple performance outcome measures can take users off track, but combined with data-based evidence, analysts more easily can discern whether the measures are providing good information or if the results are deceiving. For example, positive results can be obtained when performance measures focus on an unrepresentative group of service users. But data analytics can help to reveal whether that's been the case.

- Data analysis also can help to move from a straightforward look at comparative outcomes to a sometimes more sophisticated approach in which value added is measured. Take the comparison of two universities as an example. One may start with the cream of the crop in its student body, and show terrific educational outcomes. The other may begin with less well prepared first-year students. Simple outcomes would make the first school look better. But with the use of big data, the value added to the two student bodies can be compared and the second school may come out on top.

Why Technology Makes a Difference

Not so many years ago, when data was transferred manually from spreadsheet to spreadsheet and generating the data in the first place was extremely time consuming, states had every reason to push back at the talk of generating more and better information. But with new technology, "we're going to have a lot more state detailed information, rather than just high level," said Molliet-Ribet. "There were probably ways to do this with an asset database or a spreadsheet," she said. "But I think, obviously, technology has gotten better, faster and cheaper, and is helping make these things happen."[15]

Generating performance information also has become easier because citizens themselves can now feed into the process important pieces of information. In the past, gathering data from millions of individuals was a gargantuan task. Now with most Americans plugged into car-based GPS systems, cell phones, kiosks in selective locations and so on, they can provide information nearly effortlessly, which can be transmitted to a central location, aggregated and then disaggregated in dozens of different fashions. Not only does this ease the accumulation of data, it also means that it can be reported in real time.

What's more, according to the 2013 report "Collaboration Across Boundaries," published by the IBM Center for the Business of Government, individuals can help to build a data-based performance management system in four important ways.[16]

- "As explorer, citizens can identify, discover, and define emerging and existing problems in public services. For example, the New York-based Datakind initiative involves citizen volunteers using their data analysis skills to mine public data in health, education, environment and more areas to identify important civic issues and problems.

- "As ideator, citizens can conceptualize novel solutions to well-defined problems in public services. For example, initiatives such as *Challenge. gov* and OpenIDEO employ online contests and competitions to solicit innovative ideas to solve important civic problems.

- "As designer, citizens can design and/or develop implementable solutions to well-defined problems in public services. For example, as part of initiatives such as NYC Big Apps and Apps for California, citizens have designed mobile apps to address specific issues such as public parking availability, public transport delays, and more.

- "As diffuser, citizens can directly support or facilitate the adoption and diffusion of public service innovations and solutions among well-defined target populations. For example, physicians interacting with peers in dedicated online communities have assisted government agencies in diffusing health technology innovations."

A Helping Hand

The federal government has been leading the way for states to make progress in the use of data for performance measurement. The 2014 Data Act, for example, is shifting federal agencies to use a common data format to report their spending and to make interagency comparisons far more clear. The act is still in its beginning stages of implementation and is supposed to be fully implemented in another year. While it is focused on spending data, it may lead to more standardized performance reporting, said Kamensky. "Ultimately, after you figure out how to report financial data then you can come up with a model of how you would be able to report performance data."[17]

"I don't know of a state program that is as ambitious as the data act," said Hollister. "But I always like to point to Ohio, which has already published all of its spending transactions on one platform."[18]

The new law will largely affect states in terms of grant-related reporting, though that is still in a pilot phase. In the future, it also will likely lead the way to more standardized data generally. "I thought states and universities would find the Data Act highly intrusive," said Kamensky. But as it turns out, "I haven't heard a lot of screaming," he added. Kamensky theorizes that is because the states have discovered that technology already in place has made reporting less onerous than it would have been not so many years ago. That's good news for advocates of standardization within the states themselves.

There are other examples of the push on the part of the federal government to focus increasingly on the use of data, including the reporting that was required in the American Recovery and Investment Act of 2009 and the aggressive federal push for electronic health records. While the health record initiative has great potential for improving patients' experience when they enter the medical system, it also represents a good example of how difficult this kind of work can be.

Robert Wachter, author of a recently published book, *The Digital Doctor*, cites a number of obstacles that have been encountered along the way. For example, the technology that is geared to ease the transference of data is often designed by technology specialists who don't have a solid understanding of how the data eventually will be used. Even when medical data is more easily obtained, the users often are not trained effectively and there are many examples of routine errors in simple data entry.[19]

Wachter points to these challenges as cautionary notes, not as evidence that they won't be overcome as time goes on. He quotes from the book *Smarter than You Think* by Clive Thompson, "The past turns out to be oddly reassuring, because a pattern emerges. Each time we're faced with bewildering new thinking tools, we panic—then quickly set about deducing how they can be used to help us work, meditate and create."[20]

In all cases, the federal government can only get things rolling in the states, like pushing a hoop with a stick. The same is even true with edicts from the highest levels of state governments. "Federal and state policies can establish a supportive framework," wrote Patrick Lester, director of the Social Innovation Research Center. "But actual improvements must take place on the front lines."[21]

The Challenges to Come ...

An examination of the trend of combining big data with performance measurement doesn't only reveal the potential benefits; a number of challenges were pointed out by the men and women who are deep in the trenches of states that are trying to make this connection.[22]

For example, often the data that is collected is the easiest to collect and not necessarily the most useful. Performance measures may be selected for much the same reason. The information that is needed to measure and manage performance needs to be selected with consideration of the impact the measurements will have. Similar thought needs to go to what data is collected.

Additionally, it's critical that all the participants involved in this process understand the utility of the data they are collecting and analyzing. If the use of the data is not well understood, the individuals collecting the data may not pay necessary attention to ensuring its accuracy.

Efforts to optimize the utility and accuracy of performance measures from agency to agency "requires some sort of centralization," said Mike Lawson, former head of performance for the International City/County Managment Association (ICMA) and currently a consultant in the field.[23] But centralization can be difficult to achieve, particularly when agencies relish their autonomy and are disinclined to play together nicely. As a result, leadership from the top can be critical to ensure a focus on data and how it's going to be used.

Indiana provides a good example of leadership from the very top. Gov. Mike Pence signed an executive order in 2014 creating a "management and performance hub," in the state. "Hoosiers can benefit from a comprehensive and coordinated effort by state agencies to share data and improve and strengthen services," he wrote in the order. "Centralized data sharing, correlation and analysis capability will enable the state to achieve efficiencies in the administration of state programs."[24]

The list of other challenges to the successful use of data for performance measurement—and other purposes, as well—goes on to include lack of resources, legislators who want data and measures but are disinclined to use them to make decisions, inaccurate data that can lead to false conclusions, data overload, misinterpretations of the actual meaning of the data and the context for the measures, and unclear definitions. "When you've got all this data, people can very quickly not understand what they're looking for and that can lead to confusion and even distrust," said Kase.[25]

But, while these challenges may all play a part in slowing states down in their efforts to utilize performance measures and big data to their fullest potential, they needn't prevent them from making the effort. The benefits are so clear—and have sufficient potential for transforming the way government does its business—that the resultant accomplishments will be worth the risks and costs along the way.

Notes

[1] The Pew Charitable Trusts, Government Performance Project research.

[2] *Financial World* magazine, May 11, 1993.

[3] Authors' interview, 1995.

[4] Authors' Interview, Jan. 21, 2016.

[5] Ibid.

[6] Katherine Barrett and Richard Greene, "Measuring Performance: The State Management Report Card for 2008," *Governing*, March 2008, *http://www.pewtrusts.org/~/media/ legacy/uploadedfiles/wwwpewtrustsorg/reports/government_ performance/gradingthestates2008pdf.pdf.*

[7] Ibid.

[8] Authors' interview, Feb. 3, 2016.

[9] Authors' interview, Jan. 12, 2016.

[10] Authors' interview, Jan. 20, 2016.

[11] "Thoughts on 'Big Data' and Government Performance Management," a brief prepared for this essay by Paul Epstein, Jan. 13, 2016.

[12] Authors' interview, Feb. 2, 2016.

[13] Authors' interview, Feb. 1, 2016.

[14] Authors' interview, Feb. 10, 2016.

[15] Authors' interview, Feb. 1, 2016.

[16] Satish Nambisan and Priya Nambisan, "Engaging Citizens in Co-Creation in Public Services: Lessons Learned and Best Practices," IBM Center for the Business of Government, 2013, *http://www.businessofgovernment.org/report/engaging-citizens-co-creation-public-services.*

[17] Authors' interview, Jan. 12, 2016.

[18] Authors' interview, Feb. 10, 2016.

[19] Robert Wachter, *The Digital Doctor: Hope, Hype and Harm at the Dawn of Medicine's Computer Age*, McGraw-Hill Education, 2015.

[20] Ibid.

[21] Patrick Lester, "Building Performance Systems in Child Welfare," Social Innovation Research Center, Feb. 8, 2016, *http://www.socialinnovationcenter.org/?p=1897.*

[22] Katherine Barrett and Richard Greene, "The Causes, Costs and Consequences of Bad Government Data," *Governing*, June 24, 2015, http://www.governing.com/topics/ mgmt/gov-bad-data.html.

[23] Authors' interview, Feb. 2, 2016.

[24] State of Indiana Executive Department. Establishing the Governor's Management and Performance Hub, Executive Order: 14-06, posted by Legislative Services Agency, May 14, 2014, *http://www.in.gov/legislative/iac/20140514-IR-GOV 140139EOA.xml.pdf.*

[25] Authors' interview, Feb. 2, 2016.

About the Authors

CSG Senior Fellows **Katherine Barrett** and **Richard Greene** are experts on state government who work with *Governing* magazine, the Pew Charitable Trusts, the Volcker Alliance and others. As CSG senior fellows, Barrett and Greene serve as advisers on state government policy and programming and assist in identifying emerging trends affecting states.

Table 8.1
SUMMARY OF STATE GOVERNMENT EMPLOYMENT: 1954–2014

Year (October)	Employment (in thousands)						Monthly payrolls (in millions of dollars)			Average monthly earnings of full-time employees		
	Total, full-time and part-time			Full-time equivalent								
	All	Education	Other	All	Education	Other	All	Education	Other	All	Education	Other
1954	1,149	310	839	1,024	222	802	300.7	78.9	221.8	294	325	283
1955	1,199	333	866	1,081	244	837	325.9	88.5	237.4	302	334	290
1956	1,268	353	915	1,136	250	886	366.5	108.8	257.7	321	358	309
1957 (April)	1,300	375	925	1,153	257	896	372.5	106.1	266.4	320	355	309
1958	1,408	406	1,002	1,259	284	975	446.5	123.4	323.1	355	416	333
1959	1,454	443	1,011	1,302	318	984	485.4	136	349.4	373	427	352
1960	1,527	474	1,053	1,353	332	1,021	524.1	167.7	356.4	386	439	365
1961	1,625	518	1,107	1,435	367	1,068	586.2	192.4	393.8	409	482	383
1962	1,680	555	1,126	1,478	389	1,088	634.6	201.8	432.8	429	518	397
1963	1,775	602	1,173	1,558	422	1,136	696.4	230.1	466.3	447	545	410
1964	1,873	656	1,217	1,639	460	1,179	761.1	257.5	503.6	464	560	427
1965	2,028	739	1,289	1,751	508	1,243	849.2	290.1	559.1	484	571	450
1966	2,211	866	1,344	1,864	575	1,289	975.2	353	622.2	522	614	483
1967	2,335	940	1,395	1,946	620	1,326	1,105.5	406.3	699.3	567	666	526
1968	2,495	1,037	1,458	2,085	694	1,391	1,256.7	477.1	779.6	602	687	544
1969	2,614	1,112	1,501	2,179	746	1,433	1,430.5	554.5	876.1	655	743	597
1970	2,755	1,182	1,573	2,302	803	1,499	1,612.2	630.3	981.9	700	797	605
1971	2,832	1,223	1,609	2,384	841	1,544	1,741.7	681.5	1,060.2	731	826	686
1972	2,957	1,267	1,690	2,487	867	1,619	1,936.6	746.9	1,189.7	778	871	734
1973	3,013	1,280	1,733	2,547	887	1,660	2,158.2	822.2	1,336	843	952	805
1974	3,155	1,357	1,798	2,653	929	1,725	2,409.5	932.7	1,477	906	1023	855
1975	3,271	1,400	1,870	2,744	952	1,792	2,652.7	1,021.7	1,631	964	1080	909
1976	3,343	1,434	1,910	2,799	973	1,827	2,893.7	1,111.5	1,782	1,031	1,163	975
1977	3,491	1,484	2,007	2,903	1,005	1,898	3,194.6	1,234.4	1,960	1,096	1,237	1,031
1978	3,539	1,508	2,032	2,966	1,016	1,950	3,483	1,332.9	2,150	1,167	1,311	1,102
1979	3,699	1,577	2,122	3,072	1,046	2,026	3,869.3	1,451.4	2,418	1,257	1,399	1,193
1980	3,753	1,599	2,154	3,106	1,063	2,044	4,284.7	1,608	2,677	1,373	1,523	1,305
1981	3,726	1,603	2,123	3,087	1,063	2,024	4,667.5	1,768	2,900	1,507	1,671	1,432
1982	3,747	1,616	2,131	3,083	1,051	2,032	5,027.7	1,874	3,154	1,625	1,789	1,551
1983	3,816	1,666	2,150	3,116	1,072	2,044	5,345.5	1,989	3,357	1,711	1,850	1,640
1984	3,898	1,708	2,190	3,177	1,091	2,086	5,814.9	2,178	3,637	1,825	1,991	1,740
1985	3,984	1,764	2,220	2,990	945	2,046	6,328.6	2,433.7	3,884.9	1,935	2,155	1,834
1986	4,068	1,800	2,267	3,437	1,256	2,181	6,801.4	2,583.4	4,226.9	2,052	2,263	1,956
1987	4,115	1,804	2,310	3,491	1,264	2,227	7,297.8	2,758.3	4,539.5	2,161	2,396	2,056
1988	4,236	1,854	2,381	3,606	1,309	2,297	7,842.3	2,928.6	4,913.7	2,260	2,490	2,158
1989	4,365	1,925	2,440	3,709	1,360	2,349	8,443.1	3,175.0	5,268.1	2,372	2,627	2,259
1990	4,503	1,984	2,519	3,840	1,418	2,432	9,083	3,426	5,657	2,472	2,732	2,359
1991	4,521	1,999	2,522	3,829	1,375	2,454	9,437	3,550	5,887	2,479	2,530	2,433
1992	4,595	2,050	2,545	3,856	1,384	2,472	9,828	3,774	6,054	2,562	2,607	2,521
1993	4,673	2,112	2,562	3,891	1,436	2,455	10,288.2	3,999.3	6,288.9	2,722	3,034	2,578
1994	4,694	2,115	2,579	3,917	1,442	2,475	10,666.3	4,176.8	6,489.3	2,776	3,073	2,640
1995	4,719	2,120	2,598	3,971	1,469	2,502	10,926.5	4,173.3	6,753.2	2,854	3,138	2,725
1996	(a)	(a)	(a)	(a)	(a)	(a)	(a)	(a)	(a)	(a)	(a)	(a)
1997 (March)	4,733	2,114	2,619	3,987	1,484	2,503	11,413.1	4,372.0	7,041.1	2,968	3,251	2,838
1998 (March)	4,758	2,173	2,585	3,985	1,511	2,474	11,845.2	4,632.1	7,213.1	3,088	3,382	2,947
1999 (March)	4,818	2,229	2,588	4,034	1,541	2,493	12,564.1	4,957.0	7,607.7	3,236	3,544	3,087
2000 (March)	4,877	2,259	2,618	4,083	1,563	2,520	13,279.1	5,255.3	8,023.8	3,374	3,692	3,219
2001 (March)	4,985	2,329	2,656	4,173	1,615	2,559	14,136.3	5,620.7	8,515.6	3,521	3,842	3,362
2002 (March)	5,072	2,414	2,658	4,223	1,659	2,564	14,837.8	5,996.6	8,841.2	3,657	4,007	3,479
2003 (March)	5,043	2,413	2,630	4,191	1,656	2,534	15,116.4	6,154.4	8,962.0	3,751	4,115	3,566
2004 (March)	5,041	2,432	2,609	4,188	1,673	2,515	15,477.5	6,411.8	9,065.7	3,845	4,256	3,631
2005 (March)	5,078	2,459	2,620	4,209	1,684	2,525	16,061.6	6,668.9	9,392.6	3,966	4,390	3,745
2006 (March)	5,128	2,493	2,635	4,251	1,708	2,542	16,769.4	6,960.9	9,808.6	4,098	4,505	3,883
2007 (March)	5,200	2,538	2,663	4,307	1,740	2,566	17,788.7	7,418.9	10,369.9	4,276	4,670	4,063
2008 (March)	5,270	2,593	2,677	4,363	1,780	2,582	18,725.9	7,883.2	10,842.7	4,445	4,853	4,222
2009 (March)	5,346	2,649	2,697	4,408	1,814	2,594	19,424.8	8,278.6	11,146.3	4,565	5,007	4,320
2010 (March)	5,326	2,669	2,656	4,378	1,824	2,554	19,579.1	8,516.5	11,062.6	4,620	5,111	4,342
2011 (March)	5,314	2,704	2,609	4,359	1,847	2,512	19,971.9	8,813.2	11,158.6	4,735	5,233	4,446
2012 (March)	5,286	2,723	2,562	4,312	1,843	2,469	20,172.8	9,060.4	11,112.4	4,838	5,410	4,501
2013 (March)	5,282	2,733	2,549	4,306	1,855	2,451	20,501.6	9,285.8	11,215.8	4,933	5,525	4,580
2014 (March)	5,344	2,774	2,569	4,341	1,879	2,462	21,154.9	9,554.7	11,600.2	5,046	5,597	4,713

Source: U.S. Census Bureau, Census of Governments: Employment (1957, 1962, 1967, 1972, 1977, 1982, 1987, 1992, 1997, 2002, 2007, 2012 and the Annual Survey of Public Employment & Payroll Remaining years. For information on sampling and nonsampling errors and definitions, see http://www.census.gov/govs/apes/how_data_collected.html. Data users who create their own estimates from this table should cite the U.S. Census Bureau as the source of the original data only.

Note: Detail may not add to totals due to rounding.
Key:
(a) Due to a change in the reference period, from October to March, the October 1996 Annual Survey of Government Employment & Payroll was not conducted. This change in collection period was effective beginning with the March 1997 survey.

Table 8.2
EMPLOYMENT AND PAYROLLS OF STATE AND LOCAL GOVERNMENTS BY FUNCTION: MARCH 2014

Functions	All employees, full-time and part-time (in thousands)			March payrolls (in thousands of dollars)			Average March earnings of full-time employees
	Total	State government	Local government	Total	State government	Local government	
All functions....................................	19,255,141	5,343,688	13,911,453	73,233,899,250	21,154,853,338	52,079,045,912	4,691
Education:							
Higher education	3,212,069	2,621,119	590,950	10,591,508,310	8,929,608,421	1,661,899,889	5,612
Instructional personnel only..	1,129,598	839,863	289,735	4,889,332,168	4,014,642,342	874,689,826	7,631
Elementary/Secondary schools..	7,682,816	60,437	7,622,379	26,643,240,764	232,327,941	26,410,912,823	4,184
Instructional personnel only..	5,231,857	44,591	5,187,266	20,962,390,297	187,053,772	20,775,336,525	4,673
Libraries.......................................	185,540	728	184,812	442,090,063	2,002,222	440,087,841	3,901
Other Education	92,651	92,651	-	392,728,835	392,728,835	-	4,647
Selected functions:							
Streets and Highways..................	510,385	221,646	288,739	2,182,938,366	1,022,210,925	1,160,727,441	4,488
Public Welfare	527,621	241,355	286,266	2,046,495,146	939,983,848	1,106,511,298	4,103
Hospitals......................................	1,066,922	430,963	635,959	4,930,728,442	1,964,759,245	2,965,969,197	5,012
Police protection	963,444	103,164	860,280	5,096,373,291	582,597,852	4,513,775,439	5,755
Police Officers.........................	714,677	64,789	649,888	4,218,338,855	427,568,716	3,790,770,139	6,154
Fire protection	432,511	-	432,511	2,105,070,467		2,105,070,467	6,312
Firefighters only......................	392,779	-	392,779	1,942,386,213	-	1,942,386,213	6,378
Natural Resources.......................	190,740	146,022	44,718	760,263,396	595,889,723	164,373,673	4,570
Correction....................................	717,720	451,703	266,017	3,119,219,104	1,958,132,842	1,161,086,262	4,466
Social Insurance	78,147	77,702	445	336,461,122	333,881,820	2,579,302	4,437
Financial Admin..........................	426,202	171,645	254,557	1,840,586,919	794,429,684	1,046,157,235	4,735
Judicial and Legal.......................	431,877	178,069	253,808	2,120,545,134	959,723,830	1,160,821,304	5,251
Other Government Admin.........	412,800	58,258	354,542	1,213,730,447	254,240,793	959,489,654	4,718
Utilities	514,221	37,465	476,756	2,708,575,918	235,923,298	2,472,652,620	5,591
State Liquor stores	11,983	11,983	-	29,188,816	29,188,816	-	3,454
Other and unallocable....................	1,797,492	438,778	1,358,714	6,674,154,710	1,927,223,243	4,746,931,467	4,563

Source: U.S. Census Bureau, 2014 Annual Survey of Public Employment & Payroll.

Note: Data users who create their own estimates using these data should cite the U.S. Census Bureau as the source of the original data only. The data in this table are based on information from public records and contain no confidential data. The data in this table come from a sample of governmental units and are thus subject to both sampling and nonsampling error. Additional information on nonsampling error, response rates, and definitions may be found within the survey methodology *http://www2.census.gov/govs/apes/14_methodology.pdf>*.

Note: Detail may not add to total due to rounding.

Table 8.3
STATE AND LOCAL GOVERNMENT EMPLOYMENT, BY STATE: MARCH 2014

State or other jurisdiction	All employees (full-time and part-time)			Full-time equivalent employment		
	Total	State	Local	Total	State	Local
United States	19,255,141	5,343,688	13,911,453	16,188,581	4,341,163	11,847,418
Alabama	319,691	108,845	210,846	283,141	88,687	194,454
Alaska.....................................	62,520	29,967	32,553	54,435	27,049	27,386
Arizona....................................	336,821	96,362	240,459	287,144	78,689	208,455
Arkansas..................................	192,658	73,039	119,619	167,493	62,079	105,414
California	2,151,200	499,403	1,651,797	1,752,729	406,842	1,345,887
Colorado..................................	345,283	104,573	240,710	280,486	79,518	200,968
Connecticut	228,271	78,130	150,141	190,660	63,013	127,647
Delaware	55,990	30,818	25,172	49,042	26,135	22,907
Florida	972,226	205,161	767,065	863,896	176,990	686,906
Georgia....................................	583,460	171,526	411,934	508,642	131,916	376,726
Hawaii.....................................	91,273	72,787	18,486	74,920	58,409	16,511
Idaho.......................................	102,526	30,283	72,243	80,704	23,814	56,890
Illinois.....................................	783,361	153,788	629,573	628,231	123,001	505,230
Indiana....................................	389,514	116,625	272,889	318,963	87,692	231,271
Iowa	240,257	68,707	171,550	181,805	49,888	131,917
Kansas	241,437	61,334	180,103	195,140	49,469	145,671
Kentucky	282,216	99,534	182,682	242,987	83,409	159,578
Louisiana.................................	295,167	89,587	205,580	262,918	76,207	186,711
Maine......................................	91,206	26,871	64,335	70,717	20,990	49,727
Maryland	338,522	91,746	246,776	301,853	86,771	215,082
Massachusetts	393,597	123,661	269,936	329,701	98,985	230,716
Michigan..................................	557,215	184,889	372,326	437,560	142,057	295,503
Minnesota................................	372,642	103,575	269,067	282,992	82,223	200,769
Mississippi	213,775	65,620	148,155	192,077	56,884	135,193
Missouri...................................	377,432	107,920	269,512	316,651	88,133	228,518
Montana	72,613	27,073	45,540	57,077	20,721	36,356
Nebraska	144,074	36,921	107,153	118,556	32,101	86,455
Nevada....................................	127,300	34,235	93,065	109,862	27,236	82,626
New Hampshire	90,069	25,864	64,205	71,316	18,698	52,618
New Jersey	550,568	160,715	389,853	475,254	143,707	331,547
New Mexico	144,943	54,960	89,983	125,761	46,114	79,647
New York.................................	1,315,411	269,083	1,046,328	1,166,793	240,744	926,049
North Carolina.........................	643,544	171,073	472,471	549,747	145,187	404,560
North Dakota...........................	64,231	25,507	38,724	45,825	18,752	27,073
Ohio..	713,526	189,076	524,450	578,629	136,486	442,143
Oklahoma................................	252,056	84,091	167,965	215,278	66,939	148,339
Oregon.....................................	242,326	82,281	160,045	190,330	66,966	123,364
Pennsylvania	682,119	205,755	476,364	569,375	161,369	408,006
Rhode Island............................	57,737	24,126	33,611	47,922	18,691	29,231
South Carolina.........................	286,244	92,307	193,937	256,341	78,690	177,651
South Dakota...........................	62,017	19,036	42,981	45,382	14,625	30,757
Tennessee	368,235	97,219	271,016	323,676	79,258	244,418
Texas......................................	1,614,390	368,761	1,245,629	1,436,297	313,284	1,123,013
Utah	190,419	71,656	118,763	140,418	54,038	86,380
Vermont...................................	50,992	17,439	33,553	39,900	14,483	25,417
Virginia...................................	536,328	167,764	368,564	447,594	127,408	320,186
Washington..............................	421,067	151,617	269,450	341,924	120,091	221,833
West Virginia...........................	120,680	48,670	72,010	103,675	40,281	63,394
Wisconsin	377,428	107,932	269,496	279,515	72,960	206,555
Wyoming	61,571	15,776	45,795	51,003	13,484	37,519
Dist. of Columbia	46,993		46,993	46,244		46,244

Source: 2014 Annual Survey of Public Employment & Payroll. For information on sampling and nonsampling errors and definitions, see http://www.census.gov/govs/apes/how_data_collected.html. Data users who create their own estimates from these tables should cite the U.S. Census Bureau as the source of the original data only.

Note: Statistics for local governments are estimates subject to sampling variation.

Table 8.4
STATE AND LOCAL GOVERNMENT PAYROLLS AND AVERAGE EARNINGS
OF FULL-TIME EMPLOYEES, BY STATE: MARCH 2014

State or other jurisdiction	Amount of payroll (in thousands of dollars)			Percentage of March payroll		Average earnings of full-time state and local government employees (dollars)		
	Total	State government	Local governments	State government	Local government	All	Education employees	Other
United States	67,204,519,212	18,929,609,482	48,274,909,730	28%	72%	4,691	5,046	4,565
Alabama	962,602,832	343,733,577	618,869,255	36%	64%	3,698	4,400	3,397
Alaska..................	272,310,155	141,572,839	130,737,316	52%	48%	5,462	5,648	5,274
Arizona..............	1,087,900,108	309,324,259	778,575,849	28%	72%	4,380	4,698	4,266
Arkansas..............	546,395,362	229,878,947	316,516,415	42%	58%	3,497	4,026	3,192
California	9,361,434,942	2,227,858,641	7,133,576,301	24%	76%	6,369	6,689	6,276
Colorado..............	1,102,788,003	310,949,390	791,838,613	28%	72%	4,737	5,382	4,525
Connecticut.........	958,237,211	349,453,964	608,783,247	36%	64%	5,769	6,512	5,415
Delaware	203,138,016	104,964,537	98,173,479	52%	48%	4,673	4,515	4,855
Florida	3,252,805,378	676,050,421	2,576,754,957	21%	79%	4,098	4,252	4,060
Georgia................	1,694,568,451	456,822,169	1,237,746,282	27%	73%	3,617	3,930	3,514
Hawaii..................	314,451,689	235,981,071	78,470,618	75%	25%	4,589	4,501	4,879
Idaho...................	266,138,756	92,385,983	173,752,773	35%	65%	3,767	4,558	3,449
Illinois..................	2,831,321,403	586,810,849	2,244,510,554	21%	79%	5,195	5,749	5,067
Indiana.................	1,071,207,271	319,169,908	752,037,363	30%	70%	3,892	4,284	3,746
Iowa....................	703,422,712	247,633,456	455,789,256	35%	65%	4,701	6,183	4,160
Kansas	667,311,347	198,639,031	468,672,316	30%	70%	3,817	4,510	3,583
Kentucky	820,299,879	312,909,558	507,390,321	38%	62%	3,676	4,194	3,416
Louisiana.............	900,947,762	305,280,517	595,667,245	34%	66%	3,720	4,437	3,435
Maine..................	240,216,383	79,692,673	160,523,710	33%	67%	3,897	4,284	3,730
Maryland	1,389,376,456	390,742,801	998,633,655	28%	72%	5,213	5,008	5,297
Massachusetts	1,559,592,029	495,758,637	1,063,833,392	32%	68%	5,277	5,595	5,140
Michigan..............	1,758,037,845	636,557,654	1,121,480,191	36%	64%	4,895	5,626	4,559
Minnesota............	1,168,531,867	380,786,579	787,745,288	33%	67%	4,990	5,596	4,742
Mississippi	586,887,906	197,365,197	389,522,709	34%	66%	3,300	3,820	3,087
Missouri...............	1,038,320,939	294,591,342	743,729,597	28%	72%	3,627	3,762	3,576
Montana...............	191,375,895	72,980,103	118,395,792	38%	62%	3,999	4,324	3,822
Nebraska.............	433,232,117	112,087,322	321,144,795	26%	74%	4,209	4,193	4,215
Nevada................	489,519,607	119,577,340	369,942,267	24%	76%	5,236	4,876	5,364
New Hampshire ...	254,852,959	73,392,804	181,460,155	29%	71%	4,372	4,995	4,162
New Jersey............	2,557,091,162	798,630,097	1,758,461,065	31%	69%	5,974	6,131	5,906
New Mexico..........	450,817,486	181,903,803	268,913,683	40%	60%	3,906	4,408	3,626
New York..............	6,216,683,369	1,340,751,057	4,875,932,312	22%	78%	5,802	6,013	5,747
North Carolina......	1,982,473,958	587,297,205	1,395,176,753	30%	70%	3,987	4,634	3,766
North Dakota........	162,669,547	72,319,005	90,350,542	44%	56%	4,243	4,593	3,999
Ohio.....................	2,205,600,526	569,074,831	1,636,525,695	26%	74%	4,419	5,217	4,195
Oklahoma..............	700,212,636	243,597,873	456,614,763	35%	65%	3,512	4,107	3,260
Oregon.................	782,500,438	286,562,941	495,937,497	37%	63%	4,909	4,956	4,883
Pennsylvania.........	2,379,206,078	689,205,344	1,690,000,734	29%	71%	4,765	4,896	4,714
Rhode Island........	236,175,825	95,525,561	140,650,264	40%	60%	5,410	5,595	5,291
South Carolina.....	893,088,334	281,930,003	611,158,331	32%	68%	3,765	3,985	3,672
South Dakota.......	146,525,924	52,245,186	94,280,738	36%	64%	3,636	4,090	3,425
Tennessee	1,102,202,902	291,924,952	810,277,950	26%	74%	3,716	4,145	3,582
Texas....................	5,424,917,925	1,334,436,850	4,090,481,075	25%	75%	4,055	4,795	3,860
Utah.....................	499,039,308	215,838,443	283,200,865	43%	57%	4,301	4,686	4,048
Vermont................	151,038,701	65,704,293	85,334,408	44%	56%	4,363	4,944	4,001
Virginia.................	1,737,618,864	521,898,982	1,215,719,882	30%	70%	4,342	4,838	4,159
Washington...........	1,560,617,461	512,041,339	1,048,576,122	33%	67%	5,655	5,168	5,927
West Virginia........	330,047,534	134,872,224	195,175,310	41%	59%	3,486	3,687	3,359
Wisconsin	1,079,902,492	297,532,462	782,370,030	28%	72%	4,666	5,125	4,513
Wyoming	195,201,302	53,365,462	141,835,840	27%	73%	4,398	4,317	4,429
Dist. of Columbia	283,662,160	-	283,662,160	0%	100%	6,543		6,543

Source: 2014 Annual Survey of Public Employment & Payroll. For information on sampling and nonsampling errors and definitions, see http://www.census.gov/govs/apes/how_data_collected.html. Data users who create their own estimates from these tables should cite the U.S. Census Bureau as the source of the original data only.

Note: Statistics for local governments are estimates subject to sampling variation.

Table 8.5
STATE GOVERNMENT EMPLOYMENT (FULL-TIME EQUIVALENT) FOR SELECTED FUNCTIONS, BY STATE: 2014

		Education								Selected functions	
State	All functions	Higher education (a)	Other education (b)	Highways	Public welfare	Hospitals	Corrections	Police protection	Natural resources	Financial and other governmental administration	Judicial and legal administration
United States	4,341,163	1,744,545	85,538	216,554	237,520	397,780	442,409	101,393	132,762	168,124	173,452
Alabama	88,687	41,719	2,923	4,217	3,954	11,874	4,841	1,367	2,002	2,463	3,195
Alaska..................	27,049	5,614	275	3,188	1,934	255	2,238	696	2,409	1,113	1,503
Arizona................	78,689	33,651	2,962	2,986	5,715	7,046	9,586	1,928	1,526	2,473	2,131
Arkansas..............	62,079	25,531	1,376	3,373	3,927	6,763	5,557	1,242	1,953	1,973	1,385
California	406,842	166,584	4,285	19,680	3,653	42,416	53,397	11,347	15,619	26,100	6,355
Colorado..............	79,518	44,100	1,633	3,109	2,404	5,791	7,139	1,226	1,094	1,812	4,810
Connecticut	63,013	18,669	2,989	3,189	5,484	6,465	5,762	1,947	712	2,286	6,179
Delaware	26,135	7,974	355	1,494	1,584	1,386	2,878	1,065	514	816	1,803
Florida	176,990	62,979	2,909	6,352	9,005	3,895	23,071	4,272	8,137	6,338	19,321
Georgia	131,916	60,931	2,522	4,892	7,036	7,793	20,407	2,924	4,845	3,219	3,783
Hawaii.................	58,409	10,901	126	889	414	4,655	2,429	0	812	687	2,498
Idaho..................	23,814	9,262	357	1,468	1,767	608	2,024	488	1,851	1,305	515
Illinois.................	123,001	57,863	1,939	6,872	9,330	9,850	10,856	3,266	3,043	4,899	2,570
Indiana................	87,692	56,497	972	3,525	5,108	1,889	6,082	1,882	2,272	1,798	1,423
Iowa	49,888	22,941	1,040	2,261	2,651	7,934	2,921	943	1,594	1,027	2,282
Kansas	49,469	21,533	635	2,834	2,233	7,929	3,466	1,051	798	1,753	2,104
Kentucky	83,409	36,929	2,188	4,449	7,863	6,135	4,337	2,072	2,772	2,576	5,154
Louisiana	76,207	27,734	2,638	4,426	5,132	9,808	5,895	1,689	4,088	1,981	1,702
Maine..................	20,990	7,298	231	2,044	2,824	455	1,179	518	1,017	1,290	729
Maryland	86,771	27,829	2,036	4,528	6,654	3,666	12,559	2,272	2,025	3,143	5,186
Massachusetts	98,985	32,120	1,127	3,138	6,917	5,302	12,295	2,926	1,147	3,929	9,141
Michigan	142,057	74,408	625	2,664	11,797	16,090	12,537	2,617	3,343	4,220	1,474
Minnesota............	82,223	36,689	3,948	4,555	3,096	4,534	4,179	921	3,096	4,827	3,735
Mississippi	56,884	19,644	1,458	3,295	3,049	11,357	3,244	1,202	3,033	1,457	740
Missouri...............	88,133	30,659	1,584	5,541	6,956	10,604	12,289	2,495	2,195	2,899	4,241
Montana	20,721	7,525	379	2,121	1,769	650	1,238	487	1,540	1,041	728
Nebraska	32,101	12,495	539	2,054	2,447	3,772	2,930	842	2,161	789	748
Nevada	27,236	9,363	140	1,726	2,068	1,320	3,578	842	894	1,391	743
New Hampshire	18,698	6,992	304	1,596	1,884	571	1,071	505	354	770	764
New Jersey	143,707	35,170	2,674	5,729	8,750	16,869	8,791	3,948	1,886	5,378	12,882
New Mexico	46,114	18,580	888	2,144	1,781	7,360	3,742	526	1,049	1,107	3,246
New York.............	240,744	57,042	3,917	10,641	4,354	41,614	29,307	5,785	2,938	16,277	18,442
North Carolina......	145,187	62,259	3,843	10,828	1,120	18,505	19,830	2,869	4,031	3,257	6,293
North Dakota........	18,752	8,486	330	1,024	543	921	875	207	1,086	688	602
Ohio	136,486	70,866	1,993	6,228	3,197	15,316	13,113	2,607	2,476	6,565	3,043
Oklahoma.............	66,939	28,793	1,692	2,875	7,441	1,566	4,628	1,954	1,811	2,554	2,807
Oregon................	66,966	23,803	803	3,678	7,527	7,982	5,068	1,360	2,520	3,943	3,020
Pennsylvania	161,369	57,688	4,890	13,581	11,066	11,005	18,381	6,671	5,726	6,990	3,050
Rhode Island........	18,691	5,401	497	746	1,320	854	1,521	345	376	884	1,180
South Carolina......	78,690	31,320	2,989	4,280	4,781	6,984	8,224	2,058	2,138	3,351	836
South Dakota.......	14,625	5,708	365	989	1,730	379	871	337	948	440	635
Tennessee	79,258	34,464	1,934	3,465	7,635	3,765	7,016	1,761	3,752	3,329	2,496
Texas..................	313,284	132,397	4,425	12,815	23,657	23,206	39,899	6,797	10,687	7,694	5,733
Utah...................	54,038	24,103	1,950	1,565	2,750	8,863	3,138	868	1,267	2,425	1,544
Vermont...............	14,483	4,915	436	1,070	1,543	194	1,087	652	610	644	685
Virginia................	127,408	56,649	2,685	7,391	2,898	15,239	14,151	3,203	2,659	4,332	3,806
Washington...........	120,091	53,879	2,173	6,616	10,521	10,289	8,553	2,222	4,790	2,771	1,905
West Virginia........	40,281	14,118	1,246	5,162	3,502	1,678	3,383	1,031	1,892	1,929	1,615
Wisconsin	72,960	38,541	1,098	1,466	2,182	3,645	9,518	884	2,321	2,439	2,142
Wyoming	13,484	3,929	215	1,795	567	733	1,328	276	953	752	548

Source: U.S. Census Bureau, 2014 Annual Survey of Public Employment & Payroll.

Note: Data users who create their own estimates using these data should cite the U.S. Census Bureau as the source of the original data only. The data in this table are based on information from public records and contain no confidential data. The data in this table come from a sample of governmental units and are thus subject to both sampling and nonsampling error. Additional information on nonsampling error, response rates, and definitions may be found within the survey methodology <http://www2.census.gov/govs/apes/14_methodology.pdf>.

Key:
(a) Includes instructional and other personnel.

Table 8.6
STATE GOVERNMENT PAYROLLS FOR SELECTED FUNCTIONS, BY STATE: MARCH 2014
(In thousands of dollars)

State	All functions	Education Higher education (a)	Education Other education (b)	Selected functions Highways	Selected functions Public welfare	Selected functions Hospitals
United States	21,154,853,338	8,929,608,421	392,728,835	1,022,210,925	939,983,848	1,964,759,245
Alabama	375,462,465	192,088,092	11,418,170	14,325,020	13,745,854	50,491,771
Alaska..........................	147,708,266	29,520,828	1,566,748	18,619,656	9,287,824	1,327,426
Arizona........................	345,795,548	164,922,711	10,775,345	12,964,470	19,114,500	33,319,381
Arkansas......................	245,159,396	113,356,685	5,239,710	13,368,601	12,394,569	24,762,362
California	2,601,749,990	1,003,778,372	21,680,757	150,400,215	17,988,701	334,502,596
Colorado......................	393,436,219	226,457,087	7,364,191	14,568,912	10,393,398	25,082,754
Connecticut..................	391,539,640	109,222,603	17,905,271	17,965,242	34,767,553	41,559,591
Delaware	115,480,387	41,375,923	2,076,830	5,415,740	5,643,494	4,770,533
Florida.........................	732,442,103	327,127,572	10,373,499	27,624,411	28,429,882	13,267,375
Georgia........................	509,721,019	282,606,264	11,590,974	14,277,144	23,456,892	30,853,650
Hawaii..........................	256,070,261	52,325,904	508,552	4,136,104	1,719,546	24,460,600
Idaho...........................	103,016,155	36,848,062	2,027,628	5,578,343	6,562,527	2,015,965
Illinois.........................	674,330,605	288,293,920	9,408,196	44,068,168	53,628,150	53,251,071
Indiana........................	353,666,707	244,783,156	3,406,592	12,310,096	15,857,714	5,689,010
Iowa	271,605,540	126,691,077	5,870,849	12,432,151	13,334,192	44,320,102
Kansas	217,066,641	105,698,259	2,707,156	10,956,405	7,471,317	35,705,849
Kentucky	339,364,215	173,898,129	9,170,866	14,513,227	24,203,502	27,298,215
Louisiana......................	326,009,372	123,164,656	11,490,557	18,587,730	19,571,107	37,546,777
Maine..........................	87,791,619	31,421,084	948,208	8,421,949	10,220,217	1,880,903
Maryland	430,175,032	148,820,805	10,180,064	22,635,808	27,343,620	16,492,081
Massachusetts	544,215,247	170,178,878	7,059,837	18,364,848	38,094,318	24,143,069
Michigan......................	750,112,588	403,099,156	3,549,226	13,989,844	54,181,512	87,136,479
Minnesota.....................	431,776,369	204,062,926	20,919,787	22,575,635	11,393,134	20,609,092
Mississippi....................	211,268,855	86,977,925	4,752,208	9,933,922	10,453,252	39,339,695
Missouri.......................	320,715,063	134,811,952	5,275,822	18,207,726	19,968,503	34,848,147
Montana	84,847,911	30,081,276	1,587,690	9,542,504	6,478,393	2,304,219
Nebraska	123,965,427	50,522,488	2,335,107	7,977,492	7,389,187	14,057,590
Nevada.........................	130,556,530	51,058,792	685,034	7,431,287	7,413,909	6,044,887
New Hampshire	86,738,691	36,113,689	1,358,203	6,898,775	7,633,084	2,292,811
New Jersey	848,604,652	222,369,710	15,692,027	33,113,872	49,732,684	79,278,356
New Mexico	199,332,142	89,747,275	3,666,141	7,611,649	6,176,664	31,775,682
New York......................	1,419,468,227	310,025,002	21,399,367	59,825,659	22,219,071	231,732,153
North Carolina.............	648,744,186	303,145,376	18,181,772	41,617,263	4,123,636	77,582,996
North Dakota...............	82,606,462	39,076,805	1,327,689	5,499,806	1,804,071	2,759,897
Ohio............................	657,842,321	334,858,894	10,319,919	28,864,070	17,322,030	75,164,310
Oklahoma.....................	266,741,385	124,687,175	6,627,588	10,731,962	22,791,494	6,132,599
Oregon.........................	326,570,590	120,318,507	3,926,320	18,722,472	28,560,471	41,357,491
Pennsylvania	797,823,464	330,365,270	20,367,992	56,023,550	43,613,031	39,180,607
Rhode Island................	102,375,788	26,934,391	3,009,179	3,805,799	7,666,114	4,234,611
South Carolina.............	305,381,772	147,103,897	10,952,928	14,247,668	13,689,268	19,600,731
South Dakota...............	57,596,259	23,722,290	1,349,345	3,818,801	6,104,542	1,131,577
Tennessee	316,715,479	148,213,944	7,266,027	12,156,988	25,867,652	13,672,465
Texas	1,463,499,126	731,395,233	20,814,666	55,235,242	76,949,718	114,616,444
Utah............................	244,567,211	124,256,859	7,758,177	6,795,107	9,548,238	36,548,416
Vermont.......................	72,557,685	27,082,244	2,073,841	5,137,437	6,880,252	908,163
Virginia........................	589,836,581	290,978,797	13,034,698	35,996,018	12,420,222	65,304,223
Washington...................	603,975,691	279,260,157	10,335,824	34,698,366	45,861,066	62,585,624
West Virginia................	146,015,977	64,248,933	5,134,928	15,376,333	9,139,019	4,385,581
Wisconsin	346,399,776	186,190,080	5,131,086	7,980,707	9,168,621	14,962,006
Wyoming	56,410,703	16,319,311	1,126,244	6,860,731	2,206,133	2,471,312

See footnotes at end of table.

STATE GOVERNMENT PAYROLLS FOR SELECTED FUNCTIONS, BY STATE: MARCH 2014—Continued
(In thousands of dollars)

State	Corrections	Police protection	Natural resources	Financial and other governmental administration	Judicial and legal administration
			Selected functions, continued		
United States	1,958,132,842	582,597,852	595,889,723	794,429,684	959,723,830
Alabama	16,123,640	5,115,714	7,356,362	10,727,310	14,626,354
Alaska...........................	12,698,498	4,706,002	13,669,521	6,698,578	9,569,808
Arizona.........................	34,743,758	9,708,547	6,335,467	9,592,091	10,233,446
Arkansas.......................	17,599,249	4,697,234	6,882,821	7,307,776	5,502,193
California	393,949,904	89,050,911	92,318,331	128,780,397	42,341,954
Colorado.......................	30,357,491	6,754,972	5,691,080	9,220,026	25,105,918
Connecticut	37,117,008	13,996,366	4,102,303	13,971,144	42,779,500
Delaware	11,727,100	6,895,633	1,937,994	2,672,210	8,364,137
Florida	73,125,775	16,862,224	27,730,543	22,479,859	79,698,433
Georgia.........................	45,083,578	10,115,354	16,126,440	12,186,348	15,871,754
Hawaii...........................	11,188,836	-	3,608,528	2,803,938	11,976,332
Idaho.............................	8,803,602	2,302,669	8,549,720	6,142,461	4,257,850
Illinois..........................	66,505,628	21,765,114	14,585,133	24,558,725	22,775,840
Indiana..........................	16,997,032	8,057,736	8,161,862	7,524,746	9,092,118
Iowa..............................	14,662,096	5,394,629	8,561,367	5,203,047	12,596,589
Kansas	10,893,505	4,600,411	3,278,275	6,858,852	8,999,116
Kentucky	11,373,644	7,942,409	9,896,330	9,886,443	18,466,799
Louisiana......................	23,768,165	9,085,392	17,687,317	8,536,160	7,721,634
Maine............................	4,438,374	2,686,959	4,539,902	5,016,283	3,516,410
Maryland	56,803,916	12,678,465	10,519,336	14,351,410	28,481,481
Massachusetts	64,281,427	25,928,709	7,366,077	22,527,384	52,969,393
Michigan.......................	62,694,123	13,776,563	16,352,649	23,590,134	10,154,809
Minnesota.....................	19,108,947	4,533,739	15,015,242	28,187,590	19,588,759
Mississippi....................	8,290,969	4,040,437	9,614,538	5,446,240	4,637,183
Missouri........................	33,176,003	10,278,162	7,533,839	10,561,954	16,246,930
Montana	4,511,596	2,269,311	6,284,410	4,109,371	3,391,217
Nebraska.......................	10,373,218	4,152,106	7,434,504	3,113,000	3,637,729
Nevada..........................	15,308,546	5,102,492	4,096,798	5,203,327	5,004,074
New Hampshire	5,083,832	2,656,151	1,657,234	3,585,887	3,818,099
New Jersey	52,834,060	28,494,076	11,115,346	28,163,265	79,684,500
New Mexico	12,910,820	2,210,433	4,480,558	4,788,852	13,898,666
New York......................	178,605,610	50,170,671	16,306,915	91,326,273	134,933,665
North Carolina.............	74,459,033	17,050,387	15,221,956	14,581,784	30,081,808
North Dakota...............	3,476,552	1,103,768	4,530,907	3,011,941	3,247,541
Ohio..............................	58,122,372	13,394,359	10,683,734	35,637,312	17,929,630
Oklahoma.....................	14,420,620	8,710,438	6,389,934	10,378,240	12,785,255
Oregon..........................	24,729,280	7,303,041	11,215,737	18,056,560	15,257,040
Pennsylvania	84,538,443	41,259,550	29,267,926	30,344,958	26,410,822
Rhode Island................	9,771,485	2,506,422	2,185,236	4,883,473	6,990,978
South Carolina.............	23,327,876	7,577,748	6,642,318	11,889,944	4,017,990
South Dakota................	2,926,896	1,366,348	3,384,199	2,105,939	2,877,416
Tennessee	21,023,980	8,050,755	14,692,298	14,535,997	13,886,676
Texas............................	123,035,538	34,935,007	49,962,266	35,515,625	31,098,078
Utah..............................	11,162,243	3,570,777	4,939,952	10,664,081	7,533,426
Vermont........................	4,786,006	3,578,472	3,009,699	3,096,727	3,357,966
Virginia........................	47,139,686	15,249,322	12,634,497	18,930,686	18,445,520
Washington...................	35,816,528	11,071,984	21,705,479	14,606,768	11,446,576
West Virginia...............	8,366,946	4,173,854	6,637,164	5,895,072	7,490,619
Wisconsin	41,175,077	4,392,264	9,759,634	11,437,139	13,941,935
Wyoming	4,714,331	1,273,765	4,230,045	3,736,357	2,981,864

Source: U.S. Census Bureau, 2014 Annual Survey of Public Employment & Payroll.

Note: Data users who create their own estimates using these data should cite the U.S. Census Bureau as the source of the original data only. The data in this table are based on information from public records and contain no confidential data. The data in this table come from a sample of governmental units and are thus subject to both sampling and nonsampling error. Additional information on nonsampling error, response rates, and definitions may be found within the survey methodology <http://www2.census.gov/govs/apes/14_methodology.pdf>.

Key:
(a) Includes instructional and other personnel.

Table 8.7
STATE EMPLOYEES: PAID HOLIDAYS**

State or other jurisdiction	Major holidays (a)	Martin Luther King's Birthday (b)	Lincoln's Birthday	President's Day (c)	Washington's Birthday (c)	Good Friday	Memorial Day (d)	Columbus Day (e)	Veteran's Day	Day after Thanksgiving	Day before or after Christmas	Day before or after New Year's	Election Day (f)	Other (g)
Alabama	★	★(h)	...	...	★(i)	...	★	★	★	(k)	(k)	...	...	★
Alaska	★	★	...	★	...	...	★	...	★	...	...	...	...	★
Arizona	★	★	...	★	...	...	★	★	★	...	...	...	...	...
Arkansas	★	★(h)	...	★(i)	...	...	★	...	★	(k)	Before	...	...	★
California	★	★	...	★	...	...	★	★	★	★	...	...	...	★
Colorado	★	★	...	★	...	...	★	★	★	...	...	...	...	...
Connecticut	★	★	★	...	★	★	★	★	★	...	...	...	...	...
Delaware	★	★	...	...	...	★	★	...	★	★	...	...	★	★
Florida	★	★	...	...	...	...	★	★	★	★	...	...	...	...
Georgia	★	★	...	...	(l)	...	★	★	★	(l)	(l)	...	...	★
Hawaii	★	★	...	★	...	★	★	...	★	...	...	...	★	★
Idaho	★	★(h)	...	★	...	...	★	★	★	...	...	...	...	...
Illinois	★	★	★	...	★	...	★	★	★	...	...	...	★	...
Indiana	★	★	(m)	...	(m)	★	★	★	★	(m)	(m)	...	★	...
Iowa	★	★	...	...	...	...	★	...	★	...	...	...	...	★
Kansas	★	★	...	...	...	...	★	...	★	...	...	...	...	...
Kentucky	★	★	...	...	★(n)	...	★	...	★	★	★	★	★(t)	...
Louisiana	★	★	...	...	★	★	★	...	★	...	...	...	★(u)	★
Maine	★	★	...	...	...	...	★	★	★	★	...	...	...	★
Maryland	★	★	...	★	...	...	★	★	★	★(aa)	...	...	★	★
Massachusetts	★	★	...	★	...	...	★	★	★	...	...	...	...	★
Michigan	★	★	...	★	...	...	★	...	★	★	Before	Before	★(z)	...
Minnesota	★	★	...	★	...	...	★	...	★	★	...	...	...	★
Mississippi	★	★(h)	...	...	★	...	★(v)	...	★	(k)	(k)	...	...	★
Missouri	★	★	★	...	★	...	★	★	★	...	...	...	...	★
Montana	★	★	...	★	...	...	★	★	★	...	...	...	★	★
Nebraska	★	★	...	★	...	...	★	★	★	...	...	...	...	★
Nevada	★	★	...	★	...	...	★	★	★	★(cc)	...	...	...	★
New Hampshire	★	★(h)	...	★	...	...	★	★	★	★	...	...	...	★
New Jersey	★	★	...	★	...	★	★	★	★	...	...	...	★	...
New Mexico	★	★	...	(o)	...	...	★	★	★	(o)	...	...	(w)	...
New York	★	★	(j)	...	★	...	★	★	★	...	...	...	★	...
North Carolina	★	★	...	...	...	★	★	...	★	(x)	...	...	...	...
North Dakota	★	★	...	★	...	★	★	...	...	(p)	...	...	...	...
Ohio	★	★	...	★	...	...	★	★	★	...	...	...	...	...
Oklahoma	★	★	...	★	...	...	★	...	★	★	Before	...	...	...
Oregon	★	★	...	★	...	...	★	...	★	★	...	...	...	★
Pennsylvania	★	★	...	★	...	...	★	★	★	★	...	...	...	...
Rhode Island	★	★	...	...	...	...	★	★	★	...	...	...	★	★
South Carolina	★	★	...	★	...	...	★	...	★	★	Both	...	...	★
South Dakota	★	★	...	★	...	...	★	(y)	★	...	...	...	...	...
Tennessee	★	★	...	★	...	★	★	(q)	★	(q)	...	...	...	...
Texas	★	★	...	★	...	(r)	★	...	★	★	Both	...	...	...
Utah	★	★	...	★	...	...	★	★	★	...	...	...	...	★
Vermont	★	★	...	★	...	...	★	...	★	(dd)	...	...	...	★
Virginia	★	★	...	...	★	...	★	★	★	(ee)	...	...	...	★
Washington	★	★	...	★	...	...	★	...	★	★	...	...	...	★
West Virginia	★	★	...	★	...	...	★	★	★	★	(s)	(s)	★	★
Wisconsin	★	★	...	...	...	...	★	...	...	...	Before	Before	...	...
Wyoming	★	★	...	★	...	...	★	...	★	...	...	...	...	...
Dist. of Columbia	★	★	...	...	★	...	★	★	★	...	...	...	...	★
American Samoa	★	★	...	★	...	★	★	★	★	...	...	...	...	★
Guam	★	★	...	★	...	...	★	...	...	...	...	...	...	★
No. Mariana Islands	★	★	...	★	...	★	★	(ff)	★	...	...	...	...	★
Puerto Rico	★	★	...	★	...	★	★	★	★	...	Before	...	...	★
U.S. Virgin Islands	★	★	...	★	...	★	★	(gg)	★	...	(bb)	...	...	★

See footnotes at end of table.

STATE EMPLOYEES: PAID HOLIDAYS** — Continued

**Holidays in addition to any other authorized paid personal leave granted state employees.

Source: The Council of State Governments' survey of state personnel office websites, January 2016.

Note: In some states, the governor may proclaim additional holidays or select from a number of holidays for observance by state employees. In some states, the list of paid holidays is determined by the personnel department at the beginning of each year; as a result, the number of holidays may change from year to year. Number of paid holidays may also vary across some employee classifications. If a holiday falls on a weekend, generally employees get the day preceding or following.

Key:

★ –Paid holiday granted.

… –Paid holiday not granted.

(a) New Year's Day, Independence Day, Labor Day, Thanksgiving Day and Christmas Day.

(b) Third Monday in January.

(c) Generally, third Monday in February; Washington's Birthday or President's Day. In some states the holiday is called President's Day or Washington-Lincoln Day. Most frequently, this day recognizes George Washington and Abraham Lincoln.

(d) Last Monday in May in all states indicated, except Vermont where holiday is observed on May 30. Generally, states follow the federal government's observance (last Monday in May) rather than the traditional Memorial Day (May 30).

(e) Second Monday in October.

(f) General election day only, unless otherwise indicated. In Indiana, primary and general election days.

(g) Additional holidays:

Alabama — Mardi Gras Day (Baldwin and Mobile counties only)(day before Ash Wednesday), Confederate Memorial Day (fourth Monday in April), Jefferson Davis' Birthday (first Monday in June).

Alaska — Seward's Day (last Monday in March), Alaska Day (October 18).

Arkansas — Employee is granted one holiday to observe his or her birthday.

California — César Chávez Day (March 31), one personal holiday (employees become eligible for a personal holiday once they have completed six months of state employment).

Colorado — State employees may have César Chávez Day (March 31) off in lieu of any other legal holiday that occurs on a weekday in the same fiscal year.

Delaware — Eligible employees are granted two floating holidays per calendar year, Return Day after 12:00 noon (second day after a general election) in Sussex County only.

Florida — Full-time employees are entitled to one personal holiday each year. Personal holidays are credited to eligible employees on July 1, and must be taken by the employee by June 30 of each year.

Georgia — Confederate Memorial Day (fourth Monday in April).

Hawaii — Prince Jonah Kuhio Kalanianaole Day (March 26), King Kamehameha I Day (June 11), Statehood Day (third Friday in August).

Iowa — State employees are granted two days of paid leave each year to be added to the vacation allowance and accrued under certain provisions.

Kansas — One discretionary holiday that can be used any time during the calendar year.

Louisiana — Mardi Gras Day (Tuesday before Ash Wednesday), Inauguration Day (every four years, in Baton Rouge only).

Maine — Patriot's Day (third Monday in April).

Maryland — Service reduction days in 2013 include May 24, August 30, November 27, December 24 and December 31. Due to budget constraints, state operations are curtailed on service reduction days.

Massachusetts — Patriot's Day (third Monday in April), Evacuation Day (March 17 — Suffolk County only), Bunker Hill Day (June 17 — Suffolk County only).

Minnesota — Regular and temporary employees with at least six months of employment shall receive two floating holidays each payroll year.

Mississippi — Confederate Memorial Day (last Monday in April).

Missouri — Harry Truman's Birthday (May 8).

Nebraska — Arbor Day (last Friday in April).

Nevada — Nevada Day (last Friday in October).

New Hampshire — Employees who are employed on a full-time basis are eligible for two floating holidays.

Rhode Island — Victory Day (second Monday in August).

South Carolina — Confederate Memorial Day (May 10).

Texas — The following are partial staffing holidays: Confederate Heroes Day (January 19), Texas Independence Day (March 2), San Jacinto Day (April 21), Emancipation Day in Texas (June 19) and Lyndon Baines

Johnson Day (August 27). Staff offices are scheduled to be open on partial staffing holidays and optional holidays. An employee may observe optional holidays in lieu of any partial staffing holiday on which state offices are required to be open to conduct public business. Optional holidays include Cesar Chavez Day (March 31), Good Friday, Rosh Hashanah and Yom Kippur.

Utah — Pioneer Day (July 24).

Vermont — Town Meeting Day (first Tuesday in March), Bennington Battle Day (August 16).

Virginia — Lee-Jackson Day (Friday preceding the third Monday in January). State offices will close at noon on the day before Thanksgiving.

Washington — One additional paid holiday per calendar year.

West Virginia — West Virginia Day (June 20).

District of Columbia — Presidential Inauguration Day (January 20) and District of Columbia Emancipation Day (April 16).

American Samoa — American Samoa Flag Day (April 17), Manu'a Cession Day (July 16).

Guam — Liberation Day (July 21), All Souls' Day (November 2) and Our Lady of Camarin Day (December 8).

Northern Mariana Islands — Commonwealth Covenant Day (March 25), Citizenship Day (November 4) and Constitution Day (December 8).

Puerto Rico — Three Kings Day (January 6), Birthday of Eugenio Maria de Hostos (second Monday in January), Birthday of Luis Muñoz Marin (February 18), Emancipation Day (March 22), Birthday of Jose de Diego (third Monday in April), Birthday of Don Luis Munoz Rivera (third Monday in July), Constitution or Puerto Rico Day (July 25), Birthday of Dr. José Celso Barbosa (July 27), Discovery of Puerto Rico (November 19).

U.S. Virgin Islands — Three Kings Day (January 6), Holy Thursday (Thursday before Good Friday), Transfer Day (March 31), Easter Monday (Monday after Easter), Emancipation Day (July 3), Liberty Day (November 1).

(h) In Alabama, Arkansas and Mississippi, also celebrated as Robert E. Lee's Birthday. In Idaho, also celebrated as Idaho Human Rights Day. In New Hampshire, also celebrated as Civil Rights Day.

(i) In Alabama, celebrated as George Washington's and Thomas Jefferson's Birthday. In Arkansas, celebrated as George Washington's Birthday and Daisy Gatson Bates Day.

(j) The state has designated Lincoln's birthday as a floating holiday in 2013 for state employees in certain bargaining units.

(k) At the discretion of the governor.

(l) In Georgia, Robert E. Lee's Birthday is observed on the day after Thanksgiving, and Washington's Birthday is observed the day before Christmas.

(m) In Indiana, Lincoln's Birthday is observed on the day after Thanksgiving, and Washington's Birthday is observed the day before Christmas.

(n) In Kentucky, half day.

(o) In New Mexico, President's Day is observed on the day after Thanksgiving.

(p) In North Dakota, state offices close at noon on Christmas Eve when it falls on Monday through Thursday.

(q) In Tennessee, at the governor's discretion Columbus Day may be observed the day after Thanksgiving.

(r) In Texas, Good Friday is an optional holiday. An employee is entitled to observe optional holidays in lieu of any partial staffing holiday in which state offices are required to be open to conduct public business.

(s) Half day on Christmas Eve and New Year's Eve (closes at noon).

(t) Tuesday after first Monday in November of presidential election years.

(u) General Election Day is a state holiday the first Tuesday after the first Monday in November in even-numbered years.

(v) Also celebrated as Jefferson Davis' Birthday.

(w) Employees are allowed up to two hours paid administrative leave to vote.

(x) Three days when Christmas Day falls on Tuesday, Wednesday or Thursday; two days when Christmas Day falls on Friday or Monday.

(y) Celebrated as Native Americans Day.

(z) First Tuesday in November, even numbered years.

(aa) Observed as American Indian Heritage Day.

(bb) Observed as Boxing Day.

(cc) Observed as Family Day.

(dd) Most state offices will be closed the day after Thanksgiving.

(ee) At the discretion of the governor. A paid holiday will be granted on the day before Christmas for 2013.

(ff) Celebrated as Commonwealth Cultural Day.

(gg) Also celebrated as Virgin Islands/Puerto Rico Friendship Day.

Table 8.8
2015 STATE MILEAGE REIMBURSEMENT RATES FOR PRIVATELY OWNED VEHICLES

State or other jurisdiction	Current rate (cents per mile)	Date effective (a)
Federal Rate..........................	57.5	January 1, 2015
Alabama.............................	57.5	January 1, 2015
Alaska................................	58.5	January 2, 2015
Arizona..............................	44.5	November 15, 2006
Arkansas............................	42	March 1, 2009
California	57.5	January 1, 2015
Colorado (b)	52 to 55	January 1, 2015
Connecticut........................	57.5	January 1, 2015
Delaware	40	February 22, 2013
Florida	57.5	January 1, 2015
Georgia...............................	57.5	January 1, 2015
Hawaii................................	57.5	January 1, 2015
Idaho..................................	57.5	January 1, 2015
Illinois................................	57.5	January 1, 2015
Indiana...............................	40	July 1, 2015
Iowa	57.5	January 1, 2015
Kansas	57	July 1, 2015
Kentucky	43	July 1, 2015
Louisiana............................	51	July 1, 2015
Maine..................................	44	January 1, 2009
Maryland	57.5	January 1, 2015
Massachusetts	45	May 22, 2011
Michigan.............................	57.5	January 1, 2015
Minnesota...........................	57.5	January 1, 2015
Mississippi..........................	57.5	January 1, 2015
Missouri..............................	37	January 1, 2015
Montana	57.5	January 1, 2015
Nebraska	57.5	January 1, 2015
Nevada................................	57.5	January 1, 2015
New Hampshire	57.5	January 1, 2015
New Jersey	31	January 1, 2013
New Mexico	57.5	January 1, 2015
New York............................	57.5	January 1, 2015
North Carolina....................	57.5	January 1, 2015
North Dakota......................	57.5	January 1, 2015
Ohio	52	July 6, 2015
Oklahoma............................	57.5	January 1, 2015
Oregon................................	57.5	January 1, 2015
Pennsylvania	57.5	January 1, 2015
Rhode Island.......................	57.5	January 1, 2015
South Carolina....................	57.5	January 1, 2015
South Dakota......................	42	July 1, 2015
Tennessee	47	August 1, 2011
Texas..................................	57.5	January 1, 2015
Utah...................................	56	July 1, 2015
Vermont..............................	57.5	January 1, 2015
Virginia...............................	57.5	January 1, 2015
Washington.........................	57.5	January 1, 2015
West Virginia......................	57.5	January 1, 2015
Wisconsin	51	July 1, 2015
Wyoming	57.5	January 1, 2015

Source: The Council of State Governments Survey of State Government websites, August 2015.

Key:

(a) Most recent date the rate was updated or affirmed.

(b) CRS 24-9-104 states that on and after January 1, 2008, state officers and employees shall be allowed mileage reimbursement of 90% of the prevailing IRS rate per mile for each mile actually and necessarily traveled while on official state business and, when authorized to be utilized and necessary for official state business, 95% of the prevailing IRS rate per mile for four-wheel-drive vehicles (necessary because of road, terrain, or adverse weather conditions) and forty cents per nautical mile for privately owned aircraft.

Women in State Government: Still Too Few

By Susan J. Carroll

In recent years the movement of women into state-level offices has slowed after several decades of gains. Efforts to actively recruit women for elective and appointive positions will be critical in determining what the future holds for women in state government.

In the history of our nation, women are relative newcomers among state elected and appointed officials. Women first entered state-level offices in the 1920s following passage and ratification of the Nineteenth Amendment to the U.S. Constitution, which granted women suffrage. However, significant growth in the numbers of women in office occurred only after the emergence of the contemporary women's movement during the late-1960s and early-1970s. Since the mid-1970s, as data collected by the Center for American Women and Politics show, women have greatly increased their numbers among elected and appointed officials in state government. Nevertheless, progress has slowed in recent years, and nationwide statistics show little or no growth in the numbers of women serving in state-level offices since the turn of the century.

Governors

Since the founding of our country, only 37 women (22D, 15R) have served as state governors (Table A), and only one woman has served as governor of a U.S. territory (Puerto Rico). Almost half of the states, 23, have never had a female chief executive. Arizona is the only state to have had four female governors as well as the only state to have had a woman succeed another as governor. New Hampshire has been governed by three different women although one of the governors of New Hampshire, Vesta Roy, served for only seven days following the death of an incumbent. Connecticut, Kansas, Oregon, Texas and Washington each have had two female governors.

The first female governor, Nellie Tayloe Ross of Wyoming, was selected in a special election to succeed her deceased husband in 1925. Fifteen days later a second woman, Miriam "Ma" Ferguson, was inaugurated as governor of Texas, having been elected as a surrogate for her husband, a former governor who had been impeached and consequently was barred constitutionally from running again. Ferguson's campaign slogan was "Two governors for the price of one." The third woman to serve as a governor, Lurleen Wallace of Alabama,

campaigned on the slogan, "Let George do it," and was similarly elected to replace a husband who was prohibited by term limits from seeking an additional term in office.

The first woman elected in her own right (i.e., without following her husband) into the governorship was Ella Grasso, who presided over the state of Connecticut from 1975 to 1980. Twenty-five of the female governors, including Grasso, who have served since the mid-1970s were elected in their own right. The other nine became governor through constitutional succession; only three of these nine were subsequently elected to full terms.

Six women (3D, 3R) serve as governors in 2016, falling short of the record nine women who served simultaneously in 2004 and again in 2007. Four female governors—Mary Fallin (R-Oklahoma), Nikki Haley (R-South Carolina), Maggie Hassan (D-New Hampshire) and Susana Martinez (R-New Mexico)—were re-elected and one woman, Gina Raimondo (D-Rhode Island), was newly elected as governor in 2014. A sixth female governor was added in early 2015 when Secretary of State Kate Brown (D-Oregon) succeeded to the governorship upon the resignation of the incumbent.

Martinez, a Latina, and Haley, an Indian American, are the first two women of color ever to serve as governor of a state.

Other Statewide Elected and Appointed Officials in the Executive Branch

The states vary greatly in their numbers of statewide elected and appointed officials. For example, New Hampshire and Maine have only one statewide elected official, the governor, while North Dakota, at the other extreme, has 12.

The first woman to hold a major statewide office was Soledad C. Chacon (D-New Mexico) who was secretary of state in New Mexico from 1923–26; Delaware, Kentucky, New York, South Dakota and Texas also had female secretaries of state in the 1920s. The first female treasurer, Grace B. Urbahns (R-Indiana), served during the same time period, from 1926–32.

Table A: Female Governors Throughout History

Name (Party-State)	Dates served	Special circumstances
Nellie Tayloe Ross (D-WY)	1925–1927	Won special election to replace deceased husband.
Miriam "Ma" Ferguson (D-TX)	1925–1927, 1933–1935	Inaugurated 15 days after Ross; elected as surrogate for husband who could not succeed himself.
Lurleen Wallace (D-AL)	1967–1968	Elected as surrogate for husband who could not succeed himself.
Ella Grasso (D-CT)	1975–1980	First woman elected governor in her own right; resigned for health reasons.
Dixy Lee Ray (D-WA)	1977–1981	
Vesta Roy (R-NH)	1982–1983	Elected to state senate and chosen as senate president; served as governor for seven days when incumbent died.
Martha Layne Collins (D-KY)	1984–1987	
Madeleine Kunin (D-VT)	1985–1991	First woman to serve three terms as governor.
Kay Orr (R-NE)	1987–1991	First Republican woman governor and first woman to defeat another woman in a gubernatorial race.
Rose Mofford (D-AZ)	1988–1991	Elected as secretary of state, succeeded governor who was impeached and convicted.
Joan Finney (D-KS)	1991–1995	First woman to defeat an incumbent governor.
Ann Richards (D-TX)	1991–1995	
Barbara Roberts (D-OR)	1991–1995	
Christine Todd Whitman (R-NJ)	1994–2001	Resigned to take presidential appointment as commissioner of the Environmental Protection Agency.
Jeanne Shaheen (D-NH)	1997–2003	
Jane Dee Hull (R-AZ)	1997–2003	Elected as secretary of state, succeeded governor who resigned; later elected to a full term.
Nancy Hollister (R-OH)	1998–1999	Elected lieutenant governor; served as governor for 11 days when predecessor took U.S. Senate seat and successor had not yet been sworn in.
Jane Swift (R-MA)	2001–2003	Elected as lieutenant governor, succeeded governor who resigned for an ambassadorial appointment.
Judy Martz (R-MT)	2001–2005	
Olene Walker (R-UT)	2003–2005	Elected as lieutenant governor, succeeded governor who resigned to take a federal appointment.
Ruth Ann Minner (D-DE)	2001–2009	
Jennifer M. Granholm (D-MI)	2003–2011	
Linda Lingle (R-HI)	2003–2011	
Janet Napolitano (D-AZ)	2003–2009	First woman to succeed another woman as governor; resigned to become U.S. Secretary of Homeland Security.
Kathleen Sebelius (D-KS)	2003–2009	Father was governor of Ohio. Resigned to become U.S. Secretary of Health and Human Services.
Kathleen Blanco (D-LA)	2004–2008	
M. Jodi Rell (R-CT)	2004–2011	Elected as lieutenant governor, succeeded governor who resigned.
Christine Gregoire (D-WA)	2005–2013	
Sarah Palin (R-AK)	2007–2009	Resigned.
Beverly Perdue (D-NC)	2009–2013	
Jan Brewer (R-AZ)	2009–2015	Elected as secretary of state, succeeded governor who resigned.
Mary Fallin (R-OK)	2011–present	
Nikki Haley (R-SC)	2011–present	First Asian (Indian) American woman to be elected governor.
Susana Martinez (R-NM)	2011–present	First Latina to be elected governor.
Maggie Hassan (D-NH)	2013–present	
Gina Ramaindo (D-RI)	2015–present	
Kate Brown (D-OR)	2015–present	Elected as secretary of state, succeeded governor who resigned.

Source: Center for American Women and Politics, Eagleton Institute of Politics, Rutgers University, February 2016.

Figure A: Proportion of Women Among Statewide Elective Officials

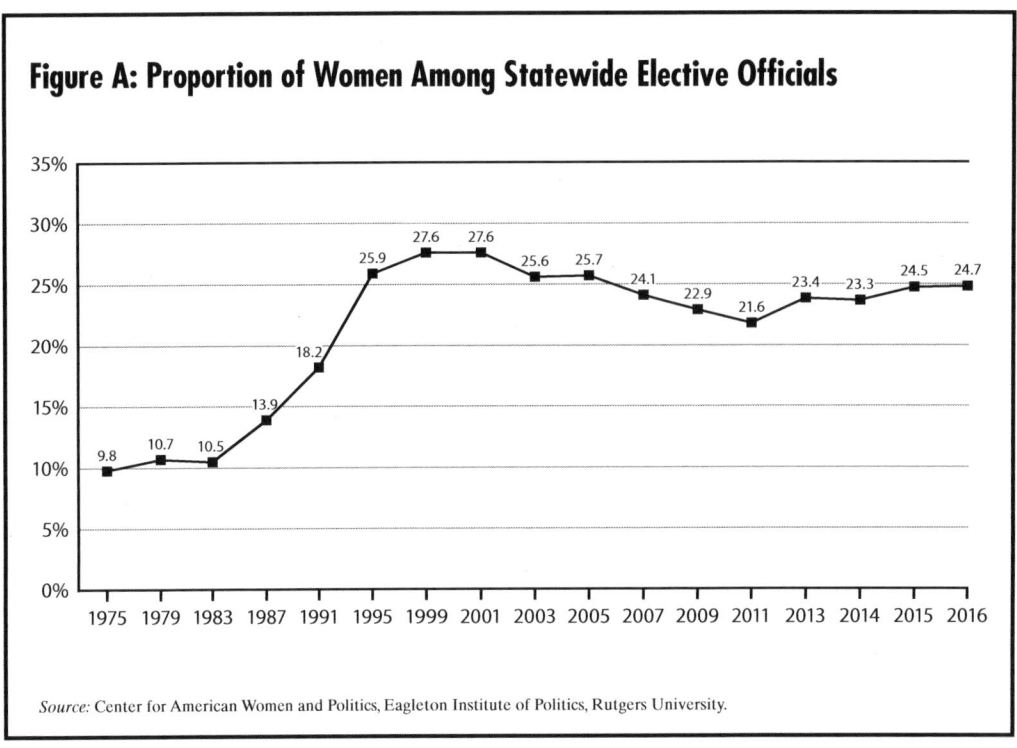

Source: Center for American Women and Politics, Eagleton Institute of Politics, Rutgers University.

Several years passed before a woman became lieutenant governor. Matilda R. Wilson (R-Michigan) served briefly as lieutenant governor of Michigan in 1940 when she was appointed to fill an expiring term. However, the first woman elected as a lieutenant governor was Consuelo N. Bailey (R-Vermont) who served from 1955–56. An additional three decades passed before a woman became attorney general of a state; the first was Arlene Violet (R-Rhode Island) who served from 1985–87.

As evident from Figure A, the proportion of women among statewide elective officials (including governor) has grown substantially since the 1970s. From 1975 to 1983 the increases were small and incremental. Then, between 1983 and 2000, there was a period of significant growth; the number and proportion of women serving statewide almost tripled, reaching a record of 92 women constituting 28.5 percent of all statewide elected officials in 2000. Since 2000, the numbers and proportions have declined. Fewer women, 77, hold statewide offices in 2016 than in 1995 when there were 84 women.

In early 2016, women hold 24.7 percent of the 312 statewide elective positions. In addition to the six women governors, 12 women (4D, 8R) serve as lieutenant governors in the 44 states that elect lieutenant governors in statewide elections. This is considerably fewer than the record high number of 19 women who served as lieutenant governors in 1995.

Other female statewide elected officials include: 13 secretaries of state (7D, 6R), nine attorneys general (6D, 3R), nine state auditors (5D, 4R), nine chief education officials (3D, 5R, 1 nonpartisan), eight state treasurers (4D, 4R), two corporation commissioners (2R), two public service commissioners (2R), two state comptroller/controllers (1D, 1R), one commissioner of insurance (1D), one commissioner of labor (R), one railroad commissioner (R), one agriculture and commerce commissioner (R), and one public utilities commissioner (R). In addition to the two women of color who serve as governors, the women serving in statewide elective office include two African Americans (the lieutenant governor of Kentucky and the state treasurer of Connecticut); two Latinas (the lieutenant governor of Illinois and the secretary of state of Rhode Island); one Native American (the superintendent of public instruction of Montana); one Asian Pacific Islander (the state controller of California); and one multi-racial individual (the attorney general of California).

Women may be slightly better represented among top appointed officials in state government than among statewide elected officials, although it is not possible to know for certain since the most recent data available are from 2007. According to nationwide data collected by the Center on Women in Government and Civil Society at SUNY-Albany, in 2007, women constituted 32.2 percent of department heads with major policymaking responsibilities (including heads of departments, agencies, offices, boards, commissions and authorities) who were appointed by governors. This proportion represented a substantial increase over 1997 when women constituted just 23.2 percent of department heads. Women were even better represented in 2007 among top appointed advisers in governors' offices, with women holding 41.9 percent of these positions—a slightly higher proportion than the 39.5 percent of these positions they held in 1997. Women of color are still a rarity among appointed officials, with women of color constituting just 6.3 percent of all department heads and top advisers in governors' offices in 2007.

Justices on Courts of Last Resort

The first woman to win election to a state court of last resort was Florence E. Allen, who was elected to the Ohio Supreme Court in 1922 and re-elected in 1928. Nevertheless, it was not until 1960 that a second woman, Lorna Lockwood of Arizona, was elected to a state supreme court. Lockwood's colleagues on the Arizona Supreme Court selected her in 1965 to be chief justice, making her the first woman in history to preside over a state court of last resort. She was followed by Susie Sharp of North Carolina who, in 1974, became the first woman to be elected by popular vote to be chief justice of a state court of last resort.

In 2003, Petra Jimenez Maes of New Mexico, who currently serves as an associate justice, became the first Latina chief justice of a state supreme court. Similarly, in 2005 Leah Ward Sears of Georgia became the first African American woman to preside over a state court of last resort.

According to the National Center for State Courts, 126—or 36.7 percent—of the 343 sitting justices on state courts of last resort in early 2016 are women. Of the 53 chief justices of these courts, 22, or 41.5 percent, are women. Women comprise a majority of justices on courts of last resort in nine states—Arkansas, California, Maryland, Massachusetts, New York, Ohio, Tennessee, Washington and Wisconsin. Women constitute at least 40 percent of the justices (but less than a majority) on an additional 21 courts of last resort.

Legislators

Even before 1920 when women won the right to vote across the country, a few women had been elected to legislatures in states that had granted the franchise to women. By 1971 the proportion of women serving in state legislatures across the country had grown to 4.5 percent, and over the years this proportion has increased more than fivefold. As Figure B illustrates, the proportion of women among legislators grew steadily throughout the 1970s and 1980s. However, the rate of growth slowed in the 1990s, and similar to the pattern for statewide elected officials, the numbers and proportions of women legislators nationwide have leveled off since the late 1990s. The proportion of women legislators has increased only about two percentage points since 1999 (Figure B).

In early 2016 women hold 444, or 22.5 percent, of all state senate seats and 1,364, or 25.2 percent, of all state house seats across the country. The number of women who serve in state legislatures in early 2016—1,808—is just under the record number of 1,809 who served in 2010.

Great variation exists across the states in the proportion of legislators who are women. (See Table B.) Colorado ranks first among the states with 42 percent among its legislators, followed by Vermont (41.1 percent), Arizona (35.6 percent), Washington (34.0 percent) and Minnesota (33.8 percent). With the exception of Minnesota and Illinois, all of the states ranked in the top 10 in the proportion of women in their legislatures are located in the west or northeast. However, despite this geographic concentration, no easy explanation exists for why these states have risen to the top, and scholars who have statistically examined the variation among the states in the representation of women in their legislatures have found no simple patterns.

At the other extreme, Wyoming, with only 13.3 percent, ranks last among the 50 states in the representation of women among its legislators. Accompanying Wyoming in the bottom five states are Oklahoma (14.1 percent), South Carolina (14.1 percent), Alabama (14.3 percent), and Mississippi (14.4 percent). Eight of the 10 states with the lowest proportions of women are southern or border states. Only one southern state, Florida, with 25.0 percent women, and one border state, Missouri, with 24.9 percent women are above the national average of 24.5 percent. As these rankings make

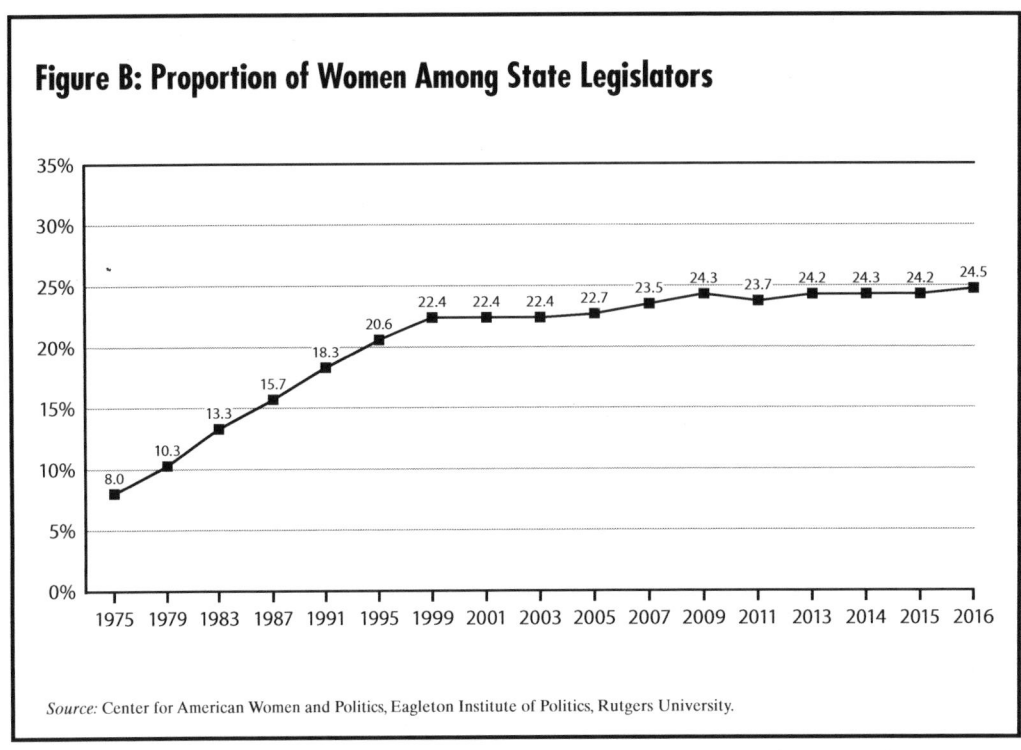

Figure B: Proportion of Women Among State Legislators

Source: Center for American Women and Politics, Eagleton Institute of Politics, Rutgers University.

clear, the south as a region lags behind the rest of the country in the representation of women within its legislatures.

Nationwide, Republicans outnumber Democrats among all state legislators regardless of gender. However, a very different pattern is evident among women legislators where Democrats outnumber Republicans. Among female state senators nationwide, 59.9 percent are Democrats; among female state representatives, 60 percent are Democrats.

About one-fifth of female state legislators, 22 percent, are women of color. Of the 102 senators and 296 representatives serving in legislatures in early 2015, all but 33 are Democrats. African American women hold 68 seats in state senates and 191 seats in state houses across 41 states. Latinas are concentrated in 26 states; they hold 20 senate and 68 house seats. Asian American women count among their numbers 12 senators and 26 representatives in 13 states while Native American women hold two senate and 11 house seats in six states.

The Future

Although women have made substantial progress over time in increasing their presence in state government, the leveling off among state legisla-

tors and slight decline among statewide elective officials since the turn of the century are troubling developments. At a minimum, these developments provide evidence that increases over time are not inevitable.

The lack of growth in numbers has implications for women's representation not only among state legislators and nongubernatorial statewide office-holders, but also among governors and members of Congress. Probably the most striking positive development for women in state government in recent years has been the increase in women governors. Of the 37 women governors across the entire history of our country, 23 have served all or part of their terms during the first few years of the 21st century. Of the six sitting governors, three held statewide elective office before running for governor—one as lieutenant governor, another as secretary of state and a third as state treasurer. In addition, four of the current women governors served in their state legislatures, where two were majority leaders and one was majority whip.

Similarly, many of the women who have run for Congress gained experience and visibility in state government before seeking federal office. Of the 84 female members of the U.S. House in the 114th

Table B: Women in State Legislatures 2016

State	Senate			House			Legislature (both houses)	
	Democrats	Republicans	% Women	Democrats	Republicans	% Women	% Women	State rank (a)
Alabama	3	0	11.4 (b)	11	5	15.2	14.3	46
Alaska	1	4	25.0	2	10	30.0	28.3	15
Arizona	6	7	43.3	11	8	31.7	35.6	3
Arkansas	3	4	20.0	6	14	20.0	20.0	36
California	8	4	30.0	11	8	25.0	25.8	20
Colorado	8	4	34.2	20	10	46.2	42.0	1
Connecticut	8	1	25.0	25	19	29.1	28.3	15
Delaware	5	1	28.6	7	2	22.0	24.2	27
Florida	6	6	30.0	13	15	23.3	25.0	23
Georgia	8	2	17.9	28	18	25.6	23.7	29
Hawaii	8	0	32.0	10	4	27.5	28.9	13
Idaho	4	6	28.6	7	12	27.1	27.6	17
Illinois	12	4	27.1	32	10	35.6	32.8	7
Indiana	3	6	18.0	12	10	22.0	20.7	34
Iowa	6	1	14.0	21	6	27.6	22.7	30
Kansas	4	9	32.5	10	17	21.6	24.2	27
Kentucky	2	2	10.5	10	8	18.0	15.9	43
Louisiana	3	2	12.8	9	8	16.2	15.3	44
Maine	5	3	22.9	30	16	30.5	29.0	12
Maryland	10	2	25.5	36	11	33.3	31.4	8
Massachusetts	12	0	30.0	29	9	23.8	25.0	23
Michigan	1	3	10.5	17	9	23.6	20.3	35
Minnesota	15	8	34.3	27	18	33.6	33.8	5
Mississippi	4	5	17.3	11	5	13.1	14.4	45
Missouri	5	1	17.6	19	24	26.4	24.9	26
Montana	12	6	36.0	21	8	29.0	31.3	9
Nebraska (c)	···Nonpartisan···		22.4	···············Unicameral···············			22.4	31
Nevada	3	2	23.8	9	7	38.1	33.3	6
New Hampshire	4	4	33.3	69	45	28.5	28.8	14
New Jersey	8	3	27.5	18	7	31.3	30.0	11
New Mexico	4	3	16.7	13	10	32.9	26.8	19
New York	7	5	19.0	37	5	28.7 (d)	25.8	20
North Carolina	7	5	24.0	14	12	21.3	22.4	31
North Dakota	4	4	17.0	11	8	20.2	19.1	38
Ohio	4	3	21.2	13	13	26.3	25.0	23
Oklahoma	3	3	12.5	5	10	14.9	14.1	48
Oregon	6	2	26.7	16	4	33.3	31.1	10
Pennsylvania	4	5	18.0	14	23	18.2	18.2	40
Rhode Island	9	1	26.3	18	3	28.0	27.4	18
South Carolina	1	1	4.4	12	10	17.7	14.1	48
South Dakota	1	6	20.0	4	11	21.4	21.0	33
Tennessee	2	4	18.2	7	9	16.2	16.7	41
Texas	2	5	22.6	16	13	19.3	19.9	37
Utah	3	3	20.1	7	3	13.3	15.4	43
Vermont	7	2	30.0	44	15	43.3 (e)	41.1	2
Virginia	7	1	20.0	14	4	18.0	18.6	39
Washington	10	8	36.7	19	13	32.7	34.0	4
West Virginia	0	2	5.9	6	12	18.0	14.9	47
Wisconsin	7	4	33.3	14	9	23.2	25.8	20
Wyoming	1	0	3.3	3	8	18.3	13.3	50

Source: Center for American Women and Politics, Eagleton Institute of Politics, Rutgers University. Figures are as of February 2016.
Key:
(a) States share the same rank if their proportions of women legislators are exactly equal or round off to be equal (AK, CT; FL, MO; IL, OR; MA, OH, WI).

(b) Includes one Independent.
(c) Nebraska has a unicameral legislature with nonpartisan elections.
(d) New York percentage includes Working Family Party (WFP).
(e) Vermont percentage includes three Independents and three Progressives.

Congress, 45 served in their state houses, 20 in their state senates and three in statewide elective offices. Of the 20 female U.S. senators, seven served in their state houses, five in their state senates and four in statewide elective offices.

Activists who are interested in increasing the number of women serving in office often refer to a political pipeline through which potential women candidates for higher office come forward from among the pool of women who have gained

Table C: Women Statewide Elected Officials 2016

State	Governor	Lieutenant Governor	Attorney General	Secretary of State	Treasurer
Alabama	★	w	★	★	★
Alaska	★	★	★		
Arizona	★		★	w	★
Arkansas	★	★	w	★	★
California	★	★	w	★	★
Colorado	★	★	w	★	★
Connecticut	★	w	★	w	w
Delaware	★	★	★		★
Florida	★	★	w		★
Georgia	★	★	★	★	
Hawaii	★	★			
Idaho	★	★	★	★	★
Illinois	★	w	w	★	★
Indiana	★	★	★	w	w
Iowa	★	w	★	★	★
Kansas	★	★	★	★	★
Kentucky	★	w	★	w	w
Louisiana	★	★	★	★	★
Maine	★				
Maryland	★	★	★		
Massachusetts	★	w	w	★	w
Michigan	★	★	★	w	
Minnesota	★	w	w	★	
Mississippi	★	★	★	★	w
Missouri	★	★	★	★	★
Montana	★	w	★	w	
Nebraska	★	★	★	★	
Nevada	★	★	★	w	★
New Hampshire	w				
New Jersey	★	w			
New Mexico	w	★	★	★	★
New York	★	w	★		
North Carolina	★	★	★	w	★
North Dakota	★	★	★	★	★
Ohio	★	w	★	★	★
Oklahoma	w	★	★		★
Oregon	w		w	w	★
Pennsylvania	★	★	w		★
Rhode Island	w	★	★	w	★
South Carolina	w	★	★	★	★
South Dakota	★	★	★	w	★
Tennessee	★				
Texas	★	★	★		
Utah	★	★	★		★
Vermont	★	★	★	★	w
Virginia	★	★	★		
Washington	★	★	★	w	★
West Virginia	★		★	w	★
Wisconsin	★	w	★	★	★
Wyoming	★			★	★

Source: Data for elected officials are current as of February 2016 and have been provided by the Center for American Women and Politics, Eagleton Institute of Politics, Rutgers University.

Key:
★ — Denotes that this position is filled through a statewide election.
w — Denotes that this position is filled through a statewide election and is held by a woman.

experience at lower levels of office. Clearly, the pipeline has worked well in recent years in the case of governors and members of Congress. But what if the pool of women candidates in statewide and state legislative offices continues to stagnate or decline? Then, the number of politically experienced women with the visibility and contacts necessary to run for governor or a seat in the U.S. House or Senate is unlikely to grow.

While several different factors may be responsible for the recent leveling off in the number of women in elective offices in the states, a lack of effective recruitment certainly is one of the most important. Statistics on the number of female candidates over time seem clearly to point to a problem with recruitment. For example, 2,528 women were general election candidates for the more than 6,000 seats up for election in state legislatures in 2014, which means more seats were uncontested by a woman than were contested. Moreover, there were 92 fewer female candidates in 2012 than in 2010 and only 70 more women than in 1992. Clearly, then, a major factor contributing to the leveling off in the number of female officeholders is a lack of greater numbers of female candidates.

Research has found that women who run for office are less likely than their male counterparts to be self-starters. Women more often than men seek office only after receiving encouragement from others. In a 2008 nationwide study of state legislators, scholars at the Center for American Women and Politics found that only 26 percent of female state representatives, compared with 43 percent of their male counterparts, said it was entirely their own idea to run for their first elective office. In contrast, 53 percent of female state representatives, compared with 28 percent of men, said they had not thought seriously about running for office until someone else suggested it. Similarly, a study of major party candidates in state legislative races conducted a few years earlier found that only 11 percent of women, compared with 37 percent of men, were self-starters who said that it was entirely their own idea to run for the legislature; in contrast, 37 percent of women, compared with 18 percent of men, reported that they had not seriously thought about running until someone else suggested it. Another recent study of people in the professions from which political candidates are most likely to emerge (i.e., law, business, politics, and education) found that notably fewer women (43 percent) than men (59 percent) had ever considered running for office.

Findings such as these suggest that the future for women in state government will depend, at least in part, upon the strength of efforts to recruit women for both elected and appointed positions. Legislative leaders, public officials, party leaders, and advocacy organizations can help by renewing their commitment and augmenting their efforts to identify and support potential women candidates, especially in winnable races with open seats or vulnerable incumbents. Recruitment efforts may well be key to determining whether the number of women officials continues to stagnate or again begins to move steadily upward as in earlier decades.

About the author

Susan J. Carroll is Professor of Political Science and Senior Scholar at the Center for American Women and Politics of the Eagleton Institute of Politics at Rutgers University. Her most recent books are *More Women Can Run* (Oxford 2013, with Kira Sanbonmatsu) and *Gender and Elections* (Third Edition, Cambridge 2014, with Richard L. Fox).

Chapter Nine

SELECTED
STATE POLICIES
AND PROGRAMS

The following tables do not appear in the 2016 printed edition of *The Book of the States*. They are available on the CSG Knowledge Center web page at: *http://knowledgecenter.csg.org/kc/category/content-type/content-type/book-states*

Political Will and Creative Approaches Needed for Future Disasters Demands

By Beverly Bell

Just like the head and tail of a coin, there are two sides to every disaster—providing help to those who need it and paying for that assistance. It's a tug-of-war that's becoming more contentious every year. Federal law requires assistance in times of disasters, but as threats grow in complexity—possible infrastructure failures, vulnerabilities from electromagnetic pulses and unforeseen consequences from hydraulic fracturing to name a few—the burden of marshalling the necessary resources and funding is an ongoing struggle.

On Sept. 11, 2001, a seismic shift occurred in the United States, one that challenged former assumptions, validated others and significantly altered priorities under the mantle of a changing world view. As the current presidential administration winds down and a new one assumes control in 2017, questions remain: What will be the next devastating incident? How will the new leadership manage it? Will it be a negative example of how something shouldn't be done? Or will future actions be the result of a disaster management structure that is adroit, adaptable and fiscally responsible? With coordination among all the key players—federal, state, tribal, local, private sector, non-profits and academia—this kind of thoughtful and resilient system is more than a pipe dream. It's the answer to providing aid and being able to pay for it.

How to Handle Rising Disaster Costs

In the 2013 Sandy Recovery Improvement Act, the U.S. Congress required the Federal Emergency Management Agency, or FEMA, to address rising disaster costs. As background, the Disaster Relief Fund is the main account used by the federal government to pay for disaster response and recovery. Managed by FEMA, the fund provides a wide variety of grants and other support to state and local governments, as well as various nonprofit entities. Congress has traditionally appropriated money to maintain the Disaster Relief Fund, or DRF, at a certain level, and then provided additional financing for assistance through supplemental appropriations following a specific large disaster. For the last several years, Congress, the Government Accountability Office, the Office of Management and Budget, and others have expressed concerns over rising disaster costs.

FEMA's latest response to tackle the problem is a proposal adding a deductible to the FEMA Public Assistance—or PA—Program. The PA program is designed specifically to help states, tribes, jurisdictions and certain private non-profit organizations after a presidentially declared disaster. It's a multi-billion dollar program paid out of the DRF and has the potential to impact every government and every jurisdiction throughout the country. The deductible proposal would function like a typical homeowner's insurance policy, requiring states to meet a certain financial commitment before qualifying for federal assistance. The deductible could be offset with credits the states would be given for mitigation and resiliency investments.

States have identified several key issues with the concept. For example, the deductible concept can't simply shift the financial burden of disasters to states, local jurisdictions, tribes, etc. It shouldn't result in ever-increasing and onerous administrative burdens, requiring more state and local personnel, more expense, and more bureaucracy. There must be ample time for implementation, both for FEMA and the states. For FEMA, this means full development of the concept, internal education and training, and the creation of understandable and consistent guidance for the states. On the state level, it will require enough time for state legislatures to be thoroughly briefed on the new requirements and plan through their budgetary cycles for additional deductible responsibilities. States also will need time for training of state personnel as well as all sub-grantees. Most importantly, any change in the program can't result in delayed assistance to those in need.

Flexible Federal Grant Funding

Politicians often call out the inefficient use of public funds. However, when it comes to the difficult task of breaking down silo grant funding, they give up because of constituent backlash. The current state of grant funding has too many programs with too many restrictions and too little funding. Several years ago, the state emergency management community put forward an idea for streamlining the grant structure. It would have allowed stakeholders to work together in identifying and prioritizing the risks to a state or region, and engage in comprehensive planning to apply the grants to buy down that risk while building long-term capabilities. Given the current fiscal and political climate, such a model is still a viable and responsible alternative. Flexible grants that include transparency and accountability allow more deliberate and cohesive planning.

National Flood Insurance Program Still in Jeopardy

Despite recent attempts to address its serious fiscal problems, the National Flood Insurance Program, or NFIP, remains $23 billion in debt. Created in 1968, this federal program provides insurance to property owners as well as businesses located in communities that are part of the NFIP. All participants agree to adopt and enforce floodplain ordinances in exchange for insurance. For years, however, policy costs have not reflected true actuarial rates. This, coupled with a decline in enrollment and revenue, as well as large payouts from recent hurricanes such as Katrina and Superstorm Sandy, has left the program dangerously underfunded. Exacerbating the situation is that the Federal Emergency Management Agency has updated flood maps to provide a more accurate picture, but some of these have been redrawn because of political pressures. Putting the NFIP on solid financial footing, along with educating citizens about the real risks of floods where they live and work, is vital to the long-term economic viability of communities faced with this hazard.

Extreme Weather Adaptation

In recent years, emergency managers have witnessed more severe and more frequent weather events. They have seen ice storms and tornadoes in the same day. These extremes represent a new normal—one that calls for a broad, inclusive approach to planning along with adequate funding to support the effort. As more states manage massive wildland fires, prolonged and repetitive flooding, and more dangerous hurricanes, adaptation planning with all subject matter experts at the table is required. This includes emergency management, which is best suited for evaluating the consequences and impacts of these serious hazards. In addition, emergency management can provide valuable expertise at the nexus of land-use questions and potential disasters.

The Critical Role of Emergency Management

Regardless of whether a disaster is natural or man-made, state emergency management acts as the central coordination point for all resources and assistance provided during the event. When a disaster strikes, emergency management remains one of the most crucial functions of state government. It also has the overarching responsibility of saving lives, protecting property and helping people recover once a disaster has occurred. Typically, emergency management comes to the forefront once an event has taken place. In reality, much of the work comes before—in the form of disaster drills and exercises, plans and programs, public warning tests, and preparedness education.

Emergency management includes four main parts, referred to as the Four Pillars:

- **Mitigation**—Activities that reduce or eliminate the degree of risk to human life and property;
- **Preparedness**—Activities that take place before a disaster to develop and maintain a capability to respond rapidly and effectively to emergencies and disasters;
- **Response**—Activities to assess and contain the immediate effects of disasters, provide life support to victims and deliver emergency services; and
- **Recovery**—Activities to restore damaged facilities and equipment, and support the economic and social revitalization of affected areas to their pre-emergency status.

On the state level, these four elements encompass many different aspects, from planning and implementation to training and exercises. A state emergency manager will interact with all sectors of the population, including other state agencies, elected officials, local jurisdictions, all public safety personnel, the private sector, volunteer organizations and the general public.

State Emergency Management Organizational Structure, Budgets and Staff

States use a variety of structures when it comes to the emergency management function. In 16 states, the emergency management office is located within

Table A: State Emergency Management: Agency Structure, Budget and Staffing

State or other jurisdiction	Position appointed	Appointed/ selected by	Organizational structure	Agency operating budget FY 2016 (excluding federal funds)	Full-time employee positions
Alabama	★	G	Governor's Office	$3,381,343	83
Alaska	★	G	Adjutant General/Military Affairs	$2,457,700	62 (a)
Arkansas	★	G	Governor's Office	$2,109,509	104 (a)
Arizona	★	ADJ	Adjutant General/Military Affairs	$3,899,518	51
California	★	G	Combined Homeland Security/Emerg. Mgt.	$140,897,321	950 (a)
Colorado	...	GHSA	Combined Homeland Security/Emerg. Mgt.	$953,147	85 (a)
Connecticut	...	PSS	Combined Homeland Security/Emerg. Mgt.	$4,889,917	78 (a)
Delaware	★	G	Public Safety	$1,971,000	37
Florida	★	G	Governor's Office	$58,034,342	157 (a)
Georgia	★	G	Governor's Office	$3,207,396	116 (a)
Hawaii	★	G	Adjutant General/Military Affairs	$2,400,000	75
Idaho	★	ADJ	Adjutant General/Military Affairs	$1,533,450	41 (a)
Illinois	★	G	Governor's Office	$32,493,200	209 (a)
Indiana	★	G	Combined Homeland Security/Emerg. Mgt.	$20,758,455	267 (a)
Iowa	★	G	Combined Homeland Security/Emerg. Mgt.	$3,694,623	74 (a)
Kansas	★	G	Adjutant General/Military Affairs	$1,576,261	47
Kentucky	★	G	Adjutant General/Military Affairs	$1,850,000	78
Louisiana	★	G	Combined Homeland Security/Emerg. Mgt.	$6,894,297	51 (a)
Maine	★	G	Adjutant General/Military Affairs	$1,105,298	29 (a)
Maryland	★	G	Adjutant General/Military Affairs	$2,218,103	74
Massachusetts	★	G	Public Safety	$12,952,030	102
Michigan	★	G	State Police	$4,959,500	71 (a)
Minnesota	★	PSS	Public Safety	$11,073,800	79 (a)
Mississippi	★	G	Governor's Office	$5,733,175	155
Missouri	★	PSS	Public Safety	$2,498,000	93
Montana	...	ADJ	Adjutant General/Military Affairs	$1,264,472	26 (a)
Nebraska	★	ADJ	Adjutant General/Military Affairs	$1,899,577	38 (a)
Nevada	★	PSS	Public Safety	$373,611	33 (a)
New Hampshire	★	G	Public Safety	$4,782,914	43 (a)
New Jersey	★	G	State Police	$22,010,000	387
New Mexico	★	G	Combined Homeland Security/Emerg. Mgt.	$2,584,700	65 (a)
New York	★	HSD	Combined Homeland Security/Emerg. Mgt.	$6,409,000	427 (a)
North Carolina	★	G	Public Safety	$12,106,590	188 (a)
North Dakota	★	ADJ	Adjutant General/Military Affairs	$9,343,329	70 (a)
Ohio	★	PSS	Public Safety	$6,027,438	94
Oklahoma	★	G	Governor's Office	$570,049	30
Oregon	★	ADJ	Adjutant General/Military Affairs	$2,051,096	42 (a)
Pennsylvania	★	G	Governor's Office	$15,290,000	173
Rhode Island	★	G	Governor's Office	$1,950,000	32
South Carolina	★	ADJ	Adjutant General/Military Affairs	$2,928,162	60
South Dakota	★	PSS	Public Safety	$777,301	20
Tennessee	★	G	Adjutant General/Military Affairs	$2,900,000	110
Texas	★	PSS	Public Safety	$5,243,369	265
Utah	★	PSS	Public Safety	$1,470,000	62 (a)
Vermont	★	PSS	Public Safety	$2,456,028	26 (a)
Virginia	★	G	Combined Homeland Security/Emerg. Mgt.	$9,830,080	155 (a)
Washington	★	G	Adjutant General/Military Affairs	$3,306,125	82 (a)
West Virginia	★	G	Military Affairs and Public Safety	$3,218,977	53 (a)
Wisconsin	★	G	Adjutant General/Military Affairs	$3,325,187	61 (a)
Wyoming	★	G	Governor's Office	$1,000,000	25 (a)
Dist. of Columbia	★	M	Combined Homeland Security/Emerg. Mgt.	$4,551,525	98 (a)
Guam	★	G	Combined Homeland Security/Emerg. Mgt.	$2,000,200*	17 (a)
U.S. Virgin Islands	★	G	Combined Homeland Security/Emerg. Mgt.	$5,134,418*	61 (a)

Source: The National Emergency Management Association, April 2016.
Key:
★ — Yes
... — No
G — Governor
ADJ — Adjutant General
DHSEM — Director of the Division of Homeland Security and Emergency Management

HSD — Homeland Security Director
GHSA — Governor's Homeland Security Advisor
M — Mayor
PSS — Public Safety Secretary/Commissioner/Director
*Territories receive only federal funding for their operating budgets.
(a) Includes homeland security and emergency management positions.

the state military department under the auspices of the adjutant general. Twelve states have it in the public safety department. In 10 states it's housed in the governor's office and in 12 states it's located in a combined emergency management/homeland security agency. The remaining states use other organizational structures.

Regardless of how an agency's daily operations are organized, most governors make the final decision on who serves as the state emergency management director. The governor appoints the state emergency management director in 34 states.

The majority of states—34—combine their emergency management and homeland security full-time equivalent positions. The total number of full-time equivalents for these states is 3,945 and averages 116 staff per state. For those states that have a stand-alone emergency management office, FTE positions total 1,966, averaging about 103 per state.

Agency operating budgets for the 2016 fiscal year range up to $141 million, with the average state agency budget at approximately $9 million, while the median is about $3.2 million.

State Homeland Security Funding and Responsibilities

The State Homeland Security Grant Program is a central federal source that supports and sustains state and local government homeland security capabilities. For fiscal year 2016, it's funded at $402 million. Eighteen states rely solely on those federal grants to fund their homeland security offices. This represents an increase from 2015, when 15 states depended totally on federal grants. Thirty-nine states receive at least 60 percent of their funding for their state homeland security office from federal sources, down from 42 percent in 2015. On average, states rely on 74.5 percent federal funding, 21.3 percent state appropriations and 4.2 percent from other sources to pay for their homeland security function.

When it comes to the state homeland security offices, responsibilities and organizational structures vary from state to state. In some cases, state homeland security directors manage grants and budgets; in others, they have very limited roles. In 19 states, a combined emergency management/homeland security office oversees daily operations of the homeland security function. Fifteen states keep the homeland security function in their public safety department and seven states have it in the adjutant general/military affairs department. Six states run it out of the governor's office. The rest of the states have other organizational structures for their homeland security function.

On the Horizon
On-Going Public Health Dangers

The Zika virus came to the public health forefront in the U.S. in 2015 with an outbreak in South America and Mexico. There are now confirmed cases of the virus, which causes birth defects, in almost every state. This latest infectious disease highlights the crucial relationship between state emergency management and health departments. These two critical agencies have been working more closely together since the 2009 H1N1 influenza pandemic. Those efforts resulted in improved information sharing and coordination that played a key role in managing the 2014 Ebola outbreak, the largest in the disease's history, which resulted in four infections and one death in the U.S. The Ebola scare was followed in 2015 by the Highly Pathogenic Avian Flu. Twenty-one states reported an outbreak in their domestic bird population and an unprecedented loss in the poultry industry occurred with the death of millions of animals. These examples show that public health risks can't be isolated to one particular country or region of the world. As a result, infectious diseases represent another area of responsibility that requires emergency management—along with their public health partners—to plan for and address.

Proactive Instead of Reactive

Mitigation represents one of the best methods in achieving resiliency while reducing the impact of future disasters. However, it has often been at the end of a typical disaster cycle, something to be tackled after the disaster has occurred and following significant response and recovery expenditures. The ideal approach places a more robust mitigation program at the beginning, before a disaster takes place. It anticipates the protection of critical infrastructure and provides incentives for the adoption and enforcement of effective building codes under an umbrella of long-term needs, clearly formulated by a community.

Understanding the Total Picture

All of the mentioned elements—the NFIP, climate change, public health threats, disaster funding, mitigation investment—are not disparate pieces. The NFIP is inexorably linked to increased flooding and sea level risings created by climate change. Climate change issues such as drought and lack

Table B: Homeland Security Structures

State or other jurisdiction	State homeland security advisor Designated homeland security advisor	Homeland security organizations Day-to-day operations under	Full-time employee positions
Alabama	Public Safety Secretary/Commissioner	Public Safety	5
Alaska	Dual Title–Emerg. Mgt./Homeland Security Director	Combined Emerg. Mgt./Homeland Security Office	62 (a)
Arizona	Homeland Security Director	Homeland Security (stand-alone office)	17
Arkansas	Dual Title–Emerg. Mgt./Homeland Security Director	Combined Emerg. Mgt./Homeland Security Office	104 (a)
California	Dual Title–Emerg. Mgt./Homeland Security Director	Combined Emerg. Mgt./Homeland Security Office	950 (a)
Colorado	Dual Title–Emerg. Mgt./Homeland Security Director	Public Safety	85 (a)
Connecticut	Deputy Commissioner	Combined Emerg. Mgt./Homeland Security Office	78 (a)
Delaware	Homeland Security Advisor	Public Safety	1
Florida	Florida Dept. of Law Enforcement Commissioner	Florida Dept. of Law Enforcement	157 (a)
Georgia	Dual Title–Emerg. Mgt./Homeland Security Director	Governor's Office	116 (a)
Hawaii	Adjutant General	Adjutant General/Military Affairs	5
Idaho	Dual Title–Emerg. Mgt./Homeland Security Director	Adjutant General/Military Affairs	41 (a)
Illinois	Public Safety Secretary/Commissioner	Governor's Office	209 (a)
Indiana	Dual Title–Emerg. Mgt./Homeland Security Director	Combined Emerg. Mgt./Homeland Security Office	267 (a)
Iowa	Dual Title–Emerg. Mgt./Homeland Security Director	Combined Emerg. Mgt./Homeland Security Office	74 (a)
Kansas	Adjutant General	Adjutant General/Military Affairs	0
Kentucky	Homeland Security Director	Governor's Office	15
Louisiana	Dual Title–Emerg. Mgt./Homeland Security Director	Combined Emerg. Mgt./Homeland Security Office	51 (a)
Maine	Adjutant General	Combined Emerg. Mgt./Homeland Security Office	29 (a)
Maryland	Homeland Security Director	Governor's Office	2
Massachusetts	Homeland Security Director	Public Safety	8
Michigan	State Police Superintendent/Director/Commissioner	State Police	71 (a)
Minnesota	Public Safety Secretary/Commissioner	Public Safety	79 (a)
Mississippi	Homeland Security Director	Public Safety	15
Missouri	Public Safety Secretary/Commissioner	Public Safety	10
Montana	Adjutant General	Adjutant General/Military Affairs	26 (a)
Nebraska	Lieutenant Governor	Combined Emerg. Mgt./Homeland Security Office	38 (a)
Nevada	Dual Title–Emerg. Mgt./Homeland Security Director	Combined Emerg. Mgt./Homeland Security Office	33 (a)
New Hampshire	Dual Title–Emerg. Mgt./Homeland Security Director	Public Safety	43 (a)
New Jersey	Homeland Security Director	Homeland Security (stand-alone office)	109
New Mexico	Dual Title–Emerg. Mgt./Homeland Security Director	Combined Emerg. Mgt./Homeland Security Office	65 (a)
New York	Division of Homeland Security and Emergency Services Commissioner	Combined Emerg. Mgt./Homeland Security Office	427 (a)
North Carolina	Public Safety Secretary/Commissioner	Public Safety	188 (a)
North Dakota	Homeland Security Director	Adjutant General/Military Affairs	70 (a)
Ohio	Public Safety Secretary/Commissioner	Public Safety	24
Oklahoma	Homeland Security Director	Homeland Security (stand-alone office)	20
Oregon	Adjutant General	Adjutant General/Military Affairs	42 (a)
Pennsylvania	Homeland Security Director	Governor's Office	6
Rhode Island	State Police Superintendent/Director/Commissioner	Public Safety	0
South Carolina	State Police Superintendent/Director/Commissioner	State Police	19
South Dakota	Homeland Security Director	Public Safety	2
Tennessee	Homeland Security Director	Public Safety	26
Texas	State Police Superintendent/Director/Commissioner	Public Safety	5
Utah	Public Safety Secretary/Commissioner	Public Safety	62 (a)
Vermont	State Police Superintendent/Director/Commissioner	Combined Emerg. Mgt./Homeland Security Office	26 (a)
Virginia	Public Safety Secretary/Commissioner	Combined Emerg. Mgt./Homeland Security Office	155 (a)
Washington	Adjutant General	Combined Emerg. Mgt./Homeland Security Office	82 (a)
West Virginia	Dual Title–Emerg. Mgt./Homeland Security Director	Combined Emerg. Mgt./Homeland Security Office	53 (a)
Wisconsin	Adjutant General	Adjutant General/Military Affairs	61 (a)
Wyoming	Dual Title–Emerg. Mgt./Homeland Security Director	Governor's Office	25 (a)
Dist. of Columbia	Dual Title–Emerg. Mgt./Homeland Security Director	Combined Emerg. Mgt./Homeland Security Office	98 (a)
Guam	Homeland Security Director	Combined Emerg. Mgt./Homeland Security Office	17 (a)
U.S. Virgin Islands	Dual Title–Emerg. Mgt./Homeland Security Director	Combined Emerg. Mgt./Homeland Security Office	61 (a)

Source: The National Emergency Management Association, April 2016.
(a) Includes homeland security and emergency management positions.

of food and potable water can result in increased public health emergencies. These events and all disasters exert more pressure on the federal budget and disaster funding mechanisms such as the DRF. A greater focus on mitigation allows smarter planning and better consequence management. The different factors demand problem solving that acknowledges the entire picture, making the most of common resources and synergetic opportunities.

About the Author

Beverly Bell is the policy and program manager for the National Emergency Management Association, an affiliate of The Council of State Governments. She assists in national policy coordination and grant implementation, while also conducting research and acting as an information clearinghouse for emergency management and homeland security issues.

Redesigning State Financial Aid to Meet the Needs of Today's Students

By Sarah Pingel, Ed.D. and Brian A. Sponsler, Ed.D.

As state leaders construct public policy to support increased educational attainment and workforce development, they need be mindful of the assumptions about college students and their attendance patterns embedded in most state financial aid programs. Reforming state aid is one necessary step to supporting student success.

Data confirms what intuition unearths—higher education looks vastly different today than it did in the 1970s. When viewed across all student groups and postsecondary institutional types, undergraduate enrollments have increased 140 percent since 1970. There also has been significant progress in racial and ethnic group participation in higher education. For example, black male participation has jumped from roughly 470,000 students in 1976 to 1.07 million in 2013, a 127 percent increase. Even greater or equally impressive gains have been made for black females (221 percent), Hispanic males (523 percent) and females (925 percent), and American Indian and Native Alaskan students (113 percent) over the same time period.[1]

In addition to marked strides in postsecondary participation by race and ethnicity, students are also increasingly likely to pass through several gateways to adulthood prior to or while enrolled in higher education. For example, approximately one in five students are working full time while enrolled, and 26 percent are raising dependents of their own. While significant work remains to ensure postsecondary access and success for all types of students, these data show that the makeup of college campuses has shifted as compared to 40 years ago.

At the same time, our progress in creating postsecondary opportunity for students from low-income households remains stymied. While half of all people from high-income families earn bachelor's degrees by age 25, just one in 10 people from low-income families attain undergraduate degrees. While a variety of factors likely contribute to a student's overall propensity to enroll in and complete college, affordability remains a persistent challenge that may be addressed through policy at federal, state and institutional levels.

States in particular stand to play a key role in crafting affordable pathways to and through college for students of a variety of backgrounds. The provi-sion of appropriations supports campus budgets in a variety of areas, such as general operating support and capital improvements. Many states also utilize tuition policy to control the maximum price that students may pay for college, whether through setting the actual tuition amount, imposing a cap on tuition increases or freezing tuition levels. Finally, 49 states provide further support for targeted populations of students through state-funded financial aid programs.

It is state financial aid programs in particular that merit new scrutiny as postsecondary institutions and the students that they serve continue to evolve in the 21st century. States have a long history of making investments in individuals seeking postsecondary education. Before the federal government created broadly accessible financial aid programs through the passage of the Higher Education Act in 1965, several states had already begun funding aid for college students. Two original state aid programs are still in operation today—California's Cal Grant, created in 1955; and Illinois' Monetary Award Program, which began in 1958. Spurred in part by a federal matching incentive, a wave of state programs were developed throughout the 1960s and 1970s, including 20 states with established programs that are still awarding aid to students today.

Continuing this historical legacy, in 2014, state financial aid programs collectively invested $11.7 billion in students, providing a significant financial benefit for individuals, institutions and, ultimately, state economies. State financial aid programs, however, tend to primarily serve students following what is often mislabeled a "traditional" postsecondary pathway: matriculating directly into a two- or four-year degree program in the fall following high school graduation. These students are more likely than their peers to attend credit-hour-based postsecondary programs, pursue their education on a full-time enrollment basis and complete their programs on time.

The Need for Reform

Education Commission of the States' research and policy analysis indicates that many of the largest state-based financial aid programs are explicitly designed to serve students following the historically traditional pathway into and through college — a challenge when trying to address the needs of today's college students. For example, among the 100 largest state-funded financial aid programs in the country:

- Twenty-nine programs will only fund students who enroll full time.

- Forty-three programs define the duration of the aid award by a set number of terms or years, as opposed to anchoring eligibility to the length of time needed to complete a program at varying enrollment intensities.

- Thirty-three programs link aid eligibility to college entrance exams, such as the SAT or ACT, or a high school grade point average — traditional college readiness measures that are of little relevance for adults returning to higher education from the workforce.

To support intentional redesign conversations, the Education Commission of the States has outlined four key principles to serve as guideposts for state policy leaders as they seek to redesign state financial aid policies and programs:

- **Principle 1: Financial aid programs should be student-centered.**
  Aid programs designed around students and their needs position students for successful outcomes.

- **Principle 2: Financial aid programs should be goal-driven and data-informed.**
  Aid programs should have clearly defined and easily understood intentions aligned with measurable state education and workforce goals.

- **Principle 3: Financial aid programs should be timely and flexible.**
  Aid programs should provide financial support to students when it can have the greatest impact on enrollment and persistence decisions.

- **Principle 4: Financial aid programs should be broadly inclusive of all students' educational pathways.**
  Aid programs need to respond to the diverse enrollment options available to today's college students.

Separately, each of the principles addresses a specific area for states to make incremental policy change. Taken together, they provide the opportunity for states to make fundamental shifts in how state financial aid programs are designed and awarded and how aid dollars impact student enrollment and persistence choices.

Applying these principles within states over the past two years has proved a rich undertaking, with many states seeking support in aid policy reform. Specifically, state policy leaders need to find ways to bridge the divide between the current reality of higher education and the design of state-funded aid programs. As we have supported states through thoughtful redesigns of aid policy, we have found that one of the largest challenges is achieving coordination among competing priorities and stakeholders, and the challenges posed by limited fiscal commitments to state financial aid programs.

Competing Priorities

First, while state legislative activity around financial aid programs is robust, it often lacks coordination with existing programs or approaches to student financial support. In 2015, 44 states considered 245 bills related to state financial aid programs. Individual states considered anywhere from one measure to 54.[2] As an indicator of legislative interest in aid, the sheer number of bills introduced by states certainly has its limitations, however, the wide reach of financial aid programs as a topic of legislation is unique across other areas of post-secondary policymaking.[3] Of the 245 measures considered in the 2015 session, one-half of these proposed bills would create entirely new state financial aid programs. These new programs would be in addition to the 559 grant, scholarship, loan forgiveness, work study, tuition waiver, and other staterun programs awarding students in 2014.[4]

To be sure, states face real challenges in providing affordable college pathways for students; legislative attention is a welcome voice in facing these challenges. However, a powerful, overarching goal should be in place to inform statewide financial aid policy development and maintenance. Through engagement within the states, we learn that program coordination can be difficult to achieve. Additionally, we find that the number of programs a state operates is likely unrelated to the total amount of funds that they devote to the programs.[5] Therefore, when new programs are enacted, they do not necessarily incite more investment in aid. In the best case, new programs may be enacted as a strategic choice to bring a state closer to its goals; in the worst case, new programs can divert resources and attention from existing approaches that may be showing promise.

Another challenge to achieving alignment around a common goal is the variety of players within a state that have a stake in financial aid policy. Figure A illustrates several of the key stakeholder groups involved in state financial aid policy development and maintenance. Within and across these groups, coalitions of support for financial aid programs have the potential to develop. On the other hand, in some state contexts, various stakeholders who are removed from key conversations have the potential to derail, distract or detract from state goals that they were not involved in developing.

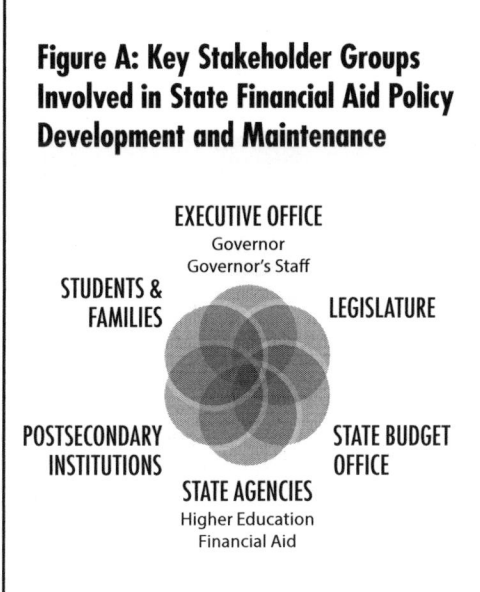

Figure A: Key Stakeholder Groups Involved in State Financial Aid Policy Development and Maintenance

EXECUTIVE OFFICE
Governor
Governor's Staff

STUDENTS & FAMILIES

LEGISLATURE

POSTSECONDARY INSTITUTIONS

STATE BUDGET OFFICE

STATE AGENCIES
Higher Education
Financial Aid

Budgetary Challenges

From a budgetary perspective, the idea of a zero-sum game can be a pervasive theme within state-level conversations surrounding aid policy. Often, decisions are made in the context of taking from one group and reallocating to another, or restricting student eligibility to stay within a certain target budget figure. In this way, the underlying assumption that states are not in a position to invest more heavily into their financial aid programs unfortunately drives many conversations surrounding financial aid redesign.

Although effective budgeting is key, it should not replace larger conversations surrounding state goals and overall program design. In other words, an exclusive focus on budgetary concerns can shift attention from developing policy based on stra-

tegic, goal-focused conversations. In their place, what may result are eligibility changes that are based on producing a certain budget outlay rather than working toward larger strategic aims.

Final Thoughts

The data bear out the changing demographics among postsecondary students as compared to 40 years ago. Unfortunately, the pace of policy adaptation to this new group of students has been slower than the changes in postsecondary participation rates. This disconnect is especially salient in state financial aid policies; policies that have the potential to remove affordability barriers for key student populations. States have begun to redesign policies to be more student-centered, goal-driven and data-informed, timely and flexible, and broadly inclusive. In the path to reform, states face a variety of challenges, not the least of which are posed by competing priorities and limited budgetary capacity. Ultimately, the ways in which states choose to face—or not face—these challenges will contribute toward their overall approach to the provision of higher education within their borders and the composition of their workforce.

Notes

[1] Snyder, T.D., and Dillow, S.A. (2015). Digest of Education Statistics 2013 (NCES 2015-011). National Center for Education Statistics, Institute of Education Sciences, U.S. Department of Education. Washington, DC.
[2] Of note, the number of bills considered in each state and in total across the nation is not a pure measure of legislative interest in financial aid programs, as it is also impacted by unrelated factors such as the number of legislative days and specific state-level legislative processes.
[3] Education Commission of the States' unpublished postsecondary tracking database.
[4] Authors' calculation. 45th Annual Survey Report on State-Sponsored Student Financial Aid. (2014). National Association of State Student Grant and Aid Programs: Washington, DC. Retrieved from *www.nassgap.org*.
[5] Ibid.

About the Authors

Sarah Pingel, Ed.D., is a policy analyst in the postsecondary and workforce development institute at Education Commission of the States, where she leads the organizations work relating to state financial aid.
Brian A. Sponsler, Ed.D., is director of the postsecondary and workforce development institute at Education Commission of the States, working with leadership across the states to develop sound public policy in support of student success.

The Adult Learner:
A Critical Ally for State Economic Development

By Wilson Finch

Critical to state education and economic goals, adult learners will represent a majority of college students in the near future, yet they are largely an untapped resource. States and higher education institutions must adequately address their unique needs, concerns and expectations with comprehensive, proactive and targeted strategies that reflect this new reality.

Since the advent of land grant institutions and the G.I. Bill, public higher education policy has focused on increasing access to colleges and universities across the United States. Recently, this emphasis has expanded to include fostering successful degree completion, with the realization that most students who enroll do not graduate in expected timeframes and many never finish at all.[1] Yet, policies for access and completion have remained primarily directed at traditional college students—full-time, first-time students ages 18 to 22). While there are notable examples of states and institutions developing policies and programs to address nontraditional students' needs,[3] including adults over the age of 24, overall these programs are viewed as extensions of existing traditionally focused programs and do not offer comprehensive support for adult learners. This is perplexing since adults over age 24 are the fastest growing population within American higher education. This article demonstrates why states and public institutions of higher education, or IHE, should focus more resources and efforts on the adult learner population, describes the unique supports and resources adult learners need, and suggests strategies to assist their enrollment, persistence and degree attainment within systems of higher education.

The Traditional Student Myth

Programs and policies directed toward traditional college students assume students have little experience in higher education, lack substantial learning experiences beyond formal education and can prioritize coursework over employment or other obligations. However, as of 2011, adult students made up 38 percent of undergraduates and are the fastest growing student population: by 2019, they are predicted to comprise 61 percent of all undergraduates.[4] Conversely, the traditional K–12-to-college pipeline population is actually in decline.[5] This is a fundamental shift in the makeup

of the college student, and nontraditional students are becoming the system's *raison d'être*. Yet, in many cases, this transformation has not provoked changes in how higher education is structured, to whom it is marketed, and what state and institutional supports are offered.

The Degree of Need

The failure of the U.S. to produce enough postsecondary graduates to satisfy future jobs is well-documented.[6] Two outcomes of this shortage are relevant to adult learners. First, the lack of potential workers with the necessary postsecondary credentials is hampering economic development within states.[7] Second, those individuals with postsecondary credentials are much more economically secure in times of economic fluctuation.[8] To address this, by 2014 26 states had adopted some degree attainment goal in order to meet their economic needs.[9] However, achieving these goals is highly unlikely if only traditional students are considered.

The Adult Equation

Take two examples: Iowa and Tennessee. In 2015, Iowa Gov. Terry Branstad set a state degree attainment goal of 70 percent of Iowans by 2025.[10] Tennessee Gov. Bill Haslam has set a goal of 55 percent degree attainment by 2025.[11] Table A shows how these goals are represented in real numbers.

Comparing the difference between the current degree attainment level and the goal level with the number of students enrolled in the K–12 system, the challenge of achieving the governors' goals is evident: Even if *every single student* in the public K–12 system graduates from high school, enrolls in college and completes a degree program, Tennessee barely would reach its goal and Iowa would fall short. However, such progressions are unlikely, as Iowa and Tennessee have relatively little room for improvement within the traditional college pipeline.

Table A: Current College Degree Attainment

	Iowa		Tennessee	
	%	Count	%	Count
Current Attainment	36%	555,220	29.7%	1,006,913
Goal	70%	1,091,725	55%	1,864,653
Difference between current count and goal		536,505		857,740
Total Public K–12 Enrollment		498,000		1,006,500

Sources:

Current Attainment
U.S. Census Bureau. "Educational Attainment 2008–2012: 5-Year Estimates." *American Community Survey*, 2012. *http://factfinder.census.gov/faces/tableservices/jsf/pages/product view.xhtml?pid=ACS_14_5YR_S1501&prodType=table.*

Goals
Carnevale, Anthony P., Nicole Smith, Artem Gulish, and Andrew R. Hanson. *Iowa: Education and Workforce Trends through 2025.* Iowa Department of Education and Georgetown Center on Education and the Workforce, 2015. *https://cew. georgetown.edu/wp-content/uploads/Iowa_Wrkfrce2025.pdf.*

Drive to 55 Tennessee. Accessed March 23, 2016. *http://drive to55.org/.*

Public K–12 Enrollment
"Enrollment in Public Elementary and Secondary Schools, by Region, State, and Jurisdiction: Selected Years, Fall 1990 through Fall 2023." *Digest of Education Statistics*, 2013. Institute of Education Sciences—National Center for Education Statistics, Fall 2012. *https://nces.ed.gov/programs/digest/d13/tables/dt13_ 203.20.asp.*

Table B: High School Graduation, College-going Rates and College Graduation Rates

Rates	Iowa	Tennessee	Best performing states
HS Graduation	90.5	87.2	90.5
College-going	66.6	62.1	78.8
College Graduation	51	41	62

Sources:

High school graduation
"Public High School 4-Year Adjusted Cohort Graduation Rate (ACGR), by Race/ethnicity and Selected Demographics for the United States, the 50 States, and the District of Columbia: School Year 2013–14." *Common Core of Data (CCD)*. Institute of Education Sciences—National Center for Education Statistics, 2013–2014. *http://nces.ed.gov/ccd/tables/ ACGR_RE_and_characteristics_2013-14.asp.*

College-going rates
"College-Going Rates of High School Graduates—Directly from High School." NCHEMS Information Center. National Center for Higher Education Management Systems, 2010. *http://www.higheredinfo.org/dbrowser/index.php?submeasure =63&year=2010&level=nation&mode=data&state=0.*

College graduation rates
"Graduation Rates." NCHEMS Information Center. National Center for Higher Education Management Systems., 2009. *http://www.higheredinfo.org/dbrowser/?level=nation&mode= data&state=0&submeasure=24.*

Even if these states match their best performing counterparts within the next few years, they would still fall short of their degree attainment goals. Furthermore, the traditional student population is *decreasing* nationwide;[12] the state goals appear to represent a naïve optimism rather than a viable policy solution if only focusing on traditional students. Yet, most state and institutional resources have been devoted to traditional students. For example, most financial aid is unavailable to adults, marketing is targeted to traditional students and great emphasis is placed on ensuring high school students have a clear pathway into higher education.

This is where the focus of such policies needs to be expanded to include adult learners. Continuing with our previous examples of Iowa and Tennessee, 54.2 percent of Iowa adults and 54.4 percent of Tennessee adults have a high school degree but not a college degree; slightly less than half of these have some college experience.[13] These individuals are likely to have college credits from previous enrollments or could earn some credit for learning gained outside of college, which could significantly reduce time-to-degree for adult degree completion. If 48.6 percent and 36.4 percent of these adult learners could be enticed to return to college and complete their degrees, Iowa and Tennessee would reach their state attainment goals even if public high schools stopped producing students.[14]

From our two examples, we can see that there are limits to improving the high school graduate-to-degree-completion pipeline, but even capturing a relatively minor percentage of adults with high school diplomas could propel a state quickly toward its attainment goals. However, state and institutional efforts often do not reflect this opportunity.

Why are states and IHE, who bemoan low-enrollment statistics or results from performance measures, ignoring this potential solution and a largely untapped pool of enrollment candidates? There are several answers to this question. Perception is a problem, particularly for the general public. When many people think of a college student, they imagine a young, full-time student, living on a university campus. However, these students only represented 15 percent of enrolled students in 2011.[15] This misperception has misdirected efforts and resources, obscured the issue and discouraged nontraditional students. Still these data can surprise even some higher education administrators.

The issue is not that these data do not exist, but rather they are buried in data systems unanalyzed and unpublished unless specifically requested. There are also political reasons: there is a certain appeal to helping young people pursue their goals that is difficult to transfer to an adult trying to return to college. It is further possible that most lawmakers were themselves traditional students, and may therefore be unaware of the issue. State and institutional inertia also contributes to the problem. While adding a few *ad hoc* supports for adults—such as childcare or online programs—may seem feasible and tangible, completely changing an institution's culture or structure to reflect a new student population reality is a much more difficult task.

In addition to these more systemic problems, attracting nontraditional students is a persistent problem requiring innovative efforts. Traditional students are a captive audience within high schools, however, adults are a more dispersed population and may be more difficult to reach. Targeting this population depends more heavily on mass marketing and creative efforts, such as outreach through employers, unemployment centers and community events.

What are the unique needs of adult learners?

The 2013 National Adult Learners Satisfaction-Priorities Report noted that achieving adult learners' expectations and satisfaction, or "fit," was key to promoting "persistence, student success, and stability," while failing to do so would lead to "higher attrition, poor performance, and fluctuation."[16]

Nontraditional students are more likely to work full time and have children, leading to multiple demands on their time. For many, education is still a priority, albeit a lower one, because they see degree attainment as directly tied to advancement in their careers or income. Accordingly, they seek programs that respect their time and money. IHE can respond to these needs with adult-specific policies and programs, such as those highlighted below. Furthermore, adult students have different learning styles, expectations and requirements (andragogy) compared to traditional students.[17]

Lastly, it is important to recognize that many adults have had previous experiences in higher education or felt it was beyond their reach. In both cases, as many studies have put it, "life got in the way" and non-academic circumstances disrupted degree attainment.[18]

Specific Adult-Focused Strategies

To meet the needs of adult learners, states and IHE should consider whether their efforts to serve this population are proportional to their representativeness in the student population. For example,

if adult students make up 40 percent of a system's student population, is 40 percent of the marketing budget used to target them? Does 40 percent of the state's financial aid go to them? Do institutions offer unique and directed supports such as prior learning assessment, accelerated courses and extended hours that recognize their substantial student enrollment numbers? Unfortunately, most institutions and states feel it is sufficient to offer only a limited number of these programs and supports, often confined to specific degree programs and rarely promoted. While helpful, their impact is limited and lacks a comprehensive effect because these efforts merely attempt to shoe-horn a nontraditional student into a traditional model. These programs and resources should be provided at all institutions with significant adult populations or adult enrollment goals, and importantly, they should be offered in all degree programs.

For decades, several exemplary institutions, and more recently, some states have begun to recognize this need. Specific programs and initiatives that are growing in popularity include:

- Adult-specific orientations, student support services, staff

- Andragogical teaching approaches—addressing the different ways adult students learn within the classroom

- Competency-based education, or CBE—a time-flexible instructional model that commonly combines assessments of prior and classroom learning with more modularized teaching

- Flexible scheduling, accelerated courses, online courses—all opportunities to adapt class times around competing obligations of adult learners

- Interdisciplinary adult degree programs—programs that speed up degree completion by finding the most favorable combination of previous credits, transfer credits and prior learning assessment, or PLA, credits when a more specific major is not necessary or desired

- Life and career planning—increasing efforts to tie major and course selections to the student's professional and life goals

- Marketing—directed specifically at adults and addressing their concerns, needs and goals

- Partnerships with local businesses—encouraging business partners to support employees' desires to return to school and make more concrete links between degree attainment and career opportunities

- Prior learning assessment—granting of college credit for learning obtained outside of the classroom[19]
- Substantial financial aid for adults—a high priority for many adults that is not met by state and federal offerings and that does not incentivize PLA and CBE
- Targeted incentives for institutions—links to performance funding, state-organized innovation programs, streamlined procedures, lowered policy barriers, shared resources and intra-state networks

Also critical to these strategies is how well they are integrated into the IHE and state systems. These efforts and initiatives should not depend upon a series of "ifs": *if* a student asks and asks the right person, *if* the student choses the right degree program, *if* the student is at the right institution with the right support structures, etc. If IHE and states are serious about boosting adult enrollment and completion, they must be more *proactive* and *comprehensive* in their efforts.

Nevertheless, it is critical to note that these supports, when done properly, do not undermine the academic integrity and rigor of degrees, but rather remove barriers, attract new students, and make components of higher education more efficient and effective, less burdensome and confusing, and more relevant to and respectful of the lives of their students. Our economy and the personal wellbeing of our students depend heavily upon *quality* and *rigorous* postsecondary credentials.

Conclusion

The economic future of the states will be heavily dependent upon how well equipped and educated its future workforce will be, and this future is too important to leave chance. A valuable and plentiful resource, the adult learner remains a highly underutilized and untapped resource for public higher education, which could boost the economic development of states while also providing increased financial stability and career advancement to these students. There are longstanding practices and new innovations that should be studied, exemplified, scaled and supported in order to develop this resource. The adult learner, rather than being an anomaly within higher education, could become its most important ally.

Notes

[1] The national fall 2006 cohort for associates and bachelors students were compared with the combined summer 2009 graduates using the most recent NCHEMS data.

"Graduation Rates." NCHEMS Information Center. National Center for Higher Education Management Systems., 2009. *http://www.higheredinfo.org/dbrowser/?level=nation&mode=data&state=0&submeasure=24.*

Further reading: American Association of Community Colleges. "National College Completion Initiatives."

"Four-Year Myth." Complete College America, 2014. *http://completecollege.org/new-report-4-year-degrees/.*

Russell, Alene. "A Guide to Major U.S. College Completion Initiatives." *AASCU Policy Matters.* American Association of State Colleges and Universities, October 2011.

[2] For examples of specific state PLA efforts, see "State Policy Approaches to Support Prior Learning Assessment: 2015 Update." *Resource Guides for State Leaders.* Council for Adult and Experiential Learning (CAEL) and HCM Strategists, 2016. *http://www.cael.org/pdfs/cael_hcm-pla-state-policy-report-2016.*

For broader, adult-oriented programs, see "Re-Enroll Adults with Some College and No Degree." *Strategy Labs: State Policy Agenda*, April 2015. Lumina Strategy Labs. *http://strategylabs.luminafoundation.org/higher-education-state-policy-agenda/action-20.*

[3] I will be primarily focusing on "adult learners," which are defined as students aged 25 to 64. However, I will also reference "nontraditional students," which the National Center for Education Statistics defines as having one or more of the following characteristics: "delayed enrollment into postsecondary education; attends college part time; works full time; is financially independent; has dependents other than a spouse; is a single parent; or does not have a high school diploma." Adult learners represent a substantial proportion of nontraditional students, and there is considerable overlap in terms of needs, expectations, and outlooks.

Pelletier, Stephen G. "Success for Adult Students." *Public Purpose*, 2010, 2–6.

[4] Hess, Frederick. "Old School: College's Most Important Trend Is the Rise of the Adult Student." *The Atlantic. http://www.theatlantic.com/business/archive/2011/09/old-school-colleges-most-important-trend-is-the-rise-of-the-adult-student/245823/.*

Wyatt, Linda G. "Nontraditional Student Engagement: Increasing Adult Student Success and Retention." *Journal of Continuing Higher Education* 59, no. 1 (2011): 10–20.

[5] Kiley, Kevin. "The Pupil Cliff." *Inside Higher Ed*, January 11, 2013. *https://www.insidehighered.com/news/2013/01/11/ wiche-report-highlights-decline-high-school-graduates-and-growing-diversity.*

[6] Baum, Sandy, Jennifer Ma, and Kathleen Payea. "Education Pays 2013." The College Board, 2013. *http://www.rilin.state.ri.us/Special/ses15/commdocs/Education %20Pays,%20The%20College%20Board.pdf.*

Carnevale, Anthony P., Nicole Smith, and Jeff Strohl. *Help Wanted: Projections of Job and Education Require-*

ments through 2018. Georgetown University Center on Education and the Workforce, 2010.

Carnevale, Anthony P., Nicole Smith, and Jeff Strohl. *Recovery: Job Growth and Education Requirements through 2020,* Georgetown University Center on Education and the Workforce, 2013. *https://repository.library. georgetown.edu/handle/10822/559311.*

[7] Ibid.

[8] "Earnings and Unemployment Rates by Educational Attainment." Bureau of Labor Statistics, March 15, 2016. *http://www.bls.gov/emp/ep_chart_001.htm.*

[9] HCM Strategists. "States with Higher Education Attainment Goals." Lumina Foundation, December 11, 2014. *http://strategylabs.luminafoundation.org/wp-content/uploads/2015/01/50StateAttainmentGoals121114. pdf.*

[10] Carnevale, Anthony P., Nicole Smith, Artem Gulish, and Andrew R. Hanson. *Iowa: Education and Workforce Trends through 2025.* Iowa Department of Education and Georgetown Center on Education and the Workforce, 2015. *https://cew.georgetown.edu/wp-content/uploads/ Iowa_Wrkfrce2025.pdf.*

[11] *Drive to 55 Tennessee.* Accessed March 23, 2016. *http://driveto55.org/.*

[12] Kiley, "The Pupil Cliff."

[13] U.S. Census Bureau. "Educational Attainment 2008–2012: 5-Year Estimates." *American Community Survey,* 2012. *http://factfinder.census.gov/faces/tablese rvices/jsf/pages/productview.xhtml?pid=ACS_14_5YR _S1501&prodType=table.*

[14] Ibid.

[15] Hess, "Old School."

[16] Noel-Levitz and Council for Adult and Experiential Learning (CAEL). "National Adult Learners Satisfaction-Priorities Report," 2013. *http://www.cael.org/pdfs/ ali_report_0713.*

[17] Knowles, Malcolm S. *The Modern Practice of Adult Education: From Pedagogy to Andragogy.* 2nd ed. Englewood Cliffs: Prentice Hall/Cambridge, 1980.

Ross-Gordon, Jovita M. "Research on Adult Learners: Supporting the Needs of a Student Population That Is No Longer Nontraditional." *Peer Review* 13, no. 1, Winter 2011. Association of American Colleges and Universities. *https://www.aacu.org/publications-research/periodicals/ research-adult-learners-supporting-needs-student-popula tion-no.*

[18] Steele, Patricia, and Wendy Erisman. "Adult College Completion in the 21st Century: What We Know and What We Don't." *Higher Ed Insight,* 2015. Adult College Completion Network. *http://papers.ssrn.com/sol3/papers.cfm? abstract_id=2622629.*

[19] Additional information about PLA and student outcomes: Klein-Collins, Rebecca. "Fueling the Race to Postsecondary Success: A 48-Institution Study of Prior Learning Assessment and Adult Student Outcomes." Council for Adult and Experiential Learning, 2010. *http://eric.ed.gov/?id=ED524753.*

About the Author

Wilson Finch has been a senior consultant at the Council for Adult and Experiential Learning (CAEL) since 2014. His primary focus has been on statewide and systemwide approaches to prior learning assessment (PLA) and higher education support for workforce projects. Previously, Wilson was the assistant director for Postsecondary Completion Initiatives for the Tennessee Higher Education Commission (THEC).

Census Data Show More Americans with Health Insurance Coverage after ACA Kicks In

By Debra Miller

A comparison of U.S. Census data for 2013 and 2014, released in early 2016, shows that a greater portion of Americans in each state had health insurance in the more recent year. Nearly 8.5 million individuals gained health insurance coverage between 2013 and 2014. In 2014, all the provisions of the Affordable Care Act designed to increase access to affordable insurance were in place for states. Some states, however, decided not to expand income eligibility for Medicaid to 138 percent of the federal poverty level as the Supreme Court ruled in 2012 was the prerogative of the states, not Congress. The states that showed the greatest increase in coverage between 2013 and 2014 were states that expanded Medicaid income eligibility.

What was the Status of Insurance Coverage in States in 2014?

The proportion of state residents with health insurance coverage in 2014 ranged from a high of 96.7 percent in Massachusetts to a low of 80.9 percent in Texas. The average health insurance coverage in the 50 states and the District of Columbia was 89.3 percent. Health insurance coverage includes employer-provided coverage, individually purchased coverage and coverage under the major

government programs: Medicaid (for people with low-incomes), Medicare (for seniors and people with severe disabilities) and TriCare (for military veterans and their dependents).

Figure A provides the top and bottom five states in terms of the proportion of residents who had health insurance coverage in 2014.

All five of the states with the highest proportion of residents with health insurance coverage— Massachusetts, Vermont, Hawaii, Minnesota and

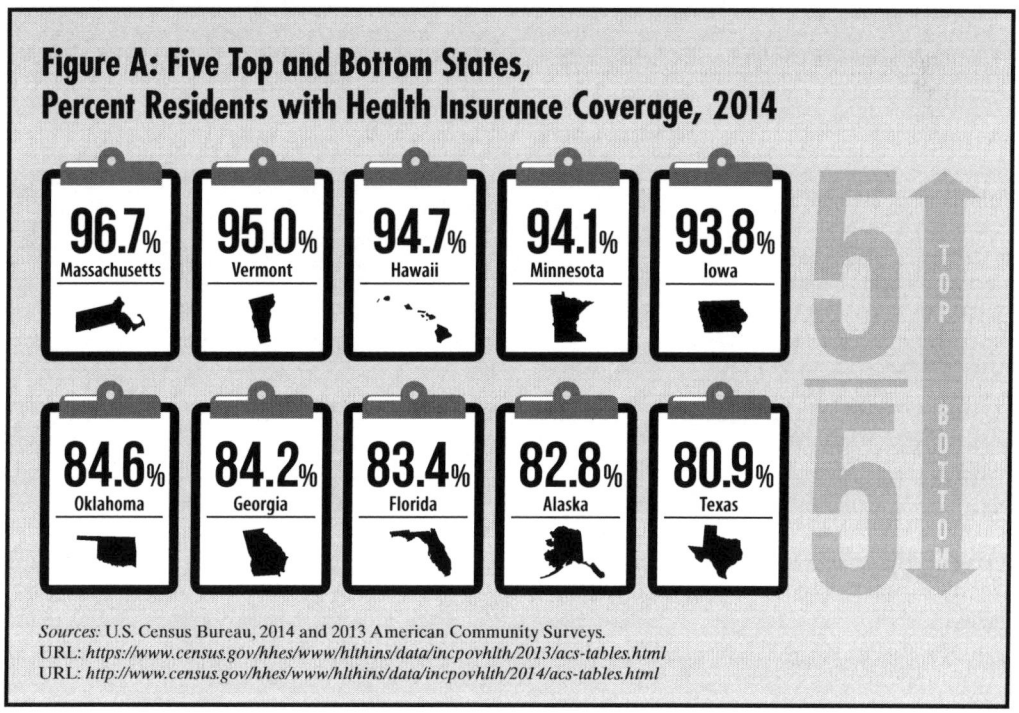

Figure A: Five Top and Bottom States, Percent Residents with Health Insurance Coverage, 2014

| 96.7% Massachusetts | 95.0% Vermont | 94.7% Hawaii | 94.1% Minnesota | 93.8% Iowa |
| 84.6% Oklahoma | 84.2% Georgia | 83.4% Florida | 82.8% Alaska | 80.9% Texas |

Sources: U.S. Census Bureau, 2014 and 2013 American Community Surveys.
URL: *https://www.census.gov/hhes/www/hlthins/data/incpovhlth/2013/acs-tables.html*
URL: *http://www.census.gov/hhes/www/hlthins/data/incpovhlth/2014/acs-tables.html*

Iowa—are states that expanded Medicaid eligibility beginning Jan. 1, 2014, as soon as allowed under the Affordable Care Act. Massachusetts had begun to expand insurance coverage, in fact mandating coverage, under then-Gov. Mitt Romney whose health reform passed in 2006.

Alaska, one of the bottom five states, did not immediately expand Medicaid. However, the state joined the expansion states on Sept. 1, 2015, and is likely to show increased coverage in the 2015 Census data. The other four states with the highest rates of uninsurance—Texas, Florida, Georgia and Oklahoma—had not expanded Medicaid eligibility as of mid-year 2016.

Did Insurance Coverage in the States Increase Between 2013 and 2014?

Without exception, in all 50 states, insurance coverage increased. The percent drop in the number of individuals not covered by health insurance ranged from 41 percent in Kentucky to 8 percent in Alaska. CSG calculated the change in the number of people insured, see Table 9.11, in order to allow for state-to-state comparison between states with widely varying population sizes.

Approximately 8.5 million Americans gained health insurance coverage between 2013 and 2014, U.S. Census data show. Another way to state this improvement in coverage is to say that nearly one in five (19 percent) of those uninsured in 2013 gained health insurance coverage in 2014.

Two major ACA policy changes went into effect between 2013 and 2014 that contributed to the increase in health coverage. First, in all states individuals were able to purchase health insurance policies through either state-run health insurance exchanges or the federal government exchange, *www.health.gov*. Families with income levels between 138 and 400 percent of the federal poverty level were entitled to federal subsidies to make the policy premiums more affordable. Second, 24 states and the District of Columbia expanded Medicaid eligibility to 138 percent of the federal poverty level on Jan. 1, 2014, the first day Congress provided federal matching funds—which for three years will cover 100 percent of expenditures for the newly eligible population. Later in 2014, Michigan and New Hampshire, on April 1 and August 15, respectively, also expanded Medicaid eligibility income levels.

Even without Medicaid eligibility expansion, other avenues to insurance coverage were opened up by the ACA. Through the exchanges, subsidies were available to make coverage more affordable. Presumably, some individuals in non-expansion states learned they were eligible for Medicaid coverage. Other provisions of the ACA provided increased insurance coverage: covering dependent children on parents' insurance to age 26, eliminating pre-existing condition exclusions, and eliminating annual and lifetime limits on coverage.

Increasing Medicaid eligibility seemed to make the biggest difference in coverage. Almost without exception, the states with expansion saw greater drops in the number of individuals without coverage than states that did not move to increase Medicaid eligibility to 138 percent of the federal poverty level.

What If All the States Had Expanded Medicaid?

CSG calculated how insurance coverage would have increased between 2013 and 2014 if the 24 states that didn't expand Medicaid in 2014 had experienced the same gains in coverage as states that did expand Medicaid eligibility. An additional 2.6 million Americans would have had health insurance coverage in 2014, bringing the number of newly insured to just over 11 million.

Since 2014, five more states have adopted policy to expand Medicaid—Pennsylvania on Jan. 1, 2015; Indiana on Feb. 1, 2015; Alabama on Sept. 1, 2015; Montana on Jan. 1, 2016; and Louisiana on Jan. 12, 2016. U.S. Census data for insurance coverage in 2015 and 2016 will presumably document the increase in health insurance coverage in those states due to this policy change.

About the Author

Debra Miller is director of health policy in The Council of State Governments' national headquarters office in Lexington, Ky. She has over 30 years of experience analyzing states' health programs for low- and middle-income children and adults. Her work has appeared in the 2010, 2012, 2014 and 2015 volumes of *The Book of the States*.

Table 9.11
HEALTH INSURANCE COVERAGE STATUS BY STATE FOR ALL PEOPLE: 2013–2014
(In thousands)

State or other jurisdiction	2013 Total population	2013 Covered	2013 Percent	2013 Not covered	2013 Percent	2014 Total population	2014 Covered	2014 Percent	2014 Not covered	2014 Percent	2013–2014 % change persons not covered by health insurance
United States	311,158	265,977	85.5	45,181	14.5	313,890	277,220	88.3	36,670	11.7	-19
Alabama	4,755	4,110	86.4	645	13.6	4,767	4,188	87.9	579	12.1	-10
Alaska**	712	580	81.5	132	18.5	712	589	82.8	122	17.2	-8
Arizona*	6,521	5,403	82.9	1,118	17.1	6,623	5,720	86.4	903	13.6	-19
Arkansas*	2,907	2,442	84.0	465	16.0	2,914	2,571	88.2	343	11.8	-26
California*	37,832	31,331	82.8	6,500	17.2	38,297	33,531	87.6	4,767	12.4	-27
Colorado*	5,173	4,444	85.9	729	14.1	5,266	4,723	89.7	543	10.3	-26
Connecticut*	3,541	3,209	90.6	333	9.4	3,541	3,296	93.1	245	6.9	-26
Delaware*	912	828	90.9	83	9.1	921	849	92.2	72	7.8	-13
Florida	19,245	15,392	80.0	3,853	20.0	19,583	16,338	83.4	3,245	16.6	-16
Georgia	9,801	7,955	81.2	1,846	18.8	9,907	8,338	84.2	1,568	15.8	-15
Hawaii*	1,345	1,254	93.3	91	6.7	1,368	1,296	94.7	72	5.3	-21
Idaho	1,592	1,335	83.8	257	16.2	1,613	1,394	86.4	219	13.6	-15
Illinois*	12,705	11,086	87.3	1,618	12.7	12,702	11,464	90.3	1,238	9.7	-23
Indiana**	6,472	5,569	86.0	903	14.0	6,498	5,722	88.1	776	11.9	-14
Iowa*	3,045	2,798	91.9	248	8.1	3,063	2,874	93.8	189	6.2	-24
Kansas	2,837	2,489	87.7	348	12.3	2,845	2,554	89.8	291	10.2	-16
Kentucky*	4,312	3,696	85.7	616	14.3	4,329	3,962	91.5	366	8.5	-41
Louisiana**	4,523	3,772	83.4	751	16.6	4,548	3,876	85.2	672	14.8	-11
Maine	1,314	1,167	88.8	147	11.2	1,316	1,182	89.9	134	10.1	-9
Maryland*	5,834	5,241	89.8	593	10.2	5,886	5,423	92.1	463	7.9	-22
Massachusetts*	6,614	6,367	96.3	247	3.7	6,668	6,450	96.7	219	3.3	-11
Michigan**	9,784	8,713	89.0	1,072	11.0	9,799	8,962	91.5	837	8.5	-22
Minnesota*	5,363	4,923	91.8	440	8.2	5,398	5,081	94.1	317	5.9	-28
Mississippi	2,925	2,425	82.9	500	17.1	2,927	2,503	85.5	424	14.5	-15
Missouri	5,931	5,158	87.0	773	13.0	5,951	5,257	88.3	694	11.7	-10
Montana**	999	835	83.5	165	16.5	1,008	865	85.8	143	14.2	-13
Nebraska	1,841	1,632	88.7	209	11.3	1,854	1,674	90.3	179	9.7	-14
Nevada*	2,757	2,187	79.3	570	20.7	2,806	2,379	84.8	427	15.2	-25
New Hampshire**	1,309	1,168	89.3	140	10.7	1,312	1,191	90.8	120	9.2	-14
New Jersey*	8,792	7,631	86.8	1,160	13.2	8,831	7,866	89.1	965	10.9	-17
New Mexico*	2,052	1,669	81.4	382	18.6	2,050	1,753	85.5	298	14.5	-22
New York*	19,400	17,331	89.3	2,070	10.7	19,500	17,803	91.3	1,697	8.7	-18
North Carolina	9,645	8,136	84.4	1,509	15.6	9,752	8,476	86.9	1,276	13.1	-15
North Dakota*	708	635	89.6	73	10.4	724	668	92.1	57	7.9	-22
Ohio*	11,398	10,141	89.0	1,258	11.0	11,421	10,466	91.6	955	8.4	-24
Oklahoma	3,770	3,104	82.3	666	17.7	3,798	3,214	84.6	584	15.4	-12
Oregon*	3,893	3,322	85.3	571	14.7	3,931	3,549	90.3	383	9.7	-33
Pennsylvania**	12,569	11,347	90.3	1,222	9.7	12,583	11,518	91.5	1,065	8.5	-13
Rhode Island*	1,036	916	88.4	120	11.6	1,040	963	92.6	77	7.4	-36
South Carolina	4,678	3,939	84.2	739	15.8	4,734	4,092	86.4	642	13.6	-13
South Dakota	827	734	88.7	93	11.3	835	753	90.2	82	9.8	-12
Tennessee	6,395	5,508	86.1	887	13.9	6,449	5,672	88.0	776	12.0	-13
Texas	25,977	20,228	77.9	5,748	22.1	26,486	21,438	80.9	5,047	19.1	-12
Utah	2,874	2,472	86.0	402	14.0	2,916	2,551	87.5	366	12.5	-9
Vermont*	621	576	92.8	45	7.2	620	590	95.0	31	5.0	-31
Virginia	8,054	7,064	87.7	991	12.3	8,115	7,231	89.1	884	10.9	-11
Washington*	6,864	5,904	86.0	960	14.0	6,955	6,312	90.8	643	9.2	-33
West Virginia*	1,825	1,570	86.0	255	14.0	1,821	1,665	91.4	156	8.6	-39
Wisconsin	5,669	5,151	90.9	518	9.1	5,685	5,267	92.7	418	7.3	-19
Wyoming	573	496	86.6	77	13.4	575	506	88.0	69	12.0	-10
Dist. of Columbia*	636	594	93.3	42	6.7	648	614	94.7	34	5.3	-19

Sources: U.S. Census Bureau, 2014 and 2013 American Community Surveys. (Numbers in thousands) Kaiser Family Foundation.

URL: https://www.census.gov/hhes/www/hlthins/data/incpovhlth/2013/acs-tables.html

URL: http://www.census.gov/hhes/www/hlthins/data/incpovhlth/2014/acs-tables.html

URL: http://kff.org/health-reform/state-indicator/state-activity-around-expanding-medicaid-under-the-affordable-care-act/

Key:
*State adopted Medicaid expansion beginning 1/1/2014.
**Later date Medicaid expansion adopted: Alaska, 9/1/2015; Indiana, 2/1/2015; Louisiana, 1/12/2016; Michigan, 4/1/2014; Montana, 1/1/2016; New Hampshire, 8/15/2014; Pennsylvania, 1/1/2015.

Table 9.12
NUMBER AND PERCENT OF CHILDREN UNDER 19 YEARS OF AGE, AT OR BELOW
200 PERCENT OF POVERTY, BY HEALTH INSURANCE COVERAGE AND STATE: 2014
(In thousands)

| State or other jurisdiction | Total children under 19 years, all income levels | At or below 200 percent of poverty | | Health insurance coverage | | | |
| | | Number | Percent | With | | Without | |
				Number	Percent	Number	Percent
United States	76,145	33,492	44	30,598	40.2	2,894	3.8
Alabama	1,150	585	50.9	553	48.1	32	2.8
Alaska................................	193	65	33.6	57	29.2	8	4.4
Arizona..............................	1,677	845	50.4	724	43.2	121	7.2
Arkansas............................	734	390	53.2	369	50.3	21	2.9
California	9,490	4,377	46.1	4,036	42.5	341	3.6
Colorado............................	1,289	473	36.7	433	33.6	40	3.1
Connecticut	805	256	31.8	242	30	14	1.8
Delaware	212	80	37.5	73	34.2	7	3.3
Florida	4,215	2,096	49.7	1,844	43.7	253	6
Georgia..............................	2,588	1,276	49.3	1,133	43.8	143	5.5
Hawaii	316	103	32.6	98	31	5	1.6
Idaho.................................	449	211	47.1	190	42.5	21	4.6
Illinois...............................	3,093	1,261	40.8	1,200	38.8	61	2
Indiana..............................	1,630	735	45.1	661	40.5	74	4.5
Iowa..................................	745	275	36.9	261	35.1	14	1.9
Kansas	747	302	40.4	274	36.8	27	3.7
Kentucky	1,038	506	48.8	478	46	29	2.8
Louisiana	1,156	582	50.4	547	47.3	35	3.1
Maine................................	263	109	41.4	101	38.4	8	3
Maryland	1,398	442	31.6	418	29.9	24	1.7
Massachusetts	1,443	433	30	422	29.3	11	0.7
Michigan............................	2,293	1,012	44.2	957	41.8	55	2.4
Minnesota...........................	1,322	442	33.4	412	31.2	30	2.3
Mississippi	765	421	55	393	51.4	28	3.7
Missouri............................	1,425	617	43.3	547	38.4	70	4.9
Montana	231	101	43.6	89	38.4	12	5.2
Nebraska............................	482	185	38.4	169	35	17	3.4
Nevada...............................	689	341	49.5	298	43.2	43	6.3
New Hampshire	279	79	28.2	74	26.6	5	1.7
New Jersey	2,091	672	32.1	621	29.7	51	2.4
New Mexico	522	289	55.3	262	50.2	27	5.1
New York............................	4,364	1,859	42.6	1,773	40.6	86	2
North Carolina....................	2,375	1,175	49.5	1,091	46	83	3.5
North Dakota	171	54	31.7	50	29.3	4	2.3
Ohio..................................	2,717	1,196	44	1,113	41	83	3
Oklahoma...........................	978	468	47.9	418	42.7	50	5.1
Oregon...............................	881	410	46.5	383	43.5	27	3
Pennsylvania	2,786	1,103	39.6	1,017	36.5	86	3.1
Rhode Island	222	89	39.8	84	37.9	4	1.9
South Carolina....................	1,125	577	51.3	537	47.7	40	3.6
South Dakota	216	87	40.1	80	37	7	3.1
Tennessee	1,545	779	50.4	725	46.9	54	3.5
Texas.................................	7,393	3,624	49	3,096	41.9	527	7.1
Utah..................................	939	344	36.6	290	30.9	54	5.7
Vermont.............................	124	44	35.5	43	34.5	1	1
Virginia..............................	1,936	669	34.5	600	31	69	3.6
Washington.........................	1,655	640	38.7	597	36.1	43	2.6
West Virginia......................	388	191	49.3	186	48	5	1.3
Wisconsin	1,338	520	38.9	483	36.1	37	2.8
Wyoming	142	49	34.9	45	31.5	5	3.4
Dist. of Columbia	119	53	44.8	52	43.5	2	1.3

Source: U.S. Census Bureau, 2014 American Community Survey.
URL: *http://www.census.gov/hhes/www/hlthins/data/incpovhlth/2014/acs-tables.html.*

Data in this table represent children under 19 in the poverty universe. Percentages are based on the total children under 19. For more information on poverty and the poverty universe see: *http://www.census.gov/hhes/www/poverty/methods/definitions.html.*

Regulating Hydraulic Fracturing in the States: Trending Issues in 2016 and Beyond

By Liz Edmondson

Due to advances in technology and drilling techniques, most notably hydraulic fracturing, vast reserves of untapped natural gas in shale formations are commercially viable, resulting in a significant increase in natural gas production over the last decade. However, this increase in production has raised concerns over environmental impacts such as water pollution, seismic activity, and air quality. This article provides an overview of some of these concerns and how state legislatures are addressing these issues.

Natural gas production has increased dramatically in the United States in recent years. Advances in hydraulic fracturing and horizontal drilling have resulted in the commercial viability of vast quantities of previously untapped gas reserves in shale formations.[1] In the past 10 years alone, production increased from 23.5 million cubic feet in 2005 to almost 33 million cubic feet in 2015.[2] However, along with this surge in production has come growing concern regarding the environmental consequences of these techniques, including water pollution, waste disposal, air quality, and seismic activity. In addition, policymakers are also increasingly addressing the interaction between federal, state, and local regulation.

The task of balancing the opportunities inherent in increased domestic natural gas production with environmental and public protection has largely fallen to state policymakers. However, the federal government does regulate some areas related to natural gas production, most notably water and air quality. Under the Clean Water Act, on-shore oil and gas extraction facilities are prohibited from discharging pollutants into surface waters in most instances.[3] In addition, the U.S. Environmental Protection Agency, or EPA, issued the first air quality standards for hydraulically fractured natural gas wells in 2012, which require reductions in volatile organic compounds. In May 2016, the EPA finalized rules to reduce methane emissions from new and modified oil and gas sources. These standards are expected to reduce methane emissions from the oil and gas sector 40 to 45 percent below 2012 levels by 2025, while also cutting volatile organic compound and air toxics emissions.[4] While the federal government is getting more involved in regulating natural gas, fracking operations are at this time still predominantly regulated at the state level.

Given the rapid and increasing development of shale gas, its controversial nature, and the limited oversight on the federal level,[5] states have taken a variety of approaches in attempting to balance environmental and public safety concerns with shale development. Indeed, states vary significantly in geology, economic conditions, geography, demographics, the extent of shale gas production and other factors, which partially contributes to the variety of regulatory approaches. However, the swift expansion of shale gas development has resulted in a patchwork of regulatory trends that states will continue to address going forward.

Outright Bans on Fracking and the Disposal of Fracking Waste

In light of the potential environmental impacts of fracking, some states have banned the practice altogether. New York and New Jersey were among the first states to act, placing moratoriums on well permitting until the environmental and health risks of the practice could be evaluated. After a seven-year review,[6] New York Gov. Andrew Cuomo announced in December 2014 that the state would ban fracking and the state issued a Findings Statement on June 29, 2015, to that effect.[7]

In contrast, while the New Jersey legislature passed a bill that would have permanently banned fracking in the state in 2011, Gov. Chris Christie issued a conditional veto that placed a moratorium on the practice for just one year, which has since expired.[8] While fracking is currently allowed in the state, no fracking operations are currently taking place.

Although Vermont has very limited deep shale deposits, the state—in a largely symbolic gesture—became the first state to ban fracking and the collection, storage, or treatment of wastewater from the practice with the passage of H. 464 in 2012.[9] In 2015, a Maryland bill banning fracking for two and one-half years, until October 2017, became law after Gov. Larry Hogan declined to veto the legislation.[10]

In addition, other states have passed legislation prohibiting the disposal of fracking wastes in their states. Fracking requires operators to inject large amounts of water into a wellhead. This process results in the production of significant amounts of wastewater that typically contains chemicals used in the fracking process, as well as salt, radioactive material and heavy metals. This water must be managed and is typically reused, treated and released, or injected underground.[11]

Some states with limited or more expensive disposal options for this wastewater have opted to transport it to other states for management. In response, both Connecticut and Vermont prohibit the storage or disposal of fracking waste in their states.[12] While New Jersey has attempted such a ban, Gov. Chris Christie has vetoed bills that would have banned the disposal of fracking waste in the state on two occasions.[13]

The District of Columbia and other communities, counties and cities across the country are also acting to regulate or restrict hydraulic fracturing. In 2014, the District of Columbia passed a resolution urging the federal government to prohibit fracking in the George Washington National Forest, a 1.1 million acre forest in West Virginia and Virginia containing the headwaters of the Potomac River, the capital's only source of drinking water.[14] In addition, hundreds of communities, towns and cities across the United States have banned fracking through local initiatives.[15]

States Ban Fracking Bans and Courts Weigh in on Localities' Ability to Regulate Fracking

In response to restrictions on fracking by these localities, various actions have been taken to hinder the ability of local governmental entities to ban fracking or the disposal of fracking wastes. At the state level, both Oklahoma and Texas lawmakers voted to limit local governments from prohibiting the practice. Oklahoma's bill, SB 809, signed into law in 2015, prohibits localities from banning fracking, but allows local governments to set reasonable restrictions on noise, traffic and fencing, and to enact reasonable setbacks for surface operations.[16] The Texas law was enacted in response to a fracking ban imposed by the town of Denton, which halted fracking activity in the town until the legislation was signed by Gov. Greg Abbott on

May 18, 2015, approximately six months after the ban became effective.[17]

In other states, courts have found fracking bans enacted by local governments illegal. In 2013, Mora County, New Mexico, was the first county in the country to ban hydraulic fracturing. Soon thereafter, various parties filed a lawsuit in federal court against the county, alleging that the ordinance was unconstitutional and infringed on private property rights. The U.S. District Court for the District of New Mexico struck down the ban, finding that it violated the U.S. Constitution's Supremacy Clause because it contained language that stripped oil and gas companies of rights protected by federal case law and the U.S. Constitution.[18] In addition, the court found that the ordinance was further illegal because it prohibited activities that are allowed under state law. Soon after the decision, Mora County rescinded the ban.[19] A similar ordinance banning fracking wastewater disposal and enacted by a Pennsylvania township was also rejected by a federal court.[20]

Similarly, states and localities continue to clash over to what extent local governments can place restrictions on fracking operations. In 2015, the Ohio Supreme Court considered whether a city could enforce its local zoning ordinances against an oil and gas company, which required local certifications and requirements in addition to the state's permitting scheme. Ohio laws, amended in 2004, give the state "sole and exclusive" authority to regulate the permitting, location, and spacing of oil and gas operations and repealed any portions of the previous law giving local governments authority to adopt regulations concurrent with the state. The city argued that the state's Home Rule Amendment to its constitution, which gives local control to all matters not of statewide interest, allowed it to impose its own permitting requirements on oil and gas operations.

However, in a 4-3 opinion, the court found that Ohio's Home Rule Amendment "does not allow a municipality to discriminate against, unfairly impede, or obstruct oil and gas activities and production operations that the state has permitted" under its oil and gas laws.[21] Because the legality of restrictions and bans on fracking largely depend on the specific way the ordinance is written, the state's constitutional provisions, and the extent to which the state regulates oil and gas operations, challenges to local attempts at regulation and restriction of fracking will be case-specific and will likely continue.

Seismic Activity: How Will States Respond?

According to the U.S. Geological Survey, the number of earthquakes in the central and eastern United States has increased significantly in recent years. Beginning in 2009, earthquakes in these areas of the country increased to an average of 99 earthquakes of magnitude 3 and above compared to only 21 M3+ quakes between the years 1973–2008. By 2014, there were 659 M3 and larger earthquakes, with rates continuing to rise.[22]

A recent article in *Science* magazine notes that many of these earthquakes are thought to be induced by the injection of wastewater into the subsurface from hydraulic fracturing operations or enhanced oil recovery. The study found that in regions prone to seismic activity, the rate of injection was the factor that most affected the probability of an induced earthquake.[23]

Oklahoma has thus far taken limited action on this issue. The Oklahoma Corporation Commission, which regulates the oil and gas industry, recently responded to the increase in seismic activity by requesting that producers located in the northwest area of the state reduce by 40 percent the amount of wastewater they dispose. In March, the agency developed a similar plan to reduce the total volume of wastewater disposed in central Oklahoma by 40 percent below 2014 levels over a two month period.[24] In addition, Gov. Mary Fallin directed approximately $1.4 million of emergency funds to addressing triggered earthquakes, which allowed the commission to add additional staff and upgrade technology.

The Kansas Corporation Commission also ordered a reduction of fracking wastewater injections in two counties that border Oklahoma as a result of increased seismic activity reported in the USGS study.[25] Ohio now requires that seismic monitors be installed for fracking operations within three miles of a known fault. If seismic activity above a 1.0 magnitude is detected, the operation must cease pending an investigation. Well operations would be suspended if a connection between the well and the seismic activity is uncovered.[26] Texas has taken a less restrictive approach and hired a full-time seismologist and requires more information from operators during the permitting process.

As seismic activity continues to increase in the central and eastern parts of the country and more research is conducted on the relationship between fracking and increased seismic activity, policymak-

ers will have to make decisions as to how to regulate disposal wells.

Conclusion

Natural gas production is expected to continue to increase in the immediate future.[27] As a result, states will continue to grapple with the economic advantages this production brings and the environmental and regulatory challenges natural gas production presents. In addition to the issues discussed above, states will address other issues such as methane emissions, severance taxes, fluid disclosure requirements and the enforceability of regulatory controls given significant revenue shortfalls in some states. In addition, the federal government is becoming more active, with the EPA engaging in studies and rulemaking that will affect the industry. State policymakers will need to be aware of the challenges in regulating fracking where local, state and federal actors are involved, in addition to being aware of the options for addressing the environmental issues surrounding the production of this booming resource.

Notes

[1] Environmental Protection Agency, "Natural Gas Extraction—Hydraulic Fracturing," available at: *https://www.epa.gov/hydraulicfracturing*.

[2] Energy Information Administration, "U.S. Natural Gas Gross Withdrawals," available at: *http://www.eia.gov/dnav/ng/hist/n9010us2m.htm*.

[3] While operators have historically handled their wastewater by injecting it into disposal wells, it has become more common for operators to utilize public owned treatment works (POTW) where disposal wells are unavailable or other wastewater management alternatives exist. At this time, there are no pretreatment standards that apply to indirect discharges from onshore oil and natural gas extraction to POTWs, which can result in wastewater from these operations being discharged to surface waters without treatment. EPA has proposed a rulemaking that would address this issue by establishing pretreatment standards. 80 FR 18557 (April 7, 2015).

[4] Environmental Protection Agency, "Reducing Methane Emissions from the Oil and Natural Gas Industry" (March 10, 2016), available at: *https://www3.epa.gov/airquality/oilandgas/pdfs/20160310fs.pdf*; Environmental Protection Agency, "EPA Releases First Ever Standards to Cut Methane Emissions from the Oil and Gas Sector" (May 12, 2016), available at: *https://www.epa.gov/newsreleases/epa-releases-first-ever-standards-cut-methane-emissions-oil-and-gas-sector*

[5] Despite the historically limited federal regulation of oil and gas development and production, the Environmental Protection Agency and the Bureau of Land Management, which governs oil and gas production on federal

lands, have been working to conduct scientific studies and update regulations for shale gas development.

[6] New York State Department of Public Health, "A Public Heath Review of High Volume Hydraulic Fracturing for Shale Gas Development" (December 2014), available at: *http://www.health.ny.gov/press/reports/docs/high_volume_hydraulic_fracturing.pdf.*

[7] New York Department of Environmental Conservation, "Final Supplemental Generic Environmental Impact Statement on the Oil, Gas and Solution Mining Regulatory Program: Findings Statement" (June 2015), available at: *http://www.dec.ny.gov/docs/materials_minerals_pdf/finding-statehvhf62015.pdf.*

[8] *http://www.state.nj.us/governor/news/news/552011/approved/20110825c.html.*

[9] H. 464 (2012), available at: *http://www.leg.state.vt.us/docs/2012/bills/Passed/H-464.pdf.*

[10] SB 409 (2015), available at: *http://mgaleg.maryland.gov/2015RS/chapters_noln/Ch_480_sb0409T.pdf.*

[11] Environmental Protection Agency, "Assessment of the Potential Impacts of Hydraulic Fracturing for Oil and Gas on Drinking Water Resources (External Review Draft) (2015), p. 8-1, available at: *https://cfpub.epa.gov/ncea/hfstudy/recordisplay.cfm?deid=244651.*

[12] Public Act No. 14-200 "An Act Prohibiting the Storage or Disposal of Fracking Waste in Connecticut" (2014), available at: *https://www.cga.ct.gov/2014/act/pa/pdf/2014PA-00200-R00SB-00237-PA.pdf.*

[13] State of New Jersey Senate, No. 1041 (2014), available at: *http://www.njleg.state.nj.us/2014/Bills/S1500/1041_R1.HTM;* Tran, Andrew Ba, "Where communities have banned fracking" *Boston Globe* (December 18, 2014), available at: *https://www.bostonglobe.com/news/nation/2014/12/18/where-communities-have-banned-fracking/05bzzqiCxBY2L5bE6Ph5iK/story.html.*

[14] *http://www.foodandwaterwatch.org/sites/default/files/frack_actions_districtofcolumbia.pdf.*

[15] Tran, Andrew Ba, "Where communities have banned fracking" *Boston Globe* (December 18, 2014), available at: *https://www.bostonglobe.com/news/nation/2014/12/18/where-communities-have-banned-fracking/05bzzqiCxBY2L5bE6Ph5iK/story.html;* Food and Water Watch, *http://www.foodandwaterwatch.org/insight/local-resolutions-against-fracking.*

[16] Oklahoma Senate Bill 809 (2015), available at: *http://www.oklegislature.gov/BillInfo.aspx?Bill=SB%20809.*

[17] Stravato, Michael, "To Quiet Calls for Fracking Curbs, Texas Bans Bans" *Newsweek* (June 12, 2015), available at: *http://www.newsweek.com/2015/06/12/quiet-calls-fracking-curbs-texas-bans-bans-339164.html.*

[18] *SWEPI v. Mora County, New Mexico, et al.*, No. 14-35, D. New Mexico (January 19, 2015).

[19] *http://www.scribd.com/doc/260405069/Mora-County-repeal-of-anti-fracking-ordinance.*

[20] *http://www.reuters.com/article/usa-energy-ban-idUSL1N12J0KQ20151019.*

[21] *State ex rel. Morrison v. Beck Energy Corp.*, 143 Ohio St.3d 271 (Ohio S.Ct. 2015), available at: *http://*

www.supremecourt.ohio.gov/rod/docs/pdf/0/2015/2015-Ohio-485.pdf.

[22] U.S. Geological Survey, "Induced Earthquakes," available at: *http://earthquake.usgs.gov/research/induced/.*

[23] Weingarten, M., et al. "High-rate injection is associated with the increase in U.S. mid-continent seismicity" *Science*, Vo. 348, Issue 6241 (June 19, 2015), available at: *https://profile.usgs.gov/myscience/upload_folder/ci2015Jun18141430 55600Weingarten_etal.pdf.*

[24] Oklahoma Corporation Commission, "Media Advisory—Regional Earthquake Response Plan for Central Oklahoma and Expansion of Area of Interest" (March 7, 2016), available at: *http://www.occeweb.com/News/2016/03-07-16ADVISORY-AOI,%20VOLUME%20REDUCTION.pdf.*

[25] Kansas Corporation Commission, "Order Reducing Saltwater Injection Rates" Docket No. 15-CONS-770-CMSC (March 19, 2015), available at: *http://estar.kcc.ks.gov/estar/ViewFile.aspx/15-770%20Order.pdf?Id=05630050-78a3-4800-a08b-85202375305a.*

[26] Ohio Department of Natural Resources, "Ohio Announces Tougher Permit Conditions for Drilling Activities Near Faults and Areas of Seismic Activity," available at: *http://ohiodnr.gov/news/post/ohio-announces-tougher-permit-conditions-for-drilling-activities-near-faults-and-areas-of-seismic-activity.*

[27] Energy Information Administration, "Short Term Energy Outlook," available at: *http://www.eia.gov/forecasts/steo/report/natgas.cfm.*

About the Author

Liz Edmondson joined the CSG national policy staff as the director of energy and environmental policy in 2015. Prior to joining CSG, Liz worked as a staff attorney for the Kentucky Resources Council where she conducted extensive research, policy analysis, and advocacy on a range of environmental and energy issues. She has also served as in-house attorney for Morgan Worldwide Consultants, where she advised federal regulators on legal and technical issues surrounding several high profile rulemakings and policy initiatives related to surface coal mining in Appalachia. After leaving MWC, Liz started her own law firm where she focused on energy and environmental law. Liz regularly publishes and speaks on coal mining, natural gas, environmental law, and energy and is the immediate past chair of the Kentucky Bar Association's Environment, Energy and Resources section. She received her B.A. in environmental and energy policy and her J.D. *cum laude* from the University of Louisville.

Solar PV Development in the U.S.: Growth, Hurdles and Opportunities

By Jeffrey Domanski

The solar PV industry provides great opportunity for creating jobs, saving energy and putting money back into local economies. However, it faces many hurdles to growth, including limited understanding of its economic and environmental benefits, project costs and the absence of best practice standards. This article discusses these impediments and progress to address them.

Solar PV basics

2015 was a banner year for solar photovoltaic, or PV, deployment in the U.S. Installed capacity increased five-fold from 2010, to over 7 gigawatts, or GW.[1] Ten times that capacity (70 GW) is expected to be added by 2020, by which time the solar industry will contribute approximately $30 billion to the U.S. economy annually.[2]

Currently, nearly all solar projects are linked to the electricity grid, and are thereby dependent on the operation of the grid system. When a grid power outage occurs, systems within the outage area do not function. Interest in "off-grid" systems that could operate independently of a regional power grid through the use of a battery storage system is strong. The introduction in 2015 of the Tesla "Powerwall" home battery module is a clear indication of the direction of efforts; indeed, there has been significant investment in battery technology research and development.

An average residential or small commercial system is about 8-10 kilowatts, or kW, and comprised of approximately 30 connected solar PV panels. Not long ago, a 30 kW solar PV system was considered large.[3] In recent years, it is common for municipal and commercial projects to be measured in megawatts rather than kilowatts, including projects on closed municipal landfills.

Solar cost trends

The national average price of a solar PV project dropped from $12 per watt in 1998 to less than $4 per watt by 2013, which includes a 50 percent cost reduction since 2010.[4] These reductions were driven in large part by drops in the cost of panels and other hardware.[5] The U.S. Department of Energy's SunShot Initiative, launched in 2011, seeks to make solar PV cost-competitive with other forms of electricity by 2020 by focusing on research, manufacturing and market solutions. The SunShot Initiative also seeks to support non-equipment, or "soft," cost reductions, including access to capital, supply-chain costs and grid connection, which now account for up to 64 percent of the cost of a residential solar installation.[6] A primary goal of this program is to help solar energy grow from less than 2 percent of the U.S. electricity supply to roughly 14 percent by 2030 and 27 percent by 2050.[7]

Investment Tax Credit extension

Federal and state incentives have been instrumental in supporting the growth of solar. A significant boon to the industry occurred in December 2015, when Congress passed a 4-year extension of the federal Investment Tax Credit, or ITC, for solar PV installations as part of an omnibus appropriations bill. The ITC covers up to 30 percent of system cost through a tax credit to the system owner. The ITC will remain at 30 percent for solar energy installations through 2019, and then drop in the subsequent two years, but will remain at 10 percent for commercial projects beginning in 2022. According to IBTS Solar Programs Manager Rudy Saporite, "This is a critically important policy development, as it provides the long-term certainty needed to continue growing the industry in a sustainable way by investing in quality solar installations that generate attractive returns for years to come, as well as fostering improved technology, establishing industry best practices, and driving down costs."

Net Metering

State-level "net metering" policies have been critical to facilitating solar growth. When a PV system's production exceeds the needs of the customer's building, the excess electricity is sent back to the electric grid. In many states, a credit is granted to the owner/leaser of the solar PV system, which is used to reduce the customer's total electric bill. The policy supporting this credit approach is commonly referred to as "net metering."

There has been notable resistance to net metering policies at the state-level. Critics of the policy contend that net metering over compensates system owners for excess power sold back to the grid and unfairly shifts the burden of paying for grid services to other, non-solar utility customers. Some states are beginning to alter or eliminate net metering programs. In December 2015, the Nevada Public Utilities Commission voted unanimously to approve a new solar net metering rate for NV Energy, reducing the credit for net-metered customers from $0.11/kWh to $0.026 by 2020. This change has essentially stopped solar development in Nevada. SolarCity alone has cut 550 jobs since this decision.[8]

The California Public Utilities Commission recently enacted a net energy metering, or NEM, successor tariff, also known as NEM 2.0. It builds upon the policy that, for the past decade, has assured net-metered customers they will earn retail-rate payments for surplus solar energy, which has helped position the state as a leader in rooftop solar.

States and Utilities

A number of states are focusing on the role of utility companies. Mississippi has a net metering policy that is more favorable to the utilities, as excess electricity from customer-sited solar projects is valued at the average wholesale rate rather than the higher retail rate. Both Minnesota and Texas have net metering policies, but investor-owned utilities in those states have the option to establish a value of solar tariff for compensating net-metered customers for generation. These tariffs require annual review and approval by the state public utility commission.

In New York, a significant, stakeholder-focused process is transforming the power-generation market. The "Reforming the Energy Vision," or REV, proceedings were initiated by Gov. Andrew Cuomo in 2014. Cuomo charged the Public Service Commission with changing the way electricity is distributed and supplied, with a focus on encouraging distributed energy resources, or DERs, including solar PV, and transitioning away from grant-based incentives toward greater use of financial and other market-based strategies. Other U.S. states and countries are watching the REV process closely.

Growth in Finance-based Strategies

A number of finance-based strategies are providing a spectrum of options for solar PV customers and fostering increased investor-community confidence in solar as an asset class. For both residential and small commercial customers, many of these tools offer no upfront-cost options, attractive interest rates and "cash-positive" structures, wherein monthly savings exceed payments thereby yielding benefit to customers from Day 1.

For customers who can afford an upfront cash outlay and/or can take advantage of federal and state tax incentives, a straightforward purchase is usually the optimal option. For customers not able to meet purchase requirements, solar PV leases and power purchase agreements, or PPAs, are widely available. Both leases and PPAs are third-party ownership models for a solar PV system. Rather than the homeowner or business owner paying for the panels and reaping the rewards of the electricity they produce, a third party owns the panels and either sells the electricity produced to the customer at a discounted rate (PPA) or requires a fixed monthly payment for a guaranteed output (lease). Either way, the third party absorbs all upfront costs while the customer receives free solar panels and typically purchases electricity at a lower rate than the local utility for the lease/PPA period (e.g., 20 years).

In California, the residential market for solar PV leasing agreements and PPAs increased from 9 percent in 2009 to 75 percent in 2012. This financing structure played a significant role in the rapid deployment of solar PV in the state. While the share of third-party ownership has since decreased due to the reduction in the cost of solar, it remains the dominant ownership model.[9] Other states experiencing rapid growth due to these models are Arizona, Colorado, Massachusetts, New Jersey, New York and Pennsylvania—all states with attractive customer incentives and relatively high electricity rates.

There are a number of finance options to support direct purchase. Banks and other lending organizations partner with an incentive provider (e.g., state authority) to provide subsidized energy project loans, which often provide financing at half of the market interest rate. In an On-Bill Financing model, a utility company allows customers to repay the cost of energy projects through their utility bill. The Property Assessed Clean Energy, or PACE, model allows commercial customers— and residential customers in some states—to finance energy projects through their property tax bill. Both On-Bill Financing and PACE projects are transferable with sale of a property and, therefore, reduce concern over personal liability and reluctance to invest. These are also considered relatively safe investments because payments on property tax and utility bills rarely default.

Investor-Community Strategies

A number of finance-based programs and instruments in place and on the horizon are focused on engaging investors in solar and other energy projects to foster growth of solar developer companies and leverage private investment.

State-level Green Banks are at the center of many of these efforts. In general, a Green Bank is a public or quasi-public institution that uses public funds to attract private-sector investment for clean energy projects through programs and financial support mechanisms. Connecticut, Hawaii and New York are leaders in this approach.

Securitization of energy project lending as an asset class was initiated in Pennsylvania as a program known as WHEEL, WareHouse for Energy Efficiency Loans, and is an innovative approach that seeks to facilitate energy project loans by the traditional finance community by pooling loan and supporting secondary investment markets.

Securitization provides a pathway to large-scale capital markets and significantly lower interest rates. This brings down the cost of solar PV to consumers, giving solar companies access to virtually limitless funds as long as these assets continue to perform. In general, to engage large-scale private investment, rating agencies must have assurances the equipment and services are rated on an equal basis through a national standard in order to evaluate the investments. To securitize solar PV leases, assets must be accurately rated by a third party against widely adopted standards.

In late 2012, the National Renewable Energy Laboratory, or NREL, initiated the Solar Access to Public Capital, or SAPC, working group, backed by funding from the U.S. Department of Energy, or DOE, to build investment community confidence in solar project instruments. This required organization of the solar, legal, banking, capital markets, engineering and other relevant stakeholder communities in order to open lower-cost debt investment for solar asset deployment. More than 400 organizations, including five rating agencies—Standard & Poor's, Moody's, KBRA, Fitch and DBRS—participated in the SAPC process to standardize contracts, develop best practices, and discern the way rating agencies perceive solar project portfolios as an investment asset class. This effort led to development of residential (2015) and commercial (2016) PV system installation best practice guides, as well as a best practice guide for operations and maintenance.[10] These guides were developed to encourage high-quality system development and operation to improve lifetime project performance.

In late 2013, SolarCity, the largest vertically integrated residential solar installer in the country, successfully sold a portfolio of solar leases into the secondary market as a unique asset class. This new solar security represents an unprecedented opportunity to lower the cost of capital and bring solar into reach for millions of homeowners.

Promoting industry best practice

Through the Solar Quality Initiative, an extension of the SAPC process, solar industry leaders continue to partner to ensure this booming industry is built on a solid foundation of quality installation and assurance, by addressing risk borne by investors, including maintenance costs, failures, and performance, and developing minimum requirements to instill investor confidence in an environment of rapid growth.

As the solar industry continues its transformation to being a provider of energy services from being a vendor of labor and hardware, the need for quality assurance, or QA, and standardized measurement has moved from a program requirement to a necessity for responsible growth and financial confidence. QA is needed to facilitate the efficient flow of capital by private investors into the market by providing confidence in the underlying economics of distributed solar energy and in the quality of the physical asset. As markets for renewable energy mature, the need is emerging for a true investment-grade quality assurance, or IGQA, system that can provide a variety of stakeholders with the data necessary to manage risk with confidence.

IGQA goes beyond traditional in-house or programmatic QA programs by providing stakeholders with the suite of data necessary for securitization and management of risk. In addition to traditional field inspections to assure work was installed to industry best practices, specifications, and building code, IGQA would tracks and reports on a broad set of metrics that includes energy production.

Conclusion

While solar PV currently represents a relatively small share of total energy production, this share is anticipated to grow substantially in coming years. As with any booming industry, growing pains are inevitable. However, the progress in policy development, the focus on industry best practices, and the associated advances in solar finance strategies and asset securitization described in this article indicate the industry is accelerating into maturity.

Notes

[1] 1 gigawatt (gW) = 1,000 megawatts (mW) = 1,000,000 kilowatts (kW) = 1,000,000,000 watts (W).

[2] SEIA, "Impacts of Solar Investment Tax Credit Extension," Research & Resources, Solar Energy Industries Association, *http://www.seia.org/research-resources/impacts-solar-investment-tax-credit-extension*

[3] U.S. Department of Energy, *Guide to Implementing Solar PV for Local Governments*, IBTS and the Solar Outreach Partnership

[4] Solar Energy Industry Association, "Tracking the Sun VI: The Installed Cost of Photovoltaics in the US from 1998–2013," *Solar Market Insight Report 2014 Q1-Q4*

[5] Feldman et al., "Photovoltaic System Pricing Trends: Historical, Recent, and Near-Term Projections, 2014 Edition" *NREL, http://www.nrel.gov/docs/fy14osti/62558.pdf*

[6] "Friedman et al., "Benchmarking Non-Hardware Balance-of-System (Soft) Costs for U.S. Photovoltaic Systems, Using a Bottom-Up Approach and Installer Survey—Second Edition," National Renewable Energy Laboratory, *http://www.nrel.gov/docs/fy14osti/60412.pdf*

[7] U.S. Department of Energy, "Energy Infrastructure Update, Federal Energy Regulatory Commission," *SunShot Vision Study, http://www1.eere.energy.gov/solar/sunshot/vision_study.html*

[8] Shallenberger, Krysti. "Nevada PUC Denies Request to Stay Solar Net Metering Reforms." *www.utilitydive.com*

[9] Schafer, Alissa Jean, "Solar financing paves the way for market growth," CleanEnergy.org, *Southern Alliance for Clean Energy, http://blog.cleanenergy.org/2015/08/07/solar-financing-paves-the-way-for-market-growth/*

[10] Solar Quality Initiative, "Solar industry best practice guides," *Commercial/Industrial, http://www.solarquality.org/commercial—industrial.html*

About the Author

Jeffrey Domanski is senior manager, energy and sustainability, at the Institute for Building Technology & Safety, or IBTS, a 501(c)(3) nonprofit established to provide services to help governments implement cost-effective services and address challenges. IBTS is also a leading solar PV quality assurance provider working to improve best practices to enhance reliability, safety and investor confidence.

A Non-Starter at the Federal Level, Gas Taxes Again the Preferred Transportation Revenue Mechanism for States in 2015

By Sean Slone

Despite concerns about the long-term solvency and sustainability of the federal highway trust fund, the Fixing America's Surface Transportation or FAST Act passed by Congress in December 2015 did not include what many said was a much needed increase in the federal gas tax, which has remained unchanged since 1993. Congress instead offset a transfer of general funds to supplement gas tax revenues by tapping a Federal Reserve surplus fund among other sources. The action came at the end of a year in which eight states did raise their own gas taxes.. With the fuel efficiency of the nation's vehicle fleet improving and the greater adoption of electric vehicles on the horizon, some states are also looking to a new revenue mechanism that some believe could one day replace the gas tax—a mileage-based user fee. Concerns about how the fees would be administered and whether it could ever be done as efficiently as the gas tax are causing doubts it will be ready in time to help fund the next long-term iteration of the federal program when the FAST Act expires in 2020.

No Gas Tax Increase for the FAST Act

On Dec. 4, 2015, President Barack Obama signed into law the first long-term federal surface transportation authorization bill approved by Congress in over a decade. The Fixing America's Surface Transportation, or FAST, Act authorized $305 billion over fiscal years 2016 through 2020.

What the legislation didn't do was something many transportation analysts had said would likely be necessary to move forward with a long-term bill.

"There's no new money (in the FAST Act) … and I think there was frankly a missed opportunity here to raise the gas tax, but I'm not a member of Congress," said Sarah Puro, principal analyst at the Congressional Budget Office.[1]

Last raised by Congress in 1993, the federal gasoline excise tax rate has remained at 18.4 cents per gallon since then, even as escalating road construction costs have eroded its buying power and improved vehicle fuel economy has limited revenues despite increases in the overall vehicle miles traveled by Americans.[2] The gas tax continues to bring $40 billion into the federal coffers every year, which is deposited into the highway trust fund, and Jeff Davis, a senior fellow at the Eno Center for Transportation in Washington, D.C., said that's likely to remain the case for the foreseeable future.

"It's projected to be ($40 billion) a year flat line indefinitely," he said. "(But) in the last three years we started $51 billion in new spending commitments out of the (highway trust fund) every year. And both the good news and bad news of the FAST Act is that over the next five years, $51 (billion) a year will rise to $59 (billion) a year while $40 billion stays put. … The perpetual imbalance of taking ($51 billion) to ($59 billion) while doing nothing whatsoever about the $40 billion we're getting from user revenues is a bad way to do business but between inertia and the vote situation, it really was the path of least resistance."

In order to keep a dwindling Highway Trust Fund solvent and help bridge a gap between how much was expected to come in to the fund and how much was required to cover transportation expenditures over the course of the five-year bill, Congress made a transfer from the general fund that was then offset with subsidies from a variety of sources including $53.3 billion from a surplus of the Federal Reserve Bank.

"We have clearly demonstrated that the votes do not exist in Congress to reduce the current $51 billion in highway trust fund spending commitments down to the $40 billion level," Davis said. "And although we haven't actually had a vote on the floor, it's pretty clear the votes are not there to increase the excise taxes on gasoline and diesel fuel in any substantial way.…We've got a situation now where the next bill is going to be problematic. It's going to (require) $120 billion for the next five-year bill at baseline."

A general fund transfer on that scale would likely be even tougher to come by than the FAST Act's $70 billion, transportation experts say, while a gas tax increase to fill the gap would need to be on the order of 20 cents a gallon, a doubling of the current rate. Such an increase would likely prove politically impossible in the current climate.

That's why Davis and others view the FAST Act as perhaps the last bill of its kind.[3]

Even as Congress was going out of its way in 2015 to avoid a gas tax increase, state governments were raising their own gas taxes to help make transportation improvements and tackle extensive backlogs of projects made longer by years of uncertainty from Washington.

Why the Gas Tax for States?

Eight states raised gas taxes through legislation approved in 2015 — Georgia, Idaho, Iowa, Michigan, Nebraska, South Dakota, Utah and Washington. There were a variety of factors that made the gas tax the preferred revenue mechanism for those states:

- One of the most important factors was the low price of gas. The price of a gallon of unleaded regular gas averaged $2.40 in 2015, about 94 cents less than in 2014. It was the lowest average since 2009, according to AAA.[4]

- States also turned back to the gas tax after failed efforts to fund transportation through other means. In Michigan, a sales tax-focused ballot measure failed to win the support of voters in May 2015.[5] Georgia voters rejected local option sales tax ballot measures to fund transportation in nine of 12 regions of the state in 2012.[6]

- Several states expressed concerns about an overreliance on either borrowing or the use of general fund dollars for transportation in recent years and a need to move back to a more user fee-driven model for transportation funding.

- In most cases, the states had gone many years without increasing their gas taxes.

- State policymakers also noted that the gas tax, unlike other potential options, was already set up, easy to understand and administer and — despite concerns about increasing fuel efficiency and the predicted eventual proliferation of electric vehicles — gas tax revenues aren't likely to erode by much in the near term.

- For states like Washington, another key advantage the gas tax had was that its revenues are

protected and dedicated for transportation by the state constitution.

- At least prior to the passage of the FAST Act late in the year, states also worried about the short- and long-term future of federal transportation funding and saw an opportunity since it appeared Congress was unlikely to raise the federal gas tax.

- In some states, the gas tax became the vehicle for increased transportation investment simply by process of elimination when negotiation processes and political compromise simply eliminated other options.

Here's a closer look at what happened in each state.

Iowa's Senate File 257

When Iowa Gov. Terry Branstad signed legislation to raise the state's gasoline and diesel taxes in February 2015, Iowa became the first state to do so that year. The state had seen its last gas tax increase in 1989.[7]

"Our fuel tax (increase) is very simple," said Rep. Josh Byrnes, chairman of the House Transportation Committee. "It's just a straight up, 10 cent a gallon increase."[8]

Byrnes' counterpart on the Senate side, Sen. Tod Bowman, said the simplicity was necessitated by a consensus process when lawmakers in the Republican House and Democratic Senate were coming up with possible solutions.

"Everything under the sun was considered," he said. "The question was 'was it politically viable?'...Multiple different ways of indexing (the fuel tax) were considered. We looked at other tools that would bring in revenue besides the fuel tax...and we kind of shied away from anything that would be too toxic."[9]

Stuart Anderson, director of the Planning, Programming and Modal Division at the Iowa Department of Transportation, said it made sense that lawmakers would turn to the gas tax to carry the load.

"In Iowa, we benefit from diversity of funding sources at the state level so that's why we weren't shy about focusing on the fuel tax at this time," Anderson said. "The fuel tax before this bill was about 32 percent of our revenue stream at the state level. After the bill, it's a little over 40 percent."[10]

Byrnes said one reason for turning to the gas tax was that the lack of available road funding had become so severe that cities and counties had become too reliant on borrowing.

"Our counties and our cities had no choice but to bond," said Byrnes. "We're a pay-as-you-go state (but) the bonding was atrocious at our county level. As a taxpayer, what's better? To have a user fee or to have these (taxpayers) paying interest… on these bonds."

In addition to providing new revenues, the Iowa legislation imposes restrictions on future debt and bonding for local road projects.[11]

Utah's House Bill 362

Rep. Johnny Anderson, who chairs Utah's House Transportation Committee, said his state faced a common problem when they took on the task of looking at transportation funding in 2013.

"The very moment that you put a cents-per-gallon fuel tax in place or you increase a cents-per-gallon fuel tax, it starts losing purchasing power," he said. "Construction costs are rising much faster than inflation in the state."[12]

Lawmakers converted the state's 24.5 cents-per-gallon tax to a 12 percent tax on the wholesale gas price, which equated to an immediate 4.9 cent increase in the per-gallon tax with the potential for that to grow in the future. Lawmakers also established a floor and a ceiling on the tax to limit price volatility.[13]

"House Bill 362 doesn't just increase the fuel tax," Anderson said. "We put in place fuel tax reform. This is the most significant transportation funding legislation in 20 years."[14]

Anderson said his state's gas tax changes were precipitated by a need to move back to a "user pays, user benefits" model for transportation funding in Utah.

"The Utah Legislature hadn't touched the fuel tax since 1997," he said. "Since then, they had been earmarking more and more of the general fund (mostly from the sales tax) to cover the shortfall. In 2014–2015, we finally got to the point that more than half of the state's investment in transportation funding was coming from the sales tax and not the user fees. Making the argument that we needed to stop raiding the general fund and require roadway users to pay for the roads was key to (the bill's) passage."[15]

Georgia's House Bill 170

Signed into law on May 4, 2015, by Gov. Nathan Deal, Georgia House Bill 170, the Transportation Funding Act of 2015, not only increased the state's gas and diesel taxes, it indexed the gas tax rate to both the Corporate Average Fuel Economy and the Consumer Price Index.[16]

One key to the passage of the measure was a concern expressed in the findings of a 2014 Joint Study Committee, said Rep. Valerie Clark, vice chair of the House Transportation Committee.

"Georgia's dependence on federal transportation funds (was) a problem due to federal funding uncertainty in the short- and long-term," Clark said.[17]

The committee noted in its final report that in its FY 2015 budget, the state relied on federal funds to cover 76 percent of capital construction project costs and 68 percent of capital maintenance project costs.

Baruch Feigenbaum, a transportation policy analyst at the Reason Foundation, said reducing reliance on the federal government proved to be a good selling point for the bill.

Feigenbaum also noted Georgia had gone more than 20 years with no significant revenue changes. A previous attempt to increase transportation revenues through local option sales taxes in 2012 had been largely a failure with voters in nine of 12 regions of the state rejecting the plan.[18]

South Dakota's Senate Bill 1

When South Dakota's leaders embarked on an effort that could raise additional revenues for transportation in 2014, Sen. Mike Vehle had an idea of the challenge that might lie ahead.

"South Dakota is the least taxed state in the nation," said Vehle, who chairs the Senate Transportation Committee. "So this was not going to be an easy deal."

It had been 16 years since the state's last gas tax increase.

"Our gas tax was 22 cents," he said. "This is what it was in 1999 and with road cost inflation it (was) worth only 11 cents. It was cut in half. We would have had to be at 45 cents to be even with 1999."

But when it came to making the decision to increase state revenues to boost transportation spending, Vehle recognized not all states are created equal.

"Florida has twice as many miles of interstates as South Dakota does," he noted. "It has 18 and a half million people to pay for them and we've got 850,000."

Lawmakers ultimately approved an increase of 6 cents to motor fuel taxes.

Even as experts warn of a future where electric vehicles dominate the roads, the gas tax made the most sense for South Dakota for right now, Vehle said. But that doesn't mean the fuel tax will continue to make sense as the primary transportation revenue vehicle for the long term, he added.

"Now is the time when we need to start thinking what are we going to do when we get to 2020, 2025, 2030, when we really start to see (gas tax revenues) come down," he said. "Let's start working on it now so we can sell it."[19]

Washington's Senate Bill 5987

Washington state House Transportation Committee Chair Judy Clibborn said a gas tax increase made the most sense for her state because it was something that everyone understood. It was also a revenue source lawmakers could be assured would go toward the purpose for which it was intended.

"Gas taxes (in Washington) are constitutionally protected for transportation so (revenues) cannot be siphoned off … (to be used for) other state services," Clibborn said.

That would not have been the case with a package that relied on general fund dollars from sales taxes or other revenues.[20]

Washington's Senate Bill 5987 is a $16 billion, 16-year transportation package that includes a gradually implemented 11.9 cents-per-gallon gas tax increase.

"Nobody likes to have a tax increase. But we haven't been as diligent on maintenance and preservation as we've needed to be," said Senate Transportation Committee Chair Curtis King. "We need to invest in that to get caught up. If we don't do it in the next two or three years, those repairs, it's going to cost us three or four times more."[21]

Idaho's House Bill 312

When Idaho considered transportation funding legislation in 2014, legislators knew it wouldn't go anywhere because it was an election year and they needed to go through an education process to make sure lawmakers and the voting public were on the same page in recognizing the need for additional investment, recalled Rep. Clark Kauffman, a member of the Idaho House Transportation and Defense Committee.

"Most people didn't realize it had been almost 25 years since there had been any increase in our use fees—fuel and registration," he said.

By the time 2015 rolled around, state transportation officials and business and industry leaders had completed the education process, legislators understood the need and leadership was on board.[22]

Signed into law on April 21, Idaho House Bill 312 increased the state gas tax by 7 cents-per-gallon.[23]

"This law became effective in July (of 2015) and was the biggest non-event of the year because gas prices have fallen and people didn't even care," said Kauffman.

Unlike measures in some other states, Idaho's law is mostly a straightforward gas tax increase.

"The gas tax was already set up and functioning," said Kauffman. "We realized that it didn't account for future inflation and some of the proposals that were brought forward would have had options to deal with inflation. Some of those ideas were provided at the last minute and didn't have proper vetting time."[24]

Nebraska Legislative Bill 610

In making a gas tax increase in Nebraska a reality, lawmakers faced a major hurdle other states did not, said Sen. Jim Smith, who chairs the Senate Transportation Committee.

"We're the only state that had to override the veto of a governor and that was the governor (Pete Ricketts) that I campaigned for and endorsed," Smith said. "It was a very public argument and debate that took place in Nebraska during the session over the gas tax."

Despite the vocal opposition of anti-tax groups like Americans for Prosperity, Nebraska's Legislative Bill 610 became law with a vote to override the Gov. Ricketts' veto on May 14. It gradually increases the state gas tax by 6 cents.

"It was something that was necessary and was the right thing to do in Nebraska," said Smith.[25]

Smith said there were a number of reasons the gas tax made sense as the revenue mechanism of choice.

"It was the most direct and explainable way to meet funding needs," he said. "Nebraska is one of only two states that do not use bonding as a source of funding and using general funds (from income and sales taxes) was not an option. … A user-type tax was the most acceptable."[26]

Michigan's Transportation Funding Package

On Nov. 3, Michigan lawmakers voted to increase the state's gas tax as part of a plan laid out in seven separate pieces of legislation. The plan is expected to generate $1.2 billion a year by the time it's fully phased in in fiscal year 2021.[27]

But unlike other states, Michigan didn't decide to have the gas tax carry the bulk of the load. Political compromise resulted in an even split down the middle between new revenues and general fund dollars.

Under the plan, the state's 15 cent-per-gallon diesel tax and 19 cent-per-gallon gas tax both will increase to 26.3 cents on Jan. 1, 2017, and generate about $400 million a year in new revenue for roads. Starting in 2022, the fuel tax rates will be indexed to inflation. Vehicle registration fee increases will bring in an additional $200 million a year.

The other $600 million in the plan would come from a gradual shift of general fund dollars used to fund other government services. The shift would start with $150 million in 2019 before building up to the $600 million level for 2021 and beyond.

But critics have said the plan is irresponsible since it doesn't spell out the programs and priorities that will be impacted by the budget shifts or cuts. Gov. Rick Snyder has said future revenue projections make him confident the state won't have to cut other areas of state government to support the plan.[28]

Looking Beyond the Gas Tax

Despite the reliance of states on the gas tax in their 2015 transportation revenue packages, many believe its days of usefulness are numbered. Increasing fuel efficiency, and eventually electric cars, will continue to erode the revenues gas taxes can bring in over time.

A more sustainable funding mechanism might be to charge motorists by the mile rather than by the gallon, some believe. The FAST Act included $95 million to fund grants to help states test alternative user-based revenue mechanisms such as those based on mileage.[29]

"That's a big deal for us," said Alex Herrgott, deputy staff director for the U.S. Senate Environment and Public Works Committee. "It's a lot of money to not actually spend on construction—to spend on these pilot programs. ... But what it's going to do is lead to a seeding in the states for individual states and municipalities to figure out a good way to do this. The best ideas that we ever harness at the federal level are always incubated in states."[30]

Oregon has been experimenting with the mileage-based user fee concept for 15 years. The Oregon General Assembly passed legislation in 2013 to create a program called OReGO under which the state will enlist up to 5,000 volunteers to pay 1.5 cents per mile they drive on Oregon roads and receive a refund for what they pay in fuel taxes. Three private vendors are supplying the measuring devices to plug in underneath dashboards to tally miles.[31] The program was officially launched in July 2015 and in January 2016, OReGO officials said volunteer sign-ups had surpassed 1,000.[32]

Meanwhile, California in early 2016 was gearing up to test a mileage-based fee of its own. As in Oregon, state officials said they would seek 5,000 volunteers for the experiment. In California's case, though, the pilot is only scheduled to last nine months and no actual money will change hands.[33]

Washington state transportation officials also have signed off on a pilot program that will give drivers the choice of having a GPS device in their car or a smartphone app that would connect to their vehicle's Bluetooth network to track mileage.[34]

Mileage-based user fee proponents say by providing participants a choice of how their mileage data is collected and who collects it, they can alleviate some of the privacy concerns that have been expressed by civil liberties advocates about the concept.

But Jeff Davis of the Eno Center for Transportation warns that mileage-based user fees may face an even more significant challenge in widespread implementation for precisely one of the reasons gas taxes proved so appealing to states in 2015.

"The problem is the gas tax is so incredibly efficient to administer," he said. "You've got less than 2,000 refinery racks paying these taxes—filing quarterly returns and paying estimated taxes that bring in $36 billion a year—and it doesn't take that many people at the IRS to process 2,000 returns a quarter and do some auditing. If you're going to continue user finance, there are three ways to do it: you can tax fuel, you can tax vehicles or you can tax drivers and either way you're going from less than 2,000 taxpayers to over 100 million taxpayers. ... Not going to happen anytime soon. Don't expect (mileage-based user fees) to ride in on a chariot and save us."[35]

Notes

[1] Remarks by Sarah Puro. Transportation Research Board Annual Meeting. January 10, 2016.

[2] Chris McCahill. "Economy, gas prices pushed driving upward in 2015, but less than in past years." State Smart Transportation Initiative Newsletter. February 29, 2016. Accessed from: *http://www.ssti.us/2016/02/economy-gas-prices-pushed-driving-upward-in-2015-but-less-than-in-past-years/?utm_source=SSTI+Community+of+Practice+*

Master+List&utm_campaign=5f400bd3c1-Newsletter_Feb_29_20162_28_2016&utm_medium=email&utm_term=0_f54dd1d9a6-5f400bd3c1-8455553

[3] Remarks by Jeff Davis. Transportation Research Board Annual Meeting. January 10, 2016.

[4] Paul Davidson. "Gas should remain a bargain in 2016." *USA Today*, KGW.com. January 2, 2016. Accessed from: *http://www.kgw.com/money/consumer/gas-should-remain-a-bargain-in-2016/10101732*

[5] Paul Egan and Kathleen Gray. "Michigan Voters Refuse Tax Hike for Roads." Tribune News Service. May 6, 2015. Accessed from: *http://www.governing.com/topics/elections/tns-michigan-voters-roads-tax.html*

[6] Ariel Hart. "Voters reject transportation tax." *Atlanta Journal-Constitution*. August 1, 2012. Accessed from: *http://www.ajc.com/news/news/state-regional-govt-politics/voters-reject-transportation-tax/nQXfq/*

[7] William Petroski. "Gas tax hike takes effect Sunday." *The Des Moines Register*. February 25, 2015. Accessed from: *http://www.desmoinesregister.com/story/news/politics/2015/02/25/iowa-gas-tax-branstad/23990671/*

[8] Remarks by Rep. Josh Byrnes. CSG National Conference. Nashville, Tenn. December 11, 2015.

[9] Telephone interview with Sen. Tod Bowman. April 2015.

[10] Remarks by Stuart Anderson. Transportation Research Board Annual Meeting. January 2016.

[11] Byrnes.

[12] Remarks by Rep. Johnny Anderson. CSG National Conference. Nashville, Tenn. December 2015.

[13] American Road and Transportation Builders Association. Transportation Investment Advocacy Center. "Utah House Bill 362 (2015)." Case Study. Accessed from: *http://www.transportationinvestment.org/wp-content/uploads/2015/07/Utah-House-Bill-362-2015-Case-Study.pdf*

[14] J. Anderson, CSG National Conference.

[15] E-mail interview with Rep. Johnny Anderson. November 30, 2015.

[16] Georgia House of Representatives. House Bill 170 (2015). Accessed from: *http://www.legis.ga.gov/Legislation/20152016/153458.pdf*

[17] Remarks by Rep. Valerie Clark. CSG National Conference. Nashville, Tenn. December 11, 2015.

[18] Remarks by Baruch Feigenbaum. Transportation Research Board Annual Meeting. Washington, D.C. January 10, 2016.

[19] Remarks by Sen. Mike Vehle. CSG National Conference. Nashville, Tenn. December 11, 2015.

[20] Remarks by Rep. Judy Clibborn. CSG National Conference. Nashville, Tenn. December 11, 2015.

[21] Rachel La Corte. "Gas tax increases by 7 cents in Washington state." *The Seattle Times*. August 1, 2015. Accessed from: *http://www.seattletimes.com/seattle-news/gas-tax-increases-by-7-cents-in-washington-state/*

[22] Remarks by Rep. Clark Kauffman. CSG National Conference. Nashville, Tenn. December 11, 2015.

[23] Idaho House of Representatives. House Bill 312. Accessed from: *https://www.legislature.idaho.gov/legislation/2015/H0312E1.pdf*

[24] E-mail interview with Rep. Clark Kauffman. November 23, 2015.

[25] Remarks by Sen. Jim Smith. CSG National Conference. Nashville, Tenn. December 11, 2015.

[26] E-mail interview with Sen. Jim Smith. November 30, 2015.

[27] AASHTO Journal. "Michigan Gov. Snyder Praises Measure Raising Billions More for Transportation." November 6, 2015. Accessed from: *http://www.aashtojournal.org/Pages/110615mich.aspx*

[28] Jonathan Oosting. "Inside Michigan's new road funding deal: fuel taxes, registration fees, tax relief and more." Michigan Live. November 4, 2015. Accessed from: *http://www.mlive.com/lansing-news/index.ssf/2015/11/inside_michigans_new_road_fund.html#incart_story_package*

[29] Andy Winkler and Sarah Kline. "10 Things You Need to Know About the FAST Act." Bipartisan Policy Center. January 12, 2016. Accessed from: *http://bipartisanpolicy.org/blog/10-things-you-need-to-know-about-the-fast-act/*

[30] Remarks by Alex Herrgott. Transportation Research Board Annual Meeting. Washington, D.C. January 10, 2016.

[31] Peter Wong. "OReGO lines up test drive for state road fee." *Portland Tribune*. July 16, 2015. Accessed from: *http://www.pamplinmedia.com/pt/9-news/266924-140766-orego-lines-up-test-drive-for-state-road-fee*

[32] William Maetzold. "Sign-ups pass 1,000 for OReGO." KTVL. January 20, 2016. Accessed from: *http://ktvl.com/news/local/sign-ups-pass-1000-for-orego*

[33] Michael Cabanatuan. "CA: California to Road-Test New Fees That Would Replace Gas Tax." McClatchy. February 18, 2016. Accessed from: *http://www.masstransitmag.com/news/12171363/california-to-road-test-new-fees-that-would-replace-gas-tax*

[34] "Leaders think pay-by-mile tax will work in Washington." KIRO 7. February 24, 2016. Accessed from: *http://www.kiro7.com/news/local-leaders-think-pay-by-mile-tax-will-work-in-washington-state/110566173*

[35] Davis.

About the Author

Sean Slone is the director of transportation and infrastructure policy at The Council of State Governments. He staffs CSG's Transportation Public Policy Committee and writes about transportation policy for CSG publications, such as Capitol Ideas magazine, the Current State E-Newsletter, the Capitol Comments blog and Capitol Research policy materials. He is the author of two CSG national reports: *Transportation and Infrastructure Finance* (2009) and *Shovel-Ready or Not? State Stimulus Successes on the Road to Recovery* (2010). He has written an article for The Book of the States each year since 2010.

Table 9.13
REVENUES USED BY STATES FOR HIGHWAYS: 2014 (In thousands of dollars)

State or other jurisdiction	Beginning balance total (a)	Highway-user revenues (b) — Motor-fuel taxes	Motor-vehicle and motor-carrier taxes	Road and crossing tolls	Total	Appropriations from general funds (c)	Other state imposts	Miscellaneous	Bond proceeds — Original issues	Refunding issues	Payments from other governments — Federal funds — Federal Hwy. Admin.	Other agencies	From local government	Total receipts
Total	87,781,482	31,698,598	24,469,072	12,264,165	68,431,835	9,644,053	10,328,694	10,132,294	22,866,541	7,844,816	39,539,315	1,884,082	3,155,136	173,826,870
Alabama	561,123	599,939	163,918		763,857	164,930	44,884	7,017			869,167	60,808	5,107	1,915,770
Alaska			72,515	48,813	121,328	487,624	235	4,300			541,204	15,333		1,170,024
Arizona	1,447,204	621,541	254,987		876,528	8,296	694,363	70,281			669,148	27,626	8,597	2,354,839
Arkansas	491,413	391,818	154,692		546,510	65,263	214,365	16,857	695,126		539,690	33,450	4,003	2,115,264
California	30,002,935	4,846,387	2,670,673	706,558	8,223,618	1,860,764	638,743	1,585,431	2,771,784	9,072	3,366,052	125,676	895,352	19,476,492
Colorado	1,058,867	556,199	975,252	23,525	1,554,976	1,200		68,138	23,449		557,827	33,808		2,239,398
Connecticut	1,374,565	363,232	155,059	804	519,095		82,216	73,138	357,729		450,560	46,248	4,661	1,533,648
Delaware	1,804,279	61,826	84,885	568,708	715,419	85,406		172,577	96,704	282,655	174,162	4,918	6,584	1,538,425
Florida	3,602,641	1,407,537	1,305,317	1,673,810	4,386,664		410,588	419,729	921,816	764,328	2,244,788	106,032	195,649	9,449,594
Georgia	2,208,946	942,368	104,690	8,305	1,055,363	199,918		114,447	32,718		1,129,150	78,706	41,162	2,651,464
Hawaii	234,539	79,877	150,972		230,849			4,385			212,997	3,761		451,992
Idaho	170,826	210,951	167,974		378,925			22,509	81,900		297,019	27,433	5,035	812,821
Illinois	2,799,596	1,142,733	1,361,673	1,025,071	3,529,477	112,774	313	49,534	2,098,108		1,409,411	26,111	1,281	7,227,009
Indiana	7,321	780,885	251,041	203,002	1,234,928	129,128		315,970	4,200		973,124	10,314	56,815	2,724,479
Iowa	318,587	425,289	884,540		1,309,829	55,618	30,313	6,142			512,741	77,401		1,992,044
Kansas	642,083	236,429	116,259	46,796	399,484		524,853	8,523	298,629	212,875	396,202	8,897	32,332	1,881,795
Kentucky	104,933	769,132	596,997		1,366,129	5,626		233,072	601,802	174,225	685,318	10,928		3,077,100
Louisiana	3,158,730	586,060	137,227	16,191	739,478	346,413	61,785	289,090	437,599	203,351	713,558	27,975	86	2,819,335
Maine (d)	152,455	236,801	82,641	133,701	453,143			16,496	22,125		176,029	4,718		672,511
Maryland	1,312,467	247,810	383,123	670,063	1,300,996	93,631	191,940	81,451	358,292		569,752	13,570	158,177	2,767,809
Massachusetts (d)	650,734	335,747	114,082	310,232	760,061	407,635	617,205	290,765	684,681		522,773	7,772		3,290,892
Michigan	1,082,521	810,182	840,455	45,046	1,695,683	261,348	65,893	154,345	20,043		902,002	18,241	15,739	3,133,558
Minnesota	1,578,950	706,962	585,442		1,292,404		513,235	76,787	362,233		752,841	18,488	194,182	3,210,170
Mississippi	188,443	344,519	158,011		502,530		43,917	5,593	98,840		544,208	15,400	155,342	1,365,830
Missouri	1,159,097	657,139	288,743		945,882	2,930	351,598	16,832	108,913	977,770	842,454	37,061	23,973	3,307,413
Montana	75,860	113,242	115,853		229,095		7,035	53,968			426,817	24,613	3,695	745,223
Nebraska	141,115	320,434	93,354		413,788	41,995	303,775	26,613			338,668	8,241	496,996	1,630,076
Nevada	218,966	266,768	220,091	791	487,650		1,148	44,278	100,673		314,833	8,512	19,011	976,105
New Hampshire	346,992	104,518	84,723	118,937	308,178	57,745		93,146	2,905		172,940	16,614	1,928	653,456
New Jersey (e)	2,146,462	372,272	852,450	1,741,567	2,966,289			344,175	4,192,490		605,967	23,712	3,849	8,136,482
New Mexico	352,321	168,603	215,202		383,805	14,070	24,832	100,432	80,642		367,029	20,647		991,457
New York	625,743	392,870	391,132	2,136,342	2,920,344	710,462	1,781,100	1,978,543	3,183,320	81,990	1,816,443	53,534	13,671	12,539,407
North Carolina	1,973,889	1,794,258	652,258	21,027	2,467,543		607,021	97,274		19,590	1,305,035	30,659	19,441	4,546,563
North Dakota	182,285	214,209	116,247		330,456	289,326		362			283,058	11,147	29,185	943,534
Ohio	2,947,195	1,697,889	791,858	268,773	2,758,520	12,542		263,907	290,416		1,544,757	18,386	84,909	4,973,437
Oklahoma	848,284	100,835	111,576	248,987	461,398		754,620	210,221	10,423	482,708	673,367	10,706	24,116	2,144,851
Oregon	3,173,937	442,035	493,289		935,324	54,596	13,964	52,228	453,473		417,329	71,680		2,481,302
Pennsylvania	4,115,765	1,515,701	511,227	1,275,839	3,302,767	893,931	20,525	390,147	955,492	771,610	1,711,119	35,806	19,689	8,101,086
Rhode Island (e)	81,894	55,740	28,784	18,806	103,330	30,990		21,233	29,500		268,248	5,185		458,486
South Carolina	383,744	502,113	254,719	22,567	779,399	102,456	3,210	19,571	101,172		622,135	11,881	30,664	1,670,488

See footnotes at end of table.

REVENUES USED BY STATES FOR HIGHWAYS: 2014 (In thousands of dollars) — Continued

State or other jurisdiction	Beginning balance total (a)	Highway-user revenues (b)				Appropriations from general funds (c)	Other state imposts	Miscellaneous	Bond proceeds		Payments from other governments			Total receipts
		Motor-fuel taxes	Motor-vehicle and motor-carrier taxes	Road and crossing tolls	Total				Original issues	Refunding issues	Federal funds		From local government	
											Federal Hwy. Admin.	Other agencies		
South Dakota.........	24,680	122,612	107,407	-	230,019	-	80,447	31,992	-	-	279,238	6,584	10,517	638,797
Tennessee..............	1,146,956	652,208	287,436	36	939,680	-	59,831	31,957	-	-	946,036	40,296	37,612	2,055,412
Texas.....................	6,936,733	2,207,420	4,439,131	549,570	7,196,121	2,541,892	43,275	1,556,508	759,892	2,952,260	3,020,814	295,685	300,261	18,666,708
Utah......................	693,706	232,080	133,040	762	365,882	63,662	448,392	74,696	250,831	-	335,197	84,176	33,503	1,656,339
Vermont.................	12,079	79,965	118,814	-	198,779	32,935	1,659	17,492	11,500	-	217,630	51,814	5,071	536,880
Virginia.................	2,689,191	531,602	865,120	64,223	1,460,945	205,674	1,366,608	126,461	321,837	297,655	1,266,343	21,772	75,463	5,142,758
Washington............	1,455,292	1,093,470	554,972	230,406	1,878,848	-	158,069	405,091	1,238,344	116,980	977,398	47,249	33,021	4,855,000
West Virginia.........	176,142	436,809	289,929	84,907	811,645	22,639	3,116	25,684	-	-	471,846	10,180	314	1,345,424
Wisconsin..............	820,189	832,588	604,713	-	1,437,301	189,057	71,695	30,756	664,308	217,482	688,613	96,081	108,243	3,503,536
Wyoming...............	52,589	72,966	43,790	-	116,756	56,909	73,400	32,109	-	-	259,849	34,521	-	573,544
Dist. of Columbia ...	46,218	14,028	30,789	-	44,817	34,668	18,526	145	142,632	-	156,429	3,726	-	400,943

Source: U.S. Department of Transportation, Federal Highway Administration, *Highway Statistics, 2014,* (Dec. 2015).

Note: Detail may not add to totals due to rounding. This table was compiled from reports of state authorities.

Key:
(a) Any differences between beginning balances and the closing balances on last year's table are the result of accounting adjustments, inclusion of funds not previously reported, etc.
(b) Amounts shown represent only those highway user revenues that were expended on state or local roads.
(c) Amounts shown represent gross general fund appropriations for highways reduced by the amount of highway-user revenues placed in the State General Fund.
(d) Amounts shown represent data reported for 2010 and 2011.
(e) Amounts shown represent data reported for 2013.

Table 9.14
STATE DISBURSEMENTS FOR HIGHWAYS: 2014 (In thousands of dollars)

State or other jurisdiction	Capital outlay — State administered highways (a)	Capital outlay — Local roads and streets	Capital outlay — Total	Maintenance and service total — State administered highways (a)	Maintenance and service total — Local roads and streets	Maintenance and service total — Total	Administration, research and planning	Highway law enforcement and safety
Total..............................	74,336,715	6,164,560	80,501,275	22,555,826	895,813	23,451,639	8,397,352	9,485,562
Alabama	1,058,602	105,657	1,164,259	40,278	-	40,278	214,815	233,369
Alaska..........................	762,425	-	762,425	225,220	-	225,220	91,998	49,409
Arizona........................	790,800	83,989	874,789	149,973	-	149,973	217,385	191,021
Arkansas......................	1,383,802	-	1,383,802	206,658	69,152	275,810	155,257	97,269
California	4,532,694	190,467	4,723,161	1,549,817	496,340	2,046,157	665,816	1,909,669
Colorado.......................	1,010,752	101,137	1,111,889	427,697	-	427,697	99,388	179,631
Connecticut	759,074	-	759,074	130,400	-	130,400	370,662	17,830
Delaware	239,521	-	239,521	299,444	-	299,444	88,519	94,505
Florida	4,501,032	105,973	4,607,005	891,715	-	891,715	297,074	381,024
Georgia.........................	1,084,816	63,897	1,148,713	317,611	-	317,611	421,490	220,074
Hawaii..........................	192,370	-	192,370	79,288	-	79,288	16,727	9,150
Idaho............................	351,260	62,814	414,074	110,996	-	110,996	29,587	43,372
Illinois	3,936,160	39,657	3,975,817	770,407	14,271	784,678	336,943	107,589
Indiana.........................	1,377,754	-	1,377,754	704,513	56,362	760,875	121,435	21,872
Iowa	869,593	-	869,593	210,115	-	210,115	127,664	127,106
Kansas	791,153	107,091	898,244	138,596	-	138,596	59,239	85,341
Kentucky	1,575,909	323,772	1,899,681	412,348	71,411	483,759	32,330	105,487
Louisiana	1,120,326	52,103	1,172,429	144,251	2,732	146,983	79,497	62,993
Maine (b)	380,032	18,435	398,467	211,599	-	211,599	20,954	25,724
Maryland	1,346,125	62,857	1,408,982	432,605	-	432,605	106,490	181,678
Massachusetts (b)........	1,064,039	281,767	1,345,806	286,495	-	286,495	274,098	203,205
Michigan.......................	1,197,718	1,001,021	2,198,739	295,263	-	295,263	130,883	243,502
Minnesota.....................	1,195,000	-	1,195,000	489,833	-	489,833	168,642	140,803
Mississippi	894,062	140,503	1,034,565	86,445	-	86,445	72,804	32,650
Missouri........................	981,717	121,553	1,103,270	484,426	-	484,426	71,796	228,219
Montana	453,399	-	453,399	134,741	-	134,741	61,237	57,693
Nebraska	445,021	348,824	793,845	194,166	108,171	302,337	48,343	66,562
Nevada..........................	340,012	-	340,012	116,546	-	116,546	144,712	103,946
New Hampshire	282,702	9,939	292,641	217,848	-	217,848	40,622	41,186
New Jersey (c).............	2,811,302	-	2,811,302	780,218	-	780,218	150,104	388,616
New Mexico	372,279	-	372,279	72,603	-	72,603	321,102	20,670
New York	4,559,881	784,719	5,344,600	1,515,455	-	1,515,455	349,395	413,669
North Carolina.............	2,441,663	-	2,441,663	943,973	-	943,973	264,623	361,361
North Dakota................	580,875	75,344	656,219	34,783	-	34,783	30,438	31,531
Ohio	2,421,432	358,547	2,779,979	497,261	-	497,261	69,545	305,552
Oklahoma......................	1,203,641	109,605	1,313,246	205,735	-	205,735	130,194	113,930
Oregon..........................	984,882	151,960	1,136,842	211,720	10,063	221,783	124,366	66,542
Pennsylvania	3,651,606	220,349	3,871,955	1,359,673	-	1,359,673	542,190	663,546
Rhode Island (c)	246,706	25,073	271,779	97,955	1,454	99,409	45,196	26,506
South Carolina.............	958,600	-	958,600	419,538	44,964	464,502	121,656	121,988
South Dakota................	412,067	61,595	473,662	75,698	-	75,698	62,987	37,147
Tennessee	1,104,827	40,216	1,145,043	335,834	-	335,834	181,800	33,502
Texas............................	10,400,653	280,255	10,680,908	2,525,319	-	2,525,319	357,285	809,175
Utah..............................	423,752	-	423,752	450,672	-	450,672	86,710	78,436
Vermont........................	192,634	60,779	253,413	125,827	792	126,619	55,401	63,621
Virginia.........................	1,765,636	-	1,765,636	1,713,829	-	1,713,829	318,416	219,275
Washington...................	2,235,256	369,699	2,604,955	728,518	1,551	730,069	193,721	299,009
West Virginia................	743,532	-	743,532	323,625	-	323,625	112,433	49,353
Wisconsin.....................	1,526,106	126,618	1,652,724	239,822	-	239,822	217,244	79,606
Wyoming	381,515	-	381,515	102,431	-	102,431	65,860	40,648
Dist. of Columbia	-	278,345	278,345	36,043	18,550	54,593	30,279	-

See footnotes at end of table.

STATE DISBURSEMENTS FOR HIGHWAYS: 2014 (In thousands of dollars) — Continued

		Bond retirement		Grants-in-aid		Balances end-of-year		
State or other jurisdiction	Interest	Current revenues or sinking funds	Refunding bonds	to local governments	Total disbursements	Reserves for current highway work	Reserves for debt service	Total
United States	8,187,761	11,622,651	7,844,816	15,129,260	164,620,316	95,937,034	1,051,002	96,988,036
Alabama	390,660	22,675	-	218,720	2,284,776	192,117	-	192,117
Alaska.........................	a 8,896	22,972	-	11,608	1,172,528	(2,504	-	(2,504
Arizona.......................	139,757	165,615	-	649,695	2,388,235	1,413,629	179	1,413,808
Arkansas.....................	29,302	73,825	-	7,027	2,022,292	584,385	-	584,385
California	458,866	132,978	9,072	4,404,632	14,350,351	35,129,076	-	35,129,076
Colorado......................	36,056	88,440	-	627,891	2,570,992	727,273	-	727,273
Connecticut	190,908	411,835	-	62,055	1,942,764	851,054	114,395	965,449
Delaware	112,801	169,581	282,655	3,743	1,290,769	1,987,863	64,072	2,051,935
Florida	599,195	602,177	764,328	395,899	8,538,417	4,513,818	-	4,513,818
Georgia........................	123,132	319,382	-	192,524	2,742,926	2,117,484	-	2,117,484
Hawaii.........................	19,530	31,470	-	48,437	396,972	289,559	-	289,559
Idaho...........................	29,832	27,020	-	153,147	808,028	175,619	-	175,619
Illinois	312,232	339,872	-	474,038	6,331,169	3,408,056	287,380	3,695,436
Indiana........................	51,214	49,045	-	231,020	2,613,215	118,585	-	118,585
Iowa	-	-	-	690,172	2,024,650	285,981	-	285,981
Kansas	68,124	115,654	212,875	148,881	1,726,954	762,690	34,234	796,924
Kentucky	146,506	102,165	174,225	1,542	2,945,695	236,338	-	236,338
Louisiana.....................	20,053	86,727	203,351	1,929	1,773,962	4,204,076	27	4,204,103
Maine (b)	35,192	13,415	-	77	705,428	119,538	-	119,538
Maryland	189,634	303,087	-	162,529	2,785,005	1,295,271	-	1,295,271
Massachusetts (b)	349,534	295,437	-	168,447	2,923,022	1,018,604	-	1,018,604
Michigan......................	104,155	129,490	280,265	36,235	3,418,532	1,077,547	-	1,077,547
Minnesota....................	61,545	119,975	-	821,675	2,997,473	1,791,547	-	1,791,547
Mississippi	39,755	47,437	-	99,055	1,412,711	120,904	20,658	141,562
Missouri	135,319	162,050	977,770	258,023	3,420,873	1,045,637	-	1,045,637
Montana	4,391	11,110	-	41,429	764,000	57,083	-	57,083
Nebraska	-	-	-	343,987	1,555,074	216,117	-	216,117
Nevada.........................	13,883	56,220	-	3,200	778,519	416,552	-	416,552
New Hampshire	34,648	50,830	-	44,343	722,118	278,330	-	278,330
New Jersey (c).............	940,015	2,258,738	-	163,174	7,492,167	2,790,777	-	2,790,777
New Mexico	72,657	106,610	-	51,634	1,017,555	326,223	-	326,223
New York......................	908,081	2,375,759	81,990	402,172	11,391,121	1,738,808	35,221	1,774,029
North Carolina.............	100,272	135,633	19,590	147,189	4,414,304	2,106,148	-	2,106,148
North Dakota...............	1,452	3,865	-	122,021	880,309	245,510	-	245,510
Ohio	102,556	262,045	-	1,133,725	5,150,663	2,769,969	-	2,769,969
Oklahoma.....................	120,936	120,230	-	875	2,005,146	987,989	-	987,989
Oregon.........................	112,165	65,888	482,708	12,272	2,222,566	3,432,673	-	3,432,673
Pennsylvania	486,572	181,725	771,610	323,195	8,200,466	3,963,632	52,753	4,016,385
Rhode Island (c).........	37,323	31,052	-	-	511,265	29,115	-	29,115
South Carolina.............	50,405	145,540	-	1,595	1,864,286	189,946	-	189,946
South Dakota...............	-	-	-	1,136	650,630	12,847	-	12,847
Tennessee	-	-	-	291,200	1,987,379	1,214,989	-	1,214,989
Texas...........................	1,037,377	886,305	2,952,260	433,282	19,681,911	5,479,447	442,083	5,921,530
Utah.............................	111,598	254,655	-	75,915	1,481,738	868,307	-	868,307
Vermont.......................	2,394	3,302	-	27,052	531,802	17,157	-	17,157
Virginia........................	152,687	194,215	297,655	654,617	5,316,330	2,515,619	-	2,515,619
Washington...................	66,380	274,223	116,980	516,667	4,802,004	1,508,288	-	1,508,288
West Virginia................	18,684	57,045	-	10,243	1,314,915	206,651	-	206,651
Wisconsin	161,087	292,554	217,482	455,751	3,316,270	1,007,455	-	1,007,455
Wyoming	-	-	-	3,585	594,039	32,094	-	32,094
Dist. of Columbia	-	22,783	-	-	386,000	61,161	-	61,161

Source: U.S. Department of Transportation, Federal Highway Administration, Highway Statistics, 2014(December 2015).

Note: Detail may not add to totals due to rounding. This table was compiled from reports of state authorities.

Key:
(a) Includes expenditures for local roads and streets under State control. Most local roads are under State control in Delaware, North Carolina, Virginia, and West Virginia.
(b) Amounts shown represent data reported for 2010 and 2011.
(c) Amounts shown represent data reported for 2013.

Table 9.15
PUBLIC ROAD LENGTH MILES BY OWNERSHIP: 2014

State or other jurisdiction	Rural mileage						Urban mileage					
	State highway agency	County	Town, township & municipal (a)	Other jurisdictions (b)	Federal agency (c)	Total rural roads	State highway agency	County	Town, township & municipal (a)	Other jurisdictions (b)	Federal agency (c)	Total urban roads
Total......................	615,767	1,597,119	561,346	50,705	153,513	2,978,451	171,617	243,477	785,861	6,652	7,648	1,215,254
United States total....	614,743	1,597,119	559,289	50,705	153,490	2,975,347	168,060	243,477	775,851	6,651	7,641	1,201,680
Alabama	8,352	60,180	6,236	169	817	75,754	2,550	2,060	20,967	0	686	26,263
Alaska	4,897	2,114	1,456	2,303	2,319	13,089	696	1,538	327	7	72	2,640
Arizona	5,573	13,702	2,486	3,955	13,668	39,383	1,249	4,205	20,146	376	234	26,210
Arkansas.................	14,086	64,602	4,643	—	2,148	85,480	2,332	1,402	12,887	—	493	17,115
California	10,312	75,461	1,707	2,078	25,152	114,709	4,786	22,589	81,337	603	1,503	110,818
Colorado.................	7,538	51,302	2,073	833	6,526	68,271	1,523	4,747	14,145	20	33	20,469
Connecticut	1,170	—	4,224	264	35	5,694	2,551	—	13,141	71	52	15,815
Delaware.................	2,852	—	51	41	72	3,017	2,548	—	755	37	50	3,391
Florida...................	5,643	26,379	2,616	82	1,789	36,509	6,472	43,869	35,077	5	459	85,883
Georgia	12,595	58,216	4,064	90	2,225	77,190	5,360	29,264	15,410	31	237	50,302
Hawaii....................	483	1,023	—	49	113	1,668	459	2,275	—	21	17	2,772
Idaho.....................	4,623	15,526	1,830	13,061	8,202	43,243	362	134	4,463	698	2	5,658
Illinois...................	10,431	13,853	71,246	407	217	96,155	5,545	2,635	41,020	377	29	49,606
Indiana...................	8,874	53,906	2,759	56	1,077	66,672	2,356	11,307	16,200	13	150	30,026
Iowa	7,692	88,075	5,458	431	110	101,765	1,030	1,633	9,526	185	28	12,401
Kansas	9,521	111,357	5,143	177	687	126,884	775	1,959	10,731	61	66	13,592
Kentucky	24,522	37,097	1,866	482	795	64,761	3,116	2,826	8,791	74	160	14,967
Louisiana	13,183	27,968	2,209	19	647	44,026	3,511	4,740	9,120	16	7	17,394
Maine	7,399	366	11,739	277	126	19,907	967	—	1,990	45	7	3,009
Maryland	2,830	9,445	361	104	721	13,461	4,259	10,677	3,383	108	95	18,522
Massachusetts	563	—	5,535	246	21	6,365	2,448	—	27,067	389	85	29,990
Michigan.................	6,853	72,821	2,799	74	1,808	84,355	2,802	16,728	18,390	7	—	37,928
Minnesota...............	10,257	43,618	58,546	1,675	2,527	116,624	1,554	2,913	17,635	40	1	22,144
Mississippi..............	9,497	50,184	2,769	629	365	63,445	1,411	2,046	8,822	13	57	12,348
Missouri..................	30,761	69,685	5,485	22	1,001	106,954	3,132	3,669	17,764	6	41	24,611
Montana	10,492	42,594	1,175	4,235	12,322	70,819	512	—	3,651	—		4,164
Nebraska	9,539	60,496	17,040	114	160	87,349	410	757	5,274	7	71	6,519
Nevada	4,662	25,893	171	18	3,238	33,981	726	2,796	5,231	56	24	8,834
New Hampshire	3,186	—	7,732	18	149	11,084	717	—	4,242	88		5,047
New Jersey	352	1,569	3,010	565	174	5,670	1,988	5,081	25,722	446	134	33,371
New Mexico	11,062	36,256	770	189	10,776	59,052	1,013	2,862	5,491		34	9,400
New York................	9,617	15,577	38,574	670	300	64,738	5,429	4,657	38,750	824	408	50,069
North Carolina.........	59,244	—	2,356	885	3,075	65,560	20,324	—	20,173	22	227	40,745
North Dakota...........	7,171	10,190	66,037	19	1,546	84,962	223	12	1,890			2,125
Ohio......................	13,562	25,037	35,699	989	172	75,458	5,669	4,055	37,457	147	97	47,426
Oklahoma	10,851	75,396	7,549	980	13	94,789	1,413	2,724	13,625	121	—	17,883
Oregon	6,430	29,173	1,247	1,379	20,252	58,481	1,229	3,927	9,719	101	22	14,998
Pennsylvania............	28,796	23	43,498	829	771	73,918	10,974	278	34,299	520	50	46,121
Rhode Island............	374	—	953	6	25	1,358	716	—	3,847	38	68	4,668
South Carolina..........	29,796	25,929	421	192	1,559	57,896	11,577	4,697	2,128	—	3	18,405

See footnotes at end of table.

PUBLIC ROAD LENGTH MILES BY OWNERSHIP: 2014—Continued

State or other jurisdiction	Rural mileage						Urban mileage					
	State highway agency	County	Town, township & municipal (a)	Other jurisdictions (b)	Federal agency (c)	Total rural roads	State highway agency	County	Town, township & municipal (a)	Other jurisdictions (b)	Federal agency (c)	Total urban roads
South Dakota	7,508	34,978	32,912	1,409	2,406	79,212	258	285	2,566	253	2	3,364
Tennessee	10,321	49,985	4,189	384	1,174	66,054	3,576	7,803	18,099	11	18	29,507
Texas	64,729	127,693	11,007	6	2,037	205,472	15,694	19,268	72,196	365	600	108,123
Utah	4,701	23,472	1,765	516	4,339	34,793	1,178	770	9,404	-	8	11,361
Vermont	2,354	-	10,209	-	149	12,712	252	-	1,268	-	7	1,526
Virginia	46,766	29	498	42	2,077	49,412	11,746	1,689	11,305	21	724	25,485
Washington	5,511	32,745	1,629	8,370	8,217	56,473	1,544	6,423	16,455	90	433	24,944
West Virginia	31,326	-	637	247	834	33,045	3,082	-	2,598	35	0	5,715
Wisconsin	9,589	19,087	62,177	115	663	91,631	2,176	1,687	19,651	21	46	23,581
Wyoming	6,295	14,116	732	1,009	3,894	26,047	466	491	1,714	254	-	2,925
Dist. of Columbia	-	-	-	-	-	-	1,375	-	-	28	100	1,503
Puerto Rico (d)	1,024	-	2,057	-	22	3,104	3,558	-	10,009	0	7	13,574

Source: U.S. Department of Transportation, Federal Highway Administration, Highway Statistics, 2014.

Key:
— Not applicable or unavailable
(a) Prior to 1999, municipal was included with other jurisdictions.
(b) Includes state park, state toll, other state agency, other local agency and other roadways not identified by ownership.
(c) Roadways in federal parks, forests, and reservations that are not part of the state and local highway systems.
(d) 2009 data

Table 9.15a
NUMBER OF HIGHWAY BRIDGES AND STRUCTURAL CLASSIFICATION

State or other jurisdiction	Number of bridges	Number of structurally deficient bridges	Number of functionally obsolete bridges	Number of deficient bridges
Totals	611,845	58,791	84,124	142,915
Alabama	16,095	1,353	2,115	3,468
Alaska.................................	1,493	148	434	582
Arizona...............................	8,056	246	673	919
Arkansas..............................	12,853	845	2,012	2,857
California	25,318	2,009	4,419	6,428
Colorado..............................	8,624	521	851	1,372
Connecticut.........................	4,225	357	1,087	1,444
Delaware	875	48	129	177
Florida	12,198	251	1,760	2,011
Georgia................................	14,790	729	1,623	2,352
Hawaii..................................	1,142	60	435	495
Idaho...................................	4,369	385	450	835
Illinois.................................	26,674	2,244	1,959	4,203
Indiana................................	19,145	1,717	2,310	4,027
Iowa	24,242	5,025	1,071	6,096
Kansas	25,047	2,303	1,791	4,094
Kentucky	14,261	1,183	3,198	4,381
Louisiana.............................	13,012	1,838	1,959	3,797
Maine...................................	2,431	361	470	831
Maryland	5,313	306	1,078	1,384
Massachusetts	5,167	461	2,231	2,692
Michigan..............................	11,086	1,299	1,745	3,044
Minnesota............................	13,301	810	375	1,185
Mississippi	17,057	2,184	1,263	3,447
Missouri...............................	24,398	3,222	3,059	6,281
Montana	5,243	411	503	914
Nebraska..............................	15,341	2,474	984	3,458
Nevada.................................	1,919	35	219	254
New Hampshire	2,470	312	453	765
New Jersey	6,686	596	1,714	2,310
New Mexico	3,960	267	359	626
New York..............................	17,461	1,990	4,698	6,688
North Carolina.....................	18,124	2,085	3,089	5,174
North Dakota.......................	4,401	692	227	919
Ohio	27,104	1,893	4,278	6,171
Oklahoma............................	23,049	3,776	1,586	5,362
Oregon.................................	8,037	417	1,437	1,854
Pennsylvania	22,783	4,783	4,319	9,102
Rhode Island........................	766	178	251	429
South Carolina.....................	9,344	1,004	848	1,852
South Dakota.......................	5,866	1,156	232	1,388
Tennessee	20,106	1,026	2,607	3,633
Texas...................................	53,209	1,008	8,928	9,936
Utah....................................	3,019	95	386	481
Vermont...............................	2,749	190	658	848
Virginia...............................	13,884	1,063	2,517	3,580
Washington..........................	8,158	385	1,719	2,104
West Virginia.......................	7,215	1,092	1,462	2,554
Wisconsin	14,134	1,282	742	2,024
Wyoming	3,085	370	279	649
Dist. Of Columbia	254	10	164	174
Puerto Rico..........................	2,306	296	968	1,264

Source: Highway Statistics 2014, *https://www.fhwa.dot.gov/policyinformation/statistics/2014/*, updated February 18, 2016.

Table 9.16
APPORTIONMENT OF FEDERAL FUNDS ADMINISTERED BY THE FEDERAL HIGHWAY ADMINISTRATION FEDERAL-AID HIGHWAY PROGRAM APPORTIONMENTS PURSUANT TO THE HIGHWAY AND TRANSPORTATION FUNDING ACT OF 2014 FOR FISCAL YEAR 2015 (a)(b) (In thousands of dollars)

State or other jurisdiction	National highway system	Surface transportation program	Highway safety improvement program	Railway-highway crossings program	Congestion mitigation and air quality improvement program	Metropolitan planning program	Appalachian apportioned total
United States total..	22,397,992	10,302,373	2,241,318	220,000	2,315,856	320,461	37,798,000
Alabama	457,293	210,341	45,720	4,532	11,397	2,980	732,263
Alaska	289,366	133,099	30,698	1,100	27,493	2,198	483,955
Arizona	413,210	190,064	42,731	2,676	51,829	5,671	706,182
Arkansas	309,421	142,324	30,242	3,761	12,302	1,665	499,714
California	1,930,325	887,889	196,843	15,280	463,638	48,493	3,542,468
Colorado	298,581	137,338	29,642	3,169	42,256	5,126	516,113
Connecticut	277,794	127,777	29,221	1,306	44,200	4,473	484,771
Delaware	95,480	43,918	9,392	1,100	11,651	1,727	163,268
Florida	1,143,438	525,946	117,189	8,464	13,585	20,068	1,828,689
Georgia	745,815	343,052	74,083	7,875	67,884	7,530	1,246,239
Hawaii	96,315	44,490	9,484	1,100	10,349	1,695	163,244
Idaho	166,697	76,675	16,542	1,777	12,802	1,569	276,061
Illinois	793,513	364,991	76,854	10,345	109,991	16,538	1,372,231
Indiana	552,613	254,185	53,355	7,372	47,071	5,073	919,669
Iowa	293,745	135,114	27,055	5,225	11,285	1,922	474,345
Kansas	225,079	103,529	18,847	5,887	9,507	1,888	364,737
Kentucky	398,221	183,169	40,108	3,653	13,686	2,455	641,292
Louisiana	421,573	193,910	42,305	4,021	11,436	4,167	677,413
Maine	105,801	48,665	10,401	1,226	10,287	1,785	178,166
Maryland	331,012	152,255	34,084	2,291	53,645	6,721	580,007
Massachusetts	327,494	150,637	33,563	2,425	63,361	8,712	586,192
Michigan	593,834	273,145	57,856	7,400	73,936	10,037	1,016,208
Minnesota	377,579	173,675	35,537	5,955	32,196	4,432	629,373
Mississippi	289,164	133,007	28,398	3,378	11,208	1,648	466,804
Missouri	563,830	259,344	56,451	5,509	23,549	5,038	913,720
Montana	241,673	111,162	24,714	1,844	14,873	1,742	396,007
Nebraska	170,138	78,258	15,133	3,563	10,278	1,606	278,977
Nevada	200,497	92,222	20,933	1,100	32,539	3,182	350,473
New Hampshire	94,020	43,246	9,232	1,100	10,339	1,532	159,470
New Jersey	539,935	248,353	55,705	3,628	103,995	12,066	963,683
New Mexico	217,521	100,053	22,289	1,614	11,402	1,560	354,440
New York	899,994	413,969	92,734	6,167	183,021	24,204	1,620,088
North Carolina	605,016	278,288	60,040	6,445	51,204	5,638	1,006,630
North Dakota	144,907	66,653	12,299	3,625	10,510	1,627	239,622
Ohio	756,020	347,746	74,490	8,589	95,666	11,228	1,293,739
Oklahoma	380,848	175,178	36,668	5,183	11,744	2,506	612,128
Oregon	292,722	134,643	29,279	2,889	19,382	3,508	482,423
Pennsylvania	934,243	429,722	96,084	6,580	104,402	12,572	1,583,603
Rhode Island	126,675	58,266	12,820	1,100	10,421	1,800	211,082
South Carolina	401,416	184,639	39,889	4,222	13,087	3,053	646,307
South Dakota	164,488	75,659	15,754	2,322	12,255	1,713	272,191
Tennessee	492,999	226,764	49,464	4,712	37,007	4,659	815,605
Texas	2,002,345	921,016	202,537	17,501	164,476	23,722	3,331,597
Utah	203,267	93,496	20,769	1,568	12,908	3,141	335,149
Vermont	115,947	53,332	11,641	1,100	11,835	2,032	195,887
Virginia	586,030	269,556	59,937	4,462	54,867	7,328	982,180
Washington	388,755	178,815	38,657	4,063	36,917	7,097	654,305
West Virginia	258,519	118,911	26,423	1,985	14,309	1,650	421,798
Wisconsin	442,348	203,466	43,000	5,610	27,372	4,431	726,227
Wyoming	149,899	68,949	15,372	1,100	10,411	1,532	247,263
Dist. of Columbia ...	90,575	41,662	8,853	1,100	10,092	1,720	154,003

Source: U.S. Department of Transportation, Map 21 Funding Tables / FHWA Notice N4510.788, February 2016.

(a) Apportioned Federal-aid highway program funds authorized for FY 2015 pursuant to The Highway and Transportation Funding Act of 2014
(b) Shows the State-by-State, program-by-program apportionment amounts, before post-apportionment set-asides, before penalties, and before sequestration) available for FY 2015.

"Stepping Up" to Beat the Mental Health Crisis in U.S. Jails

By Risë Haneberg and Karen Watts

Over the last 40 years, local jails have increasingly become de facto psychiatric treatment facilities for the millions of people with mental illnesses and substance use disorders who become involved with the local criminal justice system. Counties and states are at the breaking point, many without the resources or capacity to address this population's mental health needs while ensuring an appropriate criminal justice response and protecting public safety. The national Stepping Up movement offers state and local governments a roadmap for navigating the complicated process of addressing this urgent issue.

There was a time when news of there being more people with mental illnesses in local jails than inpatient treatment facilities in the United States would be shocking. Today, it's no surprise to hear that jails across the nation see an estimated 2 million people with serious mental illnesses each year[1]—almost three-quarters of whom also have substance use disorders[2]—or that the prevalence of people with serious mental illnesses in jails is three to six times higher than for the general population.[3] Once incarcerated, people with mental illnesses tend to stay longer in jail and upon release are at a higher risk of returning to jail than people without these illnesses.

"The United States has 5 percent of the world's population, but we have 25 percent of the world's prison population. In large part, that's because we have essentially criminalized mental illness," U.S. Sen. Al Franken (D-MN) has said. "Instead of pro-viding people with adequate access to mental health treatment, we let them fall through the cracks and languish in jail."

The human toll—and the cost to taxpayers—is staggering. Jails spend two to three times more on adults with mental illnesses that require intervention than on people without those needs,[4] yet often do not see improvements in recidivism or recovery. Despite counties' and states' tremendous efforts to address this problem, they are often thwarted by significant obstacles, such as coordinating the efforts of multiple systems and operating with minimal resources. Meanwhile, large numbers of people with mental illnesses continue to cycle through the criminal justice system, often resulting in tragic outcomes, missed opportunities to link them to treatment, inefficient use of funding and failure to improve public safety.

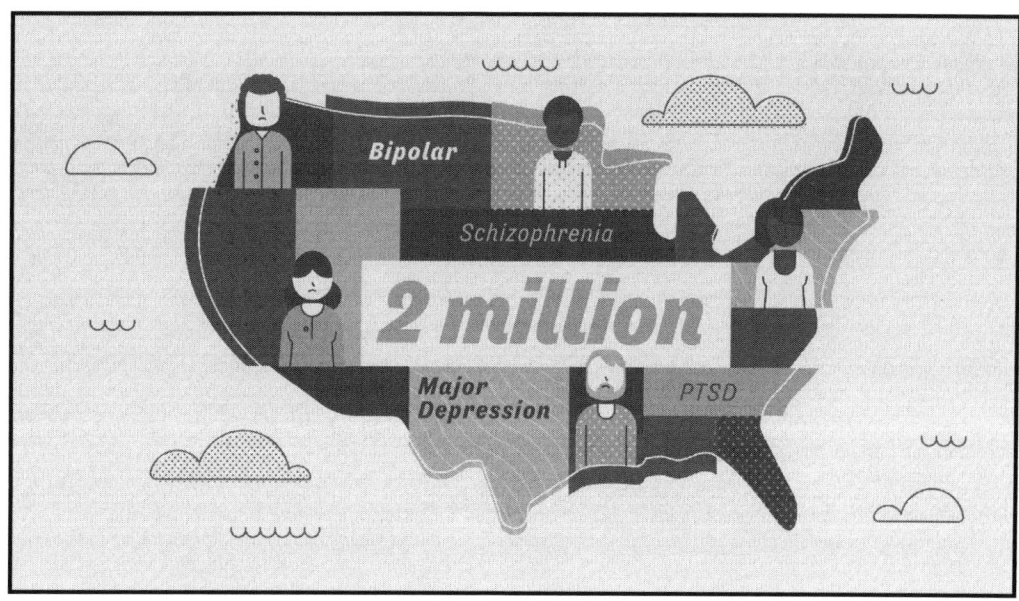

Recognizing the critical role local and state officials play in affecting change, in the spring of 2015, The Council of State Governments Justice Center, the National Association of Counties, and the American Psychiatric Association Foundation joined forces to launch *Stepping Up*, an unprecedented national initiative of county and state leaders to reduce the number of people with mental illnesses and substance use disorders in jails. With support from the U.S. Department of Justice's Bureau of Justice Assistance, the initiative builds on the many innovative and evidence-based practices being tested and implemented across the country and engages a diverse group of organizations with relevant expertise, including those representing the criminal justice system, such as sheriffs, jail administrators, judges, prosecutors, defense attorneys and community corrections professionals; and the behavioral health system, including mental health agency directors, treatment providers, and substance use experts, as well as people with mental illnesses and their families, and key advocacy groups, such as the National Alliance on Mental Illness.

The initiative challenges counties to "step up" and commit to addressing the factors contributing to the over-representation of people with mental illnesses in jails, and to using research-based strategies to drive those numbers down. It also provides counties with clear, practical direction for developing action plans to facilitate access to treatment and promote appropriate alternatives to jail. As of April 2016, 251 counties across 42 states had signed on to the initiative, and statewide *Stepping Up* efforts have been launched in California and Ohio.

At a May 2015 national *Stepping Up* kick-off event in Columbus, Ohio, mental health advocate and former Rhode Island Congressman Patrick Kennedy said, "*Stepping Up* is perfectly timed with all of these efforts in prevention, all of these efforts in treating the whole person. The only problem is, those efforts aren't being taken to scale. And that's why we're stepping up—to take the things we already know work to scale."

A growing number of law enforcement professionals—who are on the front lines of contact with people with mental illnesses in their communities—are being trained to interact with this population effectively, but lack the viable treatment options in the community that are necessary to divert many of these people from jail.

"People with mental illnesses who encounter the criminal justice system need treatment so they are put on a path to recovery," asserts Dr. Saul Levin, CEO and medical director of the American Psychiatric Association Foundation. "We need to improve the availability of community-based behavioral health care services and we, as providers, must take steps to deliver integrated substance abuse and mental health treatment."

In the months following the initiative's launch, participating counties established strategic plans to attack this challenge, specifically to reduce the number of people with mental illnesses in jail, to reduce their length of stay in jail, to increase the number of people connected to treatment in the community, and to reduce recidivism. At the summit, a draft document—"Reducing the Number of People with Mental Illness in Jail—Six Questions County Leaders Need to Ask"—was released to further guide counties in this work. The six questions are:

- Is our leadership committed?
- Do we conduct timely screening and assessments?
- Do we have baseline data?
- Have we conducted a comprehensive process analysis and inventory of services?
- Have we prioritized policy, practice and funding improvements?
- Do we track progress?

Jurisdictions that have undertaken this effort include Bexar County, Texas, where the jail is now screening everyone for mental illnesses at booking; New York City, where early diversion options have been implemented to provide treatment for people with mental illnesses and reduce their length of stay in jail; Franklin County, Ohio, where a jail liaison team has been established to ensure that people are being connected to treatment on release; and Salt Lake County, Utah, which has reoriented supervision caseloads to provide more intensive supervision to people with serious mental illnesses who are at a higher risk of reoffending.

At a national *Stepping Up* summit in April 2016, 50 select county teams from across the country met in Washington, D.C., to share and compare their strategies in this work, as well as to hear from experts in the field about how to better serve this population. The more than 250 summit participants want to radically reform how local criminal justice systems address the largest mental health crisis this country as ever seen. "We have to meet this urgent problem where it lives: in our local jails and in our communities. It's not about throwing money at the situation, it's about being smarter about recognizing who belongs in the criminal justice system and who doesn't, and redirecting resources to alternative responses that will better serve the individual and the community," said Chief Deputy Allen Jones of the Champaign County (IL) Sheriff's Office. Champaign, IL is also a current recipient of a Justice and Mental Health Collaboration Program (JMHCP) grant to develop a system-wide plan to reduce the number of people with mental illnesses in its jail.

The *Stepping Up* initiative has already seen a high level of commitment and effort to bring about real systemic change in counties and states across the country. Much of this work takes time, however, as well as a willingness to adopt new approaches and the ability to garner crucial funding. "We know more now than ever before what types of approaches can advance both recovery and recidivism-reduction goals," said Denise O'Donnell, director of the U.S. Department of Justice's Bureau of Justice Assistance. "[This initiative] leverages a broad range of strategies that improve diversion, community-based treatment, crisis intervention by police, specialty courts and supervision caseloads, reentry planning and other approaches that can be taken to the next level."

Notes

[1] Steadman, Henry, et al., "Prevalence of Serious Mental Illness among Jail Inmates." *Psychiatric Services* 60, no. 6 (2009): 761–765. Even greater numbers of people have mental illnesses that are not serious mental illnesses, but still require resource-intensive responses.

[2] Abram, Karen M., and Linda A. Teplin, "Co-occurring Disorders Among Mentally Ill Jail Detainees," *American Psychologist* 46, no. 10 (1991): 1036–1045.

[3] Steadman, Henry, et al., "Prevalence of Serious Mental Illness among Jail Inmates."

[4] See, e.g., Swanson, Jeffery, et al., *Costs of Criminal Justice Involvement in Connecticut: Final Report* (Durham: Duke University School of Medicine, 2011).

About the Authors

Risë Haneberg is a Senior Policy Advisor for The Council of State Governments Justice Center.

Karen Watts is the Deputy Director of Communications for The Council of State Governments Justice Center.

Table 9.17
PRISONERS UNDER JURISDICITON OF STATE OR FEDERAL CORRECTIONAL AUTHORITIES, BY SEX :
DECEMBER 31, 2013 and 2014

State or other jurisdiction	December 31, 2013 Population			December 31, 2014 Population			Percent change 2013–2014		
	Total	Male	Female	Total	Male	Female	Total	Male	Female
United States (a).........	1,576,950	1,465,592	111,358	1,561,525	1,448,564	112,961	-1.0	-1.2	1.4
Federal (b)...............	215,866	201,697	14,169	210,567	196,568	13,999	-2.5	-2.5	-1.2
State (a)...................	1,361,084	1,263,895	97,189	1,350,958	1,251,996	98,962	-0.7	-0.9	1.8
Alabama (c)...............	32,381	29,660	2,721	31,771	29,182	2,589	-1.9	-1.6	-4.9
Alaska (d) (e) (f)........	5,081	4,450	631	5,216	4,568	648	:	:	:
Arizona (c).................	41,177	37,402	3,775	42,259	38,295	3,964	2.6	2.4	5
Arkansas...................	17,235	15,904	1,331	17,874	16,476	1,398	3.7	3.6	5
California..................	135,981	129,684	6,297	136,088	129,706	6,382	0.1	0	1.3
Colorado....................	20,371	18,556	1,815	20,646	18,738	1,908	1.3	1	5.1
Connecticut (f) (g).......	17,563	16,328	1,235	16,636	15,510	1,126	:	:	:
Delaware (f).................	7,004	6,405	599	6,955	6,361	594	-0.7	-0.7	-0.8
Florida......................	103,028	95,757	7,271	102,870	95,567	7,303	-0.2	-0.2	0.4
Georgia.....................	54,004	50,445	3,559	52,949	49,438	3,511	-2	-2	-1.3
Hawaii (f)	5,632	4,972	660	5,866	5,198	668	4.2	4.5	1.2
Idaho (c)...................	8,242	7,176	1,066	8,117	7,080	1,037	-1.5	-1.3	-2.7
Illinois.....................	48,653	45,737	2,916	48,278	45,390	2,888	-0.8	-0.8	-1
Indiana	29,913	27,078	2,835	29,271	26,396	2,875	-2.1	-2.5	1.4
Iowa	8,697	7,983	714	8,838	8,086	752	1.6	1.3	5.3
Kansas (c) (g).............	9,763	9,026	737	9,663	8,881	782	:	:	:
Kentucky	21,030	18,717	2,313	21,657	19,084	2,573	3	2	11.2
Louisiana...................	39,299	37,071	2,228	38,030	35,955	2,075	-3.2	-3	-6.9
Maine........................	2,173	2,013	160	2,242	2,063	179	3.2	2.5	11.9
Maryland....................	21,335	20,410	925	21,011	20,100	911	-1.5	-1.5	-1.5
Massachusetts	10,950	10,143	807	10,713	9,985	728	-2.2	-1.6	-9.8
Michigan....................	43,759	41,700	2,059	43,390	41,267	2,123	-0.8	-1	3.1
Minnesota...................	10,289	9,566	723	10,637	9,901	736	3.4	3.5	1.8
Mississippi.................	21,969	20,352	1,617	18,793	17,448	1,345	-14.5	-14.3	-16.8
Missouri.....................	31,537	28,755	2,782	31,942	28,836	3,106	1.3	0.3	11.6
Montana	3,642	3,230	412	3,699	3,311	388	1.6	2.5	-5.8
Nebraska	5,026	4,656	370	5,441	5,001	440	8.3	7.4	18.9
Nevada (h)..................	/	/	/	12,537	11,452	1,085	:	:	:
New Hampshire	3,018	2,781	237	2,963	2,715	248	-1.8	-2.4	4.6
New Jersey	22,452	21,427	1,025	21,590	20,571	1,019	-3.8	-4	-0.6
New Mexico	6,931	6,276	655	7,021	6,348	673	1.3	1.1	2.7
New York....................	53,550	51,193	2,357	52,518	50,192	2,326	-1.9	-2	-1.3
North Carolina.............	36,922	34,430	2,492	37,096	34,455	2,641	0.5	0.1	6
North Dakota (c)........	1,576	1,419	157	1,718	1,514	204	9	6.7	29.9
Ohio.........................	51,729	47,579	4,150	51,519	47,311	4,208	-0.4	-0.6	1.4
Oklahoma	27,547	24,769	2,778	27,650	24,799	2,851	0.4	0.1	2.6
Oregon.......................	15,517	14,212	1,305	15,075	13,799	1,276	-2.8	-2.9	-2.2
Pennsylvania (c)..........	51,422	48,760	2,662	50,694	47,936	2,758	-1.4	-1.7	3.6
Rhode Island (f)	3,361	3,169	192	3,359	3,201	158	-0.1	1	-17.7
South Carolina.............	22,060	20,669	1,391	21,401	20,032	1,369	-3	-3.1	-1.6
South Dakota (c)	3,682	3,240	442	3,608	3,199	409	-2	-1.3	-7.5
Tennessee	28,521	26,069	2,452	28,769	26,160	2,609	0.9	0.3	6.4
Texas........................	168,280	154,450	13,830	166,043	151,717	14,326	-1.3	-1.8	3.6
Utah (c).....................	7,077	6,415	662	7,026	6,364	662	-0.7	-0.8	0
Vermont (f)	2,078	1,924	154	1,979	1,823	156	-4.8	-5.2	1.3
Virginia.....................	36,982	34,133	2,849	37,544	34,529	3,015	1.5	1.2	5.8
Washington..................	17,984	16,535	1,449	18,120	16,666	1,454	0.8	0.8	0.3
West Virginia...............	6,824	6,016	808	6,896	6,065	831	1.1	0.8	2.8
Wisconsin (g)	22,471	21,232	1,239	22,597	21,219	1,378	:	:	:
Wyoming.....................	2,310	2,050	260	2,383	2,106	277	3.2	2.7	6.5

Source: Bureau of Justice Statistics, National Prisoner Statistics, 2013–2014. *Prisoners in 2014* NCJ 248955

Note: Jurisdiction refers to the legal authority of state or federal correctional officials over a prisoner, regardless of where the prisoner is held.

Key:

/—Not reported. Estimated count added into state and U.S. jurisdictional totals.

:—Not calculated.

(a) Includes imputed counts for Alaska, which did not submit 2014 National Prisoner Statistics (NPS) Program data in time to be included in this report.

(b) Includes inmates held in nonsecure privately operated community corrections facilities and juveniles held in contract facilities.

(c) State has updated 2013 population counts.

(d) Alaska did not submit sex-specific jurisdiction counts in NPS in 2013.

(e) Alaska did not submit 2014 NPS data in time for this report, but jurisdiction totals were obtained from a report to the state legislature.

(f) Prisons and jails form one integrated system. Data include total jail and prison populations.

(g) State has changed reporting methodology, so 2014 counts are not comparable to those published for earlier years.

(h) Nevada did not submit 2013 NPS data in time for this report.

Table 9.18
NUMBER OF SENTENCED PRISONERS ADMITTED AND RELEASED FROM STATE AND FEDERAL JURISDICTION: 2013 and 2014

State or other jurisdiction	Admissions (a)					Releases (b)				
	2013 total	2014 total	Percent change 2013–14	2014 New court commitments (c)	2014 Parole violations (c)(d)	2013	2014	Percent change 2013–14	2013 Unconditional (e)(f)	2013 Conditional (e)(f)
United States (c)	629,962	626,644	-0.5	448,993	164,225	623,990	636,346	2	177,967	405,924
Federal (h)	53,664	50,865	-5.2	46,145	4,719	54,785	54,529	-0.5	53,245	431
State	576,298	575,779	-0.1	402,848	159,506	569,205	581,817	2.2	124,722	405,493
Alabama	11,265	10,912	-3.1	8,827	1,137	11,488	11,585	0.8	4,002	7,428
Alaska (c)(i)(j)(k)	3,906	3,846	-1.5	/	/	3,774	3,774	:	2,004	1,744
Arizona	13,538	14,439	6.7	11,989	2,449	12,931	13,513	4.5	2,229	10,300
Arkansas (l)	8,987	9,435	5	4,218	5,217	6,541	8,812	34.7	597	8,156
California (e)	38,295	38,765	1.2	33,497	5,268	36,353	38,559	6.1	/	/
Colorado	10,137	10,144	0.1	5,275	4,867	10,220	9,869	-3.4	1,585	8,152
Connecticut (i)(k)	5,492	5,487	:	4,532	879	5,177	5,968	:	2,936	3,017
Delaware (i)	3,142	3,349	6.6	2,711	610	4,251	4,222	-0.7	282	3,866
Florida	33,613	32,014	-4.8	30,984	114	32,855	32,754	-0.3	20,699	11,673
Georgia	19,478	18,455	-5.3	16,614	1,838	18,226	17,124	-6	7,157	9,847
Hawaii (i)	1,380	1,845	33.7	1,116	729	1,615	1,242	-23.1	306	635
Idaho	3,719	4,597	:	1,570	3,012	3,761	4,501	19.7	513	3,962
Illinois	30,959	29,678	-4.1	20,769	8,835	31,370	30,055	-4.2	4,406	25,517
Indiana	18,881	17,086	-9.5	14,442	2,347	17,959	17,866	-0.5	2,351	15,445
Iowa	5,159	5,153	-0.1	3,711	1,423	5,202	5,005	-3.8	1,121	3,835
Kansas	5,220	5,683	8.9	4,278	1,338	5,133	5,554	8.2	1,707	3,826
Kentucky	15,834	18,385	16.1	10,613	7,657	16,871	17,731	5.1	3,282	14,337
Louisiana	16,770	16,376	-2.3	11,639	4,737	17,646	17,882	1.3	1,267	16,472
Maine	929	774	-16.7	586	188	971	1,031	6.2	620	409
Maryland (m)	9,223	9,223	:	5,579	3,640	9,504	9,466	-0.4	1,306	8,075
Massachusetts	2,567	2,526	-1.6	2,268	224	2,855	2,654	-7	1,885	727
Michigan	14,417	13,834	-4	7,702	3,472	14,307	14,177	-0.9	873	11,155
Minnesota	7,687	7,866	2.3	5,095	2,771	7,808	7,642	-2.1	916	6,702
Mississippi	8,105	6,570	-18.9	5,075	1,367	8,201	9,442	15.1	1,173	8,162
Missouri	18,983	19,000	0.1	10,080	8,591	18,790	18,767	-0.1	1,525	17,115
Montana	2,382	2,448	2.8	1,888	560	2,347	2,387	1.7	272	2,099
Nebraska (h)	2,922	2,705	-7.4	2,130	495	2,583	2,284	-11.6	793	1,475
Nevada (h)	/	5,876	:	4,488	925	/	5,838	:	2,107	3,330
New Hampshire	1,659	1,611	-2.9	658	770	1,633	1,562	-4.3	68	1,489
New Jersey	9,802	9,257	-5.6	6,827	2,430	10,766	10,275	-4.6	6,095	3,931
New Mexico	3,567	3,798	6.5	2,500	1,298	3,345	3,515	5.1	918	2,573
New York	22,740	21,572	-5.1	13,054	8,427	23,382	22,927	-1.9	2,435	20,206
North Carolina	14,077	16,016	13.8	13,671	2,345	13,829	15,264	10.4	4,406	10,771
North Dakota	1,222	1,142	-6.5	953	189	1,173	1,046	-10.8	139	901
Ohio	21,998	22,189	0.9	18,301	3,868	21,235	22,399	5.5	10,062	12,209

See footnotes at end of table.

NUMBER OF SENTENCED PRISONERS ADMITTED AND RELEASED FROM STATE AND FEDERAL JURISDICTION: 2013 and 2014—Continued

State or other jurisdiction	Admissions (a)					Releases (b)				
	2013 total	2014 total	Percent change 2013–14	2014 New court commitments (c)	2014 Parole violations (c)(d)	2013	2014	Percent change 2013–14	2013 Unconditional (e)(f)	2013 Conditional (e)(f)
Oklahoma................	8,019	10,095	25.9	6,943	3,152	7,374	8,654	17.4	4,195	4,349
Oregon....................	5,532	5,330	-3.7	3,701	1,461	5,048	5,432	7.6	13	5,240
Pennsylvania	20,455	20,084	-1.8	10,252	9,074	19,632	20,555	4.7	3,268	17,138
Rhode Island (i).....	810	821	1.4	699	122	885	867	-2	638	224
South Carolina.......	6,431	6,283	-2.3	5,049	1,224	6,716	6,897	2.7	2,524	4,295
South Dakota (k).....	1,842	2,266	:	1,073	539	1,820	2,413	:	303	1,648
Tennessee	13,803	14,987	8.6	8,911	6,055	16,348	15,556	-4.8	4,974	10,500
Texas......................	76,488	75,571	-1.2	49,825	24,482	74,093	77,277	4.3	10,661	61,933
Utah........................	3,094	2,922	-5.6	1,596	1,326	2,988	2,979	-0.3	988	1,967
Vermont (i).............	1,858	1,715	-7.7	601	1,114	1,752	1,740	-0.7	274	1,459
Virginia..................	11,636	12,237	5.2	12,150	87	11,880	12,094	1.8	1,094	10,898
Washington.............	21,426	20,797	-2.9	7,642	13,153	20,861	20,898	0.2	2,233	18,609
West Virginia..........	3,573	3,544	-0.8	1,885	1,217	3,780	3,468	-8.3	1,004	2,001
Wisconsin (k)..........	7,343	6,134	:	4,129	1,975	5,475	5,433	:	252	5,105
Wyoming................	1,004	937	-6.7	752	185	895	862	-3.7	264	586

Source: Bureau of Justice Statistics, National Prisoner Statistics, 2013–2014.

Note: Counts based on prisoners with a sentence of more than 1 year.

Key:

/ – Not reported.

: – Not calculated.

(a) Excludes transfers, escapes, and those absent without leave (AWOL), and includes other conditional release violators, returns from appeal or bond, and other admissions.

(b) Excludes transfers, escapes, and those AWOL, and includes deaths, releases to appeal or bond, and other releases.

(c) U.S. and state totals by type of admission exclude counts for Alaska.

(d) Includes all conditional release violators returned to prison for either violations of conditions of release or for new crimes.

(e) U.S. and state totals by type of release exclude counts for California because the state was unable to report detailed information on releases.

(f) Includes expirations of sentence, commutations, and other unconditional releases.

(g) Includes releases to probation, supervised mandatory releases, and other unspecified conditional releases.

(h) The Sentencing Reform Act of 1984 eliminated the federal parole system but allowed courts to impose a term of supervised release after imprisonment as part of an inmate's sentence. Some persons with unconditional releases from the Bureau of Prisons may be released to community supervision.

(i) Prisons and jails form one integrated system. Data include total jail and prison populations.

(j) Alaska did not submit 2014 National Prisoner Statistics (NPS) admission or release data. Release-type data for 2014 were obtained from data submitted by Alaska to the National Corrections Reporting Program.

(k) Counts for 2014 admissions and releases are not comparable to earlier years due to a change in reporting methodology.

(l) Counts for 2014 admissions are not comparable to earlier years due to a change in reporting methodology.

(m) State did not submit admissions or release data in 2014 to NPS.

(n) State did not submit 2013 NPS data.

Table 9.19
PRISON FACILITY CAPACITY, CUSTODY POPULATION, AND PERCENT CAPACITY, DECEMBER 31, 2014

State	Type of capacity measure			Custody population	Custody population as a percent of:	
	Rated capacity	Operational capacity	Design capacity	Custody population	Lowest capacity (a)	Highest capacity (a)
Federal (b)	132,731	...	...	169,840	128	128
Alabama (c)	...	26,145	13,318	25,664	192.7	98.2
Alaska (d)	...	5,352	...	5,188	96.9	96.9
Arizona	37,681	42,961	37,681	35,181	93.4	81.9
Arkansas	15,450	15,429	15,529	15,250	98.8	98.2
California (c)	...	127,594	87,187	119,071	136.6	93.3
Colorado	...	14,502	14,502	16,687	115.1	115.1
Connecticut	/	/	/	16,167	/	/
Delaware (c)	5,649	5,210	4,161	6,730	161.7	119.1
Florida (e)	...	109,191	...	100,873	92.4	92.4
Georgia (e)	59,566	53,418	...	52,719	98.7	88.5
Hawaii	...	3,527	2,491	3,965	159.2	112.4
Idaho (c)(e)	7,010	6,858	6,858	7,497	109.3	106.9
Illinois	32,095	32,095	28,212	48,278	171.1	150.4
Indiana	...	30,517	...	28,073	92	92
Iowa (f)	7,276	7,276	7,276	8,209	112.8	112.8
Kansas	9,180	9,233	9,164	9,539	104.1	103.3
Kentucky	12,164	11,590	11,925	12,114	104.5	99.6
Louisiana (e)	18,121	15,686	16,764	18,710	119.3	103.3
Maine	2,339	2,133	2,339	2,199	103.1	94
Maryland (g)	...	23,465	...	21,236	90.5	90.5
Massachusetts	...	...	8,029	10,447	130.1	130.1
Michigan(c)(h)	44,919	43,939	...	43,359	98.7	96.5
Minnesota	...	9,454	...	9,576	101.3	101.3
Mississippi (e)	...	26,008	...	13,069	50.2	50.2
Missouri (c)	...	31,673	...	31,903	100.7	100.7
Montana	1,679	...	...	1,687	100.5	100.5
Nebraska (c)	...	4,094	3,275	5,228	159.6	127.7
Nevada	/	...	/	12,693	/	/
New Hampshire (c)	...	2,723	2,190	2,723	124.3	100
New Jersey	18,584	19,958	23,108	18,633	100.3	80.6
New Mexico	6,840	7,708	7,708	3,876	56.7	50.3
New York	51,480	51,868	50,960	52,362	102.8	101
North Carolina	...	43,815	37,503	37,348	99.6	85.2
North Dakota	1,479	1,479	1,479	1,325	89.6	89.6
Ohio	34,986	...	...	46,151	131.9	131.9
Oklahoma	16,529	18,638	16,529	19,126	115.7	102.6
Oregon	...	...	14,997	14,492	96.6	96.6
Pennsylvania	47,945	47,945	47,945	48,538	101.2	101.2
Rhode Island	3,989	3,774	3,973	3,133	83	78.5
South Carolina	...	23,269	...	20,948	90	90
South Dakota(c)	...	3,622	...	3,497	96.5	96.5
Tennessee	16,844	16,403	...	15,699	95.7	93.2
Texas (c)	159,583	153,331	159,583	139,870	91.2	87.7
Utah	...	7,191	7,431	5,307	73.8	71.4
Vermont	1,681	1,681	1,322	1,548	117.1	92.1
Virginia (i)	...	30,514	24,219	28,480	117.6	93.3
Washington(i)	...	16,744	...	17,180	102.6	102.6
West Virginia	4,647	5,923	5,097	5,867	126.3	99.1
Wisconsin (c)	...	22,918	17,181	22,572	131.4	98.5
Wyoming	2,288	2,288	2,407	2,114	92.4	87.8

Source: Bureau of Justice Statistics, National Prisoner Statistics, 2014, Prisoners in 2014 NCJ 248955.

Key:
...—Not available. Specific type of capacity is not measured by state.
/—Not reported.
(a) Population counts are based on the number of inmates held in custody of facilities operated by the jurisdiction. Excludes inmates held in local jails, other states, or private facilities unless noted.
(b) Due to differences in the dates when data were extracted, the federal custody count reported for the calculation of capacity excludes 3,990 inmates compared to the yearend custody data reported in the National Prisoner Statistics (NPS).
(c) State defines capacity in a way that differs from BJS's definition.
(d) Alaska did not report 2014 capacity or custody population data to NPS. Estimates derived from a report to the state legislature.
(e) Private facilities included in capacity and custody counts.
(f) Both capacity and custody counts exclude inmates in community-based work release facilities.
(g) State did not report 2014 capacity counts to NPS. Data are from 2013.
(h) Capacity counts include institution and camp net operating capacities and the population of community programs on December 31 because these programs do not have a fixed capacity.
(i) State has changed reporting methodology, so 2014 capacity counts are not comparable to those published for earlier years.

Table 9.20
ADULTS ON PROBATION: 2014

State or other jurisdiction	Probation population				Change during 2014		Number on probation per 100,000 adult residents, 12/31/2014 (a)
	1/1/2014 (a)	2014		12/31/2014 (a)			
		Entries	Exits		Number	Percent	
U.S. total	3,929,810	1,983,385	2,041,230	3,864,114	-65,696	-1.7	1,568
Federal	19,118	9,197	10,090	19,121	3	--	8
State	3,910,692	1,974,188	2,031,140	3,844,993	-65,699	-1.7	1,560
Alabama (b)	50,698	20,998	18,147	53,640	2,942	5.8	1,429
Alaska	7,167	5,342	5,432	7,077	-90	-1.3	1,287
Arizona	70,827	26,493	24,088	73,232	2,405	3.4	1,422
Arkansas	29,107	9,623	10,726	28,192	-915	-3.1	1,244
California	294,057	169,167	168,310	295,475	1,418	0.5	991
Colorado (b)	78,843	53,393	53,026	78,988	145	0.2	1,907
Connecticut	45,039	22,568	22,376	43,070	-1,969	-4.4	1,522
Delaware	16,039	12,227	12,601	15,665	-374	-2.3	2,131
Florida (b)	233,017	155,099	162,272	227,087	-5,930	-2.5	1,422
Georgia (c)	518,507	283,648	329,168	471,067	-47,440	-9.1	6,161
Hawaii	21,576	4,658	5,303	20,931	-645	-3	1,877
Idaho	33,062	13,212	12,848	33,450	388	1.2	2,761
Illinois	123,862	56,639	58,317	122,184	-1,678	-1.4	1,233
Indiana	123,261	78,020	82,707	118,574	-4,687	-3.8	2,356
Iowa	29,301	16,335	15,707	29,929	628	2.1	1,252
Kansas	16,446	21,050	21,168	16,328	-118	-0.7	746
Kentucky	53,350	26,728	25,971	54,107	757	1.4	1,587
Louisiana	41,761	13,658	14,440	40,979	-782	-1.9	1,155
Maine	6,710	3,195	3,335	6,570	-140	-2.1	612
Maryland	81,304	40,585	42,350	79,539	-1,765	-2.2	1,713
Massachusetts	67,784	77,736	77,246	68,274	490	0.7	1,269
Michigan (b)	179,567	98,486	96,451	180,583	1,016	0.6	2,343
Minnesota	98,267	48,033	48,639	97,661	-606	-0.6	2,330
Mississippi	31,675	9,959	6,583	34,398	2,723	8.6	1,517
Missouri	51,197	25,376	29,270	47,303	-3,894	-7.6	1,009
Montana (b)	8,362	4,171	3,889	8,621	259	3.1	1,075
Nebraska	13,545	9,108	9,812	12,940	-605	-4.5	911
Nevada	12,102	5,201	5,276	12,027	-75	-0.6	548
New Hampshire	3,994	2,736	2,820	3,910	-84	-2.1	368
New Jersey	112,598	41,600	38,300	115,898	3,300	2.9	1,667
New Mexico (b)	16,690	6,773	6,829	16,060	-630	-3.8	1,013
New York	107,730	27,984	31,460	104,254	-3,476	-3.2	670
North Carolina	94,437	54,086	56,718	90,918	-3,519	-3.7	1,181
North Dakota	4,947	3,944	3,306	5,585	638	12.9	967
Ohio (b)	243,282	119,293	121,913	238,915	-4,367	-1.8	2,660
Oklahoma	27,208	11,605	10,245	28,568	1,360	5	972
Oregon	36,957	14,454	13,488	37,923	966	2.6	1,212
Pennsylvania	171,970	100,272	95,505	176,737	4,767	2.8	1,748
Rhode Island (b)	22,988	**	**	23,595	607	2.6	2,793
South Carolina	35,300	13,652	13,856	35,096	-204	-0.6	931
South Dakota	6,262	3,674	3,133	6,803	541	8.6	1,054
Tennessee	65,751	24,133	26,802	62,950	-2,801	-4.3	1,239
Texas	398,607	150,244	160,750	388,101	-10,506	-2.6	1,938
Utah	11,188	6,090	5,295	11,983	795	7.1	583
Vermont	5,791	3,306	3,435	5,662	-129	-2.2	1,120
Virginia	54,020	28,465	28,648	54,966	946	1.8	848
Washington (b)	89,199	43,876	34,658	94,112	4,913	5.5	1,713
West Virginia (b)	7,174	**	882	7,174	/	:	488
Wisconsin (b)	46,140	**	**	46,212	72	0.2	1,034
Wyoming	4,984	2,627	2,415	5,196	212	4.3	1,165
Dist. of Columbia	7,042	4,666	5,224	6,484	-558	-7.9	1,185

See footnotes at end of table.

ADULTS ON PROBATION: 2014— Continued

Source: Bureau of Justice Statistics, Annual Probation Survey, 2014. NCJ 249057.

Note: Counts based on most recent data and may differ from previously published statistics. Counts may not be actual as reporting agencies may provide estimates on some or all detailed data. Due to nonresponse or incomplete data, the probation population for some jurisdictions on December 31, 2014, does not equal the population on January 1, 2014, plus entries, minus exits. Reporting methods for some probation agencies changed over time and probation coverage was expanded in 1998 and 1999.

Key:
** — Not known.
: — Not calculated.
/ — Not reported.
(a) Detail may not sum to total due to rounding. Reflects reported data, excluding jurisdictions for which data were unavailable.
(b) Data for entries and exits were estimated for nonreporting agencies.
(c) Counts include private agency cases and may overstate the number of persons under supervision.

Table 9.21
ADULTS ON PAROLE: 2014

State or other jurisdiction	Parole population				Change during 2014		Number on parole per 100,000 adult residents, 12/31/14 (b)
		2014					
	1/1/14	Entries	Exits	12/31/2014 (a)	Number	Percent	
U.S. total	849,359	425,134	411,694	856,872	7,513	0.9	348
Federal	109,356	45,000	45,118	109,265	-91	-0.1	44
State	740,003	380,134	366,576	747,607	7,604	1	303
Alabama	7,884	2,475	2,262	8,097	213	2.7	216
Alaska	2,303	1,072	1,165	2,210	-93	-4	402
Arizona	7,636	11,779	11,913	7,502	-134	-1.8	146
Arkansas	21,589	9,459	8,910	21,743	154	0.7	959
California (c)(d)	89,527	21,157	18,546	87,104	-2,423	-2.7	292
Colorado	10,846	8,296	9,075	10,067	-779	-7.2	243
Connecticut	2,640	2,137	2,213	2,564	-76	-2.9	91
Delaware	657	507	488	676	19	2.9	92
Florida	4,683	6,166	6,330	4,519	-164	-3.5	28
Georgia	25,931	12,002	12,386	25,547	-384	-1.5	334
Hawaii	1,647	827	934	1,540	-107	-6.5	138
Idaho	3,851	2,318	1,952	4,217	366	9.5	348
Illinois	29,586	27,094	27,036	29,644	58	0.2	299
Indiana	10,340	8,554	9,413	9,481	-859	-8.3	188
Iowa	5,595	3,574	3,400	5,769	174	3.1	241
Kansas	4,065	3,628	3,642	4,051	-14	-0.3	185
Kentucky	14,019	9,207	6,497	16,729	2,710	19.3	491
Louisiana	27,615	16,716	14,712	29,619	2,004	7.3	835
Maine	22	0	1	21	-1	-4.5	2
Maryland	12,464	5,051	5,978	11,537	-927	-7.4	248
Massachusetts	2,106	2,514	2,671	1,949	-157	-7.5	36
Michigan	18,439	10,114	10,140	18,413	-26	-0.1	239
Minnesota	5,997	6,193	5,548	6,642	645	10.8	158
Mississippi	6,901	6,529	3,547	9,883	2,982	43.2	436
Missouri	19,402	13,842	14,749	18,495	-907	-4.7	395
Montana	1,020	601	527	1,094	74	7.3	136
Nebraska	1,235	1,500	1,668	1,067	-168	-13.6	75
Nevada	5,522	4,194	3,789	5,927	405	7.3	270
New Hampshire	2,256	1,489	1,360	2,385	129	5.7	224
New Jersey	14,918	5,871	5,900	14,889	-29	-0.2	214
New Mexico	2,132	1,062	939	2,255	123	5.8	142
New York	45,039	21,063	21,213	44,889	-150	-0.3	288
North Carolina	7,171	10,975	8,014	10,025	2,854	39.8	130
North Dakota	548	1,114	1,078	584	36	6.6	101
Ohio	16,797	8,210	7,686	17,321	524	3.1	193
Oklahoma	2,554	784	778	2,560	6	0.2	87
Oregon	23,088	9,559	8,683	23,964	876	3.8	766
Pennsylvania	103,802	65,246	64,419	104,629	827	0.8	1,035
Rhode Island	435	254	221	468	33	7.6	55
South Carolina	5,477	2,361	2,613	5,225	-252	-4.6	139
South Dakota	2,577	1,579	1,545	2,611	34	1.3	404
Tennessee	13,732	4,539	4,773	13,498	-234	-1.7	266
Texas	111,302	36,213	36,103	111,412	110	0.1	556
Utah	3,265	1,964	1,917	3,312	47	1.4	161
Vermont	1,098	558	549	1,107	9	0.8	219
Virginia	1,800	446	515	1,732	-68	-3.8	27
Washington	9,500	5,515	4,789	9,880	380	4	180
West Virginia	2,553	1,977	1,781	2,749	196	7.7	187
Wisconsin (c)	20,083	**	**	20,010	-73	-0.4	448
Wyoming	753	513	551	715	-38	-5	160
District of Columbia	5,601	1,336	1,657	5,280	-321	-5.7	965

See footnotes at end of table.

ADULTS ON PAROLE: 2014—Continued

Source: Bureau of Justice Statistics, Annual Parole Survey, 2014. *Probation and Parole in the United States, 2014* NCJ 249057.

Note: Counts based on most recent data and may differ from previously published statistics. See Methodology. Counts may not be actual as reporting agencies may provide estimates on some or all detailed data. Due to nonresponse or incomplete data, the parole population for some jurisdictions on December 31, 2014, does not equal the population on January 1, 2014, plus entries, minus exits.

Key:
** — Not known.

(a) Detail may not sum to total due to rounding. Reflects reported data, excluding jurisdictions for which data were unavailable.

(b) Computed using the estimated U.S. adult resident population in each jurisdiction on January 1, 2015.

(c) Data for entries and exits were estimated for nonreporting agencies.

(d) Includes post-release community supervision and mandatory supervision parolees: 41,947 on January 1, 2014; and 21,157 entries, 18,546 exits, and 46,575 on December 31, 2014.

Table 9.22
CAPITAL PUNISHMENT

State or other jurisdiction	Capital offenses by state	Prisoners under sentence of death	Method of execution
Alabama	Intentional murder with 18 aggravating factors (Ala. Stat. Ann. 13A-5-40(a)(1)-(18)).	201	Electrocution or lethal injection
Alaska...........................	...	...	...
Arizona........................	First-degree murder, including pre-meditated murder and felony murder, accompanied by at least 1 of 14 aggravating factors (A.R.S. § 13-703(F)).	124	Lethal gas or lethal injection (a)
Arkansas......................	Capital murder (Ark. Code Ann. 5-10-101) with a finding of at least 1 of 10 aggravating circumstances; treason.	35	Lethal injection or electrocution (b)
California	First-degree murder with special circumstances; sabotage; train wrecking causing death; treason; perjury causing execution of an innocent person; fatal assault by a prisoner serving a life sentence.	746	Lethal injection
Colorado......................	First-degree murder with at least 1 of 17 aggravating factors; first-degree kidnapping resulting in death; treason.	3	Lethal injection
Connecticut	... (c)	12	Lethal injection (c)
Delaware	First-degree murder (11 Del. C. §636) with at least 1 statutory aggravating circumstance. (11 Del. C. §4209).	17	Lethal injection (d) or hanging
Florida (e)	First-degree murder; felony murder; capital drug trafficking; capital sexual battery.	401	Electrocution or lethal injection
Georgia.........................	Murder with aggravating circumstances; kidnapping with bodily injury or ransom when the victim dies; aircraft hijacking; treason.	85	Lethal injection
Hawaii...........................	...	...	...
Idaho............................	First-degree murder with aggravating factors; first-degree kidnapping; perjury resulting in death.	11	Lethal injection
Illinois.........................	... (f)	0	...
Indiana.........................	Murder with 17 aggravating circumstances (IC 35-50-2-9).	14	Lethal injection or electrocution
Iowa	...	...	...
Kansas	Capital murder with 8 aggravating circumstances (KSA 21-3439, KSA 21-4625, KSA 21-4636).	9	Lethal injection
Kentucky	Capital murder with presence of at least one statutory aggravating circumstance; capital kidnapping (KRS 532.025).	34	Electrocution or lethal injection (g)
Louisiana (e)................	First-degree murder; treason (La. R.S. 14:30 and 14:113).	85	Lethal injection
Maine............................	...	...	...
Maryland	... (h)	...	(h)
Massachusetts	...	...	...
Michigan......................	...	...	...
Minnesota....................	...	...	...
Mississippi	Capital murder (Miss Code Ann. § 97-3-19(2)); aircraft piracy (Miss Code Ann. § 97-25-55(1)).	48	Lethal injection
Missouri.......................	First-degree murder (565.020 RSMO 2000).	33	Lethal injection or lethal gas
Montana (e)	Capital murder with 1 of 9 aggravating circumstances (Mont. Code Ann. § 46-18-303); aggravated kidnapping; felony murder; capital sexual intercourse without consent (Mont. Code Ann. § 45-5-503).	2	Lethal injection
Nebraska	... (s)	10	...
Nevada..........................	First-degree murder with at least 1 of 15 aggravating circumstances (NRS 200.030, 200.033, 200.035).	78	Lethal injection
New Hampshire	Murder committed in the course of rape, kidnapping, home invasion, drug crimes; killing of a police officer, judge, or prosecutor; murder for hire; murder by an inmate while serving a sentence of life without parole (RSA 630:1, RSA 630:5).	1	Lethal injection or hanging (i)
New Jersey	... (j)	...	...
New Mexico	... (k)	2	Lethal injection (k)
New York (l)	First-degree murder with 1 of 13 aggravating factors (NY Penal Law §125.27).	0	Lethal injection

See footnotes at end of table.

CAPITAL PUNISHMENT — Continued

State or other jurisdiction	Capital offenses by state	Prisoners under sentence of death	Method of execution
North Carolina.............	First-degree murder with the finding of at least 1 of 11 statutory aggravating circumstances. (NCGS §14-17).	157	Lethal injection
North Dakota...............	...	...	...
Ohio.............................	Aggravated murder with at least 1 of 10 aggravating circumstances (O.R.C. secs. 2903.01, 2929.02, and 2929.04).	145	Lethal injection
Oklahoma (e)...............	First-degree murder in conjunction with a finding of at least 1 of 8 statutorily-defined aggravating circumstances.	48	Electrocution, lethal injection or firing squad (m)
Oregon (n)	Aggravated murder (ORS 163.095-150).	36	Lethal injection
Pennsylvania	First-degree murder with 18 aggravating circumstances.	184	Lethal injection
Rhode Island................	...	...	...
South Carolina (e).......	Murder with 1 of 12 aggravating circumstances (§ 16-3-20(C)(a)).	44	Electrocution or lethal injection
South Dakota...............	First-degree murder with 1 of 10 aggravating circumstances.	3	Lethal injection
Tennessee	First-degree murder (Tenn. Code Ann. § 39-13-202)with 1 of 16 aggravating circumstances (Tenn. Code Ann. § 39-13-204).	73	Lethal injection or electrocution (o)
Texas (e).......................	Criminal homicide with 1 of 9 aggravating circumstances (TX Penal Code § 19.03).	271	Lethal injection
Utah..............................	Aggravated murder (76-5-202, Utah Code Annotated).	9	Lethal injection or firing squad (p)
Vermont........................	...	...	...
Virginia.........................	First-degree murder with 1 of 15 aggravating circumstances (VA Code § 18.2-31).	8	Electrocution or lethal injection
Washington...................	Aggravated first-degree murder.	9	Lethal injection or hanging
West Virginia................	...	...	...
Wisconsin	...	...	...
Wyoming	First-degree murder; murder during the commission of sexual assault, sexual abuse of a minor, arson, robbery, burglary, escape, resisting arrest, kidnapping, or abuse of a minor under 16 (W.S.A. § 6-2-101 (a)).	1	Lethal injection or lethal gas (q)
Dist. of Columbia	...	...	...
American Samoa	First-degree murder (ASC §46.3513). (p)	0	Hanging (r)
Guam	...	...	...
No. Marianas Islands...	...	...	...
Puerto Rico..................	...	...	...
U.S. Virgin Islands.......	...	...	...

Sources: The Council of State Governments' survey, January 2016; U.S. Department of Justice, Office of Justice programs, Bureau of Justice Statistics, Capital Punishment, 2014 — Statistical Tables, December 2014. The United States Supreme Court ruling in *Roper v. Simmons*, 543 U.S. 551 (2005) declared unconstitutional the imposition of the death penalty on persons under the age of 18. The United States Supreme Court ruling in *Atkins v. Virginia*, 536 U.S. 304 (2002) declared unconstitutional the imposition of the death penalty on mentally handicapped persons. The method of execution of Federal prisoners is lethal injection, pursuant to 28 CFR, Part 26. For offenses under the Violent Crime Control and Law Enforcement Act of 1994, the execution method is that of the State in which the conviction took place (18 U.S.C. 3596).

Key:
... — No capital punishment statute.

(a) Arizona authorizes lethal injection for persons sentenced after November 15, 1992; inmates sentenced before that date may select lethal injection or gas.

(b) Arkansas authorizes lethal injection for those whose offense occurred on or after July 4, 1983; inmates whose offense occurred before that date may select lethal injection or electrocution.

(c) On April 25, 2012, Connecticut Governor Dannel Malloy signed into law a bill (SB 280) repealing the state's death penalty. The law replaces the death penalty with a sentence of life without parole for future cases, and does not apply to those already sentenced to death. The Connecticut Supreme Court is currently considering whether the 11 inmates who remain on death row can still be executed.

(d) Delaware authorizes hanging if lethal injection is held to be unconstitutional by a court of competent jurisdiction.

(e) The United States Supreme Court struck a portion of the Louisiana capital statute on June 25, 2008 (*Kennedy v. Louisiana*, U.S. 128 S.Ct. 2641). The statute (La. Rev. Stat. Ann. § 14:42(D)(2)) allowing execution as a punishment for the rape of a minor when no murder had been committed had been ruled constitutionally permissible by the Louisiana Supreme Court. The U.S. Supreme Court found that since no national consensus existed for application of the death penalty in cases of rape where no murder had been committed, such laws constitute cruel and unusual punishment under the Eighth and Fourteenth Amendments. The ruling affects laws passed in Florida, Oklahoma, South Carolina, Texas, and Montana.

(f) Governor Pat Quinn signed a bill (SB 3539) on March 9, 2011 that abolishes the death penalty effective July 1, 2011. He commuted all death sentences to life without parole.

(g) Kentucky authorizes lethal injection for persons sentenced on or after March 31, 1998; inmates sentenced before that date may select lethal injection or electrocution.

(h) On May 2, 2013, Governor Martin O'Malley signed into law a bill (SB 276) that abolishes the death penalty for future crimes. Gov. O'Malley announced on December 31, 2014, that he would commute the sentences of the four remaining death-row inmates to life in prison without the possibility of parole.

(i) New Hampshire authorizes hanging only if lethal injection cannot be given.

(j) New Jersey repealed its death penalty statute in 2007.

(k) Governor Bill Richardson signed a bill in March of 2009 abolishing the death penalty. The law is not retroactive and leaves two inmates on death row.

(l) The New York Court of Appeals has held that a portion of New York's death penalty sentencing statute (CPL 400.27) was unconstitutional (*People v. Taylor*, 9 N.Y.3d 129 (2007)). As a result, no defendants can be sentenced to death until the legislature corrects the errors in this statute. Efforts to restore the statute have been voted down.

(m) Oklahoma authorizes electrocution if lethal injection is held to be unconstitutional, and firing squad if both lethal injection and electrocution are held to be unconstitutional.

(n) In November 2011, Governor John Kitzhaber placed a moratorium on all executions in Oregon.

(o) Tennessee authorizes lethal injection for those whose capital offense occurred after December 31, 1998; those who committed the offense before that date may select electrocution by written waiver.

(p) Authorizes firing squad if lethal injection is held unconstitutional. Inmates who selected execution by firing squad prior to May 3, 2004, may still be entitled to execution by that method.

(q) Wyoming authorizes lethal gas if lethal injection is ever held to be unconstitutional.

(r) The last execution was in the 1920s.

(s) LB 268 banned the death penalty in Nebraska on May 27, 2015. Gov. Pete Ricketts vetoed the bill on May 26, 2015 and the law was sent back to the legislature. The Senate overturned the veto by 30-to-19 on May 27, 2015, resulting in Nebraska becoming the 19th state to eliminate the death penalty. The law is subject for removal once again as the Nebraska Death Penalty Repeal Referendum is on the November 8, 2016, ballot as a veto referendum.

Global Markets and Resources to Reach Them

By Jack Cobb and Andy Karellas

Looking to the global marketplace for economic development and paying attention to export and import trends is no longer an option for state policymakers—it is a necessity.

Less than 5 percent of the world's population lives in the United States, which means that over 95 percent of the potential customer base for American businesses lives beyond our borders. While the U.S. does hold a disproportional 20 percent of global purchasing power, our businesses can only truly succeed if they find ways to tap into consumers abroad. Unfortunately, as of 2014, only 11.7 million jobs in the U.S. were built directly on exports.[1] In addition, foreign-owned companies employ 6.1 million Americans with an additional 2.4 million employed in these firms' supply, distribution and other indirectly supported jobs.[2] Jobs from both exporting and foreign direct investment, or FDI, account for only 14 percent of the total U.S. workforce.

Looking to the global marketplace for economic development and paying attention to export and import trends is no longer an option for state policymakers—it is a necessity. As the U.S. continues to recover from the Great Recession and reinvent multiple industries, particularly manufacturing, international engagement on both exports and FDI must be a baseline activity for state trade promotion agencies rather than a best practice.

There was a time when the federal government was the gatekeeper for international trade policy and engagement. Today, states have more opportunities and resources at their disposal to drive trade policy, making it very important for state leaders to understand those policies—particularly how free trade agreements affect their state—as they craft their job growth strategies.

Free Trade Agreements

The federal government does play the predominate role in negotiating trade agreements. Although these can be contentious, free trade agreements are, at their essence, an agreement between two or more countries to abide by certain rules that affect trade and offer protections for investors and intellectual property rights. They are designed to reduce barriers to trade, protect U.S. competitive interests abroad and enhance the rule of law among partner countries.

The U.S. has completed negotiations on the Trans-Pacific Partnership agreement, or the TPP. TPP is a proposed multilateral trade agreement with 11 other nations: Australia, Brunei, Chile, Canada, Japan, Malaysia, Mexico, New Zealand, Peru, Singapore and Vietnam. These nations collectively have a market size of nearly 800 million consumers and account for nearly 40 percent of the world's Gross Domestic Product. In 2014, U.S. businesses exported roughly $726 billion in goods—or 45 percent of total U.S. material exports—and $178 billion in services to TPP countries.[3] These exports support an estimated 15.6 million direct and indirect American jobs while foreign direct investment in the U.S. from companies based in TPP countries was valued at $720 billion and employed 1.6 million people. The proposed TPP would remove 18,000 foreign taxes and barriers on U.S. goods and services in the other 11 partner nations. Under the terms of the Trade Promotion Authority, or TPA, signed into law in 2015, TPP must be reviewed and receive a vote in the House and Senate within 90 days of the agreement's formal submission by the President to the Congress.

In addition to projected increases in exports from the manufacturing and service sectors, food and agricultural exports in the U.S. reached $150 billion in 2014, supporting more than 1 million jobs. The U.S. Department of Agriculture released a report in April 2015 showing how a finalized trade agreement would benefit all 50 states. The report details the market potential for American-grown agricultural products, such as apples and wheat, in the other 11 participating TPP nations.

While the White House prepares for TPP's formal submission to Congress, a similarly ambitious trade deal with the European Union, the Transatlantic Trade and Investment Partnership, or TTIP, is in advanced stages of negotiation. This partnership would bring together two of the world's leading economies and estimates suggest the increase in bilateral trade could see a net employment gain of nearly 750,000 jobs for the U.S.

A report produced by the Atlantic Council, Bertelsmann Foundation and the British Embassy in Washington, D.C., "TTIP and the Fifty States: Jobs and Growth from Coast to Coast," suggests each state will not only see employment gains but that household income could rise by up to 13 percent per capita. According to this analysis, states that currently have the highest unemployment rates could benefit the most with better-than-average job growth. According to the report, states set to benefit the most from a transatlantic trade agreement in terms of employment are those that rank highest in population—California, Florida, New York and Texas. Some states—such as Georgia, North Carolina and Pennsylvania—will outperform the average in relation to population.

Federal and State Collaboration

Through the TPP and TTIP agreements, U.S. trade negotiators seek to eliminate foreign tariffs and reduce many of the nontariff barriers that prevent American small businesses from competing in foreign markets. A corresponding challenge is to increase the number of American businesses that export, as less than 1 percent of American companies export. According to the National Small Business Association, one of the largest challenges for small businesses is a lack of understanding about the export process. While small account for 98 percent of exporting firms, they represent only 34 percent of exports in terms of value.[4] By decreasing barriers, red tape, and overall cost of doing business, small businesses can greatly benefit from free trade agreements and realize the potential these markets offer.

A wide variety of federal departments and independent agencies provide direct assistance to firms looking to export their goods as well as indirect assistance through grants to state and local partners. Part of the challenge the National Small Business Association identified is navigating this web of resources. A step toward improving this situation has been made through the Trade Facilitation and Trade Enforcement Act of 2015, signed into law by President Barack Obama in February 2016. This Act requires the development of a framework to improve coordination between federal trade promotion offices and states in an effort to help small businesses navigate and utilize the various federal and state export promotion resources available to them.

As the federal government focuses on concluding large free trade agreements on the international front, the act's domestic work to improve federal-state coordination will ensure American businesses are better positioned to navigate the export process and capitalize as these new markets and opportunities become available.

While those efforts are underway, state trade offices vary in capability and resources as they work to develop their presence and services in a post-recession global economy. Many state offices assist American businesses by facilitating foreign trade missions and local events, providing counseling and training, as well as offering a number of technical services to identify suppliers and produce pricing analyses. The Trade Facilitation and Trade Enforcement Act also helps facilitate states' work in this area through the reauthorization of the State Trade and Export Promotion, or STEP, program.

State Trade and Export Promotion Program

Recently reauthorized and entering its fifth year, the Small Business Administration's STEP program competitively awards matching grants to state trade promotion agencies. These grants are designed to help states provide resources to small businesses so that they can more easily begin exporting and increase the value of their exports. The grants also support state efforts to help small businesses participate in, and organize their own, international trade missions. In its first four years the program awarded more than $84 million to state trade agencies, making possible the technical assistance and guidance necessary for small businesses to navigate and compete in markets around the world.

According to a survey conducted by the State International Development Organizations, or SIDO, more than 80 percent of state trade directors find STEP to be "very important" or "extremely important" to the success of their export promotion efforts. In fact, eight states report that the STEP program provides more than half of their total budget for export promotion activities. This impact is part of the reason the program was reauthorized by Congress through 2020.

According to Ann Pardalos, manager of the International Trade and Investment Office in Missouri's Department of Economic Development, "The STEP program was able to assist many states with extending their reach overseas and, in some instances, by establishing representative offices for the purpose of export and trade promotion." In 2012, Missouri received a STEP grant that was used to assist 155 small businesses engage in exporting. Overall, the STEP program has resulted in more than $26 million in export transactions for Missouri companies, while helping to create 155 new jobs.

Notes

[1] Office of the U.S. Trade Representative. "The Trans-Pacific Partnership: Economic Benefits" *https://ustr.gov/sites/default/files/TPP-Economic-Benefits-Fact-Sheet.pdf*

[2] Richards, Julian and Schaefer, Elizabeth. Jobs Attributable to Foreign Direct Investment in the United States. Office of Trade and Economic Analysis, International Trade Administration, U.S. Department of Commerce. February 2016

[3] Business Roundtable. "The Trans-Pacific Partnership Agreement: An Opportunity for America" *http://businessroundtable.org/sites/default/files/reports/TPP%20Overview%202016.pdf*

[4] "Exporting is Good for Your Bottom Line." International Trade Administration, U.S. Department of Commerce *http://www.trade.gov/cs/factsheet.asp*

About the Authors

Jack Cobb is a senior policy analyst at The Council of State Governments.

Andy Karellas is the director of federal affairs at The Council of State Governments, and also serves as director of the State International Development Organizations.

Chapter Ten

STATE PAGES

Table 10.1
OFFICIAL NAMES OF STATES AND JURISDICTIONS, CAPITALS, ZIP CODES AND CENTRAL SWITCHBOARDS

State or other jurisdiction	Name of state capitol (a)	Capital	Zip code	Area code	Central switchboard (b)
Alabama, State of	State House	Montgomery	36130	334	242-7100
Alaska, State of	State Capitol	Juneau	99801	907	465-2111
Arizona, State of	State Capitol	Phoenix	85007	602	542-4331
Arkansas, State of	State Capitol	Little Rock	72201	501	682-2345
California, State of	State Capitol	Sacramento	95814	916	445-2841
Colorado, State of	State Capitol	Denver	80203	303	866-2471
Connecticut, State of	State Capitol	Hartford	06106	860	566-4840
Delaware, State of	Legislative Hall	Dover	19903	302	744-4101
Florida, State of	The Capitol	Tallahassee	32399	850	717-9337
Georgia, State of	State Capitol	Atlanta	30334	404	656-1776
Hawaii, State of	State Capitol	Honolulu	96813	808	586-2211
Idaho, State of	State Capitol	Boise	83720	208	334-2100
Illinois, State of	State House	Springfield	62706	217	782-0244
Indiana, State of	Statehouse	Indianapolis	46204	317	232-4567
Iowa, State of	State Capitol	Des Moines	50319	515	281-5211
Kansas, State of	The Capitol	Topeka	66612	785	296-3232
Kentucky, Commonwealth of	State Capitol	Frankfort	40601	502	564-2611
Louisiana, State of	State Capitol	Baton Rouge	70804	225	342-7015
Maine, State of	State House	Augusta	04333	207	287-3531
Maryland, State of	State House	Annapolis	21401	410	974-3901
Massachusetts, Commonwealth of	State House	Boston	02133	617	725-4005
Michigan, State of	State Capitol	Lansing	48909	517	373-3400
Minnesota, State of	State Capitol	St. Paul	55155	651	201-3400
Mississippi, State of	State Capitol	Jackson	39215	601	359-3150
Missouri, State of	State Capitol	Jefferson City	65101	573	751-0290
Montana, State of	State Capitol	Helena	59620	406	444-3111
Nebraska, State of	State Capitol	Lincoln	68509	402	471-2244
Nevada, State of	State Capitol	Carson City	89701	775	684-5670
New Hampshire, State of	State House	Concord	03301	603	271-2121
New Jersey, State of	State House	Trenton	08625	609	292-6000
New Mexico, State of	State Capitol	Santa Fe	87501	505	476-2200
New York, State of	State Capitol	Albany	12224	518	474-8390
North Carolina, State of	State Capitol	Raleigh	27601	919	733-5811
North Dakota, State of	State Capitol	Bismarck	58505	701	328-2200
Ohio, State of	Statehouse	Columbus	43215	614	466-3555
Oklahoma, State of	State Capitol	Oklahoma City	73105	405	521-2342
Oregon, State of	State Capitol	Salem	97301	503	378-4582
Pennsylvania, Commonwealth of	The Capitol	Harrisburg	17120	717	787-2500
Rhode Island and Providence Plantations, State of	State House	Providence	02903	401	222-2080
South Carolina, State of	State House	Columbia	29201	803	734-2100
South Dakota, State of	State Capitol	Pierre	57501	605	773-3212
Tennessee, State of	State Capitol	Nashville	37243	615	741-2001
Texas, State of	State Capitol	Austin	78711	512	463-2000
Utah, State of	State Capitol	Salt Lake City	84114	801	538-1000
Vermont, State of	State House	Montpelier	05609	802	828-3333
Virginia, Commonwealth of	State Capitol	Richmond	23219	804	786-2211
Washington, State of	Legislative Building	Olympia	98504	360	902-4111
West Virginia, State of	State Capitol	Charleston	25305	304	558-2000
Wisconsin, State of	State Capitol	Madison	53702	608	266-1212
Wyoming, State of	State Capitol	Cheyenne	82002	307	777-7434
District of Columbia	John A. Wilson Building	...	20004	202	727-6300
American Samoa, Territory of	Maota Fono Complex	Pago Pago	96799	684	633-4116
Guam, Territory of	Congress Building	Hagatna	96910	671	472-8931
No. Mariana Islands, Commonwealth of	Capital Hill	Saipan	96950	670	664-2280
Puerto Rico, Commonwealth of	The Capitol	San Juan	00902	787	721-7000
U.S. Virgin Islands, Territory of	Legislature Building	Charlotte Amalie, St. Thomas	00802	340	774-0001

Key:
(a) In some instances the name is not official.
(b) Numbers generally come from an executive branch office, such as the office of the governor.

Table 10.2
HISTORICAL DATA ON THE STATES

State or other jurisdiction	Source of state lands	Date organized as territory	Date admitted to Union	Chronological order of admission to Union
Alabama	Mississippi Territory, 1798 (a)	March 3, 1817	Dec. 14, 1819	22
Alaska	Purchased from Russia, 1867	Aug. 24, 1912	Jan. 3, 1959	49
Arizona	Ceded by Mexico, 1848 (b)	Feb. 24, 1863	Feb. 14, 1912	48
Arkansas	Louisiana Purchase, 1803	March 2, 1819	June 15, 1836	25
California	Ceded by Mexico, 1848	(c)	Sept. 9, 1850	31
Colorado	Louisiana Purchase, 1803 (d)	Feb. 28, 1861	Aug. 1, 1876	38
Connecticut	Fundamental Orders, Jan. 14, 1638; Royal charter, April 23, 1662	(e)	Jan. 9, 1788 (f)	5
Delaware	Swedish charter, 1638; English charter, 1638	(e)	Dec. 7, 1787 (f)	1
Florida	Ceded by Spain, 1819	March 30, 1822	March 3, 1845	27
Georgia	Charter, 1732, from George II to Trustees for Establishing the Colony of Georgia	(e)	Jan. 2, 1788 (f)	4
Hawaii	Annexed, 1898	June 14, 1900	Aug. 21, 1959	50
Idaho	Treaty with Britain, 1846	March 4, 1863	July 3, 1890	43
Illinois	Northwest Territory, 1787	Feb. 3, 1809	Dec. 3, 1818	21
Indiana	Northwest Territory, 1787	May 7, 1800	Dec. 11, 1816	19
Iowa	Louisiana Purchase, 1803	June 12, 1838	Dec. 28, 1846	29
Kansas	Louisiana Purchase, 1803 (d)	May 30, 1854	Jan. 29, 1861	34
Kentucky	Part of Virginia until admitted as state	(c)	June 1, 1792	15
Louisiana	Louisiana Purchase, 1803 (g)	March 26, 1804	April 30, 1812	18
Maine	Part of Massachusetts until admitted as state	(c)	March 15, 1820	23
Maryland	Charter, 1632, from Charles I to Calvert	(e)	April 28, 1788 (f)	7
Massachusetts	Charter to Massachusetts Bay Company, 1629	(e)	Feb. 6, 1788 (f)	6
Michigan	Northwest Territory, 1787	Jan. 11, 1805	Jan. 26, 1837	26
Minnesota	Northwest Territory, 1787 (h)	March 3, 1849	May 11, 1858	32
Mississippi	Mississippi Territory (i)	April 7, 1798	Dec. 10, 1817	20
Missouri	Louisiana Purchase, 1803	June 4, 1812	Aug. 10, 1821	24
Montana	Louisiana Purchase, 1803 (j)	May 26, 1864	Nov. 8, 1889	41
Nebraska	Louisiana Purchase, 1803	May 30, 1854	March 1, 1867	37
Nevada	Ceded by Mexico, 1848	March 2, 1861	Oct. 31, 1864	36
New Hampshire	Grants from Council for New England, 1622 and 1629; made Royal province, 1679	(e)	June 21, 1788 (f)	9
New Jersey	Dutch settlement, 1618; English charter, 1664	(e)	Dec. 18, 1787 (f)	3
New Mexico	Ceded by Mexico, 1848 (b)	Sept. 9, 1850	Jan. 6, 1912	47
New York	Dutch settlement, 1623; English control, 1664	(e)	July 26, 1788 (f)	11
North Carolina	Charter, 1663, from Charles II	(e)	Nov. 21, 1789 (f)	12
North Dakota	Louisiana Purchase, 1803 (k)	March 2, 1861	Nov. 2, 1889	39
Ohio	Northwest Territory, 1787	May 7, 1800	March 1, 1803	17
Oklahoma	Louisiana Purchase, 1803	May 2, 1890	Nov. 16, 1907	46
Oregon	Settlement and treaty with Britain, 1846	Aug. 14, 1848	Feb. 14, 1859	33
Pennsylvania	Grant from Charles II to William Penn, 1681	(e)	Dec. 12, 1787 (f)	2
Rhode Island	Charter, 1663, from Charles II	(e)	May 29, 1790 (f)	13
South Carolina	Charter, 1663, from Charles II	(e)	May 23, 1788 (f)	8
South Dakota	Louisiana Purchase, 1803	March 2, 1861	Nov. 2, 1889	40
Tennessee	Part of North Carolina until land ceded to U.S. in 1789	June 8, 1790 (l)	June 1, 1796	1
Texas	Republic of Texas, 1845	(c)	Dec. 29, 1845	28
Utah	Ceded by Mexico, 1848	Sept. 9, 1850	Jan. 4, 1896	45
Vermont	From lands of New Hampshire and New York	(c)	March 4, 1791	14
Virginia	Charter, 1609, from James I to London Company	(e)	June 25, 1788 (f)	10
Washington	Oregon Territory, 1848	March 2, 1853	Nov. 11, 1889	42
West Virginia	Part of Virginia until admitted as state	(c)	June 20, 1863	35
Wisconsin	Northwest Territory, 1787	April 20, 1836	May 29, 1848	30
Wyoming	Louisiana Purchase, 1803 (d)(j)	July 25, 1868	July 10, 1890	44
Dist. of Columbia	Maryland (m)	…	…	…
American Samoa	…………………… Became a territory, 1900 ……………………			
Guam	Ceded by Spain, 1898	Aug. 1, 1950	…	…
No. Mariana Islands	…	March 24, 1976		
Puerto Rico	Ceded by Spain, 1898	…	July 25, 1952 (n)	…
U.S. Virgin Islands	…………… Purchased from Denmark, March 31, 1917 ……………			

See footnotes at end of table.

HISTORICAL DATA ON THE STATES — Continued

Key:

(a) By the Treaty of Paris, 1783, England gave up claim to the 13 original Colonies, and to all land within an area extending along the present Canadian to the Lake of the Woods, down the Mississippi River to the 31st parallel, east to the Chattahoochee, down that river to the mouth of Flint, border east to the source of the St. Mary's down that river to the ocean. The major part of Alabama was acquired by the Treaty of Paris, and the lower portion from Spain in 1813.

(b) Portion of land obtained by Gadsden Purchase, 1853.

(c) No territorial status before admission to Union.

(d) Portion of land ceded by Mexico, 1848.

(e) One of the original 13 Colonies.

(f) Date of ratification of U.S. Constitution.

(g) West Feliciana District (Baton Rouge) acquired from Spain, 1810; added to Louisiana, 1812.

(h) Portion of land obtained by Louisiana Purchase, 1803.

(i) See footnote (a). The lower portion of Mississippi also was acquired from Spain in 1813.

(j) Portion of land obtained from Oregon Territory, 1848.

(k) The northern portion of the Red River Valley was acquired by treaty with Great Britain in 1818.

(l) Date Southwest Territory (identical boundary as Tennessee's) was created.

(m) Area was originally 100 square miles, taken from Virginia and Maryland. Virginia's portion south of the Potomac was given back to that state in 1846. Site chosen in 1790, city incorporated 1802.

(n) On this date, Puerto Rico became a self-governing commonwealth by compact approved by the U.S. Congress and the voters of Puerto Rico as provided in U.S. Public Law 600 of 1950.

Table 10.3
STATE STATISTICS

State or other jurisdiction	Land area In square miles (2010)	Land area Rank in nation	Population (a) Size	Population (a) Rank in nation	Percentage change 2014 to 2015	Density per square mile	Rank in nation	Number of Representatives in Congress	Capital	Population (j)	Rank in state	Largest city	Population (j)
Alabama	50,645	28	4,858,979	24	2.6	96.0	27	7	Montgomery	200,481	2	Birmingham	212,247
Alaska	570,641	1	738,432	48	1.9	1.3	50	1	Juneau	32,406	2	Anchorage	301,010
Arizona	113,594	6	6,828,065	14	14.6	60.1	33	9	Phoenix	1,537,058	1	Phoenix	1,537,058
Arkansas	52,035	27	2,978,204	33	3.8	57.2	34	4	Little Rock	197,706	1	Little Rock	197,706
California	155,779	3	39,144,818	1	9.0	251.3	11	53	Sacramento	485,199	6	Los Angeles	3,928,864
Colorado	103,642	8	5,456,574	22	18.7	52.6	37	7	Denver	663,862	1	Denver	663,862
Connecticut	4,842	48	3,590,886	29	-1.1	741.6	4	5	Hartford	124,705	4	Bridgeport	147,612
Delaware	1,949	49	945,934	45	10.6	485.3	6	1	Dover	37,366	2	Wilmington	71,817
Florida	53,625	26	20,271,272	3	18.2	378.0	8	27	Tallahassee	188,107	7	Jacksonville	853,382
Georgia	57,513	21	10,214,860	8	11.6	177.6	17	14	Atlanta	456,002	1	Atlanta	456,002
Hawaii	6,423	47	1,431,603	40	8.0	222.9	13	2	Honolulu	350,399	1	Honolulu	350,399
Idaho	82,643	11	1,654,930	39	12.2	20.0	44	2	Boise	216,282	1	Boise	216,282
Illinois	55,519	24	12,859,995	5	-1.7	231.6	12	18	Springfield	116,809	6	Chicago	2,722,389
Indiana	35,826	38	6,619,680	16	3.3	184.8	16	9	Indianapolis	848,788	1	Indianapolis	848,788
Iowa	55,857	23	3,123,899	30	4.6	56.0	36	4	Des Moines	209,220	1	Des Moines	209,220
Kansas	81,759	13	2,911,641	34	3.1	35.6	41	4	Topeka	127,215	5	Wichita	388,413
Kentucky	39,486	37	4,425,092	26	2.8	112.1	22	6	Frankfort	25,557	13	Louisville (e)	612,780
Louisiana	43,204	33	4,670,724	25	4.7	108.1	23	6	Baton Rouge	228,895	2	New Orleans	384,320
Maine	30,843	39	1,329,328	42	-0.7	43.1	38	2	Augusta	18,705	7	Portland	66,666
Maryland	9,707	42	6,006,401	19	5.2	618.8	5	8	Annapolis	38,856	7	Baltimore	622,793
Massachusetts	7,800	45	6,794,422	15	5.8	871.1	3	9	Boston	655,884	1	Boston	655,884
Michigan	56,539	22	9,922,576	10	0.6	175.5	18	14	Lansing	114,620	6	Detroit	680,250
Minnesota	79,627	14	5,489,594	21	5.9	68.9	30	8	St. Paul	297,640	2	Minneapolis	407,207
Mississippi	46,923	31	2,992,333	32	-0.4	63.8	32	4	Jackson	171,155	1	Jackson	171,155
Missouri	68,742	18	6,083,672	18	3.3	88.5	28	8	Jefferson City	43,132	15	Kansas City	470,800
Montana	145,546	4	1,032,949	44	9.4	7.1	48	1	Helena	29,943	6	Billings	108,869
Nebraska	76,824	15	1,896,190	37	7.0	24.7	43	3	Lincoln	272,996	2	Omaha	446,599
Nevada	109,781	7	2,890,845	35	18.3	26.3	42	4	Carson City	54,522	6	Las Vegas	613,599
New Hampshire	8,953	44	1,330,608	41	2.0	148.6	21	2	Concord	42,444	3	Manchester	110,448
New Jersey	7,354	46	8,958,013	11	2.1	1,218.1	1	12	Trenton	84,034	6	Newark	280,579
New Mexico	121,298	5	2,085,109	36	-0.2	17.2	45	3	Santa Fe	70,297	4	Albuquerque	599,642
New York	47,126	30	19,795,791	4	2.4	420.1	7	27	Albany	98,566	6	New York City	8,491,079
North Carolina	48,618	29	10,042,802	9	10.3	206.6	15	13	Raleigh	439,896	2	Charlotte	809,958
North Dakota	69,001	17	756,927	47	22.6	11.0	47	1	Bismarck	68,896	2	Fargo	115,863
Ohio	40,861	35	11,613,423	7	1.4	284.2	10	16	Columbus	835,957	1	Columbus	835,957
Oklahoma	68,595	19	3,911,338	28	8.1	57.0	35	5	Oklahoma City	620,602	1	Oklahoma City	620,602
Oregon	95,988	10	4,028,977	27	14.4	42.0	39	5	Salem	161,637	2	Portland	619,360
Pennsylvania	44,743	32	12,802,503	6	0.7	286.1	9	18	Harrisburg	49,082	9	Philadelphia (f)	1,560,297
Rhode Island	1,034	50	1,056,298	43	1.3	1,021.6	2	2	Providence	179,154	1	Providence	179,154
South Carolina	30,061	40	4,896,146	23	13.8	162.9	19	7	Columbia	132,067	1	Columbia	132,067

See footnotes at end of table.

STATE STATISTICS — Continued

State or other jurisdiction	Land area — In square miles (2010)	Land area — Rank in nation	Population (a) — Size	Population (a) — Rank in nation	Percentage change 2014 to 2015	Density per square mile	Rank in nation	Number of Representatives in Congress	Capital	Population (j)	Rank in state	Largest city	Population (j)
South Dakota	75,811	16	858,469	46	6.0	11.3	46	1	Pierre	14,054	8	Sioux Falls	168,586
Tennessee	41,235	34	6,600,299	17	8.0	160.1	20	9	Nashville (g)	644,014	2	Memphis	656,861
Texas	261,232	2	27,469,114	2	18.0	105.2	26	36	Austin	912,791	4	Houston	2,239,558
Utah	82,170	12	2,995,919	31	17.3	36.5	40	4	Salt Lake City	190,884	1	Salt Lake City	190,884
Vermont	9,217	43	626,042	49	-1.2	68.0	31	1	Montpelier	7,671	6	Burlington	42,211
Virginia	39,490	36	8,382,993	12	6.6	212.3	14	11	Richmond	217,853	4	Virginia Beach	450,980
Washington	66,456	20	7,170,351	13	15.1	107.9	24	10	Olympia	49,218	24	Seattle	668,342
West Virginia	24,038	41	1,844,128	38	-2.5	76.7	29	3	Charleston	50,404	1	Charleston	50,404
Wisconsin	54,158	25	5,771,337	20	2.1	106.6	25	8	Madison	245,691	2	Milwaukee	599,642
Wyoming	97,093	9	586,107	50	3.1	6.0	49	1	Cheyenne	62,845	1	Cheyenne	62,845
Dist. of Columbia	61	...	672,228	...	-17.3	11,020.1	...	1 (h)	...	...	...	...	...
American Samoa (b)	77	...	55,519	...	-3.1 (c)	721.0	...	1 (h)	Pago Pago	3,656 (b)	3	Tafuna	9,756 (j)
Guam (b)	210	...	159,358	...	2.9 (c)	758.8	...	1 (h)	Hagatna (d)	1,051 (b)	13	Dededo (d)	44,943
No. Mariana Islands (b)	179	...	53,833	...	-22.2 (c)	300.7	...	1 (h)	Saipan (d)	48,220 (b)	1	Saipan (d)	48,220 (b)
Puerto Rico	3,424	...	3,474,182	...	-4.8	1,014.7	...	1 (i)	San Juan	395,326	1	San Juan	395,326
U.S. Virgin Islands (b)	134	...	106,405	...	-2.0 (c)	794.1	...	1 (h)	Charlotte Amalie, St. Thomas	18,481 (b)	1	Charlotte Amalie, St. Thomas	18,481 (b)

Source: U.S. Census Bureau, information available as of April 2016.

Key:
... — Not applicable
— — Not applicable
(a) July 1, 2014 Census Bureau estimates.
(b) 2010 Census Bureau counts.
(c) Population change calculations are from 2000–2010.
(d) Municipality.

(e) This city is part of a consolidated city-county government and is coextensive with Jefferson County.
(f) Philadelphia County and Philadelphia city are coextensive.
(g) This city is part of a consolidated city-county government and is coextensive with Davidson County.
(h) Represented by one non-voting House Delegate.
(i) Represented by one non-voting House Resident Commissioner.
(j) 2012 Census Bureau counts.
(k) 2012 Census Bureau counts.

Table 10.4
PERSONAL INCOME, POPULATION AND PER CAPITA PERSONAL INCOME, BY STATE, 2014–2015

State or other jurisdiction	Personal income (millions of dollars)				Population (thousands of persons) 2015 (a)	Per capita personal income (dollars)		
	2014	2015p	Percent change 2014–15	Rank of percent change 2014–15		2015p	Rank in U.S. 2015p	Percent of U.S. average 2015p
United States	14,683,147	15,324,109	4.4	-	321,467	47,669	-	100
Alabama	181,909	189,357	4.1	22	4,860	38,965	45	82
Alaska	39,793	41,312	3.8	28	739	55,940	6	117
Arizona	255,093	266,756	4.6	14	6,829	39,060	42	82
Arkansas	112,076	116,485	3.9	26	2,979	39,107	41	82
California	1,939,528	2,061,337	6.3	1	39,151	52,651	10	110
Colorado	261,735	275,107	5.1	7	5,457	50,410	14	106
Connecticut	233,293	240,519	3.1	39	3,591	66,972	1	140
Delaware	43,392	45,093	3.9	27	946	47,662	21	100
Florida	850,178	894,190	5.2	6	20,276	44,101	28	93
Georgia	393,594	414,274	5.3	5	10,216	40,551	40	85
Hawaii	65,348	68,373	4.6	13	1,432	47,753	20	100
Idaho	60,041	62,083	3.4	34	1,655	37,509	48	79
Illinois	613,672	636,281	3.7	30	12,862	49,471	16	104
Indiana	261,092	271,426	4.0	25	6,620	40,998	38	86
Iowa	139,625	140,501	0.6	48	3,124	44,971	26	94
Kansas	130,364	133,591	2.5	43	2,912	45,876	23	96
Kentucky	165,044	172,550	4.5	15	4,426	38,989	44	82
Louisiana	195,426	202,048	3.4	35	4,671	43,252	30	91
Maine	54,195	55,941	3.2	37	1,329	42,077	35	88
Maryland	323,778	337,174	4.1	21	6,007	56,127	5	118
Massachusetts	396,206	414,724	4.7	12	6,795	61,032	2	128
Michigan	403,726	421,044	4.3	18	9,924	42,427	33	89
Minnesota	267,389	277,483	3.8	29	5,490	50,541	13	106
Mississippi	103,091	106,075	2.9	42	2,993	35,444	50	74
Missouri	252,482	260,123	3.0	40	6,084	42,752	32	90
Montana	40,844	42,647	4.4	16	1,033	41,280	37	87
Nebraska	89,479	91,040	1.7	46	1,896	48,006	18	101
Nevada	115,672	121,973	5.4	4	2,891	42,185	34	88
New Hampshire	70,020	72,948	4.2	20	1,331	54,817	8	115
New Jersey	515,020	535,604	4.0	24	8,959	59,782	3	125
New Mexico	77,356	80,201	3.7	32	2,085	38,457	46	81
New York	1,098,103	1,142,485	4.0	23	19,799	57,705	4	121
North Carolina	389,513	408,364	4.8	9	10,044	40,656	39	85
North Dakota	41,265	41,166	-0.2	50	757	54,376	9	114
Ohio	489,695	504,993	3.1	38	11,615	43,478	29	91
Oklahoma	169,228	173,187	2.3	44	3,912	44,272	27	93
Oregon	163,653	173,170	5.8	2	4,030	42,974	31	90
Pennsylvania	609,679	629,710	3.3	36	12,804	49,180	17	103
Rhode Island	51,027	52,905	3.7	31	1,056	50,080	15	105
South Carolina	177,242	186,286	5.1	8	4,897	38,041	47	80

See footnotes at end of table.

PERSONAL INCOME, POPULATION AND PER CAPITA PERSONAL INCOME, BY STATE, 2014–2015—Continued

State or other jurisdiction	Personal income (millions of dollars)				Population (thousands of persons) 2015 (a)	Per capita personal income (dollars)		
	2014	2015p	Percent change 2014–15	Rank of percent change 2014–15		2015p	Rank in U.S. 2015p	Percent of U.S. average 2015p
South Dakota	38,631	38,637	0.0	49	859	45,002	25	94
Tennessee	264,965	277,707	4.8	10	6,601	42,069	36	88
Texas	1,231,085	1,284,262	4.3	17	27,474	46,745	22	98
Utah	110,842	116,992	5.5	3	2,996	39,045	43	82
Vermont	29,090	29,968	3.0	41	626	47,864	19	100
Virginia	419,185	437,111	4.3	19	8,384	52,136	11	109
Washington	350,322	366,790	4.7	11	7,171	51,146	12	107
West Virginia	66,857	68,329	2.2	45	1,844	37,047	49	78
Wisconsin	254,405	263,301	3.5	33	5,772	45,617	24	96
Wyoming	31,885	32,417	1.7	47	586	55,303	7	116
Dist. of Columbia	46,016	48,070	4.5	...	672	71,496	...	150

Source: U.S. Bureau of Economic Analysis and Bureau of the Census

Key:

p - Preliminary

(a) Census Bureau midyear population estimate. Estimates for 2014 reflect Census Bureau midyear state population estimates available as of December 2014. Estimates for 2015 are derived from the quarterly state population estimates produced by BEA based on unpublished Census Bureau data.

ALABAMA

Nickname..The Heart of Dixie
Motto..*Aldemus Jura Nostra Defendere*
(*We Dare Defend Our Rights*)
Flower ....Camellia
Bird.. Yellowhammer
Tree...Southern (Longleaf) Pine
Song...*Alabama*
Entered the Union...............................December 14, 1819
Capital..Montgomery

STATISTICS

Land Area (square miles)..50,645
Rank in Nation...28
Population..4,858,979
Rank in Nation...24
Density per square mile 96.0
Capital City...Montgomery
Population...200,481
Rank in State..2
Largest City...Birmingham
Population...212,247
Number of Representatives in Congress 7
Number of 2016 Electoral Votes...9
Number of County Governments...67
Number of Municipal Governments..................................461
Number of School Districts..132
Number of Special Districts 548

LEGISLATIVE BRANCH

Legislative Body ....Legislature

President of the Senate ....Lt. Gov. Kay Ivey
President Pro Tem of the Senate.........................Del Marsh
Secretary of the Senate .... D. Patrick Harris

Speaker of the House...................................Mike Hubbard
Speaker Pro Tem of the House ....Victor Gaston
Clerk of the House .... Jeff Woodard

2016 Regular Session.............................Feb. 2 – May 16, 2016
Number of Senatorial Districts 35
Number of Representative Districts 105

EXECUTIVE BRANCH

Governor .... Robert J. Bentley
Lieutenant Governor ....Kay Ivey
Secretary of State...John Merrill
Attorney General ....Luther Strange
Treasurer.. Young Boozer
Auditor.. Ronald Jones
(Examiner of Public Accounts)
State Comptroller ....Thomas L. White
(Comptroller)

Governor's Present Term............................ 1/2011 – 1/2019
Number of Elected Officials in the Executive Branch 7
Number of Members in the Cabinet 23

JUDICIAL BRANCH

Highest Court...Supreme Court
Supreme Court Chief Justice.............................Roy S. Moore
Number of Supreme Court Judges 9
Number of Intermediate Appellate Court Judges..............................10
Number of U.S. Court Districts...3
U.S. Circuit Court.. 11th Circuit

ALASKA

Nickname..The Last Frontier
Motto...*North to the Future*
Flower ....Forget-Me-Not
Bird.. Willow Ptarmigan
Tree...Sitka Spruce
Song...*Alaska's Flag*
Entered the Union...................................... January 3, 1959
Capital...Juneau

STATISTICS

Land Area (square miles)..570,641
Rank in Nation...1
Population..738,432
Rank in Nation...48
Density per square mile 1.3
Capital City..Juneau
Population...32,406
Rank in State..2
Largest City .... Anchorage
Population...301,010
Number of Representatives in Congress 1
Number of 2016 Electoral Votes...3
Number of Geographic Counties...16
(Number of Geographic Boroughs)
Number of County Governments..14
Number of Consolidated Governments..............................5
Number of Municipal Governments..................................148
Number of Special Districts 15

LEGISLATIVE BRANCH

Legislative Body ....Legislature

President of the Senate ....Kevin Meyer
Secretary of the Senate .... Liz Clark

Speaker of the House................................. Mike Chenault
Clerk of the House ....Crys Jones
(Chief)

2016 Regular Session...................Jan. 19 – April 17, 2016
Number of Senatorial Districts 20
Number of Representative Districts 40

EXECUTIVE BRANCH

Governor .... Bill Walker
Lieutenant Governor ....Byron Mallott
Attorney General ....Craig Richards
Treasurer... Pamela Leary
Auditor...Kris Curtis
State Comptroller .... Scot Arehart
(Director, Division of Finance)

Governor's Present Term.......................... 12/2014 – 12/2018
Number of Elected Officials in the Executive Branch.........................2
Number of Members in the Cabinet 19

JUDICIAL BRANCH

Highest Court..Supreme Court
Supreme Court Chief Justice.............................Dana Fabe
Number of Supreme Court Judges 5
Number of Intermediate Appellate Court Judges.............................3
Number of U.S. Court Districts...1
U.S. Circuit Court..9th Circuit

ARIZONA

Nickname	The Grand Canyon State
Motto	*Ditat Deus* (*God Enriches*)
Flower	Blossom of the Saguaro Cactus
Bird	Cactus Wren
Tree	Palo Verde
Song	*Arizona March Song* and *Arizona*
Entered the Union	February 14, 1912
Capital	Phoenix

STATISTICS

Land Area (square miles)	113,594
Rank in Nation	6
Population	6,828,065
Rank in Nation	14
Density per square mile	60.1
Capital City	Phoenix
Population	1,537,058
Rank in State	1
Largest City	Phoenix
Population	1,537,058
Number of Representatives in Congress	9
Number of 2016 Electoral Votes	11
Number of County Governments	15
Number of Municipal Governments	91
Number of School Districts	242
Number of Special Districts	326

LEGISLATIVE BRANCH

Legislative Body	Legislature
President of the Senate	Andy Biggs
President Pro Tem of the Senate	Sylvia Tenney Allen
Secretary of the Senate	Charmion Billington
Speaker of the House	David Gowan
Speaker Pro Tem of the House	Bob Robson
Clerk of the House	Jim Drake (Chief)
2016 Regular Session	Jan. 11 – April 23, 2016
Number of Senatorial Districts	30
Number of Representative Districts	30

EXECUTIVE BRANCH

Governor	Doug Ducey
Secretary of State	Michele Reagan
Attorney General	Mark Brnovich
Treasurer	Jeff DeWitt
Auditor	Debra K. Davenport
State Comptroller	D. Clark Partridge (Comptroller)
Governor's Present Term	1/2015 – 1/2019
Number of Elected Officials in the Executive Branch	11
Number of Members in the Cabinet	36

JUDICIAL BRANCH

Highest Court	Supreme Court
Supreme Court Chief Justice	W. Scott Bales
Number of Supreme Court Judges	5
Number of Intermediate Appellate Court Judges	22
Number of U.S. Court Districts	1
U.S. Circuit Court	9th Circuit

ARKANSAS

Nickname	The Natural State
Motto	*Regnat Populus* (*The People Rule*)
Flower	Apple Blossom
Bird	Mockingbird
Tree	Pine
Song	*Arkansas*
Entered the Union	June 15, 1836
Capital	Little Rock

STATISTICS

Land Area (square miles)	52,035
Rank in Nation	27
Population	2,978,204
Rank in Nation	33
Density per square mile	57.2
Capital City	Little Rock
Population	197,706
Rank in State	1
Largest City	Little Rock
Population	197,706
Number of Representatives in Congress	4
Number of 2016 Electoral Votes	6
Number of County Governments	75
Number of Municipal Governments	502
Number of School Districts	239
Number of Special Districts	740

LEGISLATIVE BRANCH

Legislative Body	General Assembly
President of the Senate	Lt. Gov. Tim Griffin
President Pro Tem of the Senate	Jonathan Dismang
Secretary of the Senate	Ann Cornwell
Speaker of the House	Jeremy Gillam
Speaker Pro Tem of the House	Jon Eubanks
Clerk of the House	Sherri Stacks (Chief)
2016 Regular Session	April 13 – May 12, 2016
Number of Senatorial Districts	35
Number of Representative Districts	100

EXECUTIVE BRANCH

Governor	Asa Hutchinson
Lieutenant Governor	Tim Griffin
Secretary of State	Mark Martin
Attorney General	Leslie Rutledge
Treasurer	Dennis Milligan
Auditor	Roger A. Norman
State Comptroller	Larry Walther (Director, Department of Finance & Administration)
Governor's Present Term	1/2015 – 1/2019
Number of Elected Officials in the Executive Branch	7
Number of Members in the Cabinet	44

JUDICIAL BRANCH

Highest Court	Supreme Court
Supreme Court Chief Justice	Howard Brill
Number of Supreme Court Judges	7
Number of Intermediate Appellate Court Judges	12
Number of U.S. Court Districts	2
U.S. Circuit Court	8th Circuit

CALIFORNIA

Nickname..The Golden State
Motto.. *Eureka (I Have Found It)*
Flower ....California Poppy
Bird...California Valley Quail
Tree.. California Redwood
Song...*I Love You, California*
Entered the Union....................................September 9, 1850
Capital...Sacramento

STATISTICS

Land Area (square miles)..155,779
Rank in Nation...3
Population..39,144,818
Rank in Nation...1
Density per square mile 251.3
Capital City...Sacramento
Population..485,199
Rank in State...6
Largest City .... Los Angeles
Population..3,928,864
Number of Representatives in Congress 53
Number of 2016 Electoral Votes.......................................55
Number of Geographic Counties......................................58
Number of County Governments..57
Number of Consolidated Governments...................................1
Number of Municipal Governments 482
Number of School Districts 1,025
Number of Special Districts 2,861

LEGISLATIVE BRANCH

Legislative Body ....Legislature

President of the Senate ....Lt. Gov. Gavin Newsom
President Pro Tem of the Senate....................................Kevin De Leon
Secretary of the Senate .... David Alvarez

Speaker of the House...Anthony Rendon
(Speaker of the Assembly)
Speaker Pro Tem of the House ....Kevin Mullin
(Speaker Pro Tem of the Assembly)
Clerk of the House .... E. Dotson Wilson
(Chief)

2016 Regular Session...................................Jan. 4 – Aug. 31, 2016
Number of Senatorial Districts 40
Number of Representative Districts 80

EXECUTIVE BRANCH

Governor ....Edmund G. Brown Jr.
Lieutenant Governor ....Gavin Newsom
Secretary of State...Alex Padilla
Attorney General ....Kamala Harris
Treasurer...John Chiang
Auditor... Elaine M. Howle
State Comptroller .... Betty Yee
(Controller)

Governor's Present Term...............................1/2011 – 1/2019
Number of Elected Officials in the Executive Branch.........................9
Number of Members in the Cabinet 11

JUDICIAL BRANCH

Highest Court...Supreme Court
Supreme Court Chief Justice.............................. Tani Cantil-Sakauye
Number of Supreme Court Judges 7
Number of Intermediate Appellate Court Judges...........................96
Number of U.S. Court Districts 4
U.S. Circuit Court...9th Circuit

COLORADO

Nickname...The Centennial State
Motto......................... *Nil Sine Numine (Nothing Without Providence)*
Flower ....Rocky Mountain Columbine
Bird...Lark Bunting
Tree.. Blue Spruce
Song...*Where the Columbines Grow*
Entered the Union... August 1, 1876
Capital.. Denver

STATISTICS

Land Area (square miles)...103,642
Rank in Nation...8
Population..5,456,574
Rank in Nation...22
Density per square mile 52.6
Capital City... Denver
Population..663,862
Rank in State...1
Largest City .... Denver
Population..663,862
Number of Representatives in Congress 7
Number of 2016 Electoral Votes...9
Number of Geographic Counties......................................64
Number of County Governments..62
Number of Consolidated Governments...................................2
Number of Municipal Governments 271
Number of School Districts 180
Number of Special Districts 2,392

LEGISLATIVE BRANCH

Legislative Body .... General Assembly

President of the Senate ....Bill Cadman
President Pro Tem of the Senate....................................Ellen Roberts
Secretary of the Senate .... Effie Ameen

Speaker of the House................................... Dickey Lee Hullinghorst
Speaker Pro Tem of the House ....Dan Pabon
Clerk of the House ....Marilyn Eddins
(Chief)

2016 Regular Session...............................Jan. 13 – May 11, 2016
Number of Senatorial Districts 35
Number of Representative Districts 65

EXECUTIVE BRANCH

Governor .... John Hickenlooper
Lieutenant Governor ....Joe Garcia
Secretary of State...Wayne Williams
Attorney General .... Cynthia Coffman
Treasurer.. Walker Stapleton
Auditor... Dianne E. Ray
State Comptroller .... Bob Jaros (Controller)

Governor's Present Term............................... 1/2011 – 1/2019
Number of Elected Officials in the Executive Branch.........................5
Number of Members in the Cabinet 21

JUDICIAL BRANCH

Highest Court..Supreme Court
Supreme Court Chief Justice...............................Nancy E. Rice
Number of Supreme Court Judges 7
Number of Intermediate Appellate Court Judges............................22
Number of U.S. Court Districts 1
U.S. Circuit Court... 10th Circuit

CONNECTICUT

Nickname	The Constitution State
Motto	*Qui Transtulit Sustinet (He Who Transplanted Still Sustains)*
Flower	Mountain Laurel
Bird	American Robin
Tree	White Oak
Song	*Yankee Doodle*
Entered the Union	January 9, 1788
Capital	Hartford

STATISTICS

Land Area (square miles)	4,842
Rank in Nation	48
Population	3,590,886
Rank in Nation	29
Density per square mile	741.6
Capital City	Hartford
Population	124,705
Rank in State	4
Largest City	Bridgeport
Population	147,612
Number of Representatives in Congress	5
Number of 2016 Electoral Votes	7
Number of Geographic Counties	8
Number of Municipal Governments	30
Number of School Districts	17
Number of Special Districts	447

LEGISLATIVE BRANCH

Legislative Body	General Assembly
President of the Senate	Lt. Gov. Nancy Wyman
President Pro Tem of the Senate	Martin Looney
Secretary of the Senate	Garey E. Coleman
	(Clerk of the Senate)
Speaker of the House	Brendan Sharkey
Speaker Pro Tem of the House	Linda Gentile, Bob Godfrey, Patricia Billie Miller, Bruce Morris, Linda Orange, Kevin Ryan, Peggy Sayers
	(Deputy Speakers of the House)
Clerk of the House	Martin Dunleavy
2016 Regular Session	Feb. 3 – May 4, 2016
Number of Senatorial Districts	36
Number of Representative Districts	151

EXECUTIVE BRANCH

Governor	Dan Malloy
Lieutenant Governor	Nancy Wyman
Secretary of State	Denise W. Merrill
Attorney General	George C. Jepsen
Treasurer	Denise L. Nappier
Auditor	John C. Geragosian and Robert M. Ward
State Comptroller	Kevin P. Lembo
	(Comptroller)
Governor's Present Term	1/2011 – 1/2019
Number of Elected Officials in the Executive Branch	6
Number of Members in the Cabinet	14

JUDICIAL BRANCH

Highest Court	Supreme Court
Supreme Court Chief Justice	Chase T. Rogers
Number of Supreme Court Judges	7
Number of Intermediate Appellate Court Judges	9
Number of U.S. Court Districts	1
U.S. Circuit Court	2nd Circuit

DELAWARE

Nickname	The First State
Motto	*Liberty and Independence*
Flower	Goldenrod
Bird	Blue Hen Chicken
Tree	American Holly
Song	*Our Delaware*
Entered the Union	December 7, 1787
Capital	Dover

STATISTICS

Land Area (square miles)	1,949
Rank in Nation	49
Population	945,934
Rank in Nation	45
Density per square mile	485.3
Capital City	Dover
Population	37,366
Rank in State	2
Largest City	Wilmington
Population	71,817
Number of Representatives in Congress	1
Number of 2016 Electoral Votes	3
Number of County Governments	3
Number of Municipal Governments	57
Number of School Districts	19
Number of Special Districts	260

LEGISLATIVE BRANCH

Legislative Body	General Assembly
President of the Senate	Vacant
President Pro Tem of the Senate	Patricia Blevins
Secretary of the Senate	Bernard J. Brady
Speaker of the House	Peter Schwartzkopf
Speaker Pro Tem of the House	Helene Keeley
Clerk of the House	Richard Puffer
2016 Regular Session	Jan. 12 – July 1, 2016
Number of Senatorial Districts	21
Number of Representative Districts	41

EXECUTIVE BRANCH

Governor	Jack Markell
Lieutenant Governor	Vacant
Secretary of State	Jeffrey Bullock
Attorney General	Matthew Denn
Treasurer	Ken Simpler
Auditor	R. Thomas Wagner
State Comptroller	Kristopher Knight
Governor's Present Term	1/2009 – 1/2017
Number of Elected Officials in the Executive Branch	6
Number of Members in the Cabinet	19

JUDICIAL BRANCH

Highest Court	Supreme Court
Supreme Court Chief Justice	Leo Strine Jr.
Number of Supreme Court Judges	5
Number of U.S. Court Districts	1
U.S. Circuit Court	3rd Circuit

FLORIDA

Nickname	The Sunshine State
Motto	*In God We Trust*
Flower	Orange Blossom
Bird	Mockingbird
Tree	Sabal Palmetto Palm
Song	*The Swannee River* (*Old Folks at Home*)
Entered the Union	March 3, 1845
Capital	Tallahassee

STATISTICS

Land Area (square miles)	53,625
Rank in Nation	26
Population	20,271,272
Rank in Nation	3
Density per square mile	378.0
Capital City	Tallahassee
Population	188,107
Rank in State	7
Largest City	Jacksonville
Population	853,382
Number of Representatives in Congress	27
Number of 2016 Electoral Votes	29
Number of Geographic Counties	67
Number of County Governments	66
Number of Consolidated Governments	1
Number of Municipal Governments	410
Number of School Districts	95
Number of Special Districts	1,079

LEGISLATIVE BRANCH

Legislative Body	Legislature
President of the Senate	Andy Gardiner
President Pro Tem of the Senate	Garrett Richter
Secretary of the Senate	Debbie Brown
Speaker of the House	Steve Crisafulli
Speaker Pro Tem of the House	Matt Hudson
Clerk of the House	Bob Ward
2016 Regular Session	Jan. 12 – March 11, 2016
Number of Senatorial Districts	40
Number of Representative Districts	120

EXECUTIVE BRANCH

Governor	Rick Scott
Lieutenant Governor	Carlos Lopez-Cantera
Secretary of State	Ken Detzner
Attorney General	Pam Bondi
Treasurer	Jeffrey H. Atwater (Chief Financial Officer)
Auditor	Sherrill Norman
Governor's Present Term	1/2011 – 1/2019
Number of Elected Officials in the Executive Branch	5
Number of Members in the Cabinet	4

JUDICIAL BRANCH

Highest Court	Supreme Court
Supreme Court Chief Justice	Jorge Labarga
Number of Supreme Court Judges	7
Number of Intermediate Appellate Court Judges	61
Number of U.S. Court Districts	3
U.S. Circuit Court	11th Circuit

GEORGIA

Nickname	The Empire State of the South
Motto	*Wisdom, Justice and Moderation*
Flower	Cherokee Rose
Bird	Brown Thrasher
Tree	Live Oak
Song	*Georgia on My Mind*
Entered the Union	January 2, 1788
Capital	Atlanta

STATISTICS

Land Area (square miles)	57,513
Rank in Nation	21
Population	10,214,860
Rank in Nation	8
Density per square mile	177.6
Capital City	Atlanta
Population	456,002
Rank in State	1
Largest City	Atlanta
Population	456,002
Number of Representatives in Congress	14
Number of 2016 Electoral Votes	16
Number of Geographic Counties	159
Number of County Governments	153
Number of Consolidated Governments	6
Number of Municipal Governments	535
Number of School Districts	180
Number of Special Districts	510

LEGISLATIVE BRANCH

Legislative Body	General Assembly
President of the Senate	Lt. Gov. Casey Cagle
President Pro Tem of the Senate	David Shafer
Secretary of the Senate	David A. Cook
Speaker of the House	David Ralston
Speaker Pro Tem of the House	Jan Jones
Clerk of the House	Bill Reilly
2016 Regular Session	Jan. 11 – March 24, 2016
Number of Senatorial Districts	56
Number of Representative Districts	180

EXECUTIVE BRANCH

Governor	Nathan Deal
Lieutenant Governor	Casey Cagle
Secretary of State	Brian Kemp
Attorney General	Sam Olens
Treasurer	Steve McCoy
Auditor	Greg Griffin
Comptroller	Alan Skelton
Governor's Present Term	1/2011 – 1/2019
Number of Elected Officials in the Executive Branch	8

JUDICIAL BRANCH

Highest Court	Supreme Court
Supreme Court Chief Justice	Hugh Thompson
Number of Supreme Court Judges	7
Number of Intermediate Appellate Court Judges	12
Number of U.S. Court Districts	3
U.S. Circuit Court	11th Circuit

HAWAII

Nickname... The Aloha State
Motto.. *Ua Mau Ke Ea O Ka Aina I Ka Pono*
(*The Life of the Land Is Perpetuated in Righteousness*)
Flower.. Native Yellow Hibiscus
Bird.. Hawaiian Goose (Nene)
Tree.. Kukue Tree (Candlenut)
Song...*Hawaii Ponoi*
Entered the Union.................................... August 21, 1959
Capital..Honolulu

STATISTICS

Land Area (square miles)..6,423
Rank in Nation..47
Population...1,431,603
Rank in Nation..40
Density per square mile..222.9
Capital City...Honolulu
Population..350,399
Rank in State...1
Largest City..Honolulu
Population..350,399
Number of Representatives in Congress 2
Number of 2016 Electoral Votes....................................4
Number of Geographic Counties......................................4
Number of County Governments.....................................3
Number of Consolidated Governments...........................1
Number of Municipal Governments 1
Number of Special Districts 17

LEGISLATIVE BRANCH

Legislative Body .... Legislature

President of the Senate .... Ronald Kouchi
President Pro Tem of the Senate.................... Will Espero
(Vice President of the Senate)
Secretary of the Senate ....Carol Taniguchi
(Chief Clerk of the Senate)

Speaker of the House...................................Joseph Souki
Speaker Pro Tem of the House ....John Mizuno
(Vice Speaker of the House)
Clerk of the House .... Brian Takashita
(Chief)

2016 Regular Session..............................Jan. 20 – May 5, 2016
Number of Senatorial Districts 25
Number of Representative Districts 51

EXECUTIVE BRANCH

Governor .... David Ige
Lieutenant Governor .... Shan Tsutsui
Attorney General .... Doug Chin
Treasurer .... Wesley Machida
(State Budget Director)
Auditor...Jan Yamane
State Comptroller....................................Douglas Murdock
(Comptroller)

Governor's Present Term............................ 12/2014 – 12/2018
Number of Elected Officials in the Executive Branch 2
Number of Members in the Cabinet 20

JUDICIAL BRANCH

Highest Court...Supreme Court
Supreme Court Chief Justice............................ Mark E. Recktenwald
Number of Supreme Court Judges 5
Number of Intermediate Appellate Court Judges................................6
Number of U.S. Court Districts...1
U.S. Circuit Court... 9th Circuit

IDAHO

Nickname.. The Gem State
Motto.................................... *Esto Perpetua* (*Let It Be Perpetual*)
Flower .... Syringa
Bird.. Mountain Bluebird
Tree... Western White Pine
Song..*Here We Have Idaho*
Entered the Union.....................................July 3, 1890
Capital..Boise

STATISTICS

Land Area (square miles)......................................82,643
Rank in Nation...11
Population...1,654,930
Rank in Nation..39
Density per square mile 20.0
Capital City..Boise
Population..216,282
Rank in State...1
Largest City...Boise
Population..216,282
Number of Representatives in Congress 2
Number of 2016 Electoral Votes....................................4
Number of County Governments...................................44
Number of Municipal Governments 200
Number of School Districts 118
Number of Special Districts 806

LEGISLATIVE BRANCH

Legislative Body .... Legislature

President of the Senate ....Lt. Gov. Brad Little
President Pro Tem of the Senate............................Brent Hill
Secretary of the Senate ....Jennifer Novak

Speaker of the House.. Scott Bedke
Clerk of the House ....Bonnie Alexander
(Chief)

2016 Regular Session......................Jan. 11 – March 25, 2016
Number of Senatorial Districts 35
Number of Representative Districts 35

EXECUTIVE BRANCH

Governor ....C.L "Butch" Otter
Lieutenant Governor .... Brad Little
Secretary of State.....................................Lawerence Denney
Attorney General ....Lawrence Wasden
Treasurer... Ron Crane
State Comptroller .... Brandon D. Woolf
(Controller)

Governor's Present Term.................................... 1/2007 – 1/2019
Number of Elected Officials in the Executive Branch 7
Number of Members in the Cabinet 39

JUDICIAL BRANCH

Highest Court...Supreme Court
Supreme Court Chief Justice...............................Jim Jones
Number of Supreme Court Judges 5
Number of Intermediate Appellate Court Judges..............................4
Number of U.S. Court Districts...11
U.S. Circuit Court... 9th Circuit

ILLINOIS

Nickname..The Prairie State
Motto.......................................*State Sovereignty—National Union*
Flower .... Native Violet
Bird .... Cardinal
Tree .... White Oak
Song...*Illinois*
Entered the Union......................................December 3, 1818
Capital ....Springfield

STATISTICS

Land Area (square miles).......................................55,519
Rank in Nation..24
Population...12,859,995
Rank in Nation..5
Density per square mile 231.6
Capital City...Springfield
Population...116,809
Rank in State...6
Largest City .... Chicago
Population...2,722,389
Number of Representatives in Congress 18
Number of 2016 Electoral Votes......................................20
Number of County Governments.....................................102
Number of Municipal Governments 1,298
Number of School Districts 905
Number of Special Districts 3,227

LEGISLATIVE BRANCH

Legislative Body .... General Assembly

President of the Senate ....John J. Cullerton
President Pro Tem of the Senate.......................Don Harmon
Secretary of the Senate ....Tim Anderson

Speaker of the House ....Michael J. Madigan
Clerk of the House .... Timothy Mapes

2016 Regular Session.............................Jan. 13 – May 31, 2016
Number of Senatorial Districts 59
Number of Representative Districts 118

EXECUTIVE BRANCH

Governor ....Bruce Rauner
Lieutenant Governor ....Evelyn Sanguinetti
Secretary of State..Jesse White
Attorney General ....Lisa Madigan
Treasurer...Mike Frerichs
Auditor..Frank Mautino
State Comptroller ....Leslie Munger
                                                      (Comptroller)

Governor's Present Term...........................1/2015 – 1/2019
Number of Elected Officials in the Executive Branch.........................6
Number of Members in the Cabinet 18

JUDICIAL BRANCH

Highest Court...Supreme Court
Supreme Court Chief Justice...........................Rita B. Garman
Number of Supreme Court Judges 7
Number of Intermediate Appellate Court Judges.............................54
Number of U.S. Court Districts 3
U.S. Circuit Court...7th Circuit

INDIANA

Nickname..The Hoosier State
Motto...*Crossroads of America*
Flower ....Peony
Bird .... Cardinal
Tree ....Tulip Poplar
Song...........................*On the Banks of the Wabash, Far Away*
Entered the Union....................................December 11, 1816
Capital .... Indianapolis

STATISTICS

Land Area (square miles)......................................35,826
Rank in Nation..38
Population...6,619,680
Rank in Nation..16
Density per square mile 184.8
Capital City...Indianapolis
Population...848,788
Rank in State...1
Largest City ....Indianapolis
Population...848,788
Number of Representatives in Congress 9
Number of 2016 Electoral Votes......................................11
Number of Geographic Counties.....................................92
Number of County Governments.....................................91
Number of Consolidated Governments....................................1
Number of Municipal Governments 569
Number of School Districts 291
Number of Special Districts 752

LEGISLATIVE BRANCH

Legislative Body .... General Assembly

President of the Senate .... Lt. Gov. Eric Holcomb
President Pro Tem of the Senate......................David C. Long
Secretary of the Senate ....Jennifer Mertz

Speaker of the House .... Brian C. Bosma
Speaker Pro Tem of the House ....William C. Friend
Clerk of the House .... M. Carolyn Spotts

2016 Regular Session.........................Jan. 5 – March 10, 2016
Number of Senatorial Districts 50
Number of Representative Districts 100

EXECUTIVE BRANCH

Governor ....Mike Pence
Lieutenant Governor ....Eric Holcomb
Secretary of State......................................Connie Lawson
Attorney General ....Greg Zoeller
Treasurer...Kelly Mitchell
Auditor... Paul D. Joyce
                                                   (State Examiner)
Comptroller ....Suzanne Crouch
                                                (Auditor of State)

Governor's Present Term...............................1/2013 – 1/2017
Number of Elected Officials in the Executive Branch.........................7
Number of Members in the Cabinet 16

JUDICIAL BRANCH

Highest Court...Supreme Court
Supreme Court Chief Justice...........................Loretta Rush
Number of Supreme Court Judges 5
Number of Intermediate Appellate Court Judges............................15
Number of U.S. Court Districts 2
U.S. Circuit Court...7th Circuit

IOWA

Nickname..The Hawkeye State
Motto.......... *Our Liberties We Prize and Our Rights We Will Maintain*
Flower .... Wild Rose
Bird...Eastern Goldfinch
Tree...Oak
Song..*The Song of Iowa*
Entered the Union...................................December 28, 1846
Capital ....Des Moines

STATISTICS

Land Area (square miles) 55,857
Rank in Nation...23
Population..3,123,899
Rank in Nation...30
Density per square mile 56.0
Capital City...Des Moines
Population..209,220
Rank in State..1
Largest City ....Des Moines
Population..209,220
Number of Representatives in Congress 4
Number of 2016 Electoral Votes..............................6
Number of County Governments..............................99
Number of Municipal Governments 947
Number of School Districts 366
Number of Special Districts 535

LEGISLATIVE BRANCH

Legislative Body .... General Assembly

President of the Senate .... Pam Jochum
President Pro Tem of the Senate......................................Steve Sodders
Secretary of the Senate ....Michael E. Marshall

Speaker of the House...Linda Upmeyer
Speaker Pro Tem of the House ....Matt Windschitl
Clerk of the House .... Carmine Boal
(Chief)

2016 Regular Session..Jan. 11 – April 19, 2016
Number of Senatorial Districts 50
Number of Representative Districts 100

EXECUTIVE BRANCH

Governor .... Terry Branstad
Lieutenant Governor ....Kim Reynolds
Secretary of State ....Paul Pate
Attorney General .... Thomas Miller
Treasurer.. Michael Fitzgerald
Auditor... Mary Mosiman
State Comptroller..Calvin McKelvogue
(Chief Operating Officer)

Governor's Present Term.. 1/2011 – 1/2019
Number of Elected Officials in the Executive Branch..........................7
Number of Members in the Cabinet...30

JUDICIAL BRANCH

Highest Court...Supreme Court
Supreme Court Chief Justice....................................... Mark S. Cady
Number of Supreme Court Judges 7
Number of Intermediate Appellate Court Judges 9
Number of U.S. Court Districts..2
U.S. Circuit Court.. 8th Circuit

KANSAS

Nickname... The Sunflower State
Motto.............. *Ad Astra per Aspera (To the Stars through Difficulties)*
Flower .... Wild Native Sunflower
Bird.. Western Meadowlark
Tree...Cottonwood
Song.. *Home on the Range*
Entered the Union....................................... January 29, 1861
Capital ....Topeka

STATISTICS

Land Area (square miles)................................81,759
Rank in Nation..13
Population..2,911,641
Rank in Nation..34
Density per square mile 35.7
Capital City...Topeka
Population..127,215
Rank in State..5
Largest City ....Wichita
Population..388,413
Number of Representatives in Congress 4
Number of 2016 Electoral Votes..............................6
Number of Geographic Counties.............................105
Number of County Governments..........................103
Number of Consolidated Governments............................2
Number of Municipal Governments.......................626
Number of School Districts............................306
Number of Special Districts 1,523

LEGISLATIVE BRANCH

Legislative Body ....Legislature

President of the Senate ....Susan Wagle
President Pro Tem of the Senate...Jeff King
(Vice President of the Senate)
Secretary of the Senate ....Corey Carnahan

Speaker of the House... Ray Merrick
Speaker Pro Tem of the House .... Peggy Mast
Clerk of the House ....Susan W. Kannarr
(Chief)

2016 Regular Session..Jan. 11 – April 27, 2016
Number of Senatorial Districts 40
Number of Representative Districts 125

EXECUTIVE BRANCH

Governor ....Sam Brownback
Lieutenant Governor ....Jeff Colyer
Secretary of State ....Kris Kobach
Attorney General .... Derek Schmidt
Treasurer..Ron Estes
Auditor... Scott Frank
State Comptroller..DeAnn Hill
(Director, Office of Management, Analysis & Standards)

Governor's Present Term.. 1/2011 – 1/2019
Number of Elected Officials in the Executive Branch..........................6
Number of Members in the Cabinet...14

JUDICIAL BRANCH

Highest Court...Supreme Court
Supreme Court Chief Justice.......................................Lawton R. Nuss
Number of Supreme Court Judges 7
Number of Intermediate Appellate Court Judges 14
Number of U.S. Court Districts..1
U.S. Circuit Court.. 10th Circuit

KENTUCKY

Nickname..The Bluegrass State
Motto...*United We Stand, Divided We Fall*
Flower ....Goldenrod
Bird ....Cardinal
Tree ....Tulip Poplar
Song..*My Old Kentucky Home*
Entered the Union...June 1, 1792
Capital..Frankfort

STATISTICS

Land Area (square miles) 39,486
Rank in Nation..37
Population...4,425,092
Rank in Nation..26
Density per square mile 112.1
Capital City...Frankfort
Population...25,557
Rank in State..13
Largest City ....Louisville
Population..612,780
Number of Representatives in Congress 6
Number of 2016 Electoral Votes...8
Number of Geographic Counties...120
Number of County Governments...118
Number of Consolidated Governments...2
Number of Municipal Governments 418
Number of School Districts 174
Number of Special Districts 628

LEGISLATIVE BRANCH

Legislative Body .... General Assembly

President of the Senate .... Robert Stivers
President Pro Tem of the Senate..................................David Givens
Secretary of the Senate ....Donna Holiday
(Chief Clerk of the Senate)

Speaker of the House.....................................Gregory Stumbo
Speaker Pro Tem of the House ....Jody Richards
Clerk of the House ....Jean Burgin
(Chief)

2016 Regular Session...............................Jan. 5 – April 12, 2016
Number of Senatorial Districts 38
Number of Representative Districts 100

EXECUTIVE BRANCH

Governor ....Matt Bevin
Lieutenant Governor ....Jenean Hampton
Secretary of State..Alison Lundergan Grimes
Attorney General ....Andy Beshear
Treasurer...Allison Ball
Auditor...Mike Harmon
State Comptroller ....Edgar C. Ross
(Controller)

Governor's Present Term........................... 12/2015 – 12/2019
Number of Elected Officials in the Executive Branch........................7
Number of Members in the Cabinet 13

JUDICIAL BRANCH

Highest Court...Supreme Court
Supreme Court Chief Justice............................John D. Minton
Number of Supreme Court Judges 7
Number of Intermediate Appellate Court Judges.............................14
Number of U.S. Court Districts..2
U.S. Circuit Court..6th Circuit

LOUISIANA

Nickname..The Pelican State
Motto...*Union, Justice and Confidence*
Flower ....Magnolia
Bird...Eastern Brown Pelican
Tree..Bald Cypress
Song...............................*Give Me Louisiana* and *You Are My Sunshine*
Entered the Union.. April 30, 1812
Capital.. Baton Rouge

STATISTICS

Land Area (square miles) 43,204
Rank in Nation..33
Population...4,670,724
Rank in Nation..25
Density per square mile 108.1
Capital City.. Baton Rouge
Population..228,895
Rank in State..2
Largest City ....New Orleans
Population..384,320
Number of Representatives in Congress 6
Number of 2016 Electoral Votes...8
Number of Geographic Counties...64
(Number of Geographic Parishes)
Number of Consolidated Governments...1
Number of Municipal Governments 304
Number of School Districts 69
Number of Special Districts 96

LEGISLATIVE BRANCH

Legislative Body ....Legislature

President of the Senate ....John Alario
President Pro Tem of the Senate.......................................Gerald Long
Secretary of the Senate ....Glenn Koepp

Speaker of the House...Taylor Barras
Speaker Pro Tem of the House ....Walt Leger III
Clerk of the House ....Alfred W. Speer

2016 Regular Session.. March 14 – June 6, 2016
Number of Senatorial Districts 39
Number of Representative Districts 105

EXECUTIVE BRANCH

Governor ....John Bel Edwards
Lieutenant Governor ....Billy Nungesser
Secretary of State...Tom Schedler
Attorney General ....Jeffrey Landry
Treasurer...John Neely Kennedy

Governor's Present Term... 1/2008 – 1/2016
Number of Elected Officials in the Executive Branch........................7
Number of Members in the Cabinet 16

JUDICIAL BRANCH

Highest Court...Supreme Court
Supreme Court Chief Justice...............................Bernette J. Johnson
Number of Supreme Court Judges 7
Number of Intermediate Appellate Court Judges.............................53
Number of U.S. Court Districts..3
U.S. Circuit Court..5th Circuit

MAINE

Nickname..The Pine Tree State
Motto.. *Dirigo* (*I Direct* or *I Lead*)
Flower .... White Pine Cone and Tassel
Bird..Chickadee
Tree...White Pine
Song..*State of Maine Song*
Entered the Union..................................... March 15, 1820
Capital .... Augusta

STATISTICS

Land Area (square miles)..30,843
Rank in Nation..39
Population..1,329,328
Rank in Nation..42
Density per square mile 43.1
Capital City... Augusta
Population..18,705
Rank in State...7
Largest City...Portland
Population...66,666
Number of Representatives in Congress 2
Number of 2016 Electoral Votes....................................4
Number of County Governments..16
Number of Municipal Governments.................................22
Number of School Districts...99
Number of Special Districts 237

LEGISLATIVE BRANCH

Legislative Body ....Legislature

President of the Senate ....Michael Thibodeau
Secretary of the Senate ....Heather J.R. Priest

Speaker of the House.....................................Mark Eves
Clerk of the House ....Robert B. Hunt

2016 Regular Session...................Jan. 6 – April 20, 2016
Number of Senatorial Districts 35
Number of Representative Districts 151

EXECUTIVE BRANCH

Governor ....Paul LePage
Secretary of State...Matthew Dunlap
Attorney General...Janet Mills
Treasurer...Teresa M. Hayes
Auditor...Pola Buckley
State Comptroller..Douglas Cotnoir
(Controller)

Governor's Present Term............................. 1//2011 – 1/2019
Number of Elected Officials in the Executive Branch.........................1
Number of Members in the Cabinet 16

JUDICIAL BRANCH

Highest Court...Supreme Judicial Court
Supreme Court Chief Justice................... Leigh Ingalls Saufley
Number of Supreme Court Judges 7
Number of U.S. Court Districts...1
U.S. Circuit Court..1st Circuit

MARYLAND

Nickname.......................................The Old Line State and Free State
Motto.................................... *Fatti Maschii, Parole Femine*
(*Manly Deeds, Womanly Words*)
Flower ....Black-eyed Susan
Bird...Baltimore Oriole
Tree.. White Oak
Song................................ *Maryland, My Maryland*
Entered the Union............................ April 28, 1788
Capital ....Annapolis

STATISTICS

Land Area (square miles).......................................9,707
Rank in Nation...42
Population...6,006,401
Rank in Nation...19
Density per square mile 618.8
Capital City...Annapolis
Population...38,856
Rank in State...7
Largest City..Baltimore
Population..622,793
Number of Representatives in Congress 8
Number of 2016 Electoral Votes.......................................10
Number of Geographic Counties.....................................24
Number of County Governments.....................................23
Number of County Equivalents.....................................1*
Number of Municipal Governments 157
Number of Special Districts 167

*The city of Baltimore is an Independent City and considered a
county equivalent.

LEGISLATIVE BRANCH

Legislative Body .... General Assembly

President of the Senate ....Thomas V. Mike Miller Jr.
President Pro Tem of the Senate.....................Nathaniel J. McFadden
Secretary of the Senate .... William B.C. Addison Jr.

Speaker of the House.......................... Michael Erin Busch
Speaker Pro Tem of the House .... Adrienne A. Jones
Clerk of the House ....Sylvia Siegert
(Chief)

2016 Regular Session.........................Jan. 13 – April 20, 2016
Number of Senatorial Districts 47
Number of Representative Districts 47

EXECUTIVE BRANCH

Governor ....Larry Hogan
Lieutenant Governor .... Boyd Rutherford
Secretary of State......................................John Wobensmith
Attorney General ....Brian Frosh
Treasurer...Nancy K. Kopp
Auditor..Thomas J. Barnickel
State Comptroller ....Peter Franchot
(Comptroller)

Governor's Present Term.......................... 1/2015 – 1/2019
Number of Elected Officials in the Executive Branch.........................4
Number of Members in the Cabinet 25

JUDICIAL BRANCH

Highest Court...Court of Appeals
Supreme Court Chief Justice..................Mary Ellen Barbara
Number of Supreme Court Judges 7
Number of Intermediate Appellate Court Judges..........................12
Number of U.S. Court Districts...1
U.S. Circuit Court..4th Circuit

MASSACHUSETTS

Nickname..The Bay State
Motto.......……………...... *Ense Petit Placidam Sub Libertate Quietem*
(*By the Sword We Seek Peace,but Peace Only under Liberty*)
Flower ....Mayflower (Epigaea repens)
Bird...Chickadee
Tree..American Elm
Song.. *All Hail to Massachusetts*
Entered the Union..February 6, 1788
Capital.. Boston

STATISTICS

Land Area (square miles)......................................7,800
Rank in Nation..45
Population...6,794,422
Rank in Nation..15
Density per square mile..871.1
Capital City.. Boston
Population...655,884
Rank in State...1
Largest City... Boston
Population...655,884
Number of Representatives in Congress 9
Number of 2016 Electoral Votes...............................11
Number of Geographic Counties.............................14*
Number of County Governments 5
Number of Consolidated Governments.........................2
Number of Municipal Governments 53
Number of School Districts 84
Number of Special Districts 417

*Seven counties have been abolished and are only geographic in nature.

LEGISLATIVE BRANCH

Legislative Body ....General Court

President of the Senate ....Stanley C. Rosenberg
President Pro Tem of the Senate........................Marc Pacheco
Secretary of the Senate ....William F. Welch
(Clerk of the Senate)

Speaker of the House...................................Robert A. DeLeo
Speaker Pro Tem of the House ....Patricia A. Haddad
Clerk of the House ....Steven T. James

2016 Regular Session......................... Jan. 6 – Dec. 31, 2016
Number of Senatorial Districts 40
Number of Representative Districts 160

EXECUTIVE BRANCH

Governor ....Charlie Baker
Lieutenant Governor ....Karyn Polito
Secretary of State.. William F. Galvin
(Secretary of the Commonwealth)
Attorney General ....Maura Healey
Treasurer...Deb Goldberg
(Treasurer & Receiver General)
Auditor..Suzanne Bump
State Comptroller ....Thomas Shack III
(Comptroller)

Governor's Present Term............................... 1/2007 – 1/2015
Number of Elected Officials in the Executive Branch.....................6
Number of Members in the Cabinet 10

JUDICIAL BRANCH

Highest Court...................................Supreme Judicial Court
Supreme Court Chief Justice.........................Ralph D. Gants
Number of Supreme Court Judges 7
Number of Intermediate Appellate Court Judges.........................28
Number of U.S. Court Districts..11
U.S. Circuit Court...1st Circuit

MICHIGAN

Nickname.. The Wolverine State
Motto...........................*Si Quaeris Peninsulam Amoenam Circumspice*
(*If You Seek a Pleasant Peninsula, Look About You*)
Flower ....Apple Blossom
Bird...Robin
Tree.. White Pine
Song...*Michigan, My Michigan*
Entered the Union.....................................January 26, 1837
Capital...Lansing

STATISTICS

Land Area (square miles)..56,539
Rank in Nation..22
Population...9,922,576
Rank in Nation..10
Density per square mile 175.5
Capital City..Lansing
Population...114,620
Rank in State...6
Largest City..Detroit
Population...680,250
Number of Representatives in Congress 14
Number of 2016 Electoral Votes...............................16
Number of County Governments 83
Number of Municipal Governments 533
Number of School Districts 576
Number of Special Districts 443

LEGISLATIVE BRANCH

Legislative Body ....Legislature

President of the Senate ....Lt. Gov. Brian Calley
President Pro Tem of the Senate...........................Tonya Schuitmaker
Secretary of the Senate ....Carol Morey Viventi

Speaker of the House....................................Kevin Cotter
Speaker Pro Tem of the House ....Tom Leonard
Clerk of the House ....Gary Randall

2016 Regular Session.................... Jan. 13 – Dec. 31, 2016
Number of Senatorial Districts 38
Number of Representative Districts 110

EXECUTIVE BRANCH

Governor ....Rick Snyder
Lieutenant Governor ....Brian Calley
Secretary of State.. Ruth Johnson
Attorney General .... Bill Schuette
Treasurer...Nick Khouri
Auditor..Doug Ringler
State Comptroller ....Michael J. Moody
(Director, Office of Financial Management)

Governor's Present Term............................... 1/2011 – 1/2019
Number of Elected Officials in the Executive Branch.....................5
Number of Members in the Cabinet 22

JUDICIAL BRANCH

Highest Court..Supreme Court
Supreme Court Chief Justice.................................. Robert P. Young Jr.
Number of Supreme Court Judges 7
Number of Intermediate Appellate Court Judges.............................28
Number of U.S. Court Districts..2
U.S. Circuit Court..6th Circuit

MINNESOTA

Nickname..The North Star State
Motto................................... *L'Etoile du Nord* (*The North Star*)
Flower ....Pink and White Lady-Slipper
Bird...Common Loon
Tree...Red Pine
Song..*Hail! Minnesota*
Entered the Union...................................May 11, 1858
Capital...St. Paul

STATISTICS

Land Area (square miles)................................79,627
Rank in Nation...14
Population..5,489,594
Rank in Nation...21
Density per square mile 68.9
Capital City...St. Paul
Population..297,640
Rank in State..2
Largest City...Minneapolis
Population..407,207
Number of Representatives in Congress 8
Number of 2016 Electoral Votes..........................10
Number of County Governments..........................87
Number of Municipal Governments....................853
Number of School Districts.................................338
Number of Special Districts.................................610

LEGISLATIVE BRANCH

Legislative Body ....Legislature

President of the Senate ....Sandra Pappas
President Pro Tem of the Senate.................Ann Rest
Secretary of the Senate ....JoAnne Zoff

Speaker of the House ....Kurt Daudt
Speaker Pro Tem of the House ....Tim O'Driscoll
Clerk of the House ....Al Mathiowetz
(Chief)

2016 Regular Session........................March 8 – May 23, 2016
Number of Senatorial Districts 67
Number of Representative Districts 67

EXECUTIVE BRANCH

Governor ....Mark Dayton
Lieutenant Governor ....Tina Smith
Secretary of State....................................Steve Simon
Attorney General ....Lori Swanson
Treasurer...Myron Frans
(Commissioner of Finance)
Auditor.. Rebecca Otto

Governor's Present Term...............1/2011 – 1/2019
Number of Elected Officials in the Executive Branch.........5
Number of Members in the Cabinet 25

JUDICIAL BRANCH

Highest Court..Supreme Court
Supreme Court Chief Justice............Lorie Skjerven Gildea
Number of Supreme Court Judges...........................7
Number of Intermediate Appellate Court Judges.............19
Number of U.S. Court Districts.............................1
U.S. Circuit Court...................................8th Circuit

MISSISSIPPI

Nickname..The Magnolia State
Motto..........................*Virtute et Armis* (*By Valor and Arms*)
Flower ....Magnolia
Bird..Mockingbird
Tree...Magnolia
Song...*Go, Mississippi*
Entered the Union............................December 10, 1817
Capital...Jackson

STATISTICS

Land Area (square miles)................................46,923
Rank in Nation...31
Population..2,992,333
Rank in Nation...32
Density per square mile 63.8
Capital City...Jackson
Population..171,155
Rank in State..1
Largest City..Jackson
Population..171,155
Number of Representatives in Congress 4
Number of 2016 Electoral Votes............................6
Number of County Governments..........................82
Number of Municipal Governments....................298
Number of School Districts.................................164
Number of Special Districts.................................439

LEGISLATIVE BRANCH

Legislative Body ....Legislature

President of the Senate ....Lt. Gov. Tate Reeves
President Pro Tem of the Senate............Terry Burton
Secretary of the Senate ....Liz Welch

Speaker of the House ....Philip Gunn
Speaker Pro Tem of the House ....Greg Snowden
Clerk of the House ....Andrew Ketchings

2016 Regular Session......................Jan. 5 – April 24, 2016
Number of Senatorial Districts 52
Number of Representative Districts 122

EXECUTIVE BRANCH

Governor ....Phil Bryant
Lieutenant Governor ....Tate Reeves
Secretary of State.........................Delbert Hosemann Jr.
Attorney General ....Jim Hood
Treasurer..Lynn Fitch
Auditor...Stacey Pickering
State Comptroller................................Mark Valentine
(Fiscal Management Director,
Department of Finance & Administration)

Governor's Present Term...............1/2012 – 1/2016
Number of Elected Officials in the Executive Branch.........8

JUDICIAL BRANCH

Highest Court..Supreme Court
Supreme Court Chief Justice............William L. Waller Jr.
Number of Supreme Court Judges...........................9
Number of Intermediate Appellate Court Judges.............10
Number of U.S. Court Districts.............................2
U.S. Circuit Court...................................5th Circuit

MISSOURI

Nickname..The Show Me State
Motto....................................... *Salus Populi Suprema Lex Esto*
(*The Welfare of the People Shall Be the Supreme Law*)
Flower .... White Hawthorn Blossom
Bird..Bluebird
Tree...Flowering Dogwood
Song...*Missouri Waltz*
Entered the Union...August 10, 1821
Capital .... Jefferson City

STATISTICS

Land Area (square miles)...68,742
Rank in Nation...18
Population..6,083,672
Rank in Nation...18
Density per square mile..88.5
Capital City... Jefferson City
Population..43,132
Rank in State...15
Largest City..Kansas City
Population..470,800
Number of Representatives in Congress 8
Number of 2016 Electoral Votes..................................10
Number of Geographic Counties..................................115
Number of County Governments..................................114
Number of County Equivalents.......................................1*
Number of Municipal Governments 954
Number of School Districts 534
Number of Special Districts 1,854

*The city of St. Louis is an Independent City and considered a
county equivalent.

LEGISLATIVE BRANCH

Legislative Body .... General Assembly

President of the Senate .... Lt. Gov. Peter Kinder
President Pro Tem of the Senate.........................Ron Richard
Secretary of the Senate ....Terry L. Spieler

Speaker of the House.....................................Todd Richardson
Speaker Pro Tem of the House ....Denny Hoskins
Clerk of the House ....D. Adam Crumbliss

2016 Regular Session...........................Jan. 6 – May 13, 2016
Number of Senatorial Districts 34
Number of Representative Districts 163

EXECUTIVE BRANCH

Governor .... Jay Nixon
Lieutenant Governor ....Peter Kinder
Secretary of State...Jason Kander
Attorney General ....Chris Koster
Treasurer..Clint Zweifel
Auditor..Nicole Galloway
State Comptroller ....Stacy Neal
(Director, Division of Accounting)

Governor's Present Term........................ 1/2009 – 1/2017
Number of Elected Officials in the Executive Branch..........6
Number of Members in the Cabinet 17

JUDICIAL BRANCH

Highest Court...Supreme Court
Supreme Court Chief Justice.....................Patricia Breckenridge
Number of Supreme Court Judges 7
Number of Intermediate Appellate Court Judges...........32
Number of U.S. Court Districts...2
U.S. Circuit Court...8th Circuit

MONTANA

Nickname...The Treasure State
Motto.. *Oro y Plata* (*Gold and Silver*)
Flower ....Bitterroot
Bird.. Western Meadowlark
Tree..Ponderosa Pine
Song..*Montana*
Entered the Union.....................................November 8, 1889
Capital ....Helena

STATISTICS

Land Area (square miles)...145,546
Rank in Nation...4
Population..1,032,949
Rank in Nation...44
Density per square mile 7.1
Capital City...Helena
Population..29,943
Rank in State...6
Largest City... Billings
Population..108,869
Number of Representatives in Congress 1
Number of 2016 Electoral Votes....................................3
Number of Geographic Counties..................................56
Number of County Governments..................................54
Number of Consolidated Governments..........................2
Number of Municipal Governments 129
Number of School Districts 319
Number of Special Districts 763

LEGISLATIVE BRANCH

Legislative Body ....Legislature

President of the Senate .... Debby Barrett
President Pro Tem of the Senate........................ Eric Moore
Secretary of the Senate ....Marilyn Miller

Speaker of the House...................................... Austin Knudsen
Speaker Pro Tem of the House......................Lee Randall
Clerk of the House ....Lindsey Grovom
(Chief)

2016 Regular Session.................... No 2016 Regular Session
Number of Senatorial Districts 50
Number of Representative Districts 100

EXECUTIVE BRANCH

Governor .... Steve Bullock
Lieutenant Governor ....Mike Cooney
Secretary of State..Linda McCulloch
Attorney General ....Tim Fox
Treasurer..Sheila Hogan
(Director, Department of Administration)
Auditor..Tori Hunthausen
State Comptroller .... Cody Pearce
(Administrator, State Accounting)

Governor's Present Term............................... 1/2013 – 1/2017
Number of Elected Officials in the Executive Branch..........6
Number of Members in the Cabinet 19

JUDICIAL BRANCH

Highest Court...Supreme Court
Supreme Court Chief Justice........................ Mike McGrath
Number of Supreme Court Judges 7
Number of U.S. Court Districts...1
U.S. Circuit Court...9th Circuit

NEBRASKA

Nickname	The Cornhusker State
Motto	*Equality Before the Law*
Flower	Goldenrod
Bird	Western Meadowlark
Tree	Western Cottonwood
Song	*Beautiful Nebraska*
Entered the Union	March 1, 1867
Capital	Lincoln

STATISTICS

Land Area (square miles)	76,824
Rank in Nation	15
Population	1,896,190
Rank in Nation	37
Density per square mile	24.7
Capital City	Lincoln
Population	272,996
Rank in State	2
Largest City	Omaha
Population	446,599
Number of Representatives in Congress	3
Number of 2016 Electoral Votes	5
Number of County Governments	93
Number of Municipal Governments	530
Number of School Districts	272
Number of Special Districts	1,269

LEGISLATIVE BRANCH

Legislative Body	Unicameral Legislature
President of the Senate	Galen Hadley
	(Speaker of the Legislature)
President Pro Tem of the Senate	Bob Krist
	(Chairperson of the Executive Board)
Clerk of the Legislature	Patrick O'Donnell
2016 Regular Session	Jan. 6 – May 13, 2016
Number of Senatorial Districts	49

EXECUTIVE BRANCH

Governor	Pete Ricketts
Lieutenant Governor	Mike Foley
Secretary of State	John Gale
Attorney General	Doug Peterson
Treasurer	Don B. Stenberg
Auditor	Charlie Janssen
State Comptroller	Jerry Broz
	(State Accounting Administrator)
Governor's Present Term	1/2015 – 1/2019
Number of Elected Officials in the Executive Branch	6
Number of Members in the Cabinet	30

JUDICIAL BRANCH

Highest Court	Supreme Court
Supreme Court Chief Justice	Michael G. Heavican
Number of Supreme Court Judges	7
Number of Intermediate Appellate Court Judges	6
Number of U.S. Court Districts	1
U.S. Circuit Court	8th Circuit

NEVADA

Nickname	The Silver State
Motto	*All for Our Country*
Flower	Sagebrush
Bird	Mountain Bluebird
Tree	Bristlecone Pine and Single-leaf Piñon
Song	*Home Means Nevada*
Entered the Union	October 31, 1864
Capital	Carson City

STATISTICS

Land Area (square miles)	109,781
Rank in Nation	7
Population	2,890,845
Rank in Nation	35
Density per square mile	26.3
Capital City	Carson City
Population	54,522
Rank in State	4
Largest City	Las Vegas
Population	613,599
Number of Representatives in Congress	4
Number of 2016 Electoral Votes	6
Number of Geographic Counties	17
Number of County Governments	16
Number of County Equivalents	1*
Number of Municipal Governments	19
Number of School Districts	17
Number of Special Districts	139

* Carson City is an Independent City and considered a county equivalent.

LEGISLATIVE BRANCH

Legislative Body	Legislature
President of the Senate	Lt. Gov. Mark Hutchison
President Pro Tem of the Senate	Joseph P. Hardy
Secretary of the Senate	Claire Clift
Speaker of the House	John Hambrick
	(Speaker of the Assembly)
Speaker Pro Tem of the House	John Ellison
	(Speaker Pro Tem of the Assembly)
Clerk of the House	Susan Furlong
	(Chief Clerk of the Assembly)
2016 Regular Session	No 2016 Regular Session
Number of Senatorial Districts	21
Number of Representative Districts	42

EXECUTIVE BRANCH

Governor	Brian Sandoval
Lieutenant Governor	Mark Hutchison
Secretary of State	Barbara Cegavske
Attorney General	Adam Laxalt
Treasurer	Dan Schwartz
Auditor	Paul V. Townsend
State Comptroller	Ron Knecht
	(Controller)
Governor's Present Term	1/2011 – 1/2019
Number of Elected Officials in the Executive Branch	6
Number of Members in the Cabinet	21

JUDICIAL BRANCH

Highest Court	Supreme Court
Supreme Court Chief Justice	Ron Parraguirre
Number of Supreme Court Judges	7
Number of U.S. Court Districts	1
U.S. Circuit Court	9th Circuit

NEW HAMPSHIRE

Nickname	The Granite State
Motto	*Live Free or Die*
Flower	Purple Lilac
Bird	Purple Finch
Tree	White Birch
Song	*Old New Hampshire*
Entered the Union	June 21, 1788
Capital	Concord

STATISTICS

Land Area (square miles)	8,953
Rank in Nation	44
Population	1,330,608
Rank in Nation	41
Density per square mile	148.6
Capital City	Concord
Population	42,444
Rank in State	3
Largest City	Manchester
Population	110,448
Number of Representatives in Congress	2
Number of 2016 Electoral Votes	4
Number of County Governments	10
Number of Municipal Governments	13
Number of School Districts	166
Number of Special Districts	131

LEGISLATIVE BRANCH

Legislative Body	General Court
President of the Senate	Chuck Morse
President Pro Tem of the Senate	Sharon Carson
Secretary of the Senate	Tammy L. Wright
	(Clerk of the Senate)
Speaker of the House	Shawn N. Jasper
Speaker Pro Tem of the House	Sherman Packard
Clerk of the House	Karen O. Wadsworth
2016 Regular Session	Jan. 6 – July 1, 2016
Number of Senatorial Districts	24
Number of Representative Districts	204

EXECUTIVE BRANCH

Governor	Maggie Hassan
Secretary of State	William M. Gardner
Attorney General	Joseph A. Foster
Treasurer	William Dwyer
Auditor	Jeffrey A. Pattison
State Comptroller	Gerard Murphy
	(Comptroller)
Governor's Present Term	1/2013 – 1/2017
Number of Elected Officials in the Executive Branch	1

JUDICIAL BRANCH

Highest Court	Supreme Court
Supreme Court Chief Justice	Linda Stewart Dalianis
Number of Supreme Court Judges	5
Number of U.S. Court Districts	1
U.S. Circuit Court	1st Circuit

NEW JERSEY

Nickname	The Garden State
Motto	*Liberty and Prosperity*
Flower	Violet
Bird	Eastern Goldfinch
Tree	Red Oak
Song	*I'm From New Jersey*
Entered the Union	December 18, 1787
Capital	Trenton

STATISTICS

Land Area (square miles)	7,354
Rank in Nation	46
Population	8,958,013
Rank in Nation	11
Density per square mile	1,218.1
Capital City	Trenton
Population	84,034
Rank in State	6
Largest City	Newark
Population	280,579
Number of Representatives in Congress	12
Number of 2016 Electoral Votes	14
Number of County Governments	21
Number of Municipal Governments	324
Number of School Districts	523
Number of Special Districts	234

LEGISLATIVE BRANCH

Legislative Body	Legislature
President of the Senate	Stephen Sweeney
President Pro Tem of the Senate	Nia H. Gill
Secretary of the Senate	Jennifer A. McQuaid
Speaker of the House	Vincent Prieto
	(Speaker of the Assembly)
Speaker Pro Tem of the House	Jerry Green
	(Speaker Pro Tem of the Assembly)
Clerk of the House	Dana M. Burley
	(Clerk of the General Assembly)
2016 Regular Session	Jan. 12 – Dec. 31, 2016
Number of Senatorial Districts	40
Number of Representative Districts	40

EXECUTIVE BRANCH

Governor	Chris Christie
Lieutenant Governor	Kim Guadagno
Attorney General	Robert Lougy
Treasurer	Ford M. Scudder
Auditor	Stephen Eells
State Comptroller	Philip Degnan
Governor's Present Term	1/2010 – 1/2018
Number of Elected Officials in the Executive Branch	2
Number of Members in the Cabinet	23

JUDICIAL BRANCH

Highest Court	Supreme Court
Supreme Court Chief Justice	Stuart Rabner
Number of Supreme Court Judges	7
Number of Intermediate Appellate Court Judges	33
Number of U.S. Court Districts	1
U.S. Circuit Court	3rd Circuit

NEW MEXICO

Nickname...The Land of Enchantment
Motto..*Crescit Eundo (It Grows As It Goes)*
Flower .... Yucca (Our Lord's Candles)
Bird..Roadrunner aka Greater Roadrunner
Tree... Piñon
Song..............................*Asi es Nuevo Mexico* and *O, Fair New Mexico*
Entered the Union.. January 6, 1912
Capital.. Santa Fe

STATISTICS

Land Area (square miles)...121,298
Rank in Nation..5
Population..2,085,109
Rank in Nation..36
Density per square mile 17.2
Capital City.. Santa Fe
Population...70,297
Rank in State..4
Largest City .... Albuquerque
Population...599,642
Number of Representatives in Congress 3
Number of 2016 Electoral Votes...................................5
Number of County Governments.................................33
Number of Municipal Governments 103
Number of School Districts 96
Number of Special Districts 631

LEGISLATIVE BRANCH

Legislative Body .... Legislature

President of the Senate .... Lt. Gov. John A. Sanchez
President Pro Tem of the Senate................................. Mary Kay Papen
Secretary of the Senate ....Lenore Naranjo
(Chief Clerk of the Senate)

Speaker of the House...Don Tripp
Clerk of the House ....Denise Greenlaw Ramonas
(Chief)

2016 Regular Session....................................Jan. 19 – Feb. 18, 2016
Number of Senatorial Districts 42
Number of Representative Districts 70

EXECUTIVE BRANCH

Governor ....Susana Martinez
Lieutenant Governor ....John A. Sanchez
Secretary of State ....Brad Winter
Attorney General ....Hector Balderas
Treasurer...Tim Eichenberg
Auditor...Tim Keller
State Comptroller.. Ronald Spilman
(Controller)

Governor's Present Term............................... 1/2011 – 1/2019
Number of Elected Officials in the Executive Branch.........................7
Number of Members in the Cabinet 29

JUDICIAL BRANCH

Highest Court...Supreme Court
Supreme Court Chief Justice...........................Barbara J. Vigil
Number of Supreme Court Judges 5
Number of Intermediate Appellate Court Judges.............................10
Number of U.S. Court Districts 1
U.S. Circuit Court... 10th Circuit

NEW YORK

Nickname..The Empire State
Motto... *Excelsior (Ever Upward)*
Flower ....Rose
Bird... Bluebird
Tree .... Sugar Maple
Song..*I Love New York*
Entered the Union...July 26, 1788
Capital..Albany

STATISTICS

Land Area (square miles).......................................47,126
Rank in Nation..30
Population..19,795,791
Rank in Nation..4
Density per square mile 420.1
Capital City...Albany
Population...98,566
Rank in State..6
Largest City ....New York City
Population...8,491,079
Number of Representatives in Congress 27
Number of 2016 Electoral Votes.................................29
Number of Geographic Counties.................................62*
Number of County Governments.................................57
Number of Municipal Governments 614
Number of School Districts 679
Number of Special Districts 1,174

*New York City is coextensive with the five boroughs (counties).

LEGISLATIVE BRANCH

Legislative Body .... Legislature

President of the Senate .... Lt. Gov. Kathy Hochul
President Pro Tem of the Senate....................................John Flanagan
(Temporary President & Majority Leader)
Secretary of the Senate .... Frank Patience

Speaker of the House...Carl Heastie
(Speaker of the Assembly)
Speaker Pro Tem of the House .... Jeffrion Aubry
(Speaker Pro Tempore of the Assembly)
Clerk of the House ....Laurene R. Kretzler

2016 Regular Session... Jan. 6 – Dec. 31, 2016
Number of Senatorial Districts 63
Number of Representative Districts 150

EXECUTIVE BRANCH

Governor ....Andrew M. Cuomo
Lieutenant Governor ....Kathy Hochul
Secretary of State ....Rossana Rosado
Attorney General .... Eric T. Schneiderman
Treasurer... Eric Mostert
State Comptroller..................................Thomas P. DiNapoli

Governor's Present Term............................... 1/2011 – 1/2019
Number of Elected Officials in the Executive Branch.........................4
Number of Members in the Cabinet 75

JUDICIAL BRANCH

Highest Court...Court of Appeals
Supreme Court Chief Justice...........................Janet DiFiore
Number of Supreme Court Judges 7
Number of Intermediate Appellate Court Judges.............................66
Number of U.S. Court Districts 4
U.S. Circuit Court... 2nd Circuit

NORTH CAROLINA

Nickname.............................. The Tar Heel State and Old North State
Motto......................... *Esse Quam Videri* (*To Be Rather Than to Seem*)
Flower .... Dogwood
Bird .... Cardinal
Tree ....Long Leaf Pine
Song.. *The Old North State*
Entered the Union... November 21, 1789
Capital ....Raleigh

STATISTICS

Land Area (square miles) 48,618
Rank in Nation...29
Population..10,042,802
Rank in Nation...9
Density per square mile 206.6
Capital City...Raleigh
Population..439,896
Rank in State..2
Largest City ....Charlotte
Population..809,958
Number of Representatives in Congress 13
Number of 2016 Electoral Votes 15
Number of County Governments......................................100
Number of Municipal Governments 533
Number of Special Districts 320

LEGISLATIVE BRANCH

Legislative Body .... General Assembly

President of the Senate .... Lt. Gov. Dan Forest
President Pro Tem of the Senate..Phil Berger
Secretary of the Senate ....Sarah Lang
(Principal Clerk of the Senate)

Speaker of the House ....Tim Moore
Speaker Pro Tem of the House ....Paul Stam
Clerk of the House ....Denise Weeks
(Principal Clerk of the House)

2016 Regular Session..................April 25 – mid-July 2016 (projected)
Number of Senatorial Districts 50
Number of Representative Districts 120

EXECUTIVE BRANCH

Governor ....Pat McCrory
Lieutenant Governor ....Dan Forest
Secretary of State...Elaine Marshall
Attorney General ....Roy Cooper
Treasurer...Janet Cowell
Auditor..Beth Wood
State Comptroller ....Linda Combs
(Controller)

Governor's Present Term....................................... 1/2013 – 1/2017
Number of Elected Officials in the Executive Branch 10
Number of Members in the Cabinet 9

JUDICIAL BRANCH

Highest Court..Supreme Court
Supreme Court Chief Justice.. Mark D. Martin
Number of Supreme Court Judges 7
Number of Intermediate Appellate Court Judges.............................15
Number of U.S. Court Districts 3
U.S. Circuit Court..4th Circuit

NORTH DAKOTA

Nickname...Peace Garden State
Motto........*Liberty and Union, Now and Forever, One and Inseparable*
Flower ....Wild Prairie Rose
Bird..Western Meadowlark
Tree .... American Elm
Song...*North Dakota Hymn*
Entered the Union.....................................November 2, 1889
Capital.. Bismarck

STATISTICS

Land Area (square miles).......................................69,001
Rank in Nation..17
Population..756,927
Rank in Nation..47
Density per square mile 11.0
Capital City..Bismarck
Population..68,896
Rank in State...2
Largest City ....Fargo
Population..115,863
Number of Representatives in Congress 1
Number of 2016 Electoral Votes 3
Number of County Governments.............................53
Number of Municipal Governments 357
Number of School Districts 183
Number of Special Districts 779

LEGISLATIVE BRANCH

Legislative Body ....Legislative Assembly

President of the Senate ....Lt. Gov. Drew Wrigley
President Pro Tem of the Senate........................ Dick Dever
Secretary of the Senate .... William Horton

Speaker of the House.. Wesley Belter
Clerk of the House ....Buell Reich

2016 Regular Session.................. No 2016 Regular Session
Number of Senatorial Districts 47
Number of Representative Districts 47

EXECUTIVE BRANCH

Governor .... Jack Dalrymple
Lieutenant Governor .... Drew Wrigley
Secretary of State..Alvin Jaeger
Attorney General .... Wayne Stenehjem
Treasurer..Kelly Schmidt
Auditor...Robert R. Peterson
State Comptroller ....Pam Sharp
(Director, Office of Management & Budget)

Governor's Present Term........................ 12/2010 – 12/2018
Number of Elected Officials in the Executive Branch........................12
Number of Members in the Cabinet 18

JUDICIAL BRANCH

Highest Court..Supreme Court
Supreme Court Chief Justice........................... Gerald W. VandeWalle
Number of Supreme Court Judges 5
Number of Intermediate Appellate Court Judges..............................3
Number of U.S. Court Districts..................................1
U.S. Circuit Court..8th Circuit

OHIO

Nickname	The Buckeye State
Motto	*With God, All Things Are Possible*
Flower	Scarlet Carnation
Bird	Cardinal
Tree	Buckeye
Song	*Beautiful Ohio*
Entered the Union	March 1, 1803
Capital	Columbus

STATISTICS

Land Area (square miles)	40,861
Rank in Nation	35
Population	11,613,423
Rank in Nation	7
Density per square mile	284.2
Capital City	Columbus
Population	835,957
Rank in State	1
Largest City	Columbus
Population	835,957
Number of Representatives in Congress	16
Number of 2016 Electoral Votes	18
Number of County Governments	88
Number of Municipal Governments	937
Number of School Districts	668
Number of Special Districts	841

LEGISLATIVE BRANCH

Legislative Body	General Assembly

President of the Senate	Keith Faber
President Pro Tem of the Senate	Larry Obhof
Secretary of the Senate	Vincent Keeran
	(Clerk of the Senate)

Speaker of the House	Cliff Rosenberger
Speaker Pro Tem of the House	Ron Amstutz
Clerk of the House	Bradley Young
	(Legislative Clerk of the House)

2016 Regular Session	Jan. 5 – Dec. 16, 2016
Number of Senatorial Districts	33
Number of Representative Districts	99

EXECUTIVE BRANCH

Governor	John Kasich
Lieutenant Governor	Mary Taylor
Secretary of State	Jon Husted
Attorney General	Mike DeWine
Treasurer	Josh Mandel
Auditor	David A. Yost
State Comptroller	Timothy Keen
	(Director, Office of Budget & Management)

Governor's Present Term	1/2011 – 1/2019
Number of Elected Officials in the Executive Branch	6
Number of Members in the Cabinet	24

JUDICIAL BRANCH

Highest Court	Supreme Court
Supreme Court Chief Justice	Maureen O'Connor
Number of Supreme Court Judges	7
Number of Intermediate Appellate Court Judges	69
Number of U.S. Court Districts	2
U.S. Circuit Court	6th Circuit

OKLAHOMA

Nickname	The Sooner State
Motto	*Labor Omnia Vincit (Labor Conquers All Things)*
Flower	Mistletoe
Bird	Scissor-tailed Flycatcher
Tree	Redbud
Song	*Oklahoma*
Entered the Union	November 16, 1907
Capital	Oklahoma City

STATISTICS

Land Area (square miles)	68,595
Rank in Nation	19
Population	3,911,338
Rank in Nation	28
Density per square mile	57.0
Capital City	Oklahoma City
Population	620,602
Rank in State	1
Largest City	Oklahoma City
Population	620,602
Number of Representatives in Congress	5
Number of 2016 Electoral Votes	7
Number of County Governments	77
Number of Municipal Governments	590
Number of School Districts	550
Number of Special Districts	635

LEGISLATIVE BRANCH

Legislative Body	Legislature

President of the Senate	Lt. Gov. Todd Lamb
President Pro Tem of the Senate	Brian Bingman
Secretary of the Senate	Paul Ziriax

Speaker of the House	Jeffrey Hickman
Speaker Pro Tem of the House	Lee Denney
Clerk of the House	Jan Harrison
	(Chief)

2016 Regular Session	Feb. 1 – May 27, 2016
Number of Senatorial Districts	48
Number of Representative Districts	101

EXECUTIVE BRANCH

Governor	Mary Fallin
Lieutenant Governor	Todd Lamb
Secretary of State	Chris Benge
Attorney General	Scott Pruitt
Treasurer	Ken Miller
Auditor	Gary Jones
State Comptroller	Lynne Bajema
	(Comptroller)

Governor's Present Term	1/2011 – 1/2019
Number of Elected Officials in the Executive Branch	8
Number of Members in the Cabinet	16

JUDICIAL BRANCH

Highest Court	Supreme Court
Supreme Court Chief Justice	John Reif
Number of Supreme Court Judges	9
Number of Intermediate Appellate Court Judges	12
Number of U.S. Court Districts	3
U.S. Circuit Court	10th Circuit

OREGON

Nickname..The Beaver State
Motto...*She Flies with Her Own Wings*
Flower ....Oregon Grape
Bird.. Western Meadowlark
Tree.. Douglas Fir
Song...*Oregon, My Oregon*
Entered the Union...February 14, 1859
Capital ....Salem

STATISTICS

Land Area (square miles)..95,988
Rank in Nation...10
Population...4,028,977
Rank in Nation...27
Density per square mile 42.0
Capital City...Salem
Population...161,637
Rank in State...2
Largest City ....Portland
Population...619,360
Number of Representatives in Congress 5
Number of 2016 Electoral Votes 7
Number of County Governments...36
Number of Municipal Governments 241
Number of School Districts 230
Number of Special Districts 1,035

LEGISLATIVE BRANCH

Legislative Body ....Legislative Assembly

President of the Senate ....Peter Courtney
President Pro Tem of the Senate.........................Diane Rosenbaum
Secretary of the Senate ....Lori Brocker

Speaker of the House...Tina Kotek
Speaker Pro Tem of the House ....Tobias Read
Clerk of the House ....Tim Sekerak
(Chief)

2016 Regular Session.......................Feb. 1 – March 3, 2016
Number of Senatorial Districts 30
Number of Representative Districts 60

EXECUTIVE BRANCH

Governor .... Kate Brown
Secretary of State..Jeanne Atkins
Attorney General .... Ellen Rosenblum
Treasurer..Ted Wheeler
Auditor..Mary Wenger
State Comptroller .... Robert Hamilton
(Manager, Statewide Accounting, Chief Financial Office)

Governor's Present Term......................... 2/2015 – 1/2019
Number of Elected Officials in the Executive Branch.........................6

JUDICIAL BRANCH

Highest Court..Supreme Court
Supreme Court Chief Justice..........................Thomas A. Balmer
Number of Supreme Court Judges...7
Number of Intermediate Appellate Court Judges............................13
Number of U.S. Court Districts...1
U.S. Circuit Court.. 9th Circuit

PENNSYLVANIA

Nickname..The Keystone State
Motto...*Virtue, Liberty and Independence*
Flower ....Mountain Laurel (Kalmia latifolia)
Bird... Ruffed Grouse
Tree..Hemlock
Song...*Pennsylvania*
Entered the Union...December 12, 1787
Capital .... Harrisburg

STATISTICS

Land Area (square miles)..44,743
Rank in Nation...32
Population...12,802,503
Rank in Nation...6
Density per square mile 286.1
Capital City... Harrisburg
Population...49,082
Rank in State...9
Largest City ....Philadelphia
Population...1,560,297
Number of Representatives in Congress 18
Number of 2016 Electoral Votes 20
Number of Geographic Counties...67
Number of County Governments...66
Number of Consolidated Governments....................................1
Number of Municipal Governments 1,015
Number of School Districts 514
Number of Special Districts 1,756

LEGISLATIVE BRANCH

Legislative Body .... General Assembly

President of the Senate ....Lt. Gov. Mike Stack
President Pro Tem of the Senate.............................Joseph B. Scarnati
Secretary of the Senate ....Megan Martin
(Secretary-Parliamentarian)

Speaker of the House...Mike Turzai
Clerk of the House ....Dave Reddecliff
(Chief)

2016 Regular Session.......................Jan. 5 – Dec. 31, 2016
Number of Senatorial Districts 50
Number of Representative Districts 203

EXECUTIVE BRANCH

Governor ....Tom Wolf
Lieutenant Governor ....Mike Stack
Secretary of State..Pedro Cortes
(Secretary of the Commonwealth)
Attorney General .... Kathleen Kane
Treasurer..Timothy Reese
Auditor... Eugene DePasquale
State Comptroller ....Anna Marie Kiehl
(Chief Accounting Officer)

Governor's Present Term......................... 1/2015 – 1/2019
Number of Elected Officials in the Executive Branch.........................5
Number of Members in the Cabinet 28

JUDICIAL BRANCH

Highest Court..Supreme Court
Supreme Court Chief Justice..........................Thomas G. Saylor
Number of Supreme Court Judges...7
Number of Intermediate Appellate Court Judges............................32
Number of U.S. Court Districts...3
U.S. Circuit Court..3rd Circuit

RHODE ISLAND

Nickname...Little Rhody and Ocean State
Motto...*Hope*
Flower ....Violet
Bird..Rhode Island Red
Tree...Red Maple
Song...*Rhode Island*
Entered the Union..May 29, 1790
Capital..Providence

STATISTICS

Land Area (square miles)..1,034
Rank in Nation..50
Population..1,056,298
Rank in Nation..43
Density per square mile 1,021.6
Capital City...Providence
Population..179,154
Rank in State..1
Largest City...Providence
Population..179,154
Number of Representatives in Congress 2
Number of 2016 Electoral Votes 4
Number of Geographic Counties...5
Number of Municipal Governments 8
Number of School Districts 4
Number of Special Districts 90

LEGISLATIVE BRANCH

Legislative Body .... General Assembly

President of the Senate ....M. Teresa Paiva-Weed
President Pro Tem of the Senate......................William Walaska
Secretary of the Senate ....Joseph Brady

Speaker of the House.............................Nicholas A. Mattiello
Clerk of the House ....Frank McCabe

2016 Regular Session......................Jan. 5 – late June 2016 (projected)
Number of Senatorial Districts 38
Number of Representative Districts 75

EXECUTIVE BRANCH

Governor .... Gina Raimondo
Lieutenant Governor .... Dan McKee
Secretary of State..Nellie Gorbea
Attorney General ....Peter F. Kilmartin
Treasurer .... Seth Magaziner
Auditor.. Dennis Hoyle
State Comptroller ....Marc Leonetti
(Controller)

Governor's Present Term............................ 1/2015 – 1/2019
Number of Elected Officials in the Executive Branch.........5
Number of Members in the Cabinet 27

JUDICIAL BRANCH

Highest Court...Supreme Court
Supreme Court Chief Justice........................Paul A. Suttell
Number of Supreme Court Judges 5
Number of U.S. Court Districts..1
U.S. Circuit Court..1st Circuit

SOUTH CAROLINA

Nickname.. The Palmetto State
Motto......*Animis Opibusque Parat* (*Prepared in Mind and Resources*)
and *Dum Spiro Spero* (*While I breathe, I Hope*)
Flower .... Yellow Jessamine
Bird..Carolina Wren
Tree...Palmetto
Song...................................*Carolina* and *South Carolina on My Mind*
Entered the Union..May 23, 1788
Capital.. Columbia

STATISTICS

Land Area (square miles)...30,061
Rank in Nation..40
Population..4,896,146
Rank in Nation..23
Density per square mile 162.9
Capital City.. Columbia
Population..132,067
Rank in State..1
Largest City.. Columbia
Population..132,067
Number of Representatives in Congress 7
Number of 2016 Electoral Votes 9
Number of County Governments 46
Number of Municipal Governments 270
Number of School Districts 83
Number of Special Districts 279

LEGISLATIVE BRANCH

Legislative Body .... General Assembly

President of the Senate ....Lt. Gov. Henry McMaster
President Pro Tem of the Senate..........................Hugh K. Leatherman
Secretary of the Senate .... Jeffrey Gossett
(Clerk of the Senate)

Speaker of the House...James H. Lucas
Speaker Pro Tem of the House .... Thomas E. Pope
Clerk of the House ....Charles F. Reid

2016 Regular Session....................................Jan. 12 – June 2, 2016
Number of Senatorial Districts 46
Number of Representative Districts 124

EXECUTIVE BRANCH

Governor .... Nikki Haley
Lieutenant Governor ....Henry McMaster
Secretary of State...Mark Hammond
Attorney General ....Alan Wilson
Treasurer ....Curtis Loftis
Auditor...George Kennedy
State Comptroller...Richard Eckstrom
(Comptroller General)

Governor's Present Term............................... 1/2011 – 1/2019
Number of Elected Officials in the Executive Branch.........9
Number of Members in the Cabinet 15

JUDICIAL BRANCH

Highest Court...Supreme Court
Supreme Court Chief Justice.....................Costa M. Pleicones
Number of Supreme Court Judges 5
Number of Intermediate Appellate Court Judges...............9
Number of U.S. Court Districts...1
U.S. Circuit Court..4th Circuit

SOUTH DAKOTA

Nickname ....The Mt. Rushmore State
Motto.. *Under God the People Rule*
Flower ....American Pasque
Bird..Ring-necked Pheasant
Tree...Black Hills Spruce
Song.. *Hail, South Dakota*
Entered the Union.................................... November 2, 1889
Capital ....Pierre

STATISTICS

Land Area (square miles) 75,811
Rank in Nation..16
Population...858,469
Rank in Nation..46
Density per square mile 11.3
Capital City...Pierre
Population...14,054
Rank in State...8
Largest City..Sioux Falls
Population...168,586
Number of Representatives in Congress 1
Number of 2016 Electoral Votes...3
Number of County Governments...66
Number of Municipal Governments 311
Number of School Districts 152
Number of Special Districts 547

LEGISLATIVE BRANCH

Legislative Body ....Legislature

President of the Senate ....Lt. Gov. Matthew Michels
President Pro Tem of the Senate...................Gary Cammack
Secretary of the Senate ....Jeanette Schipper

Speaker of the House.......................................Dean Wink
Speaker Pro Tem of the House ....G. Mark Mickelson
Clerk of the House .... Arlene Kvislen
(Chief)

2016 Regular Session....................Jan. 12 – March 29, 2016
Number of Senatorial Districts 35
Number of Representative Districts 35

EXECUTIVE BRANCH

Governor ....Dennis Daugaard
Lieutenant Governor .... Matthew Michels
Secretary of State..Shantel Krebs
Attorney General ....Martin Jackley
Treasurer...Richard Sattgast
Auditor...Martin L. Guindon
Auditor...Steve Barnett
(State Auditor)

Governor's Present Term...................................... 1/2011 – 1/2019
Number of Elected Officials in the Executive Branch 8
Number of Members in the Cabinet 19

JUDICIAL BRANCH

Highest Court..Supreme Court
Supreme Court Chief Justice...................David E. Gilbertson
Number of Supreme Court Judges 5
Number of U.S. Court Districts 1
U.S. Circuit Court...8th Circuit

TENNESSEE

Nickname ....The Volunteer State
Motto.. *Agriculture and Commerce*
Flower ....Iris
Bird...Mockingbird
Tree...Tulip Poplar
Song.................................... *When It's Iris Time in Tennessee*;
The Tennessee Waltz;
My Homeland, Tennessee;
My Tennessee;
and *Rocky Top*
Entered the Union..June 1, 1796
Capital .... Nashville

STATISTICS

Land Area (square miles)...41,235
Rank in Nation..34
Population...6,600,299
Rank in Nation..17
Density per square mile 160.1
Capital City.. Nashville
Population...644,014
Rank in State...2
Largest City.. Memphis
Population...656,861
Number of Representatives in Congress 9
Number of 2016 Electoral Votes...11
Number of Geographic Counties..95
Number of County Governments...92
Number of Consolidated Governments....................................3
Number of Municipal Governments 345
Number of School Districts 14
Number of Special Districts 465

LEGISLATIVE BRANCH

Legislative Body .... General Assembly

President of the Senate .... Lt. Gov. Ron Ramsey
President Pro Tem of the Senate...........................Bo Watson
(Speaker Pro Tem)
Secretary of the Senate ....Russell Humphrey
(Chief Clerk of the Senate)

Speaker of the House.......................................Beth Harwell
Speaker Pro Tem of the House ....Curtis Johnson
Clerk of the House .... Joe McCord
(Chief)

2016 Regular Session....................Jan. 12 – mid April 2016 (projected)
Number of Senatorial Districts 33
Number of Representative Districts 99

EXECUTIVE BRANCH

Governor .... Bill Haslam
Lieutenant Governor .... Ron Ramsey
Secretary of State...Tre Hargett
Attorney General .... Herbert Slatery
Treasurer...David H. Lillard Jr.
State Comptroller ....Justin P. Wilson

Governor's Present Term.. 1/2011 – 1/2019
Number of Elected Officials in the Executive Branch..........................1
Number of Members in the Cabinet 29

JUDICIAL BRANCH

Highest Court..Supreme Court
Supreme Court Chief Justice.............................Sharon G. Lee
Number of Supreme Court Judges 5
Number of Intermediate Appellate Court Judges 24
Number of U.S. Court Districts 3
U.S. Circuit Court...6th Circuit

TEXAS

Nickname	The Lone Star State
Motto	*Friendship*
Flower	Bluebonnet (Buffalo Clover, Wolf Flower)
Bird	Mockingbird
Tree	Pecan
Song	*Texas, Our Texas*
Entered the Union	December 29, 1845
Capital	Austin

STATISTICS

Land Area (square miles)	261,232
Rank in Nation	2
Population	27,469,114
Rank in Nation	2
Density per square mile	105.2
Capital City	Austin
Population	912,791
Rank in State	4
Largest City	Houston
Population	2,239,558
Number of Representatives in Congress	36
Number of 2016 Electoral Votes	38
Number of County Governments	254
Number of Municipal Governments	1,214
Number of School Districts	1,079
Number of Special Districts	2,600

LEGISLATIVE BRANCH

Legislative Body	Legislature
President of the Senate	Lt. Gov. Dan Patrick
President Pro Tem of the Senate	Juan Hinojosa
Secretary of the Senate	Patsy Spaw
Speaker of the House	Joe Straus
Speaker Pro Tem of the House	Dennis Bonnen
Clerk of the House	Robert Haney
	(Chief)
2016 Regular Session	No 2016 Regular Session
Number of Senatorial Districts	31
Number of Representative Districts	150

EXECUTIVE BRANCH

Governor	Greg Abbott
Lieutenant Governor	Dan Patrick
Secretary of State	Carlos Cascos
Attorney General	Ken Paxton
Auditor	Lisa Collier
State Comptroller	Glenn Hegar
	(Comptroller of Public Accounts)
Governor's Present Term	1/2015 – 1/2019
Number of Elected Officials in the Executive Branch	6

JUDICIAL BRANCH

Highest Court	Supreme Court
Supreme Court Chief Justice	Nathan L. Hecht
Number of Supreme Court Judges	9
Number of Intermediate Appellate Court Judges	80
Number of U.S. Court Districts	4
U.S. Circuit Court	5th Circuit

UTAH

Nickname	The Beehive State
Motto	*Industry*
Flower	Sego Lily
Bird	California Seagull
Tree	Blue Spruce
Song	*Utah, We Love Thee*
Entered the Union	January 4, 1896
Capital	Salt Lake City

STATISTICS

Land Area (square miles)	82,170
Rank in Nation	12
Population	2,995,919
Rank in Nation	31
Density per square mile	36.5
Capital City	Salt Lake City
Population	190,884
Rank in State	1
Largest City	Salt Lake City
Population	190,884
Number of Representatives in Congress	4
Number of 2016 Electoral Votes	6
Number of County Governments	29
Number of Municipal Governments	245
Number of School Districts	41
Number of Special Districts	307

LEGISLATIVE BRANCH

Legislative Body	Legislature
President of the Senate	Wayne Niederhauser
Secretary of the Senate	Leslie McLean
Speaker of the House	Gregory H. Hughes
Clerk of the House	Sandy Tenney
	(Chief)
2016 Regular Session	Jan. 25 – March 10, 2016
Number of Senatorial Districts	29
Number of Representative Districts	75

EXECUTIVE BRANCH

Governor	Gary R. Herbert
Lieutenant Governor	Spencer Cox
Attorney General	Sean Reyes
Treasurer	Richard Ellis
Auditor	John Dougall
State Comptroller	John Reidhead
	(Director, Division of Finance)
Governor's Present Term	8/2009 – 1/2017
Number of Elected Officials in the Executive Branch	5
Number of Members in the Cabinet	24

JUDICIAL BRANCH

Highest Court	Supreme Court
Supreme Court Chief Justice	Matthew B. Durrant
Number of Supreme Court Judges	5
Number of Intermediate Appellate Court Judges	7
Number of U.S. Court Districts	1
U.S. Circuit Court	10th Circuit

VERMONT

Nickname .... The Green Mountain State
Motto .... *Freedom and Unity*
Flower .... Red Clover
Bird .... Hermit Thrush
Tree .... Sugar Maple
Song .... *Hail, Vermont!*
Entered the Union .... March 4, 1791
Capital .... Montpelier

STATISTICS

Land Area (square miles) 9,217
Rank in Nation 43
Population 626,042
Rank in Nation 49
Density per square mile 68.0
Capital City ....Montpelier
Population 7,671
Rank in State 6
Largest City ....Burlington
Population 42,211
Number of Representatives in Congress 1
Number of 2016 Electoral Votes 3
Number of County Governments 14
Number of Municipal Governments 43
Number of School Districts 291
Number of Special Districts 153

LEGISLATIVE BRANCH

Legislative Body .... General Assembly

President of the Senate .... Lt. Gov. Phil Scott
President Pro Tem of the Senate ....John F. Campbell
Secretary of the Senate ....John H. Bloomer Jr.

Speaker of the House ....Shap Smith
Clerk of the House .... Donald G. Milne

2016 Regular Session ....Jan. 5 – TBD
Number of Senatorial Districts 13
Number of Representative Districts 104

EXECUTIVE BRANCH

Governor ....Peter E. Shumlin
Lieutenant Governor ....Phil Scott
Secretary of State ....Jim Condos
Attorney General ....William H. Sorrell
Treasurer ....Elizabeth Pearce
Auditor .... Douglas Hoffer
Comptroller ....Andrew Pallito
(Commissioner, Dept. of Finance and Management)

Governor's Present Term .... 1/2011 – 1/2017
Number of Elected Officials in the Executive Branch 6
Number of Members in the Cabinet 12

JUDICIAL BRANCH

Highest Court ....Supreme Court
Supreme Court Chief Justice .... Paul L. Reiber
Number of Supreme Court Judges 5
Number of U.S. Court Districts 1
U.S. Circuit Court .... 2nd Circuit

VIRGINIA

Nickname .... The Old Dominion
Motto .... *Sic Semper Tyrannis* (Thus Always to Tyrants)
Flower .... Dogwood
Bird .... Cardinal
Tree .... Dogwood
Song ....*Carry Me Back to Old Virginia*
Entered the Union ....June 25, 1788
Capital .... Richmond

STATISTICS

Land Area (square miles) 39,490
Rank in Nation 36
Population 8,382,993
Rank in Nation 12
Density per square mile 212.3
Capital City .... Richmond
Population 217,853
Rank in State 4
Largest City ....Virginia Beach
Population 450,980
Number of Representatives in Congress 11
Number of 2016 Electoral Votes 13
Number of Geographic Counties 95*
Number of Municipal Governments 229
Number of School Districts 1
Number of Special Districts 193

*In addition to the 95 counties, Virginia has 39 Independent Cities, considered county equivalents. Five cities in the Hampton Roads area were formed of entire counties and function at the county level of government. They are listed with the Independent Cities but counted as consolidated governments in Virginia.

LEGISLATIVE BRANCH

Legislative Body .... General Assembly

President of the Senate .... Lt. Gov. Ralph Northam
President Pro Tem of the Senate ....Stephen Newman
Secretary of the Senate ....Susan Clarke Schaar
(Clerk of the Senate)

Speaker of the House .... William J. Howell
Clerk of the House ....G. Paul Nardo

2016 Regular Session ....Jan. 13 – March 12, 2016
Number of Senatorial Districts 40
Number of Representative Districts 100

EXECUTIVE BRANCH

Governor ....Terry McAuliffe
Lieutenant Governor ....Ralph Northam
Secretary of State ....Kelly Thomasson
(Secretary of the Commonwealth)
Attorney General ....Mark Herring
Treasurer ....Manju Ganeriwala
Auditor ....Martha Mavredes
State Comptroller ....David Von Moll
(Comptroller)

Governor's Present Term .... 1/2010 – 1/2014
Number of Elected Officials in the Executive Branch 3
Number of Members in the Cabinet 15

JUDICIAL BRANCH

Highest Court ....Supreme Court
Supreme Court Chief Justice .... Donald W. Lemons
Number of Supreme Court Judges 7
Number of Intermediate Appellate Court Judges 11
Number of U.S. Court Districts 2
U.S. Circuit Court .... 4th Circuit

WASHINGTON

Nickname..The Evergreen State
Motto.....................*Alki* (Chinook Indian word meaning *By and By*)
Flower ....Coast Rhododendron
Bird..Willow Goldfinch
Tree... Western Hemlock
Song.................................... *Washington, My Home*
Entered the Union...................................... November 11, 1889
Capital .... Olympia

STATISTICS

Land Area (square miles)..66,456
Rank in Nation..20
Population...7,170,351
Rank in Nation..13
Density per square mile 107.9
Capital City...Olympia
Population...49,218
Rank in State..24
Largest City...Seattle
Population...668,342
Number of Representatives in Congress 10
Number of 2016 Electoral Votes................................12
Number of County Governments..............................39
Number of Municipal Governments 281
Number of School Districts 295
Number of Special Districts 1,285

LEGISLATIVE BRANCH

Legislative Body .... Legislature

President of the Senate ....Lt. Gov. Brad Owen
President Pro Tem of the Senate........................... Pam Roach
Secretary of the Senate ....Hunter G. Goodman

Speaker of the House.................................. Frank Chopp
Speaker Pro Tem of the House ....Jim Moeller
Clerk of the House ....Barbara Baker
(Chief)

2016 Regular Session....................Jan. 11 – March 10, 2016
Number of Senatorial Districts 49
Number of Representative Districts 49

EXECUTIVE BRANCH

Governor ....Jay Inslee
Lieutenant Governor .... Brad Owen
Secretary of State ....Kim Wyman
Attorney General .... Bob Ferguson
Treasurer...James McIntire
Auditor... Troy Kelley
State Comptroller ....David Schumacher
(Director, Office of Financial Management)

Governor's Present Term............................... 1/2013 – 1/2017
Number of Elected Officials in the Executive Branch 9
Number of Members in the Cabinet 25

JUDICIAL BRANCH

Highest Court...Supreme Court
Supreme Court Chief Justice....................Barbara A. Madsen
Number of Supreme Court Judges 9
Number of Intermediate Appellate Court Judges...........................22
Number of U.S. Court Districts 2
U.S. Circuit Court.. 9th Circuit

WEST VIRGINIA

Nickname....................................The Mountain State
Motto...........*Montani Semper Liberi* (*Mountaineers Are Always Free*)
Flower ....Rhododendron
Bird.. Cardinal
Tree... Sugar Maple
Song......................*West Virginia, My Home Sweet Home*;
The West Virginia Hills;
and *This is My West Virginia*
Entered the Union...June 20, 1863
Capital .... Charleston

STATISTICS

Land Area (square miles)..24,038
Rank in Nation..41
Population...1,844,128
Rank in Nation..38
Density per square mile 76.7
Capital City.. Charleston
Population...50,404
Rank in State..1
Largest City.. Charleston
Population...50,404
Number of Representatives in Congress 3
Number of 2016 Electoral Votes................................5
Number of County Governments..............................55
Number of Municipal Governments 232
Number of School Districts 55
Number of Special Districts 317

LEGISLATIVE BRANCH

Legislative Body .... Legislature

President of the Senate .... Lt. Gov. Bill Cole
President Pro Tem of the Senate........................... Donna J. Boley
Secretary of the Senate ....Clark Barnes
(Clerk of the Senate)

Speaker of the House..................................Tim Armstead
Speaker Pro Tem of the House .... Bill Anderson
Clerk of the House ....Steve Harrison
(Clerk of the House of Delegates)

2016 Regular Session....................Jan. 13 – March 12, 2016
Number of Senatorial Districts 17
Number of Representative Districts 58

EXECUTIVE BRANCH

Governor ....Earl Ray Tomblin
Lieutenant Governor .... Bill Cole
Secretary of State ....Natalie Tennant
Attorney General .... Patrick Morrisey
Treasurer...John D. Perdue
Auditor...Glen B. Ganier III

Governor's Present Term............................... 11/2010 – 1/2017
Number of Elected Officials in the Executive Branch 6
Number of Members in the Cabinet 10

JUDICIAL BRANCH

Highest Court...Supreme Court of Appeals
Supreme Court Chief Justice............................... Menis E. Ketchum II
Number of Supreme Court Judges 5
Number of U.S. Court Districts 2
U.S. Circuit Court.. 4th Circuit

WISCONSIN

Nickname	The Badger State
Motto	*Forward*
Flower	Wood Violet
Bird	Robin
Tree	Sugar Maple
Song	*On, Wisconsin!*
Entered the Union	May 29, 1848
Capital	Madison

STATISTICS

Land Area (square miles)	54,158
Rank in Nation	25
Population	5,771,337
Rank in Nation	20
Density per square mile	106.6
Capital City	Madison
Population	245,691
Rank in State	2
Largest City	Milwaukee
Population	599,642
Number of Representatives in Congress	8
Number of 2016 Electoral Votes	10
Number of County Governments	72
Number of Municipal Governments	596
Number of School Districts	440
Number of Special Districts	765

LEGISLATIVE BRANCH

Legislative Body	Legislature
President of the Senate	Mary Lazich
President Pro Tem of the Senate	Richard Gudex
Secretary of the Senate	Jeffery Renk
	(Senate Chief Clerk)
Speaker of the House	Robin Vos
	(Speaker of the Assembly)
Speaker Pro Tem of the House	Tyler August
	(Speaker Pro Tem of the Assembly)
Clerk of the House	Patrick Fuller
	(Chief)
2016 Regular Session	Jan. 12 – Dec. 31, 2016
Number of Senatorial Districts	33
Number of Representative Districts	99

EXECUTIVE BRANCH

Governor	Scott K. Walker
Lieutenant Governor	Rebecca Kleefisch
Secretary of State	Douglas La Follette
Attorney General	Brad Schimel
Treasurer	Matt Adamczyk
Auditor	Joe Chrisman
State Comptroller	Jeffrey Anderson
	(Controller)
Governor's Present Term	1/2011 – 1/2019
Number of Elected Officials in the Executive Branch	6
Number of Members in the Cabinet	16

JUDICIAL BRANCH

Highest Court	Supreme Court
Supreme Court Chief Justice	Patience D. Roggensack
Number of Supreme Court Judges	7
Number of Intermediate Appellate Court Judges	16
Number of U.S. Court Districts	2
U.S. Circuit Court	7th Circuit

WYOMING

Nickname	The Equality State and The Cowboy State
Motto	*Equal Rights*
Flower	Indian Paintbrush
Bird	Western Meadowlark
Tree	Cottonwood
Song	*Wyoming*
Entered the Union	July 10, 1890
Capital	Cheyenne

STATISTICS

Land Area (square miles)	97,093
Rank in Nation	9
Population	586,107
Rank in Nation	50
Density per square mile	6.0
Capital City	Cheyenne
Population	62,845
Rank in State	1
Largest City	Cheyenne
Population	62,845
Number of Representatives in Congress	1
Number of 2016 Electoral Votes	3
Number of County Governments	23
Number of Municipal Governments	99
Number of School Districts	55
Number of Special Districts	628

LEGISLATIVE BRANCH

Legislative Body	Legislature
President of the Senate	Phil Nicholas
President Pro Tem of the Senate	Drew Perkins
	(Vice President of the Senate)
Speaker of the House	Kermit C. Brown
Speaker Pro Tem of the House	Tim Stubson
Clerk of the House	Patricia Benskin
	(Chief)
2016 Regular Session	Feb. 8 – March 4, 2016
Number of Senatorial Districts	30
Number of Representative Districts	60

EXECUTIVE BRANCH

Governor	Matthew Mead
Secretary of State	Ed Murray
Attorney General	Peter Michael
Treasurer	Mark Gordon
Auditor	Cynthia Cloud
Governor's Present Term	1/2011 – 1/2019
Number of Elected Officials in the Executive Branch	5
Number of Members in the Cabinet	48

JUDICIAL BRANCH

Highest Court	Supreme Court
Supreme Court Chief Justice	E. James Burke
Number of Supreme Court Judges	5
Number of U.S. Court Districts	1
U.S. Circuit Court	10th Circuit

District of Columbia

Motto..................................*Justitia Omnibus* (*Justice to All*)
Flower ....American Beauty Rose
Bird.. Wood Thrush
Tree...Scarlet Oak
Song.. *Washington*
Became U.S. Capital ....December 1, 1800

STATISTICS

Land Area (square miles)..61
Population...672,228
Density per square mile 11,020.1
Delegate to Congress*...1
Number of 2016 Electoral Votes................................3
Number of Municipal Governments 1
Number of Special Districts 1

*Committee voting privileges only.

LEGISLATIVE BRANCH

Legislative Body ....Council of the District of Columbia

Chair...Phil Mendelson
Chair Pro Tem .... Kenyan McDuffie
Secretary to the Council .... Nyasha Smith
2016 Regular Session...................................Jan. 5 – TBD

EXECUTIVE BRANCH

Mayor...Muriel Bowser
Secretary of the District of Columbia .... Lauren C. Vaughn
Attorney General ....Karl Racine
Chief Financial Officer...............................Jeffrey Barnette
Auditor .... Yolanda Branche
State Comptroller...Anthony Pompa
(Deputy Chief Financial Officer)

Mayor's Present Term .... 1/2015 – 1/2019
Number of Elected Officials in the Executive Branch.......................10

JUDICIAL BRANCH

Highest Court....................................D.C. Court of Appeals
Court of Appeals Chief Justice ....Eric Washington
Number of Court of Appeals Judges.............................9
Number of U.S. Court Districts 1

American Samoa

Motto........................*Samoa-Maumua le Atua* (*In Samoa, God Is First*)
Flower .... Paogo (Ula-fala)
Plant...Ava
Song...*Amerika Samoa*
Became a Territory of the United States 1900
Capital.. Pago Pago

STATISTICS

Land Area (square miles)..77
Population...55,519
Density per square mile 721.0
Capital City.. Pago Pago
Population...3,656
Rank in Territory 3
Largest City..Tafuna
Population...9,756
Delegate to Congress*...1
Number of School Districts 1

*Committee voting privileges only.

LEGISLATIVE BRANCH

Legislative Body ....Legislature

President of the Senate ....Gaoteote P. Tofau
Secretary of the Senate ....Leo'o V. Ma'o

Speaker of the House........................... Savali Talavou Ale
Speaker Pro Tem of the House ....Fetu Fetui Jr.
Chief Clerk of the House........................... Fialupe Lutu

2016 Regular Session................................. Jan. 11 – TBD
Number of Senatorial Districts 12
Number of Representative Districts 17

EXECUTIVE BRANCH

Governor ....Lolo Matalasi Moliga
Lieutenant Governor ....Lemanu Peleti Mauga
Attorney General ....Talauega Eleasalo V. Ale
Treasurer... Falema'o M. Pili
Auditor .... Liua Fatuesi

Governor's Present Term............................. 1/2013 – 1/2017
Number of Members in the Cabinet 16

JUDICIAL BRANCH

Highest Court..High Court
High Court Chief Justice............................. F. Michael Kruse
Number of High Court Judges 6

Guam

Nickname .... Hub of the Pacific
Flower .... Puti Tai Nobio (Bougainvillea)
Bird .... Guam Rail
Tree .... Ifit (Intsiabijuga)
Song .... *Stand Ye Guamanians*
Stone .... Latte
Animal .... Iguana
Ceded to the United States by Spain .... December 10, 1898
Became a Territory .... August 1, 1950
Request to become a Commonwealth Plebiscite .... November 1987
Capital .... Hagatna

STATISTICS

Land Area (square miles) 210
Population 159,358
Density per square mile 758.8
Capital .... Hagatna
Population 1,051
Rank in Territory 13
Largest City .... Dededo
Population 44,943
Delegate to Congress* 1
Number of School Districts 1

*Committee voting privileges only.

LEGISLATIVE BRANCH

Legislative Body .... Legislature

Speaker .... Judith T. Won Pat
Vice Speaker .... Benjamin J.F. Cruz
Clerk of the Legislature .... Rennae V. Meno

2016 Regular Session .... Jan. 13 – Dec. 31, 2016
Number of Senatorial Districts 15

EXECUTIVE BRANCH

Governor .... Edward J.B. Calvo
Lieutenant Governor .... Ray Tenorio
Attorney General .... Elizabeth Barrett-Anderson
Treasurer .... Rose T. Fejeran
Auditor .... Doris Flores Brooks
Comptroller .... Anthony Blaz
(Director, Dept. of Administration)

Governor's Present Term .... 1/2003 – 1/2019
Number of Elected Officials in the Executive Branch 10
Number of Members in the Cabinet 55

JUDICIAL BRANCH

Highest Court .... Supreme Court
Supreme Court Chief Justice .... Robert J. Torres Jr.
Number of Supreme Court Judges 3

Northern Mariana Islands

Flower .... Plumeria
Bird .... Marianas Fruit Dove
Tree .... Flame Tree
Song ....*Gi Talo Gi Halom Tasi*
Administered by the United States
a trusteeship for the United Nations .... July 18, 1947
Voters approved a proposed constitution .... June 1975
U.S. president signed covenant agreeing
to commonwealth status for the islands .... March 24, 1976
Became a self-governing Commonwealth ..... January 9, 1978
Capital .... Saipan

STATISTICS

Land Area (square miles) 179
Population 53,883
Density per square mile 300.7
Capital City .... Saipan
Population 48,220
Largest City .... Saipan
Delegate to Congress* 1
Number of School Districts 1

*Committee voting privileges only.

LEGISLATIVE BRANCH

Legislative Body .... Legislature

President of the Senate .... Francisco Borja
Vice President of the Senate .... Arnold Palacios
Clerk of the Senate .... Doris Bermudes

Speaker of the House .... Joseph P. Deleon Guerrero
Vice Speaker of the House .... Rafael Demapan
Clerk of the House .... Linda B. Muna

2016 Regular Session .... Jan. 11 – TBD
Number of Senatorial Districts 9
Number of Representative Districts 18

EXECUTIVE BRANCH

Governor .... Eloy S. Inos
Lieutenant Governor .... Victor Hocog
Attorney General .... Edward Manibusan
Treasurer .... Mark Rabauliman
(Secretary of Commerce)
Auditor .... Michael Pai
Comptroller .... Larrisa Larson
(Secretary, Dept. of Finance)

Governor's Present Term .... 1/2013 – 1/2019
Number of Elected Officials in the Executive Branch 10
Number of Members in the Cabinet 17

JUDICIAL BRANCH

Highest Court .... Commonwealth Supreme Court
Commonwealth Supreme Court Chief Justice ..... Alexandro C. Castro
Number of Commonwealth Supreme Court Judges 3

Puerto Rico

Nickname...Island of Enchantment
Motto.............................*Joannes Est Nomen Ejus (John is His Name)*
Flower ....Puerto Rican Hibiscus
Bird...Puerto Rican Spindalis
Tree.. Ceiba Pentandra
Song.. *La Borinqueña*
Became a Territory of the United States ....December 10, 1898
Became a self-governing Commonwealth ....July 25, 1952
Capital..San Juan

STATISTICS

Land Area (square miles)...3,424
Population..3,474,182
Density per square mile 1,014.7
Capital City...San Juan
Population...395,326
Largest City ....San Juan
Resident Commissioner in Congress*...1
Number of School Districts 1

*Committee voting privileges only.

LEGISLATIVE BRANCH

Legislative Body ....Legislative Assembly

President of the Senate ....Eduardo Bhatia
Vice President of the Senate ....Jose L. Dalmau Santiago
Secretary of the Senate ....Tania Barbarossa

Speaker of the House...................................Jaime R. Perello
Speaker Pro Tem................................Roberto Rivero Ruiz de Porras
Clerk of the House ....Brunilda Ortiz-Rodriguez

2016 Regular Session...........................Jan. 11 – Nov. 15, 2016

EXECUTIVE BRANCH

Governor ....Alejandro Garcia Padilla
Secretary of State..............................Victor Suarez Melendez
Attorney General .... Cesar Miranda Rodriguez
Treasurer..Juan Zaragoza
Comptroller.............................. Yesmin M. Valdivieso-Galib

Governor's Present Term.............................. 1/2013 – 1/2017
Number of Elected Officials in the Executive Branch 10
Number of Members in the Cabinet 10

JUDICIAL BRANCH

Highest Court...Supreme Court
Supreme Court Chief Justice........................Liana Fiol-Matta
Number of Supreme Court Judges 7

U.S. Virgin Islands

Nickname..The American Paradise
Motto.. *United in Pride and Hope*
Flower .... Trumpetbush
Bird.. Yellow Breast or Banana Quit
Song... *Virgin Islands March*
Purchased from Denmark .... March 31, 1917
Capital..Charlotte Amalie, St. Thomas

STATISTICS

Land Area (square miles)*...134
Population..106,405
Density per square mile 794.1
Capital City..Charlotte Amalie, St. Thomas
Population...18,481
Largest City ....Charlotte Amalie, St. Thomas
Delegate to Congress** 1
Number of School Districts 1

*The U.S. Virgin Islands is comprised of three large islands (St. Croix, St. John, and St. Thomas) and 50 smaller islands and cays.
**Committee voting privileges only.

LEGISLATIVE BRANCH

Legislative Body ....Legislature

President ....Neville A. James
Vice President ....Janette Millin Young

2016 Regular Session........................... Jan. 11 – Dec. 31, 2016

EXECUTIVE BRANCH

Governor ....Kenneth Mapp
Lieutenant Governor ....Osbert Potter
Attorney General ....Claude E. Walker
Commissioner of Finance .... Valdamier Collens

Governor's Present Term.............................. 1/2015 – 1/2019
Number of Elected Officials in the Executive Branch 10
Number of Members in the Cabinet 21

JUDICIAL BRANCH

Highest Court...Supreme Court
Supreme Court Chief Justice........................... Rhys S. Hodge
Number of Supreme Court Judges 3
U.S. Circuit Court...3rd

Index

—D—

—G—

Give Your CPA Exam Score a Boost
with these Essential Study Tools

Cram Course
Boost your score by 8-10 points!

- Get a final review with this condensed CPA Exam Review supplement – the perfect complement to your full review course

- Reinforce your understanding of the most heavily tested topics on the CPA Exam

- Take the Cram Course leading up to Exam Day to refresh your mind on important topics

Audio Lectures
Maximize every minute leading up to the exam!

- Easy MP3 download – ideal for Apple or Android devices

- Turn any moment into a study opportunity! Listen to lectures on your commute, at the gym, or even as you nod off to sleep

- Immerse yourself in the most important CPA Exam topics

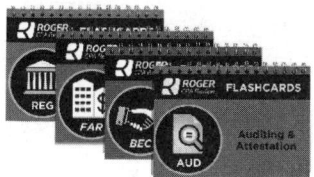

CPA Exam Flashcards
Make studying portable, accessible, and fun!

- Harness overarching CPA Exam concepts

- Create important connections to actual CPA Exam usage and application

- Make studying more exciting by involving family & friends – pull out your flashcards for a quick & interactive study method.

Share Your CPA Story

Would you like to inspire other CPA Candidates to reach their goals like you are? If so, we invite you to create a video to share your story—your successes, your painpoints, and lessons learned.

Email your video to CustomerExperience@rogercpareview.com, and you could be featured on our social channels.

As always, connect with us @RogerCPAreview